A. D. Harvey was born in 1947 in Colchester and was educated at St John's College, Oxford and University College (now Wolfson College), Cambridge. He has taught at the universities of Cambridge, Salerno, La Réunion and Leipzig. His books include *Britain in the Early Nineteenth Century* and *Literature into History*. He has also contributed to the *Daily Telegraph*, *Independent*, *Guardian*, and *Times Higher Education Supplement*.

COLLISION OF EMPIRES

Britain in Three World Wars,
1793–1945

A. D. Harvey

PHŒNIX

A PHOENIX PAPERBACK

First published in Great Britain
by The Hambledon Press in 1992
This first paperback edition published in 1994
by Phoenix, a division of Orion Books Ltd,
Orion House, 5 Upper St Martin's Lane,
London WC2H 9EA

Copyright © A. D. Harvey 1992

A CIP catalogue record for this book is available
from the British Library.

ISBN: 1 85799 125 7

Printed and bound in Great Britain by
Butler & Tanner Ltd, Frome and London

942
R48799

Contents

PART TWO
THE FIRST WORLD WAR
1914–1918

Introduction

The year of this book's first publication, 1992, was fifty years since the fall of Singapore and the victory at El Alamein, seventy-five years since the Battle of Passchendaele and the British capture of Jerusalem, 199 years since Britain was drawn into the Great War with France.

The two world wars of the first half of the twentieth century make up a natural pair. They were only twenty-one years apart, and most of the senior officers in the Second World War participated in the battles of 1914–1918 as junior officers. The experience of economic mobilization in the First World War provided crucial lessons two decades later. New tactical theories, with regard for example to the employment of aircraft and armour, were pioneered in the first war and tried out on a large scale in the second, and a similar continuity is discernible in the political sphere. It is inevitable that the two wars should be compared and contrasted.

The Great War with France of 1793–1815, separated from the twentieth century wars by nearly a hundred years, may seem out of place in such a comparison. In its time it was 'the most extensive and expensive war that ever raged,' its campaigns were on a scale 'unprecedented in the annals of the world', and the Earl of Liverpool, the Prime Minister who led Britain to final victory, later asked, 'Who that contemplated the character of the late war could for a moment think of comparing the events of that war, and the state of things growing out of it, with the events and effects of any former war?' Equally, it was on a vastly greater scale than those celebrated but essentially limited conflicts which briefly disturbed the long Victorian peace, the Crimean War and the Boer War. From the perspective of two hundred years later however the Great War with France tends to be regarded as only a logical development and continuation of the wars of the eighteenth century. Yet in a sense, at least as regards Britain, it belongs to the era of twentieth-century warfare. Britain's industrial economy, however primitive even by the standards of 1914, enabled Britain to mobilize economic resources on a scale simply not available to less developed countries. These were primarily financial resources, but the British government also had access to a labour market that was far more flexible than those of the still essentially agricultural economies of the other belligerents. Part of the story of 1914–1918 and 1939–1945 relates to economic resources and the use made of them, and that story would be incomplete without an account of the relationship between war-making and economic growth in the years 1793–1815. It was the Great War with France, moreover, that secured for Britain the position in the world which had to be defended in the first half of the twentieth century, and the assumptions behind the decision for war in 1914 and 1939 will be more clearly understood if the earlier war is taken into account.[1]

One may also compare the different styles of national and military leadership during the different wars, the developing relationship between government and public opinion, and between the armed forces and the nation at large. A degree of evolution is detectable from war to war. Partly it was a matter of the growing size and complexity of organization. The Duke of Wellington directed his battles from the saddle, riding his horse over the bodies of the slain while musket-balls whistled round his ears. General Eisenhower had never even seen a dead body till after he directed the Anglo-American invasion of North Africa – the Royal Air Force kindly flew him over a battlefield to view the carnage – and the only time he was ever in close proximity to an infantry weapon being fired in anger was when he himself, with his .45 automatic, tried to kill a rat which had invaded his private loo in his G.H.Q. at Caserta. But the evolution was not simply in terms of size and complexity and distancing between different component elements of the war-machine. The social gulf between the officers and other ranks of Wellington's comparatively small army was much greater than in the vastly more numerous British armed forces of the Second World War, though as will be shown, class prejudices continued to exert an influence even in the latter conflict. Again, though society pretended much less solicitude for the safety and welfare of the common soldier in the 1793–1815 war than in the twentieth-century world wars, Wellington husbanded the lives of his men far more carefully than did Haig, or even Montgomery.

No less interesting than comparison between the different wars is comparison between Britain's conduct of war and that of other belligerents. Again, this sort of comparison seems natural and inevitable, though it has never previously been attempted in any detail. Historians traditionally study only one country at a time, even though the result is a national historiography which does not fit together with other national historiographies. The British, for example, used to blame the inter-war slump and even the military reverses of 1941–1942 on the loss of talent involved in the blood-letting of 1914–1918, and this explanation is still not completely out of favour today. The Germans, who lost more men in the First World War, and relative to Britain very

[1] John, Earl of Sheffield *Remarks on the Bill of the Last Parliament for the Amendment of the Poor Laws* (1819) p. 80; *Annual Register* 1799 p. iii; *Parliamentary Debates* n.s. vol. 7 col. 1663 (16 July 1822).

B. R. Mitchell and P. Deane *Abstract of British Historical Statistics* (Cambridge 1962) p. 366–8, 396, 398 indicates that government expenditure in 1856 (the climax of the Crimean War) was 14 per cent of National Income, in 1901 and 1902 (Boer War) under 12 per cent, in 1814 more than 30 per cent and in the years 1916–1918 more than 50 per cent.

All books cited in the footnotes of this volume were published in London unless otherwise indicated.

many more in the Second World War, have never found the need to resort to this excuse for failure. In the following pages, utilizing archive material in five countries and printed sources in thirteen languages, I have tried to go beyond the stock assumptions of national mythologies and to make meaningful comparisons between Britain's experience and that of other belligerents.

In order to maintain a degree of coherence and clarity, the three wars are dealt with separately in chronological sequence. Each of the three wars is discussed in terms of Why, What, How and Who – Why had Britain gone to war, What resources had been used, How had these resources been employed on the battlefield, Who decided about this why, what and how. The relationship between the objectives of a war and the resources mobilized to fight it, and between the resources mobilized and the way they are applied in the front line is in itself an important issue, and of course the political conditions of the direction of a war are inevitably involved in the decision to go to war in the first place. This book compares not only war with war and belligerent with belligerent, but also particular aspects of war with other aspects. I have attempted to reduce its length by resisting the temptation to underline all the comparisons as emphatically as possible, but in dealing with 32 years of warfare, extending over 152 years, in which forty million people died I have not altogether been able to resist complication.

Certain themes may be traced from one chapter to another. In 1793, in 1914, and again in 1939 the British government was drawn reluctantly into a war that was already in progress, even though remaining neutral appeared a realistic option in the view of some politicians. In all three wars the subsequent course of British policy and the eventual outcome underline the question of how far the initial reluctance of the British government can be taken as proof of its superior moral sensibility. In any case, once Britain was at war the circumstances in which hostilities had commenced tended more and more to be forgotten in the pressure of subsequent events. In all three wars Britain was able to mobilize greater capital resources than its enemies, yet though these wars involved a vast financial, social and human burden, the first one in most respects made a profit, and the wars of 1914–1918 and 1939–1945 probably did not cost Britain more than we could afford: but all three wars caused immense damage to the economy and social fabric both of our enemies and of most of our allies, and the economic history of the wars must be regarded as one of the most significant, as well as one of the most illuminating aspects of the economic history of the western world during the last two hundred years.

In the 1793–1815 war Britain's superior capital resources were used to maintain forces that were of higher quality, though weaker in numbers, than those on the other side: in all forty-eight of the victories listed on the Duke of Wellington's monument in St. Paul's the British forces were less numerous than the armies they defeated. In 1914–1918 and 1939–1945 the emphasis was on beating the enemy in a war of production, and the stock-piling of munitions and the establishment of lines of supply was given more importance than the possibility of achieving decisive results from the skilful application of individual determination and flair. This relates to an important sub-text in the book. The 1793–1815 war was fought under the guidance of a generally weak ministry acting through a tiny bureaucracy, there were no organized military staffs in the modern sense, and ultimate success depended on the talents of individuals brought forward by luck and patronage as much as by rational assessment of their abilities.

War was managed in a vastly more professional and systematic way in 1914–1918 and 1939–1945 but the new levels of organizational complexity which this involved resulted in lost opportunities, misapplied resources and hugely increased expenditure – in 1914–1918 Britain on its own, separate from its allies, spent more than the enemy alliance of Germany, Austria-Hungary, Turkey and Bulgaria put together. Bureaucracy, which in the twentieth century seems to have expanded more rapidly in Britain than in any other European country, does not owe its present suffocating extent only to the 1914–1918 and 1939–1945 wars, but the two World Wars do provide us with some of the best-documented cases of how bureaucracy, and bureaucratically organized systems, misuse resources and promote their own growth at the expense of the objectives they were meant to achieve. The rise of bureaucracy in wartime Britain coincided with the concentration of political power in the hands of the prime minister so that by 1940, if not by 1918, a supposedly democratically-elected leader was as much the master of the state apparatus, and as much the focus and epitome of his people's political will, as any totalitarian dictator, though as will be shown this transformation was not unrelated to the pressures which had resulted in dictatorship abroad.

Nearly half a century after the end of the last of these wars it is still difficult to put these developments into perspective. The evident decline of Great Britain as a world power is less the consequence of wartime over-exertion than of the enlarged international role Britain assumed after 1945, complicated by the failure to find a way out from the effects of poor economic management in the 1950s and 1960s. The increased power of the prime minister since 1940 has not enabled any post-war prime minister to bring the system round in new directions – largely, one supposes, because no prime minister since Attlee has had a realistically constructive idea of where he (or she) wished to lead the nation. But Britain's relative failure since 1945, though built on foundations which existed in 1945, cannot be blamed on what happened during the wars. Germany, France and Japan, even Italy and Spain, have built impressively on foundations that, in any analysis, were far more shaky. Today's Britain is not the same as the Britain of the Empire era: yet much of what is being said and being done today seems to echo the sayings and doings of the past, and we cannot begin to understand where we are now without some knowledge of where we were before.

I wish to thank Dr Roy Bennett of Ashbourne, Derbyshire, Professor P.K. O'Brien of the Institute of Historical Research, London and Dr Philip Towle of Cambridge University for permission to cite their unpublished doctoral dissertations. I am also grateful to the Librarian of the University of London

Library for similar permission given in respect of dissertations by John Vincent Smith and Toby Redgrave. Material in the Liddell Hart Centre for Military Archives is quoted with the permission of the Trustees. Ann Beedell gave invaluable assistance in the preparation of the text. Amongst those who helped me with their personal recollections of the years 1939–1945 were Professor A.G. Dickens, Mr R.M. Greenwold and Dr R.B. Jones.

PART ONE

THE GREAT WAR WITH FRANCE

1793–1815

Outline: 1793–1815

France, which had been at war with Austria and Prussia since the previous spring, declared war on Britain in February 1793. The British ministers had expected this to happen but did nothing to prevent it, though they had no clear war aims. Later French successes on the continent lent credibility to claims that Britain was fighting simply to preserve national independence.

Britain's main asset in the war was her wealth. The subsidizing of European allies turned out to be of little practical benefit, but in any case represented only a small part of national expenditure. Thanks to Britain's unparalleled financial resources, highly trained forces could be transported to any part of the globe and supplied indefinitely with the food, clothing and weaponry required to maintain their fighting efficiency. Losses from disease were often staggering yet were vastly greater in the French armies. In spite of frequent blunders by the generals, especially in the 1790s, British troops were usually able to defeat numerically superior French armies simply because the ranks of the latter were constantly being depleted by starvation and disease, and filled up again with raw recruits, whereas the British units were made up of soldiers who had survived successive campaigns.

The effectiveness of both Army and Navy in the face of the enemy was however matched by deficiencies in the strategic thinking of both civilian ministers and senior officers. As it turned out, Spain and Portugal offered the ideal theatre for a relatively small expeditionary force backed up by naval power, but the British government stumbled into the Peninsular involvement almost at random. The future Duke of Wellington not only led the British forces in the Peninsula, but also made a major contribution to final victory simply by managing to persuade ministers of the strategic importance of the Peninsular campaigns.

Despite the pressure of war, British government and society was forced to restructure itself remarkably little. Having access to the financial resources of the London capital market, the government needed to make only limited demands on the manpower and industrial resources of the country. War mobilization prevented neither the spread of industrialization nor high levels of unemployment. It was as if, paradoxically, the very weakness of central government enabled Britain's human and material resources to come effectively into play. The end result was that an increasingly discredited regime in Britain made a leading contribution to the overthrow of Napoleon, and while every other country in Europe was impoverished and exhausted by the twenty-two-year-long war Britain in 1815 was richer than ever before.

1

Britain at War with France

Napoleon has taught our children to play the game of hocus-pocus with popes, priests, kings and other straw-stuffed scarecrows; they, (for we, their fathers, still cling to the rocking-horse and the rattle,) despising the toys of our times, will cast them aside for ever, and play a manlier game.

'De Ruyter', *circa* 1811, in Edward John Trelawny, *Adventures of a Younger Son* (3 vols 1831) vol. 3, p. 316.

I. Causes or Occasions

As everyone knows the storming of the Bastille in Paris on 14 July 1789 launched France into two decades of social and political experiment. After three years France's continental neighbours attempted to intervene to halt this process, though in doing so they received little encouragement from the British government. What finally brought Britain into the military alliance against France was the French declaration of war on Britain on 1 February 1793.

The ensuing struggle – 'Wars of unusual extent duration and ferocity; Anarchy and civil bloodshed, exiles, proscriptions, assassinations, and judicial murders, the worst species of the worst crime' – spread across a succession of grand coalitions, innumerable separate peace treaties and twenty-two years of marches and counter-marches, sieges, invasions and slaughter. It is consequently not easy to say briefly what the wars were *about*. Certainly the question of restoring the French monarchy was frequently forgotten amidst more urgent preoccupations. The endless twists and turns of events point to how great the distinction must be between the real *causes* of a war, the actual *occasion* of war breaking out, and the policy *objectives* of the belligerents as they settled down to the first, or fifth, or fifteenth year of global conflict.[1]

The position of Britain – or England, as it was generally called at this time – seems simpler than that of most other countries. Britain's war against Revolutionary France (1793–1801) was of course technically a separate conflict from the war against Napoleon (1803–1814, with a postscript in the Hundred Days in 1815). But the two wars had in common the themes of Anglo-French

---

[1] The quotation is from Lord Grenville 'Commentaries of my own Political Life and of Public Transactions connected with it,' Introduction c. 1810, British Library Add. 69130 p. 5.

rivalry, fears of French international policy, and continental hostility to British pretensions at sea. In 1793 a reluctant British government, despite opposition and criticism at home, was drawn into the European war which had broken out the previous year; in 1803 a much less reluctant British government backed by an unenthusiastic but resolute consensus at home promoted hostilities at a time when Europe was at peace. This might suggest a degree of development over the period as a whole, a growing national commitment to the war against France, but no such clear-cut development was evident in other countries. At various times between declaring war on Austria in April 1792 and Napoleon's second abdication in June 1815 France was at war with Russia, Austria, Prussia, Spain, Sweden, Turkey and the Netherlands. During the same period, at differing various times, Britain was at war with all these states, as well as with Denmark for seven years and with the U.S.A. for three years. Britons were frequently unwelcome in countries with which the British government was at peace, and often had to pass themselves off as Frenchmen, or at least Germans, to avoid insult. Over the period as a whole it seems that Britain was as much the 'common enemy', *l'ennemi commun*, as Revolutionary and Napoleonic France.[2]

II. The Occasion of War

Once the war was in progress it was condemned by its British opponents as a war of opinion, fought against the French Revolution. John Cartwright, the campaigner for parliamentary reform, called it 'The Rotten Borough War', and John Thelwall, the London Corresponding Society's chief speech-maker, claimed that 'the System of War and the System of Corruption have gone hand in hand'. And it is certainly true that at the time of the French declaration of war the British government was extremely disturbed by internal political developments in France and was beginning to organize measures against French-inspired revolutionary sentiment at home. But the government did not, so long as peace lasted, accept the logic of a double

---

[2] Cf R.M. Bacon *A Memoir of the Life of Edward, Third Baron Suffield* printed for private circulation Norwich 1838 p. 15–16 and T. Sadler ed. *Diary, Reminiscences, and Correspondence of Henry Crabb Robinson* (3 vols 1869) vol. 1 p. 259; Charles Theremin *Des Intérêts des Puissances Continentales relativement à l'Angleterre* (Paris an III – 1794) p. 113–4: 'Dites moi, maintenant, si ce n'est pas le gouvernement Anglais qui est l'ennemi commun de tous les peuples civilisés.' For 'England' see Donat Henchy O'Brien *My Adventures during the Late War* (2 vols 1839) vol. 1 p. 51, 62–3, 74 and especially p. 102: 'Our personal honour, as well as that of the navy – and, indeed, of the English nation in general – precluded the possibility of our attempting to escape whilst we were upon ... parole;' and *The Life and Adventures of John Nicol, Mariner* (Edinburgh 1822) p. 178, where 25 Spanish vessels were encountered at the Battle of St. Vincent on 14 February 1797: 'We were only eighteen; but we were English, and we gave them their Valentines in style.' O'Brien was Irish, born in Co. Clare, and Nicol Scots, born at Currie near Edinburgh.

offensive, simultaneously against the French Revolution's sympathizers in Britain and against the French Revolution itself beyond the English Channel. They took precisely the opposite view. Lord Grenville, the Foreign Secretary, confided to his brother his desire

> to keep my own country at least a little longer from sharing in all the evils of every sort that surround us. I am more and more convinced that this can only be done by keeping wholly and entirely aloof, and by watching much at home, but doing very little indeed; endeavouring to nurse up in the country a real determination to stand by the Constitution when it is attacked, as it most infallibly will be if these things go on; and, above all, trying to make the situation of the lower orders among us as good as it can be made . . . I trust we may again be enabled to contribute to the same object by the repeal of taxes.

This was also the opinion of Lord Auckland, the most influential British envoy on the continent, who thought Britain should '*ascertain how far it is possible to effectuate an entire cessation of hostilities* [i.e., between France and Austria] *and to leave France to the internal pursuit of her own inventions*'.[3]

At the same time Lord Grenville, at Auckland's prompting, acknowledged that it might be wise to enter into consultation with the powers already at war with France. At this stage fear of France had not overridden suspicion regarding the attitude and policy of France's enemies, and the British ambassador at Berlin was warned:

> it is not His Majesty's Intention that You should press for such communication, in such a Manner as might commit the King's Dignity. It will be obvious to remark, that the King of Prussia has, under the present Circumstances, a much stronger Interest than His Majesty to re-establish the former confidential Intercourse.

This caution was perhaps justified: both in Berlin and Vienna various excuses were made to defer an official response. Nor did preoccupation with developments in western Europe prevent Grenville from objecting to what was going on in eastern Europe, where Poland was on the point of suffering its Second Partition at the hands of Prussia and Russia. When Colonel Sir James Murray was sent on a special mission to the military headquarters of the King of Prussia he was instructed to explain His Britannic Majesty's 'entire disapprobation' of the dismemberment of Poland, 'and His determination on no account to concur in any measures which may tend to the completion of a design so unjust in itself, and so contradictory to the principles by which His Majesty has invariably been activated'. Murray was even advised that if

---

[3] John Cartwright *A Constitutional Defence of England* (1796) passim; John Thelwall *The Tribune* vol. 3 p. 107 speech 28 Oct. 1795; [Richard] Duke of Buckingham *Memoirs of the Court and Cabinets of George III* (4 vols 1853–4) vol. 2 p. 224. Grenville to Marquis of Buckingham 7 Nov. 1792; *HMC Dropmore Mss* vol. 2 p. 334 Auckland to Grenville, 15 Nov. 1792.

Poland was partitioned any military alliance between His Britannic Majesty and the partitioning powers would be out of the question:

> The interests of His own dominions may still require that He should persevere in that line towards France on which He is now acting but it must be on principles, and in a manner wholly distinct from the other Powers, in whose views, in such a case, it will be impossible for the King to concur.[4]

Though Russia was also about to seize upon Polish territories, Anglo-Russian contacts were at a more cordial level, possibly because it was the Russians who first broached the possibility of discussions. Lord Grenville informed the Russian minister plenipotentiary in London that Britain was willing to cooperate with Russia,

> not with the view of meddling in France's interior affairs or of establishing by force a particular form of government or constitution but in order to provide for their own security and for the most important interests of Europe, in opposing a barrier to their intrigues against the governments of other countries and to that spirit of aggression and aggrandisement which gives all the Powers such just cause for inquietude and jealousy.[5]

The potential victim of French aggression which most concerned the British government was the Netherlands, then officially known as the United Provinces. The French minister in London was warned:

> This government, adhering to the maxims which it has followed for more than a century, will also never see with indifference, that France shall make herself, either directly or indirectly, sovereign of the Low Countries, or general arbitress of the rights and liberties of Europe.

Yet only timorous preliminary steps were made towards coordinating British

---

[4] *HMC Dropmore Mss* vol. 2 p. 330 Auckland to Grenville 9 November 1792 and p. 332 reply 13 November 1792; Public Record Office FO 64/26 Grenville to Sir Morton Eden 13 Nov. 1792; for the dilatory Prussian response FO 64/26 Eden to Grenville 23 Nov. and 15 Dec. 1792; for the Austrians FO 7/31 Alexander Straton to Grenville 28 Nov., 5 Dec. and 22 Dec. 1792; FO 29/1 Grenville's official instructions to Murray 4 Jan. 1793.

T.C.W Blanning *The Origins of the French Revolutionary Wars* (1986) p. 158 claims 'it was concern for the Low Countries which turned British policy to active resistance to the Revolution', and it is true that the decision to approach the governments in Berlin and Vienna followed immediately on Dumouriez's victory at Jemappes (6 Nov. 1792) which made possible the rapid overrunning of the Austrian Netherlands (Belgium) by the French Revolutionary army. It might therefore be argued that Jemappes provoked a decisive reorientation of British policy. But Grenville's papers give no indication that he was conscious of shifting from one line of policy to another, and since the French had occupied Mainz on 21 October 1792 it was already clear, before Grenville's letter to the Marquis of Buckingham of 7 Nov. 1792, that the French were gaining the military advantage. Incidentally, Brussels fell on 14 November, and the news of the Battle of Jemappes was not reported in *The Times* till 22 November.

For a detailed account of the approach to war generally see John Ehrman *The Younger Pitt* (3 vols 1969 –) vol. 2 p. 206–258.

[5] Public Record Office FO 65/23 f. 259 Grenville to Woronzow (i.e., Count Semen Romanovich Vorontsov) 28 Dec. 1792.

and Dutch military resources. At the end of November 1792 Grenville asked Auckland to procure Dutch naval intelligence concerning the French fleet; early in January 1793 he asked about the size of the Dutch garrisons in the Caribbean and pointed out, 'If the war goes on, our East India fleets must sail under joint convoys'. By late January he was advising the Dutch to concert defensive measures with the Prussians, and offered the assistance of Sir James Murray, who had reached the Prussian headquarters some days earlier. Murray was instructed 'to give the strongest assurances that His Majesty is proceeding with vigour and dispatch in His naval preparations'; even at the end of December Grenville had informed the British ambassador at St. Petersburg that 'The exertions of this Country, and is some degree those of Russia will naturally be directed to a maritime War'. It was obvious that the combined British, Dutch and Russian naval forces would be overwhelmingly stronger than the French Navy, but it is not clear how, in Lord Grenville's view, this would help prevent a French invasion of the United Provinces by land. Perhaps he thought it was up to the Dutch to defend their own borders: he told Auckland on 22 January 1793, 'I am almost tired of harping on the same string of urging the Dutch Government to energy and execution'.[6]

Meanwhile Lord Grenville had come to the conclusion that, if an Anglo-French war was unavoidable, the onus of starting it should be left to the French:

> there is too much reason to believe the French are determined to drive us to extremities. A very few days must now probably decide this question, and we feel very unwilling to afford anything like a pretext which could diminish the strong impression to be expected here from so unprovoked an attack.

This was written late in November 1792 but in spite of some provocative speeches in Paris nothing was done by the French at this stage to finalize the rupture. Since Grenville thought the war was inevitable, it is slightly odd that he should leave to the enemy the choice of timing – especially since British naval preparations were far from as advanced as was pretended. Grenville's performance at this juncture was patently disingenuous. As was to be pointed out later, in order to demonstrate that Grenville's policy was 'erroneous and culpable',

> it is not in the least necessary to show that the Government of France were chargeable with no errors, or that Great Britain had no injuries to complain of; but that such explanations and reparations were offered, as would unquestionably have served, had the affairs of Britain been in the hands of wise and able Ministers, as a basis for reconciliation.

[6] *Parliamentary History* vol. 30 col. 255 Grenville to Chauvelin 31 Dec. 1792; *HMC Dropmore Mss* vol. 2 p. 341 Grenville to Auckland 26 Nov. 1792; ibid. vol. 2 p. 363 same to same 5 Jan. 1793; ibid. vol. 2 p. 371 same to same 22 Jan. 1793; Public Record Office FO 29/1 Grenville to Murray 20 Jan. 1793; FO 65/23 f. 268 Grenville to Sir Charles Whitworth 29 Dec. 1792; *HMC Dropmore Mss* vol. 2 p. 371 Grenville to Auckland 22 Jan. 1793.

And in fact Grenville assumed the opposite of a conciliatory manner. To Chauvelin, France's minister in London, he wrote just before the final breaking off of relations:

> I have examined, Sir, with the utmost attention, the paper you remitted me on the 13th of this month. I cannot help remarking that I have found nothing satisfactory in the result of it . . .

This was evidently not intended to be polite. To Auckland, at about the same period, Grenville wrote:

> You know . . . my personal and sincere abhorrence of war where it can be avoided. But I am satisfied that nothing but vigorous and extensive and systematic measures can save us now.

But even by this stage no such measures had actually been promulgated; evidently the government was still waiting for the French to make a move.[7]

The measure of the French government which finally supplied the British Cabinet with the pretext they had been waiting for was not even directed against Britain or an allied government. On 21 January 1793 Louis XVI was executed in Paris. As soon as the news reached London the French minister there, the Marquis de Chauvelin, was ordered to leave. This was no rash, instinctive gesture made under the influence of shock and revulsion: the British government had expected the French to carry out the death sentence on their ex-king and had had time to consider an appropriate response. Chauvelin had been accredited as the emissary of Louis XVI; disputes about accreditation were not unusual in this period, though they did not normally result in expulsion, but the possibility of arranging alternative diplomatic representation from the National Convention was not discussed by the British ministers. They simply waited for Louis XVI's execution as their cue to expel Chauvelin: 'The King told me yesterday he would be ready to have the Council whenever the news came', the Prime Minister informed Lord Grenville on 23 January.[8]

The British ministers fully expected that the expulsion of Chauvelin would mean war. On the same day that Chauvelin was ordered to leave Lord Grenville wrote to Auckland:

> I imagine the next despatch to you, or the next but one, will announce the commencement of hostilities. Probably the French will commence them; but if not, after all lines of communication are interrupted of necessity, and after all hope of satisfactory explanation is over, I do not see how we can remain any longer *les bras croisés*, with a great force ready for action, that force avowedly

---

[7] *HMC Dropmore Mss* vol. 2 p. 341 Grenville to Auckland 26 Nov. 1792; William Belsham *Reply to the Rev. Herbert Marsh's Vindication of a Late Work Styled a History of the Politicks of Great Britain and France* (1801) p. 3; ibid. p. 69 Grenville to Chauvelin 18 Jan. 1793 (also printed in *Parliamentary History* vol. 30 col. 266); *HMC Dropmore Mss* vol. 2 p. 367 Grenville to Auckland 15 Jan. 1793.

[8] *HMC Dropmore Mss* vol. 2 p. 372 Pitt to Grenville 23 Jan. 1793.

meant against France, and the language and conduct of that power giving every day more instead of less ground of offence to us and all the world.

The British government even issued a kind of official manifesto, in the form of a message from the King to Parliament requesting a strengthening of the armed forces,

> for maintaining the security and rights of his own dominions; for supporting his allies; and for opposing views of aggrandizement and ambition on the part of France, which would be at all times dangerous to the general interests of Europe, but are peculiarly so, when connected with the propagation of principles which lead to the violation of the most sacred duties, and are utterly subversive of the peace and order of civil society.

The French declaration of war came three days later.[9]

As the declaration of war had been made by the French, the British ministers were able to pretend that their hands had been forced. William Pitt, the Prime Minister, having loyally backed up the policy of his cousin the Foreign Secretary throughout the crisis, told the House of Commons in February:

> When war was declared, and the event no longer in our option, it remained only to be considered, whether we should prepare to meet it with a firm determination.

It enabled him also to disclaim all responsibility:

> whatever temptations might have existed to this country from ancient enmity and rivalship, paltry motives indeed! or whatever opportunity might have been afforded by the tumultuous and distracted state of France, or whatever sentiments might be excited by the transactions which had taken place in that country, his majesty had uniformly abstained from all interference in its internal government.

Certainly, in his contacts with the Russians some weeks earlier, Lord Grenville had similarly insisted that there should be no interference in French internal affairs: but a little later he confided to his eldest brother:

> I have no other view of the contest in which we are engaged, nor ever have had, than that the existence of the two systems of Government is fairly at stake, and in the words of St. Just, whose curious speech I hope you have seen, that it is perfect blindness not to see that in the establishment of the French Republic is included the overthrow of all the other Governments of Europe.

One might conclude from this that Lord Grenville at least had always thought of the war as both inevitable and necessary and that anything said that suggested a contrary view prior to the French declaration of war was intended to mislead. But to mislead whom? The war did come in for fierce criticism, but only from a dwindling minority; the ministers had no reason to suppose

---

[9] *HMC Dropmore Mss* vol. 2 p. 372–3 Grenville to Auckland 24 Jan. 1793; *Parliamentary History* vol. 30 col. 239 King's message 28 Jan. 1793.

that the war would necessarily be unpopular, and in any case they seem never to have discussed the question of whether public opinion needed to be nursed or cajoled on this issue.[10]

In 1914, there was to be the same maidenly reluctance, the same calculated waiting on pretexts, followed by the same triumphant statement of crystal clear principles showing the new enemy as unambiguously the aggressor: but even more than in 1914 there was no long-term expectation or desire for war in 1793, merely, in the end, a submission to events that somehow took on an unmistakable suggestion of cynical and inveterate opportunism.

In this instance at least the British were much less deliberately cynical than they may have appeared. The attempt at consultation with the governments already at war with France had so far reached no conclusion; the United Provinces, whose security was a major concern to the British, was not in a position to be defended. It was probably the fact that Britain's most important potential allies were *already* at war with France which explains the awkwardness of British policy. Lord Grenville was justifiably suspicious of the long term objectives of the Berlin and Vienna governments, and was reluctant to commit Britain to coalition policies over which he had only partial control. In addition, the main reason for thinking of cooperating with Berlin and Vienna was that, so far, they were *losing* the war against France; if they had been winning French aggression and aggrandizement would scarcely have been a problem. Lord Grenville's difficulty was not so much one of explaining the war to the British public as of explaining it to himself. Should Britain have joined the war at its commencement in the spring of 1792? Should greater efforts have been made to postpone British participation? Should measures have been concerted with Berlin and Vienna much earlier? Somehow the right decisions had been consistently eluding Lord Grenville; it was much easier to blame it all on the French.

III. The Ideology of the War

This aspect of the matter was not really canvassed at the time. William Wilberforce, a leading supporter of the government and one of the few close friends of the Prime Minister, later wrote of the war, 'I had but too much reason to know that the ministry had not taken due pains to prevent its breaking out'. In the debate in the House of Commons on the outbreak of war, on 12 February 1793, he 'was actually upon my legs' to speak against the war when Pitt sent him a note asking him not to speak. Consequently the war was denounced only by the Foxite opposition in Parliament and by the radical reformers out of doors, both of which groups were already so marginalized

---

[10] *Parliamentary History* vol. 30 col. 345–6 Pitt's speech 12 Feb. 1793; Buckingham *Memoirs of the Court and Cabinets of George III* vol. 2 p. 303 Grenville to Buckingham 17 Sept. 1794 (St. Just had, incidentally, been guillotined two months previously).

that few people were prepared to give serious attention to anything they had to say.[11]

In leading the country into war, the ministers obviously benefited from the growing public revulsion against the new French regime, especially after the execution of Louis XVI, but neither at the commencement nor at any subsequent stage did the British government present the war as essentially ideological. From the very beginning there were those who thought it odd that Europe's first revolutionary republic should so resolutely oppose the second. In November 1793 Captain Horatio Nelson, afterwards the hero of Trafalgar, conversed with the Bey of Tunis:

> On being told of the excesses which the French government had committed, he drily observed, 'That nothing could be more heinous than the murder of their Sovereign; and yet Sir,' added the Bey, 'if your historians tell the truth, your own countrymen once did the same.'

The essayist William Hazlitt, making the same point some years later, thought that John Bull 'will have the monopoly of rebellion and regicide to himself'. There is something in this: a major shift in the role of the monarchy in Britain, which will be discussed later, naturally involved an altered appreciation of monarchs everywhere, and those who, like George III himself, could be identified with the losing side in England's seventeenth century Civil War were still numerous and influential. But though there was no single uniform analysis within the British government few of the key ministers placed much emphasis on sentimental or ideological aspects of the war, and when the United Provinces were overrun by the French what worried the British was simply that 'The liberty of Europe was never before in such danger, nor was there since the Roman Age, so great a Prospect of Universal Empire'.[12]

Of course at the time of the declaration of war the French government seemed terrifyingly extreme in its ideology, and likely to become even more so:

> on every side beset with Foes,
> The goaded Land waxed mad; the crimes of few
> Spread into madness of the many

But in 1795 the establishment of the Directory and General Bonaparte's defeat of the insurrectionary sections on 13 *vendémiaire* brought the extremist phase of the French Revolution to an end. This was quickly recognized by the British government, which announced itself ready 'to meet any disposition

[11] Robert Isaac and Samuel Wilberforce *The Life of William Wilberforce* (5 vols 1838) vol. 2 p. 11 Wilberforce to W. Hey 14 Feb. 1801.

[12] James Stanier Clarke and John M'Arthur *The Life of Admiral Lord Nelson, K.B.* (2 vols 1809) vol. 1 p. 138 fn.; William Hazlitt 'Character of John Bull' in *The Round Table* (1817) printed in P.P. Howe ed. *The Complete Works of William Hazlitt* (21 vols 1930–34) vol. 4 p. 99; Public Record Office WO 1/302 f 393 Sir Gilbert Elliot to Henry Dundas 23 Feb. 1795.

to negotiation on the part of the enemy, with an earnest desire to give it the fullest and speediest effect, and to conclude a treaty for general peace, whenever it can be effected, on just and suitable terms'. This announcement, and a pamphlet which Lord Auckland published in October 1795 entitled *Some Remarks on the apparent circumstances of the War in the fourth week of October 1795*, provoked Edmund Burke to write his famous *Letters on a Regicide Peace*, attacking on moral and ideological grounds the very principle of negotiating with the French republic: but though Burke had his disciples in the Cabinet and had some influence on Lord Grenville he was very far from setting the tone for the ministers. According to Wilberforce, 'They by no means shared in Mr. Burke's persuasions concerning the proper object and nature of the war'.[13]

The poet Wordsworth, who if not exactly representative of his time was representative of that strain of thinking and sensibility which was to prove most durable, was shocked by the war:

> Not in my single self alone I found,
> But in the minds of all ingenuous Youth,
> Change and subversion from this hour.

He later wrote of 'A conflict of sensations without name', when, for example, attending church and hearing prayers offered for victory:

> 'mid the simple worshippers, perchance
> I only, like an uninvited Guest
> Whom no one owned sate silent . . .

Originally Wordsworth had been an enthusiastic supporter of the French Revolution and had gone to Paris after graduating from Cambridge in 1791, returning to England only a few weeks before the French declaration of war:

> else (though assured
> That I was and must be of small weight
> No better than a landsman on the deck
> Of a ship struggling with a hideous storm)
> Doubtless, I should have then made common cause
> With some who perished; haply perished too,
> A poor mistaken and bewildered offering.

Initially he had difficulty in sorting out the relative claims of ideology and of national policy (a difficulty that was to become familiar in the mid-twentieth century) and was haunted by nightmares

---

[13] William Wordsworth *The Prelude* 1805 text, book X lines 312–4; *Parliamentary History* vol. 32 col. 570, royal message of 8 Dec. 1795 and cf. Thomas Philip Schofield 'English Conservative Thought and Opinion in Response to the French Revolution 1789–1796' unpublished (London Univ. Ph.D. dissertation 1984) p. 222–236; R.I. and S. Wilberforce *The Life of William Wilberforce* vol. 2 p. 391 appendix, dated 11 Dec. 1828.

of despair
And tyranny, and implements of death;
. . . and the unbroken dream entangled me
In long orations, which I strove to plead
Before unjust tribunals.

But increasingly what isolated Wordsworth, was less his nostalgia for the departed spirit of Liberty and Progress than his conviction that national policy should have a morally coherent direction. Lord Grenville, a conventionally pious, even devout man, was too painfully aware of living in the real world to take such a view, and William Pitt was simply too busy to spare time for ideological abstractions. It was so much easier to fall back on expediency and opportunity.[14]

IV. The Objectives of the War in the 1790s

Once the French had declared war one moves from the realm of causes and occasions to that of aims and objectives: and finds that the British government had none. Despite the non-interventionist policy he had recommended in November 1792 Lord Auckland initially urged the view that 'our first and great object ought to be to destroy the Convention [i.e., the French republican regime]' A motion by Charles Grey in the House of Commons in 1794 'that the existence of the present government of France ought not to be considered as precluding, at this time, a Negociation of Peace' rallied only 90 M.Ps in its favour, to 254 against. But when in late 1795 government had accepted at least the principle of negotiating with the Directory, the objectionable nature of the French regime could no longer be imputed as an official war aim. In August 1796 Sir Horatio Nelson, as he then was, received a visit from the Dey of Algiers's 'Lord of the Bedchamber, or some such great man', and took the opportunity to ask why the Dey would not give up his marauding against Britain's allies Genoa and Naples, since they would pay tribute in exchange for a peace treaty:

His answer was, 'If we make peace with every one, what is the Dey to do with his Ships?' What a reason for carrying on a Naval war! but has our Minister a better one for the present?

Nelson himself later gave the opinion, 'The great object of the war is – *Down, down with the French!*'[15]

Though attempts to negotiate were made, all failed and the personal opinion

[14] William Wordsworth *The Prelude* 1805 text, book X lines 232–4, 266 and 272–4; 1850 text, book X lines 225–230, 402–3, 410–412.

[15] *Parliamentary History* vol. 31 col. 1204, 26 Jan. 1794; Sir Nicholas Harris Nicolas ed. *The Dispatches and Letters of Vice-Admiral Lord Viscount Nelson* (7 vols 1844–6) vol. 2 p. 236 Nelson to Sir John Jervis 5 Aug. 1796; ibid. vol. 4 p. 90 Nelson to Earl Spencer 6 Nov. 1799.

of many cabinet ministers, even Lord Grenville, was that peace with a republican regime in France was impossible. As Grenville wrote to Henry Dundas:

> In all the revolutions in that country ... the Jacobin principle has remained unshaken, the centre of all the hopes and wishes of the adherents to that principle in every other part of Europe; and so it will be, as I believe, for a hundred more such revolutions, till the principle itself be attacked and subdued in its citadel at Paris.

Burke's *Letters on a Regicide Peace* gained wide attention, and his views were circulated in a warmed-up form by William Windham, his closest discile in the Cabinet. Windham felt that there was insufficient public awareness of the consequences of 'so dreadful a catastrophe: I mean, of course, Peace with a Jacobin Republick', and occasionally waxed hysterical on the subject 'of the danger which from that moment will begin to operate against the Country'. Windham's great fear was that 'the Wives and Daughters of the first nobility and gentry of the Country' would frequent the French Embassy if it were to be reopened,

> [to] be initiated there in the doctrines of Revolutionary Morality; and be ready to take lessons in the practice from the numberless able and agreeable professors, who will attend there for that purpose.[16]

Despite the efforts of Burke and Windham however there was increasingly a shift of emphasis. In one of his rare anonymous articles William Pitt, the Prime Minister, claimed:

> our Contest is not barely for Power, or Glory, or Wealth, or Commerce, much less is it to secure some speculative advantage, to avert some remote or contingent danger. It is for present SAFETY and EXISTENCE – for the immediate Independence of the Nation, for the security of the Life, Liberty, and Property of every individual among us.

As the military power of France increased, so the ideological aspect lost what appeal it had ever had, as a pamphlet published in 1799 frankly acknowledged:

> The present War is not *now*, as has been said, a war of principle, carried on to inforce a political creed:– it is a war of self-defence, to preserve national independence.

The doctrines taught and practised by the French Republic at home were now

---

16 *HMC Dropmore Mss* vol. 6 p. 47 Grenville to Dundas 25 Nov. 1799; [Lewis Melville ed.] *Windham Papers* (2 vols 1913) vol. 2 p. 3 Windham to Burke 17 Jan. 1796 (The same idea is hinted at in his speech against the preliminaries of peace 3 Nov. 1801, *Parliamentary History* vol. 36 col. 127.) For the assumed connection between revolutionary doctrine and sexual freedom see also A.D. Harvey 'George Walker and the Anti-Revolutionary Novel' *Review of English Studies* vol. 28 (1978) p. 290–300 at p. 292, 296–7. This brand of sexual paranoia and sense of the dreadful fragility of values (especially those held by one's womenfolk) is evidently characteristic of a certain mentality – see Brian Bunting *The Rise of the South African Reich* (1969) p. 198, 313.

presented as if no concern to the British government, so long as there was no attempt to export them. Applying a sort of personification to the French Revolution Pitt told the Commons in June 1799:

> We will not leave the monster to prowl the world unopposed. He must cease to annoy the abode of peaceful men. If he retire into the cell, whether of solitude or repentance, thither we will not pursue him.

Herbert Marsh, perhaps the most influential pro-government writer on the war, asserted:

> It was a war of aggression, of injury, and of insult, on the part of France, as well in the motives which gave it birth as in the open declaration of it: and, on the part of Britain, it was just and necessary, as being strictly a war of self defence.

But perhaps the most widely noticed statement of war aims came from William Pitt; in February 1800 he told the House of Commons that the object of the war was:

> security; – security against a danger, the greatest that ever threatened the world – security against a danger which never existed in any past period of society. This country alone, of all the nations of Europe, presented barriers the best fitted to resist its progress. We alone recognized the necessity of open war, as well with the principles as the practice of the French revolution. We saw that it was to be resisted no less by arms abroad than by precautions at home, that we were to look for protection no less to the courage of our forces than to the wisdom of our counsels; no less to military effort than to legislative enactment.

Even at this late date Pitt had more than a sop to throw to those who wished to emphasize the ideological element, and he sought to imply a rather more coherent policy against domestic Jacobinism in the early stages of the war than had in fact existed; these self-congratulatory elaborations on the central theme of *security* merely underline the fact that security had not been the explicit objective in 1793, however much it came to be emphasized after four or five years of French military triumph and conquest.[17]

V. The War against Napoleon

On the basis of security a compromise peace *was* conceivable; negotiations on these terms took place in 1796 and 1797, and more successfully in 1801.

---

[17] *Anti-Jacobin; or Weekly Examiner* no. 12, 29 Jan. 1798, p. 89. (Pitt's authorship is identified in a copy in the British Library); anon. *Arguments for a Coalition against France* (1799) p. 1; *Parliamentary History* vol. 34 col. 1051–2, Pitt's speech of 7 June 1799; Herbert Marsh *The History of the Politicks of Great Britain and France, Vindicated from the late attack of Mr. William Belsham* (1801) p. 18; *Parliamentary History* vol. 34 col. 1442–3, Pitt's speech of 17 Feb. 1800; he had in fact mentioned the issue of security as far back as 12 Feb. 1793, cf *Parliamentary History* vol. 30 col. 348, but had given it much less emphasis.

The peace negotiated in 1801 and ratified as the Treaty of Amiens in 1802 broke down in the first half of 1803. Having signed a treaty with Napoleon Bonaparte the British government was no longer in a position to cite the ideological unacceptability of the French regime: at the same time those who had defended the French republic in the 1790s were dismayed by its transformation into a dictatorship; indeed the Whigs, feeling themselves somewhat compromised as formerly the pro-French party, prided themselves on their disdain for Napoleon. Fox, the opposition leader, visited Paris during the brief peace, met the young Corsican dictator and reported triumphantly, 'In conversation He found him very deficient upon every subject; no powers or extent of mind'. Later of course there was a sustained campaign of vilification against Napoleon, as for example Robert Southey's speculation as to what would have happened if Nelson had successfully intercepted Napoleon on the way to Egypt in 1798:

> A romantic obscurity would have hung over the expedition to Egypt, and he would have escaped the perpetration of those crimes which have incarnadined his soul with a deeper dye than that of the purple for which he committed them – those acts of perfidy, midnight murder, usurpation, and remorseless tyranny, which have consigned his name to universal execration, now and for ever.

But in 1803 this was still largely in the future, and though it was recognized that Napoleon was dangerous, it was not universally accepted that he was dangerous to Britain or that Britain needed in any way to become involved with him.[18]

William Pitt, temporarily out of office in 1803, urged his old theme of a necessary war of self-defence:

> It is for our property, it is for our liberty, it is for our independence, nay, for our existence as a nation; it is for our character, it is for our name as Englishmen, it is for everything dear and valuable to man on this side of the grave.

In reality most of what the British government objected to in French policy related to geographically somewhat remote issues: the annexation of Piedmont; the continuance of French garrisons in the theoretically independent Batavian Republic; and the occupation of Switzerland following the collapse of the French-modelled constitution. The British government for their part refused to evacuate Malta as arranged in the Treaty of Amiens because, as the French were officially informed, 'the possession of Malta was necessary for our security, and was rendered so not from any desire of aggrandizement on the part of His Majesty, but by the conduct of the French Government'. Probably eight years of continental war during the 1790s had helped educate the British public into an interest in European affairs that they may have lacked

[18] Kenneth Garlick, Angus Macintyre etc. ed. *The Diary of Joseph Farington* (16 vols New Haven 1978–84) vol. 6 p. 2045, 2 June 1803; Robert Southey *The Life of Nelson* (1st published 1813, quotation is from p. 137–8 of Hutchinson's cheap standard lives ed.).

previously. Wordsworth regarded the original French invasion of Switzerland in 1798 as a turning point; 'after the subjugation of Switzerland, and not till then', he claimed, the war had come 'to be regarded by the body of the people, as indeed just and necessary'; certainly the sufferings of the Swiss received an unprecedented amount of publicity in Britain. Even so Switzerland was rather a long way away and as William Wilberforce, one of the most influential parliamentary back-benchers, objected:

> we have been too apt to make ourselves principals in continental quarrels; we have been somewhat too forward to engage in wars, and above all we have continued them too long, for continental objects, contrary to the true policy and real interests of this country.[19]

On 24 May 1803 Charles James Fox, who had led the parliamentary opposition to the war in the 1790s, adopted an argument similar to Wilberforce's in one of the classic speeches of his career – it fills fifty densely printed columns of the *Parliamentary History*. But soon the opposition in Parliament began to focus much less on the justice of the war than on the fitness of the ministers to conduct it. The whole question of why Britain was at war generated comparatively little interest. Whereas the Hon. Thomas Erskine's critique of government policy *A View of the Causes and Consequences of the Present War with France* went through 35 editions in 1797, the year of its publication, the nearest corresponding works of the 1800s, *The Question – Why do we go to War? – temperately discussed* by William Burdon, fellow of Emmanuel College, Cambridge and *Considerations on the Causes, Objects and Consequences of the present War, and on the Expediency, or the Danger, of Peace with France*, by William Roscoe of Liverpool, went through three and five editions respectively. Napoleon's preparations for an invasion of England in any case rendered the original cause of the war somewhat irrelevant, and inevitably generated a flood of chauvinistic propaganda, including an attempt at the systematic indoctrination of the army with regard to

> a savage and implacable Enemy, who has the Insolence and Barbarity to aim at the Slavery of Our Persons, the extinction of Our Religion and the destruction of Our Navy, Our Commerce and Constitution, so long the Envy and Admiration of the World.

---

[19] W.S. Hathaway ed. *The Speeches of the Right Honourable William Pitt* (3 vols 1817 edit.) vol. 3 p. 302, Pitt's speech of 22 July 1803 (this passage is not in the short report printed in *Parliamentary History*); *Parliamentary History* vol. 36 col. 1334, note by Lord Whitworth, late April 1803; William Wordsworth *Concerning the Relations of Great Britain, Spain, and Portugal, to each other, and to the common enemy, at this crisis; and specifically as affected by the Convention of Cintra* (1809) 1915 edit. prepared by A.V. Dicey p. 8 (see also William Lisle Bowles's poem *The Sorrows of Switzerland* of 1801 and James Montgomery *The Wanderer of Switzerland* of 1806); *Parliamentary History* vol. 36 col. 1404, Wilberforce's speech of 23 May 1803.

Wordsworth, who already in 1802 was writing of Britain and of those

> who find
> In thee a bulwark for the cause of men

by October 1803 thought of the country as

> the only light
> Of liberty that yet remains on earth!

and wrote with would-be prophetic congratulation:

> Shout, for a mighty Victory is won!
> On British ground the Invaders are laid low;
> The breath of Heaven has drifted them like snow,
> And left them lying in the silent sun
> Never to rise again![20]

When after Trafalgar, the threat of a French invasion was removed the war became increasingly accepted as an unattractive, unavoidable but fortunately remote fact of life:

> It is not a boisterous ardour to repel the aggression, or retort the insolence of the enemy, that possesses the British people at present; it is a much more temperate and durable principle; it is a patriotic acquiescence in a state of things which, as far as it relates to foreign affairs, they know they cannot alter ... It is not that they have imbibed a love of war: but that they know very well that peace cannot alter the nature of that man [Napoleon] with whom we have to deal.

As Henry Brougham wrote in *The Edinburgh Review*, 'War has become, from its long duration, almost the natural, certainly the ordinary and habitual, state of the country'.[21]

The general mood of passive acquiescence was briefly interrupted in 1808 by Napoleon's attempt to take over Spain and the subsequent revolt of the Spanish populace: these developments caused a powerful if passing enthusiasm and had briefly the liberating effect of the Russian resistance to Hitler in 1941, more especially amongst those who had opposed the war most bitterly in the 1790s. The Whig poet Thomas Campbell wrote:

> here are my hopes, that what the French Revolution has failed in, the Spanish will achieve; and that we shall hear, in the language of Cervantes, all the great principles of British liberty laid down in the future writings of Spain.

---

[20] A figure of 48 editions of *A View of the Causes and Consequences of the Present War with France* is given in the *Dictionary of National Biography's* article on Erskine and as the British Library Catalogue shows 35 *London* editions for 1797 alone the higher figure is not implausible, but cannot be confirmed. Burdon's pamphlet came out in 1803; William Roscoe's in 1808; Devon County Record Office 152M/C 1801 OM 14; William Wordsworth sonnet 'When I have borne in memory', 1802; Wordsworth sonnet 'One might believe that national miseries', October 1803; Wordsworth sonnet 'Anticipation: October 1803'. (All these sonnets were published in 1807).

[21] *Times* 28 Oct. 1807; *Edinburgh Review* vol. 20 (1812) p. 214–5.

An article in *The Edinburgh Review* expressing the same view in a less romantic form was denounced by one ministerialist M.P. who asserted:

> though we do approve the Spanish Revolution, we have neither felt nor expressed any wish for the radical success of any people against their rulers: and God forbid that we ever should!

But according to Wordsworth, in his famous tract on the Convention of Cintra, the British army sent to the Peninsula was generally seen as engaged on a straightforward mission of liberation:

> that army had been sent upon a service which appealed strongly to all that was human in the heart of this nation ... there was scarcely a gallant father of a family who had not his moments of regret that he was not a soldier by profession, which might have made it his duty to accompany it.

Indeed Wordsworth claimed:

> there is not a man in these Islands, who is not convinced that the cause of Spain is the most righteous cause in which, since the opposition of the Greek Republics to the Persian Invader at Thermopylae and Marathon, sword ever was drawn!

In reality, few took such a high view for long, if at all, and Wordsworth himself confessed in a sonnet 'Composed while the Author was engaged in writing a tract occasioned by the Covention of Cintra' that he chose to

> weigh the hopes and fears of suffering Spain;
> For her consult the auguries of time,

while isolated from his fellow-countrymen

> in dark wood and rocky cave,
> And hollow vale which foaming torrents fill
> With omnipresent murmur, as they rave
> Down their steep beds.[22]

A perhaps more realistic view was that the British government was acting with unashamed cynicism in allying itself with the most reactionary and bigoted elements in Spanish society, for it was generally recognized that

---

[22] William Beattie *Life and Letters of Thomas Campbell* (3 vols 1849) vol. 2 p. 149 Campbell to Mayow 14/15 July 1808; Richard Wharton *Remarks on the Jacobinical Tendency of the Edinburgh Review, in a letter to the Earl of Lonsdale* (1809) p. 13 (the offending *Edinburgh Review* article, probably by Francis Jeffrey is in vol. 13 (1808–9) p. 223–234; the similarity of the French and Spanish revolutions is discussed and denied in Josep Fontana *La Crisis del antiguo régimen, 1808–1833* (Barcelona 1979) p. 18–19); Wordsworth *Tract on the Convention of Cintra* 1915 edit. p. 6; ibid. p. 13–14; Wordsworth sonnet 'Composed when the Author was engaged in writing a tract occasioned by the Convention of Cintra', first published in 1815. Wordsworth's first reaction to the Convention of Cintra had been to organize a County Meeting to vote an address of protest, but this had been vetoed by his patron the Earl of Lonsdale: see Mary Moorman *William Wordsworth: a Biography: the Later Years 1803–1850* (Oxford 1968 edit.) p. 137–8

the Spanish opposition to Napoleon was dominated by an uncompromisingly backward-looking Roman Catholicism of the type that was used to justify the denial of civil rights to Roman Catholics in Ireland. The government which hastened to assist the Spanish rising had in fact fought a general election only a year previously as the champions of anti-Catholicism, so that it seemed as if 'having experienced the efficacy of a cant phrase upon Britons . . . *no popery* is wafted across the sea, to attempt a concordance with *Catholic patriotism*'. The paradoxical relation between British foreign and domestic policy was underlined by the fact that men of Irish refugee origins were prominent in the leadership of the Spanish resistance to Napoleon, as at least one British officer recognized:

> the intolerant religious distinctions of the English Government have deprived us of some of the best blood which the United Kingdom produces; whilst, in unison with the very men thus banished from our service, we have been fighting the battles of foreign Roman Catholics.

In any case the corruption of the *ancien régime* in the Peninsula was painfully evident to the British servicemen who were sent there to defend it. The Spanish regency was seen as maintaining 'that diabolical system by which plunder has been openly licensed, and despotism and injustice towards the people, and even treachery itself, in those of a higher class, have hitherto passed with impunity'. In Portugal it was noted:

> It is melancholy to see so fair a portion of the Globe blessed with the finest climate & the richest soil – producing every thing man can desire – to see such a Country so neglected and by the iron hand of despotism, its Inhabitants so greatly debased.

This particular writer tried to persuade himself that it would be even worse if the French conquered the country:

> it is still more melancholy to reflect how great a chance there is, that it may again fall under the rod of a Barbarian crew, whose aim seems to be to renew the Ages, when Goths and Vandals buried the learning of Ages in the Dust, and established dark Ignorance over a civilised World.

But the logical conclusion was that such countries needed to be not only defended against the French but also liberated from their own corrupt governing classes; and as the war prolonged itself talk of annexation and colonization became increasingly audible.[23]

---

[23] Robert Gourlay *Letter to the Earl of Kellie, concerning the Farmers' Income Tax* (1808) p. 29; Lady Bourchier ed. *Memoir of the Life of Admiral Sir Edward Codrington* (2 vols 1873) vol. 1 p. 216 Edward Codrington to Jane Codrington 25 May 1811; W.F.P. Napier *History of the War in the Peninsula and in the South of France* (6 vols 1828–40) vol. 4 p. 489 Codrington to Henry Wellesley 1 March 1812; British Library Add. 39201 f. 62 journal of Major-General John Randoll Mackenzie 25 Jan. 1809.

VI. Unofficial War Aims

During the 1790s a certain official vagueness as to *why* the war was being fought was inevitably translated into a certain vagueness as to *how* it should be fought. Henry Dundas, the Secretary of State for War and the Colonies, told the House of Commons in 1801:

> be the causes of the war what they may, the primary object ought to be, by what means we can most effectually increase those resources on which depend our naval superiority, and at the same time diminish or appropriate to ourselves those which might otherwise enable the enemy to contend with us in this respect ... I consider offensive operations against the colonial possessions of our enemies as the first object to be attended to in almost every war in which Great Britain can be engaged.

In his confidential correspondence Dundas went even further, insisting that the question of the French Revolution and a satisfactory European settlement had to be strictly subordinated to Britain's own interests:

> if we do not manfully make up our minds to some determinate stand for the preservation of *British interests* involved in this contest, we are playing the part of spendthrift bankrupts, who for the sake of a few years' brilliant *éclat*, have made up their minds to terminate their career by a desperate suicide ... We are drove from necessity into the war from the best and wisest motives, because if we did not then interpose, the frenzy of the principles which reigned in France would have extended itself to this country, and overturned every chance we had of preserving our own constitution. I likewise feel as much as anybody that if, by the continuance of the war and the great exertions we are making for that purpose, we can contribute to the restoration of the French monarchy it is a most desirable event for the future tranquillity of this country and of Europe; but if the consequence of having successfully contributed to do so is to be an abandonment of all those possessions and all that consequent power upon which our future greatness must rest, I beg to wash my hands of such a system.

At the same time there was no interest in the possibility of annexations in Europe, and though Corsica was occupied by British troops from 1794 to 1796 and though the Corsican leaders expressed a wish to adhere to the British Crown, the cabinet were more attracted by the idea of ceding the island to Russia.[24]

At the peace settlement in 1802 the tropical colonies conquered during the 1790s were retained – mainly those taken from the Dutch and Spanish. When the war resumed in 1803 British dominance at sea quickly established an effective British monopoly of colonial produce without the necessity of annexing any more foreign colonies; indeed, once the ports of Europe were barred to British trade even the British colonies produced more than could

---

[24] *Parliamentary History* vol. 35 col. 1072–3, Dundas's speech of 25 March 1801; *HMC Dropmore Mss* vol. 6 p. 38 Dundas to Grenville 24 Nov. 1799; ibid. vol. 3 p. 261 cabinet minute 19 October 1796.

be sold. French (and Dutch) colonies in the West and East Indies came to be seen as significant chiefly in strategic terms, as potential bases for marauding against British trade, and no very high priority was given to invading them. At the same time the establishment of British garrisons in various corners of Europe, and the resulting development of British trade in these areas, gradually encouraged soldiers and travellers to think in terms of annexations nearer home, especially as the local governments were clearly incapable of conducting their own affairs. This was especially the case in Sicily, where the British second-in-command advised London in 1806:

> the possession of Sicily is a most important object, whether as a military post or as a valuable colony . . . nothing short of declaring the island English, and giving to it the advantages of British legislation, will ensure to us a friend in Sicily, or make our tenure in it of any duration.

In July 1809 Sir John Stuart, commanding the British troops in the island, burst out at his dinner table:

> As for the king of the Two Sicilies, [i.e., Sicily and Naples,] his cause is desperate; he has lost one kingdom, and he must lose the other. There is no alternative for England but to take Sicily for herself, or to abandon it altogether.

Captain Charles Pasley, in his influential *Essay on the Military Policy and Institutions of the British Empire* published in 1810, advocated annexing the whole of Italy. Wordsworth, who thought 'the true welfare of Britain is best promoted by the independence, freedom, and honour of other Nations', wrote to Pasley at length deploring his expansionist views, but the latter added further arguments in favour of annexations in later editions of his *Essay*. Some sort of protectorate was also implied in Edward Blaquiere's proposal to separate Sicily from the Neapolitan crown, though under a Catholic prince.[25]

Such views were never officially adopted by the British Cabinet though the Marquess Wellesley, when Foreign Secretary, read Pasley's book and quoted

---

[25] Sir J.F. Maurice ed. *The Diary of Sir John Moore* (2 vols 1904) vol. 2 p. 139–140, Moore to Brownrigg 27 Nov. 1806; Henry Bunbury *Narrative of some Passages in the Great War with France from 1799 to 1810* (1854) p. 378 (and cf. Public Record Office FO 70/94 Lord William Bentinck's despatch of 26 Dec. 1811); Charles Pasley *Essay on the Military Policy and Institutions of the British Empire* (1810) p. 64–8, 167–171 and footnotes on p. 152, 162, cf in later editions footnotes on p. 163 and 177; Ernest de Selincourt, Chester L. Shaver, Mary Moorman, Alan G. Hall ed. *The Letters of William and Dorothy Wordsworth* (7 vols Oxford 1967–1988) vol. 2 p. 478–480 Wordsworth to Pasley 28 March 1811 and cf. Wordsworth *Tract on the Convention of Cintra* 1915 edit. p. 150; E. Blaquiere *Letters from the Mediterranean: containing a Civil and Political Account of Sicily, Tripoly, Tunis, and Malta* (2 vols 1813) vol. 1 p. 650–1. See also letters from anonymous correspondents suggesting annexation in *Morning Post* 14 Aug. 1810 p. 2d (dated Messina 22 June 1810) and in *Anti-Gallican Monitor* vol. 1 no. 13 (21 April 1811) p. 103a (dated Palermo 9 March 1811). The general feebleness of the continental regimes allied to Britain (with special reference to Sicily) had been ventilated in Gould Francis Leckie's *An Historical Survey of the Foreign Affairs of Great Britain with a View to explain the Causes of the Disasters of the late and present Wars* published in 1808.

his ideas on some other topics with evident approval; they were however given wide circulation. John Galt, formerly engaged in foreign trade and later famous as a regional novelist, complained in his *Voyages and Travels* of 1812 of 'that ruinous infirmity of our foreign policy, which has, hitherto, led us to make conquests in war, for the express purpose of afterwards resigning them', and asked:

> By what means are we to receive and embody with our own strength, those innumerable individuals over the continent, who long to embrace and to promote our cause?

For Galt the answer was obvious:

> Only by Great Britain proclaiming her resolution to maintain an insular empire, in opposition to the continental system: to avow, that all the islands over which her jurisdiction has not yet been extended, are only not hers because she has not found it convenient to take possession of them; and that what she does take possession of, she will maintain to the utmost, and consider as integral parts of her empire, never to be ceded by treaty, never to be separated but by the sword.

These blood-curdling views were condemned by Henry Brougham in *The Edinburgh Review* though the passage about 'the ruinous infirmity of our foreign policy' was quoted in the highly laudatory and unusually lengthy four-part review of Galt's book published in *The Gentleman's Magazine*. Obviously the kind of annexationist programme recommended by Galt would hardly have fitted in with the government's policy of continental alliances but it seems probable that the ministers took annexationist propaganda more seriously than the petitions for peace which were being organized by certain anti-government groups during the same period.[26]

In 1806 Viscount Howick, Foreign Secretary in the latter part of the short-lived Ministry of All the Talents, had warned of the dangers of concentrating on purely British interests:

> Whilst we are acquiring colonies, the enemy is subjugating the Continent; and though I am by no means disposed to raise doubts of our ability to maintain the context in this manner, I cannot help fearing the effect of any system which might enable the French, either completely to subdue the remaining Powers of the Continent, or to engage them in opinion against this country. I believe a chief cause of our failure in the last war [i.e., 1793–1801] to have arisen from the want of a sufficient union amongst the members of the Confederacy against

---

[26] For Wellesley and Pasley see below p. 135; John Galt *Voyages and Travels, in the Years 1809, 1810, and 1811; containing Statistical, Commercial, and Miscellaneous Observations on Gibraltar, Sardinia, Sicily, Malta, Serigo, and Turkey* (1812) p. 130; ibid. p. 399 and p. 400; *Edinburgh Review* vol. 23 (1814) p. 41–2, 61–2 (article by Henry Brougham) and cf. *Gentleman's Magazine* espec. vol. 82 (1812) p. 253; John Rosselli *Lord William Bentinck & the British Occupation of Sicily, 1811–1814* (Cambridge 1956) p. 128–135; Antonio Capograssi *Gli Inglesi in Italia durante le campagne napoleoniche* (Bari 1949) p. 172–3.

France; and we shall be again in danger of incurring the same evil, if, whilst our allies are calling upon us for assistance, we shall appear to be pursuing separate objects of our own.

This turned out, in fact, to be precisely what happened: but as the war prolonged itself and almost the whole of Europe became organized under Napoleon against Britain and relations with the U.S. deteriorated, an increasingly vocal part of public opinion insisted that it simply did not care what foreigners thought anyway:

> She [France] says, 'England shall have no intercourse with any part of the Continent' – We must reply, 'No other power shall have any intercourse with the Continent' – The sea is ours, and we must maintain the doctrine – that no nation, no fleet, no cock-boat shall sail upon it without our permission. America declares that England must not presume to declare a port in a state of blockade, unless she can keep a force actually before that Port. England must reply, we will not condescend to mince and carve out and dwindle down our system of blockade. There is but one Navy in the world, the British Navy.

By the time these words were published – in a leading ministerialist newspaper – Britain had already captured most of France's and the Netherlands' colonies, had established a protectorate over Spain, Portugal, Sicily and those of Denmark's colonies which had not been occupied and had established a line of bases in the Western Mediterranean – Gibraltar, Minorca, Sicily, Malta, the southern Ionian Islands – which bulged menacingly towards Italy. There was, consequently, a certain disingenuousness in John Galt's complaint,

> that we are treated as an outcast from the community of nations; that our laws and usages are held to be obnoxious to the new order of things; that our efforts to maintain our independence, and to avenge the insults we have received from our old, hereditary, and particular foe, are represented by the subjugated, degraded, and, now, nominal princes of Europe, as measures inconsistent with their prosperity; and that every modification of our industry and intelligence, even justice and self-defence, are held to be pernicious to the welfare of the ruling few, and, as such, the means of the subjected many are exerted to destroy them.[27]

Contempt for foreigners even extended to a dismissal of the fundamental principles of international law:

> It cannot be too frequently repeated, that you must not suffer any of your measures to be restrained by the smallest regard to the former public code: the enemy, and his puppets, will cause it to parade in apparition before you, as if it were yet in existence; but you must only regard it as the bug-a-boo, which crafty younkers conjure up to teaze their unhacknied comrades out of their toys.

---

[27] C. Grey *Some Account of the Life and Opinions of Charles second Earl Grey* London 1861 p. 135, memo autumn 1806; *Courier* 21 Jan. 1811 (*The Courier* was the daily newspaper with the largest circulation at this time, and the one most closely identified with the government); John Galt *Voyages and Travels* p. 401.

Accordingly the British Admiralty Courts cited French violations of 'the genuine principles of maritime law' to justify such peculiar legal decisions as the charging a neutral American ship salvage after it had been captured by British vessels while in French custody, it being explained:

> France has fulminated her decrees against the commerce of the whole world, and has even compelled this country, defensively, to have resort to measures, which abstractedly and originally, would be unjust in the highest degree.

Only occasionally did British officials see the tendency of British policy to resemble that of Napoleon in certain key respects: thus the policy of the Marquis of Hastings as Governor General in India was compared to Napoleon's Continental System, in a confidential memorandum written shortly after Waterloo but not published till 1853:

> The ostensible object was to organise the great family of nations, and to promote universal peace and harmony; but the plan necessarily involved the sacrifice of national independence, and, although it seemed to embrace a multitude of arrangements, it was perfectly simple in its own nature, and reducible to one single proposition – the establishment of the well-meant despotism of a powerful state over all its weaker neighbours.

But at this stage at least the oft-celebrated principles of the British Constitution were not for export; Britain's freedom was nothing if not 'an inheritance guaranteed to her by the blood of her victorious sons, and sanctioned by the tacit confession of millions of terror-stricken foes!'[28]

In reality Britain's foes were less given to tacit confession than to extremely vocal accusation. Their complaints cannot however be understood without some reference to the economic background, for it was Britain's economic position relative to other countries in the 1790s and 1800s which determined much of the foreign policy both of Britain and of the other European governments.

---

[28] *The War as it is, and the War as it Should be; an Address to the United Administration, urging the necessity of a New Species of Warfare, and a new basis for a Treaty of Peace. By a true Englishman* (1806) p. 29, Thomas Edwards *Reports of Cases Argued and Determined in the High Court of Admiralty, commencing with the Judgments of the Right Hon. Sir William Scott, Easter Term 1808* ed. George Minot (Boston 1853) para. 255, *Acteon* case 24 July 1810 (Sir William Scott's younger brother was, incidentally, Lord Chancellor and a key figure in the Cabinet); Henry St. George Tucker *Memorials of Indian Government* ed. John William Kaye (1853) p. 233–4; William Harvey *Hours of Loyalty: or, Allegorical Political Delineations in Rhyme* (1813) p. vi.

2

The Industrial Revolution at War

He would have liked to give him some explanation involving the terms circulating-medium, currency, depreciation of currency, paper, bullion, rates of exchange, value of precious metals in the market, and so forth; but looking down at the little chair, and seeing what a long way down it was, he answered: 'Gold and silver and copper. Guineas, shillings, half-pence – You know what they are?'

Charles Dickens *Dombey and Son* (1847–1848) Chap. 8.

I. Assessing Britain's Wartime Economy

The economic power which Britain mobilized for war between 1793 and 1815 was minuscule compared to the effort of 1914–1918, let alone of 1939–1945, and as it was a world war fought with a technology of wood and leather the role of industrial output was less central. Yet except for population the British government was able to marshal economic resources far greater than those mobilized for any previous war. *The Edinburgh Review* boasted in 1807:

all our establishments are upon a scale infinitely more extensive than was ever exemplified before among such a number of people. We have a navy suitable to a population of fifty millions; and a debt, revenue, and colonial establishment greater than would belong elsewhere to an hundred million.

The war precisely coincided with the emergence of Britain as the dominant industrial power in the world; as Malthus wrote:

in no twenty-two years of our history of which we have authentic accounts has there ever been so rapid an increase of production and consumption, both in respect of quality and value, as in the twenty-two years ending with 1814.

Presumably, therefore, the way in which British economic resources were harnessed to the war effort must have had some relation to the whole process of economic development in this period.[1]

It is the extent of Britain's economic mobilization between 1793 and 1815 which makes these years a forerunner of the total warfare of the twentieth century but much of the data which historians of twentieth-century economies

[1] *Edinburgh Review* vol. 10 (1807) p. 418; *Quarterly Review* vol. 29 (1823) p. 229 for Malthus's view.

would rely on to establish a coherent view of an economic system was simply not recorded in the 1790s and 1800s. And while statistics for Britain in these years are patchy and inadequate for other countries they are all but non-existent, so that a full understanding of how far Britain differed from contemporary norms is virtually impossible.

The tendency in recent years has been for economic historians to emphasize the slackening, or at least the sluggishness, of British economic growth in this period, but early nineteenth-century commentators were almost unanimous in celebrating Britain's flourishing state during the war years. 'War, accounted in former days a season of embarrassment and poverty, assumed in the present age, the appearance of a period of prosperity', Viscount Hamilton told the House of Commons in 1808. Three years later the Earl of Rosse wrote:

> We cannot expect to carry on war without encountering some difficulties, and incurring heavy expense. But never did this country, after all, carry on a war in which it suffered so few privations.

Middle-class analysts were of the same opinion regarding 'that wonderful extension of commerce and manufactures . . . which, contrary to all former example, continued to swell as the war was protracted'. Thomas Telford, the great bridge and canal builder, did not believe, even in 1799, that 'any spot of the Earth, of equal dimensions, ever exceeded what Great Britain is now, I mean with regard to Wealth & the useful Arts'. David Ricardo's verdict was:

> Notwithstanding the immense expenditure of the English government during the last twenty years, there can be little doubt but that the increased production on the part of the people has more than compensated for it.

Of course the working classes, subject to spiralling food prices and to bouts of underemployment and unemployment arising from structural changes in the economy, must often have had a less rosy view but it was in the nature of Britain's capitalist system, then as subsequently, that it did not operate on the basis of distributing its benefits equitably; indeed one commentator noted sourly:

> There never yet was a crisis, when, in the commercial world, the march of avarice was so rapid, or its devastations so extensive upon the morals and well being of society.

But even this may be taken as indicating conditions of Thatcherite boom rather than of contraction.[2]

[2] For modern econometric studies see Glenn Hueckel 'War and the British Economy, 1793–1815: A General Equilibrium Analysis' *Explorations in Economic History* vol. 10 (1972–3) p. 365–396; Joel Mokyr and N. Eugene Savin 'Stagflation in Historical Perspective: The Napoleonic Wars Revisited' in Paul Uselding ed. *Research in Economic History* (Greenwich Connecticut 1976–) vol. 1 p. 198–259; C. Knick Harley 'British Industrialisation before 1841: Evidence of Slower Growth during the Industrial Revolution' *Journal of Economic History* 42 (1982) p. 267–289 (see especially p. 285 for Harley's 'reasonable conjectures about demand
continued

II. Population and Wealth: Some International Comparisons

Britain in the 1800s was of course a hugely unequal society in economic terms but it seems to have been considerably less unequal than other European countries. This relative social equality is one of the most important factors to be borne in mind when comparing Britain with the other economic systems of the Napoleonic period.

In terms of population Britain – from 1800 officially the United Kingdom – ranked fourth amongst the state systems of Europe. As the British census was not extended to Ireland it is uncertain even how big the United Kingdom population was, but it was probably about fifteen million in 1801. France's population has been calculated at 27,349,631 in 1801, plus 6.5 million inhabitants of territories annexed before 1803 such as the Austrian Netherlands, Liège, Namur, Savoy, Nice, Geneva, Piedmont, Elba and the Rhineland. The Russian population, dispersed of course over a very large area with inadequate communications, was not only larger than France's but growing very rapidly; Alexis Eustaphieve estimated it as 37 million in 1795 and 46 million in 1811. The territories of the Austrian Habsburgs *circa* 1800 were variously calculated at 19,439,300 or just under 25 million. Spain, not counting the South American colonies, had a population of 10,541,000 in 1797; Prussia 9,580,000. The next two most important German states after Austria and Prussia were Bavaria and Saxony each with under two million inhabitants. Sweden and Denmark-Norway both had populations under three million; the Kingdom of the Two Sicilies (southern Italy and the island of Sicily) ranked as the seventh most populous European state with just under six million.[3]

continued

growth'); Jeffrey G. Williamson 'Why Was British Growth So Slow during the Industrial Revolution?' *Journal of Economic History* 44 (1984) p. 687–712 (see especially p. 708–712 for a classic statement of the case – such as it is – for seeing the war as a retarding influence); N.F.R. Crafts *Economic Growth during the Industrial Revolution* (Oxford 1985) espec. p. 9–47. These studies tend to undervalue the significance of growth rates of under 3 per cent per annum in an economy with much lower levels of overall consumption than are characteristic of European economies today, and are prone to make up for the deficiencies of the statistics by an over-reliance on the fancy algebra of modern economic analysis. See also the 103-page introduction to the 1987 edition of François Crouzet *L'Économie Britannique et le Blocus Continental*. For contemporary opinion see *Parliamentary Debates* vol. 10 col. 38 (Viscount Hamilton's speech 21 Jan. 1808); Earl of Rosse *Observations on the Present State of the Currency of England* (1811) p. 75; William Forbes *Memoirs of a Banking-House* (1860) p. 86; Sir Alexander Gibb *The Story of Telford: the Rise of Civil Engineering* (1935) p. 58 Telford to Andrew Little 13 July 1799; David Ricardo *On the Principles of Political Economy and Taxation* (1817) p. 188; John Brown *Memoir of Robert Blincoe* (Manchester 1832) p. 36.

[3] Charles H. Pouthas *La Population Française pendant la première moitié du xixe siècle* (Paris 1956) p. 22 and Jacques Peuchet *Statistique Élémentaire de la France* (Paris 1805) p. 228; Alexis Eustaphieve (i.e. A. Eustaf'ev) *The Resources of Russia, in the Event of a War with France* (1812) p. 6 and cf. Henri Storch (i.e. Heinrich Friedrich von Storch) *Tableau Historique et Statistique de l'Empire de Russe à la fin du dix-huitième siècle* (Basel 1801) p. 252; J.G. Boetticher *A Geographical, Historical and Political Description of the Empire of Germany* . . .

continued

London in 1801 was only just beginning to spread north of Oxford Street, and places like Islington, Canonbury, Newington Green, Stoke Newington, or Tottenham were still villages linked to the metropolis by coach routes running between open fields; but with a population of over 800,000 it was already easily the largest city in Europe. Apart from the unique phenomenon of London, Britain was not more urbanized than other countries; Paris (547,000 inhabitants), Naples (400,000 inhabitants), Vienna (231,000 inhabitants), Rome (163,000 inhabitants), Berlin (153,128 inhabitants), Madrid (140,000 inhabitants), even Marseilles (111,130 inhabitants) and Lyon (109,500), were considerably larger than any British provincial city; Birmingham, Edinburgh, Manchester and Liverpool were comparable in size with third-rank European centres like Bordeaux, Rouen, Nantes, Bologna, Warsaw, Breslau, Königsberg and Danzig.[4]

While the economic structure of Ireland, Wales and upland Scotland resembled that of not particularly advanced districts on the continent, visitors to England were struck by the appearance of a much greater degree of middle-class affluence than was to be found elsewhere:

> There are in other countries as many servants kept in some houses; but the number of families who keep one or more men-servants is far greater here than in any other country.

The relatively wide distribution of wealth in England is confirmed by tax statistics. In France – after Britain the wealthiest country in Europe – the 600 or so most important tax-payers in each *département* were inscribed as *notables*: there were 66,735 in 1810. The average income of *notables* obviously varied from *département* to *département*; examination of the records of five *départements* outside Paris show that 72.5 per cent of *notables* in these *départements* had incomes under 5,000 francs (£200). On this basis it would be a generous estimate to suppose there were more than 25,000 French taxpayers with incomes over 5,000 francs (£200). The richest individual taxpayer was the Duc de Choiseul–Praslin with an income of at least 320,000 francs (about £13,000). It seems in addition that there were 165 individuals with incomes over £1,600 and 19 with incomes over £3,200. In 1801, in a tax assessment which if anything tended to underestimate incomes, 26,366 persons in England were

continued
to which are added Statistical Tables exhibiting a view of all the States of Europe (1800) p. 34 of *Statistical Tables* for population of Habsburg territories (and cf Storch p. 252) and p. 10, 14–15, 62 of *Statistical Tables* for population of the smaller states; B.R. Mitchell *European Historical Statistics 1750–1975* (1981) p. 33 for the population of Spain; Leopold Krug *Betrachtungen über den National-Reichthum des preussischen Staats, und über den Wohlstand seiner Bewohner* (2 vols Berlin 1805) vol. 1 p. 224 for population of Prussia.

[4] British census figures; figures in Pouthas *Population Française*, p. 98 for population of French cities; Harry Hearder *Italy in the Age of the Risorgimento 1790–1870* (1983) p. 96 for population of Rome and Bologna, p. 125–6 for that of Naples; *Encyclopaedia Britannica* 3rd edit. for population of Madrid, 11th edit. for population of Vienna; Leopold Krug, vol. 2 p. 62 for population of Prussian cities.

reported as having incomes over £500, and a further 42,694 with incomes over £200. One thousand and twenty persons were assessed as having incomes over £5,000, the average being £9,775 each; a further 3,657 had incomes between £2,000 and £5,000. Thus:

	France (c. 1810)	England (1801)
Incomes over £200	25,000	69,060
Incomes of at least £1,600	165	–
Incomes £2–5,000	–	3,657
Incomes of at least £3,200	19	–
Incomes over £5,000	1?	1,020

And France of course had more than three times the population of the English part of the United Kingdom.[5]

III. The Evidence of Tax Statistics

The much greater wealth of the English tax-payer needs to be taken into consideration when assessing claims that the tax-burden in Britain was three times higher than it was in France; at any rate there is no clear evidence that the burden of war-time taxation had an effect in damping down or undermining British economic growth. Nevertheless tax statistics, together with foreign trade statistics derived from the levying of customs dues, do provide the chief body of evidence for supposing that the British economy virtually stagnated during the war years, and therefore require closer examination.[6]

[5] Louis Simond *Journal of a Tour and Residence in Great Britain during the Years 1810 and 1811* (2 vols Edinburgh 1817) vol. 2 p. 185; D.M.G. Sutherland *France 1789–1815: Revolution and Counterrevolution* (1985) p. 385–6 for *notables* generally; Guy Chaussinand-Nogaret, Louis Bergeron, Robert Forster 'Les Notables du "Grande Empire" en 1810' *Annales: Economies Sociétés Civilisations* vol. 26 (1971) p. 1052–1075 at p. 1069 for the analysis of the *notables* of five *départements*; Albert Soboul 'La Grande Propriété Foncière à l'Epoque Napolénienne' *Annales de la Révolution Française* vol. 53 (1981) p. 405–418 at p. 406 for the richest individual tax-payers, and Marcel Marion *Histoire Financière de la France depuis 1715* (6 vols Paris 1927–31) vol. 2 p. 323 for the system of assessment; *Parliamentary Papers* 1852 IX p. 964, and cf. *Parliamentary Papers* 1814–15 X p. 106–7, which give a breakdown of the amounts paid by different income groups in 1812, but only for Schedule D (profits of trade and industry) and without giving the number of the taxpayers, which can only be estimated approximately from the amounts paid in each income group: in the City of London alone there were at least 800 Schedule D taxpayers with incomes over £1,500, the average being nearly £5,000 each.

[6] Peter Mathias and Patrick O'Brien 'Taxation in Britian and France 1715–1810: A Comparison of the Social and Economic Incidence of Taxes collected for the Central Governments' *Journal of Economic History* 5 (1976) p. 601–650 at p. 618, 620 tables 7 and 8 gives, in terms of the price of a hectolitre of wheat, British tax levels as three times those of France. But wheat was nearly twice as expensive in Britain as in France, and a much larger proportion of the population lived well above subsistence level (i.e. did not spend most of their income on food) so the utility of calculations in terms of the price of wheat is debatable.

The statistics for international trade, whether 'real' or 'official' values, need to be treated with care; they indicate a good deal of annual fluctuation but the longer-term picture is merely of a slackening in previously high rates of growth. Unfortunately it is not known how large a component of Gross National Product was represented by foreign trade either in 1793 or in 1815, or even what proportion of industrial manufactures were exported at any given time. In 1810 exports and imports of unwrought iron were both at about 20,000 tons a year, whereas total output (and domestic consumption) was about 400,000 tons, suggesting that in the iron industry foreign trade represented only about 5 per cent of total output and consumption, but it is generally assumed that the percentage exported was much higher in other manufacturing industries; on the other hand there is no reason to assume that the percentages remained stable between 1793 and 1815, especially since the foreign trade sector of most European economies was in a state of collapse during the war. Since it seems therefore that foreign trade cannot be taken as an index for overall economic performance, the statistics for domestic taxation take on a special importance.[7]

The Property Tax assessments show overall growth, but assessments under Schedule D, of the profits of trade, industry and professions, show no growth; rather, taking into consideration an annual rate of inflation of 3.3 per cent they show a steady dwindling; and in Lancashire, the pace-setter of the factory movement, the drop between 1803 and 1812 seems catastrophic; £2,240,347 assessed profits from trade, industry and professions in 1803, only £1,583,731 in 1812. These figures certainly bear out the most pessimistic interpretation of the effects of the war; it seems more likely however that they are the result of progressive underassessment.[8]

The Property Tax assessments suffered very considerably from an amateur bureaucracy inexperienced in handling a survey of unprecedented scope and detail. In 1801 one of the first assessments for what was then a new tax listed only 320,759 persons; in 1803 the figure was 1,246,116 and the number assessed and subsequently exempted on the grounds of low income varied from 8.7 per cent of the county total in Surrey to 49.2 per cent in Huntingdonshire, and in Wales from 2.2 per cent in Caernarvonshire to 61.8 per cent in neighbouring Merionethshire and 70.9 per cent in Radnorshire. Dr. Henry Beeke, Regius Professor of Modern History at Oxford, author of *Observations on the Produce of the Income Tax and its proportion to the whole Income of Great Britain* (1799) and an adviser to the Addington ministry on fiscal matters, wrote of the 1803 assessment:

[7] B.R. Mitchell and Phyllis Deane *Abstract of British Historical Statistics* (Cambridge 1962) p. 281–2; cf ibid. p. 275–6 for a brief discussion of the 'official' statistics and subsequent estimates; Science Museum Library Ms 371/4 f.222 (Weale Mss) manuscript Custom House return of iron imports and exports.

[8] *Parliamentary Papers* 1812–13 XII p. 305 and 1814–15 X p. 90, cf. P.K. O'Brien 'Government Revenue, 1793–1815: A Study in Fiscal and Financial Policy in the Wars against France' (unpublished Oxford D.Phil 1967) p. 242.

The returns seem to indicate that in a few Districts they have charged almost every thing come-at-able, & that in a few others the Surveyors have returned what they suppose will be the net Produce.

With regard to Schedule D, Beeke suggested:

almost every where (excepting in & near the Metropolis) the smaller trading & manufacturing Incomes must have been *totally omitted*. The Commercial Incomes of the Metropolis . . . will amount to near *twelve millions*, while *in all the rest of England & Wales* there will be no more than about sixteen millions. The latter, if all petty Retailers were included, and the Assessments had been made with equal Strictness, must have amounted to a good deal more.

My opinion was that the Metropolis would return *one fourth* part of Schedule D if every where was assessed with equal accuracy.

Analysis of later Schedule D assessments broken down by income and by county do not in fact bear out Beeke's surmise, and it is probable that he had been led astray by the notoriously erratic figures in the 1801 population census for 'Persons chiefly employed in Trade Manufactures and Handicrafts'; the number of persons assessed under Schedule D was equal in Middlesex to 31.2 per cent of those shown in the 1801 census as 'employed in Trade Manufactures and Handicrafts', but in Staffordshire and Warwickshire only 4.4 per cent and in Cheshire and Lancashire only 3.5 per cent. Nevertheless Beeke was obviously correct in supposing there was a problem with the technicalities of assessment, though the 1803 assessment was probably more accurate than later ones made when the public had had more time to perfect methods of tax evasion.[9]

The new industrial communities of the 1800s still did not have extended service sectors as in the older established provincial centres, but though large-scale employers were already common in the cotton spinning industry, weaving was only just beginning to move over from being a family business, and small workshops were still the rule in the metal goods centres, Sheffield, Birmingham and the Black Country. It is clear that there must have been many more Schedule D incomes in these areas than appeared in the assessments. In Warwickshire for example, still in tax terms a predominantly agricultural county, there were only about 4,000 schedule D taxpayers whose total property was assessed at less than £600,000. A comparison with neighbouring, less industrialized, counties suggests that two-thirds of the Schedule D assessments in Warwickshire can be attributed to the professions, trades and local industries servicing the county's agricultural sector; the remaining third, which can be attributed to the booming manufacturing industries of Birmingham and Coventry, represents less value than the profits from the ownership of houses and ironworks in the county. Though Birmingham and

[9] *Parliamentary Papers* 1812–13 XII p. 249; British Library Add 31229 f. 69 Henry Beeke to Nicholas Vansittart 6 April 1804; Add. 31229 f. 75 Beeke to Vansittart 10 May 1804; *Parliamentary Papers* 1802 VII p. 451 and 1812–13 XII p. 244.

Coventry had a combined population of 109,540 in 1811, not more than nine individuals accounted for a fourteenth of the total Schedule D assessments for Warwickshire, and at an average of under £5,000 a year even these nine were not outstandingly rich. These figures seem to confirm the view later put forward that by 1811 evasion of tax under Schedule D resulted in the concealment of 50 per cent of actual income; and it seems probable that the newer and more rapidly growing the industrial enterprise, the greater the likelihood of evading taxes.[10]

While Schedule D figures indicate stagnation or recession, certain other statistics suggest the complete opposite. Original net income of the Post Office (subject to certain deductions only) trebled during the war years – £445,632 in 1794, £1,328,266 in 1812. Revenue from newspaper stamps rose from £144,940 in 1797 to £304,962 in 1814. Revenue from Hawkers' Licences doubled in ten years, from £8,963 in 1800 to £17,898 in 1810. The duty on Fire Insurance premiums, at 2s. 6d. per £100 raised £321,154 in 1805 and £486,540 in 1814 – an increase of more than 50 per cent in ten years. House building, which had been in recession in the 1790s, boomed 1800–1813 and despite the increase of population the average number of inhabitants per house fell by 10 per cent or more in some industrial centres. There was also a massive investment in town improvements, new roads and other public works: there were 750 private Acts of Parliament to facilitate such projects 1785–1792 and 1,414 in 1801–1808, and the Clerk of the House of Commons unhesitatingly attributed the increase to 'the superaccretion of wealth'. Total expenditure on bridges by county authorities was £41,000 in 1793 and £46,000 in 1800, both normal levels for the period, but £130,000 in 1813.[11]

Some classic canal building was in progress during the war years. The aquaduct on the Ellesmere Canal at Pont Cysyllte, built by Thomas Telford between 1795 and 1805, cost only £47,018 6s. 7d. but with a waterway just under twelve feet wide carried on an iron trough 1,007 feet across the River Dee on twenty-one arches at a height of 127 feet above the river, and approached by what was at the time the largest earth embankment ever constructed, it was one of the great wonders of the world. Sir Walter Scott described it as 'the most impressive work of art he had ever seen', and it later inspired Wordsworth's lines

[10] For Schedule D assessments 1812 see *Parliamentary Papers* 1814–15 X p. 104–7; for evasion of tax under Schedule D see Phyllis Deane and W.A. Cole *British Economic Growth, 1688–1959: Trends and Structures* (Cambridge 1967) p. 328; P.K. O'Brien 'British Incomes and Property in the Early Nineteenth Century' *Economic History Review* 2nd series vol. 12 (1959) p. 255–267 at p. 261; *Parliamentary Papers* 1852 IX p. 180.

[11] *Parliamentary Papers* 1812–13 IV p. 938; 1826–7 XVII p. 24; 1844 XXXII p. 377; 1857 iv p. 213; C.W. Chalklin *The Provincial Towns of Georgian England* (1974) p. 285, 338–340; George Chalmers *Comparative View of the State of Great Britain and Ireland, as it was, before the War: as it is, since the Peace* (1817) p. 38; HMC *Dropmore Mss* vol. 10 p. 121 Lord Auckland to Lord Grenville 11 Feb. 1811; B.R. Mitchell and Phyllis Deane *Abstract of British Historical Statistics* (Cambridge 1962) p. 411.

> Nature doth embrace
> Her lawful offspring in Man's art; and Time,
> Pleased with your triumphs o'er his brother Space
> Accepts from your bold hands the preferred crown.

The Caledonian Canal, built by Telford through the Great Glen, was not completed till 1823 but it had originally been surveyed in 1801, at a time when the Armed Neutrality seemed to threaten the coasting trade of north-eastern Scotland. Telford, who may be considered as supreme amongst those whose creative talents were liberated by the challenge of the new industrial era, was by no means averse to seeing the parallel between his engineering work and the world conflict:

> My uninterrupted 30 Years Warfare seems still distant from termination. Since we parted I have travelled upwards of 2,000 Miles, Inspected the northern Roads, Bridges & Canal, examined the Harbours of Peterhead and Aberdeen, set agoing an extensive New Harbour at Dundee, arranged a Plan for a New Road between Glasgow and Carlisle, and am now preparing to proceed with vigour upon the improvement of the Communication between England and Ireland by the route of North Wales. This is my mode of subjugating Kingdoms.

Apart from Telford's work at Dundee, a new dock was built at Hull, a graving dock (for cleaning ships' bottoms) was opened on the Tyne in March 1804, and there was also a massive extension of the dock facilities at London, already the greatest port in the world: the West India, Brunswick, London, East India, Commercial and Rotherhithe docks were all opened between 1802 and 1813. There was also an attempt to build a tunnel under the Thames at Limehouse. George Chalmers, one of the most perceptive commentators of the period, wrote:

> The active spirit of domestic melioration, which existed before the war began, continued, with augmented energy, during the progress of hostilities. The world will contemplate this enterprize with wonder. Millions and tens of millions, have been raised upon the people, for carrying on an interesting war, yet they found the money, as they had the skill, and industry, to improve their island.[12]

It is impossible to estimate industrial investment in this period, but figures for the cotton industry suggest a near tripling of capacity between the mid

---

[12] John Rickman ed. *The Life of Thomas Telford, Civil Engineer, written by himself* (1838) p. 41–5; cf. Samuel Smiles *The Life of Thomas Telford, Civil Engineer* (1867) p. 159 for Scott's remark; Wordsworth's sonnet 'Steamboats, Viaducts, and Railways', no. XLII of 'Poems Composed or Suggested during a Tour in 1833'; British Library Add. 41963 f. 197 Telford to Charles Pasley 6 Sept. 1815; John Sykes *Local Records; or Historical Register of Remarkable Events which have occurred in Northumberland and Durham, Newcastle upon Tyne, and Berwick upon Tweed* (2 vols Newcastle 1833) vol. 2 p. 19–20; Walter M. Stern 'The First London Dock Boom and the Growth of the West India Dock's' *Economica* n.s. 19 (1952) p. 59–77; George Chalmers *An Estimate of the Comparative Strength of Great Britain* (1802) p. 311 – the reference is to the French Revolutionary War of 1793–1802 but is in fact even more applicable to the Napoleonic War which followed.

1790s and 1813. Iron and steel manufacturing capacity is estimated to have nearly quadrupled during the war. Much of this involved the ploughing back of profits, but the great industrialists were also investing elsewhere. The first Sir Robert Peel had, by 1796, spent £15,000 on a stake in the pocket borough of Tamworth, and £100,000 on a landed estate in Staffordshire; John Horrocks evidently spent heavily on establishing his political power base in Preston; Matthew Boulton employed the fashionable architects James and Samuel Wyatt to enlarge his entrepreneurial palace at Handsworth, Birmingham; the Crawshay family of Cyfartha acquired a property in North London now known as Clissold Park (Richard Crawshay's grand-daughter Elisa later married the local curate, Angustus Clissold, from whom the present name derives). None of this suggests recession in Britain's manufacturing industries.[13]

Separate fragments of information can provide an impression; but the missing fragments might have suggested exactly the contrary picture. There are two clusters of information which appertain to the country as a whole and which can only be interpreted as demonstrating growth. First, there was a massive increase in the money supply. In 1797 the Bank of England was instructed by the Pitt government to cease honouring bank-notes with cash. There were at the time £9,531,330 worth of Bank of England notes in circulation, and, it is estimated, £22.5 million in gold. By August 1815 there were over £27 million of Bank of England notes in circulation, while country bank-notes circulating mainly in the general neighbourhood of the issuing bank had exceeded £14 million even in 1809. (The largest denomination notes issued were of £1,000 but prior to 1812 the Bank of England also produced a number of the legendary £1,000,000 notes for internal accounting purposes). In addition coin did not entirely disappear, though it fell below £10 million; coining or uttering false coins remained a rather more common crime than forging banknotes. In the period 1812–1815 there were 212 convictions for offences involving forged notes and 621 for offences involving false money. South American dollars, valued at 4s-9d., were issued with a miniature head of George III on the head of the Spanish king. ('The Bank of England, to make their dollars pass/stamped the head of a fool on the neck of an ass') but unstamped dollars were also accepted as current and there was no check on the quantity of silver in circulation. The South American dollars were called in during 1804 and completely overstruck (the obverse of this new issue shows Britannia with FIVE SHILLINGS above and DOLLAR below) but foreign coins continued to circulate freely. It is probable therefore that the face value of money in circulation almost doubled between 1797 and 1815. Even with 3.3

13 Deane and Cole *British Economic Growth, 1688–1959* p. 185, cf. Science Museum Library Ms 371/1 f. 92 and f. 103–4 (Weale Mss) and Philip Riden 'The Output of the British Iron Industry before 1870', *Economic History Review* 2nd series 30 (1977) p. 442–459, at p. 450; A.D. Harvey *Britain in the Early Nineteenth Century* (1978) p. 32–3; Norman Gash *Mr. Secretary Peel: The Life of Sir Robert Peel to 1830* (1961) p. 15–17.

per cent per annum inflation this was a substantial net increase; moreover there were those who thought 'the rapidity of circulation has increased much more than the amount of currency'.[14]

At the same time, even allowing for inflation, there was a steady rise in the profits from the ownership and exploitation of land: approximately 50 per cent in money and 10 per cent in real terms 1803–1812. Except in Lancashire, Middlesex and Surrey, farming was still the dominant economic activity, according to the tax statistics at least. Something must have happened to these additional agricultural profits. Some of the money trickled, via the country banks, into government loans to finance the war; some of it of course went on war taxes. Some if it went on a perhaps unduly lavish investment in enclosures and drainage, for this period of high agricultural incomes was naturally enough also a period of massive investment and, it was afterwards alleged, 'cultivation was carried to the utmost border of profit, to the very verge of loss'. Some of the additional income went on playing guinea whist and mixing brandy with the wine, as the Earl of Warwick complained in 1800. But enclosures meant labourers' wages; whist and wine-with-brandy meant profits for market town card-sharpers and wine merchants. At any rate the money was recirculated in the economy. Assuredly it was not hoarded: because of the suspension of cash payments it was difficult to acquire specie to hoard. And if the money was spent, the spending must have created more employment, more incomes, more demand. The recession in the manufacturing sector indicated by the Schedule D assessments is not only controverted by the fragmentary statistical material available relating to trade and industry, but is also incompatible with the evidence of the Schedule A and B assessments showing the profits from the ownership and exploitation of land.[15]

It seems domestic consumption increased very considerably during the war

[14] *Parliamentary Papers* 1821 XVI p. 177 for the quantity of banknotes in 1797 and in 1815, and Thomas Tooke *A History of Prices and the State of the Circulation from 1793 to 1837* (6 vols 1839–57) vol 1 p. 245 for estimates of the quantity of gold; L.S. Pressnell *Country Banking in the Industrial Revolution* (Oxford 1956) p. 153; Jasper Atkinson *A Letter to a Member of Parliament occasioned by the publication of the Report of the Select Committee on the High Price of Gold Bullion* (1810) p. 94; *Parliamentary Papers* 1816 XIII p. 301, 1818 XVI p. 161. C.R. Josset *Money in Great Britain and Ireland* (Newton Abbot 1971) p. 166, 198. In 1830 the Duke of Wellington stated in the House of Lords that 'the largest sum ever known to be in circulation during the Bank Restriction' was £30 million in Bank of England notes, £23 million in country bank notes, 4 million in gold and 11 million in silver (*Parliamentary Debates* n.s. vol. 22 col. 39 4 Feb. 1830) but this seems to have been an *ex parte* calculation some time after the period referred to. At least one professional gang both counterfeited coins and forged Bank of England notes: see the interesting account in *The Trial at Large, of William Booth, and his Associates . . . at the Stafford Summer Assizes, 1812* (Wolverhampton 1812).

[15] *Parliamentary Papers* 1812–13 XII p. 305 and 1814–15 X 90 and 96 for tax assessments under Schedules A and B, using P.K. O'Brien's estimate of 3.3 per cent per annum inflation in 'Government Revenue, 1793–1815' p. 242; Sir Edward West *Price of Corn and Wages of Labour: with observations upon Dr. Smith's, Mr. Ricardo's, and Mr. Malthus's doctrines upon those subjects* (1826) p. 107; *Parliamentary History* vol. 35 col. 834 (intervention of Earl of Warwick 17 Nov. 1800).

years. It has been calculated that inland carriers based in London moved 135,996 ton miles in 1796 and 275,356 ton miles in 1816. Coastal trade also expanded enormously. There are no returns for the number of coasting vessels between 1791 and 1823 but in 1790 there were 332,962 tons of coastal shipping and in 1824 833,416; this represented 25.6 per cent of total registered shipping in 1790 and 35.9 per cent in 1824, confirming the view that domestic expansion was more rapid than the increase in foreign trade.[16]

IV. Industrialization and Boom

Contemporary commentators were generally convinced that the war promoted an economic boom. Whereas the last years of peace were 'marked by the symptoms common to an era of tranquillity – complaints of overstock in the genteel professions, and of inadequate payment in almost all of an humbler description', this situation 'was entirely altered by the war'. According to Joseph Lowe,

> the army, the navy, the public offices of government opened a career to numbers of every class, and by absorbing a very large proportion of the candidates for employment, created a corresponding briskness in agriculture, trade, and professions.

It was pointed out that 'this is precisely what is effected by the increased expenditure of government: a new and immense market is at once opened for consumption', and that 'the expenditure of government, through its various channels and subordinate agents, has occasioned a demand for almost every species of produce'. Robert Owen, capitalist, social theorist and philanthropist, even attributed the spread of industrial technology to wartime conditions:

> The want of hands and materials, with this lavish expenditure, created a demand for and gave great encouragement to new mechanical inventions and chemical discoveries, to supercede manual labour in supplying the materials required for warlike purposes.[17]

---

16 John A. Chartres and Gerald L. Turnbull 'Road Transport' in Derek H. Aldcroft and Michael J. Freeman ed. *Transport in the Industrial Revolution* (Manchester 1983) p. 64–99 at p. 85 Table 7. (Chartres' and Turnbull's figures have been challenged by Dorian Gerhold 'The Growth of the London Carrying Trade, 1681–1838' *Economic History Review* vol. 41 (1988) p. 392–410 but the estimate on p. 403, Table 3 that the increase in ton-miles hauled 1800–1808 was only 2 per cent seems scarcely plausible); John Armstrong and Philip S. Bagwell 'Coastal Shipping' in Aldcroft and Freeman p. 142–176 at p. 145 Table 15, cf *Commons Journals* vol. 57 p. 955 and *Parliamentary Papers* 1826–7 XVIII p. 209; both in the Armstrong and Bagwell article and in the *Commons Journal* and *Parliamentary Papers* sources the figure for 1790 refers to *British* shipping and the figure for 1824 to *United Kingdom* (i.e. British and Irish) shipping.
17 Joseph Lowe *The Present State of England* (1822) p. 29; William Blake *Observations on the Effects produced by the Expenditure of Government during the Restriction of Cash Payments* (1823) p. 62, 116; *The Life of Robert Owen: Written by Himself* (1857) p. 124.

Indeed, although the standard iconography of Britain during the Industrial Revolution nearly all dates from the 1830s, 1840s and even later, these were the years in which the realities evolved which only subsequently obtained classic depiction. The poet Blake's evocation of London in the early 1790s was still timeless, almost equally applicable to 1593 or 1893:

> How the Chimney-sweeper's cry
> Every black'ning Church appals;
> And the hapless Soldier's sigh
> Runs in blood down Palace walls

and as one commentator wondered, 'Who turns his attention to the second-floors, the garrets, the back-rooms, and the cellars of this Metropolis?' But foreign visitors, looking about themselves with fresh eyes, were astonished by the features of the new industrial England which Englishmen still – or already – took for granted: thus London in 1809, as described by a young Swede:

> One passes through eternally long streets, between houses all alike, all dark and smoke-begrimed. One penetrates ever deeper into an atmosphere of coal smoke in whose twilight moves an unending multitude of people, past shops without equal for splendour and abundance. In this huddle of houses one comes with amazement upon St. Paul's Church, a high colossal shape which seems to look down with indignation on the race of shopkeepers who buy and barter beneath its walls ... London has its monuments in its crowds of people, its ceaseless activity, the richness of its wares, from every quarter of the globe; and it is this, its most interesting aspect, that says to the foreigner, so soon as, in that constant hum, he is able to think: 'Thou art a city which rulest over the sea and the commerce of the world'.

And industrial Lancashire in 1814, as seen by a German:

> There are hundreds of factories in Manchester which are five or six stories high. At the side of each factory there is a great chimney which belches forth black smoke and indicates the presence of the powerful steam engines. The smoke from the chimneys forms a great cloud which can be seen for miles around the town. The houses have become black on account of the smoke. The river upon which Manchester stands is so tainted with colouring matter that the water resembles the contents of a dye-vat.

This anticipates Friedrich Engels's *Lage der arbeitenden Klasse in England* (Condition of the Working Class in England) by almost a generation; at least half the East End alleyways where Jack the Ripper lurked at the end of the century had been built by 1815.[18]

---

[18] James Peller Malcolm *Anecdotes of the Manners and Customs of London during the Eighteenth Century* (1808) p. 484; Erik Gustav Geijer *Impressions of England, 1809–1810* ed. Anton Blanck (1932) p. 82–3, 85–6, letters of Geijer to Lisa Liljeborn August 1809; W.O. Henderson *Industrial Britain under the Regency* (1968) p. 136 report of Johann Georg May, Prussian factory commissioner, May 1814.

The first of the smogs which became characteristic of London in the later nineteenth century

continued

Though the scale of British industrial enterprise would continue to grow after 1815, even by 1793 Britain was the world's leading textile and metal goods manufacturer, a major iron-ore producer, and far and away the world's greatest primary producer of copper, tin and coal. The mining industry had an importance as a leading sector of technology which has been somewhat neglected by subsequent historians – except with regard to the use of steam engines in mines – but which was much celebrated at the time. The Jarrow Colliery, which had a shaft of the then unprecedented depth of 840 feet, was formally opened in 1803 before a crowd of 10,000, to the accompaniment of military bands, a procession of the local Volunteers, artillery salutes, and an open-air collation. Wartime mining disasters were on a suitably epic scale. An explosion at Felling Colliery near Gateshead on 25 May 1812 killed and fatally injured 92, with 29 survivors: 'the noise of the explosion though dull, was heard to three or four miles distance, and much resembled an unsteady fire of infantry'; the resultant dust had the effect of an early twilight. A second explosion in the same colliery nineteen months later killed 23. On 3 May 1815, during Napoleon's Hundred Days, 75 men and boys were caught underground when Heaton Colliery flooded; it took nine months to pump the mine dry and when investigators eventually descended the shaft they found that the pit ponies, candles, and even bark from the rough-hewn pit props, had been eaten, and that the last survivor of the trapped miners had died only a few days previously. That awful, hopeless nine months entombment is perhaps the most dreadful single instance of the casual horrors which accompanied the establishment of the new industrial order.[19]

Another aspect of the economic development of the period, perhaps as remote as could be from the troglodytic sufferings of the northern miners, was the growth of suburbia. The diffusion of wealth meant also the diffusion of raised expectations of domestic comfort; better quality roads and improvements in the design of carriages encouraged the growth of dormitory towns within daily commuting distance of the larger centres, especially London. Take, for example, the area to the north of the City of London. In 1800 some of the terraced houses on the west side of Newington Green were already old, dating from the Commonwealth; they are still there

continued
and in the first half of the twentieth century hit London in the year after Waterloo, on 26 November 1816, though the first smog described as 'making the eyes smart, and almost suffocating those who were in the street, particularly asthmatic persons', was not till 12 November 1828: Luke Howard *The Climate of London, deduced from Meteorological Observations, Made in the Metropolis* (3 vols 1833) vol. 2 p. 162–3; vol. 2 p. 313; vol. 3 p. 303; but see also Peter Brimblecombe *The Big Smoke: a History of Air Pollution in London since Medieval Times* (1987) p. 59–60 for something like a classic smog as early as November 1679.

[19] John Sykes *Local Records; or Historical Register of Remarkable Events which have occurred in Northumberland and Durham, Newcastle upon Tyne, and Berwick upon Tweed* (2 vols Newcastle 1833) vol. 2 p. 16–17; ibid. vol. 2 p. 66 and R.L. Galloway *A History of Coal Mining in Great Britain* London 1882 p. 402; T.S. Ashton and J. Sykes *The Coal Industry of the Eighteenth Century* (Manchester 1964) ed. p. 40–41.

today, the house where the banker poet Samuel Rogers was born in 1763 being now a shoe-repair shop. A few fields further north was Stoke Newington, described by Edgar Allan Poe as 'a misty-looking village ... where were a vast number of gigantic and gnarled trees and where all the houses were excessively ancient'. (Poe attended a school, in the years following Waterloo, on a site just to the east of that now occupied by the public library in Stoke Newington Church Street, though the stuccoed villa of no great age which accommodated the school was transformed in his writings into a 'large, rambling, Elizabethan house'.) Despite the building of new houses Stoke Newington remained essentially an inward-looking village community and a place of retirement, but Hackney, on the other side of what had once been Ermine Street, was virtually a middle-class boom town. The population increased 31.7 per cent between 1801 and 1811 and the influx of money was testified to by the building of James Spiller's huge new church in 1792–1797 (the porch and spire were added in 1812–1813) a smart Town Hall in 1802 (just west of the tower that was all that was left when the old parish church was dismantled in the 1790s; now a branch of the Midland Bank), a chapel of ease in South Hackney in 1806 (with a church school built nearby in 1809), and the Parochial Charity Schools in Chatham Place in 1811. Some of the tombs in St. John's Churchyard record the migration of City gents northward to the leafier tranquillity of this attractive parish: 'George Patterson Esq., late Deputy Accomptant General to the *East India Company*, who died the 5th day of May, 1831, in the 75th year of his age', or 'In Memory of Elizabeth, Wife of Thos Bowerbank, Merchant of Lothbury, London, of this Parish who died the 6th Jan. 1808 aged 35 Years'; distinctly up market from 'Mr. Robert Thorne, late of Holloway, for Many Years an Eminent Letter-Founder in Fann Street Aldersgate Street' (1753–1820) or 'Mr. John Williams of this Parish, and of Saint James's Clerkenwell: Soap Manufacturer' (1755–1829) whose monuments one sees in the more modest churchyard of St. Mary Magdalene in Holloway Road a couple of miles to the west. It was Joshua Watson, a retired wine-merchant whose brother was the rector of Hackney, and the Rev. Henry Handley Norris, the rector's brother-in-law and curate at South Hackney, who became the leading figures in the group working for the revival of the High Church tradition in the Church of England; they eventually became known as the Hackney Phalanx or, less authentically, as the Clapton Sect. It was a meeting of Joshua Watson, Norris and John Bowles at Watson's Clapton home in 1811 which led to the setting up of the National Society for the Education of the Poor, which till 1870 was much the largest organizer of primary education in England and which built many of the primary schools which are still in use today. Hackney seems indeed to have been the classic suburb of the period, and the reason is easy to see from a map; it was the nearest suitable area to the City of London.[20]

[20] Poe's evocation of Stoke Newington is in his story 'William Wilson', the 'large, rambling, Elizabethan house' probably being inspired by Fleetwood House which stood further down the street from the school; it was demolished some years later; population figures are

continued

V. Mobilizing National Resources

Contemporaries were well aware of the importance of economic change to the national war-effort: they even believed that industrialization, and specifically the mechanization of manufacturing processes in the new factories, created the manpower surplus required for the huge wartime armed forces.

Some years before the war Adam Smith in *The Wealth of Nations* had stated:

> Among the civilized nations of modern Europe, it is commonly computed that not more than one hundredth part of the inhabitants of any country can be employed as soldiers, without ruin to the country which pays the expence of their service.

During the Napoleonic Wars various continental governments did force up the proportion of the population enlisted, but also managed, as Adam Smith had warned, to ruin their countries. Britain forced the proportion up to one member of the armed forces per twenty-nine inhabitants – one in eighteen if part-time soldiers are included. In 1811 Britain had a population of 12,596,803; there were 218,949 men in the regular Army, nearly all recruited in Britain despite the persistent tradition that the English employed the Irish to do their fighting, 77,159 in the permanently embodied Militia, and a naval establishment fixed at 145,000; in addition 228,418 were undergoing part-time training as local militia, and 58,647 were members of the Volunteers and Yeomanry, also part-time. This was a level achieved nowhere else, and was achieved with much less ruinous effect. But what is truly extraordinary is that this building up of the armed forces, and the extension of industrialization, was achieved with a very high level of unemployment. The poet Wordsworth attempted to give an explanation in 1811:

> How comes it that we are enabled to keep up, by sea and land, so many men in arms? – Not by our foreign commerce, but by our domestic ingenuity, by our home labour, which with the aid of capital and the mechanic arts and establishments, has enabled a few to produce so much as will maintain themselves, and the hundreds of thousands of their Countrymen whom they support in arms.

Wordsworth's neighbour and fellow-poet Robert Southey took up this notion in *The Quarterly Review*, possibly after discussion with Wordsworth:

> In one place, a large steam engine performs the manual labour of five hundred able men; in another place, a cotton mill works with all the delicacy of five

continued
of course in the 1801 and 1811 Census returns; for Joshua Watson and the Hackney Phalanx see Edward Churton *Memoir of Joshua Watson* (2 vols Oxford 1861) vol. 1 p. 96–7 and A.B. Webster *Joshua Watson: The Story of a Layman, 1771–1855* (1954) p. 18–32. The chapel of ease in South Hackney has been replaced by a Victorian structure and the Parochial Charity Schools by a typical London School Board barracks.

hundred skilful artisans; and a thousand men may thus be marched to the army without national loss.

The British Critic claimed in 1812:

> It is ascribable to the skill and science applied to the diminution of labour in this country, that we have, at this moment, little short of 600,000 men in arms.

In 1816 Robert Owen told the social expert Patrick Colquhoun – who agreed – that in the cotton industry alone machinery had replaced 'the manual labour of a population of *eighty* millions' and guessed that the figure for the whole textile industry was 200 million. Finally Southey, in his *History of the Peninsular War*, stated as a matter beyond controversy:

> The manufacturing system supplied the war with men as well as means ... we were enabled without violence or difficulty to maintain in arms a force scarcely inferior in numbers to that of the enemy with all their fivefold superiority of population.[21]

The problem with this analysis is that the process of building factories and labour-saving machines must have required manpower: vast increases of output could not have been achieved without an initial input of skilled labour. In addition, though mechanization had made impressive progress, it was still at a comparatively early stage. It has been calculated that by 1800 only 1,330 steam engines had ever been built, many of which had already ceased operating by that date. There was also, apparently, an increase in the use of water mills in the 1790s (sometimes using steam engines for pumping). Nevertheless it is clear

---

[21] Adam Smith *An Inquiry into the Nature and Causes of the Wealth of Nations* London 1776, book 5 chap.1 'Of the Expences of the Sovereign or Commonwealth', part 1 'Of the Expence of Defence' – p. 676 of Oxford 1976 edit. prepared by R.H. Campbell and A.S. Skinner; for size of armed forces 1811 see *Parliamentary Papers* 1812 IX p. 189, 201, 208 and Wm. Laird Clowes *The Royal Navy: A History* (7 vols 1897–1903) vol. 5 p. 9. These figures do not include the Irish militia or volunteers, and the tradition that the British armed forces at this period were largely recruited in Ireland seems to be somewhat exaggerated: up to 1 Nov. 1796 it was calculated that only 23, 138 Irishmen had joined the British Army and 15,515 the Navy and Marines (John T. Gilbert *Documents Relating to Ireland, 1795–1804* (Dublin 1893) p. 100–101 Pelham to Duke of York 14 Nov. 1796). In 1799 there were allegedly over 600 Irish officers in the Habsburg Army (British Library Add. 35 709 f. 179 Earl of Hardwicke to Lord Hawkesbury 26 Nov. 1804 copy) and there were many others in the Spanish and even the Russian Armies. One notes also that relatively few of the deserters from the Army listed in Public Record Office WO 25/2907 had enlisted in Ireland. For the comments of Wordsworth and others see Ernest de Selincourt, Chester L. Shaver, Mary Moorman, Alan G. Hill ed. *The Letters of William and Dorothy Wordsworth* (7 vols Oxford 1967–88) vol. 2 p. 476 Wordsworth to Charles Pasley 28 March 1811; *Quarterly Review* vol. 5 (1811) p. 407 (Southey's review of Pasley's book *Essay on the Military Policy and Institutions of the British Empire* – the review was published in May 1811 and was conceivably written at the same time as Wordsworth's letter on the same subject); *British Critic* vol. 39 (1812) p. 489; *The Life of Robert Owen: written by himself* (1857) p. 126–7; Robert Southey *History of the Peninsular War* (3 vols 1823–32) vol. 1 p. 59, (and cf. T.R. Malthus *Principles of Political Economy: considered with a view to their practical application* (1820) p. 409.)

that Britain, though far more mechanized than any other country in the 1800s, was still very largely dependent on essentially primitive sources of power. The skyline even of London was still crowded with windmills, perhaps most of which were used not for flour-milling but for land-drainage, log-sawing, even for metallurgical processes; for example a lead-grinding works at the Rosemary Branch (where today Southgate Road crosses the Regent's Canal in Islington) was powered by two giant windmills built in 1786 and 1792. In the London postal districts alone Windmill Drive, Windmill Hill, Windmill Lane, Windmill Row, Windmill Street, Windmill Walk, and *five* Windmill Roads, not to mention Mill Hill Place and two Mill Hill Roads, commemorate the sites of windmills or in some cases groups of windmills, all of them providing power for relatively small-scale enterprises with relatively crude technologies geared to irregular rhythms of working. Another source of power was human muscle: the cranes in the newly constructed London docks were powered by treadmills consisting of six or eight men running inside a drum; other machines were worked by horses. Moreover where the steam engine was used it was often to replace human muscle-power or less efficient natural power sources only in the theoretical sense: tasks such as the pumping out of deep mines simply would not have been feasible by any other means. All in all, it seems unlikely that early nineteenth-century machines resulted in any reduction in the total demand for labour.[22]

In any case industrial mechanization was only one of the dramatic economic developments of this period. To build the East India Docks, 625,000 cubic yards of earth had to be excavated by pick and shovel; to build the West India Docks twenty-four million bricks were made on the Isle of Dogs in 1801 alone; to make room for London Docks fifteen streets and 33 courts, yards and alleys had to be wholly demolished, along with parts of ten other streets; all without the aid of machinery. House-building, enclosures, road and bridge construction, all involved heavy demands on manpower. Labour gangs working on canals were numbered in thousands:

> *I shall Sir, sett out to join my Armies in the North*, Scotland first, and then Leicester, in the latter County I have had 7,000 men employed for two years past,

Telford boasted to one of his military friends. Then there were the barracks erected to house the troops mobilized for the war, and the coastal defences built against French invasion: 'incessant sinks of money; walls of immense

---

[22] J.R. Harris 'The Employment of Steam Power in the Eighteenth Century' *History* vol. 52 (1967) p. 133–148 at p. 147; G.N. von Tunzelman *Steam Power and British Industrialization to 1860* (Oxford 1978) p. 138; R. Thurston Hopkins *Old Watermills and Windmills* (1934) p. 148 cf. T.F.T. Baker ed. *Victoria County History: A History of the County of Middlesex* vol. 8 (1985) p. 73. Dockyard cranes were still operated by treadmills in the middle of the nineteenth century, cf Henry Mayhew *London Labour and the London Poor* (4 vols 1861–2) vol. 3 p. 304.

dimensions; masses of stones brought and put into piles', as William Cobbett later described them. More than forty of the hundred or so Martello Towers erected on the south and east coast, 'these monuments to the wisdom of Pitt and Dundas and Perceval' are still to be seen today, though much else has gone. These fortifications 'undertaken and executed, both at home and abroad, in a manner little checked, or protected against profusion and waste' cost over £9 million and the barracks nearly £7 million, and the number and scale of the various projects can be gauged from the fact that Dartmoor Prison, when first opened in 1809 (to house 5,000 prisoners of war) had cost only about £74,000. All of this suggests an expansion rather than a contraction of the demand for labour in these years.[23]

The high figures for unemployment introduce an element of confusion here. England, with Wales, was at this stage the only country in Europe with an effective nation-wide system of poor relief – this is in itself surely a sign of economic advancedness – but the system was by no means either efficient or uniform, especially when it came to keeping records. In 1822 it was stated:

> all former Returns have been entirely inaccurate as to the *numbers* of persons, Permanently or Occasionally, relieved. The great difficulty in keeping this account is, to avoid the repeated enumeration of persons who are relieved more than once within the year.

For what they are worth however the statistics show that in 1803 there were 693,289 persons permanently and 295,912 temporarily receiving poor relief in England – there are no statistics for Scotland and Ireland, and the Welsh statistics are best omitted because of the lower living standards and apparent prevalence of subsistence farming there. In the 1803 statistics children under fourteen are given separately in the case of outdoor relief but not in the case of those receiving assistance as inmates of workhouses; by extrapolation one can calculate a pauper population of 505,485 persons aged fourteen or over. Of these 153,571 were specified as 'above 60 Years of Age, or disabled from labour by permanent illness, or other infirmity'. If half the remainder are women this would give, at most, 175,000 able-bodied male paupers. One noticeable feature of the statistics is the proportion of children; the higher the overall incidence of pauperism in a county, the larger the proportion of children. Whereas it has been calculated that 37.5 per cent of the population was under fourteen in 1815, 48.9 per cent of those receiving outdoor relief in 1803 were under

---

[23] John Pudney *London's Docks* (1975) p. 30–31, 51 and Joseph G. Broodbank *History of the Port of London* (2 vol. 1921) vol. 1 p. 92–125; Daniel Lysons *Supplement to the First Edition of the Historical Account of the Environs of London* (1811) p. 158 fn. 2; British Library Add. 41963 f. 94 Telford to Charles Pasley 21 April 1813 – the Leicester project was presumably the Grand Union Canal opened in 1814 (for the technical assistance which Pasley gave Telford see Add. 41964 f. 63 Telford to Pasley 2 Nov. 1830); William Cobbett *Rural Rides* ed. G.D.H. Cole and Margaret Cole (3 vols 1930) vol. 1 p. 222–3 (1 Sept. 1823) Sheila Sutcliffe *Martello Towers* (Newton Abbot 1972) p. 85 and 104; *Parliamentary Papers* 1817 IV p. 107–8 and 1820 XI p. 177; Basil Thomson *The Story of Dartmoor Prison* (1907) p. 11.

fourteen; 57.3 per cent of recipients of outdoor relief were under fourteen in Berkshire and 64.3 per cent in Sussex, these being the two counties with the highest level of unemployment; in Northumberland only 29.6 per cent of those receiving poor relief were under fourteen. This was not necessarily because there was more work for juveniles in a coal-mining area; 25.8 per cent of those receiving outdoor relief in Sussex were under five years old and only 10.7 per cent in Northumberland. It seems that large families were a principal cause of pauperism in the agricultural counties, and this suggests that poor relief may have been necessary in many families as a regular supplement to poor wages and that heads of pauper families may often have been in productive employment – though productive for someone else. The fact that expenditure per head on paupers on outdoor relief was a third of the cost per head of paupers in workhouses is another indication that families on outdoor relief normally also had regular wage incomes.[24]

During the later 1790s some rural communities began to use poor relief payments to supplement low agricultural wages in times of high food prices. This was known as the Allowance, or Speenhamland, System, but it is not actually known how widely it was practised as a regular and deliberate policy. By 1830 it was thought characteristic of the southern agricultural counties, in Sussex having allegedly begun during the 1795 famine and become normal by 1801, and in the western half of Oxfordshire dating from about 1809. The statistics suggest that the determining factor was less food prices as such than the number of mouths to be fed in particular families. The Speenhamland system flourished at the time of the final stages of the abolition of serfdom on the continent of Europe and suggests the recurrent tendency towards re-enserfment that has dominated the relationship of the governing classes to the lowest of the lower orders ever since the first retreat of serfdom in the fourteenth century. Poor Relief payments represented over 7 per cent of public expenditure in 1803 (as compared to under 3.9 per cent in 1931 at the height of the inter-war slump) and were thus a transfer payment of some significance. The main beneficiaries of the system were the working farmers, whose own contributions to the poor-rate were supplemented by the contributions of land-owners who employed fewer people (and probably paid them better) on less economically farmed gentlemen's estates; since in parish communities the farmers would normally be acquaintances, if not friends and relations, of the Poor Law guardians this system of spreading the wage-bill also increased the opportunities for forcibly imposing labour discipline. It seems therefore

[24] *Parliamentary Papers* 1822 V p. 529 (p. 13 of Report on Select Committee on Poor Rate Returns); 'Poor Law Returns 1803–4', demy-folio volume 13 supplementary to *Parliamentary Reports* 1st series p. 714–5; for calculation of the age distribution of the population see R.D. Lee and R.S. Schofield 'British Population in the Eighteenth Century' in Roderick Floud and Donald McCloskey ed. *The Economic History of Britain since 1700* (2 vols Cambridge 1981) vol. 1 p. 17–35 at p. 23 Figure 2.2.

that the high figures for unemployment were largely the result of social and political sleight of hand, and that many paupers were simply people who worked for less wages.[25]

Underemployment or apparent unemployment in the agricultural south was balanced, in national terms, by maximum utilization of available labour in the industrial north, including the widespread use of child labour. The war years probably saw the greatest extent, and worst abuses, of child labour during the whole of the Industrial Revolution period; thus John Brown's classic account of the ill-treatment of child workers, *Memoir of Robert Blincoe*, is based on the experience of Robert Blincoe while serving as an 'apprentice' at Lowdham Mill near Nottingham and Litton Mill near Tideswell between 1799 and 1813; he had been born about 1792. In 1816 a Parliamentary Select Committee was told that only 17.8 per cent of the workforce in Scottish cotton mills were men over eighteen, and 38.2 per cent women over eighteen; the remaining 44 per cent were children, and 4.1 per cent of the total workforce comprised children under ten. In the Manchester area at the same date 48.3 per cent of the workforce in cotton factories was under eighteen. In Nottinghamshire, in seven out of eight factories reported on in 1816, 45.8 per cent of the total workforce was under eighteen, 6 per cent of the total under ten; adult males comprised only 17.4 per cent of the workforce (the workforce of the eighth factory was for some reason, probably technical, much more predominantly adult male). And it was claimed that the proportion of children, and especially younger children, had been much higher at the beginning of the French Wars, previous to the introduction of larger and more specialized machines requiring adult operators: the Parliamentary Select Committee was told in 1816 that 'Thirty years ago they were almost all children, and at least five times as many under ten years of age as at present'. In the years after the war, as the collection of statistics became more systematic, child labour continued to decline. By 1836 the adult male component of the employees in Lancashire cotton mills had risen to an average of 27.9 per cent. It would not be entirely justifiable to argue backwards from the change 1816–1836 but it does seem

---

[25] *Parliamentary Papers* 1834 XXVIII p. 1A evidence of D.O.P Okeden re Oxfordshire, 1833 and p. 546A evidence of C.H. Maclean re W. Sussex; Mitchell and Deane *Abstract of British Historical Statistics* p. 396, 399, 410, 418. See also J.R. Poynter *Society and Pauperism: English Ideas on Poor Relief, 1795–1834* (1969) p. 83, 189, 'Poor Law Returns 1803–4' p. 714–5 (see previous note) show that on average in-paupers cost £12.2 a year to maintain, out-paupers (counting those only temporarily on relief as half-units) £3.85. There is, incidentally, no reason to suppose that the Peace of Amiens in 1802–3 had forced up unemployment figures generally: payments for poor relief were higher in the year ending Easter 1813 than in the years ending 25 March 1815 and 25 March 1817, which were both years of peace, cf *Parliamentary Papers* 1839 XLIV p. 4–5. There were numerous complaints of the shortage of agricultural labour, not necessarily from the counties with the fewest paupers; A.H. John 'Farming in Wartime: 1793–1815' in E.L. Jones and G.E. Mingay *Land, Labour and Population in the Industrial Revolution: Essays Presented to J.D. Chambers* (1967) p. 28–47 at p. 32–3.

clear that child labour in the textile factories was more important during the
war than at any time subsequently.[26]

Wartime conditions probably also affected the employment prospects of
women. It was claimed, for example, that after 1793 'the Journeymen in such
numbers enlisted and went off, that the householders [master weavers] took
the girls and learnt them, rather than let their looms stand.' In the tailoring
trade increased demand and inelasticities of labour supply due to unionization
of the male workers (itself a sign of labour shortage) led the master-tailors
to break with tradition and to begin employing women. In the absence of
detailed information regarding the pre-war situation it cannot be stated with
any certainty that it was the war itself that was the major factor in determining
the level either of female or of juvenile labour; in general it seems to have been
more to do with the kind of machinery being operated, and the availability
of cheaper women or child workers, than with the non-availability of men.
In contrast with the world wars of the twentieth century, for example, the
manufacture of munitions remained a male preserve, at least in the government
factories; weapons manufacture was too highly-skilled a trade, and too well-
paid, to be opened to women.[27]

The use of women and children in the factories helps explain why it was that
in a period of social strain, skilled labour shortage, rising prices and political
excitement there was not more labour agitation than there was. It also explains
how in a period of increased demand for labour there were enough adult male
workers available for the more skilled and strenuous tasks such as building the
factories, constructing the machines, mining and transporting the coal and iron
– and joining the Army. It was actually believed at the time that a particularly
large proportion of the menfolk in the textile areas joined the Army, those
of them who had been factory apprentices often, it was alleged, joining up
as soon as their indentures had expired. There are no surviving registers
of recruitment but records of the place of enlistment of deserters from the
Army do not confirm this view. Nevertheless there is a detectable military
element in the style of working-class protest in the textile manufacturing

26 John Brown *Memoir of Robert Blincoe* was first published in *The Lion* in 1828 and as
a book at Manchester in 1832: see also A.E. Musson 'An Introductory Note on Robert Blincoe
and the Early Factory System' in Derby 1966 edit. espec. p. 22–6 and cf. 'Alfred' [i.e. Samuel
Kydd] *The History of the Factory Movement: from the Year 1802, to the Enactment of the
Ten Hours' Bill in 1847* (2 vols 1857) vol. 1 p. 24–6; *Parliamentary Papers* 1816 III p. 478–9
(p. 240–1 of Minutes of Evidence, taken before the Select Committee on the State of the
Children employed in the Manufactories of the United Kingdom); ibid. p. 512–3 (p. 274–5
of Minutes); ibid. p. 426, 449–451, 453–4 (p. 188, 211–3, 215–6 of Minutes); ibid. p. 581, 591
(p. 343, 353 of Minutes); *Parliamentary Papers* 1836 XLV/1 p. 56–7, cf. P. Gaskell *Artisans
and Machinery* (1836)p. 142–3.
27 Parliamentary Papers 1808 II p. 121, cf. Clive Emsley *British Society and the French
Wars* (1978) p. 75; T.M. Parssinen and I.J. Prothero 'The London Tailors' Strike of 1834 and
the Collapse of the Grand National Consolidated Trades' Union: A Police Spy's Report'
International Review of Social History vol. 22 (1977) p. 65–107 at p. 69; Public Record Office
WO 54/512 list of the workforce at Waltham Abbey powder mills etc., 1812.

districts after the end of the wars; at Peterloo in 1819 some contingents marched to the scene of the demonstration five abreast with a leader for every hundred men; they 'appeared to come in regular order . . . wheeled upon receiving the word of command . . . marched with particular precision' or, according to another account, 'marched to the sound of the bugle, and in very regular time, closing and expanding their ranks, and marching in ordinary and double quick time, according as it pleased the fancy of their leaders to direct them.' It seems that many groups had been carefully drilled by men who had been sergeants in the Army or the Militia during the war, and that the rank and file of the demonstrators included many ex-soldiers. Similarly the silk banners embroidered with slogans which appeared at Peterloo doubtless had their ultimate origin in the impedimenta of pre-Reformation popular religion but almost certainly derived some of their inspiration also from the colours presented with great publicity to local volunteer corps during the wars.[28]

VI. The Contribution of Technology

It can be seen that the spread of factory employment which was such a feature of the war years involved less serious competition with the armed forces with regard to manpower than it might have done; nevertheless the war with France was not an Industrial War in the sense that the twentieth-century wars against Germany were. Nor, though this was the classic era of new industrial technology, was it a war dominated by technical change and development in weaponry. Though many individuals rose to the challenge posed by the war in the field of mechanical invention it seems that the general level of technological sophistication was insufficient for the boldest inventions

---

[28] See e.g. John Bohstedt 'Gender, Household and Community Politics: Women in English Riots 1790–1810' *Past and Present* no. 120 (1988) p. 88–122 at p. 116–7 for women weavers' lack of involvement in the 1808 Lancashire weavers' strike; *Parliamentary Papers* 1816 III p. 443 (p. 205 of Minutes) and J. Farey *General View of the Agriculture and Minerals of Derbyshire* (3 vols 1815–7) vol. 3 p. 503–4 on military recruitment from textile areas; Public Record Office WO 25/2907; *The Trial of Mr. Hunt, Mr. Johnson, and Others, for a Conspiracy, at the Manchester Meeting, on the 16th August Last* (Leeds 1820) p. 38, evidence of William Houlton or Hulton; report of the Peterloo incident by John William Tyas in *The Times* 19 August 1819 p. 2b-c, reprinted in Raymond Williams ed. *The Pelican Book of English Prose vol. 2 from 1780 to the Present Day* (Harmondsworth 1969) p. 77–85 at p. 78 and cf. Samuel Bamford *Passages in the Life of a Radical* (2 vols Middleton 1843) vol. 1 p. 197–200. See also N. Gash 'After Waterloo: British Society and the Legacy of the Napoleonic Wars' *Transactions of the Royal Historical Society* 5th series vol. 28 (1978) p. 145–158, at p. 150–151. Sermons on the occasion of the presentation of colours to volunteer units were published by, amongst others, the Rev. Weeden Butler (Royal Pimlico Volunteers and also Chelsea Armed Association, both in 1799) the Rev. John Davies (Royal Garrison Volunteers, Portsmouth, 1799) and the Rev. C. Hayward (Clare Military Association, 1799). For the presentation of colours to the Bury Association by Lady Clerke see Staffordshire County Record Office Ms F 920 7 W80, E. Hall typescript 'Hero of Badajoz: Diary of a Soldier's Wife 1789–1814', p. 92.

to be rendered practical. Despite the promising title of his book *Torpedo Warfare and Submarine Explosions*, published in New York in 1810, Robert Fulton had little success with his experiments in manpowered underwater warfare. The French used manned balloons for observation purposes early in the Revolutionary War but with the small-scale, short-ranged warfare of the day the advantages over cavalry reconnaissance were insufficient to outweigh the organizational and technical problems involved in early ballooning; as Shelley pointed out, at about the time Wellington's army was holding the lines of Torres Vedras against Masséna's advance, 'the art of navigating the air is in its first and most helpless infancy; the aerial mariner still swims on bladders, and has not mounted even the rude raft'. Nor had steam power quite come of age; Edward Thomason made a working model of a steamship with steerable paddles, to serve as a fireship for attacks on French shipping in port, and was granted an interview by the First Lord of the Admiralty in 1796, but his design was thought impracticable and Thomason was left to employ his inventive genius in improving the design of corkscrews and designing the telescopic toasting fork. Similarly George Medhurst, a pioneer in the application of pneumatic power (something which found a number of military applications in the twentieth century) found his proposals 'met with that indifference and contempt, which usually attend all attempts to deviate so widely from established customs', and had to be content with inventing 'Baker's Patent Mangle' and the type of weighing scales that are still in use today in old-fashioned greengrocers' shops. Sir George Cayley, before inventing the aeroplane, tested pointed and finned shells, some with detachable sabots, with a 6-pounder gun borrowed from the Ordnance, at Scarborough 'about the years 1804–5', but the Ordnance failed to recognize the advantage of this kind of ammunition. The incendiary rocket developed by Sir William Congreve, though spectacularly effective on occasion, was not always so; in November 1810 Wellington wrote:

> I am no partisan of Congreve's rockets . . . It is but fair, however, to give every thing a trial, more particularly as I have received the orders of Government to try these machines.

By November 1813 he had concluded they were only of use for setting fire to towns; Wellington had himself witnessed the unprecedented level of destruction achieved with rockets in the bombardment of Copenhagen in 1807 but since for the most part he campaigned on allied territory equipment for burning down towns was of little practical utility. The 'spherical case shot' artillery ammunition invented by Henry Shrapnel, which detonated in mid-air releasing a supposedly lethal discharge of shot, had been used with excellent effect under Wellington's command at Kjøge in 1807 and at Vimeiro in 1808, but as late as March 1812 he was insisting, 'I have reason to believe that their effect is confined to wounds of a very trifling description; and they kill nobody'. Another development in artillery, the carronade, a short-barrelled naval gun, was almost universally praised but its chief importance was in strengthening the broadsides of small ships, and the great naval battles of the war were fought with conventional long guns.[29]

The British Royal Navy's equipment was often far more ingenious than that used in other countries; the mops and rammers for the cannon had flexible shafts of heavy rope and were much handier to use in the confined space of the gun decks, and the firing mechanism on the guns themselves was more up-to-date, as one French officer recalled:

> We were still using slow-matches which fired the round with an awful delay, so that if the ship was rolling very much [as at the Battle of the First of June] . . . entire salvos would pass over the masts without causing the least damage. The English had flint locks, pretty clumsy but much better than our slow-matches. Not possessing graduated elevating gear, they used their foresights which gave them direct horizontal fire.

But the flint-lock firing mechanism (operated by a lanyard) on British naval artillery had been introduced, during the American War of Independence, over a hundred years after becoming a normal part of army muskets; this, and the use of thick rope instead of wood for the shafts of the implements that had to be rammed down the gun barrels, hardly represents a triumph of advanced technology, even by the standards of 1800. And the British warships themselves were built on notoriously conservative lines. Compared to French and Spanish line of battleships, British warships were cramped and small, with the lower gun-ports too close to the waterline for convenient use in heavy seas. In the action of 29 May 1794, the prelude to Earl Howe's great victory of the First of June, the seas were so high that on Howe's flagship the *Queen Charlotte* the pumps had to be kept constantly at work to void the sea water that was being shipped through the gun ports as they were opened to fire at the enemy, and on occasion the lee ports were opened just to let the water pour out: no doubt an unnerving experience as Howe's fleet was 280 miles from the nearest dry land at the time. New principles of ship building were slow to be introduced: the first line of battleship built with diagonal trusses,

[29] Thomas Jefferson Hogg *The Life of Percy Bysshe Shelley* (2 vols 1858) vol. 1 p. 62–3; Sir Edward Thomason *Memoirs: during half a century* (2 vols 1845) vol. 1 p. 4–7, 14–5; George Medhurst *A New System of Inland Conveyance for Goods and Passengers & c.* (1817) p. 31; *Mechanics' Magazine* vol. 45 (1846) p. 60–64, letter from Sir George Cayley dated 26 June 1846; *The Despatches of Field-Marshal the Duke of Wellington* ed. J. Gurwood (13 vols 1834–9) vol. 6 p. 564 Wellington to Hon. G. Berkeley 6 Nov. 1810 and vol. 11 p. 314 Wellington to Earl Bathurst 22 Nov. 1813 on the subject of Congreve rockets; Sir John Hope employed rockets with particular effect at the crossing of the Adour in February 1814: see Roger Norman Buckley ed. *The Napoleonic War Journal of Captain Thomas Henry Browne, 1807–1816 (1957) p. 264, Feb. 1814;* for Shrapnel: *Wellington's Despatches vol. 8 p. 659* Wellington to Earl of Liverpool 12 March 1812 but cf. ibid. vol. 9 p. 65 same to same 16 April 1812 and *The Humble Petition of Henry Needham Scrope Shrapnel to the Right Honorable House of Peers and Lords* (Salisbury 1868) p. 6 Wellington [then Sir Arthur Wellesley] to Sir John Sinclair 13 Oct. 1808 and to Sir Henry Shrapnel 16 June 1809, cf. testimonials of various officers as to effectiveness of shrapnel printed p. 6–23.

a constructional principle developed during the 1790s to provide a particularly strong hull structure, was only launched in 1815. Iron 'knees' in the angle between the ship's ribs and the deck-beams began to replace oak knees in Royal Naval vessels about the time of Trafalgar; they had been in use in French warships since the seventeenth century, and in East India Company ships since the 1780s. The greatly superior sailing qualities of French privateering vessels remained a major headache for the British throughout the war: Sir Samuel Bentham, the brother of Jeremy Bentham the philosopher, designed a series of sloops and schooners, longer, shallower and more scientifically constructed than conventional vessels, but though these performed exceptionally well and might have provided an answer to the French privateers, only six vessels were ever constructed to these designs.[30]

Similarly, on land, though much of the British army's equipment was well-designed this was not the case with the most important item of equipment, the musket. Initially the very high production standards insisted on by the Ordnance Board were an obstacle in the way of acquiring sufficient arms for military needs: the Ordnance Board then went to the other extreme by standardizing the inferior East India Company model, and after the Battle of Waterloo the House of Commons was told 'it was astonishing to see the number of barrels [of muskets] that had burst and were lying on the field'. One officer recalled, twenty years after Waterloo:

> The firelocks of the British army then in use . . . were of a bad quality; soldiers might be seen creeping about to get hold of the firelocks of the killed and wounded, to try if the locks were better than theirs, and dashing the worst on the ground as if in a rage with it.[31]

---

[30] Examples of Royal Navy mops and rammers of this period are preserved at the National Maritime Museum, Greenwich, and elsewhere; Gicquel des Touches 'Souvenir d'un marin de la République' *Révue des Deux Mondes* 75ᵉ année 5ᵉ periode vol. 28 (July-Aug. 1905) p. 407–436 at p. 424; Sir Howard Douglas *A Treatise on Naval Gunnery* (1820) p. 205 (the adoption of flint-locks on naval guns is here attributed to the author's father Rear-Admiral Sir Charles Douglas: *The Dictionary of National Biography* is doubtful on this point); for conditions on 29 May 1794 see T. Sturges Jackson ed. *Logs of the Great Sea Fights 1794–1805* (Navy Records Society) (2 vols 1899–1900) vol. 1 p. 25 (Log of the master of *Queen Charlotte*) and vol. 1 p. 40 (supplementary log, possibly by the signal lieutenant) and cf. Lady Bourchier *Memoir of the Life of Admiral Sir Edward Codrington* (2 vols. 1873) vol. 1 p. 22; Robert Greenhalgh Albion *Forests and Sea Power; The Timber Problem of the Royal Navy, 1652–1862* (Cambridge Mass. 1926) p. 393 and see generally John Knowles ed. *The Elements and Practice of Naval Architecture; or a Treatise on Ship-building* (3rd edit. 1822) and Gabriel Snodgrass *Letter . . . to . . . H. Dundas . . . and the Court of Directors of the East India Company* (1797); M.S. Bentham *The Life of Brigadier-General Sir Samuel Bentham, K.S.G.* (1862) p. 106–113 and 166–9.

[31] Richard Glover *Peninsular Preparation: The Reform of the British Army 1795–1809* (Cambridge 1963) p. 52–3; *Parliamentary Debates* vol. 34 col. 1078 (speech of Colonel Charles Palmer, 11 June 1816); 'Operations of the Fifth or Picton's Division in the Campaign of Waterloo. By an Officer of the Division. 1835' *United Services Journal* 1841 part 2 p. 170–203 at p. 183.

VII. The Contribution of Industrial Production

We have no statistics either for total industrial output in this period, or for weapons production, but it seems clear that armaments manufacture represented a very much smaller share of the country's total economic effort in 1793–1815 than in 1914–1918 or 1939–1945. In 1806 it was claimed that of 305,000 tons of iron produced in a year, the government would use 56,000 tons; if this figure for government requirements is anything to go on, then it is probable that the proportion of the rapidly increasing output of the iron industry purchased by government actually fell during the wars. Government orders for cloth, not merely for the British armed forces but to supply the allies, were very considerable, but again probably represented a declining proportion of a rapidly growing output. Much of government military expenditure went on rations and pay: from April 1808 to December 1811 British forces in Spain and Portugal consumed £20,181,250 18s. 10d. in pay and only £281,117 4s.5d. in Ordnance supplies. In the same period the Spanish government received from Britain over two million pounds worth of ordnance and commissariat stores, everything from gunpowder to £833 3s. worth of bugles and trumpets. These supplies, though vital to the Spanish resistance to Napoleon, represent about one per cent of British government expenditure in the period.[32]

Bearing in mind Britain's lead in other fields of industrialization it is not surprising that British munitions output compared favourably with that of other countries. Between 1803 and 1816 the British manufactured 2,673,366 fire-arms and purchased 293,000 abroad (mainly at the beginning of the period). The French in the slightly briefer time-span 1803–1814 manufactured 2,659,397 and captured 700,000. Their manufacturing capacity seems to have been much larger than the British in 1803 but was surpassed by 1811, in which year Louis Simond saw a single steam-powered plant in Birmingham which produced 10,000 musket barrels a month. (After Waterloo surplus musket barrels were fitted together to serve as gas pipes.) Gunpowder output also expanded; in 1809 Ordnance Board powder mills produced 36,623¾ ninety-pound barrels of powder and private contractors using government-supplied saltpetre a further 24,433 ninety-pound barrels. It was the Ordnance Board powder mills at Waltham Abbey which produced the largest explosion of the period, when on 27 November 1811 No. 4 Press House and the adjoining

---

[32] For government requirements in iron see *Parliamentary Debates* vol. 7 col. 86–7 (speech of Sir John Wrottesley 9 May 1806): the Chancellor of the Exchequer's statement (ibid. vol. 6 col. 949, 29 April 1806) indicates a figure of only 25,730 tons: see also Sir Edward Thomason *Memoirs: during half a century* (2 vols 1845) vol. 1 p. 45; *Parliamentary Papers* 1812 IX p. 59, 64–5 and cf p. 142. A breakdown of the cargoes of 154 ships unloading government supplies from Britain in Spanish ports in 1809 is given in José Canga Argüelles ed. *Documentos pertencientes a las observaciones sobre la historia de la Guerra de España* (2 vols Madrid 1835) vol. 2 p. 253–7 no. LVII and see also vol. 2 p. 103 no. XXII.

Corning House blew up, killing seven workmen and breaking windows in Hackney ten miles away. As already mentioned, some of Britain's munitions output was supplied to allied governments: Portugal received in the years 1796–1801 31,500 muskets, 11,300 cavalry carbines, 3,300 pistols, 14,300 swords, 10,000 barrels of powder, 500 tons of saltpetre and twenty field guns, and a further 114,116 muskets, 600 carbines, 2,120 rifles and six field guns in the period 1808–11; Spain received 222,141 muskets, 2,600 carbines, 342 guns; Sweden in 1808 received 35,000 muskets. In 1813 the British government sent to Palermo for the use of the Austrian government 'muskets, accoutrements and ammunition' for 50,000 infantry, and carbines and accoutrements etc. for 10,000 cavalry. The claim made shortly after the war that 'the British government put into execution the gigantic plan of being the depot, the manufactory, the place of arms, and the centre of the European war' is somewhat exaggerated but is essentially true as far as Spain's and Portugal's participation in the war was concerned.[33]

Much of British munitions production was contracted out. In 1815 government viewers stationed with contractors in Birmingham received a total of £3,570 2s wages – from the amount there must have been at least twenty of them – and the London-based Inspector of Small Arms was paid £365 expenses for a stay in Birmingham, a very considerable sum of money for the period; the Assistant Inspector received £159 5s. travel expenses. At the same time the government's own installations, the dockyards, Woolwich Arsenal, and various factories run by the Ordnance Board, played a relatively larger role in war production than they did in the twentieth-century world wars. Both in size and technical sophistication government factories were in advance of anything in the private sector: Woolwich Arsenal was probably the largest covered factory area in the world at this period, and the largest of its four blast furnaces could process sixteen tons of metal at a time for high quality castings. Supply to the government was a key area in

[33] Charles Dupin *View of the History and Actual State of the Military Force of Great Britain* (2 vols 1822) vol. 2 p. 172, 175; Louis Simond *Journal of a Tour and Residence in Great Britain during the Years 1810 and 1811* (2 vols Edinburgh 1817) vol. 2 p. 120; Charles Singer et al. *A History of Technology* (5 vols Oxford 1954–8) vol. 4 p. 271; Richard Glover *Peninsular Preparation* (Cambridge 1963) p. 67; John Sherwig *Guineas and Gunpowder* Cambridge Mass. 1969 p. 137, 192, 237 fn; Public Record Office FO 70/56 Foreign Office to Lord William Bentinck 6 Oct. 1813; Dupin *Military Force of Great Britain* vol. 2 p. 171. There had been some much larger explosions before the wars: on 5 November 1772 a privately owned powder store detonated at Chester, killing 40 and injuring 56 people (*Annual Register* 1772 p. 137), and even worse loss of life resulted from the explosion of powder magazines at Crema in Italy in 1768, at Brescia in Italy in 1769, and at Abbeville in France in 1773. Other notable wartime explosions included those of powder mills at Hounslow, 14 Jan. 1796, at Dartford, 10 Aug. 1796, at Cork, 5 May 1802, and at Faversham, 7 Sept. 1802, 18 Sept. 1807, and 16 Jan. 1810.

the development of mass-production techniques. The French emigré Marc Isambard Brunel mechanized the manufacture of wooden pulley-blocks for rigging naval vessels; this involved 'forty-three machines constituting a system of machinery' capable of producing 160,000 pulley-blocks per year: a crude fore-runner of the massive specialized machine-tools and production lines of the Second World War era. Brunel then went on to design a mechanical plant for the manufacture of the army's boots, capable of producing 400 pairs a day: this was on private venture, and unfortunately for Brunel Napoleon abdicated before he could dispose of the bulk of his output.[34]

Techniques developed in the private sector were quickly adopted at Woolwich and the dockyards: the method of casting guns solid and then boring them out by revolving the barrels on huge jigs had been pioneered by the Carron company in Scotland but by 1809 the Woolwich arsenal produced 385 full-length guns – not carronades – by this process. The mechanized ropery designed by Simon Goodrich, engineer to the navy, at Portsmouth, owed its inspiration to the mechanized rope-making plant of Grimshaw, Webster, Hills & Scarth at Sunderland; but was much bigger. The use of gas-lighting in factories had been pioneered at Boulton's Soho Works in Birmingham from 1802 onwards, and in the Philips & Lee cotton factory in Manchester from 1806, but in 1807 the copper rolling mills and mechanized rope-making plant in the naval dockyard at Portsmouth went over to 24-hour round-the-clock shift work and this seems to suggest that they too were already using gas-lighting. At a time when there were no technical colleges or university engineering departments, and most engineering firms operated on a rule-of-thumb basis, the government was unique in the wealth of technical information at its disposal: Simon Goodrich, 'mechanist' in the Naval Works department (later Civil Architect and Engineer's department) compiled

---

[34] *Parliamentary Papers* 1816 XII p. 152; *Penny Magazine* no. 445 (9 March 1839) p. 90, and cf. 'Plan of the Ordnance premises [at Woolwich] 1818' Public Record Office WORK 43/160; Richard Beamish *Memoir of the Life of Sir Marc Isambard Brunel* London 1862 p. 93, p. 344 (appendix B), see also Public Record Office Adm. 106/1883, which includes several letters from Brunel, and Singer ed. *A History of Technology* vol. 4 p. 426–8 and plate 26; Beamish *Brunel* p. 133.

The actual construction of the machines Brunel designed was carried out by Henry Maudslay, who had previously supplied the tools designed by Brunel and by Sir Samuel Bentham for the Royal Carriage Factory at Woolwich. Maudslay's former employer, Joseph Bramah, meanwhile designed and built a machine to print serial numbers on all the bank-notes generated by the war – the Bank of England ordered thirty of these machines at 240 guineas each in 1808 and another eight in 1814, and from 1809 Bank of England notes were entirely printed except for the individual signature. For an important letter illustrating the relationship between Brunel and Maudslay see Science Museum Library Ms 1261 Maudslay to Brunel 14 Sept. 1805 and cf. W.T. Vincent *The Records of the Woolwich District* (2 vols Woolwich [1888–1891]) vol. 1 p. 351; Ian McNeil *Joseph Bramah: A Century of Invention, 1749–1851* (Newton Abbot 1968) p. 144–5.

78 volumes of notes and a collection of hundreds of engineering drawings – 200 for the war years alone.[35]

Nevertheless the government saw no particular need to establish its munitions supply on a new organizational basis, and much of the expertise required for the development of government munitions production came from outsiders like Brunel. Admittedly Sir Samuel Bentham, an engineer and designer of major talent, was Inspector General of Naval Works 1796–1807 and a member of the Navy Board 1808–1812 but when he was not quarrelling with his less imaginative colleagues he was on secondment in Russia – both his brigadier-general's rank and his knighthood were Russian. The officers of the Ordnance were principally field engineers, experts in entrenchment and surveying, or artillerists; one of them, Lieutenant John Bell, invented the technique of using a heavy iron ball swinging on a chain for demolition work but apart from this instance of inspired crudity, and the Shrapnel shell and the Congreve rocket, little in the way of technological inventiveness was contributed by Ordnance officers. Simon Goodrich, the Navy's mechanical engineering expert, was an official of inferior rank, and with little influence: when the prestigious civilian engineers John Rennie and James Watt Junior, and Watt's partner Southern, came to Portsmouth to make an inspection at the government's request, they found fault with everything except for the Boulton & Watt steam engines, causing Goodrich to complain to a confidant, 'How can I who am called a *Mechanist* pretend to contradict any general assertion of those who are called *Engineers*?' – a *cri de coeur* which the professional expert was to provoke often in subsequent years, though later it would generally be the expert who would be the government official and his victim who would be the private citizen.[36]

VIII. International Comparisons: External Trade

Figures for industrial output in other European countries are even less available than for Britain, and the best mode of comparing Britain's economic position with that of other nations is by examining statistics for foreign trade.

[35] *Penny Magazine* no. 445 (9 March 1839) p. 90; Science Museum Library microfilm B54/Books 72–8 & Misc. f 208 (Simon Goodrich's notebooks); William Murdock *An Account of the Application of the Gas from Coal to Oeconomical Purposes . . . read before the Royal Society, on 25th February 1808* (1808) p. 7 and John Van Voorst *An Address to the Proprietors of the Intended Gas Light and Coke Company: to which is annexed, an Epitome of the Evidence, taken before the Committee of the House of Commons* (1809) p. 47 and cf. also p. 53, 56, 62; Science Museum Library microfilm B54/Books 72–8 & Misc. f. 249 H. Vernon to Simon Goodrich 21 July 1808; E.A. Forward 'Simon Goodrich and his Work as an Engineer', Part II *Transactions of the Newcomen Society* vol. 18 (1937–8) p. 1–28 and list in ibid. vol. 19 (1938–9) p. 249–260.

[36] Vincent *The Records of the Woolwich District.* vol. 1 p. 332; Science Museum Library microfilm B54/Books 72–8 & Misc. f. 208 Goodrich to John Grimshaw 23 Feb. 1807.

The overall picture is that French and British foreign trade at the time of the French Revolution were approximately equal, that by the end of the 1790s British trade was twice France's and that despite a minor French recovery in the 1800s this remained true for the rest of the war period. And France was, because of rather than in spite of the wars, the most successful trading nation on the European continent.

An important element in France's actually rather limited success was a shift from maritime to overland trade, involving a decline in the population of the major ports but a useful development in the infrastructure of inland manufacturing and distribution centres. Something similar also occurred in Germany where Berg, Aachen, Jülich and Krefeld and several areas of Saxony developed into major textile centres. Nevertheless a shift of this kind was not possible everywhere, and the clearest picture of Britain's impact on international trading arrangements – and a justification for the bitterness against Britain which Napoleon sought to exploit with the Continental Blockade – is given by an examination of the numbers and movement of merchant shipping.

We may take as our starting point a survey made by French consular officials, on orders from Paris, three years before the commencement of the French Revolution. These figures, which are consistent with official Danish, Swedish and British data, are the only comparative estimates available for the whole of Europe.

Country	Number of ships	Ships over 100 tons burthen	Total tonnage
Spain	1,202	534	149,460
Portugal	300	–	84,843
Genoa	643	89	42,130
Two Sicilies	1,047	400	132,220
Habsburg Empire	1,141	150	84,090
Venice	418	297	60,332
United Provinces (i.e Holland)	1,871	1,498	397,709
Hanse Towns	467	433	101,347
Rostock	65	8	3,648
Sweden	1,224	626	169,279
Denmark	3,601	700	386,020
Danzig	77	74	28,857
Prussia	99	96	21,497
Russia	523	18	39,394
England	–	–	881,963 (plus 348,000 tons of colliers)
France	5,268	3,270	729,340

The British figures may be supplied from British sources as 11,719 vessels in 1789.[37]

In the thirty years that followed we may *assume* a catastrophic decline in the shipping of Genoa, Venice and the Two Sicilies as a result of those countries' unwilling involvement in the Anglo-French war in the Mediterranean; of Spain, which was at war with Britain between 1796 and 1801 and between 1805 and 1808, and of Ostend (where all the Habsburg ships over 100 tons were registered) which was annexed to France in the 1790s and shared the fate of other French ports. What happened to the French merchant marine can be assessed from the figures for entries and departures in and out of French ports in 1792 and 1801: 1,442 tons of shipping, more than half of it French, in 1792 and 699,056 tons of shipping, only about a third of it French, in 1801. Napoleon's Continental Blockade, which reduced customs receipts from 60,622,189 francs in 1807 to 11,552,152 francs in 1809, also helped reduce the incomes of French shipowners, and hence also their capacity to invest in new ships. The number of French ocean-going vessels is estimated to have been reduced from 1,500 in 1801 to 179 in 1812.[38]

The decline of the Dutch merchant navy seems to have been at least as rapid, as may be seen from figures for the number of ships passing through the Sound in and out of the Baltic:

Year	Total	British	Dutch	Swedish	Danish	Prussian
1783	11,166	?	?	?	?	?
1790	9,493	3,788	2,009	430	1,559	698
1793	9,967	3,478	887	2,295	1,508	615
1796	12,112	4,455	–	2,505	2,157	2,022
1801	8,998	2,656	–	1,632	1,527	2,049
1802	12,130	3,957	634	2,212	1,771	2,388
1804	10,579	3,507	–	2,154	1,899	2,012

In 1790 Sweden was at war with Russia, so that it is possible that much of the normal Swedish traffic to Stockholm, Åbo and other Baltic ports was diverted to Göteborg, outside the Baltic: at any rate the figures for Swedish traffic through the Sound are only a quarter or a fifth of what was normal a few years later, and it is possible that Dutch shipping substituted itself for Swedish shipping in 1790, thus inflating the pre-Revolutionary

[37] Ruggiero Romano 'Per una Valutazione della Flotta Mercantile Europea alla fine del Secolo XVIII' *Studi in onore di Amintore Fanfani* (6 vols Milan 1962) vol. 5 p. 573–591 at p. 578, 582–9.

[38] Jacques Peuchet *Statistique Élémentaire de la France* (Paris 1805) p. 495–6; Marcel Dunan 'Napoleon et le Système Continentale en 1810' *Révue d'Histoire Diplomatique* vol. 60 (1946) p. 71–98 at p. 82; Georges Lefebvre *Napoleon* (2 vols 1969) vol. 2 p. 84.

War figure. Even so the drop from 887 Dutch ships passing through the Sound in 1793 to none in 1796 is striking enough. The decline continued in the Napoleonic period. The number of ships entering the Texel-Vlie and Maas-Goeree channels, representing the bulk of landings in the Netherlands, averaged 2,700 a year before 1805: in 1806 the figure was 1,369, in 1807 1,079 and in 1810 only 259.[39]

Of course neutral shipping benefited from the obstacles placed by the belligerents in one another's way. The Swedish mercantile marine seems to have stagnated, if not actually declined, in the 1790s, and the same may also have been true for the Danish merchant fleet based at Copenhagen; but there was considerable growth in the merchant fleet sailing from ports in Norway, at that time a Danish territory.

Norwegian shipping	*Other Danish shipping*
1799 747 ships of 49,470.5 lasts and 6,336 crew	1,436 ships of 75,499 lasts and 12,564 crew
1802 990 ships of 53,753.5 lasts and 7,680 crew	1,278 ships of 66,189 lasts and 8,806 crew

one last = approx. two tons

In 1807, when Danish trade with Britain was running at record levels, the British attack on Copenhagen began seven years of war between the two countries in which 1,560 Dano-Norwegian vessels were sunk or captured by the British and receipts from transit dues at Copenhagen fell by 88 per cent. The same pattern of expansion as a result of neutrality, eventual but inevitable involvement in the war, and disastrous decline was also experienced by Hamburg, the principal Hanse port. Hamburg survived Danish occupation during the Armed Neutrality crisis of 1800–1801 with only a minor shock – 1801 seems indeed to have been a peak year for Hamburg's shipping industry – but the French occupation of northern Germany from 1806 onwards led to a rapid falling off of business. This is reflected in a decline in the size of the merchant fleet from which there was no recovery even after the conclusion of the war:

---

[39] J. Jepson Oddy *European Commerce . . . Detailing the Produce, Manufactures, and Commerce, of Russia, Prussia, Sweden, Denmark and Germany* (1805) p. 369 and Jean Pierre Catteau [i.e. Catteau-Calleville] *Tableau des États Danois* (3 vols Paris 1802) vol. 3 p. 357 foll. (Catteau's figures are not completely consistent with Oddy's or, for that matter, with figures cited on different pages of Catteau's own book; where in doubt I have followed Oddy); Simon Schama *Patriots and Liberators: Revolution in the Netherlands, 1780–1813* (New York 1977) p. 561–2.

Year	Number of trading vessels	Burden in lasts
1792	205	20,460
1801	279	30,490
1806	248	27,200
1812	145	16,250
1822	112	12,260[40]

The United States held on to its neutrality longest and benefited most; U.S. merchant tonnage grew from 558,000 tons in 1802 to 981,000 tons in 1810. There were however a whole series of checks and obstacles: a virtual state of war with France 1797–1801, a war with Tripoli 1801–5, constant friction with the British and French blockade authorities 1807–12. In the five years prior to the outbreak of the Anglo-American war of 1812, 917 American ships had been seized by British cruisers, 858 by the French and their allies. Once the war with Britain had broken out, despite the successes of American frigates against the Royal Navy, U.S. foreign trade virtually collapsed, as the statistics show:

Year	Imports	Exports	Re-exports	Net profits of carrying trade
1791	30,500,000	19,012,000	500,000	6,200,000
1807	144,740,342	108,343,000	59,644,000	42,100,000
1811	57,887,952	61,317,000	16,023,000	40,800,000
1813	22,177,812	27,856,000	2,848,000	10,200,000
1814	12,967,859	6,927,000	145,000	2,600,000[41]

During the same period the growth of the British merchant fleet was nothing less than phenomenal, especially given that it was already the largest in the world when the wars began, and had moreover to sustain the burden and disruption of its merchant seamen being systematically pressed into naval service.

[40] Oddy *European Commerce* p. 321; ibid. p. 386 and Catteau *Tableau* vol. 2 p. 358; *New Cambridge Modern History* vol. 9 p. 488 and Marius Vibaek *Den Danske Handels Historie fra den Aeldste Tider til vor Dage* (3 vols Copenhagen 1932–8) vol. 2 p. 298 and 300; Walter Kresse *Materialen zur Entwicklungsgeschichte der Hamburger Handelsflotte, 1765–1825* (Hamburg 1966) p. 70–113 Tabelle 4; ibid. p. 66–7 Tabelle 2.

[41] Bradford Perkins *Prologue to War: England and the United States 1805–1812* (Berkeley 1961) p. 29; E.R. Johnson et al. *History of Domestic and Foreign Commerce of the United States* (2 vols Washington 1915) vol. 2 p. 29–30; D.C. North *The Economic Growth of the United States 1790–1860* (Englewood Cliffs 1961) p. 221, 228, 249.

	England Only			Britain, Ireland, Colonies		
Year	Ships	Tons	Crew	Ships	Tons	Crew
1789	9,558	1,078,374	80,299	14,310	1,395,172	108,962
1792	10,633	1,186,610	87,589	16,079	1,540,145	118,286
1802	13,446	1,642,224	113,670	20,568	2,128,055	154,530
1815	17,346	2,139,301	135,006	24,860	2,681,276	177,309

Bearing in mind that all the other indications are that the global volume of seaborne trade shrank considerably during the war years, one may accept the contemporary boast that 'From being the greatest, we became the *only* commercial nation in the world.'[42]

IX. A Key Resource: Money

Ultimately however British predominance was a question of money. The general scale of British war expenditure relative to that of her allies may be seen from the fact that the Waterloo campaign cost the British – over and above ordinary army expenditure of £21,338,831 10s.8d. – £12,873,553 for extraordinary services and £11,035,297 13s 1¾d in loans, stores and advances to the allied powers. The Prussians, who claimed a half share in the defeat of Napoleon spent a mere 15,300,000 thalers – £2,353,846. Peak Prussian government expenditure in the years of the so-called War of Liberation, 1813-14, was £7,123,867, about a thirtieth of what Britain spent in the same period.[43]

The total expenditure of France can only be guessed. Records of French budgets have been published, though these are awkward to use for comparative purposes as they do not run systematically from year to year but instead cover irregular periods of, for example, fifteen months, and include allocations for paying off the excess expenditure of previous budget periods. In most years these budgets were grossly overspent, and were also supplemented by contributions from France's allies fixed by treaty but always in part – never entirely – spent on military requirements within the territory of the contributing government. Thus, for example, of the 229,127,901 Dutch gulden paid to the French by the Batavian Republic (i.e., the Dutch) up to the end of 1804, 74,065,814 gulden was for French troops stationed within the frontiers

[42] *Commons Journals* vol. 57 p. 955, vol. 59 p. 586, vol. 71 p. 804; *Edinburgh Review* vol. 32 (1819) p. 50 (article by J.R. McCulloch). See also Sir Frederick Morton Eden *Eight Letters on the Peace; and on the Commerce and Manufactures of Great Britain and Ireland* (2nd edit. 1802) p. 43–4 for the decline of shipping in previous eighteenth-century wars.

[43] *Parliamentary Papers* 1816 XI p. 201; Karl Mamroth *Geschichte der Preussischen Staats-Besteuerung, 1806–1816* (Leipzig 1890) p. 48.

of the Batavian Republic. Similarly, after the Battle of Austerlitz the Austrian government agreed to pay over 118 million francs; 27 million was spent locally by the French army, 48 million was sent to France, the rest never paid. After the Battle of Wagram the Austrian government agreed to pay 250 million francs, of which 76 million was spent locally by the French army, 88 million sent to France and the rest never paid. After the Battle of Jena, Prussia, Saxony and the minor German principalities allied to them handed over approximately 500 million francs, but while La Bouillerie, *Trésorier général du domaine extraordinaire* thought the precise amount was 470,467,387 francs, Daru, the intendant general of the army and responsible for the army's accounts thought it was 513,744,410 francs, and it is not clear how much of the money actually reached France.[44]

Napoleon himself was supremely vague about such details. In 1807 for example he ordered:

> as soon as my army has entered Portugal it must be fed, clothed and paid by the contributions which shall be levied in that country: from that moment on there must be no need for me to send another half-penny.

Both in Portugal and later in Spain, where an army of over 250,000 lived for five years principally off what could be found locally, no accounts, or even estimates, were ever produced but this system of military theft covered mainly food, fuel, transport and other services, and despite Napoleon's facilely categorical order, the fire-arms and the uniforms, and usually the soldiers' pay, had to come from France; in December 1810 we find his chief of staff Berthier writing to Masséna, commanding the army in Portugal, to say that two wagon convoys were en route, one with 2.5 million francs for soldiers' pay, the other with 2 million. One may conclude that the official budgets almost certainly represented the greater part of total expenditure, but they evidently cannot be used as a basis for calculating the exact total – and whatever the total, it was by British standards unimpressive. In 1805 the French budget was 684 million francs (£27,636,363) compared to British government income of £76,469,450 15s. 4³/₄d. and in 1813 1,150 million francs (£46,464,646) compared to British government income of £109,078,113. Thus Britain, possessing with Ireland less than half the population of the French Empire, spent at least twice as much: but even more remarkable was the differences in the way the money was raised and the effect this had on economic life generally.[45]

---

[44] French budgets are printed in [F.N. Comte] Mollien *Mémoires d'un Ministre du Trésor Public, 1780–1815* (4 vols Paris 1845) cf. Marcel Marion *Histoire Financière de la France depuis 1715* (6 vols Paris 1927–31) vol. 4 p. 333–4; G. Graaf Schimmelpenninck *Rutger Jan Schimmelpenninck en eenige Gebeurtenissen van Zijnen Tijd* (2 vols Hague 1845) vol. 2 p. 312–3 (appendix B); Marion *Histoire Financière* vol. 4 p. 319–320.

[45] *Correspondance de Napoleon 1er* vol. 16 p. 165 no. 13327 Napoleon to General Clarke 5 Nov. 1807; W.F.P. Napier *History of the War in the Peninsula and in the South of France* (6 vols 1828–40) vol. 3 p. 611 (appendix) Berthier to Masséna 4 Dec. 1810, Marion *Histoire Financière* vol. 4 p. 337 cf. *Parliamentary Papers* 1806 IX p. 3 and 1813–14 X p. 3.

Taking Europe as a whole, the bulk of the total amount of money spent in the wars of 1792–1815 was raised by taxation. The British government, reversing an earlier policy of financing war by long-term borrowing, raised 58 per cent of Britain's war expenditure from taxes, compared to only 19 per cent during the American War of Independence. It would seem that there had been a progressively increasing dependence on loan finance in wartime by the British exchequer since the wars against Louis XIV and that this policy remained in force during the first years of the French Revolutionary War, up till the financial crisis of 1797. After the suspension of cash payments by the Bank of England and a period of uncertainty about the stability of credit, it was remarked, 'It is now pretty evident, that during the remainder of this War, the supplies must be raised within the year'. This was, on balance, what actually occurred from then on. The French also counted on taxation to finance two-thirds of budgeted expenditure. The Russian government too covered most of its rapidly increasing expenditure by taxes:

Year	Tax receipts in roubles	Expenditure in roubles
1802	77,163,555	79,303,355
1806	95,252,501	108,528,755
1809	148,134,116	279,246,791
1812	258,386,087	287,541,557

Even Austria, whose finances were chronically shaky, managed to raise half of annual expenditure from taxes until the disaster of 1809; in 1799, mobilized for war, Austrian expenditure was estimated at 137,148,000 Austrian gulden and income at 74,371,000 gulden; in 1802, demobilized, expenditure at 87,324,000 gulden and income at 70,981,000 gulden; the 1799 figure for expenditure, the highest recorded for the pre-Napoleonic period, translates as £11 million. Spain too had huge deficits: in 1797, the worst year of the mid-1790s, expenditure was 1,422,690,423 reales – about £14.2 million – and income only 602,246,860 reales. The country with the biggest problem in raising taxes was probably the Netherlands. Their revenue system was in need of drastic overhaul and was of course severely damaged by the collapse of trade: in 1804 expenditure was 71,146,038 gulden (about £6 million) and income only 32,925,000 gulden; since 1795 the public debt had increased from 787 million gulden to 1,126 million, more than two-thirds of this being payments to France, and tax revenue was barely sufficient to pay the interest on this debt. Even after tax reforms in 1806 revenue seems not to have kept up to 50 per cent of expenditure, the difference being made up by recourse to the Netherlands' highly developed – but increasingly overburdened – capital market. But no other country borrowed so large a proportion of its expenditure.[46]

---

[46] P.K. O'Brien 'Government Revenue 1793–1815' p. 19 Table 6. The calculation by Sir John Bradbury in Public Record Office T 171/106, 'The Financing of Naval and Military
continued

As was to be expected in a period of spiralling government costs, there was everywhere a spate of fiscal reforms and experiments. Britain's wartime income tax, which raised £13,360,407 0s.8 ½d. in 1812 alone, was one of the big successes of the period. In Russia the duty on vodka, the most important single source of revenue, was bumped up from 27,189,690 roubles in 1806 to 93,273,633 in 1811. In France a new cadastration (survey of taxable property) in 1808 eliminated inequalities of assessment and on balance rounded down the amounts levied; in fact direct taxation declined somewhat though the new *départements* paid especially heavily and some of the *départements* in pre-1789 France paid a third less in 1813 than they had in 1791 before the wars started. It seems that Napoleon was looking to the political base of his regime, the *notables*, and was prepared to sacrifice revenue to Public Relations.[47]

Other than taxes, governments had three resources: funded borrowing (i.e., loans promoted as a long-term investment for subscribers, with a guaranteed interest); short-term borrowing, and emergency expedients primarily involving the issue of paper money.

In the eighteenth century the two countries with a developed capital market and a tradition of government dependence on a funded debt were Britain and the United Provinces (i.e., the Netherlands), though there were also important capital markets in Frankfurt, Leipzig, Hamburg, Antwerp, Genoa and even Paris; as late as 1809 Antwerp held 30 per cent of the Swedish national debt, Leipzig 13 per cent and Genoa 8 per cent, the Dutch holding most of the rest. In 1815 Barings, who had contracted for a £30 million loan in London to help finance the Waterloo campaign, were allegedly able to place so much of it in European financial centres that it was necessary to move only £1 million from Britain. Except in Britain and the United Provinces however it cannot be said that governments had made the transition to a stable funded debt

---

continued
Operations 1793–1886' 12 Feb. 1900 estimates only 47 per cent of total war expenditure 1793–1815 was raised by taxes but this calculation is based on a much narrower view of what constitutes war expenditure than that in P.K. O'Brien's much more recent and exhaustive work. According to O'Brien taxes provided 26 per cent of war expenditure 1702–13, 21 per cent 1739–48, 20 per cent 1756–63, 19 per cent 1775–83 and 10.4 per cent 1793–7; the quotation is from an anonymous letter to William Windham in October 1798, British Library Add. 37877 f. 268; Russian figures are in Add. 31230 f. 271, 273–4, paper by Sir Francis D'Ivernois *c*. Nov. 1812 based on Russian official records: for D'Ivernois's mission to Russia and his investigations and planned financial reforms see Otto Karmin *Sir Francis D'Ivernois, 1757–1842: sa vie, son oeuvre et son temps* (Geneva 1920) p. 486–98; Adolf Beer *Die Finanzen Oesterreichs im XIX. Jahrhundert* (Prague 1877) p. 390–2 (Anmerkung 1); José Canga Argüelles ed. *Documentos pertencientes a las Observaciones sobre la historia de la Guerra de España* (2 vols Madrid 1835) vol. 1 p. 11 no. V; Schama *Patriots and Liberators* p. 497 cf. Schimmelpenninck *Schimmelpenninck en eenige Gebeurtenissen van Zijnen Tijd* vol. 2 p. 312–3, 315 (appendices B and C) and James C. Riley *International Government Finance and the Amsterdam Capital Market 1740–1815* (Cambridge 1980) p. 213.

[47] *Parliamentary Papers* 1812–13 XI p. 3; British Library Add. 31230 f. 273 D'Ivernois memo; Marion *Histoire Financière* vol. 4 p. 309–10.

system. Habsburg Austria frequently defaulted. Prussia, after a determined effort, cleared off the debts incurred by Frederick the Great by 1785. France, having borrowed heavily to finance the various wars of the mid-eighteenth century, had a major debt problem before the French Revolution but the total collapse of the currency in the 1790s as a result of the over-issue of government paper money, the notorious *assignats*, meant that by the time Napoleon came to power the government had been able to discard its pre-war obligations.[48]

The French government undoubtedly made much less use of systematic public borrowing in the 1800s than was actually feasible, given that Paris remained a not unimportant capital market. Ouvrard, the great financial speculator of the period, who supplied millions of francs' worth of goods on credit and offered Napoleon numerous large loans against future taxes, afterwards wrote in his memoirs

> Napoleon did not know any source of revenue other than taxation and conquest. For him credit was an abstract concept: he saw in it only the dreams of ideologues and the hollow ideas of economists.

This was also the view of Ouvrard's German collaborator Vincent Nolte; Napoleon, he later wrote,

> never had a correct idea of what credit means, and never considered it worthwhile to make any regulations applicable to it, but looked upon bankers, merchants, and, most especially, public purveyors, as so many birds of prey.

As always, Napoleon was totally pragmatic in this matter. Though proud of his policy of not depending on credit he allowed his allies to borrow money on the Paris market. The Hanse city of Lübeck for example paid its enforced contributions to the French treasury by borrowing in Paris. Napoleon even occasionally subscribed to loans himself, for example taking up six million francs of the otherwise unsuccessful loan floated by the Saxon government to finance Saxon preparations for the invasion of Russia in 1812. In this particular instance Napoleon undoubtedly considered secret investment in the Saxon loan as the most discreet way of guaranteeing the loyalty of the Saxon government; but when Mollien, the treasury minister, talked about a national bank with something of the role of the Bank of England Napoleon fobbed him off with excuses.[49]

---

[48] Karl Åmark *Sveriges Statsfinanser* (Stockholm 1961) p. 653; [Jean-Baptiste-Honoré-Raymond] Capefigue *Histoire des Grandes Operations Financières: Banques, Bourses, Emprunts, Compagnies Industrielles, etc.* (3 vols Paris 1855–8) vol. 3 p. 29; Leopold Krug *Geschichte der preussischen Staatsschulden* (Breslau 1861) p. 30.

[49] G.J. Ouvrard *Mémoires* (3 vols Paris 1826–7) vol. 1 p. 137 (see ibid. vol. 1 p. 72–9, 119–126 for Ouvrard's advances to the French government); Vincent Nolte *Fifty Years in Both Hemispheres; or Reminiscences of a Merchant's Life* (1854) p. 69; Marion *Histoire Financière* vol. 4 p. 336–8, 357–8; Mollien *Mémoires* vol. 3 p. 325–7; ibid. vol. 3 p. 321–4 and footnotes for the Saxon loan.

It was consistent with Napoleon's views that his elder brother Joseph, when installed as King of Spain, set himself, amongst his first tasks, to eliminate the Spanish national debt inherited from the deposed Bourbons: in mid 1809 this stood at 7,194,266,839 reales (about £72 million). The means chosen was the sale of public property (*bienes nacionales* – a term obviously adapted from the *biens nationaux* sold off in France in the 1790s) and the intention was obviously to create a kind of property-owning new middle class that would be committed to the new regime, though as in France there was evidently also the idea that too much mobile capital was less desirable than a bourgeoisie rooted in real estate.[50]

Without particularly understanding the British credit system, Napoleon subscribed to the view of his own propagandists that the British funding system was vicious, unnatural, and ultimately ruinous. Even the British leaders were by no means happy with the runaway growth of the National Debt, and in the winter of 1806–1807 Lord Grenville, then Prime Minister, promoted an oddly short-sighted project to fix a limit on British loan finance. This scheme was shelved at the fall of Grenville's ministry and while the French consolidated debt grew from 45,180,624 francs – £1,825,480 – in 1804 to 63,307,637 francs in April 1814, the total British funded debt rose from £229,614,446 in February 1793 to £497,043,488 in February 1802 and £816,311,939 in February 1816. This included a £3 million loan advanced to the Austrian government in 1794 and extended to £4.6 million a year later; the Austrians defaulted and the oustanding amount, fixed by negotiation at £2.5 million, was carried on the British accounts till 1823, and corresponds approximately to the entire French consolidated debt at the time of Napoleon's first abdication.[51]

The British government was naturally reluctant to take on the debts of its allies: when in 1812 the Russian government seemed anxious that Britain should take over their £4.5 million debt on the Dutch capital market, Earl Cathcart, the ambassador to Russia, was instructed, 'Your Lordship will studiously avoid any reference to this Subject in your intercourse with the Russian Government'. At the same time nearly two-thirds of the money – £47 million – borrowed on the Irish account was actually raised in England: this incidentally gives an indication of the poverty of Ireland as compared to the sister isle. As a result of the War of 1812, the United States' debt nearly

---

[50] *Esposicion hecha a su Magestad sobre la Deuda Pública de la Nacion, con los estados de ella, por su ministro de hacienda* (Madrid 1809) p. 11; *Reales Decretos de 9 de Junio y 18 de Agosto del 1809* – a copy of this and other of Joseph's decrees are in British Library, shelf-mark T. 1545.

[51] See next chapter; A.D. Harvey 'The Ministry of All the Talents: The Whigs in Office February 1806 to March 1807' *Historical Journal* vol. 15 (1972) p. 619–648 at p. 640–643; Marion *Histoire Financière* vol. 4 p. 337 and *Parliamentary Papers* 1819–20 IV p. 112 (figures in *Parliamentary Papers* 1857–8 XXXIII p. 240–2 are slightly different, apparently because added up by years running 1 Jan.-31 Dec. instead of 1 Feb.-31 Jan. as in the earlier version: in this form the debt in 1815 is given as £861,039,049); Karl F. Helleiner *The Imperial Loans: A Study in Financial and Diplomatic History* (Oxford 1965) p. 49–50, 173.

trebled, from $45,154,189 in January 1812 to $116,490,582 in January 1817 but the latter amount merely corresponded to the portion of the Irish debt funded in Ireland. The sheer scale of British debt transactions constantly invited such belittling comparisons.[52]

As an example of a country that was unable to float major long-term loans at home, one may take Prussia. In order to finance Prussian participation in the opening stages of the French Revolutionary War, the Berlin government borrowed five million gulden on the Amsterdam market in 1793 and a further three million in 1794. In the latter year the government also managed to raise 1,227,450 thalers – £188,838 – on the domestic market. There was also a £1.2 million subsidy forthcoming from Britain, representing about as much as the borrowing at Amsterdam and at home combined. This was still not enough, and a loan of 8 to 10 million gulden was opened to subscribers at Frankfurt am Main, and princes, prelates, noblemen, etc., invited to subscribe. Only 1,387,000 gulden were subscribed. Considerably more was raised by defaulting on the government's domestic bills and by December 1804, even after various repayments, the total government debt stood at 24,780,220 thalers – £3.8 million – a bit less than normal annual revenue. The Prussian government's policy in 1805–1806 of trying to play the French off against the British involved increased spending and on 4 February 1806 an order was made for the issue of 9,093,210 thalers – £1.4 million – of Treasury bills. After Prussia's catastrophic defeat at Jena in October 1806 these notes began to depreciate: Leopold Krug, in his *Geschichte der Preussischen Staatschulden* (Breslau 1861) prints an interesting table of the fluctuations of the 100 thaler Treasury bills on the Berlin bourse. Considering the unhappy circumstances of the country, these Treasury bills kept up their value rather well, creeping down to 27 thalers for a 100 thaler bill in July 1808, rising to 74.5 thalers in December 1808, then back down to 31.5 thalers in July 1809, after Napoleon's victory at Wagram put an end to what was widely seen as an Austrian bid to liberate Germany from the French yoke, then, encouraged by the issue of an additional two million thalers' worth of bills in December 1809 which was evidently seen as a prelude to the redemption of the original issue, back up to 86.75 in February 1810. By March 1812 the 100 thaler bills were up to 90 thalers, but Prussia's re-entry into the war against France brought them down to 24 thalers in June 1813. This Treasury bill issue was actually one of the more successful and less economically disruptive expedients of the Prussian government. Total indebtedness was 54,419,149 thalers at the end of 1806 and 131,765,336 thalers at the end of 1812; the Treasury bills were only a small part of this. Most of the indebtedness came from non-payment of interest, official salaries and pensions, and from not paying for purchases and requisitions. A

---

[52] Public Record Office FO 65/78 p. 13a-b Castlereagh to Earl of Cathcart 24 July 1812; Bernard Cohen *Compendium of Finance: containing an account of the Origins, Progress, and Present State of the Public Debts, Revenue, National Banks and Currencies of France, Russia, Prussia etc.* (1822) p. 167, 173.

vast amount of negotiable paper was issued, under various titles – but all, in effect, government I.O.U.s – some of which came back as payment of taxes. The effect on trade and industry, and even on agriculture, of no-one being able to rely on being paid or, if paid, on the value of the currency they were paid in, can only have been crippling.[53]

X. The Paper System

The most spectacularly disastrous issue of paper money in this period was of course the French *assignats* of the 1790s, which eventually came to a total face value of 45,581,411,618 livres and effectively wiped out the old currency system and enabled the French government to start again from scratch. Thereafter the French currency was held stable, but other governments were forced by the exigencies of the war to follow the same route.[54]

In the Austrian Habsburg territories there were 440,549,000 gulden's worth of notes in circulation in September 1806 and 1,011,801,000 gulden's worth in July 1810 after sufficient had been printed to cover the expenses of the disastrous 1809 campaign. Napoleon was intrigued though unimpressed by the way the bankrupt Vienna government managed to maintain itself with a fiduciary issue and in September 1809, after Austria had sued for peace for the fourth time in twelve years, he ordered his minister of police to set up a secret factory to print Austrian money, explaining:

> It is with paper money that the house of Austria has been able to make war: it is with paper money that it will be able to do so again. That being so, it is my policy, in time of peace as in time of war, to destroy this paper money and force Austria to return to the system of specie, which by its nature will force her to reduce her army and the mad expenditure which has compromised the security of my states.

---

[53] Krug *Preussischen Staatsschulden* p. 33, 37–9; Sherwig *Guineas and Gunpowder* p. 47–9; Krug *Preussischen Staatsschulden* p. 67, p. 80–94 for the table showing the fluctuations of the 100 thaler Treasury bills; ibid. p. 117, 215 for total indebtedness 1806 and 1812; Mamroth *Preussischen Staats-Besteuerung* p. 48, 51–5 for the various kinds of paper issued by the Prussian government. See also Eckart Kehr ed. *Der Preussische Finanzpolitik 1806–1810: Quellen zur Verwaltung der Ministerien Stein und Altenstein*, prepared for publication by Hanna Schissler and Hans-Ulrich Wehler (Göttingen 1984) p. 36–42.

[54] The figure for the total issue of *assignats* is taken from Monbrion *De la Prépondérance maritime et commerciale de la Grande Bretagne* (Paris 1805) p. 312. The livre was approximately equal to the later franc – 1 franc = 1 livre 3 deniers (1.0125 livres) = about $\frac{1}{25}$ of a pound sterling. Under Napoleon note issue rose from a modest 34m francs in January 1804 to 87m francs in April 1805 and continued to rise more slowly to 111 million francs in 1812. There was something of a crisis of confidence in the note issue Sept.-Dec. 1805, payments in specie at the banks being limited to one note per person, but nothing like the catastrophe of the *assignat* era. A rapid reduction of the note issue during 1813 had a considerable adverse effect on trade: René Sédillot *Le Franc: histoire d'une monnaie des origines à nos jours* (Paris 1953) p. 180–187.

In February 1811, when Austrian notes were changing hands at the rate of twelve gulden paper for one gulden silver, a proclamation launched a new issue of paper, exchanging the old notes on a sliding scale of value depending on date of issue: notes of March 1799 were exchangeable at 105 for 100 gulden of new notes – not a bad offer as the old notes must have been falling to pieces at this stage in any case – while March 1807 notes were at 206 for 100 new notes, January 1809 notes at 222: 100, January 1811 notes at 500: 100. This extraordinary piece of economics was never completely acted through because of the renewal of war and financial chaos in 1813. (Interestingly enough, in view of Napoleon's sabotage scheme, this 1811 issue had a far more complicated design than was normal for paper money of the period, with a border of patterned roundels and oblongs and the denominations printed in German, Hungarian, Czech and Polish; the intention may have been to make the notes especially difficult to forge).[55]

In Denmark, the government set up a new public bank in 1791 with the object of helping to cancel the excess of paper currency already in circulation. By 1804 the notes of the new bank were already at 25 per cent discount, and the old notes at 45 per cent: by 1813 pre-1800 notes were at 1800 rixdollars per rixdollar of specie. The Danish government was probably more sensitive to commercial matters than most other European regimes but was helpless to resist the 'voracious Cancer' of inflation. They had borrowed over five million gulden on the Frankfurt and Amsterdam money markets in 1801–5, including two million gulden from Rothschild *père*, but after the commencement of the war with Britain in 1807 trade, revenue and credit collapsed in unison. The government was even reduced to commissioning Jewish currency speculators to keep up the Danish exchange rates on the international market by buying and selling against the current price trends, but with little success.[56]

The Russian government avoided the levels of inflation experienced in Austria and Denmark by adding to the currency somewhat more gradually:

[55] Beer *Finanzen Oesterreichs* p. 392–3 (Anmerkung II); Leon Lecestre ed. *Lettres Inedites de Napoleon 1er* (2 vols Paris 1897) vol. 1 p. 356 Napoleon to Fouché 6 Sept. 1809; Cohen *Compendium of Finance* p. 60; Albert Pick *Papiergeld* (Braunschweig 1967) p. 248, though cf. 1800 10 Gulden note illustrated in Deutche Bundesbank *Deutsches Papiergeld, 1772–1870* (Frankfurt 1964) (no pagination) which already has anti-forgery features in the design, but less elaborate.

There were several instances of foreign coins being manufactured in Birmingham, and the Prussian government eventually persuaded the British to prosecute Jewish immigrants involved in counterfeiting and exporting Prussian groschen: Geheimes Staatsarchiv, Preussischer Kulturbesitz, Merseburg, Rep 81 London 204, and see also Public Record Office TS 11/623/2013 and FO 33/16 p. 103 Sir James Craufurd to Lord Grenville no. 59, 23 Oct. 1798.

[56] Cohen *Compendium of Finance* p. 142–3 and cf. M.L. Nathanson *Historisk-statistisk Fremstilling af Danmarks National og Stats Huusholdning* (Copenhagen 1836) p. 124–154; Johann Georg Rist *Lebenserinnerungen* ed. G. Poel (2 vols Gotha 1880) vol. 2 p. 232 for the cancer image; Nathanson *Danmarks National og Stats Huusholdning* p. 322–4, Vibaek *Danske Handels Historie* vol. 2 p. 307–311, and Riley *International Government Finance* p. 139 Table 6–4 and p. 143.

Year	Paper roubles in circulation	Exchange rate of paper against specie
1797	163,574,840	126:100
1800	212,689,335	153:100
1803	247,624,665	125:100
1806	319,239,960	137:100
1809	533,201,300	224:100
1810	577,000,000	300:100
1817	836,000,000	?

Nevertheless the sudden drop in the value of the paper rouble when the quantity of notes issued was increased rapidly after 1806 is indicative of the public's distrust of paper money.[57]

Though these note issues included high denomination notes they directly affected the quantity – and people's confidence in – the currency changing hands in the street and market place. There was another, more sophisticated way for the government to print money, though it depended on the prior existence of an established and confident money market: the exchequer or treasury bill. The U.S. government which in 1812–85 issued 36 million worth of such instruments (confusingly designated Treasury Notes) was unusual in including in the issue bills as small as $3: generally exchequer bills were of large denomination, bearing interest, but not negotiable in small-change transactions, perhaps only negotiable at a government office; their theoretical attraction was as a kind of intermediate-term investment. The Prussian government's bill issue has already been described. Similarly the Spanish had 1,490,000,000 reales – about £14.9 million – of such bills in circulation in 1802 bearing 4 per cent interest The Spanish economy was unable to sustain this quantity and the discount rose from 15 per cent in 1802, when peace with Britain was officially concluded, to 52 per cent in 1804 when the war was resumed. In Britain on the other hand the government's use of bills was one of the keys to its wartime success.[58]

The issue of bills was essentially a technique for by-passing cash-flow problems, the gap between obtaining orders and receiving payments, and on five occasions (1793, 1797, 1807, 1808, 1811) the British government allocated Exchequer Bills for the purpose of assisting merchants to tide over their credit difficulties. The quantity of these bills – principally Exchequer Bills but also bills issued by the Navy and Victualling Boards, Ordnance Debentures, etc. – rose from £14.3 million in 1793 to £69.8 million in 1815 and at any given time for most of this period was very roughly equivalent to half annual tax revenue.

[57] Cohen *Compendium of Finance* p. 24.
[58] Donald H. Kagin 'Monetary Aspects of the Treasury Notes of the War of 1812' *Journal of Economic History* vol. 44 (1984) p. 69–88 at p. 69; Cohen *Compendium of Finance* p. 96–7.

These bills were sufficiently respected to be welcome on the British market; of £400 million Exchequer Bills issued 1797–1810 about £70 million were taken up immediately by the Bank of England. Most of the rest were disposed of by the brothers Goldsmid, the financial giants of the day, who were also involved in the consortium originally led by Walter Boyd and Paul Benfield and later by Sir Francis Baring and John Julius Angerstein which contracted for most of the government's funded loans. The bills were sought after by London banks and fire and marine insurance companies, and the Goldsmids managed a huge contact network of potential buyers up until 1808, in which year Benjamin Goldsmid hanged himself. For a time Abraham, the surviving brother, continued to flourish and in 1809 made Jewish history when he gave dinner and beds to the Dukes of Cumberland, Sussex and Cambridge (the King's three youngest sons) at his residence in Finsbury Square after they had attended a service at the Great Synagogue in Duke's Place. The following year, apparently over-extended in his dealings both in Exchequer Bills and in script of the funded debt, Abraham Goldsmid shot himself through the head in the garden of Nelson's former country seat, Merton Place, which he had purchased some time previously; the shock of this suicide caused a panic on the London money market.[59]

Up until 1813, Exchequer Bills were also the government's main means of making payments on the continent, the export of guineas being prohibited by law, and the depreciation abroad of Exchequer Bills led to a sustained attack in Parliament on the government's financial policy. Probably it was less the case that the British government's over-issue of paper had devalued the pound sterling than that the sheer vastness of British financial transactions on the continent compared to the contracted and timorous state of the European money markets made the latter unable to match British demand; Nathan Meyer Rothschild reckoned that it was the scale alone of British overseas expenditure in 1814–1815 that lowered the exchange rate 30 per cent. The fact that Parisian bankers were willing to do business with the Rothschilds in British government bills, despite the war and Napoleon's views on Britain, bankers, and bills, suggests that there was considerable confidence in the stability of the British currency even in the enemy capital, though it was later claimed that nearly £7.3 million in gold had to be smuggled from England to Dunkirk to support British credit on the French market.[60]

[59] A.D. Harvey *Britain in the Early Nineteenth Century* (1978) p. 319 for the use of Exchequer Bills to support mercantile credit; P.K. O'Brien 'Government Revenue 1793–1815' p. 495, cf. *Parliamentary Papers* 1806 IX p. 265, 1812–13 XI p. 221, 1819–20 IV p. 113 – the latter gives only figures for Exchequer Bills; P.K. O'Brien 'Government Revenue, 1793–1815' p. 48–53 and S.R. Cope 'The Goldsmids and the Development of the London Money Market during the Napoleonic War' *Economica* new series vol. 9 (1942) p. 180–206 espec. p. 188.

[60] *Parliamentary Papers* 1819 III p. 160 for Rothschild's estimate of the effect on the exchange of government spending overseas: the effect was also recognized by Jean Baptiste Say *England and the English People* (2nd edit. 1816) p. 12 fn., and see also S. Cock *An*

continued

The torrent of bills was only a part of it, however; after 1797 there was also the vast increase of paper money circulating in Britain which has already been described. The British government's role in all this was partly stimulating, partly permissive: stimulating in that funded loans and Exchequer and Navy Bills were issued, to what must have been near the limit of available credit, as a result of government decisions as regards spending; permissive in that the Bank of England and the country banks were left free to issue notes in accordance with the amount of business they found to transact. Yet even the government's spending had some of the characteristics of *laissez faire*; one of the most experienced officers on the staff of the Commander-in-Chief wrote:

I have always been surprised that the Treasury exercised so little control over the other departments in matters of expenditure. Indeed in the manner in which the business has of late years been transacted there, you might almost have at once transferred it over to the Bank of England, upon which all the great offices were to draw at pleasure: this sounds absurd, but the practice was not far short of it.

Paradoxically the financial ministries on the continent, faced with national bankruptcy and the collapse of their currency, made much greater efforts to impose some sort of grip on financial matters; it was even claimed that money loaned by the British government to the Austrians was not made available to the spending departments of the Vienna government owing 'to false ideas of economy in the Chamber of Finance, as to the mode of remittance'. These same financial authorities, in Vienna, Berlin, Copenhagen and St. Petersburg and elsewhere, were also responsible for forcing into circulation the paper currency which so quickly became devalued; the British Treasury merely *permitted* the process and left it to the market to determine the amount. It was pointed out:

Where currencies of paper have failed in other countries, it is generally where speculative men have formed the plans for establishing them ... Fortunately for this country, our currency, in the present extraordinary conjuncture, has, to this day, been left to the management of experienced traders, who, little perhaps acquainted with abstruse theories, have regulated their proceedings by the emergent wants of the time. I confess, therefore, that I feel a confidence in it far superior to what I should if it were the theoretical off-spring of the most able and enlightened politician.

Another writer stated uncompromisingly:

I am confident, that no human being, or corporation of human beings, is capable

continued
Examination of the Report of the Bullion Committee: shewing that the Present High Price of Bullion, together with the Scarcity of Gold Coin, and also The Low Rate of Foreign Exchange, are not attributable to the Issue of Bank Paper (1810): the smuggling of gold from England to support the exchange rate in Paris is in Jean Baptiste Say *A Treatise on Political Economy; or the Production, Distribution and Consumption of Wealth* (2 vols 1821) vol. 1 p. 484 fn., this being a translation of the 4th edition of Say's *Traité d'Economie* originally published in 1803.

of executing so important a trust, as that of proportioning the amount of the circulating medium to the wants of the community. It is utterly impracticable to calculate what amount of currency would be required, for the purposes of distributing the annual produce amongst its consumers.[61]

The inflation of prices during the war years has been estimated at 3.3 per cent per annum. It was not that the increased money supply in itself forced up prices. Fluctuations in foreign trade resulting from the war and several bad harvests caused periodic price rises and the increased circulation of money had the effect of smothering any tendency for overall prices to fall back to earlier levels once short-term shortages had been overcome; in other words the war and poor harvests caused upward movements, and the increased money supply eliminated any compensating downward movement between phases of price increase. But the rising prices, together with resistance to British Exchequer Bills in the disordered continental money markets, led to a widespread feeling that the economy was incorrectly managed, perhaps even on the brink of catastrophe. Relatively speaking of course this was quite untrue: the British government sustained a much higher level of expenditure than any other regime without any of the financial disasters that ruined Europe. But it was one of the paradoxes of the period that the British government's modest and partial programme of economic management was misunderstood and condemned by a developing theoretical orthodoxy which owed much of its authoritativeness to an economic achievement which it would have wished to render impossible.[62]

Parliamentary criticism of the apparent depreciation of the currency led to the setting up of a Commons committee to investigate the whole question of the restriction of specie payments and the resultant increase of paper money. This committee, soon famous as the Bullion Committee, eventually produced a report which recommended the resumption of cash payments within two years, but the proposal was voted down by the government side of the House of Commons. Although one M.P. burst out, 'Mr. Speaker, I don't like this business at all. I think it is a humbug', there was enormous interest in the question, not least amongst technical experts; the Catalogue of the Goldsmiths' Library of Economic Literature lists 194 different pamphlets, etc., on 'Finance' published in 1810–11. The leading intellectuals on both sides of politics united in condemning what had come to be called 'the paper system' – the phrase had been coined by Henry Brougham in 1803. Not only the Whig *Edinburgh Review* but also the Tory *Quarterly Review* pontificated against

[61] British Library Add. 38737 f. 340 Willoughby Gordon to William Huskisson 25 Sept. 1809; Public Record Office FO 7/43 f. 37b Sir Morton Eden to Foreign Office 10 Oct. 1795 quoting opinion of Thugut, the Austrian chief minister; Earl of Rosse *Observations on the Present State of the Currency of England* (1811) p. 88–9; William Blake *Observations on the Effects produced by the Expenditure of Government during the Restriction of Cash Payments* (1823) p. 19.

[62] For the rate of inflation see P.K. O'Brien 'Government Revenue, 1793–1815' p. 242.

paper money: not only Francis Horner, the rising light amongst the moderate Whigs and Chairman of the Bullion Committee, but also William Huskisson, the most respected economic expert on the government side, spoke against the government's policy. Another opponent of paper, who made his debut as an economic pundit on this issue, was David Ricardo, whose speculations on the stock exchange were in the process of netting him a fortune which amongst fortunes deriving from war finance was probably second only to that of the Rothschilds; after he had died in 1823 worth somewhere between £675,000 and £775,000 his brother Moses wrote of his career on the Stock Exchange:

> His complete knowledge of all its intricacies; his surprising quickness at figures and calculation; his capability of getting through, without any apparent exertion, the immense transactions in which he was concerned; his coolness and judgment, combined certainly with (for him) a fortunate tissue of public events, enabled him to leave all his contemporaries at the Stock Exchange far behind, and to raise himself infinitely higher not only in fortune, but in general character and estimation, than any man had ever done before in that house.

The vast fortune Ricardo was in the process of making on the Stock Exchange must have helped to suggest he knew what he was talking about; but despite his success in speculating in government securities Ricardo had no belief in the theoretical propriety of having government securities in the first place: 'Respecting the paying off the national debt ... I would pay it off entirely, and never allow any new debt, on any pretence whatever, to be contracted', he wrote. Indeed there seems to have been a radical contradiction in Ricardo's life, between his business employments and his intellectual devotion to theories he could not live by: as Lord Grenville noted after his death, 'The extreme caution & fairness of his mind & conduct, contrasted very strikingly with the extravagance of his *political* opinions'. It was the doctrines of theorists like Ricardo – especially of Ricardo himself – which became the basis for economic orthodoxy during the remainder of the nineteenth century: when the gold standard again became an issue after the First World War there was considerable scholarly interest in the debates of 1810–1811. Undoubtedly Ricardo and Co. had the best of the argument – as an argument. Yet closer examination of what was said and written on the other side indicates that the advantages of an expanding fiduciary currency were pretty well understood.[63]

[63] *Parliamentary Debates* vol. 20 col. 139 (intervention, 14 May 1811, by John Fuller, M.P. for Sussex, a man well-known for his parliamentary boisterousness); *Edinburgh Review* vol. 2 (1803) p. 105 cf Frank Whitson Fetter 'The Authorship of Economic Articles in the Edinburgh Review 1802–47' *Journal of Political Economy* vol. 61 (1953) p. 232–259 at p. 243 fn. 49 for Brougham's coining of the phrase 'the paper system'; Piero Sraffa ed. *The Works and Correspondence of David Ricardo* (11 vols Cambridge 1951–73) vol. 10 p. 6 (biographical notice by Moses Ricardo); ibid. vol. 10 p. 103 for estimate of Ricardo's estate; *The Correspondence of the Right Honourable Sir John Sinclair, Bart* (2 vols 1831) vol. 1 p. 372 Ricardo to Sinclair 11 May 1820; British Library Add. 38297 f. 64 Grenville to George Harrison 14 Oct. 1823; and

continued

Ricardo and even Horner were far better theoretical economists than any of their opponents, and had the advantage of being able to build on the doctrines of Adam Smith, which tended to support their views. The fact that the government victory in the final debate on the bullion issue on May 1811 was secured by the ministers' tame back-benchers served to endorse the critics' claim that they had had some sort of moral or intellectual victory. On the government side, Nicholas Vansittart, soon to be Chancellor of the Exchequer, had a faculty for immensely complicating already complicated details; it is arguable that both in his financial speeches on this issue and in his later work as Chancellor of the Exchequer he never quite grasped the main points of his business. Spencer Perceval, who actually held the Chancellorship of the Exchequer at this time as well as being Prime Minister, and Viscount Castlereagh, who also took a leading part on the government side, had no standing as financial experts. Sir John Sinclair, perhaps the most eminent economist on the government side of the Commons, was so notoriously boring that other M.P.s fled when he rose to speak. Outside the House of Commons Nathan Meyer Rothschild, who was in the process of amassing an even greater fortune than Ricardo's, seems not to have agreed with Ricardo's views but even at this comparatively late stage of the war was still quite unknown in Britain: even as late as 1814 Vansittart could still refer to him as 'a great Jew Broker named Rothschild' who 'manages the Money concerns of the Landgrave of Hesse'. Dr. Henry Beeke, Regius Professor of Modern History at Oxford and formerly a financial adviser to the Addington government, thought the report of the committee on cash payments 'one of the most *ill-founded, nonsensical, contradictory* & *mischievous* Publick Papers that I ever had the Lot to examine', and asked one of his friends in the government, 'Had you not one Person! on the Committee from your Side of the House to ask a few Common Sense Questions?' Yet the pamphlet which Beeke himself helped to write was somewhat evasive on the key question of whether there had been any big increase in the amount of the circulating medium.[64]

The official tendency was to accept the critics' view that specie was the only 'natural' circulating medium and that paper was viable only as the 'representative' of specie, and to deny that any depreciation had occurred, mainly with a view to preventing loss of public confidence in paper money. Yet the possibility that there might be a relationship between the increase of

continued

cf John Bowring *Autobiographical Recollections* (1877) p. 58 'Ricardo said that he had made his money by observing that people in general exaggerated the importance of events' i.e. with regard to fluctuations of government stock in response to political and foreign news.

[64] British Library Add. 31231 f. 14 Vansittart to Lord Clancarty 27 Jan. 1814 for Rothschild as financial manager for the Landgrave of Hesse; Add. 57415 f. 40 Beeke to J.C. Herries 27 Sept. 1810. In this letter Beeke also states that he 'gave . . . material assistance' to Jasper Atkinson whose *A Letter to a Member of Parliament occasioned by the publication of the Report of the Select Committee on the High Price of Gold Bullion* refers to the question of the circulating medium on p. 74 and p. 94.

trade and the increase of the circulating medium had been perceived by Sir John Sinclair at least as early as September 1796, when he wrote 'The increased commerce and revenue of the country, certainly demand a greater increase of a circulating medium'. The Rev. Dr. Edward Tatham, Rector of Lincoln College, Oxford, who in 1795 had claimed that 'the Public Debt, instead of a *national evil, is a national good*' because of its effect of promoting circulation, in 1797 argued with regard to the circulating medium, 'in time of war, its quantity soon becomes deficient; and particularly so, after a war of more than four years duration', though in the same year Sir Francis Baring, the then leader of the London money market, warned that the relationship between the volume of currency and the volume of trade 'remains to be proved'. Sinclair's argument was later taken up by Castlereagh when he told the House of Commons that the circulation

> does not appear to exceed what existed, previous to 1797, in a greater degree than is required by the immense increase of our trade, revenue, and manufactures, the advancement of agriculture and every other branch of internal improvement; the whole conducted under the accumulated expence of increased taxes and advanced prices of labour.

It was also the opinion of the Earl of Rosse that 'in proportion as the quantity of goods to be circulated increases, some addition will become necessary to the currency which circulates them.'[65]

Perhaps the most extreme supporter of paper was Thomas Attwood, a Birmingham businessman who was later to be prominent in the agitation for Parliamentary Reform in the early 1830s. Attwood went so far as to suggest that it was the increased supply of money in itself, not an increased demand operating on a free supply of money, which caused economic growth. He even, after Waterloo, recommended the issue of bank notes as a solution to the post-war recession, arguing that a tenfold increase of output, *if* supported by an increase of the money supply in proportion, would have the result that 'The population would have ten times more valuable articles to divide annually among them'. Evidently Attwood had overlooked some of the subtleties of

---

[65] P.K. O'Brien 'Government Revenue, 1793–1815' p. 187–193 for views of the 'representative' status of paper; Sir John Sinclair *Letters written to the Governor and Directors of the Bank of England in September 1796, on the Pecuniary Distresses of the Country and the Means of Preventing Them* (1797) p. 15: Sinclair's general views were amplified by Ambrose Weston in *A Method of Increasing the Quantity of Circulating-Money* (1799) Part 2 p. 5–8, and Sinclair himself restated his doctrine of the necessity of increasing circulation to keep pace with economic growth in *Thoughts on Circulation and Paper Currency* (1810) p. 15; Edward Tatham *A Letter to the Right Honourable William Pitt . . . on the National Debt* (2nd edit. 1795) p. 31; Edward Tatham *A Second Letter to the Right Honourable William Pitt . . . on a National Bank* (1797) p. 9; Sir Francis Baring *Observations on the Establishment of the Bank of England, and on the Paper Circulation of the Country* London 1797 p. 4–5; *Parliamentary Debates* vol. 19 col. 1002 (speech by Castlereagh 7 May 1811); Earl of Rosse *Observations on the Present State of the Currency of England* (1811) p. 78.

market forces, and also certain infrastructural constraints, but he seems to have been on to something that Ricardo and Co. wished to overlook.[66]

Generally however the supporters of 'the paper system' preferred to point to realities, not to theories. Nathan Meyer Rothschild told a Commons committee in 1819 that the paper system 'has given facilities to the war and to every business on that account; everything has gone smooth'. Another defender of paper money thought it had 'promoted an immense internal improvement in our arts and our agricultural operations'. (Certainly the work of rebuilding, modernizing and extending the Bank of England's buildings continued under the supervision of John Soane all through the war.) Vansittart went so far as to claim that the critics of paper 'either suspect some latent fallacy in their own doctrines, or think them inapplicable to practical purposes'.[67]

In retrospect the worst failures of the government in the economic sphere seem to have been their refusal to mitigate the effects of rising prices and general structural change on the poorer classes. Their innovative policies on the financial and fiscal side were so to speak balanced by their extreme Smithian handling of issues such as the control of food supply and minimum wages, and by their failure to develop any plans to handle the predictably painful transition from war to peace. Yet even in the 1914–1918 war the British government was reluctant to acknowledge the extent to which war conditions demanded an increase in the scope of government activity, and even more reluctant to accept that extended government activity in wartime might offer useful experience for the conduct of post-war government. That lesson had been learnt by the time of the 1939–1945 war but the ministers of the 1793–1815 period should not be blamed for failing to adopt the policies of 1939–1945 – especially since war left Britain in 1815 the most powerful nation in European history since the collapse of Rome rather than, as in 1945, a ruined husk.

[66] Thomas Attwood *A Letter to the Right Honourable Nicholas Vansittart on the Creation of Money, and on its Action upon National Prosperity* (Birmingham 1817) p. 17; ibid. p. 69–70 for the quotation given, and cf Thomas Attwood *The Remedy; or, Thoughts on the Present Distresses* (1816) passim.

[67] *Parliamentary Papers* 1819 III p. 158; *Phocion's Opinions on the Public Funds, on the Circulating Medium, and on the Situation of the United Kingdom, at this Critical Juncture* [1811] p. 10; *Parliamentary Debates* vol. 19 col. 920 (Vansittart's speech of 7 May 1811); see also the attack on 'theoretical projectors' at the end of George Chalmers *Considerations on Commerce. Bullion and Coin, Circulation and Exchanges: with a View of our Present Circumstances* (2nd ed. 1811) p. 212–3.

3

Britain at War with Europe

At no period of our history have we been so completely surrounded by enemies ... We see all Europe jealous of our power and greatness, rising up in arms, and preparing a general crusade against us.

William Hunter, *A Short View of the Political Situation of the Northern Powers* (1801), p. 78.

I. The European Response to British Policy

Britain's novel position, with commerce and above all *money* as the basis for international power rather than territory and population, was bitterly resented on the continent. The French of course were eager to belittle Britain's unique run of victories at sea, and even hinted that the British were somehow cheating:

> The strongest squadron needs only 15 thousand men perfectly provisioned and having not the least privation to suffer: the greatest naval battle is not equal to a skirmish on land, it costs little in blood and tears. She will regain the esteem of Europe, she will be worthy to have allies, when she presents herself at the front line with 80,000 men: and then, whatever the outcome, she would not desire everlasting war.

The British, it was said 'imagine that gold and slander are better security than the hazards of combat'. After Napoleon's fall rumours circulated in Paris that it was 'English gold', together with the Duke of Orleans, that had caused the French Revolution in the first place. The idea of Britain as a 'nation of shopkeepers' solely devoted to profit and willing to resort to the worst treachery to gain their ends was a central theme of Napoleon's propaganda: it was during his reign that the catch-phrase '*Albion perfide*' entered common usage. Even when on campaign against the armies of Austria and Russia Napoleon nursed his obsession with the British menace, denouncing the Austro-Russian coalition of 1805 simply as 'this new league which the hate and gold of England has woven' and the Russian army as 'the hired servants of England'. He instructed Fouché, his minister of police:

> Have caricatures made: An Englishman, purse in hand, entreating the various Powers to take his money, &c. This is the real direction to give the whole business.

Such caricatures were duly circulated. British commercial policy also came in for close attention from Napoleon's tame intellectuals:

> English vessels cover every sea: she sends soldiers, arms, gold, agents to the four quarters of the world; there is no colony so remote that her distant expeditions do not threaten it; there is no empire, however much a stranger to European intercourse, to which she does not labour to procure access and to secure exclusive establishments there. Countries Europe scarcely knows have received from England names which she regards as marks of ownership: those still unknown await English appellations; and as she extends the realm of nautical geography, she enlarges at the same time that of English maritime domination.

In a pioneer analysis of the British Empire as a system of economic exploitation, drawn up on behalf of his French hosts, the exiled Irish revolutionary leader Arthur O'Connor argued:

> Rome has given us an example of the extent to which dominion may be carried by exacting tribute from the nations she has vanquished; but it has been reserved for Great Britain to unite the passion for domination with the insatiable spirit of mercantile exaction.
>
> An island at one extremity of Europe, with a population of scarcely eleven millions, she bestrides the other three quarters of the earth; one foot on the vast continent of America, the other upon the Indies, she consigns Africa to eternal barbarism and slavery, that the produce of the Antilles may swell the list of her imports; collecting annually in kind, by a mixt system of commerce, exaction, plunder and tribute, to the amount of $17\frac{1}{2}$ millions from the produce of the different nations she has conquered, which she deals out to the nations of Europe at the exorbitant rate of a monopoly price; making those which are territorially free, but maritimely enslaved, feel a part of the injustice she uses to those unfortunate countries over whose liberties she exercises an uncontrouled dominion.

According to O'Connor, other European countries, by purchasing colonial goods from Britain 'are paying tribute to maintain that navy which shackles their commerce'. Similarly Charles Theremin, a Prussian diplomat of French – presumably Huguenot – origin who threw in his lot with the French revolutionary government, claimed 'England has made for herself a political and commercial monarchy in Europe like the one she has in the Indies'.[1]

---

[1] *Moniteur* 7 Jan. 1808 (vol. for 1808 p. 21–7) Commentary on British declaration of 19 Dec. 1807 p. 23: this article is attributed to Napoleon himself; Xavier Audouin *Du Commerce Maritime, de son Influence sur la Richesse et la force des États: Démontrée par l'Histoire des Nations anciennes et modernes. Situation Actuelle des Puissances de l'Europe &c* 2 vols. Paris an IX – i.e. (1801) vol. 2 p. 125. Lord John Russell ed. *Memoirs, Journal, and Correspondence of Thomas Moore* (8 vols. 1853–6) vol. 3 p. 215 journal 13 March 1821; H.D. Schmidt 'The Idea and Slogan of Perfidious Albion', *Journal of the History of Ideas* vol. 14 (1953) p. 604–616 espec. at p. 607–613, cf. R.B. Holtman *Napoleonic Propaganda* (Baton Rouge 1950) p. 3–7; *Correspondance de Napoléon* (31 vols. Paris 1858–69) vol. 11 p. 319 proclamation of 30 Sept. 1805 (8 vendémiaire an XIV) and vol. 11 p. 536 proclamation of 1 Dec. 1805 (10 frimaire an XIV) and see also French caricature 'L'Angleterre Demontée' *c*. Dec. 1805, described in
continued

Although the most seminal propaganda against British commercial hegemony was published in France by persons resident in that country, it is to be noted that at least two of the most influential writers on anti-British themes were not themselves French: Arthur O'Connor was a member of the Protestant Ascendancy in Ireland and had been deported because of his part in the struggle for an independent Ireland; Charles Theremin was of German birth, and wrote the anti-British tract just quoted while serving in London as a member of the Prussian diplomatic service. There was also a noteworthy contribution by native-born Britons living in the United States, such as James Thomson Callender and, especially, Thomas Paine. And anti-British propaganda enjoyed great popularity in other continental countries besides France. From Germany – still officially known as the Holy Roman Empire – it was reported:

> Among the other topics which assist the sale of political pamphlets and journals in the empire, there is none more universally resorted to than an indiscriminate abuse of the British Government and all its measures.

A standard opinion, according to the Prussian minister Hardenberg, was that:

> England, by her trade monopoly, the sole basis of her huge debts which she cannot abandon or even see much reduced without being lost, is the most dangerous enemy of the continent, its industry and well-being.

The minority of British sympathizers blamed French propaganda and 'ridiculous prejudices in economic matters' but even they had to admit, 'The dominant principle of all the political theorists and writers at the present moment is – jealousy of British power'.[2]

continued
Frederick George Stephens and Mary Dorothy George *Catalogue of Political and Personal Satires Preserved in the Department of Prints and Drawings of the British Museum* (11 vols. 1978) (originally published 1870–1954) vol. 8 p. 375–6 (cat. no. 10451), cf. Trotsky's Order to the Soviet Armed Forces no. 159, 24 October 1919 'On all fronts you meet the hostile plots of the English. The counter-revolutionary troops shoot you with English guns ... supplies of English manufacture ... uniforms made in England ... English explosives ... etc.' Leon Trotsky *My Life: An Attempt at an Autobiography* (Harmondsworth 1975) p. 449; Napoleon to Fouché 30 May 1805 quoted in A.M. Broadley *Napoleon in Caricature, 1795–1821* 2 vols. (1911) introduction by J. Holland Rose p. xxxiii and cf xxxiii fn; [A.M. Blanc de la Nautte] Comte d'Hauterive *De l'État de la France a la Fin de l'An VIII* (Paris an IX – i.e. 1800) p. 117–8; Arthur O'Connor *The Present State of Great Britain* (Paris 1804) p. 2–3; ibid. p. 7; Charles Theremin *De l'Interêts des Puissances Continentales relativement à l'Angleterre* (Paris an III – i.e. 1794) p. 5. For a later official polemic see *Moniteur* 1808 vol. 1 p. 21–7, 7 Jan. 1808.

    2 For Theremin see the title page of his *De l'Interêts des Puissances Continentales* where he describes himself as 'Conseiller d'Ambassade de Prusse, ci-devant employé a la Cour de Londres', and the preface. Callender was a Scot who fled to the U.S.A. in 1793 after having been arrested for publishing the first edition of his *Political Progress of Britain*: Paine, who had made his reputation during the American Revolution, came originally from Thetford in Suffolk. For propaganda in Germany see Otto Tschirch *Geschichte der öffentlichen Meinung in Preussen vom Baseler Frieden bis zum Zusammenbruch des Staates (1795–1806)* (2 vols. Weimar 1933–4) espec. vol. 2 p. 229–236. The quotations are from *HMC Dropmore Mss* vol. 281 H. Elliott
continued

The Swiss-born publicist Sir Francis D'Ivernois pointed out in 1803 that the French had published over fifty books against Britain's 'maritime despotism' while the British had not had even one book translated into another language to explain the nature and justification of their maritime rights in wartime. But the British version of the facts, when available, was rarely taken seriously in any case; as the Russian minister of marine pointed out:

> It is always the measureless ambition and cruelty of Napoleon which causes them [the British] to be more ambitious and more cruel than he ever was. It is *him* who ravages and devastates the world because everything that isn't settled by the English is a wrong done to the world whose safety they care for so much, as everyone knows. After they have set up this spectre, they apply their system.[3]

Unfortunately Britain was in the invidious position of crying 'Thief!' while becoming visibly fatter and richer at the rest of the world's expense. The wartime economic boom, together with the government's readiness to dole out subsidies to potential allies, gave credibility to the nation that the war was viewed in London simply as a business proposition. Arthur O'Connor claimed that 'the revenue and finance of Great Britain has been so imperiously and inveterately fixed by the late minister [i.e. William Pitt] on a basis of WAR that they can no longer stand on a basis of PEACE', but he grudgingly acknowledged that Britain might eventually come to recognize the economic advantages of ending hostilities:

> War affords Great Britain so many means of making the other nations of Europe contribute to defray her expences, that nothing but the inordinate expence at which she makes war could prevent her interest in making it perpetual.

But Theremin a little earlier had stated outright that 'Peace on the Continent is a calamity for her [Britain], war on the Continent is the food of her prosperity' and that Britain 'feeds her commerce with war, and war with her commerce'. This view was later taken up by Monbrion: 'war feeds war, which far from being harmful to her, on the contrary is favourable'. This interpretation was widely accepted outside France, even in official circles;

continued
to Lord Grenville 15 Aug. 1798; Leopold von Ranke ed. *Denkwürdigkeiten des Staatskanzlers Fürsten von Hardenberg* (5 vols. Leipzig 1877) vol. 5 p. 243 Erste Denkschrift Hardenbergs über den Vertrag vom 15 December 1805, 30 Dec. 1805; *HMC Dropmore Mss* vol. 4 p. 396 A. de Luc to Lord Grenville 26 Nov. 1798 and vol. 6 p. 375 memoire by Friedrich Gentz 1800. There seems however to be relatively little anti-British propaganda emanating from the Netherlands, cf W.P.C. Knuttel *Catalogus van de Pamfletten-Verzameling berustende in de Koninklijke Bibliothek* (8 vols. Utrecht 1978) espec. vols. 6 and 8.

.   [3] British Library Add. 31237 f. 36 undated memo by D'Ivernois headed 'Importance dont il serait pour l'Angleterre d'adopter & d'organiser sans delai quelque mesure qui la mette à portée de plaider sa cause au dehors de manière a s'y concilier les voeux des étrangers' – 1803 is the most probable date though 1802 or 1804 are possible; Soviet Foreign Ministry *Vnyeshnyaya Politika Rossii, XIX i nachala XX vyeka* (8 vols. Moscow 1960–72) vol. 4 p. 46 P.V. Chichagev to Alexander I 23 Aug. O.S. (4 Sept. N.S.) 1807.

in Denmark, for example, it was supposed in 1800 that the British 'had not hesitated to commit the greatest injustices in order to maintain their superiority at sea, and ... they have even striven to rekindle the war on the continent so as to attain this end'. As late as November 1813 the Austrian government attached some importance to a memorandum which, reviewing the obstacles to a general European peace, stated:

> The first and greatest of these difficulties is to be found, I think, in the superlative prosperity of England herself, or to be more precise, in the maritime and commercial preponderance which is the basis of this prosperity. The English government sees the brilliant and important position of Great Britain as the result of a system of war followed during a great many years with a constancy and activity in which it glories, and is so proud and satisfied with its work that it sees only the dangers and not the advantages of a contrary system.[4]

It was even believed that the British stirred up the Barbary States – Algiers, Tunis, Tripoli – against their trade rivals so that countries officially at peace with Britain suffered the depredations of commerce raiders acting indirectly on Britain's behalf. Theremin accused Britain of engineering Algerian attacks on American shipping in 1794, and there were similar reports with regard to Tunis in 1800 and Tripoli in 1801. These reports were taken seriously even in Britain:

> the common belief in the Mediterranean is, that we rather encourage the piracy of these freebooters, for opposing the commerce of other nations; – a most false charge undoubtedly in this extent ... If the archives of European diplomacy could be ransacked by some person of patience more than human, and of a perverted taste for the study of elaborate trifling mingled with infatuation and misconduct in great concerns, high among the monuments of incredible folly and wickedness we will venture to say, would stand the despatches touching Algerine affairs. We make no doubt that, but a few years ago, would be found 'MOST SECRET AND CONFIDENTIAL' letters reckoning upon the assistance of his Highness the Dey in provisioning a fleet or a garrison, and stating to 'your Lordship' the gratifying assurance of his continued good dispositions towards '*His Majesty*' and his hostility towards 'the persons *at present exercising the government of France*'.

In reality the Foreign Office files show that, although Britain had much better relations with the Barbary States than other European powers – which

---

[4] O'Connor *Present State of Great Britain* p. 83 and p. 82 n. 2; Theremin *De l'Intérêts des Puissances Continentales* p. 7 and p. 19; Monbrion *De la Préponderance Maritime et Commerciale de la Grande Bretagne* (1805) p. 221; Österreichisches Staatsarchiv: Staatenabteilung Danemark Paris 80. 1800 f. 94 Anton Joseph Emanuel Krauss's despatch 21 June 1800; Österreichisches Staatsarchiv: Staatenabteilung England Varia 13. Memo 'Sur le politique de l'Angleterre relativement a la paix generale'. There are two copies, one 'Écrit en Octobre 1813' and purporting to be a French translation of a memo by an American named Walsh, and the other, probably intended for wider circulation, 'Écrit le 1 Novembre 1813' and not mentioning any author. Walsh may be Robert Walsh (1784–1859) editor in 1811–12 of *The American Review of History and Politics*; he had lived in Britain and in France 1806–9.

was more the result of the intimidating strength of the British fleet in the Mediterranean than of the regular purchases of provisions in North African ports – these relations were not always altogether harmonious, and were at no time based on particularly confidential relations between British consular officials and the Barbary princes; though one should perhaps mention that in 1801 the British consul in Tripoli, when rejecting American accusations that he had encouraged the Bashaw to declare war on the U.S.A. as 'complaints of the most unwarrantable and ungrounded nature', was able to support his innocence by a signed testimonial from the Bashaw himself. Nevertheless reports of dealings with the Barbary princes inevitably contributed to Britain's reputation as an exploiter of discord, and the Americans were later to blame their bad relations with the Indian tribes in 1811–1812 on the machinations of British agents working from Canada.[5]

II. The Case for Action against Britain

Two centuries previously Sir Walter Ralegh had written:

> There are two ways in which England may be afflicted. The one by invasion . . . The other by impeachment of our trades; by which trades all commonwealths flourish, and are enriched.

Resentment of Britain's maritime power naturally encouraged continental enemies to pursue the same line of thought. The idea of some kind of concerted action against British sea-borne trade was canvassed in the French National Convention even before the French declaration of war in 1793:

> The credit of England rests on fictitious wealth . . . the whole edifice is supported by the prodigious activity of sea trade, and Asia, Portugal and Spain are the most favourable markets for the exchange of English industrial products: we must close these markets while opening them to the rest of the world.

In August 1793 a report issued on behalf of the Committee of Public Safety proclaimed:

---

[5] Theremin *De l'Intérêts des Puissances Continentales* p. 25–6; Österreichisches Staatsarchiv: Staatenabteilung Danemark 80. 1800 f. 93–4 Krauss's despatch 21 June 1800; Public Record Office London, HO 42/58 f. 294–7 Rufus King to Thomas Pelham 28 Nov. 1801; *Edinburgh Review* vol. 26 (1816) p. 45 for 'the common belief in the Mediterranean . . .' quote and cf Thomas Spence *The National Debt* [circa 1796] reprinted in G.I. Gallop ed. *Pig's Meat: The Selected Writings of Thomas Spence, Radical and Pioneer Land Reformer* (Nottingham 1982) p. 105–6 at p. 106; Public Record Office FO 76/5 f. 135 Bryan McDonough to Duke of Portland 1 Nov. 1801, cf FO 3/8, FO 8/1 and FO 77/5 passim; Bradford Perkins *Prologue to War: England and the United States 1805–1812* (Berkeley 1961) p. 283–6. Presumably the British could not be blamed for the incident during the war between Britain and Spain of 1805–8 when Spanish merchant ships attempting to evade British cruisers by sailing under Moroccan or Algerine colours were attacked by *Sardinian* privateers: Public Record Office FO 67/36 Joseph Smith 12 Nov. 1807.

one day the people brought together by the common need for liberty ... the people of the continent, tired of these islanders' oppression and this naval tyranny, will fulfil the vow of Cato: *the modern Carthage will be destroyed.* Where will she be when all the European nations – conscious at last of this monopoly of wealth, this exclusive right to trade, this monopoly of the pretended political liberty which England has so long shunned – will cry out, Let us smash the sceptre of this queen of the seas, so that they may at last be as free as the land?[6]

So long as almost the whole of Europe was united in arms against revolutionary France this rhetoric was quite empty: but by 1795 the anti-French alliance was crumbling and the Committee of Public Safety began to consider memoranda discussing the possibility of closing the ports of Northern Europe to British trade:

> If these efforts have the success which it is natural to hope for, English trade with Germany will be totally destroyed, communication will be cut off, bills of exchange will no longer arrive, disorders will break out in all the trading centres of England, the bankruptcies will multiply and the position of traders and of that part of the population who live off them will become so intolerable that the ministry will in the end be obliged to sue for peace.

The same policy was also recommended by a citizen of Frankfurt who had worked for some years in England and who thought the closure of the ports 'will give an electric shock to the whole of England' and cause 'a temporary stagnation in all the English manufactures'. In the same year there was another project 'to constrict the circulation by the extraction of guineas' by means of manipulation of the foreign exchange – this was only a few months before the British government's own foreign exchange dealings forced them to substitute paper money for gold as the main circulating currency. Economic warfare was of course only one possible means of attacking Britain: Bertrand Barère's *La Liberté des Mers, ou le gouvernement anglais devoilé* (3 vols. Paris 1798) listed ten possible ways of assailing the British government, of which closing the ports of the continent was only the first; others included ruining, or opening up to competition, the Newfoundland cod fisheries, encouraging revolution in

---

6 'A Discourse touching A War with Spain, and of the protecting of the Netherlands' in *The Works of Sir Walter Ralegh, Kt* (8 vols. Oxford 1829) vol. 8 p. 302; Guy Kersaint [i.e. Armand-Gui-Simon, Comte de Coetnempren de Kersaint] *Discours sur l'État de l'Angleterre et les consequences de la guerre maritime avec ce Pays prononcé a la séance* [de la Convention] *du premier janvier 1793* Paris 1793 (It is quite untrue that Britain then enjoyed anything like a monopoly position in trade with Spain or Asia – unless Asia is meant to mean India rather than the Levant); Bertrand Barère *Rapport Fait au nom du Comité de Salut Public le premier août 1793* (Paris 1793) p. 24.

The analogy with Carthage had at one time been applied by the British to the Dutch, as in Dryden's 'Annus Mirabilis', 1667:

> Thus, mighty in her Ships, stood *Carthage* long ...
> Yet stoop'd to *Rome*, less wealthy, but more strong ...
> (stanza 5)

India, and promoting the movement for national independence in Ireland. But outside France politicians less inveterately anti-British than the French seem to have been chiefly interested in the idea of a commercial embargo. The Spanish minister Manuel de Godoy talked in October 1796 of 'forcing England to give up her despotic domination of the seas and her monopoly of commerce'; to do this, Godoy said, 'we need to embarrass her trade on all sides'. The scheme put to the Committee of Public Safety in 1795, of barring British ships from continental ports, was commended by U.S. President Thomas Jefferson to a Danish envoy in 1801; it was, he said, 'the only means of humbling them'.[7]

Although the British had played only an auxiliary role in the fighting on the continent in the Seven Years' War, the Peace of Paris in 1763 had left them the leading colonial and maritime power in Europe; the term 'The British Empire' dates from this period. Even during the American War of Independence, jealousy of Britain had contributed to the decision of the French, Spanish and Dutch governments to intervene on the side of the American rebels, and to the decision of the Baltic powers to band together in the Armed Neutrality of 1780. Dutch bitterness against the British, dating back to the time of the Commonwealth, was exemplified by a little booklet, *Engelsche Tieranny*, published at Amsterdam in 1781 and consisting of four dialogues illustrated by woodcuts depicting English atrocities against the Dutch – the burning of Terschelling, a massacre on the Guinea coast, the plundering of St. Eustatius and so on. After the American War, the continued economic expansion of Britain and the aggressive posture adopted by the younger Pitt's government with regard to supposed British interests in remote corners of the world – exemplified by the Nootka Sound and Oczakov crises of 1790 and 1791 – made it not entirely improbable that sooner or later there would be a second and more destructive collision between Britain and a European alliance. The progress of the revolution in France, and the formation of the First Coalition to overthrow the young French Republic, intervened to prevent anything of this sort occurring. From 1792 onward a common hostility to Jacobinism united traditional enemies in alliance against France. Yet within four years various developments in the war marked the end of the general European conflict as essentially a crusade against the French Revolution and

[7] Memo by Antoine Bernard Caillard for Committee of Public Safety 1796, quoted in Bertrand de Jouvenel *Napoléon et l'Économie Dirigée* (Brussels 1942) p. 58–9; ibid. p. 60 quoting views of a Frankfurt informant passed on by the minister to the Batavian Republic 2 fructidor an IV (i.e. 19 Aug. 1796); Bertrand Barère *La Liberté des Mers* part 8 chap. 7 – the British Library has only a Spanish translation of 1841; the Library of Congress catalogue lists 5 Spanish-language editions published for the South American market 1800–26 and editions published in Spain in 1835, 1841 and 1842; Rigsarkivet Copenhagen f.u.A. Spanien II Depecher 1796 Christopher Vilhelm Dreyer's despatch 1796 no. 72, 17 Oct. 1796; Rigsarkivet Copenhagen f.u.A. Amerika II Depecher, Peter Blucher Olsen's despatch 1801 no. 10, 24 Oct. 1801, Jefferson's precise words being quoted as 'les Anglais triomphent et le feront lontems, qu'on n'adopte pas generalement le seul moyen de les humilier, celui de convenir de leur fermer tous les ports'.

reopened the question of the continental powers' attitude to British maritime hegemony.[8]

Spain, with a branch of the Bourbon dynasty enthroned at Madrid, might have been expected to be amongst the most implacable enemies of the regime which had guillotined Louis XVI. But increasing disgust with Britain as an ally combined with a string of military failures to make the war with the regicide French government unpopular. In December 1794, Antonio Valdés, the minister of marine, attacked the policy of chief minister Godoy in the council of state, urging 'how much one should mistrust her [Britain's] persuasions and advice on the subject of cooperation or secret measures, since experience had already proved that she sought to employ the Spanish navy for her own interests'. Valdès cited the instances of the allied landings at Toulon and in Corsica and 'above all' America – i.e. presumably the West Indies. Godoy himself acknowledged:

> Though we were in alliance with them, they mysteriously concealed from us all their operations; we had no share in the advantages obtained, but were always sharers in the losses.

Nor was Godoy's own enthusiasm for the alliance increased by the bumptious manner – the *'vivacité mal placé'* – of the British envoy, the *'jeune et ardent'* Francis Jackson. The British Court of Admiralty's condemnation of a Spanish ship, the *Santiago*, as a lawful prize was apparently the last straw. 'It is scarcely credible how much the animosity against the English increases daily, both at the Court and in the Country', reported the Danish envoy at Madrid.[9]

When Spain finally abandoned the coalition and made peace with France by the Treaty of Basel in August 1795, it was initially supposed that Godoy intended henceforth to maintain a policy of neutrality; but a little over a year later the Spanish government declared war on Britain, citing in justification the conquest of Corsica, 'done without any agreement with Spain', the

---

[8] Cf John Entick *The Present State of the British Empire* (1774). Horace Walpole's remark, 'We now talk of the British *empire* ... In my time it was the British *monarchy*' evidently belongs to the same period: [John Pinkerton] *Walpoliana* (2 vols. 1799) vol. 1 p. 29–30. The revolt of the American colonies almost certainly delayed the term's adoption in everyday speech. John Dee, in *General and Rare Memorials pertayninge to the Perfect Arte of Navigation* had written of 'Brytish Common wealth' and 'Brytish Impire' as far back as 1577 – see p. 8, 11, 13, 14, 28, 55, 57 – but in this as in many other things he had been out of step with his times. For the Nootka Sound and Oczakov Crises see John Ehrman *The Younger Pitt* (3 vols. 1969–) vol. 1 p. 349–350, 384–6 and vol. 2 p. 11–30. The *Engelsche Tieranny* pamphlet was reprinted in facsimile during the First World War, presumably at German instigation.

[9] Rigsarkivet Copenhagen f.u.A. Spanien II Depecher 1795, Dreyer's despatch 1794 no. 53, 31 Dec. 1794; J.B. d'Esmenard ed. *Memoirs of Don Manuel de Godoy* 2 vols. (1836) vol. 1 p. 455; Rigsarkivet Copenhagen f.u.A. Spanien II Depecher 1795, Dreyer's despatch 1795 no. 9, 4 March 1795 for both reference to Jackson and to Spanish reaction to the seizure of the Santiago.

Later, in 1802, Jackson was minister at Paris, where 'it is said openly that he is only a ninny and pig-headed'. Public Record Office FO 27/70 'Secret Intelligence from France' 15 Feb. 1802.

condemnation of the *Santiago* and 'numerous other grievances relative to the detention of Spanish vessels and property and English harassment of Spanish trade and navigation'. The manifesto issued in the name of King Carlos IV claimed of the Anglo-Spanish operations against Toulon:

> [British] bad faith had manifested itself at the most critical moment of the campaign, in the treatment experienced from Admiral Hood by my squadron at Toulon, where he only thought of destroying what he could not carry away.

Urging the war, the octogenarian Archbishop of Granada warned:

> The views of England in provoking the war are not directed against the strength of France as a European power; what she aims at and covets is the wealth of our colonies, which the treaty of Basel has rescued from her ambitious rapacity.[10]

The Spanish volte face was the first major instance of what was to be a constant theme throughout the next twenty years: denunciation of British selfishness and treachery. Even a genuine neutral could write:

> Ambition and intoxication with a unique prosperity amidst the general sufferings unfortunately makes England forget true principles and that power, which was so long the support of Europe and especially of Italy, now collaborates in its destruction by the incoherence of its plans and the inconsistency of its conduct.

The British government's betrayal of its allies was a Russian grievance in 1800 and again in 1807, and its readiness to sacrifice friends in its haste to seize illegitimate advantages was eloquently condemned by a Danish manifesto of August 1807 provoked by the British expedition against Copenhagen:

> The English government, having by a shameful inaction betrayed the interests of allies engaged in a struggle as serious as it was uncertain, suddenly deployed all its strength to surprise and attack a neutral, peaceful and offenceless state.

The eight accusations representing the standard case against Britain period which were examined in an unpublished pro-British pamphlet of 1809 included five relating to betrayal of allies, viz.:

1. England works only for her own interest.
2. She gave the initiative for each of the coalitions.
6. England does nothing for her allies.
7. England sends no troops to the aid of her allies.
8. If England had only 14,000 men to give to her allies why then did she find 45,000 so promptly for service in Portugal and Spain.

And from the other side of the Atlantic, former U.S. President Thomas

---

[10] Rigsarkivet Copenhagen f.u.A. Spanien II Depecher 1795, Dreyer's despatch 1795 no. 58, 31 Dec. 1795; ibid. Depecher 1796, Dreyer's despatch 1796 no. 69 postscript 6 Oct. 1795 and *Memoirs of Don Manuel de Godoy* vol. 1 p. 266–7 fn; *Memoirs of Don Manuel de Godoy* vol. 1 p. 475 for opinion of Don Juan Manuel de Moscoso y Peralta, Archbishop of Granada – text gives Basel as Bâle.

Jefferson wrote of England in 1810, 'it is well known she has been the least faithful to her alliances of any nation in Europe, since the period of her history wherein she has been distinguished for her commerce and corruption.'[11]

It was scarcely a mitigation that the British government had frequent cause to find Austria, Russia and, after 1808, Spain equally unsatisfactory as allies. Even before British entry into the war in 1793 Lord Grenville had found it necessary to protest, even if 'in guarded Terms' against the Austro-Russo-Prussian scheme to complete the dismemberment of Poland, warning of 'the Mischief which must result to the Common Cause from such an evident Act of Injustice brought forward at such a Period as the present'. He was not much less enthusiastic regarding the Austrian proposal to round off the deal by swapping the Austrian Netherlands for Bavaria:

> we are desirous of keeping these Ideas separate from that of the common Interest, which all Europe had, and particularly our two Courts, in opposing the Progress of France.

After six years of unsuccessful coalition warfare Grenville still felt that the Austrian chief minister had yet to perceive that the object of the war was resistance to France, not the enlargement of the Habsburg Empire:

> The thing that perplexes me most in this and in every part of my business is the conduct of Thugut. If he were paid to thwart all our measures and to forward those of France, he could not do it more effectually.

Later as one of the British ministers acknowledged resignedly:

> There is a prevailing impression abroad of the enormous Wealth of England which always tempts Foreigners to impose upon Us even in private Transactions, and much more in Dealings with the Government.

But of course it was the British failures of cooperation which were more obvious: because only Britain ever seemed to profit from the war.[12]

---

11 Joseph [i.e. Giuseppe] Greppi *Révélations Diplomatiques sur les Relations de la Sardaigne avec l'Autriche et la Russe pendant la première et deuxième coalition* (Paris 1859) p. 177 Gaetano Balbo to Carlo Emanuele IV 28 Sept. 1800 for the 'Ambition and intoxication' quote; *Vnyeshnyaya Politika Rossii* vol. 3 p. 627–8 Budberg (foreign minister) to Lord Granville Leveson-Gower 18(30) June 1807; for Danish manifesto see French-language copy in Österreichisches Staatsarchiv: Staatenabteilung Danemark 84; for the unpublished pamphlet ibid. Staatenabteilung England Varia 13: this pamphlet was supposedly written in Swedish by a Professor G—— at Uppsala, 21 Jan. 1809. The archives in Vienna have a German and a French translation. It has not been possible to identify Professor G——. The French version, entitled 'Réflexions sur quelques Imputations dirigées Contre l'Angleterre relativement à sa Conduite politique' professes to have been drawn up 'pour l'instruction de ses Écoliers et de ses Enfants', the German version is 'für Seine Kinder und Deutsche Schüler'. It is possible that during their war with France in 1809, the Austrian government contemplated publishing at least the German version for propaganda purposes. H.A. Washington ed. *The Writings of Thomas Jefferson* (9 vols New York 1853–4) vol. 5 p. 513 Jefferson to John Langdon 5 March 1810.

12 British Library Add. 34447 f. 19–21, Lord Grenville's minute of interviews with the Austrian envoy Stadion and Prussian envoy Jacobi 12 Jan. 1793, copy; Add. 34447 f. 487

continued

Spain in 1796 was merely the first state to use Britain's conduct in the war as a justification of what were essentially opportunist and pragmatic policies with regard to the European conflict. The Danish envoy at Madrid explained Godoy's anti-British policy in terms of 'national presumption, political ignorance, and the personal vanity of this minister and his *ambition de jouer un rôle*'. Yet Godoy was merely reasserting the pre-French Revolution practice in preferring national interest to ideological principle as the chief factor in determining whom to fight a war against. Thereafter, up until 1812, the continuing struggle was seen by most governments in the same light as any other war, as an opportunity for rival states to jockey for position. It was no coincidence that the foreign policy of most European governments was dictated by single individuals of unchallenged power within the state: not only Napoleon but also hereditary sovereigns like Paul I of Russia or Gustav IV Adolf of Sweden, or royal favourites like Thugut, Metternich, Acton, Haugwitz, Bernstorff, Godoy – individuals for whom each foreign policy success meant an increase of personal and political opportunities at home. The war against Revolutionary and Napoleonic France was a war not of statesmen but of politicians, and in politicians' terms a war with France might make less sense than a war with Britain, which was as greatly disliked but less obviously formidable. And it was the uncertain policy of successive British cabinets, seen in the context of daily increasing British economic power, which seemed to give both a model and an excuse for pragmatic policies.[13]

III. The Armed Neutrality of 1800

Politicians' thinking rather than statesmanship seems to have been behind the first concerted action against Britain during the war years, the Armed Neutrality of 1800. Ostensibly the Armed Neutrality declared by Russia, Prussia, Sweden and Denmark in December 1800 aimed simply at preventing British warships from searching, and often confiscating, those countries' trading vessels. But the initiative for the Armed Neutrality came from Paul I of Russia, in the form of a declaration issued on 27 August 1800 calling on Prussia, Sweden and Denmark to join in defending their mercantile trade: yet Russia seems to have had only half a dozen ships engaged in international trade and as Lord Nelson afterwards pointed out, 'it was nonsense to talk of mutual protection of trade, with a power who had none'. And while it was true that

continued

Grenville's minute of conversation with Stadion 5 Feb. 1793 and cf p. 7–8 above; *HMC Dropmore Mss* vol. 5 p. 147 Lord Grenville to Thomas Grenville 16 July 1799, cf. vol. 5 p. 281–2 Thomas Grenville to Lord Grenville 15 Aug. 1799 and Public Record Office FO 7/43 f. 32, 36 Sir Morton Eden to Lord Grenville 10 Oct. 1795; British Library Add. 31236 f. 23 memo by Nicholas Vansittart 2 Sept. 1812.

[13] Rigsarkivet Copenhagen f.u.A. Spanien II Depecher 1796, Dreyer's despatch 1796 no. 32, 19 May 1796.

Britain had been interfering with neutral shipping, so had other powers: the United States of America was virtually in a state of war with France because of the activities of French warships, and the resulting attempts by the U.S. to impose an embargo against France had strained relations between the U.S.A. and Sweden. Indeed the Swedish Consul-General in the U.S., complaining of American arrests of Swedish and Danish vessels trading with France on the pretext that they were carrying American-owned goods, compared American contraband rules unfavourably with those of the British government:

> The English who have so often been at open war with France; and whose Subjects have of course so frequently been prohibited from trading with the dominions of that Country, never have presumed to capture or bring into port the Vessels of other Nations under pretence that they might be the covered property of their own Subjects.[14]

It is probable that the origin of Paul I's anti-British policy was less his objection to British interference with neutral shipping than his irritation at the failure of the joint Anglo-Russian invasion of North Holland in 1799 and his dispute with the government in London over the possession of Malta. In addition, having left the Third Coalition against France in disgust – his armies had been defeated in Switzerland as well as doing badly in the Netherlands – he was evidently casting around for a new sphere in which to play the arbiter in international affairs. Initially he seems to have seen the Armed Neutrality as part of a larger scheme, a Northern League that would impose peace on the warring nations of Europe; later he may have regarded the confederation as a step towards an alliance with France – in January 1801 he wrote to his hitherto arch-enemy Napoleon urging him to assist the Armed Neutrality by a naval demonstration against the English coast. It has been argued that his policy was consistent, aiming at the restoration of peace, order and legitimate rights, and that he had joined the coalition against France when France seemed the main threat to the European balance of power, later abandoning the alliance only because of British and Austrian abuse of his trust. Yet however grand the terms in which Paul I explained his schemes to himself – and since he was

---

[14] Sir Nicholas Harris Nicolas ed. *The Dispatches and Letters of Vice-Admiral Lord Nelson* (7 vols 1844–6) vol. 4 p. 334 Nelson to Henry Addington 4 April 1801, recounting his words to the Prince Royal of Denmark, cf J.P. Catteau [i.e. Catteau-Calleville] *Tableau des États Danois* (3 vols Paris 1802) vol. 3 p. 360, 362–3 which shows that 6 Russian ships entered and 7 left the Baltic in 1799 and 7 entered and 6 left in 1800, out of totals of over 5,000 moving each way annually; for Franco-American relations see Ulane Bennel *La France les États-Unis et la guerre de course 1797–1815* (Paris 1961) p. 48–116 and A. de Conde *The Quasi War: The Politics and Diplomacy of the Undeclared War with France 1797–1801* (New York 1966) passim; Riksarkivet Stockholm. America 2, Richard Söderström to U.S. Secretary of State John Marshall, 24 Nov. 1800, copy – written, incidentally, in English. At this time Söderström was also representing Danish interests in the U.S.A. and the offences complained of seem to have been mainly against Danish vessels but cf his note of 25 Nov. 1800.

generally thought to be mentally unbalanced the terms were probably grand enough – the other northern governments took a strictly practical view.[15]

The adherent of the Armed Neutrality with the greatest grievance against British maritime policy was Denmark. During the 1790s Danish trade had benefited considerably from the fact that the country was at peace both with France and with the protagonists of the successive anti-French coalitions. Searches and confiscations by patrolling British warships were a constant irritation but when in 1798 the Danes began to organize their merchant shipping into convoys with armed escorts this was in defence against French rather than British molestation. In the year ending October 1799 eight Danish convoys were intercepted by British 'cruisers' but only one was forcibly searched, and the officer responsible was later disavowed. In February 1799 the British Foreign Office and Admiralty gave the Danish government permission to purchase light warships – suitable for convoy work – in Britain. But the Danes were unhappy with the general situation, and in March 1799, after the detention of some Danish vessels, the Danish minister in London complained, 'While France invades and pillages the continent, England extends her domination at sea with a most unwise despotism'. On Christmas Eve of 1799 the Danish frigate *Havfruen* (Mermaid) convoying merchantmen from Malaga, was fired on by a British naval vessel which was attempting to search ships in the convoy. Amicable feelings seem to have diminished thereafter. By June 1800 there was talk in official Danish circles of 'a quadruple alliance against England' and the Austrian *chargé d'affaires* reported:

> the hatred of the cabinet and of the public for the English is so deep rooted that at present only the military power is wanting for them to break with and cry vengeance against the people who have long since secretly been their enemies. A pamphlet exists here, on the subject of the injustices committed by the English against the Danes . . . they have so often violated the first fundamental principles of the law of nations and acted at sea like brigands and pirates.[16]

On 25 July 1800 a British squadron attempted to search a Danish convoy escorted by the frigate *Freya*: the latter resisted and there was an exchange of cannon fire lasting twenty minutes, in which two Danish and five English seamen were killed, and which ended with the *Freya* striking her colours. An official protest by the Danish minister in London was met by indignant counter-accusations. Lord Grenville, the British Foreign Secretary, wrote a strong note in the name of King George III referring to 'deliberate and open aggressions . . . The lives of his brave seamen have been sacrificed, the honour

---

[15] Cf. Hugh Ragsdale *Détente in the Napoleonic Era; Buonaparte and the Russians* (Laurence, Kansas 1980) p. 79, 111–7, 122–4 and Ole Feldbaek *Denmark and the Armed Neutrality, 1800–1801* (Copenhagen 1980) p. 70–1, 78–80.

[16] Feldbaek *Denmark and the Armed Neutrality* p. 28–9, 33; Rigsarkivet Copenhagen f.u.A. England II Depecher 1799, Fredrik Wedel-Jarlsberg's despatch 1799 no. 24, 15 Feb. 1799; ibid. 1799 no. 28, 20 March 1799; Österreichisches Staatsarchiv: Staatenabteilung Danemark 80. 1800 f. 83 Krauss's despatch 7 June 1800; ibid. 1800 f 93–4, Krauss's despatch 21 June 1800.

of his flag has been insulted, almost in sight of his own coast'. A special envoy, Lord Whitworth, was sent to Copenhagen to negotiate and a few days after his arrival a powerful British naval squadron appeared off the Danish coast to back him up. Initially the Danish government considered resistance: the Prince Regent of Denmark wrote, 'we shall be praised since we have fought for freedom, and the British will make so many enemies that they will inevitably be moving towards their fall, which would be a blessing to Europe'. But more cautious views prevailed, and on 29 August the Danish government agreed to accept the restitution of the *Freya* and the ships she had been escorting, in exchange for giving up the policy of armed convoys. The motive for the Danish concessions was perhaps less the British squadron in the Sound than the commercial advantages accruing from neutrality; as the Austrian minister in Berlin pointed out:

> Denmark has become rich during this war, in spite of the fact that a hundred of her merchant ships are taken into England's ports each year, and she does not hesitate in preferring this state of affairs, uncomfortable as it is, to an open rupture.[17]

But two days before the Anglo-Danish settlement was agreed in Copenhagen, Paul of Russia, in his capital seven hundred miles to the north-east, had issued his declaration calling for an Armed Neutrality, and the *Freya* case had been expressly cited in this declaration. On the day the negotiations were concluded in Copenhagen, he issued an order for the seizure of British property within the Russian Empire. The discovery, a couple of days too late, that powerful allies would be available in a struggle against Britain obviously affected the Danish attitude to the interim convention just signed with Britain. Perhaps a more important factor was fear of being isolated with regard to the Baltic bloc which Russia was establishing, for the Danes had good reason to be suspicious of the motives behind the policy of their Swedish neighbours. On 16 December 1800 both Denmark and Sweden signed conventions with Russia promulgating an Armed Neutrality, and Prussia followed suit two days later. If in the event Denmark appeared to be one of the more committed participants in the Armed Neutrality it was largely by contrast with the extremely ambivalent attitude of the Swedish and Prussian governments.[18]

---

[17] J.B. Scott ed. *The Armed Neutralities of 1780 and 1800* (New York 1918) p. 479 Lord Grenville to Wedel-Jarlsberg 30 July 1800; Feldbaek *Denmark and the Armed Neutrality* p. 57 quoting Prince Royal of Denmark to adjutant-general Hans Lindholm 16 Aug. 1800; Österreiches Staatsrchiv: Staatenabteilung Preussen 81. No folio no., Hudelist's despatch 12 Jan. 1801.

The Danish flag which the *Freya* was forced to strike had a uniquely mystical status: the original of this white cross on a red field, known as the *Dannebrog*, was said to have fallen from heaven during the Danish victory over the Estonians at Lyndanisse, on 15 June 1219.

[18] Scott *The Armed Neutralities of 1780 and 1800* p. 531–549 for texts of the conventions, which are identical (save for a slight rearrangement of the clauses in the Prussian convention) except that the Russo-Danish Convention contained secret clauses arranging for joint naval action.

The Swedish government had had its own grounds for complaint against Britain. In June and July 1798 two escorted Swedish convoys totalling 43 ships loaded with ore and naval stores for Portugal and Spain had been arrested by the British and subsequently condemned as prizes; this incident had been a major reason for Sweden dropping out of the Anglo-Russian invasion of North Holland in 1799 in which a Swedish contingent had been expected to participate. By June 1800 the two countries were refusing to recognize each other's *chargés d'affaires* because of a detail of protocol. Yet strained relations with Britain seem to have played little part in the Swedish government's decision to adhere to the Armed Neutrality. It seemed rather that joining the confederation was simply one more obscure manoeuvre in the complicated game of hide-and-seek which Sweden was playing with its traditional enemies, and now partners, Russia and Denmark. The Swedish envoy in London adopted a conciliatory, almost apologetic tone in his communications with Lord Grenville and even protested against Sweden being included in the British embargo against the Armed Neutrality powers, on the grounds that the Swedish government had yet to inform the British officially of its adherence to the confederation. The Swedish counter-embargo against British shipping was not promulgated till the middle of February 1801. The tenderness of the Stockholm government towards British susceptibilities was the more remarkable in view of a bitter controversy that was simultaneously being maintained with Spain.[19]

On 3 September 1800 a party of British naval personnel lurking in open boats off Barcelona under the command of Captain James Hillyar stopped a Swedish sailing vessel, the *Hoffnung*, apparently to make a routine search. Once on board, the British seamen forced the crew at pistol-point to take them past the Spanish defences into Barcelona harbour where they boarded and captured two Spanish 22-gun sloops, the *Concepcion*, alias *Esmeralda*, and *La Paz*. The Spanish government, now at the end of the fourth year of a war with Britain which was turning out as badly as the preceding war with France, was outraged, but of course not in a position to complain directly to the British authorities. Instead, though exonerating the Swedish crew of willing complicity in 'so base and lawless a proceeding', they demanded that the Swedish government should apply to the British for restitution of the captured sloops and punishment of the officers responsible. The Swedish government duly raised the matter in London, though without success, but disclaimed all liability. They also complained that the Spanish authorities permitted French

[19] Sven G. Svenson *Gattjinatraktaten 1799: Studier i Gustav IV Adolfs Utrikespolitik, 1796–1800* (Stockholm 1952) p. 167–173; Public Record Office, London FO 73/28 f. 67 J. Talbot to Lord Grenville 23 May 1800 and f. 99–102 Grenville to Talbot 20 June 1800; Seved Johnson *Sverige och Stormakterna, 1800–1804* (Lund 1957) p. 44–68; Scott *The Armed Neutralities of 1780 and 1800* p. 585–7 cf p. 563 Carl August Friherre Ehrensvard to Lord Grenville 17 Jan. 1801; Feldbaek *Denmark and the Armed Neutrality* p. 117.

ships to attack Swedish merchantmen in Spanish ports, and their note on this subject was phrased in terms of deliberately offensive sarcasm:

> His [Swedish] Majesty would have congratulated himself on the outcome of his representations, if he had observed in his favour any indication of the energy which the Government of Spain has recently displayed against him in a matter, in which he himself has nothing but grievances. Nevertheless the apparent uselessness of his demands has not caused His Majesty to depart from the tone of moderation and equity which becomes the intercourse of two friendly powers.

An official note to the Prussian government asserted that 'After all the vexations to which neutral flags have been exposed during the present war', the Spanish attempt to pressurize Sweden into obtaining satisfaction from the British was 'the most oppressive measure which they have had to endure'. Copies of the Swedish note to the Prussian government were rather freely circulated, and since Prussia was not a party in the dispute, the principal object of the note seems to have been propaganda against Spain. The particularly flagrant violation of Swedish neutrality by the British, which was the origin of the dispute, was played down, even though Sweden was on the point of joining a confederation to resist British usurpations.[20]

The Prussians meanwhile were also playing a game of their own. Having withdrawn from the original military coalition against the French Republic, Prussia had been an interested by-stander in the European war, waiting in the wings ready to seize such advantages as were offered by the turn of events. As the Austrian minister at Berlin put it.

> The Court of Berlin feels keenly the advantage of having acquired by its system of neutrality a decisive superiority in the affairs of Germany, in subduing to its influence half of that important empire.

But the Prussian government's ambitions were not confined to the minnows, the petty principalities and Imperial Free Cities that were too weak to survive the storms of international affairs. The chief obstacle to Prussia's expansion in northern Germany was Hanover, the principality belonging to George III

---

20 William James *The Naval History of Great Britain* (6 vols 1826) vol. 3 p. 73–5, cf Public Record Office FO 73/28 f. 205–7 Hillyar to ? 24 Oct. 1800, copy, where Hillyar denies having used threats, claiming merely that he intended to prevent the *Hoffnung* from getting ahead of his boats and raising the alarm and that the Swedish captain having mentioned that he had never been to Barcelona before, 'I informed him I would stand his Pilot, & show him a good berth'; cf f. 248–9, copy of the account of Martin Rudbarth, the Swedish – it seems actually Swedish Pomeranian – captain. (This seems to be the same *Hoffnung* that later figured in a painting by Caspar David Friedrich); Scott *Armed Neutralities of 1780 and 1800* p. 507–9 note by Chevalier d'Urquijo 17 Sept. 1800; ibid. p. 509–511 note by Fredrik Wilhelm Ehrenheim 22 Oct. 1800; ibid. p. 511–2 Ehrenheim to Haugwitz 1 Nov. 1800, cf Bayerische Hauptstaatsarchiv MA III 2575 – see also Public Record Office FO 73/28 f. 179 and f. 181 J. Talbot to Grenville 31 Oct. and 4 Nov. 1800 where the Prussians were careful to express their concern only *verbally*.

of Great Britain. At the same time there was enormous jealousy of British economic penetration into northern Germany:

> The towns want maritime trade and manufactures. The farflung shipping interest especially, headed by the minister responsible for such concerns, with active members amongst the people of every class, has let itself be drawn by the French party into jealousy against the English, and the feeling has spread to the public as a result of the high price of sugar, coffee and tea. These folk are infatuated with the absurd idea that there would be more maritime trade for every nation that had ports, if the French overthrew English power.

Prussian ministers claimed, 'it is impossible to make manufactures prosper, so long as Europe is flooded with goods from England'. While awaiting Prussian accession to the Armed Neutrality, Paul I of Russia urged the Prussian government to seize Hamburg, an Imperial Free City and the major entrepôt for British trade with Germany, so as 'to oblige the English to give up their pretensions against the neutral powers'. The Prussians hesitated; but a Prussian ship carrying alleged contraband had been arrested by the British Royal Navy and sent into Cuxhaven, another though much less important free city and trading centre, and the Prussian government sent troops to occupy the town. But although Prussia joined the Armed Neutrality two days after Denmark and Sweden, Haugwitz, the Prussian chief minister, assured his government's envoy in London that 'l'association maritime' had nothing to do with Paul's embargo against British shipping. 'They hate, no doubt they really loathe, the English,' it was noted, 'but the schemes of Paul I are too vast not to frighten them, and his changeableness always inspires great mistrust'. Haugwitz strove to persuade the Earl of Carysfort, Lord Grenville's brother-in-law and envoy to Berlin, that Prussia had joined the Armed Neutrality only to restrain Paul I from further excesses. Indeed Haugwitz, it was reported,

> seemed to attach great importance to the distinction he had made between the contracting powers, who had had the chief part in establishing the Armed Neutrality, and those who joined, like Prussia, or joined later: and they continue to send wheat and all kinds of grain to England from the ports of Prussia and East Friesland, these speculations making an enormous profit.[21]

The Danes on the other hand were determined to take the Armed Neutrality seriously – because of their geographical position they were obviously more afraid of being diplomatically isolated vis-à-vis Britain than, as with Sweden and Prussia, vis-à-vis Russia. The British minister at Copenhagen was told initially that Denmark's accession to the Armed Neutrality was not intended to cancel the convention of 29 August, but the notes delivered by the Danish

---

[21] Österreichisches Staatsarchiv: Staatenabteilung Preussen 80. 1800 [f. 181] Hudelist's despatch 31 March 1800; *HMC Dropmore Mss* vol. 4 p. 396 A. de Luc to Lord Grenville 26 Nov. 1798; Österreichisches Staatsarchiv: Staatenabteilung Preussen 81. 1800 f. 96 Hudelist's despatch 16 Nov. 1800; ibid. despatch 28 Nov. 1800; ibid. 12 Jan. 1801; Geheimes Staatsarchiv, Preussichev Kulturbesitz, Merseburg, Rxɪ London no. 73 Haugwitz to Jacobi f. 294, 29 Dec. 1800; Österreichisches Staatsarchiv: Staatenabteilung Preussen 81. Hudelist's despatches 12 Jan. and 12 Feb. 1801.

minister in London became progressively more hostile. That of 23 February 1801 spoke of Britain's 'outrageous proceedings' and 'violent resolutions' and ended with a scarcely veiled threat about his Danish Majesty being 'reduced to the urgent necessity of exerting those means which his dignity and the interests of his subjects will imperiously prescribe'. Prussian notes also became more threatening; and at the end of March 1801 Danish troops occupied Hamburg while Prussian forces crossed the border into Hanover.[22]

Five days after the Danish seizure of Hamburg and the publication of an official manifesto explaining how British attacks on neutral trade had led to this occupation, a powerful British squadron under Lord Nelson sailed into the roadstead at Copenhagen and cannonaded the Danish navy into submission. On the other side of the Sound, at Malmö, Swedish officials listened to their windows rattle from the gunfire and watched the pall of smoke drifting into the sky with a certain degree of complacency: though seven Swedish ships of the line left Karlskrona on 13 April to do battle with the much larger British force they scuttled back into port soon after contacting British scouting vessels and it is difficult to believe that Gustav IV Adolf had ever intended them to fight. In Russia Paul I had been murdered on 23 March – not so much assassinated as liquidated, strangled, it is said, with the sash of one of his chivalric orders – and after Nelson's victory at Copenhagen it was obvious to both the Danish and Prussian governments that their political opportunism had led them into a suicidally exposed position. Though the Armed Neutrality was not formally brought to an end till June, it had in truth been extinguished with the unfortunate Tsar ten weeks earlier.

IV. Copenhagen, 1807

'Deserted by every friend, surrounded by a host of foes, she now stands alone, to try her strength against the united efforts of Europe'. That was how Britain's position was described in an anti-government pamphlet of 1801. Nelson's victory of Copenhagen and the suddenly arranged demise of Paul I showed how flimsy the confederation against Britain really was: but the flimsiness was the result of weakness in political and military organization, not of underlying motives. Within less than seven years the project was revived under more inspired leadership.[23]

Britain's victory over Denmark was followed by negotiations with France and the signature of the Treaty of Amiens in March 1802; then, after a brief year of peace, the war between Britain and France resumed and British diplomats sought once more to mobilize a European coalition against the French. An Austro-Russian army was crushed at Austerlitz in December

[22] Feldbaek *Denmark and the Armed Neutrality* p. 106; Scott *The Armed Neutralities of 1780 and 1800* p. 583–4.

[23] William Hunter *A Short View of the Political Situation of the Northern Powers* London (1800) p. 4.

1805; the Prussians, not waiting even to regularize relations with potential allies, hastened to overwhelming defeat at Jena in October 1806:

> Another year! – another deadly blow!
> Another mighty Empire overthrown!
> And We are left, or shall be left, alone,
> The last that dare to struggle with the Foe.

Once the Russians had been beaten at Friedland in June 1807 Britain indeed stood alone, with the old complaints of British betrayal and exploitation of allies renewed and refurbished.[24]

The mutual blood-letting at Copenhagen in 1801 seems to have reduced rather than increased Danish hostility to Britain, and between 1801 and 1807 there had been an enormous though fluctuating increase in Anglo-Danish trade. Meanwhile Napoleon's campaign across northern Germany and Poland in 1806–1807 brought the reality of the French threat much closer to Denmark than it had ever been in the 1790s. Moreover by mid-1807 the Danish government could no longer count on its former allies in the Armed Neutrality; Prussia had been defeated and overrun, Russia had submitted, Sweden was in military alliance with Britain and conceivably planning the annexation of Norway, at that time part of the Danish realm. Nor was the British government sympathetic to the Danish plight; as early as January 1807 Viscount Howick, Foreign Secretary in Lord Grenville's short-lived ministry, accused the Danes of pursuing an anti-British policy. The withdrawal of their troops in Holstein and their naval rearmament programme seemed to indicate, as Howick complained,

> fears with regard to England, and security with regard to France. He declared that he saw no other way of explaining these two measures combined, and that this supposition must necessarily throw a very unfavourable light on Denmark's future intentions.

At the beginning of March, Rist, the Danish *chargé d'affaires* in London, warned his government that the Tory opposition in England was no friend to the neutral powers: 'the current fashion amongst those who pretended to energy and patriotism is to place neutrals almost in the class of enemies of England'. Three weeks later Lord Grenville's ministry fell, and these Tory patriots formed a new government, with George Canning replacing Howick at the Foreign Department.[25]

After the Russians had submitted to French terms at the Treaty of Tilsit

---

[24] William Wordsworth, sonnet 'November 1806'.

[25] Generally, see S.G. Trulsson *British and Swedish Policies and Strategies in the Baltic after the Peace of Tilsit in 1807* (Lund 1976) espec. p. 131–141 and p. 154–8; Rigsarkivet Copenhagen f.u.A. England II Depecher 1807 Rist's despatch 13 Jan. 1807; ibid. 3 March 1807, cf the remark allegedly made by Pitt in 1795 to the Spanish ambassador, 'the nature of this war does not allow us to draw any distinction between enemies and neutrals,' *Memoirs of Don Manuel de Godoy* vol. 1 p. 468.

it became quickly apparent that the new ministry in London lacked either the faith or the patience to take Denmark's continuing neutrality seriously. The British demanded that the Danes hand over their fleet for safe-keeping, and sent a powerful expeditionary force, equipped with siege artillery and incendiary rockets, to collect it. Faced with the choice of defying the British government or provoking Napoleon, the Danes wavered. On 8 August 1807 the Austrian *chargé d'affaires* at the Danish court reported:

> It seems that the government here will throw itself into the arms of England, having no other choice and being already cut off from the continent ... The French minister, in a meeting he had some days ago with Count Bernstorff, told him that he regarded the prolonged stay of the English fleet in the straits as an infraction of the neutrality of this court, and that if English vessels were permitted to station themselves on the Danish coasts and particularly in the roadstead of Copenhagen, he would be obliged to ask for his passports.

Francis Jackson, the man who had so irritated the Spanish minister Godoy in 1795, arrived on a special mission from London, hinting menacingly at evidence of Danish hostility to Britain and the unsatisfactory nature of 'the Conduct of the Court of Denmark throughout the war'. He told Bernstorff:

> It might be possible, altho' appearances were much against the Supposition, that the Danish Government did not *wish* to lend itself to any hostile views against His Majesty's Dominions and Interests ...

Nevertheless it would be necessary to prevent any possibility of the Danish fleet falling into French hands. Bernstorff protested:

> because You know or think you know that France has the Intention of wounding us in the tenderest Part, would You struggle with her for the guilty Priority – and be the first to commit the Deed?[26]

In the end the Danish government chose resistance; the British demand for the Danish fleet was too outrageous, and Jackson's tone too peremptory. The result was that, without any declaration of war, British land and sea forces bombarded Copenhagen until the Danes capitulated, igniting huge fires in the process by means of the Congreve rockets thoughtfully brought along for just such an eventuality, despite an earlier government recommendation that they should not be used against civilian targets:

> the night naturally proved unusually dark and shewed off this dreadful fire to the utmost advantage ... The light arising from it was so great as to enable me to read or write on the Quarterdeck of the Prometheus with much facility. About 8 o'clock the Batteries and Bombs [small ships armed with mortars] began to blaze away and distribute their favours very profusely, but from the light of the fire we were debarred in a great measure from seeing the shells fly

---

[26] Österreichisches Staatsarchiv: Staatenabteilung Danemark 84 Friedrich Freiherr von Binder's despatch 8 Aug. 1807; Public Record Office London FO 22/54 f. 63 Francis Jackson's despatch 7 Aug. 1807; ibid. f. 66.

through the air. Congreve transmitted many of his rockets towards the Town, which for the cause recited above did not appear so lucid as on former occasions. Could the whole of this awful scene be committed to paper by an ingenious pencil it would form an elegant transparent [type of illuminated picture] The firing was again tremendous all night, and to advert to my simile, constitutes the third act of the play, with improved scenery, machinery, &c. I recollect on perusing the history of the Riots in London in the year 1780, that an old fellow was heard to exclaim upon seeing Newgate in a blaze that he had not missed being present at a fire in the metropolis for 50 years, but he never before saw one so grand as that. What must he have said had he seen the one in question at Copenhagen?

Nearly 2,000 civilian inhabitants died; amongst the buildings destroyed was the Vor Frue Kirke and Jackson's younger brother noted, as the 390 foot high steeple toppled into the inferno, 'the distant loud hurrahs it occasioned along our line'. The Danish fleet, including 13 line of battle ships and vast quantities of naval stores, was carried off to England in triumph.[27]

The bombardment of the Danish capital sent a shock wave of horror across Europe. Even George III thought it 'a very immoral act'. William Wilberforce wrote, 'They must think us the most unjust and cruel of bullying tyrants', but though he thought 'our national character injured' he rejoiced that the British bombardment had consisted mainly of 'rockets, which set the houses on fire without injuring the inhabitants' and proposed a subscription to help the poorer Danes to rebuild their homes. To Alexander I, the young Tsar of Russia, it was 'an act of violence, the like of which history, so fertile in examples, cannot show'. This opinion was of course for public consumption, but there was an unusual note of anguished sincerity in Alexander's official eloquence:

A tranquil and peaceful Power, which by its time-honoured and unalterable wisdom had attained a position of moral dignity among the monarchs of the

---

[27] Charles Chambers 'Journal: "The Bombardment of Copenhagen 1807"' in W.G. Perrin ed. *The Naval Miscellany* vol. 3 (Navy Records Society vol. 63 1928) p. 410–11 cf. Christopher Lloyd and Hardin Craig, Jnr. 'Congreve's Rockets, 1805–1806' in Christopher Lloyd ed. *The Naval Miscellany* vol. 4 (Navy Records Society vol. 92 1952) p. 424–468 at p. 440 (Lord Howick to Lord Keith 14 July 1806) and p. 453 (Thomas Grenville to Keith 11 Oct. 1806); Lady Jackson ed. *The Diaries and Letters of Sir George Jackson, KCH from the Peace of Amiens to the Battle of Talavera* (2 vols. 1872) vol. 2 p. 212 Jackson to his mother 14 Sept. 1807; *Parliamentary Papers* 1808 IX p. 25–52 for details of vessels seized. See also Olav Bergersen *Nøytralitet og Krig* (2 vols. Oslo 1966) and for a contemporary Danish account Anton Frantz Just *Historie om Englands Overfald paa det frelige og neutrale Danmark i Aaret 1807* (Viborg 1807) and C.F. Hellfried *Outlines of a Political Survey of the English Attack on Denmark in the Year 1807* (1809) – Hellfried was the Danish postmaster general; the original Danish version of his book came out in 1808.

The unprecedented scale of the British attack on Copenhagen may be gauged from the fact that the *nine*-day bombardment of Dresden by the Prussians in July 1760 killed only 49 citizens; 416 houses in the inner city and suburbs were destroyed: M.B. Lindau *Geschichte der Haupt- und Residenzstadt Dresden von der frühesten bis auf die gegenwärtige Zeit* (2 vols. Dresden 1857–62) 2 p. 422–3.

world, found itself seized and treated as if it had been contriving dark plots and meditating the destruction of England, all for the purpose of justifying its total and immediate spoliation.

And the Bavarian *chargé d'affaires* at Berlin, writing in strict confidence to his government, expressed the same indignation:

> And what is no less worse, it enables to triumph, and crowns with the most complete success, the most abominable scheme, the most treacherous entreprise, that was ever conceived ... the most hateful, atrocious enterprise of which history offers an example. It is frightful to see that such horrors can be committed with impunity; for the general hatred and distrust which they must inspire are by no means sufficient punishment for a government which seems long since to have voluntarily given up all honourable feeling.

So whole-hearted was the condemnation expressed in his despatches by the Austrian *chargé d'affaires* at the Danish court that his official superiors in Vienna had to remind him that they did not desire to know his private opinions. As one experienced former British diplomat remarked, 'Our Court must have been very badly informed of the temper and feelings of the Continent towards us if it has yet to learn that we are everywhere detested'. In America the attack on Copenhagen was cited by Thomas Jefferson, together with the crimes of Napoleon, as proof that the 1800s were, with the Macedonian and Roman imperial eras, one of 'three epochs in history, signalized by the total extinction of national morality'.[28]

[28] A. Aspinall ed. *The Later Correspondence of George III* (5 vols. Cambridge 1962–1970) vol. 4 p. 607 fn 2 Canning to Joan Canning 26 August 1807; Robert Isaac and Samuel Wilberforce *The Life of William Wilberforce* (5 vols. 1838) vol. 3 p. 344 diary 19 Sept. 1807; ibid. vol. 3 p. 345 diary 20 Oct. 1807 and p. 348 (in reality the three days' barrage of shell and round-shot must have been one of the most intensive ever recorded prior to 1914, involving the expenditure of more than three times the quantity of gunpowder fired off at Waterloo: in addition to the mortars and howitzers and twenty 24-pounders brought with the Army, the Navy employed bomb vessels and landed lower-deck guns from some of the battleships to equip shore batteries); Scott *The Armed Neutralities of 1780 and 1800* p. 636, Alexander I's declaration of 7 Nov. 1807: George III sneered that the declaration was 'couched in language so gross & insulting that H.M. conceives it must have been framed by those who write for the Paris Moniteur & transcribed word for word at Petersburg'. *Later Correspondence of George III* vol. 4 p. 653–4 no. 3562 George III to Canning 2 Dec. 1807 but cf P. Baillen ed. *Briefwechsel König Friedrich Wilhelm's III und der Königin Luise mit Kaiser Alexander I* (Leipzig 1900) p. 169 no. 157 Alexander to Friedrich Wilhelm of Prussia 2 Nov. 1807; Bayerisches Hauptstaatsarchiv MA III 2590 François Gabriel Chevalier de Bray despatch 1807 no. 64, 19 Sept. 1807; Österreichisches Staatsarchiv: Staatenabteilung Danemark 84, Vienna chancery to Freiherr von Binder 10 Oct. 1807, draft: 'Il ne convenoit point de vous prononcer ni sur la justice de sa cause, ni sur l'injustice de celle de l'Angleterre, pareils jugements étant du ressort de la cour mais jamais de celui de son Chargé d'affaires'; C.P. Miles ed. *Correspondence of William Augustus Miles on the French Revolution, 1789–1817* (2 vols. 1890) vol. 2 p. 358 Miles to Charles Long 19 Nov. 1807; Thomas Jefferson *Memoirs; Correspondence and Private Papers* (4 vols. 1829) vol. 1 p. 87.

Even Napoleon pretended to be shocked. Fouché, his minister of police, recalled:

I hadn't seen Napoleon abandon himself to such a violent rage since the fall of Paul I. What struck him most in this vigorous coup was the promptness and resolution of the English ministry.

Metternich reported a conversation between the French emperor and the Portuguese ambassador:

'You see how the English behave: when one government permits itself such actions, the others can only to likewise in their turn: they had not even recalled their ambassador, one always used at least to begin with that before proceeding to deeds: it's terrible. Now other people will have to rush ahead just as much'.

[The ambassador replied] 'But I suppose, Sire, that you do not wish to establish this as a legal principle in Europe?'

The Emperor was a little taken aback, and after a short silence he cried out, 'But if the others do it?'[29]

But in reality this second attack on Copenhagen played directly into Napoleon's hands: fourteen years of complaints against the way Britain waged war had finally climaxed in that country's almost total moral and diplomatic isolation.

V. The Continental System

Fifteen weeks after the bombardment of Copenhagen, Napoleon issued a decree at Milan which was an important stage in the erection of what came to be known as the Continental Blockade: the exclusion of British trade from every European port under the control of himself or his allies. As we have seen the idea of a universal boycott of British trade had been canvassed in the 1790s, but it has never been entirely clear what Napoleon had in mind when establishing the Blockade, especially as the system was radically modified during the course of its operation. In itself the timing of the original Milan decree suggests nothing more than a retaliation against the British Orders in Council of 11 November 1807 which extended the existing British blockade of French-controlled ports; indeed though Napoleon instructed his minister of finance and minister of the interior, the director of customs and a member of his Council of State to make a joint examination of the British Orders in Council, their report was still on its way to him when he issued the Milan decree.[30]

[29] Louis Madelin ed. *Les Mémoires de Fouché* (Paris 1945) p. 253; Österreichisches Staatsarchiv: Staatenabteilung Frankreich 200 Klemens Graf von Metternich's despatch 22 Sept. 1807.

[30] Napoleon's Berlin Decree of 1 Nov. 1806 had banned direct intercourse with Britain and dealing in British owned or manufactured goods, but it was the second Milan Decree of
continued

Fouché recalled:

> The idea of destroying English power as the sole obstacle to his universal monarchy became his *idée fixe* ... Napoleon was convinced that by closing all her markets he would reduce her to a consumptive decline (*phtisie*) and to collapse.

But the total boycott, which became impossible to enforce and merely spawned a vast smuggling trade, was replaced after three years by the Trianon decree of 5 August 1810 which allowed colonial goods – tea, coffee, sugar, spices, raw cotton – into Europe from Britain, but subject to very high tariffs. This may have been intended to prepare the way for fiercer penalties against the importation of British manufactures. At the same time Napoleon permitted grain to be exported to Britain; this, as it turned out, helped the British to weather the effects of a particularly poor harvest, which might otherwise have resulted in the most serious economic crisis of the war period. This change in a policy which was on the point of destabilizing Britain has generally been interpreted as aiming, not at the British economy generally and indiscriminately, but at one particular key element of it, Britain's system of credit and fiduciary currency.[31]

The central role of Britain's public debt, not merely as a motive for but as a means of making war, had long been recognized and had featured even in Immanuel Kant's essay on Perpetual Peace (*Zum Ewigen Frieden*, 1795):

> But what can we think of a system of credit, the ingenious invention of a commercial people of this century, by means of which debts are accumulated without end, and yet cause no embarrassment in their reimbursements, since the creditors never make their demands all at one time. Considered as a political engine, it is a dangerous means of monied power, a treasury for war, superior to that of all other states collectively ... The abolition of the funding system must therefore be a preliminary article [i.e. of peace].

Thomas Paine's *The Decline and Fall of the English System of Finance* (1796) was also widely circulated on the continent – he threatened 'this work will be published in all languages' and it certainly appeared in German, French, Italian and Spanish. Paine argued that the funding system was inevitably doomed and stated, 'I would not give twenty shillings for one hundred pounds in the funds to be paid twenty years hence'. Similarly an essay by the Chevalier de Guer

---

continued
17 Dec. 1807 which not only filled in the last details of the Continental Blockade and extended it to the open sea but also marked the beginning of strict international enforcement; Bertrand de Jouvenel *Napoléon et l'Économie Dirigée* p. 308–9 and p. 309 fn. 1 for the precise timing of the decree.

[31] *Mémoires de Fouché* p. 246; Eli Heckscher *The Continental System: An Economic Interpretation* (Oxford 1922) p. 201–3 for the Trianon Decree. The view that the Continental System aimed to damage British credit by draining gold out of the country, rejected by Heckscher p. 340–7, was put forward in J.H. Rose *Napoleonic Studies* (1906) p. 218–9 and is still current in British universities today.

published in 1801 gave an agreeable picture of the panic that would ensue when British credit collapsed:

all the inhabitants of London plunged into despair at the sudden loss of all their money, rushing to the Bank, breaking down the doors and forcing the safes, in a vain search for the gold which was not there, and the government obliged to fight its own people when it was already too big a job to repel the enemy.[32]

Presumably the criticism of paper money which was voiced in London contributed to the belief on the continent that the British financial system was desperately fragile; at any rate one London banker's statement regarding the ruinous effect of paper currency elicited the comment, 'his book will be read with avidity in France; and it may probably produce hopes in that country, which, I trust, he does not wish to inspire'. There was certainly an awareness that the French might attempt some sort of offensive against the British financial system. An employee of the Bank of England claimed:

The enemies of our country, aware that to throw into confusion the resources of the nation, would prove a victory far more valuable to them, than the overthrow of our fleets and our armies, planned a most artful attempt to accomplish that object.

The fiendish scheme identified by this writer consisted of the manipulation of the Hamburg exchange, in conjunction with the small-scale landing on the coast of Pembrokeshire in 1797 (the latter had in reality been intended as a diversion to cover the invasion of Ireland); clearly the British understood the potential of such a strategy quite as well as the French.[33]

The common belief that the continuance of the war was necessary for the maintenance of British credit was based on an assessment of the British economy as fundamentally distorted, diseased and unsound:

the gold which England draws to herself from every part would soon overload her and stifle every type of industry if she had not, by the excessive expenses of her wars and the great luxury of her inhabitants, opened a route for it to run out with the same abandon as it ran in. In fact, if the nine thousand millions which

---

[32] Immanuel Kant, *Perpetual Peace* ed. Nicholas Murray Butler, (New York 1939) p. 5–6; this however gives 'Treasure' rather than 'Treasury' which in the context is a more appropriate translation of *Schatz*; Thomas Paine *The Decline and Fall of the English System of Finance* (1796) p. 12 for his not giving 20/- for £100 in the funds, p. 43 for promise to publish the pamphlet in all languages; Julien-Hyacinthe Marnière, Chevalier de Guer *Essai sur le credit Commercial Considéré comme Moyen de Circulation* (Paris and Hamburg 1801) p. 24–5.

[33] *Brief Observations on a Late letter Addressed to the Right Hon. W. Pitt. by W. Boyd. Esq., &c. on the Stoppage of Issues in Specie by the Bank of England* (1801) p. 10. This pamphlet is sometimes attributed to William Combe, author of *Doctor Syntax*; incidentally Walter Boyd himself, as well as his pamphlet, eventually ended up in French hands for he was in France in the outbreak of war in 1803 and was interned till 1814; T.S. Surr *Refutation of Certain Misrepresentations relative to the Nature and Influence of Bank Notes, and of the Stoppage of Issues in Specie, at the Bank of England, upon the Prices of Provisions* (1801) p. 33.

the last two wars against France cost her were still in circulation in England, wouldn't she have collapsed under the weight of her own wealth?

According to this view only the war and the opportunity it gave to enforce a commercial monopoly protected Britain from 'disastrous' or 'fatal' effects of the national indebtedness:

> so long as her commerce can sustain her power and maintain her credit, so long as her fleets are victorious and maintain the dominion of the seas, Great Britain will prosper: but as soon as one or other of these pillars which hold up the edifice of her greatness fall, she will see the end of her dominion and will be parcelled out amongst the Powers she had subjected to her yoke.[34]

Napoleon may have known the pamphlet just quoted, and was certainly acquainted with the writings of the Chevalier de Guer, though the general tendency of the latter, in advocating credit institutions on the continent, was contrary to Napoleon's own thinking. The question is whether Napoleon was materially influenced by these luridly simplistic arguments.[35]

Napoleon was by no means averse to voicing some of the economic clichés of his publicists: the British, he would say, 'need an enormous volume of trade, if their customs-houses are to pay the interest on their public debt', and 'It is the necessity of paying this, of maintaining their credit, which drives them on'. These remarks prove only his ignorance: as has already been shown he had no interest in or understanding of credit finance. The astonishing facility of his mental processes deprived him of the patience to be original, and the bias of his mind was always towards the past: 'I am the successor of Charlemagne', he would say, or 'I am a Roman Emperor: I belong to the best breed of Caesars, the founders'. Indeed his career of two decades was a re-run of the entire history of the late Roman Republic and Roman Empire, with himself playing, like a more formidable Alec Guinness, not only Augustus and Trajan but also Sulla and Pompey and Constantine and Theodosius: but most of what was really modern in his regime had been inherited from the Revolution and he had no interest in even the trappings of modernity. The essentially novel aspects of the British economy were distasteful to him, if only on account of their novelty. At the same time he liked to go into detail – 'he did not limit himself to reigning, to governing, he kept on administering, not just as a

---

[34] Monbrion *De la Prépondérance Maritime et Commerciale de la Grande-Bretagne* (Paris 1805) p. 322 and p. 355, cf also p. 328. The first passage quoted shows the shakiness of the economic theory of many of the French critics; most of the money raised to finance Britain's wars was in fact spent in Britain, both foreign subsidies and overseas expeditions requiring to be fed and paid outside the country representing only a small part of total expenditure; consequently most of the money *was* still in circulation in Britain.

[35] For the question of Napoleon's knowledge of Guer's work see Audrey Cunningham *British Credit in the Last Napoleonic War* (Cambridge 1910) p. 33–4. For an interesting attempt to trace the principles of the Continental System back to the Navigation Act passed by the Convention in 1793 Frederick L. Nussbaum *Commercial Policy in the French Revolution: A Study of the Career of G.J.A. Ducher* (Washington 1923) p. 292–302.

prime minister but in more detail than each minister' – and he generally made
a point of having informed ideas about whatever business he was engaged in.
One may assume therefore that he thought he knew what he was doing with
the Continental Blockade, but not that his thinking was necessarily derived
from the economists. The whole analysis of Britain's predicament was so
theoretical and futuristic, the promise of imminent collapse so speculative, and
Napoleon himself so little interested in economic abstractions that the illusion
of a coherent strategy of economic warfare could scarcely have tempted him
for a moment. He caused David Ricardo's pamphlet *The High Price of Bullion*
to be translated in *Le Moniteur* but was surely attracted by the pamphlet's
utility as propaganda rather than as a guide to policy. If Napoleon really did
have a systematic theory behind his policy it is inexplicable that he made no
attempt to monitor progress: had he done so he would have seen that as soon
as Anglo-French trade was permitted again in 1810, the trade balance was
established in Britain's favour and that the export of grain to England, far
from causing a drain of gold from England, was accompanied by a drain
of gold from northern Europe. It seems clear that the principal objective of
Napoleon's Continental System was not the economic ruination of Britain,
but something much more immediate, tangible and attainable.[36]

One of the features of the Continental System was the way it placed France's
political dependencies at a disadvantage vis-à-vis France itself. Even if it had
been simply a question of a Continental Blockade there would have been
a tendency for France, as the strongest European economy, to make up
most of the deficiency created by the exclusion of British products, but the
Continental Blockade as such was only part of a larger system. The export of
Spanish wool into France was prohibited. The exit duty on raw silk leaving
Italy for France was lifted, benefiting French silk manufacturers at the expense
of the Italian customs revenue, while the advantage to Italian exporters was
more than off-set by forbidding exportations to other countries for months
at a time. The decree forbidding the importation of English textiles into Italy
defined as English all textiles not bearing the mark of French manufacture, and
though Napoleon justified this enactment as a revival of a law of 10 *brumaire
an* IV (31 October 1796) the main effect was in cutting off a principal market

---

[36] Jean Hanoteau ed. *Memoirs of General de Caulaincourt, Duke of Vicenza* (3 vols.
London 1950) vol. 2 p. 148, 149 for Napoleon's *obiter dicta* on British credit; Adrien
Dansette ed. *Napoléon: Vues Politiques* (Paris 1939) p. 412 for Napoleon's self-identification
with Charlemagne and the Caesars; [F.N. Comte] Mollien *Mémoires d'un Ministre du Trésor
Public, 1780–1815* (4 vols. Paris 1845) vol. 2 p. 230 for Napoleon as administrator; *Moniteur*
24, 25, 26 Sept. 1810, pp. 1050–1052, 1054–6, 1058–60 and cf Piero Sraffa ed. *The Works and
Correspondence of David Ricardo* (11 vols Cambridge 1951–73) vol. 10 p. 374; A. Chabert *Essai
sur les Mouvements des Revenues et de l'Activité Économique en France de 1798 a 1820* (Paris
1949) p. 322 (tableau II) and p. 326 (tableau 14) cf. *Parliamentary Papers* 1840 XLIV p. 124.
The latter shows exports from France to Britain as higher in 1809 when they were forbidden
than in 1810 when they were permitted.

for Swiss and German exports. When Eugène Beauharnais, as Viceroy of Italy, protested against such policies, Napoleon wrote in explanation:

> My principle is: France before all else. You must never lose sight of the fact that, if English trade triumphs at sea, it's because the English are the strongest there, and it's therefore fitting, since France is the strongest on land, that she should make her trade triumph on land: otherwise everything will be lost ...
>
> Italy must not make calculations separate from the prosperity of France: she must pool her interests with France; she must above all make sure of giving France an interest in their alliance ... Therefore take as your motto: *France before all else.*
>
> I therefore find it somewhat odd that there is some reluctance to come to the aid of French manufactures in a measure which also aims at harming the English.[37]

This policy was quickly recognized for what it was by third parties, such as the Bavarian government:

> The general system of France as regards [freedom of trade] is no longer a mystery to anybody. They seek to cut off all communication with England in order to force her to make peace by suffocating her in the excess (*embonpoint*) of her wealth, but they wish at the same time to protect an exclusive market for French manufactures or at least to guarantee to the Empire all the contraband from Great Britain if it turns out to be impossible to destroy entirely all communication between that illustrious island and the continent.

The confusing modification of Napoleon's trade blockade in 1810, by which imports of colonial goods from Britain were permitted subject to heavy duty, was interpreted as an attempt to increase French revenue by making France the channel through which British trade entered the continent:

> The whole point of the regulations comprised under the name of the Continental System was at the same time to harm Britain and to enrich France, from whom all the goods would henceforth be supplied which previously had come through England, besides which a source of income for the imperial treasury would be opened through single individuals now and then obtaining licences for importing a number of cargoes in exchange for surrendering 30 (or 50?) per cent of the value.

This was also, in fact, the opinion of some British newspapers but it was shared

---

37 A. du Casse ed. *Mémoires et Correspondance Politique et Militaire du Roi Joseph* (10 vols. Paris 1854–5) vol. 6 p. 161 Joseph to Napoleon 30 April 1809; Evgenij Viktorovic Tarle *La vita economica dell'Italia nell'età napoleonica* (Turin 1950) p. 279; for the definition as English of all textiles not marked as French see Tarle p. 135, and Marcel Dunan *Napoléon et l'Allemagne: Le Système Continental et les débuts du Royaume de Bavière 1806–1810* (Paris 1942) p. 351–2, cf. Louis Antoine Fauvelet de Bourrienne *Memoirs of Napoleon Bonaparte* ed. R.W. Phipps (4 vols. New York 1906) vol. 3 p. 109; *Correspondance de Napoleon 1er* vol. 21 p. 70–71 Napoleon to Eugène 23 Aug. 1810. See also Ulane Bonnel *La France les États-Unis et la Guerre de course 1797–1815* (Paris 1961) p. 212–226, 232–251, 289–295 for French policy as it affected the U.S.A.

by Napoleon's treasury minister, Mollien, who saw the revised Continental System as 'appropriating indirectly, at the expense of the continent, by means of his licences, a share of England's monopoly'. It shows the crudity of Napoleon's economic thinking that he believed such a transparent measure to be practical politics.[38]

This policy eventually contributed to the breach with Tsar Alexander and the catastrophic invasion of Russia in 1812; nevertheless Napoleon seems to have originally conceived it in terms of the support it could mobilize amongst the citizens of the states under his influence or control. This was where the widespread resentment of British wealth and sea-power entered into his scheme. A common front against a universal bogey was a first-class basis for the diplomatic and psychological unification of the continent, even if the real object of this unification was a permanent French hegemony. Moreover the idea of a united front against British maritime supremacy fitted in perfectly with the policy traditions of his new allies. In announcing his breach with Great Britain in November 1807 Alexander referred respectfully to the policy of Armed Neutrality: he had previously told the Swedish plenipotentiary Stedingk that he wished 'to hold to the engagements contracted with the Swedish and Danish courts in the treaties of 1780 and 1800'. Sweden at first refused to cooperate, but after the Russian invasion of Finland and the deposition of Gustav IV Adolf the Swedes' enforced accession to the Continental System, in the spring of 1810, was presented as a revival of the Armed Neutrality of 1800–1801: 'Thus are the Northern Powers again united in the same System, and on the same fundamental principles . . . against a haughty and implacable Enemy'.[39]

The blockade of Great Britain, in providing an active organizational expression of a Europe united under Napoleon's leadership, had a powerful symbolic resonance. Napoleon seems to have consciously promoted this aspect of his policy. As early as 1805 he had inaugurated a propaganda campaign against Britain which went far beyond the customary rhetoric of wartime: writing to Fouché on the subject of the newspapers published in Paris, he ordered 'The tone of these papers ought to be directed towards attacking England, her fashions, her customs, her literature, her constitution'. At the end of 1806 he commanded that 'all letters coming from England or written in English or by Englishmen are to be sent back' – a decree that must have

[38] Michael Doeberl *Rheinbundverfassung und bayerische Konstitution* [Munich 1924] p. 65–73 (Beilage no. 6) Denkschrift Maximilian von Montgelas Jan. 1808, at p. 67; Ludwig Graf von Montgelas ed. *Denkwürdigkeiten des Bayerischen Staatsministers Maximilian Grafen von Montgelas 1799–1817* (Stuttgart 1887) p. 223 (Denkschrift 1817); *Times* 16 Aug. 1810 p. 2d, *Star* 17 Aug. 1810 p. 2a; Mollien *Mémoires* vol. 3 p. 116.

[39] Scott ed. *The Armed Neutralities of 1780 and 1800* p. 657, manifesto of Alexander I; vol. 4 p. 86 note of Nicholas Roumantsev's interview with Stedingk 24 Sept. (6 Oct.) 1807; Rigsarkivet Copenhagen f.u.A. Amerika II Depecher: Peder Pedersen to U.S. Secretary of State Robert Smith 6 April 1810, copy.

been as gratifying to the numerous French prisoners of war in Britain as to the American government. After the bombardment of Copenhagen he told Metternich, the Austrian ambassador at his court,

> I will not permit it that there should be an English diplomatic mission in Europe, I will declare war on any power whatever that two months from now still has one ... The English declare they will no longer respect neutrals at sea, I shall no longer recognize them on land.

The extravagant phrases of the Milan decree about 'the barbarous system adopted by the English government, who make laws similar to those of Algiers', in contradistinction to 'the principles of international law, which are also those of justice and honour' also suggest propaganda rather than legislation; and to make sure this propaganda was sufficiently noticed, Napoleon instructed his minister of the interior to 'write a circular to all the chambers of commerce, to make them feel the sad consequences there would be in the future from these new English laws [the Orders in Council of 11 November 1807], if they were passed over in silence'.[40]

Brilliant as it was as a pre-emptive strike, the attack on Copenhagen made Britain the Untouchable of Europe. The pro-British Friedrich Gentz, who had earlier remarked, 'Twist and turn this Danish expedition as I may, I cannot get any use out of it', was now forced to observe ruefully, 'So now, after ten years of fruitless efforts to unite even a part of the European Powers in resistance to Tyranny, we have lived to see a complete coalition against the last bulwark of freedom'. It may even have been his over-confidence in this situation which led Napoleon to overplay his hand.[41]

VI. From Isolation to Triumph

By the end of 1807 Britain had few friends in Europe. The King of Sardinia, Vittorio Emanuele I may have been pro-British, and certainly resented the French annexation of his mainland territories, which contained most of the wealth and population of his hereditary possessions; but he was in constant fear of provoking a French invasion of his barren island kingdom. The King

[40] *Correspondance de Napoléon 1er* vol. 10 p. 578 Napoleon to Fouché 1 June 1805; ibid. vol. 14 p. 34 Napoleon to A.M. Gaudin 1 Dec. 1806; Prince Richard de Metternich ed. *Mémoires Documents et Écrits Divers ... de Metternich* (8 vols. Paris 1880–84) vol. 2 p. 130 Metternich to Stadion 16 Oct. 1807; *Correspondance de Napoléon 1er* vol. 16 p. 228–9 for text of decree 17 Dec. 1807 and p. 231 Napoleon to A.M. Cretet 17 Dec. 1807. One notes that though he told Murat to get rid of his children's English governesses, apparently on security grounds, in 1805, he later expressed no surprise in seeing them still in Murat's household: Catherine Davies *Eleven Years' Residence in the Family of Murat, King of Naples* (1841) p. 4, 6.

[41] Louis von Ompteda ed. *A Hanoverian-English Officer a Hundred Years Ago: Memoirs of Baron Ompteda* (1892) p. 208–9 Gentz to Ompteda 26 Aug. 1807; *Briefwechsel zwischen Friedrich Gentz und Adam Heinrich Müller, 1800–1829* (Stuttgart 1857) p. 120 30 Nov. 1807.

of Sweden, Gustav IV Adolf, intent on seizing Norway from the Danes, maintained his alliance with London but quarrelled with London's emissaries. The Bourbons of Naples, who like Vittorio Emanuele I had been driven by the French from the more important part of their kingdom on the mainland, were kept loyal by the fact that Sicily was defended by a British garrison, though relations between the British military commander and the Palermo government were consistently poor. Portugal, whose court had been bullied by British envoys into fleeing to Brazil, soon came 'entirely under the control and direction of the British Government'. Lord Palmerston, then at the outset of his long political career, remarked cheerfully:

> by the bye is it not curious that the only two sovereigns who besides ours have shown any spirit & energy in these times should have been the King of Sweden & the Prince of Portugal who have been constantly represented by the opposition the one as a madman & the other an idiot.

It is difficult however to see much evidence of spirit and energy in the vacillating conduct of the Prince Regent of Portugal, who only submitted with the greatest reluctance and procrastination to British pressure to evacuate his capital; and the policy of the King of Sweden, even if sane, turned out to be grotesquely unsuccessful. Allies of this calibre hardly mitigated the otherwise total isolation of Britain after Copenhagen.[42]

It would take all the rashest miscalculations of Napoleon's subsequent career to rescue '*Albion perfide*' from the position it had created for itself by September 1807; and even then, even after the Bonapartist usurpation in Spain, the invasion of Russia, the burning of Moscow, the War of Liberation in Germany, the allied march on Paris, Napoleon's first abdication, his triumphant return from Elba and the final British-led victory at Waterloo, the feeling would persist that the British had somehow managed to organize the whole twenty-two years of European warfare largely for their own benefit:

> the Continental system, as they called it, and as they managed it, was promoting to the utmost extent the views of England: was, instead of impairing her commerce, securing to her that of the whole world; and was pouring into her lap the means of continuing the war, just as long as her ministers should think it expedient.

[42] For Sardinia see Public Record Office FO 67/36, Joseph Smith's despatches during 1807; for Gustav IV Adolf's Norwegian schemes see S.G. Trulsson *British and Swedish Policies and Strategies in the Baltic after the Peace of Tilsit in 1807* (Lund 1976) p. 133–4, 154–8; for Sicilian resentments see Public Record Office FO 70/44 Lord William Bentinck to Marquess Wellesley 26 Dec. 1811 and *Memoirs of Comte Roger de Damas 1787–1806* (1913) p. 413–4; for Portugal see Percy, Viscount Strangford *Observations on some Passages in Lieut. Col. Napier's History of the Peninsular War* (1828) passim – it was Strangford, as British minister at Lisbon in 1807, who negotiated the evacuation of the Portuguese court to Brazil; Kenneth Bourne ed. *The Letters of the Third Viscount Palmerston to Laurence and Elizabeth Sulivan 1804–1863* (Camden Society 4th series vol. 23, 1979) p. 97, 24 Dec. 1807.

After Napoleon's final defeat at Waterloo it was said of him:

> Great Britain is under weightier obligation to no mortal man than to this very villain; for by the occurrences whereof he is the author, her greatness, prosperity, and wealth, have attained their present elevation.

But part of the victory the British had won for themselves was that they did not even need to acknowledge this paradox.[43]

---

[43] C.F. Adams ed. *Memoirs of John Quincy Adams* (12 vols. Philadelphia 1874–7) vol. 2 p. 145, 8 Aug. 1810; F.C.F. von Müffling *Passages from my Life* (1853) p. 275 Graf Gneisenau to Müffling 29 June 1815.

4

Wellington's War

There is really such a thing as an *invincible nation*: it is only to have organisation
– it is only to have a bayonet at one end of a musquet, and at the other a *well-fed freeman*.

Robert Gourlay, *A Specific Plan for Organising the People and for obtaining Reform
Independent of Parliament* (1809), p. 171.

I. The Elusive Strategic Pattern

Although it lasted twenty-two years and extended through two peace treaties,
Britain's role in the war against Revolutionary and Napoleonic France had
a curiously simple pattern. The British government at first blundered about
seeking a strategy. Then, in response to the enemy's strategic initiatives, they
increasingly focused their attention on to a narrower field. Finally they were
able to channel the country's main resources into a single theatre which offered
a possibility of decisive victory. When the defeated Napoleon returned from
exile in Elba in 1815, it was a single knock-out blow guided by a British hand
which crushed him.

The simplicity of this long-drawn out development is apparent in retrospect
and is neatly enough focused by the elegant trajectory of the career of the
man who vanquished Napoleon at Waterloo, the Duke of Wellington: but to
contempories the design was evident only in its final stages.

The policy of blunder, lasting up until 1807 when Napoleon established
what he hoped would be a definitive pacification of mainland Europe, had
numerous causes. There was, from 1793 onwards, a failure to understand the
strength of the new French Republic and the likely duration of any war against
it. Pitt was not unique in this failure and though the Republic seemed at its
most disorganized in 1793 it remained an administrative and political shambles,
seemingly on the brink of dissolution, until the establishment of the Consulate
in 1799. There was also the failure to make durable alliances with the other
powers hostile to France: the extension of British sea-power and the British
government's commitment to a policy of colonial conquests was a source of
distrust in all London's arrangements with continental governments.

The British ministry's preoccupation with conquering France's possessions
in the West Indies in the mid-1790s could be justified by the need to defend

Britain's colonies and sea-trade by eliminating French overseas bases but in this respect the policy was substantially a failure. The force sent to invade Guadeloupe in 1794 was unable to maintain its position and had to be evacuated after eight months, and this important French colony did not come under British control till 1810; St Lucia, having been occupied, was reconquered by the French in June 1795 and required a second British invasion in May 1796. The wastage of men from disease in these rugged, overgrown, impenetrably lush and sinister islands was enormous and depressing. In the meantime, and in fact till 1810, Britain's sporadic interventions on the European mainland were either in a role auxiliary to the much larger armies of continental allies, as in Flanders in 1793–1795, and in north Germany in 1805–1806; or for strictly limited objectives as in the landing at Toulon in 1793, at the Helder in 1799, at Ferrol and Cadiz in 1800 and at Walcheren as late as 1809; or else fell aimlessly between the two as in Calabria in 1805 and 1806. A foreign diplomat might feel he had good grounds for referring jeeringly to 'some grotesque (*barroque*) plan for a landing which will get stuck like the others and cost immense amounts. They would do better to give us subsidies'. Even the campaign in 1801 to reconquer Egypt from the French, launched simultaneously though without synchronization across the eastern Mediterranean and the Red Sea, had no longer-term objective than that of securing an important bargaining counter for use in future peace negotiations, for all that it was to establish a fruitful tradition of defending British India on the coasts of the eastern Mediterranean.[1]

To some extent the British government may have been led astray by the example of how Britain's very successful participation in the Seven Years' War had been conducted by Pitt the Elder, who was after all the father of the man who was Prime Minister for most of the period 1793–1806 and uncle of the man who was Foreign Secretary till 1801. But perhaps this is too charitable: Britain had had a more reliable (because more desperate) ally in 1756–1763 and a less desperate enemy, and the different circumstances of the war against the French Republic were understood well enough:

> The war was to be viewed either as an ordinary contest between two nations, and carried on upon the usual principle of annoying and weakening your antagonist till he was brought to equitable sentiments; or we were to consider it as a new and extraordinary war, which could be carried on with a system suited to its portentous nature. Hence, therefore, it was to be carried on by attacking the enemies' colonies, capturing their ships &c., or it was to be carried on by

[1] For the foreign diplomat's opinion of British strategy see Joseph [i.e. Giuseppe] Greppi *Révélations diplomatiques sur les relations de la Sardaigne avec l'Autriche et la Russe pendant la première et la deuxième coalition* (Paris 1859) p. 139, Gaetano Balbo to Savoyard Secretary of State Domenico Simone Ambrosio Conte di Chialemberto 3 Feb. 1800; for the Egyptian expedition see [James] Lord Dunfermline *Lieutenant-General Sir Ralph Abercromby K.B.* (1861) p. 247–8 and cf Edward Ingram *Commitment to Empire* (Oxford 1981) p. 341–2, 387–401 and present author's letter in *Times Higher Education Supplement* 16 April 1982.

aiming decisive blows at the seat or centre of the system from which the true principle of the war and danger proceeded.

The real problem was perhaps the lack of any conceptual framework for planning a war on the necessary scale. The word 'strategy' did not even appear in the English language till 1810, but the lack of this word was scarcely felt for there was never, in all the twenty-two years of war, any real attempt to think out the strategic implications of Britain's position.[2]

II. The Problem of Strategic Control

In the First World War there was the War Council, later War Cabinet, system which arrived at the decision to attack Gallipoli after enough discussion to muddle the whole issue and which later achieved a stalemate lasting over a year between the views of Lloyd George and those of General Sir William Robertson. In the Second World War there was Churchill's virtuoso performance with the Chiefs of Staff, in which a not always happy compromise was worked out between Churchill's large gestures and the military's desire to avoid doing anything rash. In the 1790s there was some interesting correspondence on strategic objectives between Lord Grenville as Foreign Secretary and Henry Dundas as War and Colonial Secretary, but it never quite came to grips with practical military details and Dundas failed to learn from their joint failures 'that something more than his fiat is necessary to form a general, and that red coats make not a soldier'. Nor did the situation improve after Dundas retired and Grenville went into opposition.[3]

At this period there was always at least one general in the Cabinet, the Master General of the Ordnance – who despite his responsibility for the Ordnance was not normally an artillery officer and therefore not likely to be too well ahead on the technical problems of his department, but for that very reason potentially of value as an adviser on military affairs generally. He was never consulted. The First Lord of the Admiralty, who was also an Army general more often than an admiral, but a civilian more often than either, was also usually left out of strategic decision-making. There was no organized Army or Navy staff. The Admiralty Board always included naval members but they were normally only of captain's rank; the concept of a First Sea Lord who was professional head of the service had not yet emerged. In the 1790s this lack of a general staff system was not remarkable, as the same deficiency was to be found in the armed forces of the other European powers, but by the 1800s the concept of a general staff began to emerge rapidly on the

---

[2] *Parliamentary History* vol. 36 col. 747–8, speech by William Windham 13 May 1802.

[3] [Richard] Duke of Buckingham *Memoirs of the Court and Cabinets of George the Third* (4 vols 1853–5) vol. 3 p. 8 Lieutenant General T.G. Simcoe to Marquis of Buckingham 2 Jan. 1800.

continent: it was to be a full hundred years before the British army caught up with this development.[4]

The aspect of general staff work which is at issue here is what in the twentieth century came to be called the 'operations' department. Very crudely, the adjutant-general's staff is responsible for organizing the manpower side of of an army, the quarter-master staff is responsible for the material side, and the operations staff for the fighting side. The operations side being the most crucial and unpredictable aspect of an army's functioning, the commanding general traditionally kept this part of the business strictly in his own hands. It seems that the first officer to act like a modern chief of general staff in helping the commanding general to plan battles was Louis-Hyacinthe Boyer de Crémilles, *maréchal général des logis* – i.e. quarter-master-general – under Maurice de Saxe in the War of the Austrian Succession. In Russia the quarter-master staff, which by 1796 numbered 32 officers of major's rank or upwards, was reorganized in the late 1790s as a section of the Tsar's suite and had a particular emphasis on operations. The establishment of a distinct operations component within the Prussian and Austrian army staffs followed within the next few years.[5]

Napoleon of course had no need for an operations staff to advise him: though Alexandre Berthier was given the title *Major-Général* of the Army, implying some sort of overall organizational responsibility, in practice he functioned simply as the head of a military secretariat. In Britain there was no Napoleon, but nor was there any recognition of the need for an organized body to provide expert advice on military planning. The Royal Navy's use of written 'fighting instructions' such as Earl Howe's 31-section 'Explanation' to the 1799 Signal Book and Nelson's so-called 'Trafalgar Memorandum' of 9 October 1805, both of which had the force of orders, correspond in some respects to instructions prepared by an operations staff but were in fact drawn up by the fleet commander personally. In the Army there was nothing corresponding even with these guidelines. The Commander-in-Chief of the

---

[4] For developments in Prussia see William Görlitz *The German General Staff: Its History and Structure, 1657–1945* (1953) p. 20–22, for Austria see Gunther E. Rothenburg *Napoleon's Great Adversaries: The Archduke Charles and the Austrian Army, 1792–1814* (1982) p. 70.

In Britain the War and Colonial Department had been established in 1794 in order to manage the war with France. It was not specifically an *Army* department (the civil affairs of the army were handled by the War Office, under the Secretary at War, usually a minister below Cabinet rank). The anomaly that the Navy and the Ordnance (at this time a separate service) were represented in the Cabinet while the Army was not was effectively resolved by excluding both First Lord and Master-General from the key decision-making.

[5] For developments in Russia see A. von Drygalski *Beiträge zur Orientierung über die Entwicklungsgeschichte der russischen Armee: von ihren Anfangen bis auf die neueste Zeit* (Berlin 1892) p. 19–20 and Christopher Duffy *Russia's Military Way to the West: Origins and Nature of Russian Military Power, 1700–1800* (1981) p. 181–202, and cf Theodor von Bernhardi *Denkwürdigkeiten aus dem Leben des kaiserl. russ. Generals von der Infanterie Carl Friedrich von Toll* (4 vols Leipzig 1856–8) vol. 1 p. 17–25.

Army between 1795 and 1809 was the Duke of York, the King's second son: though he commanded the field army in Flanders in 1793–1795 and in North Holland in 1799 he had no say in operational matters when in London. In November 1805, when Prime Minister Pitt decided to send an expeditionary force to the River Weser, the Duke of York wrote to him an unsolicited letter advising against the operation on the grounds of the difficulty of the terrain in winter time, the unpreparedness of the troops and the lack of equipment: the operation went ahead nevertheless.[6]

When Grenville succeeded his cousin as Prime Minister in 1806 he attempted to run the war on a broader consultative basis. At the beginning of October 1806, after British forces acting without orders had occupied Buenos Aires, Lord Grenville and William Windham, the Secretary of State for War, began to develop a scheme to exploit this unexpected toehold in the Spanish dominions by sending an expeditionary force to the Pacific coast of South America. Troops were to be sent either direct from Britain or from India; in the latter case the force could 'first attack Manilla, and then proceed from there in the beaten track to Acapulco'. In working out this bizarre scheme for a coordinated movement on both the east and west coasts of the South American continent ('The objection obviously is, that these two attacks cannot correspond exactly in point of time') Lord Grenville made two innovations in planning procedure. First he wrote to his eldest brother, the Marquis of Buckingham, for advice. Buckingham was not a professional soldier and he had not held office since the 1780s, but he was patently jealous of his youngest brother having become Prime Minister and the latter, having deferred to the Marquis all his life, was more than anxious to placate him. Secondly, Lord Grenville consulted Major-General Sir Arthur Wellesley, newly returned from a brilliant military career in India but still regarded in Britain as a protégé of the Marquis of Buckingham. Lord Grenville and Wellesley may have discussed the South American venture as early as the time of Grenville's first communication on the subject with Buckingham; at any rate at some point Grenville asked Wellesley for a memo on the operation. It was evidently assumed right from the beginning that Wellesley's role was to be entirely consultative but, though he was at this stage a relatively junior general, there was no involvement with any more senior military figure, not even an official request for the loan of Wellesley's services; nevertheless this seems to have been the first recorded instance in which a general participated in the preliminary stages of strategic planning. This innovation must however be balanced against the fact that Buckingham, a total outsider, without military training or official status, was also being consulted; moreover the middle Grenville brother, Thomas, who

[6] [V.B.] Derrécagaix *Le Maréchal Berthier* (2 vols Paris 1904–5) vol. 2 p. 26–36 and [J.B.M.E.] Vachée *Napoleon at Work* (1914) p. 124–147; Julian S. Corbett ed. *Fighting Instructions, 1530–1816* (1905) p. 268–279, 316–320; Arthur Aspinall ed. *The Later Correspondence of George III* (5 vols Cambridge 1962–70) vol. 4 p. 367–9 no. 3159 Duke of York to Pitt, 27 Nov. 1805.

happened to be First Lord of the Admiralty, evidently felt that considering his own official standing in the matter he was not being consulted enough:

> For my own part, I am more than ever convinced that all these distant combinations are of necessity subject to so many chances, that I have little stomach to them; but in spite of my feeble opposition, our military projectors are running after one expedition, and one general with another and another, till (in military language) the batallions are all clubbed, and no man knows where to find an entire company.[7]

Soon afterwards the Grenville ministry was replaced by that of the Duke of Portland, under whom planning procedures reverted behind the veil. To this day it remains a mystery who actually thought up the attack on Copenhagen, perhaps the most elaborate and dramatic coup of the entire war; for some reason the idea is generally attributed to George Canning, the Foreign Secretary, but all his private correspondence has to say on the subject is that the King told him, 'It is a very immoral act. So immoral I won't ask who originated it. I have determined not to ask that question'. Since George III was not generally given to coyness this suggests that the King himself did not suspect Canning of being responsible. The basic concept of the Copenhagen expedition was not new, resembling in different respects the Helder expedition of 1799, the previous foray against Copenhagen in 1801 and, less auspiciously, Vice-Admiral Sir John Duckworth's forcing of the Narrows to threaten Constantinople in February 1807. The operational orders, brief, dry, to the point, and not dealing with too many steps ahead, went out over the signature of Viscount Castlereagh, the Secretary of State for War; the order for British land and naval forces to rendezvous in Danish waters were issued eleven days before the instruction was given to attack the Danish capital in the case of diplomatic measures failing, which makes it look as if the possibility of some sort of attack was envisaged well before the target was selected. No record survives of whom Castlereagh consulted, if anybody.[8]

The inadequacy of this mode of procedure was strongly felt by some soldiers. James Willoughby Gordon, the Duke of York's military secretary and a key man at the Horse Guards, carried on a regular correspondence with the leading oppositionist Earl Grey which made quite clear his poor opinion

[7] Buckingham *Court and Cabinets of George the Third* vol. 4 p. 80 Grenville to Buckingham 3 Oct. 1806 and cf ibid. vol. 3 p. 90–91 same to same 31 Oct. 1806 and *HMC Dropmore Mss* vol. 8 p. 370 Windham to Grenville 2 Oct. 1806. Wellesley's memo dated 20 Nov. 1806 is in *HMC Dropmore Mss* vol. 9 p. 485–493 and cf British Library Add. 58988 f. 3 Wellesley to Grenville 9 Oct. 1806; Buckingham ed. *Court and Cabinets of George III* vol. 4 p. 123 Thomas Grenville to Buckingham 17 Feb, 1807.

[8] Aspinall ed. *Later Correspondence of George III* vol. 4 p. 607 fn. 2 Canning to Joan Canning 26 Aug. 1807; A.N. Ryan 'Documents Relating to the Copenhagen Operation, 1807' in N.A.M. Rodger ed. *The Naval Miscellany* (1984) p. 297–329 at p. 306–7 and p. 308–311 and Public Record Office WO 6/14 Castlereagh to Cathcart 9 June, 19 July, 29 July 1807.

of the government's handling of the war, and Sir John Moore, one of the most respected generals in the Army, was of the same view, complaining:

> The military operations of Great Britain have been directed by Ministers ignorant of military affairs, and too arrogant and self-sufficient to consult military men.

But it does not seem there was much idea of how to develop an alternative system. For example William Armstrong's *Practical Observations on the Errors committed by the Generals and Field Officers Commanding Armies & Detachments*, published in 1808, sounds promising but reserves most of its extraordinarily banal criticisms for foreigners. Thomas Reide's *Staff Officer's Manual* of 1806 dealt merely with brigade majors and aides de camp. John Le Marchant, having worked to establish the military college at High Wycombe (forerunner of Sandhurst and Camberley) produced 'An Outline of the General Staff of the Army' in December 1802 which ran to 280 quarto pages and of which 200 copies were circulated in manuscript, but this barely dealt with the operations side of staff work and anyway its proposals were not implemented. Later the Adjutant-General with Wellington's army in the Peninsula, Lord Charles Stewart, told his brother, Viscount Castlereagh:

> I think both the situations of Adjt. Genl. and Qr. Mr. Genl. are not understood in our Army, nor is the business conducted through them in such a manner as to render the offices as interesting or as important as they are in most of the other Army's [sic] in Europe.

This seems clearly a complaint at the army staff's lack of involvement in the conduct of operations but the way in which Stewart refers to *both* the Adjutant-General and the Quarter-Master-General as being deprived of sufficiently interesting or important work hardly suggests that he had a clear idea of how the staff organization could be improved: responsibility for operational planning could hardly be shared between the two departments.[9]

Without a central general staff organization there was obviously no way of training and developing a staff for the different expeditionary forces, and the distance and slowness of communication between Whitehall and the various zones of operations made both forward planning and centralized control largely impossible, so that the whole issue of operational planning never quite came into focus. This encouraged local commanders to take too much on themselves: in this respect Army officers received a bad example from the Navy. The seizure of Buenos Aires in 1806 was decided on and planned by

[9] There are 590 letters from Willoughby Gordon to Grey 1806–1843 preserved in the Dept. of Palaeography and Diplomatic, 5 The College, Durham University, Durham: Grey's replies 1807–1812 are in the British Library, Add. 49477. J.F. Maurice ed. *The Diary of Sir John Moore* (2 vols 1904) vol. 2 p. 57–8, note on Général Regnier's account of the campaign in Egypt; Denis le Marchant *Memoirs of the late Major-Gen¹ Le Marchant* (printed for private circulation, 1841) p. 123–4 and R.H. Thoumine *Scientific Soldier: A Life of General Le Marchant 1766–1812* (1968) p. 102–105; J.W. Fortescue *A History of the British Army* (13 vols 1899–1930) vol. 7 p. 413 fn. quoting Lord Charles Stewart to Castlereagh 24 Aug. 1809.

Commodore Sir Home Popham, using forces that had been involved in the successful occupation of the Cape of Good Hope. At about the same period Rear Admiral Sir Sidney Smith, who had earlier shown brilliant initiative in holding Acre against Napoleon in 1799, was allowing his imagination to run away with him in his unauthorized consultations with the King and Queen of the Two Sicilies:

> Sometimes he is to be Viceroy of Calabria: at others to have the island of Lampedosa to hold as a fief from the King of Naples with the title of duke, and to go to Jerusalem and make instant war on Buonaparte in the King of Naples' name!!!

Yet the government had no real alternative to accepting the limitations on central control imposed by distance: as the Earl of Liverpool, Castlereagh's successor as Secretary of State for War, told the general commanding in Sicily,

> It is impossible to attempt to provide by Instructions, for all the different Contingencies which may arise in the Mediterranean, in a war so extensive as the present.[10]

III. Command of the Sea

The lack of long-range forward planning in the period 1793–1815 was perhaps most noticeable in the Royal Navy, because it was the most capital-intensive service. In 1918 a considerable amount of time and energy was employed in planning and preparing for the 1919 campaign, in which both tanks and gas were expected to have a decisive role, and in the Second World War the Manhattan Project – the development of the atomic bomb – employed 120,000 people over a period of years, and cost approximately 80 per cent of U.S. Federal expenditure on weapons research. There was nothing even remotely comparable in the wars against the French Revolution and Napoleon. And yet, on the naval side, these wars were fought with huge and vastly complex machines which, in relation to the everyday technology of the period, were quite as impressive as the tank or the heavy bomber.[11]

Indeed there is no greater conceptual or technical gap between air strikes by carrier-borne torpedo planes at over a hundred miles distance and naval artillery duels involving battleships fifteen miles apart than between the ironclads *Monitor* and *Merrimack*, slogging it out in Hampton Roads in 1862, and the close-range grappling of Nelson's flagship H.M.S. *Victory*

---

10 Maurice ed. *Diary of Sir John Moore* vol. 2 p. 132, 20 Sept. 1806; Public Record Office WO 6/38 f. 1 Liverpool to Lord William Bentinck 4 June 1811.

11 Cf Martin J. Sherwin *A World Destroyed: The Atomic Bomb and the Grand Alliance* (New York 1947) p. 39–40 for Manhattan Project statistics.

with the *Redoutable* at Trafalgar. The troglodytization of warship's crews, which was to reach its epitome in the stokers toiling below the waterline in the boiler rooms of a twentieth-century battleship, was already foreshadowed in the gun-crews buried within the wooden hull of the traditional sailing man of war. Nelson's *Victory*, built in 1765, was already a comparatively old vessel by the time of Trafalgar, and of course its basic concept was at least 250 years older. The *Victory* was not exactly a precision-made instrument. It needed 38 tons of ballast to correct an inbuilt but inexplicable list to starboard, and it drew nine inches more than envisaged at the design stage. The 64,104 yards of stitching on its seven tons of sails were done by hand, and the thousand-plus pulley blocks carried at Trafalgar were also carved by hand, the machine-made blocks produced by Brunel only becoming available later. Yet the idea of mass-production was already there: the twenty-odd masts and spars carried on each of Nelson's ships at Trafalgar were standardized according to the gun-rating (i.e. size) of each vessel, and many of his ships were built out of standardized timbers. At a displacement of up to 2,500 tons these line of battle ships were far larger than anything available for civilian use, and they each carried more guns than an army. The largest siege pieces used in the British army were 24-pounders. Most line of battleships carried 32-pounders, each 9 foot 6 inches long and weighing $55\frac{1}{2}$ cwt; some carried a lower-deck armament of 42-pounders. At the Battle of the First of June Howe's flagship, H.M.S. *Queen Charlotte*, in 130 broadsides fired off 25 tons of gunpowder – more than the expenditure of gunpowder by Wellington's artillery at Waterloo – and 60 tons of iron shot. The ship of the line was the period's most cherished symbol of technological achievement:

> Those who have ever witnessed the spectacle of the launching of a ship of the line, will perhaps forgive me for adding this to the examples of the sublime objects of artificial life. Of that spectacle I can never forget the impression and of having witnessed it reflected from the face of ten thousand spectators. They seem yet before me – I sympathize with their deep and silent expectation, and with their final burst of enthusiasm. It was not a vulgar joy, but an affecting national solemnity. When the vast bulwark sprung from her cradle, the calm water on which she swung majestically round, gave the imagination a contrast of the stormy element on which she was soon to ride – All the days of battle and the nights of danger which she had to encounter, all the ends of the earth which she had to visit, and all that she had to do and suffer for her country, rose in awful presentiment before the mind, and when the heart gave her a benediction, it was like one pronounced on a living being.[12]

---

[12] Arthur Bugler *H.M.S. Victory: Building, Restoration & Repair* (1966) p. 9 for the extra ballast (a total of 1148 tons was carried) p. 17 for the extra draught, p. 364 appendix XXXVIII for the sails; W.H. Long ed. *Naval Yarns: Letters and Anecdotes comprising Accounts of Sea Fights and Wrecks, Actions with Pirates and Privateers, &., from 1616 to 1831* (1899) p. 170 anonymous letter from a member of the *Queen Charlotte's* crew; Thomas Campbell *An Essay on English Poetry* (Boston 1819) p. 226–7: this is a reprint of his introduction to his *Specimens of the British Poets* (7 vols 1819).

For Britons of this period the line of battle ship also represented the supreme achievement of national prowess in warfare. The bare statistics tell the story of Britain's naval triumphs clearly enough:

Naval Losses and Captures, 1793–1815

	British warships captured	British warships lost and later recaptured	British warships lost in accidents	Enemy warships captured
98 guns or larger			4	9
80s			1	19
74s	1	3	17	87
64s			6	24
50s and 54s	1	1	5	9
Frigates	8	9	58	229

Apart from innumerable smaller skirmishes, the French were defeated at the Battle of the First of June in 1794, the Spanish at St. Vincent and the Dutch at Camperdown in 1797, the French again at the Nile in 1798 and the Danes at Copenhagen in 1801 and, in the culminating triumph of Nelson's career, the combined French and Spanish fleets were annihilated off Cape Trafalgar in October 1805. All these successes dated of course from before the beginning of Wellington's string of military victories in the Peninsula. Later the bulk of the Russian Mediterranean fleet was blockaded in the Tagus till it surrendered in September 1808. The final remnants of Venice's naval tradition were smashed at Lissa in 1811, and a succession of minor actions in 1813 and 1814 put an end to American pretensions as a naval power for at least a generation. These battles at sea were painted by Loutherbourg and Pocock and depicted in innumerable prints, but never as vividly as in the word pictures of 'Pel Verjuice's' autobiography:

> Bursting forth from the many black iron mouths, and whirling rapidly in thick rings, till it swells into hills and mountains, through which the sharp red tongues of death dart flash after flash, and mingling fire, the smoke slowly rolls upwards like a curtain, in awful beauty, and exhibits the glistening water and the hulls of the combatants beneath; while the lofty mastheads and points of yard-arms seem as if cut away from the bodies to which they belong, and sustained, or resting, on the ridges of the dense and massy vapours below. The ensigns are partially enveloped in the clouds; so much of them as is visible shivering in the multiplied concussions, as though they fluttered in the anticipation of victory, or trembled in the expectation of defeat. And ever and anon, amid the breaks of the cannons' peal, the shrieks and cries of the wounded, mingling with the deep roar of the out-poured and constantly reiterated 'hurra! hurra! hurra!' (a chorus of cataracts) sweep over the rippled smiles of the patient, passionless, and unconscious sea.

Yet except at Copenhagen, where Britain and Denmark were not even officially at war, all the major battles took place as a result of the British response to the strategic initiatives of the enemy, and the main British strategy, once the Royal Navy dominated the situation after Trafalgar, was to blockade the enemy ports so that they filled up with a succession of brand new vessels coming off the slipways with only inexperienced crews to handle them and officers who dared not risk even a trial cruise because of the blockading British squadrons which hovered relentlessly on the horizon.[13]

The memory of Nelson's victories tended afterwards to encourage the assumption that the point of sea-power was to fight big sea battles. But the real point of sea-power was to do this to an enemy port:

> The silence of death reigns there; one goes through the streets without meeting a living soul; there is as much grass here as in a field; the population which has been reduced by half for the most part remains indoors because there is nothing to do outside.

That is a description of La Rochelle in 1809: 'It's almost the same situation as one finds in once flourishing ports like Le Havre, Ostend, Dunkirk and elsewhere'. One might add Amsterdam, Hamburg and Copenhagen to the list. The key feature of Britain's part in the French wars was less the defeat of the enemy battle fleets than the driving of French and later Danish and finally American commerce from the oceans, while keeping them open for the expansion of British trade.[14]

Yet so little official attention was given to the question of the *guerre de course*, the war against trade, that it is now difficult to reconstruct how precisely it was conceived and conducted. Earl Howe's instructions on taking the Channel Fleet to sea at the beginning of July 1793 directed him to protect British and molest enemy trade, and a further missive from the Admiralty six weeks later drew his attention to the fact that British convoys were sailing from Jamaica and Lisbon and a French one from the United States, but the main battle fleets were not normally concerned with convoys. Admiralty records in the Public Record Office include a mere fifteen letter-books dealing

---

[13] Michael Lewis *A Social History of the Navy, 1793–1815* (1960) p. 345, 352, 348 Table X. R.Vesey Hamilton ed. *The Letters and Papers of Sir Thomas Byam Martin* (3 vols 1898–1902) vol. 3 p. 388 'Remarks on Naval Administration' gives 156 enemy ships of the line, 382 frigates, 662 corvettes, 2,506 armed ships and vessels 'captured and destroyed', but the discrepancy between these two sets of figures seems rather larger than the number of enemy ships actually sunk by the Royal Navy; John Fowler ed. *The Life and Literary Remains of Charles Reece Pemberton* (1843) p. 142 ('The Autobiography of Pel Verjuice', originally printed in *Monthly Repository* 1833–4, reprinted 1929, in which edition the passage quoted appears, minus a few necessary commas, on p. 199–200).

[14] Odette Viennet ed. *Un Enquête Économique dans la France Impériale (Philippe André Nemnich 1809)* (Paris 1947) p. 87 and cf 'Rapport over den Toestand van Koophandel, Fabrieken en Landbouw in het Departement Holland' in H.T. Colenbrander ed. *Gedenkstukken der Algemeene Geschiednis van Nederland van 1795 tot 1840* (22 vols Hague 1905–22) Part 5 (8th vol.) p. 606–637 esp. at p. 607–608.

with convoy work for the twenty odd years 1793–1814. The instructions recorded in these letter books are very general – at their most specific these instructions might order a captain 'to make enquiry for, and take under your Convoy, such ships as may be at the Nore' – and seem to be additional to work that was assumed to be in progress. As the warships involved are frequently not named there is no basis for any calculation of the proportion of the Royal Navy's effort devoted to trade protection – or to commerce raiding, which was often carried out by the same vessels on the same voyage. A memo by the Earl of Chatham, then First Lord of the Admiralty, in the second year of the wars refers to 'The Enemy having annihilated their own commerce, which they could not protect, that they might direct all their efforts to a predatory War against our Trade' and boasts:

> from the unremitting attention paid to their protection, all the numerous Convoys have sailed and arrived in security, excepting only the trifling one under the charge of the *Castor*, and which was retaken & burnt by Lord Howe.

The reference is to the Newfoundland convoy captured in May 1794 by five French battleships under Contre-Amiral Joseph-Marie Nielly and recaptured soon afterwards by a detachment of Earl Howe's battle fleet – and promptly destroyed, 'Howe not wishing to weaken his crews by sending the prizes into port'. This destruction of the recaptured convoy in itself hardly suggests that a high priority was given to preserving British merchant shipping. Chatham clearly felt that the Royal Navy was in fact doing too much, that the immediate requirement for convoys was now less than had been the case in the first months of hostilities, and that 'less frequent demands being necessary for Frigates for Convoys, and other Services, it may be found practicable to dismantle many of them in order to man the Line of Battle Ships'.[15]

Under Chatham's successor, Earl Spencer, it was proposed to form a small squadron of frigates and two-deckers (i.e. smaller line of battle ships) based at Cork, another of two-deckers at Spithead on the Isle of Wight and a third of large frigates at Falmouth 'to cruize constantly to the westward for the protection of the trade and annoying the enemy'. A fourth squadron of smaller vessels at Yarmouth Roads and Leith would take care of the Baltic and Archangel routes. This involved only a tiny proportion of Britain's total naval resources. Eighteen months later Dundas, the Secretary of State for War and the Colonies, forwarded to Spencer a number of complaints relating to French privateers operating in the Caribbean and a list, supplied by Jamaica planters, of 160 British merchant vessels taken in 1795 on the way to or from

---

[15] John Barrow *The Life of Richard Earl Howe, K.G.* (1838) p. 211, 213; Public Record Office Adm. 2/1103 f 136 Lords of Admiralty to Thomas Young of H.M.S. *Snake* 17 May 1809; the series of letter books referred to are Adm. 2/1097–1111; Public Record Office PRO 30/8/364 f. 2, 3–4, memo by Earl of Chatham 1794, cf William James *The Naval History of Great Britain* (6 vols 1826) vol. 1 p. 183–4. Howe's ships also recaptured and burnt half of a Lisbon convoy belonging to their Dutch allies.

Jamaica: 'I told them I could only send the papers to you and they need not doubt of your doing whatever you could for their relief'. This seems to be the only instance in the 1790s of the question of trade protection being discussed between cabinet ministers, and it does not seem that the matter was ever ventilated in the Cabinet itself.[16]

Nevertheless enemy interference with British maritime trade remained a serious problem throughout the wars. Between 1793 and 1800 2,861 British merchant ships were lost to enemy action – mostly to privateers – and the 2,218 captured enemy vessels taken over by the British shipping firms, though largely compensating for the overall loss, was of no direct benefit to the hundreds of shipowners who suffered from lost cargoes, lost crews, lost orders and the constant haemorrhage of inflated insurance premiums. Altogether between 1793 and 1814 1,031 French privateers with 9,400 guns and a total of 69,147 men as crew were captured by the Royal Navy: the peak years were 1797–1799 (134 privateers taken in 1797, 136 in 1798, 104 in 1799) but as late as 1810 67 French privateers were captured and by this time Danish (or rather Norwegian) raiders were becoming a problem, with American 'Baltimore clippers' joining in as well after 1812.[17]

The ability of French privateers to operate even in sight of British ports was largely due to the superior design of their ships, especially of their three-masted luggers; and the failure of the Royal Navy to adopt the up-to-date designs of engineers like Sir Samuel Bentham seems to suggest a lack of interest in the problem at an intermediate level as well as in the Cabinet. The poor quality of the British patrol vessels – wet, unweatherly and cramped – was pointed out in 1811 by a naval architect, Richard Hall Gower, who also urged the running down of the main battle fleet in order to provide crews for more smaller vessels; but of course the opinions of a mere pamphleteer were beneath official notice. Nevertheless it was the Royal Navy which undertook the main burden of the task both of shipping protection and commerce raiding. Although no less than 10,605 Letters of Marque were issued to privateers

[16] Julian S. Corbett ed. *Private Papers of George, Second Earl Spencer: First Lord of the Admiralty, 1794–1801* (3 vols 1913–23) vol. 1 p. 16–17 Sir Charles Middleton to Spencer late 1794; ibid. vol. 1 p. 247–255 Dundas to Spencer 22 April 1796, the quotation being from p. 248.

[17] C. Wright and C.E. Fayle *A History of Lloyds* (1928) p. 451; C.B. Norman *The Corsairs of France* (1887) p. 451 Appendix XIX. C.B. Norman gives much higher figures for captures of British vessels than Wright and Fayle: 5,158 in the years 1793–1800 and 10,871 for the whole period 1793–1814 (p. 453 Appendix XXII) but these figures presumably include small coasting vessels, ships' boats, inshore fishing vessels etc. that were not insured at Lloyds.

The most successful French privateer captain was Robert Surcouf, who took fourteen ships in the Bay of Bengal in a single three months cruise in 1807, including two English East Indiamen of 800 tons, a Portuguese vessel of 1,000 tons and a native-owned vessel of 1,150 tons. Nevertheless Surcouf and other privateers sailing out of Port Louis in Mauritius accounted for only a third in value of prizes taken by Mauritius-based raiders in the years 1803–10, the rest falling to vessels of the unusually active naval squadron operating in the area: Auguste Toussaint *Les Frères Surcouf* (Paris 1979) p. 251–9, 266, 274.

between 1793 and 1815 this was mainly for the sake of legitimizing chance pickings that might fall to heavily-armed 'runners' (i.e. ships not in convoy) which were equipped to resist French privateers and warships but were primarily engaged in carrying merchandise. Privateering had reached its peak in the American War of Independence, yet only a decade later, and for reasons that are by no means clear, there was considerably less interest in 'fitting out' private ships of war. In Bristol, for example, the newspapers had carried numerous advertisements for privateering crews in the American War, but none at all in the 1790s, and though the *Salamine* which looted Tórshavn in the Faroes in June 1808 and the *Margaret and Ann* which participated in the *coup d'état* at Reykjavik a year later were both privateers, nearly all the epic sea fights recorded between British armed merchantmen and French vessels were, on the British part, a matter simply of self-defence. Nevertheless, some of the British 'runners' were extraordinarily heavily armed – for example the *Planter* of Liverpool with twelve nine-pounders and six six-pounders outgunned most Royal Navy brigs – and especially after 1803 there were a number of serious complaints against British private ships of war, leading in the period 1803–1807 alone to the revocation of six Letters of Marque, the forcible impressment of two crews, and several prosecutions, three of them for piracy on the high seas.[18]

The Royal Navy meanwhile expanded its force of smaller vessels as rapidly as was consistent with the priority given to the battle fleet. In 1793 there had only been 42 sloops in commission; by December 1800 there were 103 sloops, 36 brigs, plus 20 hired sloops and brigs and 97 armed cutters engaged chiefly in protecting the coastal trade. By January 1814 there were 76 Royal Navy sloops and 172 Royal Navy brigs actually at sea. There had also been in 1800 93 line of battle ships, 12 fifty-gunners, and 141 frigates; in January 1814 there were 91 line of battle ships, 7 fifties and 124 frigates so that the overall proportion of sloops and brigs had increased and, it would seem, sloops had to some extent replaced frigates (which were considerably larger) as more suited for trade war.[19]

It is not clear however to what extent these smaller vessels were required simply as picket boats, fleet reconnaisance, despatch carriers etc. In the 1790s

[18] Richard Hall Gower *Remarks relative to the Danger Attendant on Convoys* (1811) p. 11–12, and for the running down of the main battle fleet p. 7–8, 17; *Parliamentary Papers* 1842 XXVII p. 379–381. For privateers generally see J.W. Damer Powell *Bristol Privateers and Ships of War* (Bristol 1930) p. 303–320 and Gomer Williams *History of the Liverpool Privateers and Letters of Marque with an Account of the Liverpool Slave Trade* (1897) p. 304–429: for 'runners' see Damer Powell p. 300 and Gomer Williams p. 304, for the *Planter* see Gomer Williams p. 374.

[19] See various issues of *Steel's Original and Correct List of the Royal Navy* and, with confusing differences of definitions of in commission and in repair, *Parliamentary Papers* 1803–4 VII p. 226–7. Roger Morriss *The Royal Dockyards during the Revolutionary and Napoleonic Wars* (Leicester 1981) p. 12 Table 1 gives even higher figures for vessels, including those laid up.

Nelson had complained bitterly of the shortage of smaller vessels to support his battle fleet:

> Was I to die this moment, 'Want of Frigates' would be found stamped on my heart. No words of mine can express what I have, and am suffering for want of them.

Two weeks before his death Nelson sent the Admiralty a list of 22 frigates and 16 sloops 'actually wanted for the Mediterranean Station', and of these only five frigates and nine sloops were required for convoy work (viz. two frigates and two sloops to convoy to Gibralter, two frigates and three sloops to protect shipping in the Straits and one frigate and four sloops to protect traffic en route for Malta). The other 17 frigates and seven sloops were required for duties related to the operations of the battle fleet. Some years later, in January 1814, the Mediterranean Fleet had the highest proportion of larger vessels of any fleet command of the time: 37 line of battle ships and fifties to 55 frigates, sloops and brigs. If the Mediterranean Fleet of 1814 is taken as possessing the bare minimum of smaller vessels needed to support a battle fleet, we find that a little more than half the smaller vessels in commission in 1800 were required for fleet duties, and just under half in 1814. But even if they were not required for fleet duties it is not clear that they were assigned to convoy work and commerce raiding. Steel's Navy List for July 1800 specifies only three out of 141 frigates and 10 out of 103 sloops as engaged in convoy service (plus two sixty-fours and a fifty escorting convoys of East Indiamen); four frigates and twenty sloops are specified as cruising, though this may have been partly in connection with fleet movements. Presumably many of the vessels not specified in the Navy List as doing anything were also engaged is snooping for blockade runners and privateers, but the general nature of their employment remains unclear.[20]

A curious side-show in this trade war, and one which illustrates its haphazard organization, relates to the fate of the world's least desirable colonies, the Danish settlements in northern waters. On 15 May 1808 the sloop H.M.S. *Clio* put ashore a landing party at Tórshavn, Faroe, spiked the eight 18-pounder guns in the fort and blew up the store of gunpowder. Within a few weeks privateers descended on the now defenceless town and seized the property of the Danish Crown Monopoly, though the British Admiralty Court subsequently refused to condemn it as a lawful prize. The following year privateers also descended on Reykjavik. They brought with them a Danish adventurer Jørgen Jørgensen but their attempt to replace the Danish governor by a pro-British puppet regime was quickly disowned by the Foreign Office. A few weeks later two Royal Navy brigs under orders

[20] Nicholas Harris Nicolas ed. *The Dispatches and Letters of Vice Admiral Lord Viscount Nelson* (7 vols 1844–6) vol. 3 p. 98 Nelson to Spencer 9 Aug, 1798; ibid. vol. 7 p. 85–6 Nelson to Admiralty, paper enclosed in letter 7 Oct. 1805; *Steel's Original and Correct List of the Royal Navy: Corrected to July 1800* and ibid. *Corrected to January 1814.*

to convoy vessels as far as North Cape (on the passage to Archangel) and then cruise westward of North Cape 'for the Protection of homeward bound Trade', made a couple of landings in northern Norway. At Hasvik a landing party got drunk and sacked the village church, for which offence five men were subsequently flogged, and at Hammerfest, the northernmost town in the world, shore batteries were bombarded for 140 minutes until the Norwegians ran out of ammunition, after which the town was looted. An English seaman, killed in the artillery engagement, was buried in the town churchyard and one Alex. Johnston, a quartermaster, subsequently received '4 dozen with a thieves Cat for having taken part of the church furniture away and also disguising it till looked for and found in his possession'. As far as is recorded, the French coast never had to submit to this kind of terrorization. The Dano-Norwegian government was later able to land twelve guns at Hammerfest to strengthen the defences there, indicating that they were still in active control of the Norwegian coastal passage, but in February 1810, following the representations of Sir Joseph Banks of the Royal Society, the Faroes, Iceland and the Greenland settlements were exempted from British attack and blockade, an indication of how total British command of the sea had become in northern waters.[21]

IV. The British Army: A Profession of Amateurs

The problems of strategic control were compounded by what can only be described as the amateurishness of Britain's senior professional officers. The only training available in the Royal Navy was practical experience on board ship: Nelson went to sea at the age of twelve and was commanding a frigate at the age of twenty, and remained till his death in some respects as naive and one-dimensional as a character in *Roderick Random* or *Peregrine Pickle*.

[21] John F. West *Faroe: The Emergence of a Nation* (1972) p. 61–5; W.J. Hooker *Journal of a Tour in Iceland in the Summer of 1809* (printed for private circulation, Yarmouth 1811) p. 310 and H.P. Briem *Sjálfstaeði Íslands, 1809* (Reykjavik 1936) passim: see also Egerton Mss in British Library; Eg.2066 consists of Jørgen Jørgensen's autobiographical 'The Adventures of Thomas Walker', Eg.2067 comprises his 'Historical Account of a Revolution in the Island of Iceland in the Year 1809' plus a memo by the Danish governor Count Trampe, Eg.2068 includes another version of Jørgensen's account and various papers, and there are various Jørgensen letters in Eg.2070; Public Record Office Adm. 53/1213 ship's log of *H.M.S. Snake* 5, 7, 22 July 1809 and Adm. 53/2137 captain's log of H.M.S. *Fancy* 22 July 1809 cf A. Hagemann *Engelskmanden under Finmarken* (Kristiana 1891) p. 63, 66, 66fn. and Jørgen Sivertsen *Hammerfest, 1789–1914* (Hammerfest 1973) p. 32–6. In July 1808 there was an attempt at something similar at Christiansund: two English frigates attempted to enter the harbour to seize shipping. There was evidently no intention of making a landing and in any case they were beaten off by the shore batteries: C.F. Wandel *Søkrigen i de Dansk-Norske Farvande, 1807–14* (Copenhagen 1915) p. 159–163; the Order in Council of 7 Feb. 1810 is in *London Gazette* no. 16340, p. 189 of 1810 volume and see also West *Faroe* p. 68 and for Greenland Louis Bobé *Den grønlandske Handels og Kolonisations Historie indtil 1870 (Meddelser om Grønland* vol. 55) (Copenhagen 1936) p. 83–8.

Orientated since the seventeenth century towards challenging the enemy's main fleets, either by blockading them or by fighting major fleet actions, the Royal Navy was satisfied by the defeats inflicted on the French, Spanish, Dutch and Danish and, once the decisive warfare shifted from the oceans to dry land, was satisfied with playing an auxiliary role, without any attempt to face up to the problem of the war as a whole. The Army, with no such stupendous victories to its credit till comparatively late in the wars, was even less interested in the problem of overall strategy, and even after long years of war retained an extraordinary peacetime ethic, as a department of the British aristocracy. At least in the Navy the prospect of prize money and the much smaller number of admirals encouraged senior naval officers to go to sea. In the Army the tendency was for senior officers to avoid active service as far as possible: General Tilney in Jane Austen's *Northanger Abbey*, attracting notice by his elegant deportment in the pump-room at Bath and 'poring over the affairs of the nation' in the library of his country house, is probably a portrait drawn from life. Visiting the army in Flanders in 1794, William Windham, the Secretary at War, reported:

> When the line was drawn out the other day, in circumstances as critical as an army ever stood in; where nothing but uncommon exertions could have ensured its success, and where the ruin of the world must have been the consequence of defeat, there was but one Major-General from one end of the line to the other, and most of the Brigades were commanded by men, too young both in age and service to be entrusted with the care of a company.

The result was that only a handful of senior army officers in the 1790s had experience of commanding in the field – Abercromby, Cornwallis, Grey, Sir Charles Stuart – and these had literally died out by the 1800s. Some of the next generation had taken pains to train themselves in the intellectual side of their profession. The Hon. John Hely-Hutchinson, who succeeded to the command in Egypt on the death of Abercromby, had spent eleven years on the continent with various foreign armies, including that of the French Republic. Robert Craufurd, though having less experience of foreign H.Q.s and staff work than his older brother Charles (whose active career was cut short by wounds), shared his brother's scientific interests and assembled an important collection of English, French, German – and some Italian and Latin – texts on the science of war. But as the military struggle began to concentrate itself, the larger size of the commands required a substantial supply of senior officers and many of those available had no real idea of how to carry out their duties. The conduct of Sir John Stuart during the Battle of Maida on 3 July 1806 – Britain's first victory over French troops on the European mainland – is described thus by his Quarter-Master-General:

> In truth he seemed to be rather a spectator than a person much, or *the* person *most*, interested in the result of the conflict. He formed no plan, declared no intention, and scarcely did he trouble himself to give an order. Perfectly regardless of personal danger, he was cantering about, indulging himself in little

pleasantries, as was his wont; and he launched forth with particular glee when a Sicilian Marquis, whom he had brought with him as an extra aide-de-camp, betook himself to shelter from fire behind a haystack. But after the charge of Kempt's light infantry, and the utter rout of the French left wing, a change came over the spirit of Sir John Stuart. Still he dawdled about, breaking into passionate exclamations, 'Begad, I never saw anything so glorious as this! There was nothing in Egypt to equal this! It's the finest thing I ever witnessed'. From that moment he was an altered man and full of visions of future greatness.

After Sir Arthur Wellesley, already Britain's most experienced field commander but still near the bottom of the list of lieutenant-generals, had been permitted to win the Battle of Vimeiro on 21 August 1808, he was superseded by Sir Harry Burrard, with Sir Hew Dalrymple arriving shortly afterwards to take over from Burrard. Wellesley complained:

> The Chiefs ask my opinion about everything, & never act according to it; & Sir Burrard by his Interference after the Battle of the 21st. prevented me from marching in pursuit of the enemy, by which he saved them from total destruction ... The General has no plan, or even an idea of a plan, nor do I believe he knows the meaning of the Word *Plan*.

During the final stages of the Battle of Vimeiro, when Wellesley had been urging the pursuit of the broken French, Burrard's contribution had been to remark:

> This is a glorious victory; we must have a plan of the ground, and the movement of the troops, to be sent off with the despatches ... I assure you the sea air has very much sharpened my appetite ... Well, I think we have done enough for one day.

Burrard himself confessed:

> I own that a great command would be the source of very anxious moments to me. Take my word for it Sir J⁰ Moore is the man who should act ... I am getting old and certainly not so active in mind or body as I have been or should be.

(He was in fact 53.) When Dalrymple took over the command Sir John Moore noted him down as an officer 'who had allowed a war of sixteen years to pass without pushing for any service except in England and Guernsey'. He turned out, in Moore's opinion, to be 'confused and incapable beyond any man I ever saw head an army'. This was also pretty much Wellesley's opinion.[22]

---

22 [Lewis Melville ed.] *The Windham Papers* (2 vols 1913) vol. 1 p. 244 Windham to Pitt 19 Sept. 1794; a copy of Leigh and Sotheby's catalogue *A Catalogue of part of the Library of the late Gen. Robert Craufurd ... To which is added the small Library of a Military Officer* is in the British Library, shelf-mark 130 k.5 (4); Henry Bunbury *Narratives of Some Passages of the Great War with France, from 1799 to 1810* (1854) p. 248–9; Charles Webster ed. *Some Letters of the Duke of Wellington to his Brother William Wellesley-Pole* (Camden Miscellany XVIII, Camden Society 3rd series LXXIX) (1948) p. 7, letters 24 and 26 Aug. 1808; [George] Landmann *Recollections of my Military Life* (2 vols 1854) vol. 2 p. 242, 244–5; British Library
continued

A year later an attack on Antwerp by the largest expeditionary force ever sent from Britain was foiled, less by the Dutch and French than by the lethargy of the Earl of Chatham, whose only recent war experience was as an adviser on the Helder expedition in 1799; but it appeared that his nomination to the command of the Walcheren expedition had been absolutely necessary because:

> it would have been impossible considering the number of troops we now have on foreign service to have found officers of sufficient standing for so large a force as was sent out, unless you took your commander in chief high up upon the list. Had Hope for instance been appointed Ld Huntley & Paget, and Ld Rosslyn could not have served, being all senior to him, and deficient as our list of generals is it would have been a great loss to have cut out such good officers. Then taking a man of Ld Chatham's standing the choice was nearly reduced to a question between him & Ld Moira . . .

And Moira, who had done rather well in the American War of Independence, was one of the leaders of the opposition, whereas at least Chatham was in the Cabinet.[23]

The inadequacies of Britain's senior officers – and there were no fewer than 261 generals and lieutenant-generals in the Army List by 1812 – seems to have been less a question of lack of opportunities to gain experience than of lack of interest in the practical and technical side of the profession. Walter Scott, an early admirer of Sir Arthur Wellesley, considered him to be the first British general of the period to grasp the secret of handling an army as a unit instead of concentrating on drill: 'We have been hitherto polishing hinges when we should have studied the mechanical union of a huge machine.' Wellesley himself insisted in later years:

> One must understand the mechanism and power of the individual soldier; then that of a company, a battalion, or brigade, and so on, before one can venture to group divisions and move an army. I believe I owe most of my success to the attention I always paid to the inferior part of tactics as a regimental officer.

This sounds eminently sensible of course: but one notes that two of Wellesley's most successful subordinate generals in the Peninsula were Sir Thomas Graham, who joined the Army – with the rank of temporary lieutenant-colonel – only at the age of 45 and received his first permanent commission, as a

continued
Add. 49485 f.3–4, Burrard to Willoughby Gordon 3 Sept. 1808; Maurice ed. *Diary of Sir John Moore* vol. 2 p. 259, 31 Aug, 1808; ibid. vol. 2 p. 270, 2 Oct. 1808; Webster ed. *Some Letters of the Duke of Wellington to his Brother William Wellesley-Pole* (Camden Miscellany XVIII) p. 9–10, letter 16 Sept. 1808.

23 Kenneth Bourne ed. *The Letters of the Third Viscount Palmerston to Laurence and Elizabeth Sulivan. 1804–1863* (Camden Society 4th series XXIII) (1979) p. 111 letter 15 Sept. 1809. In fact the obvious man to appoint would have been Viscount Cathcart, who had commanded the Copenhagen expedition in 1807 and was commander in chief in Scotland: he was a lieutenant-general senior to the Earl of Chatham.

major-general, at 61, and Sir Thomas Picton who, though on officer since the age of 15, seems never to have been in a general action till the Battle of Busaco in 1810, when he was 52.[24]

V. Military-Naval Cooperation

In some respects Britain's strategic position actually required a higher level of professional competence than was necessary in other European armies. Britain was an island, had command of the sea, and had a commitment to defend a distant colonial empire. This meant that the necessarily complex problem of military-naval cooperation was likely to have a greater role in Britain's war-making than in that of any other power.

The peculiar organizational difficulties of what would long afterwards be designated Combined Operations had been amply discussed in perhaps the most valuable work of military theory to be published by a Briton in the eighteenth century: Thomas More Molyneux's *Conjunct Expeditions that have been carried on jointly by the Fleet and Army, with a Commentary on a Littoral War* published in two volumes in London in 1759. Molyneux showed that since 1603 27 major and eleven minor conjoint operations had 'miscarried' and seven major and 23 minor had succeeded. He argued that the proportion of failure and success between major and minor operations was explained by the fact that the smaller operations were entirely in the hands of the Navy, under a single commander, whereas the larger, involving substantial bodies of troops under military commanders, were characterized by lack of understanding of the problems of this type of operation and disputes between the senior officers of the two services. Nor did Molyneux confine himself to polemical generalities. One of the questions he discussed was of particular importance for the campaigns of the 1790s: the confusion that too often prevailed when troops were landed from boats. He pointed out that 'At the very moment, the Army is required to be in Regiments most, it is least', and discussed the need to load and unload the boats in an arranged order, according to the tactical formations that would be required to fight on the beach. He even devoted several pages to the design and lay-out of specialized flat-bottomed landing craft.[25]

Forty years later Molyneux's advice still had not been attended to. There

[24] H.J.C. Grierson ed. *The Letters of Sir Walter Scott* (12 vols 1932–7) vol. 2 p. 480 Scott to J.B.S. Morrill 26 April 1811; Louis J. Jennings ed. *The Croker Papers: The Correspondence and Diaries of the Late Right Honourable John Wilson Croker* (3 vols 1884) vol. 1 p. 337, conversation *circa* 1820.

[25] Thomas More Molyneux *Conjunct Expeditions: or Expeditions that have been carried on jointly by the Fleet and Army, with a Commentary on a Littoral War* (2 vols 1759) vol. 2 p. 5–8, 39, 49, 55, 57–65. Molyneux was a lieutenant in the Foot Guards: he became M.P. for Haslemere in 1759 and died in 1776.

were some spectacular rows between Navy and Army commanders. In March 1794 Major-General David Dundas threw up his command in Corsica after Vice-Admiral Lord Hood, enraged by his reluctance to take Bastia by storm, attempted to claim an overriding authority as supreme commander; Sir Gilbert Elliot, the civil commissioner in the Mediterranean, thought 'The true cause of the final rupture is that Lord Hood is extremely sanguine and enterprising, and General Dundas has the opposite qualities of caution and backwardness', but Dundas's opinion was that 'Lord Hood was a man who never reasoned himself, nor would he listen to reason'. Non-communication also operated at a lower level. In sea-borne invasions, troops were, for the most part, put ashore any old how. Most of the landings made by British forces 1793–1814 were against very light or non-existent opposition, but the Helder landings of 27 August 1799 would have gone seriously adrift if the Batavian (i.e. Dutch) forces on hand had been willing to approach through the covering fire of the British warships, for the landing boats were so badly managed that battalions and even companies became intermixed – a serious matter for troops accustomed to fight in rigid formation shoulder to shoulder with familiar comrades – and in addition many soldiers were drowned. At Cadiz in the following year the landing was postponed at the last moment, but preparations were sufficiently advanced for it to be obvious that the naval commander had no grip on the situation:

> I found him all confusion, blaming everybody and everything, but attempting to remedy nothing . . . He said that he could not help the want of boats, and that his orders had not been obeyed.

After that the problem was taken in hand, and landing arrangements for the invasion of Egypt were carefully planned by the Hon. Alexander Cochrane of the Royal Navy and John Moore of the Army, and were even rehearsed in advance. The landing at Aboukir on 8 March 1801 was made against fiercer opposition than ever previously encountered in a beach landing but the British were able to form up and drive off the French within twenty minutes, the precision of their deployment astonishing the French, who described it as '*un mouvement d'opéra*', a ballet sequence.[26]

Moore thought conjoint operations required specialized troopships as well as specialized landing craft and training programmes. He thought that the

[26] J.H. Godfrey ed. 'Corsica, 1794 . . . from the Nelson-Hood Letters' Christopher Lloyd ed. *The Naval Miscellany* (Naval Records Society) vol. 4 (1952) p. 359–421, at p. 370–372, Hood to Dundas 6 and 7 March and Dundas to Hood 8 March: Countess of Minto *Life and Letters of Gilbert Elliot, First Earl of Minto from 1851 to 1806* (3 vols 1874) vol. 2 p. 233, Minto to Lady Minto 14 March 1794; Maurice ed. *Diary of Sir John Moore* vol. 1 p. 68, 13 March 1794; Fortescue *History of the British Army* vol. 4 p. 654–5 and cf Piers Mackesy *Statesman at War: The Strategy of Overthrow, 1798–1799* (1974) p. 194–200; Maurice ed. *Diary of Sir John Moore* vol. 1 p. 378, 7 Oct. 1800; [A.D.E.] Las Cases *Mémorial de Sainte-Hélène ou journal de la vie privée et des conversations de l'empereur Napoléon* (4 vols 1823) vol. 1 part 1 p. 242, conversations 26–30 Sept. 1815.

vessels hired by government were far too small and inadequately crewed and that the government should provide its own troopships:

> Twenty or twenty-five might carry this whole expedition, sail well, be amenable to signal, fit to carry each a couple of flat boats, and to man them when required. Unless some plan of this kind is adopted we shall not be able to avail ourselves of our naval superiority.

The unhandiness of the hired vessels employed by the government was demonstrated during the Copenhagen expedition in 1807; no less than 377 transports had to be marshalled and convoyed across the North Sea. The Royal Navy had great difficulty in keeping track of this vast armada; the Danes sank one hired transport, four were captured by French privateers, seven foundered in bad weather with the loss of more than four hundred lives, one beached itself on the Danish coast, one was rammed and sunk outside Dover Harbour and one disappeared unaccountably, leaving nine survivors but no official explanation of what had happened to their ship. With the inadequate accommodation on board hired troopships it was not surprising that senior Army officers preferred to travel on warships: in August 1807, in the Copenhagen expedition, Sir Arthur Wellesley, the later Duke of Wellington, embarked on a 16-gun fireship; in July 1808, en route for Portugal, he sailed on a 22-gun sloop, and returning to the Peninsula in the following spring, he had a 28-gun frigate. The progressive importance of the warships indicates the progressive value attached to Wellesley as a commander, but the fact that he sailed on warships may have encouraged him to overlook the problems experienced by his soldiers.[27]

By 1809 the technical problems of littoral warfare had still not been properly mastered, but the British had blundered into their epic involvement in Spain, where it was necessary to confront the problems not of coastal but of continental warfare.

VI. The Continental Commitment

Arguably Britain could and should have embarked on continental warfare much earlier. In 1810 Captain C.W. Pasley of the Royal Engineers published Part One of his *Essay on the Military Policy and Institutions of the British Empire*, a work on which he had already been engaged when sent abroad with the Walcheren expedition, in which he was wounded. There was sufficient demand for two new editions of the book in 1811 and it was reviewed at length in *The Times* (this two-part article being reprinted verbatim in *The Gentleman's Magazine*), *The Monthly Review* and *The Quarterly Review* (by

---

[27] Maurice ed. *Diary of Sir John Moore* vol. 2 p. 205 Moore to Castlereagh 8 May 1808; *Parliamentary Papers* 1808 IX p. 53–4.

Robert Southey): according to *The Times* Pasley's views had 'excited greater attention among the higher classes of Political Readers in the country than any since the time of Mr. BURKE'. Pasley ridiculed the British policy of breaking up the army into small expeditions:

> According to our unhappy mode of systematically dividing our force, as if we thought it would be taking an unfair advantage of an adversary to send more men against him than he has got ready, or can speedily assemble to oppose us with, in any part of the world; our military enterprises may be almost entirely disregarded, so that they cannot even be considered as diversions. Knowing that they hazard little or nothing by such feeble attacks as we have generally made, the French can fearlessly employ the great body of their armies in overwhelming our continental allies; which being once done by a system radically contrary to ours, the reimbarkation of the troops employed in our expeditions, after an almost useless waste of money and lives, follows as a matter of course.

For perhaps the first time since the Hundred Years' War it was seen to be possible for Britain, *alone and unassisted*, to sustain a major campaign against a great European power, for as Pasley sneeringly pointed out:

> surely we cannot boast much of the excellence of our military institutions and policy, if with such vast resources, and having nothing to fear at home, we cannot take the field, even with more than a hundred thousand soldiers, in any point abroad, when the safety of Europe, and eventually our own, may depend upon the effort.

Indeed he argued that Britain was 'strong enough to furnish a force of 120,000 men, for incessant actual service'.[28]

Pasley found an illustrious convert. He argued:

> as the talents that lead to the greatest eminence in Great Britain are of a nature principally parliamentary, that is to say, not such as to qualify the possessors for the management of a war ... our rulers at all times may generally be supposed, from the very nature of things, somewhat deficient in the skill and energy requisite for planning and conducting warlike operations upon sound principles.

---

[28] C.W. Pasley *Essay on the Military Policy and Institutions of the British Empire* (1810) p. 194, 199, 501: the 'force of 120,000 men, for incessant actual service' reference is from p. 32–3.

No subsequent parts of Pasley's essay were ever published, though a second volume was promised. Pasley's letters in the British Library (Add. 41962) indicate that any subsequent part, if it had been published, would probably have been very critical of British policy. For reviews see *Times* 11 Feb. 1811 p. 2a–d, 12 Feb, 1811 p. 3c–e, *Gentleman's Magazine* vol. 81 p. 150–154 and p. 244–7 (Feb. and March 1811) *Quarterly Review* vol. 5 (1811) p. 403–437 and *Monthly Review* vol. 65 (1811) p. 402–415; cf *Times* 11 Feb. 1811 p. 2a. Wordsworth wrote a lengthy letter to Pasley on the *Essay* cf Ernest de Selincourt, Mary Moorman, Chester L. Shaver and Alan G. Hill ed. *The Letters of William and Dorothy Wordsworth* (7 vols Oxford 1967–88) vol. 2 p. 473–482, Wordsworth to Pasley 28 March 1811 and see also p. 482–5, Wordsworth's cover letter to Richard Sharp.

This was exactly the opinion of the then Foreign Secretary, the Marquess Wellesley, whose knowledge and approval of Pasley's opinions are demonstrated by a long quotation from Pasley's book in the memo he was to write following his resignation in March 1812. In the 1790s Wellesley had organized a highly successful war in India in parallel with the mismanaged conflict in Europe and was all too aware that none of his colleagues 'had acquired much fame . . . as war ministers'. Before taking the seals of the Foreign Department, Wellesley had been on a diplomatic mission to Spain and two of his brothers were currently in the Peninsula, one as commander-in-chief of the British army, the other as ambassador to the Spanish junta. It was not surprising therefore that he began to translate Pasley's arguments into Peninsular terms. At first he merely thought that Britain should aim at:

> creating so powerful a diversion in the Peninsula as might enable the powers on the Continent to oppose the views of France, according to their respective means, so that France might be reduced to the alternative, either of relinquishing her designs in the Peninsula or elsewhere, or of making an imperfect effort in two quarters.

Later however he saw Britain's opportunity in larger and more urgent terms:

> If England could not strike at the monster's heart it was necessary for her to attempt to maim & cripple it, before it was prepared to discharge its collected strength upon her Coasts. If she could not touch a vital part, a limb might be lopped off.

Like Pasley, he condemned the strategy of raids and short-term expeditions which seemed still to be favoured by the Cabinet:

> Lord Wellesley was far from underating the combined exertions of the naval and military forces of this country or the Advantages which England possesses over all other nations in the command of such a force, but Lord Wellesley was of opinion that this great branch of our power had been misapplied when employed upon objects of a temporary nature & upon summer excursions.
>
> Such Expeditions might indeed be highly judicious and proper under certain circumstances. The Plunder of a Fishing Town, the Destruction of a Basin, and the Burning a few Ships upon the Stocks might be sufficient acts of aggression in a quarrel about a Sugar Island, and upon a balance of profit and loss between dried fish burnt Ships and Sugar might compel a hostile nation to think of Peace. In Lord Wellesley's Judgement however such operations were wholly inapplicable to the character of the present war.

What he wanted was the concentration of Britain's entire military resources in Spain. Having however resigned by the time he wrote the memo just quoted his attempt to refocus British strategy was something of a *post facto* self-justification. Amongst those who failed to be impressed was his younger brother Arthur, now Lord Wellington, the commander-in-chief in Spain. The latter informed his staff, 'Lord Wellesley knew nothing about the matter, and he had no reason to be dissatisfied with government at home'. Wellington believed he simply could not have used more troops because of logistic problems: 'all this difficulty in the detail was quite unknown at home'.[29]

VII. The Duke of Wellington

The initial stages of Britain's involvement in the Peninsula – the victory at Vimeiro, the disgraceful Convention of Cintra which permitted the French to withdraw with their booty, Sir John Moore's advance on Sahagun and his subsequent chaotic and catastrophic retreat to Coruña, the battle outside that town and the hasty evacuation of the victorious but outnumbered British army – seemed to be completely in the hit-and-miss tradition of Britain's previous adventures on the continent, complete with victories that were not exploited, allies that were not forthcoming and evacuations that looked like desperate escapes. But from 1809 onwards the British were able to maintain a growing army in Portugal and Spain and finally to march it into the South of France. This was very much the achievement – managerial and diplomatic, as well as military – of one man: Sir Arthur Wellesley, later Viscount, Earl, Marquess and finally Duke of Wellington.

For Britain it was an age of giants: Rothschild, Telford, Byron, Malthus, Wordsworth, Pitt, Canning, Turner, Flaxman, Blake. But the two figures who stand out most vividly in popular memory from this period are Wellington and Nelson.

As folk heroes they were completely unalike. One can see how, in the mid-twentieth century, Montgomery had an essential appeal to the common man's love of the commonplace, Mountbatten for the common man's love of royalty and film-star style. Nelson is rather unexpected, except for his physical courage and his staunch conservativism: he is difficult to fit into any theory of the folk hero's relation to popular expectation, though he was quite well qualified to have a place in the pantheon of great English eccentrics. Slender, sickly, dreadfully mutilated, scruffy yet over-bemedalled, 'he looked like a goose in his gait and manner'. Southey's biography captures Nelson's ardour but gives it a wholesome, healthy, public school quality which is all Southey's

[29] British Library Add. 37296 f. 273–4 for Wellesley quoting Pasley in 1812; Duke of Wellington ed. *Supplementary Despatches, Correspondence and Memoranda of Field Marshall Arthur Duke of Wellington* (12 vols 1858–65) vol. 7 p. 258–9, memo by Wellesley's confidant, Col. Meyrick Shawe; [Lewis Melville ed.] *The Wellesley Papers: The Life and Correspondence of Richard Colley Wellesley Marquess Wellesley, 1760–1842* (2 vols 1914) vol. 2 p. 45 'Notes on the General State of Europe' 15 May 1811; British Library. 37296 f. 267–8 memo by Wellesley 20 March 1812; ibid. f. 268–9; George Larpent ed. *The Private Journals of F.S. Larpent, Esq.* (3 vols 1853) vol. 1 p. 157, 1 May 1813.

The general question of the relationship between the causes of a war and the resources mobilized to fight it, which was touched upon in the arguments both of Pasley and of Wellesley, had been ventilated by Swift in his pamphlet on 'The Conduct of the Allies', as far back as 1711.

own, and almost the complete opposite of the real Nelson. His preoccupation with death or glory, or perhaps preferably both together – 'Westminster Abbey or Victory!', he would cry out as he lop-sidedly strode his quarterdeck during the heat of battle – seemed somehow more the product of a German romantic novelist's imagination than of a Norfolk parsonage. When one of his captains presented him with a coffin made from the main-mast of the French flagship *L'Orient*, which blew up at the Nile, he insisted on having it propped against the bulkhead behind his chair when he sat down to dinner. He was ostentatiously proud of his foreign titles and decorations, signing himself with his Sicilian ducal title added to his British barony – *Nelson and Brontë* – and making sure that *all* his coats had sewn on them the insignia not only of the Order of the Bath, but also of the Order of the Crescent, of the Neapolitan Order of St. Ferdinand of Merit, and even of the obscure North German Order of St. Joachim. Of course his three great victories, unprecedentedly complete and the last of them against considerable odds, were the basis of his myth: 'those two men (Buonaparte and he) divided the world between them – the land and the water', wrote the poet Thomas Moore after Trafalgar. Even Dorothy Wordsworth, the poet's sister, burst into tears when the news came of Nelson's triumphant death at Trafalgar ('William would not believe all at once, and forced me to suspend my grief till he had made further inquiries') and his myth was enduring: in the largest naval action in European waters after the Trafalgar campaign, the signal flown by the British commander to rally his squadron was 'Remember Nelson', and as it was hoisted to his signalling yards Captain Hoste could hear the cheering of the other ships' companies. Yet it is difficult to believe that if he had survived Trafalgar Nelson's reputation would have been enhanced by subsequent years of patient organization and diplomacy in the Mediterranean, or by cabinet office in Whitehall.[30]

Nelson's single encounter with Wellington – then Sir Arthur Wellesley – gives a fair impression of Nelson's strenths and weaknesses, and the account Wellington afterwards gave also suggests something of the latter's personality, his self-assurance, his caution about giving himself away, a certain stylishness in his way of assessing a situation. They met shortly after Wellesley's return from India:

> I went to the Colonial Office in Downing Street, and there I was shown into the little waiting-room on the right hand, where I found, also waiting to see

[30] Lord Broughton [J.C. Hobhouse] *Recollections of a Long Life* ed. Lady Dorchester (6 vols 1909–11) vol. 6 p. 233, 1 April 1849, conversation of 2nd Earl of Minto: 'goose' in this instance means a fool rather than a fowl; Nicolas ed. *Dispatches and Letters of Lord Viscount Nelson* vol. 3 p. 89 for Nelson's coffin; Lord John Russell ed. *Memoirs, Journal, and Correspondence of Thomas Moore* (8 vols 1853–6) vol. 1 p. 186 Moore to Anastasia Moore 2 Nov. 1805; De Selincourt et al. ed. *Letters of William and Dorothy Wordsworth* vol. 1 p. 650 Dorothy Wordsworth to Lady Beaumont 29 Nov. 1805; *Memoirs and Letters of Capt. Sir William Hosts* (2 vols 1833) vol. 2 p. 56: the action in question was the Battle of Lissa, 13 March 1811.

the Secretary of State, a gentleman, whom from his likeness to his pictures and the loss of an arm, I immediately recognized as Lord Nelson. He could not know who I was, but he entered at once into conversation with me, if I can call it conversation for it was almost all on his side, and all about himself, and really, in a style so vain and silly as to surprise and almost disgust me. I suppose something that I happened to say may have made him guess that I was *somebody*, and he went out of the room for a moment, I have no doubt to ask the office keeper who I was, for when he came back he was altogether a different man, both in manner and matter. All that I had thought a charlatan style had vanished, and he talked of the state of the country and of the aspect and probabilities of affairs on the Continent with a good sense, that surprised me equally and more agreeably than the first part of our interview had done; in fact, he talked like an officer and a statesman.[31]

Perhaps unfairly Wellington is never regarded as touched with genius as are other generals of comparable achievement. Possibly this has something to do with his aura of unrelenting technical proficiency – unlike Hannibal, Charles XII, Frederick the Great or Napoleon he was never defeated. (Fuentes d'Oñoro, of which Wellington wrote, 'We had very nearly three to one against us engaged; above four to one of cavalry . . . If Boney had been there we should have been beaten', is commemorated as a French victory on the Arc de Triomphe in Paris, presumably because except at the village of Fuentes d'Oñoro itself the British line was forced back, though it was the French who eventually withdrew). There are 48 engagements, all victories, inscribed on bronze plaques around the bottom of Wellington's monument in St. Paul's, a monument as vertiginously ugly in its vulgar parody of Baroque as the numerous complimentary épergnes on public display at Wellington's former town residence, Apsley House. Admittedly some of these 48 victories were distinctly minor, but Salamanca, Vitoria, and of course Waterloo rank with Agincourt, Pavia, Rocroi, Blenheim, Rossbach, Marengo, Austerlitz and Jena as amongst the really classic battles of military history. It was Sir William Slim after a later war who wrote of leading an army, 'the creation of its spirit and its leadership in battle give you the greatest unity of emotional and intellectual experience that a man can have'. Wellington would not have disagreed. His subsequent failure as Prime Minister in 1828–1830, when faced with the two great issues of Catholic Relief and Parliamentary Reform, has given him the reputation for poor judgement off the battlefield and tends to suggest that in stepping from Headquarters to Cabinet he passed out of his depth. This is not so. He himself boasted in later life:

that the power of rapid and correct calculation was his forte, and that if circumstances had not made him what he was, he would probably have become distinguished in public life as a financier.

He was a successful Irish Secretary, a successful supervisor of diplomatic and

---

[31] Jennings ed. *Croker Papers* vol. 2 p. 233–4, reminiscence of Wellington recorded 10 Oct. 1834.

logistic arrangements in the Peninsula, a successful commander of the Allied occupation forces in Paris, and in the Cabinet had a major voice in key decisions between 1818 and 1827. The post of Irish Secretary, which he held 1807–1809, was by far the most responsible office outside the Cabinet and was increasingly reserved for young men of outstanding promise: Castlereagh had held it before him, Peel and William Lamb, later Viscount Melbourne, after him. It is even probable that his command in the Peninsula prevented Wellington from entering the Cabinet either at the collapse of the Portland Ministry in 1809 or, if not too compromised by his brother Wellesley's falling out with his colleagues, at some point in 1812.[32]

Wellington imposed himself on the forces under his command in a quite different way from Nelson: a German officer remarked, 'the Duke exercised far greater power in the army he commanded than Prince Blücher in the one committed to his care', but he lacked the inspirational effect that enabled Nelson to move his captains to shivers of admiration and tears ('when I came to explain to them the *"Nelson touch"* it was like an electric shock', Nelson told Lady Hamilton three weeks before Trafalgar: 'Some shed tears'). Equally Wellington would not have encouraged his commanders to exclaim, 'You are, my Lord, surrounded by friends whom you inspire with confidence', and if he had, would not have recounted the details in a letter to his mistress. Yet whatever his effect on his captains, or on the overcrowded decks of his flagship, Nelson remained a remote figure, almost an icon to most of the men under his command. Wellington moved around much more, concerned himself more with details. The sense of his detailed supervision of everything that was happening in his army ensured that his troops were constantly on alert for his presence; he came, not to advertize himself, or to pose, but to inform himself; his carefulness for their progress reassured his troops and whenever battle was imminent he was was cheered wherever he went, acknowledging these cheers politely but brusquely, like a great landed magnate raising his hat to the curtsies of the milkmaids as he promenaded through one of his estates.[33]

Indeed, while commanding in Spain and Portugal Wellington strove to organize his personal life much more like an English country gentleman running his estates than like a professional soldier. Although the tall shakos and tight red coats of the standard military uniform were by no means especially suitable for the Spanish climate, and though he wrote, 'I think it indifferent how a soldier is clothed, provided it is in an uniform manner', in practice he insisted on his army being dressed according to regulations and resisted any suggestion of reform:

[32] Wellington *Supplementary Despatches* vol. 7 p. 176–7 Wellington to William Wellesley-Pole 2 July 1811; Sir William Slim *Defeat into Victory* (1956) p. 3; G.R. Gleig *The Life of Arthur Duke of Wellington* (1864) (People's Edition) p. 9 quoting Wellington's remark in conversation about his financial talents.

[33] [F.C.F. von] Müffling *Passages from my Life: Together with Memoirs of the Campaign of 1813 and 1814* (1853) p. 213; Nicolas ed. *Dispatches and Letters of Lord Viscount Nelson* vol. 7 p. 60 Nelson to Lady Hamilton 10 Oct. 1805.

Everything is now, I believe, as I found it twenty years ago; and if once we begin to alter we shall have nothing fixed, as there are no bounds to fancy.

But he regarded himself as superior to his own rules. Except on the most ceremonial occasions he eschewed the military coat with the complicated arrangement of buttons and braid which in those days denoted general's rank and instead wore only a blue or grey civilian frock-coat, and boots of his own design – the original Wellington boots – covered with non-regulation trousers and gaiters; instead of the prescribed 1803 Regulation sword with George III's cypher on the guard he carried a mameluke-hilted sabre brought back from India. He thus appeared the very archetype of the English *milord*, plainly dressed among the exceptionally large retinue of liveried retainers represented by his army. Though he objected to his officers cluttering up the army with an excess of baggage and hangers on, he campaigned in Spain with a larger entourage of servants than the Emperor Napoleon took with him in the invasion of Russia: in addition to two huntsmen for his fox-hounds, a goat boy and '3 women' (purpose unspecified but presumably for the laundry as Wellington insisted on always being fresh and spruce) he had with him in Spain three footmen (to Napoleon's four in Russia) two valets (Napoleon also had two) three cooks (the same as Napoleon) and five orderlies (presumably the counterpart of Napoleon's two butlers). Soldiers of conveniently available regiments could be used for duties such as feeding the hounds (a not unpopular duty as there was sometimes more biscuit available for the dogs than for the soldiers) but the regular servants, together with Wellington's headquarters staff, totalled 417 men by October 1813. This was probably up to 50 per cent larger than the military households of the field commanders in other European armies and included, beside Wellington's body servants, a notably high proportion of senior officers. Yet he not only shaved himself and brushed his own clothes, he also involved himself personally in every aspect of headquarters work, even the decyphering of captured French mail. And though, unlike so many British commanders in later wars, he had no time to keep a diary, he maintained an enormous correspondence, especially with the government.[34]

Wellington's position *vis-à-vis* the government in Whitehall developed and matured until in the aftermath of Vitoria his position resembled that of

[34] [John] Gurwood ed. *Dispatches of Field Marshal the Duke of Wellington* (13 vols 1834–9) vol. 8 p. 371 Wellington to Col. Torrens 6 Nov 1811; ibid. vol. 9 p. 487 Wellington to Lt. Col. Gore 14 Oct. 1812; Gleig *Life of Arthur Duke of Wellington* p. 480; John Wilkinson Latham *British Military Swords: From 1800 to the Present Day* (1970) p. 4; S.G.P. Ward *Wellington's Headquarters: A study of Administrative Problems in the Peninsula, 1809–1814* (Oxford 1957) p. 194–7 Appendix II, cf Nigel Nicolson *Napoleon: 1812* (1985) p. 65. For an eye-witness account of arrangements and daily routine at Wellington's H.Q. in 1812 see Roger Norman Buckley ed. *The Napoleonic War Journal of Captain Thomas Henry Browne, 1807–1816* (1987) p. 155–6, 200–201. Much of the captured French correspondence examined at Wellington's H.Q. is preserved in the Public Record Office, at WO 31/1–3.

Marlborough just over a century earlier, virtually the senior partner in the syndicate of theatre commander and home government. Wellington later claimed that the whole policy of the Peninsular campaigns was largely his, and that it was at his insistence that the army was maintained in that theatre year after year:

> It is quite certain that my opinion alone was the cause of the continuance of the war in the Peninsula. My letters shew that I encouraged, nay forced, the Government to persevere in it. The success of the operations of the army supported them in power.

This is not entirely true. Wellington received as much support from Lord Castlereagh up to September 1809 as he afforded in return, though it was not untypical of him that in later years he told a story of how, at the time of the scandal provoked by the Convention of Cintra, when he asked Castlereagh to give him a lift in his carriage to the King's levée, 'Castlereagh hemmed and hawed, and said that there was so much ill-humour in the public mind that it might produce inconvenience'. Wellington also complained much of Castlereagh's younger brother, Lord Charles Stewart, the Adjutant-General on his staff: 'Charles Stewart intrigued in the army against me, and with the assistance of Robert Craufurd had turned every one of the general officers against me, except Beresford'. Yet it was Castlereagh who insisted, in the aftermath of the Cintra scandal, that Wellington (or Wellesley as he then was) should be sent back to the Peninsula to resume command of the British forces. After Castlereagh resigned office in September 1809, Spencer Perceval, the new Prime Minister, was less supportive:

> Mr. Perceval was not very sanguine as to our success, and . . . from his language in the Cabinet it was to be inferred that he was not an advocate for the vigorous prosecution of the war in the Peninsula.

But as Wellington was himself aware, his military position in the Peninsula in 1810 and 1811 was hardly reassuring:

> The Government are terribly afraid that I shall get them, and myself, into a scrape. But what can be expected from men who are beaten in the House of Commons three times a week? A great deal might be done now, if there existed in England less party and more public sentiment, and if there was any Government.

To the Earl of Liverpool, Secretary of State for War, he complained directly:

> I acknowledge that it has appeared to me till very lately, that the Government themselves felt no confidence in the measures which they were adopting in this country.

Liverpool's reply was hardly calculated to soothe:

> all the officers in the army who were in England, whether they had served in Portugal or not, entertained and avowed the most desponding views as to the result of the war in that country.

Again, in January 1811 Wellington complained to his brother William Wellesley-Pole:

> I acknowledge that I doubt whether this government (I mean the existing administration in England) have the power, or the inclination, or the nerves to do all that ought to be done to carry on the contest as it might be.

In March 1811 he warned Liverpool that the withdrawal of British forces from the Peninsula would open Britain to the risk of a French invasion across the Channel. Given the immense numerical superiority of French forces in Spain the Cabinet's wavering was hardly surprising but Wellington probably knew, though he refused to acknowledge, that his own eldest brother, the Marquess Wellesley was constantly pressing, not for withdrawal but for reinforcement of the Peninsular army, and even quarrelling 'like Cat and Dog' on the subject with the Prime Minister, Spencer Perceval. The two brothers were rarely in direct communication, the Marquess Wellesley perhaps because he was too lazy, Wellington because he was too wary of becoming involved with his brother's erratic politics:

> I have always expected he would quit the government, at which period it would have been reported that he and I had been intriguing to increase the power of our family, and I wished to be able to say that I had not written him a line since he went into office.

When Wellesley did quit he wrote a memo waxing eloquent on their earlier collaboration in India and the advantage of their mutual knowledge and confidence in each other, and mentioned in a foot-note how odd it was that as Foreign Secretary he only saw those of his brother's despatches that were published. The gossip meanwhile at the British H.Q. in Spain was that 'Lord Wellington was very angry with Lord Wellesley for his resignation and hardly spoke to any one for some days after he had heard the fact'. By this stage however Wellington's position was much more secure: he had been advising Charles Stuart, the British envoy in Lisbon, on the reform of Portugal's finances, and when Viscount Melville, the President of the Board of Control for India, sent him a packet of memoranda on the proposed transfer of the East India Company's army to the Crown he promptly wrote off two long letters of helpful commentary; his almost universal competence was becoming recognized. There was something unnecessarily self-conscious, almost a note of false humility, in his letter to the Secretary of State for War in December 1813 urging the continuation of the war in the South of France rather than transferring the army to Holland but acknowledging, 'It is the business of the Government, and not my business, to dispose of the resources of the nation; and I have no right to give an opinion on the subject.'[35]

[35] [P.D.] Earl Stanhope *Notes of Conversations with the Duke of Wellington, 1831–1851* (1888) p. 83 memo by Wellington for Lord Mahon 18 Sept. 1836; Jennings ed. *Croker Papers* vol. 1 p. 344, notes of Wellington's conversation 1826; ibid. vol. 1 p. 346; Gurwood ed.
continued

VIII. Wellington's System: Logistics and Repression

Wellington would have agreed with Napoleon's dictum that an army marches on its stomach: where he would have disagreed was in how that stomach was to be filled. In 1812 Wellington's entire command, of fewer than 50,000 British troops including those in the rear and 21,377 Portuguese and Spanish troops attached to his field army and dependent on British commissariat arrangements, included 87 commissaries and 255 commissariat clerks, of whom 70 were permanently assigned to brigades and cavalry regiments. In January 1809 Maréchal Soult's army for the invasion of Portugal consisted of only 20,000 men but included 71 'employés' in the commissariat and an unspecified but presumably larger number of 'sous employés'. Pro rata Soult's commissariat service had more staff. Yet even at their best the logistic arrangements of Napoleon's armies had a minimalist hit-and-miss character, with a heavy reliance on expedients and improvisations. To take an earlier campaign, organized under Napoleon's direct supervision and ultimately crowned with epic success, instructions were given at the beginning of the 1805 autumn campaign against Austria for the preparation of 500,000 biscuit rations at Strasbourg, 200,000 at Mainz and 1,000,000 distributed between Würzburg and Ulm. The latter, left to the care of the Bavarian government, failed to materialize. Napoleon also counted on the availability of over 4,500 wagons, which in the event were not to be found. Even when

continued
Dispatches of the Duke of Wellington vol. 6 p. 21 Wellington to Vice-Admiral George Berkeley 7 April 1810; ibid. vol. 6 p. 347 Wellington to Earl of Liverpool 19 Aug. 1810; Wellington *Supplementary Despatches* vol. 6 p. 592 Liverpool to Wellington 10 Sept. 1810; ibid. vol. 7 p. 43 Wellington to William Wellesley-Pole 11 Jan. 1811; Gurwood ed. *Dispatches of the Duke of Wellington* vol. 7 p. 380 Wellington to Liverpool 23 March 1811; National Library of Wales: Coed-y-Maen Mss: Earl Temple to C.W.W. Wynn 15 Sept. 1811, cf Meyrick Shawe's memo of 1812, Wellington *Supplementary Despatches* vol. 7 p. 259, Wellesley's 'Notes on the General State of Europe' [Melville ed.] *Wellesley Papers* vol. 2 p. 44–9 and Wellesley's 1812 memo, British Library Add. 37296 f. 264–306; Wellington *Supplementary Despatches* vol. 7 p. 5 Wellington to William Wellesley-Pole 15 Dec. 1810; British Library Add. 37296 f. 276–8 and f. 278 verso, fn., Wellesley's memo of 20 March 1812; *Private Journal of F.S. Larpent* vol. 1 p. 157–8, 1 May 1813; Gurwood ed. *Dispatches of the Duke of Wellington* vol. 8 p. 358–364 memo sent to Charles Stuart 29 Oct. 1811; ibid. vol. 8 p. 614 fn. Viscount Melville Wellington 10 Feb. 1812 and ibid. vol. 8 p. 614–9 Wellington to Melville 12 and 13 March 1812. ibid. vol. 11 p. 386 Wellington to Earl Bathurst 21 Dec. 1813.

Six weeks after his letter to William Wellesley-Pole of 15 Dec. 1810, in which he said he wished to be able to say he had not written a line to the Marquess Wellesley, Wellington sent off a rather major letter to his eldest brother, cf Gurwood ed. *Dispatches* vol. 7 p. 184–9, 26 Jan. 1811. Wellesley's memo of 20 March 1812 in which he complained of only seeing those of his brother's despatches that were published may have been intended as a pamphlet: the footnote at Add. 37296 f. 278 verso expatiating on the utility of Wellesley seeing Wellington's despatches has 'We have been assured that a directly contrary procedure prevailed' altered to 'It has however been rumoured that . . .', both original and alteration being in Wellesley's own handwriting. And though it is true there was remarkably *little* correspondence between them, Wellington was in close touch with his youngest brother Henry, the ambassador to the Spanish junta, who was naturally in close touch with their eldest brother the Foreign Secretary.

Napoleon took care to instruct Bernadotte to take a week's supply of biscuit while marching through neutral Hesse-Cassel, he made no arrangements for forage for the horses. Evidently the idea was that if the troops did not carry their own food, they would be obliged to seize the granaries in the market towns, which would obviously annoy the Hesse-Cassel government, whereas the horses could be fed by turning them loose in the fields along the line of the march, which would annoy only the peasants; but marching horses require grain fodder and at that time of the year there was nothing in the fields but autumn grass.

The arrangement later made in Spain and Portugal were even more rudimentary. Napoleon's orders at the time of the first invasion of Portugal (under Junot, over a year before Soult's campaign) were:

> as soon as my army has entered Portugal it must be fed, clothed and paid by the contributions which shall be levied in that country: from that moment on there must be no need for me to send another half-penny.
>
> I don't see that, under the pretext of lack of provisions, its march need be delayed a single day: that excuse is only valid for men who don't want to do anything: 20,000 men can live anywhere, even in the desert.

The French troops simply had to make do. Soult's army for the invasion of Portugal in January 1809 had a paper establishment of 2,400 horses for supply transport plus 200 for the ambulance service: in reality there were 80 horses and 35 mules. There probably was not a great deal for them to carry anyway. Lord Grey later claimed:

> It was well known that the manufacturers of Yorkshire made the clothing of the French army; and not only the accoutrements but the ornaments of marshal Soult and his army were formed by the artisans of Birmingham.

Such rumours, though pervasive, had little foundation; but 2,582 British Army greatcoats recently captured at Coruña were distributed amongst 20,000 men. Six thousand five hundred pairs of shoes were collected from various quarters; 1,800 pairs of shoes cut out but not sewn up were also provided, leaving more than half the army to walk from France to Portugal without any new shoes at all. (When in March 1811 Wellington asked London for shoes he requested 150,000 of the largest size plus 100,000 pairs of soles and heels. The disproportion between French and British supplies reminds one of Gillray's caricature 'French Liberty British Slavery' of December 1792, with its obese British farmer carving a huge joint – the statuette of Britannia on the wall above his head has a sack labelled 'sterling' in place of a shield – contrasted with the Frenchman eating raw onions, and Cruikshank's 'French Happiness English Misery' of January 1793 contrasting a couple of guzzling Englishmen and four famished Frenchmen pulling a frog apart.)[36]

---

[36] Ward *Wellington's Headquarters* p. 83–4; Pierre Madeleine Le Noble *Mémoires sur les Opérations Militaire des Français . . . en 1809, sous le commandement du maréchal Soult Duc de Dalmatie* (Paris 1821) p. 356 Table VI; Martin van Creveld *Supplying War: Logistics from*
continued

The theoretical function of the French commissariat officials was to fix requisitions in each area the army was based in or passing through, and these requisitions were then levied as an impost by the local magistrate or paid for by money levied elsewhere, or taken in lieu of future cash contributions, the troops meanwhile enforcing local compliance by threatening, and if necessary carrying out, arrests, confiscations and house-burnings. In practice the French soldiers spent a fair proportion of their time fending for themselves, but the result was that they suffered a tremendous wastage of men, through starvation, sickness and, occasionally, assassination by the locals while dispersed in small groups hunting for food and loot. 'We could not advance 100 yards without seeing dead soldiers of the enemy, stretched upon the road or at a little distance from it, who had laid down to die, unable to proceed through hunger and fatigue', recorded one Scots soldier of the pursuit of the French forces retreating from the lines of Torres Vedras in November 1810. Wellington later estimated that over six years his forces lost from death, wounds and desertion 6,000 men per year:

> It would have been infinitely greater, but for attention to regular subsistence. The French armies were made to take their chance and to live as they could, and their loss was immense.

On another occasion he put the French loss at 83,000 a year – more than Napoleon's army at Waterloo. 'An account of the French Troops which have entered from 13 Oct 1807 to the 1st June 1812' put French losses in the Peninsula in dead and captured as 488,924 out of a total 788,847 who had crossed the Pyrenees, of whom 119,923 had already returned to France: French figures covering the period October 1807 to 30 April 1813 put the loss at 473,000.[37]

continued

Wallenstein to Patton Cambridge 1977 p. 45–50; *Correspondance de Napoléon 1er* (31 vols Paris 1858–69) vol. 16 p. 165 no.13327 Napoleon to Général Clarke 5 Nov. 1807; Le Noble *Operations du maréchal Soult* p. 61; *Parliamentary Debates* vol. 23 col.8, Earl Grey 5 May 1812; Gurwood ed. *Dispatches of the Duke of Wellington* vol. 7 p. 410–411 Wellington to Earl of Liverpool 31 March 1811.

[37] For the French system of requisitioning see Vansittart's memo with Wellington's annotations, British Library Add. 31236 f. 22–5; Duke of Wellington ed. *Despatches, Correspondance, and Memoranda of Field Marshal Arthur Duke of Wellington* [continuation series] (5 vols 1867–73) vol. 3 p. 1–53 'Memorandum on the War in Russia in 1812' p. 9–14; *Journal of a Soldier of the Seventy-First or Glasgow Regiment. Highland Light Infantry, from 1806 to 1815* Edinburgh 1819 p. 122; Francis Earl of Ellesmere *Personal Reminiscences of the Duke of Wellington* ed. Countess of Strafford (1903) p. 160, note of conversation 28 Jan. 1837 and of Stanhope *Conversations with the Duke of Wellington* p. 86, 10 Oct. 1836; National Army Museum Mss 7512–16 'An account of the French Troops which have entered Spain from 13 Oct. 1807 to the 1st June 1812'; José Canga Argüelles *Documentos pertenecientes a las Observaciones sobre la historia de la Guerra de España* (2 vols Madrid 1835) vol. 1 p. 358 num. LXXX

The official return of British casualties in Wellington's armies from 1808 to 1814 gave 9,254 rank and file (of whom 1,375 were in the King's German Legion or other foreign units in British pay) 49 drummers, 510 sergeants, 47 staff, 317 subalterns, 191 captains, 56 field officers and 10 generals killed: Public Record Office WO 79/50.

Wellington's opinion was that 'a soldier who has got through one campaign is of more service than two, or even three, newly arrived from England' and as time passed he had the advantage of deploying progressively more combat-hardened troops against progressively less experienced adversaries. The much lower rate of wastage in the British Army also meant that recruitment was rather less of a social and economic burden in Britain than in the territories controlled by Napoleon. Altogether from 1 January 1793 to 31 December 1815 the British Army recruited (essentially on a voluntary basis) 747,670 men, or an average of 32,507 a year: the French, in the shorter period 1799–1814 raised 2,015,000 French troops (mainly by conscription) or an average of 125,969 a year, plus 644,000 non-French troops (40,281 a year). Of course the population resources available to Napoleon were much greater than those controlled by the British government, but Napoleon also bit into them much more deeply, which involved not merely a greater demographic strain but also the organization of a system of conscription that probably would not have been workable, or politically acceptable, in Britain. Napoleon boasted of being able to expend (*dépenser*) 25,000 men a month, yet except in 1812, the year in which he mobilized as many men as possible for the invasion of Russia, the total *Grand Armée* was only approximately twice the size of the total British Army and even without conscription the British were able to maintain a higher proportion of national manpower under arms than was possible on the continent.[38]

The secret of the British achievement was the deployment of non-human resources. This was a world war fought with a technology of wood and

[38] Gurwood ed. *Dispatches of the Duke of Wellington* vol. 6 p. 221 Wellington to Duke of York 26 Dec, 1812; for British recruitment figures see W.B. Hodges 'On the Mortality arising from Military Operations' *Journal of the Statistical Society* vol. 19 (1856) p. 219–271, for French recruitment see Jacques Houdaille 'Le Problème des Pertes de Guerre' *Révue d'Histoire Moderne et Contemporaine* vol. 17 (1970) p. 411–423 at p. 415, Isser Woloch 'Napoleonic Conscription: State Power and Civil Society' *Past and Present* no. 111 (1986) p. 101–129 and Alan Forrest *Conscripts and Deserters: The Army and French Society during the Revolution and Empire* (New York 1989) especially p. 187–218; [Jean Antoine] Comte de Chaptal *Mes Souvenirs sur Napoléon* ed. A. Chaptal (Paris 1893) p. 341 for expending 25,000 men a month; [Etienne Denis] Pasquier *A History of my Time: Memoirs of Chancellor Pasquier* ed. Duc d'Audiffret-Pasquier (3 vols Boston 1893–4) vol. 2 p. 98 for the oppressive laws needed to back up the system of conscription.

In the parish churchyard at Pfeddersheim in Rheinland-Pfalz there is an interesting memorial to the young men of the area who were conscripted for the *Grand Armée* during the period when the Rhineland was annexed to France, indicating that military service was by no means altogether resented by Napoleon's involuntary subjects. The inscription reads:

Denkstein der Veteranen aus dem Kanton Pfeddersheim. Veteranen Verein zu Pfeddersheim. Die in Ihre Heimath Zuruckgekehrten ehemaligen soldaten Napoleons aus dem Kanton Pfeddersheim weihen ihren auf dem Felde der Ehre gefallenen Kriegskameraden dies Denkmal . . . 1847.

It is almost certain that there was no such thing as a Veteranen Verein (Veteran's Association) anywhere in Britain in the post-Waterloo years.

leather and the vast investment in complex munitions characteristic of twentieth-century warfare was still in the future. Wellington's army in the Peninsula always had proportionately less artillery than the French; what he had more of was money. If the British soldier lasted longer in the firing line than his French counterpart it was largely because he cost his country far more. The British government did not march its armies on board hired ships to carry them across the ocean at vast expense simply in order to abandon them without food and clothing on barren shores. Foreign observers were astonished at the level at which the British troops were maintained: 'Luxury has in no way declined in the English army. This vice, by multiplying their needs, renders them little capable of mobility', noted a French emigré officer in the Austrian service. One English cavalry lieutenant recorded his equipage in 1813 as three riding horses (one of them allegedly formerly 'King Joseph's'), a horse and a mule for baggage, a pony 'for the Small Breakfast Canteens', two greyhounds, a dog captured from the French ('my French Prisoner – a Faithful companion' – judging by an attached drawing probably a poodle) and, in addition to a military orderly, a valet-cook, a groom and a 'very faithful' Portuguese manservant. The common soldiers of course were less well off, but relative to the soldiers of other armies they were kept in excellent physical condition: even the Prussians admitted 'Our infantry does not possess the same bodily strength or powers of endurance as yours'. In July 1809 Major-General Robert Craufurd, leaving fifty of his weaker men behind, marched his Light Brigade 62 miles in 26 hours 'in the hottest season of the year, each man carrying from fifty to sixty pounds weight upon his shoulders'. Wellington, whose habit of deprecating others was as marked as Montgomery's, claimed to have done even better in India but Craufurd's was a record no European army could equal.[39]

Although the British soldiers received almost twice the pay of the next best paid European soldiers – and it was an event if this pay was even a few months in arrears – by 1813 only 8 per cent of expenditure in the Peninsula was for pay; 56 per cent was for supplies and a further 9 per cent was for inland transport. Yet local expenditure provided only part of the army's needs as not only weapons and ammunition but also much of the foodstuff had to be imported by sea from Britain or from countries outside the war zone; it has been estimated that most of the livestock for meat and nearly all the fodder for

[39] [J.B.L.] Baron de Crossard *Mémoirs Militaires et Historiques pour servir à l'Histoire de la Guerre depuis 1792 jusqu'en 1815 inclusivement* (6 vols Paris 1829) vol. 4 p. 9 (The despatch on which this chapter is based, written while on mission in Spain 1808–1809, is in Österreichisches Staatsarchiv: Staatenabteilung Spanien Varia 77 and contains various libellous and ridiculously prejudiced remarks which have been suppressed in the printed version); National Army Museum Mss 6807–267 [George Woodberry] 'The Idle Companion of a Young Hussar: during the year 1813' p. 29; Müffling *Passages from my Life* p. 216; W.F.P. Napier *History of the War in the Peninsula and in the South of France* (6 vols 1828–40) vol. 2 p. 407, cf Samuel Rogers *Recollections* (1859) p. 203 where Wellington claimed to have once marched troops 72 miles in 34 hours, including a stretch of 47 miles in 15 hours.

the horses was purchased by the commissariat within the Peninsula (though usually at interior depots, not in the vicinity of the fighting units) but that the proportion of bread and breadstuffs imported by sea rose from less than half up to the end of 1810 to up to 90 per cent in 1813. (In 1812 Wellington estimated the army's daily consumption of food as 200,000 lb). This level of dependence on imports would of course have been out of the question without Britain's command of the sea, but there was still a significant need for local spending power, and here Britain's financial resources were crucial. The first half of the Peninsular War was fought with British credit instruments: specifically, Exchequer Bills. It was not always easy to persuade the Spanish to accept these; the Talavera campaign in the summer of 1809 was delayed for five weeks by the need to await a supply of hard cash from England; 'I propose to commence my march as soon as it shall reach the army', Wellesley – as he then still was – told the Secretary of State for War, and five days later when it still had not arrived, he wrote:

> it was and is quite impossible to move without money . . . we can no longer obtain the supplies of the country, or command its resources for the transport of our own supplies.

After another five days, the money having finally reached the army (though 'the articles ordered are not yet arrived'), Wellesley set out, writing to the Secretary of State just before his departure:

> I believe much of this delay and failure is to be attributed to the want of experience of our Commissariat; much to the want of money, and to our discredit in Portugal.

Three years later British credit had been improved by a string of victories but the sheer quantity of Exchequer Bills saturating the market caused them to pass only at 25 per cent discount. In 1813 the British government finally produced an issue of guineas, the first coinage of gold since 1799, using melted down mohurs and pagodas imported from India, and together with French coin collected by the Rothschilds in northern Europe and surreptitiously shipped out from Helvoetsluys, over £2.5 million in coin passed through Wellington's hands in the space of a few months, considerably facilitating the final stages of his Peninsular operations.[40]

[40] British Library Add. 38272 f. 152 'General Yearly Statement of Disbursements in the Peninsula and in the South of France for the Service of the Army': total expenditure 25 Dec, 1812–24 Dec. 1813 was £14,157,311 18s. 4d: I have not counted commissariat pay with the army pay: it represented a further 1 per cent. Toby Michael Ormsby Redgrave 'Wellington's Logistical Arrangements in the Peninsular War' London Univ. Ph.D. dissertation 1979 p. 54, 63–4, 75, 104; Gurwood ed. *Dispatches of the Duke of Wellington* vol. 9 p. 224 Wellington to Dr. James McGrigor 9 June 1812 for army's daily bread requirement; ibid. vol. 3 p. 318 Wellington to Castlereagh 22 June 1809; ibid. vol. 3 p. 329–330 same to same 27 June 1809; John Sherwig *Guineas and Gunpowder: British Foreign Aid in the Wars with France, 1793–1815* (Cambridge Mass. 1969) p. 255; ibid. p. 263, Edward Herries *Memoir of the Public Life of the Right Hon. John Charles Herries in the Reigns of George III, William IV, and Victoria* (2

continued

It seems indeed that British commissariat arrangements were perfected only by the time the war was practically over. Admittedly the British Army's worst experience in the Peninsular War, Moore's chaotic retreat on Coruña, could be blamed on the Spanish:

> arrangement only was wanting, the district being capable of easily supplying a much larger force. If we had been permitted to supply ourselves by means of our Commissariat, our difficulties would have very soon vanished. In that case, all we wanted from the Junta was their Recommendation or Commands to the different Magistrates. The Detail would have been easily managed. But this would not satisfy the Junta. With a great appearance of eagerness, they insisted on supplying us with every thing . . . But when we came to the trial, their Contractors failed in every instance.

But there were soon complaints equally bitter regarding the behaviour of British officials:

> The horses starved, while ships loaded with hay and oats from England enough to furnish all the cavalry were rotting and spoiling in the Tagus . . . the commissariat, instead of being with the army, are in Lisbon, keeping their houses, horses and whores.

Yet even after Welliington had begun to impose his organizing will on the general situation, arrangements remained in some respects quite inadequate. After the wars a French expert roundly condemned the practice of bivouacking:

> It is one of the principal causes of that frightful waste of men which occurred in the last wars, when one could calculate on average that the infantryman did not last above two campaigns.

That was in the French Army. In the British Army, though tents were issued for the officers in 1809, the men were provided with them only in 1813. The preferred practice was to billet the men in houses and churches but on campaign, with tens of thousands of soldiers concentrated in an underdeveloped or rural zone, this was not always possible. A bandmaster of the Cameronians recorded for 31 July 1811:

> wet, dejected, and miserable, we sat Officers, and Men, under the cover of the trees, without as much as a blanket to throw over us, our Regiment by some mistake received no blankets on marching to join the Army nor neither did they through the whole campaign which was a shameful neglect.

On 30 August 1811 he observed the men tearing down branches to build

> a kind of wigwam which sheltered them from the rays of the sun by day, but had little or no affect in keeping the rain or dew out at night, canvas would scarsly keep out the heavy dews that fall in Portugal, in such encampments

continued
vols 1880) vol. 1 p. 85–6, and Charles Oman *A History of the Peninsular War* (7 vols Oxford 1902–30) vol. 7 p. 147, 288.

the men never took of any part of their cloths at night . . . such is the fatigues that shortens the lives of Soldiers and that occasioned the death of thousands of Britains in the Peninsula.

Even when blankets and tents were available they were not always in the right place at the right time. An officer recalled:

It frequently happened too, that after the termination of a long march, in wet weather, we had to stand for hours exposed to torrents of rain, before our camp equipage arrived from the rear.

The further the British Army advanced, the longer became its lines of supply, with the result that by the time Wellington's troops had crossed into France they found that it was no longer the case that they were better shod than the enemy:

Numbers of men were marching barefooted, and in vain did the captains of companies ride on before the line of march to the various towns in our route in order to purchase a supply of these articles, which they uniformly found had been put in requisition by the French.[41]

The French, who actually had things far worse, were at least permitted to try to make themselves as comfortable as possible. 'A French bivouac after the departure of the troops was like an old-clothes shop and a furniture store: English bivouacs were nothing like it', recollected one old soldier of the *Grande Armée*. This indiscriminate acquisitiveness was never permitted under Wellington's command. The corollary of the British Army's more comprehensive supply system was that the troops could be kept under restraint much more than the French – or even the Spanish, for as Wellington remarked, 'The Spanish armies, which are neither fed nor paid, nor clothed, cannot be kept together by the bonds of discipline, as I keep my troops'. The British Army was in fact both wet-nursed and kept in order by rigid discipline to an extent incredible in other armies – a characteristic which was to be frequently commented on also in the 1914–1918 and 1939–1945 wars. Afterwards, a Quartermaster wrote:

An English army is perhaps, generally speaking, under stricter discipline than any other in the world; but in proportion as they are held tight while they are

[41] British Library Add. 39201 f. 7 Journal of Major-General John Randoll Mackenzie; Buckingham *Court and Cabinets of George the Third* vol. 4 p. 359–360 Vice-Admiral George Berkeley to Earl Temple 10 Sept. 1809; [Joseph] Baron Rogniat *Considerations sur l'Art de la Guerre* (3rd edit. Paris 1820) p. 265–6; [John] Gurwood ed. *The General Orders of Field Marshal the Duke of Wellington* (1837) p. 289–292; British Library Add. 32468 f. 46 Journal – in fact Reminiscences – of John Westcott, bandmaster of the Cameronians; ibid. f 66–7; John Malcolm 'Reminiscences of a Campaign in the Pyrenees and South of France in 1814' *Constable's Miscellany* vol. 27 (1828) p. 235–307 at p. 288; ibid. p. 287.

For British commissariat arrangements generally see Toby Redgrave's Ph.D. dissertation cited in previous note and Gurwood ed. *General Orders of the Duke of Wellington* p. xxxiii–xl. For Spanish arrangements see Argüelles ed. *Documentos* vol. 1 p. 197–218 num. XLII and XLIII.

in hand, if circumstances occur to give them liberty, I know of no army more difficult to restrain when once broke loose.

One of Napoleon's generals noted, 'The subordination of every moment is the *sine qua non* of the existence of the English armies', and Napoleon himself raised the matter with Colonel Mark Wilks, who was Governor of St. Helena at the commencement of his exile there:

[Bonaparte] In your army and navy I recognize nothing but a blind and undistinguished obedience, and a fear of your superiors greater than I have ever observed in nations the most stigmatized for servility.

[Wilks] We have no objection to the national imputation of being the most obedient soldiers in Europe.[42]

Although other British officers also commented on the contrast between the orderly behaviour of French troops even after months of ruthless foraging for themseves, and the constant need for unrelaxed discipline within the British Army, the wet-nursing and twenty-four hour regulation of the British soldiery was largely due to Wellington's assessment of what was required. 'We are not naturally a military people; the whole business of an army upon service is foreign to our habits', he wrote. He later complained of 'the habitual inattention of the Officers of the regiments to their duty' and their relaxation rather than stricter enforcement of army regulations while on campaign. It was, he acknowledged, 'an unrivalled army for fighting' but:

Nobody ever thinks of obeying an order; and all the regulations of the Horse Guards, as well as of the War Office, and all the orders of the army applicable to this particular service, are so much waste paper.

He certainly issued a large number of orders, relating to plunder, stragglers, the collection of firewood, roll calls, and so on: units from which troops had been reported plundering were ordered to hold frequent roll calls, and in October 1811 the standing orders in Sir Thomas Graham's division were:

rolls must be called frequently and sentries must be posted in such numbers as may be necessary, and limits must be set beyond which no soldier is to go from his cantonments.

In theory such regulations were in keeping with what Frederick the Great had recommended in his well-known *Instruction Militaire* (written *circa* 1747) but in practice even the Prussian Army never achieved the sustained day-and-

---

[42] A.L.A. Fée *Souvenirs de la Guerre d'Espagne dite de l'Indépendance 1809–1813* (Strasbourg 1856) p. 287 and cf [M.S. Comte] Foy *History of the War in the Peninsula* (2 vols 1827) vol. 1 p. 159–162; Gurwood ed. *Dispatches of the Duke of Wellington* vol. 6 p. 583 Wellington to Henry Wellesley 11 Nov. 1810; William Surtees *Twenty-five Years in the Rifle Brigade* (Edinburgh 1833) p. 149; Foy *History of the War in the Peninsula* vol. 1 p. 162; Julian S. Corbett ed. *Colonel Wilks and Napoleon: Two Conversations Held at St. Helena in 1816* (1901) p. 29, 21 April 1816.

night supervision characteristic of Wellington's system. It was perhaps no coincidence that one of the most popular marching songs in the British Army at this period was 'Tom he was a piper's son' with its refrain 'And all the tune that he could play /was "Over the hills and far away"'. Nor was it particularly surprising that, as Wellington himself noted, deserters from the *Grande Armée* enrolled in units in British pay tended to desert back to the French as quickly as possible, preferring hardship and plunder to 'the comfort and plenty of the British Army, accompanied as these must be by regularity of habit and by the maintenance of strict discipline'; the 28 foreign-born soldiers executed after court-martial in Wellington's army, compared to the 52 British-born, is considerably in excess of the actual proportion of foreign-born troops under his command and subject to British military law.[43]

Wellington later explained:

> The French soldiers are more under control than ours. It was quite shocking what excesses ours committed when once let loose ... Our soldiers could not resist wine. The French too could shift better for themselves and always lived upon the country ... The French system of conscription brings together a fair sample of all classes: ours is composed of the scum of the earth.

These remarks (November 1831) tend to be taken as the customary exaggerations of a retired Colonel Blimp and though it is true that Wellington's reactionary tendencies became increasingly marked after 1815 in this case there seems to have been no alteration. In one of his rare letters to the Marquess Wellesley in January 1811 he referred disparagingly to the French political system 'which can with impunity lose one half of the troops employed in the field every year, only by the privations and hardships imposed upon them', but described the French troops as 'sober, well-disposed, amenable to order, and in some degree educated'. When in September 1812 Vansittart, Chancellor of the Exchequer suggested:

> It may be worth considering whether any useful Hint can be derived from the System by which the French Armies are subsisted, modifying it so as to strip it, as far as possible, of its Injustice and Oppression,

---

[43] For corroboration of Wellington's view see [John Stepney Cowell] *Leaves from the Diary of an Officer of the Guards* (1854) p. 103–104; Gurwood ed. *Dispatches of the Duke of Wellington* vol. 4 p. 343 Wellington to J. Villiers 5 May 1809; ibid. vol. 9 p. 575–6 circular 28 Nov. 1812; ibid. vol. 10 p. 539 Wellington to Colonel Torrens 18 July 1813; British Library Add. 32468 f. 85 Westcott's Journal, citing divisional standing orders Oct. 1811: as a conscientious N.C.O. Westcott seems to have kept careful note of such orders: 'soldier' is given as 'soldiers' in the MSS; Frederick II *Military Instructions ... for the Generals of his Army* (1762) p. 3–5 and cf Richard Fester ed. *Die Instruktion Friedrichs des Grossen für seine Generale von 1747* (Berlin 1936) p. ix–xi for the date of composition; Gurwood ed. *Dispatches* vol. 7 p. 482 Wellington to Thomas Graham 23 April 1811; John Keegan *The Mask of Command* (1987) p. 128 and cf John Green *Vicissitudes of a Soldier's Life, or a Series of Occurrences from 1806 to 1815* (Louth 1827) p. 175–6 where the public hanging of two soldiers sentenced for burglary is described.

Wellington responded:

> I am sorry to say that our Troops are not of that description, nor are they in
> the state of discipline to perform these services. They could not be trusted to
> inflict an exact measure of punishment on a disobedient Village or district. They
> would plunder it as well as the others [i.e. the French] readily enough; but their
> principal object would be to get and to drink as much liquor as they could, &
> then to destroy as much valuable property as should fall in their way.

He was quite aware that 'British troops, if deprived of their magazines, would
starve in a district in Spain in which the French army would live in plenty', but
he insisted that the British could not be permitted the same freedom. Perhaps
the very first recorded employment of his 'scum of the earth' phrase was in a
letter to the Secretary of State for War in July 1813 when he complained:

> We have in the service the scum of the earth as common soldiers; and of
> late years we have been doing every thing in our power, both by law and
> publications, to relax the discipline by which alone such men can be kept
> in order.

But it seems that from the very beginning his logistical system was based on
the belief that his men were the scourings of society, only waiting for the least
relaxation of control to give themselves over to intoxication and pillage.[44]

The fact that his soldiers were, at least by English standards, poorly paid
and subject to brutal punishments and were, nonetheless, all volunteers, tends
to support the notion that they must have been quite as mindless and depraved
as Wellington said they were. The storming of Badajoz in April 1812 was
followed by scenes of despoilment and debauch which shocked every officer
who saw it. A couple of months later Wellington announced in a General
Order that two soldiers had been found who had drunk themselves to death:
'This is not the first instance that has come to his knowledge of soldiers dying
of drink'. Next year he complained of the 'frequency of the crime of striking,
and even firing at officers in the execution of their duty' – presumably during
attempts to halt looting. He was not alone in his low opinion of his troops.
'The worst men were fittest soldiers. Keep the better sort at home', Lord
Melville – the former Secretary of State for War Henry Dundas – told the
House of Lords in 1808. The bestselling comic poem *The Military Adventures
of Johnny Newcome*, written by an officer who commanded a battalion at
Vitoria, includes the lines:

> The way I estimate a British soldier –
> He's stouter than a Frenchman, and is bolder;

[44] Stanhope *Conversations with the Duke of Wellington* p. 9, 2 Nov. 1831 and p. 14, 4
Nov. 1831 and cf also p. 18, 11 Nov. 1831; Gurwood ed. *Dispatches* vol. 7 p. 188, Wellington
to Marquess Wellesley 26 Jan. 1811; British Library Add. 31236 f. 22–3, Vansittart's memo of
2 Sept. 1812 and Wellington's responses; Gurwood ed. *Dispatches of the Duke of Wellington*
vol. 10 p. 367 observations May 1813 on General Whittingham's memo of 24 April 1812; ibid.
vol. 10 p. 496 Wellington to Earl Bathurst 2 July 1813.

> But such a set of wanton idle knaves!
> You're forced, by G-d! to treat them all like slaves.

A footnote to this passage states:

> The immorality of the British soldier is disgusting, and it is only by strict attention and severe discipline that it is at all kept within bounds.

Another footnote thirty pages on claims 'A German Soldier will sell his bread to feed his horse – a British Soldier will sell the corn to purchase drink'. Yet William Napier, who also served in the Peninsula and later wrote a classic history of the campaigns, thought the typical British soldier 'observant and quick to comprehend his orders, full of resources under difficulties, calm and resolute in danger, and more than usually obedient and careful of his officers in moments of imminent peril'. The intelligence and education of these men is indicated by the large proportion of the memoirs and reminiscences of the Peninsular campaigns published during the nineteenth century that were by men who had served in the ranks: certainly a larger proportion than of memoirs of the First World War. Moreover a significant number of these memoir-writers were Methodists, who presumably thought of other things than the next opportunity to become paralytically drunk. Though the Society for the Promotion of Christian Knowledge supplied the Royal Navy with bibles and prayer books, it was 'not in the habit of supplying the Military with Books . . . the finances & calls upon the Society do not allow them to engage in such an expensive concern'. The Chaplain-General concerned himself more with the Royal Navy too. Ten Chaplains, as majors of infantry, were in Wellington's army in November 1808, but they were obviously too few: hence perhaps the number of Methodists. It was characteristic of Wellington that he thought working-class religion almost as dangerous as working-class drinking habits:

> The meeting of soldiers in their cantonments to sing psalms, or hear a sermon read by one of their comrades, is, in the abstract, perfectly innocent; and it is a better way of spending their time than many others to which they are addicted; but it may become otherwise.

On the basis of such remarks one may judge that Wellington's attitude to his men derived from fairly specific social prejudices.[45]

---

[45] The sack of Badajoz is described in Julian Sturgis ed. *A Boy in the Peninsular War: The Services, Adventures, and Experiences of Robert Blakeney* (1899) p. 273–7; Gurwood ed. *General Orders of the Duke of Wellington* p. 104, 4 June 1812; Gurwood ed. *Dispatches of the Duke of Wellington* vol. 11 p. 166 Wellington to Major-General Barnes 6 Oct. 1813; *Annual Register* 1808 'History of Europe' p. 113, speech by Viscount Melville in the House of Lords 13 March 1808 – not in *Parliamentary Debates*; [David Roberts] *The Military Adventures of Johnny Newcome, with an Account of his Campaigns on the Peninsula and in Pall Mall* (1815) p. 112, p. 112 fn. 2 p. 144 fn. 1 and cf p. 61 fn. 1 and see also *Memoirs of the Late War: The Personal Narrative of Captain Cooke* (2 vols 1831) vol. 1 p. 87–8; Napier *History of the War in the Peninsula* vol. 3 p. 271; Archives of the Society for the Promotion of Christian

continued

Wellington, it should never be forgotten, was an Irishman. The Irishness of at least three of his brothers, the Marquess Wellesley, William Wellesley-Pole, later Lord Maryborough, and Henry Wellesley, later Lord Cowley, was frequently kept in mind by contemporaries as an explanation of their vagaries, but Wellington himself took great care that his Irishness should be forgotten. There was undoubtedly an artistic streak in him: his father had been professor of music at Trinity College Dublin and in his teens he had himself been very fond of the violin. He burnt his violin in the first summer of the wars, when he was 24, and thereafter devoted himself to a quite different artistic career, that of acting the charade of the Perfect Englishman (one recent writer describes him as 'the most perfect embodiment of the gentlemanly ideal England has ever produced').[46]

The stereotype of the Perfect Englishman was evolving rapidly in this period. The Perfect Englishman was modest, restrained in expression, to the point, instinctively honest and honourable, neat and elegant but never showy or overdressed, orderly and efficient in practical affairs, politically conservative and indeed extremely class-conscious though confident of his ability to handle the lower orders, and addicted to fox-hunting. It would be difficult to say how far Wellington personally contributed to the evolution of this stereotype but it is curious that he was not only *the* most famous Englishman of his day, but almost the only famous Englishman of his day to exhibit these characteristics. Most of the political leaders – Pitt, Lord Grenville, Fox, the Earl of Liverpool – were noted for their lack of personal elegance. Nelson, that other great English warrior of the period, was almost the complete antithesis of what an English gentleman was meant to be, his blind eye, missing arm and generally dishevelled appearance underlining the passionate, hypochondriachal, almost feminine ardency of his personality. Even on the field of battle, Wellington avoided the heroic poses which had become established in fashion (in foreign armies at least). Instead of Napoleon's vainglorious Orders of the Day with which the *Grand Armée* was inspired before combat, Wellington merely thanked his troops briefly *after* the battle. As Samuel Smiles wrote in 1859:

> Napoleon's aim was 'Glory'. Wellington's watchword . . . was 'Duty'. The former word, it is said, does not once occur in his despatches; the latter often, but never accompanied by any high-sounding professions.

continued

Knowledge (Holy Trinity Church, Marylebone Rd London) Minute Books of the S.P.C.K. vol. 35 p. 133 secretary to Capt. Oliver at Shorncliffe 9 May 1809, cf vol. 36 p. 50, 15 Nov. 1811; Gurwood ed. *Dispatches of the Duke of Wellington* vol. 7 p. 231 Wellington to Henry Calvert 6 Feb. 1811.

For Methodist memoirs see amongst others B.G. *Narrative of a Private Soldier* (Glasgow 1819), the anonymous *Story of a Peninsular Veteran* (no date) and *Memoirs of a Sergeant* (1835) and John Stevenson *Soldier in Time of War* (1841). There are also of course unpublished examples, for example the memoir of an unidentifiable soldier of the 38th Regiment of Foot in the National Army Museum, Mss 7912-21.

46 Keegan *Mask of Command* p. 142.

Yet many of his soldiers remembered him appearing, neat, dapper and repressed, elegantly mounted on a man-sized hunter (not for him Napoleon's finicky little Arab steeds and sack-of-potatoes horsemanship), unperturbed by shell and shot, often addressing steadying words to the troops – 'Now, lads . . .!' And after the victory was won whereas Nelson could begin an official despatch 'Almighty God has blessed his Majesty's Arms in the late Battle', Wellington would confine himself to writing a plain chronological recital of the facts: it was he more than anyone who made understatement an English characteristic.[47]

In his attitude to his rank and file, Wellington the Perfect Englishman may have been remembering the wonderful sobriety and orderliness and phenomenal endurance of the sepoy troops he had commanded in India but he was also responding to and reinforcing a set of specifically English social attitudes. The whole European-wide crisis of the 1790s and 1800s threw open the great question of the relations between social classes, and between the individual and public authority: and obviously this question was central to the problem of how to run a large army. Yet though many of the volunteers who joined up to serve under Wellington seem to have been inspired by national sentiment and patriotic spirit these motivations were, paradoxically, given rather less emphasis in the British Army (and especially in that part of it Wellington commanded) than in the conscript armies of the Continent. Part of the British response to the ideological crisis of these years was to reinforce and refurbish the conservative values which in other countries had been more or less discredited. Wellington participated whole-heartedly in this process. A sensible and humane man, and by no means backward in complaining of the inadequacies of his social equals, he was consistently opposed to egalitarianism. He once, when praising the N.C.O.s of the Guards, said:

> They do in fact all that the commissioned officers in the Line are expected to do – and don't do. This must be as long as the present system lasts – and I am all for it – of having gentlemen for officers; you cannot require them to do many of the things that should be done. They must not speak to the men for instance [i.e. except to give orders] – we should reprimand them if they did.

The same attitude still survived as late as the Second World War; perhaps it owed its resilience to its success in the early nineteenth century.

The social and moral dividedness of British society, and *ipso facto* of the British Army, was for Wellington a basic political and military premise which

---

[47] Samuel Smiles *Self-Help; with Illustrations of Character and Conduct* (1859) p. 157; Nicolas ed. *Dispatches of Lord Viscount Nelson* vol. 3 p. 56 Nelson to St. Vincent 3 Aug. 1798. Nelson's Nile despatch was apparently modelled on Rodney's 'It has pleased God, out of his Divine Providence, to grant to his Majesty's arms a most complete victory' after the Battle of the Saints, cf [G.B.] Mundy *The Life and Correspondence of the late Admiral Lord Rodney* (2 vols 1830) vol. 2 p. 225 Rodney to Philip Stephens 14 April 1782.

Two world wars later Wellington's understatedness would be taken to its definitive level in the opaqueness of Sir Archibald Wavell.

he never cared to question, and united by a high degree of military enthusiasm, the British troops were divided in practically every other sense. The French Army, despite the contrast of the rags of the private soldiers and the gorgeous uniforms of generals loaded down with gold embroidery like footmen at a palace ball, was much more of a band of brothers. As Sir William Napier later wrote:

> Napoleon's troops fought in bright fields where every helmet caught some beams of glory, but the British soldier conquered under the cold shade of aristocracy.

Napier was himself the grandson of a duke but the difference was noted even by common soldiers:

> How different the duty of the French officers from ours. They, stimulating the men by their example, the men vociferating, each chaffing each, until they appear in a fury, shouting to the points of our bayonets. After the first huzza, the British officers, restraining their men, still as death: 'Steady, lads, steady', is all you hear, and that in an undertone.

The French spoke of '*cet affreux silence*' of Wellington's troops in action and partly perhaps it was a matter of the English style:

> In the very height of the most desperate conflict, all was cool and collected, and every officer's word could be distinctly heard, at the slightest cessation of firing.

Yet always there was that vast conceptual distance between officers and men that went far beyond either the rigid drill imposed by battlefield tactics, or the systematic investment by the officer class in 'humbling the soldiery, that it may be respected, and the convenience of the machine not clogged with the effusions of spirit or the encroachments of sense'. At the same time this essentially conservative spirit functioned in combination with a level of logistic support which was far beyond what had been achieved in eighteenth-century warfare and which only Britain's economic resources made available: the ultimate refinement of traditional modes of warfare came together with the new style of machine-economy warfare of the future:

> the soldiers are only passive instruments, wheels which must be well greased and carefully attended to, in order that the machine may produce its effect on all occasions.

Though investing, one might say, stylistically in the traditional modes, Wellington first and foremost owed his success to the completeness of his understanding of the potential and implications of the new economic era which Britain was pioneering at this time.[48]

---

[48] Stanhope *Conversations with the Duke of Wellington* p. 17, 11 Nov. 1831, cf James Lonsdale Hodson *Home Front* (1944) p. 274, diary 4 Jan. 1943: Napier *History of the War in the Peninsula* vol. 3 p. 272; *Journal of a Soldier of the Seventy-First or Glasgow Regiment* p. 132. Russell ed. *Memoirs of Thomas Moore* vol. 6 p. 137, 8 Sept. 1830; Edward Costello *Adventures*
continued

IX. Wellington's Logistics and the Logic of Success

It follows from this that it would be misleading to present a contrast between Wellington as a conservative and traditional general and Napoleon as an innovative and inspired one: the logistic framework of Napoleon's campaigns was altogether primitive compared to Wellington's. But the logistic and material context is so often underrated and misunderstood that even contemporary experts – even Wellington's own brother, the Marquess Wellesley – failed to appreciate what was going on.

Contemporaries noted for example that the dependence of Wellington's forces on their lines of supply 'renders them little capable of mobility'. Wellington himself claimed, 'It was impossible to move at all in the Peninsula without previously concerted arrangements for the supply of the troops with provisions, means of transport, &c', and when in mid-November 1812 part of his army lost touch with its supplies some of the troops actually collapsed from starvation, while others fell out to be taken prisoner by the French. Even at the moment of victory Wellington never forgot his caution. When Masséna, unable to provision his troops in Portugal in the early spring of 1811, was obliged to retreat with his starving and disorganized army, Wellington was unwilling to follow up his advantage:

> Our chief had the option of disorganising his Army by a close pursuit without supplies, which, while it could last, must have been brilliant, – or a temporary halt, foregoing the opportunity not to return but retaining his Army in discipline, supply and efficiency.

Similarly, after Waterloo he did not press too closely on the heels of the defeated French during their withdrawal into France, explaining:

> I cannot separate from my tents and my supplies. My troops must be kept and well-supplied in camp, if order and discipline are to be maintained.

But the other side of the coin was that the British troops not only suffered much less wastage but also could be kept concentrated for much longer, and one of the reasons Wellington was consistently victorious in Portugal and Spain was that the French, despite having much larger forces in the Peninsula, were never able to concentrate their full strength against him.[49]

continued
of a Soldier (2nd edit. 1852) p. 255–6 Costello 5 May 1836 (as an officer in the British Legion in the Carlist Wars Costello was comparing the discipline with that of Wellington's army); Robert Gourlay *A Specific Plan for Organising the People and for Obtaining Reform Independent of Parliament* (1809) p. 46; Foy *History of the War in the Peninsula* vol. 1 p. 157.

One notes that the simile of the machine, as applied to armies, was establishing itself in this period. Robert Jackson *Systematic View of the Formation, Discipline, and Economy of Armies* (1804) p. 22, for example, talks of artisans as best suited for 'that part of the great machine, which operates destruction, mechanically, by the use of fire arms'.

[49] Crossard *Mémoires Militaires et Historiques* vol. 4 p. 9; Stanhope *Conversations with the Duke of Wellington* p. 82 memo by Wellington for Lord Mahon 18 Sept. 1836; Earl of Longford

continued

Whereas the Anglo-Portuguese-Spanish army under Wellington's direct command did not exceed 80,000 till the 1813 campaign, the French forces probably never fell below 200,000: the peak seems to have been 291,414 present under arms in July 1811, and even in April 1812, when 27,000 men of the Imperial Guard and various Polish units had been sent to join the forces assembling for the invasion of Russia, and reinforcements had been diverted for the same purpose, the available troops still numbered 230,187. Of course the French requisitioning arrangements and the growing incidence of guerilla attacks on the French lines of communication absorbed considerable manpower and there were also Spanish armies to be dealt with in the southern and eastern provinces; but the French had the lowest opinion of both the tactical and strategic ability of the Spanish generals and fully realized that they could be defeated in detail once Wellington had been disposed of.[50]

Part of the reason why much larger French forces were never concentrated against Wellington was that the French command in Spain was never centralized. Both Napoleon and his favoured marshals seem to have had a low opinion of the military abilities of King Joseph, Napoleon's elder brother and nominee to the throne of Spain, and of his chief of staff Maréchal Jourdan, who at this stage was the only one of Napoleon's marshals not to have been at least a duke, if not a prince. In the first part of 1810 Napoleon began to make his army commanders in Spain answerable directly to himself, but though the Army of the North (Général Dorsenne) and of the Ebro (Général Reille) were never subsequently placed at Joseph's disposal, Napoleon tacitly admitted his error when in March 1812 he gave his brother the supreme command over Soult's Army of the South (56,427 men) Marmont's Army of Portugal (52,618 men), the Army of the Centre and Suchet's Army of Aragon (60,640 men). Communications with Soult were so interrupted by Spanish guerilla activity that in April 1812 'it is not known if he has been informed that the Emperor has entrusted to the King the command of his armies', but eventually Soult did cooperate with King Joseph in trying to remedy the disaster at Salamanca. Suchet on the other hand simply refused to detach any troops and continued to run his zone of operations like a private fief. It seems very unlikely however, given the general logistic problem, that Suchet's uncooperativeness made that much difference.[51]

Even before Napoleon had given his brother overall command of the various armies, Marmont, at the head of the so-called Army of Portugal,

continued
Pakenham Letters, 1800–1815 (Printed for private circulation 1914) p. 82 E.M. Pakenham to Earl of Longford 20 March 1811; Müffling *Passages in my Life* p. 251.

50 Michael Glover *Legacy of Glory: The Bonaparte Kingdom of Spain 1808–1813* (1971) p. 212 for July 1811 figure, ibid. p. 219 for troops sent to assist invasion of Russia; [E.H.] Vicomte de Grouchy ed. *Mémoires Militaires du Maréchal Jourdan* (Paris [1899]) p. 396 for April 1812 figure.

51 Grouchy ed. *Mémoires Militaires du Maréchal Jourdan* p. 387–392 and Glover *Legacy of Glory* p. 168–171, 174, 227–8; quotation is from Grouchy ed. *Mémoires Militaires du Maréchal Jourdan* p. 389.

was complaining that 'the English army is always united and ready because it has plenty of money and plenty of transport', while the Army of Portugal 'are obliged to scatter ourselves to enormous distances and to be constantly on the move to find food'. The fate of Masséna's army before the Lines of Torres Vedras a year earlier had shown what would happen if an overwhelming force attempted to remain concentrated in an area lacking provisions. In another letter Marmont reaffirmed the point:

> The English army, provided in advance with large magazines, and adequate means of transport, lives everywhere equally well; the Army of Portugal, without magazines, with little transport, without money, can only live by spreading itself out.

Jourdan, Joseph's chief of staff, agreed: 'the Imperial armies, without magazines and without means of transport, are incapable of undertaking any major operation'. Joseph did his best: at the end of May 1812 he sent Marmont two convoys of provisions, 'draining the store-houses of Madrid', but warned Marmont against expecting much more:

> the departure of these convoys has made the price of wheat go up considerably in my capital and I have the pain of hearing every day that a great number of people are dying in the streets.

Presumably these two convoys helped Marmont to pull his army together and advance to meet Wellington's troops probing from the west: and two months later he was utterly defeated and himself badly wounded at the Battle of Salamanca. Joseph fled his starving capital while Soult collected 61,000 men and moved up from the south to help restore the situation. Although the French were able to force Wellington's withdrawal from Madrid, there was no possibility of their remaining concentrated long enough, or sustaining a campaign long enough, to bring Wellington's to battle on disadvantageous terms. Quite simply Wellington's superior logistic arrangements gave him a choice of timing and placing which was denied the French.[52]

It was for this reason that, from the spring of 1811 onwards, Wellington had no wish for the size of the army under his command to be built up to the extent observers like Pasley or the Marquess Wellesley thought feasible. It is probable that the Cabinet had only the vaguest grasp of the stupendous complexity of the commissariat arrangements developed in the Peninsula under Wellington's supervision and of the additional burden in

[52] [Auguste Marmont] *Mémoires du Maréchal Duc de Raguse de 1792 à 1832* (9 vols Paris 1857) vol. 4 p. 345 Marmont to Jourdan 26 Feb. 1812; ibid. vol. 4 p. 350 same to same 2 March 1812 and cf whole section vol. 4 p. 309–356. (The French had in fact prepared magazines in 1811 but they were completely inadequate); Grouchy ed. *Mémoires Militaires du Maréchal Jourdan* p. 386–7, memo on supply difficulties 28 May 1812 (the whole memo p. 386–394 is worth study); [Marmont] *Mémoires* vol. 4 p. 391 King Joseph to Marmont 23 May 1812. See also Jean Morvan *Le Soldat Impérial* (2 vols Paris 1904) vol. 1 p. 409–422. For Joseph's government and relation with the Spanish governing classes generally see Wenceslao Ramírez, Marqués de Villa-Urrutia *El Rey José Napoleon* (Madrid 1927) p. 31–60.

pack animals and transport vehicles each additional reinforcement involved: Wellington himself claimed that 'all this difficulty in the detail was quite unknown at home'. Nevertheless key members of the Cabinet were fully aware of the general nature of the financial problems involved in overseas expeditions. When the Marquess Wellesley complained of 'the *narrow* and imperfect scale on which the efforts in the Peninsula were conducted' and 'it was always stated to him by Mr. Perceval that it *was impossible to enlarge* that system', what Perceval had in mind was simply the financial aspect. Somewhat to Wellington's annoyance he was never invited to discuss overall strategy with the ministers but he himself, from the organizational point of view, and the ministers, from the financial point of view, were anyway in approximate agreement.[53]

The financial aspect – specifically the shortage of coin and the impossibility of forcing more Exchequer Bills on the Portuguese and Spanish money markets – also explains why, having established a rather weak army in the Peninsula to face the huge French forces that were theoretically available, the ministers then sent a much larger force to waste itself in attacking Flushing.

The Flushing – or Walcheren – expedition in the autumn of 1809 was provided with £125,000 in Spanish dollars and Dutch silver ducats and was also well-supplied with food but the Commissary General was instructed to requisition money in the Netherlands in exchange for bills drawn on the British Treasury, 'without looking for further aid from this country'. Despite the government's assurance that 'we do not possess the power of sending you from hence a single foreign coin of any sort', it was soon necessary to send a further £40,000 in dollars and to insist once more on the policy of requisitioning money locally – the Earl of Chatham, commanding the expedition, seemed to think that since Middleburg and Flushing, the only Dutch towns so far occupied, had surrendered to him he was not entitled by the laws of war to extort money from the citizenry. Since Flushing had been bombarded into ruins the said citizenry were not likely to be cooperative in any case: but it is probable that if Chatham had had more speedy success and had actually occupied Antwerp, the planned objective of the expedition, he would have had much less difficulty in passing bills on the Treasury. Equally Wellington would not have been able to cash bills on the Treasury in the Peninsula, even at 25 per cent discount, if he had been defeated at Vimeiro and Talavera.[54]

[53] *Private Journal of F.S. Larpent* vol. 1 p. 157, 1 May 1813; [Melville ed.] *Wellesley Papers* vol. 2 p. 74–5 memo Feb. 1812.

[54] Marquess of Londonderry ed. *Memoirs and Correspondence* [later volumes as *Letters and Despatches*] of Viscount Castlereagh (12 vols 1845–53) vol. 6 p. 288–90 W. Huskisson to C.H. Robinson 17 July 1809 and ibid. vol. 6 p. 305 same to same 17 Aug. 1809; ibid. vol. 6 p. 304 Castlereagh to Chatham 17 Aug. 1809; ibid. vol. 6 p. 311 same to same 29 Aug. 1809 – and vol. 6 p. 314–318 C.H. Robinson to Chatham 29 Aug. 1809. For a description of the bombardment of Flushing see *Journal of a Soldier of the Seventy-First or Glasgow Regiment* p. 100–101.

There were also at this stage – the late summer of 1809 – 4,418 troops in Malta, 18,008 in Sicily and a large fleet in the Mediterranean to pay for, financed of course by bills on the Treasury but, in effect, soaking up the foreign exchange balances derived from Britain's exports in the central Mediterranean area. Britain's various military toe-holds on the continent served as points of entry into the continental markets, despite Napoleon's Continental Blockade, and the trade that was made possible helped provide the local resources required by the British occupying forces. This meant, somewhat paradoxically, that in each zone of operations the British could be concentrated under arms more easily than the French, and with less burden on the local populace, but that the overall size of the forces deployed in each theatre was subject to limits which the French tended simply not to bother with.[55]

The only other alternative to this system would have been to accept a much higher wastage of troops as a result of poorer supply arrangements, thereby necessitating conscription and a politically unacceptable interference with individual liberty and the free movement of labour within Britain, or to have mobilized even larger quantities of food and ready money in Britain for despatch abroad, which again would have involved awkward and unprecedented government interference in the economy. The balance that was evolved, without any real analysis or prevision, seems to have been perfectly adjusted to the actual requirements of the situation, though of course it did require the military talents of Wellington to ensure that there would be a strategic dividend at the end of the day.

Whereas the more ambitious but theoretically unsound strategy of Napoleon, in its *dirigisme* and its inadequate underpinning in existing infrastructures, seems symptomatic of the era of Mercantilism – Napoleon a *physiocrate* turned war-lord – the British could be said to have fought the war according to the principles of the market economy, without unified control, with all the relevant factors, all the participating sectors, left to find their own mutual relation, and with the assumption that it was possible to rely on superior skills and energies in the market place itself. As with the market economy, such a system could only be really effective in competition with less developed rivals: and just as market economy processes were bound, sooner or later to give way to a system dominated by state capitalism, so market economy warfare was forced, in the present century, to give way to the total warfare appropriate to the era of state capitalism.

---

[55] Piers Mackesy *The War in the Mediterranean, 1803–1810* (1957) p. 399 Appendix II for number of troops in Malta and Sicily.

5

Venetian Oligarchy or Vacuum

> In the midst of a delusive calm, in Peace and prosperity such as [Europe] had never yet experienced the latent seeds of change expanded themselves, and the flame burst forth with sudden and consuming fury. Those Governments upheld only by respect and usage, were rapidly levelled to the dust: Others still totter to their foundations; And none have been wholly spared however strong in the wisdom of their institutions or in the affections of their subjects.
>
> Lord Grenville, 'Commentaries of my own Political Life and of Public Transactions connected with it'. Introduction *circa* 1810. British Library, Add. 69130 p. 3–4

I. The British Political System during the French Wars

The twentieth-century world wars are still a living or at least a second-hand memory for most adults in Britain, but few of them have any idea what role the great-grandparents of their great-grandparents had in the struggle against Napoleon. We are separated from the 1800s not merely by a gap of nearly two hundred years of social and economic change but also by the resulting differences of institutions, manners and values. One can assume – not always with justification – that the political system of 1914–1918 and 1939–1945 was comprehensible in terms of that of the 1990s, perhaps differing merely in the lesser development of the pressure groups that have become stronger in our own day, or the greater influence of conventions which are now observed to be in decline. Asquith wore a lounge suit, sometimes a frock coat and striped trousers, and risked being hit by an egg: ditto John Major, or Norman Lamont. Spencer Perceval wore skin-tight leather breeches, a white neck-cloth, and a ribbon in his hair, and was shot dead with a screw-barrel flint-lock pistol in the lobby of the House of Commons, though it never occurred to his colleagues afterwards that they should provide themselves with police bodyguards. The multiplicity of such details makes the style of those days seem to our eyes picturesque, improbable and irrecoverably remote.[1]

When attempting to reconstruct the workings of a system which now seems changed beyond recognition, one has to face the further difficulty that the French Wars lasted twenty-two years, with six major changes of government. The politics of the First World War, with two changes of government in four

---

[1] *Full and Authentic Report of the Trial of John Bellingham* (1812) p. 16,66.

years, are complicated enough: the politics of the French Wars are at least three times more complicated, and much less carefully investigated by modern scholars.

As in the twentieth-century world wars, Britain was ruled by a ministerial team which depended primarily on its majority in the House of Commons, though it was a House of Commons rather different from the twentieth-century one even in its physical associations, for in those days Parliament still met in the jumble of medieval buildings that were destroyed in the fire of 1834. The supremacy of the House of Commons was both a constitutional convention dating from the seventeenth century and an eminently practical working arrangement, for the Commons provided a kind of arena for the various conflicting and competing power groupings in the country, a market where different sectors and interests could find the weight in balance of their power. Obviously these groupings did not compete on equal terms, and the identity of the groupings was different then from what it is today, but essentially the same system operates still, however much its workings are hidden within the bureaucratic mechanisms of organized national parties. The House of Commons was an arena because what happened there had a special prominence, and gave a special opportunity for talented individuals to shape and mould events; indeed events in the House of Commons absorbed the attention of the commercial organs of public opinion, newspapers and caricature prints, to a degree unequalled in the twentieth century. Nevertheless, as with any arena, what happened off-stage, out of view, was also crucially important, and to a large extent determined the range of possible on-stage events.

The forces operating through this arena may be enumerated, very crudely, as follows: the lower classes whose willing acquiescence was necessary to provide manpower for a war and whose antagonism, if too open, would mean the kind of class strife which had broken out in so many places on the continent; the middle class, who paid a lot of the taxes, constituted the bulk of the electorate (which however numbered fewer than 400,000) and whose organizational skills and managerial experience were necessary for the stability of the regime; an aristocracy, many of the richer members of which were in the House of Lords and which dominated the House of Commons either by its virtual proprietorship of rotten boroughs or by its leadership in the county constituencies; and the monarchy.

To understand the role of the Monarchy it is necessary to understand what I here call the 'aristocracy'. It was not a hereditary titled aristocracy, though there were over a thousand heads of families with hereditary titles – dukes, marquesses, earls, viscounts, barons and baronets – of which more than three-quarters, the peers of the Scots and Irish creations and the baronets, the hereditary 'Sirs', did not have a right to seats in the House of Lords. The titled families were merely the most prominent of over 12,000 armigerous families, some of which were sunk in poverty and obscurity but others of which, though boasting of no higher title than 'Mr' were masters of vast estates, great palaces, numerous retainers and widespread influence. In economic and organizational terms this aristocracy can be identified as the 'Landed Interest', at this time much the most powerful 'lobby' in the country, for the more numerous lower echelons of the Landed Interest, the tenant and yeoman farmers, to a great extent allowed their social superiors to be their spokesmen. This elite was united by a sense of itself as essentially a community of equals: they were all 'gentlemen' and made a point of knowing which of the people they had to deal with were gentlemen and which not – someone on the borderline was often described as 'a gentlemanly sort of man' – but they were also divided in part by wealth and background, even by title. Richer commoners for whom a seat in the House of Commons – perhaps even the virtual ownership of a close borough – was almost hereditary, resented the influence of members of the House of Lords over parliamentary elections, especially in the county constituencies; the elder sons of peers, recognized as being essentially the representatives of their fathers, were either traditionally confined to only one of the two seats in each county, or else excluded from the county representation altogether. The not so rich and cosmopolitan, equally, tended to resent those whose town houses in the West End and ability to afford to dress themselves *à la mode* gave them the entrée into High Society and the Court. Those immersed in local affairs, and not rich and powerful enough to exert influence beyond the village where they had their Family Seat, resented those whose careers in Westminister and Whitehall flourished amidst pensions, jobs, salaries and increased taxes. And those whose political associations prevented them from obtaining office resented those whose offices they coveted.[2]

In international affairs Britain's ultimate success in the wars with France represented the supersession of territory by money as the basis for power, but this was not especially evident in Britain's internal affairs because of the monetarization of the aristocratic economy and the integration of the monied into the landed interest. The leaders of the London money market were also frequently M.P.s, for example Sir Francis Baring, Walter Boyd, the notorious East India nabob Paul Benfield – these last two went bankrupt in somewhat discreditable circumstances in March 1800 – and later on David Ricardo, who having made a vast fortune on the Stock Exchange accepted a seat in the House of Commons as part-repayment of a debt. Out of 658 M.P.s returned in 1802, there were 124 with major business interests, 56 of them bankers; the number of businessmen fell to 112 in the Whig-sponsored General Election of 1806 and rose again to 125 in the Tory-sponsored General Election of 1807. The Toryism common amongst the emergent manufacturing interest is exemplified by Sir Robert Peel and his son, also Robert, the future Prime Minister, and

---

[2] At the beginning of the nineteenth century there were 257 English and British peers with seats in the House of Lords, 231 Scots and Irish peers entitled to elect a small number of representative peers sitting in the House of Lords, and 651 baronets, cf A.D. Harvey *Britain in the Early Nineteenth Century* (1978) p. 6 and *Debrett's Peerage of England, Scotland and Ireland* (1803) p. 963–983.

by the Preston cotton kings, John and Samuel Horrocks, but Tory politics
and diversification into land-ownership resulted in a national business lobby
being slow to emerge.[3]

By 1914 at least party politics were the result of a symbiosis of electorate and
the people they elected. If Mr. Gladstone had not existed the Victorian middle
class would have had to invent him (and indeed they produced a fair number
of *Doppelgänger*). It would not have been quite so easy for Mr. Gladstone
to have invented the Victorian middle class if it had not existed but then he
would not have seen the necessity; but since it did exist and was already
visible a generation before Gladstone was born, it was perhaps the central
fact of his career. He helped shape its views, and its political character, as it
has come down to us, is the result of a continuing dialogue between himself
and his supporters. This symbiotic process remains the essence of politics to
this day. Yet this process only became a dominant feature after the 1832
Reform Act. Wilberforce, Burdett, even Canning in his last years as M.P. for
Gladstone's home town, attempted the Gladstonian role of popular tribune,
but as M.P.s for unusually large constituencies they were an anomaly in the
pre-1832 system, and in any case neither Burdett, with his ultra-fashionable
private life and his increasing self-distancing from his electoral caucus in the
City of Westminister, nor Canning, with his long and discreditable record of
back-room intrigue, were very convincing as tribunes of the people.[4]

Before 1832 party politics were not something first produced by the
interaction of party leaders and public opinion at the national level and then
channelled through the party machines into a confrontation in Parliament,
they were something that grew out of parliamentary confrontation. The
aristocracy dominated Parliament: party politics therefore grew from within
the aristocracy.

Before 1832 the electoral system was constituted so that the government
always won General Elections. A significant number of M.P.s saw their
first allegiance as being to the government of the day, and in addition the
government had the means to acquire, by promises of favour, the nomination
of many close boroughs, as well as directly controlling a small number of
borough seats in ports like Chatham, Dover and Queenborough where the
government itself was the largest employer. Governments therefore, though
not deaf to public opinion, were in practice invulnerable to it; and the internal
groupings both within government and amongst its parliamentary opponents
had little to do with manipulations of or responses to public mood.

Government was responsible to Parliament – that is, depended on a majority
in the House of Commons where all finance legislation was initiated – but since
it always won General Elections it was clearly not appointed by Parliament. It

---

[3] R.G. Thorne ed. *The House of Commons, 1790–1820* (5 vols 1986) vol. 1 (R.G. Thorne's
Introductory Survey) p. 318 for numbers of M.P.s with business interests.

[4] John Dinwiddy 'Sir Francis Burdett and Burdettite Radicalism' *History* vol. 65 (1980)
p. 17–31 espec. p. 30–31 proposes a quite different view of Burdett's role in radical politics
but cf Harvey *Britain in the Early Nineteenth Century* p. 222–3.

was the King who appointed governments and on occasion – 1783 and 1807 – dismissed them.

Obviously the royal choice was limited by the availability and willingness of ministers to serve, and since the Commons was not organized on party lines all ministries tended to have in them an element of coalition, with the result that a poor team might have difficulty in presenting an united front, just as was later the case in France during the Third Republic. George III had sustained his right to appoint and, effectively, to dismiss his governments ever since the beginning of his reign. The one serious exception had been the Fox-North coalition of 1783 where the two dominant cliques in the Commons formed an unexpected alliance which was initially too strong for the King to resist; nevertheless he got rid of them after a few months and the survival of his nominee, William Pitt, long enough to stage the inevitably victorious General Election, sufficed to restore the royal power. During the subsequent seventeen years of Pitt's first administration, party politics, such as they were, consisted of a single party led by Charles James Fox, who claimed for themselves the exclusive denomination of *Whigs* and who agitated against what they regarded as a clique of placemen who had been thrust into office by the King, in defiance of the Foxite interpretation of the constitution. The clique of placemen for their part did not regard themselves as a party: they were simply the Ministry, the Administration, the Government. Many of their numerous supporters regarded party politics as damaging, disloyal, perhaps unconstitutional or even treasonable; for example Wilberforce, the influential M.P. for Yorkshire, thought party was 'achieving the ruin of our country' and complained that:

> half the people are employed in the very service which the worst enemies of the country would be glad to hire agents to affect – in fermenting discontent, in damping ardour, in checking public spirit.[5]

Stable government – in the twentieth century a sign of the strength and cohesion of major parties – was thus in the late eighteenth century more a sign of royal power: despite his commanding influence in the House of Commons Pitt's position was essentially that of Thugut, Haugwitz, Bernstorff or Godoy on the continent, a royal servant surviving by royal favour.

One of the paradoxes of this period, incidentally, was that the King himself was decades older than nearly all his wartime ministers. National leadership was not provided by the twentieth century's standard crew of overweight choleric sexagenarians and aged ferrets with megaphones, but by young, vigorous and ardent personalities. Pitt, who formed his first administration

---

[5] Robert Isaac Wilberforce and Samuel Wilberforce *The Life of William Wilberforce* (5 vols 1838) vol. 2 p. 452–9 undated notes 'On Party Principles' at p. 456.

The idea that parliamentary faction weakened the state had been a commonplace of English politics at least since the time of Jonathan Swift's *A Discourse of the Contests and Dissentions in Athens & Rome*, published in 1701 – see espec. chap. 5. The classic justification of party is Edmund Burke's *Thoughts on the Causes of the Present Discontents* (1770).

at the age of 24, was one of a generation of remarkably precocious talents; during the war years none of the prime ministers survived in that office over the age of fifty, excepting only the figurehead Duke of Portland, under whom the real power was wielded by men in their thirties. Even Spencer Perceval was only 49 when he was gunned down. Nelson was 47 at Trafalgar, Wellington 46 at Waterloo – come to that Byron died at 36, Jane Austen at 42, and Walter Scott, having become a best-selling and highly-acclaimed poet gave up verse to begin his second career as a novelist at 45. The classical architecture, chastened inexpressive sculpture and stilted language of the day all suggest stabilty and poise, but in the men who dominated the period one sees instead the urgent and impetuous thrust of youth, perhaps even the adolescent awkwardness, uncouthness and ardour which Gillray customarily attributed to politicians in his caricatures. And it was not always a youthfulness which burnt itself out in a short time, for Palmerston, who was offered the Chancellorship of the Exchequer in 1809, was still in office as Prime Minister 55 years later.

II. Government and Party in the 1800s

Though he was the King's nominee in 1783 and ostensibly his servant thereafter, William Pitt was no royal stooge. He was well acquainted with Bolingbroke's *Idea of a Patriot King* which is said to have formed George III's ideas of kingship, but was not particularly impressed by this treatise: his cousin Lord Grenville recalled 'I have often heard Mr. Pitt talk of Bolingbroke, but do not think he admired him much'. Though he certainly had a taste for the exercise of power, Pitt was no natural Tory. He had no interest in tradition. 'All the Roman remains among us, and whatever related to Gothic or ancient times, he held in no great respect', Grenville recollected sadly: Pitt had laughed when Grenville had tried to prevent the levelling of some Roman earthworks at Pitt's country seat. Pitt's receptiveness to new ideas, at least up to 1793, provided one of the keynotes of his government. Whereas Fox and his clique were essentially blue-blooded and objected to Pitt's dilution of the titled nobility by new creations, Pitt seemed perfectly satisfied with the social changes over which he presided, and when the Marquess of Abercorn boasted of the stately physique of members of the House of Lords, saying 'what a fine body of men the Nobility were', Pitt responded slyly, 'That may be owing to the New *Nobility*'. He even gave peerages to two bankers. Up till the 1830s middle-class Whigs were painfully aware, in their own party, of the 'patrician exclusiveness which drove Canning to adopt early the resolution of keeping clear of a party, by whose Lordly branches he foresaw he would be overshadowed', whereas Pitt had little difficulty in attracting the support of such middle-class leaders leaders of the Industrial Revolution as Sir Robert Peel and John Horrocks. Perhaps his indifference to tradition even affected his dealings with the Court. H.R.H. the Duke of Sussex was surely expressing the opinion of at least some of his brothers, if not of his father, when he said of Pitt, 'he treated the Royal Family with more disrespect than any other person has done'. It is certainly true that Pitt paid rather less deference to court etiquette than was customary:

> He has regularly been 6 weeks in London, without going to the Levee.
> A long train of this conduct has certainly in a degree estranged the King from him and induced him to think of him with less interest.

And though the King was consulted as a matter of routine on a wide range of matters, especially appointments, honours, foreign affairs and the armed forces, his influence on administration after 1783 did not increase and may even have declined; after the French Revolution began to proceed to extremes, a section of the Whig party led by the Duke of Portland moved over to support, eventually to join, Pitt's government, and this added a perceptibly anti-royalist element to Pitt's camp which was to manifest itself after 1804.[6]

At the beginning of 1801 Pitt resigned office over a policy – the question of removing the legal disabilities of the Roman Catholics in Ireland – which he had not adequately discussed beforehand with the King and which, by the time he felt committed to it, the King, spurred on surreptitiously by some of Pitt's colleagues, felt obliged to reject. Pitt had been Prime Minister for seventeen years. Although apparently at the height of his power and prestige he was ill, demoralized by eight years of largely unsuccessful war against the French, in need of a rest; George III too, disconcerted by Pitt's intermittent bursts of progressive ardour, almost certainly welcomed the chance to appoint a Prime Minister whose conservatism was more consistently reactionary. The new government, headed by Henry Addington, was principally composed of the more narrow-mindedly right-wing elements of Pitt's following, including Pitt's elder brother, the Earl of Chatham, representing the Pitt tradition, without the talent. In spite of some private grumbling, the new ministry quickly established itself in the public mind as both more personally loyal to the Sovereign and less likely to engage in elaborate and controversial reforms; to the back-woods conservative gentry and conservative middle class therefore it was a welcome change from the well-connected Smart Alecs whom Pitt had gathered round him.[7]

Although all his Cabinet colleagues were in the House of Lords, Addington himself was the first British Prime Minister to have come from the professional

---

[6] Samuel Rogers *Recollections* (1859) p. 177; ibid. p. 189; Kenneth Garlick, Angus Macintyre, Kathryn Cave ed. *The Diary of Joseph Farington* (16 vols New Haven 1978–1984) vol. 6 p. 2436, 7 Nov. 1804; Lord John Russell ed. *Memoirs, Journal, and Correspondence of Thomas Moore* (8 vols 1853–6) vol. 7 p. 80, diary 5 March 1835; Garlick et al. ed. *Diary of Joseph Farington* vol. 7 p. 2703, 26 Match 1806; Richard Willis 'William Pitt's Resignation in 1801: Re-examination and Document' *Bulletin of the Institute of Historical Research* vol. 44 (1971) p. 239–257 at p. 256 (memo by Earl Camden).

The two bankers ennobled by Pitt were Robert Smith, created Lord Carrington, and Robert Isaac Thellusson, created Lord Rendlesham in the Irish peerage.

[7] G.C. Lewis *Essays on the Administrations of Great Britain from 1783 to 1830* (1864) p. 275.

middle class rather than from the land-owning oligarchy, and however much it recommended him to the bourgeoisie and minor gentry, being the son of a doctor was not a recommendation in the eyes of the social groups which dominated politics. As soon as Addington's appointment was announced Henry Dundas, the Secretary of State for War in the out-going ministry, wrote to Pitt:

> all the aristocracy of the Country at present cordially connected with Government and part of it under you, feel a degradation in the first minister of the Country being selected from a Person of the Description of Mr. Addington without the smallest pretension to justify it and destitute of abilities to carry it on.

It was later said:

> his ministry was the subject of ridicule with the fashionable part of London society: or as old Lord Liverpool described and pronounced it, the *biumond* . . .

Some of Pitt's younger adherents even made use of the malicious nick-name 'The Doctor'; Addington was depicted as a doctor in a caricature by C. Williams ('The Doctor administering his gilded pill') as early as March 1802.[8]

Addington was brought down by the same means as had disposed of the Earl of Shelburne in 1783: an unexpected alliance between previously opposed factions. The difference was that in 1804, unlike in 1783, one of these factions, that led by Pitt, was perfectly willing to sell out the other. Or at least Pitt himself was; many of his most influential supporters, including his cousin and former chief lieutenant Lord Grenville, who had gone further than Pitt in establishing a tactical alliance with Fox, felt obliged to insist on Fox's inclusion in a new ministry. The idea was for a no-party government united simply on the basis of pursuing the war against Napoleon. George III's idea of a no-party government was a government with nobody in it who had ever acted in a party against him. Pitt therefore formed an administration without Fox but also without Lord Grenville and his followers, including two former cabinet ministers of the Duke of Portland's group, Earl Spencer and William Windham, and also without a small back-woods rump consisting of Addington and some friends and relations who thought Park Lane had had an illegitimate revenge on the country's first bourgeois premier. Addington was not happy in opposition; for a few months he rejoined the Pitt camp, till driven out again by the attitude of Pitt and of the other ministers, notably his own former

---

[8] Public Record Office P.R.O. 30/8/157 f. 258 Dundas to Pitt 7 Feb. 1801: [H.R.V.] Lord Holland *Memoirs of the Whig Party during my Time* ed. Lord Stavordale (2 vols 1852–4) vol. 1 p. 191.

Pitt incidentally had been characterized as a doctor in a Cruikshank print of 1795: this eventually became a commonplace of political caricature.

The ground covered in the next three paragraphs is explored in greater detail in Harvey *Britain in the Early Nineteenth Century* p. 115–219.

Foreign Secretary Lord Hawkesbury, who after working to reconcile Pitt
and Addington had inexplicably turned against the latter. Then, in January
1806, Pitt died; Hawkesbury and the other ministers felt unable to continue
on their own, and Lord Grenville finally had his chance to form a no-party
government, the Ministry of All the Talents.

Partly due to the rush of events, partly due to the influence of Fox and
Addington – now Viscount Sidmouth and a member of the new coalition –
and partly due to their increasing opposition to his policies, Grenville failed
to find room in his Ministry of All the Talents for anybody who had actually
been in office when Pitt had died, other than the distinctly untalented Lord
Charles Spencer, whose continuance on the public pay-roll was desirable to
secure the support of his brother the Duke of Marlborough. Despite the
usual government success in the General Election held a few months after
taking office, Grenville resigned, after only fourteen months of coalition, for
exactly the same reason he had resigned along with Pitt six years previously:
the question of removing the legal disabilities of the Catholics in Ireland.

The new government which replaced the Ministry of All the Talents was
composed of the men who had felt too weak to form a government in January
1806. They 'held their places less by their own strength than by the weakness
of their opponents, for of all administrations, that to which they succeeded had
been the least popular'. Although generally seen as a much more of a party
government than any ministry since the 1780s, even more than Addington
in 1801 the new ministers gained popular credit for championing the King
and opposing un-English, un-Protestant reforms like Catholic Relief: indeed
it is arguable that the General Election they fought in the late spring of
1807, with the aim of undoing the result of the General Election staged by
Grenville's ministers during the previous autumn, was more influenced by
public opinion than any previous one, though of course behind-the-scenes
organization was the crucial element in ousting most of the new M.P.s brought
in by the Ministry of All the Talents. Nevertheless it was not an entirely
reactionary regime: half the new ministers actually favoured Catholic Relief
as a matter of private opinion and merely opposed forcing such a policy
on the reluctant King. Canning, the Foreign Secretary, was the brightest of
Pitt's former protégés and though, at this stage at least, mainly interested in
exercising his own ego and his taste for intrigue, responded not unfavourably
to progressive causes – and was none too keen on George III's prerogative.
The Duke of Portland, the Prime Minister – 24 years previously he had been
nominal head of the Fox-North Coalition and had later led the secession from
the Foxite Whig party to join Pitt's ministry in 1794 – had been notably
open-minded in his handling of working class unrest in the late 1790s, when
he had been Home Secretary.[9]

---

[9] They 'held their places less by their own strength . . .' is quoted from Robert Southey
History of the Peninsular War (3 vols 1823–32) vol. 1 p. 53. Portland's career at the Home
Office can be partially studied in Public Record Office HO 42/32–55.

But the fatal illness of the Duke of Portland, and the intrigues of Canning, his duel with Lord Castlereagh and the two men's resignations, caused this already weak ministry to shed much of its ministerial strength in the autumn of 1809. It struggled on under the uncharismatic Spencer Perceval, 'a short, spare, pale-faced, hard, keen, sour-looking man, with a voice well-suited to the rest', as Cobbett described him, until March 1812 when the return to office of Castlereagh and of Sidmouth and his group provided the first significant reinforcement to the government's essentially pragmatic and conservative character. As Prime Minister Spencer Perceval had steered the government with extraordinary firmness and courage, though without flair, through all the various storms since 1809: ' "He is not", said Mr. Grattan, "a ship-of-the-line, but he carries many guns, is tight built, and is out in all weathers" '. But on 11 May 1812 he was shot dead by John Bellingham, a deranged bankrupt who had gone to the House of Commons to shoot someone important by way of protesting at his bankruptcy. This event provoked extraordinary outbursts of lower-class jubilation: at Nottingham the populace paraded with flags and drums in celebration, and Bellingham was hanged to shouts of 'God bless you, God Almighty bless you'. The former Lord Hawkesbury, who had inherited the title of Earl of Liverpool, took over as Prime Minister. Wordsworth, by no means an ill-informed commentator, had no high opinion of the new government, referring to it as 'weak in parliament, but strong enough to keep things going in a languid and uninterrupted course', but in the event, Liverpool, with Lord Castlereagh as Foreign Secretary and leader of the House of Commons – his viscountcy was a courtesy title – soon established themselves as a convincing ministerial team, and of course benefited from the gathering pace of Wellington's success in the Peninsula: together they led the country for nearly ten years.[10]

After leaving office in March 1807 Lord Grenville settled down with reluctance to leading a parliamentary opposition. Fox had died the previous autumn – a few months after achieving office after twenty-two years in opposition – and his death had widened an already apparent gap between the aristocratic, socially conservative wing of his party and its more populist, democratic, perhaps demogogic, element. His death also meant that there was no senior opposition figure capable of leading the party in the House of Commons. The result was that the opposition, though much more numerous in Parliament than ever before despite government successes in the 1807 General Election, was also much more disunited, and internal conflicts increased the already detectable reluctance of Lord Grenville and of Earl Grey, the leading

[10] William Cobbett *History of the Regency and Reign of King George the Fourth* (2 vols 1830–34) vol. 1 chap. II para. 77; [H.R.V.] Lord Holland *Further Memoirs of the Whig Party, 1807–1821* ed. Lord Stavordale (1905) p. 133, referring to the Irish M.P. Henry Grattan; Cobbett *History of the Regency* vol. 1 chap. III para. 132 and Frank Peel *The Rising of the Luddites Chartists and Plug Drawers* (Brighouse 1895) p. 156–7; Ernest de Selincourt, Chester L. Shaver, Mary Moorman, Alan G. Hill ed. *The Letters of William and Dorothy Wordsworth* (7 vols Oxford 1967–88) vol. 3 p. 21 Wordsworth to Catherine Clarkson 4 June 1812.

figure amongst Fox's former following, to take office. When George III succumbed to mental disorder at the end of 1810 they had a chance of returning to power because of the Prince of Wales's becoming Regent; but the Prince of Wales, formerly a friend of Fox's, was cooling with regard to Foxite policies and allowed Grenville's and Grey's undiplomatic, uncompromising stance to persuade him to defer turning the government over to them. A year later, in February 1812, and again after the assassination of Perceval in May 1812, they were offered a chance to share in a coalition ministry which they probably could have dominated, but they turned the proposal down, essentially on points of form. The fact was they had little interest in office.

They also had little interest in opposition. Though as late as 1804 one former follower of Edmund Burke could describe Party as 'the Soul of our Constitution' public acceptance of party opposition continued to decline. It was perhaps natural that a ministerialist pamphleteer should claim that 'PARTY and CABAL are more injurious to this country than the sword of Buonaparte', and not particularly surprising that Wellington should write to his Tory elder brother William Wellesley-Pole:

> I have never felt any inclination to dive deeply in party politicks; I may be wrong but the conviction of my mind is that all the misfortunes of the present reign, the loss of America, the success of the French Revolution &c &c are to be attributed in great degree to the Spirit of Party in England.

But it was a reformer who wrote:

> By internal dissentions the independence of a country is imminently endangered, for domestic feuds unnerve the body politic ... England in particular has endured much injury from the strife of her parties.

Lord Grenville himself was all too aware of the 'odium and perhaps the self reproach, that must attend a harassing opposition in a moment when the *struggle for existence* is no longer a façon de parler but a very weak mode of expressing the real and present danger', and told Lord Grey:

> The present circumstances and temper of the Country seem to render the pursuit of minute and harassing opposition less justifiable in itself and less creditable to those engaged in it than ever.

He also thought that party rivalry played into the hands of the King:

> disunion of Public Men not only undermines their own authority, and diminishes the resources of their Country, but tends also to establish in the Crown an uncontroulable preponderance of Power.[11]

[11] Northamptonshire Record Office Milton Ms 64 Earl of Carnarvon to Earl Fitzwilliam 8 Feb. 1804; *The Fallen Angels: A Brief Review of the Measures of the late Administration* (1807) p. 5; Charles Webster ed. *Some Letters of the Duke of Wellington to his Brother William Wellesley-Pole* (Camden Miscellany XVII. Camden Society 3rd series LXXIX) (1948) p. 26–7 Wellington to Wellesley-Pole 22 Oct. 1809; *Reasoner* 30 June 1808, letter signed 'One of the
continued

The overall picture then is that while the French Revolutionary War in the 1790s was fought by Britain under a strongly supported government with an opposition in increasing disarray, but on the European mainland at least was a series of disasters, the Napoleonic War in the 1800s was fought much more successfully, even when Britain was entirely or mainly without allies, under a succession of progressively weaker and more discredited ministries, while the opposition, instead of gaining in relative credit from the weakness of the government, contrived to decline in reputation, unity and influence, and in fact in every element of strength save mere numbers. A series of sleazy scandals, commencing in 1805 with the impeachment of Lord Melville for conniving at embezzlement while Treasurer of the Navy in the 1790s and climaxing in 1809 with the investigation of H.R.H. the Duke of York for abuses in the allocation of military commissions, merely advertized the opposition leaders' inability to keep a grip on their followers. The investigation of the Duke of York case and of the Earl of Chatham's abortive Walcheren expedition – the latter enquiry moved by Lord Porchester 'to prove the incapacity and total want of system, that pervades all the military measures of his Majesty's ministers' – and crucially important select committees such as those on the Resumption of Cash Payments and the Orders in Council imposing the counter-blockade of the continent – were dominated by back-benchers and suggest, superficially, a move towards a Commons-dominated government (as distinct from a government-dominated Commons) something like the later *Chambre*-dominated governments of the French Third Republic; but this was only a temporary phase resulting from ministerial weakness. While government spending and employment under government were reaching unprecedented levels the governmental system itself, insofar as it had a foundation in Parliament, was in visible decline: 'held together by reciprocal weakness, a most harmonious band has been formed, under which our listless country marches on to its fate,' as one pamphleteer sneered. Even Lord Grenville admitted:

> The pressure of taxation excites among the middling classes on whom it necessarily falls with greatest weight, a general sourness & discontent – not so much directed against particular persons or measures, as against the general system of Government to which they attribute their distress.

Though in the 1790s Pitt had achieved, perhaps not altogether deservedly, an aura of leadership that justified Canning's song in his honour, 'The Pilot that weather'd the Storm', his eventual successors who led the country to final victory seemed to have a much less firm grip on the tiller and were so far

continued
People' dated 28 Jun. 1808; British Library Add. 41852 f. 345–6 Grenville to Thomas Grenville 13 Dec. 1807; Grey Mss. Durham University, Grenville to Grey 20 Dec. 1808; British Library, Add. 69132 'Commentaries of my own Political Life and of Public Transactions connected with it' chap. 1, p. 54–5, dated 26 Aug. 1810.

from being admired that shortly before the news came of Napoleon's return from Elba they were having their windows broken by angry mobs.[12]

III. The Structure of Public Opinion

As already suggested, great leaders have a symbiotic relationship with the public mood they channel or represent, a symbiotic relationship (more pervasive and exhilarating than the mechanical symbiosis of organized party politics) which resembles that of those artists whose great contemporary success involves a reshaping of cultural horizons. The late sixteenth century was moulded as much by Elizabeth as by Shakespeare, the nineteenth century as much by Gladstone as by Dickens: each generation bears the impress of its political myths as much as its literary ones. The 1800s however had no politically mythic figure at their centre: only at the peripheries. One can see the necessary relationship between national leadership and public opinion being invigorated and tightened up under Pitt in the 1790s, but after his death – in fact even before his death – one finds the political leadership of the country, the whole life and involvements of the political arena, moving increasingly out of synchronization with public attitudes to the wars and to the question of national mobilization. Pitt, who owed much of his wartime prestige to his pre-war successes, can only very approximately be seen as the counterpart of Lloyd George or Churchill in the twentieth-century world wars, and in the symbolic sense the war ministries after 1803 did not provide war leadership at all. They merely held office, fumbled with the levers of power and, as the public were resentfully aware, drew enormous salaries.

It was not that the ministers were uninterested in public opinion – at least at a theoretical level. William Windham, who served under both Pitt and Grenville thought:

Mankind has never yet been in circumstances that enabled the mass of them to judge correctly of any thing that required much mental exertion.

But even the effusions of ignorance were not to be ignored. The Excise Riots of 1733, the Wilkes Riots of 1768, the Gordon Riots of 1780 had long since taught the politicians not to ignore the public mood, and events on the continent from 1789 onward necessarily reinforced this sensitivity; as Burke wrote in 1794:

Opinion (never without its effect) has obtained a greater dominion over human affairs than ever it possessed and ... must grow just in proportion as the implicit reverence for old institutions is found to decline.

[12] *Parliamentary Debates* vol. 15 col. 161 speeches by Lord Porchester 26 Jan. 1810; Robert Gourlay *Letter to the Earl of Kellie, concerning the Farmers' Income Tax* (1808) p. 62; British Library Add. 59226 f. 5–6 Lord Grenville's journal 22 May 1809. For the window breaking see *Annual Register* 1815 Chronicle p. 23: Bathurst the Secretary of State for War had his windows in Mansfield St. Portland Place broken on 7 March 1815 and Castlereagh, the Foreign Secretary, had his broken in St. Jame's Square the following day: the provocation was the discussion in Parliament of the Corn Laws.

It was the heyday of the political caricature, and the works of James Gillray, Thomas Rowlandson and Isaac Cruikshank, with their monstrous outspokenness, exuberant clutter of detail and anarchic humour, suggest an established audience of considerable sophistication. Newspapers were increasing their circulation, much to the alarm of some of the upper classes:

> He was not complaining of gentlemen for saying the war was unjust and unnecessary: if they thought so they were right in so saying. But was it a desirable thing that the public at large, that the lower classes of the community from one end of the Kingdom to the other, should, from day to day be told so?

But apart from prosecuting a hundred or so extremists for sedition in the 1790s there was not much the authorities could do to prevent the free circulation of opinion, especially when an attempt to prosecute radical reform leaders for High Treason failed ignominiously. Public meetings were becoming more numerous – the Duke of York scandal in 1809 provoked over seventy county or municipal meetings to vote thanks to his accuser, Colonel Wardle. The Volunteers offered new social and even political roles for thousands of squires, small farmers and tradesmen:

> Persons of rank and prosperity mingle with manufacturers and mechanics ... ready to repress internal tumult and to guard our shores against the approach of the foe.

In 1803 there were 379,943 men enrolled in the Volunteers and Yeomanry. It was not merely that in 'this most momentous crisis ... in any Man capable of bearing Arms, whatever be his Profession, supineness must be deemed a Crime'. The notion that the vast social and psychological energies unleashed by the French Revolution could only be confronted successfully by a national mobilization that was no less all-embracing – a notion which became a commonplace amongst German nationalists after 1807 – had been formulated by British observers in the 1790s:

> Let our governors, let every man in the kingdom, that does not look forward to anarchy with pleasure reflect on the consequence of opposing the arms of France by a mere regular army, instead of rising in a mass and opposing torrent with torrent. Wherever the faithless foe has prevailed, she has had only an army to fight with – never a people. What man, that carries the heart of a man in his bosom, can bear without indignation, to see the idling crowds that fill our public places – to see Bond Street thronged with loungers, at such a moment as this?

But there was always the danger that a mobilized populace might choose a direction of its own.[13]

---

[13] *Parliamentary History* vol. 34 col. 162 speech by Windham 31 Dec. 1798; R.B. McDowell ed. *The Correspondence of Edmund Burke* (9 vols Cambridge 1958–70) vol. 8 p. 36 Burke to Windham 16 Oct. 1794; *Parliamentary Papers* 1826–7 XVII p. 24; *Parliamentary History* vol. 34 col. 161, speech by Windham 31 Dec. 1798; George Gaskin *Christian Patriotism: a Sermon, delivered in the Parish-Church of Stoke-Newington, in the County of Middlesex, on occasion*
continued

Commentators were proud to explain the essential unity of society, despite the prevailing disparities of wealth:

> The insensible gradation of ranks, the mutual dependence of the aristocracy and their inferiors, arising from the peculiar nature of our government, diffuses widely the influence of public opinion, and binds the nation into an united mass, by the firm chain of reciprocal good offices. Hence it is, that the law, which in other countries seldom obtains more than a reluctant obedience, or, at best, a cold acquiescence, is here the object of zealous and affectionate support from the great mass of the nation.

That was the theory. In practice public opinion could have no direct effect on the parliamentary seats of the vast majority of politicians and there seemed to be no real idea of what to do about organizing public support: perhaps it was not even perceived to be particularly the government's business. John Reeves, later the King's Printer, seems to have taken the initiative in launching his Loyalist Association movement late in 1792; between November 1792 and February 1793 over a thousand of these associations were formed, nearly ten times as many as the local reform societies affiliated to the London Corresponding Society, which also belong to this period. Already the majority of local authorities had organized addresses of loyalty to the Crown, and there is a paper preserved in the Home Office in-files in the Public Record Office, drawn up by the Under-Secretary of State in the Home Department and bearing the possibly sinister caption 'Counties, Cities and Towns from whence Addresses have *not* been received. 10ᵗʰ Septemʳ, 1792'. Examination of this document gives a possible clue to why the government did not persevere with the monitoring of local opinion: among the 'Counties, Cities and Towns from whence Addresses have *not* been received' were Cumberland and Westmorland (both completely under the thumb of one of Pitt's key allies, the rotten-borough-mongering Sir James Lowther), St. Mawes (a rotten borough in Cornwall owned by Pitt's cousin and supporter the Marquis of Buckingham, head of the Grenville clan), Montgomery and Denbigh (effectively under the control of Buckingham's and Lord Grenville's sister Lady Williams Wynn during the minority of her son Sir Watkin Williams Wynn), and Dover and Queenborough (rotten boroughs controlled by the Admiralty).[14]

continued
of the Attendance of the Armed Association of Stoke-Newington, and its Vicinity, at Divine Service, on Sunday, October 21, 1798 (1798) p. 20; *Parliamentary Papers* 1803–4 XI p. 3 and see J.E. Cookson 'The English Volunteers in the French Wars, 1793–1815. Some Contexts' *Historical Journal* 32 (1989) 867–892; British Library Add. 59292 f. 44 William Freeman to Lord Grenville 12 July 1803; Arthur Young *An Enquiry into the State of the Public Mind amongst the Lower Classes* (1798) p. 35 fn.

14 Earl of Selkirk *On the Necessity of a More Effectual System of National Defence, and the means of establishing the Permanent Security of the Kingdom* (1808) p. 37; Robert R. Dozier *For King, Constitution and Country: the English Loyalists and the French Revolution*
continued

The whole issue of popular loyalism has received little more systematic attention from recent scholarship than it obtained at the time. There are a number of books on the radical reform movements of the day, of which E.P. Thompson's *The Making of the English Working Class* of 1963 remains much the best known; but the amount written about the reform movements, and indeed the intrinsic interest of the subject has led to a major distortion of perspective. The largest of the reform associations, the London Corresponding Society, never had more than 4,000 members and seems to have had almost no presence amongt the working-class population of London's East End. The largest provincial societies were those of Norwich and Sheffield: at the end of 1795 Norwich produced 5,284 signatures on a petition against the so-called Pitt and Grenville Acts which forbad public meetings of more than 50 persons. Bath, a considerably smaller town, had produced 5,033 signatures on a Loyalist Association resolution a couple of years earlier and even small centres like St. Albans and Canterbury could manage loyalist petitions with well over a thousand signatures. Claims of much larger numbers involved in reform meetings have been too credulously believed: the London Corresponding Society claimed that 'upwards of Two Hundred Thousand Citizens' attended a rally in Copenhagen Fields, in the general area of what is now Camden Road, London, on 12 November 1795, but a caricature of the scene by Gillray actually suggests a rather meagre crowd; the most careful account of this meeting specifically takes issue with the London Corresponding Society's exaggerated claims:

> You may have seen in the papers of prodigious numbers being at the meeting – This is not true in the sense such accounts w^d be understood – In the course of the day many thousands were doubtless in the field; but never at one time. – I was there between 2 & 3 & I don't believe there were 500 in the field, & I saw it at the fullest time as far as I can understand.

The opponents of reform and French ideas had numbers as well as patronage and property on their side: in Lancashire a petition in support of the Pitt and Grenville Acts obtained 7,351 signatures, that opposing only 4,303; and at Manchester when two rival town meetings were held to discuss the new legislation on 7 December 1795, the loyalists moved on to break up the much weaker anti-government meeting, capturing the anti-government petition and burning it triumphantly at the Market Cross. Though the most famous loyalist, or 'Church and King', riot was that in Birmingham in 1791, well before the outbreak of war, such occurrences continued throughout the 1790s (John Bohstedt has counted eleven, 1790–1810). There were also disturbances directed against the homes of individuals who did not illuminate their

continued

(Lexington 1983) p. 61–2 and Harry T. Dickinson 'Popular Loyalism in Britain in the 1790s' in Eckhart Hellmuth ed. *The Transformation of Political Culture: England and Germany in the Late Eighteenth Century* (1990) p. 503–533, espec. p. 517–523. (Reeves' papers relating to the Association movement are in the British Library Add. 16919–16928); Public Record Office HO 42/21/474–5 paper by Evan Nepean, the then Under-Secretary in the Home Department.

house-fronts to celebrate British victories – illuminations, from a single candle in the window to elaborate transparencies for those who could afford them, were the customary mode of celebrating major public events; and while in the early evening respectable cits would promenade to view the illuminations by the end of the evening the streets would be given over to the rampaging of drunken and frequently violent gangs, lineal ancestors of today's Cup Final hooligans. One substantial disturbance was directed against a leading reform propagandist, John Thelwall, when he came to Derby in 1797 to address a meeting held in a Baptist chapel:

> a mob collected in the street with drums, horns, &c ... broke the windows, wounded several persons with bricks and stones, and threatened to destroy the chapel. Thelwall, with a pistol in his hand, declared he would shoot any person who molested him: in consequence of which he was suffered to depart without receiving any injury.

This was one of Thelwall's finer moments: from what one knows of him the pistol was almost certainly unloaded.[15]

Apart from some behind-the-scenes encouragement of the Loyalist Associations in 1792–1793 and the later adoption of the Volunteer movement, the government did little to sponsor manifestations of popular support. The procession to St. Paul's on 19 December 1797, on the occasion of the National Thanksgiving, was the nearest thing in this period to a victory parade, but it was on a very economical scale: 250 naval ratings and marines took part. The illuminations and in rural areas the feasting and bonfires which greeted the official announcement of victories overseas were all the result of simultaneous initiatives by private individuals; the largest programme of coordinated celebrations, the King's Jubilee in the autumn of 1809, was organized by the obscurest of private individuals, a Mrs. R.C. Biggs, and had almost nothing to do with the ministry, which at that point seemed on the verge of collapse.[16]

While it is obviously true that a society lacking the twentieth century's

[15] *Proceedings and Speeches at the Meeting the Seventeenth November 1795, at St. Andrew's Hall, Norwich* (Norwich 1795) p. 24; cf Dozier *For King, Constitution and Country* p. 63. Gillray's 'Copenhagen House', dated 16 Nov. 1795 is No. 8685 in M.D. George's *Catalogue of Political and Personal Satires in the British Museum* (vol. 7 p. 199–200). The description of the Copenhagen Fields meeting is from National Library of Wales Harpton Court Mss C/334, Frankland to sister 16 Nov. 1795: a longer extract of this letter is given in Harvey *Britain in the Early Nineteenth Century* p. 82 and cf Albert Goodwin *The Friends of Liberty* (1979) p. 391 fn. where Goodwin admits that claims that 400,000 people attended this meeting must have been exaggerated; John Bohstedt *Riots and Community Politics in England and Wales, 1790–1810* (Cambridge Mass. 1983) p. 120–122 and p. 14 Table 1; *Annual Register* 1797 Chronicle p. 15–16.

[16] Linda Colley 'The Apotheosis of George III: Royalty and the British Nation' *Past and Present* no. 102 (1984) p. 94–129 at p. 109–110 for victory parades, p. 112 for Mrs. R.C. Biggs, cf p. 112 fn. 59 where Ms Colley suggests that Mrs. R.C. Bigg's correspondence with Windham represented a contact with government despite the fact that Windham was a leader of the opposition.

mass-media technology was limited in what it could do in the way of centralized propaganda, much less effort was made in this direction than in Revolutionary and Napoleonic France. Even without loudpeakers it was possible to hold very large public rallies. The two largest in wartime Britain were parades of Volunteers in Hyde Park to be reviewed by George III. On the King's Birthday on 4 June 1799 8,200 men of various London Volunteer Corps – including the Loyal Hackney and Loyal Pimlico Corps – were paraded in the presence of a crowd estimated at 150,000 people. An even larger audience witnessed the review of 12,401 Volunteers on 26 October 1803:

> It presented the sublime spectacle of a Patriotic Monarch, who reigns no less distinguished in the hearts of his people than on his throne, meeting the brave citizens of his Metropolis, armed in defence of his Crown and of the British Constitution, and, with the characteristic virtue of the sons of Albion, resolved to continue free, or gloriously to fall with the liberty and independence of their country.

This gathering was however distinctly less imposing than a review held by Napoleon on 16 August 1804 when troops assigned to the conquest of England were assembled in a shallow natural amphitheatre outside Boulogne. There was a band of two thousand drums and an immense concourse of civilians is said to have surrounded the site beyond the ranks of the soldiers (though it is difficult to say where they can have come from and only a few small groups are depicted in the most readily available contemporary prints). There were certainly 80,000 troops and they responded with immense enthusiasm to Napoleon's call:

> Commanders, officers, Legionaries of Honour, citizens, soldiers; swear upon you honour to devote yourselves to the service of the Empire – to the preservation of the integrity of the French territory – to the defence of the Emperor, of the laws of the Republic, and of the property which they have made sacred.

The massed phalanxes of the soldiers yelled back in unison '*Nous jurons!*' waved their shakos and bearskins on the end of their fixed bayonets, and shouted '*Vive l'Empereur!*' A distribution of crosses of the *Légion d'Honneur* followed; the throne of Dagobert had been brought from Paris for the Emperor to sit upon and the crosses for distribution were laid out in helmets and on shields which had supposedly belonged to du Guesclin and Bayard. Despite this slightly confusing symbolism the whole affair seems considerably closer to the iconography of the Nuremberg Rallies than did George III's decorous reviews of amateur soldiers in Hyde Park.[17]

[17] *Gentleman's Magazine* vol. 69 (1799) p. 518–520 cf *Annual Register* 1799 Chronicle p. 22–3; *Gentleman's Magazine* vol. 73 (1803) p. 974–7 at p. 975: *Annual Register* 1803 p. 446–450 prints the same account; Fernand Nicolay *Napoleon at the Boulogne Camp* (1907) p. 298–306 and cf illustration in Jean Mistler ed. *Napoleon* (2 vols Paris 1968) vol. 2 p. 39; Louis Antoine Fauvelet de Bourrienne *Memoirs of Napoleon Bonaparte* ed. R.W. Phipps (4 vols New York 1906) vol. 2 p. 354–5.

IV. George III as National Symbol

It was George III nevertheless who became increasingly the focus of patriotic enthusiasm in Britain. He had been by no means popular in his early days, and as late as 1788 Sir Gilbert Elliot thought that during the constitutional crisis brought on by the King's mental illness people were more anxious about whether Pitt would stay in office than about whether the King would recover:

> Pitt is the only object the nation can perceive and the only thing they can think valuable in the world; and I rather think they would be content and pleased to set aside the whole Royal Family, with the Crown and both Houses of Parliament, if they could keep him by it.

Yet when Pitt and George III came to the parting of their ways in 1801 it was Pitt's reputation that suffered: 'Mr. Pitt is very like Bonaparte, allways restless & not knowing what he would be at', as one countryman remarked. Royalty had made an astonishing come-back.[18]

There are several reasons for this. One reason was simply a growing campaign of propaganda, though to see this propaganda as a sufficient explanation in itself is to beg the questions, why the propaganda and why was George III the subject of it. The initiative for this propaganda came not from the Court or from the government but from middle-class enthusiasts expressing an attitude that must already have existed at least amongst their own acquaintances, and from businessmen and commercial publicists who had correctly identified a promising market: thus the anthem 'God Save the King', rarely performed in theatres before the early 1780s, became a customary part of the repertoire by 1800, evidently because theatre managers thought it was what their audiences wanted. A second reason was the conservative cause underlying the whole sequence of wars against France: despite the relative indifference of the government on this point these wars were most easily to be understood and marketed as wars of legitimacy, religion and morality, and of all these things George III was an obvious symbol. He also gained much public sympathy from his problems with his spendthrift eldest son, though efforts were made to cover up many of the details of what was in many ways a rather bizarre family circle; it was said for example that Queen Charlotte was afraid to be left alone with her husband and that:

> Mr. Pitt, and the Lord Chancellor, having a strong desire to make the King and the Royal Family appear to the people to be in the best possible state, have remonstrated powerfully with the Queen on the subject.

George III's loyalty to traditional values was also highlighted by one of the

---

[18] [Emma] Countess of Minto *Life and Letters of Gilbert Elliot, First Earl of Minto from 1751 to 1806* (3 vols 1874) vol. 1 p. 248, Gilbert Elliott letter to wife 18 Dec. 1788, cf Colley 'Apotheosis of George III' *Past and Present* no. 102 p. 102–104; Devonshire Record Office Addington Papers 152,/C1804 OZ Nathaniel Bond to Addington 23 May 1804.

issues involved in his dispute with Pitt over Catholic Relief in 1801; much play was made with his Coronation Oath 'to maintain to the utmost of his power the true profession of the Gospel, and the Protestant reformed religion established by law'. One reformer claimed:

> that the king was bound by the English parliament, and that the English parliament could again set him free: – it was a mere conditional oath; and a thing only lasting while the party for whose protection it was made were willing that it should last.

But people who had been able to forgive Pitt his young man's involvement with Parliamentary Reform could not forgive his disloyalty to the Protestant Establishment, which was one of the key elements in the self-image of the eighteenth-century Englishman, and the ventilation of the Catholic Relief issue persuaded many observers to see the King as a more reliable guardian of the established order than a corrupt House of Commons controlled by parliamentary dictators.[19]

This brings us to the third and most interesting cause of George III's increasing prestige: he undoubtedly benefited from the diminishing credibility of his governments. This was recognized even during the final weeks of the Addington ministry in the spring of 1804, when one M.P. wrote:

> The power of the King not of the Crown though that is also extremely increased is far beyond what any Sovereign has possessed since the days of Elizabeth.

Whatever might be thought about the extent and proper delimitations of the King's role in government, the fact that he did have a role made him a fixed point of reference when party and faction squabbles put the rest of the system in flux. Although behind-the-scenes consultation and confidential partisanship were as much a feature of the 1800s as the 1760s, George III came to be seen as outside and above – possibly even threatened by – party politics rather than an illicit participant as he had seemed in the 1760s: he himself complained of Pitt's attempt to reshuffle Addington's cabinet in 1803, 'He desires to put the Crown in commission – he carries his plan of removal so extremely far and high that it might reach me'. Addington's resignation in May 1804 was seen as necessary to spare the King 'the outrage of having a Minister forced upon him rudely and violently, to the degradation of royalty'. The notion of 'forcing a Minister on the King' as something to be avoided at all costs

[19] Colley 'Apotheosis of George III' *Past and Present* no. 102 p. 102–103 for 'God Save the King', p. 112–6 for commercial mechanisms; Garlick et al. eds. *Diary of Joseph Farington* vol. 6 p. 2449, 20 Nov. 1804 gossip recounted by Thomas Lawrence (the reason for the Queen's nervousness probably related to George III's psychiatric problems); Robert Gourlay *A Specifiec Plan for Organising the People and for Obtaining Reform Independent of Parliament* (1809) p. 145. For the importance of the Coronation Oath cf G.F.A. Best 'The Protestant Constitution and its Supporters, 1800–1829' *Transactions of the Royal Historical Society* 5th series no. 8 (1958) p. 105–127 at p. 115–7. A distinction between government in general and a particular ministry appears at least as far back as Walpole's time, cf *The Craftsman* no. 121, 26 Oct. 1728 (vol. 3 p. 209 of 14 vol London 1731–1737 edit.)

became one of the shibboleths of the next few years; at the same time, as the governments became weaker they found it necessary to give more emphasis to their possession of royal favour and when in October 1809 Spencer Perceval was forming his ministry he freely acknowledged that:

> the principle upon which we must rely to keep us together, and to give us the assistance of floating strength, is the public sentiment of loyalty and attachment to the King.[20]

As well as providing a rallying point and a tactical weapon for the conservative side in the internecine strife between the various parliamentary factions, and a simple and convenient political platform to be publicized in the daily press for the benefit of a readership sensitized by a decade of shocking news from the capitals of Europe, the King and his constitutional role became increasingly popular with the outsiders who were beginning to force their way into politics. When, after 1807, lower-class radicalism revived, disillusion with the Foxite Whig share in the unreforming Ministry of All the Talents of 1806–1807 prevented the new wave of reformers from taking Foxite views as a starting point for their own. In rejecting the Foxite tradition, they rejected the Foxite self-presentation as champions of the People against the usurpations of the Crown:

> no part of the cant of the times seems to me more hypocritical than the declamation of party men against what they call the 'overwhelming influence of the Crown' when ... it is by the House of Commons alone that the Constitution is subverted, the prerogative of the Crown usurped, and the rights of the people trampled upon.

Many of those who rejected the aristocratical parties began to look to the King both as a national leader of more legitimate standing than the parliamentary leaders and as a fellow victim of the encroachments of aristocratic faction. A distinction began to be perceived between 'bad ministers' and the King in whose name they pretended to govern:

> they would shrink behind the Throne, and represent those who were dissatisfied with their conduct, and dared to speak out, as hostile to the Government, and unfriendly to the established order of things.

Even the Spenceans, who later plotted to murder the entire Cabinet, preached the doctrine that

> Both King and people now find themselves paralized and subjected to one of the most unfeeling powers that can exist, namely an oligarchy that degrades the crown by granting or withholding at their pleasure, and questioning, calling

---

[20] National Library of Wales NLW 4814D Williams Wynn and Southey Mss Charles Watkin Williams Wynn to Robert Southey 4 April 1804; Earl Stanhope *Life of the Right Honourable William Pitt* (4 vols 1862) vol. 4 p. 36–7; [Charles] Lord Colchester ed. *Diary and Correspondence of Charles Abbot, Lord Colchester* (3 vols 1861) vol. 1 p. 501; E. Phipps ed. *Memoirs of the Political and Literary Life of Robert Plumer Ward* (2 vols 1850) vol. 1 p. 259 Perceval to Lord Melville 5 Oct. 1809.

upon, and compelling its agents to account for every shilling in its expenditure; while they engross, possess, and enjoy the country, uncontrolled and unlimited in their acquisitions.

It is worth recalling that in Sweden, after Britain the European country most advanced towards parliamentarianism, the assassination of King Gustav III Adolf, the classic assassination of the Baroque period, was instigated by an aristocratic clique who hoped thereby to recover their privileges, and who were foiled by the masses rallying to the Crown: this as recently as 1792.[21]

The timing of these developments was also important: the war and revelations of scandals in the administration of the national war machine, and the succession of opportunist coalitions in Parliament after 1801, helped focus public attention on the political system just when it was showing up least creditably. In 1816 William Cobbett wrote:

> I will engage that there is not, even amongst the lowest of the people, a single man now to be found in England, who would not laugh to scorn any attempt to make him believe that one of the *parties* is better than the other . . . it was the disclosures made from 1805 to 1809, inclusive, that procured us this great and permanent good.

For a few years at least the King remained as the one stable point in public life. Moreover professions of loyalty to the King served as an admission ticket to the game of politics for the newly politicized. Violent attacks on 'those who fatten on corruption' could be joined to remarks such as:

> for the tranquillity which we have enjoyed in very critical times, we are in a great degree indebted to the sense which the nation at large has entertained of the private virtues of our beloved sovereign.

This was guaranteed to earn loud cheers. The middle classes were tired of the governing elite but had their own vested interest in not overthrowing the social system: George III was the symbol of that system, in contradistinction to the politicians who were simply exploiting it. In one of his innumerable uncompleted drafts, Jeremy Bentham proposed to discuss the 'Inconsistency of King-worship with the acknowledged end of Government' in terms of the survival of idol-worship and the force of custom, but this may have missed the whole point about the novel conditions of the time. What Linda Colley has called 'The Apotheosis of George III' was not entirely 'the process of state-nationalization of nationalism' resulting from the ministers'

[21] [Thomas] Earl of Dundonald *The Autobiography of a Seaman* (2 vols 1860) vol. 2 p. 263 speech by Lord Cochrane to electors of Westminster, 1812; *Star* 10 Jan. 1810 p. 2b, speech of Mr. Favell in Common Hall, London (i.e. the lower chamber of the City of London's municipal council) 9 Jan. 1810; Thomas Evans *Christian Policy the Salvation of the Empire* (2nd edit. 1816) p. 22–3 (Evans himself was not involved in the Cato Street Conspiracy to murder the Cabinet, but he was the main ideologue of the movement). For the popular reaction to the assassination of Gustav III Adolf see Robert Liston's despatches from Stockholm, Public Record Office FO 73/13, 23 March, 20 and 24 April 1792.

Thatcherite recognition of 'the value of royal ceremonial as an anodyne to national discontent': it was also in part a transitional mode of expressing that discontent.[22]

V. Alternative Symbols

Though George III symbolized British unity and will to victory as much as Lloyd George in 1917–1918 or Winston Churchill in 1940–1941, he was not the only symbol and when after 1810 he was confined as a madman at Windsor Castle, his son the Prince Regent failed to step fully into his position, yet without leaving any sensible psychological gap.

If frequency of depiction in political caricatures was any criterion one might suppose that George III was actually a less popular figure than William Pitt in the first half of the war period. In 1798 for example George III featured in 26 British prints preserved in the Print Room of the British Museum whereas Pitt featured in 46; but of course being caricatured is not necessarily a sign of esteem – Napoleon was soon an even more frequent subject – and in any case Pitt's active political involvements provided more themes for illustration than the quiet routine of the King's life. It was noticeable however that after Pitt's death no other British politician came near to rivalling the frequency with which he had been caricatured. One figure that did become extraordinarily popular at this period had only notional existence: the archetypal figure of John Bull. In 1798 he had tailed behind the King, featuring in only 21 British caricatures. In 1803, when Pitt was out of office and therefore of reduced topicality, he features in 12 caricatures, the King in 25, and John Bull in 67 (in three of these the King is actually depicted as John Bull). This was the year in which the war was renewed, and Britain confronted the threat of invasion, badly prepared and without allies; perhaps in this sudden emphasis on John Bull, the representative authentic English citizen, one may see one more sign

---

[22] *Cobbett's Political Register* vol. 30 col. 360 Letter V to the People of the United States of America, 23 March 1816; Berkshire Record Office D/EPb 025 f. 30 report of speech of Col. George Williams of the Liverpool Volunteers at a public dinner 21 April 1809; University College, London, Bentham Papers CXXVIII p. 75, September 1809; Colley 'Apotheosis of George III' *Past and Present* no. 102 p. 106, 109, 111.

Jeremy Bentham blamed George III for personally blocking his Panopticon (model prison) scheme which was favoured by Pitt and Henry Dundas: he thought the King had 'vowed revenge' on him because of his part in the *Letters of Anti-Machiavel* attacking British policy with regard to Denmark and the Russo-Swedish War in 1789: John Bowring ed. *The Works of Jeremy Bentham* (11 vols 1843) vol. 11 p. 97. By overrating his own importance in the King's eyes, Bentham overrated the active role of the King in this period. His notes written in 1831 for a 'History of the War, between J.B. & G.3, Marginalized by A.M.' [i.e. with marginal notes by Anti-Machiavel] are in the British Library, Add. 33550 f. 365 foll; it seems from f. 366 that after forty years he remembered the war at issue to be the Russo-Turkish one that led to the Oczakov crisis in 1791.

of a turning away from the traditional political leadership, as if it was felt to be inadequate to the requirements of the moment.

After Pitt's death a curious parallel to the nation's rallying round the ageing King was provided by the attempts of a section of Pitt's former supporters to rally round the memory of their dead leader. The first meeting of his partisans after the formation of the Ministry of All the Talents decided to oppose the government on 'any measures brought forward by them either in derogation from Mr. Pitt's system, or in discredit of his memory'. Later Lord Grenville confessed that he could not be satisfied while 'Pitt's best friends' were estranged from him and attempted to recruit George Canning into his ministry. Faced with the need to choose the best person to bring with him into a broader coalition ministry, Canning decided that the first criterion to consider was 'Who would carry most of *Pitt*?' After the Talents were dismissed, Pitt Clubs were opened in many cities as foci for loyalist organizations. That in London, founded in 1808, had 1,300 members by 1816, in which year there were also at least 35 provincial clubs. Dinners had been held annually since 1802 to celebrate Pitt's birthday; the verses Walter Scott wrote in 1814 'For the Anniversary Meeting of the Pitt Club of Scotland' included the lines:

> Not the fate of Europe could bend his proud spirit
> To take for his country the safety of shame;
> O, then in her triumph remember his merit
> And hallow the goblet that flows to his name.

Ten days after Pitt's death there were references to 'the late Mr. Pitt's party' but at that stage it might have been difficult to find an alternative designation; more than three years later an intriguing reference to 'The Court and Pitt's ghost parties' indicates that an alternative designation still had not emerged. (Pitt's ghost occasionally features in caricatures after 1806.) When struggling to form his Cabinet in the autumn of 1809 Spencer Perceval confessed, 'We are no longer the sole representatives of Mr. Pitt. The magic of that name is in a great degree dissolved'. But not every one thought so. Walter Scott could still write of 'the large and sound party who profess *Pittism*' and remarked, 'It is astonishing how the loss of one man has deranged the wisdom and disorganized the force of this mighty people'. On the eleventh anniversary of Pitt's death Scott exclaimed 'How we want Billie Pitt now to get up and give the tone to our feelings and opinions!' Nearly five years later, when Lord Grenville's nephews Charles Williams Wynn and the second Marquis of Buckingham threw in their lot with the Earl of Liverpool's government, *The Courier*, a leading ministerialist newspaper, announced the 'RE-UNION OF THE OLD PITT PARTY' and Canning's associate William Huskisson, though displeased, felt obliged to accept the alliance as 'an arrangement which brings together Pitt's Friends and followers'. Had he lived beyond his forty-seventh year Pitt would have undoubtedly continued to dominate British politics but perhaps this cult of his memory had less to do with a psychological gap left by his premature demise than with the requirements of political myth-making at a time of ideological uncertainty.[23]

And yet despite the uncertainty the image presented by the national leadership, for all its insubstantiality, had a coherence, an inevitableness, an avoidance of contradictions, that was not to be achieved in the twentieth-century world wars. Perhaps it was something to do with a narrower range of conceptual possibilities. Britain was led during this crisis by a hereditary elite presiding over a society the structure and values of which were only just beginning to be questioned. Part of the weakness of Pitt's position was that he had encouraged this questioning: equally part of the glamour of the Duke of Wellington was his success in brushing such issues aside. In a sense there could be no Lloyd George or Winston Churchill in the wars against Napoleon, because there was no such need for a political magician able to reconcile contradictions: what was appropriate was the colossal self-assurance of the English *milord*.

VI. The War and the Established Order

Compared to 1914–1918 and 1939–1945 one may be astonished how little Britain's institutions reorganized themselves to meet the challenge of war in the years 1793 to 1815.

The formal division of the Cabinet into an Inner or War Cabinet and the official Cabinet, which was a feature of the British government during the twentieth-century world wars, was rendered unnecessary during the French Wars because the Cabinet had not yet completely evolved as a board transacting its most onerous duties jointly. During the American war ineffectual ministers tended to shelter behind the joint decisions of an ineffectual and divided Cabinet but this mode of doing business became rare after 1783. According to surviving papers in the Windsor Archives there were between February 1793 and December 1797 only *twelve* Cabinet meetings of which the conclusions were communicated to the King in a formal minute written by Pitt; these related to such matters as occupying the Dutch

---

23 Nottingham University, Portland Mss, Canning to Lord Titchfield 20 April 1806; Harewood Mss, Leeds Public Library, Canning to Joan Canning 27 Feb. 1807: this letter has been inaccurately quoted and wrongly interpreted in Julian R. McQuiston 'Rose and Canning in Opposition, 1806–1807' *Historical Journal* 14 (1971) p. 503–527 at p. 521, cf A.D. Harvey 'The Grenville Party, 1801–26' Cambridge University Ph.D. dissertation 1972 p. 204 fn. 1; J.J. Sack 'The Memory of Burke and the Memory of Pitt: English Conservatism Confronts its Past, 1806–1829' *Historical Journal* vol. 30 (1987) p. 623–640 at p. 635; Phipps *Memoirs of Robert Plumer Ward* vol. 1 p. 259 Perceval to Melville, 5 Oct. 1809; H.J.C. Grierson ed. *The Letters of Sir Walter Scott* (12 vols 1932–7) vol. 2 p. 268 Scott to George Ellis 3 Nov. 1809; ibid. vol. 2 p. 336 Scott to Thomas Scott 13 May 1810; ibid. vol. 4 p. 384 Scott to J.B.S. Morritt 31 Jan. 1817; *Courier* 17 Dec. 1821; British Library Add. 38743 f. 58 William Huskisson to Lord Binning 6 Dec. 1821 copy.

colonies, sending the Foot Guards to the West Indies, and entering into peace negotiations with the French Republic. Later on the sudden death of two prime ministers in office, in 1806 and 1812, resulted in the Cabinet ministers conferring together before deciding to resign. But no system had yet evolved of circulating papers, not all ministers saw material that was passed on to certain outsiders; the offices of Lord President of the Council and Lord Privy Seal were regarded as honourable make-weights and the holders of these offices rarely contributed more than verbally. (The Earl of Westmorland was Lord Privy Seal for 29 years, with a 14-month break in 1806–1807, yet one almost never encounters a letter from him amongst the papers of his colleagues.) The real decision-making was left to a group of two or three ministers. The longest-enduring and seemingly most logical team was that of Prime Minister (Pitt), Secretary of State for the Foreign Department (Lord Grenville) and Secretary of State for the War and Colonial Department (Henry Dundas) between 1793 and 1801. The holders of the same three offices also managed the strategy of the Ministry of All the Talents. In the Duke of Portland's ministry which followed, the Prime Minister's infirm health prevented him from taking a prominent part in the leadership of his government. It was explained:

> There never can be the sort of acquiescence amongst us in control as there was naturally and necessarily to Mr. Pitt. Mr. Pitt ... had himself such comprehensive talents and powers that he was himself essentially the Government in all its departments ... But the present Government is constituted with so many of equal or nearly equal pretensions that it ... must, to a great degree, be and remain a Government of departments. It is not because the Duke of Portland is at our head that the Government is a Government of departments: it is because the Government is and must be essentially a Government of Departments that the Duke of Portland is at our head.

Nevertheless this Cabinet exercised more joint supervision of individual members than hitherto – Canning as Foreign Secretary had his despatches discussed and amended in Cabinet, as also happened with his successor, the Marquess Wellesley, in the Perceval Cabinet. But there was no attempt to establish the Cabinet as a forum for the discussions of long- or even medium-term strategy and the Foreign Secretary (Canning) and War and Colonial Secretary (Castlereagh), without progressing beyond a rather chilly relationship, were left to arrange matters between them. This ancephalous system progressed one stage further under Perceval, who was too involved in raising the finance for the war and battling for his government's survival in the House of Commons to be able to give much attention to external affairs.[24]

---

[24] Arthur Aspinall ed. *The Later Correspondence of George III* (5 vols Cambridge 1962–70) vol. 2 prints 12 Cabinet minutes from the period February 1793 to December 1797, though there are two more to be found in British Library Add. 59306, one dated 17 April 1793 and the other 14 January 1796: Aspinall's third volume covering the years 1798, 1799 and 1800

continued

Nor was there any significant development of administrative apparatus below Cabinet level. Compared to foreign governments the British central civil service was tiny. By 1814 there were 1,500 officials in the Paris offices of the Ministry of War and its off-shoot the Ministry of War Administration, though not all of them were very efficient: chef de brigade Villot de la Tour had been promoted to général de brigade in May 1793 but still had not been told of his promotion by the time he retired from the Army in 1811, and in the early days of revolutionary egalitarianism Jean Méquillet was promoted to général de division on the strength of his brother's dossier and then suspended when his brother was sacked for wearing epaulettes. At the same period however there were precisely *six* clerks in the War and Colonial Department in London and perhaps 150 distributed between the War Office (under the Secretary at War), the Horse Guards and the Ordnance Board. Coleridge's prophetic complaint, in his poem 'Fears in Solitude', written in 1798:

> All individual dignity and power
> Engulfed in courts, committees, institutions,
> Associations and societies

was not as yet quite justified as far as Britain was concerned.[25]

The weakness of the ministry and of its administrative apparatus meant that it was not able to use the emergency conditions of war to increase its authority at the expense of the House of Commons. Instead the House of Commons increased *its* power because of the war. Public interest and concern justified an ever increasing circulation of printed returns and statistics that had been called for by M.P.s. Committees of Enquiry were established, to investigate spending on barracks, the navy, sinecures – no war was ever fought in which its administration was subject to so much hostile enquiry. One minister – Viscount Melville, the former Henry Dundas – was impeached, that is, prosecuted in the House of Lords by a committee of the House of Commons. The Commons, sitting as a Committee of the Whole House, investigated – and publicized – the sex life of the commander-in-chief of the Army in 1809 and the bungling of the Walcheren expedition in 1810. But just as, through a concatenation of personal circumstances, the lack of the right man at the right time, the government was never able to use the war to establish a moral ascendancy of leadership in the country, so equally

continued
prints 19 minutes. British Library Add. 59306 contains Lord Grenville's Cabinet papers for the period 1791–1807, including items variously endorsed 'Read at the Cabinet' 'Note for Cabinet' 'Read & approved at the Cabinet' 'for circulation'. For the Earl of Westmorland, christened by Canning 'le sot privé' because of his intemperate habits, see letters to the Earl of Chatham in Public Record Office PRO 30/8/369; for the quotation concerning the Duke of Portland see Spencer Walpole *The Life of the Right Hon. S. Perceval* (2 vols 1874) vol. 2 p. 16 fn. Perceval to Huskisson 21 Aug. 1809.

25 C.H. Church *Revolution and Red Tape: The French Ministerial Bureaucracy, 1770–1850* (Oxford 1981) p. 270; Georges Six *Les Généraux de la Revolution et de l'Empire* (Lyon 1947) p. 11 and p. 11 fn. 2; [P.H.] Earl Stanhope *Notes of Conversations with the Duke of Wellington, 1831–1851* (1888) p. 85, 10 Oct. 1836.

the opposition in the Commons failed to produce a popular tribune who could in any way claim to represent a united public opinion against the maladministration of the office-holders. Fox, dismayed by his loss of voting strength when the Duke of Portland's group defected to the government in 1794, finally decided in 1797 to boycott the Commons just at the moment when the failure of Pitt's schemes laid him perhaps most open to criticism. The united assaults of Fox, Pitt and Windham on Addington in 1804 were felt to be justified by Addington's inadequacy but otherwise to reflect poorly on his critics' integrity. After 1807 the opposition simply lacked a spokesman in the Commons behind whom it was possible to unite, and indeed the greatest success of the Commons against the ministry, the exposure of the Duke of York's malfeasance as commander-in-chief, was stage-managed by a maverick of no standing within the opposition counsels, Gwyllym Lloyd Wardle.[26]

Though this weakness at the controlling centre had the effect of strengthening the prestige of George III, the latter was essentially passive in this process, and with his final mental collapse and withdrawal from public view at the end of 1810 the central role of monarchy was over. His eldest son George, Prince of Wales, now Prince Regent, represented with his voluptuousness, indebtedness and deceit too much the mirror opposite of what his father had stood for, and though quick-minded, clever and perceptive was too indecisive, too inconsistent, too compromised by a multitude of shabby arrangements in his past, to be able to intimidate his ministers as his father had done. They needed each other, that was all. Especially while the war lasted, the Prince Regent seemed an anomalous figure, serving mainly to advertize the too luxurious undergrowth of British eccentricity. And though the ministers prosecuted Leigh Hunt for alluding to the Prince Regent as 'a fat Adonis of forty', they could not make him popular; at the time of the state visit of the Allied Sovereigns to London in 1814 it was said that the Regent 'lives only by protection of his visitors. If he is caught alone, nothing can equal the exercrations of the people who recognize him'.[27]

Inevitably the armed forces increased their visible presence in society at this period: after all there was a war on. With the calling out of the Militia and the raising of the Volunteers Britain became physically much more militarized than at any time since the 1640s. Jane Austen, whose novels tend to provide the most durable images of social life in England in this period, seems to have almost made a point of under-representing this aspect. There was an efflorescence of captains and majors at all social gatherings, and of red coats in the streets. As in the Mississippi valley after the American Civil War 'captain' became the customary title of professional gamblers, and for the want of an adequate police force the posting of military sentries increased: in London there were 159 sentries regularly posted in 1794 and 236 ten years later.

[26] Cf. Harvey *Britain in the Early Nineteenth Century* for a more detailed discussion of the events referred to in this paragraph.

[27] Herbert Maxwell *The Creevey Papers: Correspondence & Diaries of the late Thomas Creevey, M.P.* (2 vols 1903) vol. 1 p. 196 Creevey to Eleanor Creevey 14 June 1814.

(They were mostly in the neighbourhood of the royal palaces but the Bank of England had four, and the British Museum also had four sentries from 1807 onwards.) Victories abroad were announced by the firing of artillery salutes, and by 1813, with the French being pushed back both in Spain and Germany, these salutes became a frequent occurrence: 'Our ears are now so accustomed to the sound of the Park and Tower guns that they scarcely startle us', wrote one young man. It gave people something to gossip about in their letters: 'The guns are now firing – what that can be for, I have no guess but hope to find out before I send this'.[28]

The Royal Navy, with a relatively small officer corps dominated by career officers of relatively middle-class background, remained a subject of sentimental idolization, yet essentially marginal to the main current of political life, but in the Army the system of purchasing rank, which did not operate in the Navy, meant that the upper reaches of the Army were well populated with peers and blue-blooded M.P.s and this contributed as much as anything to the failure of the Army to establish an independent influence. It was so similar to the traditional civilian society in its class structure that it manifested exactly the same features as political society. It was impossible to imagine British colonels launching a rebellion to depose the King, as happened in Sweden in 1809. Junior officers of the less fashionable regiments might immerse themselves in the minutiae of rank and precedence; on board a transport en route for Spain, it was recorded:

> A young officer had just taken possession of a birth, which he was preparing to occupy, when a brother of the profession came up and asked him the date of his commission. Upon being informed of which, he laid claim to the birth, as being the senior. The army list was referred to, and he was found entitled to precedence – his commission bearing date one day previous to that of the other.

But officers with hereditary titles used their titles rather than their army ranks: Wellington was known throughout his army as *The Marquess*, and at Waterloo, after another promotion in the peerage, he was *The Duke*. (Compare Ronald H. Laverton's pot-boiler study of the G.O.C.-in-C. of the British Expeditionary Force in 1940, *General Gort*, which omits all mention of the general's viscountcy.) The squabbles amongst army officers, and the competition for preference, had exactly the same characteristics as amongst civilians. The classic picture of toadies and job-hunters hanging around the

---

[28] A.D. Harvey *English Literature and the Great War with France* (1981) p. 9. Warren Roberts *Jane Austen and the French Revolution* (1979) p. 68–108 and espec. p. 96–105 suggests that Jane Austen's original readers would have recognized the concealed references to the war in *Pride and Prejudice* and *Mansfield Park* but it is debatable that they either would have done or would have cared: and the deliberate omissions (e.g. of references to the Yeomanry) are more striking than the perhaps unintentional intrusions; for posting of sentries cf *Parliamentary Papers* 1816 XII p. 412–3; for artillery salutes Harriot Georgina Mundy ed. *The Journal of Mary Frampton* (1885) p. 167 G.B. Wollaston to Mary Frampton Nov. 1813; ibid. p. 181 Georgina Vernon to Mary Frampton 10 April 1814.

ante rooms of the great in civil life was reproduced even at Wellington's H.Q. in Spain:

> The officers in the lower branches of the staff are sharp set, hungry, and anxious to get on, and make the most of everything, and have a view even in their civilities . . . there is much obsequious time-serving conduct to any one who is in office or is thought to have a word to say to Lord Wellington.

Despite the successful regimentation of the rank and file, the officer corps had not yet become properly professional. Wellington more than once complained of the poor quality of his officers and Sir John Moore was positively monotonous on the subject:

> The force I have is great, but is so crippled from the want of proper people either to command the different regiments or direct the departments, that the number of troops rather tends to cause embarrassment . . . The person immediately junior to me, instead of being an assistance, was a man so completely absurd and wrong-headed that I dreaded leaving the fort, though my presence in the country was necessary . . .
>
> Since I have been in the West Indies I have observed so little system, such neglect in the higher orders, and such relaxation in the lower, neither zeal nor spirit anywhere, that I am convinced the sooner we make peace the better. Against the spirit and enterprise of the Republic we have no chance. . . .
>
> The composition of the officers is horrid . . . The military spirit is now, I think, gone. The officers wish to be advanced, to get more pay and have less duty. I see none, or at least very few, who have the smallest ambition to distinguish themselves. Little can be expected by officers formed and led by such officers. They neither look up to them as officers or respect them as gentlemen.

Another general was afraid to make an unconditional offer to serve wherever he was assigned: 'such an offer would infallibly subject me to obey those of my seniors, whom I might think, neither from their private or public character, safe to act with'. On the other hand genuine professionalism was not always appreciated, as Wellington recalled in 1826:

> An Indian victory was not only no ground of confidence, but it was actually a cause of suspicion . . . Moreover they looked upon me with a kind of jealousy, because I was a lord's son, '*a sprig of nobility*' who had come into the army more for ornament than use. They could not believe I was a tolerable regimental officer.

And even Wellington had problems with the politicking of his senior officers: Lord Charles Stewart, Viscount Castlereagh's brother, he found 'a sad *brouillon* and mischief-maker'; of Robert Craufurd, one of his ablest divisional commanders, he said, 'Poor Craufurd was a dissatisfied, troublesome man, who fell quite naturally into this sort of intrigue, and I believe he pushed it to a very blameable extent'. Earlier, in the Egyptian campaign, the death from wounds of Sir Ralph Abercromby, the commander and only lieutenant-general with the army, was followed by an attempt by most of the major-generals to dictate the conduct of the campaign to the new commander-in-chief, the Hon. John Hely-Hutchinson, a military eccentric of Dickensian rather than Montgomerian proportions; only the refusal of Moore to participate scotched this intrigue. And though there was much less of the bitterness derived from faction politics that characterized the American War, the suspicion provoked by the Foxite politics of Abercromby, Hutchinson and Moore undoubtedly contributed to their professional difficulties.[29]

Abuses in the system of commissions and promotions and the revelation of H.R.H. the Duke of York's connivance in Mary Anne Clarke's trade in cut-price commissions led eventually to the biggest public scandal of the period; an early salvo in this controversy, Denis Hogan's *An Appeal to the Public and a Farewell Address to the Army* of 1808 went through nine editions in a few months and provoked at least four lengthy replies and of course the whole business was a gift to the caricaturists, who indeed had begun hinting at the scandal as early as June 1807. The military secretary of H.R.H. the Duke of Kent, the Duke of York's disgruntled younger brother, may have been involved in stirring things up. (Another of the King's military sons, H.R.H. the Duke of Cumberland was the target of Henry Foskett's *The Rights of the Army Vindicated: in an Appeal to the Public*, which went through two editions in 1811; the public tendency to sentimentalize the King certainly did nothing for his too numerous offspring.) But junior officers in the regular Army at least had the possibility of escaping bad feeling by exchanging into another regiment: this was hardly possible for militia officers who wanted to serve in their local units, amongst friends and neighbours. Positioned uneasily between the civilian and the professional, the Militia provided some curious illustrations of the psychic strains involved in subordinating the English gentleman to professional norms. Even before the outbreak of war and the embodiment of the Militia the parliamentary reformer John Cartwright – known throughout his career as *Major* Cartwright – had published *A Letter to the Duke of Newcastle . . . Respecting his Grace's Conduct in the Disposal of Commissions in the Militia*, in which he claimed that when he was passed over for promotion after attending a dinner commemmorating the Glorious Revolution of 1688, this represented the *fifth* time officers had been promoted over his head. A rather pointless quarto pamphlet of 1797, *The Present State*

[29] John Malcolm 'Reminiscences of a Campaign in the Pyreness and South of France in 1814' *Constables's Miscellany* vol. 27 (1828) p. 235–307 at p. 237; George Larpent ed. *The Private Journal of F.S. Larpent, Esq.* (3 vols 1853) vol. 1 p. 110; J.F. Maurice ed. *The Diary of Sir John Moore* (2 vols 1904) vol. 1 p. 223 (2 July 1796) p. 232 (8 July 1796) p. 236–7 (31 Aug. 1796), while commanding at St. Lucia; [Richard] Duke of Buckingham *Memoirs of the Court and Cabinets of George the Third* (4 vols 1853–5) vol. 3 p. 8, Lieutenant-General J.G. Simcoe to Marquis of Buckingham 2 Jan. 1800; Louis J. Jennings ed. *The Croker Papers: The Correspondence and Diaries of the late Right Honourable John Wilson Croker* (3 vols 1884) vol. 1 p. 342; ibid. vol. 1 p. 346–7; Henry Bunbury *Narratives of Some Passages in the Great War with France from 1799 to 1810* (1854) p. 128 and fn. for the American War see Piers Mackesy *The War for America, 1775–1783* (1964) p. 7–12, 243–5.

of the Dorsetshire Militia, edited anonymously by George Pitt, Lord Rivers, was evidently provoked by something more substantial than it reveals. Lord Rivers, who had previously come before the public with his *Letters to a Young Nobleman, upon various subjects, particularly on Government and Civil Liberty*, on this occasion published the letter he had written to Major the Hon. George Pitt in September 1793 advising him 'as your friend, your colonel and your father' to desist from parading his contempt for their regimental adjutant; the captains of the regiment after studying this letter, wrote to deny that the Hon. George had behaved incorrectly to the said adjutant: the resultant correspondence included a letter of 15 printed pages from Lord Rivers to the captains, dated 31 October 1793; then, after a respite, the controversy was resumed on the initiative of Lord Rivers's busy-body cousin, William Morton Pitt, and included a letter of 17 printed pages from Lord Rivers to William Morton Pitt, dated 30 April 1795. Evidently part of the problem in the Dorsetshire Militia was that the pen was not less mighty than the sword. A militia adjutant was also the alleged victim in a court-martial held at Berwick in September 1810: Major John Gordon of the Aberdeenshire Militia was charged with attempting 'in gratification of spite . . . to injure the professional character of the Adjutant in the opinion of the Generals' and of trying 'to deter some of the Adjutant's most approved friends among the officers from continuing to associate with him on an intimate footing'. The Major was acquitted. *The Correspondence of John Thomas Stanley, Esq. with the Earl of Stamford* (Chester 1798) related to something possibly more serious: Major Stanley of the Cheshire Militia had refused to sign a return showing children training to be drummer boys as effectives on the strength of the regiment, and Colonel Lord Grey, son of the Earl of Stamford, Lord Lieutenant of Cheshire, had never forgiven him for this, and subsequently promoted one Captain Parker to the vacant lieutenant-colonelcy over Stanley's head, whereupon Stanley resigned, urging, 'I am sure the case in question is without a precedent, but were it not so, one Act of Injustice could not justify another'. There was also bad blood in the West Essex militia between Lieutenant-Colonel J.H. Strutt on the one hand and Colonel Sir William Smyth and Major Swallow on the other. Clausewitz's axiom, that war is the continuation of politics by other means, evidently had a very special meaning in a country like Britain that was so successful in holding the war at a safe distance: the only militia troops that ever served abroad against the French were units from Buckinghamshire and Denbighshire which arrived in southern France just after Napoleon's first abdication.[30]

[30] For replies to Hogan see *A Full and Impartial Examination of 'An Appeal to the Public'*, *A Letter to Brevet Major Hogan, upon his extraordinary 'appeal'. A Short English Answer to a Long Irish Story* and Patrick Blake's *A Word to the British Army, in consequence of Mr. Hogan's pamphlet*; George, *Catalogue of Political and Personal Satires* no. 10740 Cruikshank's 'Military Leap Frog 5 June 1807' and No. 10741 William's 'The Discarded Clark' June 1807 (both vol. 8 p. 540); Mary Anne Clarke *The Rival Princes* (2 vols 1810) passim and Arthur Aspinall ed. *The Correspondence of George Prince of Wales, 1770–1812* (8 vols 1963–71) vol. 6 p. 498 Duke
continued

VII. The War and National Consensus

In more indirect ways, of course, the war had an enormous and pervasive effect. It was perhaps the most important and certainly the most strikingly obvious event in a period of major social change. By generating price increases, hastening the decay of certain productive sectors and helping to focus Establishment repression of political dissent the war contributed both to the immiseration of the working classes and the marginalization of key elements of middle-class opinion. But the reformist groups who complained of the connection between hostility to the French Revolution abroad and repression of reformism at home were always a minority, and not always a very credit-worthy one. By 1797, when the war was going badly, the national finances had almost collapsed and the fleet had mutinied, it did begin to seem that the war was harmful to society as a whole, and William Morgan, an actuary, made a considerable noise with a series of pamphlets arguing that the war was rapidly impoverishing the country. Yet from at least 1800 onwards too many people found, from their own experience, that the exact opposite was the case, and opposition to the war as such, though widespread, never became general.[31]

In 1803, even more than in 1793, there was a prevailing sense of the necessity of the war against France. This impression had worn off somewhat by 1807; the Ministry of All the Talents had attempted to negotiate with Napoleon during 1806 and certain prominent Foxites thought that further efforts should be made. A campaign to end the war began to organize itself; despite an emphasis in the propaganda on the economic burden of the war it seems that this movement was based less on the economic self-interest of those whose business was harmed by the war than on the increasing strength and self-confidence of the commercial middle classes, who, as they throve in wartime boom conditions, became ever more hostile to the corruption and inefficiency of the traditional political order which was running the war. The anti-war campaign was in effect simply another aspect of the tension between newly emergent political classes and an increasingly discredited aristocratic regime.

As anti-war feeling channelled itself into the agitation against the Orders in Council restraining belligerent trade during 1811 and 1812, a prominent

continued
of Kent to Maria Anne Fitzherbert 18 Dec. 1809; John Cartwright *A Letter to the Duke of Newcastle . . . Respecting his Grace's Conduct in the Disposal of Commissions in the Militia* (1972) p. 51; *Star* 4 Oct. 1810 p. 4a; *The Correspondence of John Thomas Stanley Esq. with the Earl of Stamford* (Chester 1798) p. 11 Stanley to Stamford 7 Feb. 1798 and cf. Jane H. Adeane ed. The Early Married Life of Maria Josepha Stanley, with Extracts from Sir John Stanley's 'Praeterita' (1899) p. 116–8, 121–2; Charles R. Strutt *The Strutt Family of Terling 1650–1873* (printed for private circulation 1939) p. 47. See generally for militia officers J.R. Western *The English Militia in the Eighteenth Century: the Story of a Political Issue* (1965) p. 303–339.

31 James Cookson *The Friends of Peace: Anti-War Liberalism in England 1793–1815* (Cambridge 1982) p. 57–8.

lead was taken by trade organizations in provincial commercial centres, particularly the American Chamber in Liverpool, the Inland Commercial Society in Birmingham and Cutler's Hall in Sheffield. Especially in the case of the American Chamber at Liverpool, which was effectively a lobby for those worst affected by the deterioration of Anglo-American relations after 1807, there was an important ground-swell of uneasiness at the vulnerability of international trade to the effects of government war policy – though it should be remembered that the trade which members of the American Chamber sought to protect largely dated from after the outbreak of war in 1793 in any case. William Roscoe, a prominent Liverpool banker and intellectual, published a pamphlet entitled *Considerations on the Causes, Objects and Consequences of the Present War, and on the Expediency, or the Danger of Peace with France* which went through five editions in 1808 and which concluded that there was no object at stake in the war worth the national effort of sustaining it: when peace came the bank he owned in Liverpool failed. In Liverpool, the main port for Anglo-American trade, the liberalizing influence of direct contact with the U.S.A. was also important; the underlying ideological and political dimension is also indicated by the prominence within the peace movement of dissenters, especially Unitarians in Yorkshire.[32]

It was also essentially a *provincial* movement, reacting against the dominant position of London, which continued to increase in importance both as a financial centre and as a port relative to other centres. In 1808 a movement in London to petition Parliament for peace was defeated by the West Indies merchants; in 1812, when the provincial centres were rallying against the Orders in Council, London remained quiescent, and the London-based caricaturists, invariably immediately responsive to the mood of the capital, bothered to produce only a couple of prints featuring the campaign against the Orders. It is possible that the nonconformist communities in London, which had made the capital a progressive force to be reckoned with since the 1640s, were by the 1800s losing cohesion. The Dissenting Academy at Hackney, formerly a great intellectual powerhouse of English Dissent, closed down in the 1790s; in the 1802 Middlesex election the Tory candidate Mainwaring obtained an unusually high percentage of the votes in Hackney, once a nonconformist stronghold, and this was not simply because they had been swamped by newcomers to the area: it seems from the Poll Book that the leading nonconformists in the north-east of London either did not vote or, like Edward Janson, a leading Quaker businessman living in Stoke Newington, voted Tory. When a controversial young minister, Robert Aspland, took over the Gravel-Pit chapel in Hackney it was found that attendance began to decline markedly, and though Aspland had succeeded in stabilizing the situation by

---

[32] Cookson *Friends of Peace* p. 188–196, 200–201, 223. The papers printed by the iron lobby in 1806 in its agitation against the excise on iron, preserved among the James Weale Mss, Science Museum Library Ms 371/1 show impressively how well some of the business lobbies were organized.

1809 the congregation, formerly one of the most prestigious in England, had difficulty financing the building of a new chapel.[33]

Anna Laetitia Barbauld, the bardess of Stoke Newington, whose husband had been Morning Preacher at the Unitarian chapel at Newington Green, demanded querulously:

> And thinkest thou, still to sit at ease,
> An island queen amidst thy subject seas,
> While the vext billows, in their distant war,
> But soothe thy slumber, and but kiss thy shore?

The majority answer seems to have been a triumphant *yes*. Many businessmen, as critical of the aristocratic regime as their pacifist brethren, complained that the government's war policy did not go far enough:

> But while the system of occasional expedients, and the molestation of points, shall continue to engage the attention of our statesmen, nothing, in this way, suitable to the private character of the nation, can be expected. In every thing that relates to mercantile concerns, all our treaties have hitherto been singular monuments of official ignorance and presumption. It is wonderful that men, versed only in files and precedents, should still have the arrogance to suppose themselves capable of arranging matters, of which, from their education, they can have little knowledge.

The poet Coleridge (another Unitarian) complained of the public's blood-thirstiness:

> We, this whole people, have been clamorous
> For war and bloodshed; animating sports,
> The which we pay for as a thing to talk of,
> Spectators and not combatants!
>   ... Boys and girls,
> And women, that would groan to see a child
> Pull off an insect's leg, all read of war,
> The best amusement for our morning-meal!

But other observers found that the prevalent attitude was one of boredom:

> War has unfolded all its splendid and terrible forms, in such a crowded succession of enterprises and battles, with every imaginable circumstance of valour, skill, and destruction, that its grandest exhibitions are become familiar to us, almost to insipidity ... It is, even after every allowance for the natural effect of iteration and familiarity, perfectly astonishing to observe what a degree of indifference has come to prevail in the general mind, at the view of events the most awful in their immediate exhibition, and the most portentous as to their consequences.

[33] Cookson *Friends of Peace* p. 222; George *Catalogue of Political and Personal Satires* no. 11876 (vol. 9 p. 105–6) C. Williams's 'Which Drowns First, or, Boney's Improved Bucket' and no. 11880 (vol. 9 p. 109–110) Elmes's 'A Rosey Picture of the Times'. For Mainwaring's high non-conformist vote in Hackney see Thorne ed. *House of Commons, 1790–1820* vol. 2 p. 260; for the Gravel-Pit meeting cf R. Brook Aspland *Memoirs of the Life, Works and Correspondence of the Rev. Robert Aspland* (1850) p. 177–8, 216, 234, 257.

This seems, in part, to be the psychological context in which Jane Austen wrote her novels. One of the most striking instances of what one might call 'internal neutrality' was the considerable volume of business sustained by those assisting the escape of French prisoners of war; of 1,105 prisoners of war on parole who made a break for freedom in the years 1803 to 1814, at least 600 reached France, usually with the help of Englishmen, some of whom, like Thomas Moore and the brothers William and George Chalkling, were criminal specialists of the utmost daring and ingenuity, though apparently devoid of any ideological motivation beyond a commitment to free enterprise and their fee.[34]

On the other hand Britain's war effort was able to rely on an extraordinary undercurrent of chauvinism. From the Adriatic one naval captain wrote to his father:

> Do not *call out* against our Ministers; you should be here and witness the Austrian Government. How I bless my stars I am of that dear little island, under a government like ours. When I see other countries and other people, I am not only proud of being an Englishman, but feel a sort of superiority, which is in no other manner to be accounted for than its being common to all Englishmen, and is inherent in them.

The successive defeat of all the other European powers by Napoleon merely confirmed the British sense of their own unique superiority:

> A province, or a kingdom, may be invaded and over-run, indeed, in certain cases, though the whole of the people may be bent on resistance: but, for an enemy to advance with post horse celerity, driving over regularly constituted armies as if it were over so many flint stones, and to take possession of cities and fortresses with as little difficulty as if they were sheepfolds, argues a total rottenness in the conquered state.[35]

During the eighteenth century condemned criminals in English prisons had sometimes volunteered for medical experiments involving amputation (of course without anaesthetic). The same unquenchable spirit was mobilized for the war. Though many of them had been press-ganged, naval ratings, for

---

[34] The verse is from Anna Laetitia Barbauld's 'Eighteen Hundred and Eleven' first published as a quarto pamphlet London 1812 and Samuel Taylor Coleridge's 'Fears in Solitude', first published as a pamphlet London 1798: in middle age Coleridge returned to orthodoxy but in the 1790s he adhered to progressive views on most subjects, and even at one period thought of becoming a Unitarian minister; John Galt *Voyages and Travels, in the Years 1809, 1810, and 1811; containing Statistical, Commercial, and Miscellaneous Observations on Gibraltar, Sardinia, Sicily, Malta, Serigo, and Turkey* (1812) p. 15: this was one of the passages quoted in *Gentleman's Magazine* vol. 82 (1812) p. 139 in the course of an exceptionally long and highly complimentary four-part review; John Foster *Contributions to the Eclectic Review* (2 vols 1844) vol. 2 p. 114–5 (originally published Dec. 1810) Roy Bennett 'French Prisoners of War on Parole in Britain (1803–1814)' London University Ph. D dissertation 1964 p. 245 Table 18; ibid. p. 201–210, 252–277.

[35] *Memoirs and Letters of Capt. Sir William Hoste* (2 vols 1833) vol. 1 p. 348 William Hoste to Rev. Dixon Hoste 24 Sept. 1809; *Cobbett's Political Register* vol. 10 col. 844 letter to Mr. Windham 29 Nov. 1806.

example, were often inspired by a naive patriotism: 'My eyes and my limbs, if I would not sooner see the barkey sink under us, than that striped rag over our jack', exclaimed one sailor when faced by the prospect of capture by superior French forces. National sentiment was bolstered by national pride:

> When every thing was cleared, the ports open, the matches lighted, and guns run out, then we gave them three such cheers as are only to be heard on a British man-of-war. This intimidates the enemy more than a broadside, as they have often declared to me.

Thomas Trotter, Physician to the Fleet, recalled, 'we have seen them cheering their shipmates, and answering the shouts of the enemy, under the most dreadful wounds, till, from loss of blood, they expired'. Captain Bayntoun of H.M.S. *Leviathan* remembered one of his men at Trafalgar having his arm amputated near the shoulder, 'during which, with great composure, smiling and with a steady clear voice, he sang the whole of "Rule Britannia"'. It was a war of songs just as much as the First World War, though with the passing of time 'The British Grenadier' and 'Lilibullero', have become stale and 'Tom he was a piper's son' has been relegated to the primary school. The authorities were not indifferent to the musical side: at Trafalgar Nelson's ships bore down on the Franco-Spanish line 'their jib-booms nearly over the others' taffrails, the bands playing "God Save the King", "Rule Britannia" and "Britons Strike Home", the crews stationed on the forecastle of the different ships, cheering the ships ahead of them when the enemy began to fire'.[36]

Writing their memoirs, old soldiers might well recall the thrill of 'the most imposing sight the world could produce':

> Our lines glittering with bright arms; the stern features of the men, as they stood with their eyes fixed unalterably upon the enemy, the proud colours of England floating over the heads of the different Battalions.

Even the elements bent to the British genius: drenched in the rain which fell all the night before Waterloo, a soldier recalled the nights before Fuentes d'Oñoro, Salamanca, Vitoria, also 'attended with thunder and lightning. It was always a prelude to our victory'. A hundred and eighty years later, most of the actors in these dramas lie in unmarked graves, whether at home among their own people or scattered on the margins of the remote beaches and battlefields where once the Union Jack fluttered under fire:

---

36 L. Radzinowicz *A History of English Criminal Law* (5 vols 1948–86) vol. 1 p. 121 and note 51; [Frederick Chamier] *The Life of a Sailor* (3 vols 1832) vol. 2 p. 33; *The Life and Adventures of John Nicol, Mariner* (Edinburgh 1822) p. 179; Thomas Trotter *Medicina Nautica: An Essay on the diseases of Seamen* (2 vols 1797–9) vol. 1 p. 37; *Naval Chronicle* vol. 15 (1806) p. 17; Wm. Stanhope Lovell *Personal Narrative of Events from 1799 to 1815* (2nd edit. 1879) p. 46–7 and cf W.N. Glascock *Naval Sketch-Book; or, the Service Afloat and Ashore* (2 vols 1826) vol. 1 p. 225–232. For a recent discussion of English national sentiment in this period see John Dinwiddy's chapter 'England' in Otto Dann and John Dinwiddy ed. *Nationalism in the Age of the French Revolution* (1988) p. 53–70 which however, possibly does not go far enough in acknowledging the extent and degree of popular support for the war.

> The warlike of the isles,
> The men of field and wave!
> Are not the rocks their funeral piles,
> The seas and shores their grave?
>
> Go stranger! track the deep,
> Free, free the white sail spread!
> Wave may not foam, nor wild wind sweep,
> Where rest not England's dead.

Only a well-connected few benefited from the scheme to establish St. Paul's Cathedral in London as a kind of National Pantheon, and the stiflingly predictable neo-classical monuments with which the socio-military elite were honoured attract little attention today from the tourists who flock to Wren's masterpiece. The memorial to Major-General Thomas Dundas shows Victory stretching across a recumbent lion to crown a bust with a wreath of laurel; the inscription repeats the wooden phrases of the parliamentary vote authorizing a public monument to this forgotten hero, '5th June 1795 Resolved, nemine contradicente etc. etc.' Opposite, one sees 'Captain Robert Faulknor who on the 5th of January 1795 in the thirty second Year of his age and in the moment of Victory was killed . . .' falling in Greek military underwear into the arms of Neptune while Victory crowns him over Neptune's neck; as with the Dundas monument the arm of Victory appears very awkward. On the other side of the cathedral nave Nelson also has a lion and George Blagdon Westcott, Captain of the *Majestic* keels over into a reeling Victory's lap. Nearby a surprisingly undressed Richard Rundle Burges Esquire surrenders his sword to Victory, having been enrolled by the British People 'high in the list of those heroes; who under the blessing of Providence, have establish'd and maintained her naval superiority: and her exalted rank among nations', Perhaps, in the days when it was still upright and intact, the statue of Ozymandias excited the ridicule of his immediate successors: but the true memorial of greatness is in altered circumstances, and what Dundas, Faulknor, Westcott, Burges, Nelson, Wellington and their generation left behind them was a position of world leadership which Britain was ready to defend in August 1914.[37]

---

[37] [John Harris] *Recollections of Rifleman Harris* ed. Henry Curling (1929) p. 37–8; [William Wheeler] *The Letters of Private Wheeler, 1809–1828* ed. B.G. Liddell Hart (London 1951) p. 170, 19 June 1815; the verses are from 'England's Dead' by Mrs. Hemans *c.* 1822. For St. Paul's see 'The Cenotaph' one of Richard Barham's *Ingoldsby Legends c.* 1837. Poor General Dundas, commanding the British forces in Guadeloupe died not on the quarterdeck or even, as more befitted a general, on the field of battle, but of fever: and shortly afterwards the French recaptured the island and ordered Dundas's body to be 'dug up and given a prey to the fowls of the air'.

Charles Williams Wynn proposed that the names of *all* the soldiers who fell at Waterloo should be inscribed on the memorial projected to commemorate the battle: *Parliamentary Debates* vol. 31 col. 1052, 29 June 1815. See also A.D. Harvey 'War Memorials' (letter) *History Workshop Journal* 20 (1985) p. 214.

Ralph Waldo Emerson acknowledges Britain's (or is it merely England's?) ascendancy in *English Traits* (1856) p. 20.

PART TWO

THE FIRST WORLD WAR

1914–1918

Outline: 1914–1918

In a sense Britain went to war in 1914 to defend the position of European leadership attained in 1815. Despite fears of German expansionism there were those who felt in August 1914 that the war which had flared up in Europe was not Britain's concern, and the degree to which the British government was bound by treaty to support victims of German aggression was debatable. But it was assumed that if there was to be a great European conflagration, Britain would have to take a part in it. It was assumed also – and this probably helped facilitate the decision to join in – that the war would be very short.

The war lasted four and a quarter years, by comparison with the twenty-two years (with a couple of brief pauses) of the French Revolutionary and Napoleonic Wars: but it was much more intense. Twice as many British soldiers died on the first day of the Somme as in nearly six years of campaigning under Wellington in Portugal, Spain and southern France. The initial assumptions that the war could be fought on the same organizational and economic basis as the French Wars gave way gradually to the almost complete mobilization of the national economy for war.

Vast manpower, backed by vast quantities of artillery and other specialist machinery, confronted the generals with the near impossibility of effectively deploying their available strength against an enemy who could always use railways to bring up unlimited forces against an troops advancing on foot. New technological developments such as the aeroplane and the tank were welcomed almost as a distraction from the insoluble problems of mass warfare.

Military stalemate, in Britain as in most other belligerent countries, fuelled the mutual antagonism of civilian ministers and military leaders, and resulted in power struggles between insecurely placed governments and the armed forces. In Britain, France and Italy the military lost out in these power struggles, largely because of their failures on the battlefield: in Germany the military won and established a covert dictatorship which, however, was unable to withstand the superior economic resources of Britain, France and the U.S.A. The question of the most effective form of war government remained unresolved.

6

Britain's Entry into the First World War: A Study in Motives

> Nothing can extenuate the enormity of the brute fact that an innocent country has been horribly devastated because her guilty neighbours formed two huge explosive combinations against one another instead of establishing the peace of Europe; but that is an offence against a higher law than any recorded on diplomatic scraps of paper; and when it comes to judgment, the outraged conscience of humanity will not have much patience with the naughty child's plea of 'He began it'.

> Bernard Shaw *Common Sense About The War*: vol. 21, p. 113 of Constable's 33-volume Uniform Edition of Shaw's works, originally published as a *New Statesman* supplement, 14 Nov. 1914.

I. Problems of Agenda

Britain's participation in the First World War seems at once much more thoroughly researched and much less ambiguous in its motivation than the earlier involvement in the wars of 1793–1815. The origins of the First World War must be the most raked over issue in history. The controversy over who was to blame is as old as the war itself: the German White Book, with 27 documents from German Foreign Office files justifying Germany's policy, was published on 3 August 1914 before Britain had even declared war; the much longer British Blue Book and the Russian Orange Book followed within four days, and the Belgian Grey, the Serbian Blue and the French Yellow Book all appeared within the next three months.[1]

The general sequence of events is familiar enough: the Austro-Hungarian government's suspicions (shared by *The Manchester Guardian* and afterwards found to be entirely justified) that the assassination of the Habsburg heir apparent Franz Ferdinand at Sarajevo had been organized by Serb officials; Germany's seeming encouragement of a strong line by Austria-Hungary, either to forestall interference by Russia and France or else to bring on a war in which Austria-Hungary would be inextricably involved as Germany's ally; Serbia's conciliatory attitude; Austria-Hungary's declaration of war on Serbia; little

---

[1] See H.W. Koch ed. *The Origins of the First World War* (1984 edit.) p. 5–7 of editor's introduction and p. 343–70 Karl Dietrich Edmann's essay 'War Guilt 1914 Reconsidered: A Balance of New Research' for a brief historiographical background and a judicious presentation of the state of play *circa* 1977; see also Sidney Bradshaw Fay *The Origins of the World War* (2 vols New York 1929) vol. 1 p. 3–7 for the variously coloured official publications in 1914.

Montenegro's declaration of war on Austria-Hungary; the mobilization of Russia's army; General Joffre's insistence on the mobilization of the French army; Germany's demand to Belgium for free passage of her troops through Belgian territory; Britain's ultimatum to Germany. There is much truth in Lloyd George's remark that 'The nations backed their machines over the precipice'. Nearly everybody expected a short and essentially clean and heroic war; if the desolating four years' reality had been better foreseen, the governments of 1914 might perhaps have considered their moves and counter-moves with greater care.[2]

Britain's involvement in the war tends to be seen as an inevitable part of the war breaking out in the first place. Chronologically Britain's declaration of war against Germany indeed belongs to the critical week following the first Austro-Hungarian artillery bombardment of the Serbian capital, Belgrade. Yet discussion of the general causes of the war obscures the question of why Britain in particular had to join in; and the conventional presentation of Britain as a passive element in a chain reaction confuses the occasion of the war with longer-term aims and objectives which were only openly avowed, or emerged, once the bloodbath began. The German historian Fritz Fischer has argued backwards, from claims and statements made after the declaration of war, to the Germans' probable pre-war motives. This form of argument could be applied also to Britain, though perhaps with as little justice. It was surely less the case that war enabled wickedly calculating statesmen to reveal and unveil their deep-laid plots; rather it enabled them to see with hallucinated clarity prospects and threats which the polite intercourse of nations had previously kept in shadow. And the decision-making was not the exclusive monopoly of the statesmen; the *why* of the outbreak of the First World War involves something more than diplomatic conversations, cunningly phrased despatches and stiff upper-lip interviews at the Wilhelmstrasse.[3]

II. Views from the Other Side

Even a week before Britain's declaration of war the Kaiser was noting in the margin of a diplomatic paper that the British government's motive for supporting France and Russia was 'petty envy, fear of our growing big. . . . it is not a question of high politics, but one of *race*. . . . for what is at issue is whether the Germanic race is to be or not to be in Europe'. German public opinion reacted to Britain's entry into the war with a bitterness that was

---

[2] See Arthur Ponsonby *Falsehood in Wartime: containing an assortment of lies circulated during the Great War* (1928) p. 43–49 and Joachim Remak *Sarajevo: The Story of a Political Murder* (1959) p. 49–57, 66–68, 77–8, 248–250 for Serb involvement in the assassination of Franz Ferdinand, and cf H.N. Brailsford in *Manchester Guardian* 28 July 1914 p. 10a. The two opposing interpretations of German policy in the last days of peace are argued in Luigi Albertini *The Origins of the War of 1914* (3 vols Oxford 1954–7) vol. 2 p. 447–53 and in Fritz Fischer *Germany's Aims in the First World War* (1967) p. 89–90. Lloyd George's comment is in his *War Memoirs* (6 vols 1933–6) vol. 1 p. 55.

[3] Cf Fischer *Germany's Aims in the First World War*.

out of all proportion to Britain's immediate military potential, and as far as propaganda was concerned Britain remained the principal enemy throughout the whole four years' conflict. Ernst Lissauer's famous *Hassgesang gegen England*, the Song of Hate:

> Wir lieben vereint, wir hassen vereint,
> Wir haben alle nur einen Feind:
> England.
> (We love united, we hate united,
> We all have only one enemy:
> England.)

neatly distinguished between German loathing of England and the more routinely warrior-like attitude towards France and Russia; though indeed as far as Russia was concerned the novelist Thomas Mann felt all proud and patriotic because Germany 'had taken upon itself to destroy the most depraved police-state in the world', and German newspapers professed to be outraged that 'England, who poses as the guardian of morality, and all the virtues, sides with Russia and assassins'.[4]

Britain was even presented as having the prime responsibility for the war. 'England has wanted the present war and is guilty of instigating it. Its power and its imperial rule based on the brutal exercise of power must be broken at any price', wrote Reichstag Centre deputy Matthias Erzberger in October 1914. Britain's key role was given official emphasis in Chancellor Bethmann-Hollweg's speech to the Reichstag on 2 December 1914; Erzberger paraphrased this speech as 'this war is England's war ... England deliberately wanted the war'. Particularly in Scandinavia and the United States this view was also held by many neutrals and it is clear that the prejudices of the 1800s had in many instances survived remarkably intact. Ernst Graf zu Reventlow's *Der Vampir des Festlandes* (the Vampire of the Continent), which went through at least nine editions in Germany in 1915–1916 and two editions in the United States in the translation by the Irish Nietzschean George Chatterton-Hill, derived most of its ideas from anti-British propaganda of the Napoleonic period, though the vampire image of the title comes from a poem by Laurence Binyon published in *The Times* on 11 August 1914, in which it is Germany that is designated the 'Vampire of Europe'.[5]

---

[4] Fischer *Germany's Aims in the First World War* p. 32–3; for various instances of anti-English feeling see Evelyn Countess Blücher *An English Wife in Berlin: A Private Memoir of Events, Politics and Daily Life in Germany throughout the War and the Social Revolution of 1918* (1920) p. 10, 14 (9 Aug. 1914) p. 62 (10 June 1915) p. 134 (28 April 1916); Lissauer's 'Song of Hate against England' was first published in Lissauer's Flugblatt *Worte in die Zeit* no. 1, 1914, Nigel Hamilton *The Brothers Mann: The Lives of Heinrich and Thomas Mann, 1871–1950 and 1875–1955* (1978) p. 159–160; [Harriet Julia] Lady Jephson *A War-Time Journal: Germany 1914 and German Travel Notes* (1915) p. 15 diary 6 Aug. 1914.

[5] *Allegemeine Rundschau* 3 Oct. 1914, quoted in Klaus Epstein *Matthias Erzberger and the Dilemma of German Democracy* (Princeton 1959) p. 107; *Der Tag* 6 Dec. 1914 Illustrierter Teil p. 1b cf. T. Bethmann-Hollweg *Seven War Speeches by the German Chancellor* (Zurich 1916) p. 13–24; For Binyon's poem see, *Times* 11 Aug. 1914 p. 7c.

The claim that British policy had been the cause of the war obviously bore little relation to the detailed minutiae of the diplomatic exchanges of late July and early August 1914 but in a larger sense appeared to the Germans to be essentially true. It was realized in German official circles that the war was, amongst other things, a 'struggle with England for world domination', an attempt to 'compete with England for world rule'. These were not the terms in which Asquith or Sir Edward Grey saw the war, at least initially, but then they do not seem originally to have had any true perception of the war in its full disastrous immensity; they were eventually joined in office by men whose alleged merit was that they saw big issues more clearly. Lord Curzon told the King of the Belgians in February 1916, 'The British people realise that they are fighting for the hegemony of the Empire. If necessary we shall continue the war single-handed'. In the long term these words were prophetic; at the time they were spoken they merely indicate that German paranoia about Britain was not without foundation.[6]

III. Voices of the People

Except possibly in Italy – and the Italian case will be discussed later – it is never supposed that the various governments were pressurized into extreme measures by the strength of popular feeling in favour of war, but the notion that the war was wildly and universally popular is sometimes cited as a palliation of ministerial blunderings, or as a gloss on the 'unspoken assumptions' behind the decision for war. It was in fact one of the myths evolved during the war, to highlight the shock and horror generated by the casualty statistics, that the war was initially greeted with popular rejoicing. Yet in France, which is the only country where systematic analysis has been carried out, the war was greeted by mass-meetings or demonstrations against war in 36 *départements* outside Paris, including 24 street marches, and in Paris itself protest meetings were held in all but four *arrondisements*. There was perhaps more general enthusiasm in Berlin, where a huge crowd gathered outside the Imperial Palace on 31 July to hear the Kaiser speak from the balcony, but Walther Rathenau, soon after taking over the economic direction of Germany's war industries, wrote, 'We must win, we must! And yet we have no clear, no absolute right to do so . . .' and 'There is a false note about this war; it is not 1813, nor 1866, nor 1870'.[7]

In London, a crowd had gathered outside Buckingham Palace 'every day since the shadow of war began to overhang the nation'. On the evening of the day war was declared, 'some 10,000' cheered and sang the National

---

[6] Fritz Fischer *War of Illusions: German Policies from 1911 to 1914* (1975) p. 549 quoting Kurt Riezler, Bethmann-Hollweg's assistant in 1916, and the book's epigraph, quoting Wilhelm Groener in 1919; R. van Overstraeten ed. *The War Diaries of Albert I King of the Belgians* (1954) p. 85 7 Feb. 1916.

[7] Jean-Jacques Becker *1914: Comment les Français sont entrés dans la guerre* (Paris 1977) p. 149; Harry Kessler *Walther Rathenau: His Life and Work* (1929)p. 177.

Anthem when King George V, the Queen, the Prince of Wales and Princess
Mary appeared on the balcony, though judging by the photographs the turn-
out was not as big as outside the Kaiser's palace in Berlin, and was hardly
remarkable for a city with a population of over seven million. Another crowd,
predominantly male, formed opposite the Houses of Parliament on 3 August,
which conveniently enough was a Bank Holiday. C.F.G. Masterman described
the throng in rather romanticized terms:

> great crowds of silent men and women crowding Whitehall, and all the way
> from Downing Street to Parliament, just waiting, hour after hour, in a kind
> of awe and expectation, to know whether the world in which they had lived
> and moved all their lives had ceased to exist.

One photograph in *The Illustrated London News* shows the crowd as about
ten deep, and prevented from stopping the traffic by four mounted policemen;
another photo shows the traffic practically blocked while a man distributing
peace pamphlets, and three policemen who have come to rescue him, are
being squeezed against the wall by the press of people; both photographs
show almost no women. These gatherings did not entirely disperse when
night fell; Arthur Ponsonby told the House of Commons that on the evening
of 2 August, 'I saw bands of half-drunken youths waving flags, and I saw a
group outside a great club in St James's Street being encouraged by members
of the club from the balcony'. The club was presumably White's. Yet there
was also an anti-war rally in Trafalgar Square on 2 August; 'a mixed crowd
of admirers, hooligan warmongers and merely curious holiday-makers', noted
Beatrice Webb: 'It was an undignified and futile exhibition, this singing of
the "Red Flag" and passing of well-worn radical resolutions in favour of
universal peace'. Anti-war demonstrations were also organized in the East
End of London; on 4 August John Burns received a telegram, 'East End
protests against war tonight meetings everywhere come and speak at mass
meeting outside East India Dock gates Poplar 8.30 you would have a [illegible]
reception'. Nevertheless one observer wrote – from the National Liberal Club
– during the last night Britain was at peace:

> I am amazed at the lack of feeling and interest about the war everywhere – even
> now I have just passed by a ring of guffawing fools sitting over their whisky
> in the smoking-room. The holiday people at Cowes and in the train simply
> didn't seem to grasp the fact that we are on the edge of the greatest abyss in
> history.[8]

According to the standard myth, popular belligerence quickly expressed

[8] See photographs (and captions) *Illustrated London News* 8 Aug. 1914 vol. 145 p. 221,
230; Lucy Masterman *C.F.G. Masterman* (1939) p. 267; *Hansard: House of Commons* vol. 65
p. 1841; Norman and Jeanne Mackenzie ed. *The Diaries of Beatrice Webb* (4 vols 1982–5)
vol. 3 p. 212, 5 Aug. 1914; British Library Add. 46303 f. 16 telegram Seymour Cocks to
Burns 4 Aug. 1914; E. Townshend ed. [F.H. Keeling] *Keeling Letters & Recollections* (1918)
p. 180 F.H. Keeling to E. Townshend 3/4 Aug. 1914.

itself in attacks on shops owned by German immigrants. There were in fact very few such incidents in the opening week of the war. Three German shops were looted at Bow, and a German baker's shop at Poplar was smashed up following some provocative remarks by the baker's wife, though the Assistant Commissioner who reported on the latter incident did not think 'that the amount of force used was sufficient to alarm any person of reasonable firmness and courage', suggesting that calm prevailed even when the businesses of immigrants were being pillaged. Some of these early incidents were far from being straightforward instances of anti-German feeling. Harry Flach's shop in North Finchley was stoned on 7 August after he had trampled publicly on the Union Jack; but Harry Flach was a Jew from Russian Poland and may have been, not unreasonably, a little upset that his country of adoption had entered the war on the side of the government whose sponsorship of anti-semitism had led him to emigrate. Later, the thirty-six hours of disturbances at Keighley on 29–30 August 1914, which began with a drunk being ejected from a German-owned butcher's shop, climaxed with a mob attempting to march on the house of Sir Prince Smith, one of his largest local employers who was currently conducting a lock-out of his workforce; as the route to Sir Prince's house was barred by police, the crowd had to confine themselves to stoning the police-station.[9]

Nevertheless there can be no doubt that anti-German feeling began to build up, encouraged by the campaign in *The Daily Mail* and the London *Evening News* against residents of German birth. There were serious outbreaks at Deptford, Camberwell and, of all places, Saffron Walden in Essex on 17 October. There was something of a German spy scare at the time; *The Times* for 17 October, as well as printing two letters on German spies, also reported the arrest of twenty Germans working for C.G. Röder Ltd, Victoria Road, Willesden, a printing business operating from premises with a reinforced concrete floor and roof resembling the platforms allegedly used by the German siege artillery at Maubeuge, and with a view right across the London conurbation. There seems to have been no other particularly distressing war news that day; one of the targets in the Deptford disturbances was the Heart of Erin public house and it was reported 'All jewellers' shops were barricaded ... The crowd, which increased when the public-houses closed, appeared to be hostile to any shop which was open'. At Saffron Walden the rioting was directed against the home of a local J.P. who was sheltering two German evacuees and whose daughters had been reported as making pro-German remarks at prayer-meetings. By 1914 it was not usual for remarks at prayer-meetings to be followed by rioting; one may be permitted to suspect that as at Keighley seven weeks earlier particular local tensions

    [9] Julia Bush *Behind the Lines: East London Labour, 1914–1919* (1984) p. 37; Public Record Office HO 45/10944/257142 file 18 report 11 Nov. 1914 of incident 6 Aug. 1914; ibid. file 5 report 26 Aug. 1914 of incident 7 Aug. 1914; ibid. file 2a report by Arthur S. Quest 31 Aug. 1914 on riots at Keighley 29–30 Aug. 1914.

contributed more to the disturbances than the international situation.[10]

The nature of anti-German feeling during the first weeks of the war (and the undercurrents of violence in British society at this time) will perhaps be better understood if one runs a little ahead. By the end of October the press campaign against Britons of German origin was beginning to have an impact even on the professional classes. Prince Louis of Battenberg, the First Sea Lord, was forced to resign on 29 October 1914; London golf clubs asked their naturalized Austrian- and German-born members to keep away, and expelled the unnaturalized ones, the same day (this was decided, with one dissenting vote, in a meeting of about fifty club representatives at the Golfers' Club). Soon Dachshunds were being kicked in the street, and German Shepherds, too large to be kicked with impunity, had their species ignominiously but topically redesignated *Alsatian*, or even *Belgian Police Dog*. But it was only after the sinking of the *Lusitania* on 7 May 1915 that popular anti-German feeling expressed itself in really serious outbreaks of violence. Most newspapers competed with one another in vitriolic denunciation of the *Lusitania* sinking, and the Stock Exchange and Baltic Exchange closed their doors to German-born members on 11 May. On the same day, at Smithfield, German-born meat traders were pelted with offal and driven off, and the crowd demonstrated their repugnance at the massacre of all those estimable Americans on the *Lusitania* by beating up an American by-stander. Next day there was rioting in several parts of London: 150 shops were attacked in Kentish Town and Camden Town, and in Poplar looters were observed taking away their booty in prams and horse-drawn carts; one looter was reported as saying, 'Here is wealth for the taking'. Photographs published in *The Daily Sketch* on 13 May give a chilling impression of calmness, order and deliberation in the looting, though *The Times* reported 'the disturbances seem to have degenerated into quite indiscriminate looting by drunken crowds'. On 13 May two coalminers were shot and wounded while attacking a shop owned by an Englishman of English ancestry during disturbances at Goldthorpe, near Doncaster. Troops had to be called out at Bury St Edmunds and at Walton on Thames, and at Neath 56 people were injured in police baton charges; none of these were places noted for their German immigrant communities. Indeed it was reported that the rioters mentioned the *Lusitania* relatively infrequently. In Liverpool the attacks were directed partly against the Chinese community, especially the Chinese laundries. Altogether 257 persons (including 107 police and special constables) were injured in these disturbances, and 866 arrests were made. In the Metropolitan Police District alone claims were eventually made for £195,000 worth of damage. During the same week, in far away South Africa, riots caused £676,314 worth of damage, mainly to property owned by persons of British or Afrikaner origin. It rather seems that the violence of the

[10] *Times* 17 Oct. 1914 p. 9d and p. 8e; *Daily Chronicle* 20 Oct. 1914 p. 5b and see Panikos Panay 'Anti-German Riots in London during the First World War' *German History* vol. 7 (1989) p. 189–207; p. 187–8; Public Record Office HO 45/10944/257142 file 12; ibid. file 16.

war served to trigger off communal violence which had its real roots elsewhere: the British soldiers actually fighting the war had cheerfully fraternized with their German opposite numbers during the informal truce on Christmas Day 1914.[11]

Many people who had personal knowledge of Germans and Germany found the whole anti-German business incredible, protesting, for example,

> We have loved your burgs, your pines' green moan,
> Fair Rhine-stream, and its storied towers,

or sneering dutifully about 'their rotten "Kultur" talk, which is like Oxford intensified ten times over'. Although Prince Louis of Battenberg and Lord Haldane, Lord Chancellor and an enthusiast for German philosophy, were driven from office, others escaped the witch hunt. Sir Eyre Crowe, whose wife's uncle, Henning von Holtzendorff became head of the German Naval Staff in the spring of 1915, was denounced by Christabel Pankhurst in *The Suffragette* and by the thriller-writer William Le Queux in a series of well-publicized speeches at Brixton and elsewhere, and had to be defended in the House of Commons by Lord Robert Cecil, Sir John Simon and even Sir Edward Grey; he remained undisturbed at his post. Major-General Stanley Von Donop, Master General of the Ordnance, was subject to anti-German sneers in private from members of the Cabinet but when Lloyd George finally obtained his dismissal (on administrative grounds) he was appointed to command the troops on Humberside, in an area where a German invasion was thought possible. Edward Graf Gleichen commanded the 37th Division of the British Army on the Western Front and ended the war as head of the Intelligence Bureau at the Department of Information, merely changing his title by Royal Warrant to Lord Edward Gleichen. Apart from Gleichen, the Army List for January 1918 included seventeen officers with *von* before their names – actually a rather meagre testimony of more than a century of Anglo-German peace, but sufficient to suggest that anti-German sentiment had little consistent influence in decision-making circles; as an example of what

[11] *Times* 30 Oct. 1914 p. 5c; ibid. 13 May 1915 p. 10a and b; ibid. 14 May 1915 p. 10b; ibid. 15 May 1915 p. 10c; ibid. 17 May 1915 p. 5a and see Panikos Panay 'Anti-German Riots' p. 192–9; Public Rcord Office HO 45/10944/257142 file 82 Chinese minister in London to Foreign Office 12 May 1915 copy; *Hansard: House of Commons* vol. 71 col. 1970 statement of Reginald McKenna on number of casualties and arrests 17 May 1915; Public Record Office HO 45/10944/257142 file 151 for claims of damage; *Report of the Select Committee of the House of Assembly on Incendiarism* (Pretoria 1916) p. xviii (copy in HO 45/10944/257142 file 171) for the disturbances in South Africa. These latter disturbances need to be seen in the context of the Rand strike of 1913 during which 21 people were killed (*Times* 10 July 1913 p. 7d) and the disturbances in 1922, in which at least 312 people died, including 74 soldiers and policemen (*Times* 11 May 1922 p. 9g). The effect of war in stimulating urban violence is however suggested by the East St Louis race riots which occurred three months after the United States entered the war in 1917: damage amounted to nearly $3m and there were almost a hundred fatalities cf E. Barbeau and Florette Henri *The Unknown Soldiers: Black American Troops in World War I* (Philadelphia 1974) p. 24–6.

went on in people's minds at a lower level is the fact that on the war memorial to the Old Boys of St John's College, Green Lanes in Stoke Newington Public Library the name E.D. Schaeffer has been mutilated.[12]

IV. The Standard Excuses: Belgium and the Entente

Britain's ostensible reason for going to war on 4 August 1914 was to defend Belgian neutrality. This was certainly not expected by the Belgian government. In 1906 talks had taken place between the British military attaché and the Belgian Army chief of staff. These talks were later interpreted by the Germans as proof of one-sided preparations by Belgium to cooperate with France and Britain in a war against Germany, but in 1909 the Belgian Army began to prepare plans for defence against a British invasion, and in April 1912 the British were informed that their assistance would not be needed if Germany invaded Belgium. In September 1912 the Belgian minister of war 'made it quite clear' to the British naval attaché 'that in his opinion the danger of a breach of Belgian neutrality lay more from England than anywhere else'. This was, perhaps, somewhat unjust; at about this period Brigadier-General Henry Wilson, the Director of Military Operations at the War Office, was advising the French army staff not to invade Belgium as it would place Britain 'in a very embarrassing situation' – though indeed the French had already considered a scheme for invading Germany across Belgian territory and had given it up on military grounds.[13]

Although a German violation of Belgian neutrality was not unexpected in British official circles, there was no agreement on the extent of Britain's

---

[12] Thomas Hardy 'England to Germany in 1914', written autumn 1914; [F.H. Keeling] *Keeling Letters & Recollections* p. 197 F.H. Keeling to C. Townshend 25 Oct. 1914; *Hansard: House of Commons* vol. 73 col. 201 (Lord Robert Cecil 26 July 1915); ibid. vol. 74 col. 522 (Sir John Simon 22 Sept. 1915); ibid. vol. 76 col. 1547 (Lord Robert Cecil, refusing to answer a Parliamentary Question 9 Dec. 1915); for Lloyd George on Von Donop's German blood see A.J.P. Taylor ed. *Lloyd George: A Diary by Frances Stevenson* (1971) p. 129 30 Nov. 1916. Thirty-five thousand Germans formerly resident in the U.K. were deported after the end of the First World War. In the January 1945 Army List there were only eight *vons* – plus Mrs D.E. von Lewinski of the A.T.S.

[13] Carl Hosse *Die englisch-belgischen Aufmarschpläne gegen Deutschland vor dem Weltkriege* (Zurich/ Vienna 1930) p. 49–51 and Anlage p. 19–24 (item 6) and J. Wullus-Rudiger *La Belgique et l'Equilibre Européen* (Paris 1935) p. 56–63 and especially p. 310–317 (Annexe No. 4) for 1906 talks; Wullus-Rudiger p. 65 and p. 318–320 (Annexe No. 5) for Belgian planning in 1909; Hosse Anlage 32–3 (item 13) and Wullus-Rudiger p. 78–82 for Bridges-Jungbluth talks in April 1912; G.P. Gooch and Harold Temperley ed. *British Documents on the Origins of the War 1898–1914* (11 vols 1927–38) vol. 8 p. 399 item 324 Captain Kelly to Sir F. Villiers *re* conversation of the former with General Michel 12 Sept. 1912, and cf. Bernard Dernburg ed. *The Case of Belgium in the Light of Official Reports Found in the Secret Archives of the Belgian Government after the Occupation of Brussels* [New York 1915] passim, Jonathan E. Helmreich 'Belgian Concern for Neutrality and British Intentions 1906–14' *Journal of Modern History* vol. 36 (1964) p. 416–427 and Samuel R. Williamson Jr. *The Politics of Grand Strategy, 1904–1914* (Cambridge Mass. 1969) p. 216–8.

obligations to Belgium, arising as they did from treaties signed as far back as 1831 and 1839, during the first days of the independent Belgian monarchy. 'The neutrality of Belgium was indeed already a by-word in the European Chancelleries for obsolete ineffectiveness as long ago as when I was myself in diplomacy (and I left it in 1870)', noted one observer. Sir John Simon, the Attorney General, argued 'that 80 years had created wholly different circumstances', and Asquith, the Prime Minister, reported to George V, 'The Cabinet consider that the matter if it arises will be one of policy rather than legal obligation'. Cambon, the French ambassador in London, was informed that the guarantee of Belgium only operated when all the parties – including Prussia – were in agreement: 'the position, in short, was one of strictly limited liability'.[14]

Till at least two days before Britain's declaration of war the majority of the British Cabinet were opposed to any British involvement. A meeting of Lloyd George, Harcourt, Beauchamp, Runciman, Simon and Pease on the morning of 2 August decided to oppose war except in the case of a German invasion of Belgium; if the latter occurred they would be prepared to reconsider the position. Hours of discussion in the Cabinet achieved only a last-minute agreement that there was no obligation to assist the French but that a German invasion of Belgium would be resisted. Simon and Earl Beauchamp resigned from the Cabinet but allowed themselves to be persuaded to stay in office; Simon, who 'pretended to a special and personal abhorrence of killing in any shape', explained later that he had withdrawn his resignation 'without in the smallest degree, so far as he was concerned, withdrawing his objection to the policy but solely in order to prevent the appearance of disruption in face of a grave national danger'. Two other Cabinet ministers, John Burns and Viscount Morley were less helpful; they not only resigned but stuck by their resignations. Clearly the majority decision to defend Belgium was not arrived at easily.[15]

The most important Cabinet member to move over from opposing the war to accepting its necessity if Belgium was invaded was the Chancellor of the Exchequer, David Lloyd George; but at dinner with some of his colleagues in the evening of 2 August he announced that he would still resign rather than agree to war so long as the Germans undertook to observe the neutrality of

[14] Wilfrid Scawen Blunt *My Diaries: being a personal narrative of Events, 1888–1914* (2 vols 1919–20) vol. 2 p. 449–450 (concluding remarks) on Belgian neutrality as a by-word; Cameron Hazlehurst *Politicians at War July 1914 to May 1915* (1971) p. 71 quoting J. Pease diary 2 Aug. 1915 for Simon's view, and H.A. Spender and Cyril Asquith *Life of Henry Herbert Asquith, Lord Oxford and Asquith* (2 vols 1932) vol. 2 p. 82 Asquith to King George V 29 July 1914.

[15] Edward David ed. *Inside Asquith's Cabinet: from the Diaries of Charles Hobhouse* (1977) p. 180 [August] for Simon's abhorrence of killing and Trevor Wilson ed. *The Political Diaries of C.P. Scott, 1911–1928* p. 103, diary 3/4 Sept. 1914 for Simon's excuse for staying in the war government.

In September 1939 Simon – apart from Runciman the only member of Asquith's Cabinet who was still in office – acted as spokesmen for the ministers who were putting pressure on Chamberlain to declare war against Hitler.

Belgium and the French Channel coast. Lloyd George was, it seems, already perfecting a pose of martyrdom to principle (and shaping up to the new challenge in his career) when he wrote to his wife on 3 August:

> I am driven to the conclusion that if the small nationality of Belgium is attacked by Germany all my traditions & even prejudices will be engaged on the side of war. I am filled with horror at the prospect. I am even more horrified that I should ever appear to have a share in it but I must bear my share of the ghastly burden though it scorches my flesh to do so.

Germany's note to Belgium, demanding the right to deploy troops through Belgian territory, was delivered that same day. Viscount Morley claimed later that Lloyd George 'found in the German ultimatum to Belgium a sufficiently plausible excuse' to support the war, and this was also the opinion of Lloyd George's girlfriend, eventually wife, Frances Stevenson: 'the invasion of Belgium was, to be cynical, a heaven-sent excuse for supporting a declaration of war'. Yet bearing in mind how much of the Cabinet's and the Foreign Office's discussion of Britain's entry into the war had nothing to do with Belgium at all, Lloyd George may not have been the only one who found the German invasion of Belgium politically convenient; the later remark concerning German policy, 'Had she gone round the Cape of Good Hope the result would have been the same', overlooks some of the constraints on decision-making within the British Cabinet system.[16]

Another version of the chain-reaction theory of British participation in the war is that it was in fulfilment of Britain's obligations to France and Russia as partners in the Triple Entente and that it was thus a result of what Zimmermann, the German under-secretary for foreign affairs, called 'this damned system of alliances, which was the curse of modern times'. But whereas Germany was harnessed to Austria-Hungary and Italy by a formal treaty, periodically renewed, the Triple Entente was an amorphous and ambiguous arrangement. The Foreign Secretary told the House of Commons on 3 August 1914, 'The Triple Entente was not an Alliance – it was a Diplomatic group'. Its origins were in the Anglo-French agreement of 1904 which had aimed at securing French recognition of British control of Egypt and British recognition of French interests in Morocco. Though Campbell-Bannerman, the then Prime Minister, authorized staff conversations in 1905, the British and French army staffs did not settle down to any detailed discussion for another five years. Russia had already had a defensive alliance with France since 1894 and various Anglo-Russian consultations over Persia from February 1907 onwards were seen by some officials as completing the triangular partnership. In no sense however could these arrangements be

---

[16] Lord Riddell *War Diary, 1914–1918* (1933) p. 4 for the dinner on 2 August; Kenneth O. Morgan ed. *Lloyd George: Family Letters, 1885–1936* (Cardiff/London 1973) p. 167, D. Lloyd George to Margaret Lloyd George 3 Aug. 1914; John Viscount Morley *Memorandum on Resignation August 1914* (1928) p. 24 and Frances Lloyd George *The Years That Are Past* (1967) p. 73–4 for Lloyd George's use of Belgium as an excuse; Jerome K. Jerome *My Life and Times* [1926] p. 265 for the Cape of Good Hope remark.

understood as a formal strategic partnership, and in practice the Entente had little significance before 1914. France failed to back Russia's opposition to the Austro-Hungarian annexation of Bosnia-Herzegovina in 1908; Russia failed to back France in the Agadir crisis of 1911; Britain failed to support Russia's protests against the appointment of the German general Liman von Sanders to a high command in the Turkish Army in 1913.[17]

This is not to say that the *idea* of a strategic alliance did not have its appeal. While the French ambassadors in Berlin, Rome and Vienna worked for their own separate *détentes* with the governments to which they were accredited, Poincaré, then French foreign minister, feared the breakdown of the rival blocs as a recipe for instability. As one of his most trusted emissaries put it:

> By upsetting the balance and by obscuring the clarity of the situation, in reality it leads to ambiguity and instability. In doing so it eventually weakens the guarantees for peace while claiming to increase them by the chimera of universal harmony.

Sazonov, the Russian foreign minister, regretted that the Entente did not have a more coordinated policy:

> This lack of homogeneousness and solidarity between the three powers of the Entente arouses our serious apprehensions, for it constitutes an organic fault of the Triple Entente which will always place us at a disadvantage in face of the solid bloc of the Triple Alliance.

From 1910 onwards the British and French army staffs, with the knowledge of only the innermost cliques of the two governments, began perfecting plans for a small British expeditionary force to assist the French army on the continent in case of war with Germany. The British Cabinet as a whole only learnt of the military collaboration with France in 1912 and as Lloyd George recalled, 'Hostility barely represents the strength of the sentiment which the revelation aroused; it was more akin to consternation'. An exchange of notes between the British and French governments in November 1912 pledging the two countries to consult with each other at times of international crisis, though described by Poincaré as 'of great value' was passed off by the British Prime Minister Asquith as of little importance, 'almost a platitude'.[18]

[17] Gooch and Temperley *British Documents on the Origins of the War* vol. 11 p. 284 item 510 Sir Edward Goschen to Sir Arthur Nicolson 1 Aug. 1914 for Zimmermann's comment; *Hansard: House of Commons* vol. 65 col. 1810 for Grey's statement 3 Aug. 1914, cf. A.J.A. Morris *The Scaremongers: The Advocacy of War and Rearmament, 1896–1914* (1984) p. 268–9 for the currency of the view that the Entente was dead and buried by the beginning of 1911.

[18] *Documents Diplomatiques Françaises 3e serie* (11 vols Paris 1929–36) vol. 3 p. 22 item 17 Comte Beaupoil de Saint Aulaire to Poincaré 19 May 1912 and B. de Siebert and George Abel Schreiner *Entente Diplomacy and the World: Matrix of the History of Europe, 1909–1914* (1921) p. 687 Sazonov to Benckendorff 12 Dec. 1913; Lloyd George *War Memoirs* vol. 1 p. 50 for British Cabinet's consternation in 1912 and cf. John W. Coogan and Peter F. Coogan 'The British Cabinet and the Anglo-French Staff Talks, 1905–1914: Who Knew What and When Did He Know It?' *Journal of British Studies* vol. 24 (1985) p. 110–131; John K.V. Keiger *France and the Origins of the First World War* (1983) p. 114–5 for the differing estimates of the importance of the Nov. 1912 agreement.

The French not unnaturally supposed these cooperative arrangements to imply some sort of commitment but this view was not held by the British Cabinet. Yet by 1914 this alliance which had never been systematically negotiated or officially promulgated had taken on the status of a mainspring of foreign policy. Sir Eyre Crowe, assistant Under-Secretary of State at the Foreign Office, had warned in January 1907 that the German government was either 'consciously aiming at the establishment of a German hegemony, at first in Europe, and eventually in the world', or at least pushing into as advantageous position as possible, 'leaving it to an uncertain future to decide' future policy. In spite of – surely it could not be because of – his German-born mother and German-born wife, Crowe continued to press the view that the Triple Entente was a substantive alliance necessitated by German hegemonic ambitions. On 24 July 1914, when the slide into world war began to become evident, he minuted:

> Whatever we may think of the merits of the Austrian charges against Servia, France and Russia consider that these are the pretexts and that the bigger cause of Triple Alliance versus Triple *Entente* is definitely engaged.
>
> Our interests are tied up with those of France and Russia in this struggle, which is not for the possession of Servia, but one between Germany aiming at a political dictatorship in Europe and the Powers who desire to retain individual freedom.

Sir Eyre Crowe's interpretation of German policy was to become almost universally accepted by Germany's enemies once war broke out, but in the last fortnight of peace Crowe encountered some official incredulity with regard to his view both of Germany and of the Triple Entente. On 31 July he explained:

> The argument that there is no unwritten bond binding us to France is strictly correct. There is no contractual obligation. But the *Entente* has been made, strengthened, put to the test and celebrated in a manner justifying the belief that a moral bond was being forged. The whole policy of the *Entente* can have no meaning if it does not signify that in a just quarrel England would stand by her friends.

And for his part Crowe had no doubt that the French were engaged in a just quarrel: 'France has not sought the quarrel. It has been forced upon her'.[19]

Sir Edward Grey, the British Foreign Secretary, was less sure: 'France is being drawn into a dispute which is not hers', he told the British ambassador in Paris. As he saw it:

> the position was that Germany would agree not to attack France if France remained neutral in the event of a war between Russia and Germany. If France could not take advantage of this position, it was because she was bound by

[19] Gooch and Temperley *British Documents on the Origins of the War* vol. 2 p. 397–420 for Crowe's memo of 1 Jan. 1907 – quotations from p. 414 and p. 417 – ibid. vol. 11 p. 81–2 item 101 for Crowe's minute of 24 July 1914; vol. 11 p. 228–9 item 369 for Crowe's memo of 31 July 1914; and cf. Arthur Ponsonby *Falsehood in Wartime: containing an assortment of lies circulated during the Great War* (1928) p. 31–42 for the French government's perception of the Entente.

an alliance to which we were not parties, and of which we did not know the terms.

Yet Grey was not seeking a pretext for British neutrality: his diplomacy had a totally different object. Quite simply, he wished to prevent the war, and his aim was to avoid encouraging France and Russia to go to war by refusing to pledge support. Arguably Grey's style of over-subtle distinctions and self-contradictory impartialities contributed mainly to confusing the issue; he had earlier been described as 'a man rather to see difficulties than to help people over them'. But if war came, in spite of all his diplomatic finesse, then Grey had no doubt that Britain had to be a participant. Quite early in the crisis he told his colleagues:

> The time had come ... when the Cabinet was bound to make up its mind plainly whether we were to take an active part with the two other powers of the Entente, or to stand aside in the general European question ... If the Cabinet was for Neutrality, he did not think that he was the man to carry out such a policy.

The Manchester Guardian, as early as 28 July, expressed surprise that Grey avoided emphasizing that Britain had no actual commitment to any ally: 'It is strange that Sir EDWARD GREY should not have referred to this fact, which is the chief source of our moral authority in Europe'. It seems however that Grey did perceive some sort of obligation, though not precisely in the terms urged by Crowe. In his speech to the Commons on 3 August 1914 Grey argued that if Britain did not intervene and Germany was victorious over France and Russia, 'our moral position would be such as to have lost us all respect', and this, despite all his virtuoso fence-sitting, seems to have been Grey's attitude from the very beginning.[20]

If Britain's contractual obligations to defend Belgium and to support France were debatable, there was much less difference of opinion about the third and most important partner in the war alliance, Russia. Those who spoke out in favour of war had nothing to say in favour of Russia, and those who opposed the war considered the prospect of being Russia's ally one of the war's most deplorable aspects. Viscount Morley told the Cabinet late in July:

> If Germany is beaten and Austria is beaten, it is not England and France who will emerge pre-eminent in Europe. It will be Russia. Will that be good for Western civilisation? ... people will rub their eyes when they realise that Cossacks are their victorious fellow-champions for Freedom, Justice, Equality of man.

[20] Gooch and Temperley *British Documents on the Origins of the War* vol. 11 p. 220 item 352 Grey to Sir Francis Bertie 31 July 1914 31 July 1914; vol. 11 p. 253 item 426 same to same 1 Aug. 1914; Roy Jenkins *Asquith* (1978 edit.) p. 152 quoting Arthur Acland's opinion of Grey from a letter to Asquith in 1905; Morley *Memorandum on Resignation August 1914* p. 2 'On or about July 24–27'; *Manchester Guardian* editorial 28 July 1914 p. 8c; see also George Macaulay Trevelyan *Grey of Falloden. Being the Life of Sir Edward Grey afterwards Viscount Grey of Falloden* (1937) p. 251–2 and [Edward] Grey *Twenty-Five Years, 1892–1916* (2 vols 1925) vol. 2 p. 158.

Inside and outside the Cabinet Morley, the foremost surviving exponent of the Gladstonian tradition in British politics, insisted:

> he cannot brook this country becoming a party to what he regards as a Slavonic movement against Teuton influence. . . . he looks upon any tendency hostile to Germany that has its roots in Slav aspirations as prejudicial to the interests of civilisation.

It was, after all, less than ten years since the last major anti-Jewish pogrom in Russia had affected 660 communities, caused 62,700,000 roubles damage and left nearly a thousand dead – 300 dead in Odessa alone. Only the year before, Russian ignorance and prejudice had put itself once again on public display in the trial at Kiev of Mendel Beiliss for the alleged ritual murder of a Christian child. 'How would you feel if you saw Germany overrun and annihilated by Russia?', Lloyd George asked his colleagues, even though he was waiting only for the Belgian excuse to come out in favour of the war. It was noted 'L.G. strongly insisted on the danger of aggrandizing Russia and on the future problems that would arise if Russia and France were successful'. Sir John Simon took a similar view:

> We have always been wrong when we have intervened. Look at the Crimea. The Triple Entente was a terrible mistake. Why should we support a country like Russia?

Anti-Russian opinions were also expressed publicly: the influential Liberal journalist, A.G. Gardiner of *The Daily News* demanded:

> Where in the wide world do our interests clash with Germany? Nowhere. With Russia we have potential conflicts over the whole of South-Eastern Europe and Southern Asia.

In the House of Commons Philip Morrell, M.P. for Burnley and husband of the famous Lady Ottoline, urged:

> Let us remember that in going to war in this way we are going to war just as much to preserve the despotism of Russia as to interfere with German ambition.[21]

[21] Morley *Memorandum on Resignation August 1914* p. 6; Sir Almeric Fitzroy *Memoirs* (2 vols 1925) vol. 2 p. 557, 28 July 1914; Salo W. Baron *The Russian Jew under Tsars and Soviets* (New York 1964) p. 69 and p. 75 for the 1905 pogrom and the 1913 blood ritual trial; Riddell *War Diary* p. 4–5, 2 Aug. 1914 for the attitude of Lloyd George and Simon; *Daily News* 1 Aug. 1914 p. 6; *Hansard: House of Commons* vol. 65 col. 1836 (3 Aug. 1914). See also *The Autobiography of Bertrand Russell* (3 vols 1967–9) vol. 2 p. 44–5 C.P. Sanger to Russell 7 Aug. 1914 and F.C.S. Schiller to Russell 19 Aug. 1914.

The Russians were often as anti-British as the British were anti-Russian. Less than ten years previously a Tsarist naval officer had written of the British in terms reminiscent of Napoleonic times:

> Horrid folk! They are Russia's eternal enemy. They are cunning, powerful at sea, and insolent everywhere. All nations hate England, but it suits them to tolerate her.

Eugene S. Politovsky *From Libau to Tsushima: A Narrative of the Voyage of Admiral Rojdestvensky's Fleet to Eastern Seas, Including a Detailed Account of the Dogger Bank Incident* (1906) p. 28.

Yet there was no coordinated resistance, either in Whitehall or at West-minster. Up till the evening of 2 August a party within the Cabinet opposed to the war appeared to be forming, but the resignations from the British government, when they came, were not organized or jointly conceived. The ever-plausible Asquith managed to persuade Sir John Simon to withdraw his resignation, and Earl Beauchamp also fell into line with the Cabinet majority. Viscount Morley, John Burns, and, outside the Cabinet, Charles Trevelyan the Parliamentary Under-Secretary to the Board of Education, stuck by their resignations but do not seem to have even consulted one another. Of Morley's threat to resign it was noted that as he had made the same threat 'about once a month for 3 years, no one took this very seriously'. Only when war had been declared did he write to Burns, 'I would fain have a chat, if you are free'. Trevelyan had written to Burns the previous day, 'I think at this moment we feel alike, and I want to talk to you', but even this note was written after the separate decisions to resign had been made, and a few days later Morley told the editor of *The Westminster Gazette* that 'the hope that I have run my course and kept the faith' consoled him for 'an isolation which is by no means splendid'.[22]

It seems in fact that both Morley and Trevelyan based their opposition to the war on a much more detailed consideration of British foreign policy than was the case with Burns, who appears simply to have objected to the war because of an objection to war in general: he told his colleagues, 'I cannot be a member of a War Cabinet'. Burns, President of the Local Government Board, was a former working-class leader and very conscious of being the only Man of the People in the Cabinet. As early as 27 July he had written in his diary:

> The outlook for war rather serious. Why 4 great powers should fight over Servia no fellow can understand . . . Apart from the merits of the case it is my especial duty to dissociate myself and the principles I hold and the trusteeship of the working classes which I carry from such a universal crime as the contemplated war would be.
>
> My duty is clear and at all costs will be done.

There seems to have been more vanity than impartial reflection in Burns' attitude: on 3 August he noted, 'Honour, Duty, Humanity all unite in my protest against this wanton war. I have resigned and three others have followed Simon Morley Beauchamp'. When Margot Asquith, the Prime Minister's pushy wife, wrote inviting him 'to drop in *just* the same' at 10 Downing Street, Burns replied:

---

[22] *Inside Asquith's Cabinet: From the Diaries of Charles Hobhouse* p. 179–180 [August]; British Library Add. 46283 f. 60 Morley to Burns 4 Aug. 1914; Add. 46303 f. 2 Trevelyan to Burns [?3] Aug. 1914; Add. 46392 f. 163 Morley to J.A. Spender of *The Westminster Gazette* 6 Aug. 1914. Morley's recollections, written in retirement and published in two volumes in 1917 do not discuss the July-August crisis, except perhaps obliquely – vol. 2 p. 366 – but his remarks on how an earlier government had blundered into the Crimean War and the subsequent sense that 'the whole Crimean enterprise had been putting money on the wrong horse' – vol. 1 p. 140–141 – were doubtless coloured by his view of what had happened in August 1914.

I never worked harder in my life during the past month, but there never was a soul more at ease nor a happier spirit than I am, with no resentment but only a noble pity for those who succumbed to the diseased ambition of writing their diaries in red instead of black.

The sadness, badness, and madness of it all, fills me with a merciful condolence rather than a blazing wrath, but the wrath will come.[23]

Whatever one might think of Burns's Christ-like pose, he was evidently perfectly honest in announcing his lack of resentment; within three days of resigning he was writing to Winston Churchill, 'the leader of the War party in the Cabinet' suggesting that Thames lightermen could be induced to volunteer for war service by guaranteeing their jobs after the war, and before the end of the year he was urging ministers to 'stop Police Recruiting and divert to "the front" what will be wasted on the streets and what is sorely needed for the new Army, strong men of good physique and commanding appearance'. With Burns as with almost everyone else, the rights and wrongs of the war were to be seen in a different perspective once hostilities had actually begun.[24]

V. Parallel Cases: Turkey

It seems therefore that Britain's participation in the war appeared by no means necessary or inevitable to many of the people in the best position to judge the matter, that there was no clearly defined popular pressure in favour of war, and that the real reasons for joining in were not precisely those that were stated. But of course the Austria- attacks- Serbia- who- is-supported-by-Russia-who-is-warned-off-by-Germany-who-fears-encirclement-by-France-whom-she-invades-through-Belgium-who-is-defended-by-Britain scenario is only the shorthand version of what happened and necessarily omits the ambiguities and un-certainties of policy from which a truer understanding of motives and intentions is to be derived.

We may get a clearer idea of what was going on in people's minds if we step aside from the usual mode of presenting Britain's entry into the war, in which Britain is seen as sharing essentially the same swept-along-by-the-course-of-events position as Austria-Hungary, Germany, Russia and France, and attempt instead to compare Britain's role to that of the other, and more numerous, belligerents who entered the war not before but *after* the British declaration of war. These other powers – Turkey, Japan, Italy, Rumania, Bulgaria, Portugal, the United States, Greece – were clearly not involved in the initial explosion;

[23] Masterman *C.F.G. Masterman* p. 265; British Library Add. 46336 f. 125 Burns's diary for 27 July 1914; Add. 46282 f. 158 'Note to a Friend Aug. 3 1914' at foot of copy of letter to Asquith 2 Aug. 1914; Add. 46282 f. 160 Margot Asquith to Burns 14 Aug. 1914 and ibid. f. 165 reply 15 Aug. 1914.

[24] British Library Add. 46282 f. 226 Burns to Churchill copy, 7 Aug. 1914; ibid. f. 176 Burns to Asquith, Kitchener and McKenna, copy, 10 Dec. 1914; cf Lord Beaverbrook *Politicians and the War, 1914–1916* (2 vols 1928–32) vol. 1 p. 31.

they jumped in deliberately once the fire was well ablaze. Their motives for joining a quarrel which evidently had not been originally theirs may perhaps throw some light on Britain's participation.

The first of what we might call the second batch of belligerents was Turkey. Turkey was by no means an obvious ally for Germany. It is true that geographical location, and a long succession of wars of aggrandizement by Russia at Turkey's expense, made Russia appear in Constantinople as long-term enemy number one. On the other hand France was a traditional ally and held 62.9 per cent of Turkey's foreign debt, and Britain was second only to France in terms of investment in the Ottoman Empire. Germany was something of an object of suspicion because of the Triple Alliance with Austria-Hungary and Italy; the former, after thirty years of military occupation, had formally annexed the Ottoman provinces of Bosnia and Herzegovina in 1908 and the latter, in 1911, had made an unprovoked attack on Turkey in Tripolitana, in what is today known as Libya. The establishment of a German military mission in Turkey to help retrain the Turkish army, and the supply of finance and civil engineering experts to build the Baghdad railway, meant only that German influence was beginning to compete with French and British, not that it was already paramount.[25]

In 1908 there had been a constitutional upheaval in Turkey and a group of young radicals generally known as Young Turks but calling themselves *Ittihad ve Terakki Cemiyeti* (Society of Union and Progress, usually translated as *Committee* of Union and Progress) had come to power. They had survived an attempted counter-revolution in 1909 but had been ousted by a rival grouping in July 1912. On 23 January 1913 a 31-year-old army officer, Mehmet Enver, revolver in hand, led a small group of radicals in storming the Seraglio in Constantinople. Opposition to *Ittihad ve Terakki* dissolved and the restored radical regime was stronger than ever before, especially after the assassination of their temporary ally Mahmoud Sevket Paşa on 11 July 1913. Though the Ottoman Sultan, Mehmet V, remained nominally head of state, the new regime had many of the appearances of a military dictatorship but Enver, while promoting himself to general's rank, taking over the Ministry of War (and imprisoning numerous service rivals in the ministerial cellars) and increasingly projecting himself as a kind of Turkish Napoleon, was not the dictator. Nor, despite the name Committee of Union and Progress, was there a governing committee; Otto Liman von Sanders, head of the German military mission in Turkey and afterwards the leading figure in the wartime Turkish Army recorded:

> To me the Committee has ever remained a mystery. I have never learned of how many members it consisted or, excepting the well known leaders, who the members were.

[25] W.W. Gottlieb *Studies in Secret Diplomacy during the First World War* (1957) p. 19–21 for foreign investment in Turkey; Djemal Pasha [i.e. Ahmed Cemal] *Memories of a Turkish Statesman, 1913–1919* [1922] p. 99 for attitude to Triple Alliance.

In fact the 'Committee' was a western mistranslation: there was a party central committee, but only a fixed number of its members were permitted to hold government office and its functions remain obscure. Perhaps even the concept of a 'Society of Union and Progress' was merely part of the movement's rhetoric. Behind the facade of rhetoric there was simply a handful of ambitious individuals, each busy consolidating separate power bases: something like the Nazi regime in Germany thirty years later, but without a Hitler. Consequently there was a certain shapelessness and incoherence to Turkish policy and it is perhaps only in retrospect that the *Ittihad ve Terakki* comes into focus as an expression of a Turkish nationalism that aimed at restoring and renovating the Ottoman Empire on the basis of the dominance of the Turkish racial element. To begin with the regime had three simpler and more immediate priorities. First, it was obviously incompatible with *Ittihad ve Terakki*'s notion of itself as a strong and progressive government that it should tolerate the anomalies of the so-called Capitulations, the one-sided arrangements guaranteeing extra-territorial rights and commercial privileges to the European powers. Secondly Turkey had been defeated, and Constantinople itself had been threatened, in the Balkan War of 1912 and there was a desire to regain some of the territory and prestige then lost. Thirdly the Turkish government recognized itself to be completely isolated diplomatically. Nothing could be done about the Capitulations or a renewed war in the Balkans without diplomatic and even financial and technical support from an ally. At the same time, without an ally there was every prospect of a bad situation becoming worse. Even the European War promised only momentary respite because there seemed every likelihood of the Ottoman Empire being seized upon as part of the spoils of the victors.[26]

Ahmed Cemal Paşa, one of the foremost *Ittihad ve Terraki* leaders, was in Paris in July 1914 seeking French diplomatic and financial help. It was not forthcoming. Feelers extended in London also failed to evoke a response. During those busy final weeks of peace, time was running out for the Old Turkey as well as for the Old Europe. In Constantinople Enver, Talât Paşa and the Grand Vizir Said Halim Paşa were pushing ahead with arrangements for an alliance with Germany. A treaty was signed on 2 August but the Turkish government was cautious enough not to publish it. The pro-German element in the regime had its hands strengthened by the British Admiralty's decision, on the outbreak of European War, to confiscate two prestige battleships that were being built to Turkish orders in British yards, the *Reshadieh* and the *Sultan Osman I*. The latter had already been paid for, with money raised by public subscription in Turkey, and had been on the point of being handed over to a Turkish crew that had been sent to Britain for the purpose. Public opinion in Turkey was, according to its spokesmen, outraged and the German government, with uncharacteristic finesse, took the opportunity

---

[26] The quotation is from [Otto] Liman von Sanders *Five Years in Turkey* (Annapolis 1927) p. 8.

to make the Turkish people a present of the battle-cruiser S.M.S. *Goeben* and its accompanying light cruiser S.M.S. *Breslau*, these two ships having sought refuge in Turkish waters after having been caught in the Mediterranean by the outbreak of war. Nevertheless Enver was negotiating with Russian diplomats within three days of the signing of the unpublished treaty with Germany. Enver's proposals were forwarded by the Russians to London and Paris by mid-August, but London was prepared only to guarantee Turkish territorial integrity and refused to make any promises about regaining lost territories, while Paris was in favour of Turkey losing a bit more, to provide the price of Greek and Bulgarian assistance against Germany and Austria-Hungary. Under these circumstances neutrality scarcely seemed a practicable option.[27]

The Turks first aggressive move was to repudiate the Capitulations: a protest drawn up by the minister of Italy (then still neutral) was signed by the envoys of all the belligerent powers, though the German and Austro-Hungarian envoys privately intimated their governments' acquiescence. Even at this stage the Entente could probably have outbid German offers but no attempt was made to do so, and Turkey finally entered the war on Germany's side at the beginning of November. The ministers of Public Works, Public Instruction and Posts and Telegraphs resigned from the government, and Cemal Paşa also temporarily withdrew, but given the Entente attitude it is difficult to see that neutrality could have been a better long-term prospect than war alongside Germany – providing of course Germany won. And if neutrality was a policy which Turkey could not risk, this was the more so for a revolutionary government whose credibility depended on success in restoring the Empire's internal and external position. Turkey's strategic isolation meant that it could not afford to stay out of the war, and the insecure position of the regime meant that it could not afford to pursue policies of passivity and caution; Turkey's declaration of war against the Entente, far from an assertion of strength, was a reflex of weakness.[28]

VI. Parallel Cases: Italy

Another belated intervention in the war was by Italy. When the Italians joined the Entente in May 1915 there were two very good reasons why they should not have done: they already had enough problems elsewhere, and they were already in alliance with Germany and Austria-Hungary. The first reason, though never much emphasized by historians, is interesting in that it suggests the same *insouciance* and lack of realism, the same facile assumption that the war would be short, easy and profitable, which seems to have characterized

[27] Djemal *Memories of a Turkish Statesman* p. 104–107; Feroz Ahmad 'The Late Ottoman Empire' in Marian Kent ed. *The Great Powers and the End of the Ottoman Empire* (1984) p. 5–30, at p. 13–15; Gottlieb *Studies in Secret Diplomacy* p. 37–8; Harry N. Howard *The Partition of Turkey: A Diplomatic History, 1913–1923* (Norman Oklahoma 1931) p. 96–100.
[28] For the by-play over the Capitulations see Gottlieb *Studies in Secret Diplomacy* p. 59.

the entry into the war of the original belligerents eight months previously.

Most of the European powers had experienced worsening class conflict in the years before 1914 but nowhere more so than in Italy. 1913 had been a year of strikes, marches, police firing on crowds, and during the summer of 1914 there had been virtually a full-scale revolt in Romagna and the Marches. Railway lines had been occupied, at Ravenna the security forces had been besieged in their barracks, and at Fabriano, a paper-making centre, a workers' republic had been proclaimed. Then, on 13 January 1915, little more than six years after the earthquake which had almost totally destroyed Messina and Reggio di Calabria and killed over 77,000 – *The Times* had called it 'the most appalling catastrophe of modern times' – there was a major earth tremor in the Abruzzi which affected 54 communes and left 20,000 dead and 100,000 homeless; the losses would have been much greater except that the epicentre was in one of the most sparsely populated mountain regions of the peninsula. Finally, just as the Italian government was settling the details of its sell-out to the Entente, armed revolt broke out in their newly acquired Libyan colony – by early August 1915 it was to be necessary to evacuate the whole of Tripolitana except Tripoli and Homs. A working class on the brink of revolution, whole provinces shattered and demoralized by vast natural disasters, colonies in revolt; it was hardly a propitious moment to join in a controversial war.[29]

Controversial the war certainly was. Italy had been a member of the Triple Alliance with Germany and Austria-Hungary since 1884. It is true that in 1908 the Swiss chief of staff Colonel Sprecher von Bernegg had foreseen the possibility of war between Italy and Austria-Hungary, and a consequent violation of Swiss neutrality by Italy, and took it upon himself to inform the Austro-Hungarian general staff of his own dispositions in this eventuality. Pursuing the same line of thought, the Austro-Hungarian chief of staff, Franz Freiherr Conrad von Hötzendorf, recommended invading Italy in the rear while the Italians were bogged down in their campaign in Libya in 1911. Conrad was sacked for making this proposal and in July 1913 Italy and Austria-Hungary signed a naval convention providing, in the event of war, for a combined fleet under Austrian command to prevent French troop transfers from North Africa to metropolitan France. At the German army manoeuvres in the autumn of 1913, Pollio, the then Italian chief of staff, discussed the use of Italian troops on the Franco-German frontier should war occur: Conrad, now reinstated, was present at these discussions. In February 1914 Pollio offered Moltke, his German opposite number, at least three corps – 100,000 men. On 27 July 1914, as Europe began to slide into war, Pollio died. His successor, Luigi Cadorna, wrote on 31 July to the King of Italy – not, be it noted, to the premier or war minister – pointing out that the French had the Franco-Italian border too well fortified for an Italian offensive in that quarter, and suggesting that the main Italian force, initially five corps,

[29] The Abruzzi earthquake is described in Antonio Salandra *L'Intervento (1915)* (Milan 1930) p. 27, cf *Times* 30 Dec. 1908 p. 3a.

should serve under German control in Alsace-Lorraine: 'To subtract from the decisive action even a single unit not indispensable elsewhere would mean contributing knowingly to diminish the probability of success in the common task'. Cadorna explained to the King that the main, if not the only, problem was that the Italian home army had degenerated into a mere base camp for Libya, with units broken up and stripped of their best equipment to feed the Libyan campaign. The day after writing this letter Cadorna was surprised to learn that his government had decided to remain neutral.[30]

Although Camillo Marchese Garroni, the Italian minister at Constantinople, told his German colleague, 'Italian abstention would cast a stain on Italian honour which would never be wiped out', the Italian foreign minister was probably quite correct in claiming, in a letter to his ambassadors at Berlin and Vienna, that the population generally was unwilling to join a war provoked by Austria-Hungary 'in opposition to liberal principles and to the principle of nationality, out of political and territorial ambitions, more or less dissimulated, and contrary to Italian interests'. Bitterness was directed less against the Vienna government than against Vienna's Slovene and Croat subjects, who were increasingly in commercial competition with Italian businessmen in the Adriatic; the Italian premier Antonio Salandra claimed later 'There was no name more hated in Italy than *Croat*'. In May 1914, just a few weeks before the assassination of Archduke Franz Ferdinand, street fighting between Italian and Slovene ethnic communities had broken out in the Austrian port of Trieste and had sparked off student demonstrations, initially in the northeast of Italy but soon spreading to Rome, where the university had to be closed. It was also noticeable that the most energetic interest in joining the war was shown by the men who rushed to enlist in volunteer units in the French and Serbian armies. (Those in the French army, led by the son of Giuseppe Garibaldi, numbered about 2,500; after a brief spell in the firing line their unit was disbanded because it was feared it was being taken over by leftists.) Few if any Italians volunteered for the Habsburg army and a considerable number of Italian-speaking Austrian subjects fled across the border to evade their military service; a *compagnia Mazzini* which wanted to fight alongside the French in red-shirts and which was disbanded by the French authorities in September 1914 was commanded by an Italian-speaking Austrian citizen from Trieste.[31]

[30] Peter Schubert *Die Tätigkeit des k.u.k. Militärattachés in Bern während des Ersten Weltkrieges* (Osnabrück 1980) p. 5–6; *Österreich-Ungarns Aussenpolitik von der Bosnischen Krise 1908 bis zum Kriegsausbruch 1914* (8 vols Vienna 1930) vol. 3 p. 346–348 item 2644 for Conrad's memo of 24 Sept. 1911; Michael Palumbo 'Italian-Austro-Hungarian Military Relations before World War I' in Samuel R. Williamson and Peter Pastor ed. *Essays on World War I: Origins and Prisoners of War* (New York 1983) p. 37–53 at p. 44–5; Albertini *The Origins of the War of 1914* vol. 1 p. 559–560; Luigi Cadorna *Altre pagine sulla grande guerra* (Milan 1925) p. 15–23 Cadorna to King Vittore Emanuele 31 July 1914.

[31] Antonio Salandra *La Neutralità Italiana [1914]: Ricordi e Pensieri* (Milan 1928) p. 149 for Garroni's remark and p. 144–5 for the Italian foreign minister's letter to his ambassadors; ibid. p. 57 for the croat remark; ibid. p. 31–2 for the riots in Trieste and the student unrest; Gino Coletti *Peppino Garibaldi e La Legione Garibaldina* (Bologna 1915) p. 16 and p. 105–6.

Apart from the fact that there was evidently more sympathy for the Entente than for the Austro-German coalition, the Italian government wished to hold back because they first needed to clarify the terms for Italian entry into the war. In 1887, when the Triple Alliance had been renewed for the first time, an additional treaty had been signed to the effect that neither Italy nor Austria-Hungary should increase its territory in the east without 'a previous arrangement between the two Powers, based on the principle of reciprocal compensation for every gain, territorial or otherwise'. This agreement was inserted into the next renewal of the Triple Alliance in 1891, as Clause Seven. Even before it became obvious, at the end of July 1914, that the war would involve more than Austria-Hungary and Serbia, the foreign minister, the Marchese di San Giuliano, advised the King of Italy of the necessity of obtaining their allies' recognition of the Italian interpretation of Clause Seven. The compensation the Italian government had in mind was 'the cession of a part of Austria's Italian provinces corresponding to her territorial gains elsewhere'. The Austrians claimed that Clause Seven referred only to the Ottoman Empire, but the Italian view that 'the East' included Serbia and Montenegro was upheld by the Germans. The Italian government also felt that, so long as the war was limited to hostilities between Austria-Hungary and Serbia, Clause Seven would operate without Italy needing to provide military assistance.[32]

While the Italians, backed by the Germans, were trying to extract the right price from the Austro-Hungarian government, the Entente quickly began to make offers of its own. The initiative for this came from Russia, though the French president, Raymond Poincaré, caught on a state visit to St. Petersburg by the rush of events, had had time to discuss the question of offers to Italy before hurrying home. On 1 August the Albanian port of Valona, almost directly across the Straits of Otranto from the Italian port of Brindisi, was mentioned; on 4 August Trento; on 5 August control of the entire Adriatic and the Dodecanese; on 6 August Trieste; on 8 August the Dalmatian coast. The British Foreign Secretary, Sir Edward Grey later said:

> We did not tempt Italy. Never asked any country to join us in the war. Both Italy and Rumania came and offered themselves, demanding certain terms. Extortionate: and we beat them down as best we could, but *could not run the risk of refusing an ally*.

Grey often appeared not to care what happened, providing his own aristocratic hands remained clean; the tempting certainly took place, through Russian agency but in the name of the Entente: and Italy was tempted. But even foreign minister San Giuliano hesitated before stabbing Italy's allies in the back:

> We cannot however hide from ourselves that such a war, which would be considered in all Europe as an act of treachery and would increase the distrust in which we are held even on the part of those who would become our new

---

[32] Salandra *La Neutralità Italiana* p. 79, 99–102.

allies, would involve for us great risks not only in the case of defeat but even in the case of victory, because our position in the Mediterranean would become exceedingly dangerous with France victorious and our current allies transformed into implacable foes.[33]

Such views were to continue in circulation even a couple of years after the Italian government had committed itself to the Entente; in May 1917 the Duke of Aosta, cousin of the King and in command of Italy's Third Army, was wondering:

> What will become of us, last minute friends (*amici dell' ultima ora*), allies only because we have Germany against us as an aggressor. Because, what are the interests that unite us to the Entente?

And Emanuele Paternò del Castello, vice-president of the Senate, argued a few months later:

> we have three formidable foes: 1. the enemy 2. the allies 3. the extremists, the subversives and the nationalists.
>   The Austrian foe is the least danger because in spite of gas, trench clubs, etc., he is known. One knows what he's worth . . .
>   With such allies, with whom we have nothing in common, what must we or can we expect?[34]

But in the first months of the European War there was a growing agitation in favour of Italian intervention on the side of the Entente. The pro-war party included romantic patriots brought up to be ashamed of the foreign help Italy had needed to achieve independence in 1859, and political refugees from Trieste and inhabitants of the border regions near Austria-Hungary for whom the issue of Austrian hostility to Italia Irredenta was still a live one. Generally however the pro-war agitation had a factitious opportunist air to it, exemplified by the activities of the ageing wonder-boy Gabriele D'Annunzio, the young Benito Mussolini, editor of the Socialist daily *Avanti!*, and the Futurist poet F.T. Marinetti, who was still trying to establish an artistic credo in which war was conceived as some sort of climactic and cathartic happening. Marinetti's first Futurist Manifesto of February 1909 had demanded 'Let us glorify War, the only hygiene of the world', and this latter phrase was adopted as the title of a collection of his poems published in 1915, *Guerra sola igiene del Mondo*. From 12 August 1914 he dedicated himself full time to 'preparing the Italian climate for war'. In October Mussolini resigned from *Avanti!* to

[33] W.W. Gottlieb *Studies in Secret Diplomacy during the First World War* (1957) p. 231–401 for an exhaustive account of the Italian negotiations, and cf. Piero Pieri *L'Italia nella Prima Guerra Mondiale* (Turin 1968 edit.) p. 37–8; Trevelyan *Grey of Falloden* p. 302 quoting conversation with Gilbert Murray 10 Jan. 1918: *1 Documenti Diplomatici Italiani 5ª Serie, 1914–1918* (11 vols Rome 1954–1986) vol. 1 p. 83 item 151 San Giuliano to Salandra 9 Aug. 1914.

[34] Angelo Gatti *Caporetto: dal diario di guerra inedito* [diary May–Dec. 1917] ed. Alberto Monticone (Bologna 1964) p. 40, diary 26 May 1917 and p. 218, 220, diary 3 Sept. 1917.

establish an interventionist newspaper, *Popolo d'Italia*; for this he was expelled from the Socialist party. Mussolini became in effect the leader, not merely of a huge propaganda campaign, but of a pressure group of phenomenonally rapid growth. Neither he nor Marinetti relied only on the pen and the telephone. On 16 September 1914 Marinetti was arrested at a tumultuous demonstration in the Piazza del Duomo in Milan at which eight Austrian flags were burnt; he was released after five days in the cells; on 19 February 1915 he was arrested with four other Futurists while demonstrating outside the Parliament building in Rome, and on 12 April 1915 he was arrested together with Mussolini, again in Rome. These incidents maintained the level of popular excitement on the war issue: indeed the pro-war demonstrations are often cited as a factor in the Italian government's decision for war.[35]

It seems difficult to believe however that the Italian government was in any sense stampeded into adopting a war policy by the antics of Marinetti and Mussolini. Despite the street demonstrations and the avant-garde rhetoric there was still a very considerable body of opinion opposed to the war, including not only the socialist movement but also the leading parliamentarian of the day, *doyen* of the ruling Liberal party and three times ex-premier, Giovanni Giolitti. From the beginning Antonio Salandra, the Italian premier, was fully aware of the contrived nature of the pro-war agitation and indeed himself contemplated organizing demonstrations and the 'enrolment of a force, perhaps an expedition, modelled on Garibaldi's Thousand, to provoke a disturbance in Trieste while it is stripped of troops; then repression by Austria and consequent agitation in Italy'. This force would be armed and controlled by the government; Salandra in fact was prepared to stoop to any sort of dirty work to get Italy into the war; the question is *why*.[36]

To some extent Italy's pretensions to being a great power made it impossible for the country to keep out of the war. Salandra's public utterances were certainly in keeping with such a view. On 3 December 1914 he received a standing ovation in the Chamber of Deputies when he announced:

> Italy has vital interests to safeguard, just aspirations to affirm and sustain . . . a status as a Great Power to maintain intact, and moreover, not to be diminished in relative terms by possible gains on the part of other states.

But the interpretation of Salandra as merely a patriot of a perhaps not very attractive type become less convincing when one sees how far, how hard, and at what potential risk to his political career, he had to push against opposing forces to bring his country into the war. The unexpected, inexplicable character of his commitment to the war was the more striking in that he had previously shown almost no interest in foreign affairs.[37]

[35] F.T. Marinetti et al *Noi Futuristi* (Milan [1917]) p. 128–130.

[36] Salandra *Neutralità Italiana* p. 237–238 Salandra to Sonnino 28 Aug. 1914 for scheme of fomenting a demonstration against Trieste.

[37] Ibid. p. 441 and cf Richard Bosworth *Italy and the Approach of the First World War* (1983) p. 34.

After arduous negotiation Italy signed a secret treaty with the Entente on 26 April 1915. The Treaty of London promised Italy South Tyrol, Trieste, Gorizia, Dalmatia, the Albanian port of Valona (which the Italians had already occupied), new territories in Africa if Britain and France annexed German colonies there, a £50 million loan from London, and the exclusion of the Pope from any peace conference. The triple Alliance was denounced – in the technical sense, i.e. repudiated – on 4 May 1915, and all that was left was to secure a parliamentary majority in favour of a declaration of war on Austria-Hungary. That was the difficult bit; the parliamentary supremacy of Giolitti had never seemed more impregnable. Anticipating a defeat in the Chamber Salandra resigned on 13 May, but the King, himself in favour of war, refused to accept his resignation and Giolitti failed to press his advantage. There was a wave of demonstrations in favour of war: but also some against. In Turin, on 17 and 18 May there was a General Strike against the policy of intervention: a clear enough indication that Salandra could not have seriously thought of war as a means of distracting attention from the country's still simmering social unrest. Yet because Giolitti failed to make a stand, the opposition to Salandra in Parliament dissolved almost overnight and on 20 May 1915 his government was voted war powers by 407 to 74.[38]

Giolitti's opposition to the war was consistent with the reputation he had long since established for sane and pragmatic policy, and his failure to press his opposition to extremities remains to this day inexplicable except in terms of his unwillingness to go against what he perceived to be the wishes of King Vittorio Emanuele. And it seems to have been the discomfiture of Giolitti as much as the glory of leading his country into a great adventure that was Salandra's basic motive. Theoretically Giolitti and Salandra – and most of the other deputies – belonged to the same party, the Liberals. This party was not organized like one of today's British parliamentary parties, with a national organization and an official and established leader who can expect to become premier when his party achieves a majority; the Liberals were a party that had always had a majority but never had a formal leadership. Giolitti however was the dominating figure and having been premier for eight of the fourteen years since 1900 had much the widest circle of contacts and clients. But he had concentrated on wooing the political elites in Rome and had no mass following in the country. The increasing necessity of a mass base in Italian politics had been shown by the rise of the Socialist party and by the activities of the Catholic Electoral Union, which in the 1913 elections had not only secured the return of 29 of its own candidates but also claimed a share in the election of 228 out of the 511 Liberals, assistance having been given in

[38] Pieri _L'Italia nella prima guerra mondiale_ p. 70–74. William A. Renzi _In the Shadow of the Sword: Italy's Neutrality and Entrance into the Great War, 1914–1915_ (New York 1987) p. 100 accepts Vittorio Emanuele's own claim that he left all decisions to his ministers: see also p. 258: but see Denis Mack Smith _Italy and the Monarchy_ (1989) p. 210–214 for the King's desire for war and his subsequent claim that he had personally secured Italy's intervention, and p. 150–151, 168 for his dislike of the _appearance_ of active interference in government.

return for pledges to support a programme of Catholic education at school, opposition to divorce, and so on. Salandra had come to power in 1914 when Giolitti had slipped up in one of his perpetual balancing acts and had been obliged to resign. Salandra knew he could not compete with Giolitti in the salons and corridors of the power market in Rome; but almost certainly he saw in the war an opportunity to establish a mass following and a national leadership which Giolitti had not needed.[39]

It has been argued that Salandra merely wished to consolidate the Liberal party's leadership of the country, feeling that it had been compromised by Giolittism and by the rise of other parties. This view presents Salandra's policy as a visionary and altruistic campaign to save the soul of the Liberal party, but it seems more likely that Salandra was more interested in his own position than that of his amorphous party. It should be noted that while Giolitti was a Piedmontese, Salandra was a southerner, the first southern premier since 1898. The South was not interested in Trento and Trieste on the distant northern borders of the country; in April 1915 the provincial prefect of Naples warned the government that at least 90 per cent of the population of the province of Naples were opposed to intervention in the war. After two generations of national independence the southerners, like most Italians, still generally understood the words for 'our country', *nostro paese, nostra patria*, to mean merely 'our home town'. Salandra had not been premier long enough to establish a real power base except for a southern prejudice in his favour, but in the view of himself and his clique the interests of 'home town' could be promoted by maintaining both Italy as a great power and Salandra as a great statesman. The war, and the agitation in favour of Italian intervention, provided Salandra with an opportunity to consolidate his own position which he was politician enough to seize with both hands.[40]

Asquith, who regarded Italy as 'that most voracious, slippery, & perfidious Power', concluded magisterially, 'I shall always think that on a great scene she has played the meanest and pettiest of parts'; but even he acknowledged 'one must not be too squeamish about the price to be paid'. This was also Lloyd George's view:

> We were only too well pleased to secure the adhesion of another Ally to scrutinise closely the proposed territorial readjustments which were the condition of the bargain. War plays havoc with the refinements of conscience.[41]

[39] Cf 'Martin Clark *Modern Italy, 1871–1982* (1984) p. 157–9.

[40] The theory about Salandra wishing to reconsolidate the Liberal bloc is in Giovanna Procacci 'Italy: from Interventionism to Fascism, 1917–1919' *Journal of Contemporary History* vol. 3 no. 4 (1968) p. 153–176 at p. 154. For attitude of Naples province see Franco Gianola 'Una Guerra Civile nel Nome della Pace' *Historia* May–June 1985 p. 29. Even in the period 1982–5 I found that my students in Salerno still understood *paese* and *patria* to refer only to the town they came from.

[41] Michael and Eleanor Brock ed. *H.H. Asquith: Letters to Venetia Stanley* (Oxford 1982) p. 501 Asquith to Venetia Stanley 23 March 1915 and p. 505 same to same 24 March 1915. David Lloyd George *The Truth about The Peace Treaties* (2 vols 1938) vol. 2 p. 765.

VII. Parallel Cases: Greece

Premier Eleutherios Venizelos of Greece, like Salandra in Italy, favoured participation in the war ostensibly to improve his country's international position. Again there seems to have been something else behind this policy: and whereas in Italy the King, while pretending to play a passive constitutional role, had been a useful ally in the prime minister's political manipulations, in Greece it seems to have been the King's constitutional position itself which emerged as the real target of the premier's policy.

It would perhaps be unjust to see Venizelos's nationalism in terms of Salandra's. The latter had grown up in an Italy which had already achieved the greater part of its territorial claims against Austria, and in a part of the country where the distant problems of the ethnic frontier loomed much less large than the presence of carpet-baggers from Giolitti's north. Venizelos on the other hand had been born a Turkish subject, had passed his childhood in exile following his father's banishment by the Ottoman authorities, and his adolescence in Crete under Ottoman rule, and had invested sufficiently successfully in the Pan-Hellenic ideal to become prime minister in Athens while his native Crete was still Ottoman territory. Though he had achieved the liberation of his native island, he still suffered with all the sympathy of shared experience for those Greeks in the outlying archipelagos who were still ruled from Constantinople. Venizelos also had anxieties regarding the policy of Bulgaria on Greece's northern border in the aftermath of the Balkan Wars of 1912–13; having first spearheaded victory over the Turks, Bulgaria had then been humiliated by a hostile confederation of its late allies and seemed likely to renew the struggle at some stage.

For Venizelos the outbreak of the European War offered the possibility of an acceptable final settlement of the Balkan frontiers: Serbia would annex Bosnia-Herzegovina and cede Macedonia to Bulgaria, thereby gratifying the territorial ambitions frustrated in 1913, while the Greeks could drive the Turks from the Aegean Islands. King Constantine, married to Kaiser Wilhelm's sister, saw of course that there was no possibility of supporting the Austro-German alliance given Anglo-French naval power in the Mediterranean though he, his foreign minister Streit and Lieutenant-Colonel Ioannis Metaxas, his pro-German confidential military adviser, all thought that Germany was fighting Slavism – which for them included Bulgarian expansionism – and as Constantine wrote to his brother-in-law, 'The Kaiser knows that my personal sympathies and political views draw me to his side'. Nevertheless the prospects held out by an alliance with a victorious Entente were tempting and early in September 1914 he permitted the British naval officer Mark Kerr, then in command of the Greek Navy, to consult with general staff officers on the subject of a possible Anglo-Greek descent on Gallipoli. When however King Constantine insisted on waiting for the Turks to provide an excuse for declaring war there was a row with Venizelos; yet the dream of sharing in the final dismemberment of the Ottoman Empire was irresistible and in March the Queen warned her brother the Kaiser that Constantine 'is completely possessed by the spectre of Byzantium'.[42]

The Entente's relations with Greece from the spring of 1915 onwards provide a curious insight into the foreign policy preoccupations of the allied powers, and are difficult to reconcile with the proud claim of Sir Edward Grey that 'the basic principle of the political harmony between the three Allied Entente Powers is the protection of the inviolability and neutrality of second-rate Powers'. A satisfactory deal with Constantine was prevented by the Russian government vetoing any suggestion of Greek control of Constantinople, or even its internationalization, because it was thought that this would in effect mean *British* control. The Entente's clumsy efforts to win over Bulgaria alarmed the Greek government and disgusted Greek public opinion, and the proposal to establish an Anglo-French base at Salonica – Greece's second city – to assist the Serbs fuelled the increasing bitterness of Venizelos's relationship with his King; though Venizelos secured an agreement for an Anglo-French occupation of Salonica he resigned a few hours before their troops arrived. On 21 November 1915 Venizelos called for a boycott of the parliamentary elections due on 19 December, because he feared that the voting would be rigged and that too many of his supporters had been mobilized in the army. Later he proposed to the allied envoys the establishment of a provisional government responsible to the June 1915 chamber. The French financed his propaganda, and at the beginning of 1916 the French military attaché tried to interest Paris in organizing a coup d'état. In August 1916 Venizelos was in the middle of planning th establishment of a revolutionary government in Crete when, on 29 August, without consulting him, his sympathizers staged a coup in Salonica. The conspirators failed to win over the Greek troops in the city and had to be installed in control at gunpoint by the French, while far away in London Sir Edward Grey belated, 'the French should be told point blank that to encourage a revolutionary movement against the King of Greece would be much resented by the Emperor of Russia'. The French military commander, Sarrail, desired to simplify matters by occupying the whole country but was warned by Lloyd George that this would be 'a repetition of what happened in Belgium, & the Germans would always hold it up against us'. In fact the developments provoked, encouraged or permitted by the Entente, culminating in the enforced abdication of Constantine in June 1917, seem to have differed from the earlier violation of Belgium only in being more protracted. Once King Constantine was out of the way, Venizelos took over the reins of power and declared war. Throughout the prolonged crisis Venizelos himself seems to have preserved a semblance of honourable consistency, but it does seem that what he had in view, besides the greatness of Greece, was the strengthening of parliamentary authority within the country at the expense of the monarchy: indeed the Greek

---

[42] George B. Leon *Greece and the Great Powers, 1914–1917* (Thessaloniki 1974) p. 29, 33, 62, 65–6, Constantine's letter to the Kaiser is quoted on p. 29, his wife's on p. 128.

experience was perhaps the clearest instance of an attempt to use the war to unite a country on a new basis which succeeded instead in generating a new degree of division.[43]

VIII. Parallel Cases: Portugal

Japan's participation in the war on the Entente side had strictly limited scope and avowedly local objectives, and in the case of Bulgaria and Rumania both countries' governments can perhaps be excused for seeing the larger conflict as merely a continuation of the Balkan conflict of 1912–1913. Rumania had been associated with the Triple Alliance since the 1880s and had renewed its treaties with each of the Triplice powers early in 1913 and there was some truth in the comment of the Russian foreign minister Sazonov:

> The position of Rumania in the Balkans recalls in many respects that of Italy in Europe. These two powers are subject to megalomania, and, not having strength enough to accomplish their projects openly, are obliged to content themselves with an opportunist policy, observing always on which side lies force, in order that they may range themselves on this side.[44]

In any case the dynastic ambitions and racial mythology underpinning Rumanian claims in Transylvania, and also Bulgarian claims in Macedonia, hardly provide a useful parallel to British foreign policy (though a typewritten propaganda sheet dropped over the British lines in Macedonia and now preserved in the Imperial War Museum comments sadly on Britain's policy of defending Belgium while oppressing little Bulgaria). Perhaps more generally illuminating is the conduct of one of the least expected participants in the war, Portugal.

In many respects Portugal in 1914 resembled Turkey: a ramshackle empire apparently on the point of disintegrating into the hands of officious neighbours, ruled over by a revolutionary regime which needed to establish

[43] Grey's words, as quoted by Benckendorff 13 Nov. 1914 are cited in Gottlieb *Studies in Secret Diplomacy* p. 69; Leon *Greece and the Great Powers* p. 134 and p. 308–9; Alexander S. Mitrakos *France in Greece during World War I: A Study in the Politics of Power* (Boulder 1982) p. 49–50; Grey's warning, to Crowe and Hardinge 1 Sept. 1916 is quoted in Leon *Greece and the Great Powers* p. 393–4; Lloyd George's warning to Sarrail is in A.J.P. Taylor ed. *Lloyd George: A Diary by Frances Stevenson* (1971) p. 136–7, 10 Jan. 1917.

[44] Sidney Bradshaw Fay *The Origins of the World War* (2 vol New York 1929) vol. 1 p. 481, quoting Sazonov to Tsar Nicholas II 23 Nov. NS/6 Dec. OS 1913; see also Harry N. Howard *The Partition of Turkey: A Diplomatic History, 1913–1923* (Norman, Oklahoma 1931) p. 152–165 for a good account of Bulgaria's move towards war and ibid. p. 166–176 for a parallel account of Rumania's policy; for a contemporary impression see M. Erzberger *Erlebnisse im Weltkriege* (Stuttgart 1920) p. 91–101 (Bulgaria) and p. 102–110 (Rumania). See also Glenn E. Torrey 'Rumania and the Belligerents, 1914–1916' *Journal of Contemporary History* vol. 1 no. 3 (1966) p. 171–191, D. Iliescu *Documente privitoare la Răsboiul pentru Intregirea României* (Bucharest 1924) p. 37–83 and Constantin Nuţu *România în anii neutralităţii (1914–1916)* (Bucharest 1972) p. 130–234 and p. 277–313.

its ideological credentials. The eventual but inevitable collapse of Portuguese authority in the country's African colonies had long been foreseen by British and German officials, and in August 1898 London and Berlin had negotiated a convention arranging to share in any loan made to the Portuguese government and to secure each share of the loan on specified parts of the Portuguese colonies, which were to be taken over by the appropriate creditor if, as rather expected, Portugal defaulted on repayment. This convention, effectively establishing German and British spheres of influence in Portuguese Africa, was revised in 1913, though in its revised form it was only initialled, not signed; Sir Arthur Nicolson, the Permanent Under-Secretary of State at the Foreign Office regarded the convention as 'the most cynical business that I have come across in my whole experience of diplomacy'. Aware of these arrangements, the Portuguese government was naturally anxious as to the future of the overseas Empire; in 1917 an interdepartmental committee in London reported:

> It is understood, in fact, that one of the determinant factors for Portugal's active participation in the war was the conviction that military co-operation against the common enemy would render it impossible for a British Government in honour to permit any encroachment on the territorial or sovereign rights of her Ally.

The fighting between German and British Imperial forces in German East Africa (today mainland Tanzania) which threatened increasingly to spill over into the Portuguese colony of Mozambique, and the consequent need to reinforce the garrison there, in themselves tended to suck Portugal into the world conflict. But in the end, of the nearly 100,000 troops despatched abroad by the Portuguese government, only 34,000 went to Africa: 65,166 were shipped to France and Belgium, to be thrown into the holocaust of the Western Front.[45]

The Corpo Expedicionário Português was undoubtedly the outcome of the newly established Portuguese republic's desire to establish its international standing. The monarchy had been overthrown in 1910 and there had followed a vaguely Jacobin period – without a Robespierre or even a Danton – in which the revolutionary Carbonaria and armed vigilantes and militia groups functioned openly, sometimes even invading army barracks to harangue the troops. On the outbreak of war there was considerable enthusiasm for the Entente – the German and Austro-Hungarian legations needed to be given police protection – but the monarchists were openly pro-German. There were some fears that the Spanish, under cover of the war, would intervene to restore stability, perhaps to reestablish the monarchy, though the Spanish

---

[45] For Nicolson's remark see Harold Nicolson *Sir Arthur Nicolson, Bart, Lord Carnock: A Study in the Old Diplomacy* (1930) p. 393; Interdepartmental 'Territorial Changes Committee', 3rd Report 28 March 1917 quoted in Wm. Roger Louis *Great Britain and Germany's Lost Colonies 1914–1919* (Oxford 1967) p. 73–4; J.D. Vincent Smith 'Britain and Portugal, 1910–1916' (London Univ. Ph.D. dissertation 1971) p. 261, 298–9; Douglas L. Wheeler *Republican Portugal: A Political History, 1910–1926* (Madison 1978) p. 129–130, 132.

government denied any such intention. Premier Bernardino Machado was especially anxious to take Portugal into the war, somewhat to the surprise of the British minister Lancelot D. Carnegie:

> I remarked that any country which could honourably keep out of the present war was to be congratulated. He [Machado] was much displeased and talked for an hour of the renaissance of Portugal and her ability and duty to take her place in the great European struggle.

Machado's ardour was checked by the more moderate Colonel Freire de Andrade who told Carnegie of a discussion with Machado:

> In a stormy interview with the latter in the course of which a duel was hinted at, he had said that though he might have to leave office he, though he was no politician, would force him – Machado – to resign too.[46]

On 25 January 1915 a characteristically disorganized military coup took place in Lisbon, with the support of the monarchists and the moderate republicans. A 68-year-old general, Joaquim Pimenta de Castro, a personal friend of the president and a man acceptable to, though not in the confidence of, the putschists took over as premier. Pimento de Castro failed to rally any grass-roots support and antagonized the republicans by amnestying royalist exiles, and in May 1915 his government was overthrown by an armed popular insurrection. Elections followed, consolidating the hold of the new democratic regime. Increasingly open identification with the British cause provoked the Germans to declare war on 9 March 1916. The despatch of the expeditionary force to northern Europe was not popular and war expenditure placed an additional strain on an economy already weak. In May 1917 ten days of bread riots in Lisbon left many dead. Finally the discredited regime was ousted by armed insurrection early in December 1917 and the New Republic dictatorship of Sidónio Pais came into being. This development provoked exaggerated rumours amongst the Corpo Expedicionário Português's British neighbours in Flanders: 'Their command has undergone change as senior officers were on the winning or losing side in the most recent revolution at Lisbon'. Throughout all these changes of regime however certain preoccupations and forms of rhetoric remained constant.[47]

There was, first of all, a fear of Spain. The welcome given to anti-Republican conspirators beyond the border had led to bitterness and fears of military intervention to restore the Portuguese monarchy and by July 1912 the Portuguese press was suggesting that the object of Spanish policy was

---

[46] Public Record Office FO 371/2105 Carnegie to Grey 12 Aug. 1914 (on popular support for Entente); ibid. Hardinge to Grey 12 Aug. 1914 (on Spanish attitude); ibid. Carnegie to Crowe 26 Aug. 1914 (on interview with Machado); ibid. same to same 31 Aug. 1914 (on interview with Freire de Andrade). See also Public Record Office WO 158/111 report on Political Situation in Portugal dated 6 Jan. 1916.

[47] Wheeler *Republican Portugal* p. 112, 127, 293 fn 61; for the rumours in Flanders see J.C. Dunn *The War the Infantry Knew* (1987 edit.) p. 444 sub 10 Feb. 1918.

not merely a royalist intervention but annexation: 'perda da nacionalidade portuguesa', loss of Portuguese nationhood. This, after all, was the 'antigo plano de nosso inimigo tradicional', the old plan of our traditional foe. Once the war broke out the German cause tended to be identified, in both Portugal and Spain, with that of political reaction while the French and British (and more remotely Russian) side were identified with the cause of democracy; the whole issue of the war thus became entwined both with the stability of the Portuguese regime and with Portugal's relationship to the Spanish monarchical government. It was also felt that, if Portuguese foreign policy was not sufficiently different from Spain's, it would be assumed abroad that Lisbon was merely an echo, diplomatically speaking, of Madrid, and that foreigners would simply fail to recognize Portugal's 'moral superiority' to 'retrograde and reactionary Spain'. 'This moment gives her an unique opportunity in her history to acquire identity (*personalidade*). If she forsakes it, she is a nation lost', it was claimed. An article in the journal *A Aguia* argued:

> Once involved in the war we shall be involved again in our old and abandoned destiny, which was a destiny of the Ideal and Spiritual. . . . an affirmation and a necessity of our historical existence.

Troops had to be sent to Flanders 'for our past, for our future . . .' [48]

Once the Corpo Expedicionário Português was installed in the war zone, representations had to be made at the highest official levels to prohibit British troops from referring to their new allies as 'Pork and Beans'. The Portuguese regime's commitment to the war inevitably has the appearance of a faintly ludicrous Bonapartist gesture: yet more clearly than in any other country, the decision for war can be seen to grow logically out of the particular forms of weakness manifested by the government. The population as a whole almost certainly wanted the war even less than the people of any other belligerent state; but that was inevitably part of the reason why it was so necessary to the intellectuals and the politicians.[49]

[48] Hipólito de la Torre Gómez *Conspiração contra Portugal (1910–1912) As relacões políticas entre Portugal e Espanha* (Lisbon 1978) p. 175–181, 208–211 on 'loss of Portuguese nationality' and 'the old plan of our traditional enemy'; Fernando Díaz-Plaja *Francofilos y Germanofilos* (Barcelona 1973) p. 115–170, 231–298; Hipólito de la Torre Gómez *Na Encruzilhada da Grande Guerra: Portugal-Espanha, 1913–1919* (Lisbon 1980) p. 98–100, p. 148–151 quoting Joao Chagas *Diario* (4 vols Lisbon 1929–1932) vol. 1 p. 132 on acquiring *personalidade* and vol. 1 p. 375 on retrograde and reactionary Spain; Hipólito de la Torre Gómez *Na Encruzilhada* etc. p. 102 quoting Augusto de Castro in *A Aguia* vol. 9 2ª serie Jan.–July 1916 p. 153 on Portugal's old and abandoned destiny; David Magno *Livro da Guerra de Portugal na Flanders* (2 vols Porto 1921) vol. 1 p. 268 on fighting 'For our past, for our future . . .'

[49] For the attempt to suppress the 'Pork and Beans' nickname see J.C. Dunn *The War the Infantry Knew* (1987 edit.) p. 443 sub. 9 Feb. 1918: evidently the attempt failed as in 1975 the British mercenaries (mostly ex-squaddies) in Angola were still referring to their Portuguese opposite numbers as 'Porks', as I am informed by Michel Parry, co-author of the memoirs of Chris Dempster and Dave Tomkins, *Firepower* (1978).

IX. Last Parallel Case: The United States

Both militarily and in terms of influence on the professed war aims of the belligerents, the most important entry into the war was that of the United States of America. In 1914 American participation must have seemed the remotest contingency: far away, intent on excluding European political influence from their own hemisphere, with a tiny professional army, and governed by a university professor who spoke like a pacifist dreamer, the neutrality of the United States seemed a foregone conclusion. Yet in Europe the war meant a vast increase in economic demand and a reduction in supply and thereby offered American business a commercial challenge it could not ignore. Initially the U.S. Secretary of State discouraged contribution to loans floated by the belligerents on the U.S. money market, stating such loans to be 'inconsistent with the true spirit of neutrality'. But this attitude was predicated on the then customary assumption that the war would be very short. From October 1914 the American government's attitude became more permissive and by September 1915 a new Secretary of State, Robert Lansing, argued in favour of allowing loans 'for our own good' to sustain export levels. Proposals for an embargo on arms supplies to the belligerents were not supported by the President on the grounds that Germany, having been better prepared for the war, had much less need to buy arms than the Entente. This official view that the Germans had a larger stock-pile of weaponry than the Russians or the French was an early success of Entente propaganda, but the factor which principally affected trading with Europe was that France and Britain had a bigger stock-pile of money and consequently could purchase much more in the U.S.; Germany could neither afford to buy nor, with the British naval blockade, arrange importation at a significant level. Since even trade with neutral Sweden eventually reached four times its pre-war level, and with Norway six times its pre-war level, American business had a real financial interest in acquiescing in the British blockade though it was bitterly resented in principle. By late 1916 Allied borrowing, and the production of semi-manufactured goods for Allied contracts, had become such an important element in the U.S. economy that President Wilson's Peace Note of December 1916, by suggesting the possibility of a negotiated peace, caused the worst fall on the New York stock market for fourteen years: Bernard M. Baruch, later head of the War Industries Board, made $476,168.47 profit from fortuitously selling in advance. At the economic level at least it was clearly difficult if not impossible for a major trading power like the U.S. to avoid being sucked into the orbit of the European conflict.[50]

---

[50] U.S. Department of State *Papers relating to the Foreign Relations of the United States: 1914: Supplement: The World War* (Washington 1928) p. 580 W.J. Bryan to Bernstorff 15 Jan. 1915 for Secretary Bryan's opposition to loans, and Ernest R. May *The World War and American Isolation, 1914–1917* (Cambridge Mass. 1959) p. 45 and Patrick Devlin *Too Proud To Fight: Woodrow Wilson's Neutrality* (1974) p. 176–7 for the assumption that the

continued

The war naturally generated great interest and controversy, as well as great fortunes, in the U.S.A. Judging matters according to their own prejudices and their own sources of information, few Americans were inclined to accept unreservedly the Entente view of the causes of the war, especially as the British maritime blockade hardly encouraged sympathy for British foreign policy. As Bernard Shaw caustically remarked:

> Our people here . . . are so full of their sweet innocence and heroic high-mindedness that they feel that everybody who is not congenitally perverse must feel that their position is one of extraordinary nobility, and that America must be proud to have her ships rifled by our cruisers.

Americans of German and Irish extraction busily exploited the ambiguities of Britain's policy. H.L. Mencken wrote to the novelist Theodore Dreiser, 'As for me, I am for the hellish Deutsche until Hell freezes over', and Dreiser replied:

> Personally I think it would be an excellent thing for Europe and the world – tonic – if the despicable British aristocracy – the snobbery of English intellectuality were smashed and a German Vice-Roy sat in London.

The British-born magazine editor Frank Harris, transferring to New York from London and the South of France, assailed Britain in a series of articles in *The New York Sun* which were republished as a book under the title *England or Germany?* in January 1915. Denunciations of British policy and 'the calculated barbarities inflicted by a haughty, perfidious race upon innocent people' also figured in two articles by the Hungarian-born swindler I.T. Trebitsch Lincoln, formerly M.P. for Darlington, published in the New York *World* in May 1915. The magician Aleister Crowley, who despite having a name rather common in Ireland was a hundred per cent English, was in America from late October 1914 and contributed to the pro-German periodical *The Fatherland* and edited the pro-German *The International*, though his anti-British ravings were perhaps somewhat tongue in cheek, as for example his account of a Zeppelin raid on London:

> A great deal of damage was done at Croydon, especially at its suburb Addiscombe, where my aunt lives. Unfortunately her house was not hit. Count Zeppelin is respectfully requested to try again. The exact address is Eton Lodge, Outram Road.

A less whimsical attitude was taken by immigrants from the Tsar's dominions whose bitter memories of pogroms and police oppression helped to fuel suspicions that the Entente was not as virtuously innocent as pretended.[51]

continued
war would be short; Charles Seymour *American Neutrality, 1914–1917* (New Haven 1935) p. 100–104 for Secretary Lansing's letter to W. Wilson 6 Sept. 1915; May *The World War and American Isolation* p. 335, 339–340 for the British blockade and Scandinavian trade aspects; Bernard M. Baruch *The Public Years* (1961) p. 35–6.

Nevertheless a considerable number of young Americans crossed the Atlantic (or the Canadian border) to enlist in the French and British forces. 'You'll just say you are an Englishman, won't you, as a matter of formality?', one young American was requested when he joined up. An anonymous writer in the *Rheinisch-Westfälische Zeitung*, who in August 1916 urged that American 'mercenaries, if taken in arms, should be treated as common robbers and Murderers,' reported 4,000 U.S. citizens in the Canadian contingent of the British Army and a total of 10,000 U.S. citizens serving in France. By the time America entered the war there had been over 200 volunteers for the Escadrille Lafayette, an American fighter squadron – partly financed by W.K. Vanderbilt – flying under French colours, and 210 American citizens flew with the British Royal Flying Corps, of whom 51 were killed. Of the six American fighter pilots who shot down more than twenty enemy aircraft during the First World War, only two actually ever served in the U.S. armed forces.[52]

---

[51] Dan H. Laurence ed. *Bernard Shaw: Collected Letters* (3 vols so far published, 1965–) vol. 3 p. 262 Shaw to Archibald Henderson 9 Nov. 1914; Robert H. Elias ed. *Letters of Theodore Dreiser: A Selection* (Philadelphia 1959) p. 181 H.L. Mencken to Dreiser 8 Nov. 1914 and p. 182 reply 10 Nov. 1914 (cf. also Knut Hamsun's Anglophobia which, though coming to a climax in the Second World War, predates 1914: see Robert Ferguson *Enigma: The Life of Knut Hamsun* (1987) p. 236–7, 325, 371–2); Philippa Pullar *Frank Harris* London 1975 p. 302–3; Bernard Wasserstein *The Secret Lives of Trebitsch Lincoln* (New Haven 1988) 109–111; for Crowley see John Symonds *The Great Beast: the Life and Magick of Aleister Crowley* (1971) p. 198. Before leaving he had written to the press urging that Cologne cathedral should be transported to Rheims 'stone by numbered stone' as 'the symbol and monument of our victory'. *Cambridge Magazine* vol. 4 p. 3 (10 Oct. 1914). Sir Roger Casement *The Crime Against Europe* 1st edit. Berlin 1915, 2nd edit. Philadelphia 1915 is also interesting in this context; for anti-Russian feeling see Gail L. Owen 'Dollar Diplomacy in Default: The Economics of Russian-American Relations, 1910–1917' *Historical Journal* vol. 13 (1970) p. 251–272 at p. 267. For anti-British feeling in the U.S. in the 1890s see Howard K. Beale *Theodore Roosevelt: and the Rise of America to World Power* (Baltimore 1956) p. 83–8.

[52] James Norman Hall *Kitchener's Mob: The Adventures of an American in the British Army* (1916) p. 4; *Rheinisch-Westfälische Zeitung* 1 Aug 1916 front page article headed *'Neutrale' Landsknechte* and beginning 'Man schreibt uns . . .', cf. Dr Edward Gros's Introduction (p. v–xviii) to James Norman Hall *High Adventure* (1918) p. ix and p. xvi and Denis Winter *The First of the Few: Fighter Pilots of the First World War* (1982) p. 153. The leading American air ace of the First World War was Captain Edward V. Rickenbacher, U.S. Army, with 26 aerial victories but he was followed closely by his fellow Americans W.C. Lambert of 24 Squadron R.A.F. (22 victories) and F.W. Gillet of 79 Squadron R.A.F. (20 victories).

Other than Americans, the best documented foreign volunteers were those from Denmark. The novelist Isak Dinesen's brother served with the Canadians but most Danish volunteers gravitated to the French Foreign Legion, cf. Harald Nielsen ed. *Danske Soldaterbreve* (Copenhagen 1917) and I. Ravn-Jonsen *Danske Frivillige i Verdenskrigen: Soldaterbreve fra Fronterne* (Copenhagen 1917). On the other hand, though Norway was generally pro-Entente, at least one Norwegian volunteered for the German army, cf Lyder Ramstad *Med Tyskerne på Vestfronten* (Oslo 1930). See also Erich Erichsen *Forced to Fight: The Tale of a Schleswig Dane* (1916) translated from *Den tavse Dansker: en Bog om dem der gjorde deres Pligt* ('The silent Dane: a book about one who did his duty', i.e., a Schleswig Dane conscripted for the German army) *The National*

continued

Yet there was little desire for participation amongst the public; and even less amongst officials. President Wilson tended to keep U.S. policy towards Europe in his own hands, and his Cabinet consisted of men who were not on confidential terms either with the President or with one another, and who had little interest in or knowledge of transatlantic affairs. Walter H. Page, the U.S. ambassador in London, described a lunch he attended in Washington with the Secretary of State, the Secretaries of War, the Navy and the Interior, the Attorney General and Sharp, the U.S. Ambassador in Paris, in the autumn of 1916:

> all the talk was jocular or semi-jocular, and personal – mere cheap chaff . . .
> Sharp and I might have come from Bungtown and Jonesville and not from
> France and England. We were not encouraged to talk – the local personal joke
> held the time and conversation . . .
> . . . The Secretary [of State] betrayed not the slightest curiosity about our
> relations with Britain.

According to some interpretations this left the way open for Wilson's *éminence grise*, Colonel Edward M. House, to inveigle his priggish and pacifist President step by step into the war. This probably exaggerates both House's cunning and his influence: at any rate by the time Wilson finally decided on war the country at large was already psychologically prepared for the decision.[53]

Nine months after the outbreak of war in Europe, American commitment to a policy of neutrality received a major shock from Germany's first attempt at unrestricted submarine warfare. The sinking of the British liner *Lusitania* off the Old Head of Kinsale on 7 May 1915 provoked almost as much anger in America as in Britain: the 1,201 dead included 128 American passengers (amongst them the millionaire Alfred G. Vanderbilt and the impresario Charles Frohman, the man who ten years earlier had brought *Peter Pan* to America). But much of the noise about the *Lusitania* was the result of newspaper propaganda and President Wilson refused to be stampeded into over-reaction. Speaking at Philadelphia on 10 May 1915, three days after the *Lusitania* sinking, he declared:

> There is such a thing as a man being too proud to fight. There is such a thing
> as a nation being so right that it does not need to convince others by force that
> it is right.

In London Asquith dismissed this as 'a speech . . . stuffed with even more than the usual allowance of swollen & sterile platitudes', but in Washington William

continued
Union Catalog listing indicates a 13th edition of the original Danish version of this sentimental, propagandist and, it seems, largely fictional work.

According to Ferdianand Kugler *Erlebnisse eines Schweizers in den Dardanellen und an der französischen Front* (Zurich 1916) p. 19–20, 12,000 Swiss – mainly German-Swiss! – volunteered for the French army but I am unable to find confirmation of this figure.

[53] Burton J. Hendrick *The Life and Letters of Walter H. Page* (3 vols 1922–5) vol. 2 p. 174–6.

Jennings Bryan, the then U.S. Secretary of State, thought Wilson's line too provocative and resigned; nevertheless U.S. diplomatic pressure secured the ending of the German campaign of unrestricted submarine warfare, and left the British blockade as the main hazard to U.S. commerce.[54]

The Americans were no more disposed to tolerate British bullying and harassment than they had been during the Napoleonic War and in September 1916 Wilson told Page, the pro-British ambassador in London:

> that when the war began he and all the men he met were in hearty sympathy with the Allies; but that now the sentiment towards England had greatly changed. He saw no one who was not vexed and irritated by the arbitrary English course.

The *New York Tribune*, normally inclined to denounce German conduct, claimed in November 1916:

> Despite widespread sympathy for France and a well-defined affection for Great Britain in a limited circle of Americans, there has been no acceptation of the Allied point of view as to the war ... The thing that the British have failed to get before the American people is the belief that the war was one in which the question of humanity and civilization was uppermost for the British.

(This was duly quoted by the German ambassador in one of his despatches to Berlin.) President Wilson's Peace Note of 18 December 1916 latched deftly on to the hollowness of British official rhetoric:

> The objects which the statesmen of the belligerents on both sides have in mind in this war are virtually the same, as stated in general terms to their own people and to the world. Each side desires to make the rights and privileges of weak peoples and small States as secure against aggression or denial in the future ...
>
> The leaders of the several belligerents have, as has been said, stated those objects in general terms. But, stated in general terms, they seem the same on both sides. Never yet have the authoritative spokesmen of either side avowed the precise objects which would, if attained, satisfy them and their people ...

The implication that there was no real difference between Britain's war aims and Germany's was not well received in London; King George V, it is said, wept tears of mortification. It would have seemed incredible, in the aftermath of Wilson's note, to imagine that within five months the U.S. would enter the war against Germany.[55]

---

[54] Arthur Link et al. eds. *The Papers of Woodrow Wilson* (55 vols so far published Princeton 1966–   ) vol. 33 p. 149, speech at Philadelphia 10 May 1915; H.H. Asquith *Letters to Venetia Stanley* ed. Michael and Eleanor Brock (Oxford 1982) p. 590, Asquith to Venetia Stanley 11 May 1915.

[55] Hendrick *The Life and Letters of Walter H. Page* vol. 2 p. 185 for Wilson's comments to Page, and vol. 2 p. 207 for George V's tears; *New York Tribune* 24 Nov. 1916 p. 8c and cf. Devlin *Too Proud To Fight* p. 631; James Brown Scott ed. *Official Statements of War Aims and Peace Proposals December 1916 to November 1918* (Washington 1921) p. 13–15.

Despite the hard words he was soon to speak about German policy, it does not appear that Wilson was ever inclined to identify the side of right as the side Britain was fighting on. Nor does it seem that he finally and reluctantly resorted to war simply because it was the only way of putting into practice his ideas about right and justice. It may be that he had invested so much, politically and psychologically, in his peace initiative of December 1916 that, once it had failed, he had either to raise the stakes or else sit around for the rest of his term of office looking foolishly impotent; but outraged professorial vanity does not explain why, when he finally chose war, he could count on obtaining widespread support.[56]

The German announcement at the end of January 1917 of the resumption of unrestricted submarine warfare – virtually a policy of attacking merchant ships on sight – was probably not merely *a* decisive factor in America's declaring war on Germany, but *the only* deciding factor. The notorious Zimmermann telegram, revealing German attempts to promote a Mexican onslaught on the territories annexed by the U.S. in the mid-nineteenth century, was made public only after the U.S. had already broken off diplomatic relations with Berlin and was important mainly as generating support for a policy already decided: as the German ambassador explained:

> The telegram was used with great success as propaganda against us; but the rupture of diplomatic relations . . . was, in view of the situation, equivalent in all circumstances to war.

It is possible that official opinion in Washington was somewhat more united on the necessity of resisting the renewal of unrestricted submarine warfare than was the country as a whole: the far west had little to do with transatlantic trade, and even Chicago was a stronghold of neutralist opinion. One imagines on the other hand that informed opinion in Washington, knowing what to expect in political life, was less shocked by the Zimmermann telegram than it pretended to be. The telegram, the text of which was made available through the not entirely disinterested generosity of the Admiralty in London, served largely to justify a decision already made.[57]

The official version was that in opposing the renewed German policy of sinking shipping on sight, the American government was seeking to defend America's rights. Indeed, in his far-ranging rhetoric President Wilson did not confine himself merely to American rights; his government, he had claimed after the sinking of the *Lusitania*, was 'contending for nothing less high and sacred than the rights of humanity'. Yet Wilson frequently referred in his public statements to an even older concept than 'rights': to national 'honour'.

---

[56] For an interesting analysis of Wilson's motives see Devlin *Too Proud To Fight* p. 675–682; but it seems unlikely that the enigma will ever be really satisfactorily explained.

[57] The quotation is from Count Johann Heinrich Bernstorff *My Three Years in America* (1920) p. 380. The crucial role of the Zimmerman telegram has been argued in Barbara Tuchman *The Zimmerman Telegram* (1959).

(He preferred the English spelling.) He told the chairman of the Senate Foreign Relations Committee, 'The honour and self-respect of the nation is involved. We covet peace and shall preserve it at any cost but the loss of honour'. To an audience at Milwaukee he announced, 'You have bidden me to see to it that nothing stains or impairs the honour of the United States'. There is of course a connection between the concept of *right* and the concept of *honour* but the emphasis and tendency of the two concepts is entirely different. Right is a matter of distributive justice and must ultimately rest on a balancing of details: honour is simply a matter of knowing what one owes oneself, without stooping to haggling or equivocating about what one owes others. As such it had served as a useful rhetorical weapon in the old-style European diplomacy which Wilson claimed to repudiate. 'Honour' was, essentially, a word for filling in or covering up.[58]

One thing which was being covered up was the degree to which the U.S. was profiting from the European War. By April 1917 the British Ministry of Munitions had nearly 1,600 staff in its mission in the States and was spending $83 million on behalf of the Entente per week. By January 1917 U.S. exports, at $613.3 million, were running at almost *four* times the 1914 figure. Total output of rolled iron and steel had increased 76 per cent in two years. America's export trade was the principal thing threatened by the German renewal of unrestricted submarine warfare. Walter H. Page, the ambassador in London, pointed out that 'It is not improbable that the only way of maintaining our pre-eminent trade position and averting a panic is by declaring war on Germany'.[59]

'We are about to put the dollar sign upon the American flag', protested Senator George W. Norris in a hopeless last-ditch stand against the declaration of war. He blamed the manipulators in Wall Street: 'Their object in having war and in preparing for war is to make money'. After the Armistice, in the general reaction to the enthusiasm of 1917, this opinion became widespread, and in the 1920s was voiced with growing frequency; indeed it is difficult to find an instance of a government's motives for entering a victorious war being subject to more hostile criticism from its own citizens. This businessman's ramp theory was given classic statement by the novelist John Dos Passos at his most passionately anti-Capitalist:

> They went over with the A.E.F. [American Expeditionary Force] to save the Morgan loans, to save Wilsonian Democracy, they stood at Napoleon's tomb and dreamed empire, they had champagne cocktails at the Ritz bar and slept with Russian countesses in Montmartre and dreamed empire, all over the

[58] Link et al. *The Papers of Woodrow Wilson* vol. 33 p. 359 draft 7 June 1915 of 2nd *Lusitania* note; ibid. vol. 36 p. 214 Wilson to Senator William J. Stone 24 Feb. 1916; ibid. vol 36 p. 57 address at Milwaukee 31 Jan. 1916.

[59] Kathleen Burk *Britain, America and the Sinews of War, 1914–1918* (1985) p. 6; Charles Gilbert *American Financing of World War I* (Westport Conn. 1970) p. 33 Table 8 and p. 206 Table 69; Hendrick *The Life and Letters of Walter H. Page* vol. 2 p. 271 Page to U.S. govt. 5 March 1917.

country at American Legion posts and businessmen's luncheons it was worth money to make the eagle scream.

In 1934 a Senate committee was established to investigate the claims that American business interests had pushed the U.S. into the war, and Senator Gerald P. Nye obtained widespread attention with his radio talks and public addresses about 'fighting to save the skins of American bankers'. In 1936 the committee was ordered to report quickly and voted only short-term funding so that in effect the investigation was stifled before anything very illuminating had transpired. Certainly J.P. Morgan Jr., who had handled the American end of the Entente's finances, did not think the course of the investigation bore out Nye's accusations: at the end of his interrogation before the committee he shook Nye's hand and said, 'I have had a fine time. I would not have missed this investigation for the world'. He most probably laughed all the way to the bank.[60]

It is in fact quite unnecessary to argue that Wilson as an individual was subject to personal influence from business interests – something for which there is anyway no substantial evidence. The way in which he handled American neutrality obviously favoured the Entente because of British superiority at sea and Britain and France's superior financial resources; and involvement with the Entente both benefited certain sectors of the American economy and won many indirect beneficiaries over to a more pro-Entente view than they might otherwise have had. Consequently any German attempt to interfere with the Entente beyond the European land mass was bound also to affect the U.S. The situation was perhaps analogous to the way in which the market economy works with differing effects on the rich and capitalist and on the poor capitalistically exploited, so that almost any attempt by the poor and exploited to alter the rules of the market appears, at least to the capitalist, as an invasion of private property. Wilson's own personal part in American free enterprise's participation in the war was to parade his fine utterances and his peace proposals while all the time his foreign policy options were being selected for him by the working of economic relations between the U.S. and the Entente. The renewal of unrestricted submarine warfare was of course a slap in the face for him personally, but it was commercial ruin for his country. Germany drove the U.S. into war: but the Americans themselves, led by Wilson, had put themselves into the position in which they faced the choice between war and capitulation.

[60] Richard L. Neuberger and Stephen B. Kahn *Integrity: The Life of George W. Norris* (New York 1937) p. 115, 117. The Dos Passos quotation is from the section 'Big Bill' in *The 42nd Parallel*, first published 1930. The 'screaming eagle' is slang for the eagle in the emblem of the U.S. government and by the Second World War the term had come to be understood as referring specifically to the U.S. government when in the act of paying out money – see Harold Wentworth and Stuart Berg Flexner *Dictionary of American Slang* (New York 1975) edit. p. 141 sub 'The day the eagle screams/shits'; for Senator Nye's committee see John E. Wiltz *In Search of Peace: The Senate Munitions Inquiry, 1934–6* (Baton Rouge 1963) espec. p. 208 and cf. Seymour *American Neutrality* p. 56, 85, 97.

X. The British Case

Comparison with other countries that were not stampeded by events but nevertheless chose eventually to enter the war suggests certain perspectives, certain hidden agendas, in the decision made in London in early August 1914.

First of all, as in the case of Italy and Portugal, it was contrary to the self-image that the British government wished to project that Britain should keep out of any general European conflict. In 1911 France and Germany almost went to war over France's sphere of influence in Morocco. At this stage the secret military discussions between the French and the British general staffs were known to only a few people, not including the majority of the British Cabinet, and the Entente as such was given less emphasis in official circles than Britain's international standing as a great power. At a speech at the Mansion House on 21 July 1911 Lloyd George – at that time popularly regarded as almost a pacifist in foreign affairs because of his opposition a decade earlier to the Boer War – proclaimed:

> I believe it is essential in the highest interests, not merely of this country, but of the world, that Britain should at all hazards maintain her place and her prestige amongst the Great Powers of the world. Her potent influence has many a time been in the past, and may yet be in the future, invaluable in the cause of human liberty ... if a situation were to be forced upon us in which peace could only be preserved by the surrender of the great and beneficent position Britain has won by centuries of heroism and achievement, by allowing Britain to be treated where her interests were at stake as if she were of no account in the Cabinet of Nations, then I say emphatically that peace at that price would be a humiliation intolerable for a great country to endure.

Lloyd George was pretty well describing the scenario of July–August 1914, but this was after all no astonishingly accurate prophecy by the Welsh Wizard, but a statement of intention.[61]

Here is another ministerial quote:

> When England and France have once taken a third Power by the hand, that third Power *must* be carried in safety through the difficulties in which it may be involved. England and France cannot afford to be baffled ... the Government of the two most powerful countries on the face of the earth must not be frightened, either by words or things, either by the name or by the reality of war.

But this statement, from the famous Lord Palmerston, refers to a much earlier crisis, the one which led eventually to the Crimean War; apart from some of the rhetorical details and the status allocated to France, Palmerston's view was essentially the same as Lloyd George's, and indeed it seems to have been a

---

[61] *Times* 22 July 1911 p. 7b. See A.J.A. Morris *The Scaremongers: The Advocacy of War and Rearmament, 1894–1914* London 1984 p. 291–2 for responses to Lloyd George's speech.

view consistently and very widely held by Britons throughout the 99 years that separated Waterloo from Sarajevo.[62]

There is not the slightest indication that Britain became generally less jingoistic in the fifty years following Lord Palmerston's death, this being the period in which the British Empire and Britain's world role were propagandized, in public school and music hall and pulpit and newspaper, as never before. The scramble for Africa had emphasized the *necessity* of Britain's international greatness, and an increasing flood of travelogues and adventure romances had advertized its glamour. The whole process had been reinforced by a growing emphasis on History – mainly *English* History – in the country's educational system, and indeed the historical memories inculcated in the class-room provided convenient parallels which, in August 1914, somehow swelled into justifications and almost took on the role of war aims:

> We are now engaged with a power greater than the Spain of Philip II, greater than the Holland of Ruyter and Tromp, greater even than the Empires of Louis XIV and Napoleon.

Thus H.A.L. Fisher. J. Holland Rose discoursed learnedly about Napoleon's desire to hang on to Belgium in 1814 – the very same Belgium that was now being violated by the German Empire – and Maurice Hewlett urged the enemy to 'remember the Corsican –

> Whom England only durst not dread
> By sea or shore, but faced alone,
> Nor stayed for pity of her dead
> Until the despot's day was done.[63]

Nevertheless Britons' sensitivities regarding their well-earned position in the cabinet of nations overlay a certain anxiety and insecurity. In 1905 Leo Amery had warned the electors of Wolverhampton East:

> Every year the competition for power among the great world states is getting

---

[62] Evelyn Ashley *The Life of Henry John Temple, Viscount Palmerston: 1846–1865* (2 vols 1876) vol. 2 p. 45 Palmerston to Earl of Aberdeen 1 Nov. 1853.

[63]H.A.L. Fisher *The War: Its Causes and Issues. Three addresses delivered at Sheffield 31 Aug., Sept. 1, and 2 Sept, 1914* (1914) p. 7; J.H. Rose *How the War came About: Explained to the Young People of all English-Speaking Countries* (1914) p. 8–9; Maurice Hewlett 'To England: Strike Quickly' *Times* 12 Aug. 1914 p. 7d. For the increased emphasis on the teaching at history at university (whence, obviously it percolated down into the schools) see C.H. Firth *Modern History in Oxford, 1841–1918* (Oxford 1920) espec. p. 16, 29–30 and footnotes, 43. A School of Law and Modern History had been established at Oxford in 1850 and from about 40 men a year passing through the School in its first two decades, numbers had risen to about 150 a year by 1914; Cambridge had established its History Tripos in 1873 and History Professors had been appointed at Edinburgh and Glasgow in 1894. Raphael Samuel 'Continuous National History' in Raphael Samuel ed. *Patriotism: The Making and Unmaking of British National Identity* (3 vols 1989) vol. 1 p. 9–17, espec. p. 11, notes the emphasis on English rather than European history. But cf. J.H. Grainger *Patriotisms: Britain, 1900–1939* (1986) espec. p. 27–47 which argues – I think incorrectly – that patriotism was relatively underemphasized in British cultural and institutional life at this time.

keener, and unless we can continue to hold our own, unless we can keep our invincible Navy, and unless we can defend the Empire at every one of its frontiers, our Empire and our trade will be taken away from us by others and we shall be starved out, invaded, trampled under foot and utterly ruined.

While 'our invincible Navy' had very much the characteristic of a symbol of Britain's present position, past achievement and future integrity, foreign navies – and especially the German Navy which was rapidly expanding after 1906 – were seen as representing, in symbolic rivalry, the threat to Britain's position. In March 1909 Sir Edward Grey warned the House of Commons of the implications of German naval expansion:

Our Navy is to us what their Army is to them ... it is not a matter of life and death to them as it is to us. No superiority of the British Navy over the German Navy could ever put us in a position to affect the independence and integrity of Germany, because our Army is not maintained on a scale which, unaided, could do anything on German territory. But if the German Navy were superior to ours, they, maintaining the Army which they do, for us it would be a question of defeat. Our independence, our very existence, would be at stake.

This view was developed and elaborated in a much-quoted speech by Winston Churchill at Glasgow in February 1912:

The British Navy is to us a necessity and, from some points of view, the German Navy is to them more in the nature of a luxury. Our naval power involves British existence. It is existence to us; it is expansion to them. We cannot menace the peace of a single Continental hamlet, no matter how great and supreme our Navy may become. But on the other hand, the whole fortunes of our race and Empire, the whole treasure accumulated during so many centuries of sacrifice and achievement would perish and be swept away utterly if our naval supremacy were to be impaired.[64]

Indeed, so vital had 'our invincible Navy' become as a defence of existence, fortunes, treasure, centuries of heroism and sacrifice and achievement, etc., that Britain could no longer afford to rely on it to look after itself. Supposing Europe came to be dominated by a single power or alliance, Sir Edward Grey reasoned in 1911, and 'we were appealed to for help and sat by and looked on and did nothing ... we should be left without a friend', and this would mean that all the navies in Europe would gang up on the Royal Navy. This was obviously a dreadful possibility and Sir Edward Grey therefore suggested:

the question might arise whether we ought to take part by force in European

[64] Paul M. Kennedy *The Rise of Anglo-German Antagonism, 1860–1914* (1980) p. 307 quoting L.S. Amery at Wolverhampton 1905; *Hansard: House of Commons* 5th series vol. 3 col. 60–61 for Grey's speech 29 March 1909; Winston S. Churchill *The World Crisis* (6 vols 1923–31) vol. 1 p. 76. Oddly enough Grey's and Churchill's views on this matter seemed to be derived from Heinrich von Treitschke's statement that Britain 'can rely upon her fleet alone as the national weapon, and need only use her Army as a second line of defence': Heinrich von Treitschke *Politik-Vorlesungen gehalten an der Universität zu Berlin* (2 vols Leipzig 1897–8) vol. 2 p. 358, English edit. 2 vols 1916, vol. 2 p. 391–2.

affairs, and if we did it would be solely because Sea Power and the necessity of keeping command of the sea, was the underlying cause and motive of our action.

And so, four years later, British command of the open sea was being fought for in the mud of Flanders, and one Cyril Rawlins was writing to his mother from his dug-out:

> We are fighting for the right, and more than this, we are fighting for our very life as an Empire and as a nation. . . . *The enemy must not take Calais!* If they did, our Empire built up for us by centuries of toil and sacrifice, our nation, would cease to exist, we should be lost as surely as if England sank beneath the sea. You in England cannot realise this as we do who live as it were shoring up a dike, holding back the pitiless sea of brutality and slaughter.[65]

XI. Psychological Crisis and the Decision for War

But as in the case of Italy, the peculiar logic of international strategy probably had less ultimate influence in Whitehall than smaller but more intimate questions: such as the survival of one's own particular clique in office.

During the last dozen years it has become fashionable to speak of 'The Primacy of Domestic Politics' when discussing the outbreak of the First World War, with the implication that the causes of the war can be traced to the various internal problems of the different belligerents. Insofar as it applies to internal politics in a general, diffused sense the Primacy of Domestic Politics argument remains unproven, little more than an unconvincing flourish. It is possible however that internal politics had a very real significance at the key decision-making level, especially if one is thinking in terms of the personal interaction of the principal decision-makers.[66]

---

[65] Gooch and Temperley *British Documents on the Origins of the War* vol. 6 p. 784, speech by Grey to Committee of Imperial Defence 26 May 1911; Malcolm Brown *Tommy Goes To War* (1978) p. 245, Cyril Rawlins to his mother 1 July 1915. Bismarck, incidentally had raved about 'the edifice of state which centuries of glory and love of country have built up, which from the ground up is cemented with the blood of our fathers', as far back as 1849 cf. Horst Kohl ed. *Die Politischen Reden des Fürsten Bismarck* (14 vols Stuttgart 1892–1905) vol. 1 p. 94, 21 April 1849, Prussian *Landtag*, Second Chamber, and see Keith M. Wilson *The Policy of the Entente: Essays on the Determinants of British Foreign Policy, 1904–1914* (Cambridge 1985) p. 73.

[66] The phrase 'The Primacy of Domestic Politics' is taken from the work of a young historian working in Weimar Germany named Eckart Kehr. A collection of his essays was published posthumously under the title *Der Primat der Innenpolitik* ed. Hans-Ulrich Wehler (Berlin 1965). In fact, though Kehr wrote critically of 'Der Primat der Aussenpolitik' (the primacy of foreign politics, or foreign policy) what he seemed to favour was *Sammlungspolitik*, i.e., collection or combination politics, perhaps the best translation would be interrelated politics: see his 'Englandhass und Weltpolitik' essay of 1928 in *Der Primat der Innenpolitik* (Berlin 1965) p. 149–175, particularly p. 175. The Primacy of Domestic Politics idea has been popularized by Arno J. Mayer, in 'International Crises and War since 1870' in Charles

continued

In Britain the key man was Herbert Henry Asquith. In 1914 Asquith, described by Lytton Strachey as 'a fleshy, sanguine, wine-bibbing, medieval Abbot of a personage', had been Prime Minister and leader of the Liberal Party for six years, had guided his government and party through several major storms, and seemed intent on continuing to do so. What these storms were precisely seemed to interest him only as a secondary issue: Lloyd George later said of him that he was 'absolutely devoid of all principles except one – that of retaining his position as Prime Minister'. Margot, his second wife, described her husband's family thus:

> The Asquiths – without mental flurry and with perfect self-mastery – believed in the free application of intellect to every human emotion; no event could have given heightened expression to their feelings.

Even when physically attacked by suffragettes Asquith did not lose his poise:

> One of the women slashed Mr. Asquith 4 times with a crop over the head, before she was seized. Luckily he was saved . . . by the brim of his stiff hat. He never seems to defend himself on these occasions but remains calm & stolid & unshrinking.

Outward impassivity was matched by vast reserves of inner patience, or perhaps more than patience: Asquith seems almost to have taken a positive delight in unravelling problems merely by the exercise of procrastination. Yet though invariably inclined to postpone the moment of decision, he cultivated a suitably statesmanlike air of always being certain of where he was going. Such an appearance of decidedness was in fact a vital part of his political stock in trade, for as Prime Minister Asquith had to deal with a whole series of highly explosive situations which could have detonated disastrously if not handled with the utmost circumspection. The crisis over Lloyd George's 'People's Budget' of 1909 and its sequel in the reduction of the constitutional powers of the House of Lords was one such crisis; the Ulster confrontation, which seemed to be out of hand and rapidly progressing towards extremities in July 1914, was another. In late July, when the international situation began to push the problem of Ulster's resistance to Irish Home Rule off the front pages, at least one Asquith-watcher immediately concluded 'Advantage is being taken of it to defer any settlement of the Irish question'. The Cabinet's decision for war

continued

L. Bertrand ed. *Revolutionary Situations in Europe* (Montreal 1977) p. 231 and in Mayer's own *The Persistence of the Old Regime* (1981) p. 314,322, where it is argued that militarization before 1914 was part of an ultra-conservative reaction which found a welcome consummation in the outbreak of war – a view which has not been, and probably cannot be, properly documented. James Joll's chapter 'The Primacy of Domestic Politics', p. 92–122 of his *The Origins of the First World War* (1984) *suggests* that the build-up of bellicose propaganda grew out of domestic tensions in France (p. 99) and Germany (p. 112–3, 116) but since not every crescendo of propaganda climaxes in world war the pre-war propaganda build-up must be taken as only a part of the background to the decision for war, not the cause of it.

at the beginning of August 1914 may however be taken as *the* classic example of Asquithian management.[67]

For Asquith the question of absolute and objective right and wrong was inevitably subordinate to practicalities, especially the practical issue of whether the Liberal Party remained in office under his leadership. Though it is possible that he had substantially made up his mind at a relatively early stage of the international crisis he was lawyer enough to look at every side of the issues at stake. He told the King that the guarantee of Belgian neutrality was no longer relevant and that 'The Cabinet consider that the matter if it arises will be one of policy rather than legal obligation'. To his colleagues he attempted to minimize the significance of German demands for free passage across Belgian territory: 'I don't see why we need come in if they only go a little way into Belgium'. Privately he confided, 'Happily I am quite clear in my own mind as to what is right and wrong', but this was perhaps no more than his usual pretence that the key policy decisions had already been made at some anterior stage. One of his colleagues recalled him at a Cabinet meeting, when Morley, Burns, Simon, Beauchamp and others began to talk of resigning, 'looking down the table over his glasses and observing "seems as if I shall have to go on alone"'. In reality carrying on alone was the one option which was not open to Asquith, and this was why he had to be careful in handling the alternatives.[68]

Perhaps the most important limitation on Asquith's scope for manoeuvre was that his was a minority government. In the second General Election of 1910 the Liberals and the Conservatives had been neck and neck in terms of M.Ps. returned (the Conservatives actually with a 2.4 per cent lead in the number of votes) and since then the trend of by-elections had been in the Conservative favour so that by July 1914 they had 25 more seats than the ruling Liberal Party. For its majority in the House of Commons the government depended on the support of the Labour Party and the Irish Nationalists, neither of which could be seen as entirely predictable on the war issue; in any case Asquith had no intention of cutting them in on decision-making so there was no way he could be sure of their attitude in advance, especially in an emergency. Another consideration was that it was only twenty years or so since the Liberals had experienced a disastrous split. Some of the Liberal Cabinet, especially Sir Edward Grey and Winston Churchill, First Lord of the Admiralty and, it was said 'the leader of the War party in the Cabinet', were certain to resist a policy of neutrality. If the government

[67] Michael Holroyd *Lytton Strachey: A Critical Biography* (2 vols 1967–8) 2 p. 197; A.J.P. Taylor ed. *Lloyd George: A Diary by Frances Stevenson* p. 129, 30 Nov. 1916; Margot Asquith *The Autobiography of Margot Asquith* (1920) p. 269; Mary Soames *Clementine Churchill* (1979) p. 84 Clementine Churchill to Winston Churchill 4 Nov. 1913; Wilfrid Scawen Blunt *My Diaries: being a personal narrative of events, 1888–1914* (2 vols 1919–20) vol. 2 p. 447, 30 July 1914.

[68] Spender and Asquith *Life of Asquith* 2 p. 82 Asquith to King George V 29 July 1914; Masterman *C.F.G. Masterman* p. 265; H.H. Asquith *Letters to Venetia Stanley* ed. Michael and Eleanor Brock (Oxford 1982) p. 146 Asquith to Venetia Stanley 2 Aug. 1914.

decided for neutrality, the Cabinet might break up, and given the Conservative lead in the House of Commons the results would have been inevitable: 'either a Coalition Government or a Unionist [i.e., Conservative] Government either of which would certainly have been a war ministry'. An approach to the Conservative leadership on the subject of coalition was in fact made, by F.E. Smith on behalf of Churchill; the Conservative leader Andrew Bonar Law rejected this initiative but wrote to Asquith on 2 August to make clear his view that 'it would be fatal to the honour and security of the United Kingdom to hesitate in supporting France and Russia at the present juncture', so Asquith could have been in no doubt as to Conservative position in the event of the government collapsing.[69]

Asquith in fact acknowledged that a coalition might be a possibility, but did so only to remind the Cabinet's waverers of the probable consequence of failing to support him. One colleague noted:

> The P.M. is anxious we should see this thing through as a Party and does not want a Coalition and says he wants as many of his colleagues to stay with him as he can get so as not to go outside the Party.

According to Sir John Simon, Asquith's view was that

> if a block were to leave the Government at this juncture, their action would necessitate a Coalition Government which would assuredly be the grave of Liberalism.

He seems to have persuaded Runciman, Harcourt and Pease that the future of the Liberal Party as the party of government was the prime consideration and that their opposition to war was 'not in itself sufficient to justify us in handing over policy and control to the Tories.'[70]

Of course a government split might in theory have been avoided by exploring the possibilities of obtaining united Cabinet support for a policy of neutrality. In July 1914 Asquith held the seals of the War Office himself, so that the only service minister he had to deal with was Winston Churchill. Asquith seems to have been genuinely fond of the younger man, and even when Churchill was in disgrace and serving at the Front in the winter of 1915–1916 he continued to see Churchill's wife; on the other hand he seems not to have taken Churchill very seriously as a politician and knew that, as a renegade from the Conservative ranks, Churchill had minimal personal influence with the Conservative leadership. The Foreign Secretary, Sir Edward Grey, was a different matter. Not only was he a statesman of European reputation, but he

---

[69] Lord Beaverbrook *Politicians and the War, 1914–1916* (2 vols. 1928–32) vol. 1 p. 31; House of Lords Record Office Samuel Mss A/157/697 Herbert Samuel to Beatrice Samuel 2 Aug. 1914.
[70] Wilson *Policy of the Entente* p. 141–2 quoting Gainsford Mss box 521, Pease to wife 3 Aug. 1914, C. Addison *Four and a Half Years* (2 vols 1934) vol. 1 p. 35 and Trevelyan Mss 33 Runciman to Trevelyan 4 Aug. 1914.

was one of Asquith's oldest political associates, and also the embodiment of all the grace and cachet of the old Whig aristocracy on which the *arriviste* Asquith had modelled himself. Grey told his colleagues repeatedly, 'I want the Cabinet to understand they are free, there are no pledges. I am not free, if this country remains neutral I must resign'. Asquith may have had reservations concerning Grey's finicking sense of personal honour in relation to the various secret discussions with the French, but he liked Grey's style. On 2 August he told Venetia Stanley 'I shall not separate myself from him'. With any other politician this would have been an indication that he was planning to do just that, but in this case Asquith kept his word.[71]

Sir Edward Grey's handling of the international crisis was a virtuoso performance that enhanced his reputation at Westminster, partly because it chimed in with the majority desire to present Britain as dragged unwillingly into war by the sheer ruthlessness and criminality of German aggression. From Asquith's point of view however Grey's brilliantly improvised self-presentation must have seemed more impressive than the actual policy lurking uncertainly behind the facade of statesmanship. The keynote of Grey's policy in late July and early August was his struggle to avoid either pledging or refusing support to France and Russia, so as to enable them to arrive at their own decision for war exactly as if Britain did not exist, while of course reminding them that Britain did. This policy of not committing Britain came rather close to a policy of keeping Sir Edward Grey's personal honour as bright as possible in a grimy world; for example he later told a colleague:

> I am glad that I did not say to the Belgian Minister that, if Germany violated the neutrality of Belgium, we would certainly assist Belgium: for then I should have been open to the charge that I had instigated Belgium to resist, and then had proved unable to save her from the immediate consequences of resistance, which she is now suffering so terribly.

The same note of resigned passivity was struck in his famous remark, 'The lamps are going out all over Europe'. Of course Grey could hardly deny that somewhere, somehow, a decision had been made that Britain should enter the war, but he insisted that he personally had no special responsibility for the decision:

> The idea that one individual, sitting in a room in the Foreign Office, could pledge a great democracy definitely by his word, in advance, either to take part in a great war or to abstain from taking part in it, is absurd.

One is reminded of Lytton Strachey's comment after reading the British Blue Book, the collection of diplomatic papers relating to the decision for war:

> It's like a puppet-show, with the poor little official dolls dancing and squeaking

[71] Masterman *C.F.G. Masterman* p. 265; Asquith *Letters to Venetia Stanley* p. 146 Asquith to Venetia Stanley 2 Aug. 1914.

their official phrases, while the strings are being pulled by some devilish Unseen Power.[72]

No doubt a man of Sir Edward Grey's type could have been got round, or got rid of, if Asquith had really wanted. But, judging matters in his usual pragmatic way, Asquith found absolutely no reason to get rid of Grey. If the advocates of war, apart from the Foreign Secretary and Sir Eyre Crowe, had consisted only of the Conservative Party and a few hot-heads like Churchill, Asquith certainly had political courage enough to defy them and confidence enough to out-manoeuvre them; but it was not simply a question of the parliamentary opposition and a few hot-heads. As may be seen from his conduct of the constitutional crisis of 1910–1912 Asquith was pre-eminent even amongst democratic politicians in his sensitivity to the mood of public opinion, though he would certainly have recognized that public opinion was not the sum of the individual opinion of every single citizen, but rather the opinion of those who make it their business and their profession to tell the public what the public thinks. This 'Public Opinion' was almost entirely on the side of the line of thought which Sir Edward Grey and his colleagues had been advertising for the past ten years. Thus *The Times's* leader of Saturday 1 August thought 'the duty we owe to our friends' was a less powerful consideration than 'the instinct of self-preservation' and argued, 'We dare not stand aside with folded arms and placidly watch our friends placed in peril of destruction', because it would be Britain's own turn next. An additional leader, headed 'The Empire and the Crisis. A democratic duty', also reprinted in the special Sunday edition, stated:

> In the first place we must stand by our friends. The Empire has no written or spoken understandings which bind it to intervene, but it has an obligation of honour which it will discharge to the full.

Two days previously *The Manchester Guardian* had claimed that *The Times's* 'influence at great crises in our foreign affairs has almost always been for evil', but in this instance *The Times* expressed no more than what the consensus of the professional classes instinctively felt. On 1 August, the day of *The Times's* leader, Sir Arthur Nicolson, the Permanent Under Secretary of State at the Foreign Office, mortified by Grey's refusal to make a commitment to France, burst out, 'You will render us a by-word among nations'. The young Vera Brittain wrote in her diary on 3 August:

> The great fear now is that our bungling Government will declare England's neutrality. If we at this critical juncture were to refuse to help our friend France, we should be guilty of the grossest treachery & sacrifice our credit for ever.

---

[72] Trevelyan *Grey of Falloden* p. 260 Grey to Lord Selborne 15 Dec. 1914; Grey *Twenty-Five Years* vol. 2 p. 20; Trevelyan *Grey of Falloden* p. 250 memo by Grey April 1915; Holroyd *Lytton Strachey* vol. 2 p. 120 Strachey to Dorothy Bussy 21 Aug. 1914. See also Mackenzie ed. *Diaries of Beatrice Webb* vol. 3 p. 216–7, 28 Aug. 1914 for a description of Grey's demeanour later in the month.

Albert Gray, a sixteen-year-old at Rugby asked on 4 August, 'Are we going in or are we [to] stay out and leave the French to their fate, and lose all our national prestige?' and next day noted triumphantly, 'War declared by England. Intense relief, as there was an awful feeling that we might dishonour ourselves'. Exactly the same response to the declaration of war was recalled by Jerome K. Jerome:

> Young men and maidens, grey-moustached veterans, pale-faced curates, dear old ladies: one and all expressed relief and thankfulness. 'I was so afraid Grey would climb down at the last moment'. 'It was Asquith I was doubtful of. I didn't think the old man had the grit'.

The Rev. Hon. E. Lyttelton wrote later, 'had England abstained while France and Belgium were being ground to powder under our very eyes, we should not have dared to look the world in the face again'. G.W. Prothero, a former history professor at Edinburgh University, editor of *The Quarterly Review* and later historical adviser to the Foreign Office, put the matter in a nutshell: 'First and foremost . . . we are fighting for our national honour'.[73]

Such opposition as there was came mainly from within the ranks of the Liberal Party itself, or from its customary supporters. Norman Angell, the leading anti-war publicist of the time, had set up a Neutrality League on 28 July, the day the Austro-Hungarian Army began shelling Belgrade, and on 5 August the League ran a full page advert in the liberal *Daily News*:

ENGLISHMAN, DO YOUR DUTY
AND KEEP YOUR COUNTRY OUT OF A
WICKED AND STUPID WAR

But like the opposition of Morley and Burns in the cabinet, and the criticisms of Liberal backbenchers like Philip Morrell in the House of Commons, the attitude of the Neutrality League and of the *The Daily News*, though regrettable from the point of view of sentimental ideas about Liberal unity, seemed irrelevant and unrealistic, merely the negative warblings of the Little Englander in the wilderness.[74]

---

[73] *Times* 1 Aug. 1914 p. 9 c and e, cf 2 Aug. 1914 p. 3f; *Manchester Guardian* 30 July 1914 p. 8c. See also *The History of the Times* (5 vols so far published 1935–) vol. 4 part 1 p. 201, 209–10. Harold Nicolson *Sir Arthur Nicolson, Bart, Lord Carnock: A Study in the Old Diplomacy* (1930) p. 419; Vera Brittain *Chronicle of Youth: War Diary, 1913–1917* ed. Alan Bishop with Terry Smart (1981) p. 84, 3 Aug. 1914; Albert Gray *Patrick Walworth Gray: The Record of a Boy's Life* (printed for private circulation 1918) p. 118; Jerome K. Jerome *My Life and Times* (1926) p. 265; E. Lyttelton *Memories and Hopes* (1925) p. 191; G.W. Prothero *Our Duty and Our Interest in the War* (1914) p. 1. See also Dudley Barker *G.K. Chesterton: A Biography* (1973) p. 224, draft letter to G.B. Shaw Aug. 1914 in which Chesterton, formerly bitterly hostile to the Asquith government, expresses surprise at being for once in agreement with the ministers.

[74] A.J. Anthony Morris *Radicalism Against War, 1906–1914: The Advocacy of Peace and Retrenchment* (1972) p. 411–2.

Thus Asquith led his country, and the Liberal government, into war but he did not lead by any means all of the pre-war Liberal movement into the war. He does not seem to have cared. In the long term his decision ruined his party and came close to ruining his country, but he was a politician, not a prophet, and in the short term he strengthened his position, just as the comparable decision in Italy strengthened – though even more temporarily – the position of Salandra. Indeed Asquith may be seen as the Salandra of Britain.

The British decision for war may also be seen, as in the case of Portugal, as an attempt to preserve an insecure status quo, and to bolster the reputation of an ailing government, or, as in the case of Wilson's United States, as the unintended but inevitable outcome of having previously sought an innocent profit in the complications of other nations' diplomacy; or even, as in the case of Venizelos's Greece, as a tactical move in a long term programme of constitutional readjustment. What it cannot be seen as is as the outcome of policies worked out at a higher plane of moral integrity and intellectual objectivity than existed in the other capitals of Europe. The more one looks at the British government's decision for war, the more it resembles the decision for war of other governments, even down to the details of rhetoric. If, as Lloyd George wrote, 'The nations backed their machines over the precipice', it was because they were all steering their metaphorical machines with one hand on their sister-in-law's knee.

7

The War against Militarism and Imperialism

We have been living in a sheltered valley for generations. We have been too comfortable, too indulgent, many, perhaps, too selfish, and the stern hand of fate has scourged us to an elevation where we can see the great everlasting things that matter for a nation – the great peaks of honour we had forgotten – Duty, Patriotism, and – clad in glittering white – the great pinnacle of Sacrifice, pointing like a rugged finger to Heaven.

Lloyd George to London Welsh at Queen's Hall, 19 Sept. 1914; *The Times*, 21 Sept. 1914 p. 12c.

I. The War against Prussianism

Once the First World War had broken out, it was necessary for the various governments to explain to their peoples not only why the war had started but also what objectives needed to be secured before it could be honourably ended. The government of Italy, which decided to join in the war only after detailed negotiations with potential allies, could point to a list – even if only a list edited for public consumption – of internationally recognized territorial claims. The government of France, which was able to present the war as a resumption of a contest in which they had been defeated more than a generation earlier, could cite the injustice of a dictated border settlement which could now be righted; indeed the reannexation of Alsace and Lorraine, the two provinces which had been lost to Germany in 1870, was specified as a war aim to the Russian ambassador on 5 August 1914 and to the Chamber of Deputies on 22 November 1914. But as far as Britain was concerned, there were no territorial claims against Germany, and it was necessary therefore to find some other, perhaps more abstract, war aim.[1]

Even in the first weeks, when it was still supposed that Germany would

---

[1] D. Stevenson *French War Aims Against Germany, 1914–1919* (Oxford 1982) p. 12, Cf Pierre Renouvin 'Les Buts de Guerre du Gouvernement Français, 1914–1918' *Révue Historique* vol. 235 (1966) p. 1–38 at p. 3–4.

The Italian Green Book published 20 May 1915 revealed that the Italian government had demanded from Vienna the cession of the Trentino, the north-eastern area as far east as Gorizia, and six islands on the Dalmatian coast, with Trieste to be established as an independent city state. These may be regarded as Italy's officially acknowledged war aims during the war itself.

be easily crushed between the Russian steam-roller and the French *ésprit d'attaque*, the Italian ambassador in London was informed by Sir Edward Grey's private secretary, 'As in the days of Napoleon England will not replace the sword in the scabbard till she has succeeded in eliminating the permanent danger of a hegemonic power in Europe'. The threatened German hegemony was objected to not merely because it was foreign but also because it seemed to embody unacceptable social and moral values: a Declaration organized by C.F.G. Masterman and signed by 52 well-known British writers, published in *The Times* on 18 September 1914, spoke with horror of 'the domination of the whole Continent by a military caste'. This military caste was of course the Prussian officer class: on 9 November 1914 Asquith told guests at a Guildhall banquet:

> We shall never sheath the sword which we have not lightly drawn ... until the rights of the smaller nationalities of Europe are placed upon an unassailable foundation, and until the military domination of Prussia is wholly and finally destroyed.

Prussianism was evidently a danger not only to the smaller nations; Lord Sydenham, formerly Secretary to the Committee of Imperial Defence, claimed:

> Now, as in 1805, we are fighting for our lives against a great military Empire fired with ambitions of world domination which could be realized only by our destruction.

More than a year later Lloyd George told an American press magnate that Britain could not accept peace until the 'final and complete elimination of Prussian militarism'; yet even by this stage definitions of the essential nature of Prussian militarism were hard to come by. Fairly typical was the obscuring rhetoric of Billy Hughes, the Prime Minister of Australia, who referred to Prussianism as 'that monstrous excrescence upon civilization which is like a cancer eating out the very vital of all that is worthy of permanence in civilization' – or perhaps he was simply referring to the German nation as such. The distinction between Prussianism and Germany was occasionally made but generally not found worth exploring.[2]

For the first year or more of the war much of the domestic propaganda within Britain not only side-stepped these problems of definition but also

---

[2] Antonio Salandra *La Neutralità Italiana [1914]: Ricordi e Pensieri* (Milan 1928) p. 158 cf *I Documenti Diplomatici Italiani 5ª serie* (11 vols Rome, 1954–1986) vol. 1 p. 59 no. 108 Imperiali to San Giuliano 7 Aug 1914 which shows that the cypher group between 'una' and 'egemonia' was indecipherable; *Times* 18 Sept. 1914 p. 3a; ibid. 10 Nov. 1914 p. 10e; ibid 21 Oct. 1915 p. 8c for Lord Sydenham's letter; David Lloyd George *War Memoirs* (6 vols 1933–6) vol. 2 p. 854; Keith A. Murdoch ed. *'The Day' – and After: War Speeches of the Rt. Hon. W.M. Hughes* [1916] p. 53–4, speech at Cardiff, 24 March 1916.

The term 'Prussianism' seems to have been current in English since the 1890s. The distinction between Prussianism and German society and culture as a whole is discussed in Cecil Chesterton *The Prussian Hath Said In His Heart* (1914) p. 3–5 but even less importance was given to clarifying this kind of distinction than in the Second World War.

concentrated on exploiting a traditional chauvinism which to a large extent served as a pretext for the avoidance of thought altogether. All the belligerent powers made extensive use of poster advertizing, mainly to promote national saving schemes, what the Americans later called Liberty Bonds; the British, without a system of military conscription for the first two years of the war, also invested massively in advertizing for volunteers for the army. Apart from some posters exclaiming 'Remember Belgium!' or showing an illustration of the 1839 treaty with the caption 'The Scrap of Paper: Prussia's Perfidy – Britain's Bond,' the typical British recruiting poster was in the mode of Alfred Leete's famous portrayal of Kitchener with his finger pointing and the slogan 'Your Country Needs You', or the homely appeals to the men of Britain to assert their masculinity – 'Women of Britain Say Go', 'What Did You Do In The Great War, Daddy?' or:

> There are THREE Types of Men
> *Those* who hear the call and obey
> *Those* who delay
> And – *The Others*
> To Which Do *You* Belong?

A Frank Brangwyn poster displayed in stations of the London Underground depicted a battle scene: 'At Neuve Chapelle. Your Friends Need You. Be a Man'; another Underground poster by Gerald Spencer Pryse, showing a platoon marching, mounted officer in the rear, past a ruined Baroque church with the captions: 'Through Darkeness to Light. Through Fighting to Triumph' was entitled in large letters. 'The Only Road for an Englishman'. These posters are only one of the forms in which the inner experience of the time was codified; the same message is to be found elsewhere, in speeches, pamphlets, even private letters. Even frontline soldiers betrayed an uneasy self-consciousness as if not entirely confident of their identity and role: 'Remember we are writing a new page of history' wrote a Captain in the Rifle Brigade to his father shortly before dying in action in October 1914: 'Future generations cannot be allowed to read the decline of the British Empire and attribute it to us.'[3]

The avoidance of objective analysis was perhaps made necessary by the

---

[3] M.L. Sanders and Philip M. Taylor *British Propaganda during the First World War 1914–1918* (1982) p. 138 and Martin Hardie, Arthur K. Sabin *War Posters: Issued by Belligerent and Neutral Nations, 1914–1919* (1920) which reproduces Pryse's and Brangwyn's posters as plates 8 and 19 and Cate Haste *Keep the Home Fires Burning: Propaganda in the First World War* (1977) figures 15 and 17 between p. 38 and p. 39 and cf p. 54, 56–7; Captain N.J.B. Leslie to Sir John Leslie, Bart In *The Rifle Brigade Chronicle for 1914* (1915) p. 188

Leete's famous 'Your Country Needs YOU', originally the cover picture of *London Opinion* 5 Sept. 1914 was issued as a poster almost immediately afterwards. The wording of early versions was 'BRITONS [Kitchener] wants YOU. Join Your Country's Army! God Save the King'. Later the pointing finger motif was imitated by German and Italian poster designers (with a young soldier pointing) and by the Americans (with Uncle Sam pointing) cf. Joseph Darracott, Belinda Loftus *First World War Posters*, (1972) p. 63–4.

identity of Britain's allies. The atrocity stories about German soldiers hacking off the hands of Belgian children seem to have derived, in some roundabout way, from reports of how, only a dozen years previously, Belgian officials in the Congo had ordered recalcitrant native children to be mutilated in precisely this way; but what had happened in the Congo could be blamed on old King Leopold who had since died. More awkward was the claim that *'We are fighting for the cause of constitutional liberty and popular government'*, which required especially deft foot-work when it came to writing pamphlets about *'Our Russian Ally'*, and *The Times* reported:

> The Stockholm newspapers ask how the relentless Russification of Finland is compatible with England's declaration that the Triple Entente is fighting for the freedom of small nationalities.

And it was all very well for the secretary of the National Union of Teachers to write:

> We fight against the German Emperor now as our forefathers fought against Napoleon, who was a very much greater man. We fight against the Kaiser because he seeks to enslave the world to Germany, as Napoleon tried to enslave the world to France;

but France was now an ally, and the French revered Napoleon as a national hero who had been shamefully treated by the perfidious English. The first Trafalgar Day after the outbreak of war saw unprecedented numbers filing past Nelson's column in Trafalgar Square: 'it is doubtful whether such large crowds have ever been seen on any previous anniversary,' *The Times* reported. Trafalgar Day remained an occasion of patrotic celebration throughout the war, but Waterloo, where Napoleon had been defeated in person and where the Prussians had figured as allies, was in effect shelved: even regimental Waterloo Day dinners ceased to be held as 'Official festivities would be out of place and likely to wound the susceptibilities of our Allies'.[4]

There were other ambiguities in the British position, which were dealt with rather sharply in Bernard Shaw's *New Statesman* supplement of 14 November 1914: reprinted as a pamphlet entitled *Common Sense About The War* this sold 75,000 copies. Less attention was given to a manifesto issued by General Manie Maritz on the borders of South West Africa on 16 December 1914:

> The former South African Republic and Orange Free State as well as the Cape

[4] For the chopping off of hands in the Congo see Brian Inglis *Roger Casement* (1973) p. 72–3 and p. 81 and cf Haste *Keep the Home Fires Burning* p. 84–7: 'the cause of constitutional liberty and popular government' is in G.W. Prothero *Our Duty and Our Interest in the War* (1914) p. 5 cf Sir Donald Mackenzie Wallace's pamphlet *Our Russian Ally* (1914); *Times* 24 Nov. 1914 p. 6c and cf. ibid. 7 Dec. 1914 p. 7f – though it seems that in fact a Russification policy was yet barely under way in Finland. Napoleon as 'a very much greater man' than the Kaiser is in Sir James Yoxall *Why Britain went to War: To the Boys and Girls of the British Empire* (1914) p. 4; *Times* 22 Oct. 1914 p. 8d; ibid. 17 June 1915 p. 5b. See also the interesting chapter on British historians and the war in Stuart Wallace *War and the Image of Germany: British Academics, 1914–1918* (Edinburgh 1988) p. 58–73.

Province and Natal are proclaimed free from British control and independent, and all white inhabitants of the mentioned areas, of whatever nationality, are hereby called upon to take their weapons in their hands and realise the long-cherished ideal of a Free and Independent South Africa.

Maritz's uprising was quickly suppressed: but it was not to be the only insurrection aimed against British government during the war.[5]

A series of articles by H.G. Wells, published in *The Daily Chronicle* and other papers during August, proposing a kind of league of nations to ensure the impossibility of future wars, was issued as a pamphlet under the catchy title *The War That Will End War* and enjoyed a large sale, indicating that Prussianism was not the only variety of militarism held in suspicion by the British public. But there were others who took a totally different view of the situation, and these were often people of more influence in official circles: people such as Leo Amery, M.P. for South Birmingham:

> While our military task is rightly to crush Germany, our political writers of all shades are forgetting our political object is the defence and welfare of the British Empire. All this harping on Prussian militarism as something that must be rooted out, as in itself criminal and opposed to the interests of an imaginary virtuous and pacific entity called Europe, in which we are included, is wholly mischievous. We are not part of Europe.[6]

II. The New Eastern Question

The entry of Turkey into the war at the beginning of November introduced a new dimension. Partly perhaps it was something in the eastern Mediterranean air, far removed from Fleet Street and the need to posture idealistically before

---

[5] Dan H. Lawrence *Bernard Shaw: A Bibliography* (2 vols Oxford 1983) vol. 1 p. 123; Brian Bunting *The Rise of the South African Reich* London 1969 p. 24: the full text of Maritz's proclamation is in Manie [i.e Salomon Gerhardus] Maritz *My Lewe en Strewe* ([Johannesburg] 1938) p. 169–172; a grammatical error in Bunting's translation has been corrected. In John Buchan's novel *Greenmantle* (1916) Richard Hannay infiltrates himself into the confidence of the Germans by posing as 'one of Maritz's old lot' – chap. 2. For the native risings in Egbaland in August 1914 and June 1918 see Akinjide Osuntokun *Nigeria in the First World War* (1979) p. 107, p. 127–9, for that in Nyasaland in January 1915 see George Shepperson and Thomas Price *Independent African: John Chilembwe and the Origins, Setting and Significance of the Nyasaland Native Rising of 1915* (Edinburgh 1958).

In February 1915 the British authorities in India pre-empted a planned rising by Sikh and Bengali revolutionary groups: 46 of those arrested were hanged and 197 transported or sentenced to long terms of imprisonment: Penderel Moon *The British Conquest and Dominion of India* (1989) p. 966 and fn. 8.

[6] John Barnes and David Nicholson ed. *The Leo Amery Diaries* (2 vols 1980–88) vol. 1 p. 119 Amery to Lord Milner 26 May 1915. Irene Cooper Willis *England's Holy War: study of English Liberal Idealism during the Great War* (New York 1928) p. 86–8 argues that the Liberal press was responsible for discovering that the war was a holy crusade against tyranny and unprincipled policy.

maiden aunts and neutral professors. Even Leo Amery remarked, passing through Athens:

> this war seemed to sink back into its perspective along with the Persian war, far greater in all it meant for mankind, or the long destructive war between Athens and Sparta which is so much more like it.

Of course the Ottoman Empire, sandwiched between the domains of the Tsar, British-controlled Egypt and British-ruled India, seemed to have little to do with all that sob-stuff about poor little Belgium. The Turkish massacre of the Armenians, though soon well-publicized in Britain, seemed reassuringly exotic, almost reminiscent of the human sacrifices perpetrated by the natives during the Ashanti and Benin wars, though also recalling in some confusing manner the great Midlothian speeches of Gladstone: in some way related to the old-fashioned wars of the nineteenth century, fought in distant parts by heroic professionals of the traditional stiff upper lip type. Even General Sir Ian Hamilton, who had been appointed by the War Office to knock Turkey out of the war and was by no means inclined to underestimate the importance of his task, found the whole business perfectly natural and healthy, almost organic:

> Once in a generation a mysterious wish for war passes through the people. Their instinct tells them that *there is no other way* of progress and of escape from habits that no longer fit them. Whole generations of statesmen will fumble over reforms for a lifetime which are put into full-blooded execution within a week of a declaration of war. There is *no other way*. Only by intense sufferings can the nations grow, just as the snake once a year must with anguish slough off the once beautiful coat which has now become a strait jacket.[7]

Although Sir Ian Hamilton was soon to show more talent for *belles lettres* than for twentieth-century warfare, and eastwards in the desert an even more self-conscious prose stylist, T.E. Lawrence, had not yet begun his guerilla campaign against the Turks, it was quickly obvious that the Ottoman Empire was unlikely to survive the war in its current form, and that it would be Britain which would contribute most to its demise. This was a major reversal of British policy: since before the Crimean War Britain had aimed to contain Russian expansion by preserving Turkey. In 1913 Sir Louis Mallet, the British ambassador at Constantinople, had written:

> I assume that it is in the interests of Great Britain that the integrity of what remains of the Turkish Empire should be maintained – a division of the Asiatic provinces into spheres of interest could not benefit us, but would seriously affect the balance of power in the Mediterranean, our position in Egypt, in the Persian Gulf, to say nothing of India, and might bring about a European war.

This was also the view of Sir Edward Grey, the Foreign Secretary. The British

---

[7] *Leo Amery Diaries* vol. 1 p. 119 Amery to Florence Amery 23 June 1915; Sir Ian Hamilton *Gallipoli Diary* (2 vols 1920) vol. 1 p. 34, given under date 18 March 1915 but most probably written a couple of years later.

government were genuinely committed to assisting Turkey to achieve practical reforms and Grey even seemed to be moving towards some sort of joint European intervention in Turkey:

> We alone can certainly not put Turkey on her feet: she would when her fears subsided resist efforts at reform and play off one Power against another unless all were united.[8]

By the spring of 1914, having survived war with Italy and with the Balkan states, Turkey was seen as facing a potentially even more serious threat from the opposite quarter of the compass. In March 1914 Sir Louis Mallet wrote to the Foreign Office about the deteriorating relations between Constantinople and the Arab leaders Hussein and Ibn Saud:

> The need for caution is apparent at the present moment, when there is evidence of a concerted movement on the part of the Arabs. If these projects should mature and if the Arabs are eventually successful in defeating the Ottoman armies the loss of the Caliphate would probably follow, when, shorn of a further large portion of territory and of religious leadership, Turkish rule, as it exists today, would presumably disappear. Europe might then be faced with the question of a partition of the Turkish Empire which might easily produce complications of a serious nature, whilst it is difficult to estimate what might be the effects in India of a prolonged struggle for the possession of the Caliphate.

Like most other British officials at this stage, Mallet exaggerated the importance of the Ottoman Emperor's claim to be official head of the Moslem world, but he was correct in seeing that the British policy of maintaining the Turkish Empire was breaking up under his feet. Within another eight months this policy had completely disintegrated.[9]

The British Foreign Office was in no particular haste to establish an alternative policy. Russia's demand for Constantinople and control of the Straits was informally conceded in November 1914, though an official agreement was not concluded till the following spring. Discussions also took place with French officials. Rivalry over oil concessions in Mesopotamia had stimulated Foreign Office concern since the very early years of the century, and had been settled by the so-called Foreign Office Agreement as recently as March 1914. Nevertheless Mesopotamian oil was only one, and rarely the principal, point at issue in the discussions with the French. The Sykes-Picot agreement of May 1916, which regulated the prospective carve-up of the parts of Asia still under Turkish rule, allocated the oil-rich Mosul region to France;

[8] G.P. Gooch and Harold Temperley ed. *British Documents on the Origins of the War, 1898–1914* (11 vols 1927–38) vol. 10 part 1 p. 901 memo by Mallet 19 June 1913; ibid. vol. 10 part 1 p. 902 minute by Grey on Mallet's memo, cf ibid. vol. 10 part 1 p. 424–548.

[9] Gooch and Temperley ed. *British Documents* vol. 10 part 2 p. 828 Mallet to Grey 18 March 1914. Bullivant talks of the possibility of a Turkish-led war of religion in chap. 1 of John Buchan's novel *Greenmantle*, published in 1916.

this was subsequently felt to have been a mistake. There were as yet no real guide lines, or even much general idea of what Britain's future role in the Middle East ought to be. In the preliminary discussion of the Sykes-Picot agreement Britain's objectives were given as 'an opportunity to develop Lower Mesopotamia', land communications with the Mediterranean, and 'influence in an area sufficient to provide the personnel engaged in Mesopotamia irrigation work with suitable sanatoria, and hill stations, and containing an adequate native recruiting ground for administrative purposes'. Though evidently taking it for granted that they should assume the role of one of the Ottoman Empire's successor states, the British seemed to bring little enthusiasm or constructive vision to bear on the matter.[10]

III. The Cause of the Small Nationalities

Meanwhile developments elsewhere had introduced a new perspective. In August 1914 the Russian commander-in-chief, Grand Duke Nicholas, had published a manifesto to the Polish people promising them autonomy under the Romanov dynasty after the war, and in November 1914 a Polish National Committee was formed under Russian sponsorship. The effect of this was rather spoilt by the memory that it was Russia which had taken the lion's share in the eighteenth-century partitions of Poland and which had repressed Polish nationalist uprisings in 1830 and 1863, and till July 1917 Józef Piłsudski, afterwards the dominant figure in the post-war Polish republic, was trying to set up a rival nationalist organization under Austrian, and later German, auspices. In Britain more attention was excited by Tomáš Masaryk, a professor at the Czech university in Prague, former deputy in the Reichsrath at Vienna, and leading propagandist in the cause of Czech nationalism. His campaign for an independent Czech state obtained widespread sympathy in Britain, not least because it offered another 'small nation' to be displayed alongside Belgium and Serbia as a victim of Germanic imperialist oppression. When Masaryk was appointed professor at the School of Slavonic Studies at King's College London, Asquith promised to take the chair at his inaugural lecture and though indisposed on the actual evening, he sent along Lord Robert Cecil with a message to be read out to the audience:

> First and foremost the Allies are fighting for the liberty of small nations, to the end that they be left in future free from the tyranny of their more powerful neighbours to develop their own national life and institutions.

[10] C. Jay Smith 'Great Britain and the 1914–1915 Straits Agreement with Russia: The British Promise of November 1914' *American Historical Review* vol. 70 (1964–5) p. 1015–1034 espec. 1031–2; Marian Kent *Oil and Empire: British Policy and Mesopotamian Oil, 1900–1920* (1976) p. 17–94 and p. 120–2; C.J. Lowe and M.L. Dockrill ed. *The Mirage of Power* (3 vols 1972) vol. 3 p. 539–543 which prints Sir Mark Sykes' memo of January 1916, the quote being from p. 540.

Masaryk himself said in this lecture:

> If this horrible war, with its countless victims, has any meaning, it can only be found in the liberation of the small nations who are menaced by Germany's eagerness for conquest and her thirst for the dominion of Asia. The oriental question is to be solved on the Rhine, Moldau and Vistula, not only on the Danube, Vardar or Maritza.[11]

But even in 1915 some Englishmen thought that the reaction to Austrian and Turkish repression of their subject nationalities was too extreme, too unrealistic; for example the Inter-denominational Conference of Social Service Unions was warned:

> Sympathy with small nationalities has led many unthinking people to a wholly unjustified admiration for small States, regardless of the fact that, for all practical purposes, they are as great an anachronism in the large-scale world of to-day as the stage-coach and the sailing-ship.

In any case Britain's pose as the champion of small nations received something of a blow in the Dublin rising at Easter 1916. This was *the* classic failed *Putsch* inaugurating an era of failed *Putsche*. As in 1798 a country at war with Great Britain attempted to land a leader of the Irish people to liberate Ireland – Casement in the role of Wolfe Tone, a German U-boat instead of a French ship of the line, the gallows at Pentonville instead of the suicide's knife at Dublin Barracks. Although the nationalist rebels gained little popular sympathy till after the rising was put down, it did not look very good abroad: and anti-British propagandists made the most of it, especially in the United States.[12]

Early in October 1916 A.J. Balfour, philosopher, ex-premier and currently First Lord of the Admiralty, drew up a memorandum on British war aims in response to a request from Asquith for his colleagues' views on this topic. Writing in a tentative and speculative tone Balfour advocated 'rendering a policy of aggression less attractive by rearranging the map of Europe in closer agreement with what we rather vaguely call "the principle of nationality"'. The publicity whipped up in Britain and the U.S. by Tomáš Masaryk in favour of an independent Czech state was acknowledged by the suggestion that the Czechs should receive independence. Poland, somewhat contaminated in

---

[11] Thomas G. Masaryk *The Problem of Small Nations in the European Crisis* (1916): Asquith's message is printed as a preface and the passage from Masaryk's discourse is quoted from p. 31. The professor's arcane reference to the European river system contrasts the issue of Belgium, Czechoslovakia and Poland with that of Dobruja (i.e. the Bulgaro-Rumanian border), Macedonia and Turkey-in-Europe.

[12] Alfred E. Zimmern *Nationality & Government: with other War-time Essays* (1918) p. 71–2 – the whole address entitled 'True and False Nationalism', originally delivered 28 June 1915, is printed p. 61–86. Zimmern, despite his name, was born in Surbiton: he was later professor of international relations at Oxford and a key figure in the founding of U.N.E.S.C.O.. For responses in the U.S. to the British repression in Ireland after the Easter Rising see Stephen Hartley *The Irish Question as a Problem in British Foreign Policy, 1914–18* (1987) p. 58–70.

British eyes by Piłsudski's attempts to do a deal with the Germans, received more ambiguous treatment: Balfour favoured 'some kind of home rule for Poland' but thought, 'The more Russia is made a European rather than an Asiatic Power, the better for everybody', so that the preferred solution would be for Poland to remain a semi-autonomous part of the Tsar's empire. Balfour also proposed that there should be no interference in the internal affairs of Germany or what was left of Austria-Hungary after Serbia and Rumania (and the Czechs) had taken their slices, but that compensation should be obtained for damage done by the German invasion of Belgium, north-eastern France and Serbia, and for the shipping (mostly British) sunk by German U-boats.[13]

Balfour's memo, with its emphasis on a European settlement, helped prepare the British Cabinet for President Wilson's Peace Note of December 1916, which called on the belligerent powers to state their war aims. On the very day Wilson's note was delivered Lloyd George told the Commons that Britain's objective was 'Restitution, reparation, guarantee against repetition'. The British cabinet were not perhaps inclined to be intimidated by the American President's lofty moral tone: Lord Curzon had earlier given his opinion that, 'His conduct throughout the war seems to me to have been singularly ignoble and un-moral'. On the other hand they could hardly, in the face of world opinion, ignore the President's not unreasonable request that they should specify the objectives for which they were at war, and a reply drafted by Lord Robert Cecil essentially followed Balfour's proposals, stipulating the 'liberation of the Italians, as also of the Slavs, Rumanes and Czecho-Slovaks from foreign domination'. The emphasis on the problem of the European nationalities was probably quite consciously determined by the need to play up to public opinion in America; when talking to politicians from Canada, Australia and New Zealand, Balfour hastened to acknowledge that 'the essential thing was the security of the British Empire and not Central European philanthropy'.[14]

The Entente reply to Wilson's note, though drafted in French by French officials, was based on Balfour and Cecil's proposals, as Balfour himself recorded:

> The Draft Note to Wilson is mainly based on a draft of mine, and a draft of Bob Cecil's, worked up by the French draftsmen, and then subjected to some

[13] Kenneth J. Calder *Britain and the Origins of the New Europe, 1914–1918* (Cambridge 1976) p. 98; Blanche E.C. Dugdale *Arthur James Balfour* (2 vols 1936) vol. 2 p. 435–442 appendix 2, memo 4 Octo. 1916. See also Harold I. Nelson *Land and Power: British and Allied Policy on Germany's Frontiers 1916–19* (1963) p. 8–17.

[14] *Hansard: House of Commons* vol. 88 col. 1335, Lloyd George 19 Dec. 1916; India Office Library Mss Eur. F 112/116 Curzon to Lloyd George May 1916; Calder *Britain and the Origins of the New Europe* p. 107, 216–7; for Balfour's words to the Dominions representatives see *Leo Amery Diaries* vol. 1 p. 147, 27 March 1917. See generally Sterling J. Kernek 'Distractions of Peace during War: The Lloyd George Government's Reactions to Woodrow Wilson December 1916–November 1918' *Transactions of the American Philosophical Society* vol. 65 pt. 2 (1975) at p. 19–31.

hours' hammering at the hands of a Joint Committee, of which I was one of the unfortunate members.

When it was published in the second week of January 1917, it excited the sarcasm of the Austrians:

> If the enemy desire above all the restoration of outraged rights and liberties, the recognition of the principle of nationalities, and the free existence of the small States, it will suffice to point to the tragic fate of the Irish and Finnish peoples, the extinction of the freedom and independence of the Boer Republics, the subjugation of North Africa by England, France, and Italy, and, lastly, the oppression of Greece, which is unexampled in history.

The Entente demands for the dismemberment of Austria-Hungary and indemnities from Germany also seem to have been a little too much for Wilson, and on 22 January 1917 he told the U.S. Senate:

> it must be a peace without victory . . . Victory would mean peace forced upon the loser, a victor's terms imposed upon the vanquished. It would be accepted in humiliation, under duress, at an intolerable sacrifice, and would leave a sting, a resentment, a bitter memory upon which terms of peace would rest, not permanently, but only as upon quicksand.[15]

Wilson soon abandoned this statesmanlike and prophetic position as a result of experiencing two revelations. The first was that he was about to lead his country into the war, a circumstance requiring a different slogan from 'peace without victory'. The second revelation was the fall of the Tsar which, by establishing a democratic regime in Petrograd, removed the anomaly of democratic Britain and France being in coalition with the Tsarist tyranny against the militarized Central Empires, and simplified the confrontation into one of 'democracy at war with autocracy'.

IV. Democracy versus Autocracy

The democratic aspect of the Russian Revolution had been quickly seized upon by the British: four days after the establishment of the Provisional Government in Petrograd, Lloyd George, the Prime Minister, told the Commons on behalf of his government:

> They are confident that these events, marking as they do an epoch in the history of the world and the first great triumph of the principle for which we entered the war, will result, not in any confusion or slackening in the conduct of the War, but in the even closer and more effective co-operation between the Russian people and its Allies in the cause of human freedom.

[15] British Library Add. 49739 f. 127 Balfour to Lord Sanderson 4 Jan. 1917 James Brown Scott *Official Statements of War Aims and Peace Proposals December 1916 to November 1918* (Washington 1921) p. 44 note 12 Jan. 1917; ibid. p. 51–2 Wilson's speech of 22 Jan. 1917.

Wilson misread the situation in exactly the same way. Within a few months a new tyranny would emerge in Petrograd, and would publish to the world the extraordinary and hitherto secret terms of the Treaty of London, signed not only by the sinister emissaries of the Tsar, but also by the official representatives of democratic Britain, France and Italy; in the meantime, in announcing that the United States had to go to war with Germany because 'The world must be made safe for democracy', Wilson took the opportunity to lecture the elected representatives of the United States on the subjects of Constitutional Theory and International Morality:

> Cunningly contrived plans of deception and aggression carried, it might be, from generation to generation, can be worked out and kept from the light only within the privacy of courts or behind the carefully guarded confidences of a narrow and privileged class. They are happily impossible where public opinion commands and insists upon full information concerning the nation's affairs.
> A steadfast concert of peace can never be maintained except by a partnership of democratic nations. No autocratic government could be trusted to keep faith within it or observe its covenants ...
> Does not every American feel that assurance has been added to our hope for the future peace of the world by the wonderful and heartening things that have been happening within the last few weeks in Russia? ... the great, generous Russian people have been added in all their naive majesty and might to the forces that are fighting for freedom in the world, for justice and for freedom.[16]

Meanwhile, in London, the Imperial War Cabinet, at the instance of the Dominions prime ministers, was deciding to hang on to the colonies seized from Germany since 1914 and to the various territories liberated from the unspeakable Turk. In Austria posters showed an Austrian soldier shaking hands across a sunset with a distinctly more martial-looking Turk, with the caption, 'Welfare aid for the Turkish troops in Galicia. Remember our Turkish brothers in arms', but the Entente was less inclined to forget Ottoman barbarities of yesteryear. The Entente reply to Wilson's Peace Note of December 1916 had mentioned 'the enfranchisement of populations subject to the bloody tyranny of the Turks; the expulsion from Europe of the Ottoman Empire.' By the following spring Lloyd George was offering his colonial colleagues the 'disruption of the Turkish Empire as an Empire' as one of the British Empire's principal war aims:

> those fair lands are a blighted desert, although once upon a time they were the richest in the world ... The Turk must never be allowed to misgovern these great lands in the future. We owe it to these countries, for the gifts with which they have enriched mankind, that we should do something to restore their glory ... Under Turkish rule they have been a constant source of irritation, and

---

[16] Norman and Jeanne Mackenzie ed. *The Diaries of Beatrice Webb* (4 vols 1982–5) vol. 3 p. 278, 18 March 1917; *Hansard: House of Commons* vol. 91 col.1537, reply by Lloyd George during question time 19 March 1917; Scott *Official Statements of War Aims and Peace Proposals* p. 89–90.

friction, and war. There has been no one cause which has been more fruitful of bloodshed in Europe than the misgovernment of the Turkish Empire and its results. I am not sure that even this war had not something to do with German ambition in the East . . .[17]

But like Wilson, Lloyd George made full use of the propaganda potential of the short-lived parliamentary regime in Petrograd. A British note supplementary to the official Entente reply to Wilson's Peace Note, dated 13 January 1917, had warned of the continued menace of 'Germany, or rather those in Germany who mould its opinions and control its destinies,' but at that point, with the Tsar seemingly still firmly in the saddle, it had not been politic to ventilate demagogic theories about the functioning of despotic governments. After the fall of the Tsar however Lloyd George felt free to emphasise the war's essential nature as a war against autocracy, and to announce, 'We can make peace with a free Germany. It is with a Germany dominated by an autocracy that we can not make any terms of peace'; and from about this time British propaganda began to devote more attention to the discussion of the historical evolution of Prussian junker leadership, in an attempt to flesh out and amplify the previously rather vague rhetoric about 'Prussianism'.[18]

Yet a certain vagueness continued to prevail. A meeting at Blackpool sponsored by the semi-official War Aims Committee in September was reported as having given 'a clear indication of the great value of emphasising the meaning of America's entry into the war as the complete and final justification of the Allied cause from a democratic point of view', but as late as December 1917 it was felt that 'the force of campaign would be greatly increased if our War Aims could be stated on something like definite terms'. It had previously been found that 'Organised Labour in nearly every constituency declines to co-operate in forming a War Aims Committee on the grounds that our Aims are not defined'.[19]

---

[17] Bernhard Denscher ed. *Tagebuch der Strasse: Wiener Plakate* (Vienna 1981) p. 122 no. 109; Scott *Official Statements of War Aims and Peace Proposals* p. 37; Lloyd George *War Memoirs* vol. 4 p. 1749–50, 1773, 1774–5. See also Asquith's condemnation of 'Turkish rule in Europe, where the Turks has always been a stranger and an intruder', at a Guildhall banquet 9 Nov. 1916, in *Times* 10 Nov. 1916 p. 10c.

[18] Scott *Official Statements of War Aims and Peace Proposals* p. 47; ibid. p. 119 speech by Lloyd George at Queen's Hall on Belgian Independence Day 21 July 1917; Sanders and Taylor *British Propaganda during the First World War* p. 140–2. For a classic description of Prussianism as 'a doctrine of authority' see Alfred E. Zimmern 'Three Doctrines in Conflict' in *The Round Table* March 1918 reprinted in *Nationality & Government: with other War-time Essays* (1918) – see especially p. 333–42. One of the most cogent discussions of Prussianism of the whole war period, Ford Madox Hueffer's *When Blood is their Argument: An Analysis of Prussian Culture*, fell rather flat when it came out in 1915: it probably would have gained more attention if it had been published a couple of years later.

[19] Public Record Office T. 102, Meetings Department Report 25 Sept. 1917; ibid. 'Report Up to 8th December, 1917'; ibid. Meetings Department Report 10 Oct. 1917 [by G. Wallace Carter] According to the 25 Sept. 1917 report 1,298 meetings had been held in 54 coastal resorts since the beginning of August.

Eventually it was the views of President Wilson, and the Fourteen Points promulgated by him on 8 January 1918, offering independence, autonomy, guarantees to subject people everywhere, which became the rallying point of the Entente and their most successful propaganda weapon within the armed forces and on the home front of the enemy. But of course it took more than Princeton rhetoric to convince good British imperialists like Leo Amery, now a leading light of the British War Cabinet secretariat. Wilson gave Congress a lecture about

> this intolerable thing of which the masters of Germany have shown us the ugly face, this menace of combined intrigue and force which we now see so clearly as the German power, a Thing without conscience or honor or capacity for covenanted peace,

and the walls of America's cities were placarded with H.R. Hopp's poster of a colossal gorilla in a German helmet clutching a terrified girl – an adumbration of *King Kong*? – with the caption *Destroy the Mad Brute*, but meanwhile Amery was noting that Naumann's *Mitteleuropa*, a tract (a best-seller in Germany) which advocated a German-dominated free-trade area in Europe, was the only book he had read in 1917 'which really mattered, and that mainly because I had thought so far in the same direction myself'.[20]

Of course, Amery was dreadfully right-wing but this seems mainly to have meant that he had no false shame about professing the prejudices which other people were influenced by but would prefer not to admit even to themselves: his views were not so unacceptable as to prevent him achieving senior cabinet rank less than five years later. He had, incidentally, been assistant secretary to an inter-departmental committee appointed in August 1916 under the chairmanship of Sir Louis Mallet to consider 'Territorial Changes'; this committee's recommendation that German East Africa should be retained after the war to provide a land link between Cairo and the Cape was endorsed by a committee of the War Cabinet in April 1917, but the German colonies were not mentioned in the Entente's reply to President Wilson's Peace Note, partly because Poor Little Belgium seemed disinclined to allow the British a completely free hand in German East Africa. Meanwhile in Italy respected writers were not ashamed to insist on the justice of a policy of annexations which would have astonished even Naumann:

> Not to realize the imperial nature of this war of ours and to reduce it merely to a vindication of the *sacred boundaries which Nature has marked for the Fatherland* means to have understood nothing of the psychological torment of a whole people during the epic May of 1915 . . .
>
> An imperial war, therefore: a war for the conquest of wealth and political prestige, for expansion, and not just beyond the unjust old borders of the Alps and the Adriatic, but for the conquest of new opportunities that can be offered

---

[20] Scott *Official Statements of War Aims and Peace Proposals* p. 194, speech by Wilson 4 Dec. 1917; *Leo Amery Diaries* vol. 1 p. 189, 31 Dec. 1917.

to the exuberant energy of sons at present dispersed in all parts of the world, to the great benefit of the prosperity and wealth of other nations, other races.

These demands did not involve the African colonies conquered from Germany, and though the possibility had been discussed with Italy's partners in the Entente it seems difficult to believe that the Italian government were genuinely convinced that 'The possession of Asia Minor is essential for the development of our country'. What the Italian expansionists particularly and urgently desired were the French and British colonies in the Horn of Africa, Djibouti and British Somaliland: their allocation to Italy would not only link up their struggling colonies in Eritrea and Somaliland and provide better harbours, but would also remove the main competition to Italian commercial exploitation of Ethiopia and to eventual Italian control of both Ethiopia and the Yemen.[21]

Once America had entered the war Italian claims were simply an embarrassment to the British government, and in the event Italy received very little of what had been promised in 1915: Trieste, Trento, South Tyrol, and eventually about half of the territory claimed beyond the River Juba in East Africa. Since the British Empire received an accession of over 800,000 square miles in the post-war settlement the Italians felt they had some cause to be aggrieved. The fact is the British ministers had gone into the war to maintain the British Empire's position and prestige (and their own) and had been as willing to give away other countries' territories to satisfy one type of ally, like Italy, as they had been afterwards ready to embrace high and wordy principles of justice and self-determination to satisfy another type of ally, represented by Woodrow Wilson. Germany's colonies were merely a side issue: 'We did not enter the war for gain', *The Morning Post* remarked piously, 'but Providence and the blood of our people have given these Colonies into our keeping'. In the event of course these colonial acquisitions were to prove one of the more durable parts of the Peace Settlement; and there was no doubt an agreeable irony in the fact that a war fought against foreign hegemony and imperialism should end by making the largest empire in the world even larger.[22]

---

[21] Wm. Roger Louis *Great Britain and Germany's Lost Colonies 1914–1918* (Oxford 1967) p. 70, 72, 82–3; ibid. p. 64–7 for dispute with the Belgians. Savinio Acquaviva *L'Avvenire Coloniale d'Italia e la guerra* (Rome 1917) p. 46–7 for quotations, p. 81, 89–91 for objectives in the Horn of Africa, cf. Orazio Pedrazzi *L'Africa dopo la guerra e l'Italia* (Florence 1917) p. 28–37. Pedrazzi p. 42–6 also outlines the Italian claim to the area between the Rivers Juba and Tana in eastern Kenya; the reference to Asia Minor is from Senator G. Franchetti's preface to Pedrazzi's book at p. v. Jubaland was ceded to Italy by a treaty signed at London 15 July 1924; various papers on the territory are in *I Documenti Diplomatici Italiani: 7ª serie* (Rome 1953–) vol 3 passim. See also Louis *Great Britain and Germany's Lost Colonies* p. 153–4.

[22] *Morning Post* 30 June 1917.

8

Towards the Economics of Total War

Imagine a Waterloo, in which the British squares are never broken or thrown back, the French squadrons never thrown into confusion, and the old guard never shaken. Imagine this going on from week to week, from month to month, from year to year, from century to century, with Napoleon and Wellington asking every three weeks or so for another 100,000 men to replace the slain.

Bernard Shaw to Austin Harrison 14 Nov. 1914, in Dan H. Laurence ed. *Bernard Shaw: Collected Letters* (3 vols so far published 1965–), vol. 3 p. 268.

I. The Scale of the War

The First World War cost more in lives and treasure than all the previous wars of Europe put together; part of the incomprehension of the politicians which exposed the nations to war in 1914 was an incomprehension of the vastness of the resources they had at their command.

Except for the British Empire and the United States all the major belligerents mobilized more than 15 per cent of their adult male population for their armed forces; Bulgaria mobilized more than 38 per cent. Altogether the Entente mobilized 48 million men against the Central Powers' 26 million; and nearly 9 million died. The dead of the British Empire alone, it was calculated, would have required four days and three nights to march four abreast past the Cenotaph erected in their honour in Whitehall. The transportation of the various armies, their feeding, and their establishment in the theatres of war in huge temporary communities, with all the lavish waste characteristic of modern military life, meant that manpower was not the only economic resource involved; and much more than any previous conflict, the Great War came to be perceived as a war of material. 'It is not a bad description of war to say that it consists in carrying heavy things from one place to another, and that victory depends on carrying them faster and more efficiently than the enemy', remarked one observer. To supply the British Expeditionary Force in France and Flanders between 9 August 1914 and 10 November 1918 over 25 million tons of supplies were shipped from England (equivalent to nearly half the total exports of Britain in a peacetime trading year). This included:

3,240,948 tons of human food
5,438,602 tons of oats and hay
5,253,338 tons of ammunition
3,922,391 tons of coal
1,761,777 tons of ordnance stores
3,962,497 tons of engineers' stores

The hay and oats were less for cavalry than for transport horses: it was estimated that a fighting division (mainly infantry) required 16 tons of food a day for the men and 41 tons for the transport horses and the men tending them. The British were also relatively well equipped with motor lorries – there were 24,835 with the British army in France in January 1918, though inevitably a disproportionate number were appropriated by the specialist branches: transferred from the staff of the R.F.C. to a divisional H.Q. Maurice Baring was surprised to find that 'Instead of having either a light tender or a lorry or a Daimler at one's disposal, one had either to ride or to walk'. To back up distribution by road, the British in France had by November 1918 laid down 4,000 miles of light railway, plus by June 1917, 1,200 miles of standard gauge, together representing 360,000 tons of steel, and a track mileage approximately equal to that of the entire Ottoman Empire in 1914. Including French domestic and military railways there were in the French theatre of war by the end of hostilities 18,718 locomotives and 551,541 wagons for standard gauge and 2,706 locomotives and 32,984 wagons for narrow gauge involved in military business; in Italy in 1918 the 3,526 standard gauge locomotives and 71,880 wagons assigned to military purposes represented 67 per cent of all the locomotives and wagons in the country.[1]

Transport was not the only technology-intensive branch of communications. In just *one* of Italy's five army zones on the Austro-Italian front there were by early 1917 5,000 kilometres of telegraph cable, 2,000 kilometres of telephone cable (plus 3,000 kilometres laid by the artillery) 3,000 telephone receivers, 200 telephone exchanges and an average daily traffic of 10,000 telegrams and phonograms. But Italy was relatively backward in this sphere: by late March 1916 over 108,000 kilometres of telephone wire had been sent to France from Britain 'for upkeep alone' and by November 1918 the American Expeditionary

---

[1] Pietro Maravigna *Guerra e Vittoria* (Turin 1938 edit.) p. 694–5 and Richard J. Crampton *Bulgaria, 1878–1918* (Boulder 1983) p. 479; Fabian Ware *The Immortal Heritage: an Account of the Work and Policy of the Imperial War Graves Commission during Twenty Years, 1917–1937* (Cambridge 1937) p. 27; T.M. Kettle *The Ways of War* (1917) p. 156; J.F.C. Fuller *The Army in My Time* (1935) p. 152: these figures are derived from *Statistics of the Military Effort of the British Empire during the Great War, 1914–1920* (1922), which also gives figures for motor transport at p. 594; Maurice Baring *Flying Corps Headquarters, 1914–1918* (1930) p. 69; Stephen Foot *Three Lives* (1934) p. 215; David Lloyd George *War Memoirs* (6 vols 1933–6) vol. 2 p. 797: Edwin A Pratt *British Railways and the Great War: Organisation, Efforts, Difficulties and Achievements* (2 vols 1921) vol. 2 p. 622 says 2,096 miles of entirely new track were laid, and 1,581 miles reconstructed, including the laying of 589 miles of new track, and cf Ahmed Emin *Turkey in the World War* (New Haven 1930) p. 85; *Report of the Military Board of Allied Supply* (2 vols. Washington 1924–5) vol. 1 pt. 1 p. 52 table 3.

Force in France had laid for its own use over 153,000 kilometres of telegraph and telephone wire.[2]

Organized and coordinated by these vast spider-webs of signal wire, the expenditure of ammunition was on a hitherto undreamt of scale.

> From about half a mile to the north, southwards as far as he could see, the whole front was a dazzling flicker of gun-flashes. It was as if giant hands covered with huge rings set with searchlights were being shaken in the darkness, as if innumerable brilliant diamonds were flashing great rays of light. There was not a fraction of a second without its flash and roar. Only the great boom of a twelve- or fourteen-inch naval gun just behind them punctured the general pandemonium at regular intervals.

In the three-day bombardment of Copenhagen in September 1807 the British had fired off 162,000 lb of powder; at the seige of Badajoz, between 3 and 10 June 1811, 139,000 lb; at Waterloo on 18 June 1815, 51,210 lb; expenditure of shell and shot at Copenhagen and Waterloo is not recorded but at Badajoz it was 15,503 twenty-four and eighteen pound round-shot, 641 twenty-four pound charges of grape-shot and 2,781 eight and ten-inch shells; at Vitoria, where the cannonade was not as heavy as at Waterloo, 6,870 rounds were fired. This is to be compared with the 2,687,653 shells fired by the British in the preliminary bombardment of the Battle of Arras 25 March – 8 April 1917, 3,561,530 shells in the preliminary bombardment of the Battle of Messines 26 May-6 June 1917 and 4,283,550 shells in the preliminary bombardment at Passchendale 17–30 July 1917; those fired at Passchendaele amounted to about 100,000 tons in weight and cost £22,211,389 14s. 4d. and in reply the German Fourth Army fired off 27 trainloads of ammunition on the first day of the offensive alone. (More than seventy years later quantities of unexploded shells are still ploughed up every autumn). The total cost of the shells produced in Britain 1914–1918 was £915,003,412 10s. This was rather more than the entire British war expenditure in twenty-two years of hostilities with France 1793–1815 and by 1918 the National Debt was increasing every four months by more than the total debt accumulation 1793–1815. The comparatively small Austro-Hungarian offensive against Italy in May 1917, requiring the stock-piling of 1,036,225 artillery rounds and 13.6 million rounds of small arms ammunition, involved 84 trains and altogether 2,923 wagons; the German build-up for the spring offensives of 1918 involved 1,884 munitions trains. Even the Italians fired off 3,525,738 rounds of artillery ammunition at the Piave, 15–25 June 1918. Total Italian production of shells, at 70 million rounds, less than a third of British, less than a quarter of French production, required 1,667,000 tonnes of steel, 411,000 tonnes of pig iron, 21,000 tonnes of copper and 1,889,000 tonnes of coal. This was approximately equal to Italy's entire

---

[2] Maravigna *Guerra e Vittoria* p. 446; Mario Silvestri *Isonzo 1917* (Turin 1971 edit.) p. 59–60; Public Record Office WO 79/73 diary of Sir Stanley Von Donop 30 March 1916, the figure being given as 68,000 miles of telephone wire; Benedict Crowell *American Munitions, 1917–1918* (Washington 1919) p. 568, the figure being given as 96,000 miles.

output of these materials in 1917 – a year of record production levels – but does not include the material either for the vehicles to transport them or the guns to shoot them; and the latter were no longer the crudely bored-out unrifled tubes of Napoleon's day but complex precision-machined engines of destruction.[3]

The front-line troops 'caught in a Frankenstein war-machine created by their fellow-countrymen' were never able to forget the industrial, mechanical, mass-production aspect of war:

> the most startling feature is the debris that is lying scattered on the surface and thick in the trenches. Sets of equipment, rifles, bayonets, shovels, shrapnel, helmets, respirators, shellcases, iron posts, overcoats, groundsheets, bombs (in hundreds) – I don't suppose there is a square yard without some relic and reminiscence of the aweful waste of war.

The fighter ace Edward 'Mick' Mannock, passing through the trenches to inspect the wreck of a plane he had shot down, was struck not merely by the 'dead men's legs sticking through the sides [of the trenches] with putties and boots still on' and the 'bits of bones and skulls with the hair peeling off' but also the 'tons of equipment and clothing lying about'. The painter Paul Nash had a similar impression of the characteristic scenery of the front line:

> The ground for miles around furrowed into trenches, pitted with yawning holes in which the water lies still and cold or heaped with mounds of earth, tangles of rusty wire, tin plates, stakes, sandbags, and all the refuse of war.

While some of Nash's war paintings have an abstract, sea-scape quality, in others – especially 'Void', 'Desolate Landscape, Ypres Salient' and 'The Menin Road' – the dreary accumulation of mechanically-made rubbish is painfully emphasized, especially if one compares these works to the more vegetable,

---

[3] Richard Aldington *Death of a Hero* (1965 unexpurgated edition) p. 320; *Parliamentary Papers* 1817 IV p. 88 for expenditure of gunpowder at Copenhagen and Waterloo, *Supplementary Despatches, Correspondence, and Memoranda of Field Marshal Arthur Duke of Wellington, K.G.* (15 vols 1858–72) vol. 7 p. 161 for Alexander Dickson's 'Return of the Ammunition expended at the Siege of Badajoz from the 3rd to the 10th June 1811', Richard D. Henegan *Seven Years' Campaigning in the Peninsula and the Netherlands; from 1808 to 1815* (2 vols 1846) vol. 1 p. 345 fn for rounds fired at Vitoria and cf comparison of shell expenditure in earlier wars in Crowell *America's Munitions* p. 27–9 figures 1 to 3; *Statistics of Military Effort of the British Empire* p. 480, 482 for First World War bombardments: Rupprecht von Bayern *Mein Kriegstagbuch* ed. Eugen von Frauenholz (3 vols Munich [1929]) vol. 2 p. 232, 1 Aug. 1917 for expenditure of shell by German Fourth Army 31 July 1917; *History of the Ministry of Munitions* (12 vols 1922) vol. 10 pt.III p. 122 Appendix V for total cost of British production; *Hansard: House of Commons* vol. 101 col.1445 statement by Herbert Samuel 29 Jan. 1918 on increase of National Debt; Gustav Gratz and Richard Schüller *Der Wirtschaftliche Zusammenbruch Österreich-Ungarns* (Vienna 1930) p. 121; Reichsarchiv *Der Weltkrieg 1914 bis 1918* (14 vols Berlin 1925–1944) vol. 14 p. 35 fn. and Beilage 39a; Luigi Einaudi *La condotta economica e gli effetti sociali della guerra Italiana* (Bari 1933) p. 68; Guido Liuzzi *I servizi logistici nella guerra* (Milan 1934) p. 351 cf B.R. Mitchell *European Historical Statistics* (1981) p. 384, 414, 421 which show that in 1917 Italy produced 1,677,000 tonnes of coal, 1,332,000 tonnes of steel and 471,000 tonnes of pig iron.

	Aircraft	Aircraft motors	Heavy tanks	Light tanks	Artillery guns	Shells	Gas (in tonnes)	Heavy machine guns	Light m-g. and sub-machine guns
France	51,700	92,000	800	2,297	23,820	289,000,000	35,302	93,300	225,000
Britain	55,093	41,034	2,374	245	20,971	217,041,000	33,072	107,402	133,104
Italy	12,021	23,979	–	–	16,000	70,000,000	–	36,567	n.a.
Russia	1,893	920	–	–	16,800	55,400,000	–	n.a.	n.a.
U.S.A. (April 1917 onward only)	15,000	41,000	–	79	2,058	17,260,000	–	129,424	52,238
Germany	47,637	40,499	20	–	n.a.	n.a.	134,116	n.a.	n.a.
Austria-Hungary	4,338	4,346	–	–	11,561	6,641,000	–	38,900	–[4]

[4] Walter Raleigh and H.A. Jones *The War in the Air* (7 vols Oxford 1922–34) appendix vol. p. 154 appendix XXXI for British, American and German aircraft and aero-engine production; Claude Carlier 'L'aéronautique militaire française dans la première guerre mondiale' *Guerres Mondiales et Conflits Contemporains* no. 145 (1988) p. 63–80 at p. 79 for French production; Rosario Abate *Storia della aeronautica Italiano* (Milan 1974) p. 136–7; Heinz J. Nowarra and G.R. Duval *Russian Civil and Military Aircraft, 1884–1969* (1971) p. 49; John H. Morrow Jr. *German Air Power in World War I* (Lincoln Nebraska 1982) p. 213 for Austrian aircraft and aero-engine production; [J.M.G.] Pédoya *La Commission de l'Armée pendant la Grande Guerre* (Paris 1926) p. 137–8, 142 for French tank output; *History of the Ministry of Munitions* vol. 12 pt.III p. 93 appendix VI: Crowell *America's Munitions* p. 157; Ernst von Wrisberg *Erinnerungen an die Kriegsjahre im Königlich Preussischen Kriegsministerium* (3 vols Leipzig 1921–2) vol. 3 p. 160; [C.A.] Reboul *Mobilisation Industrielle: des Fabrications de Guerre de 1914 à 1918* (Paris 1925) p. 39 and 50 and cf Pédoya *Commission de l'Armée* p. 76 for French artillery production: Pédoya p. 107 for production of shells; *History of the Ministry of Munitions* vol. 10 pt.I p. 96; ibid. vol. 10 pt V p. 97; Liuzzi *Servizi Logistici* p. 348, 351 N. Voznesensky *War Economy of the U.S.S.R. in the Period of the Patriotic War* (Moscow 1948) p. 70–2, cf Alec Nove *An Economic History of the U.S.S.R.* (Harmondsworth 1982 edit.) p. 275; Crowell *America's Munitions* p. 33 figure 5 and p. 55; Gratz and Schüller *Wirtschaftliche Zusammenbruch Österreich-Ungarns* p. 110; Pédoya *Commission del'Armée* p. 53–4 for French production of machine guns, *History of the Ministry of Munitions* vol. 11 pt. V p. 27; Liuzzi *Servizi Logistici* p. 349; Crowell *America's Munitions* p. 175–6; Bundesministerium für Landesverteidigung und das Kriegsarchiv *Österreich-Ungarns Letzer Krieg* (7 vols Vienna 1930–8) vol 7 Beilage 2 Tabelle 10; mutually contradictory figures for German machine gun output are given in Wrisberg *Erinnerungen an die Kriegsjahre* vol. 3 p. 8 and Major Kopf and Hauptmann Schmidt 'Maschinengewehre' in M. Schwarte *Die Technik im Weltkriege* (Berlin 1920) p. 23–33 at p. 27. Figures for poison gas production are given in L.F. Haber *The Poisonous Cloud: Chemical Warfare in the First World War* (Oxford 1986) p. 261, table 11.1.

detailed, feathery-stroked style of his pre-war paintings. For Nash, as for so many others, the Western Front constituted a rude awakening for those who had preferred romantic, pastoral fantasies to the stern realities of the machine age; the denaturing of man and of the countryside in the front line was like an Industrial Revolution taken to hideous extremes:

> all the frightfulness that the mind of man could devise was brought into the field; and there, where lately there had been the idyllic picture of rural peace, there was as faithful a picture of the soul of scientific war. In earlier wars, certainly, towns and villages had been burned, but what was that compared to this sea of craters dug out by machines? For even in this fantastic desert there was the sameness of the machine-made article. A shell-hole strewn with bully-tins, broken weapons, fragments of uniform, and dud shells, with one or two dead bodies on its edge ... this was the never-changing scene that surrounded each one of these hundreds of thousands of men.[5]

Of course much of the waste was unintentional, or at least unauthorized. In one week in mid 1915, in a single corps area on the Ypres front, 1,204 discarded rifles, 206,100 rounds of ammunition, 400 rations of preserved meat, 308 sets of equipment, a lorry, 1,329 great coats, 715 coils of barbed wire, 3,427 entrenching tools, 2,541 shovels, 15,465 sandbags and 47 stretchers were salvaged. But litter on a gigantic scale, as much as mass-production, material excess, and the mechanized communications of advanced industrial societies, were part of the essential nature of this war. If it had not been for the economic capacity to maintain huge armies indefinitely in a desolated, unproductive battle zone, to bring up huge stocks of artillery ammunition by the trainload, to transfer hundreds of thousands of reinforcements in a matter of hours whenever an enemy break-through threatened, the war could never have developed into the vast stalemate which it so quickly became.[6]

II. The Failure of Forward Planning

The reorganization of the leading industrial economies for war production involved major shifts of resources within each society and the management of

---

[5] F.P. Crozier *The Men I Killed* (1937) p. 23; Malcolm Brown *Tommy Goes to War* (1978) p. 246, quoting letter by Lance Corporal Roland Mountford July 1916; Frederick Oughton ed. *The Personal Diary of Major Edward 'Mick' Mannock* (1966) p. 119, 20 July 1917; Paul Nash *Outline: An Autobiography and Other Writings* (1949) p. 195, Paul Nash to Margaret Nash 6 April 1917. Nash's 'Void', in the National Gallery of Canada and his 'Desolate Landscape, Ypres Salient' in Manchester City Art Gallery are reproduced in Margot Eates *Paul Nash: the Master of the Image, 1889–1946* (1973) plates 10 and 18. 'The Menin Road' is in the Imperial War Museum. See also Andrew Causey *Paul Nash* (Oxford 1980). The quotation beginning 'all the frightfulness of war' is from Ernst Jünger *The Storm of Steel* (1929) p. 109.

[6] Sir Aylmer Haldane *A Soldier's Saga* (Edinburgh 1948) p. 312 for quantity of material salvaged 1915. See also the list of items of rubbish in Guy Chapman *A Passionate Prodigality* (1933) p. 267.

these shifts was one of the key political features of the war years; indeed, the lack of success in managing them adequately was a major factor in the political and social breakdown of various countries at the end of the war, and represents a failure on the political front corresponding to the failure of the generals to master the problems on the military, tactical side. Within this overall picture of shifted resources, one is struck by certain asymmetries and anomalies: the imbalance between the resources on the Entente side and those of the Central Powers; the insignificance in productive terms of Germany's allies compared to Germany itself; and the very high output of France which, despite the loss of 55 per cent of its coal and 70 per cent of its steel production through the German occupation of the north-eastern industrial areas, appears to have achieved the highest output of petrol engines, motor vehicles, light tanks and on the Entente side at least – the German figures are not available – artillery and explosives.[7]

From any point of view the war was a tragic tale of mismanaged resources. There was a general failure to anticipate that the war would last more than a few weeks, and when it was realized that the fighting would go on for years and consume unprecedented amounts of material, there was a comparable failure to evolve any balanced economic strategy.

The idea that the war would be short was based less on the military leaders' conviction of their own capacity to arrange a really decisive military victory at the first encounter than on the assumption that the loose social fabric which could sustain a Hundred Years' War, an Eighty Years' War or a Thirty Years' War was a thing of the past, and that more refined economic forms had evolved in which it was physically, socially and economically impossible for a major war to be a long one. The idea that any war between the great powers that lasted more than a few weeks would involve the total paralysis of the belligerents' economies, and consequently of their war-making capacity, had been suggested in Jean de Bloch's six volume *La Guerre Future*, 1898, part of which was published in English as *Is War Now Impossible? The Future of War in its Technical, Economic and Political Relations*. Bloch's hint was fairly quickly taken up by the German High Command; Generaloberst Alfred Graf von Schlieffen, chief of the German general staff, wrote in 1905, at the time of the Russo-Japanese War:

> Out there in Manchuria they may face each other for months on end in impregnable positions. In Western Europe we cannot allow ourselves the luxury

---

[7] Richard D. Challener *The French Theory of the Nation in Arms, 1866–1939* (New York 1955) p. 97 citing unpublished study by Lt.- Col. Charles Menu 1928–1931 for proportion of French industrial capacity lost to German occupation: percentages given in Arthur Fontaine *French Industry during the War* (New Haven 1926) p. 403–5 are lower because they relate to manpower rather than output. French explosives output peaked at 870 tonnes per day (26,970 tonnes per month) in July 1917 and was down to 400 tonnes per day in April 1918, cf Reboul *Mobilisation Industrielle: Fabrications de Guerre* p. 122, 127.

of waging a war in this manner. The machine with its thousand wheels, upon which millions depend for their livelihood, cannot stand still for so long.

Similarly, Sir Archibald Murray, Chief of General Staff to the British Expeditionary Force in 1914, thought:

the war will last three months if everything goes well, and perhaps eight months if things do not go so satisfactorily. Beyond that he thinks it impossible to feed the armies in the field and the populations concerned, and the financial strain would be more than Europe could bear.

G.H. Perris's Home University Library volume *A Short History of War and Peace*, published in 1911, claimed that war between Britain and Germany 'would destroy the sensitive mechanism of credit, on which the economic life of both countries depends', and the relatively large sale of this book ensured that in Britain at least such views were widely circulated; immediately after the war these ideas were referred to as characteristic of the mood of 1914, even in a best-selling romantic novel, Maud Diver's *The Strong Hours*. When war began to seem imminent in July 1914, the Governor of the Bank of England, allegedly 'with tears in his eyes', urged Lloyd George, 'Keep us out of it. We shall be ruined if we are dragged in'. Beatrice Webb and her associates feared not only a collapse of credit and problems with the supply of raw materials, but also severe unemployment; John Burns predicted, 'We shall see the unemployed marching down Whitehall to destroy the House of Commons'. Even John Maynard Keynes – in 1914 still some years away from formulating his General Theory – held to a view which, while apparently contradicting Bloch's doctrine, tended towards exactly the same result:

He told me that he was quite certain that the war could not last more than a year and that the belligerent countries could not be ruined by it. The world, he explained, was enormously rich, but its wealth was, fortunately, of a kind which could not be rapidly realized for war purposes: it was in the form of capital equipment for making things which were useless for making war. When all the available wealth had been used up – which he thought would take about a year – the Powers would have to make peace. We could not use the cotton factories in Lancashire to help our Navy blockade Germany; Germany could not use its toymakers' factories to equip her armies.[8]

Keynes's reference to the German toymakers' factories is the give-away: these factories, though not in fact as numerous as British commentators often pretended, were amongst those most readily converted to munitions

[8] Gerd Hardach *The First World War: 1914–1918* (1973) p. 55, quoting Schlieffen; *Journals and Letters of Reginald Viscount Esher* (4 vols 1934–8) vol. 3 p. 177, journal 13 Aug. 1914; G.H. Perris *A Short History of War and Peace* (1911) p. 238 – the whole argument is presented p. 235–9; Maud Diver *The Strong Hours* (1919) p. 3, 5; Lord Riddell *War Diaries, 1914–1918* (1933) p. 2 quoting conversation with Lloyd George 31 July 1914; Norman and Jeanne Mackenzie ed. *The Diaries of Beatrice Webb* (4 vols 1982–5) vol. 3 p. 214, *sub* 10 Aug. 1914, note written Aug. 1918; David Garnett *The Golden Echo* (1953) p. 271.

work. The dogmatic tone adopted by Keynes and other experts had less to do with detailed knowledge than with the omniscient pose expected from a respected professional; the fact was that their assumptions had almost no basis in empirical experience.

Although the Russo-Japanese War had been fought in one of the least developed zones of China, the Russian Empire had sustained a very considerable effort at the end of thousands of miles of single-track railway for over a year before its social and economic structure began to crack and rend: and Russia, even in those days, was not noted for its political and economic soundness. Japan, actually much weaker but benefiting from better communications with the war zone, had stood up to the strain of the war very successfully. The survival of the Southern Confederacy for four years during the American Civil War was another relevant example, and one by no means totally forgotten in Europe.[9]

The attraction of the economic argument for the necessary shortness of future wars seems to have been that it tied in with the military experts' already existing commitment to a strategy of instant decisive battle. The French, for example, saw that they had allowed themselves to be outnumbered in the war of 1870 and by 1914 pinned their hopes of revenge on a furious attack by the largest army the country's male population could provide: the idea that skilled industrial manpower might have a strategic role could not be accommodated within this scheme and in 1914 the mobilization of the French Army, without any system of exemptions for essential occupations, caused the shut-down of 52 per cent of French industrial plant and threw out of work 42 per cent of the militarily exempt labour force. Even the importance of the coal and iron-ore producing areas near the German frontier was overlooked by the French military planners, who wished to concentrate their efforts on a glorious encounter battle further south. The German General Staff, faced by the prospect of a simultaneous attack by the French from the west and the Russians from the east, planned to knock out France, as the enemy which would mobilize most swiftly, by a campaign of a few weeks before marching their victorious armies to the eastern frontier to deal with Russia: the rapid defeat of France was a strategic necessity but of course if the French Army could be demolished so quickly there was no logical reason why Russia should not also, in its turn, be defeated with equal facility. Because, shortly before the war, conservative army leaders who feared for the homogeneity of the socially exclusive Prussian officer corps had successfully resisted the enlargement of the peace-time Army to provide for a larger war-time mobilization, Germany had a system of selective conscription and there would have been a possibility of systematic exemption for workers in key industries; but the mentality that opposed the expansion of the Army because it would lower the social tone of the officer corps was not anxious to immerse itself in the plebeian details of

---

[9] Cf *Journals and Letters of Reginald Viscount Esher* vol. 3 p. 192–3, 9 Oct. 1914 for a comparison with the American Civil War.

national housekeeping, and as in France there was no system of reserving key workers.[10]

The professional mind had a similar success in Britain; it was assumed that the war would be over before there would be time to raise and train new troops, and prior to August 1914 there were no plans for the enlargement of the Army or for increased manufacture of artillery or ammunition. The traditional emphasis on naval power in Britain, and the greater degree of civilian control of the Army relative to Germany, favoured the establishment of some sort of strategic planning agency above the armed services level, but the Committee of Imperial Defence, established in December 1902, had difficulties in finding a role for itself, and in the last four years before the outbreak of war concentrated on preparing a War Book: this set out in complete detail all the procedures that would be necessary if war came, specifying even the wording of the telegrams that would have to be sent to every seaport to suspend the pilot's tickets of foreign-born pilots, but it gave little guidance as to what should be done if the war lasted more than a week. By 1914 the third edition of the War Book had appeared; as a piece of detailed planning it can be compared to the German General Staff's famous railway timetable for moving the army to the Western Front; but the latter was after all only the work of a subordinate department whereas Britain's War Book was produced by a body outside, independent of and theoretically superior to the armed forces, and served to advertise the vacuum existing at the point where policy-making might have occurred.[11]

The British War Book and the various mobilization timetables show that the First World War was carefully planned in advance: but on the basis of ignoring most of the factors which turned out to be crucial. Within a few weeks of the war beginning the Germans discovered that they could not, after all, count on an instant victory over France. The French had learnt that a huge army infused with the spirit of attack also needed skilful generals to lead it, and Winston Churchill was beginning to fear that 'England, without an army, with not a soldier to spare, without even a rifle to send, with only her Navy and her money, counted for little'. Everywhere the pre-war planning turned out to have been fundamentally shaped and determined by the prejudices and wishful thinking of men who had used pseudo-logic to patch over all those holes in their doctrines which they were too embarrassed to investigate. The short war doctrine derived ultimately from the fact that the military leaders, in every belligerent country, were not merely psychologically unprepared but also mentally unequipped to fight a long one.[12]

[10] Challener *French Theory of the Nation in Arms* p. 93, 98–102; Martin Kitchen *The German Officer Corps* (Oxford 1968) p. 31–5; V.R. Berghahn *Germany and the Approach of War in 1914* (1973) p. 6–8.

[11] David French *British Economic and Strategic Planning, 1905–1915* (1982) p. 26–7, 47–8, 81–2.

[12] Winston S. Churchill *The World Crisis* (6 vols 1923–31) vol. 1 p. 493. For a discussion of German staff thinking and its rootedness in specific assumptions see Jack Snyder *The Ideology of the Offensive: Military Decision-Making and the Disasters of 1914* (Ithaca 1984) p. 107–156.

III. The Evolution of the British War Economy

With their small volunteer peace-time Army, the British had to make an even bigger effort to adjust to the conditions of mass warfare than the other belligerents. The first step, taken without any real consultation or discussion, was the decision to recruit a huge army. This decision was taken, essentially on his own initiative, by Britain's new Secretary of State for War, Field-Marshal Lord Kitchener. Though he had participated in the Franco-Prussian War of 1870 and the Russo-Turkish War of 1877, Kitchener's command experience was entirely confined to colonial warfare, usually involving small forces at the end of long supply lines, and he had never had anything to do with the planning of war on a European continental scale. Perhaps for this very reason he was able to recognize certain crucial issues which more continental-minded professionals had schooled themselves to overlook. Almost immediately after taking office he told Walter Runciman, President of the Board of Trade:

> When a war of this magnitude breaks out, the President of the Board of Trade should immediately be made Joint Secretary of State for War, Supply Department ... The old-fashioned little British Army was such an infinitely small proportion of the world's demand that looking after its equipment was not much more difficult than buying a straw hat at Harrods. But now I am going to want greater quantities of many things than have ever been made before.[13]

Accordingly Kitchener recruited a businessman, George Macaulay Booth, to help with the procurement difficulties, but he did not go far or fast enough for the most energetic of his cabinet colleagues, David Lloyd George, the Chancellor of the Exchequer. While Kitchener, with a readiness to collaborate with civilians that was unequalled by any other military leader in any other country, was arranging the establishment of an Armaments Output Committee under Booth's chairmanship, Lloyd George was organizing a Munitions of War Committee, with the same task but outside military control: Lloyd George's committee was announced to the public the very day after Booth's committee had been nominated. Lloyd George told the House of Commons on 21 April 1915 that Booth's committee was 'the Executive Committee for carrying out the policy' decided by his own committee but that was only a *post facto* rationalization. A whole new Ministry of Munitions, with Lloyd George at its head, was set up in May 1915, though it was eight months before all the relevant responsibilities were wrested from the War Office.[14]

[13] Duncan Crow *A Man of Push and Go: The Life of George Macauley Booth* (1965) p. 71.

[14] Ibid p. 105–6; *Hansard: House of Commons* vol. 71 col. 323, Lloyd George's statement 21 April 1915; Lloyd George *War Memoirs* vol. 2 p. 624–633, 638 and cf Public Record Office WO 79/73 p. 22 Asquith to ? draft, 21 Nov. 1915 concerning 'further re-adjustment of functions' between Ministry of Munitions and Master General of the Ordnance. Cf A.J.P. Taylor ed. *Lloyd George: A Diary by Frances Stevenson* (1971) p. 73, 15 Nov. 1915 where it appears that Asquith, acting at the War Office while Kitchener was in the Middle East, took the opportunity to hand over the bits of the War Office Lloyd George was seeking to control.

The establishment of a Ministry of Munitions did not in itself represent the centralization of control of the war economy, and in June 1915 W.A.S. Hewins, Conservative M.P. for Hereford and former Director of the London School of Economics, lamented in his diary:

> My mind goes back to my long courses of lectures at the School of Economics in which I dwelt on these matters of organisation and the relation between military and economic efficiency, the crowds of young German students, professors, officials who attended them, their keenness, Mommsen's enthusiastic comments on my line of thought, my conversation with Von Halle and the rest of them, my pamphlet on imperialism and the way in which they took up what they called my Neo-Merkantilismus, and now, nearly 20 years after, in the middle of this great War, we find the Germans fully organised on the lines we used to discuss then, and still I can't get any hearing with the people who are responsible for the safety of the British Empire, because they are afraid that if they do listen they will have to give up what they call Free Trade.

In fact, while Lloyd George was working to gain control of munitions procurement from Kitchener, many of their cabinet colleagues continued stalwartly to deny the one important principle on which Lloyd George and Kitchener agreed, that is, the necessity of a mass army and of a huge coordinated productive effort to supply it. The orthodox liberal core of the Cabinet – Lloyd George wasn't orthodox and Kitchener wasn't liberal – did not in the least accept that the best way to utilize Britain's economic resources was to coin them into armies and artillery barrages. In August 1914 the ministers had agreed that:

> we could win through by holding the sea, maintaining our credit, keeping our people employed & our industries going – By economic pressure, destroying Germany's trade cutting off her supplies. We should gradually secure victory.

Far from recognizing that world war necessitated vast expenditure and transfer of resources, the Financial Secretary of the Treasury instructed a colleague:

> It is of the utmost importance that we limit expenditure. We do not want to encourage anybody to spend anything unless it is absolutely inevitable to provide employment for people who are out of work.

When, in the autumn of 1915, the question of military conscription began to be an issue, the opposition of Sir John Simon on the moral grounds of libertarian principle carried less weight than the arguments of Runciman and McKenna (Lloyd George's replacement as Chancellor of the Exchequer), who both feared for the undermining of the *laissez faire* economy. One of Asquith's female confidantes recorded the Prime Minister's assessment in her diary:

> McKenna isn't insisting on the pecuniary impossibility of the compulsion bill, but adopting the Runciman depletion of industry attitude, and, added the P.M. 'the Dickens is that I so agree with him'.

The journalist C.P. Scott recorded McKenna himself as saying:

Our part in the war should be to act as paymaster for the rest . . . His point all through was that munitions and goods needed for the war could not be paid for by the sale of securities but only by goods and that we alone of the Allies were in a position to produce these in adequate quantities.[15]

In December 1915 McKenna advised his colleagues:

Our ultimate victory is assured if, in addition to our naval and military activities, we retain unimpaired our power to assist in financing, supplying, and carrying for the Allies.

But he claimed that 'every increase in the army, is a further tax on the resources of our shipping', and that, moreover, the time required to turn a ship round in British ports was increasing as a result of labour shortages; in other words 'all our resources are now in commission, and every new project is not additional, but alternative, to something we are committed to already'. Lord Esher, who was in the confidence of several ministers, thought McKenna and Runciman 'quite genuinely believe in beating the Germans by financial and commercial pressure alone, the army meantime to hold the lists': Winston Churchill's wife, complaining of McKenna's 'tepid counter-jumping calculation', was under the impression that he would even have reduced the size of the Army 'if he had the power'. Whether or not it was true, as Mrs. Churchill thought, that 'His plan is to pay our allies to do all the fighting while we do all the manufacturing here', McKenna certainly opposed himself to any further investment of British resources in the strengthening of the Army. In February 1916 a Cabinet committee, which though headed by Asquith was evidently dominated by McKenna, warned of the serious effect of labour shortages on exports. It was claimed that:

The aim of the Board of Trade . . . is to keep alive the great industries which are the mainstay of the country's export trade rather than to maintain *all* trades, or to keep exports at the pre-war level

and that:

The essential difference in this matter between the needs of this country and our allies is accounted for by the position we occupy in financing the *Entente* Powers, in which process exports play an essential part.

---

[15] W.A.S. Hewins *The Apologia of an Imperialist: Forty Years of Empire Policy* (2 vols 1929) vol. 2 p. 40 diary 18 June 1915 – 'Von Halle' was presumably the economist Ernst von Halle, 1868–1909 and 'Mommsen' may have been Theodor Mommsen, the classical scholar and doyen of German scholars: no member of the Mommsen academic dynasty seems to have been a professional economist at this time. David French *British Strategy and War Aims, 1914–1916* (1986) p. 27 quoting J.A. Pease, President of the Board of Education, to Sir A. Pease 28 Aug. 1914; House of Lords Record Office, Lloyd George Papers C/1/1/29 Montagu to Samuel 1 Oct. 1914, copy enclosed in Montagu to Lloyd George 2 Oct. 1914; Roy Jenkins *Asquith* (1978) p. 390 quoting diary of Lady Scott, 13 Oct. 1915; Trevor Wilson ed. *The Political Diaries of C.P. Scott, 1911–1928* (1970) p. 145, 14–15 Oct. 1915.

The committee's report argued that labour shortages increased the need for imports, thus increasing the adverse trade balance, and that since Britain's allies had abandoned the gold standard Britain was effectively financing most of their foreign imports in addition to the country's own needs. According to Board of Trade figures only 600,000 men could be called up for the Army in the first six months of 1916 'without great Disturbances to Trade', while the War Office demanded 967,000. The report concluded:

> If we embark on a bigger programme of expenditure than we are in fact able to support, this will show itself in a growing inability to finance and carry our necessary supplies . . . the Chancellor of the Exchequer is emphatically of the opinion that we are already spending on a scale which allows of little or no margin for further expansion.[16]

The position taken up by McKenna, Runciman and the other advocates of concurrently financing the war by exports did in fact represent a retreat from a rather more adventurous policy which had seemed feasible during the first months of the war. One of the circumstances which lends credibility to German claims that it was Britain, not Germany, which had been seeking an opportunity to go to war is the eagerness with which business and official circles in London initially embraced the notion of a British takeover of German export markets. In mid-September 1914 businessmen and M.P.s met to coordinate the takeover of the world toy market, hitherto monopolized by German manufacturers. In October 1914 it was pointed out in *The Contemporary Review*:

> Never before in the world's history has such an opportunity been offered the British trader. Secure at home, and possessing free access to the world's materials, he is presented with the markets of his greatest competitor . . . It is difficult to realise that this [German] competition has suddenly ceased – that it will not exist at all for a considerable period, and that even when the war is over it will be long before it can be as fierce as in recent years.

In order to exploit this opportunity, the Board of Trade's Commercial Intelligence Branch took on a hundred new staff, rented additional premises,

16 Public Record Office CAB 37/139/140 note by McKenna on 'The Freight Question' 20 Dec. 1915 p. 1; ibid. p. 4; *Letters and Journals of Reginald Viscount Esher* vol. 4 p. 3 Esher to Sir Douglas Haig 21 Jan. 1916; Mary Soames *Clementine Churchill* (1979) p. 161 Clementine Churchill to Winston Churchill 29 Jan. 1916; Public Record Office CAB 37/142/11 'Cabinet Committee on the Co-ordination of Military and Financial Effort. Report'. p. 8–9; ibid. p. 17; ibid. p. 18. The members of this committee were Asquith, McKenna and Austen Chamberlain. McKenna's weakness on matters of detail with regard to such matters as exchange control and overseas borrowing (cf Andrew Boyle *Montagu Norman* (1967) p. 107–110) casts an unfavourable light on his doctrinaire *laissez faire* attitudes.

McKenna's arguments had already been put forward 150 years previously during the Second Dutch War: 'Sir G. Ascue chiefly spoke that the war and trade could not be supported together,' Pepys's Diary 15 Jan. 1665.

and began issuing booklets and holding meetings to publicize the new commercial possibilities created by the blockade of Germany's ports. The British Empire Industrial League published comprehensive tables of 'German and Austrian Export Trade . . . for the use of British Manufacturers, Exporters, and Merchants' under the unambiguous title *War on German Trade!* British consular officials abroad issued over 10,000 invitations to an International Trade Fair held in the Agricultural Hall in Islington in May 1915. Although, with the inevitable patriotic hyperbole of the day, the two-week fair was hailed as a wonderful success, only 285 of the 26,281 visitors were foreign buyers, and of these 77 were French and 40 Belgians – most of the latter presumably refugees seeking the means of starting new businesses in England. Foremost amongst the staples of international commerce that met with significant demand were light bulbs and china dolls' heads.[17]

In any case exports were subject to so much red tape – the necessary licences were required to pass, with decreasing momentum, through the Board of Customs, the Treasury, the War Office, the Admiralty, the Board of Trade and the Privy Council – that the export drive never really got under way. Labour shortages as a result of military enlistment and the expansion of armaments production were also a retarding factor; moreover after the long Victorian calm many British businessmen were no longer temperamentally adjusted to the buccaneering red-in-tooth-and-claw aspect of *laissez faire* capitalism, as may be seen from frequent complaints that even the vast tragedy of war had not liberated English family firms from the menace of price-cutting and take-over by Jews of presumed German origin:

> It seems to me nothing short of monstrous that while I am passing through the bitter anguish of losing two of my sons and undergoing the dread anxiety of the third and last one being in the thick of it, that this German Jew should be adding to my worry and anxiety and poignant grief.[18]

Paradoxically, the more exports declined, the more their importance came to be emphasized: not merely as a means of winning the war but as a legitimate objective of the war. The Australian premier, Billy Hughes, on a visit to Britain in March 1916, told the City Carlton Club:

> The British people . . . recognize amongst the chief causes of this war, the desire of Germany to wrest from Britain her industrial and commercial supremacy . . . we are determined that the end of this war shall see not only the downfall of Prussian military power, but of that insidious and intolerable influence which

[17] *Times* 18 Sep. 1914 p. 3c; L.G. Chiozza Money 'British Trade and the War', *Contemporary Review* vol. 106 p. 470–482 (Oct. 1914) at p. 475; French *British Economic and Strategic Planning* p. 111; ibid. p. 111–2 and *Times* 18 May 1915 p. 5d and 21 May 1915 p. 5b.

[18] British Library Add. 62175 f. 67 Leo Maxse to Northcliffe 29 Oct. 1915 quoting an unnamed correspondent.

had in very many cases reached a point when Germany actually dominated the trade both of this Empire and that of our Allies.

In July 1916 a book entitled *The Coming Trade War* – advertised as 'The Book of the Moment on the Question of the Hour' – claimed that:

Mr. Hughes's speeches have evoked intense approbation, and have been followed by such a quickening of the national spirit as perhaps no other orator since Chatham ever aroused.

According to the authors of *The Coming Trade War* it was not merely a case of:

The captivating notion of smashing the enemy's trade, and of being avenged upon the German 'dumper' with his cheap and nasty goods, and even nastier methods, and for all the undercutting and devious trading of which we have been the victims . . .

there was also:

the ideal of wresting from the German his supremacy in certain essential trades, and of so equipping our own country that our unsleeping enemy will not again have the opportunity of building up in times of peace those vast resources and almost endless reserves of war which may be used again to the detriment of civilisation, and if possible, for the destruction of Great Britain.

And if that was not enough, there was also the moral obligation to preserve Britain's war heroes from:

the fate of returning to their native land and finding that there is no place for them at the table of life, no work for their strong hands to do, and no means of livelihood except a shamefaced appeal to the charity of the passer-by.[19]

Even at this comparatively late stage the Board of Trade was still interested in boosting exports, and though the Cabinet committee report of 1916 emphasized the relation between exports and overseas expenditure on munitions, there was clearly more to this concern for exports than immediate requirements: this is shown by the fact that an official committee was appointed in March 1916 to consider the international trading prospects of the Iron, Steel, Engineering and Shipbuilding industries after the war. The selection of Iron, Steel, Engineering and Shipbuilding as industries requiring special consideration was not precisely an acknowledgement of any special difficulties experienced by these industries under wartime conditions: the truth was that these were the industries which were especially favoured by wartime demand. Scarcities of iron and steel, of engineering production capacity and

[19] Keith A. Murdoch ed. *The Day – and After: War Speeches of the Rt. Hon. W.M. Hughes* [1916] p. 40, speech to City Carlton Club 20 March 1916; *Times* 25 July 1916 advert p. 8e-f; Thomas Farrow and W. Walter Crotch *The Coming Trade War* (1916) p. 3; ibid. p. 2–3 and p. 3–4; ibid. p. 8–9.

shipping space meant enormous rises in prices and the opportunity for huge speculative profits. Amongst those alleged to be making huge profits from the national emergency was the father of the President of the Board of Trade himself – Sir Walter Runciman, senior partner of Walter Runciman & Co. Ltd of Newcastle and London, and chairman of the Moor Steamship Line. It was probably Runciman junior who was the unnamed minister in an incident recounted by Charles Masterman. The minister in question was telling his colleagues of the huge profits to be made from shipping war supplies. Asquith remarked, 'Disgusting'. The minister defended these profits as 'the normal operation of trade', concluding, 'I can see nothing disgraceful in the whole transaction':

> 'I did not say it was disgraceful,' said Mr. Asquith with a characteristic shrug of his shoulders 'I said it was disgusting.'

Wartime dislocations – especially the dislocation of prices – caused immense hardship to working people and also to many businessmen, but it seems to be precisely because it was the reverse of hardship that was experienced by the most influential sectors of the business community that McKenna and Runciman felt justified in maintaining the old, unregulated system; as far as their own departmental spheres were concerned everything was flourishing and the only real threat was the encroachment of the War Office and the Ministry of Munitions.[20]

In January 1916 an editorial in *The Observer* newspaper, calling for a greater national effort, stated:

> We talk familiarly of what our forefathers endured in the Napoleonic wars, but few of us realise even remotely the severity of the trial.

In retrospect one is struck, not by how much more severe the experience of 1793–1815 was, but by how similar McKenna's and Runciman's *laissez faire* war economy was to the economic system prevailing in the earlier conflict. The maxim that each war is fought initially with the techniques of the previous war is perhaps truer on the management than on the military side.[21]

IV. Britain and the Allies

As in the Revolutionary and Napoleonic period, considerable faith was put in the superiority of Britain's financial resources. Edwin Montagu, the Financial Secretary to the Treasury, assured a colleague in October 1914, 'the country

---

[20] *Times* 23 March 1916 p. 8d; E. Sylvia Pankhurst *The Home Front: A Mirror to Life in England during the World War* (1932) p. 91–5, 127–130, 135–141 for profiteering generally; ibid. p. 302–3 for profiteering by the Runciman family; Lucy Masterman *C.F.G. Masterman* (1939) p. 269.

[21] *Observer* 9 Jan. 1916 p. 10c.

will win in this war whose purse is the longest', and nobody doubted that the country with the longest purse was Britain. Lloyd George claimed late in 1915 that 'we were the principal banker, arsenal, manufacturer, and general purveyor of the whole Alliance'. Later Sir William Robertson, the Chief of the Imperial General Staff, informed one of his generals, '*we* finance everybody – & credit is still good . . . at present *all* British money'. In reality both France and Russia were producing greater quantities of munitions than Britain at this stage; but even the French were willing to accept British leadership in the banking and general purveying sphere. The *Commission Internationale de Ravitaillement* established in London on 17 August 1914 to control French government purchases in Britain eventually took on the responsibility for most Entente purchasing abroad, not merely in Britain; it was staffed by personnel seconded from the Board of Trade, the government department headed by Walter Runciman. The British government-sponsored Wheat Export Co. became by late 1916 the agency for purchasing in the U.S. all the wheat shipped to Britain, France, and Italy: these purchases were the largest single item in Entente dependence on the U.S. It was also British shipping which carried the bulk of the purchased goods, and British shipyards which contributed by far the most to the replacement of shipping sunk by German U-boats:

Construction of Merchant Shipping, 1914–1918

Britain	4,342,000 GRT
France	155,000 GRT
Italy	209,000 GRT
U.S.A.	3,643,000 GRT

Yet on the purely financial side Britain's contribution, though of staggering dimensions, was probably of far less practical importance than the British government liked to think – again a parallel with the 1790s despite the vastly greater scale of the investment.[22]

By the time the U.S. entered the war in April 1917, Entente borrowings amongst themselves and on the American capital market, totalled some 6.5 thousand million dollars, of which Britain had contributed well over half: $3,814.4 million. The French share of the money on loan, $514.5 million represented about 76 per cent of what the French had themselves borrowed. About 58 per cent of Entente borrowing (equivalent to only a little less than total British lending) was to or on behalf of Russia:

[22] House of Lords Record Office, Lloyd George Papers C/1/1/29 Montagu to Samuel 1 Oct. 1914 copy enclosed in Montagu to Lloyd George 2 Oct. 1914; Maurice Hankey *The Supreme Command* (3 vols 1961) vol. 1 p. 425, late 1915: Public Record Office WO 79/66 papers of the Earl of Cavan: 'Epitome of conversation with Gen. Sir W. Robertson . . . May 5 1916, Kathleen Burk *Britain, American and the Sinews of War, 1914–1918* (1985) p. 44–5; ibid. p. 51–3 cf ibid. p. 266 Appendix IV; C. Ernest Fayle *Seaborne Trade* (3 vols 1920–24) vol. 3 p. 467–8, tables 2 and 3.

British loans to Russia 1 April 1917	$1,657.5m
French loans to Russia to 1 April 1917	$ 426.5m
Loans raised in U.S. for Russia secured in the name of the Entente to 1 April 1917	$ 740m
Ditto secured in the name of Britain to 1 April 1917	$ 610m
Ditto secured in the name of France to 1 April 1917	$ 130m
Russian borrowing on their own account in U.S. to 1 April 1917	$ 233m
Total	$ 3,797m

This lavish supply of foreign money for the Russian government meant of course that it could make enormous purchases of munitions etc. abroad and that it could do so without destabilizing the Russian currency's foreign exchange value. Yet it is doubtful whether foreign supplies of war materials to Russia were ever of major significance relative to Russia's own domestic output and it seems that much of what was imported was allowed to accumulate and to decay on the wharves at Archangel, the main port of entry to Russia while the Baltic was closed by the war. A particular deficiency of Russian industrialization at this stage was on the light engineering side, so that Russian aircraft manufacturers did not even begin to rival the massive increase of output achieved in Britain, France, Italy and Germany: but importations of aircraft clearly did little to redress the balance since crated aircraft were prominent amongst the mass of decaying equipment found in the transit yards at Archangel when the British Army arrived in 1918. Nor did the supply of foreign credits assist the stability of the rouble which because of financial mismanagement found itself in difficulties more quickly than any other major currency. The chief beneficiary of the Russian loans was American big business. J.P. Morgan, who handled all the Entente's borrowing in the U.S. at 8.3 per cent commission, made $200 million profit; service and transportation costs were at least as much again as the customer price of items delivered; while borrowing in the U.S. by or on behalf of Russia was $3,797 million up to 1 April 1917, actual deliveries of American goods to Russian ports in 1916 and 1917 totalled $863,650,936, or less than a quarter of the amounts borrowed up till 1 April 1917: some of the rest was legitimately accounted for by initial investment in plant intended to produce for Russian contracts but even this in the event benefited the U.S. economy much more than the Russian war effort.[23]

[23] Figures for war borrowing generally are from Harold G. Moulton and Leo Pasvolsky *War Debts and World Prosperity* (New York 1932) p. 426 appendix A-II, those for Russian borrowing from Gail L. Owen 'Dollar Diplomacy in Default: The Economics of Russian-American Relations, 1910–1917' *Historical Journal* vol. 13 (1970) p. 251–272 at p. 266 table 2;

continued

By the time President Wilson brought the United States into the war, British financial resources were becoming exhausted. A warning against over-investment in short-term foreign securities issued on 28 November 1916 by the U.S. Federal Reserve Board (rephrased and made more forcible by President Wilson himself) caused a fall in the Stock Exchange price of Allied bonds and required the use of sterling reserves to hold up the exchange rate. Horrified, McKenna immediately stopped the placement of new orders; yet a $250 million loan floated on the American capital market at the end of January 1917 was quickly oversubscribed, showing how advantageous the Americans found investment in Entente loans. After April 1917 the U.S. quickly took over as the financial keystone of the alliance against Germany; in July 1917 the British ambassador in Washington reported:

> The situation here is much as it was in London in Canning's time when the Russian Ambassador used to call at the Foreign Office being ignorant of French and slap his pockets and say '*aurum, aurum*'.

Though Britain continued to advance loans to the other allies, it was increasingly money which had been borrowed from the U.S. By the end of the war Britain was (if only theoretically) the largest creditor of Russia and Italy, and was not far behind the U.S. in lendings to France; France, initially running behind Britain in loans to Belgium, had crept up, overtaken and become Belgium's largest creditor; but France was even more in hock than Britain:

	Total lendings	*Total borrowings from U.S.*	*Total borrowings from Great Britain*
U.S.A.	$7,077.1m	–	–
Britain	$7,014.5m	$3,696m	–
France	$2,237.6m	$1,970m	$1,682.8m

One can see how, politically and diplomatically, this simultaneous lending and borrowing made good sense, but economically and financially it only made sense for financiers like J.P. Morgan.[24]

continued
Statistical Abstract of the United States, 1917 (Washington 1918) p. 358, 387 which show 57.5 per cent of Russia's imports from U.S. in 1916 and 77.3 per cent in 1917 were shipped to European Russia, i.e. Archangel; Owen 'Dollar Diplomacy in Default' p. 268 and fn. 54.
   By the time of the Revolution Russia had manufactured 1,893 planes and 920 aero-engines and imported 1,400 planes and 3,600 engines (Nowarra and Duval *Russian Civil and Military Aircraft* p. 49); half the Russian-built planes therefore had imported engines; one could claim therefore that imports contributed significantly to Russian aviation: except that overall quantities were so small that aviation cannot be said to have had a significant part in Russia's war effort.
   [24] Burk *Britain, America and the Sinews of War* p. 84–5, 92; Lloyd George *War Memoirs* vol. 3 p. 1713, Sir Cecil Spring-Rice to Lloyd George 5 July 1917; Moulton and Pasvolsky *War Debts* p. 426 appendix A-II.

continued

These stupendous financial transactions provided a kind of smoke-screen behind which operated real-life economic processes, equally stupendous but not entirely consistent with the money side. The smoke-screen confused Winston Churchill, who informed his cabinet colleagues in June 1915:

> It is open to Great Britain now to take the necessary lead in the Allied Councils. She commands the sea . . . she wields the power of the purse. She is becoming an important arsenal of munitions . . . She only requires victory to give her the ascendancy without which no good common action is to be expected.

The victory Churchill was hoping for was at Gallipoli: and it was not won. Kitchener was more realistic, and felt that the British were not pulling their weight:

> Although France is producing two and a half times as much munitions as we are, in proportion to our population, she is putting 130 divisions into the field. We are no doubt supplying considerable sums to the allies, but so is France both in money and material.

Kitchener was perhaps the first to realize that the emphasis on the length of Britain's purse tended to distract attention from the problem of mobilizing Britain's real industrial and manpower capacity.[25]

In the event, despite complaints of 'a subordination of naval, agricultural and commercial interests to the demands of the War Office,' no effective system of economic management was ever established. The setting up of the Ministry of Munitions under Lloyd George in May 1915 made the Welsh Wizard the nearest thing there was to a War Economy supremo but the emphasis of his department's work was on output. He was a great energizer, but like that other great energizer Lord Beaverbrook, who served with similar acclaim as Minister of Aircraft Production in 1940, his tendency was to create chaos out of system rather than the other way round. As with Beaverbrook, the successes claimed by Lloyd George were open to question: Major-General Stanley Von Donop, his principal enemy at the War Office, pointed out in September 1915, 'In printed returns Ebbw Vale are shown as having delivered 948 shell off M.

---

continued

The tradition of the Russian Ambassador slapping his pockets and saying 'aurum, aurum' is marginally less implausible than it sounds in that Maximilian Alopeus, Russian envoy in London 1806–1808, was a Finn, educated at Göttingen, and Count Lieven, ambassador from 1812, and the only other Russian ambassador who could be referred to, was a Baltic German, so that unlike the majority of the Russian upper classes they would have known Latin; it seems improbable however that either of them should be ignorant of French, or, if this were the case, should have failed to notice that the English word for 'gold' is the same as the German. Alopeus in fact clearly had no difficulty in discussing complex issues with Canning, cf Arthur Aspinall ed. *The Later Correspondence of George III* (5 vols Cambridge 1962–70) vol. 4 p. 593 no. 3480 Canning to George III 20 July 1807.

[25] Churchill *World Crisis* vol. 2 p. 407, memo 18 June 1915; Sir George Arthur *Not Worth Reading* (1938) p. 249 fn. 1 Kitchener to Asquith 11 Jan. 1916.

of M. order of 29.6.15 but none off ours of March!' and in February 1916 he noted:

> The 'public' complained at our not having produced enough H.E. in April '15 when we were only asked for it on 19.11.14 yet in 8 months M. of M. have not produced a complete round.

In effect Lloyd George was able to claim credit for work done by Von Donop at the War Office prior to May 1915: what his own contribution was is less clear. By the time Churchill took over the Ministry of Munitions in 1917 he found it in organizational confusion – fifty departments with heads having direct access to the minister had to be amalgamated into ten groups in order to devolve at least some of the responsibility for coordination – yet Churchill's power to influence general policy as Minister of Munitions turned out to be much less than Lloyd George's had been. In November 1917 Churchill announced in his provisional Munitions Budget for 1918 that, 'The foundations of the Munitions Budget is Tonnage; the ground floor is Steel; and the limiting factor in construction is Labour'; yet though he had correctly identified the key factors through which any system of overall economic management would have to operate, he did not have complete control over any of them.[26]

The central importance of manpower had been recognized very early on, and as previously mentioned, had been emphasized by the anti-conscriptionists during the long, tedious and needling discussion of the question of compulsory military service in 1915 and 1916. Once conscription was decided upon however, the government failed to master the problem of relating military requirements to the manpower needs of industry. In December 1916 Neville Chamberlain was appointed Director of National Service. Of the numerous outsiders taken into government from the business world, Chamberlain was the best known, and the biggest disappointment. Son of the great Joseph Chamberlain, half brother of the Secretary of State for India, a successful business leader, Lord Mayor of Birmingham, seemingly much more the heir of his father than his stuffed shirt elder brother Austen, his failure to get a grip on the labour situation was provoking comment within three weeks of his appointment. *The Nation*, on 24 February 1917, was able to refer confidently to 'The scheme for devitalizing and misdirecting the essential strength of the nation, known as "National Service"'. Sir Auckland Geddes, the former anatomy professor who replaced Chamberlain after a few months, explained on his predecessor's behalf, 'He was asked to use a department which did not exist to solve a problem which had never been stated'. Chamberlain's inexperience of central government – exemplified by his insistence on appointing the Town

---

[26] Editorial by F.W. Hirst in *Common Sense* 9 Dec. 1916 p. 1a; Public Record Office WO 79/73, Von Donop's diary. f. 10, 8 Sept. 1915; ibid. unfoliated, 2 Feb. 1916, and for the parallel with Beaverbrook at the Ministry of Aircraft Production in 1940 see R.A.F. Museum Hendon AC/71/20/3 (Salmond Papers); Churchill *World Crisis* vol. 4 p. 298–9; ibid. vol. 4 p. 315.

Clerk of Birmingham as his chief assistant in the Directorate of National Service – was obviously a disadvantage but the main problem was that he had no effective control over the sphere he was supposed to administer: the Ministry of Munitions kept a tight hand on its existing workforce, and the Ministry of Labour, whose local network of labour exchanges would have been of major – perhaps decisive – importance in conducting a national policy, was independent of and uncooperative towards Chamberlain's Directorate, a situation which continued after Chamberlain left office. Churchill showed he had absorbed a useful lesson from this unhappy story when he came to choose a Minister of Labour in 1940; he may also have learnt at this time that Chamberlain, though a man of great ability, with real social vision and a talent for innovation, tended nevertheless to go under very quickly once out of his depth.[27]

As a result of a multiplicity of major and minor failures British munitions output only began to exceed that of France when French production levels began to slip back from their mid-1917 peak; a party of Ministry of Munitions experts visiting French factories in 1918 were struck by the simpler lay-out of the French production lines and the higher degree of mechanization, including the use of conveyor belts; ironically, the commemorative oil paintings of munitions production commissioned by firms such as Cammell Laird and John Baker & Co., evidently with the intention of celebrating munitions workers as hand-maidens of a new kind of traditional idyll, also serve to record the poor organization and inadequate mechanization of British war factories. By the end of the war the Americans, operating to even greater economies of scale than the French, were taking over the lead, especially in explosives output. The American entry into the war involved nothing less than America's assumption of the economic leadership of the alliance against Germany. A Priority Committee set up in London under the chairmanship of Austen Chamberlain passed on its decisions to an Inter-Allied Council for War Purchases and Finance which communicated with the Allied Purchasing Commission in the U.S.A., which in practice was identical to the three-man War Industries Board which was running the U.S. war economy. This submission to American leadership was not precisely a recognition of the objective facts of Entente dependence on American supplies, which were principally of raw materials and which in any case declined markedly (especially in the case of explosives) after America began mobilizing its own armed forces; rather it was a profession of faith in America's ability to rescue the Entente from the consequences of three years of organizational and military failure:

[27] David Dilks *Neville Chamberlain* (1 vol so far published Cambridge 1984) vol. 1 p. 208; *Nation* 24 Feb. 1917 p. 694; Sir Almeric Fitzroy *Memoirs* 2 vols London 1925, vol. 2 p. 660, journal 22 Aug. 1917. Chamberlain's work as Director of National Service is described in detail in Keith Grieves *The Politics of Manpower, 1914–18* (Manchester 1988) p. 90–148.

U.S. Exports (in $)

	1913	1917	1918
Brass			
(plate, steels &c)	1,177,626	121,368,019	29,440,583
Breadstuffs	211,098,339	588,983,454	633,239,856
Chemicals	26,574,519	187,890,822	180,318,954
Copper (excl. ore)	140,164,913	322,535,344	268,982,821
Explosives	5,267,566	802,789,437	373,890,863
Iron & Steel			
(incl. manufactured)	306,080,442	1,133,746,188	1,124,999,211
[of which firearms	3,971,872	95,470,009	49,159,271]

The most important element in the combined effort to remain under British control was shipping and in August 1918 it was claimed:

> Great Britain has been too diligent in looking out for her own interests as distinguished from those of the Allies as a whole, and lacking in liberality, if not fairness in many of her dealings with the Allies.

With their long tradition of jealousy of British power, the French were undoubtedly glad to see leadership of the alliance pass from British to American hands; yet despite the large claims of Lloyd George, Churchill and Co, the British had in any case never really succeeded in utilizing their country's economic advantages to establish a dominant influence within the alliance: not of course that this was fairly acknowledged at the time.[28]

V. Foreign Parallels: Russia and Austria-Hungary

Britain's failures on the economic-strategic front, compounding failures on the military front, should not be taken to suggest that other countries managed any better. The British and American system in which many of the new government departments were run by business leaders, with business leaders also supplying the heads of sections seems to have worked relatively better than the system of business organizations dominated by professional bureaucrats which evolved in Russia and Austria-Hungary, or the capitalist free-for-all under military supervision which developed in Germany and Italy.

[28] Public Record Office SUPP 10/290 p. 79, 80, 82 (reports of mission to France, April 1918); paintings by E.F. Skinner and Stanhope Forbes in the Science Museum, South Kensington; Crowell *America's Munitions* p. 103–4; Burk *Britain, America and the Sinews of War* p. 149–151; *Statistical Abstract of the United States 1918* (Washington 1919) p. 477–492 No. 284; Crow *Man of Push and Go* p. 157 Paul O. Cravath to G.M. Booth *c.* August 1918. See John F. Godfrey *Capitalism at War: Industrial Policy and Bureaucracy in France, 1914–1918* (Leamington Spa 1987) p. 71–81 for British pressure to restrict French imports, invoking French dependence on British shipping capacity.

The disorder, confusion, waste and fraud prevailing in the distribution of raw materials in Italy, where under the direction of General Alfredo Dall'Olio the initiative was left in the hands of the business bosses running the eleven regional committees, was eventually advertised in some detail. The more decorous but perhaps equally profitable manipulations of Stinnes, Duisberg, Hugenberg and other German business leaders have remained less well documented. In France the government had to defend itself against being dictated to by the cartels which dominated French industry by extending bureaucratic controls, especially during the last eighteen months of the war. Even in Britain industrialists such as Dudley Docker resisted attempts by the Ministry of Munitions to vet apparently excessive profits: but Docker's dispute with the Ministry of Munitions is only known because he failed to get away with it, whereas many of his confrères did get away with it, and very handsomely too.[29]

In Russia the Central War Industries Committee, belatedly set up in 1915 with 33 district and 220 local committees, became an important political lobby but was ignored by larger firms and was ineffective in placing contracts with the more skilled smaller firms. Yet Russia suffered less than the other belligerents (prior to 1917) from shortages of raw materials and labour and despite inadequate supplies of shells and even rifles and small arms ammunition at the front in 1915 it is possible that by late 1916 Russia was the world's leading producer of cannon and shells. As in France and Italy extensive use was made of prisoners of war and of young men inducted into the army and subject to military discipline, and the female component of the expanding industrial workforce rose from 30 per cent in 1913 to 49 per cent in January 1917: the iconological tradition of the gallant female munitions worker in her headscarf, later popularized in Britain in the paintings of E.F. Skinner and Stanhope Forbes, was pioneered in supposedly backward Russia, in a war bond poster of 1916. Nevertheless it was soon apparent that the mobilization of industry and of industrial war materials was only one of the aspects of war management that needed vigorous central direction. Another was military manpower. Numerous exemptions from obligation to military service – married men, only sons, members of minority races – caused a manpower shortage in the Army, but the draft quotas for 1916, 1917 and 1918 had all been called up before an attempt was made in October 1915 to revise the exemption system, and the new arrangements were never operated effectively, so that the Russian army was never significantly larger than the Austro-German forces opposed to it, despite both Germany's and

---

[29] Einaudi *Condotta Economica* p. 102–3, 124–9; for France see Patrick Fridenson ed. *1914–1918: Autre front* (Paris 1977) espec. Gerd Hardach 'Economie de Guerre' p. 81–109 at p. 91–3 and Alain Hennebicque 'Albert Thomas et le régime des usines de guerre, 1915–1917' p. 111–144 esp. 115–130, p. 104–117 and (with regard to the iron producers' organization, the *Comité des Forges*) p. 221–235; R.P.T. Davenport-Hines *Dudley Docker: The Life and Times of a Trade Warrior* (Cambridge 1984) p. 100–101.

Austria-Hungary's vital commitments on other fronts. Meanwhile Russia's industrial centres were expanding rapidly but with inadequate development of infrastructure so that the growing urban populations, badly paid, badly housed, disorientated and desperate, became hot-beds of criticism directed against the regime. Shortages of chemical fertilizer and of replacements for agricultural machinery cut back agricultural output, but the increasing sclerosis of the transport network, added to shortages of all consumer goods and rapid currency inflation, made the country folk reluctant to send their farm produce to market, with the result that there were increasing shortages of food in the towns. Not simply military defeat, not failure in munitions output or in the distribution of raw materials, but an overall incapacity to regulate and organize society at a period of overheated economic growth and of psychic stress brought the regime down in March 1917.[30]

Austria-Hungary was in some respects a smaller, weaker, more divided version of Russia – the validity of this comparison is supported by the claims of Hungarian scholars that it was not Russia but Hungary which experienced the most rapid growth in the industrial sector in the years leading up to 1914. Since 1867 Hungary (including Croatia and Slovakia) had had a separate domestic government from the more industrialized western half of the Dual Monarchy, and during the war was able to hold down its contributions to the common war expenditure, ultimately paying only 37 per cent of the whole. At the same time Hungarian agricultural surpluses were not made fully available to the industrial areas of Bohemia, or to Germany which was supplying the Dual Monarchy with raw materials. Even within the component halves of the Dual Monarchy war production was badly coordinated; in 1917 the Trade Ministry's General Commissariat for the War Economy and the interdepartmental War and Transitional Economy Commission were joined by a system of supervisory trade associations of the type already operating in Germany and Italy, but this merely extended the realm of red tape and fiddling. As in Russia, transportations and its organization emerged as a key problem; the failure to increase the quantity of railway rolling stock, or even the speed at which it was moved, was causing widespread local shortages of food and fuel by late 1917.[31]

[30] Norman Stone *The Eastern Front, 1914–1917* (1975) p. 201–203; ibid. p. 210–211 and cf Peter L. Lyashchenko *History of the National Economy of Russia to the 1917 Revolution* (New York 1949) p. 761–2 for the holding up of the overall output despite transfer of production to munitions. For the 1915 situation see: Basil Gourko *Memories & Impressions of War and Revolution in Russia, 1914–1917* (1918) p. 101–105. For the labour force see Peter Gatrell *The Tsarist Economy, 1850–1917* (1986) p. 95 and cf poster illustrated in Max Gallo *The Poster in History* (New York 1974) p. 205.

[31] I.T. Berend and Gy. Ránki *The Development of the Manufacturing Industry in Hungary 1900–1944* (Budapest 1960) p. 14 for Hungarian industrial growth prior to 1914; Wilhelm Winkler *Die Einkommensverschiebungen in Österreich während des Weltkrieges* (Vienna 1930) p. 234; Hardach *The First World War* p. 74.

VI. The German War Economy

Germany was perhaps quicker off the mark than any other belligerent in attempting to establish a strategic organization of the economy. On 8 August 1914 the Jewish business magnate and intellectual Walther Rathenau, prompted possibly by one of his staff, Wichard von Moellendorff, visited Colonel Heinrich Scheüch, Director of the Central Department at the Prussian Ministry of War, to warn that the war would last longer than Germany's existing supplies; and with commendable promptness, a War Materials Department (*Kriegsrohstoffabteilung*) was set up under Rathenau's direction. By early 1915 there were 25 commercial corporations under the *Kriegsrohstoffabteilung*, mostly owned or controlled by the largest companies requiring these raw materials. The raw material prices were fixed below their real cost, the materials themselves allocated on the basis of favouritism; and the government was overcharged for the final product. Because practically the whole range of industries required for munitions already existed in Germany in 1914 and were unusually concentrated, German industrial magnates were under less pressure to reinvest in increasing output than their counterparts in other belligerent countries; although plant for fixing nitrogen by the new Haber-Bosch process was built remarkably quickly, the German chemical industry, before 1914 much the largest in Europe, allowed itself to be overtaken in explosives production by France and Britain within a couple of years. There was also no attempt made to limit exportation, official restrictions on exports from Britain having opened up profitable markets in Holland and Scandinavia.[32]

Despite the prompt action in establishing the *Kriegsrohstoffabteilung*, the German government failed to give attention to two areas of the economy which were eventually to prove of decisive importance. British government expenditure, even if unprecedentedly lavish, never ran far ahead of ideas about where the money was to come from. As early as September 1915 John Maynard Keynes, then a temporary official at the British Treasury, warned:

> the limitations of our resources are in sight ... in the case of any expenditure we must consider, not only, as heretofore, whether it would be useful, but also whether we can afford it.

Yet Britain, with its vast overseas investments, uniquely developed capital market, and a higher per capita income than Germany, had considerably larger conventional financial resources than Germany. The German government by-passed this difficulty by financing the war with unsecured loans. This posed the risk of inflation: but the intention was to transfer the inflation abroad. 'We

---

[32] Harry Kessler *Walter Rathenau: His Life and Work* (1929) p. 179, cf Lothar Burchardt, 'Walter Rathenau und die Anfänge der Deutschen Rohstoffbewirtschaftung im Ersten Weltkrieg' *Tradition* vol. 15 (1970) p. 169–196; Gerald D. Feldman *Army Industry and Labor in Germany, 1914–1918* (Princeton 1966) p. 157–8 and Hardach *The First World War* p. 60–62.

hold fast to the hope of presenting our opponents at the conclusion of peace with the bill for this war that has been forced upon us', Karl Helfferich, the state secretary at the Treasury Office, told the Reichstag on 10 March 1915. A few months later, as the loans soared, he announced, 'The instigators of this war have earned this lead weight of billions; may they drag it down through the years, not we'.[33]

The effect of this policy on the German currency only became obvious at the end of the war; more immediately harmful was the failure to maintain food supplies. Whereas Britain, heavily dependent in peace time on bulky food imports, managed to increase the yield of the grain and potato harvest 40 per cent during the war, German harvests declined – grain by 29 per cent, potatoes by 21 per cent. A food board was set up belatedly in 1916 but busied itself mainly with the problem of allocating the dwindling food supplies, when the real problem was the effect of declining availability of draught animals, manpower and chemical fertilizers. By the end of 1917 official rations in most German towns were down to 4lb of bread and 7lb of potatoes per week, plus 320 grammes of meat and fat, though in many industrial areas of the Ruhr potatoes were not distributed for weeks, or were available only to certain categories of worker. Seventy-five years later, despite the national disasters that were to follow, the very old in Germany still remember the 'Turnip Winter' of 1917–1918 as one of the worst experiences of their lives. Deaths from tuberculosis increased by up to 70 per cent, miscarriages and deaths from puerperal fever also increased – there was also an increase in deaths from tuberculosis in Britain owing to the siphoning off of doctors for the army and the redeployment of T.B. sanatoria as military convalescent homes, but to nothing like the same extent – and the productivity of workers was estimated to have fallen 40 per cent. After the war it was calculated that 762,736 people – mainly the very young or the very old – had died of malnutrition in Germany during the war, 72 per cent of the total in 1917 and 1918. Officially this catastrophe was attributed to the British 'Hunger Blockade' but since less than 10 per cent of Germany's pre-war food supplies had been imported – and some of that from areas which during the war were under German military control – the 'Hunger Blockade' does not explain why, by 1918, the German population had only 64 per cent of the pre-war quantity of cereals, 18 per cent of the pre-war quantity of meat and 12 per cent of the pre-war quantity of fats. The real reason was administrative short-sightedness, arising from the same burning-the-candle-at-both-ends mentality that dominated the management of the nation's finances.[34]

[33] Robert Skidelsky *John Maynard Keynes* (2 vols 1983–) vol. 1 p. 312, memo 9 Sept. 1915; John G. Williamson *Karl Helfferich, 1872–1924* (Princeton 1971) p. 126, Reichstag speech 10 March 1915; ibid p. 131, Reichstag speech 20 Aug. 1915.

[34] Lothar Burchard 'The Impact of the War Economy on the Civilian Population of Germany during the First and Second World Wars' in Wilhelm Deist ed. *The German Military in the Age of Total War* (Leamington Spa 1985) p. 40–70 at p. 47, cf Thomas Hudson Middleton
continued

The overall supervision of the German war economy passed effectively under the control of Erich Ludendorff when, late in 1916, a War Bureau (*Kriegsamt*) under Major-General Wilhelm Groener was established: technically the *Kriegsamt* was a branch of the Prussian Ministry of War, many of whose functions it took over, but effectively it was under the control of the army High Command, the *Oberste Heeresleitung*, of which Hindenburg and Ludendorff were the heads. Ludendorff saw the political value of denigrating previous levels of achievement under civilian control, and promulgated the Hindenburg Programme of increased munitions output. Output duly increased, though not as a result of the promulgation of the Hindenburg Programme, and not as rapidly as in France or Britain. Ludendorff also saw the value of cooperating with the business magnates who shared not only his annexationist views but also his contempt for the conventional pieties of civilian government. Increasingly he became obsessed with the idea and the rhetoric of national mobilization. The controversial Auxiliary Service Law (*Hilfsdienstgesetz*), forced on the government in December 1916, was a political flourish like the Hindenburg Programme. It made war work compulsory for every male between seventeen and sixty at a time when, with an influx of women into factory work because of rising prices and the wretched army pay of their menfolk, there was no particular labour shortage other than of skilled operatives. The main practical result of forcing this law through the Reichstag was to embitter the relationship between the Reichstag and Karl Helfferich, the rising light in the civilian government and by now Secretary of the Interior. Helfferich's unpopularity was positively welcomed by Ludendorff and his industrialist friends. Any attempt to regulate the higher management of the war economy that conflicted with the interests of big business was thwarted. Alfons Horten, head of the Iron Section of the *Kriegsrohstoffabteilung*, attempted to expose the relentless overpricing and profiteering of the steel magnates and was sacked. Groener at the *Kriegsamt*, after Ludendorff the dominating intellect of the German General Staff, attempted to establish a positive working relationship with the labour unions but was resented, like Horten, for his views on the profits being reaped by the steel magnates: in August 1917 he was sent to the front to command a division. (Although George Grosz's famous caricatures satirizing the exploitation and bad faith of the militarists and the plutocrats belong particularly to the immediate post-war

continued
Food Production in War (Oxford 1923) p. 241 table XVIII; F.L. Carsten *War Against War: British and German Radical Movements in the First World War* (1982) p. 147 for German rations in 1917; A.C. Bell *A History of the Blockade of Germany and the Countries Associated with her in the Great War, Austria-Hungary, Bulgaria and Turkey, 1914–1918* (printed for private circulation 1937) p. 672–3 for effects of blockade in Germany, cf Pat Thane *Foundations of the Welfare State* (1982) p. 133, 194: J.M. Winter *The Great War and the British People* (1985) p. 120 table 4.2 shows that deaths of women from T.B. in 1917 were 15 per cent higher than the 1912–1914 average: p. 136 table 4.8 shows that puerperal mortality, slightly up in 1915, fell by the end of the war, being 3.79 per thousand births in 1918 as compared to 4.51 in 1933; for German agriculture see W.K. Hancock and M.M. Gowing *The British War Economy* (1953) p. 19–20 cf Hardach *The First World War* p. 119 table 3.

years, his later preoccupations are already evident in some of his wartime work: the Army's love affair with big business could not be kept secret.) Curiously enough this alliance between the military high command and the iron and steel kings also developed in Italy, though the precise aim and initiative of General Dall'Olio in Italy remains more obscure than the principles guiding Ludendorff's dealings with big business; it is arguable that both in Germany and Italy the experience of collaboration between industrial leaders and general staff officers during the First World War was one of the factors assisting the later establishment of right-wing dictatorship. Equally, in Britain, the exclusion of the military from the economic sphere was a key factor in the development of the British style of war leadership. The notion of the Second World War as a continuation and sequel of the First World War is certainly valid as regards economic organization: and as we shall see it holds even more true for the way in which the economic resources mobilized were used on the battlefield.[35]

[35] Martin Kitchen *The Silent Dictatorship* (1976) p. 70 and Feldman *Army Industry and Labor* p. 301–308 for labour supply situation; Williamson *Karl Helfferich* p. 176–187 for the passage of the *Hilfsdienstgesetz* through the Reichstag; Kitchen *Silent Dictatorship* p. 146, Feldman *Army Industry and Labor* p. 361, 397–9 for treatment of Horten and Groener.

9

The War of the Generals

Here was I – a brigadier and still under forty, and with another year of the war there was no saying where I might end. I had started out without any ambition, only a great wish to see the business finished. But now I had acquired a professional interest in the thing, I had a nailing good brigade, and I had got the hang of our new kind of war as well as any fellow from Sandhurst and Camberley.

John Buchan, *Mr. Standfast* (1919), p. 18–19.

I. Some Images of the Great War

A few bitter rhymes by Siegfried Sassoon may well survive in the communal memory when all the rest of the First World War's poetry is forgotten:

> If I were fierce, and bald, and short of breath,
> I'd live with scarlet Majors at the Base,
> And speed glum heroes up the line to death,

or:

> 'Good morning; good morning!' the General said
> When we met him last week on our way to the line.
> Now the soldiers he smiled at are most of them dead,
> And we're cursing his staff for incompetent swine.[1]

An earlier generation was almost as familiar with the pen-pictures of Philip Gibbs, the most widely read and widely respected of the newspaper correspondents attached to the British Expeditionary Force, and the recipient after the war of a knighthood:

> I thought of Rawlinson in his chateau in Querrieux, scheming out the battles and ordering up new masses of troops to the great assault over the bodies of their dead ... it is inevitable that the men who risk death daily, the fighting men who carry out the plans of the High Command and see no sense in them, should be savage in their irony when they pass a peaceful house where their death is being planned, and green-eyed when they see an Army general taking a

---

[1] Siegfried Sassoon 'Base Details' and 'The General'.

stroll in buttercup fields, with a jaunty young A.D.C. slashing the flowers with his cane and telling the latest joke from London to his laughing chief.

In other countries, in other armies, there was the same sense of the uncrossable gulf between the smug fantasies of the H.Q. and the realities of the front line. Paolo Monelli, for example, wrote bitterly of the Italian general who, after an unsuccessful advance,

> greets us at the gap in the wire, hard, cold, and hostile. He says too few of us got killed. He says we ought to have taken the position. . . . He stands stiff and frowning on the path looking at us pass by. Then the buzz of a motor; lounging back to his car, he goes back to his castle.

Even in the German army it was reported that troops marching up to the firing line during the Battle of Verdun were disconcerted to see their army group commander, the Imperial Crown Prince, playing tennis in a garden beside the road, and were by no means reassured when he interrupted his game to shout out *'Macht's gut Kameraden!'* ('Good luck, comrades!') and salute them with his tennis racket.[2]

For the British at least the High Command's appalling indifference was epitomized in the sternly enigmatic silences of Sir Douglas Haig:

> All to whom he was introduced he looked straight in the face. Always it appeared as if he were about to speak, but all he did was to regard the person with his clear eyes as if he sought to imprint his face forever on his memory, and then, shaking hands, would pass on, in silence, with his inscrutable gravity.

Haig, it was said,

> was a man so lacking in imagination that, in actual fact, he never saw the war; that is, as it really was. In place he saw the phantoms of past wars, and out of these spectral shadows emerged those mythological battles which to him were so real and, consequently, so necessary.[3]

The reality, 'the veritable gloom and disaster of the thing called Armageddon,' was in fact beyond imagining:

> I saw it then, as I see it now – a dreadful place, a place of horror and desolation which no imagination could have invented. Also it was a place

---

[2] Philip Gibbs *Realities of War* (1920) p. 42 (the correct spelling is Querrieu) and cf. Rupert Hart Davis ed. *Siegfried Sassoon Diaries, 1915–1918* (1983) p. 108. 25 Dec. 1916: 'I'll warrant old Sir Henry made a good dinner in his chateau at Querrieux, good luck to him and his retinue!' (For a less good-humoured reaction see the attack on G.H.Q. staff by Lord St. David's in the House of Lords, 16 Nov. 1915 – *Hansard: House of Lords* 5th series vol. 20 col 359–367; Paolo Monelli *Toes Up* (1930) [original title *Le Scarpe al Sole*] p. 25; reminiscence of Arnold Wegner passed on by his brother-in-law, Dr. R.B. Jones. See also the evocation of the staff in F. Britten Austin 'A Battle Piece: Old Style' in his collection *The War-God Walks Again* (1926) p. 93–4, 106–122.

[3] A.A. Hanbury-Sparrow *The Land-Locked Lake* (1932) p. 285–6; J.F.C. Fuller *Memoirs of an Unconventional Soldier* (1936) p. 137;

where a man of strong spirit might know himself utterly powerless against death and destruction, yet stand up and defy gross darkness and stupefying shell-fire, discovering in himself the invincible resistance of an animal, or an insect, and an endurance which he might, in after days, forget or disbelieve.

Partly it was a question of the sheer physical scale and desolation of the front line:

The stark and shattered scene: flayed tree stumps, wastes of mud and great pools of water, reminded me of an ocean floor suddenly exposed and tensed for a crashing re-engulfment. Not a sign of life anywhere – but an obsession of human eyes, watching . . .

But it was the sheer denial of human normality which forced forth the most poignant cries of pain:

Mother, we are tramping over the dead; I think there is only about 4 hundred left out of about 13 hundred. Mother, you can let Alfred know something about all this. Mother, I have some German helmets and sausages, and I am sorry that I could not send them home. Mother, if God spares me to get home safely I will have something awful to tell you. If hell is any worse I would not like to go to it.

Out of the contrast between these experiences, and the elegant lifestyles of the High Command, came the inevitable conviction that something had gone disastrously wrong.[4]

II. New Ideas and the Old Guard

Perhaps it was the entire social system that had gone wrong:

there was a dark suspicion that in this testing time the upper class had failed. It had done nothing to justify its position. It was just a lot of snobbish public school boys.

Or perhaps it was simply the military system:

I met many other generals who were men of ability, energy, high sense of duty, and strong personality. I found them, intellectually, with few exceptions, narrowly moulded to the same type, strangely limited in their range of ideas and qualities of character.

'One has to leave many gaps in one's conversation with generals', said a friend of mine, after lunching with an Army Commander.[5]

---

[4] Siegfred Sassoon *Memoirs of an Infantry Officer* (1930) p. 216–7; Malcolm Brown *Tommy Goes to War* (1978) p. 247 quoting letter by 2nd/Lt. Blake O'Sullivan Aug. 1916; ibid., p. 198 quoting letter by Fusilier Herbert Beattie 2nd Bn Royal Inniskilling Fusiliers from the Somme.

[5] Hanbury-Sparrow *The Land Locked Lake* p. 285; Gibbs *Realities of War* p. 46.

One ex-brigadier-general confessed:

As a matter of fact, to say that the Military Mind *thinks* is a misleading statement; all it does is to react along certain well-defined, stereotyped lines.

This perhaps explains the enthusiasm shown by many senior officers for correspondence courses in memory training: the Pelman Institute in the final months of the war made much of the numerous generals who had signed on for their courses, and were particularly delighted with the lieutenant-colonel who wrote in from Salonica to announce that 'As a direct consequence of Lesson Two I have got a step in rank'. But those who forget nothing tend also to learn nothing, and Major-General Sir Ernest Swinton detected

a deeply rooted bias against novel ideas, especially when they emanated from below. To some military minds indeed suggestions from juniors smack of presumption, if not insubordination.

A brigadier-general wrote of a common regular officer type:

Realizing their own shortcomings, they have a fear of anyone with ability, and therefore resort to petty intrigue for the purpose of retaining positions which they are not competent to fill.

Partly perhaps it was a question of careerism:

Since being in the War Office, I have been very much struck by the time-serving attitude adopted by so many officers. From the highest to the lowest, with few exceptions, personal advancement is the predominating factor. . . . It is rare to find officers saying what they think and acting in what manner they think best, if it goes against the pleasure of some person who might influence their chance of reward.

There was also the question of professional solidarity, as Major-General J.F.C. Fuller explained:

no criticism is allowed, for it might seem to belittle the Army in the eyes of a cynical public.
  This fear of the truth creates a discipline the aim of which is not to foster originality, but a universal damping down and standardization, which ends in creating an all-pervading mediocrity of spirit, in which genius and talent are the demons to be exorcised.[6]

Fuller even believed that intellectual tastes were likely to damage one's career: as he wrote to Liddell Hart after the latter had been placed on half-pay:

---

6 C.D. Baker-Carr *From Chauffeur to Brigadier* (1930) p. 88; E.S. Turner *Dear Old Blighty* (1980) p. 251; Sir Ernest Swinton *Eye Witness: Being Personal Reminiscences of Certain Phases of the Great War, including the Genesis of the Tank* (1932) p. 96–7; Guy Livingston *Hot Air in Cold Blood* [1933] p. 148; R. Meinertzhagen *Army Diary, 1899–1926* (Edinburgh 1960) p. 206, 11 Feb. 1917; J.F.C. Fuller *The Army in My Time* (1935) p. 16–17.

The pretext is your health. The cause is that you are a writer. Mediocrity has its back against the wall, and we who have helped to force it into this position are its first victims. . . . You are being decapitated. I am being slowly strangled. I do not know who is to be envied most.[7]

This view is echoed in the subsequent scholarly literature. The three most often-cited examples of careers ruined by excess of intellectual capacity are those of Fuller himself, Liddell Hart, and Sir Herbert Richmond in the Navy. Since Richmond rose in peacetime to the rank of full admiral before retiring early because of an official fuss about some letters he had written to *The Times*, the complaint on his behalf turns out to be that he should have been appointed First Sea Lord, i.e. professional head of the Navy, and wasn't. Missing the top job hardly represents a ruined career. In Liddell Hart's case he owed his premature retirement to a particularly lightweight Chief of the Imperial General Staff, the Earl of Cavan ('The mind of this little man is only 800 years out of date. Isn't it wonderful?', wrote Fuller to Liddell Hart). Nevertheless, the British Army was surely not unusual in that, while permitting generals to be short of breath and in need of spectacles, it did require a certain athleticism amongst its captains; even those from the Army Education Corps. Perhaps the most interesting case is that of Fuller, who was retired as major-general. One plausible objection to Fuller was not that he wrote, but *what* he wrote. One of his memos, prepared at the request of a senior staff officer at G.H.Q. after the German Spring Offensives of 1918, and entitled 'The Basic Causes of the Present Defeat', stated:

Our army is crawling with 'duds'; though habitual offenders they are tolerated because of the camaraderie of the Regular Army: an Army so small as to permit of all its higher members being personal friends. Good fellowship ranks with us above efficiency: the result is a military trade union which does not declare a dividend.

Another of his official papers waxed sarcastic on the subject of the G.H.Q.'s lack of contact with frontline troops: 'It would be a lamentable event were the C.G.S. [Chief of Staff of the British forces in France] to be killed; yet it will be a still more lamentable one if this war is lost'. Referring to the C.G.S.'s opposition to providing specialized training for certain divisions, Fuller queried: 'Is he not thinking in six-divisional terms? Is he not still mentally living in the year 1914. . . .?' Possibly Fuller's colleagues made up in sense of humour what they lacked in brains and thoroughly enjoyed memoranda of this sort. It seems unlikely. In any case it is difficult to avoid the suspicion that Fuller may have been a little too effervescent to make a universally satisfactory theatre commander or Chief of the Imperial General

---

[7] *The Memoirs of Captain Liddell Hart* (2 vols 1965) vol. 1 p. 64 Fuller to Liddell Hart 1924.

Staff. Even Hitler, who met him several times, thought he would be *unbequem* (uncomfortable) in any organization.[8]

It is even possible to wonder if Fuller had the routine technical competence of, for example, Charles Pasley, his nearest counterpart in the Napoleonic Wars. He made no secret of the muddy patches in his thinking. His first book had been the winning – in fact the only – entry in a £100 prize competition for a study of the work of Aleister Crowley, the black magician and future anti-British propagandist:

> those who would drink deeper of this magical Eucharist, spilt with due reverence in the pages of this book, they [sic] must seek it in the Sybilline verses of those books [a list follows of Crowley's publications]. . . .
>
> By which, if they have eyes to perceive, they will become sacramental and holy, through the fire-baptism of a new birth, and will hold the key of all mysteries locked in the esoteric sign of the Sabbatic Goat, the Baphormet of Mendes, the signatures of Solve and Coagula, 'The Everlasting Yea and Nay'.

A.M.E.N.

The £100 prize (offered, needless to say, by Crowley himself) was never actually paid over, but Fuller followed up this intellectual triumph by contributing various pieces to Crowley's magazine *The Equinox*, including a magical biography of Crowley which was serialized under the title 'The Temple of Solomon the King'.[9]

Fuller's instinctive leaning towards hocus-pocus also appears in his writings on military tactics, even a quarter of a century after his final break with Aleister Crowley:

> It [the tank] is a two-dimensional weapon when compared to infantry, which is a one-dimensional arm; that is, it moves in lines and fights in lines. Whilst the old tactical form of war was linear, the new is based on plane surfaces (areas) and is developed in cubic spaces – three-dimensional warfare.

By the time he wrote this Fuller had become a supporter of Oswald Mosley and a vocal anti-semite; during the Second World War he was the most prominent B.U.F. member not to be interned, this being allegedly because 'He knows too much.' Far from being the victim of prejudice, Fuller seems to have benefited from an extraordinary open-mindedness; the wonder is,

[8] Cf. Robin Higham *The Military Intellectuals in Britain, 1919–1939* (New Jersey 1966) p. 33–4, 45, 48; *Memoirs of Captain Liddell Hart* vol. 1 p. 64 Fuller to Liddell Hart 1924; Fuller *Memoirs of an Unconventional Soldier* p. 260; ibid. p. 164–8; Diana Mosley *A Life of Contrasts* (1977) p. 163.

[9] J.F.C. Fuller *The Star of the West: A Critical Essay upon the Works of Aleister Crowley* (1907) p. 6–7; John Symonds *The Great Beast: The Life of Aleister Crowley* (1951) p. 92–3, 103.

not that some of his colleagues looked askance at him, but that he was ever promoted as high as major-general.[10]

III. Careers Open to Talent

As with most other aspects of army administration, this whole question of promotion to senior rank provoked adverse comment during the First World War. Already in October 1915 Lloyd George's secretary and girlfriend noted:

> They say, too, that there is great discontent in the ranks and among the junior officers on account of the lack of brains in the senior and commanding officers.

The shock generated by the casualty lists from the Somme strengthened this sense of discontent, especially amongst those who were most alert to the social experiment involved in raising the so-called Kitchener or New Army from amongst social classes that previously had had nothing to do with the military profession. Shortly before Lloyd George became Prime Minister a group of his unofficial advisers (including a New Army sergeant wounded at the Somme) drew up a paper complaining:

> We still see position in the higher direction of our armies reserved almost exclusively to regular officers ... the Government should be at once swift to promote those who in humble positions have given proof of competence and ruthless in dismissing those in eminent positions who have not. In particular ... it should secure that the fullest opportunities of advancement to the higher commands are accessible to officers and men who have proved their efficiency in the present war, irrespective of whether they did or did not previously follow the Army as a profession.

Later Lord Milner, a member of the War Cabinet, raised the issue with Sir William Birdwood, the commander of the Australian Imperial Force, and the latter had to acknowledge that, on the basis of his experience of Australian non-professional soldiers promoted up to divisional command, 'it seemed unreasonable to suppose that units of Kitchener's Army should be unable to produce equally good men'. Early in January 1918 a deputation of Liberal Party ministers even complained to Lloyd George about promotion policy, causing the Prime Minister to discuss over lunch with Hankey, Smuts and Lord Reading 'the failure of the War Office to allow any Territorial or new army officers to reach the higher commands'.[11]

---

[10] Fuller *The Army in My Time* p. 171–2, cf Mosley *Life of Contrasts* p. 172.

[11] A.J.P. Taylor ed. *Lloyd George: A Diary by Frances Stevenson* (1971) p. 67, 13 Oct. 1915; Thomas Jones *Whitehall Diary* ed. Keith Middlemass (3 vols 1969–71) vol. 1 p. 3–4 memo early Dec. 1916 by Jones, R.H. Tawney (the ex-sergeant), J.J. Mallon, A. Zimmerman, Lionel Hitchens; [W.R.] Lord Birdwood *Khaki and Gown* (1941) p. 324; [Maurice] Lord Hankey *The*
continued

Of course one would have a pretty strange view of reality if one based it only on the impressions of politicians, and the fact was that the British Army was uniquely open as regards promoting the young and the amateur. A somewhat overgenerous German appreciation of the system was that:

> England is more practical in her organization, and is not so hemmed in by red tape as we are. She selects the best men to command irrespective of rank and age, and only according to their efficiency.

The British Army did not cast its net quite as wide as this analysis would suggest, but it must be remembered that compared to continental armies it underwent a relatively much greater expansion, and though this expansion, as elsewhere, was primarily on the basis of officers moving up a rank or two, only in the British Army did it occur that an officer might receive *five* or *six* promotions within the space of four years.[12]

The greatest rigidity in promotions was maintained in Germany, where the most important reserve of talent for the corps of general officers was felt to be sexagenarians who had either already been pensioned off, like Hindenburg or Prince Leopold of Bavaria, or who were on the point of retirement, like Mackensen. It is often assumed that the mental sluggishness of the older German generals, or the inexperience of royal appointees without real professional background like the Imperial Crown Prince or Crown Prince Rupprecht of Bavaria, was compensated for by the authoritative advice of brilliant young staff officers. It was indeed the system in the German Army for chiefs of staff to have a considerable share of the command initiative; this caused fears amongst the Kaiser's entourage that 'the authority of the Army Commanders' was being undermined, and after the war Ludendorff condemned this practice as radically defective and the cause of confusion; but the truth was that these staff officers were never particularly young. Colonels Max Hoffmann and Max Bauer, perhaps the two ablest men in this category, were both 45 years old in August 1914, and the Saxon Colonel Richard Hentsch, notorious as the man who gave the order for the German retreat at the Marne in 1914, was only a few months younger; the chief of staff assisting the Imperial Crown Prince, Constantin Schmidt von Knobelsdorf, was a lieutenant-general in his mid fifties.[13]

The stability and emphasis on seniority in the upper reaches of the German officer corps was maintained also by the circumstance that it was not found

continued
Supreme Command, 1914–1918 (2 vols 1961) vol. 2 p. 755–6, 18 Jan. 1918. The issue had been raised previously in the House of Commons, by Sir George Scott Robertson, on 18 Nov. 1915: *Hansard: House of Commons* vol. 75 col. 2009–210.

12 Evelyn Princess Blücher *An English Wife in Berlin: A Private Memoir of Events, Politics, and Daily Life in Germany Throughout the Great War and the Social Revolution of 1918* (1920) p. 177, June-July 1917.

13 Walter Görlitz ed. *The Kaiser and his Court: The Diaries Notebooks and Letters of Admiral Georg Alexander von Muller, Chief of the Naval Cabinet, 1914–1918* (1961) p. 181, July 1916; Erich Ludendorff *Über Unbotmässigkeit im Kriege* (Munich [1935]) passim.

necessary to sack incompetents and trouble-makers right, left and centre. Maximilian von Prittwitz und Gaffron was dismissed from the command of the German Eighth Army in East Prussia three weeks into the war; Moltke was quickly removed after the failure on the Marne; but the replacement of two of his army commanders, Alexander von Kluck and Karl von Bülow, was occasioned simply by the fact that they had both become bed-ridden, the one through wounds, the other through illness, and though they were never subsequently reemployed this may have been because they were both nearly seventy years old by the time they were again fit for service. Moltke's successor as Chief of Staff, Falkenhayn, being much younger received an important field command after he was removed from his post. The situation was quite different in the French and Italian Armies. By the end of December 1914, 180 French generals or colonels commanding brigades had been dismissed (*dégommés* or *limogés* in the slang of the time), including three army, 24 corps and 71 divisional commanders, leaving only three army commanders, six corps commanders and 21 divisional commanders in the same job as they had had at the outbreak of war five months earlier. In the Italian Army the purge was less sudden but more sustained, 217 generals, 255 colonels and 335 battalion commanders being sacked (or as the Italians liked to say, *silurato*, torpedoed) by General Cadorna before he was himself dismissed in the late autumn of 1917, with a further 176 generals, colonels and battalion commanders being disposed of by his successors. In May 1917 it was claimed that since Italy's entry into the war two years previously regiments had changed their C.O.s an average of six times, though the 90ª Fanteria had had no less than 18 commanding officers since May 1915. Nor did Cadorna confine himself simply to dismissals; both Giulio Douhet, former head of the air arm, and Roberto Bencivenga, former head of Cadorna's military secretariat, were imprisoned for stepping out of line.[14]

It was not quite so bad in the British Army: 'I do not want to appear as crabing [sic] my contemporaries, who were friends and splendid fellows in a tight place,' wrote Edmonds, the Official Historian of the British Army's campaigns in France and Belgium,

> but Haig told me that he had sent home more than a hundred brigadiers, but that he was forced to leave certain corps and divisional commanders in their appointments because he could not be sure of securing better ones.

Though Rawlinson managed to escape being sacked, Gough actually was, and French and Smith-Dorrien were ignominiously shuffled off to the sidelines. There do not seem to have been many others; in August 1916 King George V warned the High Command that 'much harm was being done at home by

[14] Pierre Rocolle *L'Hécatombe des Généraux* (Paris 1980) p. 262; Luigi Cadorna *Pagine Polemiche* (Milan 1950) p. 75 cf. Mario Silvestri *Isonzo 1917* (Turin 1965) edit. p. 103; Angelo Gatti *Caporetto: dal diario di guerra inedito* ed. Alberto Monticone (Milan 1964) p. 8, 10 May 1917.

the Generals who had been sent back as useless from France', but apart from Lieutenant-General J.L. Keir, who had been sacked by his army commander, Sir Edmund Allenby, and was waxing sour on the subject of the Army's domination by cavalry officers, it is difficult to be certain whom precisely is meant. At about this time a general with the inauspicious name of Hew Dalrymple Fanshawe, who had been a corps commander in France for nearly a year, was replaced and given a division training in Britain; he eventually took this division to France but after a few months was transferred to another divisional command – in Mesopotamia. One may read into such little histories of demotion and transfer the workings of more senior officers' grudges and disesteem but the surviving evidence is largely circumstantial; it was later claimed, for example, that the reason why Major-General A.R.M. Stuart-Wortley was sent to join Fanshawe in Mesopotamia after a brief stint on the Western Front was that he was in correspondence with the King, 'a privilege D.H. [Douglas Haig] intended to reserve for himself', but there is no way of satisfactorily confirming such a report.[15]

Sir Hubert Gough, perhaps the most distinguished sacking in the British Army during the war was a full general when, at the age of 47 years 7 months, he was removed from command of the Fifth Army; Erich Ludendorff had been seventeen months older when, just before the beginning of the war, he had become Germany's youngest *major*-general. Lord Kitchener, the British Secretary of State for War (then aged 65) wrote to General Sir Ian Hamilton (aged 62) 'This is a young man's war, and we must have Commanding Officers who will take full advantage of opportunities, which come but seldom'. Sir Douglas Haig, then an army commander in France and soon to be Commander-in-Chief of the British Expeditionary Force, professed to be of the same opinion:

> progress will be disappointing unless young capable Commanders are brought up to the Front. Some of the present Captains should be chosen to command Battalions, Majors Brigades, etc.

In the event the youngest general officer of the war was Roland Boys Bradford V.C. who had been commissioned as a second lieutenant in the Durham Light Infantry in 1912 and who was killed in November 1917 aged 25 years 8 months, less than three weeks after putting up the crossed sword and baton

[15] King's College London, Edmonds papers I/2B/5b Edmonds to C.N. Barclay 7 April 1950; Robert Blake ed. *The Private Papers of Sir Douglas Haig, 1914–1919* (1952) p. 158–9, diary 6 Aug. 1916 and cf. J.L. Keir *A 'Soldier's Eye-View' of our Armies* (1919); King's College London, Liddell Hart Papers 11/1929/17, note of conversation with Edmonds 31 Oct. 1929. See also Tim Travers *The Killing Ground; The British Army, the Western Front and the Emergence of Modern Warfare, 1900–1918* (1987) p. 20–23. According to Travers p. 11 both Sir Charles Fergusson and H.D. Fanshawe's younger brother Edward were moved from corps commands in 1916: but they were soon appointed to other corps in France. See also Martin Middlebrook *The First Day on the Somme: 1 July 1916* (1971) p. 250–259 for the cases of two divisional commanders, E.J.M. Stuart-Wortley and T.D. Pilcher.

insignia of a brigadier-general. Oswald Boelcke, the German fighter ace, was said to have been the youngest *captain* in the German Army at the same age; the youngest captain in the British Army was Kenneth Vernon Bailey, who after three years service as lieutenant was promoted acting captain on 8 August 1917, more than four months before his twentieth birthday.[16]

There were in fact a number of brigadier-generals under thirty in the British Army but there is a problem comparing this situation with other armies in that the rank as such (only a temporary grade in the British Army in any case) did not exist in most other armies. British divisions consisted of three brigades (each of four, later only three, battalions from various regiments) whereas continental divisions consisted of two brigades, each comprising two regiments of three or four battalions. A British brigade, though rather smaller than a continental brigade, would normally be commanded by a brigadier-general and there would thus be a major-general and three brigadier-generals per division; the larger continental brigade would be commanded either by a colonel or by a major-general so that there would normally be two major-generals in the division, including the divisional commander, though to confuse matters there were only two grades of general in the French Army, of which the junior, *général de brigade*, sounded as if it meant brigadier-general but was in fact the normal rank for a divisional commander. After the war the rank of brigadier-general was abolished on the grounds that:

> on the expansion of the Army for war there was in the British Army an excessive number of General Officers, which tended to lower the status of British Generals, and made their numbers disproportionate to the numbers in Allied Armies,

though again, since there was a relatively high proportion of junior and field officers to the rank and file in the British Army (apparently a legacy of the former system of purchasing commissions) it does not seem that there was a disproportionate number of generals as compared to, say, captains and majors.[17]

If we leave the confusing issue of the brigadier-generals we find that the youngest British commander of a division in this period was Keppel Bethell,

[16] Sir George Arthur *Life of Lord Kitchener* (3 vols 1920) vol. 3 p. 170 Kitchener to Hamilton 14 Aug. 1915; Duff Cooper *Haig* 2 vols London 1935 vol. 1 p. 251 diary 25 June 1915; Johannes Werner *Knight of Germany: Oswald Boelcke German Ace* (1933) Preface. Kenneth Vernon Bailey's career as a teenage subaltern is noted in *The Guiness Book of Records*. Fighter pilots were predominantly very young men; in both the French and German air services the top twelve fighter aces were four captains and eight lieutenants; in the British service five captains, six majors and a lieutenant-colonel.

[17] Public Record Office WO 163/4 *Minutes of the Proceedings of, and Precis Prepared for, the Army Council, for the Year 1919* [printed 1920] p. 169 [meeting 19 Dec. 1919]. It seems therefore that Adrian Carton de Wiart's claim in his autobiography – *Happy Odyssey* (1950) p. 79 – that in 1917 he was, at the age of 36, the youngest brigadier-general in the allied armies was both untrue and meaningless.

a substantive captain who became temporary major-general commanding the 66th Division on 31 March 1918 aged 35 years 6 months; Edmund Ironside became acting major-general and commander-in-chief of Allied Forces in Russia in October 1918 aged 38 years and 5 months, and H.C. Jackson was also a major-general commanding a division before he was 40; Hugh Elles, commanding the tanks in France was a major-general at 38; Maurice Gamelin, Joffre's *chef de cabinet* when commander-in-chief, was 44 when he became France's youngest *général de brigade* and divisional commander. On the eve of the great German offensive of March 1918, of sixteen divisional commanders in the French Second Army, five had been colonels and seven lieutenant-colonels in 1914, the other four majors; of twelve divisional commanders in the British Fifth Army in the same period, five had been colonels or lieutenant-colonels in 1914 (i.e. fewer than half as compared with the French proportion of three-quarters) five had been majors, one of them on the retired list, and one a captain: the twelfth had already been a major-general on the outbreak of war.

The phenomenon of the British Army officers who had been major-generals in August 1914 and who served in frontline commands for four years, without either being sacked as incompetent or promoted in step with the huge expansion of the army, will probably never be satisfactorily explained. Sir George Gorringe commanded a corps with temporary ranking as lieutenant-general in Mesopotamia, for which he received a K.C.B. and a mention in despatches, before taking over the 47th Division in France and gaining the respect of a young staff officer named Bernard Montgomery, who later became notorious for his low opinion of his professional associates. Montgomery recalled of Gorringe, 'All the Corps Commanders under whom he served were junior to him in service. But he was very unpopular and Haig would not give him a Corps'. Aubrey Herbert thought him 'one of the worst cads I have ever met in my life'. Perhaps that is the explanation for his lack of promotion. But Major-General Colin Mackenzie, an experienced staff officer who had been mentioned six times in despatches for his exploits in various colonial wars, and held the record for the highest score for the first wicket in India, served as Director of Staff Duties at the War Office in 1915, and though War Office assignments were generally the occasion for raillery or commiseration he must have had some pull and influence – also one supposes some talent for charm and personnel management – yet despite earning another five mentions in despatches and a K.C.B. commanding the 61st Division in France he never received a corps, so that one might very well suppose that someone at G.H.Q. was standing in his light.[18]

---

[18] Nigel Hamilton *Monty: the Making of a General, 1887–1942* (1981) p. 135; Margaret Fitzherbert *The Man who was Greenmantle: A Biography of Aubrey Herbert* (1983) p. 182 Aubrey Herbert to Mary Herbert 9 May 1916. For Keppel Bethell see introduction to Brian Bond and Simon Robbins ed. *Staff Officer: the Diaries of Walter Guinness (First Lord Moyne), 1914–1918* (1987) p. 16–18.

The upper, or at least upper-middle reaches of the British Army were also relatively open to amateurs, despite the politicians' complaints to the contrary. Whereas in the Habsburg Army reserve officers were not even allowed to be appointed to captain's rank till 1916, by January 1918 four divisions and 52 brigades of the British Army had been commanded by Territorial officers (i.e. men who had been part-time soldiers before the war) and seven brigades by New Army officers (i.e. men who had not even been part-time soldiers). Henry Page Croft M.P., a Territorial officer aged 34, became at the end of 1915 a brigadier-general with four regular army battalion commanders under him, two of whom were old enough to be his father. After the Battle of the Somme Page Croft resigned his command to resume his parliamentary duties; had he not done so it seems unlikely, though of course not impossible, that he would have been left with only a brigade for the remaining years of the war.[19]

In such a huge and immobile army it was arguable of course that even brigade commanders were mere cogs in the complex machine operated by the H.Q. staff; and only three Territorials and two New Army officers received the key staff appointment of G.S.O.1. (General Staff Officer Grade 1). Stephen Foot, a New Army officer who became a G.S.O. 2 at the War Office, records that when J.F.C. Fuller, as the new head of SD7, took his list of nominations for staff to the Director of Staff Duties, the latter said, 'I suppose they are all Regulars', to which Fuller responded, 'No, none of them are'; but we have already noted that Fuller was somewhat unusual.[20]

The rapid promotion even of amateurs was an indication of how the British Army was less a separate caste than a strategic, though integrated, component of the social and administrative establishment. In October 1914 Kitchener had even been prepared to give lieutenant-general's rank and the command at Antwerp to Winston Churchill, the First Lord of the Admiralty, who was at the time not quite forty and who retired from the Army over a decade previously with the rank of lieutenant: Churchill was desperate that the Antwerp command should not go to 'dug-out trash' or to 'mediocrities, who have led a sheltered life mouldering in military routine', though it appears that Kitchener was the only one of his colleagues to take him seriously. Over a year later when Churchill left the government following the Gallipoli debacle he hoped for the command of at least a brigade on the Western Front, and even ordered the appropriate uniform; but though a brigade had been promised by Sir John French, as soon as the news got out a question was tabled in the House of Commons and Asquith told French, 'the appointment might cause

[19] *Times* 30 Jan. 1918 p. 10f reporting the Earl of Derby's speech at the Aldwych Club, cf. Gunther E. Rothenburg *The Army of Francis Joseph* (West Lafayette 1976) p. 193; [Henry] Lord Croft *My Life of Strife* [?1948] p. 100.

[20] *Hansard: House of Commons* vol. 103 col. 937 statement by J.I. MacPherson, Undersecretary of State for War, 21 Feb. 1918; Stephen Foot *Three Lives* (1934) p. 221.

criticism ... Perhaps you might give him a battalion', and with a battalion Churchill had to be satisfied.[21]

It was Churchill however who had given a vital impulse to one of the most astonishing military careers of the war. Because of an apparent surplus of manpower in the Navy, Churchill while First Lord of the Admiralty decided to form a division of naval personnel dressed in khaki (though with naval rank insignia) and equipped for land warfare, and on being introduced socially to a footloose 25-year-old amateur swimming champion and dentist from New Zealand named Bernard Freyberg, pressed him to join the division. Within a year Freyberg was acting in command of a battalion in Gallipoli in spite of having been laid up for several months with wounds – he was wounded altogether nine times and at Beaucourt would have been left for dead if stretcher bearers had not heard him exclaim, 'I wouldn't mind losing an arm for a V.C.' In April 1917 he was transferred along with his V.C. to the Army to command a brigade. It began to be rumoured at about this time that he had served before the war as a general under Pancho Villa in Mexico, but in reality his only military experience before joining the Royal Naval Division had been a few weeks as a second lieutenant in the 6th Hauraki Volunteers.[22]

The most striking promotion of amateurs was in the Canadian and Australian corps, because the colonial governments particularly desired their military formations to be led by their own citizens. A Canadian militia officer, Arthur Currie, an insurance broker in civilian life, became a lieutenant-general and G.O.C. of the Canadian Corps in mid 1917, aged 41. In the Australian Imperial Force, Gordon Bennett became another boy brigadier-general before he was thirty, and the Australian Corps was eventually commanded by one of the pioneers of reinforced concrete in Australia, Sir John Monash, who was also unusual amongst British generals in being Jewish.

The Royal Flying Corps, being essentially a new departure, was also noteworthy for quick promotion. Francis Conway Jenkins joined up in

21 Michael and Eleanor Brock ed. *H.H. Asquith: Letters to Venetia Stanley* (Oxford 1982) p. 266 Asquith to Venetia Stanley 7 Oct. 1914, cf. Lord Beaverbrook *Politicians and the War, 1914–1916* (2 vols 1928–32) vol. 1 p. 54. According to Asquith the Cabinet responded to Churchill's military ambitions 'with a Homeric laugh', Brock ed. *Letters to Venetia Stanley* p. 263, Asquith to Venetia Stanley 5 Oct. 1914, Randolph S. Churchill and Martin Gilbert *Winston S. Churchill* (8 vols plus companion vols. 1966–88) vol. 3 p. 606–614, espec. p. 612 for Asquith's note to French; it seems Asquith changed his mind as a result of a parliamentary question tabled by Sir Charles Hunter; see also Blake *Private Papers of Sir Douglas Haig* p. 117, 14 and 18 Dec. 1915 and Beaverbrook *Politicians and the War* vol. 2 p. 75–6.

22 The version given of Freyberg's almost dying remarks is in I.M.G. Steward *The Struggle for Crete, 20 May–1 June 1941: A Story of Lost Opportunity* (1966) p. 49; a possibly more authentic but less dramatic version is given in Peter Singleton-Gates *General Lord Freyberg V.C.* (1963) p. 8 and 49 where it is stated that he told Petty Officer R.H. Tobin of the Naval Division, in April 1915 'I'd give my right arm to win the V.C.'; Singleton-Gates *General Lord Freyberg V.C.* p. 25–6 for rumours – and the truth – about Freyberg's pre-war military experience. Another British officer alleged to have served under Pancho Villa was a battalion transport officer in the Royal Fusiliers, cf Guy Chapman *A Passionate Prodigality* (1933) p. 93.

1914, having it is said previously been a used-car salesman, and became like Freyberg a brigadier-general before he was 30, though without the bother of getting wounded nine times or winning the V.C.: as Director of Aircraft Parks and Depots he fought from his desk. Even younger than Jenkins was A.C. Critchley who was placed in charge of the R.F.C.'s ground-training with the rank of brigadier-general at the age of 27; but at least he was a professional soldier who had been wounded in action. (After the war he introduced greyhound racing to England.) C.A.H. Longcroft, Director of Air Training, was a major-general at 34: he was probably the original protagonist of the well-known story of the young general who, piloting his own plane on a visit of inspection to a training squadron, landed so badly that the squadron C.O., seeing only a young man in a flying helmet, peremptorily order him to take off again at once and try to make a better landing. John Salmond became Director General of Military Aeronautics on the Army Council and major-general at 36, much to the disgust of 40-year-old Major-General Sefton Brancker who had already been passed over for the appointment because he was 'too young and too junior to be a member of the Army Council'. When the Royal Air Force was formed from the Army's Royal Flying Corps and the Royal Naval Air Service, Salmond took command in France while Frederick Sykes became Chief of Air Staff (i.e. professional head of the service) in London at the age of 40: his minister proposed that he should be promoted to lieutenant-general but this was apparently opposed by his colleagues on the Air Council.[23]

What did *not* happen, except in the Australian and Canadian contingents and partly in the R.F.C., later R.A.F., was that men who had been lieutenants or captains or even civilians in 1914 became corps or army commanders by 1918: but this did not happen in any other army either. Pietro Badoglio, the officer who obtained the most rapid promotion to high command in any army during the war, had already been a lieutenant-colonel when Italy entered the war in May 1915. Bearing in mind that British lieutenant-colonels and colonels were generally rather younger than their French or German counterparts and, because of colonial wars, possessed more actual combat experience, there seems no particular reason why junior officers or colonial militiamen should have been promoted over their heads. The notion that the juniors or the colonials might include some brilliant military geniuses was little more than journalistic fantasy. After the war, Liddell Hart, in his obituary of Monash in *The Daily Telegraph*, attributed to 'some of the most distinguished senior officers whom I know' the opinion that:

---

[23] For Jenkins's pre-war career see *Hansard: House of Commons* vol. 103 col. 1207 speech by Noel Pemberton-Billings 25 Feb. 1918; an early published version of the story about the young general ordered to make a second attempt at landing properly is in A. Cunningham Reid *Planes and Personalities: A Pot Pourri* (1920) p. 23 – Longcroft is not actually named however; Norman McMillan *Sir Sefton Brancker* (1935) p. 160 memo Oct. 1917; Sir Frederick Sykes *From Many Angles: An Autobiography* (1942) p. 218.

he had probably the greatest capacity for command in modern war among all who held command in the last war. If that war had lasted another year he would almost certainly have risen from commander of the Australian corps to commander of an army; he might even have risen to be Commander-in-Chief. If capacity had been the determining factor he would have done so.

This view bears little examination however. In describing the successful Australian offensives in 1918 Monash wrote:

> fixity of plan engendered a confidence throughout the whole command which facilitated the work of every Commander and Staff Officer . . . the more nearly such a battle proceeds according to plan, the more free it is from any incidents awakening any human interest . . . It is for this reason that no stirring accounts exist of the more intimate details of such great set-pieces as Messines, Vimy, Hamel and many others. They will never be written, for there is no material on which to base them. The story of what did take place on the day of battle would be a mere paraphrase of the battle orders prescribing all that was to take place.

Monash in fact made a success of the style of generalship which had failed so conspicuously and so bloodily at Passchendaele and the Somme, and had no interest in the problem that exercised the German general staff throughout the war, that of responding rapidly to unexpected emergencies and exploiting unexpected opportunities. A generation earlier the older Moltke had written:

> No plan of operations can deal at all safely with the first encounter with the main enemy force. Only the layman expects to see in the course of a campaign the consistent carrying out of a plan settled in advance, considered in every detail and adhered to until the end.

But of course, by the elder Moltke's standards Monash *was* a layman, a layman who had achieved a mastery of one kind of warfare, but still a long way from being an all-round expert on modern warfare.[24]

IV. Left-Overs from Queen Victoria's Little Wars: Kitchener and Hamilton

The career of Monash and others shows that the British Army was more open to fresh blood than most. Yet however long it seemed at the time, the war lasted only fifty-one months – less than the time it takes to get this book written and published – and the top commanders were inevitably men who had established their careers before the war.

[24] Liddell Hart in *Daily Telegraph* 9 Oct. 1931 p. 8, cf David Lloyd George *War Memoirs* (6 vols 1933–36) vol. 4 p. 2267–8, vol. 6, p. 3382; Sir John Monash *The Australian Victories in France in 1918* (1920) p. 51, 227; Helmuth Graf von Moltke *Moltkes Militärische Werke* (4 vols in 13 parts Berlin 1892–1912) vol. 4 Part 1 p. 71: written in late 1870s.

The five leading, one might say representative, personalities of the British Army during the 1914 – 1918 war form two opposed groups. Lord Kitchener, Secretary of State for War till lost at sea when H.M.S. *Hampshire* was mined off the Orkneys in 1916, Field-Marshal Sir John French, Commander of the British Expeditionary Force on the Western Front till the end of 1915, General Sir Ian Hamilton, Commander of the Gallipoli invasion in 1915, were not only generals who had made brilliant reputations before and during the Boer War but also represent different aspects of an individualistic, unsystematic conception of warfare which was absurdly inappropriate to the conditions of 1914–1918. General Sir William Robertson, who effectively replaced Kitchener as the government's military adviser and policy-maker when he became Chief of the Imperial General Staff late in 1915, and General Sir Douglas Haig who succeeded French in command of the B.E.F. at the same period were much more attuned to the era of mass organization: so well attuned indeed that they became part and symptom of it.

It was Kitchener who saw the war most clearly for what it was, yet most lacked in the ability to adjust to it. His military career had been spent almost entirely outside Europe, in backward, underdeveloped societies where distance and communication were the major impediments to military operations and where the superior skill of British or British-trained mercenaries was a key factor for all that it was in perpetual danger of crumbling under the burden of the climate. With a staff of two or three devoted and energetic subordinates he could operate a Toy Town-sized professional army hundreds of miles up the Nile, but he had no training or experience to prepare him for the task of handling armies of millions, shunted back and forth on the dense railway networks of northern Europe in accordance with schedules issued by faceless military bureaucrats. And having always commanded against troops deficient in tactical training, and being in any case an engineer officer with little tactical training himself, he had no grip on the tactical problems of war with a skilled foe who was ready to exploit the logic of the latest military technology. Kitchener saw, before anyone else in leading authority other than Douglas Haig, that it would be a long war, requiring laborious preparations that had to be set on foot at once if a victory was to be secured in the future:

> When a war of this magnitude breaks out, the President of the Board of Trade should immediately be made Joint Secretary of State for War, Supply Department ... The old-fashioned little British Army was such an infinitely small proportion of the world's demand that looking after its equipment was not much more difficult than buying a straw hat at Harrods. But now I am going to need greater quantities of many things than have ever been made before.

In drawing up his orders for Sir John French's little army on the continent, he clearly envisaged a rapid build-up of a force which from the outset was to operate in cooperation with, not under the control of, the French Army:

> I wish you distinctly to understand that your command is an entirely independent one, and that you will in no case come in any sense under the orders of any Allied General.

His decision to raise the huge citizen armies known at the time as the Kitchener Army or New Army was made without even consulting his colleagues. He saw that it would necessarily be a war of attrition, fought with the resources of whole nations till victory was achieved by exhaustion:

> It is the German people you are fighting . . . There will be no break-through. You must lean against this line, press it, hit it as hard as you can, bend it. Some day you will find it is not there, going back, but you *will not* break through.

He even understood the essential tactical problem, for all that he was unable to conceive of a tactical solution:

> the only way to make a real success of an attack is by surprise. Also . . . when the surprise ceases to be operative, in so far as the advance is checked and the enemy begin to collect from all sides to oppose the attackers, then, perseverance becomes merely a useless waste of life.[25]

Nevertheless Kitchener was temperamentally incapable of managing the machine which he was forcing into existence. Sir Ian Hamilton later wrote:

> K. hated organization with all his primitive heart and soul, because it cramped his style.
> K. was an individualist. He was a Master of Expedients; the greatest probably the world has ever seen. Whenever he saw *any* organization his inclination was to smash it.

Sir Archibald Murray, who served under Kitchener as an almost powerless Chief of the Imperial General Staff, referred to him as 'that past master of disorganisation'. Murray recorded that Kitchener never saw the Army Council, or even the three military members (himself as C.I.G.S., the Quarter-Master-General and Adjutant-General) together as a group, but instead would summon them to his room one at a time, 'telling each of them as little as possible, whilst he kept the threads in his own hands'. His long service in climates that were said to be morally debilitating, and perhaps

---

[25] Duncan Crow *A Man of Push and Go: The Life of George Macaulay Booth* (1965) p. 71; Sir Frederick Maurice *Lessons of Allied Co-Operation: Naval Military and Air, 1914–1918* (1942) p. 174; John Charteris *At G.H.Q* London 1931 London 1931 p. 137, letter diary 9 Feb 1916; Sir Ian Hamilton *Gallipoli Diary* (2 vols 1920) vol. 2 p. 1–2 Kitchener to Hamilton 11 July 1915. Kitchener's remarks in July 1915 may be compared with the verdict of the committee of senior officers under Lieutenant-General W.M. St. G. Kirke, circulated to army officers 'as a basis for thought and study' in April 1933: 'our reading of the Official Histories indicates with almost unrelieved monotony that persistence in an attack with tired and weakened units has been a failure, and that piling up infantry has merely meant piling up casualties. Generally speaking an operation which has once failed will not succeed without the introduction of a new factor, and that factor is seldom more infantry.' Public Record Office WO 33/1305 *Notes on Certain Lessons of the Great War* p. 14. Crown Prince Rupprecht of Bavaria had concluded that a breakthrough was virtually impossible as early as mid-October 1914 cf Rupprecht von Bayern *Mein Kriegstagbuch* ed. Eugen von Frauenholz (3 vols Munich [1929]) vol. 1 p. 220, 19 Oct. 1914.

also the malevolent cast in his eye, contributed to a reputation for wondrous deviousness. 'He is quite remarkably astute and untruthful, in all matters big and small', one Cabinet colleague noted, and a professional diplomat concluded that he 'was oriental in his method and if there were two ways to proceed, one straight and the other crooked always preferred the crooked one'. Osbert Sitwell saw him as 'a god, slightly gone to seed'; perhaps the truth was simply that he was an ageing colonial veteran, increasingly out of his depth.[26]

In part because he allowed himself to become involved in the Gallipoli – or Dardanelles – adventure and then could not bring himself to end it, Kitchener gained the reputation of having an unsteady grasp of strategy; but the worst of it was that with his disdain for consultation and discussion it was never very clear if he even had a strategy or grasp of strategic principles. Ironically, Kitchener's lack of directness and spasmodic mode of asserting himself enabled Winston Churchill to seize the credit – later the discredit – for the Gallipoli expedition, which was both Kitchener's departmental responsibility and, originally, Kitchener's own idea. By the second half of May 1915 Churchill was urging Asquith, the Prime Minister, 'Let me stand and fall by the Dardanelles – but do not take it from my hands.' It is true that Churchill had given the possibility of Gallipoli landing the benefit of his imagination in September 1914: 'a Russian Army Corps cd easily be brought from Archangel, from Vladivostok, or, with Japanese consent, from Port Arthur, round to attack the Gallipoli position. No other military operations are necessary.' Yet by the beginning of the year Churchill had become much more interested in some great exploit in the Baltic. Sir Mark Sykes urged him to keep Gallipoli in mind:

> Wellington's campaign in the Peninsula was no mistake in our Napoleonic war, and here is another Peninsula far easier of access with far greater prizes in it, one of course must beware of parallels but the instance is to me too striking not to mention it.

But Churchill's attention was elsewhere, and though the naval bombardment of the Dardanelles and the allocation of ground troops to assist the Navy was decided on in the War Council in February 1915 it was Kitchener on his own responsibility who decided, initially, that the role of the troops should be merely to occupy Turkish coastal positions after they had surrendered to the Navy, and then changed his mind and decided that the troops should be

[26] Hamilton *Gallipoli Diary* vol. 2 p. 238 fn. 1; Victor Bonham Carter *Soldier True: The Life and Times of Field Marshal Sir William Robertson, Bart* (1963) p. 132 Murray to Hamilton *post* 1918 and cf. criticisms of Dardanelles Commission Interim Report published in *Times* 9 March 1917 p. 10c; Edward David ed. *Inside Asquith's Cabinet: From the Diaries of Charles Hobhouse* (1977) p. 231, 23 March 1915; Public Record Office FO 800/175 Sir Francis Bertie, *aide memoire* of conversation with Asquith 17 Aug. 1916; Osbert Sitwell *Great Morning: Being the Second Volume of Left Hand, Right Hand! an Autobiography* (1948) p. 262.

used to assault the Turkish shore defences if they failed to surrender tamely once the Navy had carried out its bombardment.[27]

Kitchener's chosen instrument at Gallipoli, General Sir Ian Hamilton, had nothing in common with Kitchener except lack of the management skills necessary for handling a large army. One suspects indeed that Hamilton, whom, it was said, 'K. despises and would gladly kick round Horse Guards Parade', both bemused and bored Kitchener. There was a pinchbeck *gai sabreur* quality about Hamilton that was more likely to appeal to someone of Churchill's romantic temperament, and indeed in his journalist days Churchill had published an eulogistic book about Hamilton:

> His mind is built upon a big scale, being broad and strong, capable of thinking in army corps, and if necessary in continents, and working always with serene smoothness undisturbed alike by responsibility or danger.

When Kitchener told the War Council that he was thinking of Hamilton for the Dardanelles command, Churchill wrote to Kitchener enthusiastically endorsing his choice; but the tone of his letter shows that there had been no prior consultation between the ministers and that the selection of Hamilton was entirely Kitchener's doing. Hamilton was in fact the most distinguished and experienced general available. It is true that the Prime Minister thought he possessed 'a good deal of *superficial* charm but there is too much feather in his brain'. And it was noted that Hamilton's appointment to the Dardanelles command 'does not inspire universal confidence, but he may have qualities superior to the engaging graces for which he is principally known'. But these were civilian criticisms: Kitchener, being quite impervious to Hamilton's charm, thought only of his nominee's military reputation, which was excellent.[28]

Hamilton belonged essentially to the *fin de siècle*, that mood, rather than a movement, which in the 1890s attempted to resurrect and rehabilitate the less solid aspects of the Renaissance. Hamilton was the *fin de siècle* version of the Renaissance soldier scholar. He was thin, handsome, elegant, rather fey. A bullet through the wrist at Majuba Hill had reduced his left hand to a skeletal, semi-paralyzed fin, adding to the suggestion of effeteness and asymmetry about him. He was exceptionally brave; it was said that in the Boer War he would have been recommended for the V.C. on three separate

---

[27] Gilbert *Winston Spencer Churchill* vol. 3 p. 464 Churchill to Asquith 21 May 1915; ibid. vol. 3* p. 95 Churchill to Sir Edward Grey 6 Sept. 1914: ibid. vol. 3* p. 583 Sir Mark Sykes to Churchill 26 Feb 1915; for a good recent account of the formulation of policy in the Gallipoli campaign see Ruddock F. Mackay *Balfour: Intellectual Statesman* (Oxford 1985) p. 255–268.

[28] Brock ed. *Letters to Venetia Stanley* p. 311 Asquith to Venetia Stanley 6 Nov. 1914; Winston S. Churchill *Ian Hamilton's March* (1900) p. 135; Gilbert *Churchill* vol. 3* p. 615 for minutes of 3 March 1915 meeting of War Council, and ibid. p. 629 for Churchill to Kitchener 4 March 1915; Brock ed. *Letters to Venetia Stanley* p. 257 Asquith to Venetia Stanley 30 Sept. 1914; Sir Almeric Fitzroy *Memoirs* (2 vols 1925) vol. 2 p. 591 21 April 1915.

occasions if he had not been so senior in rank. A charming conversationalist and prose stylist, he was nevertheless an enthusiast for his profession and only partly gave the impression that his chief wish was to reduce modern war to a branch of *belles lettres*.

When Hamilton discovered that the poet Rupert Brooke was a subaltern in his army, he was eager to snap him up for his personal entourage, but Brooke died from the effect of a mosquito bite two days before the army went into action and Hamilton had to be content with a would-be unforgettable image in his diary, 'our star is to be scrubbed bright with the blood of our bravest and best'. Brooke would have been a worthy soulmate. Shortly before he died he had written to the Prime Minister's daughter:

> I've never been quite so happy in my life, I think. Not quite so *pervasively* happy; like a stream flowing entirely to one end. I suddenly realize that the ambition of my life has been – since I was two – to go on a military expedition against Constantinople.

Indeed it was dreadfully banal to despatch merely to the other side of the English Channel, like day-trippers, regiments whose battle honours included Blenheim, Salamanca, the Pyrenees, Inkerman, Balaclava. Hamilton was definitely the right man to lead what was to have the most *poetic* venture of the war.[29]

Unfortunately a certain amount of organizational grip was needed even for a march on Constantinople. Of Hamilton's staff only the Chief of General Staff, Braithwaite, had worked with Hamilton before ('Quite characteristic of K.', Hamilton noted blithely.) For some days after his arrival in the eastern Mediterranean, Hamilton was without his Quarter-Master-General, Adjutant-General and Director of Medical Services. When they finally turned up he decided to abandon them at Alexandria while establishing his own H.Q. at Lemnos, nearer to the target area. Woodward, the Adjutant-General, attempted to protest but Hamilton refused to listen. When the heads of the staff department eventually reached Lemnos, they found that 'all administrative work was in a state of indescribable chaos. . . . everything, so far as A.G.s and Q.M.Gs. work was concerned, was in utter confusion'. Next the transport on which the Adjutant-General was installed was ordered to Tenedos and once there ordered not to leave. When finally Hamilton's staff was reunited Woodward found that there was no improvement:

> Even after the A.Gs and Q.M.G.s branches of the staff joined G.H.Q. there was an utter want of harmony between them and the General Staff . . . The C.G.S. worked in a watertight compartment and not a single conference took place between him and the A.G. and Q.M.G. until July 14th and then only at my urgent representation.

[29] Hamilton *Gallipoli Diary* vol. 1 p. 125, 23 April 1915; Geoffrey Keynes ed. *The Letters of Rupert Brooke* (1968) p. 622–3 Brooke to Violet Asquith [Feb. 1915].

Since the Adjutant-General was responsible for evacuation of the wounded and, with the Director of Medical Services, for the hospital ships, there was more to these complaints than the injured pride of the military bureaucrat; and of course it was not only the already wounded who were to suffer from Hamiliton's refusal to think about orderly organization.[30]

Afterwards Hamilton pretended blandly that the logistic mess had not really been anything to do with him; referring to the officer appointed to sort out the lines of communication, he commented, 'they have put in a good fighting soldier, quite out of his setting, and merely because they did not know what to do with him in Egypt'. For Hamilton the absurdity, inefficiency and bumbling of British Army administration was merely a theme providing an artistic effect of contrast, possibly even comic relief, in the great heroic drama of the campaign: not something for which he, as Commander-in-Chief, bore the ultimate responsibility. Not of course that he was the only one at fault; one of his G.H.Q. staff wrote from the Dardanelles:

> When I look round the one thing that hits one in the face the whole time is the very small number of men who are efficient. What is the cause of it? Is it our system of education, is it something in the character that we are breeding? This is the one thing – *the one thing* – that has struck me over and over again. I am more impressed by it than I can tell you, and if only I could discern the cause of it, I would have learnt a valuable lesson.[31]

The first landings on the Gallipoli Peninsula, on 25 April 1915, were preceded by an Order of the Day in Hamilton's best style:

Soldiers of France and of the King.
> Before us lies an adventure unprecedented in modern war. Together with our comrades of the Fleet, we are about to force a landing upon an open beach in face of positions which have been vaunted by our enemies as impregnable.

It soon transpired that, where they existed, the Turkish defensive positions were indeed impregnable: but at one of the landing beaches they did not exist at all. When a British detachment established itself unopposed on Y beach, about four miles north-west of Cape Helles, Hamilton wondered whether to throw in the Royal Naval Division, and when the major landing at Cape Helles was unable to make headway against the Turkish defenders he considered transferring the forces there to Y beach. Then, inexplicably and without orders, Y beach began to be evacuated, apparently owing to a chain of misunderstandings. Hamilton wondered whether to halt the evacuation, but his staff, not much less out of their depth than he was, advised him against

[30] Hamilton *Gallipoli Diary* vol. 1 p. 19, 17 March 1915; Public Record Office CAB 19/31 'Statement before Dardanelles Commission by Maj. Gen. E.M. Woodward, D.A.G./M.E.F' p. 8–9 (p. 173–4 of folder).

[31] Hamilton *Gallipoli Diary* vol. 1 p. 366, 3 July 1915; Charles Forbes Adam *Life of Lord Lloyd* (1948) p. 73 George Lloyd to Blanche Lloyd [1915].

this: 'the staff are clear against interference when I have no knowledge of the facts', he noted, as if this were some sort of excuse.[32]

As a result of the lost opportunity at Y beach the invasion became pinned down on two widely separate beaches. There is no doubt that the British were completely surprised by the quality of the Turkish troops; but why they should have been so surprised is itself something of a mystery. A generation earlier Kitchener himself had written in almost hyperbolic praise of the soldiers who had astonished the world by their valour in the Russo-Turkish war of 1877:

> These Turkish soldiers are perfect heroes, enduring any hardships without a murmur. Always ready to fight, never conquered except by overpowering numbers, their motto might well be, 'While we have life we will fight.'

Turkey's defeat in the First Balkan War in 1912 had however altered received opinion on the fighting quality of the Turks, and it seems to have been assumed that Ottoman society was so wretchedly decadent that the Turkish Army had simply deteriorated further since 1912 rather than, as would have been expected elsewhere, taken measures to improve itself: 'The Turkish Army is not a serious modern army . . . ill-commanded, ill-officered and in rags . . . not of the quality which distinguished them forty years ago in the Shipka Pass.' On the very eve of the Gallipoli landings the Secretary of the War Council wrote, 'it is supposed that the Turks are short of ammunition and they did not fight very well in the recent Balkan wars'. But in the event they turned out to be quite as gallant and resilient as their grandfathers and fathers of 1877.[33]

Hamilton consoled himself for this disillusionment with some belle-lettristic racialism; looking over one battalion of his army, he noted:

> [they] would serve very well as picked specimens of our race; not so much in height or physique, but in the impression they gave of purity of race and distinction. Here are the best the old country can produce; the hope of the progress of the British ideal in the world; and half of them are going to swap lives with Turks whose relative value to the well-being of humanity is to theirs as is a locust to a honey-bee.

But honey bees are normally noted for their superior organizational and logistic arrangements as compared to locusts, and Hamilton had thrown

---

[32] Hamilton *Gallipoli Diary* vol. 1 p. 120, 21 April 1915 (the French contingent carried out a diversionary landing at Kum Kale on the Asiatic mainland, near the site of the ancient city of Troy); ibid. vol. 1 p. 147, 26 April 1915.

[33] 'A visit to Sophia and the Heights of Kamerleh – Christmas 1877' [signed H.H.K] *Blackwood' Edinburgh Magazine* vol. 123 p. 194–200 (Feb. 1878) at p. 200; C.E. Callwell *Field Marshal Sir Henry Wilson: His Life and Diaries* (2 vols 1927) vol. 1 p. 129–30 Oct. 1913 for 'not a serious modern army. . . . ill-officered and in rags', Public Record Office CAB 42/1/29 memo by Lord Esher 27 Jan. 1915 for 'forty years ago in the Shipka Pass'; Hankey *Supreme Command* vol. 1 p. 302, memo 11 April 1915. For the systematic underrating of the Turks see D. French 'The Origins of the Dardanelles Campaign Reconsidered' *History* vol. 68 (1983) p. 210–224.

ashore over 40,000 specimens of the imperial master race with remarkably few of the material advantages that had made Britain successful in the past. Hamilton's forces had only a quarter of the establishment of 18-pounder field guns allocated to the British forces on the Western Front and, when larger guns began to arrive in June, it was found that some of them had been used at Omdurman, that much of the ammunition was of a new type for which fuse keys and range tables were lacking, and that the gun carriages of the eight 60-pounders were too weak to stand the recoil of firing. Before leaving London, Braithwaite, Hamilton's Chief of General Staff, had asked Kitchener for aircraft: Kitchener had responded promptly 'Not one!' By the time of the first landings Hamilton had actually managed to assemble nineteen aircraft (apart from some naval seaplanes) but fourteen of them were too underpowered or worn-out to be of any operational use. Hamilton had not even been provided with the available intelligence material on the Dardanelles, though this included a detailed survey of Turkish defences made in the spring of 1914 and reports from the British Vice-Consul at Çanakkale, a town on the coast of Asia Minor directly opposite the Gallipoli Peninsula. Hamilton no doubt thought all this was Kitchener's fault: he was that sort of commander.[34]

After three months of heavy fighting, the British had still scarcely enlarged their beach heads, but the material inadequacies of the expedition were beginning to be remedied. By now about half the Turkish Army was tied down by the landings, including four battalions of its elite corps, the so-called Constantinople Fire Brigade (*Itfaiye Alai*), and it was close to the end of its resources. Although the long-suffering Turkish soldiers exclaimed cheerfully, 'this is no real war, we get something to eat every day', many of them developed scurvy as a result of their rudimentary diet, and their few available sand bags had to be used to patch worn out uniforms, clothing and webbing stripped from dead British soldiers also being used; even the Turkish staff officers had to depend on maps taken from the British dead, their own being quite inaccurate and in any case in short supply. But as the British consolidated their material superiority, the weakness of their command structure simply became more apparent. The arrival of more divi-

---

[34] Hamilton *Gallipoli Diary* vol. 1 p. 207, 9 May, 1915; ibid. vol. 1 p. 90–91 and vol. 2 p. 279–291 Appendix 1 Brigadier Gen. Sir Hugh Simpson Baikie's Statement on Artillery, at p. 281–2, 284–5 for artillery situation; ibid. vol. 1 p. 8, 14 March 1915 and vol. 1 p. 110–111, 15 April 1915 for aircraft situation; Robert Rhodes James *Gallipoli* (1965) p. 53–4.

For proto-racism in the British Army see also Colonel G.F.R. Henderson *The Science of War: a Collection of Essays and Lectures, 1892–1903* (1904) p. 126, 130. On p. 130 Henderson writes, 'that a capacity for conquest is inherent in the English-speaking race, it would be useless to deny'. Hamilton, incidentally, was later a leading appeaser and Hitler's overnight guest at Berchtesgaden in August 1938, when he was convinced that the Germans wanted peace. On 11 Feb. 1939 he told a conference of the British Legion at Caxton Hall,' there were no rulers who kept their fingers more constantly on the pulse of their people than did the dictators' (*Times* 13 Feb. 1939 p. 19g).

sions necessitated the establishment of an intermediate tier of command, at army corps level, and the choice of corps commanders was limited by the fact that Sir Bryan Mahon, who had raised and now commanded the 10th (Irish) Division, was half-way up the list of lieutenant-generals and, as he later demonstrated, was quite capable of resigning his division rather than serve under a corps commander junior to himself. Hamilton noted:

> Excluding Indians, Marines and employed men like Douglas Haig and Maxwell, there *are* only about one dozen British service Lieutenant-Generals senior to Mahon, and, of that dozen, only two are possible – Ewart and Stopford! There *are* no others.

Sir John Ewart, the G.O.C. in Scotland had 'never approached troops in fifteen years' and was thought by Hamilton to be out of the question: 'he would not, with his build and constitutional habit, last out here for one fortnight'. Consequently the Hon. Sir Frederick Stopford, commanding the Second Army, Central Force, at Tunbridge Wells, was assigned the Gallipoli theatre: his first task was to lead a new landing at Suvla Bay to coincide with a drive inland from the Anzac beach-head further south.[35]

Hamilton did not take his corps commanders into his confidence, let alone set up a conference of corps and divisional commanders, and briefings were delayed till the last possible moment so that even senior officers had little idea of what was intended. Hamilton's orders to Stopford emphasized the consolidation of a new beach head as 'your primary objective'; an advance inland was to be made only if circumstances were favourable. By skimping preliminary discussion of the operation, Hamilton failed to ensure that Stopford realized that the whole object of the new landing was to make an advance inland, and that the securing of the beach was simply a preliminary, not a required end in itself; equally Hamilton denied himself the opportunity

---

[35] Hans Kannengiesser *The Campaign in Gallipoli* [1928] p. 149; ibid. p. 192–3 for outbreaks of scurvy, ibid. p. 143–4, 157 for use of sandbags and clothing stripped from the British dead; Otto Liman von Sanders *Five Years in Turkey* (Annapolis 1927) p. 114 for use of captured maps; Hamilton *Gallipoli Diary* vol. 1 p. 306–7, 16 June 1915.

By this period armies in all westernized countries were organized in *divisions* of 12–15,000 men, usually commanded by a major-general. Two or more divisions formed a *corps*, usually commanded by a lieutenant-general. Two or more corps formed what in English is called an *army*, which must be distinguished from *army* in the sense of the whole military organization generally. Italian has two words for the two meanings of army – *armata* for the formation comprising several corps, *esercito* for the general sense. German has the word *Armee*, adopted from the French, to denote the formation comprising several corps, but this word was formerly used by the Austrians to indicate their whole land force, the Germans preferring the more ethnic term *Heer*.

Hamilton's command originally comprised, apart from a French division detached on the mainland, two normal divisions and two understrength divisions, one of each category forming the Australian and New Zealand Army Corps, the other two reporting directly to Hamilton. By August 1915 there were two more corps commanders and an additional nine divisions.

of discovering that even before the landing Stopford had no faith in the scheme of sending his men straight from the beaches into unreconnoitered hills.[36]

Hamilton spent 7 August 1915, the day of the new landing, on the island of Imbros. Next day, when he wished to visit the Peninsula to inspect the success of his great stroke, there was no ship available to convey him till 4.15 p.m. On arrival at Suvla Bay he found Stopford's army sunbathing on the beach, with no sign as yet of any significant Turkish presence inland. Hamilton urged an immediate advance; Stopford hinted at 'many tactical reasons against it, especially the attitude of his Generals who had told him their men were too tired'. In his subsequent writing up of his diary Hamilton sketched in a deft portrait of Stopford as a smug, lethargic blimp: thus when Hamilton asked to see the divisional commanders, he recorded Stopford's response as follows:

> nothing, he said, would please him more than if I could succeed where he had failed, but would I excuse him from accompanying me; he had not been very fit; he had just returned from a visit to the shore and he wanted to give his leg a chance.

Hamilton's pen-portrait is in fact consistent with Stopford's own recollection of his assessment of the situation, which considering the initial lack of substantial Turkish resistance in his sector can only be termed defeatist:

> My own opinion was, that once we failed to get through on the 7th and 8th on first landing, the chances of our getting through with only raw troops and quite inadequate field artillery were very remote.

Indeed by the morning of 9 August the opportunity was lost: the Turks had had time to bring up reinforcements. Hamilton lamented, 'What it would have meant to have had a man imbued with the attack spirit at the head of this IXth Corps would have been just – victory!', and, a little later, added the gloss, 'Mahon's seniority has been the root of this evil!'[37]

It cannot really be claimed in Hamilton's defence that his responsibility as overall commander prevented him from taking over direct command of one of his three beach heads. From his G.H.Q. at Imbros he had not been exercising any useful supervision of his other two beach heads in any case, and when he belatedly intervened at Suvla Bay he immediately began overriding Stopford's authority as corps commander, insisting on seeing the divisional commanders, ordering a night attack which Stopford considered to be on too wide a front and, according to Stopford, instructing the latter not to commit the 54th Division 'without direct orders from G.H.Q., and then the manner in which I was ordered to employ it did not appeal to me at all'. From that point on, though still nominally in command of the landing, Stopford

[36] Rhodes James *Gallipoli* p. 245–8.

[37] Hamilton *Gallipoli Diary* vol. 2 p. 58, 8 August 1915; ibid. vol. 2 p. 63 same date; ibid. vol. 2 p. 64 same date; Public Records Office CAB 19/31 Sir Frederick Stopford's statement p. 6 (p. 19 of folder): Hamilton *Gallipoli Diary* vol. 2 p. 102, 13 Aug. 1915 and p. 105, 14 Aug. 1915.

disclaimed responsibility: 'I did not have a very free hand', he complained afterwards with typical understatement. Part of the art of generalship is to do uncomfortable things before they become necessary, not afterwards: as with the mix-up on Y beach on the day of the original landing Hamilton preferred to allow the horse to bolt before betraying agitation about the stable door. His belated intervention at Suvla Bay merely underlines the fact that it had been his responsibility to set the operation up more systematically in the first place.[38]

Meanwhile, Hamilton's own personal entourage were becoming increasingly impatient with him. The failure of the original landings in late April and the confusion of the lines of communication that accompanied them had shaken his staff's confidence in him, and their dwindling esteem had communicated itself to the frontline units: by late July it was reported, 'The whole tone of the officers about Ian Hamilton is almost beyond belief'. With the failure at Suvla Bay, his staff officers gave him up for hopeless and one of them, Guy Dawnay, who had maintained influential contacts since his pre war service on the staff of the Committee of Imperial Defence, came to London in September to advise the government against accepting Hamilton's view of the situation. Dawnay later wrote:

> Sir Ian Hamilton was of the old chivalrous school, his war was to be 'run on gallantry' – the Englishman never knows when he was beaten, and all that. So he blinded himself to the truth.

Others were less inclined to speak politely of Hamilton's bias towards self-dramatizing fantasy; by the time he was replaced in October it was being said in London that 'his arrogance and fatuity have become a byword in the army'.[39]

Eventually, in December 1915 and January 1916, the Gallipoli beach heads were evacuated without loss, in a series of embarkations that were the only adequately planned and professional part of the whole campaign. There remains a question mark over the whole business, as to whether it was not from the outset quite unrealistic and overambitious, but it was certainly Hamilton's mismanagement (supplemented from a distance by the mismanagement of Kitchener) that guaranteed the failure.

V. Sir John French

The third of the military triumvirate which set the tone for Britain's contribution to the World War during 1914 and 1915 was Field Marshal Sir John French. One of those short men with a long stride, peppery,

[38] Public Record Office CAB 19/31 p. 4, 6 (p. 17 and 19 of folder).

[39] Fitzherbert *The Man who was Greenmantle* p. 164 letter of Aubrey Fitzherbert 24 July 1915; Rhodes James *Gallipoli* p. 315; ibid. p. 138; Fitzroy *Memoirs* vol. 2 p. 607, diary 2 Oct. 1915.

plethoric, mercurial, vivid, occasionally hysterical, and sporting a particularly fine example of the bushy moustache cultivated by all generals (of whatever nationality) at this period, French was perhaps temperamentally even more out of place than Kitchener and Hamilton, though on the whole was rather less disorganized in his staff arrangements; in the smooth transfer of the British Expeditionary Force to France he took with him most of the War Office Heads of Department, including the Director of Military Operations, Director of Military Training, Director General of Military Aeronautics, Director of Supplies and the head of the Intelligence section, leaving behind the administrative chaos which Kitchener evidently found so congenial. This was later characterized as 'the only amateurish feature of the whole plan . . . illogical and unpardonable', though obviously it greatly facilitated the operations of B.E.F. during the opening phases of the campaign on the Western Front. French's problem was less isolation and lack of organization than a marked disposition to show himself jealous, resentful and uncooperative towards those he had to work with.[40]

He was jealous evidently of Smith-Dorrien, one of his corps commanders, who showed a better appreciation than French himself of the tactical situation during the retreat from Mons and fought the successful rearguard action at Le Cateau; after complaining in various quarters that Smith-Dorrien's messages to him were 'wordy, "windy" and unintelligible', French sent him home in May 1915. He was also jealous of Kitchener; as the only field-marshal with a field command in 1914 French was the ranking officer in the belligerent armies but Kitchener, though holding a civilian office, was higher up the list of British Army field-marshals, and this disturbed French enormously. When Kitchener visited France at the beginning of September to urge French not to withdraw his troops too far, he came in uniform, and French complained bitterly: 'To send another FM out here to lecture me (he came in FM's uniform!) seems to me to be a sign of distrust and it *hurts* me.' Next he began complaining about Kitchener's 'worrying' letters: 'They might be written by an old woman.' Various other squabbles followed, each requiring the careful mediation of mutual friends. After one such awkwardness French remarked pompously, 'I shall do my utmost to remember that I served with Lord Kitchener in South Africa, and enjoyed his trust and confidence in a degree which I can never forget', but South Africa was probably part of the problem: at the end of the Boer War Kitchener had confessed, 'if I had felt myself strong enough with the British public I would have sent French home'.[41]

Finally, and despite his name, French got on badly with Frenchmen (though

[40] Norman Macmillan *Sir Sefton Brancker* (1935) p. 62.

[41] Richard Holmes *The Little Field-Marshal: Sir John French* (1981) p. 284; Gilbert *Churchill* vol. 3* p. 81 French to Churchill 4 Sept. 1914; Holmes *The Little Field-Marshal* p. 271; King's College London, Liddell Hart Papers 11/1931/3 note of conversation with Edmonds 1931, cf. Maurice V. Brett and Oliver Viscount Esher ed. *Journals and Letters of Reginald Viscount Esher* (4 vol. 1934–8) vol. 3 p. 244 Esher to Kitchener 23 May 1915.

he liked France and later settled in Paris). '*Au fond*, they are a low lot, and one always has to remember the class these French generals come from', he informed Kitchener. It was reported to the King that he 'has never really sincerely, and honestly concerted with the French, while they regard him as by no means a man of ability or a faithful friend, and therefore they do not confide in him'.[42]

French was genuinely distressed by the huge casualties his troops suffered, and, not being the kind of man to run an army with maps and memoranda, seemed to have difficulty coming to grips with the vast relentlessness of the new-style warfare of the Western Front. His talents were less those of a general than of a cavalry captain who has set himself to cut a dash in society. He held the 'advanced' views of the metropolitan 'fast' set on such matters as spiritualism and marital fidelity and, while he was commanding in France, a letter of condolence he wrote to a society lady whose lover had experienced 'the great change' at Ypres developed into an epistolary flirtation which was consummated in Bayswater during a brief leave in January 1915; he wrote to this lady friend from his G.H.Q almost daily, signing himself *Peter Pan*, and far from concealing from her his military plans, announced on the eve of one battle, 'Tomorrow I shall go forward with my War Cry of Winifred'. Nevertheless it is not obvious that French was, in his particular style, a less able general than his Chief of General Staff, Sir William Robertson, or his senior subordinate in the field, Sir Douglas Haig, for all that these two methodical plodders were soon making a point of magnifying his military inadequacies.[43]

From the very beginning Haig had showed himself more attuned than French to the scope and necessary planning dimensions of the new warfare. On 5 August 1914 a War Council had been held in Whitehall and Haig, stating 'we must organise our resources *for a war of several years*', urged withdrawing a percentage of officers and N.C.O.s from the Expeditionary Force to assist the training of reinforcements at home. French, counting on a quick and glorious campaign, and temperamentally unsuited to the sort of cautious, painstaking preparations which Haig considered professional, had opposed this view. This disagreement seems to have crystallized certain doubts that had been forming in Haig's mind. In a conversation with the King before leaving for France, he expressed 'doubts' as to whether French's 'temper was sufficiently even or his military knowledge sufficiently thorough to enable him to discharge properly the very difficult duties which would devolve upon him'. Privately Haig noted, 'In my own heart, I know that French is quite unfit for this great command at a time of crisis in our Nation's history'. Two days later Haig confided more thoughts on this subject to his diary: 'His military

[42] Philip Magnus *Kitchener: Portrait of an Imperialist* (1961) p. 290 French to Kitchener 15 Nov. 1914; Bonham Carter *Soldier True* p. 125 Robertson to Stamfordham (the King's secretary) Aug. 1915.

[43] Holmes *The Little Field-Marshal* p. 278–9 cf 276–7, 281 for French's wartime romance.

ideas often shocked me when I was his Chief of Staff during the South African War.' Haig also confided these opinions to his staff officers, who transcribed them faithfully in their letters home:

> He thinks French quite unfit for high command in time of crisis ... He says French's military ideas are not sound; that he has never studied war; that he is obstinate, and will not keep with him men who point out even obvious errors.[44]

Haig did not organize a whispering campaign against French – that was not his style – though he did complain to one influential visitor of his 'effete and incompetent' chief's 'jealousy and even malice', and he was probably aware that junior officers in the army were saying 'they would greatly prefer Gen. Haig as C. in C. to Sir John French who never, not even at the Battle of Ypres, came anywhere really near the firing line'. To Haig it must have been obvious that French would soon get himself into trouble with the government without the need for undignified manoeuvring by senior subordinates like himself. It seems that Kitchener was thinking of replacing French with Sir Ian Hamilton as early as 1 November 1914, more than four months before the decision was made to send Hamilton to the Dardanelles. Somewhat oddly the erratic Kitchener voiced essentially the same criticisms as the methodical Haig: French, he said, was 'not a really scientific soldier; a good capable leader in the field, but without adequate equipment of expert knowledge for the huge task of commanding 450,000 men'. Nor was it only the soldiers who were dissatisfied; by July 1915 the King was noting in his diary, 'it would be better for all concerned if the C.-in-C. were changed', and it was the King who first told Haig, not the other way round, that he 'had lost confidence' in French.[45]

Part of the King's information with regard to French's performance as field commander derived from letters written to his secretary, Lord Stamfordham, by French's Chief of General Staff, Lieutenant-General Sir William Robertson. French had not wanted Robertson as C.G.S. and had initially been distant and off-hand with him. In March 1915 he had ordered Robertson out of his

[44] Blake *Private Papers of Sir Douglas Haig* p. 69, diary 5 Aug. 1914; ibid. p. 70, 11 Aug. 1914, ibid. p. 72, 13 Aug. 1914, John Charteris *At G.H.Q.* (1931) p. 10–11, 16 Aug. 1914.
According to Gerald J. De Groot *Douglas Haig, 1861–1928* (1988) p. 148, 150, 415 n. 27 Haig's diary for 4–12 Aug. 1914, with its disparaging references to French, was not written till *after* the war: it exists only in typescript.
[45] Alan Clarke ed. *'A Good Innings': The Private Papers of Viscount Lee of Fareham* (1974) p. 140; David ed. *Inside Asquith's Cabinet* p. 221, Charles Hobhouse's diary 8 Feb. 1915 quoting a Captain Younger of the Coldstream Guards (probably Lt. J.M. Younger gazetted temporary captain 1 Sept. 1915 but perhaps already holding acting rank in February); Callwell *Sir Henry Wilson* vol. 1 p. 186, diary 1 Nov. 1914; Brock ed. *Letters to Venetia Stanley* p. 488 Asquith to Venetia Stanley 18 March 1915; Holmes *The Little Field-Marshal* p. 299 citing King George V's diary for 1 July 1915 and Blake ed. *Private Papers of Sir Douglas Haig* p. 97, 14 July 1915.

office in order to be left alone with Haig, merely so that he could tell the latter he 'meant to see his Army Commanders alone occasionally, because R. had tried to insist that F. should not see any of his subordinates unless he (R.) was present as C.G.S.!' Without any particular encouragement from Haig, Robertson had come round to Haig's opinion, which was that Haig would make a much better Commander-in-Chief than French. Matters almost came to a head at the end of September 1915 when the big offensive at Loos achieved a temporary breakthrough which could not be exploited because French was holding the reserves too far back. After a spirited exchange on the subject Haig noted bitterly in his diary, 'It seems impossible to discuss military problems with an unreasoning brain of this kind'. Robertson, visiting London two weeks later, received an unexpected phone call from Stamfordham who 'asked him by the king's orders whether he did not consider the time had come to replace Sir J. French'. Robertson saw the King, and undertook to discuss the matter with Haig on his return to France. When Robertson and Haig met for consultation the latter duly gave his opinion: 'I had come to the conclusion that it was not fair to the Empire to retain French in command of the main battle front.'[46]

Another week passed. The King visited the Expeditionary Force on the Western Front. Various corps commanders took the opportunity to complain to His Majesty about French, and Robertson gave the opinion that it was 'impossible to deal with French, his mind was never the same for two consecutive minutes'. Haig told the King:

> French's handling of the reserves in the last battle, his obstinacy and conceit, showed his incapacity. . . . it seemed to me impossible for anyone to prevent him doing the same things again. I therefore thought strongly, that, for the sake of the Empire, French ought to be removed.

Haig even wrote a detailed critique of French's handling of the Battle of Loos which was later passed on to the King.[47]

Haig may have expected Kitchener, as Secretary of State for War, to take the final initiative in replacing French; to Kitchener's assistant military secretary Haig wrote early in November 1915, with regard to the Commander-in-Chief, 'The fact is he does not understand the size or nature of the war in which we are now engaged here in France – Will he ever learn?' But it was the King himself who afterwards claimed the credit for sacking French. Kitchener was out of the way inspecting the Gallipoli position when the final decision was made. It was not Asquith's style to undertake unpleasant tasks if he could possibly avoid them; someone – and it seems most likely that it was the King, speaking on behalf of his officer corps – forced the decision through;

---

[46] Blake ed. *Private Papers of Sir Douglas Haig* p. 88, 17 March 1915 cf. Alan Clarke *The Donkeys* (1961) p. 32–33; Blake ed. *Private Papers Of Sir Douglas Haig* p. 105, 2 Oct. 1915; ibid. p. 108, 17 Oct. 1915.

[47] Blake ed. *Private Papers of Sir Douglas Haig* p. 109, 24 Oct. 1915; Holmes *The Little Field-Marshal* p. 310.

it merely fell to Asquith to summon French to a formal interview to tell him of his dismissal. The busy-body Lord Esher even told French the subject of the interview in advance, but when French and Asquith met the former refused to discuss the B.E.F. command and would only talk about how impossible it would be for him to take over as G.O.C. Home Forces with Kitchener at the War Office; he seemed to assume that his departure from France, though decided in principle, was to be postponed till some indefinite future date to avoid commotion. It finally needed a letter from the President of the Local Government Board to tell French that his resignation was required forthwith.[48]

Kitchener only learnt of French's dismissal when passing through Paris on the way home from the eastern Mediterranean. 'He knew nothing of the events at G.H.Q.!', noted Esher, 'He made no comment.' French's removal may even have been deliberately timed to coincide with Kitchener's absence: his colleagues had lost confidence in him too, and perhaps feared he would introduce some unaccountable complication into the business, perhaps appoint the wrong chap to succeed French. Or perhaps it was merely the King's and Asquith's way of warning Kitchener that they could easily envisage running the war without him. Though Kitchener remained vastly popular with the general public, opposition to him was building up in Whitehall; about this time Lloyd George was busy denigrating Kitchener to press barons like Lord Northcliffe:

> Lloyd George assures me that this man is the curse of the country. He gave me example after example on Sunday night of the loss of life due to this man's ineptitude.[49]

Shortly afterwards Kitchener was obliged to surrender his role as adviser to the Cabinet on strategy to Robertson, who was appointed Chief of the Imperial General Staff. Haig had urged that Robertson should be appointed C.I.G.S. with the sole right of advising the Cabinet on the conduct of the war, in a discussion with Lord Esher on 14 November, and Robertson had sketched out his proposed role in one of the letters he had written to Stamfordham regarding French's low reputation at G.H.Q.:

> The Govt must receive the best military advice at home (Hankey & Callwell are I suppose the chief advisors. Ridiculous!) The S. of S. for War has not the time to study matters & formulate advice, in addition to his other work. The General Staff, with a trusted & competent head, should be allowed to function & to do the work for which it was designed, & which it alone can do.

[48] George H. Cassar *The Tragedy of Sir John French* (Newark 1985) p. 279, quoting Haig to F.S. Robb 7 Nov. 1915. See ibid. p. 280–286 for a good recent account of French's removal, and also Holmes *The Little Field-Marshal* p. 310–312 and Gilbert *Winston S. Churchill* vol. 3** p. 1311 Churchill to Clementine Churchill 4 Dec. 1915.
[49] Esher *Journals and Letters* vol. 3 p. 289, journal 29 Nov. 1915; British Library Add. 62245 f. 17 Northcliffe to Geoffrey Robinson copy 30 Dec. 1915.

The King himself urged:

> important advantages would be secured by the transfer of Sir W. Robertson to the post of C.I.G.S. making him responsible only to the *War Council* for whose information and advice he and his staff would deal with all matters of strategy and conduct of war – Lord K. would as S. of S. for War be in the same position as any other member of the Council of War to criticise and collectively to accept or reject these recommendations; but *not* to interfere with the decisions of the C.I.G.S. before they reach the War Council.

Henceforth method, system, planning, staff college expertise and carefully supervised teamwork would replace the guessing and gambles and inattention to detail, and the displays of temperament, which had characterized the Kitchener- French era: henceforth the war would become truly professional.[50]

On 5 June 1916, as preparations for the Somme offensive neared their conclusion, Kitchener, the symbol of the old order, was finally removed from the scene altogether. Shut out of the strategic planning, he had undertaken to go to Russia to discuss Entente supplies to that country: three hours out of Scapa Flow the cruiser H.M.S. *Hampshire*, on which he was embarked, struck a German mine off Marwick Head, Orkney, and sank in fifteen minutes. Though in sight of watchers on land, the *Hampshire* went down in mountainous seas which prevented any attempt at rescue, or even the launching of lifeboats; there were only twelve survivors. Kitchener's body was never found. 'Anyway, thank God, he died as near to fighting as was very well possible to a man of his rank and position', remarked one staff officer. The two leading military personalities of the British Empire were now Sir William Robertson and Sir Douglas Haig.[51]

VI. The New Professionalism

The history of Britain's military effort in 1916 and 1917 is the history of the partnership of Robertson as Chief of the Imperial General Staff and Haig as principal theatre commander. Robertson was unique amongst the higher reaches of the British Army in having risen from the ranks. In contemporary memoirs he is usually depicted as dropping his aitches in conversation, like a stage cockney – he was in fact from Lincolnshire – and some of the remarks of his critics betray a disagreeable snobbishness: 'simply a man of detail, excellent

[50] Blake ed. Private Papers of Sir Douglas Haig p. 113, 14 Nov. 1915; King's College London, Robertson Papers 1/12/3 draft: David R. Woodward *Lloyd George and the Generals* (Newark 1983) p. 80 quoting Bodleian Ms Asquith 4, Stamfordham to Asquith 3 Dec. 1915. Lieutenant-Colonel Maurice Hankey of the Royal Marine Artillery was secretary of the War Committee; Major-General Charles Callwell, author of *Small Wars; Their Principle and Practice*, was Director of Military Operations (Both had temporary rank: Hankey was a substantive captain, Callwell a substantive colonel).

[51] Macmillan *Sir Sefton Brancker* p. 129.

in a grocer's shop filling up ledgers', and 'a good troop sergeant-major'. A vestige of social unease may possible explain a certain deference to the impressively pseudo-aristocratic Haig. The latter was certainly as conscious of Robertson's background as anyone else, noting in his diary, 'He means very well and will succeed I am sure. How much easier, though, it is to work with a gentleman'. Lloyd George claimed in his war memoirs that 'whenever I saw these two men together, I felt that Haig dominated, over-awed and almost bullied [Robertson]'. This appears a typical example of the sly artistic flourishes that enliven Lloyd George's careful, systematic denigration of the Robertson-Haig partnership, but may in fact have been perfectly true; at the Liddell Hart Centre at King's College London one may compare the letters Robertson sent to Sir Launcelot Kiggell, Haig's Chief of General Staff in France, with the *drafts* of the private letters Robertson sent to Haig, and one finds that the actual letters sent to Kiggell are written in a hasty and illegible scrawl, as if it were assumed that Kiggell as a mere subordinate was obliged to take pains to decipher them, while the drafts prepared for Haig, though also written very rapidly, are in a much more carefully formed and legible hand, as if Robertson was holding himself to attention whenever he sat down to write even a draft letter to Haig.[52]

Lloyd George also claimed of Robertson that his 'oracular monosyllables and grunts misled much abler men than himself'. He was preeminently one of those people who preferred to keep his mouth shut and his ears open, which may or may not have been a lower-middle-class habit formed in his earlier years as an N.C.O. and as a subaltern promoted from the ranks. When visiting Haig's G.H.Q. it was noticed that, 'Robertson was tongue-tied at dinner, neither agreeing nor disagreeing with anything anybody said. He likes to write his opinions, not discuss them'. The more articulate French generals simply grated on Robertson's nerves; for example he considered Foch 'rather a flat-catcher, a mere professor, and very talkative'. This habitual taciturnity was of course a major disadvantage in dealing with politicians, especially those who disagreed with him as consistently as Lloyd George. As Robertson himself explained:

> Where the politician goes wrong is in wanting to know the why and the wherefore of the soldier's proposals, and of making the latter the subject of debate and argument across the table. You then have the man who knows but cannot talk discussing important questions with the man who can talk but does not know, with the result that the man who knows usually gets defeated in argument and things are done which his instinct tells him are bad.

Presumably the fact that the uncommunicable knowledge was a matter of 'instinct' rather than reason did not make explanation any easier. Curiously

---

[52] *Memoirs of Captain Liddell Hart* vol. 1 p. 358, note of conversation with Lloyd George in 1932; F.P. Crozier *The Men I Killed* (1937) p. 88; De Groot *Douglas Haig* p. 214 quoting unpublished section of Haig diary 13 Feb. 1916; Lloyd George *War Memoirs* vol. 2 p. 782.

enough, the Austrian chief of staff, Franz Conrad von Hötzendorf, seems to have had exactly the same problem in his discussions with his German opposite number, General Erich von Falkenhayn; it frequently happened that after the more articulate Falkenhayn had wheedled verbal agreement out of the less verbally agile Conrad he would receive a memo from Conrad presenting a whole new set of arguments. Whether this meant that Conrad (or Robertson) knew more about generalship than Falkenhayn is however a moot point.[53]

In any case it was not Robertson's inability to talk, but his inability to stretch his staff college dogmas to the realities of a war between peoples which was the problem. For him, as with Haig, it became axiomatic that as the principal enemy was Germany the principal strength of Britain should be concentrated on the front where German strength could most readily be challenged; this was 'that fundamental principle of war which can never be neglected without serious detriment, namely, the principle of concentration at the decisive point'. But Robertson and Haig were perfectly capable of asserting the complete opposite when it suited their purpose; when Lloyd George visited French's G.H.Q. in February 1915 to broach the question of transferring troops to the Dardanelles, 'Robertson pronounced the plan to be "good strategy" and convinced French of its soundness', and in July 1916 Haig told Joffre, the French commander-in-chief, 'the rules of war clearly emphasised that you should attack where your enemy in battle had shown himself weakest and not where he was strongest'. Nevertheless the two generals insisted on a policy of battering against the strongest part of the enemy front, and united in resisting any 'sideshows' that aimed to attack the enemy at his weaker points; mainly, it seems, because they objected to the principle of subtracting anything from the forces under Haig's control. It seems however that Robertson was somewhat less steadfast than Haig in asserting that the decisive front was necessarily defined as the one where Haig commanded; when he visited Haig's G.H.Q. in June 1917 Robertson, evidently unnerved by the constantly reiterated arguments of Lloyd George, insisted on discussing the probable cost in lives of the forthcoming Passchendaele offensive and attempted to interest Haig in Lloyd George's then favourite scheme of sending heavy guns to Italy, urging, 'it is possible that Austria would make peace if harassed enough'. Haig regarded this as tantamount to betrayal; though Robertson wrote apologetically in October 1917, 'you are perhaps a little disappointed with me in the way I have stood up for correct principles', Haig later complained to his wife:

he has not resolutely adhered to the policy of 'concentration on the Western

[53] Lloyd George *War Memoirs* vol. 2 p. 779; Charteris *At G.H.Q.* p. 134, 31 Jan. 1916; Holmes *The Little Field Marshal* p. 243 (a 'flat' was slang, since *circa* 1760, for a gullible person: a 'flat-catcher' was a professional swindler); David R. Woodward ed. *The Military Correspondence of Field Marshal Sir William Robertson, Chief of the Imperial General Staff, December 1915–February 1918* (1989) p. 100 Robertson to Repington 31 Oct. 1916; A. von Cramon *Unser Österreich-Ungarischer Bundesgenosse im Weltkriege* (Berlin 1920) p. 23.

Front' – he has *said* that this is his policy, but has allowed all kinds of resources to be diverted to distant theatres at the bidding of his political masters.

Robertson later regretted his back-sliding and wrote after the war 'compromises and half-measures . . . though harmless in appearance . . . will sooner or later drag him [a C.I.G.S.] down to perdition . . . bad strategy can never be good policy'. But by then it was too late; Haig did nothing to interfere when Robertson was sacked early in 1918 and the two men had little to do with each other thereafter. Haig had no use for friends who had served their purpose: as Sir John French had already discovered.[54]

Even if it is true that Robertson took his lead from Haig, for two years it was Robertson who had the day-to-day responsibility for dealing with civilian ministers and of resisting their ill-educated attempts to find an alternative strategy. It is possible however that the whole question of an alternative strategy was regarded by the politicians as simply a means of by-passing Robertson and Haig. The issue on which Robertson was finally sacked, that of establishing a Supreme War Council controlling the entire military resources of the Entente, seems little more than a pretext; after Robertson was removed Lloyd George simply lost interest in the project. Lloyd George's unsuccessful attempt in February 1917 to subordinate Haig to the French theatre commander Robert Nivelle seems to have been a tactical expedient of the same kind. In his *War Memoirs* Lloyd George wrote of Robertson:

> From the moment he became C.I.G.S. he hindered and thwarted at every turn every effort to concentrate and distribute the aggregate power of the Allies in such a way as to achieve the surest and speediest results.

But Lloyd George's efforts to coordinate Allied strategy seem mainly to have been aimed at undermining Robertson: and yet, objectively, the complaint is entirely justified.[55]

The Central Powers – Germany, Austria-Hungary, Turkey and later Bulgaria – were much more responsive to the need for centralized military control than the Entente. This was not because the obstacles to close cooperation were any smaller on their side. Despite the identity of language the German and Austrian military had little knowledge of one another and attempts to coordinate their planning, begun only in 1909, had broken down by 1914. Conrad von Hötzendorf, the Austro-Hungarian chief of staff, disliked the Germans; Hindenburg, the German commander on the Eastern

[54] Sir William Robertson *Soldiers and Statesmen, 1914–1918* (2 vols 1926) vol. 1 p. 263 General Staff summary 1 June 1916; Taylor ed. *Lloyd George: a Diary by Frances Stevenson* p. 29, 8 Feb. 1915; Esher *Journals and Letters* vol. 4 p. 38, Haig to Joffre 7 July 1916; Blake ed. *Private Papers of Sir Douglas Haig* p. 236, 9 June 1917; ibid. p. 259 Robertson to Haig 9 Oct. 1917 and p. 283 Haig to Lady Haig 5 Feb. 1918; Robertson *Soldiers and Statesmen* vol. 2 p. 303–4.

[55] See Frances Stevenson's account of the origins of the idea of the Supreme War Council, Taylor ed. *Lloyd George: A Diary by Frances Stevenson* p. 164, 6 Nov. 1917; Lloyd George *War Memoirs* vol. 2 p. 782.

Front till 1916, despised the Austrians. Nevertheless, under the pressure of Russian attacks German units were used to stiffen Austro-Hungarian formations, and soon German chiefs of staff were being appointed to assist Austrian commanders, though this in itself involved a major problem since in the Habsburg Army the chiefs of staff functioned mainly as assistants to the commanding generals with much less share in final decision-making than was customary in the German Army. Conrad von Hötzendorf consistently opposed the appointment of German officers to staff and command positions, but the policy was as consistently supported by the Emperor Franz Joseph; in any case by 1916 the Germans constituted the numerical majority of the combined Austro-German forces on the Eastern Front.[56]

The Turks were much less dependent on the support of German troops, yet though it became increasingly apparent that they were fighting a war of racial supremacy, from the beginning they welcomed German military and technical expertise; by January 1918 the Turkish Army chief of staff, two army commanders and seven of the twelve heads of staff departments were German officers. The Germans also provided a small air component, flying machines marked with black squares since the black crosses marking German and Austrian planes on the European fronts would hardly have been suitable for an Islamic army. Few Turks spoke even mediocre German; Hans Kannengiesser, when at the head of the 9th Turkish Division at Gallipoli, found that his official interpreter was a Bosnian commissioned from the ranks who spoke both German *and* Turkish poorly. Yet the collaboration was remarkably effective; Liman von Sanders, the senior German officer in the Ottoman Army, had frequent 'unpleasant conflicts' with Enver Paşa, the Turkish war minister, and also reported 'much unpleasant friction' between the Turkish generals and German staff officers, but the Turkish officers often supported the Germans against Enver, and the Germans sometimes supported Enver against his Turkish subordinates, so that it would seem that the disagreements were more on professional than national grounds. When Generalfeldmarschall Colmar von der Goltz died of typhus in 1916 (with two German doctors in attendance) there were immediate reports in Entente press that he had been assassinated by a Turkish officer, and Liman von Sanders himself later claimed that a staff officer forced on him by Enver had tried to poison him. Yet as early as August 1916, before any agreement had been reached on the question of unified command, with the Russians at Trebizond and Erzerum, and with Kemal's premature offensive towards Muş and Bitlis still in the balance, the Turks sent two crack divisions to reinforce the Austro-German frontline south-east of Lvov, and later three divisions were despatched to Wallachia and two more to join the German-Bulgarian forces in

[56] Norman Stone 'Moltke-Conrad: Relations between the Austro-Hungarian and German General Staffs, 1909–1914' *Historical Journal* vol. 9 (1966) p. 201–228 at p. 203–4, 226–7; Hans Seeckt *Aus Meinem Leben* ed. Friedrich von Rabenau (2 vols Leipzig 1938–40) vol. 1 p. 401–2; Rothenburg *Army of Francis Joseph* p. 202.

Macedonia. Enver, with Franz Joseph and King Ferdinand of Bulgaria, also helped secure the decision, in the autumn of 1916, to unify strategic control on all fronts under the German High Command, despite the opposition of people like Conrad von Hötzendorf.[57]

On the Entente side, as early as 28 January 1915 Kitchener suggested to the War Council 'some central authority where all the Allies were represented' to coordinate strategy, and there were four Anglo-French conferences at prime ministerial level in 1915 and a further three in 1916; there was also a meeting of French and British leaders with the Italian, Serbian and Belgian premiers in Paris in March 1916, resulting in 'a great deal of talk and froth and a Press Conference'. Robertson repeatedly insisted on the need for 'one central directing authority' but seemed inclined to suppose that this directing authority should be himself – certainly not any foreigner:

> We must get a larger share in the control of the war. The attitude of the British Empire up to the present time has been lamentable. We are contributing far more to the war than any Power and we exercise less general control than any.

This was also Lloyd George's view: 'We were ... entitled not indeed to impose our ideas upon our Allies or to dictate to them, but to impress and insist much more than we did.' But since both France and Russia maintained larger armies in the field it would have been difficult to secure recognition for any British claim to acknowledged leadership of the Entente, especially as the Battle of the Marne had restored the military reputation of France to an almost Napoleonic elevation: when Rumania entered the war and was badly defeated in 1916 it was the French who provided the military mission, of 277 staff

---

[57] Ulrich Trumpener 'Suez, Baku, Gallipoli: The Military Dimensions of the German-Ottoman Coalition, 1914–1918' in Keith Neilson, Roy A. Prete eds *Coalition Warfare: An Uneasy Accord* (Waterloo Ontario 1983) p. 29–51 at p. 34 and p. 49–50 Appendix B, cf Ulrich Trumpener *Germany and the Ottoman Empire, 1914–1918* (Princeton 1968) p. 373–4; Kannengiesser *Campaign in Gallipolli* p. 129, 139 and cf. Appendix 1 on p. 271–6; Liman von Sanders *Five Years in Turkey* p. 9, 40, 112–6; *Times* 2 May 1916 p. 8c and 7 June 1916 p. 9e, cf, Hans von Kiesling *Mit Feldmarschall von der Goltz Pascha in Mesopotamien und Persien* (Leipzig 1922) p. 183–4; Rhodes James *Gallipoli* p. 254; G.E. Silberstein *The Troubled Alliance: German-Austrian Relations, 1914 to 1917* (Lexington 1970) p. 320–3, and cf [Paul] von Hindenburg *Out of My Life* (1920) p. 182.

Despite Tsar Ferdinand's cooperation on the unified command issue the Bulgarians proved the most recalcitrant of Germany's allies, refusing to conduct any major aggressive operations; Ludendorff's later remarks, 'I found it difficult to get a clear idea of the psychology of the Bulgarian people', and, 'both their language and their national sentiment remained foreign to us', seem to have been masterly understatements: Ludendorff *My War Memories, 1914–1918* (2 vols [1919]) vol. 1 p. 253, 395 and cf. Seeckt *Aus Meinem Leben* vol. 1 p. 377–8. The Germans had to accept the holding down of the Salonica front as a worthwhile use of Bulgaria's admittedly limited manpower. Ministère de la Guerre *Les Armées Françaises dans la grande guerre* (11 'tomes', numerous volumes of annexes Paris 1923–1937) 'tome' 5 vol. 1 p. 531–5 shows that on 1 April 1917 Germany fielded the equivalent of 219 divisions, Austria-Hungary 79, Turkey 48 and Bulgaria 14.

officers distributed down to regimental level, which was intended to revitalize Rumania's military effort (this was the only counterpart, on the Entente side, of the distribution of German officers through the armies of the Central Powers). Nevertheless Robertson's concentration on the Western Front and grudging acceptance of the Palestine and South East Africa campaigns meant that, after the failure of the Gallipoli adventure, the British had little to contribute in the way of ideas and resources to other European theatres in any case; the build up of troops, under French command, at Salonica was principally a defensive response to the advance of the Central Powers in the Balkans and despite some wild claims that, 'The road to Berlin passes through the Balkans, Budapest and Vienna!' was never seriously regarded as having the decisive potential that had originally been seen in the Gallipoli venture. Robertson, of course, insisted on the 'utter uselessness – of killing Bulgars'. The result of Robertson's concentration on the Western Front was not only the slaughter on the Somme and at Passchendaele but also Britain's failure to utilize those boasted advantages in financial and naval power to impose a British shape on the war as a whole; for it does seem that the nature of Britain's superiority in economic resources made an alternative to the Western Front by no means impracticable.[58]

VII. Sir Douglas Haig

Instead of the uninhibited sweep and grandeur of Winston Churchill's and Lloyd George's strategic conceptions there was the head-on slog of the Western Front with which the name of Sir Douglas Haig is indissolubly linked.

According to folk tradition Haig was a man of breath-taking stupidity. This seems a little extreme: an officer could hardly rise to the head of an army of over a million men without some sort of ability, though equally a general with such an army could hardly fail to defeat an enemy inferior in numbers and equipment unless he was not as able as he might have been. At any rate there has been some attempt to rehabilitate Haig since the 1960s, most notably

---

[58] Hankey *Supreme Command* vol. 2 p. 482, cf. Lloyd George *War Memoirs* vol. 1 p. 404; Robertson *Soldiers and Statemen* vol. 1 p. 262 General Staff summary 1 June 1916, cf vol. 1 p. 193–5, memo to C.I.G.S. 31 Oct. 1915 and vol. 1 p. 196–206 memo to Asquith 5 Nov. 1915; ibid. vol. 1 p. 287, Robertson to Lloyd George 8 Dec. 1916; Lloyd George *War Memoirs* vol. 2 p. 782; G.A. Dabija *Armata Română Răsboiul Mondial (1916–1918)* (4 vols Bucharest [1928]–1936) vol. 4 p. 27 and Alexandru Averescu *Notiţe Zilnice din Războiu (1916–1918)* (Bucharest [?1935]) p. 315–350 Anexa A, espec. p. 316–8 and p. 335–7 Anexa No. 3 to Anexa A.E. Sylvia Pankhurst *The Home Front: A Mirror to Life in England during the World War*, (1932) p. 361 quoting *Britannia*, the organ of Emmeline and Christabel Pankhurst; Public Record Office WO 79/66 Papers of the Earl of Cavan. 'Epitome of conversation with General Sir W. Robertson . . . May 5 1916'. This continues: 'Joffre and Briand got quite excited – called him an "homme terrible".'

in John Terraine's biography *Douglas Haig: The Educated Soldier* of 1963. Terraine's sub-title is a manifesto in itself. He argues for example that Haig had a genuine interest in modern military technology, what Haig himself called 'modern scientific discoveries': the phraseology does not however suggest a high degree of technological sophistication. Apparently Haig worked it out all by himself that one of the problems with tanks would be communication and control on the battlefield. He was also perhaps the first to suggest the construction of special landing craft to launch tank attacks from the sea. Terraine's view of Haig receives ample support from the contemporary who, beyond all others, could claim to be the embodiment of intellectualism in public life: Lord Haldane. Haldane, formerly Secretary of State for War and Lord Chancellor, wrote to Haig in January 1917:

> You are almost the only military leader we possess with the power of thinking, which the enemy possesses in a highly developed form. The necessity of a highly trained mind, and the intellectual equipment which it carries, is at last recognized among our people.

Other contemporaries, not of course persons like Haldane who had been driven from public office because of their high regard for the German intellect, but perhaps equally credit-worthy, had a quite different estimate of Haig's mental abilities. Lloyd George's published opinion was that, 'I never met any man in a high position who seemed to me so utterly devoid of imagination'. His private view was, more concisely, that Haig was 'utterly stupid'. Lloyd George had an axe to grind of course, and perhaps only a politician like Lloyd George who had made his way by blarney would insist that 'a man who cannot explain his ideas and is almost tongue tied, cannot possibly be a great man'. Brigadier-General Sir James Edmonds, who served on Haig's staff, eventually rising to be Deputy Engineer in Chief, and who afterwards wrote the Official History of Haig's campaigns, might be thought to be more objective, but his opinion was essentially the same as Lloyd George's:

> He was really above the average – or rather below the average – in stupidity.
> He could not grasp things at conferences, particularly anything technical.

Edmonds found the equally inarticulate Allenby much quicker on the uptake: 'He was not dull and slow like Haig, to whom at no time could one explain a matter.' Frederick Sykes, Chief of Air Staff in 1918, agreed, finding both Robertson and Haig 'slow to grasp new ideas, and devoid of imagination'. Brigadier-General Sir Hereward Wake thought that 'there is no one at G.H.Q. who has any brains or approves of brains in any one else'.[59]

---

[59] John Terraine *Douglas Haig: The Educated Soldier* (1963) p. 95–6; ibid. p. 220–1; Blake ed. *Private Papers of Sir Douglas Haig* p. 188 Haldane to Haig 4 Jan. 1917; Lloyd George *War Memoirs* vol. 4 p. 2267; *Memoirs of Captain Liddell Hart* vol. 1 p. 358, note of conversation with Lloyd George in 1932; King's College London, Edmonds Papers III/11/4 note of conversation with Lloyd George; King's College London, Liddell Hart Papers 11/1930/15

continued

Of course it did not help that Haig was a man who spoke little and did not finish his sentences; it was even said that his French improved so much during the war that it became more fluent than his English. (The French generals – even Nivelle who had an English mother and gratified Lloyd George by speaking English to him – stuck to French when talking to Haig; according to Sir Hubert Gough 'it was part of their technique never to speak English to a British officer, even if they could speak it fluently'.) Haig naturally disliked the garrulous Henry Wilson, Robertson's successor as C.I.G.S.: a 33-page memo from Wilson of 25 July 1918 'British Military Policy, 1918–19' was endorsed by Haig 'Words! Words! Words! Lots of Words! and little else'. The talkative Foch was, in Haig's opinion, merely a 'gasconading *blagueur*'.[60]

On the other hand he wrote lucidly and perspicuously, though without the belle-lettristic strivings of Sir Ian Hamilton, for all that his tutor at Oxford had been no less a person that Walter Pater. His diaries, letters and despatches, clear and to the point as they are, confirm that his was a mind of excruciating banality. They show that in this war which confronted the self-regarding conservatism and smugness of the Edwardian era with the horrors of a continent in dissolution, he was a smug Edwardian of the most thoroughbred type. His diary if full of the kind of remarks maiden aunts make in corners at Hunt Balls when the neighbourhood is going down: 'The truth is that there are not many officers in the French Staff with gentlemanly ideas'; 'Joffre has been weak and not quite straight'. General Pershing of the American Expeditionary Force was a pleasant surprise: 'I was struck by his quiet gentlemanly bearing – so unusual for an American'. But Lloyd George was an awful shock: 'How unfortunate the country seems to be to have such an unreliable man at the head of affairs in this crisis'. He told his staff as early as October 1914, 'You can't trust anyone who has ever been in Parliament'. Nevertheless he made Sir Philip Sassoon M.P. his private secretary, even though he was a Jew, because he had useful contacts in London, and he developed a considerable admiration for Asquith, whose fraudulent patrician manner evidently appealed to Haig. (Although he claimed the title of 39th Laird of Bemersyde, Haig's family owed its social position to the famous whiskey distillery business.) He

continued
note of conversation with Edmonds 8 Dec. 1930; Brian Gardner *Allenby* (1965) p. 75: but elsewhere Edmonds recalled Allenby as 'below the standard of intelligence' at Camberley: King's College, London Edmonds Papers I/2B/5a Edmonds to C.N. Barclay 7 April 1950; Sykes *From Many Angles* p. 192, cf. p. 105, 194; John Barnes and David Nicholson ed. *The Leo Amery Diaries* (2 vols 1980–1988) vol. 1 p. 213; 3 April 1918. For a recent thoughtful assessment of Haig see Travers *Killing Ground* p. 101–123.

   60 John Charteris *Field Marshal Earl Haig* (1929) p. 152: Neville Lytton *The Press and the General Staff* (1920) p. 66 also remarks on how good Haig's French was; Sir Hubert Gough *Soldiering On* (1954) p. 164, cf. Sir George Arthur *Not Worth Reading* (1938) p. 272–4; Sir James Edmonds et al., *Military Operations: France and Belgium* (14 vols plus appendix volumes 1922–48) 1918 vol. 4 p. 12; Hankey *Supreme Command* vol. 1 p. 339, 2 June 1915.

noted approvingly 'Mr. Asquith has such a clear and evenly balanced mind. Even in his cups he was never fuddled'.[61]

Haig's own life-style as commander-in-chief was one of stultifying routine, each day as much as possible like the one before, a carefully timetabled succession of paperwork, situation conferences, reports, exercise and simple, well-prepared meals: he lived, according to Major-General Fuller, 'like a mechanical monk.' It was said of the typical British H.Q., 'The atmosphere and furnishings were those of a London club in peacetime'. Not for Haig the elegant female visitors to Head Quarters who allegedly enlivened the life of the Austro-Hungarian High Command at Teschen, a thousand kilometres further east; though like the Austrian chief of staff Conrad von Hötzendorf Haig never visited the trenches, not being a man to waste time in idle curiosity or mudlarking. It was perhaps the mind-deadening repetitiveness and orderliness of Haig's style as commander-in-chief which is the measure of his attunement to the new warfare; whether he *understood* the new warfare in any intellectual sense is another question.[62]

Haig's capacity to tackle the vast responsibilities of his post was not strengthened by his tendency to surround himself with yes-men, a weakness he had complained of in Sir John French when still himself in a subordinate position. Sir Hubert Gough, Haig's youngest army commander, had a relatively high opinion of his chief: 'Haig had imagination – more ideas than most of the senior soldiers on the Western Front'. But Gough saw evidence of Haig's preference for yes-men in the mediocrity of the officers he appointed as his successive Chiefs of General Staff, Kiggell who 'served Haig as clerk, not as an executive instrument . . . no initiative or decision', and Lawrence who 'was very little better and had no grip on the situation'. Later Gough claimed 'in these vastly important directions of coordinating the operations of his five armies, Haig received little or no help from Lawrence'. Haig himself remarked complacently, 'I have to kick Lawrence along the whole time'. But that was the way Haig seemed to like it. Sir James Edmonds thought Sir Henry Horne, who was appointed to command the First Army in September 1916, 'owned his rise entirely to agreeing with G.H.Q. every time', and it was certainly Edmond's own experience that Haig did not encourage criticism; he later told Liddell Hart of an incident at one of Haig's daily situation conferences in October 1917 which both Edmonds and Lieutenant-Colonel S.W.H Rawlins of the Royal Artillery attended in the absence of their respective departmental heads – it was the period when the Passchendaele offensive was becoming bogged down:

[61] Blake ed. *Private Papers of Sir Douglas Haig* p. 136, 28 March 1916, ibid. p. 187, 20 Dec. 1916; p. 245 20 July 1917; p. 256 24 Sept. 1917; Charteris *At G.H.Q.* p. 50, 25 Oct. 1914; Blake ed. *Private Papers of Sir Douglas Haig* p. 116 Haig to Lady Haig 13 Sept. 1916. Haig's opinion of Asquith was not shared by all soldiers: 'Fancy the nation's leader being a drunken lawyer! and a liar to boot!' Imperial War Mueseum, Lt-Col. A.G. Burn diary p. 8, 4 Aug. 1915.

[62] Fuller *Memoirs of an Unconventional Soldier* p. 141, and cf Travers *Killing Ground* p. 103; John Morris *Hired to Kill* (1960) p. 47.

Rawlins frankly said to Haig that if he continued the offensive in the mud he would have no artillery left for his spring offensive next year. Haig went white, with anger, and said – 'Colonel Rawlins, leave the room'. When Edmonds ventured to say after Rawlins had gone that he was inclined to agree with him, Haig said, if less sharply, 'You go, too'. This was the only occasion when Edmonds heard anyone really stand up to Haig and tell him the truth.[63]

Of course it was not simply that no-one dared to contradict Haig: his loyal staff seemed for the most part desperately eager to encourage him in his views. Lloyd George, visiting G.H.Q. at about the time of the incident reported by Edmonds, recalled:

I found there was an atmosphere of unmistakable exultation. It was not put on. Haig was not an actor. He was radiant. He was quiet, there was no swagger. That was never one of his weaknesses, but he had the confident demeanour of a leader who was marching his army step by step surely and irresistibly, over-coming all obstacles, including good advice from Gough and Plumer [another of the army commanders] and the Prime Minister, forward to the ultimate triumph of the war. . . . The whole atmosphere of this secluded little community reeked of that sycophantic optimism which is the curse of autocratic power in every form.

This sounds a malicious exaggeration: yet one of the staff at G.H.Q. wrote of Haig after the war:

He exhales such an atmosphere of honour, virtue, courage, and sympathy that one feels uplifted like as when one enters the Cathedral at Beauvais for the first time.

If this is not an example of the sycophancy Lloyd George complained of, it would be difficult to say what it was.[64]

The self-delusion of Sir Ian Hamilton at Gallipoli had been betrayed by the scepticism of the entourage Kitchener had selected for him; Haig, having had time to assemble a staff he could trust, had much less problems with disloyal subordinates at G.H.Q., but this meant he had an even greater problem with

---

[63] *Memoirs of Captain Liddell Hart* vol. 1 p. 366 note of conversation with Gough 1935; Gough *Soldiering On* p. 159; King's College London Edmonds Papers III/14/6–7 quoting a remark of Haig's in March 1918; King's College London, Liddell Hart Papers 11/1929/15, note of conversation with Edmonds 23 Sept. 1929; ibid. 11/1938/59, note of conversation with Edmonds 26 May 1938; Lawrence had retired from the Army after the Boer War and had accumulated various directorships in the banking and gold-mining field; from 1926 he was Chairman of Vickers. His career as a tycoon suggests talents not altogether evident while Chief of Staff.

[64] Lloyd George *War Memoirs* vol. 4 p. 222–4; Lytton *The Press and the General Staff* p. 67. Even Liddell Hart, during the war years, wrote sycophantically of Haig as 'the greatest general Britian has ever owned', adding, 'We have produced fully a hundred first-rate generals': Brian Bond *Liddell Hart: A Study of his Military Thought* (1977) p. 18, and cf *Daily Express* 21 Dec. 1916 p. 4e, an article apparently by Liddell Hart under the pseudonym 'Regimental Officer'.

the recalcitrance of the facts which his subordinates loyally concealed from him. The principal concealer of facts at Haig's G.H.Q. was his Director of Intelligence, Brigadier-General John Charteris: a breezy, energetic, and elegantly cultivated Scot with the kind of subtlety of intellect which Conan Doyle had institutionalized in the detective story; Fuller described him as 'the kind of hail-fellow-well-met type; incautious, and what in slang is described as a "flat-catcher"'. Charteris had been on Haig's staff since before the war and enjoyed a symbiotic relationship with the Commander-in-Chief that was a good deal more intimate than the business partnership Haig maintained with Robertson. What Charteris gave Haig in this relationship was not merely optimism, not merely intelligence data specially tailored to suit Haig's prejudices and policies, but also the ruthless confidence of a completely unashamed mental dishonesty. Haig was of course not the only general whose staff let him down through their lack of contact with the front and through their anxiety to emphasize only intelligence material that suited their *a priori* views: this complaint was also made, for example, of the *ufficio situazione* at Cadorna's H.Q. in Italy. But Charteris's misrepresentation of reality went beyond over-selectiveness, beyond wishful thinking, even beyond conscious bias: he was quite unscrupulous about distorting the truth to suit his own purposes. His book, *At G.H.Q.*, compiled from a letter diary which, by-passing the censorship, he sent home periodically from Haig's Head Quarters, provides evidence of this. Under the dates 25 and 26 February and 1 and 5 March 1917 Charteris gives an account of how well abreast of developments he was during the sudden withdrawal of the German Army to the Hindenberg Line. Under 5 March, he writes:

> I wish it were possible to let the public know how well informed we have been on the whole matter of this retreat, and how accurate we were in our forecast of what the Germans were going to do. But that is impossible at present.

The papers of Lord Northcliffe now preserved in the British Library include the originals of several letters from Charteris at this period. On 2 March he wrote to Northcliffe:

> This sudden withdrawal of the Germans is most interesting. A great deal of it is, of course, due to the pressure exercised by our troops, but over and above this I think they must have some big plan which they are furthering by a withdrawal at the present moment.

On 14 March he wrote to Northcliffe:

> I wish it were permissible to let the British public know how well informed we have been on the whole matter of this retreat, and how accurately we now know exactly what the Germans are going to do. It is, of course, impossible to let it out because it would help the Germans.

Now people who write lots of letters often repeat turns of phrase like 'the whole matter of this retreat' – but not at nine-day intervals. The letter Charteris printed in *At G.H.Q.* as dated 5 March may have been written to his wife, or it may be an edited version of the carbon of his letter to Northcliffe, but it was not written on 5 March. On 5 March Charteris knew very little more about the German retreat than he did on 2 March: only after more than a week had passed was he able to inform Northcliffe that 'we now know exactly what the Germans are going to do'. By altering the dates he was able to pretend to the readers of *At G.H.Q.* that he had figured out the German plan significantly earlier than was really the case, thereby conveying the impression that he, and Haig's G.H.Q. generally, were much more on top of the situation than they actually were. Since Haig's G.H.Q. was itself run on the basis of pretending always that it was much more on top of the situation than was the case, one can reasonably assume that Charteris carried out his wartime duties as Director of Intelligence with as much regard for the truth as he showed later in compiling his book. One might add that Haig defended Charteris indignantly against the criticisms of Sir George Macdonogh at the War Office, complaining that Macdonogh's advice as Director of Military Intelligence was causing 'many in authority to take a pessimistic outlook, when a contrary view, based on equally good information, would go far to help this nation on to victory'.[65]

One of Charteris's motives for keeping up a correspondence with Northcliffe was to protect his own career. 'You asked me on Sunday whether I had heard anything to your detriment in Government circles', Northcliffe wrote to him on 11 December 1917 – an indication of how far Charteris's confined his attention to his military duties. Northcliffe went on:

> I have been informed indirectly that the members of Government consider that you have misled them by exaggerated statements as to decline of German morale and number of German reserves ... I am convinced that unless examples are made of those responsible and changes at once made in Head Quarters Staff the position of the Commander-in-Chief will be imperilled.

By the time Charteris received this he may already have seen a leading article in *The Times* for 12 December complaining of 'the fatuous estimates, *e.g.*, of German losses in men and *moral*, which have inspired too many of the published messages from France'. *The Times* was of course owned by Lord Northcliffe – and on the same day the Secretary of State for War wrote to

---

[65] Fuller *Memoirs of an Unconventional Soldier* p. 141, and see Ferninand Tuohy *The Crater of Mars* (1929) p. 132–4 for an account of Charteris by a member of his staff; Enrico Caviglia *La Dodicesima Battaglia [Caporetto]* (2nd edit. Verona 1934) p. 26–7; Charteris *At G.H.Q.* p. 201, 5 March, 1917 and cf p. 197–202; British Library Add. 62159 f. 149 Charteris to Northcliffe 2 March 1917; ibid. f. 164 same to same 14 March 1917 and cf King's College London Liddell Hart Papers 1/259/76 where Edmonds writes regarding Charteris's diary, 'It is whispered among the initiated that it is a fake'. (The best account of the information available to the Allies regarding the German preparations for withdrawal is Ministère de la Guerre *Armées Françaises dans la grande guerre* tome 5 vol. 1 p. 371–387); Christopher Andrew *Secret Service: the Making of the British Intelligence Community* (1985) p. 154; Michael Occleshaw *Armour against Fate: British Military Intelligence in the First World War* (1989) p. 347–8 suggests that part of the objection to Macdonogh was that he was a Roman Catholic, Papists being regarded with tribal suspicion by good Scots Presbyterians like Haig and Charteris.

Haig to say 'my view of Charteris as a public danger is shared by practically the whole of the Army'.[66]

Charteris was eventually replaced (after the war he wrote to Northcliffe asking for a job, beginning his letter artlessly, 'Possibly you may remember me. We met several times, when I was head of the Intelligence at G.H.Q.'); nevertheless, like Haig himself, he was to some extent being blamed for a whole system of which he was only a part. A good instance of the system at work is the army commanders' response to the huge casualty lists which appalled Lloyd George and indeed everyone at home. Thus General Rawlinson, G.O.C. Fourth Army, on the opening day of the Somme, which cost the British 57,000 casualties:

> The casualties have, of course, been heavy, but when we consider that 29 brigades – over 100,000 infantry – were taking part in the first assault I do not think that the percentage of losses is excessive.

It has been alleged that Rawlinson based this remark on the return of admissions to field ambulances up to midnight on 1 July 1916, which did not include the dead, the missing, or the thousands of wounded soldiers who were still lying out in the open in shell holes, and ditches; the returns showed 14,672 casualties but the real figure is stated by Rawlinson's biographer to have been 35,600, though even this is an understimate. But either Rawlinson was referring to casualties of 35,000 plus, or he had not noticed, or been informed, after two days that at least 20,000 men of his command were unaccounted for, or else he was deliberately implying a false picture. It rather seems the latter was the case. Informed observers very rapidly perceived that the Somme attack had been a catastrophe. In Whitehall Lloyd George and the secretary of the War Committee, Maurice Hankey, had concluded that it had been a costly failure by 3 July. Foch, it was reported on 5 July, 'does not think that Haig yet understands in what our attack failed, viz, not nearly sufficient concentration of fire before infantry attack'. Sir John French, now Viscount Ypres and G.O.C. Home Command, wrote in his diary:

> attempts are being made in high quarters to minimise our losses in the Somme battle . . .
>
> The results cannot be considered commensurate with the numbers engaged; the ammunition available; or the losses incurred. Attempts are being made everywhere to conceal the latter.

Amongst these attempts may be included a letter to the Queen from Lord Esher, too frequently the spokesman of G.H.Q.: 'A great deal is made of "casualties" but only a few seem to realise the tremendous achievements that

---

[66] British Library Add. 62159 f. 184 Northcliffe to Charteris carbon 11 Dec 1917; Randolph S. Churchill *Lord Derby: 'King of Lancashire'* (1959) p. 299 Derby to Haig 12 Dec. 1917.

are not to be measured by inches on the map.' Northcliffe, after a visit to G.H.Q. at the same period, told Lloyd George:

> The troops at the front do not consider the losses dear, in view of the fact that a breach in the German fortification has been made. The loss of young officers has been grievous, but compared with the disgraceful waste of life at Loos where nothing was gained, the one hundred and fifty thousand casualties of the battles of the Somme, which include many very lightly wounded men, are trivial.

Kiggell, Haig's Chief of General Staff – quite probably prompted by Esher and Northcliffe – circularized the army commanders early in August warning them that 'the casualties incurred by us last month are being grossly exaggerated'. The real casualties were, he claimed, only 120,000 over and above the normal wastage of recent months; he added 'Sir Douglas hopes that the truth can be made known quietly in conversation'. One might have thought 120,000 bad enough but in reality the killed and wounded in July were over 151,000 more than the average for April, May and June, and since the figures for June had been 78 per cent up on the figures for April it would have been truer to say that the July casualties were 160,000 up on normal wastage for recent months.[67]

Charteris, responsible not for drawing up the casualty lists but for assessing their significance relative to the enemy's situation, regarded the Somme as an unqualified success, and never once mentioned casualty figures in the letter diary reproduced in *At G.H.Q.* A year later he jotted down a curious remark:

> I have been out all day, up to the coast where we have taken a very nasty knock. It is the first German success against us since the Loos counter-attacks. . . . we have lost practically the whole of battalion, a real bad affair.

A minor German advance, involving the loss of a battalion, was 'a real bad affair;' a minor British advance involving the loss of the equivalent of *five hundred* British battalions was, in G.H.Q.'s view, a brilliant success.[68]

---

[67] British Library Add. 621159 f. 189 Charteris to Northcliffe 9 Dec. 1919, Sir Frederick Maurice *The Life of General Lord Rawlinson of Trent* (1928) p. 162, Rawlinson to Wigram 3 July 1916, cf ibid. p. 162 footnote by Maurice (who was D.M.O. during the war); Stephen Roskill *Hankey: Man of Secrets* (3 vols 1970–74) vol. 1 p. 286, diary 3 July 1916; Callwell, *Sir Henry Wilson* vol. 1 p. 287, diary 5 July 1916 (the point being that Foch had 850 heavy guns for eight miles of front, Rawlinson 629 for more than 16 miles of front); Gerald French *French Replies to Haig* (1936) p. 214–5, undated diary entries: the second entry is given in part, with the date 3 July 1916, in Gerald French ed. *Some War Diaries, Addresses and Correspondence of Field Marshall the Right Honourable the Earl of Ypres* (1937) p. 254; Esher *Journals and Letters* vol. 4 p. 45 Esher to Queen Mary 4 Aug. 1916; King's College London, Kiggell Papers V/31 copy 6 Aug. 1916, cf. Blake ed. *The Private Papers of Sir Douglas Haig* p. 157–8 Haig to Robertson 1 Aug. 1916, given under 3 Aug. 1916: it seems that G.H.Q. took several days to organize its attempts to 'whitewash' the Battle of the Somme; *Statistics of the Military Effort of the British Empire during the Great War, 1914–1920* (1922) p. 257–8.

[68] Charteris *At G.H.Q.* p. 234, 11 July 1917.

VIII. The New Warfare of the Industrial Era

The failure of the British High Command (and the French and Italian High Commands) even to *notice*, so to speak, the appalling toll of casualties resulting from their plans was of course only a part and symptom of a larger problem: the problem posed in the way industrialized society's greater power to mobilize economic resources had increased the potential scale of warfare till it had, paradoxically, immobilized itself by its own vastness.

One French general claimed:

> The Great War will appear to people in the future as an unshaped model, a first rough proof, as it were, of the industrialized war which the progress of science and industry has imposed upon the nations.

Ernst Jünger compared the 'clatter of the looms at Manchester', to 'the rattle of the machine guns at Langemarck'. C.R.W. Nevinson – before the war a cosignatory with Marinetti of 'A Futurist Manifesto' – claimed, 'To me the soldier was going to be dominated by the machine . . . I was the first man to express this feeling on canvas', and this claim is confirmed by the paintings he executed after being invalided back home from service with a medical unit in France: 'The Mitrailleuse' and 'Motor Ambulance Driver' show the individual man reduced to a robot-like component of a machine, while 'Column on the March', 'Returning to the Trenches' and 'A Dawn: 1914' show the individual absorbed into a mass of humanity that has itself become a machine-like entity. Already at the end of the nineteenth century it was being claimed that the 'soldier today is part of a great machine which we call military organization'. When the war came Ernst Toller and his fellow soldiers 'learned that the tyranny of technology ruled even more omnipotently in war than in peace time [and] discovered that in the modern war of material the triumph of the machine over the individual is carried to its most extreme form'.[69]

---

[69] Jean de Pierrefou *Plutarch Lied* London 1924 p. 180; Ernst Jünger *Der Arbeiter: Herrschaft und Gestalt* (Hamburg 1932) p. 131 – in German 'Das Klappern der Webstuhle von Manchester, das Rasseln der Maschinengewehre von Langemarck'. Langemarck, 8 Km N.N.E. of Ypres was the scene of heavy fighting on 21–24 October 1914, though what the Germans thought was the machine gun fire was for the most part rapid musketry of the British regulars. Jünger himself saw fierce action at Langemarck, in July 1917 cf. *The Storm of Steel* (1929) p. 161–189; C.R.W. Nevinson *Modern War Paintings* with an essay by P.G. Konody (1917) frontispiece, p. 35, 37, 59, 63 Konody's essay p. 8, 16–21 for Futurist influence on Nevinson; Elihu Root *The Military and Colonial Policy of the United States: Addresses and Reports* (Cambridge, Mass. 1916 – one of 8 vols. of *Addresses and State Papers* published 1916–24) p. 3 speech at Chicago 7 Oct. 1899. Ernst Toller, quoted in Hannah Hafkesbrink *Unknown Germany: An Inner Chronicle of the First World War based on Letters and Diaries* (New Haven 1948) p. 65–6.

Wordsworth had predicted part of the psychological process involved when he wrote of

> These mighty workmen of our later age,
> Who with a broad highway have overbridged

continued

Commentators were not slow to recognize the implications of this industrial era warfare: 'A war of material rather than imagination, a slow rather than a fast struggle, the weight of metal rather than the clash of spirit', as Lord Esher put it. The Italian military theorist General Giulio Douhet wrote in 1916:

> Modern armies draw their strength from the machines they possess. They are like immense factories of destruction, in which the soldiers represent the workers operating the formidable machines of destruction. Neither the genius of the captains nor the valour of the soldiers can be a substitute for lack of means: the genius of the captain must limit itself to the best employment of the machine, the valour of the soldier to its best use.

Admiral Lord Fisher made the same point, though with a different emphasis when he wrote, 'By Sea and Land this war is solely a question of "*Apparatus*"!!! but of course you mustn't have d – d fools to work the apparatus!'[70]

But as the weary months passed and people saw that 'The Navy and Army in most theatres of war are reduced to a state of comparative stagnation through the action of machine power in novel forms', it began to be suspected that nobody knew how to work the apparatus. The generals seemed 'unable to fit the national war to military art'. When Foch became generalissimo it was pointed out that:

> War has also become mechanical, and our Army a large machine, which since the Allied effort has been placed under a single commander has lost all independent volition, and merely travels along the groove assigned to it.[71]

General Fuller later offered an explanation:

> Since 1870, European nations had rapidly become industrialized; science – that is, co-ordinated thought – lay at the bottom of their development; yet Governments remained early nineteenth century in idea, and so did the armies which served them.

But Fuller also suspected that military leadership had not merely failed to progress, but had somehow shifted into a new and dangerous direction:

continued

> The froward chaos of futurity . . .
> Sages who in their prescience would controul
> All accidents, and to the very road
> Which they have fashioned, would confine us down,
> Like engines . . .
> *The Prelude* Book V lines 370–2, 380–3

[70] Esher *Journal and Letters* 3 p. 179, 20 Aug. 1914, and see also Guy Chapman *A Passionate Prodigality* (1933) p. 275 and 'Alain' *Mars: ou la guerre jugée* (Paris 1969 edit.) p. 41, sect. xiii (originally published 1936); G. Douhet *Diario Critico di Guerra* (2 vols Turin 1921) vol. 2 p. 17 memo written in 1916; British Library Add. 62159 f. 42 Fisher to Northcliffe 16 April 1917.

[71] Lord Montagu of Beaulieu in *Sunday Times* 4 Nov. 1917 p. 6f; Pierrefou *Plutarch Lied* p. 180; Keir '*Soldiers-Eye-View*' of our Armies p. 209

Sometime before the outbreak of the World War, quite unconsciously, so it seems to me, the art of soldiership slipped into a groove and became materialized. Not increasing weapon-power alone, but the same factors which in industry have led to a separation, and, consequently, to a loss of sympathy between employer and employed, have also, quite unseen, been at work in all modern armies from the year 1870 onwards. It was, I think, ever increasing size, with its concomitant complexity of control, which more than any factors created this change both in industrial and military organizations.[72]

'The art of soldiership slipped into a groove and became materialized': it is no coincidence that the man who wrote that was soon helping Sir Oswald Mosley to organize a Fascist movement in Britain, and that the one European army which attempted to break out of the mechanistic mould in the First World War and most successfully transcended it in the Second World War was the German Army. In 1917 General von Below, who had commanded the German Second Army during its heroic defensive struggle on the Somme, wrote:

In the Somme battle, wherever the enemy gained the upper hand, it was chiefly due to the perfected application of technical means, in particular to the employment of guns and ammunition in quantities which had been hitherto inconceivable. . . .

Yet the British infantry attacks had invariably broken down against undestroyed defensive positions, and had been easily thrown back by counter-attacks, leading to the conclusion that, 'In this war, which is apparently dominated by science and numbers, individual will-power is, nevertheless, the ultimate deciding factor'. Hitler, who fought in the trenches throughout the First World War, was of exactly the same opinion: 'It is not arms that decide, but the men behind them – always'.[73]

The Germans perceived that overemphasis on material led to a fatal undervaluing of the importance of élan and tactical flexibility in the infantry:

The British (and the French) believed in the effectiveness of their ingenious but stiff artillery creeping barrage which was intended to carry forward the infantry attack which advanced without any impetus of its own.

Even where, as at Gallipoli, there was relatively little artillery support, the British systematically minimized the scope of individual initiative, as Colonel Kannengiesser observed:

The English orders which we saw went exceptionally far into the smallest details. Everything was carefully thought out ahead, allowed for in advance, in short,

---

[72] Fuller *The Army in My Time* p. 166; J.F.C. Fuller *Generalship: its Diseases and their Cure: A Study of the Personal Factor in Command* (1933) p. 13–14.

[73] [Fritz Theodor Carl] von Below *Experience of the German 1st Army in the Somme Battle* [30 Jan. 1917 – translation issued by British Expeditionary Force G.H.Q. 3 May 1917] p. 6; Hermann Rauschning *Hitler Speaks: A Series of Political Conversations with Adolf Hitler on his Real Aims* (1939) p. 15, in conversation 1932.

controlled right into the enemy's lines . . . they often missed the moment which an instinctive knowledge of the position offered, provided all methods, orders, and rules of war were consciously thrown to one side, and the victory achieved by energetically driving forward.

And Kannengiesser, though serving against the British at the head of Turkish troops whose language he could not speak, drew the same conclusion as Hitler: 'Psychological power triumphed over physical, the spirit over the material'.[74]

Although very far from neglecting artillery, the Germans quickly became convinced that the British emphasis was mistaken. The stalemate of the Western Front focused their attention on the potential of individuals: their thinking became dominated by the image of unquenchable spirit showing in an infantryman's eyes under a flared bold-bossed M16 helmet, as shown in a famous poster designed by Fritz Erler. 'All aids and machines will not achieve as much as a handful of brave men', claimed Hauptmann Willy Rohr, who from the autumn of 1915 onwards began to develop the assault troop tactics based on infiltration and automatic weapons which were eventually to prove so devastatingly effective at Riga, Caporetto, and against the British in March and April 1918. Similar methods were outlined by André Laffargue, a captain in the French Army, in his *L'Étude sur l'Attaque* published by Plon, Paris 1916, but his teachings were generally ignored and the only other country which gave as much emphasis as the Germans to assault troops was Italy. A 583-man *compagnia autonoma di esploratori arditi* was established in October 1915, and by mid-1917 *battaglioni d'assalto* began to be formed. According to folklore, both then and later, the *arditi*'s main contribution to the war was in deeds of derring-do – swimming fast-flowing mountain rivers with daggers clenched between their teeth to cut the throats of Austrian sentries and so forth – but in reality the *arditi* were most important as formations of shock troops. As with their German counterparts they provided a model for the uniformed party thugs who fought in the streets to establish Fascism in the 1920s: Italo Balbo, Mussolini's most formidable lieutenant during the March on Rome had in fact been an outstanding *arditi* leader during the war.[75]

---

[74] Ralph Haswell Lutz ed. *The Causes of the German Collapse in 1918* (Stanford 1934) [extracts from twelve-volume report by Committee of Enquiry appointed by German *Nationalversammlung* and *Reichstag* 1914–1930] p. 17 German training memo winter 1917–18; Kannengiesser *Campaign in Gallipoli* p. 267–8; ibid. p. 270.

[75] John Laffin *Jackboot: The Story of the German Soldier* (1965) p. 121; p. 16 Hellmuth Grass *Die Deutschen Sturmbataillone in Weltkrieg: Aufbau und Verwendung* (Berlin 1939) p. 149 Anlage 2 gives a sample of five mornings, training programmes. After May 1916 Rohr's unit operated as a school unit but there were eventually 18 Sturmbataillone operating distributed through the first wave attack troops at a ratio of one battalion per two divisions. (ibid. p. 46–8, 99); For Laffargue see Edmonds *France and Flanders* 1917 vol. 2 p. 62 n.l; Varo Varanini *I Capi, Le Armi, I Combattenti*; (Milan 1935) p. 251, 253 (cf. Fritz Erler's poster 'Helft uns Siegen! Zeichnet die Kriegsanleihe' and Willy Stierborsky's 'Zeichnet 6te Kriegsanleihe'.)

The British were not unaware that their investment in capital-intensive warfare had led them into a tactical impasse. During the Battle of Passchendaele, in the course of which the British artillery bombardment reduced the Flanders claylands, with their intricate system of drainage, 'to its primeval condition of a water-logged bog', Sir William Robertson noted:

> Our hope is I gather, that the artillery will knock out the hostile machine-guns, but unfortunately this entails the entire destruction of the surface of the ground and renders it almost impassable, especially in Flanders. We would therefore seem to be confronted with the problem that unless we use a great deal of artillery fire we cannot get on, and if we do use it the ground is destroyed.

But Robertson was opposed to storm troop tactics:

> People who can and do push on in front of the general line seldom or ever stay there. They are usually cut off or at any rate driven back. The fact is that the whole line must go forward together. Parties pushing forward in front of the general line nearly always come to grief and have never yet on any occasion done any good, so far as I can remember.

The point was that 'soldiering today asks for the average rather than the exception in human nature. It is like a big machine where the parts are standardised'. In practice many Victoria Crosses were awarded for what in effect were storm troop tactics: for example Company Sergeant-Major Frederick Barter, 1st Battalion Royal Welch Fusiliers, won a V.C. at Festubert in May 1915 when, with eight volunteers (one a captain in the 53rd Sikhs who on the outbreak of war had enlisted as a private in order to get to the Front more quickly), he cleared 500 yards of enemy trench with bombs, cut eleven mine leads and took three German officers and 102 other ranks prisoner, also killing perhaps as many others; Sergeant Edward Cooper of the 12th King's Royal Rifle Corps won his V.C. on 16 August 1918 when he single-handedly captured a German blockhouse holding 45 men and seven machine guns which had pinned down his unit. And as A.O Pollard, author of *Fire-Eater: The Memoirs of a V.C.* proudly testified, they enjoyed doing that kind of thing. But the British High Command was too busy to explore the implications of such individual instances: it was more interested in a system. When, in 1940, the British belatedly adopted the concept of elite shock troops, in the form of Commandos, they characteristically went to the other extreme, but in the First World War all the British Army was willing to do by way of fostering the spirit of attack in the infantry was Colonel Ronald Campbell's notorious touring bayonet demonstration, and lectures on 'the aesthetic satisfaction to be obtained from plunging the bayonet into the entrails of a German'. Campbell, as a 32-year old captain in the Gordon Highlanders, had become Superintendent of Gymnasia, Southern Command, in 1910: by May 1917 he was a lieutenant-colonel and deputy inspector of the new School of Physical and Bayonet Training, based at Aldershot, and on 7 October 1918 he was promoted colonel and inspector of the school. His ardent propagandizing of 'The Spirit of the Bayonet' earned him the D.S.O., the *Legion d'Honneur*, the

Order of Avis, the Belgian Order of the Crown, the American Distinguished Service Medal and, perhaps most appropriate of all, the Siamese Order of the White Elephant. The activities of Ronald Campbell show that the British High Command never retreated from the pre-war dogma, derived from the experience of colonial warfare, 'that the bayonet charge scarcely ever fails and that the enemy will not even face it as a rule'. A standard response from front-line units was that nobody was ever killed by a bayonet unless they already had their arms raised; and Liddell Hart later claimed 'most of the German troops did not even fix their bayonets, lest the drag should disturb their aim in firing'. This pedagogic investment in counterproductive skills was later to be a characteristic of British culture: it seem to have had no particular influence on tactical planning, though doubtless of great significance at some symbolic level.[76]

IX. Learning the Lessons of War

The British emphasis on artillery ammunition (and the bayonet) and the German and Italian emphasis on the fighting spirit of their shock troops, may be seen as characteristically diverse attempts to adjust to, or bypass, the limitations of industrialized warfare. These attempts were made only under the stress of wartime conditions, were too late to save millions of casualties and, lacking sufficient time for thought and development, were never more than imperfectly successful. The excuse for this is that the problems being confronted were essentially novel and unprecedented: but in fact they weren't. Here is one of the less familiar passages from the writings of the novelist Joseph Conrad:

> The famous three-day battles, of which history has reserved the recognition of special pages, sink into insignificance before the struggles in Manchuria engaging half a million men on fronts of sixty miles, struggles lasting for weeks, flaming up fiercely and dying away from sheer exhaustion, to flame up again in desperate persistence, and end – as we have seen them end more than once – not from the

[76] Bonham Carter *Soldier True* p. 283, Robertson to Haig 15 Sept. 1917; Woodward ed. *Correspondence of Sir William Robertson* p. 64–5 Robertson to Kiggell 5 July 1916, John Buchan *Greenmantle* (1916) chap. 1; John Laffin *On the Western Front: Soldiers' Stories from France and Flanders, 1914–1918* (Gloucester 1985) p. 64–5 and John Percival *For Valour: The Victoria Cross: Courage in Action* (1985) p. 61–4; A.O. Pollard *Fire-Eater: the Memoirs of a V.C.* (1932) p. 11. C.E. Callwell *Small Wars: Their Principle and Practice* (3rd edit. London War Office 1906) p. 399; Morris *Hired to Kill* p. 41 and cf. Hart-Davis ed. *Siegfried Sassoon Diaries* p. 60 and 249, 25 April 1916 and 15 May 1918; *Memoirs of Captain Liddell Hart* 1 p. 19 fn.

  Robert Graves, in *Goodbye to All That* chap. 10 remembers Colonel Campbell as having the V.C. but this is incorrect. Richard F. Burton *A Complete System of Bayonet Exercise* (1853) p. 5–6 refers to a prejudice against bayonet training in the British Army and claims that continental armies had established formal bayonet training years earlier: this would not be the only instance where the novelties of the 1850s were the orthodoxies of the 1900s.

victor obtaining a crushing advantage, but through the mortal weariness of the combatants ... the war in the Far East has been made known to us, so far, in a grey reflection of its terrible and monotonous phases of pain, death, sickness; a reflection seen in the perspective of thousands of miles ...

Manchuria? The Far East? This was Manchuria 1904–1905; 'this nerve-destroying contest, which for endless, arduous toil of killing surpasses all the wars of history', was the Russo-Japanese War, not the Western Front ten or twelve years later.[77]

The Russo-Japanese War had inspired major interest in Europe. It was not only that it was a war between Russia, still the chief military bogeyman for most European powers, and a non-European people whose unique and miraculous transformation into the semblance of a modern state had gained widespread journalistic attention; it was also the first war between powers at the same technological and tactical level since the 1870s. It provoked much more professional military interest than, for example, the equally distant but far more emotive Vietnam War in the 1960s. Major Otto Löffler's two volume *Der russisch-japanische Krieg in seinen taktischen und strategischen Lehren* (Berlin 1905) was translated into French, and in 1906 a lengthy essay by General François de Negrier came out in an English version by E. Louis Spiers (later famous as Sir Edward Spears) under the promising title *Lessons of the Russo-Japanese War*. There were a number of lavishly illustrated multi-volume popular histories, and a twenty-five page chapter in the twelfth volume of the *Cambridge Modern History* which came out in 1910: this was written by Major F.B. Maurice who later, as Director of Military Operations, was Sir William Robertson's principal assistant at the War Office in 1916 and 1917. The three volume *The Russo-Japanese War: Reports from British Officers attached to the Japanese and Russian Forces in the Field* came out in 1908 and though the Committee of Imperial Defence's *Official History of the Russo-Japanese War* had had only two volumes out of five published by the time the World War broke out in 1914, the German General Staff's Official History appeared in a six-volume English translations by Karl von Donat in 1910.

A recent study of the impact of the Russo-Japanese War on Britain concluded 'the two Services learnt from the Russo-Japanese War only those

---

[77] Joseph Conrad *Notes on Life and Letters* (1921) p. 111–151 Autocracy and War' (originally published in *Fortnightly Review* 1905) at p. 111, 117. Incidentally, H.G. Wells in *Anticipations: Of the Reaction of Mechanical and Scientific Progress Upon Human Life and Thought* (1902) [in fact late 1901; articles already published in *Fortnightly Review* 1901] p. 178–185 had thought that because of technical improvements, e.g. of rifles, the wars of the future would be fought with more machines and fewer (though more skilled) combatants; the American Civil War of 1861–65 had however already demonstrated that improvements in communications would mean that many more men could be maintained in the firing line than previously. In the Russo-Japanese War the Japanese kept an army in the field at about the same distance from the embarkation ports as the British maintained Wellington's army during the Peninsular War – but the Japanese army was five times larger than Wellington's.

lessons which they wanted to learn'. Thus the failure of the Russians to benefit from their enormous superiority in cavalry was blamed on the attempt to use mounted infantry tactics and helped reaffirm the theory of the *arme blanche*, i.e. that the correct use of cavalry was massed charges against formed bodies of troops. The bitter experience of the Boer War had encouraged the British to adopt a more open formation for infantry attacks; the success of the Japanese with human wave attacks by massed ranks of infantry served to encourage a return to closer formation, so that Manchuria helped undo the lessons of South Africa. With regard to artillery, the war seemed to favour the advocates of High Explosive and howitzers, though in 1914 there was still an unjustified faith in shrapnel and light field guns. In fact the British observers in Manchuria seem to have been unable to agree on the part played by artillery in the fighting, for while Major J.M. Horne stated, 'The great impression made on my mind by all I saw is that artillery is now the decisive arm and that all other arms are auxiliary to it', Lieutenent-Colonel C.V. Hume found the loss of men and material from shellfire at the Battle of Mukden quite negligible and concluded sadly, 'The experiences of this war as to the material effect which artillery in the field can produce have been of a disappointing nature from a gunner's point of view'.[78]

Some of the French observers were particularly struck by the Russians' use of machine guns:

> It is above all in the defensive that these machines demonstrated their terrible efficiency, particularly at the moment when the adversaries close to a few hundred metres and the men become nervous and shoot too high. . . . Machines without nerves and without a soul, the machine guns in these circumstances simply mow down the attackers.

It was even claimed that 'The effectiveness of these machines during the war caused them to be adopted in every country'. Yet General de Negrier mentioned machine guns only once, and Major Löffler spared them only one short paragraph, though admittedly this began resoundingly enough: '*Eine recht beachtenswerte Wirkung haben die Maschinengewehre ausgeübt*' (literally, 'A right noteworthy effect have the machine guns exerted'). The reports of the British observers also showed little interest in machine guns, referring to them only in passing; this may partly have been because there were no British observers with the Russian forces besieged in Port Arthur, where machine guns fully proved their value as defensive weapons, and those British officers attached to General Kuropatkin's army further to the north-east never

---

[78] Philip Anthony Towle 'The Influence of the Russo-Japanese War on British Military and Naval Thought, 1904–1914' London University Ph. D. dissertation 1973 p. 8; ibid. p. 166, 170–172; ibid. p. 45–6, 76–90; ibid. p. 122–8 and cf Travers *Killing Ground* p. 67–8; *Reports of the British Officers attached to the Japanese and Russian Forces in the Field* (3 vols 1906) vol. 3 p. 209, J.M. Horne 'General Report on the Russo-Japanese War up to the 15th August 1904'; ibid. vol. 3 p. 609–610, C.V. Hume 'Artillery: with Special Reference to the Battle of Mukden'.

saw machine guns in action, and had the impression that they were not very numerous. (Estimates of how many machine guns there were on either side vary enormously; but in the field armies the Japanese seem to have had more than twice as many as the Russians, though since they were generally on the offensive this does not seem to have been a significant advantage.)[79]

Observers devoted much more attention to the field fortifications, especially those of the Russians who were acknowledged world-leaders in this sphere: but of course even the best fortifications had been unable to withstand the élan and disregard for losses shown in the Japanese human wave assaults and Negrier, for example, saw in the fighting not an adumbration of the coming war of continuous fronts, but a justification of his theories on the necessity of mobility:

> Against the weapons of today, mobility alone offers any means of escape from destruction. He who persists in clinging to positions without doubt shall perish utterly. In a battle with a front of some 25–30 miles, when a general has succeeded in immobilizing the enemy in his positions, victory can only be a question of hours – nothing can wrest it from his grasp.

In the event of course the opposite turned out to be true.[80]

X. The Military Mind Confronts Reality

The various commentaries on the Russo-Japanese War illustrate the ability of experts to select from complex situations only those features which confirm their previously established doctrines. After the First World War it became a commonplace that the British High Command was unable to bring an open mind to the problems of the Western Front because it was dominated by cavalry officers who, amongst army officers as a species, were the ones most committed to traditional forms of warfare. Lieutenant-General John Lindesay Keir, an artillerist, sacked from the command of VI Corps by Haig, a cavalry

---

[79] Jack Snyder *The Ideology of the Offensive: Military Decision Making and the Disasters of 1914* (Ithaca 1984) p. 79 quoting Archives Guerre, Paris 7N671 'Enseignements de la guerre russo-japonaise' note 2 'Mitrailleuses' Dec. 1905 and see also R. Meunier *La Guerre Russo-Japonaise: Historique – Enseignements* (Paris 1906) p. 495–500; Otto Löffler *Der Russisch-Japanische Krieg in seinen taktischen und strategischen Lehren* (2 vols Berlin 1905) vol. 2 p. 121; Towle 'Influence of the Russo-Japanese War; p. 97–101 examines the response within the British Army to the lessons of the war with regard to machine guns and seems to indicate that the British showed more interest than is evident in *Reports of the British Officers* vol. 2 p. 234 and vol. 3 p. 161, 276 of the latter indicates that the Russian field army had perhaps 32 machine guns distributed between three corps, and the Japanese 14 to a division; Meunier *Guerre Russo-Japonaise* p. 495 says that at the Battle of Mukden the Russians had 88 and the Japanese 200 of these weapons.

[80] [François de] Negrier *Lessons of the Russo-Japanese War* (1906) p. 54–5 (Negrier had been Inspector-General of the French Army and member of the Supreme War Council).

man, presumably at the request of Allenby, his army commander, also a cavalry man, wrote while the war was still in progress:

> The overgrowth of perpetuated privilege with its resultant power has made itself clear in the case of our cavalry, whose insistence on young and at the same time propertied officers has culminated in their holding nearly all the most important and best paid positions in the army.

He drew up a list of the key commands held during the war by cavalry men, and this list was evidently the basis of the footnote inserted by Sir James Edmonds (of the Royal Engineers) in his *Official History*, in which it is pointed out that French, Haig, Robertson, Lawrence (Haig's last Chief of General Staff) and five out of nine army commanders had formerly been regimental officers in the cavalry. The devotedly revisionist John Terraine has subsequently drawn up a rival list, showing a predominance of non-cavalry men, but his 'Top Twenty-Seven' includes Kitchener, Royal Engineers, who as Secretary of State for War held what was normally a civilian appointment, four generals who were rather briefly C.I.G.S. during the war, and five commanders-in-chief in India and Mesopotamia. Keir's original point, that the cavalry had secured more than a statistically fair share of the top jobs, remains valid. But part of Keir's and Edmonds's disgust at the way machine-age war had fallen into the hands of the horse-soldiers was due to their belief that generals with a background in the Army's technical branches would have been much more suitable. Of Lawrence, Edmonds noted:

> That he also was a cavalry man was good and sufficient reason for not appointing him to be C.G.S. – an artillery man or a engineer should have been chosen.

And part of Edmonds's low opinion of Haig derived from the fact that, 'H. had no comprehension of light railways, concrete, or other siege-war matters.'[81]

Since the stalemate of the Western Front came from the interaction of artillery and field-fortifications, it is not actually a very plausible argument that artillerists or engineers were the best qualified to undertake the radical rethinking necessary to find a way out of the impasse. The Germans attempted, and almost succeeded with, an infantry solution, and the ultimate British solution, the tank, owed much of its tactical doctrine to infantrymen like Fuller and Liddell Hart, and its greatest tactical successes, in a later war, to the leadership of ex-infantrymen like Guderian, Rommel, and, in the British Army, O'Connor. On the other hand one of the most successful British generals with an infantry background during the First World War, the Earl of Cavan, had dropped out of the army before the war in order to become

---

[81] Keir *'Soldier's-Eye-View' of our Armies* p. 5, ibid. p. 133 and Edmonds *France and Belgium* 1918 vol. 5 p. 605 fn. 3; John Terraine *The Smoke and the Fire: Myths and Anti-Myths of War, 1861–1945* (1980) p. 163, 168; King's College London Edmonds Papers III/11/1 handwritten additions to typescript memoirs; King's College London Liddell Hart Papers 11/1929/7 note of conversation with Edmonds 6 May 1929.

that epitome of horsiness, a Master of Foxhounds. It should be remembered, moreover, that cavalry officers were not obliged by King's Regulations to think only in terms of horse warfare; and they frequently didn't. In the spring of 1915 Allenby, then commanding the Cavalry Corps, and his chief staff officer were reported to be 'despondent' about the role of cavalry; it was said 'that if these two had their way, cavalry would cease to exist as such'. As the Duke of Wellington once said, 'Because a man is born in a stable that does not make him a horse'.[82]

Haig of course insisted throughout the war that, 'we cannot hope to reap the fruits of victory without a large force of mounted troops', and, when the King suggested 'the cavalry should be reduced on account of the cost of maintenance', argued that 'in order to shorten the war and reap the fruits of any success, we must make use of the mobility of the cavalry'. Lieutenant-Commander J.C. Wedgwood of the Royal Naval Division, Assistant-Director of the Trench Warfare Department, claimed in the House of Commons that Haig's cavalry background was the main reason for retaining such large reserves, and jeered, 'With one machine gun you can wipe out a brigade'; but of course Haig was not interested in the opinion of temporary officers. His final despatch, written in the spring of 1919, devoted a page and a half to 'The Value of Cavalry in Modern War' and stated categorically, 'the decision to preserve the Cavalry Corps has been completely justified'. There followed a somewhat shorter section on 'The Value of Mechanical Contrivances' consisting of six paragraphs: four of these merely state over and over again, with slight variations of phrasing, that 'weapons of this character are incapable of effective independent action'. Yet to be fair these views were also shared by officers in the German Army: Hans von Seeckt, the commander-in-chief of the German Army after the war claimed:

> The days of cavalry, if trained, equipped and led on modern lines, are not numbered . . . its lances may still flaunt their pennants with confidence in the wind of the future.

Seeckt may however have been thinking of the more open warfare of the Russian front; a booklet published after the war by the German Army Inspectorate of Training and Education on 'Cavalry in a War of Movement' devoted to the Western Front only two of its ten sections on the First World War.[83]

In any case to blame Haig's mistakes on his cavalry background is too simple. The Somme and Passchendaele were not the product of Haig's

[82] Blake ed. *Private Papers of Douglas Haig* p. 90, 11 April 1915.

[83] Ibid. p. 90, 11 April 1915; ibid. p. 147 7 June 1916; *Hansard: House of Commons* vol. 100 col. 2249–2250, 20 Dec. 1917; J.H. Boraston A. ed. *Sir Douglas Haig's Despatches (Dec 1915–April 1919)* (1919) p. 327–330, quoting from p. 327 and 329 [Hans] von Seeckt *Thoughts of a Soldier* (1930) p. 81–101, 'Modern Cavalry' at p. 107; [Rudolf Wilhelm Philipp Albert Christian Konstantin] von Borries *Heereskavallerie im Bewegungskriege* (Berlin [Heeres-Inspektion des Erziehungs-und Bildungswesen] 1928) p. 68–108 and cf. p. 5–6.

unassisted equine imagination but of the interreaction of his ideas with those
of senior subordinates like Rawlinson and Charteris who were not cavalrymen.
This is well illustrated by the disastrous tactics employed at the Somme, where
after a week-long but insufficiently effective bombardment – 1,437 guns fired
1,508,652 shells – the British infantry, loaded down with sixty pound packs,
walked forward side by side in long rows across no man's land towards the
German machine guns. In his final despatch Haig wrote proudly:

> the battle of the Somme . . . showed that the principles of our pre-war training
> were as sound as ever . . . In short, the longer the war has lasted the more
> emphatically has it been realised that our original organisation and training
> were based on correct principles. The danger of altering them too much, to
> deal with some temporary phase, has been greater than the risk of adjusting
> them too little.

Now pre-war training had never envisaged anything like the Somme. Pre-
war training had been in terms of swift, precise, skilfully orchestrated
assaults on enemy positions which had not been softened up by week-long
bombardments. Exploitation of ground cover, speed, and alternation of
advances in short rushes with pauses to give accurate covering fire with the
rifle: that was what pre-war training had been about. The classic deployment
of Wellington's day – the men standing in squares in a meadow with bodies
strewn amongst their feet, something like Custer's Last Stand only more
orderly and in red coats – had given way to flexibility and even a degree
of individual initiative. By 1914 the British Army, a *corps d'élite* of long-term
professionals, regarded itself with justice as the most tactically efficient in the
world. During the entire reign of Queen Victoria there had not been a year
without a war *somewhere* in the British Empire: as one historian has put it,
'the British temple of Janus was seldom closed, and the loud snores of the
Horse Guards were echoed in cannonades across the globe'. Even the Boer
War coincided with the finishing off of the conquest of northern Nigeria,
a campaign against the Mad Mullah in Somaliland, the last of the Ashanti
Wars, a rebellion in Borneo, an expedition of the Aden Field Force against
the Hamar tribe and, outside the Empire but also involving British troops, the
Boxer rising in China. The Boer War made up for former underexposure to
modern weapons in the hands of a skilled enemy; even Fuller acknowledged:

> It may not have been a great war, yet it was a wonderfully military spring-
> cleaning. We got the paint and varnish of eighty-five years of peace-training off
> us, coat by coat.

British military observers waxed supercilious on the subject of other European
armies which had not enjoyed the same practical training facilities:

> Once they were deployed, the French infantry displayed marked inferiority to
> our own in minor tactics. There was not the same dash nor anything like the
> same efficiency in fire direction and control. Like the cavalry, the infantry did
> not seem to realize what modern rifle fire is like.

The fire control of the Prussian and Saxon infantry was judged 'elementary and insufficient' and Austro-Hungarian tactics were found to be old-fashioned; it was however conceded that fire control in the Swedish Army was 'more up to date than that of the German Army'.[84]

An outward symbol of progressiveness was that by 1914 the British Army had given up the traditional red coat and dressed both soldiers and officers in khaki; the French were still uniformed in extravagant red pantaloons and long blue coats, and the Prussians still favoured polished and ornamented leather head coverings derived from the eighteenth century.

By the time of the Battle of the Somme however the highly-skilled peacetime British Army had been decimated in the campaigns of 1914 and 1915, and Haig's great offensive was delivered by troops who mostly, for all that they had volunteered for the army at least a year previously, had never before been in a general action. By peacetime standards it was an almost entirely untrained army though how far this was unavoidable after several months under arms is not clear; in the French Army basic training lasted twelve weeks, with a further twelve weeks to bring new formations up to combat standard. By the time of the Somme the Germans too had worked through the first-line troops of 1914 and were heavily dependent on troops who either had not been balloted or had been too young for military service before the war, but they seem to have had much less problem with maintaining levels of efficiency. Haig's G.H.Q. was well aware of the training problem and a memo issued on 8 May 1916 over the signature of Kiggell, the Chief of General Staff, entitled 'Training of Divisions for Offensive Action', concluded, 'To ensure success it is impossible to exaggerate the vital importance of thorough training of troops'. Kiggell also wrote to Rawlinson, whose Fourth Army was to bear the brunt of the Somme offensive:

> I am desired to impress upon you the urgent necessity for the closest supervision of the training of all troops detailed to take part in the attack. The degree of success obtainable depends very much on the thoroughness of previous training and instruction.

Yet G.H.Q. attempted no control of what the training should consists of or how it should be carried out – even the initiative for setting up specialist schools to give courses on the use of grenades, mortars, etc., was taken by the Third Army, with the other armies only copying this practice later. The

---

[84] Boraston ed. *Despatches of Sir Douglas Haig* p. 345; V.G. Kiernan *European Empires from Conquest to Collapse* (1982) p. 13; Byron Farwell *Queen Victoria's Little Wars* (1973) p. 364–370; Fuller *The Army in My Time* p. 104; Public Record Office WO 33/618 *Report on Manoeuvres in 1912* [printed booklet] p. 20; ibid. p. 53, 115 and King's College London, Hamilton Papers 19/11/3 on Austro-Hungarian manoeuvres 1906 and 19/12/2 on Saxon manoeuvres 1909. Edmonds even thought the teaching at the Prussian *Kriegsakademie* 'elementary' compared to the level of instruction at the Staff College at Camberley: 'hardly above the standard of the Royal Military Academy Woolwich in the 'eighties': King's College London, Edmonds Papers I/2B/17a memo on staff training.

actual conduct of training was left to the commanders of the divisions, on the assumption that they were experienced soldiers who knew their job, though, since on the opening day of the Somme offensive individual brigades chose their own tactics, it does not seem that very close supervision was in practice exercised at divisional level. In January 1918 Sir Ivor Maxse, commanding XVIII Corps, wrote of a corps through which thirty divisions had passed during the previous twelve months:

> Of these thirty divisions two were splendidly trained, a dozen were trying to train and the remainder had little if any definite system of training at all. They had, instead, a dozen excellent reasons for explaining why they remained untrained.

The situation – including, one imagines, the excuses – must have been even less satisfactory in 1916. But Rawlinson, without contradicting Kiggell's instructions as such, made it very clear to his subordinates that he did not regard a very high level of expertise to be attainable in the time available:

> We must remember that owing to the large expansion of our Army and the heavy casualties in experienced officers, the officers and troops generally do not now possess that military knowledge arising from a long and high state of training which enables them to act instinctively and promptly on sound lines in unexpected situations. They have become accustomed to deliberate action based on precise and detailed orders.

It seems indeed the excessively detailed and rigid instructions issued to units for the opening of the Somme offensive were thought necessary because of the rawness and inexperience of the New Army formations.[85]

Although some senior officers passed down the word to the men that they would only see dead Germans once the British artillery barrage lifted, that they would not even need their rifles, that they could advance smoking their pipes, this was not the view of Rawlinson himself. He anticipated strong German resistance; yet it was his concept that a mass offensive by inexperienced troops required them to advance across the ruined landscape of no man's land in rigid line abreast. Rawlinson was undoubtedly one of the more intelligent and thoughtful of Haig's commanders, and throughout the war he was experimenting with tactical expedients, but as the Somme shows his tendency was to explore models based on *a priori* concepts. The scale of the means at his disposal, and the memory of professionals he had commanded before the war, led him with infallible military logic to fall back

---

[85] Edmonds *France and Belgium* 1916 vol. 1 Appendix vol. p. 130 Appendix 17, memo 8 May 1916; ibid. 1916 vol. 1 Appendix vol. p. 83 Appendix 11, G.H.Q. Rawlinson 16 May 1916; Tim Travers *The Killing Ground* p. 111–2, 143; Public Record Office WO 158/53 Cambrai Enquiry 21 Jan. 1918, 'Note' by Maxse; Edmonds *France and Belgium* 1916 vol. 1 Appendix vol. p. 131 Appendix 18 'Tactical Notes' issued by Fourth Army May 1916: 'General Remarks'; Edmonds *France and Belgium* 1916 vol. 1 p. 294.

on the assumption 'that a standardized army might go into a standardized battle'.[86]

Haig initially resisted this view. He argued that the conventional tactic of advancing small detachments in short rushes might be more effective than Rawlinson's vision of the parade-ground rows advancing at a walk. Rawlinson and the other army commanders with infantry backgrounds objected to the use of small detachments: 'They lead to the loss of the boldest and best without result. The enemy can concentrate on these detachments. Advance should be uniform.' It was precisely because he was a cavalry man that Haig in this instance deferred to the opinion of the infantry experts; and having once adopted the view he was too loyal (or slow-witted) to recall afterwards that it had not at first been his own opinion. It seems somehow characteristic of Haig that on the one occasion he experienced a moment of superior prescience he allowed himself to be overborne, and then afterwards defended a policy which he had initially seen to be fallacious.[87]

But Haig, as already suggested, was only the leading representative of a system. For a more detailed understanding of the mechanics of this system it is useful to examine institutional responses within the British Army to the new technology which became available during the war.

---

[86] Public Record Office WO 33/1305 *Notes on Certain Lessons of the Great War* p. 26. For Hankey's hostile comment on the plan of attack see Roskill *Hankey* vol. 1 p. 266, diary 2 May 1916.

[87] Edmonds *France and Belgium* 1916 vol. 1 p. 290: Edmonds specifies 'the three Army commanders who were infantry men' – i.e. Rawlinson, Sir Herbert Plumer and Sir Charles Monro – but essentially the same point was made by Sir William Robertson during the first week of battle, see p. 353.

10

Armageddon in the Machine Age

It was the mud, I think, that made me take to flying. I had fully expected that going into battle would mean for me the saddle of a galloping charger, instead of the snug little cock-pit of a modern aeroplane. The mud, on a certain day in July 1915, changed my whole career in the war.

William Avery Bishop, *Winged Warfare: Hunting the Hun in the Air* (1918), p.1.

I. Improved Ways of Killing

Generally the military leaders favoured new or improved ways of killing people. Old weapons were revived; pikes consisting of butchers' knives 'secured with medical plaster to the end of broomsticks' and clubs were mostly made or procured on an individual basis by those who chose to believe they would be effective weapons in trench warfare; the Imperial War Museum's collection of clubs includes entrenching tool handles shod with pieces of iron apparently cast in crude home-made moulds. Fighting knives were improvised from cut down bayonets or from flattened and sharpened German barbed-wire picket posts, the looped tops of which served as a hand guard – these were called 'French Nails' – but one could buy similar weapons, manufactured by Robbins Co. of Dudley, at the Civil Service Co-operative Stores in London's Regent Street, and in the 9th Royal Welch Fusiliers Major Lord Howard de Walden purchased a supply of Welsh knives, a type of elegant double-edged machete, for the battalion's machine-gunners and bombers. Some soldiers even bought themselves body armour such as the Dayfield Body Shield marketed by the Whitfield Manufacturing Co Ltd of Sicilian Avenue, London WC1; in July 1915 *The Times* reported:

> military experts admit that a continuance of the present trench warfare may lead to those engaged in it, especially bombing parties and barbed wire cutters, being more heavily armoured than the knights who fought at Bouvines and at Agincourt.

In February 1916 the Ministry of Munitions ordered 10,000 'suits' of body armour, each consisting of 16 variously shaped plates, and a further 50,000 of an improved pattern were ordered in the autumn, but they were not popular in the trenches. There was also official investment in flame-throwers (a revival of the Greek Fire of late classical times), underground mines and hand grenades – the latter being generally referred to in the British Army as 'bombs'. The Germans first used flame-throwers against the French at Melancourt in February 1915 and against the British at Hooge in July of the same year, and the British were already testing their own devices by September 1915, but the short range of flame-throwers and the suicidal risk involved in being the operator of one meant that in the British Army they 'happily never came into general use', though portable flame-throwers were being prepared at Wembley in 1918 for the expected 1919 campaign. (This weapon found more favour with the Italians and the French, and the latter had seven flame-thrower companies available for their abortive April 1917 offensive.) Hand grenade production, a mere 2,164 in Britain in the second half of 1914, reached the wartime peak as early as the final quarter of 1915, when 9,489,765 were manufactured: the second highest trimestrial output was in the final quarter of 1916 with 8,596,871 and the falling off after these record levels suggests that, uniquely, production was well ahead of use. Mines dug hundreds of yards under the German front line were another expedient favoured by the British, and the Germans retaliated enthusiastically: in the first half of 1917 up to twelve mines a week were 'fired' under German and British positions and on 7 June 1917 nineteen mines containing 937,450lb of explosive – some of it laid as far back as April 1916 – were detonated by the British as a prelude to the successful attack at Messines (it was said that Lloyd George had given orders to be woken so that he could hear the explosion at his home in the Surrey commuter belt). Of course none of these revived traditional techniques involved a fundamental alteration of military tactics; but there were many who thought that the aeroplane, the machine gun, the tank and gas did promise a revolution in warfare, and these weapons too were gladly welcomed into the arsenals by the various High Commands.[1]

II. The Machine Gun

The thesis that in war man confronts the technology that he has invented has

[1] For pikes see Robert Graves *Goodbye to All That* (Harmondsworth 1960 ed.) p. 171. For body armour see 'Send "Him" a Dayfield Now!' advert. Nov. 1915 in Maurice Richards and Michael Moody *The First World War: Ephemera, Mementoes and Documents* (1975) illus. no. 99 and *The Times* 22 July 1915 p. 5d; Public Record Office MUN 2/30, reports of weeks ending 26 Feb. 1916, 23 Sept. 1916 (No. 60) and 4 Nov. 1916 (No.66). See also Bashford Dean *Helmets and Body Armor in Modern Warfare* (New Haven 1920) p. 110–128 for British body armour and p. 142–7 for German body armour; for flame-throwers see Christopher Addison *Politics from Within, 1911–1918* (2 vols 1924) vol. 1 p. 124 and Donald Banks *Flame over Britain: A Personal Narrative of Petroleum Warfare* (1946) p. 62 and cf Ministère de la Guerre *Les Armées Françaises dans la Grande Guerre* (1 'tomes', numerous volumes of annexes Paris 1923–37) tome 5 annexe vol. 1 p. 580; for hand grenade production see *History of the Ministry of Munitions* (12 vols 1922) vol. 11 pt. I p. 73–4 and p. 134–5, appendix XIII, and for technical development see Guy Hartcup *The War of Invention: Scientific Developments, 1914–1918* (1988) p. 61–3; for mines see Public Record Office WO 158/135 and WO 158/139. For Lloyd George and the Messines mines cf *New Statesman* 16 June 1917 p. 248b.

its classic exemplification in the machine gun. According to tradition it was the machine gun that dominated the Western Front, and it is always the German machine guns which one thinks of in connection with the suicidal advance of the raw British troops on the first day of the Somme. In reality artillery fire was much the biggest killer, and the rifle was still of major importance: in 1914 when the British Expeditionary Force was still composed of pre-war regulars who could fire fifteen aimed rounds a minute with their rifles – the record was 38 in a minute, all hitting the inner ring of a standard target at 300 yards – the Germans thought the British had far more machine guns than was actually the case. Again, despite the emphasis on machine-gunning in the powerful battle-reenactments of Anthony Asquith's and Geoffrey Barkas's *Tell England* of 1930, the Turks at Gallipoli had very few automatic weapons: at V Beach, where in a typical *Boys' Own* technological stunt the British improvised a landing ship, the *River Clyde*, but were pinned down for 32 dreadful hours and suffered catastrophic losses, the defenders had only two machine guns, another two having previously been knocked out by the British bombardment, and two 2-pounder pom-poms: it was estimated that the Turks fired 10,000 rounds of small arms ammunition a minute, not more than a tenth of which can be attributed to the two machine guns.[2]

Nevertheless, though Raymond Asquith, the eldest son of the British Prime Minister, was probably correct in claiming 'a battle is far too much like a railway accident to be susceptible of description', the staccato regularity of machine-gun fire, distinguishable in almost any din, and the hypnotic deliberateness with which a traversing machine gun swept its deadly scythe across its field of fire, were perhaps foremost amongst the details which gave the battles of the First World War such shape and form as they possessed. And the 'mad stuttering', the 'brain-fever babble of the German machine guns' was an accompaniment even to so-called quiet periods:

> As the dark gathers the horizon brightens and again vanishes as the Vèry lights rise and fall shedding their weird greenish glare over the land and [in] acute contrast to their lazy silent flight breaks out the agitated knocking of the machine guns as they sweep the parapets.

But that is the machine gun on a stable mounting, as a defensive weapon, as a contributing element in tactical stalemate. What is more interesting in the study of the military bureaucracy's adjustment to modern warfare is the employment of the machine gun as an offensive weapon, as a solvent of stalemate and a key to break-through.[3]

[2] C.H.B. Pridham *Superiority of Fire: A Short History of Rifles and Machine-Guns* (1945) p. 57 fn; C.F. Aspinall-Oglander *Military Operations: Gallipoli* (2 vols 1929–32) vol. 1 p. 221 fn. 1 and 231; John Masefield *Gallipoli* (1916) p. 38.

[3] John Joliffe *Raymond Asquith: Life and Letters* (1980) p. 195 Raymond Asquith to Aubrey Herbert 20 Sept. 1914; William Linton Andrews *Haunting Years: The Commentaries of a War Territorial* [1930] p. 107, 141; Paul Nash *Outline: An Autobiography and Other Writings* (1949) p. 196, Nash to Margaret Nash 6 April 1917.

As the British High Command demonstrated at the Somme to everybody but itself, the employment of sheer weight of numbers in attack merely guaranteed heavier losses: 'piling up infantry has merely meant piling up casualties'. The alternative was to achieve the same weight of infantry firepower while reducing the number of infantry being shot at, and the machine gun was as much the answer here as it was for the defensive.[4]

At the beginning of the First World War most major armies were equipped with machine guns working on the short-recoil principle invented by Hiram Maxim thirty years previously, firing ammunition of from 7 to 8mm calibre loaded on a continuous belt, and mounted on tripods or, in the German Army, on a cumbersome four-legged stand known as a sledge (*Schlitten*). The basic assembly weighed at least fifty pounds – the German MG 08 no less than 116.6lb – but for sustained fire over any considerable period of time it was necessary to have a water condenser, spare gun barrels, and all the boxes of ammunition that were to be fired off at 500 rounds per minute. Obviously the essential minimum crew of two would be insufficient to handle all this gear and the standard German machine-gun team for example consisted of eight men, the leader carrying a water can, condenser tube and a spare barrel, one man carrying the gun, another the sledge, and the other five the ammunition boxes. It soon became evident that a much more portable weapon, perhaps with a much inferior capacity for sustained fire, would be desirable, not so much for attack as for consolidation, that is, defending newly gained ground while the battle was still fluid, and strengthening fire power at short notice in zones liable to be attacked by the enemy.[5]

The French Army however was equipped with the Hotchkiss machine gun, which worked on a different principle from the Maxim. Whereas in the Maxim the automatic mechanism for ejecting spent cartridges and reloading was operated by part of the breach sliding back with the recoil, the Hotchkiss mechanism involved an ejector movement powered by gas from the exploded propellant being tapped from the gun barrel. This mechanism was also developed for self-loading rifles. The British Army tested the Farquhar-Hill self-loading rifle from 1908 onwards, and the German Army tested the SIG Model 1908 designed by the Mexican Manuel Mondragon, but both types were found to be too delicate for use under active service conditions. The pioneer and leading manufacturer of this form of self-loading rifle was the Danish firm of Madsen. The Germans acquired a small consignment of Madsen guns by some mysterious means after the outbreak of war and issued them to two companies in the autumn of 1915, but eventually withdrew them owing to

---

[4] Public Record Office WO 33/1305 *Notes on Certain Lessons of the Great War* – a report by a committee of senior officers under the chairmanship of Lieutenant-General W.M.St.G. Kirke, April 1933 p. 14.

[5] [Fritz Theodor Carl] von Below *Experience of the German 1st Army in the Somme Battle* [memo 30 Jan. 1917 issued by B.E.F. G.H.Q. 3 May 1917] p. 12. Maxim invented the machine gun in a building named Hatton House, today marked with a blue plaque, on the corner of Clerkenwell Road and Hatton Gardens, London EC1.

lack of replacement parts; the British ordered 900 Madsen guns but the Danish government refused to release them to a belligerent power and the order was transferred to Rumania, then still neutral; these guns too allegedly fell into German hands when Rumania entered the war and was invaded.[6]

In 1913 the Belgian Army had adopted another weapon using the gas pressure principle in its loading mechanism, the Lewis gun. This was later adopted by the British Army and manufactured in very large quantities in Britain, and became Britain's most important automatic weapon. With its air-cooler jacket the Lewis gun looked like a large and swollen rifle but at over 30lb loaded it was, though half the weight of a Hotchkiss, three times heavier than a conventional infantry rifle and far too cumbersome for use as an assault weapon: but for consolidation and back-up purposes it was ideal.

The Germans failed to develop anything to equal the Lewis gun; where the British used Lewis guns as the moveable weapon in their two-seater aircraft, the Germans had to fall back on a lightweight Maxim-pattern gun, the LMG 14 Parabellum, but on their giant 'R' bombers captured Lewis guns were the authorized standard defensive armament. For their infantry, for want of a better alternative, they took a Maxim pattern MG 08 off its sledge mounting, attached a rifle-type butt and trigger to the rear and props to the front, and produced a heavy-weight but just about portable weapon, the MG 08/15. Since the MG 08 happened to be one of the most heavy and complicated designs of machine gun then in service – it had 235 parts to the British Vickers's 144 parts – the Germans did well to reduce the weight of the MG 08/15 from 116.6lb to 37.4lb, but it remained bulkier than the Lewis gun and till the second half of 1917 the Germans seem to have concentrated on the manufacture of the MG 08; thereafter, as the war became once more essentially mobile, the lighter MG 08/15 seems to have become important as a substitute for, rather than a complement to, the MG 08 and in the last months of the war production of the MG 08/15 was at three times the level of the MG 08.[7]

The French meanwhile had adopted the CSRG or Chauchat machine gun, described authoritatively as the worst machine gun ever made. At 20lb unloaded it was *almost* light enough to be used as an assault rifle, but it employed a long-recoil mechanism which was even more cumbersome than the

---

[6] Ian Hogg and John Weeks *Military Small Arms of the Twentieth Century* (1972) p. 4.02 and 4.22; for the Madsen Guns in German service see Public Record Office CAB 42/15 note 97/G circulated for War Cabinet 22 June 1916 and Public Record Office WO 79/74 item marked 45b 'Machine Guns' *c.* 1919 and annotated 'Bingham got this from Berlin'.

[7] Major Kopf and Hauptmann Schmidt 'Maschinengewehre', in M. Schwarte ed. *Die Technik im Weltkriege* (Berlin 1920) p. 23–33 at p. 24 for number of parts in the MG 08, p. 25 Zusammenstellung 1 for weights, p. 27 graph for numbers produced, cf Ernst von Wrisberg *Erinnerungen an die Kriegsjahre im preussischen Kriegsministerium* (3 vols Leipzig 1921–2) vol. 3 p. 8. The method of converting the German MG 08 to British 0.303 ammunition involved changing the barrel and the extractor, removing the side-plate spring and filing off the small spring on the face of the feed-block: it was not necessary to substitute anything for these two springs: Seymour Rouse *Tactical Notes for Machine-Gun Drill and Training* (1916) p. 82.

short-recoil mechanism used on the Maxim – the difference relates to whether ejection of spent cartridges occurs while the moving part of the breech is sliding back (short recoil) or while it is returning forward (long recoil) and the latter involves parts of the breech separating at the end of the recoil and moving at different speeds, a process that tends to maximize vibration. Long recoil was later adopted as a standard mechanism for 20mm cannon but with small arms ammunition it resulted in a very slow rate of fire – 240 rounds per minute – and difficulty in holding the gun steady. The Chauchat also suffered from poor production standards: a grotesquely ugly weapon, like an oversized spud-gun, with its recoil mechanism extending almost as far back as the shoulder piece, and an awkward semi-circular magazine (necessitated by the tapered shape of the French *modèle* 1886 cartridges) which contained only twenty rounds and fitted along the underside of the weapon, it did nothing to bring grace and mobility to trench warfare when introduced into service late in 1915.[8]

It was the Italians who pioneered a weapon that had the potential to give substantial mobile fire-power. In 1915 A.B. Revelli developed a gun utilizing the blow-back principle previously used in automatic pistols, in which the rear of the breech is mounted not on a precision-machined slide but on a spring. Using a light bolt, a strong spring and pistol ammunition, Revelli's gun achieved an unprecedented 1,200 rounds per minute. But the gun was manufactured by Villar Perosa as a twin-barrelled weapon, weighing a mere 13.3lb exclusive of the bipod or shield with which it was usually fitted. Despite the short range and inaccuracy of its pistol-sized ammunition it was employed from fixed positions, and the twenty-five round magazines which could be fired off in one second made sustained fire impossible. Some attempt was made to use the Villar Perosa as an assault weapon, carried in front of the operator on a tray rather like that of a cigarette girl – presumably with a good deal of stopping and stumbling to reload – but the real solution was not perceived till after the Germans introduced the first true sub-machine gun, the Bergmann MP 18/1, designed by Hugo Schmeisser, which weighed only 11.55lb loaded and fired 450 rounds per minute – exactly half the rate of the single-barrelled version of the Villar Perosa designed by Tullio Marengoni and manufactured as the Beretta *modello* 18; this, the Allies' only real sub-machine gun was introduced in the last weeks of the war, too late to have any tactical impact, though it was still in extensive use with the Italian forces in North Africa in the years 1940–1943.[9]

With the Bergmann MP 18/1 the Germans had finally developed the ideal infantry assault weapon, which the Lewis gun, the MG 08/15, the Chauchat and the tray-mounted Villar Perosa were not. Small groups of shock troops, with a light, convenient weapon offering concentrated short-range fire-power, could infiltrate forward without the need even for a preparatory

---

[8] Hogg and Weeks *Military Small Arms* p. 5.13–5.14.
[9] Thomas B. Nelson *The World's Submachine Guns* (2 vols London/Alexandria Va. 1977–80) vol. 1 p. 225,227,323–5,333.

bombardment, and break open the enemy's defences. Bergmann-armed assault troops played a key role in the German spring offensives of 1918. At last, after four years of stalemate, tactical skill once more dominated the battlefield. That this would have to happen had been realized quite early on by British regular army officers who had had the fortune not to be promoted away from contact with the firing line: 'The more you gave him [the infantryman] of machine-guns and artillery, the less and less would he perceive the duty of relying on himself'. It was remarked sardonically,

> thought was numbed by the contemplation of the terrific weight of metal that was about to be hurled at the Germans, so that it was difficult, if not impossible, to realise the potential of a single clip of cartridges intelligently directed.

The Germans, with their somewhat neo-Kantian emphasis on moral factors saw the fallacy of overlooking individual skill and courage, but in the British Army the response to the machine gun followed strictly materialist and bureaucratic lines: just at the point when the machine gun's relationship to infantry tactics needed imaginative rethinking, the British departmentalized it out of infantry tactics altogether.[10]

Compared to the political heat generated by the progress of the Royal Flying Corps and its eventual transmogrification into the Royal Air Force, Britain's Machine Gun Corps came into being extraordinarily discreetly. The usual version of the story is that Major Christopher Baker-Carr, put in charge of a machine-gun training school in France in November 1914, worked out a scheme for an independent Machine Gun Corps in the course of discussions with Captain G.M. Lindsay and sent a memo on the subject to G.H.Q.; after the usual consultations the scheme was rejected but Baker-Carr managed to rescue his memo from a pile of papers marked, 'Of no further interest', which was awaiting despatch to the B.E.F.'s depository in Le Havre; the memo was then recirculated and a rapid War Office decision obtained. It is difficult to check this story on the basis of what Baker-Carr states in his memoirs, as he gives very few dates. He established his training school in November 1914 and suggests that his memo was first sent out several months later ('For several months past, Lindsay and I had been discussing the formation of a Machine Gun Corps'). He rescued his memo from the pile intended for Le Havre six pages in his memoirs after the senior officers and machine-gun personnel of the 12th Division visited his school at Wisques, which must have been sometime after the 12th Division's arrival in France late in May 1915. The Director of Military Training at the War Office first broached the idea of a Machine Gun Corps on 5 July 1915, so that the rescue and recirculation of Baker-Carr's memo, and its despatch with favourable endorsements to the War Office would have had to occur very quickly for it to have been the principal cause of the scheme being floated in Whitehall. Moreover, the file opened at the War Office following the Director of Military Training's memo does not

---

[10] A.A. Hanbury–Sparrow *The Land-Locked Lake* (1932) p. 132,191.

contain Baker-Carr's memo, or anything referring to it. It seems therefore that Baker-Carr's paper never progressed beyond Sir John French's G.H.Q., though it may have provided the thinking behind a letter French wrote to the War Office on 23 July 1915.[11]

The true origin of the Machine Gun Corps was the memo by Major-General Frederick Heath Caldwell, Director of Military Training, dated 5 July 1915. 'I am not satisfied that we are training machine gun drafts in the most economical way', he wrote. Infantry battalions received their replacement man power from depot battalions in England, and depot battalions supplying those front-line battalions which were suffering heavy losses amongst their machine-gunners did not have enough machine guns to train an adequate flow of replacements, whereas depot battalions supplying service battalions with light casualtes 'have instructors and trained men wasting their time . . . If machine-gun training could be concentrated and machine gunners pooled for drafting all these difficulties would disappear'. He suggested 'forming a machine gun corps on the lines of the Motor Machine Gun Batteries and Cyclist Corps'. There was no particular objection to establishing new corps of this kind: the Director of Organisation, living up to his title, minuted Heath Caldwell's memo with the suggestion that *two* specialist corps should be formed, one for infantry and one for cavalry.[12]

Sir John French had written from G.H.Q. in France about a month previously requesting a larger establishment of machine-gunners and on 23 July 1915 he repeated this request, concluding his letter:

> In order to meet the above requirements, and with a view of ensuring uniformity of training, I would suggest the formation of a Corps of Machine Gunners, on similar lines to the Corps of Cyclists.[13]

Heath Caldwell used this letter to press his original point of view and a conference was set up by the Director of Organisation and held in his office on 12 August: 'Present DSD, DMT, DO, and representatives from SD2, MT2, AG1, AG2a and F1'. Not represented was the Master General of the Ordnance, Von Donop, who had noted in his diary a few days earlier, 'Geddes says Ll. G [Lloyd George, Minister of Munitions] has ordered considerably more machine guns that were required as *he* wants to increase the numbers

---

[11] C.D. Baker-Carr *From Chauffeur to Brigadier* (1930) p. 102–7, 127, 134–5; ibid. p. 127–8 for the visit of the 12th Division's senior officers to Wisques and cf Edmonds *Military Operations: France and Belgium 1915* vol. 1 p. 331; and see following note.

[12] Public Record Office WO32/11239 DMT memo for DO 5 July 1915.
There were at this time two motor machine gun batteries assigned to corps in France: Captain F.E. Soames's letter to DAA & QMG 5th Corps 18 May 1915 has an official stamp with his signature: COMDG. NO.3 BATTERY/MOTOR MACHINE GUN SERVICE cf Public Record Office WO 158/288. The Motor Machine Gun Service appears under a separate heading in the October 1915 *Army List* but as part of the Machine Gun Corps in the March 1916 list. Soames, incidentally, was promoted to major before being, for some reason, returned to unit with his substantive rank of lieutenant.

[13] Public Record Office WO 32/11239, French to War Office 23 July 1915, marked '7A'.

with units'. Two days after the meeting in the D.O.'s room, a telegram arrived from French's G.H.Q. saying, 'It has been assumed that machine-gunners in future will cease to belong to battalions or regiments and will belong to machine-gun corps'. The Adjutant-General minuted this, 'Are we not going too fast about these assumptions . . .?' (later he was to be accused of refusing to supply the machine-gun arm with sufficient men). Within the next ten days three more conferences were held, approving the establishment of a Machine Gun Corps and of a training school at Belton Park, near Grantham, and the allocation of one machine-gun company per brigade. Although the official announcement of the setting up of the Corps was not made till 5 October 1915, the actual decision to establish a corps, through the ranks of which over 161,000 men were eventually to pass, was effectively made in seven weeks, which shows that British military bureaucracy was not always quite as dilatory as sometimes made out; unfortunately the utility of the decision so promptly arrived at is somewhat open to question.[14]

The Machine Gun Corps was essentially only a training and administrative body (as was the Cyclist Corps mentioned in the memos: this organizational arrangement was rather favoured by elements in the British army at this period; there was also a proposal for the establishment of a Trench Mortar Corps at about this time). The ablest senior Machine Gun Corps officers, organizers rather than field commanders, such as Christopher Baker-Carr, Frederick Sykes and G.M. Lindsay, merely passed through the corps on their way upward and elsewhere. At the end of 1916 the senior machine-gunner in France, Lieutenant-Colonel R.W. Bradley, was in charge of the Machine Gun Corps' Heavy Section (later known as the Heavy Branch) which was equipped not with machine guns but with tanks. Later a Canadian brigadier-general, Raymond Brutinel, commanding the machine guns of the Canadian Corps, was the ranking machine-gunner. Nevertheless the lack of a charismatic General Officer Commanding to establish the kind of influence with the Commander-in-Chief that was wielded by Trenchard as G.O.C. of the Royal Flying Corps, and of an H.Q. and War Office directorate to churn out meretricious memoranda, did not prevent the Machine Gun Corps from developing its own tactical doctrine. As will be shown, the Royal Flying Corps discovered that it could fight better if it ignored the requirements of the ground troops, and similarly the Machine Gun Corps discovered it could be a better corps if it severed its links with infantry; as the Canadian Brutinel put it:

[14] Public Record Office WO 32/11239 passim. DSD was the Director of Staff Duties, DMT was the Director of Military Training, DO was the Director of Organisation, SD2 was a subordinate of DSD, MT2 a subordinate of DMT, AG1 and AG2a were from the Adjutant-General's department and F1 was from Finance: Public Record Office WO 79/73 Von Donop's diary copy f.6, 7 Aug. 1915; David Lloyd George *War Memoirs* (6 vols 1933–6) vol. 2 p. 613. The number of men serving with the Machine Gun Corps 1915–1919 is taken from the inscription on Derwent Wood's Machine Gun Corps Monument ('David') in Duke of Wellington Place, London SW1.

The Machine Gun Service must be regarded as a distinctive arm *with tactics entirely its own.* In all respects it is intermediate between the Infantry and the Artillery, its tactics being radically different from the former, and approximating to but not being identical with those of the latter.[15]

The Machine Gun Corps was responsible only for the front line's Maxim-pattern Vickers guns. The Lewis gun had been left with the infantry; the 'Tactical Notes' issued by Fourth Army H.Q. in May 1916 during the run-up to the Somme had laid down the doctrine for the exploitation of the Lewis gun's mobility, stating roundly, 'The Lewis gun is an automatic rifle', but especially after the Somme, these notes seem to have been largely ignored; perhaps in any case the officers particularly interested in automatic weapons had gravitated to the Machine Gun Corps. Within the Machine Gun Corps the aspect of the Vickers gun which was most enthusiastically embraced was its relative immobility and capacity for sustained fire; to exploit these characteristics the officers of the corps evolved a technique of barrage fire, in which the guns were grouped in batteries and fired on a distant zone chosen from a map and not actually visible to the gunners, the trajectory being calculated by trigonometry in the same way as with heavy artillery. Machine-gun barrages were employed in the later stages of the Somme, and on 18 February 1917 no less than 48 Vickers guns fired an intensive coordinated barrage, allegedly with good effect. It is difficult to see how this differed in principle from the concentration of the French army's *mitrailleuses* too far back from the firing line, which is usually considered the reason for the ineffectiveness of automatic weapons when first used in the Franco-Prussian war of 1870. At any rate the development of the machine-gun barrage was regarded with suspicion by the infantry:

The command and position of these weapons had been removed yet farther from the front; less and less were they available for direct and opportune fire, and more and more were they practised on hypothetical targets on the map: it was not unknown those days for hundredweights of lead to be buried in some intervening bank or elevation.

For many of the British frontline troops barrage-fire by machine guns in their rear merely added to the multitudinous disorientating and dehumanizing features of trench warfare:

It seemed to be only three or four feet over their heads, and its curious swish caused most uncomfortable feelings; they felt as if they were stepping out of the deep trench into a stream of our own bullets, and they did not like the idea of being shot at from behind.

In order to facilitate bigger and better barrages, some of the machine-gun officers began to press for the machine guns to be concentrated into larger tactical units. The lead in this seems to have been taken by a 27-year-old major,

---

[15] For the Trench Mortar Corps project see House of Lords Record Office, Lloyd George Papers D/23/1/5 Swinton to CID, printed for Cabinet 24 Sept. 1915; for Brutinel's memo, spring 1918 see C.S. Grafton *The Canadian 'Emma Gees'* (London Ontario 1938) p. 120.

Graham Seton Hutchison, the divisional Machine Gun Officer of the 33rd Division: it is interesting to note that like that other innovative but perhaps over-imaginative military theorist, J.F.C. Fuller, Hutchison later became a Fascist. In October 1917 Hutchison persuaded his divisional commander to remove the division's four machine-gun companies from the brigades to which they were assigned and organize them as a single unit with himself, in effect, as battalion, or battery, commander. It took Hutchison from 6 p.m. one evening till 2 a.m. the following morning to convince the company commanders that this was a good idea, but within a few weeks the turn of events seemed to confirm the logic of Hutchison's scheme. After the brilliant success of the tank offensive at Cambrai late in November, the Germans counter-attacked and virtually turned the British victory into a defeat. General Sir Julian Byng, commanding the British troops in that sector, claimed:

> With very few exceptions the artillery remained fighting to the last but the machine-gunner did not appear to have the same confidence in his weapon. The cause is not far to seek. The German machine-gunners are the pick of the infantry and therefore a *Corps d'Élite*. Our machine-gunners, on the other hand, are enlisted as such and are not brought up with the same *esprit de corps* that is found in a regiment.

This opinion is not confirmed by the numerous frontline infantry officers who thought the British machine guns had performed well: but the Army needed a scapegoat. G.H.Q. established a board of enquiry, under the presidency of Lieutenant-General A. Hamilton Gordon, commanding IX Corps, and the official report of this board included a note by Lieutenant-General Sir Ivor Maxse, commanding XVIII Corps, to the effect that the British failure to withstand the German counter attack was due to:

1. Lack of battle-training in the infantry
2. Lack of battle-training and discipline in the Machine Gun Corps

Since, according to the traditional wisdom of the British army, matters like battle-training and discipline could not be satisfactorily handled at company level, the solution was obvious, and in February 1918 all the Machine Gun Corps companies in the British Expeditionary Force were reorganized as battalions.[16]

---

[16] 'Fourth Army. Tactical Notes' May 1916 in Edmonds *Military Operations France and Belgium 1916* vol. 1 Appendix vol. Appendix 18 p. 131–147 at p. 141–3 (paras. 50–60) especially para. 50a; G.S. Hutchison *Machine Guns: Their History and Tactical Employment* (1938) p. 151–2, 160–2, 185, 187; J.C. Dunn *The War the Infantry Knew* (1987 edit.) p. 201, 16 May 1916 (possibly a post-war insertion) and p. 491, 22 June 1918; G.S. Hutchison *History and Memoir of the 33rd Battalion Machine Gun Corps and of the 19th, 98th, 100th and 248th M.G. Companies* (1919) p. 35, 40: Public Record Office WO 158/54 Byng's report dated 18 Dec. 1917 and cf William Moore *A Wood Called Bourlon: The Cover-up after Cambrai, 1917* (1988) p. 184–5; Public Record Office WO 158/53 Cambrai Enquiry 21 Jan. 1918 'Note' by Sir Ivor Maxse p. 1. See also Tim Travers *The Killing Ground: The British Army, the Western Front and the Emergence of Modern Warfare, 1900–1919* (1987) p. 69 and p. 80 n. 31. In the 1930s Hutchison founded the fascistic New Worker's Party.

This reorganization was excellent for the Machine Gun Corps as an independent branch of the army; the number of lieutenant-colonels increased from 22 in December 1917 to 87 a year later, with corresponding expansion lower down, and a *Machine Gun Corps Magazine* began to be issued. As far as military efficiency was concerned, however, the reorganization was a disaster. When the Germans launched their great offensive on 21 March 1918 there was no integrated defensive system tying the new Machine Gun Corps battalions in with the infantry, and within the infantry battalions inadequate use was made of their Lewis guns because they no longer had any specialist automatic weapons officers. As the Germans advanced, the British infantry, having no direct communication with the machine-gun units in their vicinity, gave the machine-gunners no assistance in evacuating their equipment, and the machine-gunners, left behind to cover the retreat without infantry supports, suffered heavy casualties. This seems to have been the most important single achievement of four years' tactical progress.[17]

It is even possible that the Machine Gun Corps served to keep down the number of machine guns used in the British Army. Britain was the second largest single producer of tripod-mounted machine guns during the war; there were a number of transfers to various Allies but the supply to the British Army was about 97,000 weapons, compared to 80,000 to the French Army. It seems that the British maintained relatively luxurious standards in training establishments, stockpiles and replacement rates, and though the various available statistics for the number of automatic weapons at the front do not tally, they always show Britain with relatively fewer machine guns than any of the other Entente powers:

Italian and French Theatres, 31 October 1918

	Heavy machine guns (i.e. Maxim type)	Light machine guns (Lewis, Chauchat, Villar Perosa, Browning Automatic Rifle)	Rifles
France	24,475	50,988	1,692,577
U.S.	28,414	39,911	1,362,066
U.K.	5,945	34,954	915,151
Belgium	1,067	3,266	200,000
Italy	25,084	5,000	—

[17] For the establishment of lieutenant-colonels cf January 1918 and December 1918 *Army Lists*: the former, which does not show the December 1917 promotions, gives, in addition to the officer in charge of records at 91 York St., London SW1, two substantive and twenty acting or temporary lieutenant-colonels, the December 1918 list gives 69 substantive and 18 acting or temporary lieutenant-colonels. The new substantive lieutenant-colonels, though including Hutchison and 23 others promoted on 27 December 1917, include a large number of officers brought in from outside the corps. For the problems of the machine-gunner in March 1918 see Hutchison *Machine Guns* p. 273–305.

The French and Belgians – and the Germans – retained the system of machine-gun companies with each battalion; the Italians and Americans, as well as machine-gun units allocated to battalions (in the Italian Army) or regiments (in the American Army) also had brigade and divisional machine gun troops, thus having both integrated units and disposable reserves. Only in the British Army were the machine guns organized in battalions allocated to divisions.[18]

Perhaps the best commentary on the British system was that in November 1919 the Army Council decided, 'There will be no Machine Gun Corps and no Machine Gun Battalions'. In the event several infantry battalions were reequipped as machine-gun battalions, allocated to divisions, during the Second World War: they even occasionally laid down barrages with indirect fire. But the Machine Gun Corps itself was not revived.[19]

III. Gas

In the case of the machine gun the war caused the rival armies simultaneously to recognize the special value of a weapon with which they were already familiar. The use of gas was much more of a novelty but though in retrospect it seems one of the great dead ends of military history it provides useful parallels with the development of other weapons in this period.

The idea of using toxic smoke as a weapon had been considered by the great Lord Cochrane in the mid nineteenth century (at the outbreak of war in 1914 his grandson placed his outline plan at the disposal of the government). Developments in chemistry and anaesthesia since Cochrane's time inevitably encouraged interest in such schemes. Schultz's giant gun in Jules Verne's novel *The Begum's Fortune* (1879) was intended to fire shells filled with liquid carbonic acid which would vaporize when the shell burst: 'Every living thing within a radius of thirty yards from the centre of the explosion is at once frozen and suffocated'. Albert Robida, in his account of an imaginary

---

[18] Figures for total production of machine guns are given in Chapter 7. The British transferred 10,000 Vickers guns to the French, who also acquired a thousand Maxim-pattern Brownings: the French transferred 24,103 Hotchkiss guns to various Allies and dumped more than a third of the total output of the horrible Chauchat on the Americans, cf [J.M.G.] Pédoya *La Commission de l'Armée pendant la Grande Guerre* (Paris 1926) p. 53 and *History of the Ministry of Munitions* vol. 11 pt. V p. 27. Figures for weapons with front-line units are from *Report of the Military Board of Allied Supply* vol. 1 pt. 1 p. 49 Table A which however are not consistent with ibid. vol. 1 pt. 1 p. 60 table X: the figure given at vol. 1 pt. 1 p. 49 table A for 2,386, 181 riflemen in the Italian Army evidently refers not to riflemen but to everyone not firing another weapon. Hutchison *Machine Guns* p. 329–330 gives figures for some time earlier in 1918 which are too low though they also show the comparative weakness of the British in automatic weapons: Hutchison is also the source for the organization of machine gun troops in the various armies.

[19] Public Record Office WO 163/24 '*Minutes of the Proceedings of, and Precis Prepared for, the Army Council, for the Year 1919* [printed 1920] p. 163, meeting 28 Nov. 1919; personal information from Mr. Brian Awty, who served with a machine-gun battalion in Italy in 1945.

war between Australia and Mozambique published in *La Caricature* in 1883 described the use of poison gas (*'un brouillard asphyxiante'*) and of gas masks, and Ignatius Donnelly's novel *Caesar's Column: A Story of the Twentieth Century*, published in 1890, described airships dropping poison gas which 'heavier than air and yet expansive, rolls "like a slow blot that spreads", steadily over the earth in all directions, bringing sudden death to those that breathe it'. Arsenic smoke was employed, unsuccessfully, during the siege of Port Arthur in 1904. Arthur Conan Doyle's novel *The Poison Belt*, in which the entire population of the world (except of course Professor Challenger and his cronies) are apparently killed (in fact only anaesthetized) when the Earth passes in its orbit through a zone of toxic gas, was published in 1913. Initially the military perceived gas as merely a harassing weapon, a tactical device for confusing the enemy as much as disabling him. The French had a small stock of tear-gas cartridges at the outbreak of war which they had used up by November 1914 without the Germans even noticing – the fumes from exploding H.E. shells might have much the same choking effect – and similarly the French were not aware that while the autumnal weather was setting in the Germans were bombarding them with shells loaded with sneeze gas. There was also an intriguing British scheme to spray the German trenches with amyl nitrate, presumably in order to give sleepy German sentries the benefit of the short 'rush' which made amyl nitrate briefly popular in drug-taking circles sixty years later.[20]

During the 1880s a French chemist, Eugène Turpin, who had previously invented toys, artificial ivory, artificial gums for dental work, etc., offered various explosives, improvements of gun cotton and so on, to the French Ministry of War. His best effort, known as Melinite or Turpinite, seems simply to have been a more powerful and pyrotechnically more efficient nitrate-based explosive, but the Ministry of War responded oddly that his inventions were 'applicable to mindless destruction such as conceived by criminal enemies of the social order or demented partisans in a civil war' rather than to 'the reasoned and methodical destruction which must alone be employed in the operations of a regular war'. When in 1891, the frustrated Turpin published this letter the term *Turpinite* became established as referring to some sort of new weapon of unprecedented lethal power, acting on a new principle. Public interest in such weapons was revived at the beginning of August 1914, when Turpin announced that he had developed 'an invention of terrifying character

[20] For Lord Cochrane's toxic smoke scheme see Winston S. Churchill *The World Crisis* (6 vols 1923–31) vol. 2 p. 81–2; Jules Verne *Les Cinq Cents Millions de la Bégum* (Paris 1879) p. 79, cf p. 119 of 1880 London edition; H. Beraldi *Un Caricaturiste Prophète: La Guerre telle qu'elle est prévue par A. Robida* (Paris 1916) p. 27, 29; for Donnelly see Martin Ridge *Ignatius Donnelly: The Portrait of a Politician* (Chicago 1962) and cf Cambr. Mass. 1960 edit. of *Caesar's Column* p. 99; for developments up to January 1915 see L.F. Haber *The Poisonous Cloud: Chemical Warfare in the First World War* (Oxford 1986) p. 23–5.

Even Oscar Wilde predicted of future wars, in 1889, 'A chemist on each side will approach the frontier with a bottle': Arthur Conan Doyle *Memoirs and Adventures* (1924) p. 79.

which will modify all present military tactics and render all defensive measures illusory'. Later it was revealed that this invention guaranteed an instant and painless death for everyone within a radius of 400 yards. Experiments with Turpinite were apparently carried out in September 1914; one reporter, who described it as 'an explosive . . . which kills everything within reach,' saw it tested against some sheep, which afterwards 'looked for all the world as if they had been suddenly petrified; they were all quite dead, though some were still on their feet'. On 29 September 1914 *The Evening News* published Arther Machen's famous story 'The Bowmen', in which the German attacks are wiped out by phantom bowmen with, apparently, invisible arrows; the German staff attribute their innumerable unmarked dead to the use of 'Turpinite shells'. A photograph of German soldiers killed 'without a single wound' by French 'Turpinite' shells was actually published in an Australian weekly newspaper, *The Sydney Mail*, on 6 January 1915: it shows half a dozen German soldiers sitting huddled and capsized in the lee of a haystack. (They are in fact probably only asleep, their awkward postures being explained by the fact that they have dozed off during a temporary wait during a long march; or possibly they have been killed by shock waves from an exploding shell.) Although the text of 'The Bowmen', when it was published in book form in August 1915, was altered to read, 'shells containing an unknown gas of a poisonous nature', there seems to be no evidence that any of Turpin's projects were understood to involve the toxicity of gases: the lethal effect of Turpinite seems to have been believed in without any questioning of the technical principle involved in the same way as, in the 1960s, it was readily believed that a neutron bomb had been invented which would destroy people without affecting buildings.[21]

As in the Second World War, it was the Germans who put the use of lethal gas on an entirely new practical basis. On 22 April 1915 they began their attack at Ypres with the release of 150 tons of chlorine from cylinders. They also, during the next fifteen weeks, used 800 tons of chlorine against the Russians. Though very frightening, and often fatal, gas was in the event never decisive, and its tendency to blow back amongst one's own men was almost immediately recognized as a disadvantage, especially at a time when adequate gas masks had not yet been designed. The use of gas as a shell-filler was soon seen to

[21] The French Ministry of War's letter to Turpin of 9 March 1885 is printed in Eugène Turpin *Comment on a Vendu la Mélinite* (Paris 1891) p. 320–1 and in A. Hamon and G. Bachot *Ministère et Mélinite: Étude Sociologique* (Paris 1891) p. 122: the latter book gives details of Turpin's various inventions at p. 104, 115–6 fn. 1 and p. 136–7, and cf Eugene Turpin *The Truth on Melinite: Mala Fides of the Armstrong Co. of Newcastle on Tyne* (Braine-le-Comte 1890) p. 7–12: *Times* 3 Aug. 1914 p. 5b; *Pall Mall Gazette* 17 Sept. 1914 p. 4a; *Evening News* 29 Sept. 1914. 3b, cf Arthur Machen *The Bowmen and other Legends of the War* [also headed *The Angels of Mons*] (1915) p. 37; *Sydney Mail* 6 Jan. 1915 p. 10 – picture reproduced in Rudolf Hanslian *Der Chemische Krieg* (Berlin 1927) Tafel 1.

With regard to the neutron bomb, my recollection is that I heard of it as a weapon that would kill people rather than destroy buildings about ten years before encountering the explanation that the principle involved was simply that of maximizing the bomb's emission of sub-atomic particles: the buildings within a couple of miles' radius of the bomb's detonation would still be destroyed.

be more promising than the release of clouds of gas into the wind, but it took some time before shells were developed which dispersed the gas effectively, and even more time before the Germans discovered that the diphosgene they were using in shells was largely ineffective in the open air. (The French made the same mistake with hydrogen cyanide, and it was later claimed that French Vincennite [i.e. cyanide] shells did not kill a single German soldier: in the Second World War however the Germans found hydrogen cyanide perfectly effective in enclosed spaces like the extermination chambers at Auschwitz.) Mustard gas (dichlorodiethyl sulphide), first used by the Germans in July 1917, by the French in June 1918 and by the British in August 1918 (though the first major bombardment with mustard gas manufactured in Britain was not till 30 September 1918), turned out to be the only gas used in the First World War that was of real military value: it had a long-term corrosive effect on moist parts of the body that was even worse than its initial asphyxiating effect, and its contamination was persistent so that mustard gas bombardment could render an area impassable for days, and dangerous for weeks. By 1918 the Germans were too short of rubber to be able to bring an improved respirator into service, and too short of textile fibres to replace contaminated clothing, so that had the war continued into 1919 the Germans' increasing lack of the resources to take effective counter-measures against mustard gas would probably have been of decisive importance.[22]

At peak strength in 1916 gas troops – mainly for releasing gas clouds from cylinders – in all the belligerent armies together totalled only 16,000; by 1918 they were generally much reduced in number except that the Americans were building up their gas regiments, planning on a strength of 13,500 by December 1918. The U.S. Chemical Warfare Service seems to have owed much of its dynamism to the fact that it had no practical experience to interfere with its flights of theory. Although Pershing, the commander of the American Expeditionary Force, assured Lord Esher that he would rather learn from Haig than from the French, his H.Q. staff regarded it as 'defeatist' to propose learning anything from either the French or the British, and by disregarding their allies' gas training procedures the Americans succeeded in gassing much larger numbers of their own men in 1918 than was by that stage customary in other armies.[23]

Service in such an accident-prone branch was of course unpopular and in any case gas warfare never could have been glamorous, even if it had not received so much adverse publicity: consequently gas units did not pull in the dashing well-connected volunteers who helped set the air services on their feet.

[22] Haber *Poisonous Cloud* p. 34, 39; ibid. p. 87, 117–8 and cf C.H. Foulkes *'Gas!' the Story of the Special Brigade* (1934) p. 107–8 and Hanslian *Chemische Krieg* p. 15; Haber *Poisonous Cloud* p. 192, 218–9.

[23] Haber *Poisonous Cloud* p. 135, 276 and cf James Lees-Milne *The Enigmatic Edwardian: The Life of Reginald 2nd Viscount Esher* (1986) p. 304; Allan R. Millett *The General: Robert L Bullard and the Officership of the United States Army, 1881–1925* (Westport Conn. 1975) p. 315 and A.O. Pollard *Fire-Eater: Memoirs of a V.C.* (1932) p. 247–251.

Moreover the heads of various gas services were not the men to promote their own business: they all derived from the engineers' corps of their respective armies, and the engineers did not normally recruit ambitious socialites with a flair for public relations. Lieutenant-Colonel Soulié, head of the French *compagnies Z*, worked from his office in Paris – French academic physiologists wrote 750 monographs on gas defence and 984 on gas attack so he and his staff had plenty of reading to get through. Colonel, later Major-General Otto Peterson of the German *Gaspioniere* immersed himself in organizational matters and left operational control to Colonel Max Bauer, who was head of the artillery section of the *OHL* and who also had a career as a political wire-puller and *éminence grise* to think about. Colonel, later Major-General C.H. Foulkes, the ex-hockey international head of the B.E.F.'s Special Brigade – note the discreetly menacing title – and later Director of Gas Services at Haig's G.H.Q., occupied himself with technical details and the boy scout business of devising new ways to launch small harassing attacks of no significance against the Boche. On neither side, despite some interesting experiments, were gas tactics really thought through. By 1918 the main method of using gas was shell-fire; although the British were still using gas cloud attacks and also had a very successful type of trench mortar, the Livens projector, which fired a canister containing thirteen kilograms of gas, gas shells represented nearly one in twelve of all the shells fired by British artillery in the last year of the war. In the German Army gas shells comprised more than a quarter of the shells fired in 1918; these also contained a large explosive charge however. With much of the gas that was being manufactured going to make artillery ammunition, there was correspondingly less scope for the evolution of an independent tactical doctrine; though as will be argued with regard to the parallel case of air warfare, it was less the objective effectiveness of a tactical doctrine that counted in establishing organizational independence than the political effectiveness of those promoting the doctrine. In the end it was probably the sheer unattractiveness of gas warfare, rather than its ineffectiveness, which prevented it from establishing a more independent status.[24]

IV. The Tank

The role of glamour in helping establish a new tactical doctrine is exemplified in the story of the tank: a story of spectacular successes and disappointing sequels, which had its climax a generation later in the stunning victories of the German Panzers in 1940 and 1941, and which in the First World War provided Major-General J.F.C. Fuller with his most famous dramatic role, with Winston Churchill playing a memorable walk-on-and-charge-around part and supporting performances from various members of the army's menagerie of unusual colonels, including Albert Stern the merchant banker,

[24] Haber *Poisonous Cloud* p. 109, 133–4, 262–70.

Christopher Baker-Carr, and Ernest Swinton, afterwards Major-General and Chichele Professor of Military History at Oxford University. The tank was however unusual in that unlike gas and the aeroplane its development owed nothing to direct competition with devices developed by the German Army – it was originated in fact not in the British Army but in the Royal Navy – and it was perhaps because there was no necessity of keeping up with the Germans that Haig's G.H.Q. had greater success in combating the tank lobby than it had with the aviation lobby.

Late in August 1914 Winston Churchill, as First Lord of the Admiralty, had ordered the creation of armoured car units to protect the Royal Naval Air Service installations at Dunkirk against German cavalry raids – the use of machine guns mounted on armour-plated Rolls Royces was exactly the thing to appeal to Churchill – and three months later he ordered the construction of the first experimental armoured vehicle with caterpillar tracks. The French were also interested and during 1915 the armies of both countries began testing prototypes, though in both Britain and France there was some resistance. In the British case the resistance may have been because tank development was being pushed ahead by the Admiralty. Apart from Churchill himself, Eustace D'Eyncourt, Director of Naval Construction, and Commodore Murray Sueter, Director of the Air Department, were both early converts: Sueter later described himself in his *Who's Who* entry as having 'contributed in a definite degree to the evolution and adoption of the tanks'. Albert Stern, secretary of the Admiralty's Landship Committee set up by Churchill under D'Eyncourt's presidency in February 1915, later Chairman of the Tank Committee, then Director of the Tank Supply Department at the Ministry of Munitions and by 1916 Director General of the Mechanical Warfare Department at the War Office, had originally been commissioned in the Royal Naval Reserve. In a memo to Lloyd George in July 1917 Stern complained that because of the uncooperative attitude of the War Office all development and testing to date had been by the men – over 400 – lent for that purpose by the Admiralty.[25]

Sir William Robertson's rearguard action against the establishment of the Royal Air Force will be described below; it is interesting to note that it coincided with a parallel campaign against the tank. In the autumn of 1917, when the question had arisen of appointing a successor to Sir David Henderson as Director General of Military Aeronautics, Robertson had nominated Major-General Sir John Capper. Capper had been commandant of the army's Balloon School and later of the School of Military Engineering before the war and was regarded by the army establishment as their leading intellectual in matters of military technology; in later years he was said to be able to complete *The Times* crossword every day, an important matter for personal credibility in Whitehall. Although he had captained the army's first airship, the *Nulli Secundus*, in its first and last flight over London in 1907, he had had little contact with

---

[25] Albert G. Stern *Tanks, 1914–1918: the Log-Book of a Pioneer* (1919) p. 161.

developments in heavier-than-air flight, which was another recommendation as far as Robertson was concerned. Brancker, the Deputy Director General of Military Aeronautics, had managed to block Capper's appointment, even writing to the Secretary of State on the matter. Brancker was rewarded for his obstreperousness by being sent off to the Middle East; when Stern began pressing for the building of at least 4,000 tanks for the 1918 campaign, more than twice as many as thought desirable by Robertson, the latter got rid of Stern and appointed Capper to the new post of Director General of the Tank Corps. Another engineer, Colonel – later Major-General – Hugh Elles was appointed to command the tanks in France. Elles was one of the heroic figures of the war. Fuller, his G.S.O.1, was impressed by his 'flair, élan and dash', and described him as 'boyish and reckless in danger; perhaps a better soldier than a strategist . . . universally loved and trusted by his followers'. Photographs show him as a dark, saturnine version of Trevor Howard, a physical aspect which doubtless helped Fuller to see him as a modern Henri IV; but he was not a theorist or a politician. Amongst Elles's brigade commanders was Christopher Baker-Carr, whom Fuller saw as the Murat of the Tank Corps, and John Hardress Lloyd, evidently a *beau sabreur*. Partly as a result of Albert Stern bombarding Lloyd George with letters, the War Cabinet decided in March 1918 to aim for a tank army of 5,000 vehicles, but with Capper and Elles in charge there was little danger of the tank lobby establishing too much independence.[26]

In the event it might have been better for Robertson's and Haig's subsequent reputation if they had given the tank lobby more scope. The endless stories about the army's, or the War Office's, strenuous resistance to progress (either thwarted by the superior in-fighting skills of the progressives or embarrassingly exposed by the turn of events at the front) really only show that mavericks who try to make their own procedural rules get nowhere in the fastnesses of bureaucracy. Pursuing a less confrontational course Stephen Foot, a temporary officer like Stern but a mere G.S.O.2 at the War Office, not a Director General, secured the attendance of the Director of Military Operations, the Director of the Artillery, the Director of Organisation and the Director of Supply and Transport at a meeting to discuss his memorandum, 'A Mobile Army', which advocated replacing the horses used to move supplies in the front line by caterpiller tractors, and it was this meeting which led eventually, after the war, to the British Army becoming the most dependent on mechanized transport in the world. On the other hand, the military establishment's resistance to the tank theorists prevented the more extreme claims of the latter from ever being put to the

[26] See Harold Penrose *British Aviation: the Pioneer Years, 1903–1914* (1967) p. 576 for Capper's expertise with crosswords, and Macmillan *Sir Sefton Brancker* p. 157–162 for the blocking of Capper's appointment as Director General of Military Aeronautics; Stern *Tanks 1914–1918* p. 175–8, 181; J.F.C. Fuller *Memoirs of an Unconventional Soldier* (1936) p. 88, 94.

test and thereby provided them with an excellent propaganda case which they put to full use after the war.[27]

What was at issue between the tank theorists and the military conservatives was tactical doctrine. Ernest Swinton's 'Notes on the Employment of the Tank' of February 1916 fairly admitted that 'the vulnerability of tanks to artillery fire . . . represents their chief weakness', and argued that the corollary of this was that tanks should be kept secret till they could be used *en masse* for an all out surprise attack: 'Since the chance of success of an attack by tanks lies almost entirely in its novelty and in the element of surprise . . . these machines *should not be used in driblets*'. Stern, D'Eyncourt and Churchill all thought of the tank as essentially a one-time surprise weapon; Churchill felt that even the first major assault, at Cambrai on 20 November 1917, when 400 tanks were used, was on an insufficiently large scale. Yet Haig's failure to hold back till he was able to launch a surprise attack by a thousand tanks is hardly one of the best instances of that general's reactionary short-sightedness. The tanks were still subject to mechanical teething troubles; in the very first employment of tanks in action, at the Somme on 15 November 1916, of 49 tanks, seventeen failed to reach the start line, nine suffered mechanical breakdowns after the start, five became stuck in ditches or trenches, nine were unable to accelerate fast enough to overtake the infantry, who were advancing at a slow walk, and nine performed excellently. The French had also been building tanks: their Schneider type was first used at the Chemin des Dames on 16 April 1917 and out of 48 machines in one attack, eight broke down at the start, 32 were destroyed by German artillery fire or abandoned when the lead vehicle broke down and blocked a trench-crossing, and eight returned to base *'plus ou moins détériorés'*. The larger Saint Chamond type, which was inferior even to the Schneider in trench-crossing capacity, was used at Laffaux on 5 May 1917: of sixteen machines two became bogged down in a field, five broke down before the start of the attack, four more shortly afterwards, one was knocked out by German fire, two became stuck at the first German trench, one broke down while withdrawing and one managed to get back to the start line still in working order. Later makes were more reliable, but even so 163 of the 415 British tanks assigned to the 8 August 1918 offensive at Amiens suffered mechanical problems which prevented their employment on the second day of the battle. Obviously the bigger the investment in a surprise attack the more likely it was that mechanical breakdowns, or battlefield communications difficulties, would have caused it to end in a fiasco. Then of course the larger the stockpiling and the training programme, the more likely would have been its detection by German reconnaissance, and the less likely the maintenance of any element of surprise. As events in the Second World War subsequently showed, the tank did not depend in any case on surprising the enemy with the mere fact of its existence –

[27] Stephen Foot *Three Lives* (1934) p. 218: his memo 'A Mobile Army' of 24 April 1918 is printed at p. 345–9.

in 1940 and 1941 the German Panzers were outnumbered by French and Russian tanks, often of superior quality – it depended rather on the flexibility of its employment. And it was this question of flexibility which finally undermined the mass attack doctrine: it has been calculated that for the ten hours of operating by the 400 tanks at Cambrai on 20 November 1917 the British needed to lay on 28,000 gallons of petrol, 2,000 gallons of oil, 16,000 gallons of water, 6,000 gallons of gear oil and over a ton of axle grease. In 1917 the tank was an infant that was unable to run because it was still trailing its umbilical cord; the fact that its stepmother was standing on its leading strings was of secondary importance.[28]

This is not to deny that G.H.Q., in the stepmother role, was quicker to perceive the limitations of the tank than its advantages. As Haig awaited the great German offensive of March 1918, instead of using tanks to make spoiling attacks to disrupt the German preparations, or arranging for their concentration in the rear of the threatened positions, he ordered them to be distributed along over sixty miles of front to serve as defensive strong points. 'It is like turning a polo pony into a towel horse', Fuller commented sourly. Later when the British went over to the attack Haig insisted that the Whippet light tanks should always be accompanied by cavalry, should not run ahead of them and should retire when the cavalry retired: with the result that once the cavalry came under rifle fire, the tanks, though bullet proof, could not advance. But not all Tank Corps doctrine was more realistic. Giffard Martel, in a memo of November 1916, advocated an all tank army without any infantry at all, employing a variation of battle-fleet tactics (which probably explains why he recommended that tanks should be amphibious). Fuller, in his 'Plan 1919', drawn up in May 1918, made a much more important doctrinal advance when he envisaged the possibility of paralyzing the enemy's army by striking at its system of command ('the shot through the brain') and its system of supply ('a second shot through the stomach') but, as with theories of the war-winning potential of air power which were being promoted in the same period, the technology available at the time was not sufficiently advanced to make such schemes entirely feasible. Fuller's 'Plan 1919' would have required tanks with longer range and much greater mechanical reliability and capacity to withstand shell-fire: in addition to the 163 out of 415 tanks which broke down in the 8 August 1918 attack, 109 were knocked out by the German defences. Nevertheless Sir Henry Wilson, Robertson's successor as C.I.G.S.,

---

[28] James E. Edmonds *Military Operations: France and Belgium 1916* vol. 2 Appendix vol. p. 50–59 Appendix XVIII at p. 52–3 (also printed in Swinton *Eyewitness* at p. 198–214 cf Anthony John Trythall *'Bony' Fuller: The Intellectual General, 1878–1966* (1977) p. 43 for agreement of Stern, D'Eyncourt and Churchill with Swinton's views and also Churchill *World Crisis* vol. 4 p. 347–8; Clough Williams-Ellis and A. Williams-Ellis *The Tank Corps* (1919) p. 29: Ministère de la Guerre *Les Armées Françaises dans la Grande Guerre* 'tome' 5 annexe vol. 2 p. 1205 (annexe no. 1661) and cf p. 925–6 (no. 1415); ibid. p. 1564, 1569 (annexe no. 1935) Edmonds *Military Operations: France and Belgium 1918* vol. 4 p. 87; Robin Prior *Churchill's 'World Crisis' as History* (1983) p. 242.

sent Foch a proposal for an offensive in 1919 on an eighty kilometre front with 10,500 Allied tanks: this scheme, dated 20 July 1918, was based on a watered-down version of Fuller's 'Plan 1919' produced by Capper, though it retained some traces of its original; for example it stated, 'The brain and stomach of the enemy must be struck concurrently with, or in advance of, the blow at his body', though without explaining these metaphors. One wonders what it would have done for Fuller's reputation if the attempt had been made to carry out his plan.[29]

The chief weakness of the tank was its vulnerability: designed only to withstand small-arms fire – and even then the crews had to wear protective clothing against the metal splinters shooting off from the interior surface of the armour plate when struck by a bullet on the outer side – tanks were unable to withstand armour-piercing bullets, or lashed together bundles of grenades, let alone field artillery, and by late 1918 the Germans were bringing into production 13mm anti-tank rifles and 37mm revolver cannon. At their speed, and on the terrain of the Western Front, tanks would have stood no chance against such weapons. Writing his memoirs straight after the war Ludendorff showed himself completely unimpressed by the potential of the tank; Max Bauer, the head of the *OHL*'s artillery section, who took over responsibility for tank warfare from the Organization and Replacement section in mid-1918, devoted some thought to tank tactics but seems to have been more interested in anti-tank defence. Though the *OHL* ordered 900 light tanks in the summer of 1918, the only German-designed vehicles which were available before the Armistice were twenty of the cumbersome eleven-man A7V type (in addition 25 to 30 captured British machines were used at the front: the future Oberstgruppenführer und Panzergeneral-Oberst der Waffen-SS Sepp Dietrich served as an N.C.O. in captured British Mark IVs). This is to be compared with the 2,385 vehicles on strength in the British army at the end of the war and the 2,756 – mainly Renault light tanks – in the French army. King Kong met Godzilla on 24 April 1918 at Villers-Bretonneux when three A7Vs supported by infantry encountered some British Mark IVs. After driving off two of the Mark IVs of a sub-type armed only with machine guns, the leading A7V was hit by a six-pound shell fired by a cannon-armed Mark IV, ran up an embankment in order to avoid being hit again, and being too narrow for its height toppled on its side; the second A7V was then abandoned by its eleven-man crew; the third retreated, and the supporting infantry were run down by seven British Whippet light tanks which finally withdrew with their 'tracks dripping with blood'. Probably the inferiority in design of the A7V, which had nothing like the stability and trench-crossing

[29] Fuller *Memoirs of an Unconventional Soldier* p. 240, 245–6; ibid. p. 307–8; Trythall *'Boney' Fuller* p. 47–8 for Martel's proposal: according to Imperial War Museum, Clarke Mss p. 2–3 Martel was still plugging this idea in the late 1930s; Fuller *Memoirs* p. 325 and cf p. 336–8 for relation of his scheme to Wilson's letter of 20 July 1918 and Public Record Office WO 158/842 Wilson to Foch 20 July 1918, cf Bryan Cooper *Tank Battles of World War I* (1974) p. 78.

ability of the British heavy tanks, contributed to the German lack of interest in armoured warfare, but they were surely correct in thinking that anti-tank weapons would prevent the tank from becoming a decisive break-through weapon; the 900 light tanks ordered by the *OHL*, like the French Renaults, are to be seen more as a supplement to the cavalry than as a replacement for the infantry.[30]

V. The Image and Achievements of Air Power

Of all the new weapons of this war, it was undoubtedly the aeroplane which established itself most brilliantly. Tens of thousands of army and navy officers and N.C.O.s were trained as air crew. A substantial part of ground artillery was adapted for anti-aircraft functions: by the time of the Armistice the German Army deployed 2,410 heavy anti-aircraft guns of field artillery calibre, plus 366 of the new 37mm cannon. The two-fold division of the armed forces into Army and Navy which had existed for centuries was abrogated in Britain by the establishment of the Royal Air Force as a third arm in April 1918: Italy followed suit five years later, while defeated Germany was prohibited from having any military aviation at all.[31]

Air fighting provided the most glamorous images of warfare and a large proportion of the best-known heroes, including Manfred von Richthofen, the one internationally acknowledged paladin of the war. Richthofen's British rivals were less celebrated for as John Buchan explained, 'half the magic of our Flying Corps was its freedom from advertisement'; yet of the eight Royal Flying Corps and Royal Naval Air Service pilots who shot down more than fifty enemy aircraft, five received Britain's most glamorous decoration, the Victoria Cross; all three of the men awarded six British decorations for gallantry in the First World War were fighter pilots, as were six out of the nine men decorated five times. German airmen, who claimed a total of 7,425 'kills' (including 614 observation balloons) for the loss of 6,830 machines, received between them 72 Orders *Pour le mérite*; Max Immelmann, one of the earliest of the aces, had at the time of his death on 18 June 1916 been decorated with the Order *Pour le mérite*, the Iron Cross First and Second

[30] Ludendorff *My War Memories* vol. 2. 576; [Max] Bauer *Der Grosse Krieg in Feld und Heimat: Erinnerungen und Betrachtungen* (Tübingen 1922) p. 122, 228–91; Wrisberg *Erinnerungen an die Kriegsjahre* vol. 3 p. 160 (and see Charles Messenger *Hitler's Gladiator: The Life and Times of Oberstgruppenführer and Panzergeneral-Oberst der Waffen-SS Sepp Dietrich* (1988) p. 11–15), cf *Report of the Military Board of Allied Supply* (2 vols. Washington 1924–5) vol. 1 p. 49 Table A and Pédoya *La Commission de l'Armée* p. 137–8, 142; Williams-Ellis *Tank Corps* p. 172–3: an eyewitness account of this first tank battle, by F. Mitchell, is given in C.B. Purdom ed. *Everyman at War: Sixty Personal Narratives of the War* (1930) p. 231–8. Messenger *Hitler's Gladiator* p. 10 gives a quite different account, apparently from German sources.

[31] Erich von Hoeppner *Deutschlands Krieg in der Luft* (Leipzig 1921) p. 181 for German A.A. artillery.

Classes, the Order of St Heinrich, the Albrecht Order with Swords, the Order of the House of Hohenzollern with Swords, the Bavarian Order of Military Merit, the Hanseatic Cross (awarded by the City of Hamburg) and the Turkish Iron Crescent; although he had only recently been promoted to senior lieutenant his lying in state at Douai was attended by the Crown Princes of Bavaria and of Saxony and by twenty generals. Italian airmen claimed 762 'kills' including 14 observation balloons and in addition to 46 Orders of Savoy and 24 gold medals for valour, received an average of 2.2 silver medals and 1.6 bronze medals per enemy plane destroyed – and in Italy a silver medal for valour generally rated having a street named after one in one's home town. The French ace René Fonck, having been cited 27 times in Army Orders, was entitled to wear 27 *palmes* with his *croix de guerre*, requiring a medal ribbon that hung down from above his heart to his belt. Some pilots, it is said, even flew into combat wearing all their medals, though it was left to the classless Russians of the Second World War to make a custom of painting the medals awarded to an air ace on his personal aeroplane.[32]

Air fighting provided an irresistable counter symbol to the degrading horror of the trenches:

> High above the squalor and the mud, so high in the firmament that they are not visible from the earth, they fight out the eternal issues of right and wrong.

These were the words of Lloyd George, but the same idea was expressed by the German pilot who claimed:

> We still had the honourable combat of man against man, that stood out like a thing of another age amid the din and shock of mass warfare.

Another German flier told the girl he was courting:

> in this era of mass-murder through machines, technology and chemistry, which is what modern warfare has become, we are still the only ones who conduct an honest, human warfare, eye to eye with our opponents.

---

[32] For official British reluctance to publicize aces see RAF Museum Hendon MFC 71/4/750 Rothermere to Henderson 7 Jan. 1918 and Arthur Gould Lee *Open Cockpit: a Pilot of the Royal Flying Corps* (1969) p. 150–1, and cf John Buchan *Mr. Standfast* (1919) p. 24; Hoeppner *Deutschlands Krieg in der Luft* p. 174 fn. 1 and fn. 2 for German victories and losses; Georg Paul Neumann ed. *Die Deutschen Luftstreitkräfte im Weltkriege* (Berlin 1920) p. 586 for awards of the *Pour le Mérite*; Pietro Maravigna *Guerra & Vittoria* (Turin 1938 ed.) p. 641–2. Jacques Mortane *Deux Archanges de l'Air* (Paris 1938) plate opp. p. 16 shows Georges Guynemer checking an ammunition drum just before getting into his plane, wearing all his medals.

Pictures of Soviet fighter planes with their pilots' medals painted on the nose have been published in numerous illustrated histories of the Second World War; it was not uncommon for German planes to be painted with the insignia of the Knight's Cross to celebrate an award to the pilot, but this would then be painted out after the celebratory period was over. The somewhat tasteless practice of painting on rows of small symbols signifying one's 'score' does not seem to have been customary in the First World War: Major W.G. Barker seems to have pioneered this fashion by having white flashes painted on the struts of his Sopwith Camel in 1918: Bruce Robertson ed. *Air Aces of the 1914–1918 War* (Letchworth 1959) p. 29 photo caption.

The press in the Central Empires had a taste for depicting their fighter aces as birds of prey – Immelmann was *der Adler von Lille* (the Eagle of Lille), the Bulgarians called Rudolf von Eschwege *Bjelomorssko Orel* (the Eagle of the Aegean) and Frank Linke-Crawford became *der Falke von Feltre* (the Falcon of Feltre) – but it was the parallel with medieval chivalry which was most widely cherished:

> The ancient age of chivalry is past, its glory and adventure are forgotten, the glamour of its romance has faded, but from the ashes of the old *régime* has risen a new and far more daring order of knighthood – the 'Cavalry of the Air'.

According to Lloyd George, 'They are the knighthood of this War, without fear and without reproach'. Owing to the then prevailing constitutional arrangements only Bavarian and Belgian fighter pilots received titles of knighthood, though Godfrey Banfield, the Austrian flying boat fighter ace, was made a baron, but fighter pilots of all nationalities found themselves written up as 'knights of the air' and a war-time portrait of Frank Linke-Crawford (wearing a sombre Buster Keaton expression) presents him in a distinctly sixteenth-century manner, with the date ANNO DOMINI MCMXVIII in capitals above and his name FRANK LINKE-CRAWFORD in capitals below – though perhaps this kind of thing was not reserved for aviators, for one notes that John Lavery's 1916 painting of Winston Churchill as a battalion commander on the Western Front, in uniform and wearing a French helmet, seems to be modelled on Rembrandt's 'Man in a Golden Helmet'. The medieval chivalry analogy was also evidently the origin of the heraldic symbols painted on many German fighter planes and of the regularly patterned overall finish, reminiscent of a medieval knight's surcoat, favoured by some German pilots, for example the white and blue diamond pattern adopted by Hauptmann Eduard Ritter von Schleich of Jasta 5.[33]

In fact medieval chivalry provided only part of the symbolism of aerial warfare. The all-red Nieuport of Jean Navarre; the all-red Fokker Dr. 1 of Manfred Freiherr von Richthofen, the all-red Albatros of the Austro-

---

[33] *Hansard: House of Commons* vol. 98 col. 1247, speech by Lloyd George 29 Oct. 1917. Rudolph Stark *Wings of War: An Airman's Diary of the Last Year of the War* (1918) epigraph; [Edwin Böhme] *Briefe eines deutsches Kampffliegers: an ein junges Mädchen* ed. Johannes Werner (Leipzig 1930) p. 67 Böhme to Annamarie B. 18 Oct. 1916 and cf p. 59, same to same 4 Oct. 1916; the portrait of Frank Linke-Crawford referred to is reproduced in Riccardo Cavigioli *L'Aviazone Austro-Ungarica sulla Fronte Italiana, 1915–1918* (Milan 1934) p. 47: the immediate source of the pseudo-sixteenth-century format may be the *Jugendstil* mode but to say this merely begs the question of why *Jugendstil*revived this stylistic mannerism and why it was applied to Frank Linke-Crawford. The half dozen Bavarian fighter pilots who received titles of knighthood by virtue of being awarded the Order of Maximilian-Joseph included Eduard Ritter von Schleich and Robert Ritter von Greim, briefly in 1945, the Luftwaffe's last commander-in-chief. Belgium's knighted aviator was Major le Chevalier Willy Coppens de Houthulst. For more on the 'knights of the air' see Stuart Sillars *Art and Survival in First World War Britain* (1987) p. 90–91 and cf p. 96–106 for the wartime image of the exhilaration of flight.

Hungarian Godwin Brumowski, the all-white Dr. 1 of Leutnant Weiss of Jasta 10 – his name means *white* in German – Josef Jacobs's all-black Dr. 1 and the all-yellow Hanriot of the Belgian André de Meulemeester, recall not only the red knights and the black knights of medieval legend but also the bright monochrome liveries adopted by the French Navy in the early 1790s and the all black finish seen on some Spanish warships of the same period. The roundels showing the colours of the national flag in concentric rings, adopted as identification symbols by the French at the beginning of the war, were derived from the tricoleur cockades worn in the French Revolutionary period: the French term for roundel is in fact *cocarde* though the corresponding English word *cockade*, never quite established itself in this sense. (Roundels were adopted by the British after consultation with the French in November 1914: the Russians, Italians, Belgians and Americans also subsequently adopted this system.) Many pilots had their aeroplanes painted with personal symbols: Hauptmann Schlimacky of Jasta 17 has a *Sch* monogram on his plane at least as early as October 1916 (he was shot down over Malzéville on the 23rd of the month); later Frank Linke-Crawford had a hovering falcon, Charles Nungesser had the masonic motifs of skull, crossbones, coffin and candles on a black heart-shaped field (in the Russian No. 1 Fighter Group a skull and cross bones painted on the rudder was a general unit marking). Ernst Udet had the monogram LO! in honour of his fiancée Lola Zink, painted on his plane; Rudolf Berthold had a flaming sword emblem. Some Italians painted on slogans in a crude graffiti style, often in dialect. A shooting star motif, evidently adopted from the decor of fun fairs or circuses, was frequently used on German planes, though also employed in the Belgian 1st Squadron and the American 22nd Aero Squadron; the famous hat in the ring symbol of the American 94th Aero Squadron also evidently had its origin in the entertainment world. Characters from newspaper strip cartoons, later to be much favoured by the Americans in the Second World War, were to be seen, in a very small and discreet format, on the engine cowlings of some R.A.F. squadrons in 1918, e.g. No. 139 Squadron in Italy, but the R.F.C. and R.A.F. officially discouraged personal liveries and insisted on registration and unit code letters being prominently marked, as befitted the war machines of a mobilized industrial bureaucracy: a system of squadron identification symbols of circles, bars, triangles, etc. in black or white (depending on colour scheme) was promulgated in August 1917 and in France it was announced 'the G.O.C. has decided that all British machines shall be khaki . . . Gaudy colours on wheels, cowlings, etc, will not be allowed'. As will be shown later, the intellectuals of the R.F.C. staff were concentrating on a quite different and more abstract vein of fantasy.[34]

[34] There are numerous illustrated popular histories of the World Wars published in recent years which contain accurate colour drawings of the First World War aircraft. For the British adaption of roundel markings cf Public Record Office AIR 1/864/204/5/512, Henderson to Huguet 24 Oct. 1914. 'Cockade' in the sense referred to is used in the title of the Californian

continued

At the same time as these efflorescences of youthful jauntiness the most technically complex aspects of aerial warfare were being developed. The German Zeppelin L10 bombed Tyneside using radio triangulation to locate its target zone on 15 June 1915. On 12 August 1915 a Turkish steam tug was sunk in the Dardanelles by a torpedo launched from a British seaplane. Aircraft were mobilized against the other most revolutionary new weapon of the the war, the submarine: the British Royal Naval Air Service began bombing German U-boats at sea in 1915 though it did not manage to sink one by this method till 20 May 1917. (Earlier that same month a patrolling Zeppelin had been shot down in flames by a R.N.A.S. flying boat which had been guided on to its prey by radio from its base, using information from radio tracking stations which had plotted the Zeppelin's course – an anticipation, in essentials, of the ground control technique used by R.A.F. Fighter Command during the Battle of Britain in 1940.) Air to air rockets invented by Lieutenant Y.P.G. Le Prieur of the French Navy were used with some success against German observations balloons on the Somme in 1916. The first major airlift in history was during the siege of Kut in the spring of 1916 when the R.F.C. dropped saccharine, anti-tetanus serum, a millstone, buffer springs for field guns, bundles of rupees for paying local labour and personal mail of the H.Q. staff (though not of the fighting troops). A senior R.F.C. staff officer suggested in November 1917 that an air-borne assault on the German artillery positions on the Western Front could be made with 300 Caproni heavy bombers (at that time the largest aircraft available to the Western Allies) each carrying fifty troops; he even thought attacks by air-borne troops could be made against cities like Essen, with Capronis reembarking their troops after some hours of ground operations. Nearly a year later Brigadier-General William Mitchell, commanding the air component of the American First Army Group, suggested something along similar though more practical lines: a specially trained division could be parachuted down behind enemy lines and supplied by air. Meanwhile the British were developing the aircraft carrier and on 18 July 1918 seven Sopwith Camel 2F1s were launched from H.M.S. *Furious* to bomb the Zeppelin base at Tondern in Schleswig-Holstein; the idea was to

continued

Cross & Cockade Journal, founded in 1960 and appears in Claud W. Sykes's translation of [Georg] Haupt Heydemarck *War Flying in Macedonia* [1935] p. 89 – the latter is incidentally the main source for the career of Rudi von Eschwege, the Eagle of the Aegean. Hauptmann Schlimacky's *Sch* monogram is illustrated in Heinz J. Nowarra *Eisernes Kreuz und Balkenkreuz: Die Markierungen der deutschen Flugzeuge 1914–1918 (Markings of German Aircraft in WW1, 1914–1918)* (Mainz 1968) p. 77, and the Italian graffiti *motif* is shown in Giorgio Apostolo and Giorgio Bignozzi *War Birds: Military Aircraft of the First World War in Colour* (1974) p. 14; for the British regulations see Public Record Office AIR 1/1589/204/82/74, Philip Game, B.G.G.S., to Brigade C.O.s 1917.

The derivation of the shooting-star motif on one's aircraft from the decoration of the hot-rod car one had before the war, as shown in William Wellman's 1927 film *Wings*, is sheer Hollywood, as is the identification of the shooting-star motif as a personal rather than a unit symbol: it was more the case that paint jobs on sports cars after 1918 copied the motifs used on wartime fighter planes.

ditch the aircraft alongside British warships after the mission though in the event three of the pilots landed in neutral Denmark and were interned and a fourth came down in the sea out of sight of help and was drowned. The Germans for their part were experimenting by the end of the war with aircraft armed with 20mm anti-tank cannon.[35]

The truth is however, that none of these more advanced uses of the air weapon turned out to be of major importance during the war itself. The use of torpedo-carrying planes in the Dardanelles was merely an isolated series of experiments and thereafter the development of the technique was described as 'astonishing slow'. In the summer of 1917 German seaplanes carrying torpedoes sank three British freighters off the English coast and the Germans later claimed to have sunk a Russian destroyer in the Baltic by this method, but when Admiral Sir David Beatty suggested, in October 1917, a mass attack on the German fleet by 120 torpedo-carrying Sopwith Cuckoos flown off eight converted fast merchantmen, and covered by long-range Handley Page 0/400s dropping 230lb bombs, the Admiralty saw only insuperable objections; and it does seem that the aircraft of the period, especially seaplanes, were far too slow and fragile to be a practicable weapon against ships armed with machine guns. First World War aircraft also lacked the range and bombload to be very effective against submarines, and aeroplane patrols were able to contribute much less to the campaign against the U-boat than in the Second World War.

---

[35] Bill Gunston *Night Fighters: A Development & Combat History* (Cambridge 1976) p. 16; Walter Raleigh and H.A. Jones *The War in the Air* (7 vols Oxford 1922–34) vol. 2 p. 65 cf S.W. Roskill ed. *Documents Relating to the Naval Air Service* vol. 1 (1969) p. 221–3; Raleigh and Jones *War in the Air* vol. 4 p. 54: the submarine was the UL 36. In July 1917 the UL 1 and the UB 20 were sunk by R.N.A.S flying boats; Raleigh and Jones *War in the Air* vol. 4 p. 19: the Zeppelin was the L22. (The first submarine to be sunk from the air was the Russian *Akula*, off Gotland, on 22 May 1915; the British B.X. was sunk by a bomb dropped by Austro-Hungarian floatplanes while docked at the Arsenal in Venice, on the evening of 9 Aug. 1916, cf Public Record Office AIR 1/2282/209/73/2 Harold C. Swan to J.H. Towsey 10 Aug. 1916); Michael Moynihan ed. *A Place Called Armageddon: Letters from the Great War* (Newton Abbot 1975) p. 185–6 Capt. J.S.S. Martin to his mother, 1 April 1916, from Kut; Imperial War Museum P.R.C. Groves Papers 69/34/1 copy Groves to J.M. Salmond 17 Nov. 1917 (Groves, then a GSO1, became Director of Flying Operations in the Air Ministry a few months later); William Mitchell *Memoirs of World War 1* (New York 1960) p. 268; Raleigh and Jones *War in the Air* vol. 6 p. 365–7; M. Jauneaud *L'Évolution de l'Aéronautique* (Paris 1923) p. 223–4; incidentally Joseph Frantz shot down a German plane with a single shot from a 37 cannon mounted on his Voisin on 20 May 1915, and a version of the SPAD, the SPAD XII CI Canon, was developed and used successfully by George Guynemer shortly before his death in 1917. Subsequently René Fonck shot down seven German aircraft in a similar machine, though obviously the weapon required an unusually good marksman, especially as it had to be reloaded by hand after each round: D. Porret *Les 'As' français de la Grand Guerre* (2 vols Paris 1983) vol. 1 p. 1,5 and Philippe Ochsé *Les Avions de Guynemer* (Rennes 1985) p. 18, 20. The R.F.C. had taken delivery of 5 Vickers Mark III 37mm aeroplane guns by April 1916 (Public Record Office MUN 4/2883) but 250 Coventry Ordnance Works 1½-pounder 37mm aeroplane guns ordered in Aug. 1917 had not been completed by the time of the Armistice (MUN 4/2896). Two experimental DH 4s armed with C.O.W. guns sent to France in April 1918 were quickly sent back to England by Brigadier-General Brooke-Popham (AIR 1/1083/204/5/1707).

Similarly radio-guided interceptions were a rare event: most aircraft were too small to carry adequate radios, and most potential targets were faster than Zeppelins.[36]

VI. The Birth of Bombing

Even in such a major sphere as bombing, developments in theory and technique were far ahead of routine tactical practice. It was during the First World War that the word 'bomb' evolved from meaning a hand grenade or something that an anarchist might throw, to signifying something of almost unlimited destructive potential. The Germans bombed Lunéville for the first time on 3 August 1914, the outer suburbs of Paris for the first time on 14 August. Also on 14 August was the first French air-raid on the Zeppelin sheds at Metz-Frescaty. A bomb dropped by a German plane on the market at Lunéville killed 46 and injured 50 on 1 September 1914. On 22 September a Royal Naval Air Service Sopwith Tabloid achieved a direct hit on a Zeppelin hangar at Düsseldorf with a bomb that did not explode; on 7 October one of the hangars at Düsseldorf was destroyed in another raid, and Cologne railway station was also attacked. On 27 September Joffre had ordered, with splendid vagueness, that aircraft should attack the German army by throwing some sort of missiles, ('*par un lancement de projectiles quelconques*') and a bomber group was established under Commandant de Goÿs; the first French air-raid on Germany proper was at Freiburg on 4 December 1914. A single German seaplane bombed Dover on 24 December; a man suffered bruises when he was knocked by the blast from a tree where he had been gathering holly. But aircraft were at this time a scarce resource: the Germans having by March 1915 organized a force of 36 bombers for long-range use against the British were then obliged to transfer them to the Russian front; the French, having carried out a series of large-scale raids, commencing with an attack by 17 Voisons on the BASF chemical works at Ludwigshafen on 26 May 1915 and climaxing with an attack by 62 Voisins on steel works at Dillingen on 25 August, began from September 1915 onward to concentrate much more on supporting their ground troops, though they did carry out a number of reprisal raids, managing to kill 110 civilians (mainly children) and to injure a further 123 when nine of their planes bombed Karlsruhe on 22 June 1916 in retaliation for a German raid on Bar-le-Duc: one of the 40 bombs dropped scored a direct hit on a circus

---

[36] Raleigh and Jones *War in the Air* vol. 1 p. 469, Werner Baumbach *Broken Swastika* (1960) p. 93, and Friedrich Lauck *Der Lufttorpedo: Entwicklung and Technik in Deutschland, 1915–1945* (Munich 1981) p. 16: the three British freighters were the *Gena*, sunk off Lowestoft 1 May 1917, the *Kankakee*, off Harwich 15 June 1917 and the *Storm*, also off Harwich 10 Sept. 1917: Public Record Office AIR 9/26/1; Stephen Roskill *Admiral of the Fleet Earl Beatty: The Last Naval Hero* (New York 1981) p. 233–4 and John Bullen 'The Royal Navy and Air Power: The Projected Torpedo-bomber Attack on the High Seas Fleet at Wilhelmshaven in 1918' *Imperial War Museum Review* No. 2 (1987) p. 71–7.

marquee during a performance. The head of the aviation section at French G.H.Q., Commandant Joseph-Édouard Barès, was keen to press ahead with long-range bombing in conjunction with the British Royal Naval Air Service but was denounced by Haig and by Henderson, the Director General of Military Aeronautics at the War Office; they also objected to 'interference by the naval authorities with the British land forces' and insisted that as far as the employment of aircraft was concerned, bombing was 'an unimportant duty compared with fighting or reconnaissance'.[37]

At this stage most advocates of the bomber still thought in terms of strictly military targets related to the operations of the ground forces. The engineer F.W. Lanchester wrote in 1916 of attacking the enemy's lines of communication:

> Depôts of every kind in the rear of the enemy's lines would cease to exist; rolling stock and mechanical transport would be destroyed; no bridge would be allowed to stand for 24 hours.

But already the possibility of using aircraft to strike at the heart of the enemy's war economy had been envisaged, at least in Italy:

> Modern armies represent the armoured shield behind which the nations at war work to prepare the means appropriate to feed the war: the powerful aeroplane is able to pass over such armour and strike at the nation itself in its centres of production and along the lines of supply running from the country to the army. Thus it is the best weapon to strike a fatal blow. It isn't the iron club that strikes the armour and dents it, it is the stiletto which passes through a chink in the armour and cuts the carotid artery. The army represents the nation's fist, a fist which is useless if the arm and heart are useless: the fist is covered by an iron gauntlet, the arm and the heart are naked; the new weapon attacks not the fist but the heart, and cuts the nerves and veins of the arm.

This was written, probably in 1915, by Giulio Douhet who between August 1913 and February 1915 had commanded the Italian Army's *Battaglione*

---

[37] Barry D. Powers *Strategy without Slide-Rule: British Air Strategy, 1914–1918* (1976) p. 11; J. Boruet-Aubertot *Les Bombardements Aériens* (Paris 1923) p. 84; R. Martel *L'Aviation Française de Bombardement* (Paris 1939) p. 20, cf Claude Carlier 'L'aéronautique militaire française dans la premiere guerre mondiale' *Guerres Mondiales et Conflits Contemporains* no. 145 (Jan. 1987) p. 63–80 at p. 68; E.B. Ashmore *Air Defence* (1929) p. 165; J.B. Firth *Dover and the Great War* Dover [1920] p. 85. Details for the French air raids on Germany in 1915 are in John R. Cuneo *The Air Weapon, 1914–1916* (Harrisburg 1947) (vol. 2 of *Winged Mars*) p. 372–3. Archives de l'Armée de l'Air, Vincennes, A 164 deals with reprisal raids, see especially telephone message transcript no. 3070, 3 Oct. 1917. For the Karlsruhe raid cf *Heidelberger Tageblatt* 24 June 1916 p. 1c: the victims of this tragedy are buried in a group of individually marked graves which are still visible in the principal cemetery at Karlsruhe; Raleigh and Jones *War in the Air* vol. 3 p. 279, Neville Jones *The Origins of Strategic Bombing: A Study of the Development of British Air Strategic Thought and Practice up to 1918* (1973) p. 23–4, 85–98 espec. p. 92–4, and Roskill ed. *Documents Relating to the Naval Air Service* vol. 1 p. 405–412.

See also Pol Timonier et L . . . B . . . *Comment nous torpillerons Berlin avec notre escadrille d'aéroplanes dès l'ouverture des hostilités* (Paris 1913). The French were indeed the first enemy to bomb Berlin – but not till 1940

Aviatori. Douhet had encouraged Gianni Caproni to press ahead with the development of the giant trimotor biplane he had designed in 1913 and when Italy entered the war in May 1915 the Italian Army had the most advanced bomber aircraft in Western Europe; Douhet himself had been transferred away from the aviation side and was later court-martialled and imprisoned for circulating memos such as the one quoted above. Over 800 Caproni trimotors were built 1915–1918, including 25 of the Ca 4 trimotor triplane, and the most powerful versions could carry a ton of bombs 600 kilometres. But Italian air raids, the largest by 36 Capronis on Pola on the night of 2 August 1917, were of minimal strategic importance, and these giant machines were used mainly for tactical purposes in the battle zone; the Austro-Hungarians, using single-engined machines, probably caused far more disruption on the Italian home front, frequently bombing Verona, Venice, Padua (where a single bomb killed 86 civilians in the Rotunda on 11 November 1916) and attacking even the central railway station at Milan. Meanwhile Capronis of the 18° Gruppo di Bombardamento were sent to France to attack German cities though in the event most of the crated machines were left at the Gare de Lyon for months and after assembly distinguished themselves only by the frequency with which they crashed.[38]

Even more advanced than the Caproni in 1915 was Russia's Sikorski I.M type four-engined biplane. The Tsarist Army reactivated a retired officer, M.V. Shidlovski, who was running the factory building these machines, to command a special bomber force which operated on the Eastern Front from February 1915 till the Revolution. Sikorski I.M.s carried out 442 raids, in strengths of up to 25 machines; only three were lost in action, though 40 German aircraft were claimed destroyed by the defensive machine guns which they carried. The most powerful version, the I.M Ye of August 1916 had four Russian-built 225 h.p. Renault motors and carried 1,764lb of bombs and seven Lewis guns: it also had electric lights, a lavatory and a balcony. But only 73 of the entire series were built and on that scale the Sikorski I.Ms had little more than propaganda value.[39]

[38] F.W. Lanchester *Aircraft in Warfare: The Dawn of the Fourth Arm* (1916) p. 187–8 (this book reprints older material but the section quoted was specially written for the 1916 volume: the other three arms are infantry, cavalry and artillery); G. Douhet *Diario Critico di Guerra* (2 vols Turin 1921) vol. 2 p. 20–1: cf *Times*, 26 April 1909, p. 19a for Lord Montagu warning the National Defence Association that 'the "nerve centres" of a highly civilised nation like ours' were vulnerable to 'a single well-directed blow'. For the Caproni trimotors see Rosario Abate *Storia della Aeronautica Italiana* (Milan 1974) p. 103–4, 108, 137. An interesting photographic record of the Austro-Hungarian air raids on north-east Italy may be found in Giovanni Scarabello *Il Martirio di Venezia durante la Grande Guerra e l'opera di difesa della Marina Italiana* (2 vols Venice 1933) and Andrea Moschetti, *I Danni ai Monumenti e alle opere d'arte delle Venezie nella Guerra Mondiale MCMXV–MCMXVIII* (Venice 1932). For the Capronis in France see Abate *Storia della Aeronautica Italiana* p. 107, Pédoya *La Commission de l'Armée* p. 164 fn. and A.R. Kingsford *Night Raiders of the Air* [1930] p. 129.

[39] Heinz J. Nowarra and G.R. Duval *Russian Civil and Military Aircraft 1884–1969* (1971) p. 33–5, 41, 52 and Public Records Office AIR 1/713/27/19/12 'Technical Conditions to be Fulfilled by Russian Aeroplanes [i.e., I.M.s] ... 5.12.15' p. 8–12.

Germany and Britain also developed multi-engined bombers during the war and produced bigger and bigger bombs. On 16 February 1918 a bomb weighing one tonne, dropped by a four-engined Zeppelin-Staaken RV I, destroyed the north-east wing of the Royal Hospital at Chelsea; this wing was afterwards rebuilt and blown up a second time, by a V 2, on 31 January 1945. The British had a 1,650lb bomb by the time of the Armistice: an example, like a small boiler with rocket fins and lots of bolt heads very close together, is on display in the Imperial War Museum; four such bombs were dropped by Handley Page 0/400s on Kaiserslautern in October 1918.[40]

The city attacked over the longest period was Paris. The first raid on the city centre, on 30 August 1914, killed one person and injured four: seven more raids killed a total of ten people by the end of the year. The attacks did not in fact become really serious till 1918. Altogether during the war 242 Parisians were killed by bombs from aircraft, 25 by bombs dropped by Zeppelins, and 256 by shells from ultra-long-ranged guns – 88 of these when the roof of St Gervais church collapsed on a congregation of worshippers after a direct hit on 29 March 1918. The bombing of England, while not quite as prolonged, was on a rather more serious scale. London the greatest city in the world, with a population larger than that of Berlin, Munich, Leipzig and Hamburg combined, was of course an irresistible magnet; the possibility of bombing London had featured in correspondence in *The Times* only three months before the outbreak of war. Altogether, in 51 Zeppelin and 52 aeroplane raids on London and other cities of England, 1,414 civilians were killed and 3,416 injured, though these figures scarcely reflect the degree of panic and disruption caused.[41]

The attacks on England may be seen as falling into three major phases. The first, in 1915 and 1916, when the Zeppelin was still the main threat, caused far more nuisance and excitement than physical damage. It was estimated that following an airship raid 90 per cent of the work force in affected areas would be late for work the next day, of whom 20 per cent would stay away altogether. In the Cleveland area disruption caused by air raid alarms (including the dowsing of blast furnaces) cost a sixth of pig iron production in 1916. Zeppelin raids on London caused outright panic: it was afterwards remarked, 'the morale of the people of the East End in 1940 was incomparably better than it had been in 1915'. By late 1916 however the Zeppelin had proved vulnerable to fighter attack – when the first one to be successfully intercepted over England was brought down on the night of 2–3 September 1916 cheering crowds filled the streets of north London to watch it descending in flames –

---

[40] Raleigh and Jones *War in the Air* vol. 5 p. 117–8: the plaque commemorating the two bombs, just inside the London Gate at the Chelsea Royal Hospital, states that the bomb of 16 February 1918 was only of 500lb but I have preferred to follow Raleigh and Jones.

[41] Frank Morison *War on Great Cities: A Study of the Facts* (1937) p. 174–5, 180 and H.W. Miller *The Paris Gun: The Bombardment of Paris by the German Long-Distance Guns and the Great German Offensives of 1918* (1930) p. 66–7; *Times* 27 April 1914 p. 7d, 30 April 1914 p. 7c; Raleigh and Jones *War in the Air* vol. 5 p. 153 and 157.

and experience had shown how to minimize the disruptive effects of air raid precautions.[42]

On 28 November 1916, hours after two more Zeppelins had been shot down over England, London suffered its first heavier-than-air attack: a single LVG dropped six small bombs and subsequently crash-landed near Boulogne, behind Allied lines: two people were injured. This was merely a foretaste of what was to come. In another raid on London by a single-engined plane on the night of 6 May 1917, one person was killed in a block of flats still to be seen today, Newington Green Mansions at the south end of Green Lanes, only a half a dozen streets away from Cowper Road where the Zeppelin had claimed its first victims just two years previously. Then on 13 June 1917 fourteen twin-engined Gothas bombed London in broad daylight, killing 162 people and injuring 432: the fatalities included nineteen people who were killed outside Fenchurch Street Station when the façade of an office building fell on them after a direct hit, and eighteen children mostly aged six or younger, who were killed at a London County Council school in Poplar. The only government installation of any importance to have been damaged was the Royal Mint, though the bombers also managed to ruin the flag day collection being held on behalf of the Armenians who were being massacred by Germany's Turkish allies. On 7 July 1917 a second daylight raid by 21 Gothas set fire to a temporary structure on the roof of the Central Telegraph Office at St Martin-le-Grand, creating vast and terrifying billows of smoke, and a heavy A.A. barrage, though failing to have any visible effect on the neat German formations, showered the city with shell fragments, killing ten people and injuring 55 in addition to the 44 killed and 125 injured by the German bombs. Ninety-five British aircraft attempted to intercept the raiders (only thirty of them fighter types however) and two of these defending planes were shot down; one of the Gothas came down in the sea off the Kent coast, and four more crashed in the high winds over Belgium, though this was not known in Britain till much later.[43]

This second raid, carried out virtually with impunity, and in clear view of the people of London (who, because of the unaccustomed size of the German bombers thought they were flying much lower – and more slowly – than was

[42] Raleigh and Jones *War in the Air* vol. 3 p. 246, and see generally Public Record Office AIR 1/2132/207/121/1, 'General Effect of German Raids on Industry during the late War', 16 March 1922; John Slessor *The Central Blue* (1956) p. 15.

[43] Morison *War on Great Cities* Appendix p. 208, 215; ibid. p. 216–7 and p. 120, 124 for the Poplar and Fenchurch St. incidents; for the ruined Armenian flag day of the advert in *Times* 28 June 1917 p. 4e-f; Ashmore *Air Defence* p. 170 and Raleigh and Jones *War in the Air* vol. 5 p. 36–7, and cf Greater London Record Office FB/WAR/1/188, where a normal formula for Fire Brigade reports in June and July 1917 was 'bombs and anti-aircraft shells dropped in connection with this Raid'.

The Gothas had no electrical heating, no automatic pilot and no power-assisted controls, and after several hours flight the pilot would be physically exhausted, so that problems in controlling the planes during the final stages of the return flight were quite usual: with the even larger 'R' bombers the physical strain on the pilots was even greater.

actually the case) caused tremendous excitement. That evening there were riots in Holloway, Hackney, Dalston, and Bethnal Green in which thirty shops were attacked, mostly of alleged German ownership, and fourteen policemen injured. The mob in London Fields was estimated as about two thousand strong. The disturbances continued till 10 July. As with the riots sparked off by the sinking of the *Lusitania* these disturbances were something more than merely a spontaneous overflow of anti-German feeling. At 102 Pownall Road, Dalston, a mob of five hundred people attacked Geo. Latham Storey's bakery and stole two hundred loaves and several bags of flour; in Boleyn Road, Stoke Newington, where a single bomb falling in the street had killed nine people, including a German-born shopkeeper, a police inspector was assaulted; outside the police station in Dalston Lane a crowd attacked police in an attempt to rescue rioters who had been arrested, shouting, 'You're nothing else but bloody Germans'; in the course of this disturbance a sixteen-year-old boy and three teenage girls were arrested. Ten days after the air raid King George V changed the family name of the royal dynasty from Saxe-Coburg-Gotha to Windsor – the fact that German heavy bombers were also called Gotha was an unfortunate coincidence which obviously could not be allowed to persist – but this symbolic repudiation of German connections scarcely touched the heart of the matter, and the discontent in the poorer areas of England's inner cities continued to simmer.[44]

Further massed air raids on southern England were met with increasingly effective A.A. and fighter opposition and in September 1917 the Germans switched to night bombing. The final, and perhaps most effective, phase of the German bomber offensive, the night raids by Gotha and giant 'R' bombers, continued till May 1918. British casualties were considerable – a single bomb exploding in a drill hall full of sleeping naval ratings at Chatham killed 107 and injured 55 – and there was a continuing sense of shock and disgust that the war was being brought so close to home: 'what was perfectly natural in a rubble-heap like Ypres or Arras seemed an outrage here'. There was also a major impact on the morale of an increasingly war-weary populace resulting in a massive loss of output in factories in the London area, including Woolwich Arsenal. H.M. Selby, Managing Director of Schneiders & Sons, 'the largest Clothing Manufacturers in England', explained the 87.5 per cent drop in the output of the East End factories thus:

a) 90% of the employees were women, easily frightened and liable to panic.

---

[44] *Times* 10 July 1917 p. 3a; *Hackney & Stoke Newington Recorder* 13 July 1917 p. 5c-d; Public Record Office HO 44/10944/257142 file 187. It may be observed that the press reported air raids in much more detail in 1917 than in 1940.

On the afternoon of Saturday 28 July 1917 the district conference of the London and Home Counties' Workers' and Soldiers' Council, meeting in the Brotherhood Church in Southgate Road, just to the south of Stoke Newington, was broken up by a mob which included Canadian soldiers on leave, cf *Times* 30 July 1917 p. 31, and Ken Weller *'Don't be a Soldier!' The Radical Anti-War Movement in North London, 1914–1918*, London 1985 p. 87–9. The recent bombing in the neighbourhood almost certainly contributed to the violence of this outbreak.

b) The other 10% were alien Jews, who were even more liable to panic than the women.

Government officials cheerfully accepted statements that it was Jewish immigrants rather than real true-blue Englishmen who were demoralized by the bombing, though it was noted 'that the gentlemen interviewed appeared only to be separated from the class they so vigorously denounced by the narrow margin of wealth'. When, during an air raid on the night of 28 January 1918, fourteen people were crushed to death in the crowd seeking shelter at Liverpool Street underground station (then generally known as Bishopsgate station) the coroner attributed the tragedy 'to panic almost entirely on the part of persons who might be called foreigners', and the *East London Advertiser* carried the headline, 'Cowardly Aliens in the Great Stampede'. The death of 28 people as a result of a direct hit on a public shelter in the same raid gained rather less attention. There was at this period a widespread belief that foreign-born Jews were evading military conscription, and this seems to have been behind the destructive rioting directed against Jewish property which occurred at Leeds on 2–5 September 1917, but the similar outbreaks in the East End of London three weeks later (23–24 September) may be attributed more to the hysteria generated by the German bombing. There were, incidentally, no anti-Jewish riots at this time in Germany, in spite of what was to come later.[45]

The Germans seem to have underestimated the effect on morale of their night bombing raids and after a final raid with a record 43 aircraft on the night of 19 May 1918 their bombing force was redeployed for duties on the Western Front. The German bombing attacks had however been important in converting the British government and (with much heel-dragging) even the

---

[45] John Buchan *Mr. Standfast* (1919) p. 187; Raleigh and Jones *War in the Air* vol. 5 p. 86–7; Public Record Office AIR 1/2132/207/121/1 'General Effect of German Raids on Industry during the late War', 16 March 1922 p. 14 and 16: *Times* 2 Feb. 1918 p. 3d; Julia Bush *Behind the Lines: East London Labour, 1914–1919* (1984) p. 182 (where the number dead at Liverpool St. is given as 17); Colin Holmes *Anti-Semitism in British Society, 1876–1939* (1979) p. 130–132, 136 cf Egmont Zechlin *Die deutsche Politik und die Juden im Ersten Weltkrieg* (Göttingen 1969) p. 516–557.

Panicking Jews were later to be blamed for the Bethnal Green tube disaster in 1943, *cf Ian McLaine Ministry of Morale: Home Front and the Ministry of Information in World War* (1979) p. 168 and Tony Kushner *The Persistence of Prejudice: Antisemitism in British society during the Second World War* (Manchester 1989) p. 125–6, though note James Lansdale Hodson *Home Front* (1944) p. 154, 19 August 1942: 'I asked if the Jews behave as well in the Blitz as English folk. They said, Yes they do'. The location of the 28 January 1918 panic is usually referred to as Bishopsgate Station: a station of that name on the Metropolitan Railway was opened in 1875 but renamed Liverpool Street in 1909, and a deep-level station on the Central London Railway (now Central Line) was opened nearby in 1912. It was presumably the latter station which was being used as a shelter, the superseded but evidently still current name for the Metropolitan Railway station having presumably been transferred in common parlance also to the Central London Railway station. I am grateful to Oliver Green, Curator of the London Transport Museum, for assistance on this point.

British Army to accept the logic of some sort of long-range bomber offensive against Germany. In 1916 Royal Naval Air Service and French Army doctrine, such as it was, focused on the possibility of damaging specific industries, and Lord Montagu's proposal to the Air Board on 29 May 1916 that Essen should be bombed 'with about 1,000 aeroplanes' also implied a concentration on industrial targets. A Royal Naval Air Service wing based at Luxeuil had begun carrying out air raids on Germany in conjunction with French units on 12 October 1916, using single-engined aircraft. Nine raids had been carried out by the Luxeuil wing by 1 March 1917 when the first twin-engined Handley Page 0/400 heavy bombers (designed to a R.N.A.S. specification) arrived, but later in the month the wing was ordered to be disbanded. The last raid, an attack on Freiburg by 25 R.N.A.S. and 15 French bombers, was staged on 14 April 1917.

Haig had opposed the R.N.A.S.'s bombing offensive from the very beginning; though he had claimed control of the R.N.A.S. bombing missions only on his own army front, not on the French Army front as well, he had insisted that long-range bombing had 'a quite inferior military effect' and had complained bitterly when the French Colonel Barès was invited to discuss the matter with the Air Board in London. Within a couple of months the Gotha raids on London reopened the whole question, and, what was worse from Haig's point of view, brought a number of influential outsiders into the discussion of how the air weapon might best be used. Most influential of all was General Jan Smuts, South Africa's Minister of Defence and representative to to War Cabinet, who argued:

> the day may not be far off when aerial operations with their devastation of enemy lands and destruction of industrial and populous centres on a vast scale may become the principal operations of war, to which the older forms of military and naval operations may become secondary and subordinate ... next summer, while our Western Front may still be moving forward at a snail's pace in Belgium and France, the air battle-front will be far behind on the Rhine, and ... its continuous and intense pressure against the chief industrial centres of the enemy as well as on his lines of communication may form an important factor in bringing about peace.

Civilian morale began to be seen as a possible (and legitimate) target. Lord Rothermere, head of the newly established Air Council, began to talk of successive waves of a hundred or a hundred and fifty bombers laying the Rhine valley cities 'level with the ground ... It is estimated that, among a people ravaged by hunger and despair, the panic will be instantaneous and complete'. Sir Hugh Trenchard, commanding the R.F.C. in France and Haig's right hand in aviation matters, told Haig, 'the Air Board are quite off their heads as to the future possibilities of Aeronautics for ending the war'. Haig himself warned the government against setting up an Air Ministry 'with a belief in theories which are not in accordance with practical experience'. But the Germans had given the government in London a practical demonstration

that was far more convincing than anything Haig could say and they went
ahead with their plans to establish aviation as an independent arm.[46]

After some initial squabbling, and the resignations of both Lord Rothermere
and Trenchard, who had been appointed the new R.A.F.'s first Chief of Air
Staff, the Air Ministry came under the control of a Secretary of State and a
Chief of Air Staff who both favoured the strategic use of bombing aircraft.
Lord Weir, the Secretary of State, one of Lloyd George's recruits from the
business world, assured Trenchard, 'I would very much like it if you could
start up a really big fire in one of the German towns'. Major-General Frederick
Sykes, Trenchard's replacement as Chief of Air Staff, acknowledged that, 'The
present war certainly can only finally be won on the land', but argued for 'a
vigorous offensive against those root industries upon which depends the entire
naval and military endeavour of the Central Powers'.[47]

Theory was one thing: practice another. Both of the officers with operational
control of Britain's bombers, Major-General John Salmond, commanding the
R.A.F. in France, and Trenchard, who had been appointed head of the new
Independent Force intended for the strategic bombing role, were out of
sympathy with Weir's and Sykes's ideas, and in any case heartily despised
Sykes. Salmond, the thirty-six-year-old former Director General of Military
Aeronautics, may have been anxious to prevent his rival Trenchard drawing
off resources from his own command, but his objection that bombing was
hopelessly inaccurate was difficult to counter:

> Material damage from day bombing is, I am afraid, very small and must remain
> so as long as it is necessary to bomb from great heights at which an error of
> 1,000 yards is not at all excessive. Material damage from night bombing is
> undoubtedly greater on suitable nights, but all experience in this war shows
> that it is very seldom vital.

The Germans certainly achieved some spectacular individual results: on two

---

[46] Public Record Office AIR 6/1 Air Board Minutes, Meeting No.4, 29 May 1916: Jones
Origins of Strategic Bombing p. 113–5, 122–3; Public Record Office AIR 6/3 Air Board Minutes,
Meeting No.9, 8 June 1916 p. 2 and C.R.F.C. 2218 (G), 3 June 1916 which is given as Appendix
B to the minutes of this meeting; India Office Library Mss Eur. F. 112/116 Paul Harvey to
Curzon 8 Nov. 1916 reporting Haig's complaints about Barès – AIR 6/3, meeting No.26, 24
Oct. 1916 shows that Barès's remarks at the Air Board were not especially provocative; Raleigh
and Jones *War in the Air* vol. 7 p. 10–11 Appendix II, General Smuts's memo 17 Aug. 1917
– this was actually drafted by Lancelot Storr, assistant secretary of the Committee of Imperial
Defence and it has been argued, not entirely convincingly, that it owes as much to Sir David
Henderson's thinking as to Smuts's; Sir Almeric Fitzroy *Memoirs* (2 vols 1925) vol. 2 p. 667–8,
diary 28 Dec. 1917 for Rothermere's notion of laying German cities 'level with the ground' and
cf Jones *Origins of Strategic Bombing* p. 107–110, 154–7, 158–160, 162–3; Robert Blake ed. *The
Private Papers of Sir Douglas Haig* (1952) p. 273, diary 16 Dec. 1917; Raleigh and Jones *War in
the Air* vol. 6 p. 14, vol. 7 (Appendix vol.) p. 15 Appendix III, Haig to C.I.G.S. (Robertson)
15 Sept. 1917.

[47] W.J. Reader *Architect of Air Power: The Life of the First Viscount Weir of Eastwood,
1877–1959* (1968) p. 76 – see also p. 65–6, 71–6; Frederick Sykes *From Many Angles* (1942)
p. 544–7 Appendix V, 'Review of Air Situation and Strategy for the information of the Imperial
War Cabinet 27 July 1918', at p. 546.

successive nights, 20–21 and 21–22 May 1918, they bombed and detonated 6,000 tons of ammunition in a British dump at Blarges and 5,600 tons of ammunition (including 69 million rounds of small arms ammunitions) at Saigneville, and on the evening of 11 August 1918 they bombed and set fire to No. 2 Base Mechanical Transport Depot at Calais, destroying spares for nearly 20,000 vehicles, equivalent to almost half the British mechanized transport in France. The British never achieved anything to rival this, one reason being that the Germans responded much more promptly to the threat posed by aerial incursions: as early as June 1915 an R.F.C. flier recorded in his diary:

> It is quite noticeable coming behind our lines how much more is going on. Behind the Bosche's there is hardly ever anything doing. All their movements are done by night.

Even when, at the climax of the great land battles, German ground movements became more visible, the R.F.C. and later R.A.F. failed to cause significant disruption. Of bombing attacks during the Battle of the Somme it was acknowledged 'the total effect as regards holding up reinforcements was practically nil as far as we know'. During the Passchendaele offensive a year later the R.F.C. dropped 7,886 bombs in September alone, compared to 969 dropped by German aircraft, again with no visible benefit. In June, July and August 1918 R.A.F. bombers failed to disrupt German troop movements by rail, though in the Ypres-La Bassée sector 80 tons of bombs were dropped on railway targets in less than two weeks. A post-war survey of the results of dropping 6,359 bombs on the docks at Bruges and a further 353 on La Brugeoise munitions works – a total of 275.1 tons of bombs – between February 1917 and November 1918 showed that there had been no resulting cutback in activity or output, though the 213 bombs which had hit the residential area of Bruges had killed 104 Belgian civilians: however the Germans did feel obliged to provide the submarine pens they had built at Bruges with two-metre thick roofs, though none of these were ever actually hit by a bomb.[48]

Better results might possibly have been achieved by a more sustained effort, in some specific area or another, but it seems that Trenchard largely ignored

---

[48] Raleigh and Jones *War in the Air* vol. 7 (Appendix vol.) p. 112 Appendix XXXI memo by Salmond June 1918; ibid. vol. 6 p. 424–5, 429–431; Imperial War Museum, Diary of Wing Commander D.L. Allen (then Lieutenant R.F.C.) section 2 p. 26, 27 June 1915; Raleigh and Jones *War in the Air* vol. 7 p. 112 Appendix XXI, memo by Salmond June 1918; ibid. vol. 4 p. 201–2; ibid. vol. 6 p. 409–411 and Public Record Office AIR 1/678/21/13/2137 p. 11–18; AIR 1/2115/207/506/1 'Report of the Aircraft Bombing Committee appointed by the Air Ministry to enquire into the effects of bombing in Belgium . . . March 1919' [printed] p. 8, 19, 29, 31 cf Raleigh and Jones *War in the Air* vol. 4 p. 104.

Most of the material in this paragraph refers to attacks on the rear-lines of the opposing armies but it is relevant to the question of attacks on 'strategic' targets in the Douhet sense: in any case Trenchard seems to have had little interest in the distinction between tactical and strategic targets.

Air Ministry directives instructing him to concentrate on attacking industrial targets in Germany:

Targets attacked by Independent Force	June 1918	August 1918
Chemical Industry	14.0%	8.0%
Iron and Steel Plant	13.3%	7.0%
Aerodromes	13.3%	49.5%
Railways	55.0%	31.0%

Trenchard subsequently attempted to minimize the value of aiming at specific targets:

> At present the moral effect of bombing stands undoubtedly to the material effect in a proportion of 20 to 1, and therefore it was necessary to create the greatest moral effect possible.

Even his *bête noire* Sykes did not entirely disagree. In a 'Review of Air Situation and Strategy for the Information of the Imperial War Cabinet', dated 27 June 1918 Sykes wrote of:

> widespread attacks to obtain dislocation, the aims of such attacks being to sow alarm broadcast, set up nervous tension, check output, and generally tend to bring military, financial and industrial interests into opposition ... The wholesale bombing of densely populated industrial centres would go far to destroy the *moral* of the operatives.

It is possible however that by this stage even the Air Ministry was beginning to lose interest in bombing German cities. A proposal from Captain W.R. Read, Chief Instructor at No. 1 School of Navigation and Bomb Dropping, that Berlin should be attacked by Handley Page 0/400s flying from Dunkirk was considered, in view of the distance and uncertainty regarding the necessary fuel margins, as 'a risk far out of proportion to the possible moral effect which they will produce', and it was pointed out, 'The war had now got to a point when the really useful must take the place of the merely theatrical'. A month later Sykes 'laid down that this scheme was not [to] be discussed in writing', probably to prevent there being any authentic documentation that might be leaked to the press. Later Read, by now promoted to major, was assigned to command a squadron of 0/400s that was to be sent to Prague to carry out raids on Berlin from the south, but the Armistice came before the squadron could leave England. The Armistice also aborted a plan to send two of the new four-engined Handly Page V/1500s on a round-trip to Berlin from Norfolk; they were allegedly bombed up ready to leave on 9 November but the mission had to be postponed owing to poor weather. In terms of actual measurable damage a long distance-raid on Berlin, like the penetrations of up to 150 miles that were carried out against industrial targets such as Frankfurt am Main and Stuttgart, would no doubt have had a very minor impact; yet as subsequently transpired the night bombing of German cities had a considerable effect in causing absenteeism and loss of production, just as it had in London. Altogether 746 German civilians were killed and 1,843 injured by Anglo-Franco-Italian air raids during the war, and though the collapse of the German home front, when it came in autumn of 1918, came first in areas outside the active range of Allied bombers, air raids must have added considerably to the depression of civilian morale in western Germany during these final months of the war. Yet from having been overemphasized in the autumn of 1917, the issue of civilian morale seems to have been progressively pushed into the background by the experts just as the means of attacking this morale were becoming more available.[49]

VII. Aeroplanes and the War of the Trenches

By the time of the Armistice on 11 November 1918 it was still by no means clear that bombing was the most effective use of air power, and indeed part of the reason for the failure of the bomber aeroplane to mature as an independent weapon in the 1914–18 war was the competing attractions of other types of aircraft performing other types of air warfare roles.

Originally military aviation had been conceived as a form of cavalry. Shortly before the war the engineer F.W. Lanchester had claimed:

> there is scarcely an operation of importance hitherto entrusted to cavalry that could not be executed as well or better by a squadron or fleet of aeronautical machines . . . the number of flying-machines eventually to be utilized by any of the great military Powers will be counted not by hundreds but by thousands, and possibly by tens of thousands.

Even long-range strategic bombing had derived some of its rationale from cavalry tactics as they had evolved during the nineteenth century; the word *raid* had been introduced into current English from medieval Scots by Sir Walter Scott, but the concept of the *raid* in modern warfare was popularized by the long-distance 'raids' carried out by Confederate cavalry under Jeb Stuart during the American Civil War – the word *raider* is an American coinage not found before 1863. Nevertheless this aspect of the cavalry analogy became less evident as the bomber aeroplane's potential for weight, precision, method and repetition in attack became more developed. The other uses of

---

[49] Jones *Origins of Strategic Bombing* p. 190; Raleigh and Jones *War in the Air* vol. 6 p. 136 quoting Trenchard's despatch of 1 Jan 1919; Sykes *From Many Angles* p. 551 Appendix V; Public Record Office AIR 1/474/15/312/183, notes by Lord Tiverton, the Under-Secretary of State at the Air Ministry; Chaz Bowyer *Handley Page Bombers of the First World War* (Bourne End 1992) p. 93, 132, Raleigh and Jones *War in the Air* vol. 6 p. 152–3. The report in the Public Record Office on 'moral effect of an attack on a Blast Furnace' circa July 1918 at AIR 1/1986/204/273/113 seems to represent a transitional phase, half way between attacking German morale and attacking German industry.

aircraft in the First World War were more obviously comparable to cavalry, and retained the cavalry spirit to a much larger degree.[50]

By 1914 perhaps the most vital, most dangerous and least dramatic function of cavalry was reconnaissance, and reconnaissance was precisely the function for which military aviation had originally been conceived as most suitable. In 1914, it was later recalled,

> the work of aeroplanes in war was limited practically to a simple duty – that of performing such reconnaissance work over enemy country as our cavalry were prevented from carrying out owing to the enclosed nature of the ground.

Initially, while the fighting in France and Belgium was still fluid and mobile, aircraft performed excellently in this role. Sir John French fully acknowledged this in his first official despatch to Lord Kitchener:

> I wish particularly to bring to your Lordship's notice the admirable work done by the Royal Flying Corps under Sir David Henderson. Their skill, energy and perseverance have been beyond all praise. They have furnished me with the most complete and accurate information which has been of incalculable value in the conduct of operations.

The air arm was less successful however in adjusting to the new conditions of a war of position, when the fighting became stabilized on the trench lines in the later autumn of 1914: though this was by and large not the fault of the airmen at all.[51]

Reconnaissance did not become less important in the new conditions of static warfare but it took its place as one amongst several key elements in the system of longer-term preparation and forward planning which the new format of warfare seemed to require. By the time of the Armistice on 11 November 1918 British aircraft had taken over half a million photographs of enemy ground positions. Spotting for artillery was also important as more and more heavier and longer-ranged guns were brought into service; in September 1917 the British R.F.C., as well as taking 14,678 photos, helped range artillery on 9,539 targets. Yet though a vast amount of aerial reconnaissance was carried out over the trench lines the army staffs frequently made poor use of the information gathered. At Neuve Chapelle in March 1915 the British had a complete map of the German trench system made up from aerial photographs and 1,500 copies

---

[50] F.W. Lanchester *The Flying Machine from an Engineering Standpoint* (1916) p. 8 – this was written in March or April 1914 for a lecture to the Institution of Civil Engineers in May 1914, cf P.W. Kingsford *F.W. Lanchester: A Life of an Engineer* (1960) p. 127. Incidentally, of the best-known fighter aces, Richthofen, Bishop, Nungesser, Werner Voss, the Italian Baracca and the Russian Alexander A. Kazakov had all originally been in the cavalry, and Mannock, McCudden, Hawker and Fonck in the engineers; Boelcke had been commissioned in a Telegraph Battalion, and Immelmann in a Railway Regiment, though he had resigned his commission before the war to study engineering at the Dresden *Technische Hochschule*. Both Rickenbacker and (less professionally) Nungesser had been racing-car drivers in civil life.

[51] 'Flight Commander' *Cavalry of the Air* (1918) p. 267; *The Despatches of Lord French* (1917) p. 3–13 Despatch 7 Sept. 1914 at p. 12.

of this map were issued to each corps; this careful preparation probably gave significant assistance to the initial attack but the advance was eventually held up on previously unmanned reserve positions further back which had been identified from the air but judged by the staff to be of no importance. At Festubert in May 1915 aerial reconnaissance reported the construction of a new German front line almost as soon as work began; G.H.Q. however took three more days to register that the Germans had established themselves in this position. At the beginning of 1918 aerial reconnaissance gave the British Expeditionary Force two months warning of the great German offensive of 21 March yet the ineffectiveness of the B.E.F.'s defences and the failure to organize reserves convinced Ludendorff that the British had been taken by surprise. In April 1918 British G.H.Q. decided that the preparations for a new attack on the Ypres front, which were visible from the air, were only a diversionary ploy, and once again a major German offensive achieved spectacular success against inadequately prepared British defences.[52]

With regard to artillery spotting, the Germans themselves acknowledged that the early British successes at the Somme in 1916 were due to the excellent liaison between aircraft and artillery, but since the vast expenditure of high explosive and of human life failed in the end to achieve a significant advance the best that can be said is that first-rate artillery spotting contributed to a worse than second-rate result. If there had been a real breakthrough on the Somme it is probable that the standard of the artillery spotting would have rapidly declined; at least this was the German experience in 1918 when it was repeatedly found that the usefulness of the air arm fell off after the first two days of an attack owing to the lack of forward bases and deteriorating liaison between artillery and observer air crew lacking experience in the problems of mobile warfare. It is possible in any case that by the later stages of the war new techniques such as 'flash-spotting' and 'sound-ranging' were overtaking aerial observation as the most useful procedure in counter-battery work. Trenchard's successful resistance, even in 1916, to the subordination of artillery spotting aircraft to corps C.R.A.s (i.e. the officers in charge of artillery in each corps) hardly promoted refinements in the technique of artillery-aircraft liaison: it was not till 1942 that artillery commanders in the British Army exercised tactical control over their own spotter planes.[53]

All the armies attempted to use aircraft during advances to report on the

[52] Raleigh and Jones *War in the Air* vol. 1 p. 6: for the organization of French aerial photography see André-H. Carlier *La Photgraphie Aérienne pendant la Guerre* (Paris 1921) p. 17, 58–9; Raleigh and Jones *War in the Air* vol. 4 p. 202; ibid. vol. 2 p. 92; ibid vol. 2 p. 113–4; ibid. vol. 4 p. 270; ibid vol. 4 p. 367–8 and p. 367 fn.1

[53] Raleigh and Jones *War in the Air* vol. 2 p. 172; Hoeppner *Deutschlands Krieg in der Luft* p. 157–8; Peter Mead *The Eye in the Air: History of Air Observation and Reconnaissance for the Army, 1785–1945* (1983) p. 101, cf Guy Hartcup *War of Invention* p. 69–76 for the development of sound ranging. There was some question however as to whether sound-ranging was much use if several guns were firing at the same time, cf Hartcup p. 75; Raleigh and Jones *War in the Air* vol. 3 p. 307–8 and Mead *Eye in the Air* p. 108–9.

progress of the forward line so that artillery in the rear would not fire short. By 1917 each German division was supposed to have up to twelve planes allocated to this task. There is no systematic record of how often these contact patrols were successfully carried out, but it seems from the memoirs of infantrymen that being shelled by one's own artillery was an occurrence of depressing frequency. (In one German dug-out advancing American troops found a placard saying, 'We fear no one but God and our own artillery'). The ground troops were often too busy fighting to send up the necessary recognition flares, and at Arras, for example, British troops were deterred by the fear of attracting the attention of patrolling enemy aircraft.[54]

Both German and British staffs stressed the important psychological effect of the presence of aircraft immediately above the fighting zone. Trenchard wrote of 'the moral effect produced by a hostile aeroplane, which is out of all proportion to the damage it can inflict', and it was later claimed, 'the moral effect on our own troops of our own aerial ascendancy is most marked'. The German staff noted that

> in the defence, the appearance of battle aeroplanes affords visible proof to heavily engaged troops that the Higher Command is in close touch with the front, and is employing every possible means to support the fighting troops.

Equally, captured German letters testified to the disheartening effect of constantly seeing British planes overhead. But moral effects are by their very nature difficult to assess and it was some time before either side began to work for physical, material results by systematically directing aerial attacks against troops on the ground.[55]

Ground attack on troops had been envisaged by W. Joynson-Hicks in an article entitled 'The Command of the Air' published in *The National Review* in April 1912; at the First Battle of Ypres in October 1914 such attacks were carried out by Avro 504 two-seaters armed with Lewis guns. 'I cannot understand why it was not done more extensively', recalled one of the aircrew involved: 'Later on, it was not so popular when German machines became more aggressive'. The possibility of armouring aircraft employed in

---

[54] Peter Gray and Owen Thetford *German Aircraft in the First World War* (1962) p. xiii; Theodore Roosevelt *Average Americans* (New York 1920) p. 151–2; Raleigh and Jones *War in the Air* vol. 3 p. 358.

[55] Raleigh and Jones *War in the Air* vol. 2 p. 473 Appendix IX memo by Trenchard headed 'Future Policy in the Air'; ibid. vol. 3 p. 399 Appendix XI memo March 1917 entitled 'Fighting in the Air'; ibid. vol. 4 p. 433–4 Appendix XII German memo dated 20 Feb. 1918; ibid; vol. 2 p. 252 for material from captured German letters. See also document from German sources dated, 20 Feb. 1918 in Archives de l'Armée de l'Air, Vincennes A 089.

In the Second World War too it was frequently remarked that low-level attacks on ground positions, even when involving heavy bombs, had a psychological impact out of all proportion to the physical damage caused: Public Record Office WO 106/1905 'British Operations in Norway: Lessons from Campaign in Central Norway' paras 4 and 10 and Douglas Gillison *Royal Australian Air Force, 1939–1942* (Canberra 1962) p. 325, referring to experience in Malaya.

the ground-attack role, to protect them from small arms fire from the ground, had been canvassed in September 1914, and in April 1916 Lieutenant-Colonel Maurice Hankey, secretary to the War Committee, proposed the use of low-flying armoured planes in support of tank attacks. Sir David Henderson, Director General of Military Aeronautics, thought the suggestion impractical, and later Trenchard's H.Q. in France began to employ its usual ingenuity to obstruct and obfuscate what would otherwise have seemed a promising idea:

> superiority and supremacy over low-flying aeroplanes can only be obtained by a superior offensive carried out by our low-flying aeroplanes in the enemy's area . . .
> The victory over such low-flying aircraft will be obtained, as is the case in other arms, by the superiority, the *offensive* superiority of our own weapon.

Even the writer of this memo may have suspected that the ground troops would not be satisfied by this waffle as an alternative to the development of a practical ground-attack doctrine, but suggested urbanely, 'The remedy for this is a closer co-operation between the two arms and a more widely-spread education with regard to the functions of the newer weapon'. It was left therefore to the Germans and Italians to develop ground-attack as a form of air warfare.[56]

If we pursue our cavalry analogy, ground attack by aircraft corresponds to the use of shock tactics by heavy cavalry in order to break up infantry squares, but in First World War terms a better analogy is the development of infantry shock troops, also by the Germans and the Italians in the same period as the evolution of the technique of ground attack by aircraft. German aircraft had carried out some random strafing during the Battle of the Somme – the word *strafing* though already current slang in English in something like its original German sense of 'punish' was not in fact generally used in relation to ground attack till the Second World War, though 'ground-strafeing' was allegedly accepted R.F.C. usage by the end of 1917. The R.F.C. carried out some strafing sorties on 11 May 1917 but this seems to have been an inconclusive experiment; the Italians, less distracted by enemy air activity, used no less than 109 planes in a low-level ground attack on the Carso on 23 May 1917, and 130 planes in similar attacks next day. On 10 July 1917 the Germans used about 40 aircraft to attack ground position near Nieuport,

---

[56] W. Joynson Hicks 'The Command of the Air' *National Review* vol. 59 (April 1912) p. 347–358 at p. 353; Joynson Hicks was actually thinking more of the use of large darts (which were indeed briefly experimented with in 1914) but the principle is essentially the same as the use of anti-personnel bombs; L.A. Strange *Recollections of an Airman* [1933] p. 75; Lanchester *Aircraft in Warfare* p. 31 (section first published in *Engineering* 25 Sept. 1914); M. Hankey *The Supreme Command, 1914–1918* (2 vols 1961) vol. 2 p. 497, diary 29 April 1916 and of Ernest Swinton *Eyewitness: Being Personal Reminiscences of Certain Phases of the Great War Including the Genesis of the Tank* (1932) p. 235; Maurice Baring *Flying Corps Headquarters 1914–1918* (1930) p. 243–8, memo 23 Aug. 1917 at p. 245; ibid. p. 247. Baring's phrasing recalls that of a comparably wrong-headed paper by Carlyon Bellairs on 'Commerce and War' in *The Naval Annual (Brassey's)* 1904, p. 155–75; see especially p. 169.

on the Ypres front. The real inauguration of the technique however was on 30 November 1917 when German ground strikes contributed significantly to their successful counter-attack at Cambrai; the Germans were so pleased by the results of their ground attack missions that they began developing specialized units for this work, and by November 1918 had 38 ground attack squadrons (*Schlachtstaffeln*) totalling 228 aircraft: the machines were mainly Halberstadt CL IIs or CL IVs but amongst the designs developed for this role was the Junkers-Fokker CL I, an all-metal low-wing monoplane which, except for its rather typical Fokker tail, had a strikingly modern appearance and represented one of the most important conceptual advances in aircraft design of the period.[57]

Although the British did not attempt systematic ground attack on key defensive positions till August 1918 it was later calculated the British airmen alone fired off twelve million rounds of machine gun ammunition at ground targets; but though the Germans had achieved great success in attacking ground positions at Cambrai on 30 November 1917, the British failed to obtain worthwhile results. Ground support attacks at Amiens on 8–11 August 1918 were later cited as an instance of minimal results achieved at the price of heavy losses. Generally the intensity of ground attack bore no comparison with the use made of much more heavily armed aircraft in the Second World War. The largest single concentration of air power in the First World War

[57] Willy Coppens de Houthulst *Days on the Wing* [1934] p. 201, footnote by the translator, A.J. Insall, for the 'ground-strafeing' usage in 1917; David Brown, Christopher Shores, Kenneth Macksey *The Guinness History of Air Warfare* (1976) p. 40–41; Manlio Molfese *L'Aviazione da Ricognizione Italiana durante la Guerra Europea* (Rome 1925) p. 40–42; Paul Deichman *German Air Force Operations in Support of the Army* (New York 1968) p. 5; Swinton *Eyewitness* p. 235 fn. 1; Deichman *German Air Force Operations* p. 5, cf Gray and Thetford *German Aircraft in the First World War* p. 140–141, and see also J.E. Gurdon edition/translation of Georg Paul Neumann ed. *The German Air Force in the Great War* (1921) p. 44–6, 204–211. For a description of a ground strafing mission see Stark *Wings of War* p. 38–9.

It may perhaps be as well to elaborate on the cavalry analogy. By the seventeenth century charges by armoured cavalry that were pressed home were no longer usual in European warfare – the practice in the English Civil War was unusual in this respect – and by the early years of the eighteenth century new types cavalry were beginning to take on elite status: dragoons who had originally merely been mounted infantry, and hussars, originally mounted skirmishers. The use of the cavalry charge pressed home against formed infantry was revived by Frederick the Great, though little distinction was made between the different branches of the cavalry – the classic charge at Hohenfriedberg which dispersed 20 battalions of Austrian infantry was delivered by the Bayreuth Dragoons. Distinguished use of the massed charge by cavalry was also made during the second half of the Napoleonic War. After 1815 tactical doctrine began increasingly to emphasize separate roles for different categories of cavalry: heavy cavalry, consisting of large men, often with breastplates, mounted on big horses, to charge and break up infantry formations; mounted infantry (generally despised by purists) and light cavalry for reconnaissance, skirmishing and, especially, running down foot soldiers once the heavy cavalry had scattered their formations. Under battlefield conditions it was difficult to maintain the theoretical distinction – at Balaclava the Light Brigade was sent in first with the Heavy Brigade being held back in reserve – but in so far as aircraft were perceived as cavalry, the differentiated functions of cavalry entered into the perception.

was the massing of 1,476 American, French, Italian and British planes under the command of the American Brigadier-General Billy Mitchell to support the attack by 400,000 U.S. troops on the St Mihiel salient on 12 September 1918. This was a unique effort and all it achieved was an advance of a couple of miles against an overwhelmingly outnumbered defence: a result which probably could have been secured without any air support whatever.[58]

The final months of the war produced 'three classic examples' of air attacks on 'an already broken enemy': the retreat of the Turkish Seventh and Eighth Armies after the Battle of Megiddo, the withdrawal of the Bulgarian Second Army in the Kosturino Pass, and of the Austro-Hungarian Isonzo Army after the Battle of Vittorio Veneto were all allegedly turned into routs by ground strafing and bombing. Pursuing a broken enemy was exactly the kind of work for which Haig had been maintaining his cavalry reserves throughout the long months of slog on the Western Front. The problem however was to break the enemy first – and this was never achieved by aircraft alone in the First World War, any more than it was achieved by cavalry.[59]

VIII. The Battle for Air Supremacy

The fact was in any case that aircrew had little real commitment to ground support. The classic image of First World War aviation, the brightly painted biplane fighters wheeling and turning in thrilling acrobatic dogfights, largely corresponds to the airmen's own ideal. As Ludendorff pointed out immediately after the war:

> A battle high up in the air, with the chance of high honours and a mention in Army Orders, was decidedly more exciting and wonderful than ranging for the artillery. Comprehension of the great importance of artillery-ranging work was only gradually inculcated.

As already mentioned, the first British experiments at ground strafing ceased as soon as German aircraft began to offer an alternative challenge. Similarly one airman recalled of the service in the R.F.C. in the early months of 1915:

---

[58] Raleigh and Jones *War in the Air* vol. 1 p. 6; Public Record Office CAB 21/903 Air Staff memo 'Bomber Support for the Army' 18 Nov. 1939 p. 7; William Mitchell *Memoirs of World War I* (New York [1960]) p. 234–244. See also J. Armengaud *L'Atmosphère du champ de Bataille* (Paris 1940) p. 31–2.

[59] Public Record Office CAB 21/903 Air Staff memo 'Bomber Support for the Army' 18 Nov. 1939 p. 3. For the harassing of the Turkish Armies after Megiddo see the chapter 'Nine Miles of Dead' in L.W. Sutherland *Aces and Kings* (Sydney 1935) p. 234–263. It should be emphasized that defeated armies customarily retreat in confusion: the ground-strafing merely added to the disorder, and judging by photos of e.g. the Kosturino Pass after the Bulgarian withdrawal, the ground attacks did not add very much. The British especially were inclined to exaggerate the effects of their ground attacks: it is often said that R.A.F. attacks on the Piave bridges in June 1918 significantly contributed to holding up the Austro-Hungarian advance but these attacks are not even mentioned in the Italian Official History.

I spent a lot of time on photography . . . I was greatly interested in the work, but its draw back was that it did not give us many chances of chasing Huns.[60]

From the very beginning young men of the type given classic definition in the early Biggles stories were thrilled by the possibility that aeroplanes might shoot at one another. Sir John French's first despatch, dated 7 September 1914, claimed on behalf of the R.F.C. pilots, 'by actually fighting in the air, they have succeeded in destroying five of the enemy's machines', but this seems to refer to German aircraft being forced (or frightened) into landing and being destroyed on the ground, for it was not till 5 October that a French Voisin piloted by Sergeant Joseph Frantz became the first aeroplane ever to shoot down another aeroplane in actual combat.[61]

In February 1915 Roland Garros shot down four German aircraft with a Morane-Saulnier Type L 'Parasol' monoplane equipped with a Hotchkiss machine gun firing through the arc of an armour-plated propeller. Garros was soon forced down behind German lines and an examination of his captured aeroplane, according to tradition, inspired the Germans to employ Anthony Fokker to design an interruptor gear for a machine gun and to develop a fast monoplane to carry the modified weapon. By the autumn of 1915 Max Immelmann, flying a Fokker E 1, was making a name for himself as fighter pilot. Previously air fighting had been simply one of several professional tricks whereby the British Army attempted to impose its traditional moral superiority over the enemy, and now that the Germans were coming out ahead the British felt particularly threatened. They already had in service – since February 1915 – the Vickers FB5, a pusher biplane with a forward firing gun and a performance to match that of the Fokker E 1; before the war this Vickers type had been offered for sale to the Germans as 'intended for offensive action in the air against other planes and dirigibles'. There were also a small number of Bristol Scouts, an attractive biplane of conventional lay-out armed with a Lewis gun firing at a 45° angle from beside the cockpit, outside the arc of the propeller; Lanoe J. Hawker won a V.C. by shooting down two German planes in such a machine on 25 July 1915. Nevertheless the German Fokkers seemed to dominate the skies over the Western Front in the autumn of 1915 and a senior R.F.C. officer, Lieutenant-Colonel H.R.M. Brooke-Popham was writing about 'the real struggle for air supremacy' as early as August of that year.[62]

The phrase 'Air Supremacy' became a cliché sufficiently quickly for there to be a wartime advertisement showing a pilot (complete with flying helmet)

---

[60] Ludendorff *My War Memories, 1914–1918* vol. 1 p. 270; Strange *Recollections of an Airman* p. 93.

[61] *Despatches of Lord French* p. 12, Sept. 1914 cf Raleigh and Jones *War in the Air* vol. 1 p. 329; Charles Lafon *Les Armées Aériennes Modernes* (Paris 1916) p. 207–8, and Marcel Jauneaud *L'Évolution de l'Aéronautique* (Paris 1923) p. 195.

[62] C.F. Andrews *Vickers Aircraft since 1908* (1969) p. 57; Peter Lewis *The British Fighter since 1912* (1974 edit.) p. 47–8; Raleigh and Jones *War in the Air* vol. 2 p. 144.

flashing his white teeth through the caption 'Supremacy! Gibb's Dentifrice 6d & 1/- Fragrant As The Lofty Air', but the origins of the concept are not entirely clear. The phrase 'Command of the Sea' (and its theoretical implications) appears to have been popularized by Julian S. Corbett's *England in the Seven Years' War* of 1907 and the same author's *Some Principles of Maritime Strategy* of 1911; the highly influential works of Captain A.T. Mahan, twenty years previously, had not employed the concept, and referred to 'control of the sea' and 'sea power' only in a rather general sense. H.G. Wells's *Anticipations*, published nearly ten years before *Some Principles of Maritime Strategy*, had actually referred to 'the command of the air' but the phrase seems not to have caught on at the time: not surprisingly since the first aeroplane flight was not until two years later. An article by Captain C.J. Burke in *The Aeroplane* referring to 'a struggle for the supremacy of the air' was quoted in Parliament in December 1911. In April 1912 William Joynson-Hicks published his 'Command of the Air' article in *The National Review* but this was probably more inspired by a crude analogy with Corbett's theory of naval warfare than by H.G. Wells's prophecies. An article by F.W. Lanchester published in *Engineering* on 27 November 1914 referred to both 'command of the air' and to 'air supremacy'; in another article in the same series a week later Lanchester wrote of an air fleet operating with the prime objective of challenging the enemy air fleet, and this line of thought quickly gained influential adherents amongst senior R.F.C. officers.[63]

At this stage the R.F.C.'s aircraft were alloted to mixed general purpose

---

[63] A copy of the Gibbs poster is preserved in the Imperial War Museum, catalogue no. 2398; Julian S. Corbett *England in the Seven Years' War: A Study in Combined Strategy* (2 vols 1907) vol. 1 p. 308 and same author *Some Principles of Maritime Strategy* (1911) p. 87–104, cf A.T. Mahan *The Influence of Sea Power upon History, 1660–1883* (1890) and *The Influence of Sea Power upon the French Revolution and Empire* (1892); H.G. Wells *Anticipations, of the Reaction of Mechanic and Scientific Progress upon Human Life and Thought* (1902 [actually 1901]) p. 195. (The phrase 'command of the air' had probably been used for the first time in history by Major J.D. Fullerton R.E. in his paper 'Some Remarks on Aerial Warfare' read at the International Engineering Congress at the Chicago World Columbian Exposition in 1893, cf Alfred E. Hurley *Billy Mitchell: Crusader for Air Power* (Bloomington 1975) p. 142. The phrase later appears in an army staff memo of 11 July 1910: 'German writers make no secret of the hope that the command of the air which they are striving to obtain will also give them command of the sea': S.W. Roskill ed. *Documents Relating to the Naval Air Service* vol. 1: p. 16.) *Hansard: House of Commons* vol. 32 col. 2674, G.J. Sandys, 14 Dec. 1911 citing by Captain Burke in *the Aeroplane* 23 Nov. 1911 p. 582. This was a transcript of paper given by Burke at the United Service Institution on 5 Nov. 1911. (Burke, the first man to pilot on aeroplane owned by the British government, commanded the Central Flying School at Upavon in 1916 but then took over an infantry battalion on the Western Front and was killed in the Battle of Arras, 9 April 1917.) Lanchester *Aircraft in Warfare* p. 87–8 (section first published in *Engineering* 27 Nov. 1914); ibid p. 91 (section first published in *Engineering* 4 Dec. 1914). The preface to *Aircraft in Warfare* was written by Major-General Sir David Henderson. See also Michael Paris *Winged Warfare: the Literature and Theory of aerial warfare in Britain, 1859–1917* (Manchester 1992).

formations, though the French had already begun concentrating their aircraft into squadrons according to type of machine and range of functions, and both they and the Germans had specialized bomber units. Although No. 11 Squadron became the first R.F.C. squadron to be equipped with only a single type of aeroplane in July 1915, by the end of the year the principal organizational distinction in the R.F.C. was between corps wings and army wings, the latter having better and more versatile equipment. It was only during 1916, during the battles of Verdun and the Somme, that the various air services began to concentrate their fighters in what were conceived as specialized fighter units. By the late summer of 1916 the first French fighter *groupe, Les Cicognes*, and the first German *Jagdstaffel, Jasta* 2, had been formed – the latter under Oswald Boelcke – and in the R.F.C. fighters had been concentrated in the army wings. New tactics began to be developed; for the first time groups of aircraft began to operate in close formation. 'I always give them some instructions before we take off and deal out severe criticism after every flight, and especially after every fight', Boelcke wrote of his *Staffel*; he told his men, 'everything depends on sticking together through thick and thin'. The machine age, which had created mass warfare, had also created the opportunities for individual heroics; but Boelcke was foremost amongst those who worked to subordinate even the fighter plane to the organizational principles of mass warfare – though he had no embarrassment about indulging in the distinctly primitive and individualistic custom of keeping a personal tally of the planes he had shot down, a custom which quickly became standard amongst fighter pilots.[64]

The most influential theoretician of the fighter's independent tactical role seems to have been Commandant Paul-Fernand du Peuty, commander of the air element of the French Tenth Army, who favoured using fighters to make offensive patrols in order to deny the enemy the initiative. In April 1916 du Peuty wrote to Trenchard, the C.O. of the R.F.C. in France:

> Aircraft can be divided into two: army machines [i.e. aircraft attached to ground formations] and combat machines. And these aircraft can be employed in two separate ways: either by using the combat machines to protect the army machines, or by letting the latter fend for themselves so that the combat machines can do their real job of fighting.

Pressure from the corps commanders in the Tenth Army soon forced du Peuty to give up his offensive schemes and concentrate on protecting his reconnaissance planes. The Germans too did not allow themselves to be distracted by the glamour of aerial duelling:

[64] Raleigh and Jones *War in the Air* vol. 2 p. 147–8, 166; André Van Haute *Pictorial History of the French Air Force* (2 vols 1974–5) vol. 1 p. 45; Nowarra *Eisernes Kreuz und Balkenkreuz* p. 37; Johannes Werner *Knight of Germany: Oswald Boelcke, German Ace* (1933) p. 213 Boelcke to parents 8 Oct. 1916 cf [Böhme] *Briefe eines deutschen Kampffliegers* p. 66 Böhme to Annamarie B. 18 Oct. 1916 defending the custom of keeping a score, which Annamarie had evidently found objectionable.

The main object of fighting in the air is to enable our artillery registration and photographic reconnaissance to be carried out, and at the same time to prevent that of the enemy.

In the British Expeditionary Force however attempts by corps commanders to obtain more direct control of aircraft in their corps areas, with a view to securing the use of these aircraft for purposes related to the ground fighting, were successfully resisted by Trenchard, who wished to keep operational control in his own hands.[65]

Following the practice worked out by du Peuty in the Battle of Verdun, Trenchard began concentrating on offensive patrolling over German-held territory during the Battle of the Somme. The Germans themselves later acknowledged that 'the first weeks of the Somme battle were marked by a complete inferiority of our own air forces'. Ironically one of the measures they took to counter this was to devolve operational command to a *Fliegergruppenführer* with each corps: effectively what Trenchard refused to do in the British Army. Trenchard's tactics provided wonderful sport for the German *Jasta*: the reputation as a fighter pilot of Oswald Boelcke is as indissolubly linked with the Battle of the Somme as that of the arch-individualist Jean Navarre is linked with the Battle of Verdun. Manfred von Richthofen, whose career as a pilot began under Boelcke's auspices in the Somme campaign, later wrote:

> In the morning, as soon as I had got up, the first Englishman arrived; and the last disappeared only long after sunset. Boelcke once said that this was the El Dorado of the flying man.

Trenchard, on the other side of the line, saw the whole business completely the other way round. An R.F.C. Advanced Headquarters memo of September 1916 announced:

> we know that, although the enemy had concentrated the great part of his available forces in the air on this [the British] front, the work actually accomplished by their aeroplanes stands, compared with the work done by us, in the proportion of 4 to 100.

Bogusly precise figures of this sort were soon to become a hallmark of R.F.C. – and later R.A.F. – staffwork. It was about this time that Major-General Sir David Henderson, Director General of Military Aeronautics at the War Office, admitted, 'As a matter of fact, there are no experts in military aeronautics', but this was not the view of Trenchard's Advanced H.Q. in France and from the Autumn of 1916 the R.F.C. began to develop a systematic bias towards fighter aircraft which distinguished it from the air arms of other countries and which

---

[65] Andrew Boyle *Trenchard* (1962) p. 169; Cuneo *The Air Weapon, 1914–1916* p. 268–9; Below *Experience of the German 1st Army* p. 24; Raleigh and Jones *War in the Air* vol. 3 p. 307–8.

was justified by an insistence on theoretical doctrines which found little favour outside the R.F.C.[66]

The build up of the R.F.C.'s fighter strength began in the autumn of 1916 when Haig, prompted by Trenchard, requested the War Office for twenty extra fighter squadrons, the concept being to raise the proportion of fighter to reconnaissance squadrons to a ratio of two to one. By mid 1918 the proportions of front line aircraft in various arms was as follows:

Country	Fighter (% of Total)	Reconnaissance (% of Total)	Bomber (% of Total)
Britain [Western Front]	52	29	19
France	37	49	14
Italy	39	50	11
Germany	47	39	14
[French air component in Rumania 1917]	37	53	10

If it had not been for a recent build-up of bomber strength in the British air arm the proportion of fighters would have been even higher; and it is probable that the relatively high proportion of fighters maintained in the front line by the Germans was essentially a response to British fighter strength. By this stage the British Army, having lost organizational control of the British air arm, was complaining bitterly of the deteriorating quality of reconnaissance and liaison.[67]

The Italians were certainly as conscious as the British of the glamour of aerial combat but it is instructive to read the directive, 'The Aeroplane and its Employment in Modern War', issued by the Italian High Command in December 1917 and frequently reissued thereafter:

Air action involves first reconnaissance, whether tactical or strategic: and secondly the artillery battle in the tactical sphere and bombing in the strategic sphere. Recently in the tactical sphere one has found a further use for the aeroplane: it has been used for accompanying and liaising with *infantry during battle.*

The fighter arm [*L'aviazione da caccia*] impedes enemy aircraft from investigating the terrain occupied by our troops.

[66] Below *Experience of the German 1st Army* p. 23; Manfred Freiherr von Richthofen *The Red Air Fighter* (1918) p. 78; Raleigh and Jones *War in the Air* vol. 2 p. 473 Appendix IX memo headed 'Future Policy in the Air', 22 Sept. 1916; Henderson's preface to Lanchester *Aircraft in Warfare* p. vi.

[67] Raleigh and Jones *War in the Air* vol. 2 p. 325; ibid. vol. 7 (Appendix vol.) Appendix XL between p. 162–3, giving breakdown of 3,149 French and 1,652 British warplanes, cf Molfese *L'Aviazione da Ricognizione Italiana* p. 103 fn. 1, Cavigioli *L'Aviazione da Ricognizione Austro-Ungarica* p. 265 and fn., Gray and Thetford *German Aircraft in the First World War* p. xxi, G.A. Dabija *Armata Română in Răsboiul Mondial (1916–1918)* (4 vols Bucharest [1928]–36) vol. 4 p. 24; Raleigh and Jones *War in the Air* vol. 4 p. 21–9 and 294 and vol. 6 p. 399 for complaints of deteriorating quality of air reconnaissance in 1918.

That last sentence, in a directive of twenty pages, is the only reference to fighter aircraft. Essentially the same emphasis was given by the commander of a French fighter unit in a paper dated 3 July 1917:

infantry and artillery aircraft . . . must be considered as the basic ingredient of aviation.

Fighter aviation has the role of reconnoitring for them, protecting them, creating around them the most extensive zone of security possible.[68]

Nearly half of the 1,400 or so pilots who claimed to have shot down more than five enemy aircraft in the First World War were British, including eight of the thirteen who claimed to have shot down more than fifty: this in itself shows the British emphasis on fighting. (Lest it be thought that the British had a special talent for this form of warfare, it should be pointed out that Edward Mannock, the leading British ace, despite his sinister-sounding Anglo-Saxon name and the fact that it was his great uncle George who had first taught the Prince of Wales to play billiards, was three-quarters an Irishman, four of the other top-scorers were Canadians, and another a South African–the latter incidentally was one of the smallest officers in the British Army and was killed while stunt flying after the war when the cushions he needed to sit on became mixed up with his controls.) The British aviators' victories over the Germans were however gained at the cost of enormous losses; Trenchard's insistence on the offensive meant that much of the air-fighting was over German-held territory so that any pilot who was shot down and survived became a prisoner. It was later estimated that the British offensive policy was four times as costly in casualties as the German defensive posture. As the British, unlike the Germans, were not supplied with parachutes the British casualties also involved a higher proportion of fatalities; it was not unknown for pilots whose planes had caught fire to be seen jumping out of their aircraft in mid-air to obtain a quick end rather than stay to be fried in their cockpits while their burning machines spiralled picturesquely down to earth, and Edward Mannock always carried a revolver so that he could shoot himself if ever his plane caught fire. The reason for not issuing parachutes was partly a desire to achieve a minimal saving of weight, resulting in a slight increase of offensive range, partly the consideration that aircrew shot down behind enemy lines were as much a loss to the national war effort whether they were killed or merely captured, but mainly the experts' slowness in developing suitable chutes. The high rate of wastage, taken together with a too rapid expansion of the British fighter arm, meant that new pilots had to go into action with inadequate training; and the generally more experienced German pilots, who were operating over their own territory and could afford to choose the conditions of combat, were able to make up for inferior overall numbers by superior skill. In No.1

[68] Molfese *L'Aviazione di Recognizione Italiana* p. 111–131 Appendix 'L'Aeroplano e il suo impiego nella guerra moderna' at p. 111; Archives de l'Armée de l'Air, Vincennes, A 089 paper by commander of G.C. 11 (? Duseigneur?) 3 July 1917: filed under 'Aviation de Combat: Emploi.'

Squadron R.F.C., Major Philip Fullard recalled, 'In six weeks following my arrival, 84 pilots passed through the squadron, many of them not having unpacked their kit before they were casualties'. This is equivalent to the entire squadron complement of pilots being replaced every nine days or so. (Fullard himself was an exception; he shot down 53 German aeroplanes, then broke his leg playing football on the aerodrome, and spent most of the last year of the war in hospital or on crutches.) In some squadrons at least, it was forbidden to mention casualties or to enquire about missing colleagues at mealtimes. Trenchard's policy of 'continuous offensive' was deplored by Salmond, and by Percy Groves, Director of Flying Operations at the Air Ministry; Sykes, no admirer either of Trenchard or Haig, was surely correct in identifying the former's offensive tactics with 'the battering-ram tactics beloved by G.H.Q.' and it certainly appears that Trenchard and Haig saw eye to eye on such matters.[69]

The Germans were forced to respond to the British fighter offensive by concentrating their own fighters in larger units. Manfred von Richthofen's 'Fying Circus' made its first appearance on 30 April 1917 though it was not till July that it was given formal organizational establishment as *Jagdgeschwader 1*. Three more *Jagdgeschwader*, one of them Bavarian, were formed in 1918: each consisted of four *Staffeln*, each of about ten pilots, and corresponded therefore to the *Gruppe* of the Luftwaffe in the Second World War, rather than with the *Geschwader* of three *Gruppen* which was the standard organizational unit in 1939–45. Though endlessly celebrated, in story if not in song, Richthofen's 'Flying Circus' was probably not an entirely efficient unit: one notes that *Jasta* 11, which was Richthofen's own *Staffel* before the formation of the

[69] Brown, Shores and Macksey *Guinness History of Air Warfare* p. 29 and Stanley M. Ulanoff's edition of William A. Bishop *Winged Warfare* (New York 1981 edit.) p. 252–8 both give exhaustive lists of aces: but Brown, Shores and Macksey give 784 aces in the British service whereas Ulanoff, p. 252, mentions the existence of 'more than 550 British fliers who down at least five enemy aircraft'. The eight British aces who claimed more than 50 victories were the Irishman Edward Mannock V.C., the Canadians William Bishop V.C., Raymond Collishaw, Donald MacLaren, William Barker V.C., the South African A.W. Beauchamp-Proctor V.C., and two Englishmen, James McCudden V.C., and Philip Fullard: for Mannock's great uncle see James M. Dudgeon '*Mick*': *The Story of Major Edward Mannock* (1981) p. 24. For Mannock's revolver see '*McScotch*' *Fighter Pilot* (1936) p. 88; amongst those who died jumping from a burning plane in combat was the American ace Raoul Lufbery. Of the 130 men aboard the planes shot down by Richthofen, only 36 survived. For the disadvantage of fighting over the German lines and the additional losses involved see Raleigh and Jones *War in the Air* vol. 5 p. 471 and cf P.R.C. Groves *Behind the Smoke Screen* (1934) p. 124–133; Arthur Gould Lee *No Parachute: A Fighter Pilot in World War 1* (1968) p. 219–225 Appendix C 'Why No Parachutes?'; but cf Public Record Office AIR 1/1079/204/5/1681 which makes it clear that slowness of development was the major factor: there was an Air Ministry 'Parachute Committee' under a brigadier-general, and of the brigade commanders in France C.A.H. Longcroft was especially keen for the early introduction of parachutes; Public Record Office AIR 1/2387/228/11/41 P.J. Fullard's account of his wartime experiences f.2 and cf McScotch *Fighter Pilot* p. 27; Groves *Behind the Smoke Screen* p. 127; Sykes *From Many Angles* p. 220. For a general discussion of the offensive policy see Malcolm Cooper *The Birth of Independent Air Power: British Policy in the First World War* London (1986) p. 71–6.

Geschwader, consisted of eight regular army lieutenants and four reserve lieutenants, whereas the other three *Staffeln* in the 'Flying Circus' comprised one regular army senior lieutenant, four regular lieutenants, twenty reserve lieutenants (two of them commanding *Staffeln*), two 'deputy officers' and six sergeants, indicating that *Jasta* 11 was (at least socially) more of an elite unit than the others. It might also be noted that the British and French also resorted to larger organizational groups in 1918, but principally to side-step the problem involved in the poverty of tactical doctrine: the French established a *Division Aérienne* under General Duval consisting of two *Groupements* (later called *Brigades*), one of three *Groupes* of fighters and three bombers, the other of three *Groupes* of fighters and two of bombers; Commandant Joseph Vuillemin, who later commanded *l'Armée de l'Air* in 1940, led 120 planes from this formation in a mass attack on 4 June 1918. In the R.A.F. the 80th Wing, consisting of five squadrons of, respectively, Sopwith Snipes, Sopwith Camels, SE 5As, Bristol Fighters and DH 9 Bombers, was also supposed to operate as a unit: though it is difficult to see how, and one of its pilots thought that even attacks in squadron strength 'were regarded rather in the nature of "stunts", than as orthodox R.A.F. duties'.[70]

The dreadfully solid scores clocked up by the 'aces', usually within a few short months, testify to the fierceness of their daily combats, but military conservatives were surely correct in supposing that the glamour or aerial combat was in inverse proportion to its contribution to winning the war, and during the crisis of spring 1918 Foch, the Allied generalissimo, ordered:

> At the present time, the first duty of fighting aeroplanes is to assist the troops on the ground, by incessant attacks, with bombs and machine guns, on columns, concentrations, or bivouacs. Air fighting is not to be sought except so far as necessary for the fulfilment of this duty.

[70] Gray and Thetford *German Aircraft in the First World War* p. xxxi. The names and ranks of the original members of the Richthofen *Geschwader* are given in Karl Bodenschatz *Jagd in Flanderns Himmel: aus den sechzehn Kampfmonaten des Jagdgeschwaders Freiherr von Richthofen* (8th edit. Munich 1943) p. 61–2: the two 'deputy officers' (a wartime expedient) were an *Offizierstellvertreter* and a *Feldwebelleutnant*. It might be noted in passing that very few R.F.C. pilots were N.C.O.s in the First World War; for the French *Division Aérienne* see Brown, Shores, and Macksey *Guinness History of Warfare* p. 52, and Archives de l'Armée de l'Air, Vincennes. A022 file 'Division Aérienne': see also the accompanying file 'Escadres de Combat et Groupes de Combat' which gives the impression of a desire to form larger units without a clear idea of their possible function. For 80th Wing see Strange *Recollections of an Airman* p. 159–160, 187–8: Strange was the C.O. of this formation, and cf 'Roger Vee' [Vivian Voss] *Flying Minnows* (1935) p. 277: Strange is called Colonel Napier in this book but is identified in the 1977 reissue.

The word *Staffel* was later taken up by the Nazis – the initials S.S. stand for *Schutz Staffeln* – but before 1916 it was one of those military jargon words of no particular application, equivalent to 'echelon'.

Geschwader, like *Escadrille* and *Squadriglia* had, prior to the war, a specifically naval application. The English word 'squadron' was used for both naval vessels and cavalry, so that it would be difficult to say from which of the older services the term was adapted in the aviation arm.

Having emancipated themselves organizationally from the army, the staff of the R.A.F. inevitably resisted this attempt to relegate them to a role auxiliary to that of the ground forces, and in July 1918, when the Allies were preparing to go over to the attack, R.A.F. senior officers were informed:

> The G.O.C. wishes Brigadiers to aim at using Bristol Fighters purely for fighting. It is recognized that this is not always possible at present, and that they may have to do part of the reconnaissances and bombing. This should not be considered their normal work, however, and they should only be called upon to do it in order to relieve D.H. Squadrons.

At all costs, it seem, tactical collaboration with other services was to be minimized: the air arm was to operate according to its own doctrine, not according to the requirements of the army. This insistence on going its own way was to be taken to further extremes in the next war.[71]

IX. The Air Lobby

The ability of the R.F.C. and later the R.A.F. to establish its own independent tactical doctrine, for example, the special emphasis given to aerial combat, related to the particular organizational and institutional development of the British air arm.

At the outbreak of war the British Royal Flying Corps was the only military aviation organization in the world to have a general officer as administrative head, and the appointment of Brigadier-General David Henderson as Director General of Military Aeronautics in charge of an independent War Office department in September 1913 must partly be explained in terms of the British Army's general staff being a brand-new set-up which had no time to settle into an organizational rut – unlike the army as a whole. The Royal Naval Air Service had an administrative head of more junior rank, responsible to the Admiralty Board of which different members controlled personnel, procurement and so on. On the continent the various air arms had commanders only at unit level. The rapid expansion of air services on the outbreak of the war obviously necessitated more elaborate command structures.

The first thing was to have an officer with responsibility for aircraft in the battle zone. Trenchard allegedly favoured having a senior officer appointed to the army G.H.Q. as C.R.F.C., corresponding to the C.R.A. administratively responsible for artillery and the C.R.E. responsible for engineers, and this was in fact the procedure adopted in the French, and slightly later, the German and Austro-Hungarian Armies, with a more senior officer holding the fort in Paris and Vienna, though not in Berlin. As Joseph-Édouard Barès, the

---

[71] Raleigh and Jones *War in the Air* vol. 4 p. 458 Appendix XVIII, Order of General Foch no. 4; Public Record Office AIR 1/860/204/5/425, 'Minutes of Brigadiers' Conference Held at H.Q. R.A.F. on 30th July 1918'. The Bristol Fighter was an exceptionally successful two-seater with both fixed forward-firing and movable rear armament: it could also carry bombs. The 'D.H. Squadrons' were those equipped with DH 4 and DH 9 single-engined bombers.

aviation chief at French G.H.Q. from September 1914 and Hermann von der Lieth-Thomsen, *Chef des Feldflugwesens* (or *Frontflugwesens*) from March 1915 both had only the rank of major, it may be assumed that they had little influence on their respective High Commands. (One notes that a paper prepared by Barès in November 1914, insisting on the 'frankly offensive' nature of the air weapon, 'whether in the hunt after enemy aircraft or in the destruction of troops, cantonments and fortifications by means of projectiles', was quickly toned down by colleagues on the staff.) In any case there were officers of similar rank attached to each army headquarters in the field and separately responsible for the aviation of each of the half dozen or so armies into which the French and German forces were divided: nevertheless Barès's eventual resignation, in February 1917, may have been due to resentment at losing what independence he had to senior officers in Paris who wished to bring the front under direct control. In the R.F.C. Henderson pressed for the appointment of a General Officer Commanding, with a separate headquarters, and this was the arrangement adopted. Initially Henderson was himself the G.O.C., with Sykes his deputy and General Staff Officer in France and Sefton Brancker running the Directorate of Military Aeronautics at the War Office. The H.Q. staff quickly established the tradition, later taken over by the R.A.F., of constantly looking over their shoulders; as early as September 1914, when supernumary officers were recalled from France to organize training at home, 'Everyone was indignant. Some people said: "They are trying to start a rival show in England. They are taking away our best men"'. And of course there were professional feuds. When Henderson was posted to command a division Trenchard, then commanding a tactical wing, refused to serve under Sykes and eventually succeeded as G.O.C. He commanded the R.F.C. in France till the beginning of 1918.[72]

[72] Sykes *From Many Angles* p. 144; Van Haute *Pictorial History of the French Air Force* vol. 1 p. 29–30, 52, 54; Cuneo *The Air Weapon, 1914–1916* p. 292–3; Archives de l'Armée de l'Air, Vincennes, A 088 'Org. et emploi de l'aéronautique' various drafts Nov. 1914; Maurice Baring *Flying Corps Headquarters, 1914–1918* (1930) p. 46; The French *Inspecteur de l'Aéronautique Militaire* was initially Général de Brigade Bernard, soon replaced by Général Hirschauer; Hirschauer was replaced by Régnier in January 1917: it was because of Régnier's desire to extend his control in the front zone that Barès resigned. The head of the Austro-Hungarian *Luftfahrtruppen* in Vienna was Oberst Emil Uzelac. (Amongst his staff was Alexander Löhr, commander of the Austrian airforce 1934–8, and of *Luftflotte* 4 of the Luftwaffe from 1939. As an Army Group Commander in the Balkans 1943–5 he held a more important appointment under Hitler than any other former Habsburg officer. In February 1947 he was hanged by the Yugoslavs for having given the order to bomb Belgrade in April 1941). Till the end of 1916 the Belgians also had separate administrative and front commanders for their aviation but then both posts were combined under Major Roland van Crombrugge. The Russian air service (except the heavy bomber units) were under the Grand Duke Alexander Mikhailovich who, although a General A.D.C. by virtue of his membership of the imperial family, was actually an admiral by profession: although theoretically operating from the H.Q. of his cousin the Grand Duke Nicholas (whom he loathed) he seems to have also been responsible for administration on the home front, but his memoirs *Once a Grand Duke* (1932) though extremely interesting on other topics, and evincing considerable intellectual ability, say little about his work leading Russia's air force, thereby suggesting a certain dilettantism in this sphere of his public life.

In order to reorganize the German air arm after the Somme, Generalmajor Ernst von Hoeppner was appointed *Kommandierender General der Luftstreit-kräfte – Kogenluft* for short – on 8 October 1916 with Lieth-Thomsen (who had wanted an independent Air Department established in Berlin) as his chief of staff. This effectively brought the German air arm into line with the headquarters arrangement already established in the British Expeditionary Force, but since the team of Hindenburg and Ludendorff acted as directors not merely of the army at the front but effectively of the whole country, there was not the same bureaucratic flowering in Berlin as there was in London: for example it was Hoeppner's H.Q. which handled the troublesome business of dealing with the aeroplane manufacturers. Only the Americans, confronted with even greater problems of distance than the British, reproduced the British system of a Direc-tor of Military Aeronautics in the national capital and a commanding general in the war zone. The Italians went to the opposite extreme: during the period April 1916 to April 1917there was a unified command for artillery-spotting planes (*Commando delle squadriglie per l'artiglieria*) but otherwise, till 1918, there was only an aviation commander assigned to each individual army (initially as the unit commander of the aviation group allocated to each army; later as *Commando di aeronautica d'armata*); a *Commissariato Generale per l'Aero-nautica* was established in Rome in January 1918 and two months later a *Commando Superiore d'Aeronautica* was created at the front; its first head was General Luigi Bongiovanni who had distinguished himself by losing his army corps at Caporetto.[73]

The establishment of a degree of *political* independence for the air arm was initiated, though perhaps half-heartedly, in France, when René Besnard was appointed under-secretary for military aviation on 13 September 1915. Besnard attracted much hostile criticism, and following a Zeppelin raid on Paris on 29 January 1916 he was sacked and his post abolished. It was revived in March 1917 with first Daniel Vincent, then Jacques Dumesnil as under-secretary. In Britain, Lloyd George talked to Clementine Churchill on 4 February 1916 about how Winston might have liked 'the "Air"', and in a subsequent letter

---

[73] Molfese *Aviazione du Recognizione Italiana* p. 3, 15, 34. Felice Porro *La Guerra nell'Aria* (Milan 1966 edit.) p. 152. There were of course air commanders for each component army in the German, British and French armies, but except temporarily in the French case they never achieved much independence: in the British army the commanders of the R.F.C. brigades assigned to each army seem to have been kept under especially close supervision by R.F.C. H.Q. According to Cuneo *The Air Weapon 1914–1916* p. 292–3 the particular problem between Régnier and Barès seems to have been that the former saw no need for a front commander for aviation: evidently the holder of such a post tended to complicate dealings between the administrative centre and the aviation commanders with individual armies, who had tactical control. The American arrangement, with Major-General William L. Kenly Director of Military Aeronautics in Washington, Major-General Mason M. Patrick (formerly Chief Engineer on the Lines of Communications) head of the Air Service in France and Brigadier-General William Mitchell, commanding the aviation in the First Army Group, exercising actual tactical control, seems to have been necessitated by the fact that the A.E.F. acquired its frontline aircraft in France, from French manufacturers, so that administrative supervision of procurement from Washington would hardly have been practical.

to her husband Mrs. Churchill referred to the possible appointment of an 'Air Minister'. Nine days later, on 16 February, William Joynson-Hicks, moving an amendment to the Address in the House of Commons, called publicly for an 'Air Minister' and was supported by several other M.P.s. On 23 February 1916 the Earl of Derby was appointed to head a Joint War Air Committee, to deal particularly with procurement for the Royal Flying Corps and the Royal Naval Air Service. The fact that there were two rival air services in Britain both complicated and made more urgent the problem of establishing military aviation on a coherent institutional basis; in the event the R.F.C. and R.N.A.S., having so little idea of their separate functions or the demarcation between them, showed no interest in pooling resources and Derby, lacking any executive power to break through the resulting impasse, resigned after seven weeks. Next an Air Board, under Lord Curzon, the Lord President of the Council, was established; Sir Paul Harvey, later famous as the compiler of the *Oxford Companion to English Literature*, was appointed secretary. The Air Board enraged Trenchard and Haig by interviewing the French aviation commander, Colonel Barès, on bombing policy, and infuriated the Admiralty by circulating provocative memoranda about the R.N.A.S.; the First Lord of the Admiralty, Balfour, counter-attacked in November with a memo stating, 'I do not suppose that in the whole history of the country any Government Department has ever indulged so recklessly in the luxury of inter-Department criticism'. In January 1917 a new Air Board was established under Lord Cowdray – Brancker, the Director of Air Organization, later Deputy Director General of Military Aeronautics, had advised Lloyd George against appointing Churchill – but Cowdray, entering government for the first time from the business world, had much less pull than Curzon and had little influence on the War Cabinet's decision, on 24 August 1917, to establish a completely independent air service.[74]

In May 1916 'Colonel Churchill', newly returned from exile in the trenches, had spoken in the House of Commons of the need for:

one unified, permanent branch of Imperial defence, composed exclusively of men who will not think of themselves as soldiers, sailors, or civilians, but as airmen, as servants of a new arm, as servants of an arm which, possibly at no distant date, may be the dominating arm of war.

[74] Van Haute *Pictorial History of the French Air Force* vol. 1 p. 36, 52, 59, and Cuneo *the Air Weapon, 1914–1916* p. 290, 292; Mary Soames *Clementine Churchill* (1979) p. 165, 167 Clementine Churchill to Winston Churchill 4 and 7 Feb. 1916 and cf *Observer* 6 Feb. 1916 p. 8e; *Hansard: House of Commons* vol. 80 col. 94, cf ibid. vol. 80, cols 126, 131, 138, 141, 152; Raleigh and Jones *War in the Air* vol. 3 p. 268–9: the date given by Raleigh and Jones for Derby's appointment is a week earlier than its announcement in the press, which cannot be quite correct; Blanche E.C. Dugdale *Arthur James Balfour* (2 vols 1936) vol. 2 p. 159, memo Nov. 1916; India Office Library Mss Eur. F. 112/116 Derby to Curzon 1 Jan. 1917 for Brancker's opposition to the appointment of Churchill to head the Air Board. For a reassessment of Curzon's Air Board see Cooper *The Birth of Independent Air Power* p. 56–70.

The immediate instigation of the War Cabinet's decision in August 1917 was not however the parliamentary eloquence of the ex-First Lord of the Admiralty but a report by Jan Smuts commissioned by the War Cabinet, which prophesied victory through air power in even more glowing terms. Lloyd George, having won great acclaim by setting up an entirely new department, the Ministry of Munitions, in 1915, was not disinclined to repeat the experiment, and both he and his War Cabinet colleagues were ready to fall in with any war-winning scheme that was sufficiently dramatic and innovative, provided it was guaranteed a good press: but the chiefs of both the Army and the Navy were appalled.[75]

It is at least symptomatic of the atmosphere prevailing at the War Office and the Admiralty in 1917 that the staff officers most involved with the air services felt that their superiors regarded them with enmity because of their supposed sympathy with ministerial proposals regarding an independent air force. 'I encountered almost open hostility to the new policy and to my staff generally', claimed Brancker, the Deputy Director General of Military Aeronautics; when he asked to see Sir William Robertson, the C.I.G.S., to discuss the matter Robertson refused to give him an interview. Soon afterwards Brancker was appointed to a command in the Middle East, though he learnt of this not through regular War Office channels but through reading it in *The Times*. 'They have got me all right at last', he wrote bitterly to Trenchard. Commodore Murray Sueter, who had been Director of the Air Department at the Admiralty at the outbreak of war, and who had later been moved sideways to be Superintendent of Aircraft Construction, had also shown too much interest in an independent air service, and Lord Curzon believed that Sueter's superiors held it against him. In the spring of 1917 he was banished to command R.N.A.S. units in the central Mediterranean, despite Curzon's intervention on his behalf with the First Lord of the Admiralty. From Taranto Sueter wrote, 'I do not quite know why I was exiled. I think it was for backing Lord C. and *not* the naval people'; and after the war Curzon wrote to him:

> I remember the bold and courageous fight that you made for sound principles of Air Administration when we were associated in 1917, and also how you suffered for it.[76]

One of Brancker's last achievements at the War Office was to persuade the Secretary of State against appointing Robertson's nominee, Major-General

[75] *Hansard: House of Commons* vol. 82 col. 1588, 17 May 1916; for the Smuts report see above p. 399.

[76] Norman Macmillan *Sir Sefton Brancker* (1935) p. 164, cf also p. 157; Boyle *Trenchard* p. 242, Brancker to Trenchard [Oct. 1917]; India Office Library Mss Eur. F. 112/116 Lord Sydenham to Curzon 1 Jan. 1917, Major John Baird to Curzon 10 and 17 Jan. 1917 and Sir Edward Carson, First Lord of the Admiralty to Curzon n.d. – all relating to Sueter's undesired transfer, cf Murray F. Sueter *Airmen or Noahs: Fair Play for our Airmen* (1928) p. 222, 226, 230–231, 239; Roskill ed. *Documents Relating to the Naval Air Service* vol. 1 p. 477 Sueter to Lord Montagu of Beaulieu 19 April 1917; Sueter *Airmen or Noahs* p. 243, Curzon to Sueter 21 June 1922.

John Capper, as Director General of Military Aeronautics in succession to Sir David Henderson: Brancker thought he ought to have the job himself. In the event it went to Major-General John Salmond. When Salmond took over the Directorate, Trenchard wrote to him from France, 'Remember in your dealings with the War Office that we are part of the Army and that we are not trying to run a separate show at their expense'. The decision already made by the War Cabinet to establish a Royal Air Force as an independent service was of course a total repudiation of this view. When Trenchard was appointed to be professional head of the new service, with the title of Chief of Air Staff, he attempted to limit what he saw as the damage but quickly ran into difficulties with the new minister, Lord Rothermere, proprietor of *The Daily Mirror* and *The Sunday Pictorial* and formerly Director General of the Royal Army Clothing Department; Rothermere's opinion of 'that dud Trenchard' was that:

As Chief of Air Staff he was simply a Gargantuan joke. If he is the kind of man Haig surrounds himself with I am not surprised we have done so badly in France.[77]

Both Trenchard and Rothermere soon resigned. Trenchard's successor was Major-General Frederick Sykes. As a captain Sykes had been the original commander of the Royal Flying Corps when it had been first set up, and had commanded it briefly in 1914 during Henderson's absences from Advanced H.Q. He was an able administrator and careerist (he later chaired various government committees and became Governor of Bombay) but seems to have had more talent for bureaucratic intrigue than for original military thought and was held in notably low esteem by the other senior officers of the R.F.C. Since 1915 he had helped form the Machine Gun Corps and had been on the staff of Robertson's *bête noire* the Supreme War Council at Versailles. His return to aviation as Chief of Air Staff was not universally welcomed: Sir David Henderson resigned as Vice-President of the Air Council because of his 'very unfavourable opinion of Major-General Sykes and . . . my previous relations with that officer'.[78]

Sykes may be taken as epitomizing the tendency of the R.A.F. to become a haven for desk-bound whizz-kids. Of all the varieties of bureaucracy, military bureaucracy has always been amongst the worst. The vast expansion of the wartime army had necessitated a corresponding expansion of the staff at the War Office and inevitably added something of civilian careerism to the military careerism already perhaps too prevalent: and this had been especially the case in the Royal Flying Corps where the totally novel types of problem being dealt with meant that military background and experience of military procedure

[77] Macmillan *Sir Sefton Brancker* p. 168 and cf Cooper *The Birth of Independent Air Power* p. 112–3 Boyle *Trenchard* p. 242; Reginald Pound and Geoffrey Harmsworth *Northcliffe* (1959) p. 638 Rothermere to Northcliffe [20 May 1918].

[78] Lord Beaverbrook *Men and Power, 1917–1918* (1956) p. 379 Appendix IV/12 Henderson to Rothermere [second half of April 1918].

was less requisite than in other departments. The rise of Francis Conway Jenkins from second-lieutenant to brigadier-general, C.B.E., Commander of the Russian Order of St Stanislas in four years, without ever being in action, was simply the most dramatic example of this phenomenon. One of Jenkins's admirers recalled the mood amongst the temporary officers at the Air Board:

> There was great elation when we learnt that a big scheme of expansion was going through and that we would all move up in the hierarchy. We pored over blue prints showing the future organisation of our Directorate throughout the country. Every head of department wanted to out do his neighbour. Happy indeed was he who had three G.S.O. 1s under him while his rival had only two!

Frontline soldiers were inclined to describe what was going on in rather stronger terms:

> the day of the theorist and the faddist, fatuous and dangerous, has come. And everywhere one sees or hears of the same things – great numbers of people out only for pelf, or place and its emoluments; public money and time diverted to individual self-advancement: self-seekers assailing administration without, and eating it up within.

After resigning as Chief of Air Staff, Trenchard had reluctantly accepted the command of the Independent Force assigned to bomb Germany, and observed this process of bureaucratic growth with helpless dismay. On 13 July 1918 he noted in his diary:

> It is curious to think that all the people who are so keen on bombing Germany are actually reducing the amount of bombing that could be done and largely increasing the personnel required to do so.

Two and a half weeks later he recorded, 'Still more staff have arrived, but no more bombs have been dropped on Germany'. His verdict, jotted down on the day of the final cease-fire was:

> A more gigantic waste of effort and personnel there has never been in any war. The Force has done splendidly. It would have done just as splendidly had it remained under the command of the Expeditionary Force with half the number of officers and men it has been necessary to employ here to do the work and it would have been better looked after with regard to its administrative services.

On that day, 11 November 1918, the personnel of the R.A.F. numbered 291,175; that of the French air service, still part of the Army, was 127,630. Yet as recently as June 1918 the French air service had had 47 per cent more front-line aircraft. This, rather than any warlike triumphs, was the real achievement of the new-formed Royal Air Force.[79]

[79] John Evelyn Wrench *Struggle: 1914–1920* (1935) p. 244; J.C. Dunn *The War the Infantry Knew* (1987 edit.) p. 452–3, 19 March 1918 and cf R. Meinertzhagen *Army Diary, 1899–1926* (Edinburgh 1960) p. 206–7, 11 Feb. 1917; H. Montgomery Hyde *British Air Policy Between the Wars, 1918–1939* (1976) p. 43–4, Trenchard's diary for 13 and 30 July and 11 November 1918; Raleigh and Jones *War in the Air* vol. 7 (Appendix vol.) Appendix XXXV and Appendix XL between p. 162–3.

It was not merely in institutional sense that the British led in creating an independent air service: the overall detachment of aviation from any meaningful military purposes was a process forced ahead by Britain more than any other power. Despite the pioneer work in fighter tactics by Immelmann and Boelcke, bravura manifestations such as Richthofen's Flying Circus and the daylight raids on London, and the spectacular local successes of German bombers against British military targets in France, the Germans and their allies were invariably at a disadvantage because of their inferior productive resources in light engineering; even in April 1918 when the Germans concentrated their squadrons to achieve a local superiority over the British they were outnumbered three to one on the Western Front as a whole. Because the Russian air service was relatively small and inefficient the Germans and the Austro-Hungarians employed only a small part of their air strength on the Eastern Front, even though the open nature of the warfare, the larger distances involved, and the great number of cavalry units employed by the Russians offered significant opportunities for the use of air power. It was on the fronts where they were generally on the defensive, the Franco-British and Italian fronts, that the Germans and Austro-Hungarians concentrated their warplanes. Militarily this was perhaps quite unnecessary; the Italians derived no special advantage from their overwhelming superiority in numbers and equipment over the Austro-Hungarians, and the intensity of the air fighting on the Alpine Front was much less than in France and Belgium; the Germans suffered air-crew casualties of altogether 5,833 killed and 10,053 injured, the Austro-Hungarians, up to August 1918, of 358 killed and 554 injured. Perhaps it would have made no difference if the Austro-Hungarians had made no attempt to compete with the Italians at all. But with Austria-Hungary, as with other countries, it seems that the main determinant of how the air weapon was to be used was what the enemy was doing.[80]

X. The Mind and the Machine

It is evident that the essential problem experienced during the First World War with regard to the integration and exploitation of new weaponry was one of properly understanding the potential, and also the limitations, of the new technology and that, if anything, the error was in placing too much, not too little, reliance on the schemes proposed by technical experts of comparatively junior rank and limited tactical experience. The problem of handling the new technology was however only one aspect of a larger problem of tactical and strategic management, and in sponsoring Trenchard's policy of the continuous fighter offensive, for example, Haig was to a large extent adopting a games-

---

[80] Raleigh and Jones *War in the Air* vol. 4 p. 349–350 for relative strengths on the Western Front in April 1918; Hoeppner *Deutschlands Krieg in der Luft* p. 174 fn. 1 and Cavigioli *L'Aviazione Austro-Ungarica* p. 51 for German and Austro-Hungarian casualties.

manship stratagem to divert attention from his inability to make more dramatic progress in the ground fighting; similarly the quasi-offensive aspect of employing machine guns in barrage fire was probably one of the reasons why machine-gun barrages were acceptable at H.Q. level. The new weapons probably had more impact on the political and public relations side of the war than on the battle front. If the First World War had been fought, like the American Civil War, with railways but without aircraft, tanks and machine guns, it is unlikely that it would have assumed a significantly different shape and pattern.

The problem of establishing a tactical method and enforcing tactical control are shown up more clearly perhaps in the war at sea than in the war on land, with only two brief and dramatic encounters on the North Sea deserving the name of major battles instead of the four obfuscating years of deadlock on the various continental fronts. At the encounter between British and German battle cruisers at Dogger Bank on 24 January 1915, the British, having crippled the German armoured cruiser *Blücher*, misunderstood their admiral's flag signals and allowed the German battle cruisers to escape while they finished off the *Blücher*. Poor signalling was also a factor in the mediocre performance of the British Grand Fleet off Jutland on 31 May 1916 but perhaps the real problem was that Admiral Sir John Jellicoe, while commanding a fleet consisting of many more individual ships than were ever commanded by Nelson, and distributed over a much larger area of the sea, nevertheless insisted on a degree of centralized control, and a degree of renunciation of individual initiative by his captains, that was simply unworkable.

The Battle of Jutland represented one of the few occasions that the British Royal Navy fought a major battle with an enemy that was significantly weaker in strength: and losing three battle-cruisers to Germany's one hardly qualifies as a victory. Like the huge armies on the Western Front, the huge British fleet of 1916, with its heavy artillery capable of sinking vessels barely visible on the horizon, was simply a machine that was too large for one man to handle. Yet whereas part of the problem on the Western Front was the unprecedented size of the armies and the complications involved in the employment of unfamiliar weapons, Jellicoe's fleet at Jutland was the product of decades of evolution and expert calculation, and the task it failed to carry out was precisely the one it had always been intended for.

The blowing up of three British battle cruisers at Jutland – so much grander and more expensive in lives and equipment than the famous detonation of the French flagship *L'Orient* at the Nile in 1798 – had been prefigured in H.G. Wells's *The War of the Worlds* when the torpedo ram *Thunder Child* was blown up by a Martian heat-ray: 'with a violent thud, a blinding flash, her decks, her funnels, leaped upward etc., etc.' Equally the fact that the three British battle-cruisers lost at Jutland could all have been saved by better precautions against chain-reactive explosions within their magazines seems reminiscent of the loss of four British warships because of their highly combustible electrical circuitry during the Falklands War in 1982: the more complex the technology, the easier it is to overlook weak points that in retrospect seem obvious. Even at the most rudimentary technical level modern weaponry can hardly be said to have been perfected, either today or at the time of the First World War. But the relative novelty or crudity of new weapons is less important than the ability of the military organism to adjust to such potential as they have, and it seems that in the First World War at least the degree of adjustment, whether to new weaponry of land warfare or to the older technology of the battle fleet, was cruder than the weaponry itself: not so much because of the reluctance of the military organism to adjust, as because of its insensitivity to practical detail and its readiness to be diverted by theoretical gimmicks. The same thing was to happen, but with more sophisticated theoretical gimmicks, in the Second World War.

11

The War of the Transitional Dictatorships

The present disaster will, in the course of years, decades, and centuries, emit a sanguinary radiation, in the light of which future generations will view their own fate, just as Europe has hitherto sensed the radiation of the great French Revolution and of the Napoleonic wars.

Leon Trotsky *circa* 1916, quoted in Isaac Deutscher, *The Prophet Armed: Trotsky, 1889–1921* (Oxford 1971 edit.), p. 231.

I. The Instability of the Old Order

The names of the battles of the 1914–1918 war echo like a bell tolling national disaster – Tannenberg, Ypres, Verdun, Caporetto, the Somme – but tolling too the passing of an age that was unprepared for its own demise and died hard. It was only in retrospect that it was perceived how ripe the old order was for dissolution.

In 1914, despite a decade of spiralling military expenditure, war took by surprise a Europe which in the hundred years since Napoleon had erected the semblance of a stable political system on a scaffolding of compromise and privilege. Even the most rickety parts of this structure survived the gales of war for nearly three years, but the truth is that all the regimes which went to war in the late summer of 1914 were fragile and delicately balanced. For the most part limited monarchies – a constitutional system covering a range of practices, from Britain where the King sought to be politically neutral to Russia where the Duma was still unfamiliar with its potential to challenge the autocratic power of the Tsar – these governments presented the essential paradox embodied in the phrase 'limited monarchy': everywhere social classes and interest groups were in uneasy and unequal competition. The political and social conflicts of the first half of the nineteenth century, diverted after 1848 by rising living standards and nationalist ideology, had in the final quarter of the century, reemerged, fuelled by the economic changes experienced during the years of truce and calm. A great deal of deft political footwork had avoided any irremediable clash but everywhere by 1914 the subterranean vibrations were building up to a crescendo.

Four European sovereigns were assassinated in the years 1900–1913: Umberto of Italy, Alexander of Serbia, Carlos of Portugal and George of Greece – the latter regarded as an outstandingly successful constitutional monarch. In addition the U.S. President McKinley was killed in 1901 by a Detroit-born anarchist of central European parentage. In the fourth attempt on the life of the 21-year-old Alfonso XIII of Spain, staged during his wedding on 31 May 1906, a bouquet containing a bomb killed 23 and injured 99, showering blood on the new queen's bridal gown of white and silver satin. In Russia there were 2,691 deaths from terrorist attacks in the years 1906–1909 alone: between 1902 and 1911 three ministers of the interior were assassinated as well as Grand Duke Serge, uncle of the Tsar and commander of the troops in Moscow, and Count Shuvalov, the prefect of Moscow. The repression of political dissidence after 1905 had had only a temporary effect; in April 1914, following a wave of political strikes and lock-outs, there was a general strike in St. Petersburg. In the German Empire there was the strongest Socialist party in the world, and the antagonism between an *ancien régime* self-transformed into an alliance of generals and capitalists, and a progressive movement of intellectuals and blue-collar workers threatened a rapid erosion of the common ground on which any political system needed to be based. In Italy agrarian and urban lower-class unrest flared periodically into murderous street battles with the police, culminating in the *Settimana Rossa* (Red Week) of 7–13 June 1914 when the security forces were besieged in their barracks at Ravenna and a workers' republic was proclaimed at Fabriano, a centre of the Italian paper-making industry situated in the mountains between Ancona and Perugia. In Britain the reactionary Tories were fighting a bitter and prolonged rearguard action on a complex of related issues, including the legislative power of the House of Lords and the Union with Ireland. In France, much the largest of Europe's only three republics, a variety of tensions and divisions rankled: the Paris Commune and the other embittering experiences of 1870–1871 which had accompanied the fall of Napoleon III and the establishment of the Third Republic had not been left behind, though the role of Aristide Briand, formerly apostle of the General Strike, in crushing the great railway strike of 1910 indicated the paradoxical resilience of the French system. All over Europe, in that last delayed summer of the nineteenth century, members of the social elites, immaculately dressed by their servants and effortlessly enriched by ever more complex forms of expropriation, looked forward to an endless vista of international tranquillity, decorated rather than disturbed by far-off blood feuds in Ruritania, while all the while the unemployed loitered hungrily at street corners and factory workers passed anti-boss tracts from hand to hand.[1]

When, in Lloyd George's phrase, the governments backed their machines over the precipice in late July and early August 1914, the first apparent reaction everywhere was a toning up, a drawing together of the socio-political organism. Socialists in Germany announced their *Burgfrieden* (emergency

[1] For the attempt on Alfonso XIII see *Times* 20 June 1906 p. 7b; for Russia see Alex de Jonghe *The Life and Times of Grigorii Rasputin* (1982) p. 88. There was also an attempt on the life of the British Viceroy in India, the Earl of Minto in November 1909, and another on his successor Lord Hardinge, in December 1912.

political truce); the Slovenes rioted against the Serb enemies of the Habsburg monarchy; and Sigmund Freud was suddenly proud because 'for the first time for thirty years I feel myself an Austrian and feel like giving this not very hopeful Empire another chance'. The men of Britain jostled aside the few cranks distributing peace tracts and went to queue on the pavements outside the recruiting stations: the French parliamentary deputies of rival factions struck identical tragic poses as they fled to the hotels of Bordeaux. Yet within a few months all the belligerent regimes were sliding into political crisis: and in every country the crisis had similar features.[2]

II. Opposition to War Governments

After four years of war, with time-hallowed regimes toppling like dominoes, it became easy to believe that the war had loosened the cement between classes, and between the national components of multi-national states such as Austria-Hungary – perhaps not loosened cement but given a final catastrophic shove to structures from which the cement had already fallen away. In reality it took nothing like three or four years for the cracks to begin to appear. On 18 March 1915 Berlin women demonstrated against the government outside the German Reichstag and on May Day 1915 red posters appeared in the streets of Dresden bearing the slogan:

> Is the mass murder going to continue? In the name of humanity raise your voices and demand Peace! Peace! Peace!

During the Berlin 'butter riots' of November 1915 two hundred women paraded in Berlin's Unter den Linden shouting *'Frieden! Frieden!* (Peace! Peace!) and had to be dispersed, cossack-fashion, by sending in cavalry. In St. Petersburg there were mob attacks on the police in August 1915 and during the following month the prorogation of the Duma provoked serious strikes. In Britain rioting generally deflected itself against foreign immigrants but from the very begining a part of the violence was directed against the police and other symbols of class authority.[3]

There were a number of food riots during the war involving not merely shouting in the streets and window breaking but attacks on police stations, as at Cologne and Bonn in March 1916; in the 'Potato riots' in Amsterdam in the neutral Netherlands, on 2 and 3 July 1917 the military fired on the crowd, allegedly killing five people; but the characteristic, most widespread and ultimately the most effective form of social protest during the war was the

---

[2] Hilda C. Abraham and Ernst L. Freud *A Psycho-Analytic Dialogue: The Letters of Sigmund Freud and Karl Abraham* (1965) p. 186 Freud to Abraham 26 July 1914.

[3] F.L. Carsten *War against War: British and German Radical Movements in the First World War* (1982) p. 42–3; Evelyn Countess Blücher *An English Wife in Berlin: A Private Memoir of Events, Politics, and Daily Life in Germany throughout the War and the Social Revolution of 1918* (1920) p. 90–91, diary 15 Nov. 1915; Kenneth Young ed. *The Diaries of Sir Robert Bruce Lockhart* (2 vols 1973–80) vol. 1 p. 24–5, 28 August, 17 and 27 Sept. 1915.

industrial strike. A series of strikes in Austria, beginning at Wiener Neustadt on 14 January 1918, spread to Berlin and other great German cities and helped make clear to the German military leadership, in the final weeks before their spring offensive, how little time they had left to win the war. The general strike in Turin in late August 1917, in the course of which fifty people were killed in street fighting, was ostensibly about the price of bread but coming only nine days after a delegation from the Russian Provisional Government had been welcomed by rapturous crowds shouting *Viva Lenin!* clearly represented some degree of mobilization by those opposed to the existing form of government. Yet it was Britain, the European belligerent which sustained the burden of the war with the least overall strain, which experienced the highest level of strike activity:

Strikes, 1915–1918

	No. of strikes	No. of strikers	No. of days lost
Britain	3,227	2,694,522	17,838,804
France	1,608	520,755	2,741,504
Germany	1,469	1,165,601	3,598,661

Not only were there more strikes and strikers in Britain, but they stayed out comparatively longer – on average 7.5 days as compared to 3.08 days in Germany. Moreover the strikes became a serious problem at an earlier stage in the war:

Strikes, 1915

	No. of strikes	No. of strikers	No. of days lost
Britain	706	452,571	3,038,134
France	98	9,344	44,344
Germany	137	11,639	41,838[4]

[4] Countess Blücher *English Wife in Berlin* p. 127, March 1916; *Times* 4 July 1917 p. 5b and 5 July 1917 p. 5b: and see also the very full accounts in *De Telegraaf* 3 July 1917 p. 2b of morning ed., all of p. 5 evening edition, 4 July 1917 p. 2b-f, 4b of morning edit., 6 July 1917 p. 2c-d of morning edition; William Oualid and Charles Piquenard *Salaires et Tarifs: Conventions Collectives et Grèves* (Paris 1928) p. 330, 370–1, cf George Sayers Bain, Robert Bacon, John Pimlott 'The Labour Force' in A.H. Halsey ed. *Trends in British Society since 1900: A Guide to the Changing Social Structure of Britain* (1972) p. 97–128 at p. 127 table 4.4 which gives slightly lower figures for Britain, while slightly higher figures for Germany are cited in, Carsten *War against War* p. 42, 124. Oualid and Piquenard *Salaires et Tarifs* also give statistics for Austria (sic – not Austria-Hungary, though it is not made clear if the post-1918 Austrian Republic or pre-1918 Cisleithanian Austria is referred to) and Italy (these latter statistics being somewhat implausible and for that reason possibly not worth quoting). In 1940 there were 922 strikes in Britain involving 299,000 workers and the loss of 941,000 days and in 1944 (the worst year of the Second World War for industrial conflict) 2,194 strikes involving 821,000 people and the loss of 3,960,000 days: H.M.D Parker *Manpower: A Study of War-time Policy and Administration* (1957) p. 504–5.

The French administration seems to have benefited from the fact that some of the industrial areas with the strongest labour organization were overrun by the Germans, and they also made extensive use of immigrant labour and of military conscripts subject to military law; by the time of the Armistice French civilians represented only 38 per cent of the adult male work force in the French war industries. In Germany the unions, in any case not as strong as in Britain, seem to have been seriously affected by conscription and by the socialist leadership's desire to support the war; while in Britain union membership grew steadily during the war, from 23 per cent of potential membership in 1914 to 35.7 per cent in 1918, in Germany it dropped from 13 per cent of potential membership in 1914 to 6.2 per cent in 1916 and made only a partial recovery in 1918.[5]

Initially the British authorities attempted to dragoon the men back to work in the manner that soon became normal in Germany; John Maclean, the Clydeside leader, was sentenced to three years jail for sedition in April 1916. In April 1917 the government attempted to repudiate the Trade Card system – i.e. the system of exempting from conscription men who were employed in war production – and this led to the largest 'unofficial strike' in British history, with over 200,000 engineering workers downing tools for a total of 1,500,000 days in 48 centres: only the Clyde and the Tyne were not affected. Thereafter the government sought to avoid a showdown: since even the Metropolitan Police went on strike on 30–31 August 1918 for more pay and union recognition, and the Grenadier Guards posted in Whitehall fraternized with the strikers, this was probably the wisest policy; in Britain at least there were men of influence who, like Lord Esher, recognized that the workers 'are educated and not helots' and that, 'The old oligarchic methods will not do.[6]

Industrial strikes in wartime indicate at least a degree of scepticism regarding the national priorities laid down by government; John Maclean, the Clydeside leader, an associate of several of the Russian refugees who had fled to Britain after the 1905 failed revolution, consistently opposed the war, and when not

---

[5] [C.A.] Reboul *Mobilisation Industrielle: des Fabrications de Guerre de 1914 à 1918* (Paris 1925) p. 170–171. In Italy the same system was used, and only 46 per cent of the adult male workforce in Italian war factories were Italian civilians: Luigi Einaudi *La Condotta economica a gli effetti sociale della guerra Italiana* (Bari 1933) p. 110–111. The Italians made relatively less use of women, children and foreigners than the French. For union strengths see George Sayers Bain and Robert Price *Profiles of Union Growth: A Comparative Statistical Portrait of Eight Countries* (1980) p. 37 table 22:1, p. 133 table 6:1; see also p. 142 table 7:1, showing the growth in neutral Sweden of union membership from 9.9 per cent of potential membership in 1914 to 20.6 per cent in 1918, indicating the effect on memberships of wartime pressure on real wages in a country where the political conditions were less oppressive than in Germany.

[6] Walter Kendall *The Revolutionary Movement in Britain 1900–21: The Origins of British Communism* (1969) p. 126, 130, 133; ibid. p. 157 and p. 371 fn 98; *Times* 31 August 1918 p. 6d, *Spectator* 7 Sept. 1918 vol. 121 p. 242, and Gerald W. Reynolds and Anthony Judge *The Night the Police Went on Strike* (1968) p. 2–5, 44–70; Maurice V. Brett and Oliver Viscount Esher ed. *Journals and Letters of Reginald Viscount Esher* (4 vols 1934–38) vol. 4 p. 225 Esher to C.D. Williamson 5 Feb. 1918 and ibid. Esher to Hankey 15 Feb. 1918.

in prison gave lessons in economics to labour leaders, clearly with a view to a long-term campaign against the existing economic structure. Through the influence of Winston Churchill when Minister for Munitions, David Kirkwood, another strike leader, was appointed to manage a factory belonging to the firm in which he had led the workers' struggle; he doubled the output of munitions but addressed peace meetings in his spare time. But in Britain as elsewhere the established anti-government movements were generally slow to mobilize themselves against the war. Even the British Socialist Party (an ultra-left group which maintains its marginal existence even today) supported the war until an anti-war faction gained control of the executive in 1916. Most of the self-appointed leaders of opinion rallied, as if panic-stricken, to the Government. Goldsworthy Lowes Dickinson, of King's College, Cambridge, was horrified by the university intellectuals' refusal to stand back from, let alone stand up against, the lemming-like rush:

> Like the rest, move by passion, by fear, by the need to be in the swim, those who should have been the leaders followed the crowd down a steep place . . . All discussion, all pursuit of truth ceased as in a moment. To win the war or to hide safely among the winners became the only preoccupation.

That there was a deep and widespread undercurrent of antagonism to the war is indicated by the fact that *The Daily News* which opposed the war at the beginning and remained passionately critical of the government throughout – the British embassy in Madrid even informed the Spanish press that it was pro-German – nevertheless increased its circulation during the war years and in fact became the largest circulation daily newspaper in the country. On a much smaller scale, *The Cambridge Magazine*, a university weekly normally published only during term-time, also increased its circulation by becoming a forum for independent opinion on such matters as war aims and conscription, even appearing during the vacation, and the Independent Labour Party's organ *Labour Leader* doubled its circulation between August 1914 and October 1915 in spite of an attempt by the authorities to prosecute it in August 1915.[7]

---

[7] Kendall *Revolutionary Movement in Britain* p. 109–110, 112–3, 131; David Kirkwood *My Life of Revolt* (1935) p. 167–8; E.M. Forster *Goldsworthy Lowes Dickinson* (1934) p. 162, quoting Lowes Dickinson's 'Recollections'; Stephen Koss *Fleet Street Radical: A.G. Gardiner and the Daily News* (1973) p. 227, 235; for a particularly outspoken contribution to *The Cambridge Magazine* see vol. 5 p. 159, (4 Dec. 1915) under the ironic heading 'The Effect of Shell Fire'; Carsten *War against War* p. 55–6. Public Record Office T 102 contains a number of 'Speaker's Daily Report' cards from speakers for the semi-official War Aims Committee *c.* Aug–Sept. 1917 which frequently mention the absence of opposition, indicating a degree of nervousness on this point.

As is well known Bertrand Russell, having just been sentenced in the courts to a £100 fine, was dismissed from his lectureship at Trinity Cambridge, effectively for opposing conscription, though in practice it was fairly normal in those days to dismiss university teachers who had been in trouble with the police. There was certainly no counterpart in Britain of the purge of professors who opposed the war, which was carried out in American universities: Carol

continued

The most important cause of opposition to the government in Britain was the issue of conscription. Compulsory military service was rejected by the Labour Party Conference in January 1916 (though in the event some Labour M.P.s remained loyal to the coalition government) and the Military Service Act, together with the Defence of the Realm Act and the Munitions Act was the target of a demonstration on 8 April 1916 in Trafalgar Square, attended by 20,000 people. This issue caused no problems in other European countries, where compulsory service in the army was regarded as normal, but provoked even more opposition in the Antipodes. In New Zealand the Scots-born Peter Fraser was sentenced to a year's jail for sedition, officially for having said, 'No longer will we be the dupes of the crowned heads of Europe and their satellites', but in effect for leading the opposition to conscription, and in Australia John Curtin, secretary of the Anti-Conscription League, was also jailed. These two men were later, as prime ministers of their respective countries, to introduce conscription in New Zealand and Australia in the Second World War; Fraser's associate Robert Semple, who was sentenced to three years in jail for sedition in 1916 ('All I was doing was addressing the people from the top of a urinal', he told a friend) became New Zealand's Minister of National Service in 1940, and in 1942, perhaps more appropriately, Minister of Rehabilitation. The opposition of these men in 1916 to legislation for which they took responsibility a quarter of a century later indicates something of the difference between the two World Wars.[8]

In Australia two referendums were held on the conscription issue with a small majority against compulsion both times; in Britain, with more directly at stake in the struggle with Germany, one imagines that if there had been a poll the majority would have favoured compulsion. But even this presumed majority must have included many who were appalled by the efforts of the authorities to misrepresent and pressurise Conscientious Objectors who refused to submit to the Military Service Act once it became law. A total of 5,600 Conscientious Objectors were court-martialled and 1,500 'absolutists' who refused to accept noncombatant duties or to undertake work officially deemed of national importance spent most of the second half of the war in prison. Alice Wheeldon, a former suffragette who had busied herself with helping Conscientious Objectors, was so disgusted with this persecution that she plotted with her school teacher daughter Winnie and her son-in-law Alfred George Mason to poison Lloyd George, whom they identified as 'the cause of millions of innocent lives being sacrificed'; though Lloyd George's life was

continued

S. Gruber *Mars and Minerva: World War I and the Uses of Higher Learning in America* (Baton Rouge 1975) p. 174–206. These dismissals were publicized in England in *The Cambridge Magazine*.

[8] Norman and Jeanne Mackenzie ed. *The Diary of Beatrice Webb* 4 vols (1982–5) vol. 3 p. 245, 6 Jan. 1916: E. Sylvia Pankhurst *The Home Front: A Mirror of Life in England during the World War* (1932) p. 304–7, cf *Times* 10 April 1916 p. 5c. I am indebted to Greg Palmer for passing on Robert Semple's remark, which he had from his father, a personal friend of Semple's.

never really in danger the three conspirators were sentenced to a total of 22 years in jail.[9]

Was Mrs Wheeldon's conspiracy the First World War's nearest counterpart to the 20 July plot against Hitler a generation later? At about the same period Fritz Adler, son of an Austrian Social Democrat leader, himself a party official and friend of Leon Trotsky, gunned down the Austrian minister-president Karl Graf Stürgkh in a fashionable restaurant, crying out 'Down with Absolutism! We want peace!' as he pulled the trigger: but he seems to have been working on his own. It might nevertheless be useful at this point to examine developments in Austria-Hungary and to see what light they shed on the question of opposition to the various governments.

III. The Case of Austria-Hungary

It was Austria-Hungary which suffered one of the most complete political disintegrations of the war years, but the paradigmatic quality of this break-down tends not to be recognized because of a facile assumption that the Habsburg Empire, with its ill-assorted mosaic of races, was a special case, irremediably doomed to dissolution even while all of the other belligerent states survived.

Prominent amongst the great clichés of history is the picture of the effete, feckless, mongrel, decadent, waltzing Vienna regime, presided over by the senile whiskered emperor for whose death everyone was waiting so that they could then shrug off the system without guilty feelings of impiety; it was of course a reaction against this tired hotch-potch of Holy Roman Empire, Enlightened Despotism and international cabaret which both started the war and produced, in the new ethnic states of post-war central Europe, its most striking end-products.

If this picture of the Habsburg regime were true, however, the remarkable thing would have been the fact that Austria-Hungary lasted so long. It was Austria-Hungary that suffered the most catastrophic defeats of the First World War, at the hands of Russia: but it was Russia, twenty months sooner, which first collapsed into social revolution. It was Austria-Hungary that was the first of the Central Empires to lose a city to the Western Allies when, in August 1916, in the first all-Italian conquest from an all-foreign enemy, Görst – Goriza – was occupied by the Italian Army; but it was the Austro-Hungarians who nearly two years later, on the Piave, launched the Central Empires' penultimate offensive of the war.

No amount of revisionist investigation will show otherwise than that Austria-Hungary was much the worst administered and most ineffectually mobilized of the major belligerents, with the exception of Turkey. Only

[9] Carsten *War against War* p. 68–9; *Times* 7 March 1917 p. 7b and cf Tony Bunyan *The History and Practice of the Political Police in Britain* (1976) p. 115–7.

an Austrian archduke could have fallen victim to a second assassination attempt in one day: and that was only the beginning. And of course it is true that nationalist sentiment had weakened the Habsburg polity before the war, and gained ground during the conflict. Austria-Hungary had since 1867 been divided into two roughly equal halves: Austria (Cisleithania) and the Kingdom of Hungary. There were two separate governments, but the Foreign and War ministers were common, which meant in effect that there was no united central government agency able to coordinate the whole monarchy other than those involved with external affairs; the unfortunate Graf Stürgkh was merely minister-president of Austria, not prime minister of the Habsburg Empire. The separate economic arrangements of the two halves of the Empire were to hinder war mobilization considerably. Each of the two halves included areas populated by large ethnic minorities. Austria had Italians in the south and Poles in the north-east. Austria also had the Czechs, while Hungary had the linguistically related but less economically developed Slovaks. Austria had the Slovenes while Hungary had the linguistically related Croats. Hungary also had some Ruthenians, related to the Tsar's Ukrainians, and Rumanians who claimed descent from Trajan's legions. There were nationalist movements amongst all these populations, and as might be expected they were strongest in the area where social and economic development had generated the largest educated middle class, namely Bohemia, the more westerly of the two Czech provinces; but they were not especialy strong in the Slovene districts, the second most developed Slav area, as the Slovene middle class felt less threatened by Habsburg overlordship than by Italian commercial competition and Serb imperialism.

The Austro-Hungarian Army was undoubtedly officered predominantly by men from the German language community. In 1915 the figures for the different linguistic groups were as follows:

	Percentage of regular officers	Percentage of reserve officers	Percentage of other ranks
German	76.1	56.8	24.8
Hungarian	10.7	24.5	23.3
Czech	5.2	10.6	12.6
Slovaks, Slovenes, Poles, Croats and Serbs	6.0	6.1	23.2
Rumanians	1.0	0.7	7.0
Italians	0.8	0.8	1.3
Ruthenes	0.2	0.5	7.8

Of course many of the German-speaking professional officers were of non-Germanic origin but of families which had been in the Army for generations and had little connection with ethnic minorities other than in their family names. Many of the German-speaking reserve officers (and some of the professionals) were Jews. It will be noted that despite the political autonomy of Hungary, the Hungarian-speakers were only slightly better represented, *pro rata*, in the officer corps than Czechs and Italians. Given the unequal social development of the Empire these figures do not demonstrate systematic bias within the Army itself. On the other hand they do suggest a language problem.[10]

It seems to have been their German allies who identified lack of linguistic homogeneity as a particular weakness of the Austro-Hungarian Army. The menfolk of Prussia's Polish, Kashube and Sorb minorities had had German knocked into them at school and German regiments were generally raised on a territorial basis so that even the problem of dialect was minimized; effectively there was no language problem in the German Army. In this respect it was unique. In the British New Army an attempt to forbid the Welsh language in units raised in Wales provoked an early quarrel between Kitchener and Lloyd George; at the same time troops recruited even in English working-class districts were often unintelligible to their public-school-educated officers, while in Britain's Indian Army the white officers mostly had only an elementary text-book knowledge of their men's language. Britain's allies had similar problems. Allusions to the peculiar dialects of the common soldiers are a particular feature of memoirs written by city-bred Italian officers, while in the French Army Parisian N.C.O.s like the historian Marc Bloch might find themselves assigned to Breton units where the men could not even understand one another's Breton dialects, let alone French. In the Belgian Army the rank and file were predominantly Flemish, the officers predominantly French-speakers, and even in the American Expeditionary Force Theodore Roosevelt Jr. found that some of his troops in the 26th Infantry Regiment were recent immigrants to the United States who 'did not even speak the English tongue with ease'. Even if this problem was at its worst in the Austro-Hungarian Army the fact was that most Austro-Hungarian soldiers served alongside men of their own language: Hungarian territorial (*Honvéd*) divisions, where the language of command was Hungarian, were generally Magyar right up to the level of the commanding general, though there were also two predominantly Rumanian and five predominantly Croat *Honvéd* regiments. It is not clear in any case how necessary it is for military efficiency that officers and men should speak the same language fluently: in the period of the Napoleonic War, when Habsburg officers mostly spoke only German, it does not seem to have occurred to anyone that there was a nationalities problem in the Army.[11]

---

[10] Österreichisches Bundesministerium für Heereswesen *Österreich-Ungarns Letzter Krieg, 1914–1918* (5 vols Vienna 1930–4) appendix vol 2 Beilage 1 Tabelle 5.

[11] A.J.P. Taylor ed. *Lloyd George: A Diary by Frances Stevenson* (1971) p. 7, 30 Oct. 1914; John Keegan *The Face of Battle* (1976) p. 221; Marc Bloch *Memoirs of War* (Ithaca N.Y. 1980) p. 156–7; [Adiel Debeuckelaere] *Open Brieven van de Vlaamsche Frontpartij in het jaar 1917 en Vertoogschriften van het Vlaamsche Frontverband* (Brussels 1919) p. 3–13 'Open Brief aan Albert I, koning der Belgen' 11 July 1917 at p. 5; Theodore Roosevelt *Average Americans* (New York 1920) p. 133; Richard Georg Plaschka, Horst Haselsteiner, Arnold Suppan *Innere Front: Militärassistenz, Widerstand und Umsturz in der Donaumonarchie 1918* (2 vols Munich 1974) vol 2 p. 335–352 Appendix, giving ethnic breakdown May 1918; Alan Sked *The Survival of the Habsburg Empire: Radetzky, the Imperial Army and the Class War, 1848* (1979) p. 52.

Nor is it clear that Austria-Hungary's ethnic minorities were necessarily deficient in fighting enthusiasm. Up to 31 December 1917 the Empire's military losses averaged 2.39 per cent of the population; in German-speaking areas it was 2.91 per cent, with Slovenes, Slovaks and Croats also above 2.67 per cent; the Magyars were just above average with 2.48 per cent losses, the Bohemian Czechs just below average with 2.25 per cent. The lowest death rate was amongst the proverbially gallant Poles (1.62 per cent) but this was obviously because, having been driven out of Galicia by the Russians, the Austrian authorities could not maintain recruitment there; the low figures for Austrian Serbs, mainly from Dalmatia, at 1.7 per cent and Italians and Ladeinisch-speakers at 1.83 per cent may indicate political unreliability but may also be the result of these populations supplying much of the manpower for the Imperial Navy, which suffered relatively few casualties. Figures for individual towns suggest that even the statistics for the different communities were affected by the chance circumstances of where units that suffered heavy losses had happened to be recruited: according to the records Miskolcz, with a population of 50,642 suffered not a single war casualty, and Székesfehérvár lost only 0.26 per cent of its population, whereas the records show that 19.6 per cent of the population – practically all the men of military age – of Pettau in Styria died at the front, 15.3 per cent of the population of Varasd (now Varaždin) in Croatia and 11.4 per cent of the population of Ung-Hradisch (now Uherské-Hradiště) in Moravia.[12]

Whereas the Croats and the Moravians lost comparatively heavily there were occasions when the Bohemians were detectably backward in sacrificing themselves. Bohemian exiles were active in lobbying the Entente governments and the inclusion of Czecho-Slovaks in the Anglo-French demand for 'the liberation of Italians, of Slavs, of Roumanians and of Czecho-Slovaks from foreign domination', in their reply to President Wilson's Peace Note, was a major break-through for the exile movement, though a cruel embarassment to the Czech nationalists in Prague who merely wanted federation under Habsburg rule. The surrender *en masse* of the Czech 28th Infantry Regiment at Štebnika Huta on 3 April 1915 inevitably increased Vienna's nervousness with regard to the loyalty of the Czech population (it is said the men of the regiment were singing the Czech hymn *Hej Slované* as they went over to the Russians) and Czech prisoners of war subsequently showed themselves much more willing to enlist for service against the Habsburgs than any of their Slav fellow-subjects. Nevertheless this willingness had its limits. Though over 80 per cent of Italy's 17,000 Czech prisoners of war volunteered to fight the Habsburgs in April 1918, only about 31,000 of the 200,000 Czech prisoners of war in Russia had done likewise when a Czech Corps had been established during the previous August. This was however a much better response than that of the Slovenes and Croats: in mid-1916, of 5,365 volunteers for a South

---

[12] Wilhelm Winkler *Die Tötenverluste der öst-ung. Monarchie nach Nationalitäten* (Vienna 1919) p. 38–44 table III; ibid p. 14, 16.

Slav Corps raised amongst prisoners of war in Russia, only 85 were Croats and Slovenes and though the numbers gradually increased, in April 1917, when volunteers who disagreed with the aims of the Corps were given the opportunity to resign, 41.9 per cent did so, including 76.9 per cent of the Croats and 71.2 per cent of the Slovenes. Altogether of the 1,961,333 prisoners of war, predominantly Habsburg subjects, held by the Russians on 1 September 1917 only 39,278 joined units organized to fight the Central Powers. Though there was undoubtedly a growing interest among the minorities in the possibility of national independence, especially in 1918 when it was fostered by Entente propaganda, the statistics really do not suggest that this was in itself the reason for Austria-Hungary falling apart; if Austria had the Czechs the British had the Irish, and the 'popular' risings characteristic of the final stages of the war were pioneered on the quays of Dublin during Easter 1916, not in the back streets of Prague.[13]

The whole issue of the particular demoralization of the Austro-Hungarian Army serves to distract attention from the demoralization that was pretty general throughout *all* the belligerent armies:

> men were bullied and bundled about, not like human beings, but like dumb beasts, and in a thousand ways injustice, petty tyranny, hard work, degrading punishments for trivial offences, struck at their souls, and made the name of personal liberty a mockery. From their own individuality they argued to broader issues. Was this war for Liberty? . . . Was it not rather that the masses of men engaged in slaughter were serving the purpose of powers above them, rival powers, greedy for each other's markets, covetous of each other's wealth, and callous of the lives of humble men?

This was written by Philip Gibbs, perhaps the most respected British war correspondent of the time. And it was not just a case of being bullied and bundled about. Whereas the Germans carried out only 48 capital court martial sentences during the First World War, the British carried out 291 on the Western Front alone: 14 for murder as compared to 11 for murder in the German army. Victor Silvester, later famous as a dance band leader, served on five different firing squads at the depot at Étaples in 1917. The British were however perhaps the most lenient of the Entente armies – to their own men at least (whereas the mutiny at the British base at Étaples in September 1917 was finally broken up by the ex-stockbroker's clerks and athletic accountants of the Honourable Artillery Company, armed with staves, disorderly Chinese

13 Victor S. Mamatey 'The Union of Czech Political Parties in the *Reichsrat,* 1916–1918' in Robert A. Kann, Béla K. Király, Paula S. Fichtner ed. *The Habsburg Empire in World War I: Essays on the Intellectual, Military, Political and Economic Aspects of the Habsburg War Effort* (New York 1977) p. 3–28 at p. 12–13; Rowan A. Williams 'The Czech Legion in Italy during World War I' in Samuel R. Williamson and Peter Pastor ed. *Essays on World War I: Origins and Prisoners of War* (New York 1983) p. 199–214 at p. 204, cf Z.A.B. Zeman *The Break-up of the Habsburg Empire 1914–1918* (1961) p. 132; Stanislas Kohn 'The Vital Statistics of European Russia during the World War' in Stanislas Kohn and Alexander F. Meyendorff *The Cost of the War to Russia* (New Haven 1932) p. 1–154, at p. 38.

labour battalions in the British rear areas were pacified with volleys of rifle fire, a total of 27 dead and 39 wounded resulting from two incidents in the first half of September 1917 alone). The French imposed 629 death sentences merely in the period 1 June-31 December 1917; the Italians executed at least 750 soldiers after conviction by military tribunals but hundreds more were summarily shot, including significant numbers of Czech volunteers caught attempting to desert back to the Austro-Hungarian Army. The Italians believed that, 'Austrian discipline is very severe, and the officer's revolver is ever quick to maintain it', but what evidence there is suggests that the discipline in the Austro-Hungarian Army was fairly mild by Italian standards, though certainly photographs survive of executions by firing squad within the Imperial-Royal Army. While the Austro-Hungarian Army may well have had the lowest levels of martial enthusiasm and patriotic commitment of any in the war, it clearly differed not in kind but only in degree: and modern warfare depends in any case on other factors besides the boyish enthusiasm of young conscripts.[14]

IV. Civil and Military Rule in Germany and Austria-Hungary

The cohesion of the lower ranks and the population at large was only belatedly recognized as a key problem and was to receive much more official attention in the Second World War. What was more immediately obvious in the 1914–1918

---

[14] Philip Gibbs *Realities of War* London 1920 p. 435; Martin van Creveld *Fighting Power: German and U.S. Army Performance, 1939–1945* (1983) p. 113 table 9.3; Julian Putkowski and Julian Sykes *Shot at Dawn* (Barnsley 1989) p. 18; William Allison and John Fairley *The Monocled Mutineer* (1979 edit.) p. 56 (material not in first edition 1978); Douglas Gill 'Mutiny at Étaples Base' *Past and Present* 69 (1975) p. 88–112 at p. 102–3 and cf G. Goold Walker ed. *The Honourable Artillery Company in the Great War, 1914–1919* (1930) p. 99–100; Guy Pendroncini *Les Mutineries de 1917* (Paris 1967) p. 194: Alberto Monticone *Gli Italiani in uniforme, 1915–1918* (Bari 1972) p. 216; *Times* 13 July 1916 p. 7a for 'Our Military Correspondent's' account of the sixgun-toting Austrian officers – they were in reality mostly armed with Steyr automatics; Ernst Friedrich *Krieg dem Kriege* (Frankfurt 1980) (1st published 1924) photo on p. 154. See Keegan *Face of Battle* p. 52–3, 72–4, 277–9 for some illuminating remarks on the cohesion of military units under combat conditions.

Various figures have been given for the numbers of executions in the British army: one H.V. Clarke claimed there were 37,900 in France alone (Pankhurst *Home Front* p. 312–3: there was an H.V. Clarke who appears as a lieutenant in the Royal Engineers in the *Army List* for 1917 and 1918); Lord Peel told the House of Lords on 28 April 1920 that from 4 August 1914 to 31 Dec. 1919 there had been 3,076 capital sentences and 343 actual executions (*Hansard: House of Lords* vol 39 col. 1107–8). Captain S.W. Roskill, who as the Official Historian of the Royal Navy after 1945 was on the staff of the Cabinet Office and must have heard some interesting gossip, wrote to *The Times* 8 May 1972 p. 13g 'I cannot explain why I recall it, unless it be because of the horror of the whole proceedings, but 187 is the figure I believe I was given on good authority years ago' – see also the Rev. John Foster's letter in *Times* 2 May 1972, p. 15g. Lord Peel's figure almost exactly corresponds with Putkowski and Sykes's figure of 291 soldiers plus 55 others persons in British pay and subject to military law (such as Chinese labourers, 9 of whom were executed for murder in 1918). Those shot for cowardice included a second-lieutenant and a sub-lieutenant in the Royal Naval Division.

war was the problem of the cohesion of the upper reaches of the socio-political pyramid. As Lord Esher, warned Sir William Robertson in June 1917:

> This war is so new a fact, and its circumstances are so altogether different from those of the past, that the relation of the Sovereign to his Ministers, of the Government to Parliament, and of Parliament to the People, have to be considered, if fatal mistakes are to be avoided.[15]

In the first place all the belligerent governments, with the exeption of Wilson's in America and the Society of Union and Progress regime in Turkey had problems in securing their parliamentary base. In Britain, France and Italy the governments which took those countries into the war were all discredited by failures in the conduct of hostilities and had to be reconstructed in order to allay the discontents channelled through parliament. Even in Russia the government reshuffle of August 1915 was aimed at stilling the discontent of the Duma, though afterwards the Duma was prorogued for six months; even in neutral Sweden the ministry was defeated in the Riksdag not because of dissatisfaction with the general policy of neutrality but because of doubts as to the manner in which this policy was being handled. All the new governments were coalitions, but they were more than temporary governments of National Unity brought into being by the extraordinary emergency of world war: firstly they were all riven by ideological feuds and secondly they involved an irreversible dissolution and reformation of previous political loyalties, mirroring shifts in the balance of political power – shifts generally apparent even before the war, but highlighted by the war and destined to dominate events after the war. The entry into office of the first socialist ministers in Britain and Italy (and in neutral Sweden) and of the first minister from the Catholic bloc in Italy are examples of this bending to the forces of change; in Russia the appointment of no less than four premiers, four war ministers and six ministers of the interior between 1915 and 1917 suggests indeed that the forces of change were already causing the entire system to break up. These ministries were regimes not of wartime truce, not of interregnum, but of transition.[16]

---

[15] British Library Add. 4971 f. 286 Esher to Robertson copy 20 June 1917: this passage is omitted in the printed version of Esher *Journal and Letters*.

[16] For the reshuffle of the Russian government in August 1915 see George Katkov *Russia, 1917: The February Revolution* (1967) p. 133–6. The parallel between the situation in Russia and that in other belligerent countries is obscured by the weak constitutional status and prestige of the Duma and by the existence of a kind of shadow, parallel composite parliament known as the Voluntary Organizations, consisting of the *zemstava* (county meetings), municipalities, the Russian Red Cross and the Central War Industry Committee – all of which were at odds with the Tsar's government, cf Katkov *Russia, 1917* p. 5–11, 39–44.

In Turkey, the Society of Union and Progress dominated parliament which in any case rarely met, legislation being by sultan's decree or by ministerial fiat. At the same time Enver Paşa, the dominant figure in the government, also controlled the army. See Stanford J. Shaw and Ezel Kural Shaw *History of the Ottoman Empire and Modern Turkey* (2 vols Cambridge 1976–7)

continued

The situation in Germany and Austria-Hungary was a variation of that prevailing in the western Entente countries. Centre party politicians like Matthias Erzberger in Germany may have consolidated their electoral base but initially the Reichstag was inclined to accept the leadership of ministers appointed by the Kaiser. Later the political campaign against Bethmann-Hollweg and against Michaelis, his successor as Chancellor, in the summer and autumn of 1917 gave a superficial impression of the Reichstag's independent strength but eventually served merely to emphasize that the Reichstag was too inexperienced and uncoordinated to secure a Chancellor of its own choice, so that the ultimate beneficiaries of the activities of Erzberger and his like were extra-parliamentary forces, especially the Army High Command (*OHL*) and the business cartels. In Austria-Hungary there were two parliaments, one in each capital: that in Budapest was under ministerial control but disinclined to fight Vienna's war: that in Vienna had been prorogued indefinitely in March 1914 because of the obstructionist tactics of the Czech nationalist deputies; in the early days of the war Graf Stürgkh, the Austrian minister-president, is said to have boasted while driving past Vienna's parliament building that 'the greatest thing my ministry has done is to have turned that edifice into a military hospital'. From early 1915 onward there was a clamour to recall the Austrian parliament both in the Vienna press and in the Vienna city council but when it was pointed out that the government had less political weight while it was without parliamentary support, Stürgkh claimed that various party leaders had told him that the assembly 'could not be expected to take up an attitude worthy of the dignity and interests of the state' and that therefore keeping it prorogued was 'the lesser of two evils'. After Stürgkh's assassination, the Austrian parliament was recalled by his successor, Clam-Martinic, but the latter resigned office on realizing that his government's budget was about to be thrown out by the deputies, and as in Germany confused relations between civilian ministers and parliamentary representatives simply left the initiative increasingly to the military.[17]

All the wartime governments had problems with their military High Commands, though of course the forms these problems took varied with the existing political situation in each contry. (Where the country had been overrun by the enemy attractively simple solutions might be found: King Albert of the Belgians took control of both the civilian administration and of the army, while Prince Regent Alexander of Serbia, in exile with his defeated army in Corfu and later Salonica, first sacked his High Command

---

vol. 2 p. 298–9. It would not be true to say, however, that the Turks had resolved the problems of leadership that troubled other belligerents: rather that political development in Turkey was so retarded that these problems had not yet come into focus.

[17] Klaus Epstein *Matthias Erzberger and the Dilemma of German Democracy* (Princeton 1959) p. 193–313, 221–231; Arthur J. May *The Passing of the Habsburg Monarchy, 1914–1918* (2 vols Philadelphia 1966) vol. 1 p. 291 which however gives 'building' in the original: Stephen Count Burian *Austria in Dissolution* (1925) p. 246.

and then had the more restless senior officers tried on trumped-up charges and, in two cases, shot). In Germany and in Austria-Hungary, where the ministers were not leaders of national parliamentary parties but essentially administrators who had risen to the top through successful careers in the bureaucracy and at court, there was normally a large common ground with the generals in social and political attitudes – in fact Stürgkh's brother Joseph *was* a general – except that the military men tended to be more extreme, as military men generally do: for example the Austro-Hungarian chief-of-staff, Franz Freiherr Conrad von Hötzendorf had had to be sacked in 1911 for insisting too vehemently that the war between Italy and Turkey was a not-to-be-missed opportunity for a pre-emptive strike against Italy, despite the fact that there was an alliance between Italy and Austria-Hungary. (He was reinstated in time to add his penn'orth of impatience in the July 1914 crisis.) Once the war broke out the civilian ministers, as one lot of career experts, were inclined to accept the military, as another lot of career experts, as the best-qualified to manage the war. This management was of course only in part a question of strategy in the land campaign. The Austro-Hungarian Army High Command (*AOK – Armeeoberkommando*) was given administrative and judicial authority in Galicia because it was a war zone, and a later decree established the same arrangement on the Italian front. A War Surveillance Office (*Kriegsüberwachungsamt*) was established to monitor popular discontents throughout the Empire. After areas of Croatia temporarily overrun by the Serbian army were reoccupied 120 collaborators were shot and there were numerous deportations. Later there were a number of mass hangings of disloyal civilians, including priests, and snapshots were taken of grinning executioners posing with their victims. An *AOK* memorandum of 25 April 1915 referred to the 'unreliability and lack of patriotism of a large part of the population'. Although Stürgkh believed that the civilian government should be placed entirely at the disposal of the *AOK*, Conrad von Hötzendorf pressed for his replacement by someone more energetic; whether Conrad really wanted a more energetic civilian government seems unlikely however, since in June 1916 his staff, acting on his personal orders, refused to tell the ministers even the number of divisions that had been deployed. Meanwhile the *Kriegsüberwachungsamt* rapidly extended its activities, developing into an incompetent military dictatorship which did much to generate the discontent and separatist opposition which it had been set up to monitor. Strict censorship, prompt dispersal of gatherings in the street, and controls on the movements of individuals prevented the development of any unified Austro-Hungarian sense of the crisis in which the Empire was placed. For its time Austria-Hungary's was the completest expression of that form of military and secret police dictatorship which had ebbed and flowed in southern and eastern Europe since the time of Napoleon: the war was a period of shortages, prohibitions, rumours and the chilling grip of institutional terror more in the Habsburg lands than anywhere else. It the clash of the military and civilian leadership was less evident than in other countries it was largely because the civilians had abdicated, without the military ever developing any constructive view of their own role; when in March 1917 Conrad was transferred to a field command (in part because of his poor relations with the new emperor, Karl) there was no real improvement; the mould had already rigidified.[18]

In Germany the approximate consensus of sympathy between civilian ministers and army chiefs meant that the first rifts took the form of a three-cornered struggle between the Chancellor Bethmann-Hollweg, and the rival military factions of Falkenhayn, chief of the Army High Command (*OHL – Oberste Heeresleitung*) and effectively theatre commander in the West, and Hindenburg, with his chief of staff Ludendorff, commanding in the East. Bethmann-Hollweg failed in his attempt to oust Falkenhayn in January 1915 but succeeded after a renewed struggle of some weeks in August 1916. Once established through Bethmann-Hollweg's efforts at the head of the *OHL* Hindenburg and Ludendorff then turned on the Chancellor. 'There are two political centres, Main Headquarters and the Government. The Imperial Chancellor hangs between them', one of the Reichstag deputies told the Imperial Crown Prince: perhaps rather confusingly. Hindenburg and Ludendorff simplified the situation. In the final two years of the war Germany – people as well as army – was to all intents and purposes ruled from Main Headquarters. When negotiating with the Russians at Brest-Litovsk in the early months of 1918 General Max Hoffmann one of the leaders of the German delegation, declared uncompromisingly, 'I do not represent the German government here, but the German High Command'. Ludendorff claimed later that the *OHL*'s take-over of an increasingly wide range of government functions was forced on him by the ineptitude and passivity of the civilian government. Almost as much as the *AOK* he was shocked

---

[18] Both the Belgian and Dutch constitutions allowed the sovereign extraordinary powers in time of war: whereas Queen Wilhelmina of the Netherlands did not exercise these powers in 1940–1945, Albert of the Belgians in 1914–1918 most emphatically did. For the Serbs see Boghitchévitch [Micloš Bogičevič] *Le Procès de Salonique: Juin 1917* (Paris 1927) p. 14, *Times* 25 June 1917 p. 5c, 28 June 1917 p. 5b; for the *AOK* Joseph Redlich *Austrian War Government* (New Haven 1929) p. 80–86; Zeman *Break-up of the Habsburg Empire* p. 59; Fredrich *Krieg dem Kriege* photos on p. 138–143; Gunther E. Rothenburg *The Army of Francis Joseph* (West Lafayette 1976) p. 192, cf Redlich *Austrian War Government* p. 88–91; G.E. Silberstein *The Troubled Alliance: German-Austrian Relations 1914–1917* (Lexington 1970) p. 315–6.

In Bulgaria Alexander Stamboliski the Peasant leader was arrested prior to Bulgaria's entry into the war but though he was sentenced to death (commuted to life imprisonment) his supporters remained active. One of them, Tsanko Tserkovski, met the commander-in-chief Nikola Zhedov during a parliamentary inspection of the front in September 1917 and set up a meeting of the opposition leaders and the commander-in-chief to discuss the German alliance and the possibility of replacing premier Vasil Radoslavov. Having obtained the oppositionist proposals in writing Zhedov passed them on to Radoslavov. (John D. Bell *Peasants in Power: Alexander Stamboliski and the Bulgarian Agrarian National Union, 1899–1923* (Princeton 1977) p. 121) It is difficult to say what Zhedov was trying to achieve – conceivably he was trying to undermine the position of Tsar Ferdinand – but as an instance of military interference in the political forum this incident rivals anything in other belligerent countries.

by the lack of commitment to the war evident on the Home Front, writing in July 1917:

> The *moral* of the public at home has fallen to a low ebb . . .
>
> At home shameless profiteering and pleasure-seeking, the gambling spirit, pessimism and forgetfulness of duty – not to mention sheer selfishness – are rampant and endangering the issue of the war.

At the end of the war he identified lack of strong national leadership as perhaps Germany's greatest wartime weakness:

> With an iron will Gambetta in 1870–71, and Clemenceau and Lloyd George in this war, enrolled their peoples in the service of victory . . . Berlin had learned nothing from history. They only felt their own impotence in the face of the enemy's spirit; they lost the hope of victory and drifted . . .
>
> Reichstag and People found themselves without the strong lead which, generally speaking, they longed for, and slid with the Government down the slippery way . . .

In retrospect Ludendorff concluded that his whole role in the First World War had been misconceived; his position as Hindenburg's subordinate, even though he himself took the iniative and made the decisions, was, he decided, an 'utterly unsound relationship'. In war, he thought, there should be a commander-in-chief with total and complete authority, over the state as well as over the field army. His views on this matter became influential during the Nazi period, but the balance between the military and the civilian remained unresolved under Hitler as it had been under Ludendorff. Like Hitler, Ludendorff seems to have taken on too many responsibilities at once and in his bending and warping of established institutions lost sight of their constructive potential – but perhaps the whole point was that they no longer had any.[19]

V. Civil and Military Rule in the West

The contest between civilians and the generals was more prolonged and more bitterly divisive in the western Entente countries, and this was not merely because the Entente armies started off with lower prestige and

[19] Erich Ludendorff *The General Staff and its Problems* (5 vols 1920) vol. 2 p. 468, conference of Reichstag Deputies with Imperial Crown Prince 12 June 1917; Leon Trotsky *My Life: An Attempt at an Autobiography* (New York 1930) p. 374 for Hoffmann's remark; Erich Ludendorff *My War Memories, 1914–1918* (2 vols [1919]) vol. 1 p. 7; Ludendorff *The General Staff and its Problems* vol. 2 p. 398 memo 31 July 1917; Ludendorff *My War Memories* vol. 1 p. 5; Erich Ludendorff *The Nation at War* [London 1936] p. 171 (originally published Munich 1935 under the title *Der totale Krieg* which popularized a phrase much used with reference to the Second World War). The same view regarding the error of giving operational control to the chief of staff also appears in Ludendorff's untranslated *Über Unbotmässigkeit im Kriege* (Munich 1935). For Ludendorff's contribution to the theory of total war see Jutta Sywottek *Mobilmachung für den totalen Krieg: die propagandistische Vorbereitung der deutschen Bevölkerung auf den Zweiten Weltkrieg* (Opladen 1976) p. 13–19.

needed more time to build up to a final decisive confrontation with the 'frock-coats'. Developments in Britain, France and Italy show indeed how far the conditions of world war played politicaly into the hands of the military leadership but also suggest that the civilian politicians – who in each case won out at the end – were much more alert to the political threat facing them than was Bethmann-Hollweg, let alone Stürgkh. The reason why the civilian ministers were psychologically more prepared for such a contest in the western Entente countries was, quite simply, the tradition of confrontational democratic electoral politics. In Britain, France and Italy political leaders made speeches, not to inform and to explain as in Germany or Austria, but to cajole and to promise and, when advantageous, to deceive. The generals regarded this system with exaggerated disdain: Haig said, 'You can't trust anyone who has ever been in Parliament'. This view was shared by certain civilians, especially those like Lord Milner whose careers in Whitehall and in the colonial service in some respects followed the pattern that was customary for German or Austro-Hungarian ministers. In his letters Milner complained bitterly of 'the pressure of parliamentary necessities, of Party, of a rotten public opinion', of 'this effete and dislocated Body Politic', and later of 'the Augean stable at Westminster'. He insisted 'the system is wrong . . . the system is hopeless'. One of his closer associates during the first World War was F.S. Oliver, a leading figure in the firm of Debenham & Freebody, who wrote on Boxing Day 1914:

> Democracy is not going to win this war or any other – if we win it will be because the spirit of the small remnant who hate and despise democracy and all its works will save the country in spite of its democratic government . . . Democracy has already in five months . . . proved its utter incapacity to prepare for and conduct war.

Milner himself, once put to the challenge, was unwilling to go that far:

> Some of our 'Moot', I think, like Oliver, really have an aversion for Democracy . . . I myself am perfectly indifferent. I regard it, like any other form of Govt. as a necessary evil. Democracy happens to be the inevitable form for my country & the Empire at the present time. Therefore I accept it, without enthusiasm, but with absolute loyalty.

Later Milner was to prove this loyalty, but as one of his disciples wrote afterwards:

> In every fibre of his being he loathed the slipshod compromises, the optimistic 'slogans', the vote-catching half-truths with which democracy seemed to compromise the majestic governing art.

Many men in the professional and administrative classes felt similarly; but of course the career politicians were that much more aware of this attitude and the threat it posed; they had looked into the eyes of their permanent officials and their constituency chairmen and seen the voids within; they had understood the logic behind the sly badinage in the Athenaeum and at White's. Another way of expressing it would be to say that electoral politics in Britain – and, equally, in France and Italy – had achieved some sort of uneasy balance as a result of contests fought out mainly in public, whereas the cracks and fissures within the social systems of Germany and Austria-Hungary had been papered over or cordoned off. The public nature of conflict in Britain, France and Italy had clarified divisions and in general these divisions had tended to set military and civilians, and different cliques of military and civilians, at odds with one another even before the war broke out. In Britain the Army did not like the Liberal government's policy with regard to Home Rule in Ireland – a bitter feud on the subject was in progress right up to the very eve of the war – and it was not reassured by the Liberal policy on redistributive taxation and reduction of the powers of the House of Lords, for though few of the military had really large private fortunes and even fewer had seats in the House of Lords, they had no particular sympathy for the denizens of urban slums or street-corner politicians or the M.P.s who rose to the Cabinet by using these as an electoral base. In France the divisions were of a somewhat older standing but had been refurbished and re-embittered by the Dreyfus case, in which the progressives and the Jews had won a stunning victory over the army and the aristocratic and Catholic interests. In Italy there was the same Catholic *versus* lay division as in France, and also a north *versus* south dimension. Thus though the rhetoric of unity was as loud in the Entente capitals in Berlin or Vienna, the Entente politicians were psychologically much better prepared for an internal struggle.[20]

In part because of the assumption that any major war would be dramaticaly brief, there had been no attempt anywhere before 1914 to establish the details of civilian-military relations. The only nation with previous experience of successfully fighting a major war under the direction of a civilian government with an electoral base was Britain: Lord Esher, a kind of universal *éminence grise* of the period, once tried to explain to Kitchener 'the methods by which the Seven Years War and the Napoleonic Wars had been carried on by the English Ministry of the day'. It was simply assumed that, despite the much greater speed of communications, the commander-in-chief in the field would have virtual autonomy, as Wellington had had in the Peninsula. In Italy (as in Germany) it was assumed that the Head of State would command in the field, in conjunction with the army chief of staff, and that the civilian government would be able to carry on in the rear more or less as normal. In France, where precisely this system had been defeated ignominiously in 1870, the Republic had not yet decided on an alternative model.[21]

[20] John Charteris *At GHQ* (1931) p. 50, 25 Oct. 1914; Cecil Headlam ed. *The Milner Papers (South Africa), 1897–1905* (2 vols 1931–3) vol. 2 p. 446 Milner to Lady Edward Cecil 1903; vol. 2 p. 447 same to same 24 April 1903; A.M. Gollin *Proconsul in Politics* (1964) p. 314 Milner to Lionel Curtis 27 Nov. 1915; ibid, p. 247 F.S. Oliver to unknown 26 Dec. 1914; ibid p. 314 Milner to Curtis 27 Nov. 1915; Philip Kerr, obituary tribute in *Nation and Athenaeum* 23 May 1925 vol. 37 p. 227b.

[21] Esher *Letters and Journals* vol. 3 p. 236, journal 16 May 1915.

Joffre, the French *général en chef*, seems in fact to have regarded himself, once war was declared, as possessing an authority parallel, not subordinate to that of the ministry: indeed Poincaré, the President of the Republic, complained that 'G.H.Q. considered itself as a separate government to which the government itself had to be subordinated'. Joffre himself later explained:

No-one has ever doubted my loyalty with regard to the government, nor my profound attachment to the Republic ... But it is precisely because of my respect for the institutions of my country and the responsibilities of which I had assumed the burden before and during the war that I had always opposed myself to a confusion of powers which could only do harm to my authority, of which I was legitimately jealous, to discipline, and in consequence, to the conduct of our affairs.

Poincaré was initially disposed to commiserate with his premier Viviani, to whom he wrote;

G.H.Q. considered itself, in times of war, as completely independent of the government and ... acknowledged as superior to it only the nominal and powerless authority of the President of the Republic.

But soon the logic of the French ministry's essential weakness, as much as Poincaré's own personal ambition, led him to push to increase his own power and influence as President of the Republic, and before long he was leading the civilian counter-attack on Joffre. When the question arose of sending French troops to the eastern Mediterranean, Joffre declared roundly, 'Never will I consent to allow a particle of our forces to be taken from the front, because it is here that the decisive action will take place', and when Poincaré reminded him that he would have to obey orders, Joffre responded, 'Alors, monsieur le Président, there's nothing left but for me to get myself killed at the head of my troops'. It took another eighteen months before the French government solved the problem of Joffre, by establishing a system of zone commanders under Joffre's authority and then, a week later, issuing a decree making them the immediate recipients of the government's instructions: when Robert Nivelle was appointed to command both the principal zones in eastern France, Joffre resigned. Only a few months previously a parliamentary deputy had declared of Joffre, 'he disposes of an absolute power such as no-one has ever had in France', but as was soon clear the victory of the civilians required no more than timing and tact.[22]

In Italy the inert leadership and invincible reticence of King Vittorio

[22] [Emile Emmanuel] Herbillon *Du Général en Chef au Gouvernement* (2 vols Paris 1930) vol. 1 p. 136, diary 3 April 1915 (Herbillon was G.Q.G's liaison officer with the government); [Joseph Jacques Césaire] Joffre 'La Guerre et la Politique' *Revue des Deux Mondes* CIIᵉ année 8ᵉ période tome XI (Sept. 1932) p. 46–58 at p. 47; Raymond Poincaré *Au Service de la France* (10 vols Paris 1926–33) vol. 5 p. 169 conversation 24 Aug. 1914; ibid. vol. 6 p. 124, 21 March 1915; Ch. Bugnet *Rue Saint Dominique et G.Q.G en les trois dictatures de la guerre* (Paris 1937) p. 326 citing deputy Abel Ferry in secret session 17 June 1916. See J.M. Bourget *Gouvernement et Commandement* (Paris 1930) p. 144–153 for the alterations of the command structure.

Emanuele had the same effect as the uncertain constitutional arrangements of the French Third Republic: a power vacuum appeared which the acting head of the army promptly filled. When in February 1916 the war minister, General Vittorio Zupelli, dared to pen a memo critizing the strategy of Cadorna, the army chief of staff, the latter insisted on his dismissal. Premier Salandra resisted, citing constitutional law and *lo Statuto fondamentale del Regno*. In this instance Vittorio Emanuele backed the civilians, though a press campaign whipped up by Cadorna's sympathizers drove Zupelli to resign in any case. A year later Vittorio Emanuele actually asked Cadorna to nominate a successor to the then incumbent of the war ministry. Soon after the Caporetto disaster Cadorna's nominee, General Gaetano Giordano, was replaced by General Vittorio Alfieri, who was known to have a grudge against Cadorna, and the latter's dismissal soon followed. Cadorna's speech to his H.Q. staff following his dismissal indicates the extent to which his position had gone to his head.

> I don't care if they bring me down: I know what I am worth. I, by my will, with my fist, have created and held together in my hand this organization, this army of three million men, until yesterday. If I hadn't been there, we would never have had a voice in Europe . . .

The Italian government took care to replace him with one of the obscurest generals they could find: Armando Diaz, hitherto a mere corps commander.[23]

Both Joffre and Cadorna made no real effort to establish good relations with their key subordinates; in June 1915 Poincaré was surprised to find Joffre did not have regular meetings with his army commanders, and Cadorna's position in 1917 was undoubtedly weakened by rumours of his deteriorating relationship with Luigi Capello, commanding the Italian Second Army. Cadorna also did himself a disservice by the way he reduced the power and responsibility of his assistant chief of staff and his chief of operations, while depending unduly on the advice of the head of his secretariat Roberto Bencivenga, a mere lieutenant-colonel; it was rumoured that Cadorna's decision to recommend Gaetano Giordano for the war ministry had resulted from his going through the *annuario* with Bencivenga standing over him and rejecting all the other names as they came up. Civilian resistance to the military was undoubtedly assisted by the lack of solidarity on the military side which these command methods inevitably fostered.[24]

VI. Civil and Military Relations in Britain

With certain local peculiarities the contentious relationship between civilian

23 Piero Melograni *Storia Politica della Grande Guerra, 1915–1918* (Bari 1969) p. 181–3; Angelo Gatti *Caporetto: dal diario di guerra inedito* [diary May–Dec. 1917] ed. Alberto Monticone, (Bologna 1964) p. 110–111, 15 June 1917, and p. 317, 6 Nov. 1917; ibid. p. 332, 7 Nov. 1917.

24 J.M. Bourget *Gouvernement et Commandement* p. 137; Piero Pieri *L'Italia nella Prima Guerra Mondiale* (3rd edit. Milan 1968) p. 138–9; Gatti *Caporetto* p. 110–111, 5 June 1917.

government and military high command experienced in other countries was also found in Britain: indeed Sir John French, despite rather poor personal relations with Joffre, entirely sympathized with the latter's predicament:

> We are both hampered by our respective governments. They are the greatest 'thorn in the side' a general in the field can suffer from.[25]

Sir John French's particular problem was that his own boss was not an uninformed rabble-rousing civilian: on the contrary the difficulty was that the British Secretary of State for War, Lord Kitchener, was a field-marshal like French himself, and tactless enough to visit the army in France wearing his uniform. The future protagonists of the military team in the military-civilian struggle, Sir Douglas Haig and Sir William Robertson, were at this stage merely wondering how to ditch French. In the meantime Kitchener, while losing reputation in the eyes of the Army because of the various deficiencies of the War Office, was failing to convince his civilian colleagues that he was the kind of soldier they needed; Lord Selborne found him 'a strange mixture of streaks, genius and stupidity', and Balfour noted that his 'conversation was at times incredible in its folly'. The first major challenge to civilian control came in fact not from the Army but from the Navy, when Lord Fisher, the First Sea Lord (i.e. professional head of the Navy) quarrelled with Churchill, the civilian – ex-cavalry – First Lord of the Admiralty, and demanded 'complete professional charge of the war at sea ... absolutely untrammelled'. Lord Selborne, himself an ex-First Lord, pointed out:

> Like every other part of the British constitution the powers of the First Lord of the Admiralty and the position of the Sea Lords is not only a question of law, but also of custom and tradition.

Fisher's tone in making his demands made his assault on 'custom and tradition' easy enough to shrug off, though one or two members of the cabinet may have wondered why they had previously paid so much attention to someone who had clearly outlived his better judgement. It was only when, at the end of 1915, Haig replaced French as G.O.C.-in-C. in France and Robertson replaced Murray as Chief of the Imperial General Staff that the real struggle between civilians and professionals began.[26]

Robertson, in insisting on complete control of operational policy and thereby relegating Kitchener to the civil side of his department, brought Britain into line with Germany, Austria-Hungary, Italy and, effectively, with France, where Joffre as *général en chef* had established the same autonomy of

[25] Richard Holmes *The Little Field Marshal: Sir John French* (1981) p. 280 French to Winifred Bennett 24 June 1915.

[26] George Boyce ed. *The Crisis of British Unionism: Lord Selborne's Domestic Political Papers, 1885–1922* (1985) p. 186; Ruddock F. Mackay *Balfour: Intellectual Statesman* (Oxford 1985) p. 269 Balfour to Lord Robert Cecil 16 April 1915; Randolph S. Churchill and Martin Gilbert *Winston S. Churchill* (8 vols 1966–88) vol. 5 p. 452; British Library Add. 49708 f. 246 memo by Selborne enclosed in letter to Balfour 19 May 1915.

action as that enjoyed by Falkenhayn, Conrad von Hötzendorf and Cadorna as chiefs of staff. Robertson was unique however in that while the other army chiefs also acted, in effect, as principal theatre commanders, he remained in the national capital in daily contact with the politicians, and including East and West Africa had campaigns in no less than seven separate theatres to supervise. On the other hand he was in the closest communication with Haig, his principal theatre commander, and until just before Robertson's dismissal the two soldiers consistently backed one another against the Cabinet; from the beginning Robertson made no secret to Haig of his sense of the distance between themselves and the politicians and his opinion:

> that practically anything may happen to our boasted British Constitution before this war ends and that the great asset is the army – whose value will be fixed largely by the extent to which we at the top stick together and stand firm.[27]

Perhaps the most extraordinary aspect of the general's hostility to the civilians was their attempt to deny the politicians access to the detailed information required to make any significant decision. Within a month of the outbreak of war Joffre wrote to General Galliéni, then commanding the Paris sector but soon to be minister of war:

> I shall be grateful if you do not send to the government information relevant to operations. In the reports I send I never let them know the object of operations in progress, nor my intentions, or at least, in what I say, I indicate the parts which must remain secret. In doing otherwise, certain operations could come to the knowledge of the enemy in time to be of use to him.

Similarly in the summer of 1915 French told Haig not to discuss plans for the Loos offensive with Kitchener, in case he passed the information on to Cabinet colleagues who might be indiscreet. The insulting implication was that civilians were more likely to give away secrets than staff officers, but it was soon to become clear that the object was less to starve the Germans of espionage intelligence than to stifle domestic criticism.[28]

The Duke of Wellington, who in the Peninsular campaigns had had a political position almost analogous to that of the army chiefs in 1914–1918, had frequently complained of the French army's dependence on intelligence published in the London newspapers but insisted, 'I cannot think of preventing officers from writing to their friends'. And indeed at a time when even junior officers, through their social position, often had direct access to political leaders and when the only available form of censorship was prosecution for common

[27] William Robertson *Soldiers and Statesmen, 1914–1918* (2 vols 1926) vol. 1 p. 181; David R. Woodward ed. *The Military Correspondence of Field Marshal Sir William Robertson, Chief of the Imperial General Staff, December 1915–February 1918* (1989) p. 41 Robertson to Murray 8 March 1916; the original is in Add. 52461 and the draft of the identical letter sent to Haig is in King's College London, Roberstson Papers 1/22/30.

[28] [J.S. Galliéni] *Memoires du Général Galliéni: Défense de Paris 25 Août-11 Septembre 1914* (Paris 1920) p. 172 Joffre to Galliéni 7 Sept. 1914; Gerald J. De Groot *Douglas Haig, 1861–1928* (1988) p. 205.

or seditious libel, any attempt to silence indiscretion or complaint would have been inconceivable. In any case, though having a greater diplomatic role than a twentieth-century theatre commander, Wellington did not have complete military authority over many of the personnel exercising staff functions under his command; the commissariat for example was answerable to, and in direct communication with, the Treasury. A hundred years later however, despite or perhaps because of the much greater openness of information under peacetime conditions, it quickly became established that the sole source of information coming out of a theatre of operations in wartime should be the G.H.Q.[29]

Military security was only the pretext. The French parliament established commissions to inspect the Army; their right even to visit the front was not acknowledged till June 1916 and they were prevented altogether from investigating the April 1917 mutinies. The right of commission members to come and go at will, merely notifying the war ministry of their movements, was not established till October 1917. It seems that amongst the considerations which most disturbed French G.H.Q. with regard to these commissions was the circumstance that the most active member of the *Chambre*'s commission, Pédoya, was a retired general and therefore particularly dangerous as a source of informed criticism. On the other hand Joffre attempted to prohibit even Millerand, the then war minister, from visiting the front in May 1915 despite Millerand's cooperation in keeping the parliamentary commissions away from the zone of operations. In March 1917 General Lyautey, then minister of war, refused to speak in a secret session of the *Chambre*, explaining – in open session, for the benefit presumably of newspaper reporters – 'even in Secret Committee I consider, in full responsibility, that the National Defence is exposed to risks': the session had to be suspended, to shouts of 'The Germans are at Noyon!' and 'Vive la République!' and Lyautey resigned the same evening: 'I fancy Lyautey must have had enough of them', commented Haig sympathetically. In Italy, it was the criticisms of war minister General Vittorio Zupelli which instigated Cadorna to press for his dismissal, and General Giulio Douhet, the pioneer theorist of strategic bombing, was prosecuted and jailed by a military tribunal for the crime of addressing a memorandum to a cabinet minister. In the British Army, a letter describing conditions at Gallipoli, addressed to the Prime Minister from the English war correspondent Ellis Ashmead-Bartlett and entrusted to the Australian newspaper man Keith Murdoch, was confiscated by officers of British military intelligence when Murdoch landed at Marseilles, Sir Ian Hamilton the G.O.C.-in-C. at Gallipoli

[29] J. Gurwood ed. *The Despatches of Field-Marshal the Duke of Wellington* (13 vols 1834–9) vol. 7 p. 357 Wellington to Earl of Liverpool 16 March 1811, and cf ibid. vol. 6 p. 325 Wellington to Thomas Graham 10 Aug. 1810 and [J.] Gurwood ed. *The General Orders of Field Marshal the Duke of Wellington* (1837) p. 199–200, order of 10 Aug. 1810.

The first systematic attempt to control the flow of information coming out of a war zone seems to have been during the Russo-Japanese War of 1904–5. The practice was extended to the universal censorship of all mail from the front area in 1914: in the British army the officers had to censor the letters written home by their men.

having requested Sir John French, the G.O.C.-in-C. in France to do him this favour. It is true that the British had, in Lord Esher, a figure who had no counterpart in other country, a roving elder statesman who was trusted by almost everyone. The favourite of William Johnson Cory at Eton, the friend and confidant of General Gordon, of three successive British monarchs and innumerable politicians, a brilliant Permanent Secretary at the Office of Works, Esher had at various times turned down the editorship of *The Daily News*, the governorship of the Cape, the War Office and the Viceroyalty of India. He had chaired the committee which led to the establishment of the Imperial General Staff. He was trusted by the King, by the Army and by Asquith, who sent him on an ill-defined permanent mission to France; and yet one finds that even Esher, a man of remarkable insight, allowed himself to become a mouthpiece of the generals, who exploited his sympathy while effectively concealing from him much of what was going on.[30]

The object seems to have been not merely to circumvent civilian criticism and interference but also to ensure that an increasingly disastrous war should be presented to the general public in as favourable light as possible. Comparing German and British newspapers one is struck by how much more detailed the war reporting is in the latter: yet as the British newspapers actually had far fewer successes to report the barrage they supplied of circumstantial but frequently inaccurate detail served mainly to misrepresent what was happening. This was by no means contrary to the wishes of the High Command. Lord Esher, who though only an honorary colonel in the Territorials advertized his self-identification with the military by always wearing uniform when he whisked back and forth between London, G.H.Q. and Paris, put forward the idea that John Masefield should write up the Somme:

> Masefield's book on Gallipoli will prove hereafter to be one piece of permanent literature on the subject. It is on a level with Tennyson's 'Charge of the Light Brigade', only it is in prose ... What I propose he should do is work of a permanent value in the domain of high literature.

Charteris, Haig's chief of Intelligence, seized on this suggestion with enthusiasm and also began thinking of bringing over leading artists:

> It is not for propaganda, it is in the interests of art after the war. Sooner or later, someone will have to paint the big picture of the war, as well as someone write the big book of the war.

Despite his consistent moral obtuseness Charteris really did have his eye

[30] Pierre Renouvin *The Forms of War Government in France* (New Haven 1927) p. 133–4; Jere Clemens King *Generals & Politicians: Conflict between France's High Command, Parliament and Government, 1914–1918* (Berkeley 1951) p. 92; ibid. p. 48–9, 57 and see also [J.M.G.] Pédoya *La Commission de l'Armée pendant la Grande Guerre* (Paris 1921) p. 7–40; André Maurois *Marshal Lyautey* (1931) p. 243–4; Robert Blake ed. *The Private Papers of Sir Douglas Haig* (1952) p. 214, diary 16 March 1917; Melograni *Storia Politica della Grande Guerra* p. 201–3; Desmond Zwar *In Search of Keith Murdoch* (Melbourne 1980) p. 28–9, 48.

on posterity – hence the long diary letters to his wife which he arranged to be smuggled home without being censored, evidently intended from the beginning to be the basis for a post-war best-seller – but it seems he also had a more immediate priority, that of boosting the prestige of G.H.Q. Charteris had already realized, when Kitchener's dismissal had first been rumoured, that it would be possible, in effect, to appeal to public opinion over the heads of the politicians:

> The real thing that matters is what the nation thinks. I feel sure they would stand by and for K. against any or all of the politicians.

And as the months passed, and the military failures accumulated, it became more and more a question whether the public at large – the newspaper-reading, letter-writing, M.P.-lobbying public – would stand by the generals or by the politicians who sought to order them about.[31]

VII. National Leadership

Part of the problem was of course that the politicians were as much at sea in directing the war as the generals were, and inclined to make much less secret of the fact. The war, in its scale and complexity, involved a quantum jump in the problems of decision making. Lord Esher noted:

> Twenty very able gentlemen in England, and about an equal number in France of similar age and habits are trying to do something which long life, sedentary occupations, leisurely habits of mind render ludicrously impossible.

Even the apparent exceptions did not help; in September 1914 Clementine Churchill told her husband, who was not quite forty:

> You are the only young vital person in the Cabinet. It is really wicked of you not to be swelling with pride at being 1st Lord of the Admiralty during the greatest War since the beginning of the World.

Winston Churchill duly swelled with pride; but it did neither him nor his country much good at this stage. A German general who examined the published official material on the Gallipoli campaign after the war was astonished by the way the British government transacted its business:

> Conversations, minutes and reports always preceded the decisive meetings, which again continually postponed the vital decision ... The leadership of a war cannot be entrusted to a limited liability company.[32]

[31] Esher *Letters and Journals* vol. 4 p. 57–8 Esher to Charteris 16 Oct. 1916; Charteris *At GHQ* p. 176, 30 Oct. 1916; ibid. p. 137, 9 Feb. 1916.

At this time German newspapers circulated within a relatively restricted local area: consequently, though numerous they had small and not particularly gifted reporting staffs and contained little news that did not derive from official sources.

[32] Esher *Journals and Letters* vol. 3 p. 249, journal 18 June 1915; *Winston S. Churchill* vol. 3 p. 92 Clementine Churchill to Winston Churchill 26 Sept. 1914; Hans Kannengiesser *The Campaign in Gallipoli* [1928] p. 267.

As much as military organizations, civilian governments needed some sort of effective structure of decision-making and control. In Britain there was a proliferation of high-level committees; in August 1914 Hankey, Secretary of the Committee of Imperial Defence, organized a Directory of Committees (i.e. at cabinet and inter-departmental level) there being then twenty; by December 1916 there were 102 and by October 1918 there were 165. But the central committee at the top required to direct the whole machine and to give direction to this proliferation of sub-committees took a painfully long time to evolve. The original War Council had, in November 1914, eight members: Asquith, Grey, Lloyd George, Churchill and Kitchener from the Cabinet, Fisher and Murray from the services, and Balfour, as an elder statesman and Tory leader, as a non-departmental member. The Marquess of Crewe, Secretary of State for India, Lord Haldane, ex-Secretary of State for War and currently Lord Chancellor, and Sir Arthur Wilson, another of Churchill's ageing admirals who was at this time serving without pay as a supernumerary First Sea Lord, had been added by early January 1915: the ubiquitous and indispensable Hankey acted as secretary. There was no agenda, few memoranda were circulated, and sessions were infrequent – once eight weeks passed between meetings. War Council members were not even kept posted on the developing military situation; Lloyd George recalled:

> The Prime Minister and Mr. Churchill knew a good deal more about the situation than we did. But they were not fully apprised of the facts. Casualties were scrupulously withheld. In fact, there was no considered statement submitted to the War Council on the military position showing the relative strength of the Allies and the Central Powers in men and machinery. I often doubt whether anyone inside the War Office had taken the trouble to make a careful survey.

At the beginning of November 1915 the War Council was reconstructed as a War Committee of only three members but these soon grew into nine and the practice of referring decisions to the full Cabinet, which met less regularly, created additional problems.[33]

But the real weakness was perhaps less a matter of structure than of personality. Churchill – 'clever, but quite devoid of judgement' – the increasingly unfathomable Kitchener, and Lloyd George – 'very clever, with vision, prevision, driving power and courage in wonderful combination [but] he would leave anyone in the lurch' – together had the makings of an interesting rather than reliable team but their smooth coordination and direction would have required a Prime Minister of unusual firmness and vision: and this Asquith was not. Certainly he 'looked the part of Prime Minister as no one has since Mr. Gladstone', even if, as a young acquaintance wrote, 'he has a mind of

---

[33] [Maurice] Hankey *The Supreme Command, 1914–1918* (2 vols 1961) vol. 1 p. 226; ibid. vol. 1 p. 238; David Lloyd George *War Memoirs* 6 vols London 1933–6 vol. 1 p. 420, referring to *c.* February 1915; Hankey *Supreme Command* vol. 2 p. 441.

granite and the soul of a rather bad bridge party'; and his majestic handling of the constitutional crisis of 1909–1911 might have suggested precisely the kind of firmness of grip and large views that the direction of the war required. It seems however that he was much more at home with the problems of constitutional and domestic public opinion posed by pre-war crises than with events after July 1914; and Balfour wrote privately:

> I doubt whether he possesses any influence with either K. or Churchill in military matters, or whether, if he does possess such influence, he would care to exert it.

The flair he had shown earlier soon became identifiable as only a hollow pretence; even the President of the Board of Agriculture was unimpressed:

> At cabinets he is calm and urbane – but as for ruling his colleagues or abridging idle or wasteful discussions he is hopeless: I have never heard him say a wise or strong thing at the Council table, though in the House his mastery of language indicates a decision which I believe to be non-existent.

Lord Sydenham could say as a matter of course in a *Times* article 'We have no Pitt in our hour of need', and Lord Selborne noted that the Prime Minister had 'no ounce of drive in his composition, not a spark of initiative'. Lloyd George, whose private complaints against his chief became more frequent from the autumn of 1915 onward, went even further: 'He just sits there and uses the whole of his crafty brain to quash any plan of action that is put forward'. Lloyd George's girlfriend Frances Stevenson noted in her diary in February 1916, 'The P.M. will accept *anything* which will lull his conscience, and allow him – as D. puts it – to enjoy his dinner'. (D. was Lloyd George.)[34]

Lloyd George probably concluded sometime in 1915 that he would make a better war leader than Asquith, though it was some months before he began to hint as much to his associates. He only broached the matter with Arthur Lee, his Parliamentary Military Secretary at the Ministry of Munitions at the end of March 1916:

> Today, L.G. and I had much interesting talk – mainly about the hopelessness of winning the War with our present Government – and the chances of getting rid of it.

He may have said as much to others at the same period: it had come to Asquith's ears by mid-April 1916. But the increasingly frequent tendency of

[34] Boyce *Crisis of British Unionism* p. 186–8: sketch of cabinet 1916: Boyce prints 'precision' for 'prevision'; John Maynard Keynes *Essays in Biography* (1933) p. 48 for the reference to Gladstone and Margaret Fitzherbert *The Man who was Greenmantle: a Biography of Aubrey Herbert* (1983) p. 155 Aubrey to Mary Herbert 1915 for 'the soul of a rather bad bridge party'; British Library Add. 49693 f. 185 Balfour to Bonar Law 26 Sept. 1914 copy; John Vincent ed. *The Crawford Papers* (Manchester 1984) p. 363, Earl of Crawford's diary 4 Nov. 1916; *Times* 21 Oct. 1915 p. 8d; Boyce *Crisis of British Unionism* p. 185; *Lloyd George: a Diary by Frances Stevenson* p. 68, 12 Oct. 1915, quoting Lloyd George; ibid. p. 101, 23 Feb. 1916.

Asquith's acquaintances to speak of him as principally interested in hanging on to office seems to have emerged earlier than, and independently of, any professed desire to replace him and seems to have derived from something in his style of leadership rather than from his resistance to giving up the premiership. As early as 3 September 1915 the journalist C.P. Scott recorded a private conversation with Lloyd George:

> In Churchill's phrase, said Lloyd George a little maliciously, 'The Prime Minister is the man in the "howdah" – wherever the elephant goes he will go'. Like Palmerston in his later days nothing to him matters so much as that he should stay where he is.

Certainly Lloyd George was not backward in saying such things whenever it was unlikely to get him into trouble: later Frances Stevenson noted in her diary:

> D. says that the P.M. is absolutely devoid of all principles except one – that of retaining his position as Prime Minister.

But the same thing had been expressed earlier, and in stronger language, by Lieutenant-General Henry Wilson, who thought Asquith 'a perfectly callous man of no principle bent on remaining P.M.' Lytton Strachey, a connoisseur of moral decadence if ever there was one, was probably not even aware that a change of premier had been mooted when he wrote after meeting Asquith socially in May 1916:

> I've rarely seen anyone so obviously enjoying life, so obviously, I thought, *out* to enjoy it; almost, really, as if he'd deliberately decided that he *would*, and let all the rest go hang.[35]

For the first months of the war, indeed, Asquith seemed less interested in his public duties than in a young lady, the Hon. Venetia Stanley, with whom he maintained a voluminous correspondence – in spite of the fact that she was concurrently being pursued (and with more success) by one of his younger colleagues, Edward Montagu, the Chancellor of the Duchy of Lancaster: a noteworthy feature of the Cabinet held on 19 April 1915 to discuss Greek, Italian and Bulgarian affairs was that both Asquith and Montagu, though sitting only a few feet from one another at the council table, spent most of the meeting writing love letters to the same woman – Montagu signed his, 'Yours very disjointedly and disturbedly (Winston is gassing all the time)'. One wonders whether there is not something sublimely fine and grand and

---

[35] Alan Clark ed. *'A Good Innings': the Private Papers of Viscount Lee of Fareham* (1974) p. 147 Lee to Ruth Lee 31 March 1916; David R. Woodward *Lloyd George and the Generals* (Newark 1983) p. 88; Trevor Wilson ed. *The Political Diaries of C.P. Scott, 1911–1928* (1970) p. 132, 3 Sept. 1915; *Lloyd George; a Diary by Frances Stevenson* p. 129, 30 Nov. 1916; George H. Cassar *Kitchener: Architect of Victory* (1977) p. 438 quoting previously unpublished passage in Henry Wilson's diary for 16 Dec. 1915; Michael Holroyd *Lytton Strachey: A Critical Biography* (2 vols 1967–8) p. 197, Lytton Strachey to James Strachey May 1916.

tragic in this spectacle of the ageing statesman at the greatest crisis of a classic career, besotted with and abandoned by the most intelligent girl of her generation; or whether it was not in essence the usual story of the sucker who should have been concentrating on his job, taken for a ride by a jilt who couldn't be bothered even to sleep with him. Though one might console oneself that Britain had the most interesting personalities of the world crisis – Asquith, broken by the war, Kitchener the great soldier who lost the trust of his colleagues, Churchill, the wayward unathletic Apollo of Whitehall – a rich mixture of Galsworthy, Conrad and Quiller Couch (how irremediably tight-lipped and colourless Bethmann-Hollweg and the awful Ludendorff seem by comparison) – one does wonder if a few deliberately and determinedly unromantic types like Wellington might not have been more serviceable.[36]

Asquith did not even seem to care, initially, that his Cabinet was falling apart around him. Some of Churchill's antics smacked perhaps of personal disloyalty but

> H.H.A. has not the courage or perhaps the energy to tackle W.S.C. who amuses him – and whom he thinks will not really be dangerous in his time.

When, eventually, Asquith woke up to the fact that his own lethargy was resulting in policy-making passing out of his hands, he went to the other extreme. Though by no means decided in his own mind on the question of compulsory military service he quickly recognized it as perhaps the most crucial and potentially divisive issue of wartime domestic policy; and he also identified Kitchener, with his continuing popularity out of doors and his political isolation within the cabinet, as a useful potential ally. To Kitchener he wrote therefore, on 17 October 1915, with regard to the conscription issue:

> I should like you to know that what is now going on is being engineered by men (Curzon and Lloyd George and some others) whose real object is to oust you. They know well that I give no countenance to their projects, and consequently they have conceived the idea of using you against me.

But Asquith was by this stage too lazy and too out of his depth as to policy issues either to consolidate a faction within the cabinet – the reorganization of the government as a coalition with Tory members in May 1915 had made this difficult in any case – or to reorganize the machinery for the central direction of the war. Beatrice Webb wrote of him:

> He has become senile from self-indulgence. The breakdown of British war administration is due to Kitchener's ignorance of civil life and Asquith's apathy and rooted disinclination to trouble about anything until it has become a public

---

[36] Michael and Eleanor Brock ed. *H.H. Asquith: Letters to Venetia Stanley* (Oxford 1982) P. 555 Montagu to Venetia Stanley 19 April 1915 cf ibid. p. 552 Asquith to Venetia Stanley same date. Interesting light is shed on Venetia Stanley's stature as letter-writer and lover in Artemis Cooper ed. *A Durable fire: the Letters of Duff and Diana Cooper 1913–1950* (1983) p. 57, 92–3 Diana to Duff Cooper 13 May and 9 Aug. 1918.

scandal. Slackness has become a national vice. The Englishman is as able as the German, but he has a shockingly low standard of work.[37]

Lord Esher, whose remarks as a detached observer are usually most interesting, noted that:

Throughout our armies and those of France, throughout our government and that of France, from the chiefs to the administrative heads of departments, the men are lacking in the enthusiasm, inventiveness, boldness of conception and action essential in war.

Nevertheless Esher suspected that the rule of mediocrity might not be necessarily such a bad thing: 'It was not Canning but Castlereagh who pulled us through the Napoleonic imbroglio'. In any case it was necessary to make do with what was available:

Neither the French nor ourselves have developed a great leader. All our best people are too old! Asquith, Balfour, Lansdowne, French, Fisher, etc., and the younger men seem unable to force their way to the front, so I suppose they are not first rate.

But Esher had underestimated both the general dissatisfaction with the management of the war, and the degree to which Lloyd George had already, by mid-1916, forced himself forward. As Asquith's premiership ran out of time, suggestions and proposals for restructuring the political leadership began to flow thick and fast. Lord Robert Cecil proposed 'a Cabinet Committee on civil organization' of three members, one of whom would be on the War Committee, with responsibility for mobilizing industry and the home front; the consensus seemed to favour 'two small committees, one for the actual conduct of the War, the other for business necessary to the War'. Asquith himself preferred simply to blame the failures of the existing War Committee on the civil servants and the soldiers:

there is delay, evasion, and often obstruction, on the part of the Departments in giving effect to its decisions . . . it is often kept in ignorance by the Departments of information, essential and even vital, of a technical kind, of the problems that come before it.

It was Lloyd George however who touched on the crux of the matter when on 1 December 1916 he proposed a War Committee which would not include Asquith. The latter might even have acquiesced but the scheme was leaked to the press at an inconvenient moment and he decided to stand on his prerogatives. There was a brief struggle:

All the perfectly useless members of the Govt. – some 16 or 18 out of 23 – are clinging round H.H.A.'s knees and beseeching him not to give in. No thought of what is happening to the country – you may observe. It is just *their* positions.

---

[37] Edward David ed. *Inside Asquith's Cabinet: from the Diaries of Charles Hobhouse* (1977) p. 238, 21 April 1915; Randolph S. Churchill *Lord Derby: 'King of Lancashire'* (1959) p. 449–450 Asquith to Kitchener; *Diary of Beatrice Webb* vol. 3 p. 236, 22 July 1915.

The Tories, who admired Lloyd George's energy and would have been willing to serve under him even when the coalition was first formed in May 1915, refused to back Asquith. He bowed that noble head of his to the inevitable. To Mrs. Hilda Harrison, who had replaced the unfaithful Venetia Stanley – now Venetia Montagu – as the recipient of his confidences, he wrote:

> I saw I could not go on without dishonour and impotence . . .
> The King offered me the Garter, but of course I refused . . .
> I am glad you are reading the book of Job: I think I must refresh my memory of it.[38]

Lloyd George, who became Prime Minister on 7 December 1916, immediately transformed the structure of the government. Bonar Law, the Tory leader, who had backed Lloyd George through the succession crisis, was left in charge of Parliament, and to run the war Lloyd George teamed up with the two Tory hierarchs who might have seemed most personally antipathetic to him: Lord Curzon, former Viceroy of India, the very epitome of snobbishness and embodiment of the exclusive hereditary principle which Lloyd George had spent much of his career attacking; and Lord Milner, the instigator of the Boer War which Lloyd George had so bitterly denounced in its time. Curzon, 'pompous, dictatorial and outrageously conceited . . . pig-headed, pompous and vindictive', as Hankey described him, was an indefatigible administrator but perhaps not as original or as large-viewed as he himself and his fan club supposed; Milner, no less indefatigible but probably more gifted than Curzon, seems to have travelled a very different route to arrive at a view of government disconcertingly similar to Lloyd George's, and when, soon after taking over the premiership, Lloyd George established his notorious private secretariat to facilitate the coordination of government policy, some of its members, such as Philip Kerr and Waldorf Astor, were Milner's disciples and nominees. He also secured the ultra-right-wing Imperialist Leo Amery's entry into the War Cabinet secretariat.[39]

Amongst those who sensed the implications of Lloyd George's restructuring of the government was A.G. Gardiner, who had been foremost amongst journalists in opposing Britain's entry into the war in 1914. Of Lloyd George, Gardiner wrote in February 1917:

[38] Esher *Journals and Letters* vol. 3 p. 249, journal 18 June 1915; ibid. vol. 4 p. 9 Esher to Haig 29 Jan. 1916; ibid. vol. 4 p. 24 Esher to Earl of Moray 15 May 1916; H.H. Asquith *Memories and Reflections* (2 vols 1928) vol. 2 p. 133 (Lord Crewe's account of the breakup of Asquith's govt., 20 Dec. 1916) and cf p. 147–9 (Cecil memo 27 Nov. 1916); Lloyd George *War Memoirs* vol. 2 p. 984 Asquith to Lloyd George 1 Dec. 1916; Gollin *Proconsul in Politics* p. 363 Milner to Lady Edward Cecil 3 Dec. 1916 (for a full account see Roy Jenkins *Asquith* (1964) p. 428–460); [H.H. Asquith] *Letters of the Earl of Oxford and Asquith to a Friend* (2 vols 1933–4) vol. 1 p. 13 Asquith to Hilda Harrison 10 Dec. 1916.

[39] Stephen Roskill *Hankey: Man of Secrets* (3 vols 1970–74) vol. 1 p. 272, diary 12 May 1916; Gollin *Proconsul in Politics* p. 376–8 and see also John Turner *Lloyd George's Secretariat* (Cambridge 1980) p. 18–20, 190–192.

Ostentatiously dissociating himself from Parliament, he commits its leadership to a gentleman of inferior capacity and a very limited record of public service. A new double screen of bureaucrats is interposed between the War Directorate and the heads of Departments, whose responsibility to Parliament has hitherto been direct.

The Prime Minister's new secretariat were, according to Gardiner, 'rather of the class of travelling empirics in Empire, who came in with Lord Milner and whose "spiritual home" is fixed somewhere between Balliol and Heidelberg'. As for Milner himself, Gardiner addressed him directly in 'A Letter to Lord Milner' in *The Daily News* on 12 May 1917:

> You are one of the three autocrats of this country, and the most powerful of the three. You are our master . . . You are a solitary, alien figure in our midst, not so much a man with feelings like ourselves as an embodied idea, a philosophy in a frock coat, a political system incarnate. You have come to power without a vote from the electorate – for you have never succeeded in an electoral contest – without the sanction of Parliament, without the support of a party. You represent no-one. You are the negation of democracy. You are the symbol that Parliament and Constitution have been set aside.

But of course it was not Milner himself who was responsible for his promotion to the War Cabinet, but Lloyd George; on the other hand an alliance with a man like Milner was a possibility that could scarcely have suggested itself to Lloyd George prior to the outbreak of war in 1914, whereas Milner, with rare prophetic insight, had foreseen something of the sort at least as early as 1903. In April of that year he had written privately:

> Perhaps a great *Charlatan* – political scallywag, buffoon, liar, stump orator and in other respects popular favourite – may some day arise, who is nevertheless a *statesman* – the combination is not impossible – and who, having attained and maintaining power by popular art, may use it for national ends.

In Lloyd George Milner must have thought he had found his man.[40] Many years later Leo Amery was to note:

> Ll. G. was a constructive Radical, with essentially the same kind of outlook, allowing for differences of upbringing, as Joe [Chamberlain] or Milner, or for that matter myself.

Lloyd George himself wrote of Milner, 'in constructive power and fertility of suggestion he surpassed them all . . . by inclination and conviction a State Socialist'. In immediate retrospect the six years of Lloyd George's premiership,

---

[40] A.G. Gardiner in *Nation* 1917 vol. 20 p. 696; *Daily News* 12 May 1917; Headlam ed. *Milner Papers* vol. 2 p. 447 Milner to Lady Edward Cecil 24 April 1903.

Milner had been born in Giessen in Hessen, his father's mother being German, and attended a *Gymnasium* in Tübingen for three years: otherwise his background and education were entirely English, including a brilliant career at Balliol. He had been unsuccessful Liberal candidate at Harrow in the 1885 general election.

founded as it was on his alliance with men like Milner, seems so dissociated from what had occurred before in Britain, so at odds with what came after, that the period seems the product of some kind of spell or enchantment by which the Welsh Wizard wrenched the political system from its accustomed grooves and shaped it to his own fantastic and fevered pattern. A longer view, incorporating the dictatorships and the war regimes of 1939–1945, suggests otherwise. Beatrice Webb wrote of Lloyd George:

> His one serviceable gift is executive energy. He sees that things are done and not merely talked about. Unfortunately, he does not care whether or not they are thought about.

But arguably Lloyd George and Milner understood better than the Webbs what lay behind the apparatus of parliamentary and bureaucratic institutions: certainly they seem to have understood the necessity of change created by the war better than the leaders of the other belligerent nations.[41]

VIII. Lloyd George and the Generals

Not everything changed of course: at Frinton-on-Sea wounded soldiers were banned from the Promenade lest their mutilations upset wealthy patrons of Britain's most snobbish seaside resort. Yet even at Frinton one could hear the guns from across the North Sea, rattling the windows in a manner half-prophesied in a little poem by Thomas Hardy, written only four months before the war:

> That night your great guns, unawares,
> Shook all our coffins as we lay,
> And broke the chancel window-squares,
> We thought it was the Judgement day.

Beatrice Webb heard it, in the midst of the Sussex countryside, during the Battle of the Somme: 'the dull noiseless thud beating on the drum of the ear, hour after hour, day after day, telling of the cancelling out of whole populations on the battlefield'. In central London itself, the hub-bub of traffic, already mainly motorized, drowned out the distant vibrations; yet even in central London the war never seemed very far away:

> There are camps of soldiers in the parks and the squares, in the streets there is always the sound and sight of soldiers marching by. The big white trains painted with the red cross swing into the railway stations carrying their sad burdens and often at the same time other trains leave crowded with boys in khaki, cheering and singing on their way to the front. At night London, usually so bright with lamps and electric signs, is darkened and huge searchlights sweep the sky and

[41] John Barnes and David Nicholson ed *The Leo Amery Diaries* (2 vols 1980–88) vol. 2 p. 1034, 26 March 1945; David Lloyd George *The Truth about the Peace Treaties* (2 vols 1938) vol. 1 p. 261; *Diary of Beatrice Webb* vol. 3 p. 300, 1 March 1918.

hundreds of London newspaper boys run up and down the streets like black crows shouting, 'War! Latest news of the War! War!'

London it seemed, was

a beleaguered city, walled in with a wall of blue water beyond which strong men made sorties and did not always come back. And the wind of the flail that winnowed us came to us from Flanders on intermittently flapping squalid sheets of garbled or censored news.

More than any previous war its course resounded to the names of cities lost, taken, raped, liberated, defended: Liège, Louvain, Maubeuge, Erzerum, Lemberg, Przemysl; then, early in 1915 London itself became the front line, 'the nightmare assumed a concrete form – that of the Zeppelins. The sound of their motors was like a steam locomotive in the sky.' Artillery on high-angled mountings was distributed amongst the London parks, and for the first time since Tudor times the streets of the metropolis echoed to the clatter and crash of battle actually within the city boundaries.[42]

Amongst those acutely aware of the colossal social and domestic dimension of the war was of course Lloyd George: later he was to speak of the war as 'by far the greatest event of modern times'. Despite his earlier passionate opposition to the Boer War, Lloyd George found the whole frightful business intensely interesting, full of fascinating possibilities; and he hated having to share it with the dyed-in-the-wool professionals who failed to see its potentialities. One of the things which most closely links the pre-war demagogue with the war-leader of 1917 and 1918 was Lloyd George's recognition that it was, or ought to be, a People's War. Of Kitchener's New Army – an army formed of young professional and sub-professional types like his former self, of independent thinkers, readers of Thomas Hardy and H.G. Wells – he wrote at the beginning of 1915:

It is a force of a totally different character from any which has hitherto left these shores ... In intelligence, education and character it is vastly superior to any army ever raised in this country, and as it has been drawn not from

---

[42] James Agate *Ego: the Autobiography of James Agate* (1935) p. 370, 1 May 1934 (he does not actually name Frinton but refers to 'a little east-coast resort, well known for its snobbery', which doesn't sound like Walton-on-the-Naze or West Mersea); Thomas Hardy 'Channel Firing'; *Diary of Beatrice Webb* vol. 3 p. 262, 2 July 1916; Vincent O'Sullivan and Margaret Scott ed. *The Collected Letters of Katherine Mansfield* (2 vols so far Oxford 1984-   ) vol. 1 p. 139–140 Katherine Mansfield to Laura Kate Bright 21 Sept. 1914 (printed in *Wellington Evening Post* 6 Nov. 1914); Violet Hunt and Ford Maddox Hueffer *Zeppelin Nights: A London Entertainment* (1916) p. 2–3; ibid. p. 6.

I have not been able to ascertain the furthest distance at which the sound of guns was claimed to have been heard: John Masefield said he could hear the guns at Boar's Hill outside Oxford, roughly twice the distance from Ypres as Frinton; Carliss Lamont and Lansing Lamont ed. *Letters of John Masefield to Florence Lamont* (1979) p. 75 Masefield to Florenece Lamont 24 Jan. 1919. In 1666, according to Samuel Pepys's diary for 4 June of that year, the much less powerful guns of the English and Dutch fleets engaged in the Four Days' Battle off Dunkirk could be heard in St. James's Park, in Westminster, but not at Dover or Deal.

the ranks of those who have generally cut themselves off from home ties and about whose fate there is therefore not the same anxiety at home, the people of this country will take an intimate personal interest in its fate of a kind which they have never displayed before in our military expeditions.

Many of his colleagues seemed quite indifferent to this aspect of the war: Frances Stevenson was almost certainly echoing Lloyd George's opinion of Churchill's role in the Gallipoli failure when she wrote in her diary:

> It is the Nemesis of the man who has fought for this war for years. When the war came he saw in it the chance of glory for himself, & has accordingly entered on a risky campaign without caring a straw for the misery and hardship it would bring to thousands in the hope that he would prove to be the outstanding man in this war.

As the months passed and the street-corner shrines multiplied in the slum districts and black ties, black armbands and black hat trimmings became everywhere a kind of civilian uniform, Lloyd George's rhetoric became larger and perhaps looser:

> We are undoubtedly losing the War, and nothing can save us but the nation itself. The people do not realise how grave the situation is. I feel they ought to be told.

He saw – as Ludendorff saw a little later – that it was not enough to revitalize the existing directing organs of the country: war leadership meant revitalizing and redirecting the energies of the nation as a whole. He sensed both the reserves of energy in the country, and the risks of not taking them under control; more than any other politician of his day, he was familiar with mobs and knew how close even Britain was to the arbitrament of the streets.[43]

At the same time – and unlike Ludendorff – Lloyd George had no idea of how to manage the military side of a war, though he had, by 1914, developed a taste for conducting public business as an art in itself. As Chancellor of the Exchequer he had progressed from the ardent crusader for redistributive taxation to the confidant of bankers and stockbrokers: in August 1914 his prompt handling of the financial crisis brought on by the outbreak of war was regarded as a masterpiece, not least by himself. He told his wife:

> My arrangements to save a financial panic have been a complete success – a real triumph – the first great British victory of the war.

After this great feat it was natural for him to seek some other war-related sphere of economic administration which might benefit from his mastery. Possibly his instinctive suspicion of Lord Kitchener, with his ram-rod back, moustaches like an insect's antennae and the 'ominous cast' in his eye, directed

---

[43] Sylvester *Life with Lloyd George* p. 104 14 January 1934; Lloyd George *War Memoirs* vol. 1 p. 369 memo 1 Jan 1915; *Lloyd George: A Diary by Frances Stevenson* p. 50, 15 May 1915; Lloyd George *War Memoirs* vol. 2 p. 766 memo 17 June 1916.

his attention to the War Office, though in any case the War Office had inevitably become the key sector of government expansion. Accordingly, just as Kitchener was beginning to develop the supply and procurement side of his department, Lloyd George swooped and a Ministry of Munitions was set up, with himself as minister, in May 1915.[44]

It is interesting to speculate what might have happened if Lloyd George had not jumped on the munitions issue in the spring of 1915, if for example he had been too busy being a brilliant Colonial Secretary or Foreign Secretary or somehow otherwise engaged on the non-economic side of government business. He was not alone in seeing how important munitions would be – Kitchener, whom he had shouldered out of the way, had seen it even sooner, and so also, in Germany, had Walther Rathenau. But in Germany, and also in Italy, and in the Second World War in Japan, the munitions sector provided one of the key mechanisms whereby the military infiltrated its influence into civilian affairs: equally, by snatching munitions from the Army, Lloyd George opened up an important route for civilian intervention in military affairs.

The importance of his personal role in this is underlined by the relative insignificance of the Ministry of Munitions once he had abandoned it for pastures new. In France Albert Thomas, often regarded as Lloyd George's counterpart as armaments supremo, was only a *sous-secrétaire*, for artillery and munitions, till December 1916 and when finally elevated to the French cabinet lasted only another nine months in office; even during his brief period in the cabinet he never managed to drag his department from out of the shadow of the older-established ministry of commerce. It was the latter which retained control of raw materials allocation and which battled to subordinate the iron magnates to the political objectives of the regime; but overall there was rather less clamour and publicity about weapons manufacture in France than in Britain.[45]

Lloyd George's Ministry of Munitions quickly found itself up against the War Office's Ordnance Board and the ensuing struggle was a dress-rehearsal for his more celebrated contest with Robertson and Haig in 1917 and 1918. Lloyd George's principal antagonist at the Ordnance Board was Major-General Sir Stanley Von Donop, Master-General of the Ordnance. In dealing with this grandson of a Westphalian baron, Lloyd George did not particularly press the anti-German line which had served to displace Prince Louis of Battenberg, the First Sea Lord, and the Göttingen-educated Lord Haldane, and which was used later against Lord Milner; the following remarks on Von Donop recorded in Frances Stevenson's diary were only for private consumption:

On every possible occasion he has done his best to obstruct the output of

[44] Kenneth O. Morgan ed. *Lloyd George: Family Letters, 1885–1936* (Cardiff/London 1973) p. 168 Lloyd George to Margaret Lloyd George 7 Aug. 1914.

[45] Cf John F. Godfrey *Capitalism at War: Industrial Policy and Bureaucracy in France, 1914–1918* (Leamington Spa 1987) p. 186, 228–230.

munitions for the Allies. D. says that either he is deliberately trying to help the enemy, or else it is his German blood unconsciously asserting itself.

But Lloyd George had no particular need to fight dirty; Von Donop's only real supporter was Kitchener, who had to be physically restrained from walking out of the Cabinet Room when Lloyd George insisted on Von Donop's exclusion from the Munitions Committee which immediately preceded the establishment of the Ministry of Munitions. Kitchener offered to resign when, later in 1915, the Ordnance Board was wound up during his absence on a tour of inspection at Gallipoli, but by that stage Kitchener was scarcely able to defend his own position, let alone that of his subordinates. Lloyd George was backed by *The Times*, which at the first hint of supply shortages trumpeted:

> The real remedy is to deal with the muddle at the War Office, and to put an end to the tradition that only soldiers can control war manufactures.

The Tory ex-premier Balfour also took Lloyd George's side, referring in one letter to 'Von Donop, whose incapacity in my opinion, is one of the chief causes of the present mess'. In addition Lloyd George found some eminent parliamentary stooges to denounce Von Donop in the House of Commons: when on 1 July 1915 Sir Henry Dalziel told the House, 'this Ordnance Department is responsible for the failure of the late Government and . . . is responsible for all our real blunders in regard to the War', he was eagerly supported by Sir Charles Henry and Sir Richard Cooper, the latter of whom, as chairman of a chemical manufacturing firm, had a particular interest in the allocation of contracts for explosives.[46]

Von Donop complained bitterly in private of Lloyd George claiming credit for the Ordnance Board's achievements while covering up the failures of his own Ministry of Munitions. His diary for 8 September 1915 notes: 'In printed returns Ebbw Vale are shown as having delivered 948 shell off M. of M. order of 29.6.15 but none off ours of March!' In February 1916 he recorded:

> The public complained at our not having produced enough H.E. in April '15 when we were only asked for it on 19.11.14 yet in 8 months M. of M. have not produced a complete round.

Von Donop's sense of persecution may have been justified for as late as June 1916 Lloyd George was making a point of blaming the large numbers of dud

[46] *Lloyd George: A Diary by Frances Stevenson* p. 129, 30 Nov. 1916; Jenkins *Asquith* p. 356 and Cassar *Kitchener* p. 427–9; *Times* 10 April 1915 p. 9b; Mackay *Balfour* p. 269 Balfour to Lord Robert Cecil 16 April 1915; *Hansard: House of Commons* vol. 72 col. 2091–5, cf Cassar *Kitchener* p. 384–6.

Von Donop was the son of Vice-Admiral Edward Pelham Brenton Von Donop of the Royal Navy and grandson of Georg Freiherr von Donop from Wöbbell in Westphalia. There were three von Donops in the Prussian army in 1914.

The post of Master General of the Ordnance, which had had Cabinet rank, had been abolished in 1855 but the title had been revived in 1904 for the fourth ranking member of the Army Council, who had responsibility for the procurement of artillery and ordnance stores.

shells reported from the front on Von Donop's choice of fuses. Though intellectually and temperamentally equipped for one of the paper wars soon to be characteristic of civilian-military interfacing, Von Donop lacked support of the right kind and was never able to get his version over; thus, after the war, when Lloyd George was Prime Minister, the War Office informed Von Donop:

> The authorities regard your Notes prepared for Sir George Arthur's use in connection with the Life of Lord Kitchener as not suitable for publication, in that they constitute in substance an attack on the Ministry of Munitions and this will inevitably lead to controversy between Departments which will be detrimental to the public service.

By that stage Lloyd George was being hailed as the great war-winner and peace-maker, and career-conscious bureaucrats had no wish to encourage criticism.[47]

Having dealt to his satisfaction with Von Donop (relegated to command the garrison of the Humber). Lloyd George was enabled by the death of Kitchener to take over the War Office and to begin his quest for bigger game. J.F.C. Fuller, then a staff officer in France, expressed what was apparently a widely held view amongst professional soldiers: if Lloyd George 'were only a gentleman he might do well enough, but he is such a little bounder that I am afraid he will be rather out of his depth'. Arthur Lee, Lloyd George's Parliamentary Military Secretary at the Ministry of Munitions, was convinced that no good would come of his boss's transfer to the War Office:

> He has the wildest and most dangerous ideas about altering all the chief Commands in the field, and about interfering in things which he does not understand and which require the highest technical knowledge of soldiering.

A similar impression prevailed at G.H.Q. in France: Charteris wrote:

> He dislikes D.H. [i.e. Haig] and I cannot imagine that he likes Robertson. The first thing he will do will be to look about for somebody to succeed one or both of them.

Esher noted of Robertson in September, 'He is consumed by suspicion of Lloyd George'. Yet, though he had been doubtful of the generals' competence since almost the beginning of the War, and though horrified by the casualties of the Somme, Lloyd George seems to have tried manfully to work with Robertson and Haig even if only on the basis that he, not they, was in charge of policy. It was not until mid October 1916, when he had been at the War Office for four months, that the question of sending reinforcements to the Balkans caused his first major disagreement with Robertson; the idea was to

---

[47] Public Record Office WO 79/73 (Copy of Von Donop's diary) f 10, 8 Sept. 1915; ibid. unfoliated 2 Feb. 1916; House of Lords Record Office Ll.-G D/17/16/4 Lloyd George to Edwin Montagu 5 June 1916; Public Record Office WO 79/74 marked Pbb RW, [? or RH for Sir Reginald] Brade to Von Donop 23 Oct. 1919.

assist Rumania but Robertson of course maintained that whatever happened to Britain's allies, there should be no diversion of military effort from the Western Front. Hankey urged caution:

> I warned him that he was not dealing now with munitions workers . . . but with armies led by the most conservative class in the world, forming the most powerful trades union in the world.

But perhaps this was exactly the kind of advice that excited Lloyd George to keep going.[48]

The reason for Lloyd George's clash with the generals was undoubtedly in part temperamental. The generals, while sharing Milner's suspicion of parliamentary democracy, were unable to follow Milner's line of thought with regard to 'the great *Charlatan*'. While Lloyd George was, in effect without realizing it, moving to the right in politics, some of Haig's men at G.H.Q. reportedly believed that he was working for the United Kingdom to go 'Red' with himself as President of the British Republic, and that he feared Haig as a potential General Grant – whatever that implied. Haig himself recorded his deep distrust of Lloyd George in his diary and Robertson wrote of Lloyd George as 'an under-bred Swine' and told Haig, 'I can't believe that a man such as he can remain for long head of any government. Surely some honesty and truth are required'. Lord Esher, playing middle man as usual, perhaps did not help matters by explaining, after some routine malfeasance of the press barons:

> Democracy means government by cads like Northcliffe and Rothermere. But patriotism means that gentlemen obey the cads rather than set an example of disobedience.[49]

It is somewhat suspicious, to say the least, that in his *War Memoirs*, while

---

[48] Anthony John Trythall *'Boney' Fuller: The Intellectual General, 1878–1966* (1977) p. 38–9 J.F.C. Fuller to father 20 June 1916; Clark *Good Innings'* p. 155 and espec. p. 156, diary of Ruth, Lady Lee 14 June 1916; Charteris *At G.H.Q.* p. 148, 15 June 1916; Esher *Journals and Letters* vol. 4 p. 55, journal 25 Sept. 1916; *Lloyd George: a Diary by Frances Stevenson* p. 17, 16 Dec. 1914 and cf Lloyd George's 'bread and butter' letter to Haig, 21 Sept. 1916, written after his first visit to the front as War Secretary, approving of his conduct of the campaign: Duff Cooper *Haig* (2 vols 1935) vol. 1 p. 355–6; Roskill *Hankey* vol. 1 p. 312 diary 1 Nov. 1916. By March 1917 Hankey was trying to restrain Lloyd George from trying to sack Haig, cf P.R.O. CAB 63/19 Hankey to Lloyd George 7 March 1917.

[49] King's College London Edmonds Papers III/11/3–4: this extraordinary view of Lloyd George's policy was shared by – perhaps even originated with – the King's equerry Clive Wigram cf Woodward *Lloyd George and the Generals* p. 150 quoting Sir Henry Rawlinson's diary 12 March 1917; Woodward ed. *Correspondence of Sir William Robertson* p. 213 Robertson to Kiggell 9 Aug. 1917; Robert Blake ed. *The Private Papers of Sir Douglas Haig* (1956) p. 256, diary 24 Sept. 1917; Churchill *Lord Derby: 'King of Lancashire'* p. 249 Robertson to Haig 28 Feb. 1917; Peter Fraser *Lord Esher* (1973) p. 393 Esher to Haig 29 April 1915.

It might be noted however that Lloyd George struck up a friendship with Major-General Robert Hutchison, Director of Organization at the War Office, who after the war became a Liberal M.P. and eventually Liberal Chief Whip.

emphasizing the invincible obtuseness of Haig and Robertson, Lloyd George categoricaly denied that they were on bad terms personally:

> My relations with Robertson were always pleasant and as for Haig, during my many visits to his Headquarters in France, he received me with the greatest courtesy and always made me feel a welcome guest.

In reality, even on his first visit to France as Secretary of State, Lloyd George had managed to infuriate Haig and his staff with his unpunctuality and his indiscreet questioning of the French general Foch. Sir Philip Sassoon, Haig's secretary, assured Lord Northcliffe:

> Of course as you know Sir D.H. is much too broad minded to mind anything of that sort but I could see that he was terribly disappointed in him . . . it is my private opinion that he has neither liking or esteem for the C. in C. He has certainly conveyed that impression to all.

This is quite as disingenuous as Lloyd George's own later account: far from being 'too broad minded to mind anything of that sort', Haig even complained to his wife about Lloyd George's unpunctuality. In subsequent encounters tempers frequently became frayed, and voices were raised even on matters that were more social than strategic; there was something of a row for example when Lloyd George discovered that J.A. Spender, a partisan of Asquith, had been visiting G.H.Q. – this was after Asquith had been driven from office and was making no secret of his resentment:

> Ll.G. charged Haig with entertaining his 'personal enemies' at Headquarters, and Haig retorted warmly that he had no knowledge of Ll.G.'s personal feuds and would choose his guests at his own discretion.[50]

G.H.Q.'s dealings with the press did indeed give Lloyd George considerable grounds for doubting both Haig's good will and his good sense. The two newspapermen most consistently critical of civilian interference in the military side of the war were H.A. Gwynne of the *The Morning Post* and Charles à Court Repington, who was military correspondent for *The Times* till forced to resign in January 1918, whereupon he joined Gwynne's team; their counterpart in the French press as regards attacking civilian interference was, incidentally, the proto-Fascist Charles Maurras of *L'Action Française*, which indicates something of the political implications of their stand. Gwynne's and

---

[50] Lloyd George *War Memoirs* vol. 6; British Library Add. 62160 f. 12 Sir Philip Sassoon to Lord Northcliffe Sept. 1916, cf Blake ed. *Private Papers of Sir Douglas Haig* p. 166, Haig to Lady Haig 13 Sept. 1916; British Library Add. 46392 f. 300 memo by J.A. Spender *c.* 1919

See A.J. Sylvester *Life with Lloyd George: The Diary of A.J. Sylvester, 1931–1945* ed. Colin Cross, (1975) p. 105, 18 Jan. 1934 and especially p. 111–112, 3 Oct. 1934 for some illuminating remarks made by Lloyd George while writing his *War Memoirs*:

> He said that he was very sick that Haig and Robertson were not alive. He intended to blow their ashes to smithereens in his fifth volume. Unfortunately, he could not get at them personally. He could not even *send* them a book . . .

Repington's indiscretions resulted in their being prosecuted and fined under the Defence of the Realm Act and when Repington attacked Milner in *The Morning Post* he found himself the victim of a vilificatory press campaign arranged by Waldorf Astor at Milner's personal request and launched with an extraordinary onslaught in Astor's Sunday paper *The Observer*:

> private enmity ... sheer faction and mutiny are rendering more assistance to the enemy than he has ever yet received from this country ... Weakness of character, defects of temperament, a fatal strain of hysterical instability in the whole nature and imagination of the man have gradually dulled and perverted gifts that were once so brilliant ... Fundamental want of balance and good sense ...

and so on for four entire columns.[51]

In addition to becoming involved in this sort of thing, the military High Command more than once exposed themselves to the accusation of deliberate dishonesty. It was not simply that

> they did not so much oppose of quarrel with you as paralyse you. You gave orders and you soon found that innumerable detailed obstacles arose in the way of their execution.

There seems to be little doubt that Lloyd George was justified in his later surmise that the opposition of Pétain and Foch to the Passchendaele offensive in mid 1917 was concealed from him and that the reason for this was that Lieutenant-General Henry Wilson, en route to London from French G.H.Q. to report their views, met Haig on the way and responded to some sort of bribe offered or at least hinted at by the latter. Lloyd George obviously overstated his case in claiming:

> In Palestine and Mesopotamia nothing and nobody could have saved the Turk from complete collapse in 1915 and 1916 except our General Staff. The real citadel of the Ottoman Empire was neither at Achi Baba, Baghdad nor Jerusalem – but in Whitehall.

And his additional suggestion that after the fall of Jerusalem General Sir Edmund Allenby's 'caution was not due to any fear of being beaten by this miserable remnant of a defeated army, but rather by his dread of the consequences of brushing aside the restraining hand from Whitehall' is ludicrous applied to a man of Allenby's character, and ignores the transfer of two of Allenby's divisions to France and their replacement by raw Indian troops who had to be trained before they could be used. On the other

---

[51] Cf King *Generals & Politicians* p. 40–41 and Woodward *Lloyd George and the Generals* p. 100, 110–111, 115 fn 69, 223, 266, 279 fn 55; *Observer* 12 May 1918 p. 4c-f, quoting from 4c, cf Gollin *Proconsul in Politics* p. 516–7.

Note Charteris's and Sasson's correspondence with Lord Northcliffe, the greatest press magnate of the day: Northcliffe's letters to Sassoon of 22 Feb. and 13 Dec. 1917 (British Library Add. 62160 f. 87–9, f. 101–2) warning of the campaign building up against G.H.Q. indicate that G.H.Q. used their press contacts to monitor developments in government policy.

hand Robertson's handling of the suggestions of the civilian ministers on strategic matters indicates some excessively deft footwork. Before the war, as Commandant of the Staff College, he had written on an overly political essay by young Archibald Wavell:

> The discussion of questions of policy and political matters generally leads to no practical result nor benefit of any kind to the soldier, nor is it his business.

But in the summer of 1915, when it seems he already suspected that he was in the running for appointment as Chief of the Imperial General Staff, he wrote, in a memorandum which was evidently aimed at recommending himself to the politicians:

> It is also necessary that those responsible for formulating military opinion should recognize that war is nothing but an instrument of policy, and that its conduct, while conforming to strategic principles, should also conform to the political object of the Government . . .
>
> Moreover, Commanders-in-Chief in the field must receive guidance as to the broader aspects of military policy before they can suit their operations to the political object.

Once C.I.G.S. however he consistently reversed the emphasis, insisting on the primacy of military considerations: as Frances Stevenson complained when he refused to contemplate sending help to prevent the overrunning of Rumania:

> being a soldier he does not look at the political side, nor does he realise what loss of prestige following upon such a catastrophe would mean to the conduct of the war.

But perhaps he did realize, and simply preferred to pursue other policy objectives, against the wishes of his political masters.[52]

It should be noted, moreover, that Lloyd George's dissatisfaction with the generals was shared by colleagues who had less of a social chip on their shoulders. Lord Curzon told the King's secretary in March 1917:

> Independent opinion shows that without question the French Generals and Staff are immeasurably superior to British Generals and Staff, not from the point of view of fighting but from that of generalship, and of the knowledge of the science and art of war.
>
> The War Cabinet did not consider Haig a clever man.

By 'War Cabinet' Curzon actually meant himself and Lloyd George. Milner seems to have retained some faith in Haig longer than his colleagues but in

---

[52] Thomas Jones *Whitehall Diary* ed. Keith Middlemas (3 vols 1969–71) vol. 1 p. 41 31 Dec. 1917 quoting Lloyd George; Lloyd George *War Memoirs* vol. 4 p. 2141–8 and Sylvester *Life with Lloyd George* p. 81, 24 Sept. 1932; Lloyd George *War Memoirs* vol. 4 p. 1804; ibid. vol. 4 p. 1840; John Connell *Wavell: Scholar and Soldier: to June 1941* (1964) p. 65; William Robertson *Soldiers and Statesmen, 1914–1918* (2 vols 1926) vol. 1 p. 162; *Lloyd George: Diary by Frances Stevenson* p. 116, 12 Oct. 1916.

1918 he was so anxious for Robertson's dismissal that he threatened to resign if the C.I.G.S. was not replaced.[53]

Robertson was eventually sacked and his job was given to compliant clever-clever Henry Wilson, who was unable to separate the interests of the Empire from his own and who was essentially no more than the politician's typical corrupt purchase – though after his experience with Haig and Robertson Lloyd George had some excuse for his increasing fondness for such people. After Robertson's departure from the War Office his partisans attempted one last counter-attack: Major-General Sir Frederick 'Putty Nose' Maurice, who as Director of Military Operations had been Robertson's No. 2 on the strategic side, wrote to *The Times* claiming that Lloyd George had publicly misrepresented the strength of the British forces in France, and Asquith eagerly took up the matter in Parliament. Maurice had, needless to say, no encouragement from Wilson: 'he is incredibly inaccurate . . . what the man is thinking of I can't imagine. Nor can any of us.' Hankey took seriously the War Office gossip that Maurice was 'not *compos mentis*'. Even Haig was less than gratified: 'D.H. thinks Maurice's letter very ill advised. It offends all his ideas of discipline.' Both for Asquith and for the cause of military supremacy in the strategic direction of the war, the so-called Maurice Debate in the House of Commons was a final forlorn hope, repelled by Lloyd George in his best style. By early summer of 1918 Lloyd George stood at the pinnacle of power.[54]

IX. The Source of Political Authority

The real significance of the struggle between Lloyd George and the generals, as something more than merely a dispute over strategy, or an excuse for Lloyd George's civilian critics to attack his war leadership, is indicated by the similarity of the developments in other belligerent countries. Poor relations between government and military were parallel, often responsive to, poor relations between government and parliament. Both had their part in the larger question of the ultimate source of political authority in the various countries.

France, till 1917 the only republic amongst the major belligerents, witnessed a curious though incomplete shift in the location of power from parliamentary government to presidency. French ministries were necessarily coalitions of

[53] Woodward *Lloyd George and the Generals* p. 146 quoting memo of conversation between Curzon anf Stamfordham, Royal Archives Geo. V 1079/6, cf Reginald Pound and Geoffrey Harmsworth *Lord Northcliffe* (1959) p. 520 Northcliffe to Haig 21 Feb. 1917; Gollin *Proconsul in Politics* p. 479. For a day by day account of the final stages of the campaign to dump Robertson 8–19 Feb. 1918 see Woodward *Lloyd George and the Generals* p. 262–275.

[54] Keith Jeffrey ed. *The Military Correspondence of Field Marshal Sir Henry Wilson, 1918–1922* (1985) p. 43 Wilson to Allenby, 9 May 1918; Roskill *Hankey* vol. 1 p. 545 diary 10 May 1918; Charteris *At G.H.Q.* p. 308, 7 May 1918.

fissiparous groups – of the Third Republic's 94 governments 1879-1940, 40 inherited over half of their members from their immediate predecessor, so that while governments changed ministers tended to remain the same, though since they needed constantly to attend to their personal grip on the situation they were kept busy lobbying members of the *Chambre* and *Sénat*, both within and without their own factions. The war ministry's obstruction of the army commissions in 1914-1917 may be seen as an attempt to liberate itself from *Parlement* so as to be free to conduct the war. The *président du Conseil* – prime minister – had till 1934 no staff or patronage as such and normally held another portfolio: in any government he was always the minister most likely to lose his job and his political leverage was in no sense comparable to that of a British Prime Minister.[55]

Raymond Poincaré had become *président de la République* in 1913 after a year as prime minister. He was in his early 50s and was to be once more a minister and finally prime minister again in the 1920s and it may very well be that he chose to become President of the Republic with the intention of enlarging the presidency's directing role in government. He was entitled by the constitution to attend the sessions of the council of ministers, and from the end of July 1914 onwards he not only attended, and often presided, but was also generally the chief voice in transacting and deciding business. In the council of ministers the successive *présidents du Conseil*, Viviani, Briand, Ribot and Painlevé were not strong enough in their grasp of business to challenge Poincaré's usurpation, though of course there were clashes, especially when Briand replaced Viviani. Poincaré even drafted many of the government's official communiqués. He also, in the course of August 1914, took the initiative in broadening the membership of Viviani's ministry, and the resulting negotiations took place in his official residence, the Élysée Palace.[56]

Yet Poincaré was prevented both by bad luck and by his own deficiencies as a politician from achieving a final decisive shift from cabinet to presidential government. His popularity was probably at its height on the very eve of the declaration of war: when he and Viviani, the then *président du Conseil* returned from their luckily timed visit to St. Petersburg on 29 July 1914 they were greeted with shouts of *Vive Poincaré! Vive l'Armée!* But though he opposed the temporary withdrawal of the government to Bordeaux Poincaré was generally blamed for this apparently cowardly and certainly premature retreat, and his frequent visits to the front mainly served to advertise his charmlessness, lack of common touch, or even common flair – Lloyd George dismissed him as a 'fussy little man who mistook bustle for energy', and suggested, 'His was the triumph of commonplace qualities well proportioned,

[55] Theodore Zeldin *France, 1848–1945* (2 vols Oxford 1973–7) vol. 1 ('Ambition, Love and Politics') p. 586–9.

[56] Gordon Wright *Raymond Poincaré and the French Presidency* (Standford 1942) p. 162–4; ibid. p. 144–6.

well trained and consistently well displayed', which does nor sound like the stuff folk heroes are made of. Poincaré's leadership also inevitably suffered from the failures of the military; indeed it was his backing of Robert Nivelle against the criticisms of the other generals and of Paul Painlevé, the then war minister, that was decisive in permitting Nivelle's disastrous offensive of April 1917 to go ahead. Moreover, precisely because he was *président de la République* he could not personally work sufficiently effectively to secure his parliamentary base. In November 1917 Georges Clemenceau, a fierce critic of slackness and failure in the prosecution of the war became *président du Conseil* and the reins of power were, almost instantly, snatched from Poincaré's hands. The council of ministers now met only weekly, and as Clemenceau headed the war ministry himself and personally dominated Stephen Pichon the foreign minister, the most important government business was kept in Clemenceau's hands, with Georges Mandel, his *chef de cabinet* becoming effectively the second man in the government.[57]

Lord Esher thought that the ascendancy of Clemenceau in France and that of Lloyd George in Britain represented a transformation of the structure of power in the two countries, with both the French *Chambre* and the British House of Commons losing their key role:

> Both these bodies are mere mass meetings of persons who have arrogated to themselves, by resolutions prolonging their self-ordained privileges, the power to sit and discuss measures, that have been placed before them by officials, under the authority of Mr. Lloyd George in England and M. Clemenceau in France. The democratic dictatorship of these statesmen has been confirmed, not by free assemblies representing the people, but by the assent of the people themselves, given informally and passively, and registered by the Press as the vocal organ of popular opinion . . .
>
> A constitutional change that may prove to be permanent has been brought about by a combine between the Prime Minister of the day, and the organs of public opinion other than the elected representatives of the people.[58]

The other belligerents had more established constitutional systems than the Third Republic in France but they too experienced the same tendency to produce a power vacuum that Poincaré had attempted to exploit.

In all the belligerent monarchies the king was regarded as having a special relationship with the army. This was in part historical tradition but was also enshrined in constitutional practice: in Italy and Germany the sovereign was head of the army and the professional head of the service had the title of chief of staff; in Austria-Hungary the *Armeeoberkommandant* till 1916 was

[57] Wright *Poincaré* p. 134; ibid. p. 219–220 and cf Lloyd George *The Truth about the Peace Treaties* vol. 1 p. 249–250; Wright *Poincaré* p. 200–203; D. Stevenson *French War Aims Against Germany, 1914–1919* (Oxford 1982) p. 95–6. See also Esher's account of Poincaré 24 April 1916 quoted in James Lees-Milne *The Enigmatic Edwardian: The Life of Reginald 2nd Viscount Esher* (1986) p. 286.
[58] Lord Esher *After the War* (1918) p. 56–7, 59–60.

an ageing member of the imperial family who, again, left the real control to the chief of staff; – when Kaiser Karl succeeded to the throne he appointed himself to this essentially formal position; in Russia the Tsar's cousin Grand Duke Nicholas was commander-in-chief at the front till the Tsar himself took his place in September 1915. In all the monarchies the army officer corps was dominated by a social elite of which the royal family was the natural apex, and the army high command, being theoretically subordinate to the monarch did not consider itself to be subordinate to the war ministry – in fact this independence had been established on an official basis in Germany in 1883. The relationship between army and government was at least that of co-equals, so that even in Britain the monarch was able to assume something of a liaising and coordinating function.

There was also, separate from his relationship with his army and with his ministers, the monarch's identity and role as a symbolic national figurehead. This function had, as I have argued, grown in importance in Britain during the 1800s precisely because of the weakness of the ministers; and it is possible to see a parallel between George III *circa* 1807 and Franz Joseph of Austria-Hungary *circa* 1914: both had survived so long that they were commiserated upon rather than blamed for the inadequacies of their ministers. George V and Kaiser Wilhelm II had not been around long enough to accumulate all the personal benefit of a sustained tradition of nationalist-royalist propaganda, and the political divisions in Britain and Germany involved a certain amount of ambiguous popular feeling in their regard; nevertheless even if not universally cherished their figurehead role was one of the polite conventions of public life. In Italy the dwarfish Vittorio Emanuele, despite his want of charisma, was not markedly unpopular, though unlikely to forget that his father King Umberto had been assassinated during a period of political disorder, and he was vital to the politicians as the symbol of a national unity that was nowhere very visible at grass-roots level. In all these countries, especially with a succession of weak and divided ministries, it was for the monarch to epitomize and personify the nation's unanimous will for victory.

At the outbreak of war the five principal monarchs of Europe all had different degrees of constitutional power, which they used in different ways according to individual temperament, and with markedly different effect.

In Russia Nicholas II, who retained the greatest constitutional power, involved himself with the running of the war, eventually assuming the supreme command in the field. There is a well-known photograph of him passing on horseback amongst his reverentially kneeling troops, brandishing an icon, which perfectly epitomizes the idea of the monarch as national symbol in wartime. Even if he had been no more than a symbol Nicholas might well have been swept away in the collapse of the old order: but Nicholas was much more than a symbol. 'Ah my love, when at last will you thump with your hand upon the table & scream at [whoever it was] when they act wrongly?' his wife demanded, and Nicholas did his ineffectual best to assert himself. The result was that military defeat and worsening social conditions in wartime

Russia did not merely expose to criticism the system he represented; his own personal activity advertized that responsibility for failure was his own; and he himself, as much as his regime, became totally discredited. 'The real monarch has destroyed the idea of the monarch', Trotsky had declared prematurely in 1905: by 1917 this had become true. The February Revolution of 1917 marked not merely the failure of autocracy but also the personal failure of the autocrat. It would perhaps have needed a much greater Tsar not to have failed: but only a little more insight and intelligence would have enabled Nicholas to have side-stepped some of the blame for failure and to have perhaps retained a little more influence over affairs after 1917.[59]

In Austria-Hungary the octogenarian Franz Joseph had long been a symbol of a conservatism, tradition, hallowed values and much else that the Empire needed to escape from if it was to survive. The sorry performance of his armies in Poland, and the imposition of military rule at home, gave no-one the impression of a decisive and wholesome grip, and contributed to the belief that Franz Joseph was, if not positively senile, of little account in ruling circles. In reality it was his support for the idea of a unified inter-allied command that seems to have been decisive in securing the participation of Austria-Hungary, which was practically the only constructive decision of his government during the entire war. When Franz Joseph died late in 1916 his successor, young Karl I, was a little more of one's idea of a young, dashing, enthusiastic, inspiring war figurehead: except that he was anxious to bring the war to an end. Though he managed to oust Conrad von Hötzendorf from the *Armeeoberkommando* Karl was unable otherwise to exert much initiative in the running of the war; the situation had already passed outside the control of anyone in Austria-Hungary and in any case Karl was not one of the abler members of his dynasty, not a Joseph II or a Leopold, but rather a Franz I who lacked a Metternich.[60]

It was perhaps in Germany that the sovereign's role changed most markedly and unexpectedly during the war. Before August 1914 Wilhelm II's martial posing and sabre-rattling speeches, his direct lineal descent from Frederick the Great, his title as *Oberster Kriegsherr* (Supreme Warlord), the photos of him striding down Unter den Linden with his six strapping sons, all in uniform, made him the very personification of German militarism. In the crisis leading up to the outbreak of hostilities he played an active, if not always coherent, part. Once war was declared his eldest son, originally assigned to command the 1st Guard Infantry Division, was appointed at the last moment to command the Fifth Army and later became the head of an army group, as did also Rupprecht, the Crown Prince of Bavaria – it is piquant to note that

[59] Sir Bernard Pares ed. *Letters of the Tsaritsa to the Tsar, 1914–1916* (1923) p. 106, Alexandra to Nicholas 22 June 1915; Isaac Deutscher *The Prophet Armed:Trotsky, 1879–1921* (Oxford 1970 edit.) p. 115.

The photograph of Nicholas and his troops may date from 1905 but this aspect of his rule had certainly not changed by 1914.

[60] Gunther E. Rothenburg *The Army of Francis Joseph* (West Lafayette 1976) p. 198–9.

the latter, commanding the German front opposite the British Expeditionary Force, was not only heir to the Bavarian throne but also eldest son of the Stuart Pretender to the thrones of England and Scotland. Other than in the case of Belgium and Rumania, where King Albert and King Ferdinand actually commanded in the field – perhaps one should also mention the Prince Regent Alexander of Serbia who took over command of the Serbian army when it already no longer existed, and when he himself was too ill to stand – the senior commands held by the Imperial and the Bavarian Crown Princes represent a more marked and successful royal participation in the war than occurred in any other belligerent monarchy; in the British case the person closest to the throne to come under fire was Prince Albert, the future George VI, who was present at the Battle of Jutland not as a senior officer but as a sub-lieutenant. And yet Wilhelm's own position faded almost immediately into insignificance. He abdicated the possibility of retaining civilian and national leadership by leaving Berlin to establish his military headquarters at various inconvenient locations – Luxembourg, Charleville, Pless, Bad Homburg, Spa – and at the same time abdicated the possibility of any influence on military affairs by taking an increasingly passive role in his consultations first with Falkenhayn and than with the team of Hindenburg and Ludendorff; and sometimes he did not even see the army chiefs for weeks. It was not even his decision to appoint Hindenburg and Ludendorff: it was Bethman-Hollweg who forced him to relinquish Falkenhayn, and there was little he could do but weep beforehand and sulk afterwards.

Why someone as egregiously self-assertive and as cock-surely familiar with military trivia should have allowed himself to be relegated to such a position is a mystery. He knew far more about uniforms than about strategy but he had had plenty of opportunity to pick up some sort of military education: he must for example have been better informed than his playboy son the Imperial Crown Prince, yet though Ludendorff noted sourly that 'Duke Albrecht of Württemberg . . . was of a more pronounced soldierly temperament than the two Crown Princes', they were more than mere figureheads at their respective army H.Q.s. (After the war the Bavarian Crown Prince published a glossily produced edition of his war diaries and one is struck by how much more absorbed in military affairs and how much less abreast of affairs in the capital he was than Sir Douglas Haig: when Falkenhayn was superseded he even repeated the Headquarter gossip that Falkenhayn was going to Berlin to replace Bethmann-Hollweg as chancellor.) The Kaiser may have been better informed as to political developments but he was not even a figurehead. He acted as if the war had broken his heart, and even if one discounts the view that he had been planning an eventual war since early in his reign this does seem a rather peculiar response for the successor of Frederick the Great. After his triumphant announcement of the outbreak of war from the balcony of the Berliner Schloss he disappeared from the public eye, except for a few uninspired and uninspiring visits of inspection and reviews and a meeting with Kaiser Karl at which they appeared ritually clothed in one another's uniforms, the German Emperor as an Austrian officer and the Austrian Emperor as a German one. By 1916 Hindenburg had become the living symbol of the German nation's will to win: titanic wooden statues of him were erected in German city centres so that the patriotic could pay to drive carpet tacks into the wooden body; the statues were however more important than the money raised or the strange suggestion of ju-juism. It was behind the shielding reputation of Hindenburg that Ludendorff planned and manipulated; the Emperor had become an irrelevancy even as a faççade, though of course he continued to be caricatured by *Punch* and after the war Ludendorff took care to adopt an exaggeratedly reverential tone whenever referring to the Kaiser in his memoirs. A not unjust verdict was that of Prince von Bülow, once the Imperial Chancellor: 'in peace the Kaiser was a war-lord, in war he evaded taking decisions, and in defeat he fled'.[61]

Vittorio Emanuele survived the war rather more successfully. Of all the monarchs, he had perhaps the most crucial part in involving his country in hostilities: he did not merely participate in the Gadarene rush to destruction, he also first sent away the swineherd. It was Vittorio Emanuele's desire that

[61] For the Bavarian Crown Prince Rupprecht as Stuart Pretender see Marquis de Ruvigny and Raineval *The Nineteen Descents of His Royal Highness Prince Robert from his late Sacred Majesty King James I and VI* (1901) which shows Rupprecht as being 10th in descent from James I through his mother and 12th through his father. For Albert see R. van Overstraeten ed. *The War Diaries of Albert I King of the Belgians* (1954) espec. p. 26–28: by 1918 Albert was commanding an allied army group. For Ferdinand see Alexandru Averescu *Notiţe Zilnice din Războiu 1916–1918* (Bucharest [c. 1935]) p. 58 and p. 382 Anexa No. 5 to Anexa B. For Wilhelm's resistance to the appointment of Hindenburg and Ludendorff see Walter Görlitz ed. *The Kaiser and his court: The Diaries, Note Books and Letters of Admiral George Alexander von Müller Chief of the Naval Cabinet. 1914–1918* (1959) p. 198–9, 28 and 30 Aug. 1916; [Erich] Ludendorff *My War Memories, 1914–1918* (2 vols [1919]) vol. 1 p. 225 cf Rupprecht von Bayern *Mein Kriegstagbuch* ed. Eugen von Frauenholz (3 vols Munich [1929]) for criticisms of Falkenhayn, vol. 2 p. 3 (30 Aug. 1916) for Falkenhayn as chancellor, and vol. 1 p. 494 (2 July 1916 for Rupprecht's political contacts: see also Wilhelm of Prussia *My War Experiences* [1922]. For German senior officers' attitude to the Kaiser generally see Gotthard Breit *Das Staats- und Gesellschaftsbild deutscher Generale beider Weltkriege im Spiegel ihrer Memoiren* (Boppard am Rhein 1973) p. 94–104; John Wheeler Bennett *Wooded Titan: Hindenburg, in Twenty Years of German History, 1914–1934* (1936) p. 77 and cf photo opposite p. 108: there is another photo, showing the wooden statue apparently after it had been freshly painted in Kunstamt Kreuzberg, Berlin *Weimarer Republik* (3rd edit. Berlin 1977) p. 241. Paul Lindenburg *Das Buch vom Feldmarschall Hindenburg* (Berlin 1920) p. 209 says the Berlin statue was erected in the Königsplatz opposite the *Siegessäule* in September 1915 and cf photo p. 210. For the ju–ju analogy see the British propaganda leaflet *c.* 1917 'The Wooden Idol of Berlin' which shows a drawing of the statue alongside three photos of African ju–ju idols: the shelf-mark of the British Library copy is 1879 cc 4; for Bülow's summing up see John Wheeler–Bennett *Knaves, Fools and Heroes* (1974) p. 184.

In addition to the royal warriors mentioned in the text, Archduke Karl commanded an Army Group on the Eastern Front prior to succeeding to the Habsburg throne, but he seems to have had a less active and determining role than the two German Crown Princes, cf Hans von Seeckt *Aus meinem Leben* ed. Friedrich von Rabenau (2 vols Leipzig 1938–40) vol. 1 p. 398–402. The Duke of Aosta, Vittorio Emanuele's cousin, commanded an army on the Alpine Front: like Duke Albrecht of Württemberg he was a career officer.

Italy should enter the war at the side of Britain and France which proved decisive when the majority of the liberal deputies declared their opposition to Salandra's war policy in May 1915; Salandra's failure to rally support gave Giolitti an opportunity to form his fourth government and it was Vittorio Emanuele who deterred him from trying. Giolitti's withdrawal from the scene was acquiescence not in the general population's desire for war (which despite the demonstrations in the streets of Rome itself Giolitti had neither wish nor reason to believe in) but in the King's hopes for a greater and stronger Italy. Thereafter the King abandoned Rome to the politicians, rather as Wilhelm abandoned Berlin – though Italy and Germany being different, Wilhelm lost credit and the power to influence by absenting himself from Berlin while Vittorio Emanuele merely distanced himself from the miasma of Italian public life. The appointment of his cousin Tommaso, Duke of Genoa, as Regent during his absence at the front served to advertize his departure rather than to bring into play a rival personality; and, unlike Wilhelm, Vittorio Emanuele did not hide in a military headquarters at a safe distance from the battlefield, but haunted the frontline endlessly and obsessively, taking photographs ceaselessly with a huge box camera which he carried everywhere hanging round his neck, receiving reports, saying as little as possible and looking daily sadder and sicker. 'Things are not difficult, only men', he was to confess later. Glimpses of his gold-braided cap, squashed down between the shoulders of his entourage in the back of a Hispano racing along the mountain roads, or the apparition of his stunted figure in a military cape somewhere overlooking a battlefield were a regular experience for his suffering soldiers, possibly one of the less agreeably surrealistic accompaniments of their ordeal. Whether it made him more popular with the citizenry pressed into his armies seems doubtful; but at least he managed to share the army's defeat at Caporetto without being seen to share the responsibility for it with the vainglorious Cadorna.[62]

George V's constitutional power, a matter of traditional restraints rather than of relatively recent constitutional enactments, was less than that of his brother monarchs yet he too had his influence and his opportunities. His giving up alcohol for the duration and his frequent visits (in field marshal's uniform) to the theatre of war in France were well publicized. The predominantly symbolic function of the monarchy was already well established in Britain, and he performed it admirably, while a fond public made the traditional loyal noises. Yet it was appreciated that the time-honoured ways of doing things, the long-cherished pieties, might not be able to withstand the stress of war. This was especially so after the February Revolution in Russia; one American diplomat commented, 'everybody is feeling the working-class volcano under his feet'. Lord Esher for one realized how much the King had at stake in the successful outcome of the war:

---

[62] 'Things are not difficult, only men' is from Harold Macmillan *War Diaries: Politics and War in the Mediterranean, January 1943 – May 1945* (1984 p. 220) report to War Cabinet 16–17 Sept. 1943.

If we fail to beat the enemy and have to accept a compromise peace, then we shall be lucky if we escape a revolution in which the Monarchy, the Church and all our 'Victorian' institutions will founder.

Esher thought indeed that George V was in a position to extend his powers, suggesting for example that he should 'endeavour to influence the directive policy of his Ministers, whenever and wherever the liberties of the people are threatened. This would enhance the popularity of the throne'. Perhaps wisely, George V did not involve himself in this ambiguous course; later, rereading royal letters from the time of the King's father, Esher noted, 'How well King Edward stands out compared with our poor little King, who is of so small account'. In a small volume of 'reflections upon political mechanics' entitled *After the War* published in 1918, with a preface addressed to Robert Smillie, chairman of the Scottish Miners' Federation and I.L.P leader, Esher discoursed eloquently on the adaptability of old traditions and the need 'to transform social habits and remould political institutions, in tune with the dreams and aspirations of all that is best in England', though one suspects he was none too optimistic as far as the monarchy was concerned. Nevertheless George V did assert himself occasionally, if only to expedite decisions which were already in the making. Two days before Robertson produced his memorandum urging that the C.I.G.S. should be the sole source of military advice to the Cabinet, Lord Stamfordham, who was the King's secretary and wrote in his name, told Asquith:

But His Majesty does believe that important advantages would be secured by the transfer of Sir W. Robertson to the post of C.I.G.S. making him responsible only to the *War Council* for whose information and advice he and his staff would deal with all matters of strategy and conduct of war – Lord K. would as S. of S. for War be in the same position as any other member of the Council of War to criticise and collectively to accept or reject these recommendations: but *not* to interfere with the decisions of the C.I.G.S. before they reach the War Council.

Clearly the King, through Stamfordham, was prepared to act as Robertson's spokesman on this matter. He also took the initiative in sounding out senior officers as to Sir John French's fitness to continue in command in France, and in then pressing for his removal; and in November 1916 he summoned French, now in command of Home Forces, to tell him to stop trying to undermine Haig. He also took Haig's and Robertson's side when Lloyd George tried, at the Calais Conference of February 1917, to subordinate Haig to Robert Nivelle: he had in fact something very much like a row with Lloyd George over this.[63]

[63] Arthur Walworth *Woodrow Wilson* (2 vols New York 1958) vol. 2 p. 164 quoting A.H. Frazier to Col. Edward House; Esher *Journals and Letters* vol. 4 p. 137 to Stamfordham 24 Aug. 1917; British Library Add. 49719 f. 286 Esher to Robertson 20 June 1917, copy sent to Balfour: passage omitted in the version of this letter printed in Esher *Journals and Letters*
continued

Asquith, who had found the King useful as a referee before the war, was not ill-disposed towards George V's occasional interventions, and when Sir Edward Carson, the most troublesome of the Tory leaders, wanted to resign from the coalition government in October 1915 Asquith asked him to talk it over with the King first. Lloyd George was less interested in cooperation, especially as he saw that it was the King, as much as *The Globe* and *The Morning Post* and vocal elements in Parliament, who provided Haig and Robertson with their real power base. He probably knew that the King did not like him (when Sir Henry Wilson remarked that Lloyd George and Robertson could not get on, the King exclaimed, 'No wonder, Robertson was too honest and too straight to get on with him'). Lloyd George made rather a habit of referring to the King in private as 'your little German friend', and more than once drove His Majesty to protest at his freedom in offering decorations and even peerages without the normal courtesy of first consulting the monarch in whose name they were given. He also ignored the King's opposition to the replacement of Lord Bertie, ambassador at Paris, by the Earl of Derby, when Lloyd George was seeking an honourable means of ejecting Derby from the War Office in the spring of 1918. Lloyd George claimed that Balfour had once remarked, 'Whatever would you do if you had a ruler with brains?' In fact George V was not without percipience. The decision not to admit the deposed Tsar into Britain originated with the King himself, and indicated that he put being sensible about political realities before romantic loyalty, even to his own relatives. Though never as passive as his son George VI, George V knew he had to accept being shouldered out of the limelight as symbolic national figurehead, and in the two years between becoming Prime Minister and the coming of the Armistice Lloyd George became as much the leader of the nation as Churchill was in 1940. Later he was to say of the King, 'I owe him nothing; he owes his throne to me'.[64]

In many repects Erich Ludendorff was the German counterpart of Lloyd George and Clemenceau, however different the career route he took to arrive at that position, and however much he sheltered behind Hindenburg's aura of massive self-assurance and universal competence. At least in retrospect Ludendorff realized more clearly than anyone else – more clearly even than Lord Esher – that the crisis of world war, and the crisis of nationhood which lay at the heart of world war, needed a new kind of regime; and it was regimes of this new kind which were to fight the Second World War.

continued
vol. 4 p. 125–6; Lees-Milne *Enigmatic Edwardian* p. 310, Esher's journal of 7 July 1918; Esher *After the War* p. 78 and cf p.x; David R. Woodward *Lloyd George and the Generals* (Newark 1983) p. 80 quoting Bodleian Ms Asquith 4 Stamfordham to Asquith 3 Dec. 1915 cf Robertson *Soldiers and Statesmen* vol. 1 p. 168–170; Richard Holmes *The Little Field Marshal: Sir John French* (1981) p. 328; Fraser *Esher* p. 357, citing memo by Stamfordham 12 March 1917.

   64 Gollin *Proconsul in Politics* p. 310; Lees-Milne *Enigmatic Edwardian* p. 311 cf Roskill *Hankey* p. 283, diary 10 June 1916; *Lloyd George: A Diary by Frances Stevenson* p. 25, 25 Jan. 1915; Kenneth Rose *King George V* (New York 1984) p. 207–8; Sylvester *Life with Lloyd George* p. 94, 4 April 1933.

PART THREE

THE SECOND WORLD WAR

1939–1945

Outline: 1939–1945

In September 1939, as in August 1914, Britain was again defending an international status quo with which the nation's leaders felt identified, though by now Britain's independent strength was recognized to be much less and had to be buttressed by a much firmer system of alliances than had existed in 1914. The sheer aggressiveness of German policy, and the increasingly horrific nature of Germany's internal organization, meant that the necessity of the war was much less frequently questioned than in 1914, let alone 1792–1793, but certain ambiguities remained, especially with regard to Britain's treatment of colonial territories and willingness to collaborate with regimes potentially as tyrannical as Hitler's.

Having learnt the lessons of the First World War, the British government mobilized the national economy for war with unparalleled thoroughness and efficiency, though the by now vastly greater manufacturing capacity of the United States meant that, even with a considerably less elaborate economic mobilization, American munitions output significantly exceeded Britain's.

The First World War had given the British – ministers, generals and public alike – an aversion to the large-scale slogging matches that had characterized the generalship of 1914–1918, and the expulsion of British forces from the European mainland in 1940 as a result of the capitulation of France meant that a strategy of maintaining the largest possible land forces in western Europe was in any case no longer immediately feasible. The campaign in North Africa, like that in the Peninsula in Wellington's day, utilized British advantages in naval power to maintain a relatively small high-quality force on the enemy's flank, though in fact the conditions of distance and transportation were this time much less in Britain's favour, but Britain's main strategic expedient was to mobilize national technological and industrial resources in order to attack Germany massively from the air.

Britain's unfavourable military position in 1940, and the personal dynamism of Winston Churchill, meant that conflict between civilian and military leadership was much less an issue in Britain in the Second World War than in the First. Churchill, and Roosevelt in the U.S.A., were virtually as all-powerful within their own countries as Hitler and Mussolini or Stalin. It was as if transitional, interim conditions that had prevailed in the First World War had come to a kind of maturity, with the political systems of the various belligerents adapting themselves to the logic of total war as efficiently as their economies.

12

Right against Right

Never in the course of history had there been a struggle in which the issues were so clearly defined.

Richard Hillary, *The Last Enemy* (1942), p. 208.

I. Cross-Currents

The Second World War was even more vastly destructive than the First World War, but there has been much less controversy over who started it. Discussion of the origins of the First World War is still largely within the original framework of assessing Austria-Hungary's and Germany's war guilt, even if the allocation of blame no longer seems as straightforward as it did seventy years ago. Discussion of the origins of the Second World War on the other hand has displaced itself into an analysis of timing and opportunities; the question of responsibility is scarcely an issue as such. In Germany there are competing 'intentionalist' and 'functionalist' interpretations of Hitler's decision in August 1939 to attack Poland – the difference relates to the degree of emphasis to be given to Hitler's personal priorities as distinct from socio-economic conditions creating pressure for an aggresive policy – but there is no fundamental challenge to the view that the international phenomenon of Fascism was bound sooner or later to boil over into war. In the Anglo-Saxon world A.J.P. Taylor's provocative account of Hitler as a perfectly rational opportunist statesman has stimulated controversy, but the academic revisionists have failed to engage satisfactorily with a consistently plausible tradition that sees the war as an element in what is perhaps *the* ideological confrontation of the twentieth century, or with folk memories in which the war is a great epic of good against evil – folk memories kept alive for later generations by the miraculous survival in remote jungles of mythic figures like Dr. Mengele.[1]

[1] See Richard Overy 'Germany, "Domestic" Crisis and War in 1939' *Past and Present* no. 116 (1987) p. 138–168 at p. 138–9 and for responses to the A.J.P. Taylor theses see Wm. Roger Louis ed. *The Origins of the Second World War: A.J.P. Taylor and his Critics* (New York. 1972). Two best-selling novels inspired by the Dr. Mengele archetype were William Goldman *Marathon Man* (1974) and Ira Levin *The Boys From Brazil* (1976); both were made into successful films. There is also the tradition that the Third Reich, defeated in this world, survives and flourishes in another dimension, as in Philip K. Dick *The Man in the High Castle* (1962) and Deane Romero *Flight From Time One* (1972).

The Second World War began with Hitler's attack on Poland on 1 September 1939, but since Poland vanished from the political map within one month it was the British declaration of war on 3 September, transforming Hitler's intended short sharp conquest on his eastern borders into a confrontation of super-powers, which marked the real beginning of the world conflict. Britain was thus much more forward and active in making the war than in 1914; France – also soon to be overrun – merely followed Britain's lead.

Although Britain's build-up of armaments did not begin till 1936, it had been decided in 1932 that war within the next ten years was a possibility. Initially the coming war was foreseen mainly in terms of a defensive struggle to preserve Britain's extended position as a transoceanic world power. Privately the First Sea Lord confessed, 'we have got most of the world already, or the best parts of it, and we only want to keep what we have got and prevent others taking it away from us'. In public the emphasis was slightly different. The Defence White Paper of March 1935 announced:

> The National Government . . . can no longer close its eyes to the fact that adequate defences are still required for security and to enable the British Empire to play its full part in maintaining the peace of the world.

But it was not immediately clear where the prime threat to world peace was most likely to come from and Sir Warren Fisher, head of the Treasury, wrote to the Secretary of the Committee of Imperial Defence:

> I regard it as of the first importance to say clearly that our resources would not enable us to engage simultaneously in two first-class world wars on widely distant fronts.
>
> In other words we are done if we so mis-manage affairs as to be involved in war at the same time with Germany and Japan.

This was a prophetic warning; but in the short term the increasing activity of Hitler, and passivity of the French government, and the Japanese pre-occupation with their conquest of China, focused official attention in Whitehall more and more exclusively on the threat to international stability posed by the Nazi leader. The Munich settlement, which sacrificed Czech independence to Hitler in the autumn of 1938, was an attempt to achieve a lasting European settlement, yet in January 1939 only four months later Whitehall felt obliged to warn the British Embassy in Washington that a major war provoked by Nazi Germany was still regarded as a distinct likelihood, even the possibility of a surprise aerial bombardment of London not being ruled out.[2]

---

[2] Christopher Thorne *The Limits of Foreign Policy: The West, the League and the Far Eastern Crisis of 1931–1933* (1972) p. 48 quoting Sir Ernle Chatfield to Sir Warren Fisher 4 June 1934; Defence White Paper, Cmd 4827 p. 4 (*Parliamentary Papers* 1934–35 XII p. 803–812 at p. 806); Public Record Office CAB 16/109 p. 431–2 Sir Warren Fisher to Sir Maurice Hankey 12 Feb. 1934 (For the background to Sir Warren Fisher's letter see James Neidpath *The Singapore Naval Base and the Defence of Britain's Eastern Empire, 1919–1941* (Oxford 1981) p. 13–14, 28–9, 77–8, 215.); David Dilks ed. *The Diaries of Sir Alexander Cadogan O.M., 1938–1945* (1971) p. 141–4.

After Hitler violated the Munich agreement by occupying western Czechoslovakia in March 1939 the British Government began to prepare an unprecedented and hitherto unthinkable measure, the introduction of military conscription in peacetime, and also proclaimed its intention of guaranteeing the territorial integrity of Poland; it was this guarantee which led in due course to the world war. The Polish guarantee was perhaps less a belated attempt to intimidate Hitler than a tactic of Prime Minister Neville Chamberlain to regain the ground lost in the eyes of his right-wing critics. Chamberlain himself wrote after the German occupation of Prague, 'I want to gain time, for I never accept the view that war is inevitable'. It may be that right up until the German invasion of Poland he would have been ready to arrange another 'Munich' to settle the Polish question, but the pace of events combined with the threat of a Cabinet revolt stampeded him into a declaration of war; nevertheless the country as a whole accepted, however unenthusiastically, that Britain was irretrievably committed to resisting German aggression in eastern Europe, and it seems that Chamberlain's appeasement policy was chiefly important, not in placating Hitler or postponing war, but in giving the British public enough time to be persuaded of its obligation to lead the struggle against Hitlerism. There is in fact a parallel with the circumstances of 1914; in neither case did Britain actually initiate the fighting but in both cases there was an almost general consensus that *if* there was a war, Britain would have to be a leading protagonist.

To begin with some of the statements justifying British entry into the war emphasized the need to defend Britain's international position. In *The Spectator* Harold Nicolson wrote, 'we are fighting to maintain our own position as a Great Power, our own possessions, and eventually our own independence'. Another of Nicolson's claims, 'Our power *is* our freedom', was quoted approvingly in a Foreign Office minute. But from the very beginning an ardently moral, almost apocalyptic note was struck which went far beyond the denunciations of Prussian militarism in 1914. In his broadcast to the nation announcing the war, Chamberlain explained, 'It is the evil things that we shall be fighting against: brute force, bad faith, injustice, oppression and persecution. Against them I am certain that right will prevail'. And if that was too high falutin', R.H. Tawney, answering the question, 'How do the mass of plain people in Great Britain view the present conflict?', explained to readers

---

³ Peter Dennis *Decision by Default: Peacetime Conscription and British Defence, 1919–1939* (Durham N.C. 1972) p. 206–225; Simon Newman *March 1939: The British Guarantee to Poland: A Study in the Continuity of British Foreign Policy* (Oxford 1974) p. 174–204; Keith Feiling *The Life of Neville Chamberlain* (1946) p. 401 Chamberlain to his sisters 19 March 1939; Maurice Cowling *The Impact of Hitler: British Politics and British Policy 1933–1940* (1975) p. 293–312 for the view that in August–September 1939 Chamberlain was thinking in terms of another Munich; Donald Cameron Watt *How War Came; The Immediate Origins of the Second World War, 1938–1939* (1989) p. 578–89; see also account in [F.W.F.] Earl of Birkenhead *Halifax: The Life of Lord Halifax* (1965) p. 446–7.

of *The New York Times*, 'We are fighting, they would say, if they expressed their convictions (which, of course, they don't) to preserve a way of life which we value above life'. In Australia Sir Earle Page, ex-premier and leader of the Country Party, told the Australian House of Representatives:

> If ever a race of people entered unwillingly and with a clear conscience upon war, it is the British people who do so now . . . When the history of this period is written, the record of British policy in the last twenty years will stand out in letters of gold as the epic of a race which strove with the utmost might to abolish the spectre of war from the earth. The greatness of the greatest empire the world has known is not in the proud story of its growth as much as in its attainment to the position where even its enemies concede it to be the strongest influence for peace. Its commanding sense of right and wrong and its love and devotion to that, Emerson says, is the Imperial trait which arms the Anglo-Saxon people with the sceptre of the globe. Only such an empire could have risked its prestige as this Empire has in recent years in the cause of peace.[4]

Such was the British government's faith in the irresistible glamour of its anti-Nazi mission that from the very beginning it refused to hamper itself with the usual conventions of civilized warfare. Winston Churchill, appointed First Lord of the Admiralty after ten bitter years in the political wilderness, explained:

> No technical infringement of International Law, so long as it is unaccompanied by inhumanity of any kind, can deprive us of the good wishes of neutral countries . . . Small nations must not tie our hands when we are fighting for their rights and freedom.

The operation which Churchill promoted to lay mines in Norwegian coastal waters at the beginning of April 1940 startled even officers in the Royal Navy. 'We deliberately infringe international waters and therefore the law', commented the Director of Operations (Home) of the Naval Staff: 'I thought we were fighting for international law and order.' The German foreign minister Joachim von Ribbentrop told press correspondents that the British action 'compares with the British bombardment of Copenhagen in 1807'. The German government could at least pretend that it served as some sort of justification for the invasion of Norway and Denmark on 9 April 1940. The German occupation of Denmark served in turn to justify the British seizure of Iceland, at that time still a Danish dependency; a British offer of 'assistance' was turned down by the administration in Reykjavik but a month later the

---

[4] Harold Nicolson 'People and Things' *Spectator* 1 Sept. 1939 p. 324; the quotation from Nicolson is in Public Record Office FO 371/22986/C19495, minute by William Strang (assistant Under Secretary of State) dated 8 Dec. 1939 on Vansittart's memo 'The Origins of Germany's Fifth War', Nicolson's original statement having possibly been in a B.B.C broadcast. R.H. Tawney *The Attack, and Other Papers* (1953) p. 71–8 'Why Britain Fights' (originally published in *New York Times* 21 July 1940) at p. 71 and 73; *Commonwealth of Australia: Parliamentary Debates* vol. 161 p. 42, speech by Sir Earle Page 6 Sept. 1939.

British landed troops, accompanied by a Foreign Office emissary who was relieved to report, after meeting the Icelandic administration, that his 'reception was more friendly than I had anticipated'. Once Churchill had moved from the Admiralty to 10 Downing Street and the country found itself facing the greatest challenge of its history, the no-holds-barred policy which Churchill favoured found new opportunities. The scheme to seize the French fleet at Oran following France's defeat by Germany was described by one admiral as 'the biggest political blunder of modern times and I imagine will turn the whole world against us'. (The Germans again trotted out the comparison with the bombardment of Copenhagen in 1807). A few weeks later Churchill was toying with an even more outrageous and unnecessary project:

> I am increasingly attracted by the idea of simply taking the Azores one fine morning out of the blue, and explaining everything to Portugal afterwards. She would certainly have every right to protest.

Of the British invasion of Persia in 1941 he later remarked complacently, 'Inter armes silent leges' – laws are silent in the presence of weapons.[5]

Such flagrant violations of neutral rights suggest that Britain's role in the war by no means fitted neatly into the morally absolute framework announced by Chamberlain on 3 September 1939. Mussolini gave a different emphasis when he proclaimed early in 1943: 'this is a war of religion and ideas. Today all territorial objectives take second place', but this too was not exactly true: while within each separate warring nation there was at least an official or consensual ideology, each of these warring nations was grouped in alliances with other societies having antagonistic ideologies. 'Sympathy here was for the Nazis,' noted General Joseph W. Stilwell when visiting the capital of America's Chinese allies: 'Same type of government, same outlook, same gangsterism.' Equally, when Finland sided with the Nazis German officials were not exactly thrilled to find that the Finnish head of state was pro-British and, as one might expect from an ex-bank president, high up in the Masons. To argue that these ideological inconsistencies were of little real significance and explicable entirely

[5] Winston S. Churchill *The Second World War* (6 vols 1948–54) vol. 1 p. 432–3 Cabinet note 16 Dec. 1939; Stephen Roskill *Churchill and the Admirals* (1977) p. 101 quoting diary of Capt. R.A.B. Edwards, Director of Operations (Home) 5 April 1940; William L. Shirer *Berlin Diary* (1941) p. 245, 9 April 1940; Donald F. Bittner *The Lion and the White Falcon: Britain and Iceland in the World War II Era* (New York 1983) p. 48 and cf. Solrun B. Jensdottir Hardarson '"The Republic of Iceland", 1940–44: Anglo-American Attitudes and Influences' *Journal of Contemporary History* vol. 9 (1974) no. 4 p. 27–56; Somerville Papers, Churchill College Cambridge 3/22, Admiral Sir James Somerville to Lady Somerville 4 July 1940; *Royal Institute of International Affairs: Review of the Foreign Press 1939–1945:* Series B no. 42 (15 July 1940) p. 2 quoting *Deutsche Diplomatisch-Politische Korrespondenz*; Public Record Office FO 371/24515 f, 220, Churchill note 24 July 1940 (for British plans to seize the Canary Islands at this period see Luis Pascual Sanchez-Gijon *La Planificacion Militar Britanica y España 1940–1942* (Madrid 1984), p. 89–105 and for the Spanish side Victor Morales Lezcano *Historia de la No-Beligerancia Española durante La Segunda Guerra Mundial (VI, 1940–X, 1943)* (Las Palmas 1980) p. 157–167); for the Latin tag see Churchill *Second World War* vol. 3 p. 428.

in terms of local circumstances would be to insist on a crude caricature of what was evidently a complex situation.[6]

II. The Question of Fascism and Anti-Fascism

One over-simplification that needs to be avoided is that, unifying all the conflicting and incompatible elements, there was a general framework of Fascism *versus* Anti-Fascism. Such a view seems to beg important questions about what Fascism was precisely, and whether there ever was in fact a single phenomenon which manifested itself in joint action under this label.

From its very beginnings National Socialism in Germany was identified as a local variety of the Fascism already flourishing under Mussolini's leadership in Italy; as early as 1924 a swastika labelled *Faschismus* was shown being smashed by a clenched fist under the caption *Tod dem Faschismus!* – Death to Fascism! – in a German Communist poster designed by John Heartfield. It is clear also that the sociological roots of Italian Fascism and German National Socialism were analogous both in terms of the social groups mobilized in the mass movements preceding the seizure of power and in the precise historical conjuncture of post-war disillusion, administrative break-down and Bolshevik menace in which the movements first appeared. The styles of regimentation adopted – the jack boots, the Roman salutes, the helmets masking the individuality of the wearers, the strangely epicene uniforms, the incantatory titles of the leaders, *Duce* and *Führer* – seem analogous too, the *Jugendstil* iconography of the swastika a Germanic counterpart of the more *art nouveau* symbol of the *fascio*.[7]

Nevertheless attempts to compare, or differentiate, or typologize these movements according to lists of supposed characteristics are simply mis-

---

[6] F.W. Deakin *The Brutal Friendship: Mussolini, Hitler and the Fall of Italian Fascism* (1962) p. 131, speech by Mussolini to Party Directorate 3 Jan. 1943; Theodore H. White ed. *The Stilwell Papers* London 1949 p. 131, diary of Joseph W. Stilwell 10 July 1942 (in January 1939 the permanent head of the British Foreign Office had told Mussolini to his face that he was like Chiang Kai-Shek, apparently by way of flattering him: *Diary of Sir Alexander Cadogan* p. 137; see also A. Whitney Griswold *The Far Eastern Policy of the United States* (New Haven 1938) p. 382 for Chiang's 'fascist dictatorship'); *Documents on German Foreign Policy, 1918–1945* series D (11 vols Washington 1949–64) vol. XI p. 763 Wipert von Blücher to Foreign Ministry 2 Dec. 1940, cf. Wipert von Blücher *Gesandter zwischen Diktatur und Demokratie* (Wiesbaden 1951) p. 283–5 for the dinner celebrating Marshal Mannerheim's 75th birthday in July 1942 when Hitler, self-invited, sat down for a convivial evening with Mannerheim, President Ryti and the Prime Minister, Jukka Rangell – all three of them apparently freemasons.

[7] The Heartfield poster is reproduced in Richard Hiepe, Michael Schwarz et. al *Widerstand statt Anpassung: die Kunst im Widerstand gegen den Faschismus, 1933–1945* (Berlin 1980) p. 22. With regard to the linguistic awkwardness of describing the *fascio* as an *art nouveau* symbol, there is no counterpart of the latter term in Italian, though the influence of the movement itself may occasionally be detected: in the *Enciclopedia Italiana*, published under Mussolini's auspices, the only material referring to *Art Nouveau* and *Jugendstil* is a brief article under *Secessione*.

conceived, resulting for example in Eugen Weber's heavy-handed distinction between Fascism as essentially pragmatic, aiming at power simply for its own sake, and National Socialism as much more a matter of theory, or doctrine. It seems in fact that the only leading Nazi who sincerely believed that National Socialism was a political doctrine rather than a praxis was Alfred Rosenberg, who never actually exercised any real power in the movement. There was not even a consistent style in the praxis; much of the weirder mystic element in National Socialism was injected into the ensemble by Heinrich Himmler (with a dash of Anthroposophism from Rudolf Hess), and much of the social radicalism by Joseph Goebbels: no less influential was the arch-pragmatist Hermann Göring who shortly before his death boasted, 'I joined the Party because it was revolutionary, not because of the ideological stuff'. Those who have not been entirely seduced by Albert Speer's winsome self-portrait, in his memoirs, as the naive, apolitical technocrat marooned amongst the cannibals, will see Hitler's architect and armaments supremo as also representing a significant strand of Nazi development. The fact that such different men were able – just about – to work together shows that National Socialism was more than a set of ideological positions, and owed its cohesion not to the logical consistency of its doctrines but to the pervasive nature of the fears and threats to which it was a response. Self-conceived from the very beginning as the opponents of Bolshevism, National Socialism and Fascism were in fact a gut reaction to the phantoms evoked by the apparent shift of political power into the hands of the masses and of the marginalized. Part of this gut reaction was the creation of a new psychic identity, but it was characteristic that this sense of identity, having taken form under conditions of the utmost stress, should oscillate between acknowledging similarity with parallel movements and denying it.[8]

Hitler was often generous to Italian Fascism: 'When I read the history of Fascism, I feel as if I am reading the history of our movement', he told his entourage. To Mussolini he wrote: 'What separates us are only those racial characteristics, whose imprint is given us by blood and history and by the limits of vital space defined by geopolitics.' Mussolini too was gratified by 'the political, ideological and military solidarity which unite the two revolutions, the Fascist and the National Socialist, and the future of the two peoples'. Yet it is doubtful if he quite approved some of Hitler's emphases. In February 1943 Hitler wrote to him:

Quite irrespective of which emerged victorious, Western plutocracy or Eastern Bolshevism, International Jewry would triumph in the end and would spare no

[8] See Eugen Weber *Varieties of Fascism* (Princeton 1962) p. 141–3 for the artificial distinction cited at the beginning of the paragraph, and cf Bernt Hagtvet and Reinhard Kuhnl 'Contemporary Approaches to Fascism: A Survey of Paradigms' in Stein Ugelvik Larsen, Bernt Hagtvet, Jan Petter Myklebust eds. *Who Were the Fascists? Social Roots of European Fascism* (Bergen 1980) p. 26–51. For Göring's remark see Douglas M. Kelley *22 Cells in Nuremberg* (1947) p. 53. For Rosenberg see Joachim C. Fest *The Face of the Third Reich* (1970) p. 163–5 and Kelley *22 Cells in Nuremberg* p. 38–9, 42.

effort to extirpate our races, especially their elite. European culture would be doomed to destruction and ultimate annihilation.

Somehow Mussolini never quite managed to think in these cataclysmic terms: his was a much smaller vision. As Goebbels noted:

> One might almost say that Fascism has reacted upon the creative life of the Italian people rather like sterilization. It is, after all, nothing like National Socialism. While the latter goes deep down to the roots, Fascism is only superficial.

Developing the distinction made by Ferdinand Tönnies between *Gemeinschaft* and *Gesellschaft*, Otto Ohlendorf, the leading Nazi expert on Italian Fascism, argued:

> National Socialism and Fascism were totally opposed to each other ... Fascism began by deifying the state and refusing to recognize those human communities which were based on nature; but National Socialism itself was based on those natural communities and on the men who belonged to them ... [one] has only to look at the Germanic community or at the feudal state with its mutual obligations to realize that the totalitarian state is un-Germanic.

Mussolini's associates, on the other hand, 'consider that National Socialism is a poor imitation of Fascism, based on a misunderstanding'.[9]

Nazism's emphasis on racial community – and also, though to a lesser extent, Fascism's emphasis on the State – explains what would otherwise be one of the greatest paradoxes of the Nazi-Fascist phenomenon: its fratricidal tendency. There were, from first to last, five complete, genuine, autonomous, ideologically self-conscious Nazi or Fascist regimes in Europe. That in Austria, weakened almost at its commencement by a German-inspired *Putsch*, was

---

[9] H.R. Trevor Roper ed. *Hitler's Table Talk, 1941–1944* (1953) p. 614 5 Aug. 1942; Deakin *Brutal Friendship* p. 39, quoting Hitler to Mussolini 21 Oct. 1942; *Opera omnia di Benito Mussolini* (35 vols Florence 1951–62) vol. 29 p. 230 order of the day adopted by 181st meeting of the Fascist Grand Council 4 Feb. 1939; Deakin *Brutal Friendship* p. 183 quoting Hitler to Mussolini Feb. 1943; Louis P. Lochner ed. *The Goebbels Diaries (1942–3)* (1948) p. 35, 6 Feb. 1942; Felix Kersten *The Kersten Memoirs, 1940–1945* (1956) p. 207, quoting conversation with Ohlendorf 29 Aug. 1943, cf. Ferdinand Tönnies *Gemeinschaft und Gesellschaft: Abhandlung des Communismus und des Socialismus als empirische Culturformen* (Leipzig 1887). After completing his doctorate Ohlendorf had spent a year in Italy studying Fascism. He objected to the lack of restriction on Mussolini's dictatorial power in Italy; on the other hand he confessed after the war, 'I don't believe Hitler wanted a dictatorship'. Himmler used to tear up Ohlendorf's reports personally: see *Trials of War Criminals before the Nuernberg Military Tribunals under Control Council Law No. 10* [i.e. American prosecutions of industrial, administrative and military leaders etc.] (15 vols Washington 1950) vol. 4 p. 224, 233, 282 and Heinz Höhne *The Order of the Death's Head: The Story of Hitler's S.S.* (1969) p. 234–7, 422–4; the insistence on the racial community rather than the state as the focus for nationalism was also central to the ideology of the Rumanian Iron Guard cf Klaus Charlé *Die Eiserne Garde: der Volkischen Erneuerungsbewegung in Rumänien* (Berlin 1939) p. 77, 81; for National Socialism as a poor imitation of Fascism see *Kersten Memoirs* p. 157, quoting Ciano 12 Dec. 1940.

overthrown at the orders of Hitler in 1938; that in Rumania lasted only a few months before Hitler connived and cooperated in its replacement by a more traditional military dictatorship; that in Greece was conquered and suppressed by a military coalition of Italy and Germany in 1941.

There were also in this period nine ultra-conservative ultra-nationalistic regimes based ultimately on the power and prestige of the armed forces: Poland, Bulgaria, Hungary, Spain, Rumania (both before and after the short-lived *Gardă de Fier* regime), Lithuania, Latvia and Estonia (these three till the Soviet take-over in the summer of 1940), and Vichy France. There was also a transitional type, Portugal; Salazar's New Order had much in common with the Clerico-Fascism of the Dollfuss-Schuschnigg regime in Austria from 1934 to 1938, and its ultimate origins lay in the military dictatorships of the 1920s, but the fact is that Salazar depended on mass-politicization or military support far less in the 1930s and 1940s than any other dictator, and tended to give a totalitarian emphasis to conventions and traditions of a type which Mussolini, for example, pretended to repudiate:

The Constitution . . . begins by establishing morals and justice as being outside the limits of its power . . .

We are the sons and agents of a thousand-year old civilization which has come . . . from the shaping of men by the dominance of the spirit over matter, by the dominance of reason over the instincts.[10]

Even in the Salazar regime the nominal Head of State till 1951 was a general, Oscar Carmona, who had perhaps a more than nominal role in securing the acquiescence of the armed forces, and the difficulty of a too mechanistic distinction between the different types of rightist dictatorship is indicated by the fact that Ion Antonescu headed both the fascistic *Gardă de Fier* (Iron Guard) dictatorship established in Rumania in the autumn of 1940 and the military regime with which he replaced it; a comparable transformational process had been earlier apparent under Schuschnigg in Austria. Nevertheless the traditional-style dictatorships exhibited a common pattern in that the mobilizing of mass-support was avoided and even, as in Spain and Rumania and to some extent in Estonia, confronted as a threat to political stability. Similarly in Vichy France Pétain consistently resisted the influence of right-wing populists like Doriot and Déat. Yet in all of the traditional-style military or crypto-military dictatorships the

---

[10] The two quotations are from Antonio de Oliveira Salazar *Doctrine and Action: Internal and Foreign Policy of the New Portugal, 1928–1939* (1939) p. 231, address 26 May 1934, and Antonio de Oliveria Salazar *Discursos e notos políticas, 1928–1943* (3 vols Coimbra 1959–64) vol. 2 p. 178, 14 Aug. 1936. Neil Bruce *Portugal: The Last Empire* (Newton Abbot 1975) p. 30–33, 36–8 emphasizes the army's support of Salazar, but though General Oscar Carmona, as president, had the power to appoint and dismiss the premier there is little evidence of the military having any significant influence on Salazar's regime, though cf. next paragraph in text. Marc Ferro *Pétain* (Paris 1987) p. 215–217 argues that of all contemporary regimes it was Salazar's which had the most influence with Pétain.

notion of ethnic community was of first importance, going in most cases to the lengths of racial persecution at home and irredentist foreign policy abroad; in fact two of the complete Fascist dictatorships (and Salazar's) were far less racially orientated than the ultra-conservative militaristic regimes; in the case of Italy for example the penal legislation against Jews, when eventually introduced a decade and a half after the establishment of the regime, failed to elicit significant rank-and-file support. Clearly the emergence of the Fascist regimes must be seen in the context of the ultra-conservative regimes where mass-mobilization, the defining characteristic of Fascism, did not occur, for these ultra-conservative regimes were in other respects clearly responding to a similar social and political challenge.[11]

The anti-semitism and anti-bolshevism of the Polish military *junta* no more preserved it from Nazi aggression in 1939 than did the Fascism of the Austrian dictatorship in 1934 and 1938, or the Greek dictatorship in 1941. In National Socialism-Fascism ideology took second place to *Realpolitik*. Perhaps Hitler's most startling piece of pragmatism was the August 1939 Non-Aggression Pact with the Soviet Union, which left even Mussolini staggered: to Hitler he wrote bitterly some months later:

> Voi non potete abbandonare la bandiera antisemita e antibolscevica che avete fatto sventolare per 20 anni e per la quale tanti vostri camerati sono morti: – You cannot abandon the banner of anti-semitism and anti-bolshevism which you have held aloft for twenty years and for which so many of your comrades have died: you cannot go back on your gospel in which the German people have blindly believed . . . Up till four months ago Russia was world enemy no. 1: it cannot have become and is not friend no. 1. All this has deeply disturbed the Fascists in Italy and perhaps also many Nazis in Germany.

But Hitler simply was not interested in the opinions of foreign rightists; for him international Fascism was as much a danger as an opportunity. 'I am firmly opposed to any attempt to export National Socialism', he said in 1942. 'If other countries are determined to preserve their democratic systems and thus rush to their ruin, so much the better for us.' On another occasion he said, 'it was a mistake to export ideas such as National Socialism. To do so

---

[11] Much the best documented of these rightist regimes seem to be France and Hungary: for the former see Robert Aron *Histoire de Vichy* (Paris 1954), Robert O. Paxton *Vichy France: Old Guard and New Order, 1940–1944* (1972), Raymond Tournoux *Pétain et la France: La Seconde Guerre Mondiale* (Paris 1980) and Philippe Pétain *Actes et Écrites* ed. Jacques Isorni, (Paris 1974) espec. p. 470–478; and for the latter, C.A. Macartney *October Fifteenth: A History of Modern Hungary, 1929–1945* (2 vols Edinburgh 1961) and Andrew C. Janos *The Politics of Backwardness in Hungary, 1825–1945* (Princeton 1982) p. 238–312. Also suggestive is Leonas Sabaliūnas *Lithuania in Crisis: Nationalism to Communism, 1939–1940* (Bloomington 1972). The difficulty of characterizing the Austrian regime, especially under the feeble Schuschnigg, is discussed in John Rath and Carolyn W. Schum 'The Dollfuss-Schuschnigg Regime: Fascist or Authoritarian?' in Larsen et al. eds. *Who Were the Fascists?* p. 249–256.

I omit the dictatorships of Ante Pavelić in Croatia and Josef Tiso in Slovakia because they were able to instal themselves in power only with the help and permission of the Germans.

would only lead to a strenghtening of nationalism in other countries . . . and thus to a weakening of his own position'.[12]

Mussolini had originally been of the same opinion, saying, 'Fascism is not merchandise for export', but in 1933 and 1934, in a bid for prestige abroad, he had turned towards Fascist Internationalism. Sir Oswald Mosley's British Union of Fascists began to receive subsidies (eventually totalling over £100,000 in bundles of used notes of various currencies) and the Montreux Conference, organized under Mussolini's auspices, had delegates from thirteen countries, though it was boycotted by Germany. Internationalist fantasies were also a weakness of the Dutch National Socialist leader Anton Mussert: he wanted a Groot-Nederlandsch Staat to include the Flemings (the Walloons could go and join up with the French) and a great colonial empire (the Belgian Congo clearly belonged much more to the Flemings that the Walloons), but he also thought in terms of a Germanic League consisting of Germany, the Netherlands, Scandinavia and England, headed by Hitler not as *Reichskanzler* but as League President and Germanic *Führer*, and with the Dutch having a key role as bridge between the English and the Germans. These dreams show of course the concessions to power realities which Dutchmen and other citizens of small states always accepted and Germans did not: but they also show a commitment to the idea that both race and racist ideology could transcend existing national and linguistic boundaries.[13]

Even Hitler's associates were often too immersed in Nazi doctrine to perceive the virtues of opportunitism. During the four days of civil war in Bucharest in January 1941 the German military, at Hitler's orders, cooperated with Antonescu's military putschists while local Nazi functionaries, not important enough to have received instructions from Berlin, backed the *Gardă de Fier* (Iron Guard). The German minister at Bucharest had referred contemptuously in November to 'the anarchists and experimenters of the Guard' and informed his colleagues in the foreign ministry in Berlin:

My main pedagogical task consists in making it clear to the Guardists that there is no place in the new Europe for an isolated revolutionary laboratory and that the Guard will be working in a vacuum unless it finds its way to the nascent German Reich and recognizes the law of development of the new Europe.

One might have thought this a fair presentation of Hitler's attitude; but Goebbels complained after Antonescu had ousted his Guardist subordinates that the marshal was 'a tool of the freemasons' and later noted, 'The generals and the freemasons rule. Quiet as a graveyard. The ideal state so far as our

---

[12] Adolf Hitler and Benito Mussolini *Lettere e documenti* Milan 1946 p. 37–8 for Mussolini's letter of 3 Jan. 1940; *Hitler's Table Talk* p. 490, 20 May 1942; Albert Speer *Inside the Third Reich* (1970) p. 122.

[13] Michael Arthur Ledeen *Universal Fascism: The Theory and Practice of the Fascist International, 1928–1936* (New York 1972) p. 104–5; Nicholas Mosley *Beyond the Pale: Sir Oswald Mosley and Family, 1933–1980* p. 30–32; Ledeen *Universal Fascism* p. 114–5; Rijksinstituut voor Oorlogsdocumentatie *Het Proces Mussert* (Hague 1948) p. 139–140.

diplomats are concerned, for they have always preferred political sterility.'
Hitler on the other hand was pleased with the success of Antonescu's *Putsch*
and later remarked: 'Of all our allies, it is Antonescu who has the greatest
breadth of vision. He is a man of real personality.' According to Hitler's
interpreter, Antonescu was 'the only foreigner from whom Hitler ever asked
for military advice when he was in difficulties . . . antibolshevik and anti-
slav to the marrow. . . .' It seems that Hitler was not even perturbed by
the militant Christian orientation of the Antonescu regime; the Rumanian
vice-president of the council claimed for example that Rumania's soldiers
were 'fighting on the cursed plains of Russia for the Cross'; but after the
massacre of hundreds of Jews by the Rumanian police at Jassy during the
night of 28–29 June 1941 the Nazis were evidently willing to accept that
organized Christianity in Rumania was very different from what it was in
Germany; in any case the cross seemed to serve a distinctly secular symbolic
function on the Eastern Front, being used in various forms and colours as
the identification markings of all the aircraft of the anti-Soviet coalition.
Meanwhile Horia Sima, the defeated and ousted Iron Guard leader, under
sentence of death in Rumania, was given refuge in Germany, his followers
enjoying semi-privileged status as detainees at Buchenwald and Dachau; when,
finally and inevitably, Antonescu let Hitler down in the late summer of 1944,
Horia Sima was brought out of cold-storage to head a short-lived puppet
government.[14]

The summer of 1944 also saw the installation in Budapest, with German
backing, of a regime headed by Ferenc Szálasi of the Nazi-style *Nyilaskeresztes
Párt* or Arrow-Cross Party. The previous regime, headed by Admiral Miklós
Horthy had been regarded by the Nazis as much the most feudal and

---

[14] *Documents on German Foreign Policy* series D vol. XI p. 628–9, Neubacher to Clodius
19 Nov. 1940 (Höhne *Order of the Death's Head* p. 290–291 attributes the unofficial German
support for Horia Sima to the emissaries of Reinhard Heydrich of the S.S.); Fred Taylor ed.
The Goebbels Diaries, 1939–1941 (1982) p. 232, 13 Feb. 1941 and p. 256, 6 March 1941; *Hitler's
Table Talk* p. 694, 6 Sept. 1942; Paul Schmidt *Hitler's Interpreter* (1950) p. 206; Mihai A.
Antonescu *Warum wir Kämpfen* (Bucharest 1942) p. 9; Martin Gilbert *Final Journey: The Fate
of the Jews in Nazi Europe* (1979) p. 44–6 and cf the account in Curzio Malaparte *Kaputt*
(1960 edit.) p. 77–103; Andreas Hillgruber *Hitler, König Carol und Marschall Antonescu: die
Deutsch-Rumänischen Beziehungen, 1938–1944* (Wiesbaden 1954) p. 227.

With regard to the use of the cross symbol on the Eastern Front, the Italians, as well as the
triple *fasci* on the wings of their aircraft, had a white cross on their rudders; the Hungarians
a white cross on a black square on wings and fuselage, the Rumanians a yellow cross *fourché*
outlined in blue and with a red yellow and blue roundel at the centre, on wings and fuselage,
the Slovaks – three squadrons of Slovak Avia B-534 fighters served on the Kiev front in 1941
– used a blue cross with white outline very like the German cross though with a red disc at
the centre; the Croats had a stylised sycamore-leaf symbol in black on a white ground, also
very like the German cross at first glance; the Bulgarians (not actually at war with the Soviet
Union, only with the Western allies) used a black X on a white field; and the Finns retained
their pre-war aircraft markings of an upright blue swastika on a white field.

The most successful Hungarian fighter-pilot of the war, incidentally, was surnamed St. George
(Szentgyörgy – pronounced more or less as its English counterpart – Christian name Dezsö). He
was officially credited with destruction of 34 Soviet aircraft.

retrograde amongst their allied governments, but they had previously held aloof from Szálasi not merely because of doubts whether he had any significant mass-following but also because of a classic conflict of nationalist megalomanias: while Szálasi dreamt of a *Kárpát-Duna-Nagyhaza* (Carpatho-Danubian Great Homeland), the Nazi party's Hungarian experts planned to clear the Magyars from the Danube valley altogether. It was precisely *because* of the similarity of their policies that cooperation between the Nazis and the *Nyilaskeresztes Párt* could only be a temporary expedient.[15]

In retrospect it can be seen that Hitler's various dealings with non-Germans who held political views analagous to his own were only one element in a diplomacy of *Realpolitik*: the Pact of Steel with Italy was succeeded by the Molotov-Ribbentrop pact and the failure of Italy either to enter the war or to secure armaments from Germany; the Berlin-Rome-Tokyo Axis a year later was within a few months a dead letter because of Japan's refusing to attack the Soviet Union and attempting to do a deal with the U.S. Yet the Nazis' opportunism as regards collaboration with foreign rightists was not always recognized at the time, and the existence of a united National Socialist-Fascist front, hell-bent on international aggression, seemed to be undeniable from a relatively early stage.[16]

Perhaps the key evidence in any claim that there was ever a combined Nazi-Fascist strategy is provided by the Italo-German intervention in the Spanish Civil War in 1936. Since by October 1936 the Soviet Union was providing assistance on the other side it was inevitable that leftists were soon talking of a Fascist versus Socialist war, but it was not only leftists who took the view that Italo-German support for the Spanish Nationalist leader General Franco was simply the beginning of a long-term campaign: Basil Liddell Hart, in a memorandum prepared for the British Secretary of State for War in March 1938, stated uncompromisingly, 'The second Great War of the 20th Century began in July 1936 . . .' The question is whether the intervention was the beginning of a war of ideology or a war of *Realpolitik*.[17]

It must be remembered that in assisting Franco, Hitler was not assisting a Fascist revolution but a military coup against a radical government – an eventuality he may well have feared at home – and that he was placing himself alongside not merely the volunteers from Salazar's Portugal, the

[15] Macartney *October Fifteenth* vol. 1 p. 434–5 and 435 fn. 1, vol. 2 p. 195. In the 1939 Election the *Nyilaskeresztes Párt* had won 31 seats, being especially strong in the Budapest area, cf Miklós Lackó 'The Social Roots of Hungarian Fascism: The Arrow Cross Party' in Larsen et al eds. *Who Were the Fascists?* p. 395–400, at p. 398–9.

Like Baw Maw, Japan's puppet dictator in Burma, Szálasi was half-Armenian, which may paradoxically explain the ardour of his racialist ideology; similarly many of the apostles of *Germanentum*, not least Hitler himself, may have been compensating for deep-seated insecurity as to whether they themselves were altogether German.

[16] For the effective breakdown of the Berlin-Rome-Tokyo axis see Paul W. Schroeder *The Axis Alliance and Japanese American Relations 1941* (Ithaca 1958) p. 126–53.

[17] *The Memoirs of Captain Liddell Hart* (2 vols 1965) vol. 2 p. 142, memo 15 March 1938.

Italian Blackshirts, the handful of Irish Greenshirts, and the growing Falange movement within Spain itself, but also alongside Catholic Action, the Carlists, and old colonial hands who saw no objection to using African troops against Europeans – the latter something the Germans claimed to find morally reprehensible in both world wars. Significantly enough, when making his decision to assist Franco, Hitler seems to have consulted only Göring, the leading opportunist in the Nazi party, Blomberg, the minister of war, not a Nazi but a traditional German militarist, and possibly Canaris, the future anti-Nazi plotter. The chief benefit apparently expected from assisting Franco was the opportunity to increase imports of strategic raw materials from Spain. It also seems, from the astonishing rapidity with which the first German ground troops were despatched from Hamburg, that the German government expected that the military conspirators would establish their new regime within a short time; had it seemed from the start a question of sustaining Franco in a long and arduous crusade there would have been good reason to spend more time in preliminary preparations, and had it seemed a question of hastening to rescue Franco from the consequences of his own rashness, Hitler probably would not have bothered. The speed with which German assistance arrived suggests more than anything else an eagerness to earn the gratitude of a potential trading partner who was on the point of winning anyway.[18]

Hitler's pragmatism worked the other way against the Fourth of August regime in Greece. General Ioannis Metaxas, King Constantine's close associate in the bitter years of the First World War, had come to power in 1936 without the backing either of the army or of a mass-movement, though with the support of Constantine's son, King George; the latter however confided to the British minister at Athens, 'There is only one real solution and that is that Greece should be taken over by your civil service and run as a colony'. The British minister may have agreed, for he was not at all impressed by Metaxas's dictatorship:

It has nothing behind it, it is merely the chance product of a local paralysis, whereas the genuine dictators have everything behind them and are the product of historical destiny. They are all firmly based on passionate 'ideologies' but the

---

[18] Peter Monteath 'Hitler and the Spanish Civil War: A Case Study of Nazi Foreign Policy' *Australian Journal of Politics and History* vol. 32 (1986) p. 428–442 at p. 434–6, basing argument on H. Abendroth *Mittelsmann zwischen Franco und Hitler: Johannes Bernhardt erinnert 1936* (Marktheidenfeld 1978) claims that Hitler saw Franco's position as essentially *in*secure and that the meeting with Blomberg and Göring – according to Monteath Canaris was not present – took place *after* Hitler had made up his mind to intervene; cf. Gerhard L. Weinberg *The Foreign Policies of Hitler's Germany: Diplomatic Revolution in Europe, 1933–36* (Chicago 1970) p. 288–91. It seems uncharacteristically quixotic of Hitler to risk giving assistance to someone who had been foolish enough to launch a coup without having sufficient resources to guarantee success. For Göring's emphasis on the economic benefits of intervention see Alfred Kube *Pour le Mérite und Hakenkreuz: Hermann Göring im Dritten Reich* (Munich 1986) p. 164–6, and cf. Glenn T. Harper *German Economic Policy in Spain During the Spanish Civil War, 1936–1939* (Hague 1967) p. 17–19.

theories that General Metaxas has been proclaiming are not a basis for action, they are merely adventitious drapery, and patchwork at that.

This is in fact less than just to Metaxas. Though his regime was established after those of Mussolini and Hitler (and of Salazar and Dollfuss) he had seen the totalitarian future within the matrix of the *ancien régime* long before Hitler and Mussolini, writing as early as 1917:

> The unit of energy today is the group ... For the individual to maintain his freedom and self-sufficiency within the group is perfection. Only German society was able to produce the group in a more perfect form than any other society. For this reason the victory of Germany is inevitable and necessary.

Once in power, Metaxas's pronouncements often had a Nazi rather than an Italian Fascist ring: 'The Government is not based upon a single governing party; it is based upon the whole of the Greek people', and 'We owe it therefore to revert backwards in order to discover ourselves'. But his attempts to establish a mass base for his regime, for example by making membership of the national youth movement EON compulsory, failed to generate popular enthusiasm: in the spring of 1939 Lord Lloyd, Chairman of the British Council, persuaded Metaxas to put the athletic training of EON in British hands, a counsel of despair if ever there was one. Like Salazar, moveover, Metaxas was inclined by natural temperament towards a low-profile, perhaps even self-effacing, public persona: although a general and as keen on goose-stepping parades as the other dictators, he normally wore a lounge suit, though he met the greatest crisis of his career, the Italian declaration of war on Greece in October 1940, wearing a dressing-gown and slippers. British diplomats, accustomed to judging men by their tailors, could perhaps be forgiven for their condescending estimate of his dictatorship.[19]

Metaxas considered that only Germany, Italy, Spain, Portugal and Greece were democracies and that the peculiarities of parliamentary procedure at Westminster were simply a device to enable British plutocrats to dominate a vast colonial empire. During the late 1930s German financial influence on Greece was increasing: already by 1937 Germany was taking 35 per cent of Greek exports and loans were made available to finance Greek purchases of German armaments. When the Second World War broke out Metaxas identified the struggle as one between dictatorship and capitalism

---

[19] John S. Koliopoulos *Greece and the British Connection, 1935–1941* (Oxford 1977) p. 8; Public Record Office FO 371/20390 f. 365 Sir Sidney Waterlow to Foreign Office 18 Dec. 1936; I. Metaxas *Το προσωπικο ἡμερολογιο (To prosopiko hemerologio)* ed. C. Christidis, P.M. Siphnaios, P. Vranas (4 vols Athens 1951–64) vol. 2 p. 452 quoted in George B. Leon *Greece and the Great Powers, 1914–1917* (Thessaloniki 1974) p. 70; John V. Kofas *Authoritarianism in Greece: The Metaxas Regime* (Boulder 1983) p. 59, 62; and see p. 52–97 generally for an account of Metaxas's government; Colin Forbes Adam *Life of Lord Lloyd* (1948) p. 291; see also [Lincoln MacVeagh] *Ambassador MacVeagh Reports: Greece, 1933–1947* ed. John O. Iatrides (Princeton 1980) p. 97–165 for the American ambassador's observations on the Metaxas regime.

masquerading behind a mask of pseudo-democracy, and he did not expect his own dictatorship to survive a German defeat. But he recognized that British command of the sea was an inescapable fact of life and had to be catered for: there was in any case no indication that Greece would benefit if British command of the sea was replaced by Italian. 'It is natural for maritime countries like ours to be friendly with Britain,' he noted in his diary '. . . the difference of regime does not count.' Accordingly, when war broke out, Metaxas 'at once made it clear' to the British minister of Athens 'not only that his sympathies were entirely with us, but that he knew that the interests, indeed the very existence of Greece as an independent state, were bound up with our victory'. Metaxas's real opinion was somewhat different, and less positive: 'If the Germans prevail we shall become their slaves. If the British prevail we shall become their slaves. If neither, Europe will collapse. It will collapse anyway.'[20]

Metaxas's somewhat disingenuous policy eventually assumed the appearance of heroic stature when, on 28 October 1940, without provocation, Mussolini launched the invasion of Greece for no better reason than that, in spite of its fascistic government, it looked like the easiest to conquer of all Italy's neighbours. On this occasion Metaxas assured the British minister that:

> he was determined to pursue the war, side by side with us, not only against Italy, but also against Germany, without whose defeat he recognized and declared that there could be no real peace.

Mussolini, in deciding to invade Greece, gave no attention at all to the ideological issue, and for his part, Hitler had not the least compunction in backing Mussolini. The Italian invasion of Greece – and its failure – was regrettable as a diversion and as offering opportunities to the British to establish themselves in the southern Balkans, but Hitler had no objection to promoting the overthrow of Greek Fascism.[21]

In fact one of the geographically most widely distributed ideas relating to a combined Fascist front may be seen as aimed *against* Germany. The fall of France in June 1940 was received with mixed feelings in Spain and Portugal. The French defeat was seen as proof that democracy, with 'its absurd myths, its raving delusions, its false idealisms', was a luxury no country could afford. 'A sorry advertisement for democracy, this war fought in its name and lost to demonstrate its incapacity to govern', sneered the Portuguese daily *O*

---

[20] H. Cliadakis 'Le régime de Metaxás et la deuxième guerre mondiale' *Révue d'Histoire de la Deuxième Guerre Mondiale* no. 107 (1977) p. 19–38 at p. 35; Kofas *Authoritarianism in Greece* p. 170–174, 179; Cliadakis 'Régime de Metaxas' p. 34–5; Koliopoulos *Greece and the British Connection* p. 132 fn. 2 quoting Metaxas *Το προσωπικο ἡμερολογιο* vol. 4 p. 467, 6 May 1940; Public Record Office FO 371/29839 f. 103 Sir Michael Palairet to Foreign Office 1 Feb. 1941; Koliopoulos *Greece and the British Connection* p. 132 fn 2 quoting Metaxas *Το προσωπικο ἡμερολογιο* vol. 4 p. 484, 14 July 1940 – I have altered Koliopoulos's English slightly.

[21] Public Record Office FO 371/29839 f. 103 Sir Michael Palairet to Foreign Office 1 Feb. 1941.

Comercio do Porto. But the French were neighbours and cousins, whereas Germany was outside the Latin family, and the turn of events raised the issue of 'Latinity', the common characteristics of the Latin peoples, their common inheritance of the traditions both of Rome and of Roman Catholicism, and pointed to 'the formidable task of Latin reconstruction and unification'. From Madrid the British ambassador reported the growing feeling in favour of 'a Latin bloc'; later the Spanish foreign minister Serrano Suñer met Mussolini to urge 'the necessity of a close Italo-Spanish understanding at the present moment as well as in the future in order when the moment came to face up to the encroachments of Germanism'. (Serrano Suñer's visit to Rome was even said to have been sponsored by Salazar.) In Bucharest, during the Iron Guard period, Spanish-Rumanian relations were discussed by the press in terms of a common hostility to Jews, freemasons and communists. In 1941 Renato Bova Scoppa, the Italian ambassador in Bucharest, canvassed the possibility of a 'Latin Axis', with Mihai Antonescu, the Rumanian vice-president of the council and foreign minister: it was to include Spain, Portugal and France. The Rumanians were inclined to take a more practical view: they held an isolated position in the far east of Europe; relations with Hungary remained strained; the Finns showed conspicuously little interest in Rumania's share in the great crusade against Bolshevism, and brushed aside any approaches regarding closer links; Germany was not only the most powerful, it was Rumania's *only* friend in eastern Europe. Any idea of a Latin bloc had necessarily to be subordinated to the collaboration with Germany:

> only the Alliance of Creeds and the Union of Germanity (*Germanentum*) with Latinity can still save Europe ... we must fight because our Latin mission alongside the Latin people of the continent must unite its exertions with the great civilizing mission of Germanity in the East.

No Latin bloc emerged; in any case the Germans would have vetoed it if it had ever developed beyond the stage of vague talk. Nevertheless the idea was there, and even if it was no more than a response to the claims of German racial mythology, it was the nearest thing to a truly internationalist idea amongst Germany's client states.[22]

[22] *Royal Institute of International Affairs Review of the Foreign Press* Series B no. 47 22 Aug. 1940 p. 5 quoting *Diário da Manhã* 22 June 1940; ibid. loc. cit. quoting *O Commercio do Porto* 23 June 1940; ibid. p. 6 quoting *Jornal do Porto* 4 July 1940; Samuel Hoare *Ambassador on Special Mission* (1946) p. 84 Hoare to Halifax 8 July 1940; Ramon Serrano Suñer *Entre les Pyrénées et Gibraltar: notes et réflexions sur la politique espagnole depuis 1936* (Geneva 1947) p. 275, referring to a conversation in the spring of 1942. For the story of Salazar's role behind the scenes see Public Record Office FO 371/31114/C 7784 and FO 371/31114/C8577 David Walker to Michael Stewart 19 August 1942; *Cuvântul* 22 Dec. 1940 p. 1 a–b, editorial by P.P. Panaitescu; Deakin *Brutal Friendship* p. 137, Blücher *Gesandter zwischen Diktatur und Demokratie* p. 241 – according to Mihai A. Antonescu *Im Dienste des Vaterlandes* (Bucharest 1942) p. 132 Rumania had since June 1941 played host to 62 German, 51 Italian, 22 Slovak, 14 Spanish, 6 Swiss and 2 Japanese journalists: and one from Finland. The Hungarian press apparently sent no journalists to Rumania at all. For 'the Alliance of Creeds' see Mihai A. Antonescu *Warum Wir Kämpfen* (Bucharest 1942) p. 25–6.

III. Isolated Ideologues

Of course there were individuals who were sufficiently taken in by the rhetoric – sometimes their own – to believe the war was one of ideology rather than of race and nationalism. Fascism in Italy and National Socialism in Germany had grown out of the internal crisis of those countries, and similar elements of crisis prevailed to a lesser or greater extent in nearly all other European states. In every country which the Germans overran, tensions and frustrations which had previously been underestimated became high-lighted. It was not simply a case of obscure Fascist vermin slithering out of the woodwork. In some instances leading figures in the political order which had been defeated now called for collaboration. In Belgium for example Hendrik de Man, president of the *Parti Ouvrier Belge* and former finance minister, told his fellow socialists:

> The war has led to the debacle of the parliamentary regime and of the capitalist plutocracy of the so-called democracies.
> For the working classes and for socialism, this collapse of a decrepit world is, far from a disaster, a deliverance . . .
> Prepare to enter into the ranks of a movement of national resurrection, which will include all the vital forces of the nation, its youth, its veterans, in a single party.

There is also a case for arguing that de Man's former opponents, the Belgian industrial magnates, attempted to use the German occupation of their country as a means of forcing ahead the modernization and rationalization of heavy industry, at the expense of the living standards of their workers, in a classic partnership of expediency between Big Business and Fascism. Contrary to the usual stereotype of patriotism, military defeat and occupation may even have encouraged new internationalist and ideological perspectives, channelling into new directions energies stimulated by the vast crisis of nationalisms which had Europe in its grip. The announcement, on the fourth day of the German invasion of the Soviet Union in June 1941, of 'The European Crusade against Bolshevism' was widely approved – though not by Mussolini, who tended to be six months either ahead or behind Hitler and on this occasion protested, 'It is false to speak of an anti-Bolshevik struggle. Hitler knows that Bolshevism has been non-existent for some time. No code protects private property like the Russian Civil Code'. The Nazis, still relative new-comers to power, probably sensed more clearly than Mussolini how many people there were in the conquered countries with old scores to settle, old hungers to assuage, new careers to make, or simply yearnings aroused by the subliminal message readable in the flickering hooked cross at the centre of the crimson Nazi flag which streamed triumphantly above so many city centres.[23]

---

[23] Peter Dodge ed. *A Documentary Study of Hendrick de Man: Socialist Critic of Marxism* (Princeton 1979) p. 327–8, reprinting de Man's manifesto to the *Parti Ouvrier Belge* published
continued

At the end of the war, in France, Belgium, the Netherlands, Denmark and Norway, over 160,000 collaborators received prison sentences, and 11,139 were condemned to death, over a thousand executions being carried out. Although the majority of the executions were in France, there were relatively fewer jailings in that country than elsewhere; fewer than one person in a thousand received prison or capital sentences, despite there having been no fewer than three Fascist groups – Marcel Déat's R.N.P. Jacques Doriot's P.P.F. and Joseph Darnand's *Milice* – which obtained significant popular support; whereas in Norway, where Quisling conspicuously failed to generate any grass-roots enthusiam, more than six people in every thousand received jail sentences. It seems therefore that if the incidence of punishment had been more equal as between countries the total figure for imprisonments and capital sentences could have reached one million.[24]

These prosecutions must take their place with the courtroom charades of Stalin's purges, the Riom trials in Vichy France, the Verona trials in Mussolini's *Repubblica Sociale Italiana*, the atrocious proceedings of the People's Court in Nazi Germany after the 20 July plot, and the International Military Tribunals at Nuremberg and at Tokyo, as defining the trial, the travesty trial, as one of the central and most sinister symbols of the 1930s and 1940s. The symbol can be read in more ways than one: ritual and repression, as also in the uniforms and the parades, but also an allegory of impossibly absolute commitment at a time of unprecedented confusion of values and moral principles.

Even in Britain there were minorities to be oppressed, minorities comprising individuals who placed doctrine before the official claims of their government; in view of the mockeries of injustice perpetrated elsewhere it was perhaps just as well that the British authorities preferred to proceed by bureaucratic fiat rather than by court-room drama. Nevertheless several members of the British Union of Fascists were prosecuted in the courts, including a violinist,

continued
in *Gazette de Charleroi* 3 July 1940. In 1917 de Man had travelled from Finland to Petrograd in the same railway compartment as Leon Trotsky and a brief, unfriendly, but oddly prophetic conversation took place, de Man asking, 'Do you recognize us?', and Trotsky replying, 'I do – although people change a lot in time of war': Leon Trotsky *My Life: An Attempt at an Autobiography* (Harmondsworth 1975) p. 297. For the proposed restructuring of Belgian industry see John Gillingham *Belgian Business in the Nazi New Order* (Ghent 1977) p. 27–31, 164–177 though cf. Gerhard Hirschfeld *Nazi Rule and Dutch Collaboration: The Netherlands under German Occupation, 1940–1945* (Oxford 1988) where it is argued that in the neighbouring Netherlands industrialists generally sought to maintain their distance from the Nazis; for Mussolini and the Soviet Civil Code see Malcolm Muggeridge ed. *Ciano's Diary 1939–1943* (1947) p. 365, 1 July 1941.

[24] Peter Novick *The Resistance versus Vichy: The Purge of Collaborators in Liberated France* (1968) p. 185–6 and p. 187 fn. 7, and cf. Bertram M. Gordon *Collaborationism in France during the Second World War* (Ithaca 1980) for an excellent account of the various cross-currents of French Fascism during the German occupation. Incidentally a local farmer who once gave me a lift during a visit to western Norway assured me that he had had a wonderful time as a boy during the German occupation: the social amenity of the remoter parts of rural Norway was evidently greatly improved by the presence of German troops.

who was sentenced to seven years imprisonment for posting up small stickers in telephone kiosks advertizing the wavelength of the German-based 'New British Broadcasting Service' and a farm labourer who received a fourteen year sentence for volunteering his services to the German minister in Dublin. A Plymouth dockyard worker who associated with the German-born wife of an R.A.F. sergeant under the impression she was an enemy agent also received fourteen years. During the war itself four Britons, including one from Gibraltar and one with German-born parents who had lived most of his life in France, were executed as spies, along with twelve foreigners; an Isle of Wight lodging-house landlady who was sentenced to death at Winchester Assizes late in 1940 was reprieved when it transpired that she had made up her confession, and her sentence was commuted to a mere fourteen years in prison. There were also eleven prosecutions for assisting the enemy, and no less than 385 for sabotage, though since all but 24 of the latter were dealt with by magistrates courts they were evidently not regarded as too serious or sinisterly motivated.[25]

Numerically more significant was the detention, from 23 May 1940 onwards, of 750 or so British fascists who were held without trial under Defence Regulation 18B, plus 102 persons with dual British-Italian nationality who were allegedly members of the *Partito Fascista Italiano*; amongst the latter was Celeste Sperni who, according to official opinion, 'has risen to his present position by a career of fraud and corrupt practice', a career which included being mayor of St. Pancras. Sir Oswald Mosley, leader of the British Union of Fascists, had proclaimed before his arrest:

> Every one of us would resist the foreign invader with all that is in us. However rotten the existing government, and however much we detested its policies, we would throw ourselves into the effort of a united nation until the foreigner was driven from our soil.

Indeed it was slightly odd that Mosley and the more prominent Blackshirts were denied the right to wear uniform like everyone else in wartime because they had insisted on wearing uniforms, of their own invention, in peace time. Even odder was the fact that the detainees included not only Church of England clergymen but people like John Mason, a Sheffield shop steward, who had been denounced for his leftist, not rightist, tendencies, and Graham Greene's cousin Benjamin Greene, a Quaker and pacifist who had been active in helping German refugees and who in 1924 had been Ramsay MacDonald's private secretary (though he was later involved in an insignificant radical right group, the British People's Party he continued to be a member of

[25] Nigel West *MI5: British Security Service Operations, 1909–1945* (1981) p. 120, 130–1; Cmd 7227 p. 22 and 25 (*Parliamentary Papers* 1946 – 7 XV p. 802 and 805). The sentencing to death of all five German prisoners of war who murdered a fellow prisoner at Comrie, Perthshire because he was anti-Nazi, was surely politically motivated; their execution at Pentonville was 'the first time in modern British penal history that five people have been hanged in one morning': B.D. Grew *Prison Governor* (1958) p. 123.

the Labour Party till after Munich). Although Maxwell Knight, the MI5 operative who framed Benjamin Greene, was dismissed from the Security Service at the end of the war and forced to make a new career as Uncle Max on B.B.C.'s Children's Hour, the detentions under Defence Regulation 18B were generally approved of. In November 1943, when there were still 355 fascists under detention, the release of Sir Oswald Mosley provoked more than twenty anti-Mosley rallies and a large demonstration, degenerating at times into a violent riot, in Trafalgar Square – *The Daily Mirror* claimed a crowd of 20,000 which from the photograph they published may well have been accurate; and nine days later 'men and women, described as delegates from war industries' – according to *The Daily Mirror*, 'several hundred war workers' – demonstrated against Mosley's release outside Parliament. The sacking of a worker who shouted, 'What about Mosley?', during the B.B.C.'s live broadcast of its 'Works Wonders' programme from a Vickers Armstrong factory seems however to have been accepted by the anti-fascist working-class movement as right and just.[26]

It is illuminating to compare developments in Britain with what happened in the White Dominions. In Australia and New Zealand, where organized Fascism was not a visible phenomenon, the governments assumed emergency powers similar to those of the British government, but in order to use them against the Left. In Australia nine communist periodicals were banned on 24 May 1940 and the Communist Party itself was declared an illegal organization on 15 June 1940. In New Zealand the communist *People's Voice* was suppressed but though the government also took the power to outlaw organizations it showed its more delicate sense of priorities by banning only the Jehovah's Witnesses. In South Africa the government had rather different problems. In September 1939 the Prime Minister of the Union of South Africa, General J.B.M. Hertzog, speaking in his native Afrikaans, told a restless House of Assembly in Capetown that he could see no case for a war against Adolf Hitler:

> I have carefully followed his actions step by step, and I have asked myself where is the proof that this man is out for world domination ... With what justification can one ask me and South Africa to take part in a war because Hitler and the German nation will no longer suffer this humiliation? ... We

---

[26] *Hansard: House of Commons* vol. 362 col. 581 reply by Sir John Anderson to question 27 June 1940; Public Record Office HO 45/25747 file captioned 'Defence Reg 18B – Prominent persons detained under'; Diana Mosley *A Life of Contrasts* (1977) p. 168 quoting article by her husband in *Action* 9 May 1940; *Daily Telegraph* 1 July 1940 p. 3b; Richard Croucher *Engineers at War* (1982) p. 92–3; Anthony Masters *The Man Who Was M: The Life of Maxwell Knight* (Oxford 1984) p. 142–5 and cf. questions in Parliament, *Hansard: House of Commons* vol. 377 col. 441, 904–5, 1225–7, 1575–6, 22 and 29 Jan, 5 and 12 Feb. 1942, and a note in *New Statesman* 24 Jan 1942 (vol. 23) p. 50 cf Richard Thurlow *Fascism in Britain: A History, 1918–1985* (Oxford 1987) p. 172; ibid. p. 231; *Times* 29 Nov. 1943 p. 2d, *Daily Mirror* 29 Nov 1943 front page lead story; *Times* 8 Dec. 1943 p. 2b and *Daily Mirror* 8 Dec 1943 p. 5; *Daily Mirror* 9 Dec. 1942 p. 1, 5.

are asked to plunge ourselves into that war. We have no right to do so, and if we do so the Afrikaans-speaking people outside will get such a shock that it will take them years and years to get over it.

He resigned, but not everybody was happy to be led into the war by his replacement General Smuts. Over 20,000 people attended anti-war rallies in various parts of the Transvaal on 29 June 1940, and on 31 January-1 February 1941 there were riots involving attacks by armed members of the ultra-right *Ossewa Brandwag* (Ox-wagon Fire Brigade) organization, aided by the police, on unarmed soldiers awaiting shipment to the battle zone in North Africa. By January 1942 hundreds of police had been arrested, some of them on treason charges; 58 *Stormjaers* (storm troopers) of the *Ossewa Brandwag* were also charged with treason, though in the event the main crown witnesses 'disappeared' before the trial. Although Oswald Pirow, who had become an open convert to Nazism while serving as South Africa's Minister of Defence in the 1930s, was left at large, hundreds of *Ossewa Brandwag* members were interned, including B.J. Vorster, the future premier, who went on hunger strike. Although carrying out numerous acts of sabotage, the *Ossewa Brandwag* was much more than a Boer resistance to South Africa's involvement in Britain's imperial war; in a booklet published in Johannesburg in 1943 J.F.J. van Rensburg, leader of the *Ossewa Brandwag*, denounced the perniciously divisive party system – *die volksverdelende parlementêre stelsel van partye* – and called for an anti-capitalist republic in which political parties would be replaced by the 'union of the [Boer] People in an all-inclusive People's Front (*die eenheidsorganisasie van die Volk in n'allesomvattende Volksbeweging*)'. Premier Smuts was unable to take measures to suppress Boer nationalist extremists for fear of totally alienating organized Boer opinion, even within his own party, and in 1945, when the process of denazifying Germany began, numerous persons in South Africa holding Nazi-type views were released from detention, to be welcomed home by their neighbours as honourable victims of the world Jewish plot.[27]

Amongst the executions carried out in Europe at the end of the war was that of John Amery, at Wandsworth on 20 December 1945. The son of Leopold Amery, the Secretary of State for India in Churchill's wartime government, John Amery had tried to recruit a British SS Regiment from amongst the prisoners of war in German P.O.W. camps. A tract which Amery wrote in 1943 entitled *England Faces Europe* was a fairly routine piece of fascist

---

[27] Paul Hasluck *The Government and the People, 1939–1941* (vol. 1 of Series 4 of [Official History] *Australia in the War of 1939–1945*) (Canberra 1952) p. 589; F.L.W. Wood *The New Zealand People at War: Political and External Affairs* (*Official History of New Zealand in the Second World War, 1939–45*) (Wellington 1958) p. 154; *Die Transvaler* 29 June 1940, front page lead story; *Union of South Africa: Debates of the House of Assembly* vol. 36 col. 21–3, speech by General Hertzog 4 Sept. 1939; Brian Bunting *The Rise of the South African Reich* (1969) p. 93–8; J.F.J. van Rensburg *Die Vooraand van ons Volkseie Sosialisme* (Johannesburg [1943]) p. 23–4.

paranoia about Jews and plutocrats and conspiracies and 'anti-national persons that at present exerce [sic] their control and dictatorship over Englishmen and British destinies'. In his preface Amery described himself as 'Neither Fascist or [sic] Socialist but just *English*' and the short bibliography he appended included – besides Gibbon's *Decline and Fall of the Roman Empire*, T.E. Lawrence's *Seven Pillars of Wisdom* and Louis Céline's *L'École des Cadavres* – a collection of his father's speeches published in 1928 under the title *The Empire in the New Era*. John Amery's patent crime in attempting to assist the King's enemies turned out to be useful in distracting attention from the views he shared with some of the King's ministers.[28]

IV. Right against Right in Britain

Besides those prosecuted or interned there were numerous Britons who contributed patriotically to their country's war effort while expressing political views that might have seemed more consistent with working for the other side. Even in a supposedly ideological war it was perhaps inevitable that the political views of admirals and generals would be out of step with most other people's; although one former head of Naval Intelligence and of the War College was detained under Defence Regulation 18B, Labour Party ministers had to put up with the Vice-Chief of Naval Staff – allegedly 'the best brain in the navy' – ranting on about Franco as 'the only man who, in modern times, has been able to make Spain strong'; and the Commander-in-Chief, Middle East, could advise the Chiefs of Staff, on the subject of political warfare in Italy, 'We should *not* criticise unreservedly the Fascist regime, which has many tangible and material achievements to its account'. Lower down in the military hierarchy, Lieutenant-Colonel W.P. Scott, who was in charge of German and Italian internees being deported to Australia aboard the S.S. *Dunera* and who was later court-martialled for his part in their scandalous ill-treatment, found the Jewish refugees amongst the internees to be 'subversive liars, demanding and arrogant ... They will quote any person from a Prime Minister to the President of the United States as personal references, and they are definitely not to be trusted in word or deed', whereas the Nazi-party members were 'a fine type, honest and straightforward, and extremely well-disciplined'. Amongst the rank and file of the British Army the Army Education Corps found that a not uncommon reply given to recruits to the question why one was fighting was, 'I am fighting because Jewish international financiers wanted a war'. This may also have been the opinion of Sir Oswald Mosley's brother-in-law, a pro-Nazi since his student days in Berlin in the 1920s: he requested a transfer

[28] There is a photostat of the original typescript of John Amery's *England Faces Europe*, produced *circa* 1945, in the British Library; the quotation about 'anti-national persons' is from chap. 3 p. 44.

to the Far East, rather than take part in the invasion of Germany, and died in Burma.[29]

Sometimes it seemed that the traditional solidarity of the British ruling classes outweighed any other consideration; shortly after being released from detention under Defence Regulation 18B the anti-Imperialist and British People's Party activist Harry St. John Philby lunched with Colonel Valentine Vivian, assistant Head and Director of Security at MI6, in order to clinch the appointment to the Intelligence Service of his son Kim, already a Soviet agent; when Vivian raised the question of Philby Junior's left-wing views while at Cambridge Philby Senior quickly reassured him: 'all schoolboy nonsense'. Later Victor Cavendish-Bentinck, chairman of the Joint Intelligence Committee, detected that something was not quite right about Philby Junior:

> I recollect saying as he left the room: 'That's a queer fish. What's his background?' I received the answer, 'He's old St. John Philby's son', to which I said: 'I suppose that accounts for it', and moved on to the next item.

Due allowance must also be made for the famous British tradition of tolerating upper-class eccentricity; for example, Randolph Churchill, the cherished only son of the Prime Minister, 'talks of world domination as the greatest ideal and says he admires the Germans for desiring it'.[30]

Of course Winston Churchill can no more be blamed for Randolph's ravings than Leo Amery can be blamed for *his* son's attempt to raise an SS regiment, but he himself had once professed himself an admirer of *Il Duce*. Intially he had been disturbed by Mussolini's coarse extremism – 'What a swine this Mussolini is. I see Rothermere is supporting him!' Then in 1927 Churchill had travelled to Rome, though only partly 'to see Mussolini (while he lasts)'. When

[29] The former head of Naval Intelligence and of the War College who was interned was Admiral Sir Barry Domville; on the other hand Major-General J.F.C. Fuller, a prominent Mosleyite, was not arrested, allegedly because 'He knows too much': Diana Mosley *A Life of Contrasts* (1977) p. 172. The brilliance of the V.C.N.S., Sir Tom Phillips is noted in John Colville *The Fringes of Power: Downing Street Diaries, 1939–1955* (1985) p. 134, 18 May 1940 and the example quoted of it is in Ben Pimlott ed. *The Second World War Diary of Hugh Dalton, 1940–45* (1986) p. 43, 19 June 1940; J.R.M. Butler, John Ehrman, N.H. Gibbs, J.M.A. Gwyer, Michael Howard *Grand Strategy* (6 vols 1956–76) vol. 4 p. 456 for memo by General Sir Henry Wilson 14 May 1943 on political warfare in Italy and the achievements of Fascism: this may be an instance of Wilson's disconcerting communications on political problems which Harold Macmillan refers to in his *War Diaries: Politics and War in the Mediterranean, January 1943 – May 1945* (1984) p. 425, 19 April 1944: 'In fact, the old boy just signs the telegrams which are written by his rather strange personal entourage – his son, General Davy [Wilson's D.M.O.], Lady Ranfurly and Lady Ranfurly's sister.' For Lieutenant-Colonel Scott see Peter and Leni Gillman *'Collar the Lot!' How Britain Interned and Expelled its Wartime Refugees* (1980) p. 254; for the Jewish international financiers see James Lansdale Hodson *Home Front* (1944) p. 303, 23 Feb. 1943; Mosley *Life of Contrasts* p. 206.

[30] Andrew Boyle *The Climate of Treason: Five who Spied for Russia* (1979) p. 220; Patrick Howarth *Intelligence Chief Extraordinary: The Life of the Ninth Duke of Portland* (1986) p. 163; Colville *Fringes of Power* p. 265, 13 Oct. 1940. In July 1939 Philby Senior had been the British People's Party candidate in the Hythe by-election, cf. Thurlow *Fascism in Britain* p. 180.

he met the Italian dictator he was evidently impressed, for afterwards he told a press conference:

> It is perfectly absurd to suggest that the Italian Government does not rest upon a popular basis, or that it is not upheld by the active and practical assent of the great masses . . .
>
> If I had been an Italian, I am sure I should have been whole-heartedly with you from the start to finish in your triumphant struggle against the bestial appetites and passions of Leninism. But in England we have not yet had to face this danger in the same deadly form. We have our own way of doing things. But that we shall succeed in grappling with Communism and choking the life out of it – of that I am sure.

Leo Amery, who had first encountered Mussolini at a Downing Street dinner and 'made good friends over the Macugnaga', also visited Rome and found Mussolini 'quiet, humorous, wise and very attractive'.[31]

It is interesting to see what Leo Amery and Winston Churchill made of the most publicized of the wartime statements of principle, the Atlantic Charter of August 1941. To the Viceroy of India Amery described the Charter as 'several useful points of substance, much meaningless platitude and some dangerous ambiguities'. The third clause about the right of 'all people to choose the form of government under which they will live' was paraphrased by Amery as 'no desire to democratize those who prefer other forms of constitution – this has greatly cheered Brazil, Portugal'. He went on to explain:

> The point was, after all, inserted primarily as reassurance that we are not out to democratise countries that prefer a different form of government. If Italy prefers, after we have got rid of Mussolini, to retain the corporative and functional basis of government, there is no reason why she should not so do, and Point Three has already given substantial comfort to Salazar in Portugal and friendly dictators elsewhere.

Meeting Salazar had indeed convinced Amery's fellow Tory, Sir Samuel Hoare, formerly Secretary of State for Air, India, Foreign Affairs, Home Affairs etc., of the 'unsuitability of the British parliamentary system for most continental countries' and the same opinion was expressed more forcibly in the House of Commons by the M.P. for Basingstoke:

> I have always upheld our particular form of democracy in this country, constitutional monarchy, and I have always believed in it, but I have never

---

[31] Martin Gilbert *Winston S. Churchill* (8 vols 1966–88) vol. 5 companion vol. * p. 60 W. Churchill to Clementine Churchill 5 Sept; 1923; ibid. vol. 5 p. 222; ibid. vol. 5 p. 226, and cf Robert Rhodes James ed. *Winston S. Churchill: His Complete Speeches, 1897–1963* (8 vols New York 1974) vol. 4 p. 4126 speech at Rome 20 Jan. 1927, John Barnes and David Nicholson ed. *The Leo Amery Diaries* (2 vols 1980–88) vol. 1 p. 311, 9 Dec. 1922 and p. 409, 27 April 1925. Macugnaga is a small, rocky commune in the Italian Alps, now a winter sports centre; the sort of place which produces mineral water, but Amery seems to be referring to some other sort of beverage.

expressed the belief that democracy in a Latin country has ever been other than corrupt and incompetent.

It was not simply that many of the British leaders had no sympathy with John Stuart Mill notions of democracy as the most moral and efficient system of government; they had lost faith in the concept even as a political slogan. In December 1940 Sir Alexander Cadogan, the Permanent Under Secretary of State at the Foreign Office, had warned Lord Halifax of the need to be cautious in stating war aims:

> Difficulty that I see is that to proclaim 'democracy' and 'liberty' enables the enemy to say that we stand for the 'Front Populaire' and the 'Red' government in Spain. And millions of people in Europe (I would not exclude myself) think that these things are awful.

There was also the colonial aspect, and the War Cabinet decided:

> The Charter was directed to the nations of Europe whom we hoped to free from German tyranny; it was not intended to deal with the internal affairs of the British Empire or the relations, for example, between the United States and the Philippines.

Or as Churchill expressed it more succinctly to Amery, it was not intended 'that the natives of Nigeria or of East Africa could by a majority vote choose the form of Government under which they live'.[32]

Nor did Churchill intend to let the Indians run their own affairs, and even Amery found Churchill's resistance to the Indian independence movement short-sighted: he thought Churchill had a 'complex against anything that looks like letting Indians have their own way' and 'as regards India has never got beyond the early Kipling stage'. Despite Lloyd George's conviction that the half-American Churchill had negro blood ('Look at his build and slouch . . . when he gets excited he shrieks: again the nigger comes out'), the latter was instinctively racist as far as coloured people were concerned. When Viscount Cranborne complained to the Cabinet that a black official at the Colonial Office had been forced to discontinue lunching at a certain restaurant because it was now patronized by U.S. officers, Churchill promptly responded, 'That's all right: if he takes a banjo with him, they'll think he's one of the band'. Perhaps Churchill's doctor had the explanation when he wrote, 'it is when he talks of India or China that you remember he is a Victorian'. But Churchill's High Victorianism also had its positive side: at least he exhibited none of the

[32] India Office Library Mss Eur F 125/10 vol. 6. of printed series p. 150–151 L.S. Amery to Marquis of Linlithgow 18–20 Aug. 1941; Hoare *Ambassador on Special Mission* p. 125; *Hansard: House of Commons* vol. 374 col. 1712 speech of Squadron Leader Patrick Donner, M.P. for Basingstoke 21 Oct. 1941; *Diaries of Sir Alexander Cadogan* p. 338, 4 Dec. 1940; Llewelyn Woodward *British Foreign Policy in the Second World War* (5 vols 1970–76) vol. 2 p. 207 (Woodward's paraphrase). Churchill said more or less the same, less succinctly, in the House of Commons 9 Sept. 1941 *Hansard: House of Commons* vol. 374 col. 68–9; Gilbert *Winston S. Churchill* vol. 6 p. 1163 Churchill to Amery 20 Aug. 1941.

cheap anti-semitism which had infected the professional classes in Britain as in other parts of western Europe from the late nineteenth century onwards.[33]

The 'extreme Zionism of the Prime Minister' with regard to the question of Jewish settlement in Palestine was commented on by Whitehall officials and was encouraged by one of Churchill's most valued associates, the South African premier Jan Christian Smuts. In July 1943 for example Smuts telegraphed:

> If we continue to forget or ignore Jewish claims we shall fail in our larger efforts on behalf of a fair and just general settlement at the end of this war.
>
> Jewish weakness should not make us forget moral strength of their case which goes to the root of the whole issue in this war. If we fail the Jews it means Hitler's triumph in the fundamental item of his satanic creed.

Yet in this area Churchill came up against the prejudices of the officials through whom he was obliged to work. The anti-semitism of the administration in Palestine was roundly denounced in Parliament by a former minister, and Churchill himself wrote to the Colonial Secretary:

> It may be necessary to make an example of these anti-Semite officers and others in high places. If three or four were recalled and dismissed, and the reason given, it would have a very salutary effect.

At home officials of the Foreign Office sneered at the open anti-semitism of their opposite numbers in the Colonial Office:

> One has, in dealing with matter emanating from the Middle Eastern Department of the Colonial Office, to take account of Mr. Downie's inward and spiritual conviction that illegal immigration [of Jews into Palestine] is only the outward and visible sign of a worldwide Jewish scheme to overthrow the British Empire. It is only if one realises that he regards the Jews as no less our enemies than the Germans that certain features of this draft [policy statement] become explicable.

Yet the first reports from Europe that the Jews were being systematically exterminated were explained away by the Foreign Office with a few dark hints at the unreliability of Jews as a source of information, and in September 1944, after the gas ovens at Auschwitz and Treblinka had completed the greater part of their programme of extermination, a Foreign Office official minuted, 'In my opinion a disproportionate amount of the time of the Office is wasted on dealing with these wailing Jews'. In another Foreign Office department a certain Dwight Chaplin was inspired to enliven an official file with rhyming couplets – the D-Day landings had taken place only three days previously and evidently there was still little pressure of business in his section, which was

[33] India Office Library Mss Eur F 125/10 vol. 6 p. 215 Amery to Linlithgow 25 Nov. 1941. Colin Cross ed; *Life with Lloyd George: The Diary of A.J. Sylvester, 1931–45* (1975) p. 77, 27 May 1932; *Diaries of Sir Alexander Cadogan* p. 483, 13 Oct. 1942; Lord Moran [C.M. Wilson] *Winston Churchill: The Struggle for Survival 1940–1965* (1966) p. 131, diary 24 Nov. 1943.

responsible for the post-war resettlement of Germany. The particular matter at issue was a letter from a Herr S. Sass, formerly managing director of a steel factory in the Rhineland, now a refugee in Columbia, but willing to return to Germany to collaborate with the British in reorganizing the German steel industry:

> From Africa's shore, from Colomb's sun-scorched strand
> Urgent there streams an eager Hebrew band. . . .
> Loose them like vultures on the German scene
> And hope they will not pick the carcass clean
> Or, worse, revert to type and aid the Hun
> To germanize the world with tank and gun?
> Prudence invites we leave them where they are
> And hitch our wagon not to David's star.

A minute by another, unidentifiable, official in the same file notes 'Discussed with Mr. Turner, who agrees with the policy so elegantly defined by Mr. Chaplin'.[34]

This kind of thing was obviously a long way away from the anti-semitic chain letters and the *Perish Judah* and *Kill the Jews* stickers which had proliferated on pillar boxes and in public urinals during the first months of the war, but scholarly research into the official response to information coming out of occupied Europe on the subject of the extermination of the Jews, and into the subsequent cursory and half-hearted attempts by the British occupation authorities to identify and bring to justice those who had actually carried out these and other enormities, reveals a depressing picture of the British official classes in action. In the same context one might mention the relentless maintenance by administrative organs up to the highest level of a policy of not enlisting or granting commissions in the British armed forces to coloured people, even after government had publicly stated there would be no colour discrimination. Indeed there is something in the note of sniggering smart aleckry in so many departmental documents dealing with contentious realities of this kind, something in the inevitableness with which any ministerial initiative which appeared wholesome and constructive was sterilized and diluted as it filtered down through the Whitehall departments, that makes one almost suspect that British officials would have continued functioning under monstrous dictatorships quite as placidly as their continental counterparts. But perhaps the unconcealed racism of subordinate officials is not so very

---

[34] Bernard Wasserstein *Britain and the Jews of Europe, 1939–1945* (1979) p. 33 quoting Lord Moyne to Sir Harold MacMichael 25 April 1942; Public Record Office CAB 95/14 p. 73 Smuts to War Cabinet July 1943; *Hansard: House of Lords* vol. 122 col. 210 speech by Lord Wedgwood 10 March 1942; Public Record Office PREM 4/51/9 f. 938 Churchill to Cranborne 5 July 1942; Public Record Office FO 371/27132 minute by R.T.E. Latham 22 April 1941; Martin Gilbert *Auschwitz and the Allies* (1981) p. 99. 150; ibid p. 312 quoting minute by A.R. Dew 1 Sept. 1944; Public Record Office FO 371/40816/U5266 minutes on letter from S. Sass dated 12 May 1944 cf Tom Bower *Blind Eye to Murder: Britain, America and the Purging of Nazi Germany – a Pledge Betrayed* (1981) p. 149–150.

surprising in view of the attitude towards foreigners betrayed by permanent heads of the Foreign Office such as Sir Robert Vansittart (head 1930–1938), whose considered view was that, '80 per cent of the German race are the moral and political scum of the earth ... they are a race of bone-headed aggressors', and his successor, Sir Alexander Cadogan, for whom the Italians were simply 'dirty ice-creamers'.[35]

Crude tribalism is perhaps not quite the same as racism; but both are equally a matter of unjust stereotypes. One finds that even the Ministry of Information, despite its complement of trendily progressive intellectuals, never succeeded in developing an intelligent line in anti-Nazi, as distinct from racist anti-German, propaganda. In part this was because of an understandable perplexity regarding the nature of the relationship between the German population and the Nazi Party, and the processes by which the latter had achieved and consolidated power: Nazism was clearly not something totally alien to German political sociology, to be accepted as an alibi for a whole society. But the failure to come to grips with this problem was mainly a failure of goodwill. At the beginning of the war Chamberlain had insisted that the war was against the Nazis rather than the German people, and the distinction was emphasized in the official letters of British diplomats formerly on German postings which were published in October 1939 in the British government's first tentative statement on Nazi atrocities, a Command Paper entitled *Treatment of German Nationals in Germany 1938–9*: thus, for example, the consul-general at Frankfurt am Main on the *Kristallnacht* disturbances directed against Jewish premises on 9 November 1938:

> Recent events have revealed to me a facet of the German character which I had not suspected. They seemed to me to have no cruelty in their make-up. They are habitually kind to animals, to children, to the aged and infirm. The explanation of the outbreak of sadistic cruelty may be that sexual perversion, and in particular homo-sexuality, are very prevalent in Germany. It seems to me that mass sexual perversity may offer an explanation for this otherwise inexplicable outbreak. I am persuaded that, if the Government of Germany depended on the suffrage of the people, those in power and responsible for those outrages would be swept away by a storm of indignation if not put up against a wall and shot.

Exiled German socialist leaders were even given the opportunity to discuss propaganda matters with the Director General of the Ministry of Information.

[35] Gisela C. Lebzelter *Political Anti-Semitism in England, 1918–1939* (1978) p. 46 and cf Public Record Office INF 1/292 Home Intelligence Reports for 30 Sept.–9 Oct. 1940 para I/5 and for 7 – 14 Oct. 1940 I/5. Perhaps the most illuminating books on the question of British officials' attitude to the Nazi Final Solution are Bower *Blind Eye to Murder*, Wasserstein *Britain and the Jews of Europe* and Gilbert *Auschwitz and the Allies* all cited in the previous note; Marika Sherwood *Many Struggles: West Indian Workers and Service Personnel in Britain (1939–45)* (1985) deals with the treatment of West Indians who tried to join up in Britain; Public Record Office FO 371/24418/C5304 Vansittart memo 11 March 1940; *Diaries of Sir Alexander Cadogan* p. 333, 28 Oct. 1940.

But increasingly public opinion hardened against the Germans. In September 1940 a *Times* leader stated:

> Such contribution as the German people have made to European civilization has dwindled and died away since 1870, till now after two generations of the almost uninterrupted cult of war they stand revealed as a force working solely for destruction.

Churchill himself was in sympathy with such views: 'I never hated the Germans in the last war,' he told his guests at dinner in July 1940, 'but now, I hate them like ... well, like an earwig.' Earl Winterton, M.P. for Horsham and formerly a member of Chamberlain's appeasement government, referring to a speech of Churchill two evenings previously and to a speech by Leslie Hore-Belisha just preceding his own, told the Commons in June 1941:

> The Prime Minister, to my great delight – and surely this applies almost to every Member of the House – referred to the Germans, as they should be referred to, as Huns, but throughout the speech of the Right Hon. Gentleman [Hore-Belisha] there was a reference to 'Hitler's Germany'. I do not recognize any difference between Hitler and the Germans at the present time.

At the same time it was not felt inappropriate to adopt the opening bars of the undoubtedly German Beethoven's Fifth Symphony as a kind of musical slogan in broadcasts to German-occupied Europe (Da-da-da-daaa corresponds in morse to the letter V, which the British were attempting to promote as an anti-German symbol). In November 1941, a file was opened at the Foreign Office on the subject of 'Propaganda to Germany: Distinction between Nazis and German People', which shows that the issue was still regarded as open: but the file remained comparatively thin.[36]

In a memorandum drawn up for the Foreign Office in November 1939 Sir Robert Vansittart had written:

> Let us make no further mistake about it: we are fighting the German Army, and the German people on whom the Army is based. We are fighting the *real*, and not the 'accidental' Germany. That the real Germany contains many good individual Germans is, of course, incontestable. The trouble is that they are never there corporately on the Day.

Such views came eventually to influence even the Labour Party. William

---

[36] Ian McLaine *Ministry of Morale* (1979) p. 142–6; Cmd 6120 p. 20 (*Parliamentary Papers* 1938–9 XXVII p. 448) R.T. Smallbones to Sir G. Ogilvie-Forbes 14 Dec. 1938: in reality prosecutions in Germany for homosexual offences had rocketed from 3,261 in 1931–4 to 29,771 in 1936–9 – see Richard Grunberger *A Social History of the Third Reich* (1971) p. 121 – and the most celebrated homosexuals in the Nazi regime were those like Röhm who were liquidated in 1934; Anthony Glees *Exile Politics during the Second World War: The German Social Democrats in Britain* (Oxford 1982) p. 37–9; *Times* 12 Sept. 1940 p. 5b; Colville *Fringes of Power* p. 192, 12 July 1940; *Hansard: House of Commons* vol. 372 col. 982 speech by Earl Winterton 24 June 1941 (Winterton had been Chancellor of the Duchy at the time of Munich); Asa Briggs *The History of Broadcasting in the United Kingdom* (4 vols 1961–79) vol. 3 p. 371; Public Record Office FO 371/30928/C647/118/18; see also FO 371/30928/C13125/118/18.

Gillies, the International Secretary of the Labour Party – 'the little dwarf-like Gillies', as Beatrice Webb described him – was initially sympathetic to the German socialist exiles; but after a while he began to tire of their persistent talk of participating in a democratic government in Germany after Hitler had been toppled, and finally he set to work to draw up a careful catalogue of the historical failure of the *Sozialistische Partei Deutschlands* before, during, and after the First World War, emphasizing their collaboration with class enemies, their divisions, and their strident nationalism. When judiciously circulated, Gillies's notes horrified members of the Labour Party, which at least had no taint of strident nationalism in its record, and despite opposition from more liberal-minded members, the distinction between Germans and Nazis was dropped from the official statement of Labour Party policy in 1943. This brought the Labour Party into line with the views of *The Sunday Express*, which on 7 March 1943 proclaimed in large type 'ALL GERMANS ARE GUILTY!' The government however continued to drag its feet on this issue: in the House of Lords on 10 March 1943 George Bell, the Bishop of Chichester, took up a point made by Stalin in a speech the previous November, when he had spoken of destroying not Germany but the Hitler regime: the bishop, regarded by the Foreign Office as 'one of the leading proponents of the "good Germans" theory', asked, 'Do His Majesty's Government make the same distinction as does Premier Stalin between the Hitlerite State and the German people?' Vansittart – elevated to the House of Lords after his final retirement in 1941 – made one of his characteristic speeches about the need to 'destroy Germany utterly and for ever as a military power' and 'to make an end for ever of all German pretensions, intrigues and efforts to gain the economic hegemony of Europe, which is only another road to Germany's intolerable tyrannies'. It had already been noted in Whitehall that 'Lord Vansittart is always a gift to Dr Goebbels'. The Lord Chancellor, Viscount Simon, steered by the Foreign Office 'between the Scylla of Lord Vansittart and the Charybdis of the Bishop of Chichester', reaffirmed the government's commitment to the distinction between the Germans and the Nazis. So long as the war lasted, however, this distinction could be given no practical expression, and a great deal of government activity seemed as if conducted on the assumption that no such distinction existed: for example the bombing of German cities.[37]

[37] Public Record Office FO 371/22986/C19495/15/18 Vansittart memo 'The Origins of Germany's Fifth War' 28 Nov. 1939 – for an introduction to the literature attacking Vansittart's views see Norman Rose *Vansittart: Study of a Diplomat* (1978) p. 252 fn.; Glees *Exile Politics during the Second World War* p. 103–144 and T.D. Burridge *British Labour and Hitler's War* (1976) p. 60–67 cf. Norman and Jeanne Mackenzie ed. *The Diaries of Beatrice Webb* (4 vols 1982–5) vol. 3 p. 303, 20 March 1918; *Hansard: House of Lords* vol. 126 col. 536 (Bell) col. 549 (Vansittart) col. 573–81 (Simon) 10 March 1943; Public Record Office FO 371/30928/C 13125 D. Allen minute 6 Jan. 1943, G. Jebb minute 11 Jan. 1943, cf FO 371/30928/C 3219 G.W. Harrison minute 31 March 1942. See also Willi A. Boelcke *The Secret Conferences of Dr. Goebbels: October 1939 – March 1943* (1970) p. 219, meeting of 26 March 1942 and p. 238, meeting of 22 May 1942; *Hansard: House of Lords* vol. 126 col. 536 (Bell), col. 549 (Vansittart), col. 573–581 (Simon) 10 March 1943.

The general willingness to blunt moral distinctions with regard to the Germans coincided with a similar process, though with an opposite tendency, whereby Stalin's bolshevik empire, of which Churchill had been a leading denouncer, was transformed into a heroic ally of the democracies. Three days before Hitler's invasion of the Soviet Union the British War Cabinet discussed the public line to be taken in such an eventuality; Churchill's colleagues 'took note' of his suggestion that the emphasis should be placed on presenting Germany as having attacked the Soviet Union to obtain the raw materials to carry on the war against Britain. Three days later, when the first reports came through that German forces had crossed into Soviet-controlled territory, Churchill and Eden, the Foreign Secretary, allowed themselves to be carried away by their enthusiasm at the extension of the scope of the war, and Churchill broadcast to the British people that evening hailing the Soviet Union as an ally:

> No one has been a more consistent opponent of Communism than I have for the last twenty-five years. I will unsay no word I have spoken about it. But all this fades away before the spectacle which is now unfolding. The past with its crimes, its follies and its tragedies, flashes away.

Neutral opinion was somewhat startled by this volte-face: the Swedish newspaper *Västra Nyland* wrote:

> When one of the leaders of democracy goes lyrical in his sympathy with the Soviet dictatorship one must refuse to follow. One must only hope that this is a diplomatic smoke screen intended to hide unfeigned delight in the destruction of the Soviet regime that is now unavoidable.

But Churchill was quite sincere: when Colonel J.T.C. Moore-Brabazon, the Minister of Aircraft Production, expressed the hope at a private luncheon that the Germans and the Russians would simply destroy each other, Churchill defended him in Parliament but took care to drop him from the government at the next major ministerial reshuffle.[38]

At least in retrospect the alliance with Stalin came to be seen by many right-wingers as a cynical and ultimately self-defeating expedient: as one contemporary later wrote, 'after June 1941 the war ceased to be a fight to maintain ideals, and became a war of nations against nations. The allies

---

[38] Elisabeth Barker *Churchill and Eden at War* (1978) p. 226–7; Robert Rhodes James ed. *Winston S. Churchill: His Complete Speeches* (8 vols New York 1974) vol. 6 p. 6429 22 June 1941; *Västra Nyland* quoted in Public Record Office FO 371/29352/N4010 Vereker to Foreign Office 22 July 1941 *Hansard: House of Commons* vol. 374 col. 295–8 for Churchill's defence of Brabazon 11 Sept 1941 but cf Lord Brabazon [J.C.T. Moore-Brabazon] *The Brabazon Story* (1956) p. 207–9 which shows that Brabazon himself attributed his dismissal in February 1942 to this incident. It was left to President Risto Ryti and other Finnish politicians to continue denouncing Russia and Bolshevism in terms similar to those used by Churchill since 1918, cf Risto Ryti *Stunden der Entscheidung: Reden des Finnischen Staatspräsidenten* (Leipzig [1943]) p. 101–2 speech on Finnish Independence Day 6 Dec. 1941 – the day Britain declared war on Finland.

were determined to crush not merely Nazism, but Germany for the benefit, as things turned out, of Bolshevism.' The long rear-guard action fought by the B.B.C. against playing the *Internationale* on the radio suggests that even in June and July 1941 there were those who refused to follow Churchill's lead. But generally there was enormous sympathy and admiration for the Russian people in their struggle against the invaders: the German attack evidently 'released a lot of instinctive, but repressed, class-consciousness' and the alliance with the Stalin regime, far from being seen by most people as a betrayal of principle, was welcomed as introducing a populist, egalitarian, progressive element into the struggle against Nazism which had hitherto been wanting. It was supposed to be a war of the common man – perhaps there was even a suggestion of this in the baggy shapeless battledress of the British Army in contrast with the elitist elegance of German uniforms – but till the German invasion of Russia the common man had lacked a convincing egalitarian model to identify with. Now not only twenty years of anti-Bolshevik propaganda, but also the objective truth about Stalin's regime could be stood on its head: the Archbishop of Canterbury told the House of Lords:

> We are now comrades with the Russian Armies and people, not only in resisting the unscrupulous and reckless ambitions of Hitler, but also in the struggle against a power of evil which is perhaps greater than has ever before appeared in human history. I do not think these words are mere rhetorical exaggeration. I honestly believe them to be true. Has ever such a mass of misery on so vast a scale been inflicted on the human race as that which now oppresses all the nations which have been compelled to come under German rule?[39]

V. The Myth of the Master Race – Anglo-Saxon Version

Yet antipathy towards the Germans was ultimately circumscribed by an awareness of a common racial and historical origin: the racism of Vansittart and others was cultural rather than ethnic. 'The only reliable good Germans I ever met were those who had been brought up in English schools and universities', minuted one official: this suggested at least that the Germans were not a *completely* hopeless case. But the Japanese, by thrusting themselves into the white man's war, introduced a new dimension.[40]

Just before the outbreak of the Pacific War, premier Tojo was warned by one of his colleagues that 'the entire Aryan race' – including Germany – might rally against Japan, and Tojo had responded, 'I will be careful to avoid the war's becoming a racial war'. In the event the Japanese's own racialist

[39] James Lees-Milne *Another Self* (1970) p. 136; Asa Briggs *The History of Broadcasting in the United Kingdom* vol. 3 p. 389–91, 394; Tom Pocock *1945: The Dawn Came Up Like Thunder* (1983) p. 150; *Hansard: House of Lords* vol. 120 col. 391 speech by Cosmo Lang, Archbishop of Canterbury 23 Oct. 1941.

[40] Public Record Office FO 371/46973/C 7090 minute by R.W. Selby (ex-Eton and Christ Church) 18 Oct. 1945.

prejudices and their incomplete adjustment to Western values gave the lie to Tojo's bland assurances; but Japan's enemies met the Japanese more than half-way. Britain's Empire had been buttressed by a racial myth as entrancing as that of the Nazis. G.B. Malleson, whose *History of the Indian Mutiny* went through ten editions between 1878 and 1910, explained the final British victory over the more numerous Indian rebels quite simply: 'It was a question of race'. Race was a favourite theme with the Canadian poet Wilfred Campbell, who in 1913 defined British loyalty thus:

> It is founded upon loyalty to God, race, flag, throne, constitution and country. It teaches that service, not power, is the greatest thing – that to serve well the race and the state is the supreme ideal.

Later of course the attitudes had become less rigid, or at least more ambiguous, as is shown by E.M. Forster's *A Passage to India* (1924), but old habits of mind die hard. One hears the assumption of racial superiority in the complaint of Sir Robert Craigie, the British ambassador at Tokyo prior to Pearl Harbor, 'I am so nauseated with being polite to the little blighters ... the dirty little bastards'. And in the British response to the Japanese the suspicion of the unknown underlying all prejudice was reinforced by the fact that the Japanese seemed more remote and alien than any enemy the British had ever previously fought, for never before had the British fought a non-European ethnic group which they had not previously employed on a large scale as servants or at least as slaves; the Japanese seemed closer to the extra-terrestrials led by the sinister Emperor Ming, combated by the eminently Anglo-Saxon Flash Gordon in the pre-war cinema serials, than anything encountered earlier:

> We knew the Nazis were nasty, but in the war we were always on the lookout for the Good German ... the fighter ace, shot down ... and entertained to dinner in the local R.A.F. Officers Mess. The compassionate U-boat commander; the shot-down bomber-gunner who was no more than a young lad, and was given a cup of tea. Nobody ever looked for a good Jap.[41]

Fairly typical of the European response to the Japanese was Lord Louis Mountbatten's private description of the Japanese delegation which signed the capitulation at Singapore in 1945:

> I have never seen six more villainous, depraved or brutal faces in my life. I shudder to think what it would have been like to be in their power. When they

---

[41] Nobutaka Ike *Japan's Decision for War: Records of the 1941 Policy Conferences* (Stanford 1967) p. 237, 239 Conference 5 Nov. 1941; G.B. Malleson *History of the Indian Mutiny* (4th Edit. 1892) p. 410, and cf Penderel Moon *The British Conquest and Dominion of India* (1989) p. 840–841, 860, 881. (For an early statement on the inherent superiority of white races see W. Lawrence *Lectures in Physiology, Zoology and the Natural History of Man* (1819) p. 475–501 espec. 489.) Wilfred Campbell ed. *Poems of Loyalty by British and Canadian Authors [1913]* p. vi; Hallett Abend *My Years in China, 1926–1941* (1944) p. 333; Robert Westall ed. *Children of the Blitz: Memories of Wartime Childhood* (Harmondsworth 1985) p. 228 quoting a boy from Tyneside.

got off their chairs and shambled out, they looked like a bunch of gorillas, with great baggy breeches and knuckles almost trailing on the ground.

The ape image was perhaps the commonest propaganda treatment of the Japanese in allied publications – though General Joseph W. Stilwell, who was supposed to like orientals, described the Japanese as 'these bowlegged cockroaches'. And what was especially disquieting about these allegedly deformed Japanese was that they were dressed in what appeared to be an obscene parody of European uniform.[42]

This racist attitude towards the Japanese was the more untimely in that the Japanese attack on Pearl Harbor – and even more, their rapid conquest of Malaya, Singapore and Burma – opened up the whole question of the white people's relationship with coloured populations. In Europe the war could be presented as a stand against Nazi – or was it simply German? – aggression. The same view, stripped of doctrinal ambiguities, was put forward in Asia:

> above all we must never forget that we are not fighting for this form of government or that, not for this ideology or that, but – whether we are British, Indian, American, Chinese, or of any other nation ranged together as 'The Allies' – for our own freedom, in fact for our lives.

This view achieved its classic statement in Sir William Slim's memoirs of the war in Burma:

> If ever an army fought in a just cause we did. We coveted no man's country; we wished to impose no form of government on any nation. We fought for the clean, the decent, the free things of life, for the right to live our lives in our own way, as others could live theirs, to worship God in what faith we chose, to be free in body and mind, and for our children to be free. We fought only because the powers of evil had attacked these things.

Unfortunately it did not necessarily seem that way to the natives of the countries fought over.[43]

Once the Japanese had overrun a former white colony, their administration was generally unintelligent, unsympathetic, unsuccessful and unpopular, and their establishment of puppet regimes in Manchukuo, Nanking China, Burma and the Philippines was little more than a transparent strategy aimed at encouraging a rising in India, at driving a diplomatic wedge between Britain and the U.S.A. and at establishing anti-Western feeling as a basis for Japanese

---

[42] Philip Ziegler *Mountbatten* (1985) p. 303; John W. Dower *War Without Mercy: Race and Power in the Pacific War* (1986) p. 84–8 and cf cartoons reproduced on p. 182–7 and see also Michael S. Sherry *The Rise of American Air Power: The Creation of Armageddon* (New Haven 1987) p. 242–8, Bernard F. Dick *The Star-Spangled Screen: The American World War II Film* (Lexington 1985) p. 230–231 and McLaine *Ministry of Morale* p. 158–9; *Stilwell Papers* p. 68 Joseph W. Stilwell to Winifred Stilwell 1 March 1942.

[43] Imperial War Museum Irwin Papers 2/2 circular to officers down to company commander entitled 'Eastern Army Operations 1942–3' 15 May 1943; Sir William Slim *Defeat into Victory* (1956) p. 183, cf the monument to the Empire dead at Kohima with its inscription, 'For Your Tomorrow They Gave Their Today'.

hegemony. The Japanese rising sun emblem was less hypnotic than the swastika because even more patently exclusive. Yet the Japanese really did see themselves as the champions of Asia against white domination. A booklet issued to the troops scheduled to invade Malaya, captioned 'Read This Alone – And The War Can Be Won', explained:

> four hundred and fifty million natives of the Far East live under the domination of less than eight hundred thousand whites ... Once you set foot on the enemy's territories you will see for yourselves only too clearly, just what this oppression by the white man means. Imposing, splendid buildings look down from the summits of mountains and hills on to the tiny thatched huts of the natives.

The booklet was evidently not aimed at making the Japanese soldiers behave so agreeably that they would be welcomed as liberators, for it made clear that no useful cooperation could be expected from any of the local populations: in addition to the laziness induced by the heat and by the fertility of the soil,

> after centuries of subjection to Europe and exploitation by the Chinese, these natives have reached a point of almost complete emasculation.
>   We may wish to make men of them again quickly, but we should not expect too much.[44]

The Japanese attack occurred at a time when nationalist movements in Burma and India were growing in strength. Burma had been separated administratively from the Indian Empire in 1935. The next few years saw riots between the Burmese and Indian immigrant workers, and student disorders. Ba Maw, leader of the Proletarian Party, who was prime minister from 1937 to 1939, considered that his ministry had been sabotaged by the British Governor in conjunction with foreign business interests and after the outbreak of the war in Europe began to favour a possible resort to armed resistance. An uprising was also advocated by Aung San, who had been elected president of the university of Rangoon's student union in 1938 and had later become general secretary of the small and extremist Thakin Party. During the summer of 1940, Ba Maw's party conference voted him dictatorial powers and as dictator he promulgated orders for an armed struggle. He was arrested on 6 August 1940; Aung San escaped to Japanese-controlled territory a few days later. In October 1940 U Saw, the current prime minister, travelled to London to demand Dominion Status for his country, and on the way home stopped off at Lisbon to make contact with Japanese diplomats. Lisbon was notoriously full of spies: perhaps

---

[44] For Japanese occupation policy see F.C. Jones *Japan's New Order in East Asia: Its Rise and Fall, 1937–45* (1954) p. 368–9, 373–5, Saburo Ienaga *Japan's Last War: World War II and the Japanese 1931–1945* (Oxford 1979) p. 154–5, 171–80 and Christopher Thorne *The Issue of War: States, Societies and the Far Eastern Conflict of 1941–1945* (1985) p. 156–159; for the Co-prosperity Sphere see W.G. Beasley *Japanese Imperialism, 1894–1945* (Oxford 1987) p. 233–250; 'Read This Alone – And The War Can Be Won' is printed as an appendix to Masanobu Tsuji *Singapore: The Japanese Version* (1960) p. 295–349, quotations being from p. 301, 306, and cf Thorne *The Issue of War* p. 144–6.

mainly British ones. U Saw was arrested when he reached Haifa in the course of his journey back to Burma and spent the rest of the war in British captivity. Ba Maw, who was in prison in Burma itself, was liberated by the Japanese invasion in 1942 and was subsequently installed as head of a puppet government, with Aung San as leader of the Burma National Army, having graduated from student militant to revolutionary generalissimo in a mere three years. Sir Reginald Dorman Smith, the British Governor whom the Japanese drove out, noted ruefully:

> It is definitely disappointing that after all our years of occupation of both Lower and to a lesser degree Upper Burma, we have not been able to create that loyalty which is generally associated with our subject nations.[45]

In India, there had been at the outbreak of war devolved self-governing ministries in eleven provinces, in accordance with legislation enacted in 1935, and eight of these had resigned in protest at being dragged into Britain's war. Two Indian ministries were eventually reconstructed: the other six provinces were governed by British officials without the encumbrance of democratic organs. Their lack of cooperation on this point was as much as the Indian nationalists could manage against the Raj. The cultural dividedness of the sub-continent, Mahatma Gandhi's authoritative commitment to a strategy of non-violence and, perhaps most important of all, the mere fact that the Japanese failed even to try to conquer India, prevented the independence movement in India having quite the same impact as in Burma: but amongst Indians too the leading collaborationist with the Japanese was a man of established national status. Subhas Chandra Bose had come fourth in the British Civil Service exam in 1920 but had soon resigned his employment in disgust at the Amritsar massacre when protesting Indians had been shot down by British-commanded troops. Bose became a notable maker of inflammatory speeches and was frequently arrested, there being only four years between 1924 and 1937 which he did not spend either wholly or partly in jail. Though known as an opponent of Gandhi's non-violent strategy, Bose was elected President of the Congress Party in 1938 but was forced by Gandhi to resign in April 1939. He was arrested again in July 1940, released after a hunger-strike in December 1940, and fled to Afghanistan. From there he made his way to Germany, where he raised three battalions from Indian prisoners of war for employment by the Wehrmacht.[46]

In February 1943 Bose left Kiel aboard a U-boat, and after being transferred

[45] Public Record Office FO 371/31809/F2247 Dorman Smith to Burma Office 8 March 1942, cf Ba Maw *Breakthrough in Burma: Memoirs of a Revolution, 1939–1946* (New Haven 1968) passim.

[46] For Bose's career generally see Hugh Toye *The Springing Tiger: A Study of a Revolutionary (Subhas Chandra Bose)* (1959); for his anti-climatic meeting with Hitler in May 1942 see Milan Hauner *India in Axis Strategy: Germany, Japan, and the Indian Nationalists in the Second World War* (Stuttgart 1981) p. 484–7.

to a Japanese submarine 400 miles S.S.W. of Madagascar reached Tokyo on 13 June 1943. Already 40,000 Indian prisoners in Japanese prisoner-of-war cages had pledged themselves to join an Indian National Army, but their leaders had wanted Congress Party approval before making any open alliance with the Japanese and their general uncooperativeness regarding Japanese schemes had led to the dismissal and arrest of Mohan Singh, the original head of the movement. Subhas Chandra Bose was installed in Mohan Singh's place. Although both Mohan Singh and Bose based their propaganda on the nationalist creed, it is probably true to say that there had been relatively little nationalist disaffection amongst the Indian troops: they were after all an elite volunteer fighting force, raised in country districts from amongst families which had traditionally sent sons to the Indian Army, and largely without previous political education. But the monotony and humiliation of imprisonment, and even more the shock of witnessing the astonishing collapse of the British imperial system they had served, caused many to pay heed to I.N.A. propaganda: Mohan Singh himself seems to have made his decision to assist the Japanese against the British during the four days of wandering through the Malayan countryside which elapsed between his unit being cut off by the Japanese advance on 11 December 1941 and his giving himself up on 15 December. Resentment at the 'prejudice and lack of manners' shown to them by British officers and their wives also contributed to the disillusion felt by many Indain commissioned officers who fell into Japanese hands. Subsequently the more impatient and ambitious amongst the I.N.A's recruits, eager to escape from imprisonment under appalling conditions and without other hope of release, put pressure on their fellow prisoners to join up. The success of Mohan Singh and Subhas Chandra Bose, at least as recruiting officers, proves less the unpopularity of the British Raj than the complete flimsiness of the foundations on which it rested.[47]

VI. The American Angle

These distressing signs of structural rot in the Empire coincided with pressures from another quarter. The Americans were not in general any less racist than the British. President Roosevelt talked airily of sterilizing Germans and Puerto Ricans and assigned the task of establishing 'why the Japanese were as bad as they were' to the Curator of the Division of Physical Anthropology at the Smithsonian Institute, whose researches showed that 'the skulls of these people were some 2,000 years less advanced than ours'. (Perhaps the best comment on

[47] Gerald H. Corr *The War of the Springing Tigers* London 1975 p. 72–4 for an account of Mohan Singh; p. 117–22 for a discussion of various motives for joining the I.N.A.; Philip Warner *Auchinleck: The Lonely Soldier* (1981) p. 194 memo by Sir Claude Auchinleck to army commanders in India.

this is Ezra Pound's claim, in a broadcast from Fascist Italy in March 1942, that 'F.D.R. is below the biological level at which the concept of honor enters the mind'.) In Detroit 34 people died in race riots in June 1943. Coloured soldiers – even the few coloured commissioned officers – were subjected to insult, petty persecution and ostracism. At one Army Air Force training camp in Michigan the colonel in command shot a black soldier, explaining, 'I repeatedly gave instructions that I did not want a colored chauffeur'. A German prisoner of war on the run from a P.O.W. camp in the Southern States gave himself away by his behaviour on a long-distance bus; not only did he seat himself in the Colored People Only section at the back, but he then gave up his place to an elderly black who was having to stand. In Britain an immediate response to the news of the Detroit riot was a shoot-out between black G.I.s and white military police at Bamber Bridge in Lancashire. West Indian immigrant workers were beaten up by white Americans in Liverpool and there were numerous incidents when white G.I.s were provoked by the sight of negroes dancing with English girls who had never previously had the opportunity to meet a coloured gentleman, though admittedly nothing occurred in Britain to equal the case of the South African who, after the liberation of Abyssinia from the Fascists, threw the coloured Governor of Addis Ababa out of a nightclub because he had been chatting up a white girl. Nevertheless there had been during the 1920s and 1930s a growing hostility in the United States to British Imperialism, due partly to the unattractive spectacle of British resistance to the nationalist movement in India, partly to the incidental anti-imperialist message embodied in publicity in support of China's resistance to Japanese aggression, partly to a growing sense of America's own superior international morality: the Tydings-McDuffie Act of 1934 which promised complete independence to the Philippines by 1946 enabled Cordell Hull, the U.S. Secretary of State, to hold up American policy in the Philippines as 'a perfect example of how a nation should treat a colony or dependency'.[48]

British officials were not intimidated by such pretensions. They perceived the economic imperialism underlying American policy, or at least American attitudes, and resented the American pose of ethical superiority: one official

---

[48] Christopher Thorne *Allies of a Kind: The United States, Britain and the War against Japan, 1941–1945* (1978) p. 167–8 fn. 28 quoting Sir Ronald Campbell to Sir Alexander Cadogan 6 Aug. 1942; E. Fuller Torrey *The Roots of Treason: Ezra Pound and the Secret of St. Elizabeth's* (1984) p. 162; Alfred McClung Lee and Norman D. Humphrey *Race Riot (Detroit 1943)* (New York 1968) p. 2; Mary Penick Motley *The Invisible Soldier: The Experience of the Black Soldier World War II* (Detroit 1975) espec. p. 194–257; Alan M. Osur *Blacks in the Army Air Forces during World War II: The Problem of Race Relations* (Washington 1977) p. 54; Daniel Costelle *Les Prisonniers* (Paris 1975) p. 148; Graham Smith *When Jim Crow Met John Bull: Black American Soldiers in World War II Britain* (1987) p. 86–7 and 142–3; Edward Ward *Number One Boy* (1969) p. 169; Wm. Roger Louis *Imperialism at Bay, 1941–1945* (Oxford 1977) p. 180 quoting Hull to William Phillips 19 Nov. 1942.

responded to American criticism of French colonial policy with the sour comment, 'I have never heard that the Indo-Chinese were any more unhappy than the share-croppers of the Southern United States'. Even the U.S. State Department's Far East adviser recognized that, 'Any principle has a tendency to smack us as a boomerang', with regard to Guam, Hawaii, Alaska, even the southern negro problem. In the end, despite Foreign Office fears that 'President Roosevelt is suffering from the same megalomania which characterised the late President Wilson', no consistent U.S. policy on colonial affairs was ever promulgated. But the Japanese conquest of Malaya, Singapore and Burma shifted the issue from the theoretical to the practical realm, for it was soon obvious that the main burden of the war against Japan was to be borne by the Americans, and the American public, or at least its newspapers, had some embarrassing questions to raise. 'An Open Letter from the Editors of LIFE to the People of England' asked, 'In the light of what you are doing in India, how do you expect to talk about "principles" and look our soldiers in the eye?', and stated categorically, '*one* thing we are sure we are *not* fighting for is to hold the British Empire together'. A joke current amongst Americans serving in India and Burma interpreted the letters S.E.A.C as standing not for South East Asia Command but for Save England's Asiatic Colonies. Patrick Hurley, U.S. ambassador to China, raised the same issue in the last weeks of the war: 'The question is, will we now permit British, French and Dutch imperialists to use the resources of America's democracy to re-establish imperialism in Asia?'[49]

There were indeed a number of startling ambiguities exposed by the British establishment's attempt to present the last war of the Empire as a crusade for freedom and justice. Clement Attlee, leader of Britain's Labour Party and Deputy Prime Minister from May 1940, had no hesitation in seeing that the moral issue of a war against dictatorship also involved the question of imperialism:

> it was not so long ago in my own life time when our Press used to be filled with the same kind of arrogant boasting which one hears from Hitler ...
>
> We must be prepared to bring all our colonial territories under the mandatory principle and to extend and widen the scope of international control. We must rid ourselves of any taint of imperialism. Only so can we put ourselves into a position to ask for a world organized on the democratic principle.

But this was not the view of either Churchill or the Tory majority in the Cabinet: Before the war Churchill had written to the Viceroy of India, 'my ideal is narrow and limited. I want to see the British Empire preserved for a

[49] Public Record Office FO 371/35921 minute by V.F.W. Cavendish-Bentinck 22 Dec. 1943; Louis *Imperialism at Bay* p. 165–6 quoting Stanley K. Hornbeck; Thorne *Allies of a Kind* p. 456–7 and cf Cavendish-Bentinck's minute of 22 Dec. 1943; *Life* 12 Oct. 1942 p. 32; *Foreign Relations of the United States 1945* (9 vols Washington 1967–9) vol. 7 p. 107 Hurley to President Truman 20 May 1945.

few more generations in its strength and splendour'. During the war, even after the U.S.A. had come in as Britain's ally, he insisted on proclaiming the same ideal: 'I have not become the King's First Minister in order to preside over the liquidation of the British Empire', he told a Lord Mayor's luncheon at the Mansion House in December 1942. Leo Amery, whom Churchill appointed to the India Office, thought that, 'After all, smashing Hitler is only a means to the essential end of preserving the British Empire and all it stands for in the world', and argued:

It will be no consolation to suggest that Hitler should be replaced by Stalin, Chiang Kai-Shek or even an American President if we cease to exercise our power and influence in the world. What I think is needed to-day more than anything else is a vigorous reaffirmation of our faith in our destiny as an Empire and of our determination to make good that destiny afterwards, regarding the war merely as a step in that process.[50]

It was the degree to which Britain relied on American support for the achievement of final victory which undercut the policy Amery advocated, especially as it was left to the Americans in the Far East to avenge the most shattering of the Empire's defeats at the hands of the Japanese. Paradoxically it was Churchill, who was perhaps the most inflexible of his Cabinet on the subject of India, who was also the most whole-hearted amongst his colleagues in his reliance, one might almost say emotional dependence, on the friendship and support of the U.S.A. He said after the war, 'No lover ever studied every whim of his mistress as I did those of President Roosevelt'. Himself half-American by parentage, he had little sense of the conflicting interests and attitudes which divided the two nations. Lord Beaverbrook, who as a Canadian had a certain distrust of the U.S.A., tried to warn Churchill against excessive enthusiasm for the American alliance:

in seeking that friendship, we should aim, with an equal consistency, at maintaining and strengthening our own position as a world power ... we shall approach the nearer to a sound ... and lasting relationship with the United States in so far as we are able to build up our own prestige and safeguard our own inherited interests in the economic as well as the political and military spheres.

In the event the conflict of ideals was never resolved nor, so long as the war lasted, permitted to become divisive: the struggle embarked upon in September 1939 in an attempt to preserve Britain's position of leadership in Europe ended with the United States in a position of acknowledged predominance, without the swapping of roles being properly perceived, at the time at least, let alone

---

[50] Kenneth Harris *Attlee* (1982) p. 169, quoting B.B.C. broadcast 3 Feb. 1940; Martin Gilbert *Winston S. Churchill* vol. 5 p. 886 Churchill to Marquis of Linlithgow 3 Nov. 1937; *Winston S. Churchill: The Complete Speeches* vol. 6 p. 6695, 10 Nov. 1942; Public Record Office CO 825/35/55104 Amery to Viscount Cranborne 26 Aug 1942.

systematically discussed. The Stop Hitler/Right against Wrong version of British war aims, with all its ambiguities and inconsistencies, was more than one of those 'schoolboy stories in which England is always St. George'; it was also a flight from a reality which the British political system could no longer shape to its own advantage.[51]

[51] Colville *Fringes of Power* p. 624, 2 May 1948; A.J.P. Taylor *Beaverbrook* (New York 1972) p. 555 Beaverbrook to Churchill 21 Feb 1944; the phrase about 'schoolboy stories in which England is always St. George' is from a review by Edmund Wilson of one of Harold Nicolson's books, *New Yorker* 1 Jan. 1944.

Churchill went through a phase of anti-Americanism in the 1920s – see David Irving *Churchill's War: The Struggle for Power* (1987) p. 10 – but this was seemingly only the prelude to a love-affair with America which lasted the rest of his life.

13

The War of the Super-economies

We went for a couple of days' holiday in a village near Bethesda in North Wales.

A German bomber came over our heads and crashed into the mountainside. The crew got out, and in good English they explained how they had just eaten in a Paris restaurant which was very nice.

They said the war was tragic and useless and would result in decadence, if we did not accept a 'Plan' for Europe.

Girl aged 17 in 1940, quoted in Robert Westall ed., *Children of the Blitz: Memories of Wartime Childhood* (Harmondsworth 1985), p. 203.

I. Learning from the Past

Karl Marx did not always get it right. In the Second World War history repeated itself, not as farce but as an even vaster tragedy – though one may if one chooses detect some of the characteristics of farce, hideously inverted, in the way the more gratuitously atrocious features of the First World War were reproduced on an even grosser scale in the Second World War, for instance the archaic tumult of the Armenian massacres in Asia Minor westernized and mechanized into the assembly-line death camps at Auschwitz, Treblinka and Sobibor. As far as the economic history of the Second World War is concerned, the most striking feature is how the earlier superiority of economic organization on the Entente side was now reproduced as an even greater lead for the Allies, matched by an even greater failure to utilize this material advantage, while on this occasion the naturally weaker enemy compounded its weakness by economic strategies which followed the logic not of wartime realities but of an increasingly eccentric political vision.

In the First World War every country was taken by surprise by the economic demands posed by the war: and we may contrast the regimes where the transition to a war economy simply highlighted the social and economic dislocations of pre-war society – Austria-Hungary, Germany amongst the Central Powers, Italy and especially Russia on the Entente side – and the countries which transformed themselves organizationally in ways which represented a major revision of the preexisting social and political structure. During the 1920s, under Baldwin and Ramsay Macdonald in Britain and the Republican Presidents Harding, Coolidge and Hoover in the U.S.A., the two nations which had emerged from the First World War with the strongest economies retreated from their wartime managerial experiment, but they were ready, by 1940, to put into practice, on an even larger and more comprehensive scale, the lessons learnt just over two decades previously. Germany and Japan however had learnt something quite different from the same lessons: not that modern war could only be won by overwhelming weight of economic output, but that the secret of modern war was to defeat the enemy before he had time to mobilize his full weight of output. The necessity for a Schlieffen Plan which would settle world history for a hundred years in one short and heroic campaign was for the Axis Powers reaffirmed, not refuted, by the experience of 1914–1918.

It does not seem however that this conclusion was arrived at by any process of careful and reflective thought. General Alfredo Dall'Olio, Italy's war economy supremo in the First World War and till August 1939 head of the *Commissariato generale per le fabbricazioni di guerra (Fabbriguerra)*, constantly warned of the necessity of preparing Italian industry for an eventual war. Mussolini largely ignored him, and though forced to cite Italian economic unpreparedness as a reason for not entering the war at Hitler's side in September 1939, made no attempt to turn Italian industry over to a war footing. Once Germany had defeated France, economic and logistic factors lost all influence on *Il Duce*'s fevered imagination and even by 1943, with the country starving at home and everywhere defeated abroad, there was still no overall attempt to channel national resources into war production. In the case of Japan there was a certain plausibility in the objective of gaining an island barrier in the Pacific which would hold American forces permanently at a distance, but the problem of supplying the garrisons of the island barrier in the face of a probable submarine blockade was not considered. In Germany the logistic difficulties of an invasion of Russia were underrated, as were the potential munitions output of Soviet industry and the size of the Soviet forces actually in existence at the time of the great German invasion. It is not merely hindsight that tells us that the Axis never had a serious chance of victory: their whole strategy was a patchwork of gambles and gestures in defiance of objective realities.[1]

II. The Blitzkrieg Economy in Germany

It is the German war-economic strategy which has received most scholarly attention. After the German collapse the Americans assembled as many

---

[1] For Dall'Olio see Pietro Maravigna *Come Abbiamo Perduto la Guerra in Africa* (Rome 1949) p. 406; for the Italian war economy generally see Stephen Harvey 'The Italian War Effort and the Strategic Bombing of Italy' *History* vol. 70 (1985) p. 32–45 at p. 34–36 and cf Kesselring's remarks in Donald S. Detwiler ed. *World War II German Military Studies* (24 vols New York 1979) vol 14 pt. 1 (Kesselring, 'View of the African War') p. 11.

German generals as they could find in a large hotel which quickly took on the style of an academic research institute, tempered by the austerities and, one suspects, the bullying of a prep school. The hotel was located at Mondorf in Luxembourg; it produced ample chapter and verse for what might accordingly be called the Mondorf thesis, or alternatively the Halder thesis (after Franz Halder, chief of staff of the German Army till 1942 and later its most influential apologist). The Mondorf thesis presented the German generals as cultured, intelligent, thoughtful and of course well-bred men forced to undertake policies they knew to be unworkable by that horrid guttersnipe Adolf Hitler, and hypothesizes that if only the generals had been allowed to have their own way there would have been no Nazi regime, no war on two fronts, no pointless hanging on to indefensible positions, in short, no defeat. There is something in this: but not very much. The German military establishment, without enthusiasm, produced a plan for the 1940 invasion of France which had much less decisive potential than the one finally adopted by Hitler, and the modifications Hitler made to their plans for the invasion of Russia were much less catastrophic than their own professional failure in underestimating Soviet military strength. It is arguable also that Hitler, in taking charge of the Wehrmacht's campaigns after 1942, merely made himself responsible for a defeat which no other leader or commander could have prevented anyway: as General Alfred Jodl, his closest military collaborator, later suggested, Hitler after Stalingrad 'could no longer come to a strategic decision. But perhaps there was no longer one to be reached'.[2]

The corollary of the Mondorf or Halder thesis on the economic side is that Germany's war economy simply responded to the orders of a deranged amateur and was never properly thought out, but in recent times the economic version of the Mondorf thesis has largely been replaced, or at least by-passed, by what we may call the Milward thesis, which concentrates less on unassimiliable differences of *Weltanschauung* at the top than on an academic economist's model of war and government as rational decision-making exercises. Professor Milward has argued that Hitler deliberately chose a so-called *Blitzkrieg* strategy which had a perfectly coherent rationale and which, till November 1941, worked with outstanding effectiveness. The basic concept of this *Blitzkrieg* strategy was that one would prepare one's armed forces for a quick knock-out blow, with the maximum of man-power and equipment in the front-line and minimal reserves, and then, after the knock-out blow had succeeded, lie low for a few months quietly digesting the spoils (rather like a python after it has swallowed a piglet) and then prepare for the next sudden rapid lunge.[3]

More recently still, Richard Overy, while accepting the principle that the

---

[2] Percy Ernst Schramm *Hitler the Man and the Military Leader* (1972) p. 195–204 Appendix II 'Memorandum Dictated in 1946 on Hitler's Military Leadership' by Alfred Jodl, at p. 204.

[3] Alan S. Milward *The German Economy at War* (1965) p. 11 Milward's argument is a fleshing out of an idea given sketchily in Nicholas Kaldor 'The German War Economy' *Review of Economic Studies* vol. 13 (1945–6) p. 33–52 at p. 47, 48.

Nazis had intended, at least initially, to manage the German war economy on some sort of rational basis, has rejected the Milward *Blitzkrieg* thesis in its essential form. The Overy thesis is that Hermann Göring, as plenipotentiary for the Four Year Plan, was working on the systematic build-up of large-scale munitions industries capable of sustaining a long war. Since, even as Hitler was attempting to conquer the oil-fields and ore deposits of Russia, Göring was continuing to channel lavish investment into synthetic fuel development and low-yield iron ore processing plant, both of which would have been redundant if the conquest of southern Russia had succeeded, the rationality of Göring's master plan is somewhat elusive. At the same time, and even though one cannot easily believe that Göring was the man to have thought through the relationship between his industrial empire-building and the strategy of the war, it remains true that until 1942 he was the minister with the leading responsibility in the economic sphere: not that Hitler seems to have discussed the war economy with him in any particular detail. The imputation of rational planning processes which the Milward and Overy theses share seems to be refuted by what is known of the *political* history of the Third Reich, which fits in much better with the economists' version of the Mondorf thesis.[4]

Yet there was certainly an awareness of the problem of economic mobilization. From the mid 1920s the German army had favoured the establishment of a *Kriegsamt* (War Bureau) similar to, but even more powerful than, the one which had existed during the First World War. After the Nazis came to power the Army Ordnance Bureau proposed, in the event of war, the establishment of a *Wehrmachtrüstungsamt* (Military Armaments Bureau) under the chief of the Army Ordnance Bureau, to control the economy, but of course the Nazi leadership had no intention of replacing itself with a dictatorship of military bureaucrats; in Italy, where the *Commissariato generale per le fabbricazioni di guerra* (Commissariat of War Production), was controlled by army personnel and had at least theoretically the powers called for by the Ordnance Bureau in Germany, it was totally ineffectual, partly perhaps because of the difficulty of integrating an army bureau into a party dictatorship. Schacht, the Minister of Economics, was appointed Plenipotentiary for the War Economy in 1935 but was effectively replaced by Göring with the establishment of the Four Year Plan in the following year; the Reich Defence Law of September 1938 made Keitel, as *Chef der OKW* (head of the Armed Services High Command) responsible for the war economy, with the Minister of Economics, now Walter Funk, acting as Plenipotentiary under OKW authority, but this new arrangement remained inoperative, in part because neither Keitel nor Funk dared to interfere in

---

[4] R.J. Overy *Goering: The 'Iron Man'* (1984) p. 107 for Göring's long-term plans to develop an economy capable of sustaining a long war: R.J. Overy 'Mobilization for Total War in Germany, 1939–1941' *English Historical Review* vol. 103 (1988) p. 613–39 suggests p. 625–9 that Germany was already completely mobilized for war production by 1941: it is not clear how far this contradicts earlier Overy theses.

Göring's administration of the all-pervasive Four Year Plan. Within the context of these undefined and unacted-upon mandates, the Army was permitted only to establish a *Wehrwirtschaft- und Waffenwesen* (Defence Economy and Weapons Department) with no executive powers beyond the control of an extensive local network of inspectors and comptrollers. The head of this organization – later upgraded to *Wehrwirtschaft-und Rüstungsamt*, replacing the vague *-wesen* with the more specific-sounding *-amt* – was a somewhat colourless and donnish colonel named Georg Thomas. In an article published in 1937 in *Militärwissenschaftliche Rundschau* entitled 'Breite und Tiefe der Rüstung' (Breadth and Depth in Armament), Thomas defined breadth as numbers of front-line units and depth as potential material back-up, but the main point he seemed to wish to make was:

> an arms programme can only be set up if the general staff officer concerned with economic questions has previously completed his labours of research ... the closest collaboration between the general staff concerned with operational matters and the general staff concerned with economic matters, even in the preparatory stages of an arms programme, is thus a prerequisite of the success of an armaments programme.

As Thomas's labours of research brought him into close collaboration with the opposition to Hitler within the general staff it is not surprising that his ideas had little appeal for the Nazis; indeed he was very much like the typical British staff intellectual, with a mind attuned to long vistas of caution and postponement, and Hitler was only interested in goods that could be delivered in a hurry.[5]

Essentially Hitler's economic miracle of the 1930s was to solve Germany's huge unemployment problem by a massive public-spending programme – mainly on armaments and military installations – for which the country lacked not merely the money but, even more inescapably, the material resources: even, it turned out, a sufficient supply of labour. Georg Thomas estimated that by March 1939 munitions output was nearing the levels of 1918, though since Speer later claimed that 1918 output was only exceeded in 1944 there was evidently a measure of fantasy or of self-advertisment in either Thomas's or Speer's calculations. What was more certain was that private consumption in 1938 represented only 59 per cent of national income, as compared to 83 per cent in 1932, and that while per capita output in Germany was only 3 or 4 per cent less than in Britain, per capita consumption was 27 or 28 per cent less. There was considerable discontent over low pay and high food prices. Consumer goods were often simply not available: though the Autobahn building programme and the publicity given to the Volkswagen

---

[5] For the *Wehrwirtschaft-und Waffenwesen* see B.A. Carroll *Design for Total War* (Hague 1968) p. 108–110. *Amt* means office or bureau; *Wesen* means being, or essence, but is often used in military terminology to indicate a section or department but without the implications of departmentalization. For the passage quoted see Georg Thomas 'Breite und Teife der Rüstung' *Militäwissenschaftliche Rundschau* vol. 2 (1937) p. 189–197 at p. 196–7.

made the motor car one of the more positive symbols of pre-war Nazi society, there were actually very few cars for sale; only fifty Volkswagen were built before production ceased at the outbreak of war, though over 200,000 people had handed over the RM 1,000 purchase price. In fact pre-war output of motor vehicles in Germany, even combined with that of Italy and Japan, was still less than that of Britain, and German industry was incapable even of supplying the Wehrmacht adequately, so that in February 1940, with routine wastage of trucks running ahead of deliveries, the general staff was forced to consider demotorizing the Army. Having suffered even more severely than Britain or France in the interwar slump, German industry simply could not handle the demands for tanks and planes and military trucks involved in Hitler's rearmament drive; it is even probable that the emphasis on the speedy elimination of unemployment combined with controls on civilian consumption arising from rearmament resulted in a smaller industrial base and a workforce less adapted to the requirements of industrial-era war than might have been the case with less drastic policies.[6]

Nor, despite the quantity of weaponry produced, was its quality very impressive. Hitler happened to come to power on the very eve of an exponential leap in the technical quality of both tanks and aeroplanes, and for the first five years of his dictatorship his factories were churning out military equipment that was already obsolescent. Thus, although the first production models of the PzKw III and PzKw IV medium tanks had been completed in 1936, by September 1939 there were still only 309 of these vehicles on strength, as compared to 2,886 older models, mainly fast but undergunned and underarmoured PzKw Is and PzKw IIs but also a number of Škoda tanks taken over from the Czech Army after the occupation of Bohemia-Moravia six months previously. There were shortages even of small-arms and light artillery: at the outbreak of war fifty divisions had no sub-machine guns or light A.A. guns. And after only six years of power the Nazis had no opportunity to train the larger part of the country's male population of military age: including part-trained Class II reservists fewer than two million men had

---

[6] David E. Kaiser *Economic Diplomacy and the Origins of the Second World War* (Princeton 1989) p. 167–8, 268 for labour shortages; Overy *Goering* p. 84 for Thomas's comparison of munitions output in 1918 and 1939, cf Albert Speer *Inside the Third Reich* (1970) p. 213 and n. 19 on p. 538 (it is possible that Thomas's figures are based on a total cash value of a large range of munitions including items like tanks and planes which cost relatively much more in 1939 and that Speer's figures are based on a comparison of aggregate numbers of specific traditional items like rifles and artillery); Overy *Goering* p. 83 Table 5; A.J. Brown *Applied Economics* (1947) p. 24; Marlis G. Steinert *Hitler's War and the Germans: Public Mood and Attitude during the Second World War* (Athens Ohio 1977) p. 31–3; Ferry Porsche with John Bentley *We at Porsche* (Yeovil 1976) p. 131, 133; Larry H. Addington *The Blitzkrieg Era and the German General Staff, 1865–1941* (New Brunswick N.J. 1971) p. 93–5 cf R.J. Overy *The Air War* (1980) p. 151 for the possibility of demotorizing the army; Richard Overy 'Unemployment in the Third Reich' *Business History* 29 (1987) p. 253–281 at p. 278 for the question of the effect of over-rapid rearmament on the industrial base and the quality of the workforce.

received any military training since 1918. Of course the goose-stepping army parades and the fly-pasts looked big, and were made to look even bigger by the newsreel cameramen, but there were no reserves either of trained men or of stock-piled modern weaponry to sustain any kind of military attrition or momentum; the Luftwaffe had less than 33 per cent equipment reserves, for example, the British and French air forces over 100 per cent.[7]

The weakness of Germany behind the well-publicized iron façade was pointed out cogently enough by the socialist exile Fritz Sternberg in a book published in English in October 1938 and in Dutch, Swedish and German editions in 1939 (the German edition under a Paris imprint). The English version was entitled *Germany and a Lightning War*: the German-language version is merely called *Die Deutsche Kriegsstärke* ('German War Strength') but used the word *Blitzkrieg* on p. 11:

> How long can Hitler wage war?
> As long as is necessary for a lightning war.
> (*Lange genug, wie es für einen Blitzkrieg notwendig ist*)

Hitler later claimed 'The expression *Blitzkrieg* is an Italian invention. We picked it up from the newspapers', but the authors of the *Dizionario Etimologico Italiano* state that the counterpart Italian term *guerra-lampo* is simply '*calco del ted. Blitzkrieg*' ('copy of German *Blitzkrieg*'). As a term for a very rapid military campaign Blitzkrieg was first used in English after the defeat of Poland. Sternberg however was using it in a Milwardian sense to refer to a type of war, not a style of campaigning: he argued that 'a protracted war is the greatest danger for the National Socialist régime in Germany . . . Unless German Fascism wins quickly it cannot win at all'.[8]

Confusingly enough, however, there were by the eve of the invasion of Poland a number of major weapons-building programmes that aimed to peak circa 1944. By 1944 it was intended to have a small fleet of long-ranged battleships armed with 15-inch guns, aircraft carriers, a fleet of two thousand Heinkel He 177 heavy bombers backed up with Junkers Ju 88 attack bombers, twenty motorized divisions, a modernized railway system, and so on. How under peacetime government Germany was to be capable of sustaining the social and economic strain of developing this arsenal, and how Germany was to avoid a major war in the interval, was not really considered, least

---

[7] Matthew G. Cooper *The German Army, 1933–1945* (1978) p. 155 for quality of tanks, p. 164 for shortages of submachine guns and light A.A.; Overy *Air War* p. 23 Table 2 for reserve levels in different airforces.

[8] Carlo Battisti and Giovanni Alessio *Dizionario Etimologico Italiano* (5 vols Florence 1950–57) vol. 3 p. 1890: vol. 1 p. 543 gives *Blitzkrieg* itself though Italian is noticeably less receptive to loan words than French or German: cf Hugh Trevor-Roper ed. *Hitler's Table Talk, 1941–1944* (1953) p. 172, 3–4 Jan. 1942; the first recorded use in English is in *The War Illustrated* 7 October 1939 p. 108: 'the German military machine was engaged in *Blitz-Krieg* – lightning war – with a view to ending as soon as possible'; Fritz Sternberg *Germany and a Lightning War* (1938) p. 13, 14.

of all it seems by Hitler. Before the invasion of Poland Hitler assured his generals that the campaign would be localized; Britain and France would make threats but would not declare war. He referred to 'England's war of nerves against Germany: England's land and air rearmament just beginning. France: psychology of the Maginot Line'. But it seems unlikely that Hitler had committed himself to a timetable as far as five years ahead or that if he had, he would have jeopardized his timetable by invading Poland only a few months after Britain had publicly guaranteed the inviolability of the Polish borders. What Hitler said to his generals had exactly the same status, as far as Hitler himself was concerned, as the construction programmes drawn up under the Four Year Plan; he saw no necessity of having his intuitions cramped either by anything he had said himself or by anything that had been planned on his behalf; the main thing was to keep moving forward.[9]

Once Britain and France had declared war, confusion reigned in the management of Germany's munitions industries. Thomas immediately urged the establishment of production priorities and Hitler obliged by announcing priorities on 7 September and revising them twice in October and a third time in November: the priorities decided were insufficiently specific to be much guidance in any case. There was confusion in extending planning procedures to cover relevant firms and certain industrial companies in bad odour with the Nazi party, including Opel and MAN, failed to receive war contracts for which they were eminently suitable. Men with key skills were called up into the armed forces and instead of permitting the establishment of a comprehensive system of exemptions and deferments Hitler confined himself to asking the War Ministry for the military service papers of prominent musicians and actors so that he could personally tear them up: these were the only type of civilian worker that he was concerned to protect. Göring had apparently counted on a massive drafting of female labour into munitions factories once war broke out but Hitler decided this was politically and ideologically undesirable; the woman's place was in the home, raising the large families favoured by Nazi doctrine. Hitler was simply not interested in the problems existing arrangements were causing, or their inadequacy with regard to future demands; as the parallel but even more extreme failures of omission in Italy were soon to show, dictatorship, as well as reducing the influence of the public officials best capable of engineering the transition from peacetime economy to a war footing, tended to disguise even the necessity for a systematic transition because of the strained abnormality of the conditions already existing before the war, and the distorted vision with which these conditions were perceived.[10]

[9] Overy *Goering* p. 85; Winfried Baumgart 'Zur Ansprache Hitlers von den Führern der Wehrmacht am 22. August 1939' *Vierteljahrshefte für Zeitgeschichte* vol. 16 (1968) p. 120–149, at p. 149 quoting Admiral Conrad Albrecht's diary.

[10] Carroll *Design for Total War* p. 192–6; Overy *Goering* p. 84, 98–9, but cf Overy 'Mobilization for Total War' *English Historical Review* vol. 103 p. 625–9.

III. Planning the German War Economy

Germany's economic performance during the war years may be considered under three heads, each of them related intimately to aspects of the Nazi ideology and regime: the belated and inadequate moves towards a unified and planned total war economy; the exploitation of conquered territories; and the utilization of Germany's unquestionably high levels of scientific and technical know-how – the last item being reserved for the next chapter.

In March 1940 Hitler appointed his Autobahn builder Fritz Todt as Minister of Armaments. One of Todt's most important measures was to promulgate a policy of 'self-responsibility' in industry, giving the allocation of contracts to the industrialists themselves. This policy, which was taken over by Albert Speer when he succeeded Todt as Minister of Armaments in 1942, was in general concept a revival of the First World War practice and was opposed by the overtheoretical Otto Ohlendorf (from early 1943, second state secretary at the Ministry of Economics) because it in effect meant the replacement of 'an objective state' by 'individual hyenas and monopolists'. In this as in other matters Ohlendorf underestimated his own Nazi associates: whereas in the First World War industrial self-responsibility had been a blank cheque for unscrupulous business magnates like Duisberg, Hugenberg and Stinnes, in the Second World War the proprietors were under a variety of pressures from Göring, the SS, the Gestapo and the Gauleiters, while Speer himself succeeded in establishing a fairly positive relationship with the management echelons of German industry – at least partly because they realized that they had a choice between cooperating with the well-bred, well-behaved Speer or having to deal with some more typical party boss. Hugh Trevor-Roper's judgement in his brilliant *The Last Days of Hitler* that, 'Speer was a technocrat . . . To the technocrat, as to the Marxist, politics are irrelevant', rather takes Speer too much at his own word: during the war the German industrialists knew that he was one of Hitler's right-hand men and deferred accordingly. Essentially the great German industrial concerns belonged to the old society, the partly rehabilitated ruins of Wilhelmine Germany which the Nazi party had taken over in 1933, and they simply did not have the resilience to defend themselves against a man of Speer's position and possessing Speer's undoubted gifts of leadership and intellect.[11]

At the same time the atmosphere of the regime tended to make government officials passive and isolated, and paralyzed initiative: James Burnham's verdict in 1941 that 'Germany is today a managerial state in an early stage', i.e. a

---

[11] Carroll *Design for Total War* p. 222–3; Speer *Inside the Third Reich* p. 209; *Trials of War Criminals before the Nuernberg Military Tribunals under Central Council Law No. 10* [i.e. U.S. prosecution of industrial, administrative and military leaders etc.] (15 vols Washington 1950) vol. 4 p. 239, statement by Ohlendorf; H.R. Trevor-Roper *The Last Days of Hitler* (1947) p. 84; Overy *Goering* p. 152–3.

front-runner in his 'Managerial Revolution', missed certain vital characteristics of the Nazi government system. Speer fully shared in the period's love-affair with the ideal of planning and even set up an agency with the resounding, almost mythic, title of Central Planning (*Zentrale Planung*) with responsibility for the allocation of raw materials, but his neat and symmetrical organization charts, to which he devoted more than a little attention, tended to translate into confusion at ground level: for example the organization of producers of end-products into committees and of component manufacturers into 'rings' led one official to note contemptuously:

> Many factories did not know whether they belonged at all to a committee or to a ring, and conversely there were only a few committees and rings which had a clear picture of the numbers of their component firms and which could direct them accordingly.

Even Speer could not halt the growing gap between rhetoric and reality which was an inevitable feature of totalitarian dictatorship; indeed his attempts at centralized control had much of the appearance of a reflex to preserve self-image and self-respect in the face of the systematic disorganization of the regime – almost a kind of counter-style.[12]

This confusion was of great comfort and assistance to Hermann Göring and Heinrich Himmler. Both these men aimed to build up huge autonomous industrial empires, Göring mainly in Czechoslovakia and Austria, Himmler anywhere that was suitable for a concentration camp, but especially in Poland. The general idea was to establish an industrial system that would replace the inherited capitalist set-up and, to some extent, the traditional problem of the political unity and independence of a concentrated industrial work force in a free labour market. Himmler's empire, in which cheap concentration camp labour was a key element, was part of his dream of the SS as a state within a state, with its own armed forces, economic resources and *Weltanschauung*, though in its practical details it owed much to Himmler's subordinate Oswald Pohl. Göring, as ambitious as Himmler, and more gifted, lacked the latter's dreadful, dreary singleness of purpose and the assistance of men of Pohl's sinister organizational vision, and though he was occasionally tempted by the idea of the Luftwaffe also as a state within a state, with its own land troops, and though he retained control of Luftwaffe procurement till mid-1944, he failed to tie in the organization of his industrial empire, the *Reichswerke Hermann Göring* with the running of the Luftwaffe. It may even be that the more his real grip on the Luftwaffe weakened the more he devoted himself to the Harold Robbins-style stratagems of confiscation, bribery and blackmail by which the component companies forming the *Reichswerke Herman Göring* were

[12] James Burnham *The Managerial Revolution: What Is Happening in the World* (New York 1941) p. 239; Speer *Inside the Third Reich* p. 221–2; quotation given in Carroll *Design for Total War* p. 244.

assembled. By 1944 he controlled an enterprise larger than all the other state enterprises put together, with 50 per cent of Germany's iron ore production, 20 per cent of its coal and 12.5 per cent of its steel. By this time of course Göring's personal influence with Hitler was minimal and there was little he could do to resist Speer's efforts to bring his empire within a coordinated war economy. With Himmler on the other hand Speer could only huff and puff:

> While we lack not only iron and wood but also manpower to construct armaments works for the immediate needs of the front lines, I saw during my inspection of the concentration camp at Mauthausen that the SS is carrying out plans that strike me as more than generous given today's conditions.[13]

Amongst Speer's other problems were the Gauleiters, the regional party bosses who also, in most cases, held office as heads of the provincial administrative system inherited from pre-1918 Germany. With very few exceptions Hitler always supported the Gauleiters and Speer, a newcomer in the Nazi hierarchy, fumed helplessly at their insistence on diverting scarce resources to the building of private bunkers and special trains, and protecting rug and picture-frame manufacturers or whatever – even Göring and Goebbels (himself Gauleiter of Berlin) saw the need to curb the local bosses. Speer's biggest headache of all was the Gauleiter of Thuringia, Fritz Sauckel, who was also Plenipotentiary for labour. Labour being the key resource in any economic strategy, Speer simply was not master in his own house as long as Sauckel had control of this sphere; and not only did the two men not get on, but Sauckel had no real understanding of his responsibilities other than in the doctrinaire ideological sense and, for example, maintained the party policy of not encouraging women to work in the war factories.[14]

In 1942, when Speer took office, he found the production of consumer goods was down only 3 per cent on pre-war levels. In 1943 Germany was still producing 12,000 tons of wallpaper and 4,000 tons of hair-tonic annually. Almost till the very end Speer was uncovering small firms or even not so very small firms which were churning out items that to his mind were quite unnecessary; in 1944 he found that a Leipzig firm was still producing the maps and phrase-books ordered in 1942 when an invasion of Persia had seemed a possibility. In that same year 150,000 electric cushions, 364,000 spurs and 800 tons of piano wire were manufactured. The Army,

---

[13] For Oswald Pohl see Rudolf Höss *Commandant of Auschwitz* (1959) p. 221–2; for *Reichswerke Hermann Göring* see Overy *Goering* p. 136; for Luftwaffe procurement see Speer *Inside the Third Reich* p. 332, 349–50, 553 n 3, 554 n 5; the quotation is from Speer's letter to Himmler 5 April 1943, given in Albert Speer: *The Slave State: Heinrich Himmler's Masterplan for SS Supremacy* (1981) p. 43

[14] Speer *Inside the Third Reich* p. 216–7 and Peter Hüttenberger *Die Gauleiter: Studie zum Wandel des Machtgefüges in der NSDAP* (Stuttgart 1969) p. 185–7. For Göring and Goebbels (and Ley and Funk) and their discussion with Speer in March 1943 regarding the revival of the Council of Ministers for the Defence of the Reich as a means of curbing the Gauleiters see Louis P. Lochner ed. *The Goebbels Diaries* (1948) p. 235–7, 18 March 1943.

though increasingly unable to protect its cherished suppliers of prestige goods, undoubtedly acted to encourage conservative suppliers who wished nothing more than to continue producing high-quality notepaper, china and officers' spurs; and of course colour film and high quality paper continued to be available for the Wehrmacht's prestigious illustrated magazine *Signal*. Leni Riefenstahl's film of the opera *Tiefland* was held up because of its low priority, yet Riefenstahl was able to pull strings to get sound tables refused by Speer. The Nazi hierarchy, even at the centre, was also active in this area. Goebbels campaigned to have Göring's favourite Berlin restaurant, Horcher's, closed because of the excessively luxurious standards it maintained – he even hired thugs to break the windows – but he insisted that production of components for household radios should continue so that the great German public could listen to the programmes broadcast under his auspices as Minister of Propaganda and Public Enlightenment, even though the same factories were needed to produce radar for the war against British bombers; and he had a total of 187,000 soldiers diverted from the front in successive relays to serve as extras in *Kolberg*, an epic of the War of Liberation of 1813, filmed in 1943–1944 and, on its release four months before the German surrender, allegedly seen by fewer people than had acted in it.[15]

Even where the right items were being produced, they were not produced in the most economical way. In contrast with the First World War, when the industrial magnates had salted away huge profits instead of expanding plant, the tendency in the Second World War was to circumvent restrictions on profit by investing in new plant and floor space instead of maximizing the use of existing plant by shiftwork. In 1942 only about one in ten of the workers in the tank, motor transport, small-arms and artillery sectors worked in second shifts; in the aero industry it was just over a third; the normal working week, for machine tools as well as their operators, was 48–49 hours, and up to 60 in key industries. The company pride of competing armaments firms and the technical obsessions of the armed forces's weapons experts occasioned further waste of effort in delaying standardization; in 1942 delays caused by design modifications was estimated to have reduced output of the aircraft industry by 20 per cent. In 1940 Germany spent 58 per cent more

---

[15] Speer *Inside the Third Reich* p. 222 cf Charles Webster and Noble Frankland *The Strategic Air Offensive against Germany, 1939–1945* (4 vols 1961) vol. 4 p. 481 Appendix 49xi; Milward *German Economy at War* p. 107; Speer *Inside the Third Reich* p. 238; J.R.M. Butler, N.H. Gibbs, John Ehrman, J.M.A. Gwyer, Michael Howard *Grand Strategy* (6 vols 1956–76) vol. 6 p. 6–7; Overy *Goering* p. 162; David B. Hinton *The Films of Leni Riefenstahl* (Folkestone 1978) p. 85 and Glen B. Infield *Leni Riefenstahl: The Fallen Film Goddess* (New York 1976) p. 196; Rudolf Semmler *Goebbels: The Man next to Hitler* (1947) p. 78, diary 18 March 1943 (it was in a *chambre separée* at Horcher's, incidentally, that Albert Speer first heard about the A-bomb from Friedrich Fromm, cf Speer *Inside the Third Reich* p. 225); Carroll *Design for Total War* p. 242; Patrick Robinson *The Guinness Book of Film Facts and Feats* (1980) p. 94 (there were a mere 120,000 extras in the Russian *War and Peace* of 1967).

on armaments than Britain but produced considerably smaller quantities of aircraft and certain key weapons because of excessive complexity of design and lack of standardization: in some respects they still regarded weapons manufacture as a craft rather than a matter of mass-production. Another factor occasioning waste of effort was over-confidence: Hitler's belief that Russia would be very quickly defeated led to a considerable slow-down of shell-production during the final months of 1941, though to be fair the Allies made exactly the same mistake two and a half years later and had to make a drive to boost shell production when Germany had still not surrendered in November 1944.[16]

IV. The Pillage of Europe

Speer's attempts to improve efficiency in output and the standardization of products is the economically conventional and respectable half of the story of Germany's huge increase in armaments output after 1942: exploitation of occupied territories and slave labour is the other half.

Till 1941 the chief economic importance of Hitler's conquests was in raw materials (especially those already stockpiled in the conquered countries) and captured arsenals. At the outbreak of war, calculating estimated monthly requirements against shortfalls in monthly domestic output, Germany had less than a year's supply of lead, less than seven months' stock of copper and nickel, less than three months' stock of tin. Over the next fifteen months there were additional supplies from the Soviet Union and from Japan, the latter making a somewhat cursory attempt to purchase strategic raw materials on the international market on Germany's behalf. Booty was at least as important. Yet though the conquest of France extended Germany's depleted stocks into 1941 the exploitation of France's stock-piles was poorly organized and only the rarer items like wolfram and quicksilver were shifted at all quickly – and even then 129 out of 484 tons of captured wolfram were still in France by the end of August 1940. The occupation of Norway secured that country's output of titanium, and though nickel from Petsamo in Northern Finland (now Pechenga in the U.S.S.R.) was not actually transported through German-occupied Norway the establishment of German occupation forces in northern Norway just across the border from Petsamo effectively guaranteed these supplies. Later, when western Russia was occupied, a vital source of manganese was acquired. The British Ministry of Economic Warfare had

[16] Burton H. Klein *Germany's Economic Preparations for War* (Cambridge Mass. 1959) p. 218; David MacIsaac ed. *The United States Strategic Bombing Survey* (10 vols New York) 1976 vol. 1 'The Effects of Strategic Bombing on the German War Economy' p. 35 and 43; ibid. p. 47; Overy *Goering* p. 159; W.N. Medlicott *The Economic Blockade* (2 vols 1959) vol. 2 p. 5 cf Butler et al. *Grand Strategy* vol. 6 p. 25–6.

counted on German stocks of these rarer metals, so necessary for alloys, being exhausted by the end of 1943, by which date, in reality, they were higher than in September 1939.[17]

Except in Czechoslovakia, which was one of the main centres of Hermann Göring's private empire, exploitation of the industrial potential of the occupied territories had a less vital role. The Dutch metallurgical industry increased its labour force by more than 15 per cent between 1941 and 1944 because of German contracts and the radio industry (in which the Philips Company was of course a world leader) also exported major quantities to the Reich. Similarly in Belgium by 1943 three-quarters of national output in the metallurgical industries was for German orders, though the total was only two-thirds – iron and steel only one half – of pre-war output, which anyway had been at a depressed level. Only a small part of these supplies was actually paid for – by the end of 1944 Germany owed the Netherlands $2,309 million and Belgium $3,327 million for unpaid goods – so presumably there was little reinvestment or renewal of deteriorated plant. Again, France supplied 90 per cent of its national production of lorries to Germany in 1942–1943 – 51,954 vehicles – but output levels were falling markedly. One reason for falling output was that pre-war France had been the world's greatest importer of coal (12 per cent of total needs coming from Britain which of course discontinued supplies in June 1940) and the German government failed to establish any overall strategy for coal distribution in Europe. On paper the coal supplies available to the Reich nearly doubled between 1938 and 1943 but relatively little was imported from the occupied areas, while the necessity of increasing supplies for Italy, for the synthetic oil and chemical industries, and even for domestic and office consumption (which rose by a fifth between 1938 and 1943) and resulted in actual shortages. These shortages naturally made themselves more seriously felt in France than in Germany. The German decision to pillage France rather than foster economic re-expansion was a principal reason for the failure of Pierre Laval to establish his collaborationist regime on any real popular base in 1942. By September 1943 when Speer had talks with the French industry minister Jean Bichelonne with a view to increasing French output, especially

[17] Georg Thomas *Geschichte der deutschen Wehr-und Rüstungswirtschaft, 1918–1943/5* (Boppard am Rhein 1966) p. 186; Johanna Menzel Meskill *Hitler and Japan: The Hollow Alliance* (New York 1966) p. 130–132; Harold Winkel 'Die "Ausbeutung" des besetzen Frankreich' in Friedrich Forstmeier, Hans-Erich Volkmann ed. *Kriegswirtschaft und Rüstung, 1939–1945* (Düsseldorf 1977) p. 333–374 at p. 340, Tabelle I cf Thomas *Wehr-und Rüstungswirtshcaft* p. 245; for Norwegian titanium see Alan S. Milward *War, Economy and Society, 1939–1945* (1977) p. 147; for Russian manganese ibid. p. 149; Klein *Germany's Economic Preparations for War* p. 120 Table 36 and generally p. 119–121. The Ministry of Economic Warfare's estimates of the imminence of Germany's collapse for want of raw materials had leaked out and been the subject of adverse comment in the British press by mid-1941, cf James Lansdale Hodson *War in the Sun* (1942) p. 44.

of consumer goods, it was too late, for by this stage the money, the manpower, the materials, even the will were lacking as far as France was concerned.[18]

There was a similar short-sighted, *ad hoc* style in the exploitation of captured arsenals. Standardization of weaponry throughout an army is desirable from the point of view not only of efficiency in manufacture but also of supply and movement of military formations under war conditions. Yet in some areas Germany went much further than any other major power in using confiscated or captured equipment. After the fall of France 140,000 of the French Army's 152,000 motor vehicles were seized. The French railways were still, in December 1947, trying to secure an account of 1,430 locomotives and 160,011 goods wagons removed by the occupation authorities. Although the Wehrmacht used Czech tanks in the invasion of France, captured French tanks, though of superior design, seem to have been utilized only for training purposes, but thousands of captured Russian 76.2mm M1936 (F22) field guns were converted for use with German ammunition and employed in the front line under the designation 7.62cm PAK 36(r), and Russian 85mm AA. guns were rebored to take the standard German 88mm Flak ammunition. By contrast the Luftwaffe's aircraft procurement experts seem to have been excessively reluctant to adopt captured material, though Italian-built fighters were pressed into use with second-line units engaged in operations against the *maquis* in France. The reason for not using captured aircraft seems to have had less to do with low opinion of foreign technology than with the failure of anybody at senior level to recognize an obvious possibility: towards the end of the Polish campaign in September 1939 the equivalent of three squadrons of Polish P.37 bombers were evacuated by their Polish crews to Rumania and with Rumanian-built Savoia-Marchetti S.M. 79-JR and German-built Heinkel He 111H-3 machines represented the mainstay of *Corpul Aerian* medium-bomber units serving in Russia after June 1941, till replacement types of German design and manufacture began to arrive in 1943: somehow the possibility of reequipment with French material never seems to have been considered, at least on the German side. The Finns were able to obtain 44 Curtiss Hawk 75As captured in France and Norway but perhaps only because the German found them still in their crates ready for transit. Equally, except initially in Czechoslovakia, there was no interest in foreign-designed military equipment actually being manufactured to German contracts, even though the Germans left all but a small part of the necessary

---

[18] Henry L. Mason *The Purge of the Dutch Quislings: Emergency Justice in the Netherlands* (The Hague 1952) p. 26–7; Milward *War Economy and Society* p. 147; Nicholas [Miklós] Kallay *Hungarian Premier: A Personal Account of a Nation's Struggle in the Second World War* (New York 1954) p. 301 for amounts owed by Germany for unpaid goods; Alan S. Milward *The New Order and the French Economy* (Oxford 1970) p. 132 Table 15; ibid. p. 38; Overy *Goering* p. 141 and Klein *Germany's Economic Preparations for War* p. 121–3 and cf John Gillingham *Belgian Business in the Nazi New Order* (Ghent 1977) p. 131–9 for the failure to exploit Belgian coal resources; Milward *New Order and French Economy* p. 155–8.

machine tools in their original locations and even gave the French permission to continue manufacture of war planes for the reduced armed forces maintained after the June 1940 armistice. In the later stages of the war, German-designed planes began to be built in Hungary and other places outside the Reich, but of a total non-German production in 1944 of 2,329 planes, only 244 were combat machines, and of these 74 were Messerschmitt Me 210s, a type which had been discontinued in Germany because of its bad handling characteristics. One is left with the impression of no overall plan or policy.[19]

Much more important was the exploitation of European agricultural resources. By 1943–1944 22 per cent of German grain consumption, 26 per cent of fats, and 29 per cent of meat derived from imports. The implementation of Nazi policies – mass-murder and labour drafts – caused a fall of output in Poland and Bohemia-Moravia and despite the need of Belgium and Norway to import food themselves half of Geman food imports derived from the occupied territories of western Europe. The single most important source of meat for example was Denmark.[20]

Initially however Germany's main benefit from overrunning half of Europe was *money*. German government expenditure exceeded domestic revenue from 1940; by 1943 domestic revenue was less than 45 per cent of expenditure and for political reasons tax levels were not raised any higher than they already were till March 1945. The German government obtained considerable advantage by holding down the exchange rate of the Reichsmark in its dealings with satellite nations, apparently with a view to preventing the accumulation

---

[19] Commandement en Chef Français en Allemagne: Groupe Français du Conseil de Contrôle *List of Property Removed from France during the War, 1939–1945* [also in French, German and Russian] (5 vols Berlin 1947–8) vol. 5 p. vii; ibid. vol. 5 p. 3; for Polish aircraft in Rumanian service see Jerzy B. Cynk *Polish Aircraft, 1893–1939* (1971) p. 196–7 and cf Alberto Borgiotti and Cesare Gori *Il Savoia Marchetti S.M. 79, 1935–1945* (Modena 1984) p. 270 fn. 92 and Ion Gudju et al. *Aripi Românesti: Contributii la Istoricul Aeronauticii* ([Bucharest] 1966) [in the British Library catalogue under Constantin Sendrea, Mihai Firu] p. 160. The Rumanians also had two squadrons of Bloch 210 medium bombers and two of Potez 633 light bombers but these represented pre-war purchases, and were perhaps the least effective of the machines available in Rumanian service. It does seem however that the Germans passed on some French fighters to the Rumanians, but too few to equip frontline units. For the Curtiss Hawks see William Green *War Planes of the Second World War: Fighters* (4 vols London 1960–1) vol. 4 p. 42. Commandement en Chef Français *List of Property* vol. 1 includes only about a thousand 'lathes for serial production' but cf Speer *Slave State* p. 30 where Speer refers to 2,000 machine tools (type unspecified) confiscated from France being promised for the SS factory at Buchenwald: he does not say they were actually delivered, only that 'their lack was felt elsewhere'; Webster and Frankland *Strategic Air Offensive* vol. 4 p. 499 Appendix 49 xxvi for manufacture of German designs outside Germany. Before going over to the manufacture of German designs the Czech firm Avia built twelve Czech-designed B 135 fighters for a Bulgarian contract: one of these attacked and damaged an American B-24 Liberator which entered Bulgarian air space after the raid on Ploesti of 1 August 1943.

[20] Karl Brandt, with Otto Schiller and Franz Ahlgrimm *Management of Agriculture and Food in the German-Occupied and Other Areas of Fortress Europe* (Stanford 1953) p. 610–614, Table 46 and charts 9–12 and cf ibid. p. 289–91.

of Reichsmark balances in counties which exported more to Germany than they imported; thus despite Hitler's personal esteem for Antonescu, Rumania did consistently worse in its economic transactions with Germany than the other satellite powers because its oil exports to Germany were so important, though in any case Germany consistently defaulted on its payments – it will be remembered that this had already been a revenue expedient of the Prussian government in the 1800s. Even more important were the occupation costs levied on the conquered nations: by 1943 they represented 38.4 per cent of German treasury income, and the RM10,850,000 paid by France in that year represented 60 per cent of French government expenditure. Including defaults on payment for goods, financial transfers from France in 1943 represented approximately twice the value of French exports of manufactured goods, agricultural produce and raw materials. In 1944 of course French financial contributions declined as a result of the Anglo-American invasion, but RM8,400,000,000 was extracted from northern Italy.[21]

At their peak in 1944 occupation costs represented about 17 per cent of German government expenditure: taking the war years as a whole they were less than 13 per cent of total expenditure. As more than half of wartime government spending in Germany was not covered by revenue at all, the levying of occupation costs seems to have had less significance in the financing of German war production than in hampering economic activity in the occupied countries and reducing their potential assistance to Germany as manufacturing centres. More important to the German domestic economy (and perhaps a little less immediately disastrous to the economies of the occupied countries) was the transfer of labour.[22]

Other than organizational problems labour was the main limitation on German output. In contrast particularly with the British war economy, women were virtually unaffected by war mobilization in Germany. Indeed there was a slight drop in the number of women in industry between May 1939 and May 1942 because of minor cut-backs in non-essential industries: from 2.62 million to 2.58 million. The 'German Women work For Victory' campaign promoted by Goebbels's propaganda ministry in March 1941 was not a success, and despite Goebbels's call for women to volunteer for war production in his

---

[21] For German non-payment of debts arising from import surpluses see David B. Cohen 'Le Pillage de l'Économie Bulgare par les Allemands' *Revue d'Histoire de la Deuxième Guerre Mondiale* année 18 (1968) no. 72 p. 44–66 at p. 66, N.N. Constantinescu 'Exploitation et le pillage de l'économie roumaine par l'allemagne hitlérienne dans la période 1939–1944' *Révue Roumaine d'Histoire* vol. 3 (1964). 92–114 at p. 102–5 and I.T. Berend and Gy. Ránki *The Development of the Manufacturing Industry in Hungary, 1900–1944* (Budapest 1960) p. 137. According to Kállay *Hungarian Premier* p. 302 import prices for Hungary's trade with Germany rose 180 per cent 1939–1944 whereas those for Rumania's imports from Germany rose 614 per cent. For occupation costs see Milward *War, Economy and Society* p. 138–140, Brandt *Management of Agriculture* p. 616 and Fritz Federau *Der Zweite Weltkrieg: Seine Finanzierung in Deutschland* (Tübingen 1962) p. 33.

[22] Federau *Zweite Weltkrieg* p. 33, 59

resoundingly well-received Total War speech at a special rally at the Berlin *Sportpalast* on 18 February 1943, attempts to implement decrees promoting the employment of women caused widespread complaint: and the average hours worked by women actually declined. Afterwards Speer estimated that proportionately more German women worked in the munitions industries in the First World War than in the Second. More plentiful supplies of food in the Second World War meant that women were not actually driven by sheer want to enter the factories, as had been the case in 1917 and 1918, but the commitment of the Nazi party, from Hitler downwards, to the ideal of the German housewife's home-making and child-rearing role also had its influence. One notes that in the Wehrmacht female personnel, as well as being relatively less numerous than the British A.T.S., W.R.N.S. and W.A.A.F., were subject to less drill and discipline, and did not have to salute, so that even within the armed forces the femininity and decorativeness of women, rather than their potential as substitutes for men, was emphasized.[23]

In any case Hitler had quickly seen the possibility of using the conquered populations of Europe to take the place in the factories of German menfolk conscripted into the Wehrmacht. His directive of 8 December 1941 ordering the replacement of essential workers of military age by prisoners and Russian civilians inaugurated the systematic exploitation of third-class citizenry which became a dominant feature of the Nazi economy. The use of slave labour made possible the reconciliation of two of the Nazis' more contradictory visions – that of the sturdy Aryan peasantry in their simple pastoral communities and that of the automaton-like workers labouring with feverish ant-like singleness of purpose in gigantic munitions factories. By 1944 alien workers (including prisoners of war) totalled over seven million, representing 22 per cent of the agricultural, 16 per cent of the handicraft, 17 per cent of the transportation and 29 per cent of the industrial work force – the percentage was as high as 46 per cent in the giant IG Farben chemical company and 59 per cent in the *Reichswerke Hermann Göring*, and overall non-German labour provided more than a third of the work-force in the German munitions industries.[24]

The whole system was psychologically underpinned by the concentration camp. In January 1943 there were, in addition to foreign workers and prisoners of war employed under surveillance, 123,000 detainees in concentration camps theoretically available for government work, and the numbers were pushed up to 524,000 by August 1944. Despite the slogan *Arbeit Macht Frei* (Work Liberates) above the entrance gates, few of the camps were in any way organized for modern industrial output and the appalling conditions and rapid turnover of detainees ensured that their significance in the overall picture of the

[23] Willi A. Boelcke ed. *The Secret Conferences of Dr. Goebbels* [1970] p. 120 ed. note under 13 Feb. 1941; Steinert *Hitler's War and the Germans* p. 199; Speer *Inside the Third Reich* p. 220–1; Arthur Geoffrey Dickens *Lübeck Diary* (1947) p. 121–2, 17 June 1945.

[24] Edward L. Homze *Foreign Labour in Nazi Germany* (Princeton 1967) p. 235, 239 Tables XVI and XVII.

war economy was largely, and in an appropriately negative sense, symbolic. Oswald Pohl, who organized the business side of the SS's internal empire, was interested at least theoretically in improving living conditions as a means of raising productivity, but his colleagues were more concerned to speed up the flow of detainees into the camps, even though this meant further deterioration of conditions. In the first six months of 1944, at a time when they had only the very vaguest suspicion of a nation-wide plot against Hitler and the regime, the various branches of Himmler's state security apparatus arrested 32,000 Germans for political, religious and labour offences, and 204,000 foreigners, usually on the most trivial pretexts. Speer's officials saw this as a calculated attempt by the SS to tap the labour supply of the war economy in order to increase the supply of labour within the camps. Since most of the industrial units within the camps were owned not by the SS but by large industrial combines the advantage to the SS was largely a matter of book-keeping, and to the industrial combines non-existent, since much of the concentration camp labour supplied by the SS would have been previously employed more productively in their own factories on the outside; the activities of the SS were thus mainly important for increasing the problems of holding together a skilled labour force. If not arrested, the foreign worker lived under a merely intensified version of normal wartime restrictions: recruited by various kinds of overt or covert pressure if not compulsion, housed in special barracks or calculatedly inferior billets, subject to restriction of movement by pass checks and to a degree of social ostracism by German neighbours, it was something like the existence of the workers in Fritz Lang's film *Metropolis* of 1925–1926; nevertheless the foreign worker was not necessarily worse off than he would have been in his own country, where economic recession and shortages of food and fuel were the normal consequences of German occupation policies; but the concentration camp was always there in the background, as both ultimate organizational model and ultimate menace.[25]

The Janus-faced and incoherent character of Nazi administration came out most clearly in the utilization of prisoners of war. On the eve of the invasion of the Soviet Union Germany held 1.3 million prisoners of war. The bulk of the Polish, Dutch and Belgian armies had been sent home, only the officers being kept in detention, and though there were several thousand British prisoners of war the greater part of the total number – probably over one million – was French. The latter were retained as a means of exerting pressure on the Vichy government. They were a very useful accession to the supply of labour (over half a million working in agriculture) and by 1943 some of them were being given leave, while others were being exchanged with the Vichy government at the rate of one prisoner of war for three civilian volunteers

[25] Joseph Billig *Les Camps de concentration dans l'économie du reich hitlérien* (Paris 1973) p. 72; Höss *Commandant of Auschwitz* p. 221–2; Homze *Foreign Labour in Nazi Germany* p. 256 cf MacIsaac ed. *United States Strategic Bombing Survey* vol. 3 'The Effects of Strategic Bombing on German Morale' p. 87; Speer *Inside the Third Reich* p. 374.

for work in Germany. By 1944 releases of French prisoners of war had been largely made up by accessions of British prisoners, of whom the majority, as other ranks, were obliged to work – the officers were exempted from useful employment under the Geneva Convention and were left to devote themselves to their legendary escape and theatrical exploits. The total numbers of working prisoners of war in 1944 was 1,830,000, less than twice the 1941 total. Yet in the interval no less than 5,160,000 Soviet military personnel had been captured by the Wehrmacht. The fate of these prisoners was a horror exceeded only by the murder of the Jews in the extermination camps. Up to 1 May 1944 818,000 Russian prisoners of war had been released to civilian or military status (including the pro-German forces raised by General Vlasov), 1,981,000 had died in prison camps and 1,308,000 had escaped, been shot, or had died in transit – mainly shot because too weak to continue the endless march westward, or left to die from exhaustion. Of the 1,053,000 left, 875,000 were working, mostly under appalling conditions. Rudolf Höss, the commandant of Auschwitz, later recalled that the starving Russians frequently ate one another: even if this claim is not credited there is no reason to disbelieve his statement that of the 10,000 Russian prisoners of war assigned to build the extermination camp at Auschwitz-Birkenau at the beginning of 1942 there were only 163 alive by mid-August of the same year.[26]

The foreign workers seem to have contributed their share of the detectable breakdown of law and order in the bomb-ravaged urban centres of Germany in 1944 and 1945, and in other respects they were not an accession of strength. Although a considerable proportion of German workers were too old or otherwise unfit for military service, foreign workers reported sick twice as often. Their productivity was low, too: various figures have been given; one set for 1944 gives the Italians as having only 70 per cent of the productivity of German workers and the Danes and Dutch even less. Though actual sabotage was rare, since stringent quality controls made gestures of this kind suicidal, the low productivity of Dutch and Danish workers whose background and

---

[26] Homze *Foreign Labour in Nazi Germany* p. 49 for prisoners of war June 1941; ibid. p. 187–8 for French prisoners of war 1943; ibid. p. 83 Table VII for Soviet prisoners of war, cf Christian Streit *Keine Kamaraden: die Wehrmacht und die sowjetischen Kriegsgefangenener, 1941–45* (Stuttgart 1978) p. 244 gives 5,734,528 Soviet P.O.W's by February 1945, of whom 3.3m had died or been killed in captivity and 500,000 escaped or recaptured by the advancing Red Army. See also Alfred Streim *Die Behandlung sowjetischer Kriegsgefangener im Fall Barbarossa: eine Dokumentation* (Karlsruhe 1981). The starvation of the Russian prisoners is examined in Streit p. 137–162, 249–253, and cases of cannibalism (punished by summary shooting) referred to in Streit p. 55 and Streim p. 132, 202 cf Höss *Commandant of Auschwitz* p. 124 fn 1. For the deaths of Höss's Soviet workers at Auschwitz see ibid. p. 123

James Bacque *Other Losses: An Investigation into the Mass Deaths of German Prisoners of War after World War Two* (1990) p. 187 claims that more than three-quarters of a million German soldiers died in U.S. captivity after the German capitulation, and perhaps a quarter of a million in French captivity. Though these figures have obtained little credence they do serve as a reminder of the problems which fighting units encounter in handling really large-scale mass-surrenders.

education (unlike the Italians) was as similar as could be to the Germans indicates that ways of cheating the system were not wanting.[27]

But of course the system cheated itself. Taking German-occupied Europe as an economic unit – which was precisely the view the Nazis claimed to take – the utilization of available labour, as also the exploitation of, for example, coal and financial resources, was about as inefficient and oppressive as it could have been. One can hardly say that it was worse than a crime, it was a blunder – the criminality was too gross and too deliberate for that – but certainly the badness of the management was equal in scale to the evil of the policies. The much-vaunted managerial achievement of Albert Speer, the Great Accessory of the Third Reich, was little more than part of the rhetoric of a system that set itself up in opposition to material reality.

V. The Japanese War Economy

A strain of megalomaniac fantasy was also characteristic of the Japanese war effort. It comes as something of a surprise, with Japan's vast productive capacity today, to find that in the 1940s Japanese industry was not even in the British or German league, let alone the American: admittedly the Japanese manufactured 6 per cent more aircraft than the British in 1944 but by weight this was only 52 per cent of British production because of British output of four-engined bombers, and the Japanese aircraft industry had been expanded at the expense of practically everything else. If Japanese film propaganda of the period gives far less emphasis to military hardware then German documentaries, it is at least in part because there was considerably less hardware to emphasize.[28]

Essentially Japan was still in the throes of industrialization in the 1940s. Previous to 1914 half of Japan's exports had been silk and cotton and half the country's iron and steel requirements had to be imported from abroad. During the First World War Japan had enjoyed a huge export boom; European trade with Asia declined, assisting Japanese export initiatives, and there were ammunition contracts and demand for Japanese merchant shipping from the Entente powers. Partly assisted by the wartime boom there was a massive expansion of iron and steel output – 225,000 tonnes in 1913, 5,800,000 tonnes in 1937. There was also rapid advance in technical processes; but it was only in the 1930s that Japan became capable of quantity production of large turbines, boiler tubes and large steel castings, and throughout the Second World War Japanese aero-engines and air-frames were plagued with faulty components, partly owing to the failure to exploit the manganese, tungsten etc. required

---

[27] Homze *Foreign Labour in Nazi Germany* p. 253, 260.

[28] Jerome B. Cohen *Japan's Economy in War and Reconstruction* (Minneapolis 1949) p. 199. For Japanese war films of the period cf Ruth Benedict *The Chrysanthemum and the Sword: Patterns of Japanese Culture* (1967) p. 135.

for ferro-alloys which were available in the newly-conquered territories but perhaps mainly owing to inadequate production processes resulting from too rapid an attempt to adopt advanced techniques, and insufficient attention to quality control.[29]

By the late 1930s the Japanese industrial sector was still comparatively small, suffering various symptoms of overexpansion, ill-placed for further growth, and manifesting curious features of imbalance due to specifically Japanese conditions. Firstly, potential for growth was limited by the needs of agriculture which though very highly developed required disproportionate investment both of labour and chemical fertilizer: in 1940 44 per cent of the employed population was in agriculture, fishery and forestry sector – over 14 million workers – and 105lb of chemical fertilizer was needed per acre of arable land, compared to 56lb in the U.S.A. Secondly big business sought higher profits by investment in Korea and Manchuria at the expense of broadening the industrial base in the Home Islands and, in collaboration with the Army, had committed the country to war with China. Military expenditure, which had been 29 per cent of total government expenditure in 1931, rose to 75 per cent in 1938. The level of armaments expenditure led to shortages of skilled labour, foreign exchange problems and domestic price rises, and since there was very little slack in the economy these signs of overheating were even more ominous than in Germany in the same period. By the time war with the Anglo-Saxon powers began to seem unavoidable in 1941, the economy was seriously overstretched: even stock-piles were beginning to run down. Any war against the West was unthinkable unless extremely brief.[30]

Japan's political structure had evolved by the late 1930s to something like a caricature of Imperial Germany at the beginning of the First World War. The Emperor was an even more formidable presence, though in practice even more of a figurehead. Real power was divided, in indeterminate proportions between an Army that had arrogated to itself the right to judge the best strategic interests of the country, a civilian administrative and governmental grouping which claimed constitutional rights while increasingly conscious that it had no real power base, and a conspiratorial front of monopoly capitalists. The big business combines (*zaibatsu*) were controlled either by a council of the founder's heirs, as in Mitsubishi, or by the managers, a kind of industrial shogunate, as in Mitsui. Their tendency to develop laterally into ever more diverse sectors of the economy and their penetration into banking gave them

---

[29] G.C. Allen *A Short Economic History of Modern Japan* (1981) p. 82, 96, 100–101, 265 Table XVII. For the failure to utilize available raw materials see Cohen *Japan's Economy in War and Reconstruction* p. 124–7; for technological progress in the 1930s see ibid. p. 155 and G.C. Allen 'Japanese Industry: Its Organization and Development to 1937' in E.B. Schumpeter ed. *The Industrialization of Japan and Manchukuo, 1930–1940: Population, Raw Materials and Industry* (New York 1940) p. 477–786.

[30] For labour statistics see Allen *Short Economic History of Modern Japan* p. 251, for chemical fertilizer see Cohen *Japan's Economy in War and Reconstruction* p. 365; for policy with regard to Korea, Manchuria and China, military expenditure and stockpiles see Cohen p. 5, 36, 41, 48 and cf Allen p. 147–8.

both the taste and the resources for economic imperialism, while their own financial resources, by limiting the influence of the Bank of Japan, also limited the power of the Tokyo government to restrain them by financial controls. Once war with Britain and America had commenced, the Navy, which hitherto had exercised little direct influence on national policy, began to exert itself to maintain its munitions supplies, while the Army, in spite of having installed one of its leading personalities, General Hideki Tojo as premier, failed to establish itself as a unifying factor in the management of the war economy so that for four increasingly disastrous years there was an aimless four-cornered struggle between Army, Navy, *zaibatsu* and civilian government.[31]

As in Germany and Italy during the First World War, manufacturing companies were given control of raw materials; various control associations were set up, though some not till late 1942: by 1944 there were 314 such associations, often headed by former presidents of the dominating firm in that sector and operating through a joint-stock company owned by interested firms. There was no *Zentrale Planung*, no Speer, to keep these groups in order: not even a Dall'Olio. In 1943 a weekly Supreme Wartime Economic Council was set up, consisting of premier Tojo, the ministers of the economic departments and seven business leaders, but this produced only talk. A few months later Tojo took the title of Minister of Munitions, suppressing the existing Ministry of Commerce and Industry and making its ex-minister his own deputy in the munitions field. The object seems to have been to strengthen the government's hand in dealing with the rivalry of the Army and Navy, which however soon attained new heights of the ridiculous. The new Ministry of Munitions also joined the Army and Navy in refusing to cooperate in the preliminary survey of manpower which was being attempted by the Ministry of Welfare, which theoretically had responsibility for manpower deployment. The armed forces also frequently by-passed the whole network of control associations: the Army had an effective monopoly of all the raw materials in occupied areas on the Asian mainland, and the Navy those on the islands and also the necessary shipping, which placed them in a good position to deal directly with the arms manufacturers; this may be seen as another version of the 'military-industrial complex' which had developed in Germany and Italy in the First World War and which also became apparent in the U.S.A. after Pearl Harbor.[32]

The rivalry between the Japanese Army and Navy had already been evident before the war when Army and Navy were supplied by Mitsubishi with two completely different types of twin-engined medium bomber. At the time of Pearl Harbor the two services also had completely different single-seat fighter planes, which was not unreasonable as the Army had no need for deck-landing capability and had chosen a machine that was considerably cheaper to

[31] Allen *Short Economic History of Modern Japan* p. 59–61, 136–140.
[32] Cohen *Japan's Economy in War and Reconstruction* p. 59–60, 71, 74, 274. For the 'military industrial complex' of Christopher Thorne *The Issue of War: States, Societies, and the Far Eastern Conflict of 1941–1945* (1985) p. 255.

build than the Navy's famous Zero, but even more manoeuverable. But faced with the challenge of faster, heavier American fighters both services began to order fast, heavily-armed land-based fighters, of comparable performance – but of different designs. They had less choice with radar because there were fewer suppliers, but Nihon Musen, the principal manufacturers of radar, were obliged to divide their radar factory into two halves, and engineers working on contracts for the Navy were not permitted to enter the half of the factory where work for the Army was being carried out. The radar sets were then erected in two separate early-warning systems, so that the Japanese ended by trying to defend their Home Islands against the American Superfortress bombers with two completely autonomous and dissimilar home defence establishments, neither of which worked properly. The only air-borne radar available was installed in naval JINI-S night fighters which were slower and inferior in rate of climb to the Army's night fighters. The main initiative in the direction of establishing a single system was the Army's attempt to conscript factory workers employed on Navy contracts. Evidently fearing future non-cooperation by the Navy, by the end of the war the Army was building its own cargo-carrying submarines: it already had its own aircraft carrier.[33]

Although plagued with quality-control problems and inferior materials, the Japanese aeroplane industry was the only one which maintained technical levels and output comparable with those of the other belligerent powers: indeed in their use of combat flaps (later types functioning automatically by means of manometers) they were world leaders. At the outbreak of the Pacific War the technical quality of Japanese military aircraft took the British and Americans completely by surprise: the Japanese had given minimum publicity to their aircraft industry and as late as 1945 the only photographs of certain standard Japanese aeroplane types available in the West had been taken in combat by camera guns on board Allied planes. Aircraft like the A6M2 Zero fighter epitomized the Japanese war economy in their structural lightness, cramped provision for the pilot, lack of armour and other protective devices, and fearsome effectiveness. Aesthetically Japanese aircraft design was outstanding, there was an indefinable Japanese look – perhaps still recognizable in Japanese motor car design more than a generation later – something in the harmony between the generally triangular tail fins and the long simple ovoids of the fuselages that was distinctly different from the suggestion of perpendicularity and squareness about most German designs, the clumsy fuselages of Soviet types, and the suggestion given by so many British marks of having been designed in separate sections and only afterwards put together as an ensemble. Clearly the Japanese aero-industry was in no sense backward. Production was highly concentrated: Mitsubishi's Nagoya plant

[33] Ibid. p. 241, 303; the submarines are noted on p. 73. For the Japanese army's aircraft carrier, the Akitsu Maru see R.J. Francillon Japanese Aircraft of the Pacific War (1970) p. 148–9.

at 4,250,000 square feet, was one of the largest aeroplane factories in the world, even if less than two-thirds the size of Ford's Willow Run plant in Michigan.[34]

Japan's aircraft output rose from 5,088 in 1941 (just over a quarter of British output) to 28,120 in 1944 (rather more in numbers, though not in total weight, than British output for that year). Workers in the aircraft industry increased by 285 per cent 1941–1944, indicating a handsome increase in productivity. Nevertheless efficiency was only 44 per cent of the US aircraft industry's in 1941 and 26 per cent in 1944. This was partly due to a reliance on general purpose rather than specialized machine tools (the distinction relates to the degree of complexity of the automated processes involved, special purpose machine tools not only having higher output but carrying out a longer sequence of processes with less human labour), but the German aircraft industry which also used mainly general purpose machine tools was over 70 per cent more efficient (81 per cent of US efficiency 1941, 45 per cent in 1944) and in fact the Japanese aero-industry had more manpower though smaller output than the German by 1943. Part of the problem was in the quality of the manpower, for large numbers of women, students, Koreans and other unskilled workers were drafted into the industry and there was also, by 1944, a disastrous decline in the physical health of the entire population, which inevitably affected productivity. Another cause if inefficiency was the attempt to build too many different types of aircraft, a fault frequently attributed to the German aircraft industry but much more markedly the case with the Japanese; by the autumn of 1944 the Japanese aircraft industry was attempting to mass-produce – in addition to the Navy Mitsubishi A6M Zero series and the Army Nakajima Ki-43 Hayabusa which had already been in service at the time of Pearl Harbor – three completely different newer single-seat fighter designs for the Army, two for the Navy, and two Army and two Navy twin-engined night fighter types.[35]

Aircraft production was seriously affected by the Army's stalwart refusal to exempt skilled workers from conscription. Though by the end of the war shortage of imported raw materials was the most usual cause of falling output, in the top priority machine-tools sector it was lack of skilled labour which prevented second shifts being worked till 1944, and even when initiated,

---

[34] For pictures of Japanese aircraft filmed in combat cf Jane's *All the World's Aircraft, 1945–1946*: the photos of the Kawanishi H8K2 ('Emily') are also to be found in Bill Gunston *Japanese and Italian Aircraft* (1985) p. 28–9, where their provenance is indicated. The photos in *Jane's* of the Aichi E13A ('Jake') and Mitsubishi A6M2-N ('Rufe') appear to have the same origin. For Mitsubishi's Nagoya plant see Cohen *Japan's Economy in War and Reconstruction* p. 209 cf Donald M. Nelson *Arsenal of Democracy: The Story of American War Production* (New York 1946) p. 220.

[35] Cohen *Japan's Economy in War and Reconstruction* p. 210, 219; Overy *Air War* p. 171 Table 16, for Japanese aircraft types see Francillon *Japanese Aircraft of the Pacific War* passim; for the Luftwaffe's excess number of aircraft types see Werner Baumbach *Broken Swastika* (1960) p. 48–9.

second shifts could be manned in only a small minority of machine shops. In terms of sheer numbers the Japanese had no real shortage of labour: the population increased 20 per cent in the period 1930–1944, reaching 77,044,000 in the latter year, and the proportion in employment also increased a couple of per cent. Till the extravagant conscription programme of 1944 the army was in relative terms by no means large, despite the disruptive effect of its unselective call-up procedures. Manpower was drifting, or was being impelled, from the land; the percentage of the male labour force employed in agriculture and forestry fell from 41.2 per cent in 1930 to 30.3 per cent in 1944; in 1945 the rice crop was the worst since 1909 and there were also many extraordinarily bad floods in rural areas, suggesting that the cut-back of the agricultural labour force had been at the expense of effective land-use. Labour was also transferred by order from less essential industries; output of electric lightbulbs fell from 167 million in 1940–1941 to 4 million in 1944–1945 and of candles from 43 million pounds in 1940 to one million pounds in 1945. New sources of labour were also tapped. There were relatively few prisoners of war in the Home Islands and no more than 18,000 were employed as labour. Much more important were Koreans (667,684 were brought in, theoretically on two-year contracts), women (39 per cent of the labour force in 1940, 42 per cent in 1944) and children. Japanese exploitation of juvenile labour went far beyond Germany's use over twenty-seven months of a total of 200,000 teenage boys below draft age to help man Flak guns: by July 1945 3,433,000 Japanese 'students' were working in industry, of whom only 195,000 were university students; half the rest were from primary schools. The student labour scheme had been inaugurated late in 1943 and it had been originally envisaged that the students would work for 30 days, with six hours of lessons per week; the object may have been less economic than civic and educational, as with the compulsory physical labour for intellectuals during China's Cultural Revolution. Though the children were paid (according to school grade) the money was issued in the first instance to the schools, which made various deductions. Eventually the work period was extended to 120 days, and the lessons were given up altogether in July 1944.[36]

The question of children's pay was important because, with spiralling prices and increasing shortages, the final two years of the war saw the physical immiseration of the entire population to a degree unparalleled even in the Soviet Union. Absenteeism was at 20 per cent of the workforce in 1944 and

[36] Cohen *Japan's Economy in War and Reconstruction* p. 271–2; ibid. p. 203 for machine tool industry; ibid. p. 288 (table 33) and p. 289 for population; ibid. p. 367, 407 for agricultural labour force; ibid. p. 411 for lightbulbs and candles (in rural areas at least oil lamps were still the normal form of lighting; but by 1945 there was no available mineral, vegetable or animal oil); ibid. p. 209 for prisoners of war; ibid. p. 322 and p. 323, Table 42 for child labour and p. 326 for Koreans, cf Hans-Dietrich Nicolaisen *Die Flakhelfer: Luftwaffenhelfer und Marinehelfer in Zweiten Weltkrieg* (Frankfurt 1980) p. 11. In Britain older schoolchildren were often released for 'potato picking' weeks and some schools organized farm camps but there was no national system of juvenile service.

rose to 34 per cent even in unbombed factories in 1945, and the principal reason seems to have been malnutrition: in August 1944 30 per cent of the women and child workers at the Mitsubishi glass factory at Tsurumi were suffering from beri beri. One may assume that little attention was given to official assurances that the 'heavier our bodies, the higher our will and spirit rises above them' or to radio programmes recommending callisthenics as a means of making up for lack of food. By 1945, with the massive extension of military conscription and restrictions on labour mobility, a veritable black-market in labour developed, with the Army and Navy taking a lead in encouraging it; utilizing their monopoly access to food and clothing they offered these as bribes to potential workers, many of whom were already employed in other sectors of war production. This black market in labour also increased absenteeism: prohibited from leaving their jobs, many munitions workers simply reported sick and then clocked in, on more favourable terms, at a munitions factory elsewhere. In Japan, as elsewhere, the war provided a strange commentary on the logic of the capitalist economy.[37]

VI. The British War Economy

The war effort of Germany and Japan may be summarized as ostentatiously brilliant campaigning within the context of a totally schizoid conception of means and objectives. Britain's performance was almost the mirror opposite.

Already in 1929 the Manpower Sub-Committee of the Committee of Imperial Defence was outlining the need for control of prices, wages and consumption during the next war and in 1932 it was agreed that the war in question might come within the next ten years; another Committee of Imperial Defence sub-committee was established to consider the extent and timetabling of the necessary wartime controls and the choice of government departments to administer them. In March 1933, a few weeks after Hitler came to power, the government shrugged off Winston Churchill's call for a build-up of British air defences but during the following year the staffs of all three armed services acknowledged that Germany was the most probable future enemy; the corollary was only accepted in Germany in September 1939. Except therefore in the field of actual weapons manufacture Britain had at least a five years lead over Germany in preparing organizationally for the Second World War. Nowhere was 'Planning' more of a vogue word than in Britain: 'In the world today the word "planning" is almost on everybody's lips: planned distribution, planned finance, planned transport,

---

[37] Cohen *Japan's Economy in War and Reconstruction* p. 273–4 for the black market in labour, p. 342–4 for the effects of malnutrition, cf R.H. Havens *Valley of Darkness: The Japanese People and World War Two* (New York 1978) p. 114–132. For official exhortations and the recommendation of callisthenics cf Ruth Benedict *The Chrysanthemum and the Sword: Patterns of Japanese Culture* (1967) p. 17.

planned power', Israel Sieff told a meeting of P.E.P. (Political and Economic Planning) in March 1933; he might also have added, planned warfare.[38]

Not all the detailed schemes had been completely worked out by September 1939, and some analyses and proposals drawn up by certain committees had been rudely savaged by other committees in the knockabout sixth-form debating society style practised by the British Civil Service, but the blueprints for the management of Britain's war economy were mostly ready when the German _Panzer_ spearheads crossed the Polish border. The bill to establish the new government departments needed for the war, Home Security, Economic Warfare, Information, Food, and Shipping, having been drafted well in advance, could be rushed through all its stages in the House of Commons on 1 September 1939, two days before Britain actually declared war, whereas Hitler, acting by decree, took till 17 March 1940 to establish a Ministry of Armaments and till 12 March 1942 to establish any sort of official relationship between the Ministry of Armaments and Göring's Four Year Plan office.[39]

The Nazis' conquests in western Europe prevented a repetition of Germany's principal failure on the economic front in the First World War, the inadequate supply of food; but the overall management of the German economy in the Second World War resembles that of the First in its lack of plan compounded by expressionistic botching. In Britain on the other hand the chief lessons had been thoroughly learnt and digested; amongst the results of the arduous committee work of the 1930s was that military conscription (first introduced in 1916) was reintroduced in May 1939 and that ration books (first used in 1918) were already printed ready for distribution in September 1939. Although control over the entire supply of labour was not achieved till 1942 a Schedule of Reserved Occupations, established in 1922 and since then constantly updated, prevented conscription of men wanted in industry right from the beginning.[40]

Britain's armaments production had begun to increase markedly from 1936. In April 1938 the limit of Royal Air Force rearmament was fixed for the first time in terms of plant capacity rather than available finance; Germany was still employing conventional financial accounting procedures and nine months later Schacht, the former Nazi finance minister and still president of the Reichsbank, refused to extend credits to the government on the grounds that the country was, in book-keeping terms, bankrupt. Peacetime rearmament in Britain helped warm up rather than, as in Germany, overheat the economy; income tax was raised from 4s.6d. (22.5p) in the pound in 1934 to 7s.6d. (37.5p) in 1939 and a £400 million armaments loan floated in 1937 was raised

[38] W.K. Hancock and M.M. Gowing _British War Economy_ (1953) p. 47–9, 63–4; Israel Sieff _Memoirs_ (1970) p. 164. P.E.P. set up in 1931, began issuing a broadsheet entitled _Planning_ on 25 April 1933.

[39] Hancock and Gowing _British War Economy_ p. 89, 124–5.

[40] Ibid. p. 57 for conscription, p. 52, 175–6 for rationing, p. 58 for reserved occupations.

to £800 million in 1939 so there was some pressure on private spending, but nothing like what there was in Germany. On the other hand unemployment remained at over one million even in late 1940. By the end of 1939 Britain was beginning to overtake Germany in output in certain categories of weapon. Even in the manufacture of rifles, where the Germans produced 589,400 to Britain's 45,500 in the first eight months of the war, the British made up by *reconditioning* over half a million rifles from existing stock piles.[41]

Yet Britain's productive effort was less of an assistance to first line strength than the Germans'. Tanks for example were of inferior performance, and some models of combat aircraft were continued in production simply in order not to interrupt output while replacement types were held up at the development stage – 'many, perhaps most' of the Armstrong Whitworth Whitley heavy bombers built during the war never left Aircraft Storage Units. Clearly planning sense did not always make economic sense, let alone military sense: the objective often seemed to be to maximize mobilization, with the defeat of the enemy only a side issue – a squinting of focus perhaps to be expected from a civilian-minded regime.[42]

Moreover the British military leaders took a much longer-term view of the war than their German opposite numbers, the latter evidently having a somewhat casual attitude to what one British general called, 'the fundamentals of war – that soldiers must be trained before they can fight, fed before they can march, and relieved before they are worn out'. Thus while R.A.F. front-line strength was just over half that of the Luftwaffe in September 1939, the reserves were very much greater. A massive training programme was already under way; in 1940 65.6 per cent of the military aircraft produced in Germany were fighters and bombers but only 53.2 per cent in Britain, training aircraft accounting for much of the rest. British spending on home defence was proportionately very high – for the year ending March 1939 £13 million was spent on the anti-aircraft defences of Britain and £22 million on the field army. What might be called the material infrastructure of the armed forces received massive investment. In 1940 Britain produced 6,000 armoured vehicles other than tanks to Germany's 500 and 113,000 military trucks to Germany's 88,000, which meant that the much smaller British Army was relatively much more motorized.[43]

Although a Director General of Manpower was not appointed till June 1941, and although it was not till late 1942 that the manpower budget covered all sectors of the economy, it was realized (on the basis of the First World War experience that was shrugged off by the Nazis) that manpower would be the key to war production. Perhaps the effect of Britain's vast wartime munitions

[41] Edward R. Zilbert *Albert Speer and the Nazi Ministry of Arms: Economic Institutions and Industrial Production in the German War Economy* (East Brunswick N.J. 1981) p. 99, cf M.M. Postan *British War Production* (1952) p. 18; Postan p. 12.

[42] M.M. Postan, D. Hay, J.D. Scott *Design and Development of Weapons* (1964) p. 12.

[43] Sir William Slim *Defeat into Victory* (1956) p. 164; Postan *British War Production* p. 109; Klein *Germany's Economic Preparations for War* p. 99 Table 28.

output was spoilt by the fumbling use to which this weaponry was put, and in any case it was much less than that of the U.S.A. with its much larger industrial base, but the degree of coordination of social mobilization in Britain was one of the outstanding achievements of the war, and to a large extent it was due to the leadership of Ernest Bevin, General Secretary (and creator) of the Transport and General Workers' Union, whom Churchill appointed Minister of Labour in May 1940. Despite Churchill's efforts to induce Beaverbrook to establish an overall control of war supply in 1941 – efforts thwarted by opposition to Beaverbrook on the part of Bevin, amongst others – each of the three services retained their own procurement ministries throughout the war (the Ministry of Supply for the Army, the Admiralty for the Navy, the Ministry of Aircraft Production for the R.A.F) so that alongside and within the Lord President's Committee which attempted to coordinate the home front Bevin was the real economic supremo, the work of his ministry being far more crucial than the national income framework of accounting established by Keynes at the Treasury, which has been held up by some economic historians as the greatest triumph of managerial technique of the war years. Bevin was one of the great men of the war. Coarse, touchy, truculent, transparent, natural, vain, uninhibitedly relishing power – 'Like Churchill . . . he seemed a visitor from the eighteenth century', wrote *The Times* after his death – he guaranteed that Britain's economic mobilization was more human and humane than under Lloyd George a generation earlier, let alone than under Albert Speer with his organization charts and his committees and his prefiguring of Corporation Man; and yet the humanity was of the back room and the tea break, reassuringly cosy and familiar yet essentially dingy and banal, for Bevin, though a man of vision, had little poetry. The common man image which Bevin represented was much celebrated at the time:

> Today, the high-pitched cry of 'Up Guards and at 'em!' has been replaced by the dogged slogan 'Go to it!', addressed no longer to soldiers on the field of battle, but to men in the mines and women in the factories. The age of heroics is over. The artist's subject-matter is no longer confined to the battlefield: he must look for it in the blast furnace, the shipyard or the village street.

Certainly his wartime alliance with Churchill was one of the more improbable partnerships of the war; during a visit to Chequers it was noted, 'He was a little on his guard in these unaccustomed surroundings, but soon became more at ease and even ate honey with his knife': Bevin eating honey with his knife at the Prime Minister's country residence may be seen as symbolizing the apparent fusion of classes in wartime Britain, a fusion to which no man made a greater contribution.[44]

[44] For example of the emphasis on national income accounting see Robert Lekachman *The Age of Keynes* (1967) p. 122–6; *Times* 16 April 1951 p. 5b (first leader); the longer quotation is from Eric Newton's introductory text to an illustrated pamphlet *War Pictures at the National Gallery* (1942); John Colville *The Fringes of Power: Downing Street Diaries, 1939–1955* (1985) p. 221, 12 Aug. 1940

Within the overall picture of the British war economy the most striking success was the mobilization of women. 'In no other country are women so thoroughly organized for war', boasted the commentator in Roy Boulting's documentary epic *Desert Victory*. The labour conscription of women through the National Service Act of December 1941 and the operation of the Registration of Employment Order during 1942 accelerated rather than caused women's movement into the jobs vacated by men. Taking the male population from 14 to 64 (of whom nearly two-fifths would be either too young or too old for military service) we find that in June 1939, out of 14,650,000 men, just under half were in the armed forces or the key manufacturing, mining, agricultural, transport or utilities sectors, in which there also worked just over one million women. Four years later, in June 1943, 83.4 per cent of males 14–64 years old were in the armed forces or manufacturing, mining, agriculture, transport and utilities, and in addition there were more than three and a quarter million women (more than twice as many as in 1918). In addition to the huge expansion of the armed forces, total employment in manufacturing, mining, agriculture, transport and utilities had risen from 7,770,000 to 10,250,000. The slack of unemployment, of strategic unemployment in the less essential or service industries which were being squeezed out by pressure from the Board of Trade and the Ministry of Labour, of idleness on inherited income, all contributed to the war effort, but the largest single source of extra manpower was womanpower.[45]

One of the areas where women contributed was agriculture, where the addition of 150,000 women to an approximately stable male labour force helped increase output by 28 per cent, enabling Britain to survive, in good health even if somewhat hollow-cheeked, on less than half pre-war food imports. With changes in crops, net output of calories increased 91 per cent: in Switzerland, equally beleaguered, the increase was only 17 per cent. Part of this achievement was the result of the growing use of tractors, of which there were 56,200 in 1939 and almost four times as many – 203,400 – in 1946. By 1946 they provided nine-tenths of draught power on farms: some were imported from America, 1942 being the peak year with 27,056, but the majority were turned out by factories in Britain.[46]

It is probable that the war encouraged nostalgia for traditional sex roles; the fashion of the day was for women to have long hair, red lips, padded shoulders, tight waists; even the uniforms of the women's services seemed to emphasize femininity (or would have done if they had been made to fit). Yet in Britain there was nothing like the note of passive, primitive, helpless acceptance which was evoked by an archetypal Italian wartime poster,

[45] The script for *Desert Victory* was by James Lansdale Hodson; for the rest of paragraph Hancock and Gowings *British War Economy* p. 28, 78.

[46] Edith H. Whetham *British Farming, 1939–1949* (1952) p. 101, 105, 141; Milward *War, Economy and Society* p. 253, 255 cf Keith A.H. Murray *Agriculture* (1955) p. 242; ibid. p. 275 and *Statistical Digest of the War* (1951) p. 158 Table 138.

showing a rather 1890-ish woman dragging a thumb-sucking toddler, with a charging Bersagliero in the background and the caption, 'The Italian woman, with her self-denial and sacrifices, marches alongside the fighting men'. The assertions of femininity in wartime Britain were in the context of a strenuous commitment to women's role in the war. The productive effort of the girls in the factories was celebrated in one of the classics of wartime cinema, Frank Launder's and Sidney Gilliat's *Millions Like Us* (1943) which starts with Patricia Roe, who wants to be an A.T.S (member of the women's army) being told, 'The men at the front need tanks, guns and planes. You can help your country just as much in an overall as you can in uniform these days'. But perhaps the most striking evocation of the British woman worker at war is the scene in the documentary *Night Shift* where girls in a munitions factory waltz during their midnight lunch break, the foreman, who plays the piano, being almost the only man there. Meanwhile, a thousand miles away across the blacked-out continent, even the workshops in the concentration camps stood idle . . .[47]

VII. Elements of Unbalance

It was not inappropriate that the British soldier in his baggy khaki and shaving-bowl helmet looked perhaps the least military of all the European soldiery of this war: equipped, fed and supported by the huge social effort just described, the British armed forces turned out to be something of a blunt instrument. In 1941 it was found that the divisional slice – the troops in a division plus its share of corps, army, G.H.Q and communications formations – was 42,000, well over twice the field strength of a division. Outside 735,000 men in actual tactical formations the army had over a million men on ration strength in H.Q., A.A., transport depots, other kinds of depots, etc. It had moreover already been supplied with 20 million pairs of trousers and plans were in hand to step up production. Nor was it only trousers which were in excess supply. A division of 18,347 men was allocated 4,505 motor vehicles, compared to the 2,012 vehicles per division of 14,253 men in the U.S. Army

---

[47] Harold L. Smith 'The Effect of the Second World War on the Status of Women' in Harold L. Smith *War and Social Change: British Society and the Second World War* (Manchester 1986) p. 208–229. The poster captioned 'La donna italiana colle sue rinunce e col suoi sacrifici marcia insieme ai combattenti' is reproduced in Zbynek Zeman *Selling the War: Art and Propaganda in World War II* (1978) p. 75.

In the British A.T.S., girls directing anti-aircraft fire wondered why they weren't ever allowed actually to fire the guns: D. Parkin 'Women in the Armed Forces, 1940–5' in Raphael Samuel ed. *Patriotism: The Making and Unmaking of British National Identity* (3 vols 1989) vol. 2 p. 158–170 at p. 169. Only the Soviet Union used women in combat situations, though one notes that their most successful all-female aviation unit, the 588th Bomber Regiment (later the 46th Guards Regiment) specialized in carrying out 'nuisance' raids at night in PO–2 two-seater biplanes – the air war counterpart of nagging.

(representing capacity for twelve times daily transportation needs) and the 543 motor and 726 horse-drawn vehicles in a German division. Churchill was astonished and infuriated by this lavish scale of establishment and let his military colleagues know it:

> Winston began one of his long harangues stating the Army was certain to crowd in 'dental chairs' and Y.M.C.A. institutions instead of bayonets into the landing in France. What we wanted, he said, were combatants and fighting men instead of a mass of non-combatants. We argued with him that fighting men without food, ammunition and petrol were useless.

And though the divisional slice was reduced somewhat in the war in Europe – to about 38,000 in the Mediterranean theatre – the dreadful conditions of South East Asia and the special problems this entailed of logistic and medical support pushed it up in Burma to 56,000, enabling Slim's Fourteenth Army to be celebrated in Roy Boulting's film *Burma Victory* (1945) as 'the largest single army in the world'.[48]

The sheer scale of British (and American) support for their fighting troops complicated the problem of movement on land, let alone of sea-borne invasions, in a way which has never been calculated but which, it may be suggested, prolonged the war by at least a year. Even in 1941 Air Vice-Marshal Coningham claimed, 'it's like a pyramid – you need about 1,000 tons behind to get 1 ton forward'. And the larger the organization, the greater the probability of bottle-necks: by mid-September 1944 the British and Americans had landed 2,168,307 men and 460,745 vehicles across the Normandy beachheads and a further 380,000 men and 69,312 vehicles in the South of France, but by October eight out of Eisenhower's 56 divisions were unable to advance owing to lack of transport.[49]

The industrial effort to support the considerably smaller but more capital intensive Royal Air Force was nearly as great in manpower terms as for the British Army, and if anything the R.A.F had even more problems with the complexities of marshalling its resources. In April 1941 there were 26,600 R.A.F personnel in the Middle East of whom 1,175 were pilots: but there were only 292 first-line aircraft (out of a total of 1,044) and there was a serious shortage of ground crew. Meanwhile in Britain Bomber Command had a surplus of ground crew – in November 1941 52,000 more ground crew than

[48] Hancock and Gowings *British War Economy* p. 288–290; R.F. Harrod *The Prof: A Personal Memoir of Lord Cherwell* (1959) p. 206; Walter Scott Dunn *Second Front Now – 1943* (Alabama 1980) p. 170; Arthur Bryant *Triumph of the West, 1943–1946* (1959) p. 217–8, diary of Sir Alan Brooke 14 June 1944; Butler et al. *Grand Strategy* vol. 5 p. 49. In 1945 Goebbels complained that with 1.5 million men in the West, Rundstedt managed to field only 60 'full-strength' divisions: Hugh Trevor-Roper ed. *The Goebbels Diaries: The Last Days* (1978) p. 127, 13 March 1945. Slim, with three-quarters of a million men, fielded twelve divisions and three independent brigades in 1944.

[49] James Lansdale Hodson *War in the Sun* (1942) p. 207, 22 Nov. 1941; Butler et al. *Grand Strategy* vol. 6 p. 30 cf Russel F. Weigley *Eisenhower's Lieutenants* (1981) p. 356.

required by equipment levels, half of them fitters; by February 1942 a surplus of 42,000 fitters. For nearly two years the statistical experts of the R.A.F. were able to pretend that the problem was not overrecruitment but shortfalls in aircraft deliveries, but after May 1944 men began to be transferred from the R.A.F to the other services. And despite the surplus of fitters approximately every twelfth plane on the establishment was awaiting spares in 1941; this was reduced to one in forty by 1944. It was calculated that on average six Lancasters could be repaired for the same cost and effort as building one new machine: by 1944 when 36.5 per cent of all heavy bombers issued to units came from repair shops the distribution of industrial labour between building new machines and manufacturing spares was as follows:

	New Machines	Spares
Airframes	450,000 workers	100,000 workers
Engines	175,000	90,000
Undercarriage	45,000	30,000
Propellers and accessories	18,000	17,000
Turrets	17,000	3,000
Guns	18,000	7,000
Other (including instruments)	190,000	190,000

Of course certain types of spares were repaired for routine maintenance within flying units: but if one-third of bombers issued to units were from repair shops and a repaired machine cost a sixth of a new machine and nearly a fifth of workers even in the airframe sector were producing spares, it is evident that far too many spares, or spares of the wrong kind were being produced. Nor were the planes, once built or renovated, necessarily put to very effective use: in 1942, at the height of the Battle of the Atlantic, Coastal Command planes carried out an average of one sortie a week.[50]

The scale, and disproportionate material lavishness of British war production necessitated another feature of the British war economy: its dependence on the U.S.A. In the First World War Britain had obtained a wide range of munitions from America but domestic supply had always been in far greater quantities, with the single exception of motor cars – 20,350 foreign-built (mainly Ford) cars and vans had been imported and 13,450 cars and vans built in Britain. Even the motor trucks employed by the British armed forces in the First World War had been predominantly British – 38,045 British to 20,955 foreign.

[50] Winston S. Churchill *The Second World War* (6 vols 1948–54) vol. 3 p. 669 Churchill to Chief of Air Staff, 5 April 1941; John Terraine *The Right of the Line: The Royal Air Force in the European War, 1939–1945* (1985) p. 462; ibid, p. 605; Postan *British War Production* P. 321 and Table 44; ibid, p. 317 Table 43, p. 318 and Public Record Office AVIA 10/269 DDGS 7 June 1944 'Estimated Distribution of M.A.P. Labour in Production of New Aircraft Build [sic] and for Spares'; Guy Hartcup *The Challenge of War: Scientific and Engineering Contributions to World War Two* (Newton Abbot 1970) p. 83.

In the Second World War however more than half of the British armed forces' trucks – and these of superior type – were American-built: 744,195 to 700,746 British-built vehicles. The U.S.A. also supplied most of Britain's tanks and transport aircraft from 1942 onwards, and the need to ship over training aircraft was avoided by the expedient of sending the aircrew to North America to be trained there. Even the 20mm cannon which became a feature of R.A.F. fighter planes were often of American manufacture, 45,129 being imported from the U.S.A. And whereas in the First World War British imports of raw or semi-processed materials had fallen with the important exception of petroleum, chemicals, meat and tobacco (the latter two exhibiting only a marginal increase however), in the Second World War British dependence on American raw materials was much greater: for example imports of pig iron, steel ingots and finished and semi-finished steel, which were 1,228,000 tons from all sources in 1938, more than trebled to 4,028,700 tons, nearly all from the U.S.A., in 1941. And to process this raw material 118,108 machine tools were imported from the U.S.A. 1940–1944 (more than half in 1940 and 1941 alone). During the same period 374,048 machine tools were made in the United Kingdom (representing more than half the total inventory in 1943) but the British-made machine tools were mainly simpler and cheaper types; for example in 1942, when imports of American machine tools were about one-quarter of domestic output, the majority of automatic and turret lathes, vertical drillers and boring machines were imported. Thus even when munitions were made in Britain to British designs they were often made with American materials on American machines.[51]

VIII. The U.S.A. as Arsenal of Democracy

There was almost a love affair with quantity in wartime Britain. The R.A.F. Film Production Unit film *Towards the Offensive* (1943) has as its constant refrain, 'More men, more machines, more power'. A poster showing a marine diesel hovering above a sea crowded with tank landing craft shouted in progressively larger letters, 'More! MORE! MORE! MORE! Engines'. Leslie Howard's *The First of the Few* (1942), a biopic of Spitfire designer R.J. Mitchell, shows a Nazi aviation expert early in the Hitler era boasting, 'Ve shall have more guns, more tanks, more planes', with the implication that Britain would be able to do just that when the time came. In the event however

[51] *History of the Ministry of Munitions* vol. 12 Part IV p. 51 cf Correlli Barnett *The Audit of War: The Illusion & Reality of Britain as a Great Nation* (1986) p. 165. Levin H. Campbell *The Industry-Ordnance Team* (New York 1946) p. 320; C. Ernest Fayle *Seaborne Trade* (3 vols 1920–24) vol. 3 p. 478 Appendix C Table IX; *Statistical Digest of the War* p. 169 Table 149; W. Hornby *Factories and Plant* (1958) p. 330–331. MacIsaac ed. *United States Strategic Bombing Survey* vol. 1 'The Effect of Strategic Bombing on the German Economy' p. 44 gives the total British machine tool inventory as 740,000.

it was the United States which came out ahead as the country with more of everything.[52]

In America the lavish scaling of the British war economy was reproduced on an appropriately vaster scale. The Manhattan project which designed and built the atom bomb epitomizes the U.S. war effort: in less than three years $2,000 million (about 80 per cent of Federal funding for weapons research) was spent on a project employing 120,000 people and involving the building of 37 installations in 19 different states of the Union. The U.S.A. also recruited the largest armed forces – larger even than in the Soviet Union – though these included what was also the largest proportion of uniformed non-combatants. At its peak the U.S. Army (excluding the Air Corps) had 8,200,000 men, of whom less than 1,800,000 were combat troops. There were 4,541 medical personnel alone allocated to a division of 14,253 combatants, about eleven times the allotment for the slightly smaller German division. The huge numbers frequently resulted in foul-ups of demographic proportions: in late 1942 for example 140,000 young soldiers were sent to university under the Army Specialized Training Program in order to pursue courses of study useful to the army; in February 1944, because of a shortage of front-line manpower, the scheme was abolished and the soldier-students were distributed amongst combat formations, where they served in the ranks, which was about the least effective use conceivable for a group which had been picked out because of its intellectual aptitude.[53]

The United States' greatest advantage of course was in population. In 1944 Britain's armed forces were 24 per cent of the country's labour force: the much larger U.S. armed forces only 18 per cent of theirs. Taking British output as representing 100, actual U.S. output, and U.S. output scaled to relative population was as follows:

	Actual	*Scaled to population*
Aircraft	259	94
Tanks	200	73
Wheeled vehicles	399	145
Artillery over 20mm	142	56
Small arms	224	82

[52] A photo of the More! More! More! More! poster may be found in Public Record Office INF 2/71 p. 3. The screenplay of *The First of the Few* was written by Anatole de Grunwald and Miles Malleson. The Nazi aviation expert, played by Erik Freund, appears in the credits as Messerschmidt [sic] but scarcely resembles the youthful and cadaverous Willy Messerschmitt: more a cross between Ernst Heinkel and Claudius Dornier.

[53] Martin J. Sherwin *The World Destroyed: The Atomic Bomb and the Grand Alliance* (New York 1947) p. 39–40 for research expenditure: Dunn *Second Front Now* p. 180 for medical personnel; Henry L. Stimson and George Bundy *On Active Service in Peace and War* [?1949] p. 245. At the end of 1943 the armed forces of the Soviet Union numbered over 7 million, of the U.S.A. nearly 12 million, so that despite the enormous casualties suffered by the Red Army it is possible that even the total number enlisted 1941–45 was higher in the U.S.

But of course the U.S.A. also contributed raw materials, machine tools, the bulk of new shipping, landing craft, and food, so that the figures for American contribution in military effort or munitions considerably understates the overall position.[54]

In 1939 America seemed by no means especially well-prepared for a war of industrial production. Despite the efforts of the Roosevelt administration there were still 8,750,000 unemployed (one-fifth of the number actually in work, as compared to an unemployment level of one in fourteen in Britain). The Americans had maintained its world lead in car design and production – in 1939 they had produced 78 per cent of the world's passenger cars and 63 per cent of the world's trucks – but other key industries were less flourishing. American aircraft design was excellent, but production was significantly under capitalized; in 1939 capital investment per employee was only $800 in the aircraft industry as compared to $2,600 in the Chevrolet automobile firm; in 1937 output per employee had been $4,400 in the aircraft industry and $15,000 in the automobile industry.[55]

Such was the natural wealth of the country and its business leaders' adjustments to the necessary scale that, by absorbing the unemployment and a sizeable natural increase of the work-force, and a huge and already market-impelled accession of female labour, the U.S. economy was able to expand on all fronts, including private consumption. Civilian employment increased 17 per cent while in Britain it declined 7 per cent; Gross National Product per capita was 10 per cent above British levels in 1938, 50 per cent above in 1944. It was not even necessary to impose manpower controls, though there was an Office of Economic Stabilization and later one of War Mobilization; in 1944 it was found that of several thousand firms investigated by the Office of Price Administration, 57 per cent were violating price controls, from which it appears that more regulation would have been ineffective or counter-productive in any case. Industrial growth was especially rapid in California, where the population increased by more than a quarter 1940–1944, mainly through interstate migration. Film, as the most industrial of all art forms, was inevitably responsive to the psychological impact of industrial boom; one may see in such classics of the *film noir* genre as *This Gun For Hire, Shadow of a Doubt, Mildred Pierce, Double Indemnity* and *Farewell My Lovely* (also known as *Murder My Sweet*), which date from this period and have Californian settings, something of the mood of opportunism, moral disorientation, disillusion and boundless appetite which characterized these years. The portrayal of women in these films as predatory, manipulative and independent is particularly noteworthy in view of the huge expansion of

[54] H. Duncan Hall *North American Supply* (1955) p. 473 Table 30; ibid. p. 419 Table 13.

[55] Nelson *Arsenal of Democracy* p. 53 for car and truck output 1939; Harless D. Wagener *The U.S. Machine Tool Industry from 1900 to 1950* (Cambridge Mass, 1968) p. 237 for levels of capitalization.

women's career opportunities during the war and of the doubling of the rate of divorce between 1940 and 1946. In retrospect the wartime boom appears as one of the most crucial economic developments of this century, corresponding, though on a much vaster scale, with Britain's economic expansion during the French Wars – the two are unique in the annals of war as examples of a really large-scale war generating wealth, the American instance is also interesting in that the experience of 1917–1918 had by no means encouraged one to expect it. War expenditure 1917–1920 had been at only one-sixth of the daily level of 1942–1946, peaking at 21.2 per cent of G.N.P in 1918 as compared to 39.6 per cent of the much larger G.N.P in 1945. Yet in the First World War there had been several signs of malaise. American entry into the war in 1917 had put an end to the economic boom generated by export sales to the Entente: rolled iron and steel output increased 76 per cent 1914–1916 and declined 3.7 per cent 1916–1918; copper output increased 67.6 per cent 1914–1916 and declined 1 per cent 1916–1918. Labour productivity also declined. G.N.P. stagnated and at 1914 prices was fractionally down in 1920 from 1916 levels. Yet the American war economy was not substantially more scientifically planned in 1943–1945 than it had been in 1917–1918; compared to other countries it seems to have been a triumph not of planning but of consensus.[56]

IX. Lend-Lease

Like Britain in the war against Napoleon, but on a much larger scale, the U.S.A. provided crucial economic support for the Allies, in the form of Lend-Lease. In terms of the balance of power and influence within the Grand Alliance it was probably Britain that was the most important Lend-Lease partner. The transfers were not an entirely one-way process. The U.S.A. provided $30,073 million of aid to the British Empire and received $7,567 million back, including services, construction work (especially in the building of bases in Britain, Australia and India), military stores and petrol. Practically all the tyres and inner tubes used by the U.S. Forces in the South Pacific were by 1944 manufactured in Australia with rubber from Ceylon, only the cotton and carbon black coming from America. New Zealand actually supplied more aid to the U.S.A. than was received in return; and mutual aid represented 9.8 per cent of New Zealand National Income in 1944 compared to a total U.S. mutual aid involvement representing only 5.8 per cent of American National Income in the same year. As far as Lend-Lease to the British Empire was

---

[56] Brown *Applied Economics* p. 55–6, 60–61; Charles Gilbert *American Financing of World War I* (Westport Conn. 1970) p. 224–5 and Table 81; ibid p. 202 Table 66, p. 204 and 206 Table 69; Geoffrey Perrett *Days of Sadness, Years of Triumph: the American People, 1939–1945* (New York 1973) p. 303. For divorce rates 1940 and 1946 see *Statistical Abstract of the United States of America: 1949* (Washington 1949) p. 81 no. 92. The increase was actually below the national average in California, but in neighbouring Nevada, where many Californians went to get divorced, the already high rate more than trebled.

concerned the Americans got good value for money. President Roosevelt, who shared Churchill's taste for large words and large gestures, may have seen Lend-Lease as an act of generosity; the State Department did not, and having exaggerated the benefits of the preferential tariff system operating within the British Empire, and desiring to promote free trade in the post-war world, American officials made good use of the negotiation of the details of the Lend-Lease Agreement to forward their objective of dismantling the economic ramifications of British Imperialism. At the same time British dependence on American supplies of tanks, transport aircraft, and, especially, landing craft, taken together with the generally poor performance of the British army prior to November 1942, enabled the Americans to assume the role of senior partner in the strategic direction of the war. Meanwhile Anglo-American supplies to the Soviet Union, did absolutely nothing to promote the U.S. State Department's influence in the Kremlin, but though worth only a third of Anglo-American mutual aid were probably much more important in actually winning the war.[57]

Russia suffered economically from the German invasion much more than in the First World War – much more even than France in the First World War – and by the end of November 1941 had lost control of the bulk of the modern industrial plant which had featured so hypnotically in pre-war documentaries about the Five Year Plans: 63 per cent of pre-war coal production, 68 per cent of pig-iron production, 58 per cent of steel, 60 per cent of aluminium. Under these circumstances Russia did remarkably well in raising arms output in 1943 to more than twice the fairly high 1940 level. No less than Britain and the U.S.A., the Soviet Union fought the mad-dog idealism of the Nazis with weight of material and machines, out-producing even the U.S.A. in tanks and artillery: the Russians produced 29 times more ordnance 1941–1945 than in 1914–1917; three times the quantity produced by Britain and the U.S.. There was also the huge economic effort involved in the transfer of vast factories from the threatened western regions to the Urals and beyond: by 1942 war production was five times the 1940 level in the Urals and 27 times the 1940 level in western Siberia.[58]

---

[57] R.G.D. Allen 'Mutual Aid Between the U.S. and British Empire, 1941–1945' *Journal of the Royal Statistical Society* vol. 109 (1946) p. 243–271 at p. 258 Table 11; Campbell *Industry-Ordnance Team* p. 326; Allen 'Mutual Aid' p. 260 Table 12 and p. 262 Table 13; Warren F. Kimball 'Lend-Lease and the Open Door: The Temptation of British Opulence, 1937–1942' *Political Science Quarterly* vol. 86 (1971) p. 232–259.

[58] Alex Nove *An Economic History of the USSR* (Harmondsworth 1982) p. 273; N. Voznesensky *War Economy of the USSR in the Period of the Patriotic War* (Moscow 1948) p. 70–2 cf Hall *American Supply* p. 419 Table 13. Voznesensky *War Economy* p. 65. Hall gives 70,000 guns manufactured in the U.S. December 1941-June 1944 and 64,000 in the U.K. September 1939–June 1944: the figures for British output in artillery 1940–1944 given in Webster and Frankland *Strategic Air Offensive* vol. 4 p. 469 Appendix 49 iii are almost twice as high as in Hall; in both cases the figures are for guns above 20mm: the Soviet figure for 489,000 may include 20mm weapons but in any case the usual light cannon of the Soviet armed forces was of 23mm calibre.

Up to March 1946 the British supplied the Soviet Union with £308 million worth of military goods and £112 million worth of raw materials, food, machinery and medical equipment, and the U.S.A. supplied rather more than four times the British total, plus investing heavily in developing supply routes through Persia and Alaska. This aid included three-quarters of the Soviet supply of aluminium and copper and nearly four-fifths of Soviet trucks: while the Russians produced 110,000 trucks, the U.S.A. gave them 427,284, retaining a mere 2,166,093 for the use of their own Army: they also provided the Russians with 634,000 jeeps. In adition the Americans supplied 2,670,371 tons of petroleum products, including blending agents (socialist gasoline tended to gum up the motors of trucks manufactured by free enterprise in America) and approximately 100,000 machine tools.[59]

Lend-Lease may have been the Soviet Union's main source of advanced electronic goods; Britain supplied 1,474 army and 329 navy radar sets: the Russians had no air-borne radar of their own design till 1945. The bulk of the munitions however simply supplemented Russia's own output: 9,600 guns from Lend-Lease, 489,000 from domestic production, 10,800 tanks from Lend-Lease, 102,500 from domestic production, 19,116 planes from Lend-Lease, 136,800 from domestic production. Up till April 1944 over 45 per cent of Lend-Lease tanks were British and the Russians, who were then world leaders in tank design, were particularly critical of the British vehicles. The aeroplanes were a little better appreciated, especially the American Bell P-39 Airacobras and P-63 Kingcobras which were armed with a 37mm cannon and were ideal in the ground-attack role; the P-39 was also the plane favoured by Aleksandr Pokryshkin and Grigori Rechkalov who with 59 and 58 aerial victories respectively were the second and third highest-scoring Soviet (and Allied) fighter aces. Altogether 4,764 P-39s (nearly half the total produced) and 2,421 P-63s (four-fifths of the total produced) were sent to Russia: most of the remaining P-63s were used as armoured flying targets in the U.S.A. The only instances of Stalin descending to details about equipment in his correspondence with Churchill and Roosevelt were in October 1942 when he told Churchill, 'What we particularly need is Spitfires and Airacobras', and asked Roosevelt for modern fighters, '– such as Airacobras', adding, 'It should be borne in mind that the Kittyhawk is no match for the modern German fighter'. Nevertheless the Russians received 2,097 of the unwanted P-40 Kittyhawks and only 1,331 Spitfires, the latter being mostly worn-out models handed on from R.A.F units. The British also contributed 2,952 Hawker Hurricanes; these were generally condemned as being too slow, and

---

[59] John Beaumont *Comrades in Arms: British Aid to Russia, 1941–1945* (1980) p. 202–3; John Erickson *The Road to Berlin* (Boulder Colorado 1983) p. ix for Soviet truck production, John H. Deane *The Strange Alliance* (1947) p. 93 for U.S. supplies of trucks to Soviet Union and Richard M. Leighton and Robert W. Coakley *Global Logistics and Strategy* (2 vols Washington 1955–68) vol. 2 p. 832–3 Appendix C2 for US army procurement; Deane *Strange Alliance* p. 94 for petroleum products; Wagoner *U.S. Machine Tools Industry* p. 383 Table 24.

the models armed with 0.303 machine guns had to be equipped with more effective armament. Especially in 1942, Anglo-American aircraft supply helped tide over an awkward gap between the phasing out of the Polikarpov 1-16 and the introduction of the Lavochkin La-5 and Yakovlev Yak-9: the LaGG-3 and MiG-3, the scheduled replacements of the 1-16, had the same poor rate of climb and inadequate performance at altitude as the Kittyhawks. Nevertheless even the aircraft supplied by Lend-Lease were much less significant than less glamorous items like trucks.[60]

Although Lend-Lease trucks made up nearly 80 per cent of the Soviet motor transport, the British and Americans retained nearly 90 per cent of their trucks for their own use: a fair index of the different material levels at which the Anglo-American and the Soviet forces expected to operate. War is waste: but the British and Americans raised waste – both waste of human effort and waste of resources – to unprecedented levels of material profusion. More than half of the 22 million jerry cans moved into France in the twelve weeks following D-Day simply vanished within the same period and it presumably required at least a couple of shiploads to replace them: there was so much equipment that it was simply thrown away. It is surely no coincidence that the preoccupation with litter as a problem of urban and suburban civilization began to be evident in the immediate post-war period. A discarded refrigerator in a road-side ditch somewhere in the Home Counties is perhaps as much a consequence of the way the Second World War was fought as the forty-five-year sojourn of the Soviet troops in Berlin.[61]

---

[60] Beaumont *Comrades in Arms* p. 205 Table 9 cf Bill Gunston *Aircraft of the Soviet Union: The Encyclopaedia of Soviet Aircraft since 1917* (1983) p. 317; Nove *Economic History of the USSR* p. 275, which however gives 18,700 planes supplied by Lend-Lease whereas Heinz J. Nowarra and G.R. Duval *Russian Civil and Military Aircraft, 1884–1969* (1971) p. 140 gives 19,116 planes broken down by types. For the use of the P-63 as an armoured target in the U.S. see William Green *War Planes of the Second World War: Fighters* (4 vols 1960–1) vol. 4 p. 15; *Correspondence between the Chairman of the Council of Ministers of the USSR and the Presidents of the USA and the Prime Ministers of Great Britain during the Great Patriotic War of 1941–1945* (Moscow 1957 – London edition, printed in Moscow, published under title *Stalin's Correspondence with Churchill, Atlee, Roosevelt and Truman, 1941–45*) vol. 1 p. 70 Stalin to Churchill 3 Oct. 1942, vol. 2 p. 35 Stalin to Roosevelt 7 Oct. 1942; Alfred Price *The Spitfire Story* (1982) p. 139–140: it appears that one of the Spitfires supplied to the Soviet Union had served with four different R.A.F. squadrons and had been rebuilt following a serious crash; P.R.O. AIR 46/26/34A (29 May 1942) para. 53 and AIR 46/26/71A (3 June 1943) para. 46 for inferiority of Hurricane, and piece 34A paras 49 and 52 and Appendix B for rearming of Hurricanes

[61] For the missing jerrycans see Martin van Creveld *Supplying War: Logistics from Wallenstein to Patton* (Cambridge 1977) p. 221.

The Soviet troops have of course now left Berlin: the discarded refrigerators remain.

14

The War of Technology

I was in Vienna, where I met an American Jew. He said: 'Maxim, hang your electrical machines and your chemistry! If you want to make a lot of money, invent something that will enable these Europeans to cut each other's throats with greater facility.' This set me thinking.

Sir Hiram Maxim to Captain Seymour Rouse, 1916, in Seymour Rouse, *Practical Notes for Machine-Gun Drill and Training* (1916) p. 7–8.

I. The Question of Technological Superiority and Military Advantage

The Second World War was much more of a technological war than any previous one. Even Churchill recognized that, 'This was a war of science, a war that would be won with new weapons'.[1]

The rapid advance of arms technology in the nineteenth century provoked much speculation regarding wonder weapons that would transform war but only occasionally led to one army having a technical advantage over another; in the war of 1870 the Prussians were still using the model 1841 *Zündnadel* rifle against the French model 1866 *Chassepot* with twice the range and the French also had the *mitrailleuse*, a multi-barrelled automatic gun; for all that the Prussians won. In the First World War there was remarkably little technical disparity between the opposing sides. British and German machine guns were very similar and their artillery, though having disparate characteristics, was not qualitatively unequally matched; the British 18-pounder (84mm) field gun had a range of 9,300 yards whereas the German 77mm fired a two-pound lighter shell 600 yards further, and so on. In 1879 Jules Verne had written of an incredibly long-ranged gun in his novel *The Begum's Fortune*; one of the characters had pointed out that the gun would begin to be impaired after four or five shots, and when in 1918 the Germans bombarded Paris with an incredibly long-ranged gun, the short life of the barrel turned out to be the main difficulty. The German Zeppelin and flame-thrower were also spectacular rather than entirely practical weapons. In H.G. Wells' novel *The War in the Air* German airships had easily disposed of the U.S. Atlantic Fleet, apparently with

[1] John Colville *The Fringes of Power: Downing Street Diaries, 1939–1955* (1985) p. 238, 1 Sept. 1940.

no important survivors. 'Bert Smallways saw the first fight of the airship and the final fight of those strangest things in the whole history of war: the ironclad battleship.' The real life transition was by no means as easy as that. H.G. Wells also foretold the tank, though as 'a large and clumsy insect, an insect the size of an ironclad cruiser, crawling obliquely to the first line of trenches and firing shots out of port holes in its back'. It had previously featured as *locomotives blindés de route ou de railway*, armoured engines running on road or rail, with enormous guns, in Albert Robida's account of a war between Australia and Mozambique, in *La Caricature*, October 1883. The real thing, as introduced in 1916, was more modest though still formidable, but although it seemed to give the British and French a significant technical advantage the increasing availability of anti-tank weapons by the end of 1918 would probably have put these slow, unwieldy, thinly-plated machines out of business in 1919. In the air, the Fokker scourge of 1915 was much celebrated, and the Albatros was seen as an equally serious threat in 1916, but it was the R.F.C. practice of using recce planes over the German lines which made them tactically so vulnerable, and even when the Germans had the greatest advantage in air fighting it was never because the British and French lacked machines as potent as the enemy's. The Germans were also able to take advantage of the proximity of London to their Belgian airbases, but the aircraft with which they bombed the British capital were not technically in advance of Allied types. If the unimaginable had happened and the war had dragged on for another eighteen months, probably the main development on the technological warfare side would have been Germany inability, for want of rubber and textiles, to deal adequately with mustard gas, which they themselves had been the first to introduce.[2]

The role of chemical technology in the First World War illustrates some of the recurrent paradoxes of technical competition. In 1914 chemical engineering was a relatively new area, and one in which German experience and expertise was dominant. On the eve of the outbreak of war the German chemical industry had three times the number of employees as the British, and four times the value of output. The Haber-Bosch nitrogen-fixing process, which relieved Germany of dependence on imported nitrates for fertilizers and explosives, had been perfected shortly before the war; by 1918 it was providing Germany with half of its nitrate requirements. The plant required for the Haber-Bosch process, which was erected with impressive rapidity, was technologically far in advance of what British industrial chemists of the day regarded as feasible. Though Allied experts who inspected German explosive and poison gas plant in the Rhineland after the war were not generally impressed, the Germans avoided the spectacular death toll from slow poisoning or sudden devastating

[2] See chap 10 and cf. Ian Hogg *The Guns of World War II* (1976) p. 13, and Jules Verne *Les Cinq Cents Millions de la Begum* (Paris 1879) p. 78, cf. p. 117 of London 1889 edition; H.G. Wells *The War in the Air* (1908) p. 167 cf. p. 161, 166; H.G. Wells 'The Land Ironclads' *Strand Magazine* vol. 24 (1903) p. 751–764, at p. 755: H. Beraldi *Un Caricaturiste Prophète: La Guerre telle qu'elle est prevue par A. Robida* (Paris 1916) p. 20.

explosions which accompanied the expansion of the chemical munitions industry in the Entente countries and in America. In Britain 96 workers in T.N.T. factories died of toxic jaundice in 1916 and 1917. One hundred and six died in an explosion at the munitions factory at Faversham on 2 February 1916; 73 were killed and 1,022 injured when Brunner Mond's Silvertown plant blew up on 26 January 1917, breaking windows 87 miles away in King's Lynn; and 134 died in an explosion on 1 July 1918 at a shell-filling factory at Chilwell, Nottinghamshire, 'where powerful explosives were milled and mixed like so much sugar' in 'machines originally used for coal crushing, stone pulverising, sugar-drying, paint-making, sugar-sifting'. Yet British experts thought their safety standards much higher than in France where, it was reported, 'Practically no precautions . . . are taken'; about a hundred died in France's worst chemical blast at La Pallice on 2 May 1916; three months earlier 45 had been killed at an explosion at Saint-Denis. Similarly in the U.S.A. over a hundred people died in the explosion of the T.A. Gillespie Co. plant at South Amboy, New Jersey in October 1918. In Germany on the other hand the worst wartime explosion, that in the shell-filling plant at Leverkusen in January 1917, though it broke windows 30 miles away at Krefeld, killed only eight people. The Germans also avoided the problem which afflicted several of the Entente navies: the spontaneous combustion of the shell magazines on board warships owing to the deterioration of cordite in hot weather. Apart from a couple of pre-Dreadnoughts, at least three modern battleships were lost this way: the Italian *Leonardo da Vinci* at Taranto in August 1916; the British H.M.S. *Vanguard* at Scapa Flow in July 1917 – there were only three survivors of the immediate explosion, one of whom died soon afterwards; part of the main derrick, weighing two tons, was found a mile away – and the Japanese *Kawachi* in Tokuyama Bay in July 1918. The German Navy, fully aware of the risks of storing cordite, had given up employing it as an artillery propellant, using instead nitrocellulose with a diphenylamine stabilizer; they lost no ships in this way.[3]

[3] L.F. Haber *The Chemical Industry, 1900–1930* (Oxford 1971) p. 108, 135 for comparison of British and German chemical industry in 1912 and 1913; ibid p. 202–3 and p. 200 Table 7.1 for the Haber-Bosch processing plant; L.F. Haber *The Poisonous Cloud: Chemical Warfare in the First World War* (Oxford 1986) p. 171 for inferiority of German poison gas processing; David Lloyd George *War Memoirs* (6 vols 1933–6) vol. 2 p. 592 for deaths from toxic jaundice, and see E. Sylvia Pankhurst *The Home Front: A Mirror to Life in England during the World War* (1932) p. 341–3; Lloyd George *War Memoirs* vol. 2 p. 597 for the description of the Chilwell shell-filling factory: a copy of the official report on the Chilwell explosion is in Public Record Office MUN 4/5177; it appears that the most likely cause of the explosion was a piece of metal falling into a mixer; about 16 tons of T.N.T. and amatol detonated in the Mixing House and its extension, which 'were completely destroyed, no portion of either remaining on the site'; apart from the 71 workers 'blown to pieces' in the Mixing House, 63 were killed by the collapse of the surrounding buildings. A detonation at the National Filling Factory at Crossgates, near Leeds, which killed 35 on 5 December 1916 is dealt with in MUN 4/4893; for the British experts' opinion of French safety precautions see Public Record Office MUN 5/186/11/1 p. 8 report 10 Nov. 1915 and SUPP 10/290 p. 79 report April 1918; Hans Joachim
continued

Yet the crucial point was that both British and French explosives output equalled that of Germany by 1916 and that by the end of the war U.S. production of propellant was well ahead of combined Anglo-French output and production of High Explosive was almost equal combined Anglo-French output. Despite their experience, the superiority of their processes, and their greater availability of trained chemists, the Germans also fell behind in research. The British began preparing a test range for poison gas at Porton Down in January 1916; the Germans began work on their test facility at Münsterlager only in April 1918 and it was still incomplete by the time of the November armistice. Consequently, though the Germans maintained a lead in the actual production of poison gas, they were extremely slow in discovering that the diphosgene they used to fill gas shells was relatively ineffective and that, on the other hand, mustard gas was much more damaging, though in a different way from that expected; intended to affect the eyes and respiratory tract, mustard gas had an even more lasting and disabling effect in contaminating clothes and equipment, lingering in puddles of greasy liquid which could cause serious skin burns months after it had originally been released. As the Germans were desperately short of textiles they were much less able to deal with the contaminating effect of mustard gas than the Allies, and they might have thought twice about introducing it into service if they had had the facilities to test it properly.[4]

During the Second World War the Germans sustained three separate long-term technically dependent offensive campaigns against the Allies: on land, where despite the triumphs of 1940 and 1941 the initiative was lost by 1943; at sea, where the submarine campaign was only defeated in 1944; and in the air. There were three successive technologically pioneering bombing offensives against Britain: massed conventional bombers guided by electronic navigational aids, then pilotless aircraft – the general commanding Britain's A.A. defences called this 'the first battle of the robots' – then supersonic rockets. The rocket offensive was only ended by the overrunning of the launch sites in 1945, and indeed, the more technologically advanced the form of offensive, the longer the Germans were able to keep it up.[5]

---

continued
Flechtner *Carl Duisberg: vom Chemiker zum Wirtschaftsführer* (Düsseldorf 1960) p. 276–7 for the Leverkusen explosion; Rodrigo Garcia y Robinson 'Failure of the Heavy Gun at Sea' *Technology and Culture* 28 (1987) p. 539–557 at p. 553 for the risks of ageing cordite and the use of diphenylamine; Geoffrey Cousins *The Story of Scapa Flow* (1965) p. 93 for the explosion of H.M.S. *Vanguard*. Germany's relative immunity from explosions did not continue after the war: an ammonium nitrate plant blew up at Oppau on 21 Sept. 1921 killing 600, see Eugen Rugel *Die Katastrophe von Oppau: Schlaglichter auf Zeit und Menschen* (Mannheim 1921).

   [4] Benedict Crowell *America's Munitions, 1917–1918* (Washington 1919) p. 103–4 cf Leo Grebler and Wilhelm Winkler *The Cost of the World War to Germany and to Austria* (New Haven 1940) p. 41; Haber *Poisonous Cloud* p. 119–120, cf ibid. p. 87, 192–3, 211–2 for effects of mustard gas.

   [5] Sir Frederick Pile's phrase 'the first battle of the robots' is quoted in Arthur Christiansen *Headlines All My Life* (1961) p. 235.

As well as making outstanding progress in the areas of submarine and rocket design, the Germans kept abreast of Allied technical progress in other fields. Contrary to what is often supposed they had an initial lead in radar design and by 1939 had provided their warships with gunnery ranging radar while the Royal Navy was still in the process of introducing a fixed transmitter system giving range but not direction. When a British radar set was captured in France in the summer of 1940 German experts found it much inferior to their *Freya*. The British in their turn were so impressed by the German 'Giant Würzburg' radar receivers that after the war they erected several sets for use as radio telescopes. On the other hand the British saw much sooner than the Germans the need to use radar in a systematic network involving highly complex procedures for processing information. As always, the virtue of a technologically superior device is not in its technical novelty but in its mode of employment. Essentially it was in the area of development and employment that the Germans were surpassed by the Allies: just as the French had been in 1870s and the Germans themselves, at least with regard to mustard gas, in 1918. In weapon technology as in other areas, the Nazis lost a major advantage simply as a result of their style in tackling organizational problems.[6]

II. German Science at War

Entirely characteristic of the conditions under which German technology had to operate was the failure to exploit their lead in developing the turbo-jet. A trial jet aircraft had been flown in 1938 and the world's first jet fighter, the Heinkel He 280, was first flown on 2 April 1941. Because Ernst Heinkel was thoroughly disliked by Milch, Göring's No. 2 in the Luftwaffe and Air Ministry, the project was cancelled. The heavier and more advanced Messerschmitt Me 262 first flew on 18 July 1942 but in this instance it was Hitler's interference which delayed progress: he insisted that the plane should be manufactured as a bomber. The Me 262 came into service – as a bomber – only in July 1944, by which time the R.A.F. was already receiving deliveries of the Gloster Meteor jet fighter; the Meteor was initially used in home defence against the V 1 flying bombs, the first instance of a V 1 being shot down by a jet coming ten days after the first Allied sightings of Me 262s over Europe, and even when serving in western Europe in 1945 the Meteor never came into action against manned German jets.[7]

Much attention has been given to Hitler's role in holding up the deployment of the Me 262 as a fighter but in the technical sense it was actually brought

---

[6] Alfred Price *Instruments of Darkness* (1967) p. 74 for the superiority of *Freya*; R.V. Jones *Most Secret War* (1978) p. 230 for post-war use of the 'Giant Würzburg'; ibid. p. 199, cf Price p. 121, 136–7 for the British coastal radar network.

[7] William Green *War Planes of the Second World War: Fighters* (4 vols 1960–1) vol. 1 p. 125, 185–6.

into service far too hastily. Although the Meteor I was considerably slower and less manoeuvrable than the Me 262 and even the Meteor II superior only in its initial climb rate, the jet engine developed by Sir Frank Whittle in Britain was considerably better than the German Jumo 004. It had first been bench-tested in April 1937, four months ahead of the Germans, but four years of development had followed before it was flight-tested. Though coming into service at the same time as the Me 262, the Meteor had first flown eight months after the Me 262, but development had been sufficiently thorough to enable production orders to be placed even before the prototype had flown. The Germans on the other hand, as Whittle later explained, 'had embarked on quantity production long before they had reached a state of development which would have been considered satisfactory in Britain'. The Jumo 004 motor used in the Me 262 had 40 per cent higher fuel consumption than Whittle's W2/700 jet and a life of 25 hours between major overhauls compared to 125 hours for the British engine. The inferiority of the metals used in the Germans turbines, partly due to shortages of rarer metals but perhaps also partly due to inadequacies in the Jumo design staff, astonished Whittle; he wrote later, 'it was in the quality of high temperature materials that the difference between the Germans and British engines was most marked'. Compared to the Gloster Meteor the Me 262 had far higher wing loading, which meant higher take-off and landing speeds; since throttle response was poor, with a tendency for the compressor to stall, it was difficult to accelerate for another circuit when trying to land, and since the Me 262 was often flown off motorways in wooded country (for want of suitable unbombed runways) even the most skilled pilots had difficulty in landing the machine without a pile-up.[8]

As the turbo-jet has many fewer moving parts than the piston engine it was seen as offering the possibility of a cheap mass-producible secret weapon which might turn the tide of the war at the last minute. A single-jet fighter, the Heinkel 162, was designed and forced into production so quickly that, though intended to be flown by pilots with only the most elementary training, it was practically unflyable even by experts. Large numbers of He 162s, in various stages of assembly, were found by Allied ground forces as they overran Germany; it was never encountered in the air.

In its exploitation of the possibilities of cheap mass-production the He 162 concept was analogous to that of the earlier and much more celebrated V 1 flying bomb. The V 1 was powered not by a turbo-jet but by a form of ram jet, a much cruder concept which depended on existing forward velocity for compression of the fuel-air mixture; consequently it had to be launched either with the assistance of rockets or from an aeroplane in flight. Apart from this complication the V 1 was a concept of brilliant simplicity. The crude

---

[8] Sir Frank Whittle *Jet: The Story of a Pioneer* (1953) p. 93, cf. Green *War Planes: Fighters* vol. 2 p. 54. For criticisms of the Meteor's heaviness, lack of manoeuvrability and general unsuitability for the fighter role see Roland Beaumont *Testing Years* (1980) p. 52.

chug-chugging jet motor was of a type which had been patented in 1908 and its gyroscopic auto-pilot had been in use in the First World War. Its lack of technical sophistication, initially its greatest attraction, turned out ultimately to be the V 1's greatest weakness, for it was only fractionally faster than the latest piston-engined fighters and its constant speed and direction made it an easy target for anti-aircraft fire; a more powerful engine and a throttling device for varying the speed at random intervals would have reduced losses enormously. One R.A.F. pilot, Squadron Leader Joseph Berry, shot down 60 V 1s in just over eleven weeks. A typical piece of authoritative-sounding statistical fiction produced by the D.D.I.3. section of the British Ministry of Home Security estimated that the V 1 campaign cost the Germans 641,060 man-months to the Allies 2,442,779 (nearly half the latter arising from the largely unsuccessful attempts to bomb the V 1 launch sites). Compared to the ratio between German man-months expended in resisting the western Allies and total Anglo-American man-months expended in defeating Germany this 1:4 ratio between German and Anglo-American investment makes the V 1 offensive one of the Germany's least economic campaigns: in any case it failed.[9]

The Germans also devoted considerable effort to weapons powered by liquid-fuel rockets. Initially it was the Russians who had the lead in the field of rocket-powered fighter planes, their prototype B 1 rocket first flying in May 1942, over a year before the German Messerschmitt Me 163B rocket fighter. After the B 1 crashed, killing its test pilot, the Russians decided that the whole business was too dangerous and lost interest; they were probably aware in any case that tactically speaking their weakness vis-à-vis the Luftwaffe was in the quality of their aircrew, not of their aircraft. The Germans too eventually concluded that the rocket fighter was simply too dangerous for routine use, but the decision to convert rocket fighter units to the Me 262 was only made after 279 Me 163Bs had been delivered to the Luftwaffe, and after a large number of fatal accidents. The Me 163B was responsible for a score of only nine American aircraft, one pilot, Feldwebel Siegfried Schubert, accounting for three of these. It is, incidentally, only fair to say that the Me 163B was aerodynamically far more advanced than the Russian B 1; but the Americans developed a rocket flying wing, the Northrop XP-79, which was yet more advanced still; they also had the scientific objectivity to give up this project as impractical at a much earlier stage of investment.[10]

The most dramatically successful rocket weapon was the A 4, better known as the V 2. After the atom bomb, the V 2 was undoubtedly the supreme

[9] Ferry Porsche with John Bentley *We at Porsche* (Yeovil 1976) p. 168; Public Record Office HO 192/1637 report by D.D.1.3, 4 Nov. 1944, entitled 'Economic Balance of the Flying Bomb Campaign'.

[10] William Green *Rocket Fighter* (1970) p. 49, 53 for the B.1., ibid. p. 149 for the conversion of Me 163B units to Me 262s and total production figures; ibid. p. 82–3 for the Northrop XP-79.

technological achievement of the Second World War, almost justifying the elaborate mythopoeia of Thomas Pynchon's 1970s novel *Gravity's Rainbow*. First successfully test-launched on 3 October 1942, the V 2 was so advanced that even in June 1943 British experts monitoring reports of German rocket development were still thinking in terms of a solid-fuelled rocket, like a giant firework, and supposed that, in order to attain useful range and bomb-load, it would have to consist of a forty-ton steel carcase filled with cordite. The principle of reaction propulsion, utilizing liquid fuels, had in fact been published as long ago as 1903 and stories featuring rocket ships had been appearing in magazines like *Amazing Stories* and *Astounding* since the late 1920s. The V 2 offered the enemy no possibility of defence or warning and, after – admittedly a long way after – the atom bomb was the most lethal bombing device of the war. A direct hit on the Cinema Rex at Antwerp during a performance on 16 December 1944 killed 567; ironically the worst V 2 incident in Britain, a direct hit on Woolworths in New Cross High St. during the Saturday shopping rush on 25 November 1944, which killed 160 people, involved fewer fatalities than the disaster at Bethnal Green Tube Station on 3 March 1943 in which 173 people – 62 under sixteen years old – were crushed to death in a panic caused by the launching of a salvo of solid fuel A.A. rockets in nearby Victoria Park; it will be recalled that it was the British who had first introduced the rocket into European warfare as an anti-civilian weapon. Despite the spectacular effect of the sudden detonations of its one-ton warheads, the V 2 only came into service when the bombing of enemy cities had ceased to be something happening in isolation from the general military situation, and the V 2 offensive was defeated eventually by the advance of Allied ground forces. Albert Speer later claimed that a much more promising area of rocket design was the *Wasserfall*, a twenty-five foot liquid-fuelled anti-aircraft rocket carrying a 660 lb. warhead along a directional beam up to 50,000 feet; by January 1945 220 scientists were working on this as compared to 2,210 on the V 2 and its derivative the A 9. It was typical of Nazi war-making to ignore Allied superiority in fields where it might have been combated in order to concentrate on new and unfamiliar areas of violence, as if to outflank or perhaps overtrump the stronger enemy.[11]

III. German Science and Nazi Organization

As with war production generally, the Nazi leadership seem to have realized that scientific endeavour needed to be mobilized to meet a crisis only after

[11] Jones *Most Secret War* p. 343 for the notion of a forty-ton steel carcase filled with cordite; a report by Laurence R. Dunne on the Bethnal Green Tube disaster was published as Cmd. 6583 (*Parliamentary Papers* 1944–5 IV p. 37 foll.) and the minutes of evidence are in Public Record Office H O 45/25121; for Speer on *Wasserfall* cf. Albert Speer *Inside the Third Reich* (1970) p. 365 fn.: material on *Wasserfall* captured in 1945 is in Public Record Office AVIA 40/2284–4465.

three or four years of war. Industrial companies, which often had research establishments of outstanding quality, too often attempted to keep their scientific and technical break-throughs secret so as not to help potential competitors; this, and the rivalry between various government bureaus and between Army, Navy and Luftwaffe, frustrated attempts to coordinate research centrally. Professor Carl Wilhelm Ramsauer, director of the research institute of the giant AEG company and chairman of the *Deutsche Physikalische Gesellschaft*, reported in May 1943 on the Anglo-American lead in the application of physics to warfare and recommended amalgamating institutes and increasing the numbers of physicists; but a year later Dr Werner Osenberg, director of the *Reichsforschungsamt* (Reich Research Bureau) was still struggling to secure the release of 5,000 scientists from the armed forces.[12]

Research staffs were by no means small; the Luftwaffe alone had eight major research establishments with 200–2,000 staff each. The equipment and lay-out was of the highest standard: an American expert described the Luftwaffe establishments after the war as 'the most magnificent, carefully planned, and fully equipped that the world has ever seen'. He also claimed that the army's weapons testing installations, with their 75-ton travelling cranes, mobile towers, special laboratories for filling projectiles, buried circuits for measuring points of impact, were 'the finest proving grounds in the world'. But he was also struck by the shortage of technical assistants, who were evidently even harder to save from conscription than the graduate scientists; this left the scientists themselves to do much of the routine work and in some establishments at least this was the major single cause of wasted effort. This same expert was further struck by the lack of liaison and integration between different research teams, the inadequate investment in development – i.e. the translation of basic research into mass-producible weaponry – and the lack of any institutional mechanism to establish priority of effort and optimum lines of design and development according to scientific criteria – weaknesses which reduced the effectiveness of German research 'to between one-tenth and one-half of what it otherwise might have been.'[13]

The lack of coherent overall direction was of course the obvious consequence of the Social Darwinistic atmosphere pervading the upper echelons of government and the armed forces during the Nazi period; the inadequacy of the development side was perhaps a consequence of over-rapid and poorly-planned expansion of military research facilities and of the elimination of Jews from the

[12] Louis P. Lochner ed. *The Goebbels Diary* (1948) p. 299–300, 15 May 1943 for Ramsauer's report: Leslie E. Simon *German Research in World War II* (New York 1947) p. 104–5 for Osenberg.

[13] Simon *German Research in World War II* p. 22, 75–7 for staffing of Luftwaffe establishments; ibid. p. 12 for their magnificence, and cf photographs on p. 13–21; ibid. p. 31 for army proving grounds; ibid. p. 22 for shortage of technical assistance; ibid. p. 206, and generally p. 194–206 for poor institutional structures as regards establishing priorities, and inadequate attention to development.

longer-established academic and industrial laboratories. The Nazis dismissed 1,200 academics, approximately one in ten, but including one in every four physicists and one in every five mathematicians, and by a combination of propaganda and financial constraint encouraged a steady drift into alternative employments; yet despite a 34 per cent fall in the total number of academics in the 1930s there was a lowering of the age of first appointment and a relative increase in the number of academics from lower-class backgrounds so that it is clear that as well as contracting, the profession was restructuring itself internally along lines favoured by the Nazis. After the German surrender 4,300 academics, perhaps one in every two, were subject to denazification procedures. Within the context of Nazi thinking in many pseudo-scientific areas, the altered promotion prospects of non-Jewish and especially actively Nazi scientists must have had an effect in encouraging a drift to the more glamorous and topical areas of basic research at the expense of more mundane and practical concerns such as development. The generally pointless and theoretically unsound medical experiments carried out in concentration camps were only the most extreme demonstration of how the Nazi shake-up of the scientific community provided especially favourable opportunities for charlatans and intellectual light-weights, and clearly the overall process even had its effect in the field of weapons technology.[14]

Yet the Nazis were themselves the symptom as much as the cause of the peculiarities of German social and intellectual history. The mismanagement of German scientific resources was already detectable during the First World War, and during the Second World War was mirrored by mismanagement of skill resources in areas less immediately responsive to the Nazi *Weltanschauung*.

---

[14] Richard Grunberger *A Social History of the Third Reich* (1971) p. 304–323 generally and p. 308 and fn 2 for Nazi dismissals of academics and later denazification of academics who survived the Nazi period: he estimates the figure of 4,300 as about one in every three, which appears not to allow for the contraction of the profession; David Schoenbaum *Hitler's Social Revolution: Class and Status in Nazi Germany, 1933–1939* (1967) p. 263–5 for reduction in size of the academic profession and increased youth and proletarian elements; Alan D. Beyerchen *Scientists under Hitler: Politics and the Physics Community in the Third Reich* (New Haven 1977) p. 44 for dismissals of physicists and mathematicians; ibid. p. 115–122 for Johannes Stark's attempts to 'take over' German physics 1933–6. Edward Yarnall Hartshorne Jr. *The German Universities and National Socialism* (1937) p. 98 gives the number of dismissals by subject: according to his figures on p. 93–4 Nazi dismissals represented more like one in seven of the academic community before the Nazis took power. In 1931 there were 103,900 students in German universities and 22,300 in *Technische Hochschulen*, in 1938 only 43,000 at university and 9,600 at *Technische Hochschulen* cf Fritz K. Ringer *Education and Society in Modern Europe* (Bloomington 1979) p. 292 Table V. It would not be true to claim that German science virtually collapsed: in the period 1947–9 Allied Control's Field Information Agencies, Technical, published 44 volumes of 'Accounts of Investigations and Advances made by German Scientists'; but see Alexander Mitscherlich and Fred Mielke *Doctors of Infamy: The Story of the Nazi Medical Crimes* (New York 1949) p. xix–xx for the unscientific nature of the medical experiments in the concentration camps, and p. xxxi–xxxiii for the professional motives of the doctors responsible, and cf Robert Jay Lifton *The Nazi Doctors: Medical Killing and the Psychology of Genocide* (1986) p. 270–283, 357–9, 367–8.

One example was crew-training in the Luftwaffe. Despite the experience gained during the extraordinarily rapid expansion during the 1930s, the Luftwaffe simply failed to recognize the need for a major investment in pilot-training. Although much German pilot-training after 1943 involved flying gliders, the average number of hours flown by trainees prior to qualification was only half that in Britain and America; even so, by 1944 there were insufficient aircrew to hand to fly the combat aircraft available: in December 1944 for example there were only 599 crews available for 913 serviceable night fighters. Jeschonnek, the Luftwaffe chief of staff, said some time before he killed himself in frustration and despair, 'First we have to beat Russia, then we can continue training'. Young, technologically-orientated, ambitious in his career, Jeschonnek was, like Speer, one of the blue-eyed boys of the regime but his attitude to training related less to Nazism than to the corner-cutting restlessness, and impatience with the boring old-fashioned ways of doing things, which Nazism found to build on: a culture of instant results which was as unhelpful to scientific development as it was to maintaining an air force.[15]

IV. Technology and the Japanese War Effort

In the technological as in the economic field, much of what happened in wartime Japan was simply a more extreme version of what happened in Nazi Germany: more extreme mainly because, except in the aviation industry, Japan was much the most technologically backward of the major belligerents.

The Japanese leaders – especially Admiral Isoroku Yamamoto of the Combined Fleet – had realized from the very beginning that the productive capacity of the Japanese munitions industry could not compete with that of the far more technically advanced industrial sector in the U.S.A., though they could not possibly have guessed how great their inferiority would be. Coal output per miner was 164 tonnes in Japan and 1,021 tonnes in the U.S. in 1940, and in 1944 it had fallen to 119 tonnes in Japan while rising to 1,430 tonnes in the U.S. High Explosive output per man-hour was only 3.68 per cent of American levels, propellant powder output an incredible, humilating 0.54 per cent – *pro rata* one American working a 44-hour week produced eight times more propellant than fifteen Japanese working a 67-hour week. Even more important however was Japan's inability to keep abreast of Anglo-American

[15] Charles Webster and Noble Frankland *The Strategic Air Offensive against Germany, 1939–1945* (4 vols 1961) vol. 4 p. 502 App. 49 XXVIII for night fighter and night fighter crew availability; Jeschonnek's 'First we have to beat Russia, then we can continue training' is quoted in Horst Boog, 'Higher Command and Leadership in the German Luftwaffe, 1939–1945' in Alfred E. Hurley and Robert C. Erhart ed. *Air Power and Warfare* (Washington 1979) (U.S.A.F. Academy Symposium 1978) p. 128–158 at p. 142 and cf Horst Boog *Die Deutsche Luftwaffenführung 1935–1945: Führungsprobleme; Spitzenliederung; Generalstabsausbildung* (Stuttgart 1982) p. 19–23.

progress in the actual design of weapons systems. Even if the Germans could have made better use of their technology, they remained abreast and in some areas ahead of Britain and America till the very end; the Japanese simply fell disastrously behind. For example, they produced 11,942 radar sets in 1944, 2,959 of the air-borne type, but the quality was extremely poor and attempts to copy the design of captured American sets were totally unsuccessful. The Germans tried to help as much as they could, sending 32 blockade runners to Japan up till 1944; only sixteen got through, and the Germans came to rely on cargo-carrying submarines, of which twenty reached Japan from Europe, 1943–1945. While the return traffic from Japan consisted mainly of strategic war materials such as rubber, animal fats, wolfram and tin, the German supplies comprised mainly high technology goods: heavy A.A. guns, 20mm aircraft cannon, industrial diamonds, radar, electronic range-finder and fire-director systems, stabilizers for ships guns. Apart from the industrial diamonds and the 20mm cannon, which were fitted as standard equipment to the Kawasaki Ki 61–1a fighter which came into service in 1943, most of this equipment was intended to serve as models for Japanese manufacture, and it is also believed that the Germans handed over one of their type D-IX U-boats so that the Japanese could copy it, but the German designs almost invariably proved far too complex for Japanese manufacture.[16]

Ironically the Mauser MG 151 20mm cannon, though useful, were an example of one of the few areas of technology in which the Japanese themselves excelled, and could easily have been dispensed with; it is also worth noting that the German weapon the Japanese showed most interest in was the Me 163B rocket fighter. The example sent in a U-boat from Germany was lost at sea, together with the blue-prints, and the Japanese did a very creditable

---

[16] Jerome B. Cohen *Japan's Economy in War and Reconstruction* (Minneapolis 1949) p. 349 for coal; ibid. p. 351 for explosives. In the Second World War Japan was the only country to lose a battleship by the spontaneous combustion of its propellant magazines in hot weather: the 34,000 ton *Mutsu* blew up in this fashion on 8 June 1943 off Hashira-jima in the Inland Sea. Japanese chemical engineers even managed to regress on the safety record of the Entente in the First World War: 350 workers are believed to have died in the manufacture of poison gas for use in China, cf. Saburo Ienaga *Japan's Last War: World War II and the Japanese, 1931–1945* (Oxford 1979) p. 187. For Japanese radar see Cohen p. 191 and Bill Gunston *Night Fighters: A Development & Combat History* (Cambridge 1976) p. 131–4. For German supplies to Japan see Johanna Menzel Meskill *Hitler & Japan: The Hollow Alliance* (New York 1966) p. 139–141, 150–3; for the D-IX U-boat see Cohen p. 261–2. Seventy aerial torpedoes shipped from Japan to Germany in the autumn of 1942, after the Japanese successes in aerial torpedo attacks, turned out to be in no way superior to the German torpedoes and were handed over to the navy to be used in E-boats: Friedrich Lauck *Der Lufttorpedo: Entwicklung und Technik in Deutschland, 1915–1945* (Munich 1981) p. 32–33.

A non-stop air link between Japan and its allies had been pioneered by the Italians: on 2 July 1942 a Savoia-Marchetti S.M. 75 Marsupiale tri-motor flew non-stop from Rhodes to Rangoon. On 7 July 1943 a twin-engined Tachikawa Ki 77 experimental ultra-long range monoplane of the Japanese Army left Singapore bound for Berlin, but was lost somewhere over the Indian Ocean. The three four-engined Junkers JU 290 A-3s allocated by the Luftwaffe for non-stop flights to Manchuria in January 1944 seem to have been diverted to other duties before any intercontinental missions could be undertaken.

job of designing the whole plane from scratch, simply on the basis of a rocket motor and an instruction manual which had got through on another U-boat: the result, the Mitsubishi J8M1 made its one and only flight in the last weeks of the war: true to its German forbears, it crashed and killed its test pilot. It might have been more useful if the Germans had concentrated on sending larger quantities of specific items of equipment – such as radar – which the Japanese needed but which they could not successfully manufacture themselves, but it is possible that Japan's real needs were not identified in time; besides which a submarine route half-way round the world was hardly the most practical way of acquiring munitions which could not be mass-produced at home.[17]

By the time the first atom bomb was dropped on Hiroshima Japan had already been completely defeated by conventional weapons; nearly all the major cities had been laid waste, most of the merchant fleet was at the bottom of the sea, and the surviving factories stood idle for want of raw materials. This disastrous situation was the result, more than anything, of Japan's deficiency in radar technology. Despite its speed, size and robustness, and the poor quality of Japanese ground control, the unescorted B-29 Superfortress bomber suffered serious losses in the daylight raids on Japan in 1944–1945 and this contributed to the decision to abandon high-level precision attacks in favour of night-time area bombing with incendiaries. Flying from bases thousands of miles from the factories which had produced them, the American B-29 offensive against Japan involved an even greater investment per ton of bombs dropped than the R.A.F.'s strategic air offensive against Germany, and was less able to sustain a high rate of loss in combat: but most of the Japanese night fighters carried no radar, and the B-29s were able to burn down Japan's cities with relative impunity. The Japanese Navy's leading night fighter ace seems to have been Sachio Endo, who shot down seven B-29s in a radar-equipped (but underpowered and underarmed) JINI-S over a period of five months, which may be compared with the achievement of the Luftwaffe's Martin Becker, who shot down seven R.A.F. bombers over Nuremberg on the night of 30 March 1944, and nine over Wuppertal on the night of 14 March 1945. Even more crucial was the lack of effective anti-submarine radar; although the Japanese Navy did employ radar-carrying aircraft on the anti-submarine role the equipment was so poor that the crews generally relied on the naked eye,

[17] For the J8M1 see R.J. Francillon *Japanese Aircraft of the Pacific War* (1970) p. 404. The Germans also supplied examples of the Bf 109 and FW 190 which the Japanese used for comparability tests. Before the war the Japanese had purchased twelve Heinkel He 112B (the unsuccessful trials competitor of the Bf 109) but seem not to have been greatly impressed by German aircraft design, though the Ha 40 engine used in the Kawasaki Ki 61 fighter was modelled on the DB 601 motor. The only aircraft of foreign design and manufacture employed by the Japanese in the Second World War was the Fiat B.R.20 bomber, 85 of which were employed by the army in China in 1940 and 1941. Though the Mauser MG 151s had twice the rate of fire of the Japanese Army's then standard Ho 3 cannon, it was inferior to the Ho 5, which was available only after the Ki 61 began production: the German cannon provided a stop-gap, but arguably the Ho 3 would have been adequate in any case cf. Francillon *Japanese Aircraft* p. 115, 528–9.

and anti-submarine vessels depended mainly on hydrophones, an invention of the 1890s. The submarine blockade of the Home Islands was of decisive importance in keeping down Japanese war production; by the time the B-29 bombing offensive got into its stride there was so much excess capacity in industry because of shortages of imported raw materials that the bombing of factories had only a short-term disruptive effect before production was switched to previously idle plant; 58 per cent of Japanese shipping lost was lost as a result of attacks by American submarines.[18]

Altogether a total of 4,859,634 tons of Japanese shipping was sunk by submarine attacks for the loss of 44 American submarines. These figures – representing 110,446 tons of shipping sunk per submarine lost – may be compared with the 11,089,186 tons of Allied shipping sunk for the loss of 178 German and seven Austro-Hungarian submarines in the First World War (about 59,941 tons of shipping sunk per submarine lost) and 14,687,231 tons of Allied shipping sunk for the loss of 817 German, 86 Italian and 127 Japanese submarines in the Second World War (14,259 tons of shipping per submarine lost). The Japanese lacked the advantage the British had with regard to signals intelligence; a large part of German submarine losses after November 1942 can be attributed to the fact that the British were able to decypher German radio communications, and could concentrate their anti-submarine patrols in areas where German U-boats were known to be lurking; but equally the Germans had benefited from being able to decypher the British and Allied Merchant Shipping Code, and in neither case would superior intelligence have been enough without the backing of advanced weaponry and sophisticated tactics. The Battle of the Atlantic, the Anglo-American struggle against the U-boat, ended in Allied victory after a series of protracted and bitter campaigns; the Battle of the Pacific was by comparison a easy triumph for the American submarines; and yet there can be little doubt that the German U-boats and their tactics were markedly superior to those employed by the American submariners. British and American – mainly British – technology won a decisive victory in the Atlantic; it was because the Japanese failed to develop new anti-submarine weapons (or tactics) that they were as decisively defeated in the western Pacific.[19]

---

[18] Cohen *Japan's Economy in War and Reconstruction* p. 104, cf. p. 137; David MacIsaac ed. *The United States Strategic Bombing Survey* (10 vols New York 1976) vol. 9 ('The War against Japanese Transportation'. 1941–1945) p. 47 figure 44.

[19] Theodore Roscoe *United States Submarine Operations in World War II* (Annapolis 1949) p. 498 gives a total of 52 American submarines lost from all causes; Samuel Eliot Morison *History of the United States Naval Operations in World War II* (15 vols Boston 1947–1962) vol. 12 p. 414 gives 41 to 44 American submarines lost in action against the Japanese. Allied merchant shipping losses for the First World War are in A. Laurens *Le Blocus et la Guerre Sous-marine 1914–1918* (Paris 1924) p. 210, for the Second World War in S.W. Roskill *The War at Sea, 1939–1945* 3 vols (1954–1961) vol. 3 pt. 2 p. 479 Appendix ZZ; submarine losses are in R.H. Gibson and Maurice Prendergast *The German Submarine War, 1914–1918* (1931) Appendix III p. 351–2, 388 and Friedrich Ruge *Sea Warfare, 1939–1945: A German Viewpoint*
continued

One of the major factors impelling Japan to go to war with the U.S. and Britain in 1941 had been the fear that vital oil supplies from the Netherlands East Indies would be withheld if they remained outside Japanese control. Once the Netherlands East Indies were overrun however insufficient effort was made to boost output, which fell from 65 million barrels in 1940 to 50 million in 1943. Of the latter only 10 million barrels of crude, plus 5 million of refined, actually reached Japan; in 1944, with the American blockade closing in, only 1.6 million barrels of crude and 3.3 millions barrels of refined reached Japan. Problems of this sort had been partially envisaged before the war and in 1937 work began in a project to produce 14 million barrels of synthetic oil a year (about two-fifth of total requirement) by 1943. Actual production in that year was a mere 8 per cent of the target; synthetic oil was clearly an area where the Japanese would have benefited from more systematic technical assistance from the Germans, who were the world leaders in this field. To help make up for the failure with synthetic oil a scheme was launched to distill four million barrels of crude a year from pine roots. 34,000 simple stills were prepared, but in the end only 3,000 barrels of aviation gasoline was produced, and this was so resinous that it glued up the aeroplane motors after a few flights. One gallon of crude required two-and-a-half-man days and enough fuel to heat a still for twelve hours; the contrast between the technical concept of the project and the sophistication of the fourteen-and eighteen-cylinder twin-row radial engines the oil was meant to power was almost surrealistic.[20]

Another project in the same vein, sponsored by the Army, was the establishment of 160 small blast furnaces using cheap materials and unskilled labour: the result was a small quantity of pig iron of such poor quality that it had to be resmelted. This particular project is reminiscent of Mao Tse-tung's Great Leap Forward, though its nuttiness would also have appealed to Heinrich Himmler. The underlying notion was that it would be possible to by-pass

(1957) p. 314; Morison *History of the United States Naval Operations* vol. 12 p. 413–4 for ineffectiveness of Japanese counter-measures. The two most successful submarine captains of all time were Kapitänleutnant Lothar Arnauld de la Perière of the U-35 who sank 448,024 tons of Allied shipping, mostly in the Mediterranean, in about 30 months 1915–1918 and Kapitänleutnant Walter Forstmann of the U-39 who sank 399,604 tons, also mostly in the Mediterranean, in about two years 1915–1917 cf. Arno Spindler *Der Handelskrieg mit U-Booten* (5 vols Berlin 1932 – Frankfurt 1966) vol. 5 p. 374–5 Anlage 5 and passim in text. This is to be compared with the 266,629 tons sunk September 1939-March 1941 by Kapitänleutnant Otto Kretschmer, and the 94,409 tons sunk by Lieutenant-Commander E.B. Fluckey of the U.S.S. *Barb* in 1944–5: Lieutenant-Commander R.H. O'Kane of U.S.S. *Tang* sank 93,824 tons of Japanese shipping in eight months in 1944: Roscoe *United States Submarine Operations* p. 528, 558. In the First World War the ships attacked were of much smaller average size: Kretschmer sank 44 merchant ships, Arnauld de la Perière 194.

20 W.G. Beasley *Japanese Imperialism, 1894–1945* (Oxford 1987) p. 249 for Japanese oil imports; Cohen *Japan's Economy in War and Reconstruction* p. 137 for synthetic oil; ibid. p. 146–7 for distilled oil from pine roots, and cf. Albert Speer *The Slave State: Heinrich Himmler's Masterplan for S.S. Supremacy* (1981) p. 148–50 for Himmler's interest in copying the pine root project.

material disadvantages by mobilizing traditional wisdom, folk ingenuity and moral fervour. Another example of impractical low-cost ingenuity was the attempt to rain incendiaries on the forests of western America from small balloons launched in the Home Islands and carried across the North Pacific by air currents; this too was a flop.[21]

The ultimate and perhaps most characteristic of these expedients was the campaign of *kamikaze* or suicide attacks in 1944–1945. This was nothing less than a profession of faith in the superiority of spirit over matter: the Luftwaffe idea of ramming B-17 Fortress bombers was similar but with the proviso that if one was a skilful enough flier one would escape alive – rather like riding a Harley Davidson into a brick wall – whereas for the Japanese kamikaze pilots part of the symbolic point was to get themselves killed. The Okha concept, a manned bomb to be air-launched from a conventional bomber but equipped with a solid-fuel rocket booster, was developed by Ensign Mitsuo Ohta and friends at Tokyo University's Aeronautical Research Institute during the summer of 1944 and the first production orders were placed by the Navy in September 1944; the Army's much less advanced Nakajima Ki 115, basically a crude, clumsy propeller-driven monoplane designed to take off and crash, but not to manoeuvre or to land, was the result of an order placed on 20 January 1945. The majority of human bomb attacks however were carried out in conventional combat planes. From 6 April to 22 June 1945, at the peak of the kamikaze campaign, 1,665 aircraft were utilized in kamikaze attacks, sinking 26 U.S. ships and damaging 164, which suggests that 88 per cent of the attackers were either shot down in the course of their attacks or simply missed. These suicide tactics, even more terrifying for the intended victims than for the young zealots carrying them out, were clearly insufficient to stem the triumphant American advance towards Japan, though they undoubtedly contributed to the decision to use the atom bomb on Hiroshima and Nagasaki rather than risk the mutual bloodbath of an invasion.[22]

---

[21] Cohen *Japan's Economy in the War and Reconstruction* p. 121–2; for the balloon bombs see *Times* 12 May 1947 p. 3e, Robert C. Mikesh *Japan's World War II Balloon Attacks on North America* (Washington 1973) and Yasushi Hidagi 'Attack against the U.S. Heartland', *Aerospace Historian* vol. 27 (1981) no. 2 p. 87–93.

[22] For German plans to ram U.S. bombers see Peter Henn *The Last Battle* (1954) p. 169–172 and Adolf Galland *The First and the Last: The German Fighter Force in World War II* (1955) p. 264–5. On 7 April 1945 180 virtually untrained Luftwaffe pilots attacked American bomber formations, their radios tuned in to a female choir singing, 'Deutschland über Alles', with voice-overs urging them to die for Führer and Vaterland: 70 were shot down, for the loss of only 7 B-17 bombers: David Irving *Göring: a Biography* (1989) p. 458, and cf Hugh Trevor-Roper ed. *The Goebbels Diaries: The Last Days* (1978) p. 136, 14 March 1945, p. 317, 4 April 1945, p. 323, 8 April 1945. For the Okha and the Ki 115 see Francillon *Japanese Aircraft* p. 241, 476–7: for statistics for 6 April–22 June 1945 period see Rikihei Inoguchi, Tadashi Nakajima and Roger Pineau *The Divine Wind: Japan's Kamikaze Force in World War II* (1959) p. 141 and 142 fn.1. On the Russo-German front Soviet pilots carried out more than 200 ramming attacks on German aircraft, one pilot destroying four enemy planes in this way: Von Hardesty *Red Phoenix: The Rise of Soviet Air Power, 1941–1945* (Washington 1982) p. 28.

V. Design and Engineering in Britain

Leaving aside America's construction of the atom bomb (developed in any case with British scientific assistance), Britain's technological record was overall perhaps the best of any belligerent in the Second World War. Yet as a result of Britain's increasingly ignominious economic performance since 1945, the question of inadequate scientific and design input has attracted a certain amount of attention. Deficiencies in this field were remarked even before the war: in November 1936 the Vulcan Foundry was given an order to prepare designs for the Matilda II tank; six months later it was still employing only two draughtsmen, and a year after the original order only eight. The Boeing Corporation in America had a design staff representing 8 per cent of company personnel – and a third of them were college-trained engineers – while in the average British aircraft company the percentage represented by design staff would be nearer 1 per cent and the proportion of graduates even lower. In fact Britain simply did not produce as many qualified engineers as leading competitors. *Circa* 1937–1938 there were 149 technical colleges in England and Wales with about 9,000 full-time students compared to 303 *Fachschule* in Germany with 26,056 students; at university level Britain produced 700 engineering graduates a year to Germany's 1,900; even Japan with less than 40 per cent of Britain's industrial output had 9,137 engineering students at technical colleges in 1938, and 4,467 at university level. On the other hand many of Britain's most gifted designers showed that advanced academic training was not a prerequisite for advanced design. R.J. Mitchell, who designed the Spitfire – the best, and technically one of the most progressive designs of its day – had left Hanley High School at sixteen to be apprenticed to a locomotive building firm (with evening classes at Wedgwood Burslem Technical School) and became chief designer at Supermarine at the age of 24, about the age of a university-trained engineer in Germany would obtain his diploma; he repeatedly told his son that, 'Good technical know-how but without common sense usually only resulted in mediocrity'. Sydney Camm, who designed the Hurricane, the Typhoon and Tempest and the post-war Hawker Hunter, had been trained as an apprentice wood-worker. F.G. Miles left school at thirteen to start his own business: he became the outstanding designer of advanced training aircraft but also, in only nine weeks in the summer of 1940, designed and built a fighter plane superior to the Hurricane in nearly every respect and to the Spitfire in cost, range and ammunition capacity. James Martin, later famous as the inventor of the ejector seat, designed between 1937 and 1944 three outstanding fighters – the last, the MB 5, described authoritatively as 'possibly the finest all-round single-set piston-engined fighter ever produced'; as a lad Martin had had an interview at Queen's University Belfast but had decided he already knew more about engineering than the lecturers could teach him. Henry Rolls of Rolls Royce had moved via locomotives and artillery to being chief engineer for the installation of street lighting in Nottingham at the age of 19. Major Frank Halford, whose

24-cylinder H-format Napier Sabre engines represents the culminating triumph of liquid-cooled piston-engine design and who later became a distinguished designer of jet motors, also had a Nottingham connection, having failed to complete an engineering course at the university there.[23]

Of course there were *some* college-qualified aircraft designers in the British aeroplane industry. Geoffrey de Havilland, who designed the DH 4 in the First World War and had overall responsibility for the Mosquito in the Second, had done three years at Crystal Palace Engineering School. Roy Chadwick, who designed the Avro Lancaster, had studied at Manchester College of Technology. Perhaps the best qualified in academic terms was W.E.W. Petter who had got a first in Mechanical Sciences in Cambridge: but of Petter's designs immediately before or during the war only the misconceived Lysander was placed in really large scale production, his most effective design, the Westland Whirlwind, being used to equip only two R.A.F. squadrons. Academic qualifications were very much less exceptional amongst German designers but the greatest German designer and engineer of all, Ferdinand Porsche was largely self-taught, like so many of his British counterparts. As for the Unites States, it is agreeable to learn that the man the North American Corp. employed for fourteen months with the title Assistant Chief Designer, with the responsibility for sorting out the technical problems of the P-51 Mustang, though claiming the unique qualification of a B.Sc. from the Sorbonne, Paris, France, besides a B.Sc. from Yale, had in fact only done one semester (of English, History and Philosophy) at the University of Pennsylvania and, what is more, had flunked Ethics.[24]

Of course this whole question of design, involving as it does thousands of experts engaged in hundreds of projects over a period of let's say ten years, is enormously complex. One area where Britain did conspicuously badly was tank design. From 1936 Britain, unlike Germany, had evolved two separate lines of development in the medium tank: the infantry tank which was slow and heavily armoured (Matildas, later Valentines, later still Churchills) and the cruiser, which was fast and lightly armoured. A foreseeable problem was that it would be difficult to combine and integrate tank units with machines capable of widely different speeds: perhaps less foreseeable was that German tank tactics, which were particularly favoured by the empty terrain in North

---

[23] M.M. Postan, D. Hay and J.D. Scott *The Design and Development of Weapons* (1964) p. 319 for the Vulcan Foundry; ibid. p. 39–40 for staffing in aircraft industry; Barnett *The Audit of War* p. 204–5 for British and German technical colleges and engineering graduates; Yuzo Morita (Director of Statistics Bureau of the Prime Minister's Office) ed. *Statistical Abstract of Japan 1950* (Tokyo 1950) p. 155 Table 191 and p. 157 Table 196; the background of British designers is to be found in *Who's Who* and other biographical directories; Mitchell's opinion of technical know-how is quoted in his son's preface to Alfred Price *The Spitfire Story* (1982) p. 7, and see ibid. p. 61–5, 69 for the technical, management and organizational problems involved in bringing the Spitfire into production; the assessment of the MB 5 is quoted from Peter Lewis *The British Fighter since 1912: Sixty Years of Design and Development* (1974) p. 303.

[24] Geoffrey Wolff *The Duke of Deception: Memories of my Father* (1969) p. 43, 61, 67–8 for the Assistant Chief Designer at North American.

Africa, provided little scope for the use of slower vehicles. All British tanks were initially undergunned; in addition the cruiser tanks were mechanically unreliable, so that till 1942 the best tanks available to the British were the trustworthy and shell-proof, but snail-like, infantry tanks. The problem of installing heavier guns caused unnecessary headaches. A report of August 1942 discussing the new 6-pounder (57mm) gun asserted, 'If the potential value of this gun had been appreciated when it was first designed it could have been tested and put into production at least 12 months earlier than was actually the case'. It took 26 months to produce the first model and once it had been adopted a further six to ten months were lost – depending on tank type – in making the necessary design alterations to the tanks, simply because of poor forward planning. Professor A.V. Hill, scientific adviser to the War Cabinet and to the Ministry of Supply and also M.P. for Cambridge University, Secretary of the Royal Society and winner of the Nobel Prize in Physiology – his main qualification in engineering apart from masses of practical experience was his authorship of a book entitled *Living Machinery* – denounced the whole business in a letter to *The Times* in July 1942: 'Too many disasters have been due either to technical mismanagement or inefficient use of available weapons, resources or materials.' Increasingly the British had to rely on American medium tanks for their higher-speed formations and concentrated on production of the Churchill infantry tank, which however continued to be plagued with mechanical failures: of the first 1,200 built, 1,000 had to be 'reworked' and even then often failed the acceptance test, and a report of March 1944 referred to the demoralizing effect on workers in tank factories of seeing completed tanks being broken up on the premises and the parts piled up to be taken away as scrap metal. It was only in the last months of the war that a reliable and effective British medium tank, the Cromwell, became operational, though with the customary irony of history, the Centurion which came into service almost immediately after the war became one of the classic designs of tank history and was still in use as the spearhead of the triumphant Israeli offensive in Sinai in 1967.[25]

Even the American Sherman tank, which became standard in both the U.S. and British armies, was somewhat inferior to the German Panther and markedly undergunned and fragile compared to the German Tiger tank. This undoubtedly had an intimidating effect on tank crews – being inside a tank which 'brewed up' after a direct hit was an awful way to die – but modern warfare is not like a duel between two equally-matched Sumo wrestlers and Allied armoured formations after 1942 invariably made up for

---

[25] Postan, Hay, Scott *Design and Development of Weapons* p. 309–10; Report by the Select Committee on National Expenditure: War Time Tank Production: 26 August 1942 printed in Cmd. 6865 (*Parliamentary Papers* 1945–6 VIII p. 311 foll.) p. 5–6; *Times* 1 July 1942 p. 5e; Report dated 11 March 1944 in Cmd. 6865, at p. 33. In the earlier part of the war the different marks of cruiser tank were distinguished by numbers – Cruiser A 9, Cruiser A 10, Cruiser A 13; there then followed the Crusader A 15. Examples of these and the more famous infantry tanks are preserved at Bovington Camp, Wareham, Dorset.

inferior material by their greater numbers. Significantly enough in 1942 and 1943 it was the Russian T-34 which was both the most numerous *and* the most effective tank in the world – Ferdinand Porsche horrified his colleagues by suggesting Germany should copy the design – but despite the inferiority of their PzKw IIIs and PzKw IVs in both quality and quantity the German Panzer formations frequently held their own against the Russians, showing that there are limitations to the materialist theory of military history.[26]

Another area of mechanical competition in armaments, and one which because of laymen's interest has attracted a great deal of mythologizing, is aircraft design. In reality there was only the most indirect kind of competition because the whole process of aircraft design was so complex and lengthy that to imitate enemy aircraft already in service would simply involve having a machine out of date by the time it was in production. All the aeroplanes used in the Second World War took at least two years, and sometimes four, from commencement of design to entry into operational service. The Spitfire required 339,400 man-hours to design, plus 800,000 man-hours for retooling and rejigging per variant. And of course not all planes were designed at the same time, or with the outbreak of war in September 1939 in view, so that it was rather a question of good luck than of good judgement if the right plane was in service at the right time, especially since design was developing very rapidly in the 1930s and 1940s. When Germany invaded the Soviet Union the standard Soviet fighter, on the eve of replacement, was the Polikarpov I-16, extremely heavily armed (more than twice the fire power of the Messerschmitt Bf 109E), extremely manoeuvrable but, with its stubby body, flat unaerodynamic nose and great wing span, too slow to deal effectively with German fighters: but the design was two years older than that of the Bf 109, the first prototype having flown in December 1933, before design work had even started on the Bf 109 and 22 months before the first Bf 109 prototype flew. Similarly the Focke-Wulf FW 190 which entered Luftwaffe service in 1941 gave R.A.F. Fighter Command a nasty shock as its standard equipment, the Spitfire, was a three years older design; but later in 1941 the Hawker Typhoon, of the same vintage as the FW 190, came into service and provided in some respects an even better performance.[27]

The Germans tended to be unimpressed by Soviet aircraft design and a case could be made for arguing that the Soviet aeroplane industry had been crippled by Stalin's purges. Between 1934 and 1941 450 aircraft designers and aircraft engineers were arrested, of whom fifty were executed and a hundred died in prison or labour camps: the survivors, including A.N. Tupolev, former head of the Experimental Design Section and chief engineer of the Chief Directorate of the Aircraft Industry, were obliged to work in N.K.V.D. workshops. One apparent indication of Russian backwardness was that until

---

[26] Porsche and Bentley *We at Porsche* p. 147, 150.

[27] Postan, Hay, Scott *Design and Development of Weapons* p. 161–2 for man-hours in Spitfire manufacture; generally Green *War Planes: Fighters* passim.

1944 all the standard Soviet fighter types were partly – in most cases *mainly* – of wooden construction; on the other hand it had been decided that wood was not only cheaper but facilitated maintenance work under primitive front-line conditions, and metal sections of airframes had been replaced by wood wherever possible, so that the Russian delay in producing an all-metal fighter was not entirely proof of lack of technical sophistication. It was in fact the Russians who had built the world's first all-metal, inline-engined, low-wing monoplane fighter with retractable undercarriage, the Polikarpov I-17, which first flew on 1 January 1934, again 21 months ahead of the Bf 109: perhaps because of poor workmanship it was inferior in performance to the I-16 and was produced in only small quantities 1937–1939, serving against the Hungarians in southern Russia in 1941 and 1942. Incidentally the first country to have its front-line fighter units entirely equipped with home-produced all-metal monoplanes – admittedly with fixed undercarriage and radial engines – was Poland, back in 1933.[28]

But airframe design was only part of the whole business. The British undoubtedly had a major advantage in their Rolls Royce Merlin engine: although the German Daimler Benz DB 601 incorporated certain more advanced features such as fuel injection it was heavier and bulkier for the same power and offered less scope for modification; when in 1968 Harry Saltzman made his film epic *Battle of Britain* he had to use Merlin-powered Bf 109s acquired from the Spanish government as there were no Bf 109s with the original DB 601 available. The Merlin is of course inseparable from the memory of the Spitfire, but it was also veritably the making of the Mosquito and the P-51 Mustang, two aircraft which deserve to be regarded as amongst the three or four absolutely outstanding machines of the war because of their all-round superiority over all other aircraft of the same vintage. On the other hand Italian fighter-plane design suffered from lack of a suitably powerful inline engine and R.A.F. pilots regarded Italian fighters as little more than attractive toys – 'I remember thinking that it seemed almost a shame to shoot down such pretty machines', reported one R.A.F. squadron leader. But once German DB 601 motors were available, the underpowered Macchi M.C. 200 was redesigned as the C. 202, which on entering service in July 1941 quickly established its superiority over the R.A.F. Hawker Hurricanes in North Africa.[29]

There were also the guns which aircraft carried. In retrospect the R.A.F.'s decision to adopt the Browning 0.303 machine gun seems unfortunate and they were perhaps too quick to reject the 0.50 machine gun as combining

[28] Alexander Boyd *The Soviet Air Force since 1918* (1977) p. 99 for effect of purges; ibid. p. 195–6 for wooden construction; Green *War Planes: Fighters* vol. 3 p. 166–7 for the I-17; Jerzy B. Cynk *Polish Aircraft, 1893–1939* (1971) p. 151 and cf for British monoplanes of comparable design in 1929, Lewis *British Fighter since 1912* p. 197–200. The First Soviet all-metal fighter, the Yak 9U of 1944 was in fact merely a variant of an earlier type built partly of wood.

[29] The quotation is from E.B.B. ed. *Winged Words* (1941) p. 196 'A Squadron Leader' December 1940.

the disadvantages of both rifle-bore machine guns and the 20mm cannon. But the initial rejection of the 20mm cannon was entirely justified by its excessive vibration when firing unless braced between the cylinder heads of the aeroplane's engine – an expedient for which the Rolls Royce Merlin was unsuitable. A prototype Spitfire with two wing-mounted cannon was in action on 13 January and 22 February 1940, but on both occasions one of the cannon jammed, and when cannon-armed Spitfires were issued to No. 19 Squadron in August 1940 there were so many malfunctions that after a few weeks the squadron received permission to swap their planes for older, machine-gun-armed models which had been withdrawn from the front line and relegated to an Operational Training Unit. Since many German aircraft in 1940 carried little armour the R.A.F.'s small bore ammunition was not always a fatal disadvantage in any case; moreover the MG FF cannon on the Bf 109E, though much lighter than the British Hispano cannon and firing a fractionally heavier round, had only 70 per cent of the Hispano's muzzle velocity and half the rate of fire, and with its poor ballistic performance was by no means effective against small and rapidly moving targets. The eight-gun Spitfire and Hurricane could fire 10lbs of projectiles in a three-second burst; the Bf 109E 13lbs at two different muzzle velocities; the Hurricane, incidentally, was a much steadier gun platform and was able to absorb more damage than either the Spitfire or the Bf 109.[30]

Even after the R.A.F. fighters were armed with cannon the bombers retained the 0.303 machine gun, which was pitiably ineffective against briefly glimpsed night fighters. It was not initially realized that a bullet fired at an angle to the axis of a plane's flight retains some of the forward momentum it had before being fired and when fired does not go in a straight line, the larger the angle and the faster the plane the more convoluted being the trajectory of the bullet; moreover during a three-second burst from the turret of a bomber flying at 240 m.p.h. the gun barrel moves three hundred yards, and since the bullets are not coming out straight the effect is more like firing a shotgun than anything else. Replacing the machine guns with slower-firing cannon would have further reduced the chances of hitting anything but would at least have made a much larger hole in anything hit. Unfortunately the power-operated gun turret, though originally a French concept, was taken up by the R.A.F. with excessive enthusiasm, even being installed as the sole armament on a twin-seater fighter, the Boulton Paul Defiant, but the complexity of these turrets made it difficult to convert them to larger weapons and a mid-upper

---

[30] On the decision to reject the 0.50 gun see C.H. Keith *I Hold My Aim* (1946) p. 89: Keith had been Assistant Director of Armament Research and Development in the R.A.F. The 0.50 was twice as heavy as the Browning 0.303, and had half the rate of fire; on the other hand the bullet it fired was five times heavier. For the first cannon-armed Spitfires see Public Record Office AIR 19/164/7/5A and Price *The Spitfire Story* p. 78; for the MG FF and the weight of projectiles in a three-second burst see Alfred Price *World War II Fighter Conflict* (1975) p. 78. For the Hurricane's particular advantages see Beaumont *Testing Years* p. 11–12, 14 and Adrian Stewart *Hurricane: The War Exploits of the Fighter Aircraft* (1982) p. 66–7.

turret for a 20mm cannon which had been under development in 1940 was cancelled on the direct orders of Lord Beaverbrook when Minister of Aircraft Production. The power-operated turret remained to some extent a British speciality throughout the war; the Germans for example relied on defensive machine guns moved by hand on simple pivots (not very easy physically as the gun barrels projected into the slipstream) and fed not by continuous belts of ammunition but by heavy, but soon exhausted, drum magazines; and the most heavily-armed variant of the American B-17 Fortress had five gun positions operated by hand to four operated on power, one of which had only a restricted field of fire. But whether hand or power-operated, the odds were against the defensive armament of a bomber ever actually managed to shooting down an enemy fighter.[31]

VI. The British Boffin at War

Design is only one of the engineering problems in aircraft manufacture: another is the organization of production. The Americans with their purpose-built aircraft factories and special purpose machine tools had a notable advantage here, but between Britain and Germany there was probably little difference in productive efficiency. Correlli Barnett, in his provocative *The Audit of War: The Illusion and Reality of Britain as a Great Nation* (1986) cites a Ministry of Aircraft Production document which quoted German official figures for the man-hours needed to build the Heinkel He 111 and Messerschmitt Bf 109G and calculated on the basis of weights and dimensions the man-hours required by a British factory to build the same planes. The figures, which Correlli Barnett uses to back his sustained attack on Britain's industrial record during the war, are 4,300 man-hours to build a Bf 109G in Britain to 3,900 in Germany and 17,000 man-hours to build a He 111 in Britain to 12,000 man-hours in Germany. The document itself, in the Public Record Office, tells another story. Its writer queried the German statistics – the figure of only 22 per cent of total man hours per plane being required specifically for the air frame 'appears so fantastic to me that I think it must be a misquotation' – and in any case the main subject of the document is the reorganization of

[31] For the cancellation of the mid-upper turret for 20mm guns see Chaz Bowyer *Guns in the Sky* (1979) p. 53. The power-operated 20mm mid-upper gun on the French Lioré et Olivier Leo 451 had proved in May–June 1940 to have too narrow a field of fire and an inadequate supply of ammunition: Pierre Pasquier and Joseph-Marie Tonon *L'Aviation française au combat: le groupe de bombardement II/12* (Paris 1947) p. 159–160.

Perhaps the greatest success of defensive fire relative to losses to attacking fighters was achieved by R.A.F. Bomber Command in the raid on Berlin on the night of 23–24 December 1943 when six German night fighters were downed for the loss of eleven bombers: Martin Middlebrook *The Berlin Raids: R.A.F. Bomber Command Winter, 1943–44* (1988) p. 195. During the attack on Magdeburg on the night of 21–22 January 1944 Major Heinrich Prinz zu Sayn-Wittgenstein, then Germany's leading night fighter ace with 83 victories, shot down four R.A.F. bombers before falling to the rear-gunner of a Lancaster: ibid. p. 231.

the production of the Bf 109G to reduce man-hours from 6,500 to 3,900 (i.e. from 51 per cent more than the theoretical British factory would need to 9 per cent less). It is pointed out that, 'The difference between the 6,500 man-hours before, and 3,900 man-hours after, reorganization of Me 109 production is comparable with the difference between Spitfire man-hours at Supermarine and Castle Bromwich' i.e. the difference between an old-established factory using tools originally installed to produce something else, and a factory specially designed and equipped to produce Spitfires. A hand-written note comments:

> On the whole, I think the figures suggest that German methods may produce airframes slightly more cheaply than British methods, but the possibilites of non-comparability of the bases of assessment justify, I think, a verdict of 'Not Proven'.[32]

Documents of this sort which offer a rich and evidently indigestible diet for historians like Correlli Barnett were a special feature of the war and relate to one of the period's dominant images, of the bespectacled boffins or back-room boys, with their slide-rules and their mechanical calculators and their endless stream of statistical memoranda proving that 'black's white to three places of decimals' – an image subsequently enshrined in films such as *The Dambusters* and the cinema version of Nigel Balchin's wartime novel, *The Small Back Room*. Britain, despite having invested less lavishly in scientific and technical education before the war than Germany, invested much more in boffinry during the course of hostilities; but the results were not always commensurate with investment.

Perhaps the most dramatic but most claustrophobic area of research was that carried out in the abstruser realms of mathematics by the code-breaking establishment at Bletchley Park, which by intercepting German machine-coded radio transmissions enabled the British leadership to know what the Germans were up to as quickly as the middle echelons of the German military command structure. Originally it had been Polish Military Intelligence which had discovered that the Germans were using an encoding machine known as Enigma: in July 1939 the Poles handed over to the British an example of the machine which they had acquired but the mathematical problems of breaking machine-code were so complex that it was not till April 1940 that British experts were able to decypher any of the German Enigma transmissions, and even then only those of the Luftwaffe. Ultra – this was the British code name for the material derived from breaking the Enigma codes – was of course not the only form of intelligence derived from tapping enemy signal traffic. The Germans themselves cracked the British and Allied Merchant Shipping Code in use until 1943; the British cracked the Italian naval code and were for example aware of Admiral Iachino's movements and dispositions at the time of the Battle of Matapan in March 1941. Admiral Isoroku Yamamoto

---

[32] Barnett *Audit of War* p. 321 fn. 24 cf. Public Record Office AVIA 10/269 note 'Planned Man-hours on German Aircraft' by A.D. Stats 3, 16 Feb. 1944.

was shot down by U.S. interceptors in April 1943 while flying an itinerary known to the Americans through reading Japanese codes. But breaking the Enigma codes was not only scientifically the most difficult feat but also perhaps the most important for securing Allied victory, for by enabling the Allies to locate the German U-boat packs it made a key contribution to the Battle of the Atlantic.[33]

With regard to the war on land Ultra achieved the very occasional classic success, such as forewarning the Americans of the intended German offensive in the Avranches sector on 7 August 1944 and giving time for appropriate dispositions to be made. But the more frequent botching was more typical. By means of Ultra Wavell was able to monitor the build up of Rommel's forces in Libya in early 1941 but concluded that no German attack would be possible till May; this being one of the reasons why Rommel's offensive in April was such a success. In May 1941 Freyberg, though not in the secret of Ultra, was fed with very detailed Ultra information regarding German preparations to attack Crete, but though expecting an air-borne assault in conjunction with a sea-borne landing he gave too much importance to the latter, with the result that his preparations to withstand the decisive air-borne invasion were inadequate, and his forces were driven ignominiously from the island. In November 1942 Montgomery, when pursuing Rommel to Tripoli after the Battle of El Alamein, had detailed information from Ultra regarding Rommel's strength and intended movements but advanced with such caution that his troops on occasion lost contact with the much weaker Italo-German forces. Ultra also provided adequate information concerning German strength in the Arnhem sector when, in the autumn of 1944, it was Britain's turn to use an air-borne army, but in this instance the British utilized all their precise information to underestimate all the risks, instead of, as was more customary, to overestimate them.[34]

In the war at sea Ultra provided enough information to predict the dash of the German battle-cruisers *Scharnhorst* and *Gneisenau* up the English Channel from Brest to Kiel in February 1942: it did not tell the British Admiralty the precise hour of raising anchor or point out how to take effective counter measures, but the British only *acted* as if taken by surprise. In July 1942, Ultra intelligence indicated that Germany's only surviving first-rate battleship, the *Tirpitz*, had *not* left its base in northern Norway to attack convoy PQ 17 which was en route for Murmansk with Lend-Lease supplies. Sir Dudley Pound, the First Sea Lord, chose not to believe this intelligence and ordered the convoy to scatter so as not to provide a concentrated quarry for the

[33] Cf. Nigel Balchin *The Small Back Room* (1943) p. 104 for 'the chap who proves that black's white to three places of decimals'; Ronald Lewin *Ultra Goes To War: The Secret Story* (1978) p. 44, 60, 195; ibid. p. 139 for the Italian naval code; Ronald Lewin *The Other Ultra* (1982) p. 187–191 for the interception of Admiral Yamamoto; Lewin *Ultra Goes To War* p. 213–220.

[34] Lewin *Ultra Goes To War* p. 335–340; ibid. p. 160–162 ibid. p. 156–9; ibid. p. 348–350; Correlli Barnett *The Desert Generals* (2nd edit. 1983) p. 310–312.

German battleship; as a result, of the 34 merchant ships which fled from one another and from their naval escorts, 23 were picked off by U-boats and aircraft. The whole story of Ultra simply underlines that information is only an aid to judgement – not a substitute for it. Ultra helped disperse the fog of war from the horizon: it could not clear it from inside the heads of the Allied commanders. One recalls that in the First World War the British always had much better aerial reconnaissance than the Germans . . .[35]

Another area of boffinry was operational research, which was described subsequently as 'one of the chief scientific features of the war'. Operational Research dealt with what actually happened when a weapon was put to use – obviously an important concern with ever newer and more complex weaponry. Operational Research had a feature that was most useful in a period when technical skills were in great demand: the experts who observed the weapons did not necessarily have to be capable of designing them. In Nigel Balchin's wartime novel *The Small Back Room* the legendary Reeves gun is examined by a technical sub-committee consisting of a crystallographer, a vital statistician, an embryologist and 'one of the best-known organic chemists in the country'. This is scarcely a novelist's exaggeration: Professor A.V. Hill, the grand old man of the art – he had directed the Anti-Aircraft experimental section in the Ministry of Munitions in the First World War – was a physiologist, and Solly Zuckerman, who became the leader in the field in the Second World War, was an anatomist who had branched into animal behaviour while working for the London Zoological Society. As far as I know the methods of Operational Research have never been applied to Operational Research itself, and the impression one has is that, in spite of some very high quality work, it served mainly to reinforce an already existing tendency towards over-kill, over-spending, over-optimism, and over-scaling of safety margins. In any case some of the most important work in Operational Research should have been done already by the design engineers who subsequently failed to respond to the problems pointed out to them: for example the R.A.F.'s Operational Research Section reported in September 1942 that bombers were occasionally blowing up when trying to land because of the volatility of the petrol vapour in half-emptied petrol tanks, but though the principle of purging tanks by charging them with an inert gas like nitrogen had long been familiar to chemical engineers and was even adopted for use on Soviet Pe-2 light bombers from 1943 onwards, the problem persisted in the R.A.F. till the end of the war.[36]

The scientific field in which Britain established a really significant leadership

---

35 Lewin *Ultra Goes To War* p. 221-7.
36 Balchin *The Small Back Room* p. 107. Balchin, a businessman before the war, rose by 1945 to be a brigadier and Deputy Scientific Adviser to the Army Council. J.G. Crowther and R. Whiddington (on behalf of the Department of Scientific and Industrial Research) *Science at War* (1947) p. 91; Ronald W. Clark *The Rise of the Boffins* (1962) p. 222-3 cf Jean Alexander *Russian Aircraft since 1940* (1975) p. 300.

was that of radar and associated electronic devices. As far as the construction of instruments was concerned, Britain was by no means a front-runner in this area; development of radar began in the U.S. in 1930, in Germany in 1933, but in Britain only in 1935. Moreover until the introduction of the cavity magnetron in 1942 German sets were individually better than British sets; from the very beginning the Germans managed without the groups of 350-foot high pylons which were characteristic of British radar stations. Yet though the Germans were the first to intercept an air-raid detected in advance by radar (at Wilhelmshaven on 18 December 1939), it was the British who were the first to erect a chain of radar stations giving complete and systematic early warning coverage of an entire coast line. The British radar network on the southern and eastern coasts, though possibly operated on an unnecessarily complex principle, effectively abolished any advantage of tactical surprise that might have been expected in raids on coastal regions.[37]

The British also pressed ahead with air-borne radar, but though the first 21 Blenheim night fighters with A.I.II radar were delivered by September 1939, and a further sixty with A.I.III within the next nine months, it was not till the night of 22–23 July 1940 that a night bomber was successfully intercepted by radar and shot down. The night raids on London during September and October were virtually undisturbed by R.A.F. night fighters; only in November did German bombers begin to be struck down in ones and twos over London, and then largely as a result of the fast and heavily-armed Beaufighter coming into service. The Germans were slower in starting development but soon caught up. Their first night interception using a pair of ground stations tracking hunter and hunted was on 16 October 1940 and the first successful night interception using the air-borne Lichtenstein radar equipment was on 9 August 1941.[38]

One of the most striking examples of German promptness in the electronic field was their use of radio-navigational aids to assist bombing. As far back as 15 June 1915 the Zeppelin L10 had used radio-triangulation to bomb the Tyne. The necessity of such aids for long-range night bombing tended to be denied by the R.A.F., which preferred to make exaggerated claims for the navigational skills of its specialist night-bombing crews: the Luftwaffe, primarily a tactical air force with relatively little night-bombing experience, saw the usefulness of electronic aids much sooner. As early as June 1940 the Germans were trying out a navigational aid known as *Knickebein* (Dog Leg) with which any number of bombers could follow a radio beam till it was intersected in the target area by a second beam from a separate transmitter. R.V. Jones of the Air Ministry figured out the system almost immediately, though jamming was not generally successful till February 1941; thus already in that second winter of the war

[37] For the development of the cavity magnetron see Guy Hartcup *The Challenge of War: Scientific and Engineering Contributions to World War Two* (Newton Abbot 1970) p. 89–92; Bill Gunston *Night Fighters* p. 35–8.

[38] Gunston *Night Fighters* p. 51, 60; Jones *Most Secret War* p. 223, 280.

we are in a world where aircraft were both guided and hunted through the darkness by blind machines. The degree of bombing concentration achieved on an inland target like Coventry in November 1940 would have been quite impossible without electronic aids; later on, though jamming could not save London since it was clearly identifiable at the head of a large estuary, it achieved some notable successes in preserving inland targets, for example on 8–9 May 1941 when British jamming, in conjunction with decoy fires, caused a Luftwaffe raid on Derby and Nottingham to miss Derby altogether, and Nottingham almost entirely.[39]

The British also pressed ahead with electronic aids for their own bombers: the first, Gee, was used on 8 March 1942 and the second, Oboe, in December of the same year. Oboe involved transmissions from the aeroplane to the tracking station, which severely limited traffic-handling capacity, and was used only for Pathfinder aircraft; but most of the other devices could be made standard equipment and by the end of 1943 many R.A.F. bombers were carrying a formidable (and vastly expensive) array of electronic gear: Gee; H_2S, a high-definition radar employing the cavity magnetron valve, which gave an image of the ground below the aeroplane; Identification Friend or Foe, (I.F.F.) a device for identifying British planes on the screens of British radar; Monica, a radar device for warning of approaching enemy nightfighters; blind landing approach gear; and often some sort of transmitter for jamming German transmissions. While to the physical eye the dark-painted night bombers of the R.A.F. betrayed themselves at night only by the muted glow of the specially cowled exhaust manifolds on their engines, electronically they were lit up like cruise liners: the I.F.F. device was often left on over Germany because of a rumour that it confused German night fighters, and by mid 1944 the Germans could even intercept H_2S transmissions. The value of limiting electronic output, together with the use of long-range night fighters to prey on German air-borne transmitters, was pretty well understood by the later summer of 1942. There was also a constant experimentation with jamming techniques. In December 1942 air-borne radar jammers, known as 'Mandrel', were in use, and German radio-telephone communication was jammed by broadcasting engine noise on German frequencies. 'Moonshine', a device for amplifying radar echoes to indicate much larger formations, was also used for a period.[40]

The simplest and most successful jamming device was 'Window', which consisted of strips of paper covered on one side with silver foil. It was developed early in 1942 and was loaded for use in an air-raid in May 1942 but off-loaded at the last minute before take-off; Derek Jackson, R.A.F. Fighter Command's Air-borne Radar Officer, Sir Robert Watson-Watt, the country's leading radar expert, and Lord Cherwell, Churchill's scientific adviser, all

[39] Gunston *Night Fighters* p. 16, Denis Richards and Hilary St George Saunders *Royal Air Force, 1939–1945* (3 vols 1953) vol. 1 p. 216–7.
[40] Jones *Most Secret War* p. 290–291, 295, 465–6, 469.

feared that till higher resolution radar sets had been perfected, the introduction of 'Window' might rebound on the British. On 18 June 1942 Cherwell met with Air Commodore O.G.W.G. Lywood of R.A.F. Signals to discuss the matter: that morning's instalment of the Buck Ryan strip cartoon in *The Daily Mirror* featured a fiendish enemy plot to use box-kites with metal frames to confuse and dislocate British Anti-Aircraft radar. In the final cartoon frame the A.A. officer remarks, 'Yes. And it *might* have worked twelve months ago, Ryan but *not today*'. This was perhaps premature, and it later transpired that not only *The Daily Mirror*'s cartoonists but also German scientists had figured out the 'Window' principle all on their own. The Germans had been afraid of the R.A.F. using Window ever since February 1942, and this became known to British Intelligence by October 1942; but while in Britain work was pushing ahead on higher resolution radar, in Germany Göring simply suppressed the whole issue, forbidding the development of counter-measures or even discussion of the matter. The R.A.F. finally used 'Window' for the first time in the devastating attacks on Hamburg in July 1943: the Germans did not develop a ground radar effective against this form of jamming till April 1945.[41]

The Buck Ryan strip cartoon indicated one of the incidental risks of running a science-fiction war in a science-fiction-reading society; Göring's veto on discussion of 'Window' points to a more important aspect of scientific warfare and its contrasting styles in Britain and Germany. Hitler had an autodidact's interest in conventional weapons but understood nothing of physics; Göring liked hunting rifles and knew how to clear the breach of a machine gun in mid-air while holding the control column between his knees, but that was his technical limit; Speer was an architect who seems to have judged scientific projects in terms of what can only be called committee viability; Himmler was instinctively attracted by the bogus and half-baked. In the jungle of Nazi war-mobilization there was nobody really pushing for science. In Britain it was quite otherwise: scientists were encouraged to speak out authoritatively in meetings of the military High Command (e.g. Zuckerman); in Parliament (e.g. A.V. Hill); even in the War Cabinet, where on one occasion the twenty-nine-year-old R.V. Jones was invited to address the nation's leaders. Churchill, despite his old-fashioned values, was capable of grasping new concepts quickly, and he had the true Victorian's generalized faith in technological progress, even if he did know less about technical minutiae than Hitler: he seems, incidentally, to have been the first British Cabinet minister to be interested in playing with Meccano. Moreover one of Churchill's closest advisers was Frederick Lindemann, Professor of Physics – or Experimental Philosophy as they called it – at Oxford. Lindemann, created Lord Cherwell in 1941, seems to have been the original of Sir Lewis Easton in

---

[41] Jones *Most Secret War* p. 292–3, 299; Alfred Price *Instruments of Darkness* (1967) p. 118–9.

Nigel Balchin's *The Small Back Room*: 'simply a social climber who happened to choose the science ladder.' His support of the area bombing policy gave an unjustified scientific respectability to a strategy that was as discreditable as it was ineffective; moreover he seems to have devoted most of his energy to giving advice on economic rather than scientific questions and by 1940 had as his assistants eight economists and only one scientist; his 'S Branch' (S for Statistics) was responsible for much of the wartime efflorescence of statistics – 'The choice when to use quantities, when percentages, when averages, etc. was all important. The Prof. himself had great skill in devising the right mode of presentation.' Nevertheless he was there to give more purely scientific advice when the occasion arose. Nor was Cherwell alone in promoting the role of the scientific mind in modern war-making. Though one may feel that traditional democratic processes became weaker in Britain during the war, agencies of control and influence which had flourished in peacetime were at least permitted to maintain themselves in wartime, and some were promoted to greater power; in particular the superstructure of scientific committees and consultative bodies was extended. Professor A.V. Hill's call in Parliament, in July 1942, for a central technical staff seems slightly odd in that he was himself already a member of the War Cabinet Scientific Advisory Committee, of the Ministry of Supply's Scientific Advisory Council, of the Department of Scientific and Industrial Research's Advisory Council, and an associate member of the Ordnance Board, quite apart from being involved in running the Royal Society, the University Grants Committee and the National Physical Laboratory.[42]

If anything, while there was not enough scientific consultation and organization in Germany, in Britain there was too much. Indeed, if in the First World War there was a kind of imbalance between generalship and the new material scale of warfare, in the Second World War the imbalance was between the military imagination and the limitless possibilities offered by the scientists: as will be shown in the next two chapters.

---

[42] See John Spencer Churchill *Crowded Canvas* (1961) p. 32–3 for Churchill's involvement with Meccano while Minister of Munitions in 1917; Balchin *The Small Back Room* p. 86; Earl of Birkenhead *The Prof. in Two Worlds* (1961) p. 211–261 for Cherwell's wartime career generally and R.F. Harrod *The Prof: A Personal Memoir of Lord Cherwell* (1959) p. 179–180, 191 for Cherwell's assistants and statistical work. Hill spoke urging a central technical staff on 14 July 1942, *Hansard: House of Commons* vol. 381 col. 1151, cf his letter in *the Times* 1 July 1942 p. 5e.

15

The Strategy of Long Views and Wide Margins

He refilled our glasses several times and then, I suppose inevitably, we found ourselves in each other's arms in an unrestrained embrace. Our ties came off. Our jackets came off. Buttons were unbuttoned. It was as if we were frantic. And we were.

But this was not what I had expected. Wearily, we slowly calmed down. He snuggled his face into the hollow between my neck and shoulder and said, 'Oh God, Kay, I'm sorry. I'm not going to be any good for you'.

'I'm the one who should apologize,' I said, 'I should have known how exhausted you were'.

Kay Summersby Morgan, *Past Forgetting: My Love Affair with Dwight D. Eisenhower* (1977), p. 27–8 (relating an incident in 1944).

I. Axis Underestimates

It is a truism that the victorious side in any war is the one which makes the fewest mistakes. This would be absolutely true, as well as being a truism, if wars were fought between parties of effectively equal strength but in the Second World War (as in most other conflicts) this was not the case, and it seems that the stronger side can afford to make more mistakes in proportion to its greater strength. Or to turn the axiom round, the Axis didn't get away with its mistakes whereas the Allies, with their enormous superiority in human and economic resources, did.[1]

The fundamental mistake of the Axis powers in the Second World War was of course to underestimate the human and economic resources available to their opponents – at least this was essentially true of Germany and Japan; the Italians, in a much more favourable strategic position vis-à-vis potential enemies, simply overestimated their own strength.

One has only to visit the cemetery in any country town in Germany to be reminded of the scale of the German miscalculation and of the resultant catastrophe. If one skirts the token plaque inscribed *Den hier ruhenden Opfern nationalsozialistischer Justiz zum ehrenden Gedenken* ('In honour

---

[1] It was a favourite saying of Hitler's that, 'The loser of this war will be the side that makes the greatest blunders'. Albert Speer *Inside the Third Reich* (1970) p. 229. The remark, 'The greatest general is he who makes the fewest mistakes' is attributed to Napoleon.

of the victims of Nazi justice buried here'), and the monuments erected by the exiled survivors of the Final Solution, one comes to the neatly ranked testimonies of a tragedy from which contemporary Germany still suffers even more deeply than from the mass-murder of its ethnic minorities: family graves marked with Maltese crosses for those family members who died in action, inscriptions in the customary telegraphese of the German graveyard: *verm. im Osten; unserem lb. in Russland vermissten Sohn u. Bruder; gef. 18.12.1941 bei Jerschowa – Russld; gef. 13.8.1942 bei Orel; verm. 1942 in Stalingr.; verm. in Stalingrad; verm. seit Stalingrad Februar 1943;* one notes the almost total annihilation of families – *Rudolf 1913–1943 Wilhelm 1917–1943 Hermann 1919–1943 in Russland gefallen,* or *zum Gedenken an unsere lieben 2 Söhne u. 5 Töchter in Russland gefallen u. gestorben 1943 + 1947.* One sees the gazetteer of Nazi advance, retirement and collapse: *vermisst v. Moskau; gefallen vor Charkow am 15.5.42; bei Charkow; gefallen bei Woronesch; gef. 30.6.43 im Kubanbruckenkopf; 1943 im Osten; vermisst in den Karpathen 1944; verm. 1944 in Rumänien; verm. 10.1.1945 bei Warschau; gef. 3 Jan. 1945 in Nagy-Körtenburg; gef. 4 Jan. 1945 Ödenburg/Ungarn; gefallen in Ostpreussen; gef. 12.1.1945 in Daken/Ostpr; vermisst 1945 i. Osten; verm. seit Jan. 1945 in Posen; vermisst in Pommern seit März 1945; verm. 1945 bei Berlin.* Finally the aftermath of humiliating captivity: * 24.2.1928 Gest. 10.10.1945 in Usbekistan in russ. Gefangenschaft; In stillen Gedanken an uns. lieben Sohn u. Bruder . . . geb. 28 Nov. 1924 – gest. Jan. 1947 in russ. Gefangensch. – Sibirien; dem Gedächtnis meines Lieben Mannes Karl-Wilhelm Specht General d. Infanterie *22.V.1894 + 3.XII.1953 in Woikova-Russland.*[2]

But Russia was only the nemesis of a consistently hubristic style of campaigning. The German invasion of Poland in September 1939 (with the theoretical possibility of a French counter-blow in the German rear), of Norway in April 1940 (in the teeth of Britain's naval superiority) and of France in May 1940 (with none of the numerical advantage supposedly needed by the attacking side) were all stylish gambles, relying on superior tactics and speed rather than on accurate calculation: in northern Norway the Anglo-French counter-attack was far more powerful than anticipated, and having been driven out of Narvik the German forces in the far north were saved from having to capitulate only by the Allied decision to withdraw in early June following the German victory in France; in September 1940 the Germans were planning a sea-borne assault on England after having failed to locate 14 out of 29 British divisions within 30 miles of their actual location, and after having

---

[2] All these inscriptions are taken from the Bergfriedhof, Heidelberg, but might be matched anywhere in western Germany. Inscriptions commemorating men killed in action in the First World War are almost as common in English cemeteries as in German but this is not the case with regard to the Second World War; this is mainly because Britain's military casualties were perhaps one fifth of Germany's. *Gefallen* means killed in action; *gestorben* means died, *vermisst* means missing, *Russland* is of course Russia; *im Osten* is 'on the Eastern Front'; *Gefangenschaft* is captivity.

identified eight extra divisions that did not exist; in April 1941 the Germans overestimated the power of the Yugoslavs to resist, which was fortunate as they had failed to anticipate the stiffness of the Greek defence further to the south. Nevertheless, up till and including the early months of the invasion of Russia, these slipshod methods of planning paid off handsomely.[3]

The original scheme for the invasion of the Soviet Union drawn up by General Erich Marcks was based on intelligence information that the Red Army had 151 infantry and 32 cavalry divisions and 38 motorized brigades and assumed that 'the Russians no longer possess the superiority of numbers they had in the World War'. In April 1941 the intelligence estimate was revised upward to 247 divisions or motorized brigades of which, on 21 June 1941, $216\frac{1}{2}$ were supposed to be in western Russia. The British, with less contact with the Soviet Union, estimated Red Army strength at 177 infantry and 44 cavalry divisions and 79 tank brigades – 300 major formations – and this seems to have been nearer the truth. German intelligence also miscalculated the proportion of Red Army strength which was in the Far East and Caucasus; instead of the great majority of Soviet units being in western Russia, exposed to the first onslaught, only a little over half were, which meant that the Soviets had enormous reserves outside the immediate danger zone to draw on: not $30\frac{1}{2}$ major formations outside western Russia as German intelligence thought, but more like 140. German intelligence also vastly underestimated Soviet ability to raise and equip new units, and failed to give warning of the quality of the latest Soviet tanks, and the availability of new-fangled weaponry such as the Katushka multiple rocket-launcher.[4]

Hitler nearly got away with it through the brilliance and élan of his Army. In the summer and autumn campaigns of 1941, in seven major and thirteen lesser encirclement battles, the Red Army lost nearly three million men – the equivalent of 150 strong divisions – 14,287 tanks and 25,512 guns. This was about three times the quantity of tanks and guns that the German Army had at the start of the invasion. It is unreasonable to canvass the various mistakes in strategy and management which Hitler and his generals later made without acknowledging the huge initial advantages which nobody could have dared predict which the same Hitler and the same generals had secured in 1941. But in the end the German armed forces (and their allies of the Rumanian, Finnish, Hungarian, Slovak and Italian Armies and the Spanish *División Azul* or Blue

---

[3] For German assessments of British strength in 1940 see Peter Fleming *Invasion 1940* (1957) p. 179.

[4] Matthew Cooper *The German Army, 1933–1945* (1978) p. 261; Barry A. Leach *German Strategy Against Russia, 1939–1941* (Oxford 1973) p. 168, 250–4,270 Appendix IV, cf Public Record Office WO 33/1684 'Order of Battle of the Military Forces of U.S.S.R. [March] 1941' p. 2–3. *The Great Soviet Encyclopedia* 3rd edit. vol. 4 p. 335 gives a total of 303 Soviet divisions, possibly counting armoured brigades as divisions since they are not shown separately. For location of Soviet formations cf Andreas Hillgruber *Hitlers Strategie: Politik und Kriegführung, 1940–1941* (Frankfurt 1965) p. 510.

Division – altogether an additional half-million men) were simply not strong enough for the vast task they had undertaken. The enemy was not simply Russian numbers but Russian distances: the battle zone in August 1941 was twenty times larger than in France in May 1940. The Wehrmacht started the campaign on 22 June 1941 with 500,000 trucks; by November 1941 150,000 had been written off and 275,000 needed repair.[5]

The experience of Japan from December 1941 onwards was essentially similar: the Japanese Imperial forces conquered as far as they could reach but the enemy did not surrender, leaving the victors to settle down to a war on a geographical and economic scale which they were simply unable to handle.

Whereas the Germans in Russia underestimated the capacity of the Soviet war machine to survive in a physical and material sense, the Japanese error was in misjudging the enemy's *will* to fight. The Japanese were uncomfortably aware of their own economic weakness. In June 1940, when the Japanese economy was already overstrained by the Imperial Navy's Third and Fourth Replenishment Programmes, involving four battleships and three carriers, the U.S. Congress passed the Two Ocean Naval Expansion Act providing for seven battleships and eighteen carriers. This meant that Japanese naval strength relative to American would fall from 75 per cent, in early 1942, to 30 per cent in 1944. But whereas Hitler proposed to strike at the continental heart of the Soviet Union, and to overrun at least its westernmost third, the Japanese never had any intention of invading the American or British homelands and meant only to strike at the peripheries of the white powers' colonial empires. The Japanese naval staff did not even think in terms of maintaining command of the sea, only of preventing enemy command. There was no idea of destroying the American or even the British economic capacity to launch distant expeditions sustained by transoceanic lines of supply stretching halfway round the world; the idea was simply to make such expeditions, relative to their potential result, prohibitively costly and difficult, and against the overstretched British this policy was indeed largely effective.[6]

The Japanese nevertheless underestimated the British and, particularly, American determination to avenge attacks on their overseas territories. In

[5] Cooper *German Army* p. 240–291 cf Hillgruber *Hitlers Strategie* p. 537 fn. 4 which gives German equipment at the outset of the campaign as 3,580 tanks and 7,184 guns. The Spanish Blue Division belonged officially to the German Army and had German equipment: it served in the Novgorod sector and later south of Leningrad and was not in contact with the troops of Germany's allies, cf Gerald R. Kleinfeld and Lewis A. Tambs *Hitler's Spanish Legion: The Blue Division in Russia* (Carbondale 1979) p. 35,41. For the Italian *CSIR.*, later the 8ᵃ Armata, see below. The largest and most effective, though possibly worst equipped, allied contingent was provided by Rumania, and consisted of two armies. For size of war zone and wastage of trucks see Cooper *German Army* p. 270,334. The invasion force also had over 600,000 horses.

[6] H.P. Willmott *The Barrier and the Javelin: Japanese and Allied Pacific Strategies February to June 1942* (Annapolis 1983) p. 7–8, 16–19, 28–32.

fact they seem to have thought out only the opening phases of their campaigns. This enabled them to simplify logistic arrangements enormously; such arrangements usually consisted of very little more than the supply of a few days' rice and a few weeks' ammunition. They were unable to afford the luxury of doing things on a better-organized scale but were proud to meet the challenge that this entailed. Their soldiers were prepared to die for their country, even if only of untreated wounds; and the Samurai mentality did not concern itself with the rescue and restoration of the damaged. Their fighting formations had no stretcher bearers, no first-aid teams, hardly any medical supplies, and no base hospitals to provide back-up. Even if Japanese treatment of white prisoners of war was characterized by psychotic brutality and malicious caprice, American and British indignation at the Bataan Death March and the horrifying working conditions on the Burma-Siam railway was largely misplaced: for every five white prisoners who died working on the Burma-Siam railway between November 1942 and October 1943 there died three of the Japanese soldiers assigned to supervise and guard them. The results of this cavalier attitude to logistics was already beginning to have its effects on Japanese fighting power by October 1942, when Japanese troops on Guadalcanal, as well as having much less ammunition than the Americans, were beginning to die of starvation. In the Guadalcanal fighting American casualties were 1,979 dead and about 6,000 wounded: the Japanese lost over 32,000 dead, more than half from want of medical assistance. Later, in the Imphal-Kohima battles in Burma, it was estimated that nearly half the Japanese army of 115,000 died through lack of food and medical care; later still, in the Philippines they were reduced in their extremity to cannibalism.[7]

II. Strategy as Fantasy: The Italian Case

The style of the Italians' participation in the war differed from that of their allies. Instead of the megalomaniac gambles with which Germany and Japan stunned the world there were only wild uncoordinated gestures which covered Mussolini's regime with ridicule.

The substitution of rhetoric for calculation may be entirely attributable to Mussolini himself:

Italy will not truly be an independent nation so long as she has Corsica, Bizerta,

---

[7] R.B. Pal *International Military Tribunal for the Far East: Dissentient Judgment* (Calcutta 1953) p. 649–651; F.C. Jones *Japan's New Order in East Asia: Its Rise and Fall, 1937–45* (1954) p. 347 and fn 3; Saburo Hayashi *Kōgun: The Japanese Army in the Pacific War* (Quantico Va. 1959) p. 60; Fletcher Pratt *The Marines' War: An Account of the Struggle for the Pacific from both American and Japanese Sources* (New York 1948) p. 116–7; Sir William Slim *Defeat into Victory* (1956) p. 378; Louis Allen 'Japanese Literature of the Second World War' *British Association for Japanese Studies* vol. 2 (1977) Part 1 p. 117–152, Appendix III at p. 149–152.

Malta as the bars of her Mediterranean prison and Gibraltar and Suez as the walls . . .

Italy cannot remain neutral for the whole duration of the war without resigning her rôle, without disqualifying herself, without reducing herself to the level of a Switzerland multiplied by ten.

The problem then is not of knowing if Italy will or will not enter the war, because Italy can do no less. It's a matter only of knowing when and how.

But though the rhetoric was Italian, the overextension and division of effort bears an uncomfortable resemblance to that of Britain, and this invites closer examination.[8]

Italy had entered the war in June 1940 during the last days of the victorious German campaign in France. While Hitler confronted Britain across the few miles of choppy grey sea which separate north-eastern France from Kent and Sussex, Mussolini found himself with British colonies along more than two thousand miles of the border of his recently pacified African empire. Libya was very powerfully garrisoned and was close enough to be reinforced quickly, though possibly Mussolini should have spared a thought for Ethiopia and Eritrea which, even though in no immediate danger from Britain's weakly garrisoned East African colonies, would be cut off from assistance when Britain, with easier sea communications, built up offensive forces in East Africa. Mussolini by no means counted on Britain being knocked out of the war immediately, for preparations were set in train in September to send aviation units to Belgium to join in the Battle of Britain and since these could only be expected to be in action late in October, after the season for sea-borne invasion across the Channel had passed, it would seem that Mussolini envisaged the war lasting well into 1941. Nevertheless Mussolini seems to have assumed that Britain would generally maintain a passive stance. His own imagination meanwhile had become excessively active. Hitler had invaded six European countries (not counting Austria, Czechoslovakia and Luxembourg): Mussolini wanted to invade at least one. The only problem was deciding which one.

Mussolini's first choice was Yugoslavia. On 9 August 1940 the German government was requested to permit transit of Italian troops through Austria, and to provide other assistance, in case of a possible invasion of Yugoslavia. The request was refused; Germany was receiving significant imports of metal ore from Yugoslavia, the country was coming increasingly under German economic and diplomatic influence, and it was completely against Germany's interests that Italy should seize control of Yugoslavia's resources or, even worse, wreck and disrupt them in the course of a prolonged, destructive and strategically pointless campaign. Mussolini nevertheless continued to dream of invading Yugoslavia well into September. An invasion of Greece seemed

---

[8] *Opera Omnia di Benito Mussolini* (35 vols Florence 1951–1962) vol. 29 p. 365–6 'Memoriale panoramico al re' 31 March 1940.

merely a second-best alternative, but though the Germans tried to discourage ambitions in this direction too they had less involvement with Greece, and no common frontier, so their cooperation was less necessary. The movement of German military units into Rumania made a decision seem all the more urgent: Mussolini was reportedly provoked to exclaim:

> Hitler always faces me with a fait accompli. This time I am going to pay him back in his own coin. He will find out from the papers that I have occupied Greece. In this way the equilibrium will be reestablished.[9]

It is something of a mystery how much Hitler knew in advance of Mussolini's plans to attack Greece. The two dictators met at the Brenner early in October, before Mussolini had divulged his intentions to his military chiefs, and it is possible that the invasion of Greece was discussed tête-à-tête, without anything going into the official record. Alternatively German officials may have been informed after Mussolini's meeting with his generals on 15 October 1940, though Hitler himself is traditionally supposed to have known nothing till a couple of hours after the invasion had actually started. At any rate the invasion of Greece was essentially Mussolini's idea and Mussolini's decision.[10]

At the meeting on 15 October to arrange the details of the invasion, Badoglio, chief of staff of the armed forces, did not oppose the scheme but asked for three months to build up sufficient troops; a couple of days later, in private conversation with Foreign Minister Ciano, he was outspokenly critical of the whole project. The invasion itself was planned in a mood of unreality and overconfidence, and with only two weeks' notice. It was in fact assumed that the Greeks would simply fall over when pushed. Instead their fierce counter-attacks soon drove the Italian forces back into Albania. By mid December the Italians were significantly outnumbered – 135 Greek battalions to 105 Italian, the latter also having a smaller establishment of machine guns per unit.[11]

It is conceivable that Italian superiority in the air could have helped to redress the balance – though close-support flying in the rain and low cloud of a Mediterranean winter was not to be relied on – but Italian air superiority, though considerable, was not on a scale to make up for the inadequacies of

[9] Martin L. van Creveld *Hitler's Strategy, 1940–1941: The Balkan Clue* (Cambridge 1973) p. 3, 12–13; MacGregor Knox *Mussolini Unleashed, 1939–1941: Politics and Strategy in Fascist Italy's Last War* (Cambridge 1982) p. 165–7, 171–2, 180–181; ibid. p. 176–7; Malcolm Muggeridge ed. *Ciano's Diary, 1939–1943* ed. Malcolm Muggeridge, (1947) p. 297, 12 Oct. 1940. It evidently amused Ciano to believe that Hitler had no advance notice of the invasion of Greece, but in fact Mussolini probably had not told his Foreign Minister how much he had divulged to Hitler.

[10] Knox *Mussolini Unleashed* p. 202, 222–3, 229–30, cf Creveld *Hitler's Strategy* p. 39–49.

[11] Mario Cervi *The Hollow Legions: Mussolini's Blunder in Greece, 1940–1941* (New York 1971) p. 78, 322; Knox *Mussolini Unleashed* p. 213–4; Cervi *Hollow Legions* p. 107, 196.

the ground troops. The same was found to be true in Libya, when Lieutenant-General Richard O'Connor launched his sudden offensive against the Italian army in North Africa early in December, six weeks after the Italian attack on Greece. In November 1940 the Italian air force, the *Regia Aeronautica*, had 194 bombers and 161 fighters stationed in Albania and Puglia (the 'heel' of Italy) and 129 bombers, 53 assault/army cooperation planes and 139 fighters in Libya – many of them grounded as a result of inadequate servicing and repair facilities. The Greeks at the time of the invasion had about 35 Bristol Blenheim, Fairey Battle and Potez 63 light bombers and 47 fighters, including nine French Bloch MB 151s which were faster than anything the Italians had available, and 36 Polish-built PZL P.24Fs and P.24Gs which though slow were very heavily armed compared to Italian fighters. The R.A.F. soon turned a dozen or so Gloster Gladiator fighters over to the Greek Air Force (*Elleniki Vassiliki Aeroporia*) and sent three squadrons of Blenheim bombers and a squadron of Gladiators from Egypt. For the Libyan campaign the R.A.F. retained in Egypt 116 bombers, 48 fighters and thirty or so cooperation planes, mainly Westland Lysanders. Even including their high quota of unserviceable aircraft, the *Regia Aeronautica* forces had less than a two to one advantage in numbers, with generally inferior aircraft, in the whole eastern Mediterranean theatre; the 80 bombers and 98 fighters of the *Corpo Aereo Italiano* ostentatiously despatched to Belgium to carry the triple fasces symbol into English airspace would have been an important reinforcement. In December it was necessary to transfer fighters from Puglia to Libya, and after two unimpressive skirmishes over Harwich and the South Foreland on 11 and 23 November part of the fighter component of the *Corpo Aereo Italiano* in Belgium was also transferred to Libya. Thus within two months of attacking one of the poorest and least populous countries in Europe Mussolini was having to shuttle around scarce resources.[12]

Hitler eventully bailed Mussolini out in Greece and sent Rommel to assist in North Africa, where the British had given the Italians a reprieve by transferring their energies to Greece. The bombers of the *Corpo Aereo Italiano* were withdrawn from Belgium in February 1941, having carried out a grand total of 102 combat sorties, mainly by night – their only success was an attack on the Co-operative Wholesale Society's canning factory at Waveney Drive, Lowestoft late on 29 November 1940 which severely damaged the factory and killed three people. Two squadrons of fighters remained till April, carrying out 662 sorties over Belgium, in the course of which they failed to encounter

[12] Giuseppe Santoro *L'Aeronautica Italiana nella Seconda Guerra Mondiale* (2 vols Rome 1957) vol. 1 p. 116, 141–2; Jerzy B. Cynk *Polish Aircraft, 1893–1939* (1971) p. 211; Denis Richards and Hilary St. George Saunders *Royal Air Force, 1939–45* (3 vols 1953–4) vol. 1 p. 256; I.S.O. Playfair C.J.C. Molony and W. Jackson *The Mediterranean and Middle East* (6 vols 1954–1988) vol. 1 p. 262 cf John Terraine *The Right of the Line* (1985) p. 314; Santoro *Aeronautica Italiana* vol. 1 p. 302, 356.

the R.A.F. even once. In view of the massive build-up of British resources in Egypt and the failure of the Italian economy to go over to a war footing – at this time Italian output of aircraft and tanks was perhaps one seventh of Germany's – the elimination of Greece and the return of the *Corpo Aereo Italiano* from Belgium hardly represented the reestablishment of the balance of military power in Italy's favour as far as the Mediterranean theatre was concerned; and in June 1941 Hitler's invasion of the Soviet Union presented Mussolini with a new distraction.[13]

Hitler had informed Mussolini of his intention of attacking the Soviet Union when they met at the Brenner on 3 June, though without entering into details. Mussolini, Cavallero (Badoglio's successor as chief of staff of the armed forces) and the German military representative Rintelen discussed the despatch to Russia of an Italian contingent a week before the invasion was launched on 22 June. The *Corpo Spedizionario Italiano in Russia (CSIR)* began its movement by rail to the Ukraine on 11 July 1941: it included an aviation command of 51 Macchi M.C. 200 fighters and 32 Caproni Ca 311 light bombers and again would have constituted a useful reinforcement in North Africa. On the vast Russian front on the other hand the *CSIR* represented merely a drop in a bucket and on 2 June 1942 Mussolini informed Giovanni Messe, the commander of the *CSIR*, that political reasons made it necessary to enlarge the expeditionary corps:

> We cannot be less than Slovakia and other minor states. I must be at the side of Hitler in Russia just as the Führer was at my side in the war against Greece and as he is today in Africa. The destiny of Italy is intimately bound up with that of Germany.

Messe protested that all the difficulties of the *CSIR* would be multiplied if it was enlarged to army strength and argued:

> Our scarce and antiquated weaponry, the total lack of suitable armoured equipment, the great insufficiency of vehicles, the serious problems with transport and supply, all rendered more difficult by the incomprehension and irreducible selfishness of the Germans, create for the army problems that are truly insoluble.

Mussolini did not want to hear any of this and responded blandly, 'My dear Messe, at the peace conference the 200,000 men of the army will weigh that much more than the 60,000 men of the *CSIR*'.[14]

[13] Basil Collier *The Defence of the United Kingdom* (1957) p. 500 Appendix XXVIII, cf R. Douglas Brown *East Anglia 1940* (Lavenham 1981) p. 137; Stephen Harvey 'The Italian War Effort and the Strategic Bombing of Italy' *History* vol. 70 (1985) p. 32–45 at p. 33 for Italian war production.

Note that the Italian attack on the CWS factory at Waveney Avenue, Lowestoft on 29 November 1940, in knocking out a canning factory producing rations for the forces, was a classic of strategic air warfare as formulated by Douhet.

[14] Fred Taylor ed. *The Goebbels Diaries, 1939–1941*, (1982) p. 395, 423, 3 and 22 June 1941; Giovanni Messe *La Guerra al Fronte Russo* (Milan 1954) p. 20; ibid. p. 177–8.

Meanwhile the Italian armed forces were belatedly preparing for a vast air- and sea-borne assault on Malta which, lying athwart the sea-lanes to Libya, had been vital to the British as a base for attacking the Italo-German line of supply to the North African theatre – so vital that Mussolini would have done well to have made the island's conquest his first priority in 1940, instead of attacking Greece. In March 1942 six Italian divisions and various other units began to be lined up for an attack during the period beginning 1 August 1942; a German parachute division was also made available and in an unique instance of tripartite cooperation the Japanese naval attaché at Rome was brought in on the planning. Ultimately 61,805 men were assigned to the task of conquering Malta, of whom 35,805 were to be landed on the first day. Malta's garrison consisted of eleven British and four Maltese infantry battalions, about 12,000 men (plus ten British and five Maltese regiments of field, coastal and anti-aircraft artillery). Since, in conjunction with the Luftwaffe, the *Regia Aeronautica* had almost complete command of the air, the assault had excellent prospects of success – providing it was pressed home. But Cavallero, chief of staff of the Italian armed forces, was inclined to think it better to concentrate on defeating the British in North Africa, and Rommel's astonishing successes there in the summer of 1942 encouraged a belief that a decisive victory was possible in northern Egypt provided material was not diverted to what was essentially a subsidiary operation against Malta. The Malta operation was finally shelved on 27 July, by which time the Italian parachute troops and the landing ships had already been despatched to Libya.[15]

That was Mussolini's last chance for a strategically significant victory: by the end of the year his outnumbered and poorly equipped armies both in North Africa and in southern Russia had been overwhelmed and were in precipitate retreat, and the R.A.F., based in Britain, was launching shatteringly destructive raids against the industrial centres of northern Italy, almost without loss. His dictatorship had only a few more months to survive.[16]

III. The Strategy of Wishful Thinking:
Britain and the Mediterranean

Mussolini's grotesquely ill-conceived strategy must of course be seen in the context of his regime's failure to increase output of modern armaments to a level at which the Italian armed forces could sustain simultaneous and

---

[15] Gabriele Mariano *Operazione C3: Malta* (Rome 1965) p. 219; Romeo Bernotti *Storia della Guerra nel Mediterraneo, 1940–43* (Rome 1960) p. 213–4, 242–3; F.W. Deakin *The Brutal Friendship: Mussolini, Hitler and the Fall of Italian Fascism* (1962) p. 19 emphasizes Hitler's initiative in shelving the Malta assault but it is clear that this simply accorded with the views already formed in Rome.

[16] Harvey 'Italian War Effort' *History* vol. 70 p. 39–41.

costly campaigns in several different theatres at once. Between January 1940 and April 1943 Italy manufactured 10,545 aircraft: Britain produced 15,049 in 1940 alone. And in the period 1939–1943 Italy produced 3,419 tanks as compared to 26,900 produced in Britain 1940–1944. Britain was very far from suffering Italy's limitation of resources; but made up for this by distributing what was available even more maladroitly. With Italy it was always too little; with Britain it was always either too little or too much. The results were generally rather similar.[17]

Whereas Mussolini's strategy was dominated by his personal anxiety to appear on the world stage as the equal of Hitler, Churchill's strategy, at least until America's entry into the war, was constructed around the idea that Britain was a great world power, leading some sort of alliance against Nazi aggression; and surely only the cruellest cynic would see in Churchill's thinking an element of delusion identical to that in Mussolini's. Not the most celebrated but perhaps the most far reaching aspect of Churchill's Grand Concept was the bizarre conviction that Turkey would enter the war on Britain's side.

Even before Churchill rejoined the Cabinet in September 1939, government officials had recognized the significance of Turkey in Britain's contingent war plans. A Deputy Chiefs of Staff report of June 1939 entitled 'Relative Strategic Importance of Countries Requiring Arms from the United Kingdom', after brief discussion of Egypt, Poland, Rumania and Greece, stated:

> We regard Turkey in an entirely different light from our other potential allies ... next to France, we consider Turkey as potentially our most valuable military ally in Europe.

Reference was made both to 'a steadying effect on the Arab-speaking countries' and 'much needed stiffening to the Balkan bloc'. It was appreciated that the main burden of Turkey's participation in the First World War in 1915–1918 had been carried by Asia Minor rather than by the subject territories hived off in the peace settlement, and Kemal Atatürk's efforts to modernize the new, slimmed-down Turkey had received excellent publicity in Britain: it was not perhaps sufficiently understood that Turkey had been so backward under the Ottoman Emperors that even twenty years of inspired guidance could not bring the country up to date. Turkey had certainly gone through some of the motions of being a resurgent power, remilitarizing the Straits in 1936 and in July 1938 occupying Alexandretta; and the government in Ankara had managed to conceal its intention of avoiding military involvement in European affairs at all costs.[18]

In October 1939 Turkey, France and Britain entered into a military

---

[17] Harvey 'Italian War Effort' *History* vol. 70 p. 33–4.
[18] Public Record Office CAB 54/7 p. 61–6 Deputy Chief of Staff no. 108, 24 June 1939 quoting from p. 63.

alliance, generally referred to as the Treaty of Mutual Assistance. It was widely supposed that Turkey's entry into the war against Germany would follow in due course: a poster advertizing war bonds which was widely circulated in France, captioned *Nous vaincrons parce que nous sommes les plus forts*, showed a map of the world with Germany in black, occupied Poland, Czechoslovakia and Austria in grey, and Germany's enemies and their colonies – most strikingly their vast colonies – in red: Turkey was included in one red Levantine bloc with French-controlled Syria and Lebanon and British-controlled Palestine. During consultations with their new allies the Turks seemed less interested in fighting Germany than in concerting measures against the Italians, whose control of the Dodecanese and Albania they resented, especially as it brought Istanbul within easy range of Italy's large and well-publicized bomber force, but when Italy declared war on Britain and France in June 1940 and the British and French governments called on the Turks to carry out the terms of the Treaty of Mutual Assistance, the latter merely announced their non-belligerency and their intention of continuing 'to perfect our military preparations for the defence of our country'.[19]

The Turks had the excuse that they were short of modern weaponry. Late in 1939 they demanded 115 million rounds of small arms ammunition and 6,500 sub-machine guns: the French offered two million rounds of small arms ammunition and 200 sub-machine guns a month from January 1940, plus 500 mortars to be delivered over six months and fifty anti-tank guns and thirty Morane Saulnier MS 406 fighter planes originally allocated to a Polish government order. The British were even more generous: up till November 1940 they sent Turkey about eighty 3.7 inch anti-aircraft guns, nine 75mm anti-aircraft guns built to a Latvian order – Latvia was occupied by the Soviet Union some time prior to delivery – 1,400 anti-tank rifles, 5,000 Hotchkiss machine guns, 21,000,000 rounds of small arms ammunition, 100,000 boots, 30 Fairey Battle light bombers, 10 Bristol Blenheim bombers, 30 Hawker Hurricane fighters, three Spitfires, 36 Westland Lysander army cooperation planes, and various other supplies including 397 parachutes and thirty sets of R.A.F.-pattern wading suits with brogues. The British also sent a staff mission which concerned itself mainly with studying the problem of building the airfields and roads in western Turkey needed to provide the infrastructure necessary for participation in a modern war: there was no discussion of any possible joint campaign and the Turks seemed principally interested in free development aid. Even before the final capitulation of France the Germans were secretly informed that, 'Obviously the Turkish Government feels that the collapse of France releases it from any obligation to make a statement

---

[19] Frank G. Weber *The Evasive Neutral: Germany, Britain and the Quest for a Turkish Alliance in the Second World War* (Columbia 1979) p. 40–44, 49–50; Public Record Office FO 371/25015/R6510 Halifax to Knatchbull-Hugesson (British ambassador at Ankara) 11 June 1940 and ibid. Knatchbull-Hugesson to Foreign Office 27 June 1940 quoting the Turkish premier's declaration to the National Assembly 26 June 1940.

on its attitude and dissolves the alliance', but the Turks were careful to avoid breaking off their profitable relationship with Britain and at the end of 1940 were lobbying for British support for the eventual repossession of the Dodecanese, Albania, Bulgarian Thrace and Salonika. Churchill meanwhile was more than ready to sympathize with Turkey's lack of modern armaments. On 31 January 1941 he offered the Turkish government 'at least ten squadrons of fighter and bomber aircraft' with which to threaten the Ploesti oil fields in Rumania (by then under German control) and pointed out:

> Nothing will more restrain Russian from aiding German, even indirectly, than the presence of powerful British bombing forces which could attack the oilfields of Baku . . . Further, we are prepared to send you a hundred A.A. guns, which are now either in or on their way to Egypt.

The prospect of eventual Turkish support seemed even stronger after Anthony Eden, the British Foreign Secretary, visited Ankara in February. Eden reported:

> Turkey undertakes in any event to enter the war at some stage. She will of course do so immediately she is attacked. But if she is given time by Germans to re-equip herself she will take advantage of it, and will then make war at a moment favourable to the common cause, when her weight can be used with real effect.[20]

Shortly afterwards Iraq, virtually a British protectorate, rose in revolt against British tutelage, and the Germans hastened to organize support for this unexpected ally. The Turks hinted to the Germans that they might provide active assistance in return for a Turco-German non-aggression pact, but even after the Iraq revolt collapsed discussion of the pact continued: it was concluded and signed on 18 June 1941.[21]

Four days later Germany invaded the Soviet Union. This enabled the Turks to present their pact with Germalny as a brilliant coup benefiting the Anglo-Turkish alliance; the British ambassador in Ankara telegraphed the Foreign Office on the fifth day of the German invasion of Russia:

> Minister for Foreign Affairs is in an awkward mood. He even told me today that he was disappointed that you had not expressed gratitude for his action in bringing about Russo-German war.[22]

[20] René Massigli *La Turquie devant la Guerre: Mission à Ankara, 1939–1940* (Paris 1964) p. 307–8; Public Record Office FO 371/25016, annexes to paper 'Armaments for Turkey' 28 Nov. 1940 p. 173–5, 178–189; FO 195/2464/186; *Documents on German Foreign Policy, 1918–1945* Series D (13 vols Washington 1964) vol. 9 p. 595 no. 464 Franz von Papen (German ambassador at Ankara) to Berlin 17 June 1940; Weber *Evasive Neutral* p. 60; Winston S. Churchill *The Second World War* (6 vols 1948–1954) vol. 3 p. 31 Churchill to Inönü 31 Jan. 1941; ibid. vol. 3 p. 86 Eden to Churchill 28 Feb. 1941.

[21] Weber *Evasive Neutral* p. 101–3; cf ibid. p. 81–106 generally for Turkish policy during the Iraq revolt.

[22] Public Record Office FO 371/30092/R6581 Knatchbull-Hugesson to Foreign Office 27 June 1941.

The Turkish government watched the progress of the German invasion of Russia with interest. In July Marshal Çakmak, Chief of the Turkish General Staff, told the British air attaché in Ankara:

> We hope Germany will be so exhausted in the war with Russia that the United Kingdom, America and Turkey all [?will] gain valuable time for preparing the final victory.

But in September 1941 Nuri Paşa, an industrialist, half-brother of the late unlamented Enver Paşa, visited Berlin. He was understood by the German government to be an unofficial envoy of the Turkish regime and had three meetings with Ernst Woermann, Director of the Political Department in the German Foreign Ministry; in the course of these consultations he stated Turkey's claim to protectorate over the Crimea, Transcaucasia, Azerbaijan, Daghestan, the area between the Urals and the Volga, the Tatar Autonomous Republic, bits of Syria, Iraq and Iran and, so as not to appear too modest, western Sinkiang.[23]

During 1942 and 1943 the Turks imported armaments from both sides, concluding a favourable credit treaty with Germany in September 1942 to finance the replacement of their British aircraft with more up to date German types, but also hosting a secret visit by Churchill to Adana, a provincial town in south-eastern Turkey not far from the Syrian border, in January 1943. It was only very gradually perceived that the Turkish armed forces lacked the administrative capacity to absorb all the modern weaponry that was being imported and that a good proportion was being left to rot in the open in the back lots of various ports.[24]

Even after the Ango-American conquest of the entire North African littoral and the occupation of southern Italy, the Turks remained coy. Ismet Inönü, president of Turkey and permanent chairman of the Republican People's Party, visited Cairo to meet Churchill in December 1943 and skilfully evaded Churchill's blandishments. Churchill's own commitment to a Turkish alliance was embarassingly obvious:

> He has persuaded himself that he can bring Turkey into the war and keeps turning over in his mind the consequences just as if it had already happened. He does not stop to ask what the Turks themselves are thinking.

It was clear enough to many others that what the Turks were thinking had nothing to do with Churchill's vision of a Grand Alliance:

> The Turkish General Staff have never made any secret of the fact that their desire for modern armaments arose, not from any wish to be strong against

---

[23] Public Record Office FO 371/30092/R6912 Knatchbull-Hugesson to Foreign Office 9 July 1941; Weber *Elusive Neutral* p. 113–6; *Documents on German Foreign Policy* Series D vol. 3 p. 571–5 memo by Woermann 26 Sept. 1941. As Fevzi Paşa, Çakmak had commanded the Seventh Army in Palestine in 1918.

[24] Weber *Evasive Neutral* p. 172.

the Germans, but rather that they might be fresh and strong to hold the Near East on our, and their, behalf at the end of the war when Russia might become troublesome.

Turkish military unpreparedness being what it was this elegantly Levantine argument does not seem to be quite the explanation either. Turkish policy was most probably based on the view that if they wished to remain neutral they would have to arm themselves to the teeth to discourage potential aggressors – a view also acted on, though with their own money, by Switzerland and Sweden.[25]

The Turks' utility as allies, though as illusory as their willingness to enter the war, remained an idée fixe with Churchill. It was as if he could never forget how his political career, in its opening triumphant phase, had been shipwrecked on the unyielding resistance of the Turkish infantry in the gullies and hollows of Gallipoli.

Churchill's obsession with Turkey provides the context for what may well be regarded as the biggest strategic blunder on the British side during the whole war: the intervention in Greece in the spring of 1941.

When Mussolini launched his invasion of Greece late in October 1940 Churchill's immediate reaction was that Britain could not afford to permit another Axis success: 'no answer would really help if another small ally was overwhelmed', he told the War Cabinet on 4 November 1940. The Chiefs of Staff warned however that the whole invasion of Greece might be no more than an Axis ploy to lure British forces into a dangerous dispersal of resources and opposed anything other than limited naval and air support. The British military mission in Athens was instructed not even to hint at the assistance of British ground troops. Even before the Italian invasion the British minister in Athens had been advised by London:

> The greatest assistance that we can give to Greece is to knock Italy out of the war, and to do so we must bring the maximum pressure to bear on Italy at the decisive time and place. Any dispersion of our forces would not assist towards achieving this object.

The perfect soundness of this view is demonstrated by the rapidity with which it became apparent that Italy's own resources were painfully overextended; but instead of profiting from Italy's error, the British chose to imitate it.[26]

---

[25] [C.M. Wilson] Lord Moran *Winston Churchill: The Struggle for Survival, 1940–1965* (1966) p. 145 diary 5 Dec. 1943; British Library Add. 52571 memo by Admiral Sir Howard Kelly at Ankara, 1 Dec. 1943. For the strained relations between Turkey and the U.S.S.R. after 1941 see George Kirk *The Middle East in the War* (1952) p. 443–466.

[26] Public Record Office CAB 65/16 p. 8, J.R.M. Butler, M. Howard, J. Ehrman, J.M.A. Gwyer, N.A. Gibbs *Grand Strategy* (6 vols 1956–1976) vol. 2 p. 368; C. Cruikshank *Greece, 1940–1941* (Newark 1979) p. 59–61; John S. Koliopoulos *Greece and the British Connection, 1935–1941* (Oxford 1977) p. 183; Public Record Office FO 371/244909 Foreign Office to Sir Michael Palairet (minister in Athens) 17 Aug. 1940.

The Greek Army's success in driving back the Italian invasion and the increase of German influence and military presence in Rumania and Bulgaria persuaded the British War Cabinet that a more active role in the Balkans was desirable; but undoubtedly the Turkish mirage played a part in this. In January 1941 General Sir Archibald Wavell, the British commander-in-chief in the Middle East, visited Athens and offered the assistance of British land forces. Metaxas, the Greek dictator, turned this offer down: 'If only the British had even five divisions and plenty of equipment', he noted in his diary, 'but they have next to nothing'. But Metaxas was dying; his successors were to prove that they lacked his judgement and strength of purpose.[27]

Early in February Lieutenant-General Richard O'Connor rounded off his brilliant campaign in Libya with a stunning victory over the Italians at Beda Fomm; the propaganda film *Wavell's 30,000* announced 'Dunkirk had been avenged in North Africa'. O'Connor (who had been decorated for valour by the Italians in the First World War) hoped next to advance on Tripoli; if he had reached that port it would have secured the capitulation of all the remaining Italian forces in Libya. The loss of Libya, together with the critical situation in Albania and in Somaliland and a possible intensification of the bombing of northern Italy from England, might well have rocked Mussolini's regime, which was to be overturned in similar circumstances only two years later; but by the time Dorman Smith, O'Connor's Brigadier General Staff, reached Cairo to discuss the advance on Tripoli with Wavell, the latter was already immersed in plans to send an army to Greece.[28]

After the war O'Connor claimed that the advance on Tripoli would have been perfectly feasible. Wavell was less sure, and later stated, 'we could not have advanced to Tripoli without much further reinforcement'. Major-General John Kennedy, Director of Military Operations at the War Office thought an advance on Tripoli did not rule out sending troops to Greece as only a small force would have been necessary, 'The diversion of such a force would not have affected his [Wavell's] ability to operate in Greece'. The truth was that O'Connor's tanks were worn out and a dash of over five hundred miles along the North African coastal road would have required a great deal of improvisation and utilization of captured Italian equipment; though this kind of improvisation was not customary with the overequipped British Army, O'Connor was probably just the man to handle such a business, and the smallness of his forces would have made it that much easier to organize. In

---

[27] Koliopoulos *Greece and the British Connection* p. 207 quoting I. Metaxas Το προσωπικο ἡμερολογιο (*To prosopiko hemerologio*) ed. C. Christidis, P.M. Siphnaios, P. Vranas (4 vols Athens 1951–64) vol. 4 p. 559, 15 Jan. 1941.

[28] John Connell *Wavell* (1964) p. 326–7; also R.W. Thompson *Gereralissimo Churchill* (1973) p. 107–8. John Monck's film *Wavell's 30,000* does not, incidentally, mention O'Connor by name, claiming instead that the campaign was a 'victory won by General Sir Archibald Wavell'. Presumably the reason for this was that in the meantime O'Connor had become a prisoner of war.

his old age O'Connor wrote, 'I blame myself greatly for not going on, &
telling GHQ I had done so'. Wavell for his part tended to be conservative in
his margins and expectations. Despite the huge Italian surrenders, O'Connor
was still outnumbered and it had happened before that over-bold British
commanders had run into difficulties from which they could not extricate
themselves.[29]

After Beda Fomm the British leaders also underestimated the likelihood
of an Axis counter-offensive in North Africa, so that the danger of leaving
Italy with a base in western Libya was not appreciated. Kennedy noted after
talking to Churchill, 'He would not admit the importance of Tripoli except
as a stepping stone to Sicily'. But of course the lure of Greece was the real
reason for not carrying on to Tripoli.[30]

Churchill had warned Wavell as early as 10 January 1941 that, 'Destruction
of Greece will eclipse victories you have gained in Libya, and may affect
decisively Turkish attitude', but Wavell seems to have accepted the necessity
of sending an expeditionary force to Greece before the government in London
had actually finalized its policy. On 10 February 1941 he proposed the advance
to Tripoli to the War Office and Sir John Dill, the Chief of the Imperial
General Staff, replied next day, 'General feeling is that assistance to Greece
and/or Turkey must come first apart from strain on Navy and R.A.F.
which advance to Tripoli would involve'. Wavell seems thereupon to have
concentrated on planning the details of sending troops to Greece, but it was
not till a week later that Dill and the Foreign Secretary, Anthony Eden, flew
out to Cairo to discuss the Greek project with him, and Churchill instructed
Eden, 'Do not consider yourselves obligated to a Greek enterprise if in your
hearts you feel it will only be another Norwegian fiasco'. By now the *political*
desirability of propping up the Fascist regime in Greece was taken for granted;
the Chiefs of Staff in London argued:

---

[29] Francis de Guingard *Generals at War* (1964) p. 23; Earl Wavell 'The British Expedition
to Greece, 1941' *Army Quarterly* vol. 59 (1949–50) p. 175–185 at p. 184; John Kennedy *The
Business of War: The War Narrative of Major-General Sir John Kennedy* ed. Bernard Fergusson,
(1957) p. 139, memo June 1941; King's College London, O'Connor Mss 15, notes *circa* 1970.
For an example of Wavell's caution and low expectations cf Public Record Office WO 193/971,
Wavell's comments 19 Aug. 1941 on 'Report by an Interservice committee on Operations in
Crete' G.H.Q.M.E. June 1941.

[30] Kennedy *Business of War* p. 80, diary 16 Feb. 1941. Of course the Italians, if driven
out of Tripoli, might have retreated into Tunisia, as the Italo-German forces were to do in
1942–3: in most respects Tunis was a much more convenient bridgehead in North Africa than
Tripoli or Benghazi. At the end of 1942 however the Germans were no longer inclined to
ask the Vichy government for permission before crossing the border whereas in the spring
of 1941 it would still have been desirable to negotiate with the Vichy government – which
would certainly have objected to an exclusively Italian army establishing itself in Tunisia. It
is also doubtful whether there would have been any Italian army left by the time the Tunisian
border had been reached.

The effect on public opinion throughout the world, particularly in America, of our deserting a small nation which is already engaged in a magnificent fight against one aggressor and is willing to defy another would be formidable.

But it seems that the Public Relations exercise was aimed at other Balkan states, and especially Turkey, as much as at America, and in that direction intervention would only have a positive effect if crowned with military victory. On this score Dill, the C.I.G.S., Cunningham, commanding British naval forces in the Mediterranean, the British military mission in Athens and even Wavell's Joint Planning Staff and Directorate of Military Intelligence in Cairo all had serious doubts, and the final decision to go ahead was determined by Wavell's personal and individual opinion that the scheme was practicable and that sufficient troops could be made available. But though Churchill had called for a 'precise military appreciation', Wavell seems to have made up his mind on political as much as military grounds, and never afterwards attempted to justify his view in terms of strictly military criteria; after the war he claimed that the decision to send troops to Greece 'was the only one consistent with the political requirements of the moment, with military strategy and our national honour', but these were precisely the points which it was Eden's and Dill's job to decide: Wavell's business had been simply to decide on the military feasibility of the venture, and this he seriously miscalculated.[31]

After the Cairo discussions Eden moved on to Athens where he persuaded Metaxas's successors to accept a British expeditionary force. Almost immediately disapproval of the Greek Army's dispositions caused London to have doubts regarding the military aspect of the whole business, and while the Joint Planning Staff at Wavell's Cairo H.Q. began to busy themselves with planning the evacuation from Greece of an army which had not yet even arrived there, Eden was invited to consider the possibility of British withdrawal from the commitment just made, but decided that:

> No doubt our prestige will suffer if we are ignominiously ejected, but in any event to have fought and suffered in Greece would be less damaging to us than to have left Greece to her fate.

[31] Churchill *Second World War* vol. 3 p. 17 Churchill to Wavell 10 June 1941; Connell *Wavell* p. 326; Churchill *Second World War* Churchill to Eden 20 Feb. 1941; Public Record Office CAB 66/15: WP (41) 39, 24 Feb. 1941; Koliopoulos *Greece and the British Connection* p. 228–9 cf Guingand *Generals at War* p. 23, 41–3; Wavell 'The British Expedition to Greece' *Army Quarterly* vol. 59 p. 182, and cf *Memoirs of General the Lord Ismay* (1960) p. 197–9.

[32] Guingand *Generals at War* p. 34–6; Churchill *Second World War* vol. 3 p. 93, Eden to London 7 March 1941; Randolph S. Churchill and Martin Gilbert *Winston S. Churchill* (8 vols 966–1988) vol. 6 p. 1048 Churchill to acting premier of Australia 30 March 1941. Gilbert ibid. vol. 6 p. 1012–4, 1026 suggests that Churchill was won over to the Greek adventure by Eden and Dill, but though he clearly had his reservations it does seem that he was attracted by the general concept of the operation.

From this point onward the whole business began to take on the appearance of a romantic gesture rather than a serious strategic initiative: Churchill described it as 'a rather bleak military adventure dictated by *noblesse oblige*'.[32]

When the inevitable German onslaught came, Churchill forgot his earlier lack of enthusiasm and permitted his imagination to run away with the idea of a last-ditch stand at Thermopylae; as he wrote shortly after the war, 'The intervening ages fell away. Why not one more undying feat of arms?' Why not indeed? The British Army's defeat in France could be blamed on the French collapse and had to some extent been redeemed by the evacuation of over 330,000 allied troops from Dunkirk; the blundering efforts to check the German occupation of Norway had belatedly achieved success in the Narvik sector just before the Anglo-French forces had to be withdrawn because of the defeat in France; it was the retreat in Greece, the evacuation, the successful German air-borne assault on Crete, and the first triumph of Rommel's *Afrika Korps* against the denuded British defences in Libya that first promoted the questioning of the British Army's battleworthiness and these reverses all stemmed from the decision to thin out Britain's resources by taking on the Greek venture. As Hitler wrote, 'Only this capital error on the part of the British Command made it possible for our efforts to be crowned with the reconquest of Cyrenaica'.[33]

Germany's victories in the first half of 1941 were a defeat for Italy as well as Britain. Italy was left in a secondary role in the Balkans, in Greece, even in North Africa where Rommel and his *Afrika Korps*, though nominally under Italian command and fighting on what was nominally Italian territory, were universally recognized as the dominant factor in the theatre. Consequently Mussolini was in a poor position to influence or benefit from the Axis's joint endeavours.

Britain, although in an increasingly unfavourable strategic position in the Mediterranean, was able, by means of the vast economic mobilization at home and throughout the Empire, to consolidate and to prepare a counter-blow; but this process of consolidation involved lengthy shipments of supplies round the Cape of Good Hope, a route which made Libya twenty times further from Britain than it was from Italy and which was proudly advertized as 'the longest line of supply that the history of war has ever known'. This enormous disadvantage meant that the build up of British strength in the Middle East bore little relationship to the massive output of munitions in Britain's industrial centres.[34]

---

[33] Churchill *Second World War* vol. 3 p. 228 [passage written *circa* 1949]; Deakin *Brutal Friendship* p. 19, Hitler to Mussolini 23 June 1942. 'Cyrenaica' is the eastern coastal area of Libya, of which Benghazi is the principal town.

[34] See James Lansdale Hodson, script for film *Desert Victory*, directed by Roy Boulting 1943 for 'the longest line of supply that the history of war has ever known'.

Wavell's failure to conclude the North African campaign in the spring of 1941 probably ranks with the fall of Singapore a year later as a decisive contribution to Britains failure to dominate and determine the overall strategic pattern of the Second World War. The Greek diversion, by giving the Axis a second chance in North Africa, meant that for two years British strength had to be divided between two widely separated theatres, northern Europe and the Mediterranean. Because the economic structure in Egypt could not sustain a modern army, the fighting troops needed to be backed up by a vast array of non-combatant personnel. Churchill for one never understood the vast disproportion between the troops under muster in the Middle East Command and the much smaller number in the firing line. In April 1941 for example he queried the fact that there were 26,600 R.A.F. personnel in the Middle East, 1,175 pilots, 1,044 aeroplanes – but only 292 aeroplanes available for operations and not enough ground crew to handle the new planes that were arriving. By January 1943 there were 400,000 tons of ammunition stockpiled in the Middle East; the first month of the campaign inaugurated by the El Alamein offensive, which involved expenditures of ammunition unprecedented in the theatre, had used up no more than 25,000 tons of ammunition. By this stage there were nearly three-quarters of a million British service personnel in the theatre, of which Montgomery's field army numbered about one third. The greater part of these men and supplies had come round the Cape of Good Hope, involving a vast expenditure of manpower and shipping that might conceivably have been put to better use elsewhere.[35]

The level of investment in North Africa meant that Britain's resources, though actually greater even than Germany's, remained stretched, and came perilously near to snapping when the Japanese entered the war in December 1941. One ultra-right-wing critic, Sir Archibald Southby, M.P. for Epsom, claimed after the fall of Singapore, 'One month's supply of aircraft sent to Russia could have saved Malaya'. But the Russians were receiving only 200 aircraft a month, which though very handsome by Singapore standards was not a very large proportion of British output, and of course the Russians were not being sent air crew or station personnel. These were being sent to the Middle East. When the Japanese attacked, the R.A.F. in the Far East was qualitatively the weakest of the three allied air forces in the area: the diversion to the Far East of four squadrons of fighters en route to the Middle East represented a doubling of R.A.F. fighter strength in the area.

[35] Churchill *Second World War* vol. 3 p. 669 Churchill to Chief of Air Staff, 5 April 1941; *Grand Strategy* vol. 4 p. 292. Between January 1941 and September 1942 6,611 aircraft were sent to the Mediterranean theatre: Playfair and Molony *The Mediterranean and Middle East* vol. 2 p. 362–3 App. 7 and vol. 3 p. 458–9 App. 10.

*First Line of Strength of Air Forces in
Malaya/Philippines Area c. 8 December 1941*

	Single-seat fighters	Multi-engined bombers	Flying boats
R.A.F. (with R.A.A.F.) Malaya	60	59	3
Militaire Luchtvaart van het K.N.I.L. (Dutch)	48	54	
Nederlandse Marine Luchtvaartdienst			60
U.S.A.A.F. in the Philippines	159	53 (including 35 four engined B-17s)	
U.S. Navy			28
Japanese Army A.F. (Malaya theatre)	150	130	
Japanese Army and Navy A.F.s (Philippines theatre)	254	242	24
(R.A.F. in North Africa – mid-November 1941)	c.250	c.140[36]	

[36] *Hansard: House of Commons* vol. 378 col. 69 Sir Archibald Southby 24 Feb. 1942; *Grand Strategy* vol. 3 p. 317. For air strengths in the Far East on 7 Dec. 1941 see S. Woodburn Kirby *The War Against Japan* 5 vols 1957–1969 vol. 1 p. 511 App. 9; *Royal Air Force Flying Review* vol. 14 no. 3 (Nov. 1958) p. 9–11 (and cf William Green *Warplanes of the Second World War: Fighters* (4 vols 1960–1) vol. 4 p. 32, 76–7); Louis Morton *United States Army in World War II* [series 5] *The War in the Pacific* [vol. 1] *The Fall of the Philippines* (Washington 1953) p. 42 Table 3; and p. 91 Ministerie van Oorlog *Nederlands-Indië contra Japan* (7 vols Hague 1949–61) vol. 4 p. 58; R.J. Francillon *Japanese Aircraft of the Pacific War* (1970) p. 34, 42; Playfair, Molony, Jackson *The Mediterranean and Middle East* vol. 3 p. 18.

The long-range flying boats (Consolidated PBY Catalinas, and in the Dutch service also Dornier Do 24s) carried more bombs than the R.A.F.'s Blenheim and Hudson bombers, which were also inferior in this respect to, as well as slower than, the Dutch Glenn Martin 166 and American Boeing B-17 land-based bombers. Most of the American fighter squadrons, and two of the four Militaire Luchtvaart fighter squadrons also had better equipment than the Brewster Buffalo fighters flown by the R.A.F., though the Militaire Luchtvaart also had two squadrons of these planes.

Sir Robert Brooke-Popham, the R.A.F.'s commander in the Far East estimated in September 1941 that the Japanese had 108 land-based fighters, 285 reconnaissance and light bombing planes and 196 heavy bombers 'available for new commitments including action against Russia' and that only 72 fighters, 72 reconnaissance and light bombing planes and 96 heavy bombers could be accommodated on existing bases in Indo-China and southern Thailand (King's College London, Brooke-Popham Papers V/4/31 Brooke-Popham to Chiefs of Staff 16 Sept. 1941). These underestimates explain the apparent complacency of the Allies before 7 Dec. 1941 but not the speed and completeness of the debacle which followed. Half of the U.S.A.A.F.'s most modern planes in the Philippines and of the R.A.F.'s planes in northern Malaya were put out of action by Japanese air raids in the first 24 hours.

The overinvestment in the Middle East did not of course cease immediately Rommel's forces were decisively defeated: the vast stockpiles of ammunition, the huge base camps, the telephone exchanges and the N.A.A.F.I. clubs could be transferred to another theatre of operations only by the same expenditure of effort as had brought them to North Africa in the first place. The fact that it required 21 British and U.S. divisions to finish in May 1943 a business that O'Connor had nearly concluded with two divisions over two years earlier left the Allied much stronger in the Mediterranean than was strategically desirable and committed them to maintaining the Mediterranean theatre as a key area of operations even after the invasion of northern France in June 1944.

George C. Marshall, the U.S. Army Chief of Staff, had favoured an invasion of north-west France in April 1943 with 30 U.S. and 18 British divisions; the British had out-argued him on this and the American landings in north-west Africa in November 1942 were essentially a substitute for the invasion of Europe in 1943. Doubtless the experience gained in North Africa was of vital assistance in helping the U.S. forces prepare for the D-Day landings of June 1944: amongst the weaknesses noted in North Africa were slackness, indiscipline, poor infantry tactics, road-boundedness, poor integration of arms, and physical softness, and General Dwight D. Eisenhower confided to a friend one month after the U.S. army went into action:

> I think the best way to describe our operations to date is that they have violated every recognized principle of war, are in conflict with all operational and logistic methods laid down in text books, and will be condemned in their entirety, by all Leavensworth and War College classes for the next twenty-five years.

Meanwhile Sir Alan Brooke, the British Chief of the Imperial General Staff, was exerting all his formidable energy to promote a clever-sounding scheme for stretching and ever extending German resources by threatening Europe from the south as well as from the north-west, and continued to insist that the invasion of north-western France was premature:

> It is our firm intention to carry out [invasion of northern France] at the first moment that conditions are such that the operation will contribute decisively to the defeat of Germany. These conditions may arise this year, but in any case it is our firm belief that they will arise next year. They can be created only by the Russian Army.

The idea that the German Army would use itself up on the Russian front turned out to be nonsense: in July 1943 the Germans had 14 first-line divisions in France; in June 1944 they had 27 (with *Panzer* divisions being increased from three to ten); they also had 23 divisions in Italy. The whole arithmetic of trying to overwhelm Germany's interior lines by campaigning centrifugally at the end of long sea-routes was in any case absurd (and at this period millions of Britain's Indian subjects were starving to death in Bengal and the Argentinians were burning their surplus grain as a substitute for coal, because of a world shipping shortage). The whole case for attacking the 'soft underbelly' of Europe could not have been argued convincingly if Allied forces had not already been so overwhelmingly strong in the Mediterranean; Brooke's idea of stretching and overextending German resources could in fact be put into operation with less delay than would be involved in transferring the Anglo-American armies from North Africa to England for a descent on France; yet the invasion of Italy, far from stretching German resources, actually provided them with a vital additional resource, in the shape of a landscape perfectly adapted to defensive warfare: Brooke himself later said, 'the terrain defies description. It is like the North-West Frontier; a single destroyed culvert can hold up an army for a day'.[37]

The result of the Mediterranean bias of Britain's strategy was that when the invasion of northern France eventually came – perhaps ten months later than conceivably necessary – it was not only an American-led operation but consisted predominantly of American troops which, combined with American suspicions that the British had been opposed to the whole business all along, prevented the British shaping the conduct of the operation as much as they might have liked. It was not greater strength, and certainly not greater military skill, which enabled the Americans to establish themselves as senior partners in the Anglo-American alliance in Europe, but Britain's consistent policy of directing its resources against the points where they would have the least effect.[38]

IV. Sclerosis of the System

Even more than the unending slog on the Western Front in the First World War, Britain's war-prolonging Mediterranean strategy, and the polemical brilliance with which it had to be defended, seem to have been symptomatic of a complex institutional sclerosis which had invaded the British war machine.

In retrospect one British officer could write, 'there is little doubt that the German army of 1914–18 was basically considerably superior to that of 1939–45'. The first British reverses, in Norway and France, could be glibly attributed to the British tradition of amateurism: thus Richard Hillary could look back on an Oxford rowing-crew's victory over German crews in 1938

---

[37] *Grand Strategy* vol. 3 p. 576. 637–8; Alfred D. Chandler et. al. eds. *The Papers of Dwight David Eisenhower* (11 vols so far published Baltimore 1970–1984) vol. 2 p. 904–5 no. 770 Eisenhower to Russell P. Hartle 15 Jan. 1943; ibid. vol. 2 p. 811 no. 698 Eisenhower to Thomas T. Handy 7 Dec. 1942; Arthur Bryant *The Turn of the Tide, 1939–1943* (1957) p. 551; *Grand Strategy* vol. 4 p. 423; statement at 2nd Washington Conference 13 May 1943; Walter Scott Dunn *Second Front Now – 1943* (Tuscaloosa 1980) p. 262 for increase of German strength in France; Playfair, Molony, Jackson *The Mediterranean and Middle East* vol. 6 pt. 1 p. 68; Nigel Nicolson ed. *Harold Nicolson: Diaries and Letters* (3 vols 1966–8) vol. 2 p. 348, 10 Feb. 1944.

[38] See in this context *Grand Strategy* vol. 6 p. 36, 89–90 and Nigel Hamilton *Monty: The Field Marshal, 1944–1976* (1986) p. 327–357 for disputes about the organization of the Anglo-American advance into Germany January–February 1945.

as 'a surprisingly accurate pointer to the course of the war. We were quite untrained, lacked any form of organization, and were really quite hopelessly casual. We even arrived late at the start . . . we won the race by two-fifths of a second'. Even after the debacle in Greece an American military observer considered 'that the fighting in Greece proved conclusively that the British were superior definitely man to man over the Germans'. ('Let us have no more nonsense about the superiority of our troops "as man to man"', demanded Edward Hulton in *Picture Post*, 'Armies have not met as man to man since Crécy'.) But by the spring of 1942, with the triumphant Japanese advances in Malaya and Burma coinciding with Rommel's victories in Libya, it finally began to be acknowledged even in British government circles that a major problem of the British war effort was that the British army was no good. 'Our generals are no use', Sir Alexander Cadogan, permanent head of the Foreign Office, wrote in his diary: 'Our army is the mockery of the world'. Harold Nicolson, M.P. for West Leicester, noted, 'Our whole Eastern Empire has gone . . . But I should not have minded all this so much if we had fought well'. But it was the army's leaders who had to take the failure most to heart:

Defeat is bitter. Bitter to the common soldier, but trebly bitter to his general. The soldier may comfort himself with the thought that whatever the result, he has done his duty faithfully and steadfastly, but the commander has failed in *his* duty if he has not won victory – for that *is* his duty . . . He will recall the look in the eyes of the men who trusted him. 'I have failed them', he will say to himself, 'and I have failed my country!' He will see himself for what he is – a defeated general. In a dark hour he will turn in upon himself and question the very foundation of his leadership and his manhood.

Brooke, the Chief of the Imperial General Staff, noted in his diary with something like panic:

I have during the last ten years had an unpleasant feeling that the British Empire was decaying and that we were on a slippery decline. I wonder if I was right? I certainly never expected that we should fall to pieces as fast as we are.[39]

---

[39] C.N. Barclay 'British Generalship: 1914–18 and 1939–45 – A Comparison' *Army Quarterly* vol. 59 (Jan. 1950) p. 236–244 at p. 239; Richard Hillary *The Last Enemy* (1942) p. 21–2; Public Record Office FO 371/29821 f. 91 copy of letter from Mr. Earle, U.S. minister in Sofia to U.S. Embassy, London 17 June 1941 quoting Major Craw, U.S.A.A.C. observer in Greece; *Picture Post* 21 June 1941 p. 13; David Dilks ed. *The Diaries of Sir Alexander Cadogan O.M., 1938–1945* (1971) p. 433, 9 Feb. 1942; *Nicolson: Diaries and Letters* vol. 2 p. 221, 30 March 1942; Slim *Defeat into Victory* p. 121; Bryant *Turn of the Tide* p. 304 11 Feb. 1942.

T.N. Dupuy *A Genius for War: The German Army and General Staff, 1807–1945* (1977) is a somewhat heavy-handed and unperceptive study of the question of how 'the Germans, uniquely, discovered the secret of institutionalizing military excellence'. H. Rosinski 'The French and German Soldier' *Spectator* 1 Sept. 1939 p. 316–7 is suggestive.

Curiously the British found themselves at a disadvantage not only against the Germans but also against the Japanese, who were held in notably low esteem by the German general Alexander von Falkenhausen, German military representative to the Kuomintang government in 1937–38: he wrote, 'I do not exaggerate when I say that I am convinced that two or three

continued

Simultaneously however the search for excuses began. Nicolson recorded Westminster gossip about 'the badness of our army. The cream of our officers and men have been drained off by the R.A.F. and the Commandos. What remains is pretty poor'. Brooke blamed it all on the First World War:

> it is lamentable how poor we are in Army and Corps commanders; we ought to remove several, but Heaven knows where we shall find anything very much better ... The flower of our manhood was wiped out some twenty years ago ...

In his post-war 'Notes on my Life' Brooke elaborated:

> The First World War had unfortunately taken the cream of our manhood. Those that had fallen were the born leaders of men, in command of companies or battalions. It was always the best who fell by taking the lead. Those that we lost as subalterns, captains and majors in the First World War were the very ones we were short of as colonels, brigadiers and generals in the Second World War.

The loss of the national pool of talent caused by the First World War had it seems been a cliché before the war: even Baldwin had claimed 'that one of his problems in appointments was due to the gap occasioned by the million men of our country who were killed in World War I'. The problem with this interpretation was that Britain's inferiority was most marked relative to Germany, and Germany had of course lost even more heavily in the First World War. In any case the relationship between brilliance as a subaltern and brilliance as a general is notoriously problematic: one notes that amongst the very young officers who commanded brigades in the First World War and survived to serve as field commanders in the Second World War, only Sir Harold Alexander can be said to have lived up to his initial promise, and he was so laid back that it has never been clear whether there was any real ability behind that cool, imperturbable charming façade; Slim, who served under him during the Burma debacle, later said, 'I don't believe he had the faintest idea of what was going on', and Brooke noted, 'The more I see of him the more I marvel at the smallness of the man. I do not believe he has a single idea in his head of his own!' At least Alexander was never found out. Sir Bernard Freyberg V.C., on the other hand, though gaining a reputation as the army's premier fighting general and earning a third bar to his D.S.O.,

---

continued
German divisions could drive the Japanese out of China in a short time': Hsi-Huey Liang *The Sino-German Connection: Alexander von Falkenhausen between China and Germany, 1900–1941* (Assen 1978) p. 132, report 1 Feb. 1938 – cf Slim *Defeat into Victory* p. 121 and p. 537, Evans F. Carlson *Twin Stars of China* (New York 1940) p. 31–2, 151, 275, 301–2 and Pratt *Marines' War* p. 118. Generally Japanese infantry tactics were a version of those employed by the Germans in 1918: infiltration by small groups depending on light machine guns for fire power and reliance on forward pressure and on the reluctance of an army under attack to redeploy laterally; the jungle, and poor British intelligence, provided a counterpart to the vast imbroglio of the Western Front in that troops in the front line between points that had been attacked tended to become jumpy from fear of encirclement.

was ignominiously defeated in his only independent command, the defence of Crete. (Evelyn Waugh glimpsed him during the evacuation of the island, 'composed but obtuse', signing photographs of himself for departing New Zealand soldiers.) Although there was no public recrimination afterwards the War Office evidently agreed with Montgomery's view that, 'He has no great brain power and could never command a Corps', for they left him in charge of his division of New Zealanders till the end of the war. Gordon Bennett, another boy brigadier from the First World War, abandoned his division in Singapore in order to treat the Australian government to some personal tips on how to deal with the Japanese: he was not given another field command.[40]

Other experts thought the problem was not the decimation of leadership talent in the First World War but the general lack of physical toughness. Wavell, though not keen on 'post mortems' – 'these sort of investigations do no one any good' – acknowledged 'lack of vigour in our peace time training, the cumbersomeness of our tactics and equipment . . .', but felt that, 'the real trouble is that for the time being we have lost a good deal of our hardness and fighting spirit'. And by hardness Wavell meant 'soldiers capable of marching thirty miles a day for a number of days running, and missing their full rations every second or third day'. Brooke accepted Wavell's point: 'I agree with you that we are not anything like as tough as we were in the last war'. And Kennedy, the Director of Military Operations at the War Office, chipped in with some Social Darwinism of the sort that Himmler would have liked:

> we are undoubtedly softer as a nation, than any of our enemies, except the Italians. This may be accounted for by the fact that modern civilization on the democratic model does not produce a hardy race, and our civilization in Great Britain was a little further removed from the stage of barbarity than were the civilizations of Germany, Russia and Japan.

Since Italy at that time was neither particularly democratic nor particularly

[40] *Harold Nicolson: Diaries and Letters* vol. 2 p. 270, 31 Dec. 1942; Bryant *Turn of the Tide* p. 239, diary of Sir Alan Brooke early 1942; ibid. p. 158; Donald Portway *Militant Don* (1964) p. 30 for Baldwin quote and see generally Jay M. Winter 'Die Legende der "verlorenen Generationen" in Grossbritannien' in Klaus Vondung ed. *Kriegserlebnis: der Erste Weltkrieg in der literarischen Gestaltung und symbolischen Deutung der Nationen* (Göttingen 1980) p. 115–45; Hamilton *Monty: The Making of a General 1887–1942* (1981) p. 495; Nigel Hamilton *Monty: the Field Marshal* p. 346 quoting Brooke's diary 12 Jan. 1945, and see also p. 616; Michael Davie ed. *The Diaries of Evelyn Waugh* (1976) p. 489–517 'Memorandum on LAYFORCE; July 1940–July 1941' at p. 500, 507; Hamilton *Monty: Making of a General* p. 836 Montgomery to Brooke 1 Nov. 1942; Frank Legg *The Gordon Bennett Story* (Sydney 1965) p. 265–301.

Alexander's official rank at the end of the Great War had been acting lieutenant-colonel but he had been acting in command of his brigade in April 1918. His memoirs, edited by John North, 1962, hardly clarify the mystery of his ability. Either he had a major talent for stylized self-presentation or else he had one of those essentially neat, clear, elegant, understated, economical intellects traditionally characteristic of a certain type of woman novelist. See also Nigel Nicolson *Alex: The Life of Field Marshal Earl Alexander of Tunis* (1973) p. 235–242.

luxurious this argument does not really wash either; and indeed Napoleon, over a century previously, had proved that these racial stereotypes were a myth, even in the Italian case: 'Before my day the character of the Italians was held to be impracticable for military purposes', he said on St. Helena: 'I made them the very best soldiers in Europe'. Nevertheless the cultural–racial interpretation gained some currency. 'Are we too soft, are we too civilized, are we touched with the French infection?', asked one Foreign Office mandarin after the surrender of Singapore. The precedent of the French collapse in 1940 was of course unforgettable; as the British army fell back in Burma the same official noted, 'Many disturbing resemblances with the fall of France'.[41]

The natural remedy was seen by some as more P.T. in the forces, an expedient familiar from the First World War but one which had scarcely ever occurred to Wellington or his contempories. Montgomery became notorious as a physical fitness fanatic and even the aristocratically languid Alexander (a champion miler in his youth) was filmed giving a pep talk on the theme, 'Fighting Fit and Fit to Fight'.[42]

The conspicuously unathletic Churchill thought the problem was more one of leadership, and signalled Wavell during the Japanese assault on Singapore:

> Commanders and senior officers should die with their troops. The honour of the British Empire and the British Army is at stake. I rely on you to show no mercy to weakness in any form. With the Russians fighting as they are and the Americans so stubborn in Luzon [Philippines], the whole reputation of our country and our race is involved.

Even Brooke toyed with the possibility that some kind of moral overhaul at the top was called for; he approved a draft circular which stated:

> Too many officers have been, and are being, promoted even to high command because they are proficient in staff work, because they are good trainers, because they have agreeable personalities, or because they are clever talkers

In the event this circular was never issued, perhaps because it was difficult to establish what precisely were the criteria for command suitability other than skills as a staff officer, trainer or conversationalist. One of the few people who thought he knew was General Montgomery, whose correspondence was full of dismissive judgements such as:

[41] Kennedy *Business of War* p. 198 memo by Wavell 17 Feb. 1942 cf King's College London, Brooke-Popham Papers V/5/67 Wavell to Brooke-Popham 10 April 1942; Bryant *Turn of the Tide* p. 229 Brooke to Wavell 5 July 1942; Kennedy *Business of War* p. 198, notes by Kennedy: a similar view is put forward by Norman Mailer's fascistic General Cummings in his novel *The Naked and the Dead* (1948) chapter 12; Julian S. Corbett ed. *Colonel Wilks and Napoleon: Two Conversations held at St. Helena in 1816* (1901) p. 30, 21 April 1816 and cf *Gli Uomini d'arme nelle campagne napoleoniche* in the series *L'Opera del genio italiano all'estero* published by Ministero degli Affari Esteri (Rome 1940); John Harvey ed. *The War Diaries of Oliver Harvey* (1978) p. 100, 22 Feb. 1942; ibid. p. 117, 16 April 1942.

[42] Alexander's pep talk is in Roy Boulting's film *Desert Victory* 1943: he does not sound especially convinced by his own slogan.

Lumsden is out of his depths with a Corps . . . He is a good trainer and would do for a Corps District in England, but nothing more . . . He is very excitable and highly strung and I had to calm him down on many occasions. He was a 1st class unit commander; a very good Brigadier; a good Divisional Cmd. He is a good trainer. He is young and may come along later. At present he is quite unfit for a Corps Command,

or:

Anderson is completely unfit to command an Army; he must be far above his ceiling and I should say that a Divisional Command is probably his level.

After the Battle of Alamein Montgomery noted:

The great lesson of the battle so far is the need for firmness of the Commander in charge of the battle, and the need to have to apply ginger almost continuously to weak Commanders. It is amazing how many weak Commanders we have.[43]

Many of Montgomery's remarks are reminiscent of complaints made by Wellington from the Peninsula in the 1800s. 'They are both respectable officers as commanders of regiments, but they are neither of them very fit to take charge of a large body', was written by Wellington, but it might as easily have been written by Montgomery. But in his own day Montgomery was almost unique in his hundred per cent commitment and self-application to the problems of modern generalship. His contemporaries in the Army often seemed not quite at home with the martial aspect of soldiering. Wavell confessed, 'My trouble is I am not really interested in war' (Churchill said of him, 'I always feel as if I am in the presence of the chairman of a golf club'). Brooke, as Chief of the Imperial General Staff, dreamed of giving up his post and fishing 'continuously for three months without stopping if my body stands up to it'. Alexander did his best to run his campaigns in the style of a country gentleman hosting a shooting party and as Harold Macmillan noted, 'likes to talk of other things – politics, ancient art (especially Roman antiquities), country life. He hates war'.[44]

One aspect of the general malaise was the age of senior commanders. In 1937 Liddell Hart had pointed out in *The Times* that the average age of the

---

[43] Churchill *Second World War* vol. 4 p. 88; Kennedy *Business of War* p. 199 draft by Kennedy: Nigel Hamilton *Monty: Master of the Battlefield, 1942–1944* (1983) p. 46 Montgomery to Brooke Nov. 1942; ibid. p. 215 Montgomery to Alexander 17 March 1943; Nigel Hamilton *Monty: the Making of a General 1887–1942* (1981) p. 797.

[44] [J.] Gurwood ed. *Despatches of Field-Marshal the Duke of Wellington* (13 vols 1834–9) vol. 8 p. 417 Wellington to Torrens 2 Dec. 1811; Brian Bond ed. *Chief of Staff: The Diaries of Lieutenant-General Sir Henry Pownall* (2 vols 1972–4) vol. 2 p. 95, March 1942; for Churchill's comment on Wavell see R.A. Butler *The Art of the Possible* (1971) p. 89: Robert Rhodes James *Anthony Eden* (1986) gives an alternative and possibly more authentic version, in which Wavell is said to resemble 'a good chairman of a Tory Association'; Bryant *Turn of the Tide* p. 529 fn. 1; Harold Macmillan *War Diaries: Politics and War in the Mediterranean, January 1943–May 1945* (1984) p. 374, 29 Jan. 1944.

army leadership was markedly higher than on the eve of the First World War: the G.O.C.s of the Aldershot, Eastern, Southern and Northern Commands (corresponding to corps commands in the field) averaged 58 years 11 months at first appointment as compared to 53 years at first appointment in the case of the officers holding the same commands in 1914; divisional commanders averaged 54 years 6 months at first appointment in 1937 as compared to 50 years 10 months in 1914. On the whole Britain's High Command remained elderly throughout the war; Churchill of course was in his mid-sixties when he became Prime Minister (Lloyd George had been more than ten years younger) and both Sir Dudley Pound, the First Sea Lord and Sir John Dill, head of the vital military mission in Washington, continued to serve till they died on the job, well into their sixties. Even Sir Alan Brooke, Chief of the Imperial General Staff from late 1941, who radiated virile dynamism, energy and force of personality throughout the war, was 62 when it ended. The Navy was particularly geriatric: Sir Dudley Pound, the First Sea Lord, born 1877, was probably 'past it' as early as 1940; Lord Cork, who commanded British naval forces in the Norwegian campaign, had been born in 1873; Sir Roger Keyes, Director of Combined Operations in 1940–1941, had been born in 1872; although he told the House of Commons, 'this is a young man's war', to Churchill he would complain, 'Why do you so continually dwell on my age?' and would refer to how St. Vincent had taken over the Channel Fleet at the age of 71. Sir Bertram Ramsay, a comparative youngster born in 1883 – when Churchill had been a subaltern in the 4th Hussars Ramsay's father had been his colonel and Churchill had 'often seen him as a child on the Barrack Square at Aldershot' – was twice summoned from retirement, once in 1939 to command at Dover and a second time in 1943 to organize the naval side of the D-Day landings. Sir Frederic Dreyer, once the Navy's most influential gunnery expert and author of *How to get a First Class in Seamanship*, born in 1878 and retired in 1939, was appointed Chief of Naval Air Services in 1942, though in this instance even Churchill was scandalized and secured his replacement after six months. Sir Andrew Cunningham, Pound's eventual successor as First Sea Lord, noted ruefully in his diary in 1944, 'The war has now been going on nearly five years and we are still employing officers who were flag officers & captains in the last war'.[45]

Occasionally there was a tendency to veer to the other extreme. the R.A.F. naturally prided itself on its youth: Sir Charles Portal was appointed Chief of Air Staff at only 47, and his close collaborator Sir Wilfrid Freeman assured him:

[45] Liddell Hart, *Times* 16 Sept. 1937 p. 6d; *Hansard: House of Commons* vol. 376 col. 662, Sir Robert Keyes speech 25 Nov. 1941; Paul G. Halpern ed. *The Keyes Papers* (3 vols 1972–81) vol. 3 p. 207 Keyes to Churchill 4 Oct. 1941 and cf vol. 3 p. 268 same to same 22 Aug. 1943; Churchill *Second World War* vol. 2 p. 240; Stephen Roskill *Churchill and the Admirals* (1977) p. 231–2; British Library Add. 52577 f. 8 Sir Andrew Cunningham's diary 17 April 1944.

My opinion is that the RAF have done better than the Army in this war only because the average age of their senior officers between the wars was some 10 to 15 years lower than that of their opposite numbers.

Donald Bennett became an air-vice-marshal (equivalent to major-general in the army) at 33, and the fighter ace Brendan 'Paddy' Finucane was a wing-commander (equivalent to lieutenant-colonel) at the age of 21 years 8 months: he could easily have been the grandson of Matabele War veteran Wing Commander L.F.W. 'Sos' Cohen D.S.O., M.C. whose work as an air gunner in Coastal Command earned him the D.F.C. just before his seventieth birthday in February 1944. In the Army Archibald Nye, an officer even younger than Portal, was spoken of as a possible Chief of the Imperial General Staff: he was said to be favoured by Churchill but as Sir Alan Brooke, who got the job, noted:

> he would, however, have had the very serious handicap of being on the junior side and would consequently have had some difficulty in handling men such as Wavell, Auchinleck, Alexander, Monty and Paget who were considerably senior to him.

Evidently such considerations did not apply to the post of Director of Combined Operations which was transferred in 1941 from the 69-year-old Keyes to the 42-year-old Lord Louis Mountbatten and then to the 36-year-old Major-General Robert Laycock. When Mountbatten left Combined Operations to become theatre commander in South East Asia his low age, as much as his film star good looks and his aura of brilliance, energy and royal cousinhood, was an important recommendation for an appointment that Churchill hoped would 'command public interest and approval, and show that youth is no barrier to merit'.[46]

Mountbatten nearly had foisted on him, as his key subordinate in the G.O.C. Burma appointment, an even younger man, 40-year-old Major-General Orde Wingate. The story of Wingate contains much instructive matter illustrating both the stuffiness of the British army and the methods of sweeping overkill with which some politicians attempted to overcome it. Sir

---

[46] Denis Richards *Portal of Hungerford* (1977) p. 221 Freeman to Portal 24 Nov. 1944; Bryant *Turn of the Tide* p. 264 and fn.; Philip Ziegler *Mountbatten* (1985) p. 220, Churchill minute 11 Aug. 1943.

The Germans never got their hands on the septuagenarian Sos Cohen but they must have been surprised by a body recovered from the rear gun turret of a R.A.F. bomber shot down near Dunkirk on 31 May 1940. It was a grey-haired man wearing the rank badges of a Pilot Officer (the most junior commissioned rank in the R.A.F.) and three rows of medal ribbons; in the topmost row the D.S.O., normally the highest decoration worn by aircrew, came fourth. It was Sir Arnold Wilson, K.C.I.E., C.S.I., C.M.G., D.S.O., Member of Parliament for Hitchin and a leading appeaser before the war. 'I do not wish to live behind the rampart of the bodies of a million corpses ... of the youth of England and France', he had told a Hitchin newspaper in October 1939.

Henry Pownall, Mountbatten's chief of staff in the Far East, thought Wingate mad. Leo Amery, Secretary of State for India, thought him 'another Lawrence, but more virile and sane'. The Middle East Command army staff, opposing Wingate's promotion, noted that, 'lieutenant-colonels' posts are for officers commanding battalions for which from G.H.Q. knowledge of him Wingate is not qualified'. Nine months later Churchill suggested Wingate for G.O.C. Burma, minuting:

> He is a man of genius and audacity, and has rightly been discerned by all eyes as a figure quite above the ordinary level. The expression 'the Clive of Burma' has already gained currency. There is no doubt that in the welter of inefficiency and lassitude which has characterized our operations on the Indian front, this man, his force and his achievement stand out; and no mere question of seniority must obstruct the advance of real personalities to their proper stations in war.

Sir William Slim, under whose command Wingate conducted his air-lifted operations in the Japanese rear, was less impressed:

> I found Wingate stimulating when he talked strategy or grand tactics, but strangely naïve when it came to the business of actually fighting the Japanese. He had never experienced a real fight against them, still less a battle.

The opportunity conclusively to prove himself was snatched from Wingate's grasp by his death in a plane crash at the beginning of his largest operation. He remains to this day a controversial figure, and it is arguable that the whole concept of his Chindit operations, paradoxically combining dependence on the sophisticated technology of air-supply with reliance on the extreme physical toughness of the ground units, belongs more to the realm of symbolism than to serious warfare; with their rudimentary lines of supply the Japanese in Burma simply did not worry very much about air-dropped armies materializing in remote jungle fastnesses far to their rear.[47]

Although the Germans, as in the First World War, employed some quite elderly generals – notably Gerd von Rundstedt who celebrated his 69th birthday a few days before his troops launched the Ardennes offensive – they overtook the British in their favouring of youth. Otto-Ernst Remer, who as commander of the *Grossdeutschland* battalion was instrumental in putting down the 20 July 1944 Putsch, was rewarded with promotion to *Generalmajor* at the age of 32. Kurt Meyer was promoted *SS-Brigadeführer* and *Generalmajor der Waffen-SS* at 33. In the last days of the war Erich Bärenfänger was promoted *Generalmajor* at 27. Dietrich Peltz of the Luftwaffe was appointed *Generalmajor* and *Angriffsführer England* at 29; the fighter ace Adolf Galland, *Generalmajor* at 30, was *Generalleutnant* (equivalent to

[47] Pownall *Chief of Staff* vol. 2 p. 126, 128, 25 and 29 Dec. 1943; Public Record Office PREM 4/51/9 p. 928 copy Amery to Cranborne 3 July 1942; PREM 4/51/9 p. 901 Grigg to Ismay 20 Oct. 1942; PREM 3/143/8 Churchill to Ismay for Chiefs of Staff 24 July 1943; Slim *Defeat into Victory* p. 218.

air marshal) in the Luftwaffe at 33. Hans Jeschonnek was chief of staff of the Luftwaffe two months before his fortieth birthday. The Luftwaffe, because of the Nazi managerial style favoured by Göring, was in many ways extraordinarily open and egalitarian. Werner Baumbach, in August 1941, treated Göring and Jeschonnek to an impromptu lecture on the subject of how units should be led from the cockpit, not from the desk, and was promoted to captain, and a lengthy memo to Jeschonnek complaining of the poor quality of the staff and command in Fliegerkorps II in Sicily secured him the appointment of Inspector of Bombers. Göring even met gatherings of frontline commanders without senior staff being present, in order to hear their criticisms. Yet it was more a matter of style than substance: the psychological egalitarianism of the Third Reich could be neither a substitute for its material deficiencies nor a modifying factor in its megalomaniac strategy.[48]

Nevertheless the egalitarianism and impatience with rules which underpinned Nazi ideology made many German officers particularly aware of the essentially conservative structure of the British Army. This had been remarked upon even in the First World War: 'After they were captured, the English retained their strict discipline. Maintained by a severe code of punishment, it was in their blood'. It was not merely the 'rigorous discipline, of the Prussian type', but an overall lack of flexibility. Rommel wrote of the British 'immobility and rigidity', of 'the ultra-conservative structure of their army' and of 'the machinery of command – a terribly cumbersome structure in Britain'. Of a British operational order captured at Dieppe Rundstedt commented, 'According to German ideas this order is not an order, but an aide-memoire or a scheme worked out for a map exercise' – i.e. it gave too much detail, and insufficient scope for the unit commander to choose his own method of operation. Similarly the British timetable for the withdrawal from Dieppe was drawn up *mit einem kampffremden Schematismus* – translated in the Canadian Official History as 'in a theoretical manner reflecting inexperience of battle' but meaning more literally 'with a battle-alien schematicism'. (It might be noted that these were exactly the weaknesses the Germans had complained of in their Austro-Hungarian allies in the First World War.) As late as 1944 in the Italian campaign, Sir Harold Alexander confessed:

> one of the reasons why the enemy has been able to foil us so far of victory in the battle for Rome is that he is quicker than we are: quicker at regrouping his forces, quicker at thinning out on a defensive front to provide troops to close gaps at decisive points, quicker in effecting reliefs, quicker at mounting attacks and counter-attacks, and above all quicker at reaching decisions on the battlefield.

[48] Werner Baumbach *Broken Swastika* (1960) p. 58, 66, 137–141, cf David Schoenbaum *Hitler's Social Revolution: Class and Status in Nazi Germany, 1933–1939* (1967) p. 59–71, 259–261, 299 for the Nazi emphasis on equality without reference to economic or official status.

In other words, the enemy was less stuck in a professional rut.[49]

Of course egalitarian feeling was at least as strong in Britain as in Nazi Germany, and with the build up of democratic propaganda the outward signs of privilege and social divisiveness came under attack. Obviously some forms of hierarchy and inequality were ineradicably traditional, even essential, in the armed forces: gradations of status were represented visually not merely by insignia of rank and cut of uniform but also by such things as medal ribbons ('14–'18 ribbons being potent indicators of veteran status at the outset of hostilities), collar badges denoting regiment or corps, not all of which were by any means equal in prestige, and, in the Royal Navy, the intertwined or wavy stripes indicating rank which distinguished different categories of reserve officer from colleagues whose permanent commissions entitled them to the traditional straight stripes. Nevertheless it was felt that the living conditions and social amenities of different ranks should not differ too markedly. John Colville, formerly Churchill's private secretary, on board a troopship bound for South Africa where he was to be trained as air crew, described to Churchill the dreadful cramped and deprived conditions of the other ranks who 'would gaze upwards to "A" deck and see officers leaning over the bulwark, deep in conversation with a pretty WAAF or nurse in intervals of dancing to the ship's orchestra': as a result of this letter, Colville found that when he travelled home as a newly commissioned officer, 'All ranks were subjected to an equally dreary austerity'. Politicians, if nobody else, were thrilled by the symbolic improvement since the days of the Somme:

> Then a general was a remote, Blimpish figure in white moustache, faultlessly tailored tunics, polished boots and spurs, emerging occasionally from a luxurious château, and escorted as a rule in his huge limousine Rolls by a troop of lancers. Now an Army commander is a young man, in shorts and open-neck shirt, driving his own jeep, and waving and shouting his greetings to the troops as he edges his way past guns, tanks, trucks, tank-carriers, etc. in the crowded and muddy roads which the enemy may actually be shelling as he drives along.

But the real basis of inequality in modern society, inequality of responsibility, was if anything fostered by the sheer meritocratic middle-classness of the new egalitarian ethic. On the one hand – and in contrast with developments in the

---

[49] Denis Winter *Death's Men: Soldiers of the Great War* (1978) p. 44, quoting a German officer; L.K. Truscott Jr. *Command Missions: a Personal Story* (New York 1954) p. 555; B.H. Liddell Hart ed. *The Rommel Papers* (1953) p. 262, 298, 520; C.P. Stacey *Official History of the Canadian Army in the Second World War* (3 vols Ottawa 1955–66) vol. 1 p. 391, cf Erich Ludendorff *My War Memoirs* (2 vols [1919]) vol. 1 p. 75; Nicolson *Alex* p. 232.

Senior German officers also noted the rigid social divisions in the armies of their allies, cf Donald D. Detwiler ed. *World War II German Military Studies* (24 vols New York 1979) vol. 14 'Italy as a Military Ally' p. 11–13, and Erich von Manstein *Lost Victories* (1958) p. 207 (with reference to the Rumanians). This egalitarian military style derived in part from the First World War: in G.W. Pabst's film *Westfront 1918* (1930) the battalion commander is even shown shaking hands with one of his privates who has just returned from leave.

German armed forces – the emotionally charged *rapport* between subalterns and men that had been one of the most persistent memories of the First World War was never really regained in the British army; officers suffered, as Anthony Powell has suggested, from 'what might be termed an Orwellian sense of guilt in being set above what was in general an overwhelmingly different class' and either retreated bureaucratically into their official status or assumed the role of social workers. A standard justification given by egalitarian-minded intellectuals for taking a commission was, 'I thought that as an officer I'd be able to do something for the men', whereas in the previous war people like R.H. Tawney and Ben Keeling had thought it more consistent with their political viewpoint to refuse commissioned rank. On the other hand, in matters other than daily routine, the officers tended to do too much:

> The British Army with its large number of officers tended to wet nurse the men mentally with the result that the rank and file never thought for themselves and all, including warrant officers and NCOs, lacked initiative.

As Samuel Smiles had pointed out a century earlier, 'where men are subject to over-guidance and over-government, the inevitable tendency is to render them comparatively helpless'. This process operated not merely in the relations of other ranks to junior officers, but also in the relations of junior officers to senior, and of operational units to the enormous H.Q. staffs which increasingly became characteristic of the British military machine.[50]

At least as far as Britain was concerned it was a staff officers' war, (the generals, where differentiated as characters, were uninteresting as personalities, and though the frontline fighters occasionally gained V.C.s – Montgomery, it was said, was 'not in the least impressed by the mystique of that particular award' – it was usually in battles that in retrospect have little individual importance.) The growth of military staffs was of course part of a long-term

---

[50] John Colville *Footprints in Time* (1976) p. 123, but cf Edward Behr *Anyone Here Been Raped And Speaks English? A Foreign Correspondent's Life Behind the Lines* (1981) p. 14 describing his voyage on a transport that was still very 'class-ridden' even at the end of the war: James Lansdale Hodson *War in the Sun* (1942) p. 7–59 gives a diary of a voyage to Durban on a converted liner carrying R.A.F. personnel in the summer of 1941: there were no W.A.A.F.s or orchestra but plenty of bridge and (p. 49) dinners of up to eight courses: Hodson, a journalist who made something of a parade of his egalitarian politics, was impressed that 500 of the Other Ranks were in cabins 'some of them First Class cabins' (p. 16) but he never investigated where the rest of the O.R.s were. Macmillan *War Diaries* p. 529, 22 Sept. 1944 – the passage quoted was written after a jeep ride with Lieutenant-General Sir Oliver Leese; Anthony Powell *Faces in My Time* (1980; vol. 3 of Powell's Memoir); J. Maclaren-Ross *Memoirs of the Forties* (1965) p. 230 cf ibid. p. 89 and see also A.D. Harvey 'Social Work: The Middle Class's Revenge?' *Socialist Commentary* (May 1977) p. 17–18: for the First World War attitude see [E. Townshend ed.] *Keeling Letters & Recollections* (1918) p. 185 Keeling to E. Townshend 24 Aug. 1914, p. 195 same to same 9 Oct. 1914, p. 201 Keeling to C. Townshend 27 Nov. 1914 and Richard Aldington *Death of a Hero* (1965 edit.) p. 237; John Prendergast *Prender's Progress: a Soldier in India, 1931–47* (1979) p. 56; Samuel Smiles *Self Help* (1859) p. 1.

trend that was not limited to the armed forces. Between 1914 and 1928 for example the personnel of the Royal Navy declined by 31.5 per cent but the number of officials at the Admiralty increased by 78.5 per cent. The whole war machine sucked manpower into its offices: the Colonial Office, which had 450 officials in London in 1939, had 817 by 1943, by which time some of the most important colonies had been lost to the Japanese. At its peak the Ministry of Supply, handling the procurement business of the Army, had 5,090 permanent and 63,406 temporary non-industrial civil servants (plus 346,008 industrial civil servants in government factories and installations): about 17,000 of the non-industrial civil servants, including about 200 of the elite administrative grade, were in the central offices. The Army had begun adjusting to the rhythms of exponentially growing bureaucracy even during the First World War, possibly assisted by the relatively static conditions of warfare in France and Belgium: the regulation establishment was for one Orderly Room clerk per battalion but the 4th Battalion Black Watch, while in the trenches, had *six* Orderly Room clerks, all kept very busy, and it was recalled, 'At times we began to think that in the opinion of higher formations, the paper war was more important than the flesh-and-blood war'. It was during the 1914–18 period that the word 'bumf', originally meaning lavatory paper, became popular in the sense of unwanted documents: one of the First World War's more durable gifts to English slang. The Army continued in the same direction after 1939, eventually securing an allotment of 25,000 tons of paper a year, as compared to the 20,000 tons of paper thought sufficient for the entire publishing trade.[51]

One of the most notable offenders in sponsoring the inflation of military staff was the keen, youthful, innovative Lord Louis Mountbatten. It was remarked of his command arrangements in the Far East:

> In these days when man-power is the one vital thing it does make one wonder if it is right that one Commander should collect together 7,000 able-bodied men and women to plan and supervise operations the scale of which is not yet settled and so far as I can gather is likely to be distinctly *less* than was contemplated when the staff was estimated at 4,000. When one hears that it includes such things as a private band one wonders still more

Eventually Mountbatten's staff grew to 10,000 and even Sir Henry Pownall, the arch military bureaucrat, complained of 'the unnecessary numbers of

[51] Anthony Powell *The Military Philosophers* (1968) p. 180; C. Northcote *Parkinson's Law: Or the Pursuit of Progress* (1958) p. 11; ibid. p. 13; Olier Shewell Franks *The Experience of a University Teacher in the Civil Service* (1947) p. 1; William Linton Andrews *Haunting Years: the Commentaries of a War Territorial* [1930] quoting p. 167 and cf p. 173–4, and cf the demands of the American army staff for coloured maps and coordinates from the frontline, described in Theodore Roosevelt *Average Americans* (New York 1920) p. 152–160; Eric Partridge 'Byways of Soldiers' Slang' in Conal O'Riordan, Eric Partridge et al. *A Martial Medley: Fact and Fiction* (1931) p. 127–133; Norman Longmate *How We Lived Then: A History of Everyday Life during the Second World War* (1971) p. 447.

his personal staff, the number of his uniforms; his car bedecked with *four* flags . . .'[52]

Larger staffs meant of course that larger numbers of clever young men were cut in on the responsibility of deciding how to win the war. 'A Military Assistant Secretary, like Kenneth, can have quite an influence on policy – in a sense on the whole course of the war – if he plays his hand well', remarks a character in Anthony Powell's novel *The Military Philosophers*. The war even provided an opportunity to update some of the traditional ploys of the social elite; the term Old Boy Network which became current in the 1950s seems to have had a wartime origin as the Old Boy Net – net in the sense of an army wireless communication link-up – as used by people on sufficiently close social terms to enable them to address one another as 'old boy' when begging favours. Those who objected to these developments were seen as rocking the boat; Harry Hylton-Foster, later Speaker of the House of Commons but in 1944 a deputy judge-advocate with the British army in Italy, wrote indiscreetly to a colleague in Sicily concerning the growth of administrative staff and the opportunities this gave for promotion, and was reported by the censor, with the result that he was sent back to North Africa in disgrace. Sir Roger Keyes, after he had been sacked from the Directorate of Combined Operations, denounced the self-reproducing staff structures:

> Inter-Service committees and sub-committees which have sprung up since the last war and have flourished exceedingly in peace-time have, in this war, become almost the dictators of military policy instead of the servants they should be of those who really should bear the responsibility.

But though Keyes spoke of 'the negative power which controls the war-making machine in Whitehall', it also frequently happened that in moments of crisis the staffs in the war zone failed to provide guidance, as if the Operations side of staff work, having barely emancipated itself conceptually from the Quarter-Master and Adjutant-General aspects, had become once again submerged in problems of logistics, manpower and paper. During the Battle of Crete in May 1941, for example, as Evelyn Waugh recorded, 'We did not once in the five days' action receive an order from any higher formation without going to ask for it'.[53]

It is arguable of course that the greater part of the staffs were needed to plan future operations, not to monitor operations already in progress. This

---

[52] British Library Add. 52571 f.101 Geoffrey Layton to Andrew Cunningham 7 Feb. 1944; Pownall *Chief of Staff* vol. 2 p. 203, Jan. 1945 cf Ziegler *Mountbatten* p. 279: see also Hamilton *Monty: the Field Marshal* p. 432–3.

[53] Anthony Powell *Military Philosophers* (1968) p. 20 (Powell spent most of the war at the War Office, but was at the Cabinet Office for nine weeks in 1943: Powell *Faces in My Time* p. 156–8); Tim Heald *Networks: Who We Know and How We Use Them* (1983) p. 16–17; Elwyn Jones *In My Time: An Autobiography* (1983) p. 71–2; *Hansard: House of Commons* vol. 376 col. 664 Sir Roger Keyes speech 25 Nov. 1941; ibid. col. 663 *Diaries of Evelyn Waugh* 'Memorandum on LAYFORCE' p. 502.

would perhaps be the explanation for the gap which quickly developed between planning and reality. Ever larger numbers of experts reflecting ever more systematically on the problems of three-dimensional warfare in the mid twentieth century tended to multiply problems and the resources necessary to deal with them. It was not that the planners were stupid: rather the contrary. Victor Cavendish-Bentinck of the Joint Intelligence Committee thought the Joint Planning Staff 'were head and shoulders above' his own military colleagues in intellectual ability: 'They were the highest calibre of people I have ever worked with'. But evidently they had some of the traditional failings of intellectuals. 'The Chiefs of Staff won't attack for 10 years if it is left to them', a Foreign Office official noted bitterly: 'They will never think they are sufficiently prepared.' American experts, themselves imbued with the philosophy of overkill, remarked on the excessive caution of their British opposite numbers: 'Like most British officers, McNabb took the pessimistic view in planning. He believed in wide margins of error.' Though the Americans had even larger staff establishments, one British observer thought that:

> the Americans at their best were quite uninhibited by their staff when they really got going. Without staff-work at all they would move a Division a hundred miles, commit it to action and contrive to supply it, while the British 'Q' staff of our Movements Control Section would still be proving that the movement was impossible.

This elephantine deliberateness was the more noticeable – and, to begin with, the more disadvantageous – against enemies like the Germans and Japanese who erred too much the other way: as Wavell wrote in his diary in 1943, 'I pointed out many times that the Japanese would never have invaded Malaya or got anywhere if they had planned on our conservative lines'.[54]

A wartime newsreel of the crossing of the Sangro in November 1943 includes film of huge lorries churning their way one at a time through mud reminiscent of Passchendaele while the newscaster chortles enthusiastically: 'How anybody could launch an offensive under these conditions is a mystery but the Allies have done it'. Evidently careful forward-planning did not result in a more sophisticated handling of petty details such as whether the roads would be passable or not. In fact British caution, reliance on superior material effort, and allowance for large margins of error did not always prevent humiliating slip-ups. The intervention in Norway in April and May 1940 and in Greece a year later both involved enormously costly and enormously complex support operations across the sea (in the Greek case, across the sea from a distant base)

---

[54] Patrick Howarth *Intelligence Chief Extraordinary: The Life of the Ninth Duke of Portland* (1986) p. 166; *War Diaries of Oliver Harvey* p. 119, 25 April 1942; Truscott *Command Missions* p. 144: the reference is to C.V.O'N. McNabb, Brigadier General Staff to General Anderson in North Africa; Robert Henriques *From a Biography of Myself* (1969) p. 62–3. Henriques was attached to Patton's H.Q. before and during the Casablanca landings; Penderel Moon ed. *Wavell: The Viceroy's Journal* (1973) p. 15 26 August 1943.

which simply were not able to sustain sufficient strength in the front line against an enemy using staging bases backed up by much handier overland communications. The appointment of Sir Alan Brooke as C.I.G.S. late in 1941 brought no real improvement. Brooke, described by one admirer as 'a dark, incisive, round-shouldered Irish eagle', used all his force of personality and intellect to steer Churchill away from his wilder projects and turned down the offer of a field command because 'by remaining on as C.I.G.S., I was able to render greater services to my country than if I had accepted the more attractive alternative'. Victor Cavendish-Bentinck, chairman of the Joint Intelligence Committee, recalled:

> Brooke was a powerful personality. He used to gobble like an irate turkey. He was very difficult and could be pig-headed. He got an idea into his head and it required a great deal of intelligence and facts to dislodge it. Even then it wasn't altogether dislodged.

One of Brooke's *idées fixes* was the strength of the German armed forces relative to the British, even after the disasters in Russia. Yet though he was ardent and vigorous chiefly in urging caution and delay, the Salerno operation in 1943 and the Anzio landing in 1944 were both nearly disasters for the same reasons as the campaigns in Norway and Greece failed; both involved armies depending on long sea communications pitted against defenders with handier overland communications. Later in 1944 at Arnhem a sizable army was transported at vast expense by air, to meet defeat at the hands of troops much better supplied with heavy equipment which they had been able to bring up by road. The second Chindit operation, at the beginning of which Wingate was killed, was the only major operation employing the superiority of Allied transport resources in order to strike where the enemy lacked relatively easy facilities for deploying his local strength; but precisely because the road communications in the Burmese jungle were so poor the Japanese could afford not to over-respond to the British air-borne offensive and could leave the Chindits to dissipate their strength against outposts, up-country garrisons of second-line troops, and the dreadful conditions of the jungle itself.[55]

The Anglo-American ability to rely on their superior transport facilities, combined with the huge margins of error allowed for in their planning, also tended to multiply distribution problems. Early in October 1943 for example the British Eighth Army in southern Italy was down to its last 21 tons of petrol while a few miles to the west the 10th corps of the American Fifth Army had a stockpile of 6,000 tons. A classic instance of how combined overkill in destruction and supply effort paralyzed movement occurred in France in the summer of 1944; the French railway networks had been so

---

[55] The newsreel cited is included in the Ministry of Information short *Food for Thought*, 1943; General Sir David Fraser on Brooke in *Dictionary of National Biography, 1961–1970* (Oxford 1981) p. 148; Bryant *Turn of the Tide* p. 447; Howarth *Intelligence Chief Extraordinary* p. 164–5.

extensively destroyed by having 71,000 tons of bombs unloaded over it – despite the opinion of many experts that simply knocking out the railway bridges would have been more effective as well as more economical – that it took five days for the first train to reach Paris after the liberation of the French capital, and 70,000 tons of cargo piled up at Cherbourg for want of the means to carry it away. At this time the 22 American divisions in France had transport available for 3,350,000 ton/miles of forward lift compared to 2,860,000 ton/miles required on paper: the actual need was more like 1,500,000 ton/miles. The huge non-combatant tail of the Anglo-American forces, including all the mechanics and repair shops for the trucks that were not actually needed, the guards and maintenance men for the ammunition dumps that were fired off at targets that need not have been destroyed, the medical staff needed to tend those injured in traffic accidents that would not have happened if the roads had been less overcrowded, also multiplied the size of any operation and increased the logistical problems of staging it. Allied strategy in 1944 was seriously constricted by shortages of landing craft, for example: not that they were not available in huge numbers, but they were insufficient for the vast scale of landings that it was felt necessary to make.[56]

Part of the reason for the overscaling of operations was a tendency to substitute quantity for quality, to use superiority of resources to make up for inferiority of skill. Sir Claude Auchinleck, as G.O.C.-in-C. Middle East, acknowledging that 'I am not satisfied that the tactical leadership of our armoured units is of sufficiently high standard to offset German material advantages', argued that 'our armoured forces as at present equipped, organized and led must have at least two to one superiority'. In fact the Germans had no overall advantage in quality of equipment and Field Marshal Lord Carver later emphasized the Eighth Army's 'inherent deficiencies in organization, training and command which meant that the army's full power was never fully developed'. Hitler's opinion was that, 'It is not arms that decide, but the men behind them – always', and it was central to military thinking both in Nazi Germany and in Japan that the fighting spirit of the soldier, and the brilliance of the commanders, would prevail over almost any material disadvantage. The bureaucratic, matererialist mentality in Britain and America distrusted individual spirit and brilliance, as if it was felt that military flair was incompatible with the true freedom of democratic societies; it seems never actually to have been stated that the relative inferiority of the British and Americans as frontline soldiers demonstrated their moral superiority, but as so often Soviet Russia provided images that could be held up for imitation without any risk that their truth or relevance would be too closely interrogated: the refrain 'Generals may win campaigns but people win wars', in Anatole Litvak's

---

[56] Hamilton *Monty: Master of the Battlefield* p. 422; Russell F. Weigley *Eisenhower's Lieutenants* (1981) p. 60, 269; Martin van Creveld *Supplying War: Logistics from Wallenstein to Patton* (Cambridge 1977) p. 315.

film *The Battle of Russia* – number 5 in the official American *Why We Fight* series – was surely intended primarily as a text for the Anglo-Saxon peoples.[57]

Cripplingly conservative margins were insisted on by British and American military planners in spite of the fact that the Allies, along with all their other material and organizational advantages, generally had much better Intelligence than the Axis. The Germans were reckoned by the British in North Africa to have rather less effective Intelligence than the Italians, and the Germans themselves had a traditional conviction of British superiority; the Gestapo's secret *Informationsheft G.B.* drawn up in 1940 saw British Intelligence as 'a mechanism of diabolical potency' and wished Germany could build up something half as effective, and in 1945 an American Intelligence officer noted that the bookcases in the offices of the German security services 'seemed to be lined with spy novels about the diabolically clever British'. It sometimes seems that the Germans simply failed to appreciate the importance of Military Intelligence; from 1942 onwards the Intelligence section at Wehrmacht H.Q. in France consisted of nine people under an officer who spoke no English and almost no French. Intelligence staffs in other sectors were probably equally exiguous. Certainly the Germans completely underestimated British strength in Greece in April 1941 and Soviet strength in June 1941; and the Japanese made the same mistake in Malaya and the Philippines early in 1942; but in all these cases poor Intelligence was made up for by operational brilliance. With the British and Americans it was usually the other way round: brilliant Intelligence was wasted by operational incompetence. The story of the breaking of the German Enigma codes has already been briefly outlined. The failure to capitalize fully on the advantage of vastly superior Intelligence may be attributed to the same organizational defects as characterized other aspects of the Anglo-American military machine. The theoretical advantage, rather than the practical benefits derivable from it, became an end in itself. Similarly expensive gadgetry deflected attention away from mediocre results in Britain's Royal Navy, which failed initially to gain proper advantage from its possession of the electronic searching device Asdic: prior to the war no attempt had been made to adopt suitable anti-submarine tactics; instead 'hundreds (if

---

[57] Churchill *Second World War* vol. 4 p. 29 Auchinleck to Churchill 31 Jan. 1942; Michael Carver *Tobruk* (1964) p. 260 cf Michael Carver *Dilemmas in the Desert War: A New Look at the Libyan Campaign, 1940–1942* (1986) p. 141; Hermann Rauschning *Hitler Speaks: A Series of Conversations with Adolf Hitler on his Real Aims* (1939) p. 15; Anatole Litvak's film *The Battle of Russia*, 1943.

The British and South African Official Histories, Playfair, Molony, Jackson *The Mediterranean and Middle East* vol. 2 p. 134–4 Appendix 5 (and cf vol. 3 p. 436 Appendix 8) and J.A.I. Agar-Hamilton and L.C.F. Turner *The Sidi Rezeg Battles* (Cape Town 1957) p. 31–42 show that at the beginning of 1942 the Germans had a clear superiority only in anti-tank guns, though some of their tanks carried extra armour: their 50mm tank guns were superior to the British 2 pounder (40mm) only with special ammunition at short range. The British, as well as having more tanks, also had much stronger field artillery.

not thousands) of records and analyses had been "flogged" to cover inefficiency and to present an outward appearance of smooth competence'. The more complex the institutional structure, the more difficult it is to monitor which parts are actually working; and the more people there are with a professional vested interest in preventing a systematic analysis of the institution as a whole. The truth of this principle seems to be epitomized by the history of the British military effort in the Second World War.[58]

At the same time, even in the 1940s, Britain remained a pioneer in institutional and organizational structures. Even if, from the perspective of forty years of post-war decline, Britain seems to have fought the Second World War with all the agility and panache of an old-age pensioner, in one area of war-making Britain took a decisive lead. A counter-argument to the analysis presented in the previous pages, or possibly a confirmation, is provided by the story of Britain's experiment in the strategic use of air power.

---

[58] David Hunt *A Don at War* (1966) p. 39–40, 70–3, Fleming *Invasion 1940* p. 194; Eric Larrabee *Commander in Chief: Franklin Delano Roosevelt, his Lieutenants & their War* (1987) p. 500; Military Intelligence Division U.S. War Dept. *German Military Intelligence, 1939–1945* (Frederick Maryland 1984) [written 1945–6] p. 274 and cf p. 273–295 passim; Alistair Mars *Court Martial* (1954) p. 37–8.

16

The Correct Use of Air Power

Flying! The dream of ages! The legend of the bird-man: Icarus's fall, the
punishment of over-weening pride. The witches astride their broom-sticks.
Leonardo watching the flight of birds, dissecting their wings, imagining and
designing machines which should carry a man through the air. I remember the
thrill of the early triumphs, of Blériot's crossing of the Channel. Now these
young pilots, getting into their cockpits to sail into the clouds, seemed unaware
of anything miraculous. Legend had become fact.

William Rothenstein, with Lord David Cecil, *Men of the R.A.F.* (1942) p. 13.

I. Images of War in the Air Age

In the French wars stiffly regimented men confronted the enemy face to face
across levelled muskets, and just before the Battle of the Pyrenees the Allied
commander-in-chief Wellington saw his opposite number, Marshal Soult, 'so
distinctly as to know him instantly when I met him afterwards in Paris'; in
the trenches in the First World War it was more a case of a fixed-position
rifle and a distant helmet glimpsed through a trench periscope; in the Second
World War one generally saw the enemy only in machines. The aeroplane was
the definitive weapon of the machine age. It provided the classic visual images
of the war: not the deliberately tedious and by now hackneyed abstraction
of Nash's painting, *Totes Meer*, but rather the cine film of the boys running
baggy-legged across the English grass to the Hurricanes crouched humpbacked
on an airfield 'somewhere in southern England'; the tangled vapour trails high
above the dome of St. Paul's cathedral; the young mother and child raising
radiant apprehensive faces to the drumming of innumerable motors in the
sky as massed bomber squadrons set out for Cologne or Essen. And then
those other images: the terrified columns of fugitives scattering down the
embankments as the Messerschmitts strafed the roads leading west and south
in May 1940; the aerial photos of towns, as clear as street maps but with
the bombs visible pirouetting down in one corner; the silent ravaged cities
of Germany which confronted the Anglo-Saxon invaders in 1945:

imagine a journey from Chelsea to Whitehall through nothing but ruins. They
seemed eternal: dunes of rubble stretching away amongst the towering and
tottering walls of tall buildings eviscerated by fire. Main roads had been cleared,

their sides embanked with rough walls of broken bricks beyond which rose steep screes of broken masonry, pitted cliffs of ornate façades and, here and there, bared steel girders like warped climbing-frames in a children's playground.

And, finally and conclusively, the blossoming of the mushroom clouds over Hiroshima and Nagasaki.[1]

Much more than even the tank, the aeroplane is the most expressive symbol of the Second World War. One thinks of Colonel Count von Stauffenberg's nail-biting three-hour journey by air from Rastenburg to Berlin on 20 July 1944, of Hess's deluded flight to Scotland in May 1941, of Skorzeny and Mussolini's escape from Gran Sasso in a tiny plane, even of Chamberlain's flying to Munich a year before the war broke out. In the French wars the directing personalities were depressed and disconcerted by the vast distances across which they had to struggle: when the French seized Amsterdam at the beginning of 1795 the British Viceroy in Corsica burst out, 'nothing I can say on the subject can be material. It happened a month ago, and it will be a month before this letter is read'. But the vaster distances of the Second World War were bound together within hours by the magic of the aeroplane. Winston Churchill's prime-ministerial jaunts to America, North Africa, the Middle East, Russia, were mostly by air. New Zealand's premier Peter Fraser travelled – mainly by aeroplane – 80,000 miles between October 1939 and August 1944, visiting London three times and Washington twice: his health suffered considerably and that of his wife, who generally accompanied him, broke down completely: she died in March 1945. This was just one aspect of the war's combination of vast geographic extent and tight centralized control. Amongst those normally remote from the carnage who died in air crashes were General Władysław Sikorski, head of the Polish government in exile, Subhas Chandra Bose, head of the Indian National Army, the Right Hon. Arthur Blaikie Purvis, Director General of the British Purchasing Commission and then Chairman of the British Supply Council in North America, Fritz Todt the German armaments minister, General Sir Brudenell White, chief of the Australian general staff, together with his army minister Brigadier G.A. Street, air minister J.V. Fairbairn and Sir Harry Gullett, vice-president of the Executive council in the Australian government, all killed when the R.A.A.F Hudson carrying them crashed near Canberra on 13 October 1940, Christoph Prince of Hesse, brother-in-law of the Duke of Edinburgh and, as head of the Nazi wire-tapping agency, the most powerful survivor of the German *ancien régime* in Hitler's new order, V.M. Petlyakov the Soviet aircraft designer, Admiral Mineichi Koga, commander of Japan's Combined Fleet, Vice-Admiral Lothar Arnauld de la Perière, the First World War U-boat ace, Vice-Admiral Sir Bertram Ramsay; Air Marshals Sir Trafford Leigh-Mallory and Sir Peter Drummond, Air Vice-Marshals Charles Blount

---

[1] The description of bomb damage in Berlin in 1945 is from Tom Pocock *1945: The Dawn Came Up Like Thunder* (1983) p. 176.

and Wilfred McClaughry, Generals Hans Hube, Eduard Dietl, Vyvyan Pope, Orde Wingate, Frank M. Andrews (killed in a crash at Reykjavic en route to taking up the command of American forces in the European Theatre of Operations in May 1943) and Herbert A. Dargue (on his way to take command of the Hawaiian Department shortly after Pearl Harbor), H.R.H. the Duke of Kent, Amy Johnson the famous pre-war solo flyer and latterly with the Air Transport Auxiliary, Glen Miller – Major Glen Miller U.S. Army – and actress Carole Lombard, whose plane crashed at Las Vegas in January 1942 on her way back from selling War Bonds at Indianapolis. Generalfeldmarschall Walther von Reichenau, already near death after a heart attack, was finished off in an air crash on the way to hospital. It was merely put about that Ernst Udet, head of the Luftwaffe's technical office, had been killed in a crash, but his successor Carl August Freiherr von Gablenz really was. Admiral Isuroku Yamamoto, Koga's predecessor in command of the Japanese Combined Fleet, Air Vice Marshal R.P. Musgrave Whitham, Director of War Organization at the Air Ministry in London, and the actor Leslie Howard were killed when their transport planes were shot down; Lieutenant-General William Gott survived being shot down but was killed when his wrecked plane was strafed by German fighters; in terms of targeting appropriate victims these incidents clearly represent a major technical advance on the mining of the cruiser carrying Lord Kitchener in 1916.[2]

One should perhaps also mention Marshal Balbo, shot down and killed by his own Anti-Aircraft at Tobruk, and Lieutenant-General Lesley J. McNair, commanding general U.S. Army Ground Forces, killed by a bomb from an American plane on the first day of his visit to the front line in France in July 1944.

The aeroplane also provides a symbol of the way material effort became schizophrenically detached from military reality in the Second World War. Behind the horror and the heroism of aerial combat were young intellectuals in strange pale uniforms weaving complicated expensive plans to change the

---

[2] Cf Public Record Office WO 1/302 f. 393 Sir Gilbert Elliot to Henry Dundas 23 February 1795; For Peter Fraser see James Thorn *Peter Fraser: New Zealand's Wartime Prime Minister* (1952) p. 167, 191, 196, 215–6, 219–220, 222–4, 226. Harold Macmillan *War Diaries: Politics and War in the Mediterranean, January 1943-May 1945* (1984) gives a vivid picture of the endlessness and tedium, the cold, discomfort, minor crashes, tyre bursts and engine failures which were inseparable from wartime air travel. During the Second World War the U.S.A.A.F. lost 52, 173 aircrews in combat and 35,946 in 'non-combat situations' – mostly flying accidents (Michael S. Sherry *The Rise of American Air Power: the Creation of Armageddon* (New Haven 1987) p. 204–5). Other victims of aeroplane accidents include the 76 people (51 children) killed when a U.S. Eighth Air Force bomber crashed into a village school at Freckleton, near Preston on 23 August 1944 and the thirteen who died when the pilot of a B-25 fulfilled every airman's dream by crashing into the Empire State Building in New York on 28 July 1945.

The only senior officer killed in a plane crash in the First World War was J.P. Michielson, commanding the Netherlands East Indies Army, killed in a seaplane crash on 14 February 1916.

shape of war. Even the dashing Adolf Galland, who seemed to epitomize the fighter pilot's physical and living style – though perhaps he was upstaged in his famous encounter with the newly captured R.A.F. ace Douglas Bader, for whereas Galland was merely virtually blind in one eye, Bader had had the extravagance to fly after having both legs amputated – even Galland wrote his memoirs with a practised style which told of long hours working behind a desk. Under the influence of the airmen-intellectuals the Second World War was a rerun of the First World War as regards the way air power was at same time overestimated and too clumsily applied – but on a much huger scale.[3]

II. The Air Weapon in Ground Warfare

Towards the end of the campaign in Poland Neville Chamberlain, then still British Prime Minister, wrote:

> To my mind the lesson of the Polish campaign is the power of the Air Force, when it has obtained complete mastery in the air, to paralyse the operations of land forces. The effects in this direction seem to me to have gone much beyond anything that we were led to expect by our Military Advisers.

Amongst those who should have been surprised was Sir Robert Vansittart who, as permanent head of the Foreign Office, had noted in 1937, 'The Germans and Italians have learned from the Spanish experience that infantry is still the dominant factor ... The German army can quite certainly not be stopped by Air Forces alone, & everyone knows that elementary fact'. But the question, as both Vansittart and Chamberlain conceived it, was not one which the Royal Air Force cared to discuss: the R.A.F. view was that:

> The true function of a bomber aircraft in support of an army is to isolate the battlefield from reinforcement and supply, to block or delay the movement of reserves; and generally to create disorganisation and confusion behind the enemy front ... But neither in attack nor in defence should bombers be used in the battlefield itself ... All experience of war proves that such action is not only very costly in casualties but is normally uneconomical and ineffective compared with the results of the correct employment of aircraft on the lines described above.

What had happened in Poland was excluded from 'all experience of war' by the R.A.F. staff officer who wrote this memo on the grounds that 'the relatively

---

[3] The meeting of Bader and Galland is described in Adolf Galland *The First and the Last: The German Fighter Force in World War II* (1955) p. 122–4: this book has a foreword by Bader which acknowledges 'It is always absorbing to hear the other chap's point of view' ibid. p. xi.

few occasions on which the Luftwaffe had given "really close support"' had simply been due to Polish weakness.[4]

The result of R.A.F. thinking was that at the outbreak of war, whereas the Luftwaffe and French *Armée de l'Air* both had different types of aircraft for the ground-attack, general-purpose close-support and artillery observation roles, the R.A.F. had only a single type, the Westland Lysander, which was supposed to be able to carry out all the different functions involved in aerial support of a ground army. The Germans for example had the Junkers Ju 87 Stuka dive-bomber for pin-point attacks on tactical targets; the French had developed a much faster, cannon-armed twin-engined type, the Bréguet Br 693, to carry out much the same function and later in the war, when the Ju 87 had been found too vulnerable to fighter interception, fighter bombers developed in the tradition of the Br 693 concept became the queens of the battlefield (though only the Americans imitated the Br 693 in staying with the twin-motor format). The French had also made a heavy investment in the Potez 63 general-purpose close-support type which proved to be too unspecialized to be very effective, but the German artillery observation plane, the Fieseler Fi 156 Storch, turned out to be a remarkable success: it had less than one third of the horsepower and half the weight and speed of the Westland Lysander and was of course much cheaper, but it was even better adapted to artillery spotting, which turned out to be the only one of its intended roles which the Lysander was really suitable for. (The Lysander's remarkably short landing and take-off run – short, that is, for a plane weighing three tons – was later to be utilized in landing and picking up secret agents in remote corners of occupied Europe and it is to this that the Lysander owes its comparative fame rather than to any of the functions it was designed for.) The R.A.F. also, in 1940, had a large number of Fairey Battle single-engined bombers but though their performance was in some respect similar to that of the Stuka they were not intended for close support, having been built merely as a stop-gap pending the introduction of larger, multi-engined types.[5]

In October 1939 the British Army called for 'a new type of light aeroplane to improve the application of artillery fire' and also for 'specially designed aircraft for "direct support"'. The former was pushed ahead, it being perceived that something could be developed on the model of light sporting aircraft without much trouble or expense, and trials of such aircraft were just beginning in

[4] Chamberlain to Churchill 16 Sept. 1939 quoted in David Dilks 'The Twilight War and the Fall of France: Chamberlain and Churchill in 1940' in David Dilks ed. *Retreat from Power* (2 vols 1981) vol. 2 p. 36–65 at p. 43; Public Record Office FO 371/20746/C928/928/18 marginal notes by Vansittart on CP 41(37) 'Role of the British Army' 28 January 1937 p. 3,8; Public Record Office CAB 21/903 Air Staff memo 'Bomber Support for the Army' 18 Nov. 1939 p. 2, 4.

[5] The general area of army cooperation aviation has not been systematically studied though Peter Mead *The Eye in the Air: History of Air Observation and Reconnaissance, 1785–1945* (1983) covers what is perhaps the most important aspect. The twin-engined American attack bomber was the Douglas A-26 which survived in service for many years after the war.

France at the time of the German attack in May 1940. Nevertheless when the R.A.F. established an Army Co-operation Command in December 1940, one of the first things the Air Officer Commanding wanted to do was to close down the development programme for light spotting aircraft, and when Auster spotting planes finally came into action in Algeria in November 1942 it was with pilots and observers supplied by the Royal Artillery: only the ground crew were Royal Air Force.[6]

The question of 'specially designed aircraft for "direct suport"', was evaded more successfully. In reality there was no need for 'specially designed' aircraft, as conventional fighters fitted with bomb-racks and carrying armour-piercing ammunition were the perfect weapon for close-support – i.e. shooting up enemy ground troops already deployed and in contact with one's own ground forces. Whereas the French had already started manufacturing armour-piercing 20mm ammunition by May 1940, it was only in April 1941 that the British Chief of Air Staff began even to wonder about the possibility of using armour-piercing 20mm ammunition as a last-ditch weapon against tanks in the case of a German invasion: 'The need is obvious and extremely urgent. If the Army cannot stop the German armoured fighting vehicles, then we must.' Trials with Spitfires carrying armour-piercing 20mm ammunition were carried out in June 1941 and with Hurricanes and Whirlwinds in August 1941. Sir Alan Brooke was most impressed by those trials: 'Left to their own devices they could destroy long columns even spaced out at 150 yards between vehicles', he noted. But the Royal Air Force did not want to play his game. All through 1941 and 1942, in the fighting in North Africa, close support for ground troops was conspicuous by its absence. 'While our sorties are sporadic Jerry is always in the air watching every movement and attacking every target worth while', reported one disgusted army officer from North Africa. Even a year later the numerically superior R.A.F. failed to intervene in the ground fighting in Libya in spite of the fact that the defeated Eighth Army was being bombed and strafed by German and Italian aircraft; 'there were some in the War Office who were fond of telling us how much better the Luftwaffe was at Army support than the R.A.F.', the Assistant Chief of Air Staff (Policy) noted sourly. Later, when the *Afrika Korps* was defeated at El Alamein the R.A.F. did little to prevent the Germans retreating a record 800 miles in nineteen days along a single main road. By this time the R.A.F. in North Africa had had Hurricane IIDs armed with a pair of 40mm cannon for nearly six months, and other versions of the Hurricane II which could carry bombs; the problem was that Air Vice-Marshal Arthur Coningham, the R.A.F. commander in the Middle East, had no interest in close support. When Harry Broadhurst, Air Officer Commanding, Western Desert, began to order close support missions, Coningham sent his S.A.S.O. from his H.Q. at Algiers to remind Broadhurst

    [6] Public Record Office CAB 21/903 'Air Requirements for the Army' memo by Secretary of State for War (Hore-Belisha) 17 Oct. 1939; H.J. Parham and E.M.G. Belfield *Unarmed into Battle* (Winchester 1956) p. 16; Mead *Eye in the Air* p. 163.

that since his permanent rank was only Squadron-Leader, he would be advised to toe the line: 'One kick up the arse and you've had it'. Far from the North African theatre providing a forcing-ground for the development of ground-air cooperation it was only in 1943 that Coningham's command began to catch up with the techniques being developed in Britain.[7]

After the war Sir John Kennedy, the wartime Director of Military Operations at the War Office, felt justified in writing:

> We were never able to harness our air power to the war effort in the most effective way ... we found ourselves in 1944 saddled with a force which was sadly deficient of types of aircraft suitable for close co-operation with the Army, and of airmen trained for that role.

American officers had the same opinion:

> Until the final campaign in northern Italy, close air support for ground troops was never as it should have been and was often entirely missing.

Needless to say this was not the view of the R.A.F.'s own experts. By 1945 the clean innocent Art Deco lines of the pre-war designed aircraft had become encrusted with turbocharger inlets, cannon barrels and threatening bulges but the ideas of the Air Staff's intellectuals retained a streamlined glibness and a reductionist simplicity redolent of halcyon afternoons at staff college in the early rearmament period. The bitter experience gained by others during the intervening years could be shrugged off with a self-deprecating quip: referring to his pre-war volume *Air Power and Armies* (1936) Group Captain John Slessor, Director of Plans at the Air Ministry, acknowledged:

> I have been considerably ragged after the Battle of France, and no doubt shall be again after Greece, for writing a book of which the main theme was The Bomber is not a Battlefield Weapon.

But of course one saw a little further into things than the uninitiated. The German defeat in southern Italy – i.e. the fact that it took eight months to hustle an outnumbered German army back to a line north of Rome – was recognized by Slessor to be a triumph of the correct principles of air power:

> The power of the defence on land has not been overcome by the tank or by improved artillery techniques, but by air-power ... if there had been no Air Force on either side, the German Army could have made the invasion of Italy

---

[7] [F.] d'Astier de la Vigerie *Le Ciel n'était pas vide, 1940* (Paris 1952) p. 182 for first attacks on German tanks by MS 406 with armoured piercing ammunition on 20 May 1940; Public Record Office AIR 19/164/1/1A Portal to Beaverbrook 14 April 1941 and cf AIR 16/440; Arthur Bryant *The Turn of the Tide, 1939–1943* (1957) p. 237; Public Record Office AIR 8/631 Lt.-Col. Lord Apsley to Chancellor of the Duchy of Lancaster 20 June 1941 copy; Sir John Slessor *The Central Blue: Recollections and Reflections* (1956) p. 424; Nigel Hamilton *Monty: Master of the Battlefield, 1942–1944* (1983) p. 56, 63; ibid. p. 199–200; Charles Carrington *Soldier at Bomber Command* (1987) p. 121–2. It might be noted however that Rommel's H.Q. column was strafed by two machine gun-armed Hurricanes as early as May 1941: Heinz Werner Schmidt *With Rommel in the Desert* (1951) p. 54.

almost impossible except at a cost in national effort and human life which the Allies would have been unwilling to face.

Evidently the building of aerodromes, the establishment of aircraft repair shops and the shipping in of vast quantities of complex equipment and large numbers of expensively trained personnel was not to be counted as part of the national effort. Slessor contrasted the system briefly employed in Tunisia, where air power had been subordinated to the demands of the ground commanders according to local circumstances, with the superior system in Italy where a much larger air force attempted the complete interdiction of *all* enemy troop and supply movements. The fact that the Germans had nevertheless managed to keep eighteen divisions in action was 'little short of a miracle'. In the end of course, the Germans had been driven back:

> The surprising thing is, in the circumstances, that the remains of the shattered divisions were able to disengage at all or to preserve any sort of entity as units. It speaks volumes for the discipline and fighting quality of the German soldier that they were able to do so even to the limited extent that they were.

It might have been more straightforward for Slessor to admit that the Allied air forces had simply failed to carry out their self-allotted task, but according to the R.A.F.'s way of thinking, failure to provide any visible assistance to the ground troops was a sign not of failure but of achievement: as Sir Herbert Richmond recalled of his time as head of the Imperial Defence College in the late 1920s, 'the Airmen were fixed in the delusion that the Air should fight a war of its own independently and without the least connection with the other services'. Or as the U.S. military attaché in London noted of the air war experts of his own service:

> They have a peculiar idea that they are the priests of some sacred mystery which may be sullied or tarnished or abused if it is put at the disposal of any ordinary commander who has not himself been a pilot. This is nothing more than the way all cavalrymen used to feel and also all artillerymen when artillery was a sacred mystery itself. The more one questions people . . . who are thoroughly indoctrinated with the idea, the more it becomes apparent that all they want is to follow their own line without interference from anyone.[8]

[8] John Kennedy *The Business of War: The War Narrative of Major-General Sir John Kennedy* ed. Bernard Fergusson, (1957) p. 325; L.K. Truscott Jr. *Command Missions: A Personal Story* (New York 1954) p. 554; Public Record Office AIR 8/631, memo by J. Slessor entitled 'Use of Bombers in Close Support of the Army' 6 May 1941; Slessor *The Central Blue* p. 581 memo by Slessor for H.H. Arnold 1944; ibid. p. 566–7; ibid. p. 582; ibid. p. 584 ('The surprising thing is . . .'); Paul G. Halpern ed. *The Keyes Papers* (3 vols 1972–81) vol. 3 p. 252 Richmond to Keyes 4 July 1942; James Leutze ed. *The London Observer: The Journal of General Raymond E. Lee 1940–1941* (1971) p. 137, 21 Nov. 1940.

R.A.F. officers were not unaware of the older services' low opinion of them. In December 1943 a R.A.F. officer in Russia reported of the Soviet Air Arm:

> Its status is equivalent to the artillery, tanks, engineers etc. It is probably most undesirable therefore in the opinion of the General Staff that their Army Air Force should become tainted with R.A.F. propaganda and learn the advantages of a free independent air force.

Public Record Office AIR 46/26 piece 93A para D iii.

III. The Battle of Britain and the Air Ministry

One may feel that the airmen brought to the issue of cooperating with the ground forces all the ingeniousness in evading the main point which professional groups generally display when they feel themselves under threat, but they had their own way because both the most brilliant – or at least the most publicized – victory of the war and the longest and most elaborate campaign were classic examples of strategic air warfare. Whatever the contribution of poor air support might have been to the less than dashing victory over a weaker foe in North Africa, and later in Italy and France, the fact is that no land campaign was quite comparable to the Battle of Britain in strategic importance, or to the Strategic Air Offensive against Germany in terms of necessary long-term investment.

From the very beginning the Battle of Britain – officially announced to the American public as the 'First Great Air Battle in History' – belonged as much to myth as to the history of warfare. Fought in the late summer and autumn of 1940 following the defeat of France, it was a fable of modern knights on their mechanical chargers, defending the Right high above the chequered farmlands and suburbia of the Home Counties, in the tract between the vast magnet of the Imperial Capital and those coastal features now once again, as in 1588 and 1804, transformed by the evil enchantments of war into frontline bastions against the invader – Portland Bill, Dungeness, Beachy Head, the Isle of Sheppey, the White Cliffs of Dover.[9]

It is worth noting however that it has never been precisely established what the Germans were trying to do, whether they could have succeeded, or even to what extent or in what way they failed. Hitler issued his orders for the invasion on 21 July 1940, just six days after he had ordered the construction of 372 U-boats by the end of 1941, and five days before he told his generals that he intended to invade the Soviet Union. The invasion of Russia was at least initially presented by Hitler as a means of denying the British their last potential ally in Europe; the U-boats were also evidently intended for use against the British, presumably in 1942. It seems therefore that Hitler was not necessarily counting on carrying out the cross-channel invasion. Again, the relation of the aerial assault on southern England to the proposed invasion was not clear. The opening stages of the Battle of Britain seemed to be aimed at securing command of the air over the English south coast, but there seemed to be uncertainty as to how this was to be achieved; the R.A.F., both on the ground and in the air, was the Luftwaffe's principal target for only about three weeks and this phase's most brilliant success, achieved on 24 August, consisted of forcing the R.A.F. to withdraw from Manston, a secondary

---

[9] *The First Great Air Battle in History* is the title of the American edition of Hilary St. George Saunders's pamphlet *The Battle of Britain, August–October 1940: An Air Ministry Record of the Great Days from 8 August-31 October 1940*. There were also editions in Polish, French, Dutch and Afrikaans.

aerodrome in Kent. By early September, when disruption of the fighter bases and of the ground-control system was at last beginning to erode the R.A.F.'s defensive capacity, the Luftwaffe transferred its energies to the bombardment of London. Though of course nobody in Britain knew it at the time, the invasion was postponed on 17 September 1940, and finally cancelled on 12 October; it remains uncertain whether Hitler had ever intended to carry it out against organized defences. The plan adopted by the German Army, which involved sending barge-loads of soldiers across the Channel in the face of the unreduced strength of the Royal Navy, and landing 125,000 men over a period of three days, under coverering fire from naval guns on the French coast, was wildly over-optimistic: unless it is seen as contingent on Britain simply collapsing at the onset of Luftwaffe air raids. It had never happened previously that a country had collapsed simply as a result of a demonstration of air power, but Hitler was in an optimistic mood in July 1940: and he had come a long way in ten years simply by gambling on the feebleness of his enemies' responses.[10]

Britain did not collapse: nor did the English Channel part like the Red Sea. There was no land battle in which the Luftwaffe could perform gloriously in contributing to a decision forced by the armoured spearheads, no R.A.F. light bombers throwing themselves away in suicidal attempts to halt the advance of the German land forces. There was in fact only an aerial battle of attrition: and as the American Eighth Air Force discovered over Germany in 1943 and 1944, in a battle of attrition the attacker can only prevail against the inherent advantages of the defence by a vast and sustained superiority of output in aircraft and trained crews. This superiority the Germans simply did not have in 1940. They began the Battle of Britain with a handsome numerical advantage which to a considerable extent bled away during the campaign; by December 1940 the Luftwaffe was at only 80 per cent of establishment strength and Britain had established a clear lead both in aircraft manufacture and in aircrew training.[11]

The German failure to achieve the impossible does not mean that the R.A.F. could not have improved their own performance. The R.A.F.'s ground-control system was probably too rigid and complex, and by attempting to guide the defending fighters on to Luftwaffe bomber formations by telling them where the Germans were relative to their own planes rather than relative to the ground, involved a time lag of up to four minutes – sixteen miles of flight. If the R.A.F. pilots managed to be in the right place at the right time, their attacks were generally delivered in tight formations more suitable for a peacetime air display than a high-speed battle, and a case can be made for supposing that the eight 0.303 machine gun armament carried by their Spitfires and Hurricanes was inadequate or effective only at the closest range. In any

[10] For German invasion plans see Ronald Wheatley *Operation Sea Lion: German Plan for the Invasion of England, 1939–1942* (Oxford 1958) p. 155–9, 165–6.

[11] Williamson Murray *Luftwaffe: a History, 1933–44* (1985) p. 95.

case most R.A.F. fighter pilots were notably inaccurate in their shooting – only 15 per cent of Fighter Command pilots actually managed to shoot down an enemy plane, and only seventeen pilots shot down more than ten planes in a campaign lasting from July to October.[12]

There is also the question of the overall tactical handling of R.A.F. Fighter Command – a question of vital significance for the reputation of Fighter Command's Air Officer Commanding in Chief in 1940, Air Chief Marshal Sir Hugh Dowding.

Fighter Command was divided into Groups of which No. 11 Group, under Air Vice-Marshal Keith Park, covered the area south of London which was principally subject to German air attacks. Park, who had shot down twenty German aircraft over the Western Front in the First World War, was an inspirational commander, resembling Montgomery with his vanity, flair for publicity, parsonical manner and bird-like eagerness of face, though perhaps a little more *macho*. Despite the early warning provided by the network of radar stations along the south coast, he fought his campaign in an apparently *ad hoc* manner, launching squadrons to intercept German formations as and when their course and target became apparent: whether he should have done more in the way of anticipating the German attacks, bearing in mind the short flight-endurance of his Spitfires and Hurricanes and the necessity of conserving his pilots' physical energies, is a complex technical question. Trafford Leigh-Mallory, commanding No. 12 Group to Park's north, thought that Park should have made better use of the time between Luftwaffe formations being first reported and their appearance over England, and towards the end of the Battle of Britain Leigh-Mallory helped promote a campaign of criticism which led to both Park and Dowding being removed from their posts.

The criticism centred on Park's failure to adopt Leigh-Mallory's 'big wing' policy. This was not originally Leigh-Mallory's policy but an idea pressed on him by one of his squadron-leaders, Douglas Bader, who on occasion led three, or even five, squadrons into battle as a single formation. Flying from No. 12 Group bases north of London and not immediately at risk from Luftwaffe air raids, the thirty to sixty Spitfires and Hurricanes of Bader's wing had plenty of time to form up, and though the claims registered of enemy aircraft shot down turned out to be exaggerated their entry into battle had a dramatic effect on German bomber formations. Bader was a godsend to Leigh-Mallory. He was a brilliant fighter pilot, brave as a lion, stubborn, possessing dog-like loyalty to his commanding officer – i.e. Leigh-Mallory – and incapable of appreciating anyone else's point of view. He was also, though only recently promoted squadron-leader, somewhat old for a fighter pilot, having been invalided out of the R.A.F. after losing both legs in a flying

[12] H.R. Allen *Who Won the Battle of Britain?* London (1974) p. 64–5, 85–91, 168–170, and cf K.W. Mackenzie *Hurricane Combat: The Nine Lives of a Fighter Pilot* (1987) p. 31,71. For the problem of accurate shooting in air combat see Gron Edwards *Norwegian Patrol* (Shrewsbury 1985) p. 171–176.

accident in 1931 and having been readmitted to the service only in 1939; he thus managed to combine the professional Cranwell-trained career officer with something of the independent folk hero. Leigh-Mallory was one of the R.A.F.'s committee-room heroes: Double Third at Cambridge, instructorship at the Army Staff College, three years at the Air Ministry, some reflected glamour from an elder brother who had died almost on the peak of Mount Everest, no real ideas about tactics but a flair for discovering the doctrines that would advance his career: probably a good deal cleverer than Bader as well as vastly more experienced in the art of political manipulation.

There were a number of senior officers in the R.A.F. who shared Leigh-Mallory's style of career-making. Park was not one of them; and still less was Dowding. A strikingly uncharismatic, almost melancholy, figure, Dowding had risen steadily through the service until, perhaps in late 1936, a behind-the-scenes campaign began to build up against him. In February 1937 Dowding, already A.O.C.-in-C. Fighter Command, had every reason to suppose that his next appointment would be as Chief of Air Staff, the professional head of the R.A.F.; Ellington, the current Chief of Air Staff, and Bowhill, the Air Member for Personnel at the Air Ministry, had already told him as much. But it was not to be. Perhaps too many of the up and coming younger senior officers were unhappy with the idea of someone so dour, tetchy, uninspiring, in a word *depressing*, being head of the world's most glamorous armed service; perhaps it was suspected that Dowding, doing his second tour of duty as head of the nation's fighter defences, would be ideologically unsound on what was still felt to be the R.A.F.'s primary mission, stategic bombing. Perhaps it was simply that Sir Cyril Newall, the man who actually got the Chief of Air Staff job when Ellington retired, knew something that Dowding didn't about making friends and influencing people: in 1934, when Newall had been A.O.C.-in-C. Middle East, he had travelled with Sir Philip Cunliffe-Lister, the Colonial Secretary, from Cairo to Nairobi, flying in stages between airstrips improvised in the bush; Cunliffe-Lister had noted that 'Newall was a popular and efficient Commander-in-Chief and an agreeable companion', and afterwards, when Cunliffe-Lister became Secretary of State for Air (as Lord Swinton) he was delighted to have Newall as his subordinate as Air Member for Supply and Organization. Swinton was still at the Air Ministry when Newall was appointed Chief of Air Staff.[13]

Having become chief of the service over the head of the more senior Dowding, Cyril Newall did not exert himself to make himself agreeable to the older man. In June 1938 he told Dowding his 'services would not be required after the end of June 1939'. In February 1939 Dowding was told over the telephone that he was to stay at Fighter Command till December 1939. A month later he was told that he would be retired at the end of March 1940. On 30 March, when Dowding's retirement plans were presumably at an

[13] Robert Wright *Dowding and the Battle of Britain* (1969) p. 60–61; Lord Swinton *I Remember* (1948) p. 91.

advanced stage, he was told to stay at Fighter Command till 14 July; on 5 July he was told to stay till October, and on 12 August, just as the Luftwaffe was building up to its main onslaught, he was told he was required to stay on indefinitely. These constant postponements of his retirement seem almost to have been deliberately insulting and must have played havoc not only with Dowding's private and personal plans but also with the working out of any ideas he might have had about long-term developments in Fighter Command. Dowding gave some indication of his resentment in a letter he wrote to Newall on 7 July 1940:

> Apart from the question of discourtesy, which I do not wish to stress, I must point out the lack of consideration involved in delaying a proposal of this nature until ten days before the date of my retirement . . .
> I would therefore suggest that I should not be called upon to retire otherwise than at my own request before the first retiring date given to me, viz. April 24th 1942 or the end of the war, whichever is the earlier.

Thereafter Dowding's dealing with his professional superiors show an ever growing recalcitrance and uncooperativeness; having previously had a reputation for stubbornness, he now became almost unmanageable, and within the upper echelons of the service it became increasingly felt that he had outlived his usefulness.[14]

Until late in 1937 the R.A.F. had been committed to the policy that its main function would be to launch heavy bombing attacks against a continental enemy; aerial defence against the enemy's bombers was thought likely to be ineffective and was given low priority. In December 1937 however Sir Thomas Inskip, Minister for the Coordination of Defence, urged the view, quickly adopted by the Cabinet, that the emphasis in R.A.F. expansion should be given to home defence. Fighter Command under Dowding thus became the beneficiary of a major shift of emphasis (and of investment finance) in spite of the Air Staff's preference for concentrating on the bomber arm. Dowding was not backward in insisting on the importance of his command. In the first weeks of the war for example he had informed the Air Staff:

> I must put on record my point of view that the Home Defence Organisation should not be regarded as coequal with other Commands, but that it should receive priority to all other claims.

The potential switch of emphasis away from strategic bombing had inevitably caued some bitterness and heart-searching amongst Dowding's colleagues, and his attitude was not calculated to make the new policy more popular. Leigh-Mallory, who had commanded No. 12 Group since 1937 and may be assumed to have had his ear to the ground, made no secret of his irritation

---

[14] Wright *Dowding and the Battle of Britain* p. 68, 72, 76, 95–6, 137, 157; Public Record Office AIR 19/572/1A Dowding to Newall 7 July 1940 copy: another copy is amongst Dowding's papers in the R.A.F. Museum, Hendon at AC 71/17/2: both this file and AIR 19/572 as a whole make curious reading.

with Dowding; in February 1940, according to Park, who was then Dowding's Senior Air Staff Officer, Leigh-Mallory one day 'came out of Dowding's office, paused in mine and said in my presence that he'd move heaven and earth to get Dowding removed from Fighter Command'. A man as canny and ambitious as Leigh-Mallory does not say such things in public unless sure that it will not be held against him by people who really count.[15]

Discussion of Dowding's role at Fighter Command was not confined to R.A.F. senior officers. On 6 July Churchill wrote to Sir Archibald Sinclair, Secretary of State for Air, urging that Dowding should be kept on at Fighter Command:

> Personally I think he is one of the very best men you have got ... I have greatly admired the whole of his work in the Fighter Command ... In fact he has my full confidence ... I hope you will consider whether it is not in the public interest that his appointment should be indefinitely prolonged while the war lasts.

Presumably Sinclair paid rather more attention to this letter than to an anonymous paper (quite possibly emanating from no less a person than Lord Beaverbrook, the Minister of Aircraft Production) stating that Dowding 'has definite personality but unfortunately has inadequate mental ability and a very slow brain. He is also a classic example of a complete non-cooperator with the Air Ministry or any other authority'. In August Irene Ward, M.P. for Wallsend, told Churchill, with regard to the appointment of a new Chief of Air Staff, 'My information is that the R.A.F. would consider it a disaster if the Commander in Chief of Fighter Command was given the supreme office'.[16]

By this stage the Battle of Britain was at its height and Park's poorly laid-out instructions to his sector controllers and the fact that he had only a map of his own Group area displayed at his H.Q. was providing Leigh-Mallory with polemical material, not only against Park but also against Dowding, who was allegedly leaving too much responsibility to Park despite the latter's supposedly self-evident lack of grip and vision. In September the adjutant of Bader's squadron, who conveniently happened to be an M.P., obtained a private meeting with Churchill to discuss the question of using larger fighter formations. Leigh-Mallory either knew of this or was mobilizing similar contacts of his own: he told a close friend that he was trying to enlist Churchill's support against Dowding. By mid-October the latest official gossip was that Wing-Commander Gerald Maxwell, a First World War flying ace and Stock Exchange personality, had been 'given a kind of roving commission to size up the situation in the Fighter Command' and had written

[15] Charles Webster and Noble Frankland *The Strategic Air Offensive against Germany* (4 vols 1961) vol. 1 p. 76–7. Public Record Office AIR 16/190 report on 'Fighter Policy' September 1939–May 1940; letter by Sir Keith Park in *Auckland Star* 4 July 1968 p. 3c.

[16] Randolph S. Churchill and Martin Gilbert *Winston S. Churchill* (8 vols 1966–88) vol. 6 p. 658 Churchill to Sinclair 6 July 1940; Denis Richards *Portal of Hungerford* (1977) p. 168; Public Record Office PREM 4/3/6 p. 239–240 Irene Ward to Churchill 17 Aug. 1940.

a report for Churchill which 'pointed out an extremely dangerous situation in the Fighter Command, in which it would seem that dour, dogmatic, stuffy old Dowding has managed to lose the confidence of all the fighter pilots'.[17]

By this stage the Air Staff were becoming increasingly concerned about Dowding's handling of night fighter defence and his stubborn refusal to accede to their official suggestions on the subject, and must have been increasingly aware of the extent to which Dowding's uncooperative temperament was an obstacle to the implementation of new policy. Nevertheless it was the conduct of the daylight battle which received the main emphasis. On 17 October a meeting was held at the Air Ministry to discuss Fighter Command tactics. Leigh-Mallory brought along Douglas Bader who put forward the argument for his 'big wings' with customary forcefulness. It was of course not normal to introduce uninvited junior officers into high-level conferences, though Sholto Douglas, the Deputy Chief of Air Staff, who chaired the meeting, made no objection; Park, who could have brought along a dozen squadron-leaders as experienced as Bader, had had no idea that Leigh-Mallory intended to do anything so irregular. Sholto Douglas was, according to Park, a 'bosom friend' of Leigh-Mallory; he was in favour of the 'big wing' policy. His summing up of the discussion was to the effect that, 'The employment of a large mass of fighters had great advantages, though it was not necessarily the complete solution', but Leigh-Mallory and Bader were enabled to put their point of view on record, while Park and Dowding, for their part, did not realize that one of the objects of the meeting was simply to provide ammunition for their enemies.[18]

At the beginning of November the executive of the 1922 Committee, the influential Conservative back-bench organization, met to discuss Dowding, and Sir Reginald Clarry M.P., who chaired this gathering, wrote to Churchill:

> I was requested to represent to you the lack of confidence in which Sir Hugh Dowding is held in certain quarters of the personnel of the Force, and the grave concern felt by my Executive.

[17] John Frayn Turner *The Bader Wing* (1981) p. 56–8; Wright *Dowding and the Battle of Britain* p. 201–2; Geoffrey Keynes *The Gates of Memory* (Oxford 1981) p. 269; Leutze ed. *London Observer* p. 94, diary of Raymond E. Lee, 16 Oct. 1940.

[18] See Public Record Office AIR 6/60 no. 46, report of committee under Sir John Salmond on night defence 17 Sept. 1940; ibid. no. 50 letter (adopting committee's suggestions) from Air Council to Dowding 25 Sept. 1940, ibid. no. 59 Dowding's unhelpful response 27 Sept. 1940, and ibid. no. 66 discussion of issue by staff officers 1 Oct. 1940. Night defence was also discussed at the famous meeting of 17 Oct. 1940, cf Public Record Office AIR 2/7281/19A. The importance of the night defence issue was originally pointed out by Mr. Sebastian Cox of the Air Historical Branch of the Ministry of Defence at a paper read at the London University Institute of Historical Research on 28 Feb. 1989 and I have profited from subsequent discussions with him. For Sholto Douglas and Leigh-Mallory cf Park's letter in *Auckland Star* 4 July 1968 p. 3c and Sholto Douglas with Robert Wright *Years of Command* (1966) p. 85–6, 89–90; John Terraine *The Right of the Line: The Royal Air Force in the European War, 1939–1945* (1985) p. 217. For a good recent account of the 'big wing' controversy see Vincent Orange *Sir Keith Park* (1984) p. 120–135.

Churchill's reply was brief and to the point:

> I do not think it would be at all a good thing for the 1922 Committee to become a kind of collecting house for complaints against serving Commanders-in-Chief and other important officials.

As for Dowding, he was simply too naïve to perceive what was going on. After Harold Balfour, the Under-Secretary of State for Air, had visited Bader at his base at Duxford and produced a memo echoing his views, Dowding told Balfour:

> a good deal of ill-feeling which has been engendered in this controversy has been due to young Bader, who, whatever his other merits, suffers from an overdevelopment of the critical faculty.

Dowding was inclined to think it might be a good idea if Bader was posted out of the way. Sinclair, the Secretary of State, who knew rather more than Dowding about the developing campaign against the A.O.C.-in-C., took fright at this and phoned Dowding to instruct him not to take any disciplinary proceedings against Bader – and also to tell him that he was to give up Fighter Command 'within the next day or so'.[19] Park's removal followed soon afterwards: his replacement was none other than Leigh-Mallory. Dowding's job went to Sholto Douglas.

Dowding later said of his dismissal that it was 'as if something had to be hushed up'. One thing to be covered up may have been the conduct of Bader, but a larger issue was that though Bader and Leigh-Mallory evidently succeeded in winning over the civilian ministers Sinclair and Balfour to their view – big wings and legless war heroes were of course just the things to appeal to politicians – it could on no account be acknowledged that the Park-Dowding policy of sending fighter units into action piecemeal at the last minute was in any way wrong. The whole propagandist presentation of the Battle of Britain turned on what a miraculously close-run business it had been, and of course it couldn't have been close-run if it had been won in spite of Dowding and Park pursuing disastrously mistaken tactics. In this connection it is significant that the Air Ministry attempted to avoid giving Dowding any credit for the victory. When the Air Ministry brought out their pamphlet on

---

[19] Gilbert *Winston S. Churchill* vol. 6 p. 909 fn. 1 Clarry to Churchill 6 Nov. 1940; Public Record Office PREM 4/3/6 p. 210 Churchill to Clarry 8 Nov. 1940 (Clarry's actual letter of 6 Nov. 1940 is in this file at p. 216); Robert Jackson *Douglas Bader* (1983) p. 83–4; Vincent Orange *Sir Keith Park* p. 133; Wright *Dowding and the Battle of Britain* p. 241 and cf account p. 225–240.

The classic account of a 'conspiracy' against an undesirable and unwanted team leader is in Leon Trotsky *My Life: An Attempt at an Autobiography* (Harmondsworth 1975) p. 453–468, 509–539 – see espec. p. 534. One notes that it seems difficult to keep a note of paranoia out of such accounts: neither Dowding nor Park made much secret of their bitterness but neither wrote his memoirs; when in his eighties however Dowding, deciding that it had become 'necessary to find some way in which I could say what I wanted to say', cooperated with Robert Wright in the writing of *Dowding and the Battle of Britain* (cf p. 10 and 16).

'The Battle of Britain', *The Daily Herald* pointed out that Dowding's name was not even mentioned. Churchill wrote to Sinclair in some concern:

> Your admirable pamphlet 'The Battle of Britain' is remarkable for the fact that it avoids mentioning the name of the Commander-in-Chief in this battle. Perhaps you have noticed the scathing article in the DAILY HERALD on this about a week ago.

Churchill was not at all impressed by the Air Ministry's bland explanation. Sinclair had been his adjutant during his brief stint as a battalion commander on the Western Front in 1916, and Churchill wrote to him with the frankness of old acquaintance:

> The jealousies and cliquism which have led to the committing of this offence are a discredit to the Air Ministry, and I do not think any other Service Department would have been guilty of such a piece of work ... It grieves me very much that you should associate yourself with such behaviour.

But Sinclair seems to have been hardened to rebukes of this kind – 'The abuse and insults Winston heaped upon him were unbelievable', one Cabinet colleague later recalled – and only a few weeks later he helped block Dowding's appointment to A.O.C.-in-C. Middle East. Though still only 58, Dowding was finished as far as the Air Ministry was concerned; when he was sent to America to get him out of the way it was under Ministry of Aircraft Production auspices.[20]

Later in the war Lord Beaverbrook, claiming of Churchill that 'no man is more ruthless in getting rid of enemies or more bitter and unforgiving in his private hates', cited Dowding's removal as a proof of this. As we have seen however Churchill defended Dowding before his dismissal and demanded honourable treatment for him afterwards, and as Beaverbrook, then Minister for Aircraft Production, was in a position to know this, his accusation against Churchill may be taken as confirmation of his own shady part in the business, though he pretended to be infuriated by Dowding's removal. Beaverbrook also denounced the part played by the new Chief of Air Staff, Sir Charles Portal. Portal – in Beaverbrook's opinion 'a trade unionist' – was certainly active in preventing Dowding's reemployment. But this does not mean that he was

---

[20] Wright *Dowding and the Battle of Britain* p. 246; *Daily Herald* 28 March 1941; Public Record Office AIR 19/258/2A Churchill to Sinclair 3 April 1941; Gilbert *Winston S. Churchill* vol. 6 p. 1061, 12 April 1941 – original letter is AIR 19/258/6A; Lord Brabazon [J.C.T. Moore-Brabazon] *The Brabazon Story* (1956) p. 206: Gilbert *Winston S. Churchill* p. 1101 fn. 2. One notes incidentally that when Dowding reached America Slessor wrote to Portal from Washington urging that it was 'in the national interest' that he should be recalled: Richard Hough, Denis Richards *The Battle of Britain: The Jubilee History* (1989) p. 322. When Dowding returned to England the Ministry of Air Production was quite as anxious to get rid of Dowding as the Air Ministry had been: Public Record Office AIR 19/572/8A and 11A Lord Brabazon to Sinclair 19 and 23 May 1941. Sinclair at this point recommended Dowding to Churchill as a possible Governor of Southern Rhodesia: AIR 19/572/10A Sinclair to Churchill 22 May 1941 copy.

responsible for his sacking. In 1944 Sir Wilfrid Freeman, the Vice-Chief of Air Staff and Portal's closest confidant, asked Portal:

> Why did we get rid of Dowding, who did something, and retain a number of inefficients a little junior to him who have nothing whatsoever to their credit?

Freeman went on to suggest that the fault might be Sinclair's, but essentially his question was rhetorical; if there had been a simple and reasonable answer Freeman would have already known it; at the same time the mere fact of asking the question does suggest that it was not a matter in which Portal himself had taken any sort of lead. It often appears that the British counterpart of the German, 'I was only obeying orders', is to pretend that responsibility is located mysteriously elsewhere in the organization one belongs to, but it does seem that in this instance it really was true that the removal of Dowding and Park resulted not from the initiative of those with the nominal responsibility for directing affairs but from a consensus at a slightly lower level.[21]

In some way Dowding and Park seem to have been outsiders in the R.A.F. of 1940. Park was a colonial, and though Dowding had been educated at Winchester he was not exactly the public school type; he had then gone on to Woolwich and had been commissioned into the Royal Artillery whereas Leigh-Mallory and Sholto Douglas had gone from second-rate public schools to minor Oxbridge colleges of the type that specialize in perpetuating snobbishness. It seems difficult to believe however that thirty or so years further on in one's career these factors could have had much influence; for example there were plenty of other colonials in the R.A.F., including Arthur Harris and Arthur Coningham, who both flourished during the war. Again, both Dowding and Park – but especially Dowding – had difficult personalities, but as the career of Arthur Harris indicates being stubborn and difficult to deal with was not in itself an obstacle to a successful career as a senior R.A.F. officer. It seems that what set Park and Dowding apart was their point of view. Studies such as Peter M. Blau's *The Dynamics of Bureaucracy: A Study of Interpersonal Relations in Two Government Agencies* emphasize the relationship between conformity to a group and social acceptance but do not advance beyond the issue of 'conformity to the basic norms, which protect the most valued collective interests' to an assessment of the status of professional doctrine in what is after all essentially a political process. Nevertheless there is a good case for supposing that professional doctrine was at the bottom of the objection to Dowding and Park.[22]

---

[21] Kenneth Young ed. *The Diaries of Sir Robert Bruce Lockhart* (2 vols 1973–80) vol. 2 p. 256, 5 Sept. 1943; Arthur Christiansen *Headlines All My Life* (1961) p. 227; Richards *Portal of Hungerford* p. 221 Freeman to Portal 18 March 1944. In June 1943 Dowding reportedly blamed his dismissal on Lindemann and his influence on Churchill: William Armstrong ed. *With Malice Toward None: A War Diary by Cecil H. King* (1970) p. 223, 15 June 1943.

[22] Cf Peter M. Blau *The Dynamics of Bureaucracy: A Study of Interpersonal Relations in Two Government Agencies* (Chicago 1972 edit.) p. 199–204.

continued

Most of the senior officers of the R.A.F. had never wanted to fight the Battle of Britain. They had never wanted a strong home defence force; instead they had wanted the R.A.F. to be a massive weapon of attack. The emphasis of investment was only changed, as a result of the Inskip Report and against the wishes of the Air Staff, late in 1937. For the consensus of the R.A.F. leadership the Battle of Britain was a dead end: what was important was to go over to the offensive, and on as large a scale as possible. And it was clear that the penny-packets which had been employed so successfully by Park in the Battle of Britain would be no use in large-scale offensive operations.[23]

On taking over as A.O.C.-in-C. Fighter Command Sholto Douglas urged his Group commanders to 'get away from the purely defensive outlook'. Leigh-Mallory for one responded enthusiastically, and his conception of offensive operations is reminiscent, even in its phraseology, of Trenchard's policy of perpetual offensive in 1916–1918: 'daily "tip and run" operations ... will materially affect the morale of the German Air Force', he told his sector station C.O.s, and to Sholto Douglas he wrote:

> I feel most strongly that the 'Circus' operations should be continued at every possible opportunity, with a view to bringing the GERMAN fighters into action over NORTHERN FRANCE and gaining moral superiority over them

(A 'circus' was a raid by a small number of bombers with a very large number of accompanying fighters – the term was obviously adapted from Richthofen's 'Flying Circus' of 1917–1918.) Sholto Douglas too felt that First World War experience offered valuable lessons: commenting on one particularly costly offensive mission, he told Leigh-Mallory:

> I am certain that the main trouble is that we are going over too low. In the last war, when we had these big offensive sweeps, we always went over very high.

In fact it is clear from the reminiscences of the fighter pilots themselves that the atmosphere and feel of these operations was identical to that of the fighter battles of 1917 and 1918.[24]

---

continued
On 30 May 1943 *The Sunday Pictorial* announced 'Air Chief-Marshal Sir Hugh Dowding, the Man Who Led our Fighter Pilots in the Battle of Britain, Declares that His Boys who Died in the Glorious Epic are Living On in a Future World', and ran a two page spread on alleged communications from former Fighter Command air crew from the 'other side'. Eccentric religious opinions have never been very unusual amongst senior officers and in 1940 Dowding's belief in spiritualism could not have been widely known in any case: by 1943 he was on the retired list. See Hugh Dundas *Flying Start: A Fighter Pilot's War Years* (1988) p. 99 for 'the macabre effect on the company' of Dowding's first public revelation of his spiritualist views at a commemorative dinner at the Savoy in October 1942.

[23] Harvey B. Tress *British Strategic Bombing Policy Through 1940: Politics, Attitudes, and the Formation of a Lasting Pattern* (Lampeter 1988) p. 58–60.

[24] Basil Collier *The Defence of the United Kingdom* (1957) p. 290; Public Record Office AIR 16/366/1A preamble of circular from Leigh-Mallory to No. 11 Group sector station
continued

Operations of this kind were carried on, with heavy loss but with little effect in diverting Luftwaffe energy away from more critical fronts, till late in 1943. It is probable that they would have been initiated – though possibly not maintained so long – if Dowding and Park had remained in charge. Park had issued orders to prepare to carry out offensive sweeps by up to three squadrons on 21 October 1940, and issued a new order to the same effect on 8 December, shortly before being transferred to No. 23 Group, Training Command. Less than a week after taking over No. 11 Group Leigh-Mallory issued his own orders, much more elaborately set out and specifying 'not less than six Fighter Squadrons'. The difference was principally one of scale and emphasis: Park had clearly not been intending to remain on the defensive when there were no German attacks to be defended against. At the same time his lack of interest in large formations bore out the impression that he considered the Spitfire and Hurricane to be not particularly suitable for these kind of operations. The fact that he was correct in this opinion possibly made his doctrinal error all the more unforgiveable.[25]

Park and Dowding had, it seems, committed what in intellectual professions is regarded as the most heinously subversive of professional crimes: they had dared to go against the doctrines of their peers and what was worse, had come close to demonstrating conclusively the superiority of their independent judgement. For crimes of dogma there could be no pardon: the fact that they had won the Battle of Britain was not a mitigation but an aggravation.

IV. The Blitz

'If they declare that they will attack our cities on a large scale – we will rub their cities out!' Hitler announced on 4 September 1940, and after 7 September, though daylight raids continued for some weeks, the Luftwaffe began to shift its effort to the night bombing of London; 15 September, which saw one of the largest daylight battles and which has since been commemorated annually as Battle of Britain Day, turned out to be the Luftwaffe's last really serious attempt to engage Fighter Command. The 'Blitz' had begun. London was

continued
commanders 21 Dec. 1940; AIR 16/373/46A Leigh-Mallory to Douglas 20 Jan. 1941; AIR 16/373/74A Douglas to Leigh-Mallory 12 Feb. 1941. For the First World War atmosphere of fighter sweeps over France see Pierre Clostermann *The Big Show* (1951) p. 25–52 and J.E. Johnson *Wing Leader* (1956) p. 79–118. See also Norman Gelb ed. *Scramble: A Narrative History of the Battle of Britain* (1986) p. 218–9 for some interesting remarks by Squadron-Leader George Darley on the 'big wing' controversy in the context of later offensive practice, and ibid. p. 225 for a comment by Squadron-Leader Tom Gleave.

[25] Public Record Office AIR 16/373/1A (Park's order of 21 Oct. 1940); AIR 16/373/16A (Leigh-Mallory's order of 24 Dec, 1940).

Altogether 524 R.A.F. fighters were lost in sweeps 1941–3: 731 German aircraft were claimed destroyed: the Luftwaffe's actual loss was 103: Doug Stokes *Paddy Finucane: Fighter Ace* (1983) p. 112–3.

bombed nightly from 7 September till 13 November (with a break on 3 November) after which various provincial cities were pounded in turn, with London being attacked less frequently but with increasing intensity until the night of 10–11 May 1941. Though the most spectacular raid was that of 29–30 December, 1940, which ignited a larger conflagration than the Great Fire of London and burnt out three-quarters of the City of London, the heaviest German raids of the entire war were those of 16 and 19 April 1941, involving respectively 685 and 712 sorties against London, with many crews making double or even treble sorties during the course of both nights; on the 19 April over a thousand tons of bombs were dropped, and 1,200 people were killed; but of the total of 61 heavier raids between 19 February and 12 May 1941 only seven were directed against London: 46 were directed against provincial sea ports.[26]

The American military attaché in London, Raymond E. Lee, was undoubtedly echoing R.A.F. opinion when he noted in December 1940 that:

> The whole bombing campaign against England has been so erratic and so varied in its objectives that I cannot believe it is being directed by a trained soldier or airman.

In fact it is difficult to say who was directing the offensive. Göring and Jeschonnek, the Luftwaffe chief of staff, left France for East Prussia in November, and Milch, Göring's state secretary, and Hoffmann von Waldau, Jeschonnek's chief of operations, thereafter received orders dictated over the telephone by Christa Gormanns, Göring's nurse. Göring's return to the zone of operations in March was mainly with the object of hunting down art treasures in Paris and Amsterdam. Apart from a six-hour conference in February to discuss air support in the invasion of Russia, contact with Hitler was minimal. The precise objectives of the bombing programme seem to have received only the most cursory discussion at the higher levels. Jeschonnek, the Luftwaffe chief of staff, 'Wants free hand in attacking residential areas', to which Hitler's response was, 'As long as there is still a strategic target left we must concentrate on it . . . Bombing calculated to create mass panic must be left to the last'. After the war, Göring, the head of the Luftwaffe, spoke as if attacks on residential areas had nevertheless been given undue emphasis:

> it was always my contention that attacks on the British war industries would have been much more valuable. I argued that it was no use to us to have another hundred houses go up in flames. I wished for attacks on the aircraft plants in the South of England and around Coventry, the shipping yards, Glasgow, Birmingham and the ports . . .

On the other hand, in the wet, cloudy nights of an English winter, and flying

---

[26] Max Domarus ed. *Hitler: Reden und Proklamationen* (2 vols Munich 1965) p. 1580, 4 Sept. 1940; For the 16 and 19 April 1941 raids see Denis Richards and Hilary St. George Saunders *Royal Air Force, 1939–1945* (3 vols 1953–4) vol. 1 p. 214 and cf Collier *Defence of the United Kingdom* p. 504–5, App. XXX and T.H. O'Brien *Civil Defence* (1955) p. 416.

at over three miles' altitude, it was not possible to aim bombs very precisely at specific strategic targets. The Germans in fact used large quantities of incendiary devices and also naval mines descending on parachutes (and sometimes drifting considerably on the way down) and clearly had no objection to broadcasting the death and destruction as widely as possible: nevertheless the extent of the bomb damage (in some cases still detectable today) around the principal London railway stations and the docks indicates that they did aim *generally* in the direction of strategic targets.[27]

It is often claimed that despite the immense damage inflicted and the 40,000 civilians killed the German night Blitz failed because the Luftwaffe, essentially a tactical air force, simply was not prepared or equipped for attacks of this kind. This is not really true. Prior to 1940 strategic bombing had been a favourite doctrine at the Luftwaffe Air War College at Gatow, in the historical section of the Luftwaffe High Command (*OKL*), and amongst Luftwaffe contributors to the prestigious journal *Militärwissenschaftliche Rundschau*. This indeed explains the perhaps excessive readiness with which the Luftwaffe slipped into a would-be strategic role in the autumn of 1940. It also explains why the Luftwaffe, unlike other air forces, had invested in providing itself with the electronic navigational aids that were necessary to make a long-range strategic bombing campaign practicable. R.A.F. Bomber Command, much more exclusively trained for strategic bombing, did not have such aids in 1940 because it had been able to concentrate more on developing its crews' navigational skills – though in the event these turned out to be quite inadequate. Nor did Bomber Command in 1940 have aircraft that were better suited for night bombing than the Luftwaffe's Heinkel He 111; the first of the four-engined heavy bombers, the Short Stirling, was only just beginning to come into service in the autumn of that year. If the Blitz did not succeed in knocking Britain out of the war it was for the same reason as the much heavier, costlier and more protracted R.A.F. onslaught on Germany failed – or, according to its defenders, achieved merely a somewhat qualified success. The failure, as also in the Battle of Britain, was a function of the disparity between the objective aimed at and the practical means available. Indeed, compared to the R.A.F.'s much greater effort later, the German Blitz was remarkably effective, in spite of the Luftwaffe being the pioneer of bombing

[27] Leutze ed. *London Observer* p. 163 Raymond E. Lee diary 7 Dec. 1940; David Irving *Göring: A Biography* (1989) p. 307–318; Franz Halder *The Halder Diaries* (8 vol. typescript for limited circulation Washington 1950) vol. 4 p. 195, 14 Sept. 1940; Richards and Saunders *Royal Air Force* vol. 1 p. 209. Klaus A. Maier, Horst Rohde, Bernd Stegemann, Hans Umbreit *Die Errichtung der Hegemonie auf dem Europäischen Kontinent* (Stuttgart 1979) (vol. 2 of *Das Deutsche Reich und der Zweite Weltkrieg*) p. 394–5 shows the confusion and variety of the Luftwaffe staff's ideas concerning the objectives to be aimed at during the night offensive, and the failure to establish a clear policy: it is not quite clear who made the actual choice of targets. *The Memoirs of Field-Marshal Kesselring* (1953) p. 79 state 'The C. -in-C. Luftwaffe [i.e. Göring] kept in his own hands the direction of operations of the 2nd and 3rd Air Commands against Britain', but this seems to have been true only in a general sense.

on such a scale and thus without the R.A.F.'s subsequent advantage of being able to learn lessons from the enemy's mistakes.[28]

Before 1939 there had been the most credulous estimates of the probable detruction and dislocation to be expected from air raids. The impact of the relatively small German raids of 1917 and 1918 had not been forgotten, and the Nazis had been in power only a few months before publicists in Britain began reminding people of what probably lay ahead. Liddell Hart wrote in *The Daily Telegraph* on 7 November 1933 of terrified populations fleeing from bombed cities; T.H. Wintringham's penny pamphlet of 1934, *Air Raid Warning! Why the Royal Air Force is to be Doubled* had a couple of pages on the effects of air raids, and the same author's book *The Coming World War*, published the following year, devoted eight pages to the subject, though at this stage he was still mainly worried about gas attack. (The use of gas against a massed civilian population had been described in Stephen Southwold's novel *The Gas War of 1940*, published in 1931, and remained a preoccupation throughout that decade.) Winston Churchill spoke in the House of Commons of millions without food and shelter following air raids on London. The film *Things to Come* of 1936, written by H.G. Wells and directed by William Cameron Menzies, featured devastating air raids involving both high explosive bombs and poison gas. Air Commodore L.E.O. Charlton contributed three classic texts on the subject: *War over England*, published in 1936, *The Menace of the Clouds*, published in 1937, and Part One, 'The New Factor in Warfare', in the Penguin Special *The Air Defence of Britain*, issued in October 1938. Frank Morison's historically orientated *War on Great Cities: A Study of the Facts*, published in 1937, had a 25-page chapter entitled, 'Looking to the Future'. Further publicity was provided by the statements of politicians such as Neville Chamberlain:

> Let me say at once that we cannot too strongly condemn any declaration on the part of anybody, wherever it may be made and on whatever side it may be made, that is should be part of a deliberate policy to try to win a war by the demoralization of the civilian population through a process of bombing from the air.

Until about the time of Munich the Conservative Party discouraged speculation both about the possibility of war and about the possible nature of any future war, and it tended to be opponents of the government who campaigned to keep the issue before the public. The Labour Party set up an Air Raid Precautions Committee in 1937 with Herbert Morrison, leader of the London County Council, Ritchie Calder, J.D. Bernal and J.B.S. Haldane among its members: the last two were prominent left-wing scientists. The Munich era produced not only the Penguin special already mentioned and J.B.S. Haldane's *A.R.P.* and John Langdon-Davies's *Air Raid: The Technique of Silent Approach – High Explosive – Panic*, but also a sudden awakening of interest on the part of hitherto staider members of the professional establishment. A letter

[28] Murray *Luftwaffe* p. 1–12, 21–2.

from the historian A.G. Dickens, then a don at Oxford, published in *The Daily Telegraph* on 29 September 1938 called for the provision of adequate air-raid shelters and a break away 'from this present A.R.P. mentality compounded of gas-masks, gum-boots, vacuum cleaners and high-minded voluntary principles'. This letter stimulated not only three abusive letters addressed privately to Dr. Dickens ('Dear Bloody Mr. Dickens, I hope you will be able to get into your funk hole when the time comes') but also an editorial in *The British Medical Journal* which was followed in turn by a flood of correspondence, over thirty letters on Air Raid Precautions being published in *The British Medical Journal* over the next two months – an unusually sustained debate that was the more striking in that the issue was hardly a medical one except in the most general sense. Many of these letters called for the provision of deep shelters; thus Cyril Helm, who had won the D.S.O. and M.C. as an army doctor on the Western Front in the First World War, wrote in to say:

> I think that the issue of gas masks in remote country villages is a waste of money which should be spent on providing deep shelters for everyone in our large cities.

In January 1939 21 doctors in city centre hospitals wrote to the press stating that it would be impossible to deal with the casualties that would result from bombing unless adequate shelters were provided. Nor was it only doctors who were worried. A group of engineers, architects and surveyors set themselves up as The Air Raid Protection Institute on 11 October 1938 under the presidency of Oliver Simmonds, Conservative M.P. for Birmingham Duddeston, member of the 1922 Committee, and formerly a member of R.J. Mitchell's design team at Supermarine. The Institute published a journal, each issue carrying from six to sixteen pages of commercial advertizing relating to civil defence – itself a testimony of the interest in the general topic. Early in 1939 an Air Raid Defence League was launched, the chairman of it its 'Formation Committee' being Sir Ralph Wedgwood, a railway magnate and former President of the National Confederation of Employers' Organizations. Thus by the beginning of 1939 a wide spectrum of public opinion was beginning to face up to the prospect of a disaster of colossal magnitude.[29]

[29] Churchill's warning is in *Hansard: House of Commons* vol. 295 col. 859, 28 Nov. 1934 and Chamberlain's disclaimer is in ibid. vol. 337 col. 938, 21 June 1938. A.G. Dickens's letter (*Daily Telegraph* 29 Sept. 1938 p. 11b) and some of the subsequent press correspondence were brought together in a pamphlet entitled *A.R.P.: A Campaign for a Protective Policy, September 1938–August 1939* (printed for private circulation Walton on the Naze [1939]); I am grateful to Professor Dickens for allowing me to see his copy of this rare item and also for his reminiscence of the abusive mail he received after his original letter was published. A.R.P. of course was one of the best-known abbreviations of the 1930s: it stands for Air Raid Precautions. For *The British Medical Journal* correspondence cf *B.M.J.* 1938 vol. 2 p. 810–2, 862, 914–5, 965–6, 1015–6, 1064–5, 1114, 1175, 1227–8, 1283–5; Cyril Helm's letter is *B.M.J.* 1938 vol. 2 p. 915, 29 Oct. 1938; for the 21 city doctors' letter of *Times* 13 Jan. 1939 p. 9b. See generally Uri Bialer *The Shadow of the Bomber: The Fear of Air Attack and British Politics, 1932–1939* (1980).

That the bombing of Britain's cities would involve catastrophic dislocation and loss of life – unless countered by adequate precautions – was scarcely questioned. Both J.B.S. Haldane's *A.R.P.* and John Langdon-Davies's *Air Raid: The Technique of Silent Approach – High Explosive – Panic* emphasized the vulnerability of civilian morale but also gave figures for the casualty rate per ton of bombs dropped in air raids in the First World War and in the Spanish Civil War. Haldane estimated that in 1917–1918 837 British civilians were killed by 71 tons of German bombs – i.e. twelve victims per ton of bombs. In a series of raids on Barcelona, between 16 and 19 March 1938, during the Spanish Civil War Italian planes had come in from the sea with their engines cut, dropping 41 tons of bombs and allegedly killing 1,300 people – 32 people per ton. The death toll was soon revised down to 912 people – 22 per ton – and it was later announced in *The Journal of the Air Raid Protection Institute* that in the whole of March 1938 the death toll in Barcelona *and* Tarragona was 973 from about 173 tons of bombs – less than six dead per ton. (The final and official figures were that in the course of the Spanish Civil War 730 tons of bombs were dropped on Barcelona killing 3.5 and injuring 13.7 people per ton.) An even more frightening statistic derived from the Japanese invasion of China was never publicly revised: according to Oliver Simmonds two 500lb Chinese bombs, aimed at Japanese ships offshore but falling in what must have been an exceptionally crowded street in Shanghai's International Settlement, killed 1,660 outright and fatally injured 857. The authorities were not inclined to dispute these figures; official planning was on the basis of a figure of 50 casualties per ton of bombs established by the Air Staff in 1924 and it was estimated that 2.8 million hospital beds and 20,000,000 square feet of seasoned coffin timber per month would be required once the bombing started. In April 1939 the Ministry of Health distributed one million burial forms to local authorities.[30]

---

30 J.B.S Haldane *A.R.P.* (1938) p. 40, 285, cf Oliver Simmonds 'Civil Defence: A Protective Habit of Mind' (Presidential Address) *Journal of the Air Raid Protection Institute* vol. 1 no. 3 p. 165–177 at p. 168–9 for later revision down to six fatalities per ton of bombs and Richard M. Titmuss *Problems of Social Policy* (1950) p. 14 fn. 2 for final figure of 3.5 fatalities per ton. The Shanghai statistics are given in Simmonds's Presidential Address 'Civil Defence' *Journal of the Air Raid Protection Institute* vol. 1 no. 3 p. 169: *Times* 16 Aug. 1937 p. 10a gives only 450 dead and 850 wounded by the two bombs. The incident occurred on 14 Aug. 1937; for official British policy cf Titmuss *Problems of Social Policy* p. 21 and p. 21 fn 3.

The fatalities per ton of bombs in the First World War were relatively high as very few people were taking shelter during the early air raids and there were a number of single incidents in which a large number of people were killed by the same bomb (see p. 396). The figures reported from the Shanghai incident bear no relation to anything experienced in Europe; it is theoretically possible that two bombs about a hundred yards apart and detonating at about twenty feet above the roadway might kill everybody in a two hundred yard stretch of the street, but the Chinese did not have bombs which detonated in mid-air and in the case of a bomb exploding against the roadway the bodies of those nearest would protect those further away from fatal injury.

During the London Blitz the general rate was just over one fatality per ton of bombs: on the night of 10–11 May 1941 which saw the heaviest loss of life of any raid on Britain, 1,436

continued

Public opinion surveys showed that 70 per cent of people wanted deep shelters in February 1939 and that in May 1939 53 per cent of people disapproved of the government's decision not to build underground public bunkers. Although some pundits came forward to warn against encouraging a 'shelter mentality' – that is, they feared that if warm dry underground shelters were provided the working classes would abandon their slum dwellings, set up house in the shelters and refuse to come out to man the war factories – the main reason for not building extensive underground shelters was lack of funding and shortages of labour, of steel and of cement; the latter however was largely a figment of the statisticians' imagination. Much cheaper trench-shelters and brick surface shelters (small brick cabins with thick concrete roofs, often in somewhat exposed situations) were provided instead, and in 1940 were found to offer very poor protection, especially as, owing to a misunderstanding arising from the putative cement shortage, 5,000 of the surface shelters in the London region alone were built with a lime and sand mortar containing no cement at all, and were barely strong enough to withstand a direct hit from a free-wheeling bicycle. Their fragility was quickly noted by the people of the neighbourhood; a Ministry of Home Security report in the spring of 1941 observed that 'out of thirty cases of destroyed [surface] shelters of which we have detailed information twenty-two were wholly unoccupied' – a pencilled marginal note in the typed office copy of this report asked, 'What happened in the other 8?' but the records supply no specific answer to this inopportune question.[31]

The actual provision of air-raid shelters, and the establishment of A.R.P. organizations was the reponsibility of the municipal authorities (assisted by central government grants) and by the fifth week of the London Blitz the Foreign Secretary was writing, 'I am afraid the administration of the London County Council and some of the Boroughs has been badly exposed'. Perhaps as Ritchie Calder pointed out, 'To leave local officials to deal with the battle situation was like leaving the Mayor of Dunkirk to evacuate the British Expeditionary Force'.[32]

continued
people were killed and 1,800 people seriously injured by 711 tons of H.E. bombs, which was approximately double the normal rate. The largest number of people killed *and* injured by a single bomb in London was at Druid Street Arches, Bermondsey on 25 Oct. 1940 when 105 shelterers were killed and 75 injured by a 50kg bomb which penetrated the arch of the massive railway viaduct under which people were sheltering and exploded within a confined space which maximized the effect of the blast: this would be equivalent to 2,100 fatalities and 1,500 injuries per ton of bombs but this incident was quite exceptional.

[31] Hadley Cantril ed. *Public Opinion, 1935–1946* (New Jersey 1951) p. 9; O'Brien *Civil Defence* p. 192, 540 and cf James Lansdale Hodson *Towards the Morning* (1941) p. 170, diary 5 March 1941; O'Brien *Civil Defence* p. 191–2 and C.M. Kohan *Works and Buildings* (1952) p. 49, 168–9, 357; Kohan *Works and Buildings* p. 358 and Public Record Office HO 205/222/265/1 'Third Appreciation of Air Raids, with Special Reference to London' p. 12 of printed version, f.8 of annotated typescript.

[32] India Office Library Mss Eur. F 125/152b Viscount Halifax to Marquess of Linlithgow 12 Oct. 1940; Ritchie Calder *The Lesson of London* (1941) p. 37.

At the outbreak of war the government had divided the country into civil defence regions and when the bombing had started the Commissioners in the London Region began to hold (and make a point of attending) regular meetings with the Town Clerks of the boroughs of the region: the Town Clerk was the permanent official who headed the executive administration of each borough and in most cases was also A.R.P. Controller. The meeting held on 23 October 1941 is the earliest for which the minutes are preserved; it was apparently the 54th meeting, indicating that the first meetings had been in October 1940. This meeting of 23 October 1941 was held at what for London was a quiet period of the war: it was attended by 16 Town Clerks, though there were over 40 borough administrations in what might be called the London target zone. On 20 June 1944, after the Germans had begun bombarding London with robot bombs, 18 Town Clerks came to the meeting. The Town Clerks of Poplar, Islington and Shoreditch seem to have been regular attenders; those of Hackney, Stoke Newington, Finsbury and West Ham appear never to have attended. This seems to indicate fundamental differences of attitude in different boroughs. Poplar appears to have been an outstanding example of organization and commitment, initially under the leadership of Alderman William Key. Key had been Mayor and leader of the famous Poplar rates strike in the 1920s, and had written of this in his book *Red Poplar*, published in 1925. It is said to have been due to the preparations made under his leadership that Poplar had the lowest death toll per weight of bombs of any East End borough, and his achievement was recognized by the government in his appointment as a Regional Commissioner in January 1941. At the other extreme was West Ham, where some Labour councillors had opposed even setting up an A.R.P. Committee till it was known how much money the central government would contribute. Once West Ham's A.R.P. Committee was established, spending on civil defence preparations was stinted because it was felt that the government should cover the entire cost. When the bombing started the Mayor proved to be a notably ineffective A.R.P. controller, and when a new Mayor was appointed he was a councillor who had not previously been on either the A.R.P. or the Emergency Committee and was consequently scarcely qualified to take over an organization in the midst of a crisis. The Regional Commissioners suggested that the Town Clerk should take over as A.R.P. Controller, but the council preferred to appoint the Mayor, with the Town Clerk as his deputy. After a month this arrangement was dropped and the Deputy Town Clerk took over as A.R.P. Controller; as one of the council said:

> The Council had some right to govern its own household. This has been a matter of intrigue for the past 12 months . . . They were fighting dictators abroad and creating them at home.

After a brief trial with yet another unsuccessful A.R.P. Controller and a threat from the Regional Commissioners that they would intervene and impose direct control, West Ham finally appointed the Rev. Wilson Paton, a 39-year-old

Presbyterian minister from Glasgow whose church in the Tidal Basin had been one of the first victims of the bombing; he had been a councillor (left-wing) since 1938 and had been serving with great credit as chief shelter marshal. He was an excellent A.R.P. Controller: except that he was only appointed after the worst of the bombing was over.[33]

Both Poplar and West Ham were Labour-controlled councils. The Metropolitan Borough of Stoke Newington claimed to be one of the few local authorities run on non-party lines, though the council was in fact dominated by the United Ratepayers Party. Stoke Newington at this time was a prosperous London suburb which still preserved much of the ambience of a small country town, and, unusually for a Ratepayer regime, it had invested quite extensively in community buildings during the 1930s, including blocks of council flats, a swimming pool and a new Town Hall which had been opened by no less a personage than the Lord Mayor of London just two years before the war. Unfortunately the council proved to be more concerned with preserving this civic investment than with protecting the rate-payers. Although the Town Hall and the Public Library (an older building adjacent to the site of Edgar Allan Poe's old school) were masked by commercial buildings of similar height on the opposite side of a rather narrow street, money was wasted painting camouflage on them (this is still visible today) while half a mile away an unstrengthened cellar under a block of flats named Coronation Avenue, in Stoke Newington Road, was made to serve as a public air-raid shelter – until the evening of 13 October 1940 when a bomb (possibly only a medium-sized one of 250kg) exploded in a ground-floor premises just above the shelter and caused the party walls of the basement to collapse, killing 161 people, most of whom died, it is said, as a result of flooding and leaking domestic gas. Most of the victims are named on an economical civic memorial over the mass grave in a disused and now subsiding roadway in nearby Abney Park Cemetery, and one can see how many of the victims were couples or sisters – Aurichs and Coopersteins and Danzigers and Edelsteins, Golda Moscow and Hilda Muscovitch, the names of the diaspora brought together with the grandchildren of George Eliot's England, Hephzibah Elizabeth Towells and Walter Abraham Wilson. That some night the Town Hall was almost miraculously spared from a direct hit by two different sticks of bombs, one of which stomped its way north-westwards across the borough from Palatine Road (about 300 yards south of Coronation Avenue), wrecked the two churches in Stoke Newington Church Street, one of which is only thirty paces from the Town Hall, and ended with an unexploded bomb in the tennis

---

[33] Public Record Office HO 186/2443 for the minutes of the London Regional Commissioners' meetings with town clerks; *Stratford Express* 15 Nov. 1940 p. 8d (meeting of West Ham Council 9 Nov.), 29 Nov. 1940 p. 5d (meeting 23 Nov.) 27 Dec. 1940 p. 5a (meeting of 21 Dec.) and 2 May 1941 p. 5a (meeting of 26 April 1941), cf. E. Doreen Idle *War Over West Ham: A Study of Community Adjustment* (1943) p. 59–64. The quotation is from a speech by Alderman Hollins at the council meeting of 9 Nov. 1940 (*Stratford Express* 15 Nov. 1940 p. 8d).

court of Clissold Park; the other stick fell almost simultaneously but on a more northerly line from Cowper Road, intersected the first stick in Albion Road, and ended with another unexploded bomb directly across the street from the Town Hall itself. At the meeting of the Emergency Committee next day the Coronation Avenue incident was not mentioned (they had only just begun to bring out the bodies) but discussion about camouflaging the Town Hall was renewed; at a subsequent meeting two days later camouflaging the Town Hall came on the agenda immediately before a report on the Coronation Avenue disaster.[34]

Perhaps on balance the United Ratepayers' regime in Stoke Newington didn't do too badly. The Ministry of Home Security had had to intervene and nominate its own A.R.P. Controller in Stepney as early as 4 October 1940 – and also had to replace him ten weeks later. When Southampton was bombed

[34] *Stoke Newington: Official Guide* [1938] p. 23; London Borough of Hackney Archives Department SN/EMER/2 p. 179 (meeting of Emergency Committee held 18 Sept. 1940) p. 196 (27 Sept.) p. 217 (14 Oct.) p. 221 (16 Oct.) p. 267 (8 Nov. 1940) for discussion of camouflaging town hall – the block of council flats immediately to the rear was also to be painted but the brickwork has been completely cleaned since the war and no trace of paint is now visible. It was not only in Stoke Newington that municipal worthies sought to camouflage themselves: the Mayor of Lowestoft had twice been in trouble with the authorities because of the military camouflage he had painted on his official car: *Hansard: House of Commons* vol. 365 vol. 199 intervention by P.C. Loftus. Public Record Office HO 205/222/265/1 'Third Appreciation of Air Raids, with Special Reference to London' p. 20 of printed version gives a figure of 157 fatalities at Coronation Avenue: nine of the bodies in Abney Park Cemetery are recorded as unnamed on the monument and Imperial War Graves Commission *1939–1945: Civilian War Dead in the United Kingdom* (7 vols 1954–7) vol. 4 p. 1541 – 8 lists 152 names, indicating a total of 161. Hackney Archives Department SN/A/32 contains ten CWD forms ('Death Due to War Operations') for bodies unidentified at Coronation Avenue, specifying cause of death as falling masonry in six cases, multiple injuries (i.e. probably from the direct effect of the bomb) in three cases and drowning in one case; I have been told by local residents that others amongst the dead had died from the effect of leaking domestic gas. See also note by Andrew P. Hyde in *After the Battle: The Blitz Then and Now* (2 vols 1987–8) vol. 2 p. 181. The local tradition is that the shelter was never completely cleared of bodies because of flooding but I think this unlikely: similar rumours are to be found in other cases of major bomb disasters (cf A.D. Harvey letter 'The Night the Bomb Dropped on Girl's School . . .' *Islington Gazette* 8 April 1988). The track of two sticks of bombs which narrowly missed the Town Hall can be worked out from Hackney Archives Department SN/A/37 and checked by what is visible today; one stick destroyed 46–8 Palatine Road (rebuilt), 70–74 Brighton Road (rebuilt), 84–6 Walford Road (now an open space), 41 Nevill Road (rebuilt), 6–7 Knebworth Steet (street demolished: council flats built over site on a new ground plan) and 12 Sandbrook Road (terrace demolished: new council flats). The track of the bombs then intersected that of the other stick in Albion Road where nos. 151, 184, 186, 217 were hit; these and adjacent houses were subsequently demolished and council flats and a drill hall built on the sites. The first stick went on to straddle the churches in Stoke Newington Church Street and ended with a dud in Clissold Park. The second stick of bombs was more widely spaced. The first came down in Cowper Road, where the first Zeppelin bomb fell in 1915: this street has since been completely demolished. Three more bombs fell at 49 Londesboro Road, 44 Barbauld Road and 2–4 Kingsway – directly opposite the Town Hall – but none of these buildings show any damage; the bombs reported may have been duds; nevertheless these addresses are at appropriate intervals on a straight line running from Cowper Road to Stoke Newington Church Street through the devastation in Albion Road.

it was found that the Town Clerk (and A.R.P. Controller) was 'entirely unsuited to cope with emergencies', that the Mayor was 'a poor creature' and that the Chief Constable went sick after the second night's bombing: for a period a group of R.A.F. officers, acting without official instructions, took over the management of Southampton's civil defence and later Robert Bernays, M.P. for Bristol North and a Deputy Regional Commissioner, was appointed by the Commissioners of the Southern Region to take charge of coordinating the civil and military authorities in the city. There were also signs of incompetence at Liverpool; at Coventry, while the elected leaders of the community were said to be excellent ('although curiously enough the majority of the Council are very advanced Labour and the Chairman of the Emergency Committee, Alderman Hallwell is, or at any rate was, a Communist') the Town Clerk, in the Regional Commissioner's opinion, 'is a joke and a nonentity, and no one pays the smallest attention to him'.[35]

The inadequacies of the local authorities was exacerbated by lack of direction from central government. A reasonably thick file compiled by the Ministry of Home Security labelled 'Relationship between Central Department & Local Authorities (withholding grants etc.)' indicates concern for theoretical guidelines but contains no evidence that the Ministry ever considered tackling individual instances of the problem, prior to the onset of heavy bombing: the communications from central government with the boroughs are typified by a letter of 27 October 1939 from the Ministry of Health to the Town Clerk at Stoke Newington on the subject of the attractively designated 'Civilian Death Squads':

> one driver and two men for collecting the bodies from the streets [would] be adequate for a mortuary capable of accommodating 60 to 100 bodies . . . the Minister would not regard it as essential under existing conditions to maintain more than a skeleton staff on duty at each mortuary.

Indeed, though the establishment of a Ministry of Home Security had been projected before the war, the Ministry was in fact an off-shoot of the Home Office, with the same ministerial head, and the government department which continued to handle most of the transactions between central and local government was the Ministry of Health, which was however by no means well equipped to exercise the functions of a Ministry of the Interior in wartime. Nor was much guidance available from the War Office, which might have been supposed to have some experience of dealing with war situations, but which was unable even to organize the removal of shattered glass from its own corridors for two weeks after its windows were broken by blast. (It took still longer for the windows to be boarded up.) The Regional Commissioners,

---

[35] Public Record Office HO 186/634 illegible to Harold Butler 13 Dec. 1940; Tom Harrisson *Living through the Blitz* (1976) p. 153–4 and cf Anthony Brode *The Southampton Blitz* (Newbury 1982 edit.) p. 12–26 and HO 186/634 Harold Butler to William Lewis, Mayor of Southampton, 3 Dec. 1940; Harrisson *Living through the Blitz* p. 242–3; HO 186/634 Earl Dudley to Sir Will Spens 27 Dec. 1940.

being a new concept with no established role, were also poorly placed to provide leadership. H.U. Willink M.P., a Deputy Regional Commissioner for the London Region, told the Commons that representatives of three foreign governments had asked his office for information on how to deal with air raids – possibly the U.S., Portuguese and Swiss – but that not a single British local authority had ever asked 'for any general information on the way London attempted to deal with these problems'. It is not clear why the Ministry of Home Security or the Regional Commissioners should have expected the local authorities to have taken the initiative in this, especially bearing in mind how small and poorly qualified town hall staffs were in those days. Yet the fact is that some local authorities had taken the initiative and had been rebuffed; when the Borough Engineer of Stockton on Tees mentioned that several northern towns had sent informal delegations to London and suggested a properly organized visit under official sponsorship, the proposal was brusquely vetoed by the Ministry of Home Security.[36]

It is also worth noting that till a city was actually bombed, wartime censorship guaranteed that the city officials remained in almost complete ignorance of what was in store for their communities. The attack on London on the evening of 13 October 1940 was not a particularly heavy one: the War Office estimated about 188 planes flying at 15,000–20,000 feet. The Coronation Avenue incident, which involved the highest death toll from a single conventional bomb (in Britain at least) during the whole of the war, occured at 9.20 p.m., about 25 minutes after a direct hit on Bounds Green tube station had caused hundreds of tons of earth to cave in on a tunnel where people were sheltering, killing 25. The stick of bombs which wrecked the two churches in Stoke Newington Church Street also killed three people at 41 Nevill Road and there were other fatalities in Hackney, in Paddington, where the Metropolitan Line Station in Praed Street received a direct hit, and various other parts of the metropolitan area. Excluding the Coronation Avenue disaster, casualties in the London area were initially estimated as 163 dead and 243 injured; yet *The Times* reported on the morning of 14 October, 'In one London district two bombs damaged nine houses ... Two houses were wrecked in a square in London, and it was feared some people were trapped'. The 'square in London' possibly refers to Coronation

---

[36] The file is Public Record Office HO 186/2516; Hackney Archives Department SN/A/26 Ministry of Health to Town Clerk of Stoke Newington 27 Oct. 1939, and see also Public Record Office HLG 7/435; King's College London, Davidson Papers O diary of F.H.N. Davidson Dec. 1940–June 1941 p. 47 'Reflections after One Month at W.O.'; *Hansard: House of Commons* vol. 372 col.381 speech by H.U. Willink 12 June 1941 cf *Index to the Correspondence of the Foreign Office 1940* vol. 2 p. 33 for visit of U.S. experts, *Index to the Correspondence of the Foreign Office: 1941* vol. 1 p. 97 for Swiss visit and Public Record Office FO 371/26815/C1998 for arrival of Portuguese military mission, including Capt. Gomes Marques, head of the Lisbon Fire Brigade, 20 Feb. 1941; Public Record Office HO 205/222/265/3 letter from A.S. Knolles 24 Oct. 1940 regarding officially sponsored visits from northern cities to view A.R.P. work in London.

Avenue, which consists of long blocks of flats looking at each other across a
yard – not what one would normally regard as a London square though difficult
to describe briefly in any other phrase. The Coronation Avenue incident
was successfully concealed from the neutral press, and though the Bounds
Green incident leaked out its seriousness was minimized and the Swedish
paper *Dagens Nyhter* reported that 'the number of victims fortunately was
considerably smaller than at first feared'. Two nights later a public shelter at
Dame Alice Owen's Girls' School received a direct hit. *The Times* reported,
'A number of casualties are thought to have occurred when a school building
in a London zone was struck. Scholars and teachers left the school for another
place some time ago'. Only the next day, after another night's bombing, was
it admitted that 'a big death toll is feared'. The actual number of dead at
Dame Alice Owen's Girls' School was over one hundred: and the fact that
an even larger number had died in a public shelter at Coronation Avenue
only two days previously was not even hinted at. Though local casualty lists
could be posted up in Town Halls, 'the reproduction of these figures in the
press, either individually, or in the aggregate', was strictly forbidden, and at
the end of October one well-informed air-raid warden at Shepherd's Bush,
only seven miles to the west of Stoke Newington, could refer to the death of
fifteen people in a Shepherds Bush public house which received a direct hit
during a sing-song as 'a very horrible incident . . . one of the worst smashes
London has had'.[37]

Much of the shelter accommodation, in large commercial basements or in
the London Underground, had not actually been approved for public use by
the local authorities, and was simply taken over by the populace without
official encouragement or permission. Three of the largest community shelters

[37] Public Record Office WO 166/2106 Intelligence Report no. 14 13–14 Oct. 1940 and cf
Collier *Defence of the United Kingdom* p. 495 Appendix XXVI; Public Record Office HO
20513, Intelligence Summary No. 815, 14 Oct. 1940; *Times* 14 Oct 1940 p. 4f: almost exactly
the same details were given in the *Daily Telegraph* and *News Chronicle*, indicating that the
information was from an official hand-out; *Dagens Nyheter* 14 Oct. 1940 p. 7d–e; *Times* 16 Oct.
1940 p. 4e: this may of course be a separate incident: it is reported in greater detail in the *Daily
Telegraph*; *Times*; 17 Oct. 1940 p. 4d; Imperial War Graves Commission *1939–1945: Civilian
War Dead in the United Kingdom* vol. 3 p. 1077–1088 names 91 dead while London Borough
of Islington: Finsbury Library: Finsbury archives L.3/163 [list of incidents] shows 17 bodies
unidentified, of which one was identified later. For policy on casualty figures and localities
attacked see Public Record Office HO 199/263 Public Relations Department, Circular No. 2
late July 1940 and INF 1/845 passim cf. Xan Fielding ed. *Best of Friends: The Brenan-Partridge
Letters* (1986) p. 151 Gerald Brenan to Ralph Partridge 27 Oct. 1940.

Death tolls larger than that at Coronation Avenue are frequently reported at other incidents:
Joanna Mack and Steve Humphries *The Making of Modern London: 1939–1945: London at War*
(1985) p. 50 (photo caption) say for example that 400 died when a bomb hit a reception centre at
South Hallsville School, Agate St., West Ham on 10 Sept. 1940: *1939–1945: Civilian War Dead
in the United Kingdom* vol. 1 p. 229–268 names about seventy; Millicent Rose *The East End of
London* (Bath 1973 edit.) p.v mentions 200 dead at Columbia Market: *1939–1945: Civilian War
Dead in the United Kingdom* vol. 3 p. 973–990 names fewer than forty killed 8 Sept. 1940 when
a German bomb penetrated the cellars under the market area where people were sheltering.

in West Ham were forced by the public in this way, as was the so-called Tilbury Shelter, actually the L.M.S. Goods Depot under Commercial Road and Cable Street. The Underground was by no means as safe as generally supposed. On 14 October 64 people were killed at Balham Station by a bomb which blew a hole in Balham High Road into which an abandoned bus rolled; the bus at least was the subject of some famous photos. On 12 November 42 died at Sloane Square when a bomb wrecked the booking office and the rear of a departing train: perhaps the majority of the dead were travellers rather than shelterers. On 11 January 1941 a bomb hit Bank Station and the number of fatalities is often given as 111, but was evidently much fewer; 44 victims were eventually identified by name and the returns from the City of London mortuary at Golden Lane show only one unidentified female from Bank and a 'Collection of Human Remains from all Incidents (Pieces) Bank, Cheapside, Liverpool St.'; small bits of bone were still being handed in at the mortuary from the vicinity of Bank in June but are unlikely to represent any additional victims. The highest estimate of shelterers in the Underground was 177,000 on the night of 27 September 1940: the February 1918 peak had been 300,000. In early November it was calculated that only 9 per cent of Londoners were passing the night in official shelters, 4 per cent in the Underground, 27 per cent in household shelters. Despite the banshee ululations of the sirens and the racket, especially of the high-velocity A.A. guns, the remaining 60 per cent preferred to stay in bed or in their living-room armchairs. Public shelters and favoured underground stations were very crowded, and without adequate toilets, and the provision of household shelters was less than sufficient. By the summer of 1940 two million free Anderson shelters had been issued – corrugated iron contraptions which had to be dug into the back garden – but many had not been erected and boroughs like Hackney were exceptional in organizing teams to help with erection. Even in theory they were not popular: in the northern part of Finsbury 260 householders had refused to have Anderson shelters by the beginning of April 1940. As winter closed in the prospect of passing nights on a pit lined with galvanized iron in the garden became less attractive: 'I'm not going in that thing', vociferated the mother of playwright John Osborne, 'Catch your bloody death of cold, you will. Rather get bombed'. She was not alone in this view.[38]

---

[38] Harrisson *Living through the Blitz* p. 117–126, cf Doreen Idle *War over West Ham: A Study of Community Adjustment* p. 109; Constantine Fitzgibbon *The Blitz* (1957) gives the figure of 111 fatalities at Bank whereas O'Brien *Civil Defence* states it as only 38, but cf *1939–1945: Civilian War Dead in the United Kingdom* vol. 3 p. 867–880 and Corporation of London Records Office CDI -4 Part 4 return of Golden Lane Mortuary [n.d. ?11 Jan. 1941] and Part 3 Thomas Steggles to M.O.H. 26 June and 1 July 1941. One of the victims was the fifteen-year-old sister of a three-year-old girl killed at Columbia Market on 8 Sept. 1940; for numbers of shelterers see O'Brien *Civil Defence* p. 508, Harrisson *Living Through the Blitz* p. 112, Edwin A. Pratt *British Railways and the Great War: Organisation, Efforts, Difficulties and Achievements* (2 vols 1921) vol. 1 p. 420. Though half a dozen stations had been closed in the intervening years this had been more than made up for by the construction of new platforms
continued

Lack of comfortable shelters surely helped encourage a feeling that it was anyway ignominious to cower in a 'funk hole'. Whereas German radio stations closed down whenever R.A.F. bombers were in the vicinity – on 21 October only four German or German-controlled radio stations were not driven off the air for long periods – the B.B.C. had installed low-powered transmitters which could be switched off as raiders approached, leaving listeners to pick up more distant stations transmitting on the same wavelength: this involved only a slight loss of volume and quality and the B.B.C. never went off the air. Listeners even heard a bomb exploding in Broadcasting House while Bruce Belfrage was reading the nine o'clock news on 4 October 1940; admittedly it was a bomb which had fallen half an hour earlier and which had detonated when someone tried to roll it out of the music library, but the public, not knowing the details, felt most encouraged by this show of sang-froid.[39]

Members of the ruling class seem to have made a special point of carrying on as if nothing was happening. This was perhaps even understandable when the Boche was merely bombing the East End and the docks:

> From the roof of the Café Royal got a fine view of the blaze, the Tower Bridge being cut out like fretwork. In one corner of the foreground a large flag fluttered, making the whole thing look like one of those posters of *A Royal Divorce*, Napoleon's cavalry against a background of red ruin.

But later, as the bombing moved further west, the casualness became something of a deliberate show, a display of the proper true British grit et cetera. The Director of Military Operations, Major-General John Kennedy reported of one evening:

> While I was at dinner a bomb demolished the Carlton Club, two hundred yards away . . . Later, as we sat drinking coffee in the smoking-room, another bomb fell in Waterloo Place; a shower of bricks and broken glass fell among us, and we were covered with soot and cinders from the fireplace . . . The crash and thud of bombs, and the banging of guns, went on through most of the night, and the walls of my bedroom sometimes shook unpleasantly . . . I thought to myself that this was really too much; it was bad enough having to put up with the horrors of life at the War Office, without having the horrors of war as well.

---

continued

and the extension of old ones: I am grateful to Oliver Green of the London Transport Museum for guidance on this point. The percentages are in O'Brien *Civil Defence* p. 508; for Anderson shelters ibid. p. 368 and cf London Borough of Islington: Finsbury Library: 'Minutes of the Proceedings of the Council of the Metropolitan Borough of Finsbury for the Year ended 31 March 1941' p. 35, 9 April 1940; John Osborne *A Better Class of Person* (1981) p. 108. The dreadful conditions in the large public shelters were observed even by the Prime Minister's wife cf Mary Soames *Clementine Churchill* (1979) p. 297–8; O'Brien *Civil Defence* p. 508–9 suggests that in provincial cities people preferred to 'trek' into the surrounding countryside rather than use shelters.

[39] Asa Briggs *The History of Broadcasting in the United Kingdom* (4 vols 1961–1979) vol. 3 p. 297; Bruce Belfrage *One Man in his Time* (1951) p. 111–112 cf Stuart Hibberd *This – Is London* (1950) p. 193–4.

Sir Robert Bruce Lockhart jotted down some notes on his evening at the United Service Club on 14 October 1940, the night of the Balham Station bomb:

> During dinner one crash fairly close – all diners including generals ducked to floor – room shook – glass off chandelier – but no damage. Went into smoking room – Brooks and I by window. Before our coffee came – a whizz – again on floor – bomb just outside back window – crash – blinding smoke – I had a minor cut – but curtains saved glass – covered with grime – hair – clothes – face. One naval captain stood erect in middle of room with a glass of port – held out – never shook – asked me if hurt – then 'Thank God, that did not spill'.

Doubtless many members of the United Service Club remembered their better days, when they had been bombarded in their dug-outs at Ypres and on the Somme. The atmosphere at the Dorchester was somewhat more civilian, as Cecil Beaton recorded:

> There the noise outside is drowned with wine, music and company – and what a mixed brew we are! Cabinet ministers and their self-consciously respectable wives; hatchet-jawed, iron-grey brigadiers, calf-like airmen off duty; tarts on duty, actresses (also), *déclassé* society people, cheap musicians, and motor-car agents. It could not be more ugly and vile, and yet I have not the strength of character to remain, like Harold Acton, with a book.

A Canadian diplomat found the Dorchester 'like a luxury liner on which the remnants of London society have embarked in the midst of this storm . . . It is a fortress propped up by money-bags'. At the Savoy, close to two railway terminals, it was found more difficult to exclude the uproar outside:

> Pretty bad blitz, but not so bad as Wednesday. A couple of bombs fell very near during dinner. Wall bulged a bit and door blew in. Orchestra went on playing, no one stopped eating or drinking.

But Churchill's son-in-law, the entertainer Vic Oliver, found that the sound of bombs exploding often spoilt the effect of his jokes in the cabaret which he performed nightly at the Savoy during that winter.[40]

---

[40] James Agate *Ego 5: Again More of the Autobiography of James Agate* (1942) p. 25, 7 Sept. 1940; Kennedy *Business of War* p. 59–60; *Diaries of Sir Robert Bruce Lockhart* vol. 2 p. 80, 14 Oct. 1940; Richard Buckle ed. *Self-Portrait with Friends: The Selected Diaries of Cecil Beaton, 1926–1974* (1979) p. 76, 12 Oct. 1940; Charles Ritchie *The Siren Years: Undiplomatic Diaries (1937–1945)* (1974) p. 73 and 78, 16 Oct. and 17 Nov. 1940. Graham Payn and Sheridan Morley ed. *The Noel Coward Diaries* (1982) p. 6, 19 April 1941; Vic Oliver *Mr. Showbusiness* (1954) p. 138.

It might be noted however that Montagu Norman, Governor of the Bank of England, slept in the vaults of the Bank when he was in London.

The most prominent individuals to fall victim to the Blitz seem to have been Viscountess Charlemont, the recently divorced wife of the former Northern Ireland education minister, killed at Praed Street tube station on 13 October 1940; Lionel Hichens, once a leading member of Milner's kindergarten in South Africa, latterly chairman of Cammell Laird & Co., killed in

continued

Symbolic bravado may have seemed the more appropriate as military counter-measures against the night bombing were totally ineffective at the beginning of the Blitz and still only minimally effective after six months of regular bombardment. The British had the best anti-aircraft gun of the day, the 3.7 Mk 1, which fired a 28lb shell with a time-fuse to 41,000 feet – still well above the level at which the German bombers flew. In September 1940 an average of 20,000 rounds were expended for every German bomber shot down, but by February 1941 only 3,000 rounds, which was rather better than the German rate later in the war. But there were not really enough guns; in May 1941 there were 1,691 heavy A.A. guns for the whole country as compared to a pre-war approved scale of 2,232 and an August 1940 scale of 3,744; in July 1941 Moscow alone was defended by 796 heavy guns, and the Germans later attained much larger establishments. On 11 September 1940 there were only 207 guns in the London district, and with most of the guns stationed on the outskirts of the metropolitan area the defence of central London consisted of half-batteries of four guns each in Hyde Park and Finsbury Park and on Primrose Hill, Hampstead Heath and Clapham Common: but smallness of numbers was partly made up for by the astonishing display they made, for the noise of their firing drowned out even the giant foot-treads of the falling sticks of bombs and their elongated muzzle flashes, together with the white fingers of the searchlights, outdazzled the momentary shimmer of exploding houses.[41]

The first marks of air-borne radar were too short-ranged and attempts to carry out intruder operations over the German bases were ineffectual, as were attempts to bomb the radio installations transmitting the navigational beams along which the German raiders flew. Interfering with, or 'bending' the beams was more successful, especially in conjunction with decoy fires – by March 1941 108 decoy fire sites had been constructed. Beam-bending and decoy fires achieved a signal success on the night of 8–9 May 1941 when a raid on Derby and Nottingham completely missed Derby and caused only a small amount of damage in Nottingham, but the usual effect of these measures was merely to blunt the effect of the German attacks: for example the 12–13 March raid on Liverpool involved 500 fires and hundreds of civilian fatalities even though two-thirds of the German bombers were prevented from finding the target.[42]

continued
Great Smith Street Westminster the following night; Léon Dens, former Belgian war minister, killed at the Savoy on 16 November 1940; Lord Stamp, the most brilliant bureaucrat of his generation, and his eldest son, nominally the second Lord Stamp, killed simultaneously at home in Kent on the night of 16–17 April 1941; and the Earl of Kimberley, killed at 48 Jermyn St. Piccadilly on 17 April 1941.

[41] Ian V. Hogg *The Guns of World War II* (1976) p. 91; Richards and Saunders *Royal Air Force* vol. 1 p. 213; Collier *Defence of the United Kingdom* p. 278, cf Alexander Boyd *The Soviet Air Force since 1918* (1977) p. 128; Collier *Defence of the United Kingdom* p. 479 Appendix XXII cf Public Record Office WO 166/2106.

[42] Alfred Price *Blitz on Britain: The Bomber Attacks on the United Kingdom, 1939–1945* (1977) p. 110, 112, 114, 115, 118, 120.

Improved air-borne radar, carried in the new, heavily armed and relatively fast Bristol Beaufighter, began to achieve a certain degree of success in the late winter. In January 1941 night fighters claimed three bombers shot down to the A.A.'s twelve: in March 22 to the A.A.'s 17. With over 3,000 bomber sorties a month the Luftwaffe could not have found this very intimidating. In the end the main pressure on the Germans was the hazardousness of night-flying in winter conditions, combined with the necessity of replacing crews lost in the Battle of Britain by inexperienced personnel fresh from training:

Luftwaffe Bomber Losses 1940

	May–June 1940	October–November–December 1940
Total bombers lost	521	384
By enemy action	84%	36%[43]
By accident on ops	10%	50%
By accident not on ops	6%	13%

V. The Empire Strikes Back

While the Luftwaffe was pounding Britain, the R.A.F. was bombing Germany and, to a much lesser extent, Italy. If this counter-Blitz was less dramatically horrific than the German bombing of Britain it was partly because of the differences in the distances involved: London was about 200 kilometres from the Luftwaffe bases in occupied France whereas Berlin was 900 kilometres from R.A.F. Bomber Command's bases in East Anglia, and this of course involved big differences in bombload, flying time, and strain on air-crew. Then of course Bomber Command was relatively small and still concentrating on a programmed build-up of strength, so that while the largest German raid of November 1940, that against Coventry, involved 449 bombers, the R.A.F.'s largest effort, against Hamburg, involved only 131. Moreover, having mistakenly placed its faith in its high standards of pre-war navigational training, the R.A.F. permitted itself to be amused by the Luftwaffe's reliance on electronic navigational aids, with the result that Bomber Command crews generally failed to identify their targets correctly in the dark; the first R.A.F. attack on Berlin, carried out by 81 aircraft on the night of 25–26 August, succeeded in damaging no more in the Berlin area than a single suburban summer house.[44]

[43] Richards and Saunders *Royal Air Force* vol. 1 p. 214–5; Murray *Luftwaffe* p. 44 Table III and p. 60 Table XI.

[44] John Terraine *The Right of the Line: The Royal Air Force in the European War, 1939–1945* (1985) p. 268 says 131 bombers: Martin Middlebrook and Chris Everitt *The Bomber Command War Diaries: An Operational Reference Book* (Harmondsworth 1985) p. 104 gives 130 bombers and state fatalities inflicted on the German population as two; for the first Berlin raid see Middlebrook and Everitt *Bomber Command War Diaries* p. 77.

A good deal was made of these early raids. In a broadcast on 11 September 1940, Churchill referred to Hitler and the first raids on London, and told the nation, 'He has lighted a fire which will burn with a steady and consuming flame until the last vestiges of Nazi tyranny have been burnt out of Europe', and it is clear that a large part of the British public wanted to hear about Germany burning. Only later was it possible to bring back film of the astonishing abstract art effect of night bombing seen from above, with the brilliant splashes of the bombs exploding against the dark ground and the squiggle of searchlights, like a picture by Jackson Pollock; to begin with the public had to make do with B.B.C. radio broadcasts of air crew describing what they had done and seen over Germany's cities. 'A Flying Officer in a Heavy Bomber Squadron' recounted in September 1940 how, 'About a quarter of an hour after we had left, we could still see the reflection of the fire in the sky, and about this time we made out another terrific explosion'. 'A Pilot Officer of a Heavy Bomber Squadron' described how, 'coming back, the rear gunner said he could see fire reflected in the sky forty to fifty miles away'. 'A Sergeant Pilot' recalled, 'The tail-gunner was reporting every little while and he was still reporting the fire when we were a hundred miles on our way home'. Another Sergeant Pilot, in January 1941, told B.B.C. listeners:

> When we were still about sixty miles away we could see a red glow in the sky, and thirty or forty miles off we could actually see flames rising above Bremen . . . When [after dropping the bombs] we were about ten miles away I turned to give the crew a look back over Bremen. The whole place seemed ablaze. Then when we were about a hundred miles away I turned again and even from that distance I could still pick out a red glow in the sky from the direction of Bremen.[45]

In *The Times* the R.A.F.'s raids on Germany were reported alongside the reports of the Luftwaffe's attacks on Britain, with headlines of similar size but with much more detail, most of it (as one now realizes) wishful thinking. In reality the first attack on Germany to achieve anything resembling the scale and effect of Luftwaffe raids was one on Kiel on two successive nights in April 1941, 229 bombers being sent out on 7–8 April and 160 bombers on the night following. Two hundred and thirteen people were killed, 484 injured, the town's electricity failed, and Goebbels noted, 'Inhabitants' morale very depressed. Particularly the women. Come evening, thousands head for the woods surrounding the city'. But it was almost a year before the R.A.F. contrived another such result.[46]

Even at this stage, though it ought to have been clear that the R.A.F. was not achieving very much, it was not even clear what it was that it was trying

[45] Robert Rhode James ed. *Winston S. Churchill: His Complete Speeches, 1897–1963* (8 vols New York 1974) p. 6277; 'E.B.B.' ed. *Winged Words* (1941) p. 100–101, 106, 161, 230–231. See also Public Record Office INF 1/64 memo by J.H. Brebner headed 'News Division' winter 1940–41.

[46] Fred Taylor ed. *The Goebbels Diaries 1939–1941* (1982) p. 319, 17 April 1941.

to achieve. Although no clear policy on the objectives of strategic bombing had been evolved during the First World War the experience of that war had indicated the vulnerability of civilian morale and this aspect was generally emphasized by, for example, airmen who wrote articles on air war in the *Journal of the United Service Institution* in the 1920s. An Air Staff paper of October 1925 which anticipated 8,750 casualties on the first 48 hours of massed attacks on London (presumably, at that point, by the French) and 2,500 casualties daily thereafter nevertheless emphasized that the 'moral effect' would be 'out of all proportion greater than the material results achieved' and went on to state:

> While ... serious material damage may be expected from bomb attack, the most probable cause of chaos in the community will be the *moral* collapse of the personnel employed in the working of the vital public services, such as transport, lighting, water and food distribution.

It had however already been decided that:

> the French in a bombing duel would probably squeal before we did ... The nation that would stand being bombed longest would win in the end.

This remained essentially the policy in 1940, except that the Germans had been substituted for the French – the fact that this substitution involved new complications of distance and urban geography seems barely to have been noticed. The only significant updating of R.A.F. doctrine prior to the outbreak of the Second World War was the decision in the mid-1930s to concentrate on building very heavy, very long-distance aircraft instead of the lighter bombing machines previously thought adequate; it was not till the summer of 1940 that the R.A.F. abandoned the assumption that most of its bombers would operate by daylight, and it was something like two years before all the practical implications of this change of policy were absorbed.[47]

The fall of France was a godsend to those who put their faith in strategic bombing; except against Italy in Africa there simply wasn't an Army front any more, consequently no problem about having to integrate bombing attacks tactically with the operations of the Army. Moreover Churchill, and enthusiast

---

[47] Barry D. Powers *Strategy without Slide Rule: British Air Strategy, 1914–1939* (1976) p. 192–8; Webster and Frankland *Strategic Air Offensive against Germany* vol. 1 p. 63; ibid. vol. 4 p. 62–70 App. 1, minutes of Air Staff Conference 19 July 1923; ibid. vol. 1 p. 72 fn. 1. See also H. Montgomery Hyde *British Air Policy between the Wars, 1918–1939* (1976) p. 409–413 and Malcolm Brown *British Air Strategy between the Wars* (Oxford 1984) p. 180–197. Public Record Office AIR 14/1930 memo Robert Saundby as ACAS(T), 'Note on Future Bombing Policy' 9 May 1940 and Portal to Sholto Douglas 19 May 1940 show continued interest in daylight bombing and a desire to believe that the heavy losses inflicted on R.A.F. formations attacking Germany naval bases in December 1939 would not be typical of a more sustained campaign: the experience of the Battles of France and Britain, and Bomber Command's continuing dependence on the slow Armstrong Whitworth Whitley heavy bomber, forced a surreptitious change of mind by the time the bomber offensive against Germany began to get under way.

for the air weapon since the early days, quickly identified the bomber as Britain's principal war-winning arm:

Should he [Hitler] be repulsed here or not try invasion, he will recoil eastward, and we have nothing to stop him. But there is one thing that will bring him back and bring him down and that is an absolutely devastating exterminating attack by very heavy bombers from this country upon the Nazi homeland. We must be able to overwhelm him by this means, without which I do not see a way through.

Thus Churchill a couple of weeks after the surrender of France. Two months later he amplified his ideas:

The Navy can lose us the war, but only the Air Force can win it. Therefore our supreme effort must be to gain overwhelming mastery in the air. The Fighters are our salvation, but the Bombers alone provide the means to victory. We must therefore develop the power to carry an ever-increasing volume of explosives to Germany, so as to pulverise the entire industry and scientific structure on which the war effort and economic life of the enemy depend, while holding him at arm's length from our island. In no other way at present viable can we hope to overcome the immense military power of Germany.[48]

The Air Staff were not adverse to thinking on this kind of large scale, and had its own prose stylists to press the point:

We must first destroy the foundations upon which the war machine rests – the economy which feeds it, the morale which sustains it, the supplies which nourish it and the hopes of victory which inspire it. Then only shall we be able to return to the continent . . . It is in bombing, on a scale undreamt of in the last war, that we find the new weapon on which we must principally depend for the destruction of German economic life and morale.

But of course the R.A.F.'s operational directives needed to be rather more specific than this. As early as May 1940 oil supply had been identified as a particular weakness of the German economy and the directive of 21 September 1940 decribed attacks on German oil installations as 'the basis of our longer term offensive strategy'. By the time of the 15 January 1941 directive the destruction of seventeen specific synthetic oil plants had become the 'sole primary aim' of Bomber Command. In retrospect the formulation of these directives seems to have been largely an academic exercise. The carrying out of Air Staff directives was naturally subject to operational circumstances which in practice gave the A.O.C.-in-C. wide latitude to do what he liked. For example Sir Charles Portal, the A.O.C.-in-C. Bomber Command during the Battle of Britain, thought air raids should be aimed at 'the will of the German people to continue the war', and though raids on Luftwaffe bomber bases were suggested in the directive of 4 July 1940 and were given equal top priority with attacks on

---

[48] Winston S. Churchill *The Second World War* (6 vols 1948–1954) vol. 2 p. 567 Churchill to Beaverbrook 8 July 1940; ibid. vol. 2 p. 405–6 memo by Churchill 3 Sept. 1940.

barge and shipping concentrations in the invasion ports in the directive of 13 July 1940, the bombing of aerodromes was carried out only on a minor scale in spite of the contribution such attacks might have made to weakening the Luftwaffe in the Battle of Britain.[49]

Before the war Churchill had spoken eloquently of the uselessness as well as the immorality of bombing cities rather than 'aerodromes and air bases and factories and arsenals and dockyards and railway focal points' and other targets of immediate military relevance:

> this horrible, senseless, brutal method of warfare, which we are told is the first great military step that would be taken, the killing of women and children, would not be comparable, as a military measure, with an attack upon the technical centres and air bases of an enemy power.

The experience of the Blitz on Britain's cities seemed to confirm this. Even Hitler considered that the Luftwaffe had achieved its most useful effect in its attacks on British shipping and armaments factories:

> The least effect of all (as far as we can see) has been made upon the morale and will to resist of the English people . . . No decisive success can be expected from terror attacks on residential areas.

By September 1941 Churchill was urging a similar opinion on the Chief of Air Staff:

> It is very disputable whether bombing by itself will be a decisive factor in the present war. On the contrary, all that we have learnt since the war began shows that its effects, both physical and moral, are greatly exaggerated. There is no doubt the British people have been stimulated and strengthened by the attack made upon them so far.[50]

The R.A.F. took the view however that even if it was merely a question of paying the Germans back for what they had done to Britain's cities, this would be a significant contribution to the war. At the beginning of the war R.A.F. bombers dropped leaflets warning the German population, 'Remember Britain never gives way. Her nerves are tougher, her sinews of war stronger than yours', and in 1941 the Chief of Air Staff assured Churchill that 'the consensus of informed opinion is that German morale is much more vulnerable to bombing than our own'. After the war Sir Arthur Harris, A.O.C.-in-C. Bomber Command from 1942, wrote, 'there were special circumstances which led us to believe that production would not recover so quickly [after

---

[49] Webster and Frankland *Strategic Air Offensive against Germany* vol. 1 p. 180–181 Chiefs of Staff memo 31 July 1941; ibid. vol. 1 p. 146, 153, full text vol. 4 p. 126; ibid. vol. 1 p. 154, full text vol. 4 p. 132; ibid. vol. 1 p. 154; ibid. vol. 4 p. 118, 120–121.

[50] *Hansard: House of Commons* vol. 275 col. 1825, speech by Churchill 14 March 1933; H.R. Trevor-Roper ed. *Hitler's War Directives, 1939–1945* (1964) p. 56–57, no. 23, 6 Feb. 1941; Webster and Frankland *Strategic Air Offensive against Germany* vol. 1 p. 182 Churchill to Portal 27 Sept. 1941.

bombing] in Germany as in England'. These special circumstances may have included lack of emergency food reserves and of surplus transportation and building labour, but seem mainly to have been totally unjustified assumptions about the nature of German society under the Nazis. On the German side Jeschonnek, the Luftwaffe chief of staff, assured Göring, 'British morale is more brittle than our own', but only very occasionally was it hinted in London that Germany might be a *less* rather than *more* vulnerable target than Britain:

> Germany industrial areas might be less vulnerable than ours, both because of better fire precautions and better structure. On the other hand, our much heavier scale of attack may more than counterbalance these factors.

But Harris was able to dodge this issue because, unlike some of Churchill's other advisers, he had never regarded either morale or the physical structure of German factories *as such* as his principal target. What Harris was aiming at was something both less tangible and more pervasive: and perhaps more easily harmed.[51]

The Air Staff memo of October 1925 which has already been quoted had claimed that 'the most probable cause of chaos in the community will be the *moral* collapse of the personnel employed in the working of the vital public services'. Just as the emphasis in this memo on the 'moral effects' which were out of all proportion to physical effects seems derived from internal R.F.C. propaganda concerning ground-support operations, *circa* 1916, so the idea of the particular vulnerability of the public services of a large city seems to have been adapted from J.F.C. Fuller's 'shot through the brain' in his 'Plan 1919'; but the specific antecedents of the idea of paralysing a city by disrupting its public services is not especially important, for it did not immediately become part of R.A.F. doctrine and does not seem to have played any part in Bomber Command thinking in 1940 and 1941. Only after Harris took over as A.O.C.-in-C. Bomber Command in the spring of 1942 was this concept revived: not however in order to justify a new tactical departure, but rather in order to explain the continuance of a policy which already seemed to be failing.[52]

According to his memoirs, Harris's choice of target was not the enemy's factories or the people who worked in them but the infrastructure of the communities in which the factories were located and in which the factory workers lived, shopped and commuted to their jobs. In Coventry, Harris later claimed,

[51] Norman Longmate *The Bombers: The R.A.F. Offensive against Germany, 1939–1945* (1983) p. 75; Webster and Frankland *Strategic Air Offensive against Germany* vol. 1 p. 183 minute by Portal 21 Oct. 1941; Arthur Harris *Bomber Offensive* (1947) p. 87; David Irving *Göring: A Biography* (1989) p. 296; Public Record Office HO 199/453, Air Ministry commentary dated 5 May 1942 on Ministry of Home Security Report on Effects of Air Raids 8 April 1942.

[52] Webster and Frankland *Strategic Air Offensive against Germany* vol. 1 p. 63 Air Staff paper of Oct. 1925 and see p. 384, 406.

loss of production was almost entirely due to the interruption of public utilities, the dislocation of transport, and the absenteeism caused by the destruction of houses ... there was very heavy damage, for example, to sewers, water supply pipes, electric cables, gas pipes and so forth, and this had an immediate effect on production.

This analysis was dressed up with the pretence of statistical rigour which was such a feature of the R.A.F.'s war-making style: 'a definite correlation was found between acreage of concentrated devastation and loss of man hours; the one was a function of the other'.[53]

It seems however that these conclusions, and the murderous policy which emerged from them, were not the result of careful expert analysis. Harris's theory involved assumptions about geography, town-planning and micro-economics, and experts in these fields were not consulted. The expert economic advice provided by the Ministry of Economic Warfare, with the backing of the Air Staff, was dismissed by Harris with impatience: the production bottle necks drawn to his attention, and sometimes given high priority in official directives, were regarded by him as 'panacea targets'. As it happened the expert advice was frequently misinformed and misconceived. The Ministry of Economic Warfare consistently underestimated German reserves of raw materials and of manufactured stocks except in the crucial area of petroleum products, and the material supplied to the Air Ministry by the Ministry of Home Security was often extraordinarily fatuous. A Ministry of Home Security proposal for a 'Social and Economic Study of the Effects of Air Raids on Towns' was eagerly taken up by the Air Ministry: it was based on one factory in Birmingham and on the transportation network in Hull and must be considered as possessing minimal scientific value. Derby was included at a late stage as a kind of control, being 'a town which has not suffered heavy raiding' and was monitored by checking 'the number of National Health Insurance prescriptions dispensed between January 1938 and December 1941'. Another Ministry of Home Security scheme for measuring the impact of bombing was to persuade Local Education Authorities to instruct their school teachers to set school essays on the subject of local air raids; it was later noted:

We have received some thousands of school children's essays and they seem to be of the utmost value ... Zuckerman & Co. are trying to devise a means of extracting statistical information out of them.[54]

'Zuckerman & Co.' refers to the team led by Solly Zuckerman of the Department of Human Anatomy, Oxford University, who at a later stage of the war was on the staff of the Combined Strategic Targets Committee and concluded,

[53] Harris *Bomber Offensive* p. 87.
[54] For M.E.W. underestimates see p. 541–2, 701; Public Record Office HO 199/453 R.E. Stradling, Chief Scientific Adviser, Ministry of Home Security, draft proposal 29 Sept. 1941 and A. Street to Harold Scott 11 Oct. 1941; ibid. Harold Scott to Sir John Maude 5 Feb. 1942; ibid. R.E. Stradling to Harold Scott 27 Feb. 1942.

far from having brought scientific method to bear on the selection of targets, they had obstructed it, and so prolonged the agony of war, both for the victors and for the defeated.

Harris himself did not allow any committee to interfere with his personal selection of targets, but to a large extent he operated behind a smoke-screen of spurious scientific expertise. Military aviation had taken over from the artillery as the most scientifically – or at least mathematically – orientated branch of the fighting services; even navigating an aeroplane was a question of complex computation, and the pilot had to watch more gauges and dials than a marine engineer. This aspect of air warfare encouraged R.A.F. officers to look upon themselves as scientists: 'I had been trained to think objectively about power; I had to think of the military effect of destruction of economic resources by bombings', wrote one of them. Their delusions of scientific rigour were reinforced by an influx of academic physicists and mathematicians into Whitehall. Even before the war civilian and service personnel at the Air Ministry had already manifested 'considerable development of skill in making wishful thinking plausible, giving it legal or learned form, and making it forcefully persuasive'. The statistical methods promoted by Lord Cherwell and other roving empirics from academe assisted this process, for statistics gave 'those who employ these techniques a sense of dealing in "hard facts"'. Critics of 'the new Cherwell non quantitive statistics', including Cherwell's professional rival Sir Henry Tizard, found themselves unpopular in Whitehall. C.P. Snow recalled:

> The atmosphere was more hysterical than is usual in English official life; it had the faint but just perceptible smell of a witch hunt. Tizard was actually called a defeatist.

Yet though Cherwell was all in favour of massed air raids aimed at destroying the housing in German industrial areas, it was not his arguments which influenced Harris, for Harris was not interested in other people's arguments; the main practical effect of the memos Cherwell produced on 'dehousing' Germany, was to provide a political climate in which Harris could pursue his own fantasies.[55]

It is possible indeed that, despite a considerable amount of unpublicized

---

[55] Solly Zuckerman *Apes to Warlords* (1978) p. 356; Victor Goddard *Skies to Dunkirk: A Personal Memoir* (1982) p. 196. The quotations referring to 'skill in making wishful thinking plausible' and a 'sense of dealing in "hard facts"' are from Alexander H. Leighton *Human Relations in a Changing World: Observations on the Use of the Social Sciences* (New York 1949) p. 153, 142: this book was clearly written with wartime experience in mind. For Cherwell and Tizard see C.P. Snow *Science and Government* (Cambridge Mass. 1961) p. 50.

A comparable example of an institutional group rallying in defence of an arguably untenable position, complete with discreet victimization of dissidents, is the attempt by the U.S. Army and Navy staffs to conceal the degree to which Washington had advanced warning of the Pearl Harbor attack: Kimmel and Short, the commanders at Pearl Harbor, were it seems, sacrificed to preserve the reputation of Roosevelt and Marshall, cf John Toland *Infamy: Pearl Harbor and its Aftermath* (1982) espec. p. 106 fn 118–9, 321–4.

controversy in Whitehall during the time the bombing of Germany was actually in progress, Harris's ideas on the subject were less clearly in focus than they became after the war when he sat down to write his memoirs. The notion of attacking the service infrastructure of German cities is emphasized in his memoirs but difficult to trace in his wartime pronouncements. The orders issued from Harris's H.Q., for example, state the objectives of particular raids to be 'To cause maximum destruction in an industrial area' or 'To destroy a railway junction' or 'To cause the maximum damage to an industrial centre', or 'To destroy an engineering factory'. Occasionally the language is varied: that of 10 May 1942 states the objective as being 'To ravage an industrial centre'; and one may detect a certain relish in the order for the first Thousand Bomber raid: 'Object: To destroy the City of Cologne'. In October 1943 Harris urged the Air Ministry to make clear to the public that the bomber offensive aimed at 'the destruction of German cities, the killing of German workers and the disruption of civilised community life throughout Germany', and in December 1943 he tartly reminded his superiors that, 'The German economic system, which I am instructed by my directive to destroy, *includes* workers, houses, and public utilities'. The particular importance of the utilities is only occasionally hinted at; the emphasis seems different from his post-war apologia, and the reason for this is clearly that he did not have to pretend till after the war that his methods were the most humane and economical available. Nevertheless the implication is that he was not entirely clear what he was trying to do at the time, however much clarity he obtained in retrospect.[56]

Whatever the rationale of the bombing offensive, it was difficult to square with Chamberlain's undertaking at the beginning of the war that:

> Whatever be the lengths to which others may go, His Majesty's Government will never resort to the deliberate attack on women and children, and other civilians for purposes of mere terrorism.

This remained the official public policy: a 'Squadron Bombing Leader' told B.B.C. listeners in September 1940 of the difficulties of pin-pointing targets accurately:

> For an hour and a half we flew around trying to make sure. Of course we could have unloaded on Berlin at any time we liked: but – as you know – we don't do indiscriminate bombings.

---

[56] Public Record Office AIR 25/116 includes teletyped orders from Bomber Command H.Q. to No. 5 Group, those quoted being dated 15 April 1942, 30 April 1942, 3 May 1942, 4 May 1942, 10 May 1942 – the use of the word 'ravage' is typical of Harris. The order for the Cologne raid is missing but the report on the raid begins with the order; Ian McLaine *Ministry of Morale: Home Front Morale and the Ministry of Information in World War II* (1979) p. 161–2 quoting Harris to Air Ministry 25 Oct. and 23 Dec, 1943.

German civilian morale was emphasized by Cherwell and by Smuts, another staunch advocate of the offensive (cf J.C. Smuts *Jan Christian Smuts* (1952) p. 437) and there is no doubt that they *thought* this was the objective of the offensive: but this does not necessarily mean that that was Harris's view.

A Ministry of Information pamphlet of 1943, announced in capitals BRITAIN CONTINUED TO SET HER FACE AGAINST TERROR BOMBING. At this stage, with the bomber offensive now in full swing, Harris was by no means happy with official propaganda that suggested that the total obliteration of German cities was *not* the object of the raids carried out on his orders; he complained in a letter to the Air Ministry that his air crew 'had begun to think that they were being asked to do something of which the Air Ministry was ashamed'. The Air Ministry, anxious to place on record an acceptable view of its policy, prepared several drafts of its response to Harris: one draft stated:

> It is nevertheless a point of far reaching public importance, since it is vital that the aims of the bomber offensive should be presented in a way which will avoid so far as is possible the creation of a violent controversy in a matter so closely allied to the military effort of the United Nations.

A later draft argued:

> It is, in any event, desirable to present the bomber offensive in such a light as to provoke the minimum of public controversy, and so far as possible to avoid causing offence to religious and humanitarian opinion. Any public protest, whether reasonable or unreasonable, against the bomber offensive could not but hamper the Government in the execution of their policy and might affect the morale of the aircrews themselves.

This, with 'offence to religious and humanitarian opinion' toned down to 'conflict with religious and humanitarian opinion' was the version finally adopted. But Harris did not give up, and eventually the Air Ministry had to inform him that their directives did not 'mean that the destruction of cities *as such* must be your objective'. They advised him:

> The destruction of German city which does not contain any military installations or any war production or organisation potential would not fall within the terms of your directive . . . while in the case of cities making a substantial contribution to the German war effort, the practical effects of your Command's policy cannot be distinguished from those which would accrue from a policy of attacking cities as such, the [Air] Council cannot agree that it is impossible to draw a clear distinction between these two policies. This distinction is in fact one of great importance in the presentation to the public of the aim and achievements of the bomber offensive.[57]

In 1941 a group of Quakers had established a Bombing Restriction Committee, which early in 1943 issued a pamphlet captioned, 'Stop Bombing Civilians'. A later pamphlet written for the committee by Vera Brittain, entitled *Seed of Chaos: What Mass Bombing Really Means*, cited evidence of

[57] *Hansard: House of Commons* vol. 351 col. 750 reply by Chamberlain 14 Sept. 1939; 'E.B.B.' ed. *Winged Words* p. 96; McLaine *Ministry of Morale* p. 161 cf Public Record Office AIR 2/7852 Harris to Air Ministry 25 Oct. 1943 and Portal's memo of 28 Oct. 1943; AIR 2/7852/12A, 19A and 21A (15 Dec. 1943) for successive drafts; AIR 2/7852/29A, A. Street to Harris 2 March 1944.

at least intermittent public criticism of the policy. Even *The Times* published a letter from Brigadier-General C.F. Aspinall-Oglander, official historian of the Gallipoli campaign, regretting 'that our official broadcasts, when reporting these acts of just retribution, should exult at and gloat over the sufferings which our raids necessitate . . . Let us at least preserve the decencies of English taste'. Richard Stokes, M.P. for Ipswich, warned the House of Commons, 'there is an ever-growing volume of opinion in this country which considers the indiscriminate bombing of civilian centres both morally wrong and strategic lunacy'. The Bishop of Chichester also publicly denounced the bomber offensive, notably in the House of Lords on 9 February 1944 when he was supported by Cosmo Lang, the former Archbishop of Canterbury. Churchill himself was by no means altogether happy with the offensive; one evening at Chequers in June 1943, while watching film of recent air raids on Germany he 'suddenly sat bolt upright and exclaimed, "Are we beasts? Are we taking this too far?"' It does not seem, however, despite the pretended fears of Harris and the Air Staff, that the men of the Bomber Command were especially worried about the moral issue. At the staff level, officers were so immersed in the technical minutia of the offensive and in writing memos likely to be acceptable to their seniors that they were scarcely able to take an objective over-view of the general policy of the bombing offensive, and Freeman Dyson, who worked in Bomber Command's Operational Research section and who afterwards became Professor of Physics at Princeton University's Institute of Advanced Studies, later wrote, 'Bomber Command might have been invented by some mad sociologist as an example to exhibit as clearly as possible the evil aspects of science and technology'. The aircrew who actually made – and saw – the German cities burn had even more immediate preoccupations such as staying alive in the face of progressively more effective German counter measures:

> Six miles from earth, loosed from its dream of life
> I woke to black flak and the nightmare fighters.
> When I died they washed me out of the turret with a hose.

The awesome scale of the bombing attacks seemed in any case to dwarf any merely human dimension:

> The nethermost pit of hell itself could scarcely have appeared more frightful. The over-all spectacle was virtually indescribable, the product of bursting shells, a vast enclave billowing fire and smoke below, searchlights groping in slow frenzy, their beams rendered anaemic by the glare of hundreds of flares slowly descending on their parachutes – with additional rows of fresh ones being seeded far above . . . vicious shock waves from the high explosive raining down rippled and tore across the heart of the city creating an effect like bursting bubbles in boiling porridge, and the thousands of spreading smaller fires began merging into giant unquenchable conflagrations.

One bomb-aimer noted in his diary after his first bombing mission to Germany that he had experienced a 'faint niggling at the back of my mind' about civilian casualties, but five weeks later, after a second attack on the same target, he recorded, 'No faint niggling this time; didn't even give it a thought'. The public at large, which in spite of the Air Ministry's and the Ministry of Information's campaign of misinformation had a pretty accurate idea of what was going on, was also largely indifferent. In October 1940 an opinion poll found that 46 per cent of people opposed retaliatory bombing and the same percentage favoured it; by April 1941, after most of the larger centres of Britain had been bombed, 55 per cent favoured retaliatory bombing and only 36 per cent disagreed with it. In December 1943, during the so-called Battle of Berlin, another poll found 40 per cent of people thought the bombing of Germany was important for its effect in upsetting German civilian morale. The woman who told her air-gunner husband that 'the sight of me makes her sick because I have murdered innocent people' was sternly rebuked by *Woman's Own. The Sunday Dispatch* undoubtedly spoke for most of its readers when it announced:

> Bomber personnel, often in miserable weather, and under attack by vicious fighters, try to hit their targets. Any attempt to persuade them to worry unduly about civilians is an attempt to impair their military value.

Such views were not likely to be altered by the realization that the targets involved comprised the entire central areas of the cities under attack. In the United States the critic Edmund Wilson noted, 'We are bombing Berlin to cinders, but nobody talks about it. We meet it mainly with a mixture of competitive satisfaction and a mental evasion of the matter'. The documentary film *Target Germany*, released in 1945, 'in sixteen languages for the liberated people of Europe', in its final horrific sequence of panning shots over the devastated cities of the Reich concentrated as much on bombed-out houses and apartment blocks as on wrecked factories: there seem to have been no protests.[58]

[58] Jean C. Greaves *Corder Catchpool* (1953) p. 37; Vera Brittain *Seed of Chaos: What Mass Bombing Really Means* (1944) p. 97–101: for the Bishop of Chichester see Andrew Chandler 'The Church of England and the Obliteration Bombing of Germany in the Second World War' *English Historical Review* vol. 108 (1993) p. 920–946; *Times* 1 May 1942 p. 5e; *Hansard: House of Commons* vol. 389 col. 1731 R. Stokes, 27 May 1943, question time. Lord Casey *Personal Experience, 1939–1946* (1962) p. 166; Freeman Dyson *Disturbing the Universe* (1981) p. 29 and cf the discussion of 'Technological Fanaticism' in Michael S. Sherry *The Rise of American Air Power: The Creation of Armageddon* (New Haven 1987) p. 226–236, 251–5; Randall Jarrell 'The Death of the Ball Turret Gunner' – this was the U.S.A.A.F. rather than the R.A.F. version, of course – though n.b. Jarrell's war service consisted of being a member of the ground staff at a training base in Arizona, and he never went overseas; Murray Peden *A Thousand Shall Fall* (1981) p. 251, 264; Campbell Muirhead *The Diary of a Bomb Aimer* (Tunbridge Wells 1987) p.38. 13 June 1944 and p. 96, 19 July 1944 – the city in question was Gelsenkirchen; Hadley Cantril ed. *Public Opinion, 1935–1946* p. 1067; *Women's Own* 12 Feb. 1943 p. 22c (Leonora Eyle's 'Life and You' column); *Sunday Dispatch* 21 March 1943, front page article by J.D.S. Alan and cf McLaine *Ministry of Morale* p. 163; Edmund Wilson *The Forties: From Notebooks and Diaries of the Period* ed. Leon Edel (New York 1983) p. 43, winter 1943–4.

Michael Sherry's theory of 'Technological Fanaticism' and Freeman Dyson's claim that,

continued

It was only after the event that the moral evasions were made public. Following the war Portal, the Chief of Air Staff, denied 'that our bombing of the German cities was really intended to kill and frighten Germans'. He insisted:

> Any such idea is completely and utterly false. The loss of life, which amounted to some 600,000 killed, was purely incidental and in as much as it involved children and women who were taking no part in the war we all deplored the necessity of doing it.

Harris went even further: 'In spite of what happened at Hamburg, bombing proved a comparatively humane method'. It was more humane, Harris argued, than the Hunger Blockade which had finally broken Germany in 1918:

> Whenever the fact that our aircraft ocassionally killed women and children is cast in my teeth I always produce this example of the blockade.

These self-justifications must be seen in relation to the fact that, militarily speaking, the bombing offensive was a stupendous waste of Britain's war-making resources. Indeed the two aspects of the question can hardly be separated: the same corporate tunnel vision which rationalized the moral implications of the air offensive out of existence also blinded itself to the truth about the strategic uselessness of the the campaign.[59]

VI. The New War of Attrition

Part of the reason why the bomber offensive policy, such as it was, was slow to achieve major success was that the same doctrinaire habit of mind which hindered thinking through the moral and strategic aspects also had its effect on the development of tactics.

There was, first of all, an emphasis on *quantity* rather than quality. The strategic air offensive was a huge economic operation. Over 8,000 bombers were lost and 47,268 aircrew died – more than the Luftwaffe's total wartime

continued

'Through science and technology, evil is organized bureaucratically so that no individual is responsible for what happens', (*Disturbing the Universe* p. 30) are attractive but the fact is that the professional indifference to moral issues exists independently of, and previous to, bureaucratization of science. In July 1940 the Chemical Warfare Officer of No. 4 Group Bomber Command sent a memo to sector stations saying, 'It is true that we signed a protocol at Geneva in 1924 agreeing not to use gas unless it was first used by the enemy, but Italy signed this also and has since used it against Abyssinia . . . I am not suggesting that we should use it against the enemy's civilian population –', at this point someone at Bomber Command H.Q. wrote in the margin, 'Why not?', Public Record Office AIR 14/609/33A.

In 1940, when A.O.C.-in-C. Bomber Command, Portal had forbidden his crews to machine-gun people running out of the factories they were bombing on the grounds 'that these people are civilians and that the object of our bombing is to destroy the plant and not to kill the work people'. Public Record Office AIR 14/1930 Portal to Sholto Douglas 12 Aug. 1940.

59 Richards *Portal of Hungerford* p. 167; Harris *Bomber Offensive* p. 176.

losses on all fronts. The worst night was that of the attack on Nuremberg on 30–31 March 1944 when 94 four-engined bombers were shot down and twelve more reached home damaged beyond repair; on that night more R.A.F. personnel died than in the entire Battle of Britain, while German casualties were 110 civilians, 59 foreign workers and 19 military personnel killed. In the course of the campaign a single German night fighter pilot, Heinz-Wolfgang Schnaufer, shot down 121 R.A.F. bombers, including nine on the night of 21 February 1945, accounting for more than 800 R.A.F. crew. According to Harris, each Bomber Command crew member cost £10,000 to train, including, very often, a two-way trip to North America for air training in Canada or the U.S. Even after training, Bomber Command operations involved something like a succession of advanced lectures, in the form of mission briefings, staged simultaneously in identical Nissen huts in dozens of idyllically named aerodrome campuses all over the eastern counties, and in retrospect suggest as much as anything a mass continuation programme of technological education. The investment in hardware was in proportion. It was calculated not long before D-Day, when once again British land forces were about to grapple with the foe on the mainland of northern Europe, that more people were working to build heavy bombers than to equip the entire Army. The same point was suggested in a poster by Zec, 'Women of Britain COME INTO THE FACTORIES' which shows a woman munitions worker with arms opened wide in an expansive gesture, either signalling or stretching, with a factory and two tanks behind her skirt and an endless line of multi-engined aircraft winding into the sky in the background. Truly the bomber offensive seemed to dwarf the rest of the economy; when in March 1942 the basic petrol ration, about five gallons a month for private cars, was abolished a Lancaster bomber might be using as much as 2,000 gallons in a single mission to Germany.[60]

'Early this morning we heard the bombers going out', Ed Murrow said in one of his broadcasts. 'It was the sound of a giant factory in the sky'. He might equally have likened it to an army in the sky. The heaviest ever air raid, carried out by daylight on Dortmund on 12 March 1945, involved 1,107 four-engined bombers; the crews were the equivalent of two army brigades and the 4,899 tons of bombs dropped equalled the weight of a small cruiser. (The Eighth U.S.A.A.F. carried out an attack on Berlin six days later with an even larger number of aircraft each with a larger crew but the bombload was perhaps half that dropped in the Dortmund raid). The ground crew necessary to put such a large force into the air would have been equivalent to at least

---

[60] Longmate *The Bombers* p. 29; Harris *Bomber Offensive* p. 98; *Hansard: House of Commons* vol. 397 col. 1602, speech by Sir James Grigg 2 March 1944 cf K. Hancock and M.M. Gowing *British War Economy* (1949) p. 351 and William Hornby *Factories and Plant* (1958) p. 251; Norman Longmate *How We Lived Then: A History of Everyday Life during the Second World War* (1971) p. 315–6.

A rudder from Major Schnaufer's Messerschmitt Bf 110C night fighter, with the symbols and dates of his 121 aerial victories, is preserved in the Imperial War Museum, London.

two army corps, even without counting support, repair and training units.[61]

But this massive war machine took a painfully long time to build up. In November 1940 Bomber Command flew 1,894 night sorties; in November 1941 only 1,713. When *The Daily Express* called for the more vigorous bombing of Berlin the editor received an official rebuke from Downing Street: 'You ought to know perfectly well that the work of building up a great bomber force takes a long time, maybe years'. In November 1941 average daily availability of aircraft with crews in Bomber Command was 506 but in May 1942, with the twin-engined bombers mostly phased out, it was only 417 and in January 1943 still only 515. The thousand-bomber raids on Cologne, Essen and Bremen in May and June 1942 were largely stunts, involving the use of crews from Operational Training Units and the consequent disruption of training schedules; soon afterwards Harris was demanding that bombers should be recalled to his command from the Middle East and that an approach should be made to Stalin to transfer his bomber force to Britain. It was not till the spring of 1944 that normal availability of bombers stood at over a thousand.[62]

The cost-effectiveness of the bomber offensive had already been queried by Sir John Wardlaw-Milne in the House of Commons, shortly before the first thousand bomber raid:

> when I think of the enormous number of man-hours required in the construction of these great machines, their heavy cost and, far more important, the loss of valuable trained lives, I wonder whether this policy is going to return a dividend as against that we might have received from other types of aircraft to prevent disasters in other parts of the world.

Yet even the aircraft being manufactured for the bomber striking force were not entirely suitable for their intended role. The R.A.F. consistently argued, with their infallible statistical logic, that the heavier the payload of the individual bomber, the more efficient the operation. Bomber Command

---

[61] Edmund Bliss Jr. ed. *In Search of Light: The Broadcasts of Edward R. Morrow, 1938–1961* (New York 1967) p. 81, 6 June 1944. The simile is in fact borrowed from a poem entitled 'London' by the Norwegian writer Nordahl Grieg, who was aboard a R.A.A.F. Lancaster shot down on 2 Dec. 1943. An English translation of his war poems appeared in 1944.

The Boeing B-17, which carried a crew of ten, was a somewhat older design than the British heavy bombers and whereas the latter carried their bomb-load in a long compartment along the bottom of the fuselage the B-17 carried its bombs in a compartment taking up the entire cross-section of the fuselage directly behind the flight deck – access to the rear of the plane, which housed half the crew, was by a cat walk between two racks of hanging bombs. The 'basement' arrangement on the British bombers provided stowage for up to six tons of bombs of any size: the B-17 normally carried about two tons and was unable to accommodate the larger bombs employed by the R.A.F.

[62] Webster and Frankland *Strategic Air Offensive against Germany* vol. 4 p. 431 Appendix 40; Christiansen *Headlines All My Life* p. 190; Webster and Frankland *Strategic Air Offensive against Germany* vol. 4 p. 428 Appendix 39; ibid. vol. 1 p. 341 Harris to Churchill 17 June 1942.

employed a small number of fast, unarmed De Havilland Mosquito twin-engined bombers (58 to 985 heavies in March 1944; 203 to 1440 in April 1945). Though they could carry a 4,000lb bomb these Mosquitos had less than one third of the bombload of the Avro Lancaster – but they also cost less than a third to build. The Lancaster was fractionally more economical on crew, for although it carried seven men to the Mosquito's two, four of them had a less advanced training than the Mosquito's pilot and navigator/bomb aimer. But during the Battle of Berlin in the winter of 1943–1944, 1,047 heavy bombers had been lost in 20,224 sorties (5.2 per cent) and only 10 Mosquitos in 2,034 sorties (0.5 per cent), which made the Mosquito ten times less likely to be shot down than a four-engined bomber: it was also easier to bail out from as the hatches on the Lancaster were too small for a man wearing a flying suit and parachute. If rate of loss (and resulting crew wastage) was entered into the calculation, the Mosquito was far more cost-effective than Bomber Command's favoured four-engined heavies.[63]

The overall scale of the offensive and the losses endured suggest a parallel with the British armies on the Western Front in 1914–1918 – a parallel noted by Major-General J.F.C. Fuller in an essay entitled 'Bomb Mind is the Somme Mind'. The numbers of men actually under fire in the air offensive was of course significantly smaller than in Haig's campaigns, though the expense of the equipment and the levels of skill required to operate it were much higher, and the higher technology served to focus the sacrificial slaughter of the country's youth on to the most intellectually and technically gifted sections of it, in a sophisticated piece of racial suicide. In both cases however the military machine organized itself for mass war on the basis of taking as many men as it could handle, training them to a text book standard and then putting them into action, either till they got themselves killed, as in 1914–1918, or till they had completed a fixed number of missions, as in Bomber Command from May 1943 onward. Theoretically of course these men were provided with training to the normal professional standard – which in the R.A.F. circa 1943 was a much higher standard than that of the training available in the Luftwaffe – but in no sense did the British New Army subaltern on the Western Front or the Bomber Command crewman cease to be other than civilians in uniform; the whole system was relentlessly geared to the average and the reasonably attainable, with no allowance for the exceptional or the inspired. (It is probably only the Anglo-Saxons who believe that the military ideal is represented by uniformity and teamwork rather than by individual gallantry and leadership.) The German emphasis on individual fighting spirit had been reinforced by the Nazi ideology of struggle; the average and the normal were not good enough. The difference of approach was underlined by what might appear a sensible

---

[63] *Hansard: House of Commons* vol. 380 col. 146, speech by Sir John Wardlaw-Milne, 19 May 1942 (see also Admiral Sir R.P. Ernle-Erle-Drax's article 'The British War Effort' in *Journal of the Royal United Service Institution* vol. 87 p. 319–325 (Nov. 1942) espec. p. 320–321); Webster and Frankland *Strategic Air Offensive against Germany* vol. 2 p. 201 fn. 1; ibid. vol. 2 p. 198 fn. 2 and 3, and p. 199.

and even humane measure, the limitation of tours of duty in the R.A.F. An Air Ministry circular of May 1943 fixed night bomber crews' tours of duty as thirty operations for the first tour and twenty for the second; no third tour would be theoretically possible. (Fighter tours were fixed at 200 hours of operations.) German aircrew, though given plentiful leave, skiing holidays and the like, kept on indefinitely. By the end many German airmen must have had well over 2,000 hours of operational flying; there were fifteen Luftwaffe fighter pilots who shot down more than 200 enemy aircraft each, and Hans-Ulrich Rudel destroyed 519 tanks and the Soviet battleship *Marat* in his career as a *Panzerknacker* or tank-buster; after being wounded for the second time in six months he had his leg amputated but was back in action before the stump was ready to be fitted with an artificial limb, and in all clocked up 2,530 operational flights. Hans-Georg Baetcher carried out 658 missions in multi-engined bombers. Of course the Luftwaffe's wartime recruits suffered disproportionately heavy casualties because of inadequate training, and there must also have been many of the type who in Bomber Command struggled painfully, but with dignity, through the regulation fifty ops. but who in the Luftwaffe were constrained to go on and on, not improving as pilots and with increasingly ragged nerves, till overtaken by death or disabling injury. The Germans indeed set themselves an unreasonably high standard – both the unreasonableness and the establishment of new standards of achievement were part of the Nazi message – but arguably the British aimed too low. The adoption by Bomber Command of the one-pilot crew, sensible and business-like as far as it went, also meant that, in Air Vice-Marshal Donald Bennett's words, 'the inexperience of the captains meant that almost all of them were relatively ineffective for a large part of their tour'. The whole system failed to gear itself to extending the skill level of the force as a whole; it was a mass force, geared to accommodate only the average.[64]

[64] Fuller's essay appeared in *Evening Standard* 8 Feb. 1943 p. 6a-f and was reprinted in *Watchwords* (1944) p. 28–30. For R.A.F. tours of duty see John Terraine *The Right of the Line: The Royal Air Force in the European War, 1939–1945* (1985) p. 527: this book devotes some attention to the question of crew morale; Edward H. Sims *The Fighter Pilots: A Comparative Study of the Royal Air Force, the Luftwaffe and the United States Air Army Force in Europe and North Africa, 1939–1945* (1967) p. 177; Hans Ulrich Rudel *Stuka Pilot* (Dublin 1952) p. vii (introduction by Johannes Rudel) and passim; D.C.T. Bennett *Pathfinder* (1958) p. 176.

The enormous numbers of 'kills' claimed by German aces seem incredible, especially compared to the 38 enemy aircraft credited to the R.A.F.'s official top-scorer, 'Johnnie' Johnson: but the Canadian top-scorer, George Beurling, accounted for 27 aircraft destroyed, eight damaged and three probably destroyed in just *fourteen* days of action over Malta, spread over a period of four months. He was at the time only 20 years old. He spent most of the remainder of the war on ground duties, even though he wanted nothing better than to continue as a frontline pilot. In 1948 he joined the nascent Israeli Air Force and was killed in an air crash at Rome while preparing to join the battle then raging in Palestine. His father commented, 'I've long expected him to go in a blaze of smoke from the thing he loved best – an aeroplane' (*New York Times* 21 May 1948 p. 4a). If he had been in the Luftwaffe he would have been allowed to kill himself much sooner but might have taken a couple of hundred of the enemy with him. His friends called him 'Screwball'.

This investment in mediocrity was sponsored by complacency as to the effectiveness of the attacks carried out. In his memoirs Harris sneered at the Luftwaffe's handling of the Blitz:

> Had they known anything about the exercise of air power – and they certainly knew very little – they would have known that night bombing requires not only a vast amount of specialised training, for which they had left themselves no time at all, but also very special aircraft and equipment, which they had made no attempt to produce.

This is actually far more applicable to Bomber Command, especially as regards technique and special equipment. The Germans had a variety of electronic navigational devices available even in the summer of 1940 and in the first major attack on a relatively small inland target, that on Coventry on 14 November 1940, a special elite force, K.Gr. 100, was employed to go in first to start fires that would guide the successive bomber waves which were to follow afterwards. The R.A.F. required much longer-ranged navigational aids and ones which could not be jammed or distorted – as was managed relatively easily with the German navigational beams – and though the first British device, *Gee*, was introduced into service in August 1941 it was not till 1943 that more sophisticated navigational aids such as *Oboe* and H₂S air to ground radar began to make any substantial difference to the R.A.F.'s target finding. A specialized Pathfinder Force, on the unacknowledged model of the Luftwaffe's K.Gr. 100, was belatedly set up in August 1942, and then only as a result of Air Ministry pressure on the stubbornly reluctant Harris, who denied the desirability of such an elite force. No. 617 squadron, formed in the spring of 1943 to carry out missions of special difficulty, also made important contributions to the development of technique, pioneering both low-level target marking and the Master Bomber concept (in which an ultra-experienced pilot remained over the target throughout an attack, supervising and monitoring its progress). These techniques, dangerous but not involving any particularly advanced technology, made at least as much improvement to the accuracy and effect of R.A.F. bombing as the new electronic navigational aids available in 1943. One might wonder why it should have taken till 1943 to apply to mass air raids the standards of personal skill that were already available in 1940: Leonard Cheshire, No. 617 Squadron's most innovative commander, later recalled of the standard Bomber Command raid:

> Everything was wound up and pre-set like an alarm clock hundreds of miles from a target, as though all the unknown factors could be predetermined infallibly and the raid conducted by the remote control of unseen experts.

It was essentially the same concept as at the Somme, with 'a standardized army' going into 'a standardized battle'.[65]

---

[65] Harris *Bomber Offensive* p. 85–6; Webster and Frankland *Strategic Air Offensive against Germany* vols 1 and 2 passim; Andrew Boyle *No Passing Glory: The Full and Authentic*
continued

Even in 1940 Winston Churchill had heard reports that Bomber Command was failing to carry out bombing missions effectively and urged the Secretary of State for Air, 'I hope you will address yourself further to the matter, which causes me a good deal of anxiety, and also the Cabinet'. Naturally these anxieties were concealed from the public: Philip Noel-Baker told the House of Commons on 20 May 1941, 'we can see now what a tremendous mistake Marshal Goering made when he failed to bring up his training for night bombing to the same pitch of technical perfection as ours'. It was not till the so-called Butt report of August 1941 that Bomber Command itself began to admit that there was something fundamentally wrong. It subsequently transpired that in 33 raids on Cologne between June 1941 and February 1942, involving over 2,000 sorties, 6,600 high explosive bombs and 147,000 incendiaries had been dropped by crews claiming to have bombed the city, of which only 1,100 bombs and 12,000 incendiaries were counted by the Germans within the city boundaries, (a total of 138 civilians had been killed and 277 injured, and 947 homes destroyed or seriously damaged in an effort equivalent to ten nights' bombing of London in October 1940). Up to March 1943 Essen was attacked on 132 nights, on 58 of which the city was not actually hit, though bombs fell within Essen's city limits on 34 nights when it was not the target. The first thousand-bomber raid on Cologne on 30 May 1942 was for its time an outstanding success, with 474 killed, over 5,000 injured, 45,132 rendered homeless, and 328 factories damaged, of which 36 had to cease production altogether; but London had been struck as grievously on several occasions in the Blitz of 1940–1941. (Though Goebbels insisted that 'between 250 and 300' bombers had been involved in the attack, the Luftwaffe put the number at only 70.) According to the Operations Record Book of No. 3 Group the fires at Cologne were visible from the Dutch coast and, 'It was generally thought by the crews that a second visit to Cologne would be unnecessary'. But the R.A.F.'s own reconnaissance photos, taken early in June, showed the Humboldt Deutz Motoren Werke, producing diesel engines for U-boats, as 90 per cent untouched, and the Vereinigte Deutsche Metallwerke, which 'has 10 sheds gutted' as 80 per cent intact. Six hundred acres – about 18 per cent – of the total built-up area of the city had been destroyed: it took several more raids to bring the total area wrecked up to 1,994 acres by 1945. The two subsequent thousand-bomber raids, on Essen and Bremen, were moreover much less successful, though 'earning great headlines for the R.A.F. while we lose our possessions, our trade and our troops' in the Mediterranean and Far East. Like the management of any other badly-run large corporation the staff of Bomber Command worked hard to present mediocre performance

continued
Biography of Group Captain Leonard Cheshire V.C., D.S.O., D.F.C. (1972 edit.) p. 223 cf Public Record Office WO 33/1305 *Notes on Certain Lessons of the Great War* p. 26.

Something like the master-bomber concept was already employed by Soviet night bombers before its introduction in the R.A.F., cf Public Records Office AIR 46/26 piece 79A (report of visit to Soviet night-bomber station at Monino 8/9 June 1943) para 13.

as major achievement; when a map was produced after a raid on Frankfurt showing the bombs plotted within a three-mile radius of the aiming point, the W.A.A.F. who had prepared the map was told, 'Awfully few bombs inside the circle. You'd better change that to a five mile circle before it goes in'. When an expert photographic analyst prepared a memorandum on the inaccuracy of targeting, the Air Vice-Marshal commanding that Group scrawled on it in red, 'I do not accept this report'. It was not till October 1943 that Bomber Command even realized that pound for pound the German bombs were nearly twice as powerful as their own.[66]

The choice of targets left to the A.O.C.-in-C. himself: when Harris took over as A.O.C.-in-C. he would announce his selection at a daily meeting, designated 'Morning Prayers', at his H.Q. at High Wycombe. While his staff officers cringed before his baleful glance and his horrendous mispronunciation of German place names, he would hear the weather report and, with scarcely a glance at the different folders containing details of various potential targets, would state the target, 'Mayns' it might be, or 'Botch'em' or 'Orgsberg'. The weather was generally the only material factor given much consideration; there seems to have been no other basis for choosing between different German cities other than the whim of the moment.[67]

Although he permitted various small-scale stunts, such as the daylight raid by Lancasters on the MAN diesel works at Augsburg on 17 April 1942 and the famous attack on the Möhne and Eder dams by No. 617 squadron on the night of 16–17 May 1943, Harris was reluctant to make any effort against specific economic targets suggested by the Air Ministry and Ministry of Economic Warfare, and it was left to the Americans to carry out very costly missions against the Rumanian oilfields at Ploesti on 1 August 1943 and against the German ball-bearing factories at Schweinfurt on 17 August and 14 October 1943; both targets were damaged but because of reserve stocks and reserve capacity German war production was not affected (thus confirming Harris's scepticism) though in both cases a more sustained series of attacks could have eventually achieved the desired effect. Harris also held out as long as possible against the Air Ministry's insistence that he collaborate in the campaign against German oil production in 1944. As the Americans also turned increasingly

[66] Public Record Office PREM 3/14/2 p. 139 Churchill to Sinclair 30 Dec. 1940; *Hansard: House of Commons* vol. 371 col. 1431 speech by Philip Noel-Baker; Webster and Frankland *Strategic Air Offensive against Germany* vol. 4 p. 205–213 Appendix 13 gives full text of the report by D.M. Butt of the War Cabinet secretariat and cf vol. 1 p. 178–180; ibid. vol. 1 p. 304; Werner Wolf *Luftangriffe auf die deutsche Industrie, 1942–45* (Munich 1985) p. 32; Webster and Frankland *Strategic Air Offensive against Germany* vol. 1 p. 485; Michael Balfour *Propaganda in War, 1939–1945: Organisations, Policies and Publics in Britain and Germany* (1979) p. 265; Public Record Office AIR 25/52; AIR 14/1378; Paul G. Halpern ed. *The Keyes Papers* (3 vols 1972–1981) vol. 3 p. 253 Sir Herbert Richmond to Sir Roger Keyes 4 July 1942; Dyson *Disturbing the Universe* p. 26. Constance Babington Smith *Evidence in Camera: The Story of Photographic Intelligence in World War II* (1958) p. 101; Longmate *The Bombers* p. 168.

[67] See account of 'Morning Prayers' in Max Hastings *Bomber Command* (1979) p. 248–9.

to area bombing in Europe the policy of causing economic breakdown by attacking a production bottle-neck was not really systematically attempted in the war against Germany; by the time the belated bombing of their oil industry began to cause the Germans serious shortages, they were already fighting on German soil. It was only later, in the U.S. Twentieth Air Force's attacks on Japan, that bombing made a contribution to economic breakdown by its impact on a strategic bottle-neck, in this case raw materials imports. Harris's lack of interest in enemy morale as such also led him to order fewer attacks on Italy than might have been feasible. The relatively light raids on northern Italy in the autumn of 1942 and spring of 1943 made a major contribution to undermining Mussolini's regime and in December 1942 Portal, the Chief of Air Staff, was described as 'stating his plans on the assumption that Italy is No. 1 bombing target'. But there was considerable doubt at Cabinet level as to the advisability of doing anything so controversial as bombing Rome itself; Eden, the Foreign Secretary, thought it should be 'left until a moment when we have reason to believe that Italian morale had reached breaking point'. Though the decision not to bomb Rome was essentially a political one – 'Bomb Rome' was the kind of slogan that Britain's Leftists chalked on walls in the black-out, even if not as popular as 'Second Front Now' – nevertheless the contrast between Harris's constant agitation for ever greater efforts against Germany's cities and his lack of interest in Italy provides part of the context in which the decision was made. The fragility of the Fascist regime and the extreme inadequacy of Italian anti-aircraft and civil defence organization made Italy much the most vulnerable of the Axis partners: but Harris, like Haig and Robertson in the First World War, regarded attacking the enemy at his strongest rather than weakest point as the acme of strategic sophistication.[68]

Even in choosing between potential targets in Germany Harris made no attempt to distinguish between the German cities that might be more vulnerable and those that involved special problems of location and urban structure. On 28–29 March 1942 an incendiary raid on Lübeck achieved major success – with the possible exception of the Kiel raids almost a year previously it was the first attack on a German city seriously to worry the Nazi leadership, though it was noted after the war that, 'The docks and the industrial belt, ostensibly our real targets, seem almost untouched'. Late in April a series of fire raids were also carried out on Rostock. There were a number of similar

[68] For Harris's resistance to the oil offensive in 1944 see Webster and Frankland *Strategic Air Offensive against Germany* vol. 3 p. 81–94. For the American turn to area bombing see Ronald Schaffer *Wings of Judgment: American Bombing in World War II* (New York 1985) p. 67–8, 74–6, 80–106; David McIsaac ed. *The United States Strategic Bombing Survey* 10 vols New York 1976 vol. 8 p. 28–30, 41–52; Stephen Harvey 'The Italian War Effort and the Strategic Bombing of Italy' *History* vol. 70 (1985) p. 32–45 at p. 41–5; Public Record Office AIR 19/215/6A note by R.H. Melville 2 Dec. 1942; AIR 19/215/15A Eden to Sinclair 12 Dec. 1942. In the event the first air raid on Rome, on 19 July 1943, was carried out by the Ninth U.S.A.A.F. flying from North Africa: Mussolini was deposed by his colleagues less than a week later.

targets in northern Germany which would have been equally vulnerable but instead Harris turned his attention to his thousand-bomber publicity stunt. For over a year after the Lübeck and Rostock raids bombing attacks continued with increasing intensity (though with little increase of accuracy) against more awkward inland targets, enabling Bomber Command to develop a significant body of skill and experience, but also providing a similar facility for the German night fighter defences; the first of Heinz-Wolfgang Schnaufer's 121 victories against R.A.F. night bombers was on 2 June 1942, and on 17 November 1942 Hauptmann Reinhold Knacke shot down five bombers in one night, a feat frequently equalled in the next three years. But only in the spring of 1943, with the introduction of Oboe and then H_2S, was any really substantial damage inflicted: a raid on Wuppertal-Barmen on 29–30 May 1943 which killed 2,450 and left 118,000 homeless – in fact obliterated 90 per cent of the Barmen section of Wuppertal – was the first R.A.F. raid on Germany to exceed by any significant margin the worst of the Luftwaffe raids on Britain in the winter and spring of 1940–1941.[69]

Then between 24 July and 3 August 1943 a series of raids were carried out on Hamburg. During the second night of the bombing certain peculiarities of atmospheric conditions combined with the accuracy of the bomb-aiming to cause a fire-storm, something which had occurred previously in the City of London on 29 December 1940 and at Rostock, though on a rather smaller scale. A number of very large fires within a comparatively small area caused updraughts which by sucking in air laterally generated winds of more than hurricane force. Although there were over 10,000 firemen available, including four motorized *Luftschutzabteilungen* belonging to the Luftwaffe, an area of four and a half square miles with a street frontage of 133 miles was burnt out in five hours. It has been estimated that 2,000,000,000,000 tons of air were drawn into the firestorm, 25 times more than was needed to burn everything. Temperatures were generated that were unprecedented on anything like such a scale. At least 30,000 people died on just that one night, a twentieth of Germany's total casualties from five years of bombing. In his diary Goebbels recorded the raid as 'a catastrophe the extent of which simply staggers the

---

[69] Arthur Geoffrey Dickens *Lübeck Diary* (1947) p. 32, 20 May 1945. Middlebrook and Everitt *Bomber Command War Diaries* p. 395 suggests that the Barmen casualties were five times the previous highest loss of life inflicted in an R.A.F. raid, cf Webster and Frankland *Strategic Air Offensive against Germany* vol. 2 p. 131–2. The previous record was 693 at Dortmund on the night of 4–5 May 1943. Perhaps for reasons of euphony Webster and Frankland and most writers who have used their work refer to the target as Barmen-Wuppertal which in German usage would indicate the Wuppertal section of the commune of Barmen: it was in fact the Barmen section of the commune of Wuppertal, hence Wuppertal-Barmen. It was, incidentally, the birth place of Friedrich Engels. For photographs of Wuppertal before and after the bombing see Hermann Plankermann *Wuppertal: so wie es war* (2 vols Düsseldorf 1975) and cf Norbert Krüger 'Die Zerstörung Wuppertals. Ein Überblick über die Luftangriffe im Sommer 1943' in Klaus Goebel ed. *Wuppertal in der Zeit des Nationalsozialismus* (Wuppertal 1984) p. 163–177.

imagination. A city of a million inhabitants has been destroyed in a manner unparalleled in history'.[70]

After the war Albert Speer, Hitler's armaments minister, claimed:

We were of the opinion that a rapid repetition of this type of attack upon another six German towns would inevitably cripple the will to sustain armaments manufacture and war production.

When, on the night of the final Hamburg raid, leaflets were dropped on Berlin calling on all women and children to leave at once it was reported, 'The railway stations are being beseiged by seething mobs. There is an air abroad as though the end of the world were imminent'. But Harris was not the man to be distracted from his chosen course by stunning success, any more than he was to be perturbed by failure. Instead of concentrating on really vulnerable targets which offered optimum results, he turned his attention on Berlin.[71]

Obviously Berlin was a major prestige target, irresistable to proponents of strategic air warfare. The French Navy had bombed the city on the night of 7–8 June 1940 using a converted Farman 223.4 airliner, and on 7 and 11 August 1941 the Soviet naval air arm (VVS-VMF) had carried out attacks in rather more than squadron strength, suffering on the second occasion heavy loss. Like the R.A.F.'s first attacks on Berlin, these raids were little more than gestures, but by the autumn of 1943 Harris was confident of obtaining more solid and significant results. 'We can wreck Berlin from end to end if the U.S.A.A.F. will come in on it', he told Churchill: 'It will cost between 400–500 aircraft. It will cost Germany the war'. This boast turned out to be accurate only as to the number of aircraft that would be lost. The German capital had exceptionally strong defences, and could only be reached after a long, anxious period of flying inside German-controlled airspace; and though it was an important industrial centre it covered a large area, with extensive open spaces, and being an administrative and cultural centre had far more reserve transportation and labour infrastructure than was required simply to sustain its industrial output. Between November 1943 and March 1944, in the so-called 'Battle of Berlin', 9,111 sorties by heavy bombers were carried out against other targets, usually also involving deep penetration of German

---

[70] For an interesting technical discussion of the Hamburg firestorm see Gordon Musgrove *Operation Gomorrah: The Hamburg Firestorm Raids* (1981) p. 102–113: the details quoted are from p. 110, 113 (see also Hans Brunswig *Feuersturm über Hamburg* (Stuttgart 1978) especially the dreadful photographs on p. 231, 236, 238, 275, 277, 278); For fatalities cf Hans Rumpf *The Bombing of Germany* (1975) p. 82–3; Louis P. Lochner ed. *The Goebbels Diaries* (1948) p. 333–4, 29 July 1943.

[71] Webster and Frankland *Strategic Air Offensive against Germany* vol. 4 p. 378, Appendix 37, testimony of Albert Speer 18 July 1945; H.G. von Studnitz *While Berlin Burns: the Diary of Hans Georg von Studnitz, 1943–1945* (1964) p. 93, 3 Aug. 1943: I have not been able to identify these leaflets in Public Record Office AIR 14/580 fol. but AIR 14/581 contains a specimen of a 'proclamation' under the Royal Arms 'An die Zivilbevölkerung der deutschen Industriegebiete' warning of an increase in intensity of attacks, dropped over Germany from Sept. 1943: cf also AIR 20/4865.

air-space, but only Berlin was attacked repeatedly. The result of these raids was by no means negligible. Bare statistics scarcely represent the ordeal of nights spent in bunkers cowering from the pandemonium overhead and days darkened by the smoke, ash and dust of still burning streets, but according to the records in Berlin itself 6,166 people were killed, 18,431 injured, one and a half million people rendered homeless, three and a half square miles of built-up area destroyed; 43 out of 103 factories listed as of major importance were damaged. Fire appliances had on occasion to be rushed from as far away as Hamburg and Breslau, a distance of 180 miles (even in the great fire of 29 December 1940 London had received help only from within a 60 miles radius). On the other hand, relative to what had been achieved with less effort elsewhere, these results were disappointing, and indeed the Air Staff began to conclude that the offensive against Berlin was a failure as early as December 1943. A single raid on Kassel on the night of 22–23 October 1943 indicated what might have been attempted if it had not been for Harris's obsession with Berlin: another fire storm was ignited, and out of a population of 228,000, 9,200 died (70 per cent by suffocation as the air was sucked out of their bunkers) and 91,000 were left homeless. Kassel was, in effect, the closest Bomber Command came to following up the success of Hamburg; fire storms on this scale were not created again till that of Dresden on 13–14 February 1945 when the defeat of Germany was already in sight.[72]

The paralysis of Hamburg and Kassel as centres of production, though in fact only temporary, shows that Harris's theory of attacking the infrastructure

---

[72] Paul Comet 'Sur Berlin avec Daillère' *Icare* no. 61 (1972) p. 92–101; Alexander Boyd *The Soviet Air Force since 1917* (1977) p. 70; Webster and Frankland *Strategic Air Offensive against Germany* vol. 2 p. 48 Harris to Churchill 3 Nov. 1943; Rumpf *Bombing of Germany* p. 117 and cf description in *The Berlin Diaries of Marie 'Missie' Vassiltchikov* (1985) p. 103–111, 23, 24 Nov. 1944 and Lochner ed. *Goebbels Diaries* p. 425–441, 24–29 Nov. 1943; ibid. p. 430, 25 Nov, 1944 and cf commentary to Ministry of Information film *The Fire of London* 1945 for the question of fire engines coming from out of town; F.H. Hinsley *British Intelligence in the Second World War: its Influence on Strategy and Operations* (3 vols 1979–1988) vol. 3 pt. 1 p. 302 for Air Staff opinion of the offensive. For the Kassel fire storm of Webster and Frankland *Strategic Air Offensive against Germany* vol. 2 p. 267–8: these authors give civilian fatalities as 5,248, the higher figure being in Rumpf *Bombing of Germany* p. 156–7. Martin Middlebrook *The Berlin Raids: R.A.F. Bomber Command Winter, 1943–44* (1988) p. 321 (cf p. 71, 83, 87) gives a total of 10,214 deaths, including 1,590 in three earlier raids at the end of August and beginning of September.

The term *Feuerturm* seems to be used in Germany quite generally for a fire ignited by incendiary bombing which rages out of control: it should be understood however that the firestorms at Hamburg and Dresden, and *probably* at London (29 Dec. 1940), Rostock and Kassel differed not only quantitatively but also *qualitatively* from any other very large fire on account of the meteorological conditions which the fire itself generated. The huge fire which almost totally destroyed Heilbronn as a result of the R.A.F. raid on the night on 4–5 Dec. 1944 and the fire at Tokyo started by the Twentieth U.S.A.A.F. 9–10 March 1945 were made worse by high winds which were already blowing when the attacks started. Other probable firestorms were at Krefeld 21–22 June 1943, at Darmstadt 11–12 Sept. 1944 and at Pforzheim 23–24 February 1945. In the Pforzheim raid 17,600 people were killed.

supporting the German munitions industry was not completely fallacious: one really could halt the 20 per cent (or whatever) of a community's economic activity that was vital to war production if one obliterated half the remaining 80 per cent of the city. In the case of Berlin however the threshold point at which so much of the city had been destroyed that the rest of the community became paralyzed was never approached. Berlin's output of munitions actually increased considerably during the Battle of Berlin.

Harris knew little of the structure of modern economic systems, and did not trouble to find out more. In Germany as in Britain the tendency since the mid-nineteenth century had been for large-scale industry to disperse itself to the outskirts of large cities and to small towns where ground rents were lower and traffic access easier. Consequently 57 per cent of German industry was in communities which were never even bombed and much – and generally the most modern part – of the remainder was on the outskirts of the cities and suffered much less heavily than the city centres: thus the Hamburg raids destroyed an estimated 61 per cent of the city's housing, 45 per cent of the smaller factories and 35 per cent of the larger (and generally more modern) factories. In Hamburg of course the level of destruction obviously disrupted the labour force in the 65 per cent of larger factories which remained intact but Hamburg was an extreme case and even there war production was soon resumed. Despite Harris's theory the general tendency of the raids he ordered was to knock out the parts of the community which were contributing least to munitions output and to affect the war industries only as a kind of side effect. A survey by British experts immediately after the war even suggested that the bombing facilitated the Nazi government's efforts to redirect resources away from the non-munitions sector and concluded:

> As the offensive progressed, the Germans were able to divert the effects of town area attacks more and more on to the civilian sector of industry, so that the effect on war production became progressively smaller.[73]

Post-war investigation showed that in 1944 only 6.5 per cent of Germany's machine tools were destroyed or even damaged by bombing – since the Ministry of Economic Warfare's experts grossly underestimated Germany's machine tool inventory (in 1943 it stood at 2,150,000 machine tools but was assessed by the M.E.W. at only 981,000) it was possible just as well more was not attempted in the way of destroying factory plant; but these figures

---

[73] Matthew Cooper *The German Air Force, 1933–1945* (1981) p. 300; Public Record Office AIR 10/3870 'Report on the Effects of Strategic Air Attacks on German Towns by the Towns Panel of the BSSU' p. 17 para. 50. This document prints, p. 83–103, various wartime departmental estimates of the impact of the bombing of Germany and considers them with one exception much exaggerated: p. 41 para. 136. For an account of the British and American post-war investigations see Webster and Frankland *Strategic Air Offensive against Germany* vol. 4 p. 40–56 Annexe V 'The British and United States Surveys of the Strategic Bombing Offensive'. For the recovery of Hamburg and other industrial centres see Webster and Frankland *Strategic Air Offensive against Germany* vol. 2 p. 259–260.

indicate the scope for reorganizing and redeploying resources after part of an industry had been affected by bombing. Goebbels thought that physical damage was anyway less important than the 'fact that bombed cities undergo pretty bad dislocations of public life, as a result of which the workers often stay away from their workbenches for weeks'. He cited the case of a factory in Mannheim which, two weeks after it was ready to go back into production, still only had 60 per cent of its workforce back at work. Goebbels thought that was 'the reason why the English are more interested in destroying cities than in destroying the munitions industry'. Except that his emphasis was on morale and psychological cohesion rather than on physical infrastructure, Goebbels's analysis was remarkably close to Harris's; but the fact remained that German weapons output did not peak till July 1944 and continued almost to the very end at more than twice the 1942 level despite the progressive devastation of the nation's urban centres.[74]

VII. The Cost to Germany

It took three years of increasingly heavy bombing to destroy 15 per cent of Germany's housing, whereas Japan lost 24 per cent in a mere seven months – 2,502,000 units by bombing, 614,000 units by demolition to create fire breaks, 563,000 units from accidental fires, floods and earthquakes. In material terms Germany proved remarkably resilient to air attack. In the London Blitz casualties were far below pre-war estimates: just over one fatality per ton of bombs. German civilian fatalities were only half that rate, largely because of better public shelters, better shelter discipline and a more systematic policy of evacuating families with young children; nevertheless they totalled 600,000. But of course the actual destruction resulting from the rain of bombs was only part of the cost of the air raids to the German war effort.[75]

[74] McIsaac ed. *United States Strategic Bombing Survey* vol. 1 'The Effects of Strategic Bombing on the German War Economy' p. 45; ibid. p. 44; Lochner ed. *Goebbels Diaries* p. 372, 21 Sept. 1943, cf Wolf *Luftangriffe auf die deutsche Industrie* p. 62–6. Production indices are in Webster and Frankland *Strategic Air Offensive against Germany* vol. 4 p. 466–7, Appendix 49. Public Record Office AIR 10/3870 'Report on the Effects of Strategic Air Attacks on German Towns by the Towns Panel of the BSSU' p. 41 para. 133 concludes, 'It is clear that the attempt to break the morale of the German industrial workers as a whole was not achieved, and consequently loss to war production on this account did not reach significant dimensions'.

[75] Jerome B. Cohen *Japan's Economy in War and Reconstruction* (Minneapolis 1947) p. 407–9. There is a large quantity of unpublished material relating to the destruction of German cities: in the case of Leipzig for example the records of the municipal Amt für Kriegssachschaden in the Stadtarchiv comprise 220,000 files, and there are also 592 files on casualties in the Polizei Präsidium records in the Staatsarchiv. For details and photographs of blitzed medieval buildings see *Works of Art in Germany (British Zone of Occupation) Losses and Survivals in the War* (1946).

Though German munitions output grew exponentially it is possible nevertheless that the bombing may have prevented it growing even faster. The degree to which the bombing helped to energize and to release resources is impossible to estimate; the degree to which it diverted resources is better documented. Speer, the armaments minister, claimed that eventually one and a half million workers were engaged in repairs and reconstruction, and there was also a colossal programme of shelter building on a much larger scale and to a much higher standard than in Britain, and including massive surface structures designed to withstand direct hits. In addition to city and local fire services there were by 1945 30,000 men in mobile motorized emergency fire units, the Luftwaffe providing 53 *Luftschutzabteilungen* and the *Feuerschutzpolizei* a further nine. In 1944 30 per cent of the artillery produced by German factories was for anti-aircraft functions, over 50 per cent of electronics output consisted of radar or communications equipment for anti-aircraft defence, and 33 per cent of output of the optical equipment industry was for the same purpose. By February 1945 there were over 12,000 heavy anti-aircraft guns stationed in Germany. Ammunition was fired off at an amazing rate: the average 3,343 rounds of 88mm Flak ammunition needed to down an alled bomber cost RM 267,440. The manpower required to operate the guns and searchlights was also enormous, though from February 1943 200,000 boys were conscripted from high schools to serve part time as *Flakhelfer*.[76]

The air raids also put an enormous pressure on the Luftwaffe's air strength. It is not always easy to distinguish between mobilization against R.A.F. raids by night and against the American Eighth Air Force by day as during 1943 especially night fighters were sometimes pressed into service against American B-17 formations and single-seat fighters were often used at night, the R.A.F. bombers generally showing up in silhouette against the cloud over their targets once the searchlights had come on and the fires had started, facilitating interceptions without radar. It seems however that though the Americans were responsible for only 395,000 tons of the total of 1,350,000 tons of bombs dropped on Germany they probably contributed more to the erosion of the Luftwaffe's strength; flying by daylight in vast staggered formations, and often attacking specific industrial zones, the Americans were a more obvious threat, and combatting them seemed initially to require less specialized investment. In May 1943 the Luftwaffe had 930 day and night fighters in western Europe, and 626 on the Eastern Front: a year later 1,690 in the West and only 505 in the East. From August 1944 they simply withdrew all fighters from the

[76] Webster and Frankland *Strategic Air Offensive against Germany* vol. 4 p. 377, 381 Appendix 37 testimony of Albert Speer 30 May and 18 July 1945; McIsaac ed. *United States Strategic Bombing Survey* vol. 2. Civilian Defense Division Final Report p. 75, 77, 81; Webster and Frankland *Strategic Air Offensive against Germany* vol. 4 p. 383 Appendix 37 testimony of Albert Speer 18 July 1945; Cooper *German Air Force* p. 359; Rumpf *Bombing of Germany* p. 147; Hans-Dietrich Nicolaisen *Die Flakhelfer: Luftwaffenhelfer und Marinehelfer im Zweiten Weltkrieg* (Frankfurt 1981) p. 11.

Italian front – all that enormous Allied air superiority in Italy was matched against ground forces defended only by Flak and a late autumnal flourish by about a hundred fighters of Mussolini's *Aeronautica Nazionale Repubblicana*. Since the Russians, despite their staff doctrines, never in practice attempted air superiority tactics the hugely outnumbered Luftwaffe units in the East continued to give a good account of themselves against both Soviet aircraft and Soviet ground formations; fourteen of the fifteen Luftwaffe pilots who shot down more than 200 enemy planes served on the Eastern Front, including Erich Hartmann who shot down 352 and Gerhard Barkhorn who shot down 301; Walther Nowotny shot down 167 planes in four months on the Eastern Front in 1943, and Wilhelm Batz downed fifteen Soviet planes in seven sorties on one day, 13 May 1944. As the figures show however all the Germans' increased production of aircraft was drawn into the air battle in the West, though without ever coming close, after 1943, to achieving even a temporary superiority: indeed by the end of 1944 Flak was accounting for more American bombers than the Luftwaffe's fighters.[77]

The Allied raids also stimulated the depletion, dispersal and misapplication of the Luftwaffe's increasingly exiguous bomber resources. Many German night fighter units were equipped with converted bomber types, either the Junkers Ju 88 or the less successful Dornier Do 217. These, slowed down by their massive external radar aerials, were nothing like as fast as the British Mosquito night fighter, and from December 1943 onwards 236 German night fighters (of all types) were shot down by R.A.F. night fighters on intruder missions. (The R.A.F. heavy bombers also occasionally accounted for German interceptors, but their 0.303 machine guns were not very effective and in any case the doomed crews often never saw the enemy aeroplane which sneaked up under them rip them apart with its multiple 20mm or 30mm cannon.) The R.A.F. raids also persuaded Hitler to order strategically pointless campaigns of reprisal bombing in April-June 1942 (the so-called Baedeker Raids) and in January-March 1944 ('the Baby Blitz'). The Baedeker Raids were specifically directed against the kind of historic centres which were bound to contribute

[77] Rumpf *Bombing of Germany* p. 245 Appendix but cf Webster and Frankland *Strategic Air Offensive against Germany* vol. 4 p. 454–6 Appendix 44; Webster and Frankland *Strategic Air Offensive against Germany* vol. 2 p. 295 fn. 2; Cooper *German Air Force* p. 362; Nino Arena *L'Ultimo Confronto: Evoluzione del Combattimento aereo in Italia, 1943–1945* (Modena 1975) p. 27, 44 writes of the Repubblica Sociale Italiana's air arm having a sustained frontline strength of at least a hundred Macchi C. 205V, Fiat G. 55 and German-built Messerschmit Bf 109G fighters, responsible for the shooting down of 230 Allied planes: W.F. Craven and J.L. Cate *The Army Air Forces in World War II* (7 vols Chicago 1948–1958) vol. 3 p. 470–471 write of three Martin B-26s shot down near Rovereto on 5 Nov. 1944 and heavy interdiction strikes on Italian bases less than two weeks later. According to Christopher Shores *Fighter Aces* (1975) p. 112 Major Adriano Visconti, who had shot down 19 aircraft prior to the Armistice, shot down a further 7 for the Repubblica Sociale Italiana; Captains Mario Bellagambi and Ugo Drago shot down 11 each; Sims *Fighter Pilots* p. 177; Edward H. Sims *Fighter Exploits* (1970 ed.) p. 192–3; Cooper *German Air Force* p. 358.

least to the war, notably Canterbury and Exeter, though the worst raid, that on Bath on 26–27 April 1942 which killed nearly 400 people, accidentally missed the older part of the city while igniting major fires in the more industrialized section. The Luftwaffe also felt obliged to carry out occasional tip-and-run raids which sometimes achieved spectacular though militarily useless results simply because British civilians were no longer taking precautions against what had ceased to appear a serious threat; 94 people, mainly children, were killed by a direct hit on a crowded cinema in East Grinstead on 9 July 1943, and 73 people, including many service personnel, were killed by a 500kg bomb hitting the Palace Dance Hall, Putney High Street on 7 November 1943: in both cases an air-raid alert had been given in time for the victims to disperse. Even 'the Baby Blitz' caused no particular concern – the British public found the V 1 campaign which followed in June 1944 vastly more disconcerting – and the Luftwaffe could well have used these bombers more effectively in Russia.[78]

VIII. The Legacy of Sir Douglas Haig

J.K. Galbraith, who worked on the post-war United States Strategic Bombing Survey and later became internationally renowned as an economist, wrote of the American contribution to the air offensive against Germany:

> The aircraft, manpower and bombs used in the campaign had cost the American economy far more in output than they had cost Germany. However, our economy being much larger, we could afford it.

That was the American perspective. According to the same mode of reasoning the British economy, not being much larger, could not afford it.[79]

This kind of equation had been made early in the war when Professor Frederick Lindemann, later Lord Cherwell, had quashed one exaggerated estimate of future requirement of anti-aircraft shells by 'showing that the resources required for their production would be many times as great as the damage the enemy bomber could, in the most pessimistic assumption, inflict'. Unfortunately Cherwell was one of those particularly in favour of bombing German morale:

> Investigation seems to show that having one's house demolished is most damaging to morale. People seem to mind it more than having their friends or even relatives killed.

[78] For intruder missions by R.A.F. nightfighters see Webster and Frankland *Strategic Air Offensive against Germany* vol. 3 p. 149; Public Record Office HO 192/1042 file RE/B22/87/2 report 23 Sept. 1943; ibid. HO 192/412 unfoliated report 14 Nov. 1943.

[79] J. K. Galbraith *A Life in our Times* (1981) p. 226: the view that, 'The actual effort in manpower and resources that was expended in bombing Germany was greater than the value in manpower of the damage caused', had earlier been voiced by Sir Henry Tizard cf C.P. Snow *Science and Government* (Cambridge Mass. 1961) p. 51.

As the Prime Minister's scientific adviser Cherwell was prominent amongst those who evaded the issue of what was the most cost-effective way of pursuing the war against Germany.[80]

The Americans were confident that, with their almost unlimited resources, they could build up huge air fleets to bomb both Germany and Japan while simultaneously conducting a vast amphibious campaign in the Pacific and an invasion of northern France. The British were much less boldly ambitious and seem to have regarded the strategic air offensive not as a supplement but an alternative to a full-scale invasion of German-occupied Europe. A Chiefs of Staff paper of early September 1940 talked airily of a 'general offensive in all spheres and in all theatres with the utmost possible strength in the spring of 1942' but there was no specific mention of the British Army as a factor in bringing down Hitler, or any enumeration of how many different theatres were expected to exist in 1942. Perhaps in the circumstances of 1940 this might be seen as demonstrating a commendable realism, but even in 1942 the Americans felt that the British view was that ground forces would be needed only to occupy Europe once bombing had brought about the final German collapse. Partly this was the result of growing scepticism about the quality of the British Army: in 1941 Churchill reportedly said, 'I do not believe our generals could manage a major raid. They have not got beyond Crécy and Dettingen'. The Dieppe raid proved him right. More generally, memories of the Western Front in the First World War, of Passchendaele and the Somme, exercised an inhibiting influence. As early as 1937 General Sir Edmund Ironside noted of the politicians:

> They are all frightened to death at the prospect of our being ready to make an enormous Continental Army again. The cry is that we squandered men in the last war.

When the American Army Chief of Staff General George C. Marshall urged a speedy invasion of France, Lord Cherwell told him, 'It's no use – you are arguing against the casualties on the Somme'. Churchill was warned by Trenchard that the alternative to a sustained bombing offensive would be a land campaign, which would be 'to revert to 1914–18', and he later spoke to the U.S. Assistant Secretary of War, John McCloy, of 'the hecatombs' of the First World War and his desire to avoid any repetition. But it was not just the politicians: in the Norwegian campaign General Mackesy had fears of the 'snows of Narvik being turned into another version of the mud of Passchendaele', and Admiral Sir Robert Keyes told Churchill in 1941, 'the

---

[80] R.F. Harrod *The Prof: A Personal Memoir of Lord Cherwell* (1959) p. 201; Earl of Birkenhead *The Prof in Two Worlds* (1961) p. 249–250. (In fact investigation seemed to indicate the opposite: bombed out families in London were reported as showing 'an astonishing degree of readjustment' – Public Record Office INF 1/292 Home Intelligence Report 7–14 Oct. 1940 para II/1.)

Generals of to-day shrink from running any risk of repeating the slaughter for which the generals of 1914–1918 were responsible'.[81]

It is possible that the British public, like the German, would in fact have willingly accepted a repeat performance: an opinion poll in May 1942 put the question whether it would be worth incurring extra losses by invading France in the summer of 1942 rather than waiting for an easier campaign in the summer of 1943 and found that 49 per cent of people agreed and only 17 per cent disagreed. In any case, as already argued, the style of Harris's offensives was very similar to that of Haig's for all that the technology was so different: instead of the privates and corporals walking forward into the fire of the undestroyed German machine guns they stayed at the bases as mechanics and mess-waiters, leaving to their sergeants and officers the exclusive honour of dying inefficaciously for their country. The waste of blood was much less, the waste of above-average personal ability at least as great, the waste of overall economic resources much greater.[82]

The thinking behind these two great exercises in slaughter was superficially very different in style, yet fundamentally very similar. The monosyllabic grunts of Robertson and the faltering unfinished sentences of Haig seem very unlike the confident articulateness of Portal and Harris, and whereas the appeal of the Robertson-Haig strategy was the monolithic obviousness and simplicity of its logic, part of the attraction of the strategic air offensive was its futuristic, theoretical, abstract, enormously complex quality. Yet both strategies were essentially based on stock dogmas, a refusal to be side-racked by tactical minutia, and an insistence that the nature of professional expertise was to be infallibly right. After the war Solly Zuckerman remarked:

> Once there is no scarcity of bombs or aircraft, the tendency is to use more rather than fewer on a given task. The frequency with which the principle of economy of force has been violated in the past makes one wonder in what sense it constitutes a principle of real military action as opposed to something to talk about at staff college.

---

[81] J.R.M. Butler, M. Howard, J. Ehrman, J.M.A. Gwyer, N.A. Gibbs *Grand Strategy* vol. 2 p. 343–4, cf vol. 2 p. 212–5 Chiefs of Staff to War Cabinet 27 May 1940; R.A. Butler *The Art of the Possible* (1971) p. 89; R. Macleod and D. Kelly ed. *The Ironside Diaries* (1962) p. 121 [n.d. –1937]; James Leasor and Sir Leslie Hollis *War at the Top* (1959) p. 173; Churchill *Second World War* vol. 4 p. 495 memo by Trenchard 29 Aug. 1942; Gilbert *Winston S. Churchill* vol. 7 p. 760; T.K. Derry *The Campaign in Norway* (1952) p. 152; Halpern ed. *Keyes Papers* vol. 3 p. 206 Keyes to Churchill 2 Oct. 1941.

[82] Cantril ed. *Public Opinion* p. 1062: and see also p. 1064. Harris even boasted of the serviceman's lives he had saved; following one of his congratulatory messages it was noted in the Operations Record Book of No. 83 Squadron: 'We all [sic] given to understand that our last few raids have done more to end this war and save thousands of "Brown Jobs" than anything so far'. Public Record Office AIR 27/687 'Summary of Events' 27 July 1943. Terraine *Right of the Line* p. 682 points out that 47,268 Bomber Command crew died on operations (plus 8,305 in flying accidents when not on operations) compared to 38,834 British Army officers killed 1914–1918.

The way in which intellectual theory tends to become a smoke-screen for mindless profusion and misapplication of resources seems indeed to be a characteristic of organization man in the twentieth century: and in this as in so much else it was Britain's proud destiny to lead the way.[83]

[83] Solly Zuckerman *Scientists and War: The Impact on Science of Military and Civil Affairs* (1966) p. 103.

17

The War of the Plebiscitary Dictatorships

Even though daring plans in the field of strategy and operations, exemplary military performance, and several other imponderables may offer favourable prospects to the weaker party during the course of hostilities, the entire war potential of a nation is in our time the decisive factor. This potential is composed of quantities which must be computed with mathematical precision.

Walter Warlimont, 'Reflections on High Command Organization: The Unification Problem', in Donald S. Detwiler ed., *World War II German Military Studies* (24 vols New York 1979), vol. 6, p. 11.

I. Social Cohesion in the Third Reich: Supervision

The difference between the regimes of the 1914–18 era and those of the 1939–45 era was nowhere more strongly marked than in Germany. In November 1918 the German state disintegrated at a time when German troops stood everywhere on foreign soil: in May 1945 most of Germany had already been occupied before the government agreed to surrender.

As Detlev Peukert has pointed out, the survival of the Nazi regime to the very end can be explained in terms of 'a seduction theory, or of a supervision theory' – that is, in terms of a whole population won over to the support of a Nazi *Götterdämmerung* or of a whole population intimidated by the Gestapo into fighting and dying for a doomed cause. The Allies tended to favour the latter interpretation for they had always been inclined to believe that the stability of the Hitler regime depended essentially on force and fear. This was not simply a question of self-image in the Anglo-American side – the democratic societies of free, reasonable men, voluntarily united in their opposition to dictatorship, Gestapo, brainwashing, expropriation and coercion. It was also a deduction from the recent past, and a hope for the immediate future. In 1918, as Winston Churchill himself had written:

The mighty framework of German Imperial Power, which a few days before had overshadowed the nations, shivered suddenly into a thousand individually disintegrating fragments.

It was not unnatural to hope that the same might happen again, especially as this time Britain and the U.S. were investing vastly greater energies in the undermining of the German home front. But it did not happen.[1]

The difference between the manner of the two defeats, in 1918 and in 1945, is in itself an important historical question; but the resilience of the Nazi dictatorship in 1944–1945 also poses vital questions about the nature of the Nazi regime and its common ground with other governments of the day.

The whole nature of total war meant that regimentation and coercion were by no means confined to the so-called dictatorships. Control of the civilian population was more extensive in Britain than in any other belligerent country except the Soviet Union. Rationing, the labour conscription of women, restriction of entry into certain areas and so on, were backed up by the law courts. New crimes were invented: during the six years of hostilities 332 people were sent to jail and no less than 898,300 fined for offences against British Government black-out regulations. On the other hand the key feature of Mussolini's wartime dictatorship in Italy was in its failure to extend its regulatory activities beyond peacetime levels, or even to enforce existing regulations once they came under pressure. By the autumn of 1942 food riots had become a frequent occurrence in southern Italy and in at least one instance the disturbances culminated in an arson attack on a *carabinieri* barracks. Clandestine broadsheets denouncing the Fascist leadership began to appear immediately after the renewal of R.A.F. bombing raids on northern Italy late in October 1942, and in March 1943 there was a manifestly political strike throughout the industrial centres of the north. After the return to work 875 individuals were proceeded against legally, which was not very many considering the numbers of strikers: during the First World War the Italian military authorities alone had court-martialled an average of 1,400 civilians a month, not including those who tried to evade the call-up. Between 1940 and 1943 there were in Italy a grand total of *seventeen* executions of individuals sentenced by the Special Tribunal for the Defence of the State. When one compares this with what happened under Hitler one begins to see that *dictatorship* means different things in different cultures.[2]

Not including the Jews and Gypsies who were sent to extermination camps, it is estimated that 1,650,000 persons passed through Nazi concentration camps between 1933 and 1945. The camp population stood at 21,000 in September 1939, 115,000 in August 1942, 224,000 a year later, 524,000 in August 1944

---

[1] Detlev J.K. Peukert *Inside Nazi Germany: Conformity, Opposition and Racism in Everyday Life* (1987) p. 67; Winston Churchill *The World Crisis* (6 vols. 1923–31) vol. 4 p. 540. For the influence of this view of Nazi society of the R.A.F.'s strategic bombing offensive see e.g. Anthony Verrier *The Bomber Offensive* (1968) p. 320, 360fn.

[2] *Parliamentary Papers* 1946–7 XV p. 783 (Cmd. 7227 p. 13); Nicola Gallerano 'La disgregazione delle basi di massa del fascismo nel Mezzogiorno e il ruolo delle masse contadine' Gianfranco Bertolo et al. *Operai e Contadini nella Crisi Italiana del 1943/1944* (Milan 1974) p. 435–496 at p. 461; Nicola Gallerano et al. 'Crisi di regime sociale', Bertolo et al. *Operai e Contadini* p. 3–78 at p. 67, cf Stephen Harvey 'The Italian War Effort and the Strategic Bombing of Italy' *History* vol. 70 (1985) p. 32–45 at p. 43–4; Martin Clark *Modern Italy, 1871–1982* (1985) p. 233.

and 714,000 in January 1945. The number who died in camps like Buchenwald, Bergen-Belsen and Dachau from starvation, ill-treatment, torture and disease probably exceeds one million, and though the proportion of detainees who were foreign nationals increased progressively, it is possible that more than a third of these million victims were German citizens of unexceptionable racial origin. In addition the population of 226 major prisons rose from 108,685 on 30 June 1939 to 195,636 on 31 October 1942: thereafter the increase was minimal simply because there was no more space.[3]

There were also something in the region of 27,000 death sentences handed down by civilian and military tribunals – and there were no reprieves. The figures for executions show the same tendency to rise progressively as the statistics for imprisonment: 306 civilian executions in 1940, 5,764 in 1944; 519 military executions in the first twelve months of the war, 4,118 in the fourth. The commonest reason for being executed in the Wehrmacht was probably desertion. Amongst civilians, very minor pilfering from bombed-out houses or from the homes of soldiers absent at the front sometimes resulted in the death penalty; nevertheless of 2,042 executions carried out between 22 August 1940 and 20 April 1945 in Brandenburg Penitentiary, the main penal establishment for the Berlin region, 498 were for High Treason, and 558 for sedition – including 21 clergymen and 22 students and schoolchildren. At Brandenburg alone 75 persons under twenty years old were executed (the youngest only sixteen) and 78 over sixty; six pairs of fathers and sons went to the scaffold. In the final months of the war there were also numerous summary executions by the SS of military and civilian personnel accused of desertion or other manifestations of disloyalty. In addition a number of social deviants were given lethal injections on 'medical' grounds: Bruno Lüdke, who confessed to murdering 85 women between 1928 and January 1943, was disposed of by this method in a Vienna clinic in April 1944, but other victims of Nazi medicine's efforts to purify the race included people suffering from 'incurable communism'.[4]

[3] Joseph Billig *Les Camps de Concentration dans l'économie du Reich hitlérien* (Paris 1973) p. 91; ibid. p. 72 and Wolfgang Ruge and Wolfgang Schumann *Dokumente zur Deutschen Geschichte, 1939–1942* (Frankfurt 1977) p. 142–3.

[4] Ruge and Schumann *Dokumente* p. 143 and Günter Weisenborn *Der lautlose Aufstand: Bericht über die Widerstandbewegung des Deutschen Volkes, 1933–1945* (Hamburg 1953) p. 259; Richard Grunberger *A Social History of the Third Reich* (1971) p. 124; Weisenborn *Lautlose Aufstand* p. 258; Alice Platen-Hallermund *Die Tötung Geisteskranker in Deutschland* (Frankfurt 1948) p. 76. Omer Bartov *The Eastern Front, 1941–45, German Troops and the Barbarisation of Warfare* (Basingstoke 1985) p. 27–31 shows that the Wehrmacht dealt severely with looting and rape during the campaigns of 1939 and 1940 but that in Russia looting and rape, though frequent, were rarely prosecuted: instead there were numerous executions for such offences as self-mutilation and neglect of duty.

The American authorities estimated that out of 380,000 German P.O.W.s in camps in the U.S.A. 167 were clandestinely executed by their fellow-prisoners following secret trials: seven P.O.W.s were executed by the Americans for involvement in two of these liquidations. When it was decided to segregate anti-Nazi prisoners from the rest they were initially estimated at 10–12 per cent of the total: Danielle Costelle *Les Prisonniers* (Paris 1975) p. 63–71.

To set the figure of 27,000 judicially authorized executions in some kind of comparative context, one might note that in the whole of Germany 1914–1918 there were 411 convictions under the treason laws, of which 243 were foreigners or Alsace-Lorrainers; in the army there were 150 death sentences handed down by courts martial, of which 48 were actually carried out.[5]

Clearly there is no truth in the commonly held prejudice that the Germans, having some sort of natural taste for discipline, fell unresistingly into line behind the Nazi leadership. Nor was Nazi propaganda entirely effective in maintaining commitment to the regime, for the psychological dissent of the younger generation – precisely those most intensively and comprehensively exposed to Nazi indoctrination – shows up more clearly in the documentation than that of any other social group. It was perhaps inevitable that the disruptions of wartime should boost juvenile delinquency – in Britain the juvenile crime rate nearly doubled 1938–1945 – but in Germany youth dissent also took the form of involvement in a variety of subcultural groups which had no counterpart in Britain till the emergence of the Teddy Boys some years after the war, and which can only reasonably be interpreted as expressions of conscious resistance to the values of Nazi society. One strand of the youth subculture was that of the *Swing-Jugend* in centres like Hamburg and Frankfurt am Main. The authorities, not well-informed on the technicalities of the matter, referred to those young people as imitating English fashions, though the music that the *Swing-Jugend* favoured was evidently American *Negermusik* and *Jazzmusik*. After the Haarlem Klub in Frankfurt was closed down by the police in the spring of 1939, an Ohio-Klub and a Cotton-Klub started up – again the names show the American rather than English orientation of these young people's tastes. Later the British began broadcasting 'American jazz with a German flavour' over the bogus German forces radio network *Soldatensender Calais*, which was eagerly listened to by thousands of Wehrmacht personnel in western Europe who had official access to radio receivers. The Swing movement also reappeared amongst the schoolboy *Flakhelfer* in the last two years of the war; though officially members of the *Hitler Jugend*, the *Flakhelfer* frequently took their auxiliary service as an opportunity to escape from normal *Hitler Jugend* activities and increasingly formed a distinct subcultural group within which American jazz was highly esteemed.[6]

---

[5] W. Nicolai *The German Secret Service* (1924) p. 217; Martin van Creveld *Fighting Power: German and U.S. Army Performance, 1939–1945* (1983) p. 113 table 9.3.

[6] *Parliamentary Papers* 1946 XV p. 796 (Cmd. 7227 p. 16); Detlev Peukert *Die Edelweisspiraten: Protestbewegungen jugendlicher Arbeiter im Dritten Reich* (Cologne 1983) p. 201–203; Peter Bleuel *Strength through Joy: Sex and Society in Nazi Germany* (1973) p. 243; Ellic Howe *The Black Game* (1982) p. 174–5; Willi Bucher and Klaus Pohl ed. *Schock und Schöpfung: Jugendästhetik im 20. Jahrhundert* (Darmstadt 1986: catalogue of exhibition organized by Württembergischer Kunstverein Stuttgart) p. 320–323, 326–330, 383–390; Michael H. Kater *Different Drummers: Jazz in the Culture of Nazi Germany* (New York 1992) p. 153–62, 195.

Generally more proletarian in social origin were a number of teenage gangs which modelled themselves less on jazz culture than on the *Wandervögel* groups of the earlier years of the century. They adopted various names: *Meuten* (dog packs) in Leipzig, *Stadtbadbrühe* (town baths broth) at Chemnitz; but the most famous were the *Edelweisspiraten* – or EP – originating in Düsseldorf but later spreading to Cologne. One of their customs (rather disturbing in a police state) was to walk or hitch-hike all over the Greater German Reich, either in small groups or quite alone, sleeping rough and often pilfering food. The Edelweiss Pirates were also involved in small-scale crime in Cologne and a number were eventually tried for such offences and hanged.[7]

The *Swing-Jugend* and the *Edelweisspiraten* were in a sense *the* typical expressions of dissent in Nazi society. There seems to have been remarkably little politically-informed dissent at the general level, though it does appear that many people half-expected *other people* to become involved in open resistance: the courageous protests of Hans and Sophie Scholl at Munich university were soon inflated by rumour into large student demonstrations and mass executions, though in fact there were only six death sentences (and eleven jail sentences) imposed in connection with the Scholl outbreak and the only student demonstrations in Munich at this time was one staged by 3,000 young Nazis in support of the regime. The only Nazi policies which provoked widespread opposition were those that directly conflicted with the religious prejudices of the population, such as the removal of crucifixes from school classrooms, the expulsion of monks from monasteries, and the euthanasia programme for congenital defectives – the latter of course was objectionable to a wide spectrum of lay opinion but was also in the event the principle instance of the Roman Catholic church mobilizing opposition to the regime. On the other hand there was remarkably little public concern regarding the Nazis' Jewish policies; the order of 1 September 1941 that Jews should wear the Star of David seems generally to have been welcomed as clarifying the situation in some way. Despite SS security and of course a total clamp-down on media publicity the mass-murder of the Jews began to be talked about in Germany at approximately the same time as the details began to reach Britain and America, though the scale and comprehensiveness of the programme and the systematic use of cyanide gas was rarely suspected. Deportation of Jews led to disturbances in Berlin early in March 1943 when working-class women barracked SS troopers escorting Jews, shouting, 'Go to the front where you belong!', but what was objected to was probably less the maltreatment of

[7] Peukert *Edelweisspiraten* p. 35, 42, 188–9, and Bleuel *Strength through Joy* p. 242; Peukert *Edelweisspiraten* p. 68–70, evidence of Joseph M., 15 Dec. 1942 and cf text and photos in Bucher and Pohl ed. *Schock und Schöpfung* p. 308–325 – especially p. 316–8. See also Peukert *Inside Nazi Germany* p. 154–169.

In 1945 the Allies were seriously concerned by the threat posed by Nazi-indoctrinated youth groups operating as urban guerillas under the denomination 'Werewolves'. The threat failed to materialize.

old women and children than the sight of fit well-fed young men carrying out Nazi party stunts when other young men were fighting for their country in Russia and North Africa. Even well-informed people hid themselves from the realization of what lay ahead for the deportees: when in December 1944 Swiss newspapers finally published the full truth about Auschwitz and copies were circulated in Germany, one reader responded in agony, 'Must I believe this horrible report? It exceeds the worst imaginings. It simply can't be true'. On the other hand one rather feels that if people had been less anxious to avoid facing the obvious many Germans would have realized much earlier that more was involved in the deportations than reduced rations and the occasional unimportant massacre.[8]

A similar mental passivity may be read into the anti-Hitler plot which culminated in the unsuccessful 20 July 1944 *Putsch*. Since the war this conspiracy has been much celebrated in Germany, and it is only just to point out that no conspiracy of anything like comparable proportions ever developed in Italy or Japan, let alone in Britain, or the U.S.A. or the Soviet Union. Nevertheless the 20 July plot was essentially half-baked, and the involvement of prominent and widely respected individuals like Generaloberst Ludwig Beck, the former Army chief of staff, and Carl Goerdeler, former Oberbürgermeister of Leipzig and Reich Prices Commissioner in the early days of the Hitler regime, demonstrates less the stature of the plot than the weaknesses of the ruling elite which Hitler had brushed aside so contemptuously in the 1930s. Admittedly the plotters were the counterpart of the upper professional classes still holding hegemonic power in Britain – Adam von Trott zu Solz, one of the more prominent 20 July plotters, had even read Politics, Philosophy and Economics at Balliol College, Oxford – but the conspiracy may be taken simply as yet another indication of how inept such groups are at moments of real challenge unless given leadership by self-made wild men like Lloyd George or Churchill. Goerdeler was anti-democratic, ultra-nationalistic, too basically decent perhaps to be a Nazi, but saved from being a quasi-fascist only by the junk of nineteenth-century constitutional theory he had taken on board in his youth. After serving with the German occupation authorities in Western Russia in the last months of the First World War he had involved himself with the resistance to the setting up of Danzig as a Free City and with a plot to attack the newly-formed Polish republic in order to prevent the cession to Poland of the corridor between East Prussia and Pomerania. As Prices Commissioner he seems to have served with more

---

[8] Marlis G. Steinert *Hitler's War and the Germans: Public Mood and Attitude during the Second World War* (Athens, Ohio 1977) p. 207, cf Christian Petry *Studenten aufs Schafott: die Weisse Rose und ihr Scheitern* (Munich 1968) p. 130, 195–7; Steinert *Hitler's War and the Germand* p. 134–5; ibid. p. 141–4 for rumours of the extermination of the Jews but cf Gitta Sereny *Into that Darkness: from Mercy Killings to Mass Murder* (1974) p. 159 citing diary of Hubert Pfoch, Aug. 1942; Ursula von Kardoff *Berliner Aufzeichnungen, 1942–1945* (Munich 1976) p. 37–8, diary 3 March 1943; ibid. p. 215–6, diary 27 Dec. 1944.

satisfaction to himself than to his Nazi colleagues, and though his appointment was not renewed in 1935 he continued to submit memoranda till one of them fell foul of both Göring and Goebbels in the autumn of 1936. In 1937 he resigned at his post as Oberbürgermeister of Leipzig in protest at the removal of a statue of the composer Mendelssohn (member of a famous Jewish family) but it seems that what he found most objectionable in the Hitler regime was its wild deficit finance and its assault on local municipal autonomy. When he first made contact with British officials in December 1938 with a view to organizing resistance to Hitler Sir Alexander Cadogan of the Foreign Office noted, 'He had already sent us a "programme", which we couldn't subscribe to – too much like "Mein Kampf"'. At one time he favoured a Reichstag consisting partly of members nominated by professional groups and by compulsory trade unions, but later favoured a combination of direct elections and nominations by annually held provincial councils which were themselves to be elected by county (*Kreis*) councils derived from a combination of direct and indirect election: a complicated system designed to minimize the effect of shifts in public opinion, and indicative of how far he was from being a democrat.[9]

As for Beck, his political sophistication was demonstrated by his proposal, early in 1943, that after the *Putsch* there should be a ruling triumvirate, which would include Hjalmar Schacht, Hitler's former finance minister and a man whom the Allies were later to put on trial as a Major War Criminal. Other plotters favoured cooperation with the grandchildren of the Kaiser and there was also some hope of using the national crisis to arrange the confessional unification of the German Roman Catholic and Protestant communities, so as to bring to an end four centuries of un-German ecclesiastical dividedness. People like Konrad Adenauer who were known to favour the breaking up of Germany into autonomous regions were not asked to join the eager debate concerning the shape of the post-Hitlerite Germany. (This is why Adenauer was still alive to become the first post-Hitlerite Chancellor after the war.) And it was only because of the initiative of the young army officers led and inspired by Claus Graf Schenk von Stauffenberg that any contact was made with socialist groups.[10]

It was in fact mainly due to Stauffenberg that the plot progressed beyond

[9] Gerhard Ritter *The German Resistance: Carl Goerdeler's Struggle against Tyranny* (1958) p. 19 and Eberhard Zeller *The Flame of Freedom: The German Struggle against Hitler* (Coral Gables 1969) p. 47–8 for Goerdeler's career at the end of the First World War; Ritter *German Resistance* p. 34–5 for Goerdeler's career as price commissioner and Zeller *Flame of Freedom* p. 49 for the nature of his objections to the Nazi regime circa 1937; David Dilks ed. *The Diaries of Sir Alexander Cadogan, 1938–1945* (1971) p. 128, 10 Dec. 1938. Goerdeler's constitutional views are discussed in Ritter *German Resistance* p. 183–5, Hans Mommsen 'Social Views and Constitutional Views of the Resistance', in Hans Mommsen, Joachim Reichardt, Ernst Wolf *The German Resistance to Hitler* (1970) p. 55–147 at p. 114–127 and Peter Hoffman *The History of the German Resistance, 1933–1945* (1977) p. 184–190.

[10] Otto John *Twice through the Lines* (1972) p. 102; ibid. p. 88–9, 109. Material dealing with Adenauer is extremely coy on the subject of the 20 July plot and I am grateful to Dr. R.B. Jones for suggesting the explanation given here.

fantasy at either the political or the practical level. It was finally left to Stauffenberg to handle relations with the socialists as well as personally assassinate Hitler at his *Wolfsschanze* H.Q. near Rastenburg in East Prussia and, simultaneously, lead the military uprising in Berlin. By means of split-second timing Stauffenberg managed to get away from Hitler's East Prussian H.Q. just before his bomb exploded and to fly to Berlin in time to lead the coup; if the plan had not required him to be in both places at once perhaps he would have been able to make a better job of killing Hitler.

The 20 July conspiracy was not the only anti-Nazi plot. At the end of 1942 a Dr. Kumerow, a section head at a wireless factory in Berlin was executed for planning to blow up Goebbels with a radio-controlled bomb placed under a bridge leading to the latter's private villa on Schwanenwerder Insel, Wannsee; Kumerow was a neighbour and may have suspected the notoriously randy propaganda minister of tampering with his womenfolk: at any rate the political ramifications remain obscure. There were also a number of conspiratorial communist cells which the Gestapo found relatively easy to penetrate; perhaps the most important of these was the '*Rote Kapelle*' spy-ring, in connection with which 118 people were arrested in September 1942. The key member of this group in Berlin was a Luftwaffe officer, Harro Schulze-Boysen, whose combination of social elitism and ultra-left politics made him a kind of heterosexual counterpart of Britain's Burgess and Maclean; but since he had stepped out of his social class to become a Soviet agent, Schulze-Boysen's activities were evidently easier to detect than those of the more exclusively upper-class Stauffenberg-Goerdeler circle. The latter involved a large range of contacts – its existence must have been known to literally hundreds of people – and was pursued with the laxest security. 'One of the most astonishing things about the 20 July assassination plot was that so many people – not all of them discreet – knew about it, and yet the police never had an inkling', wrote one woman who herself knew all about the plot from her sister, even though neither had any allotted role in the organization. No attempt was made even to avoid compromising the security of Stauffenberg, who was the only plotter with regular access to Hitler and therefore indispensable for the assassination; only five weeks before the day of the *Putsch* Stauffenberg attended a final conference of the plotters in a hotel: Goerdeler and the socialist leader Julius Leber were amongst those who attended even though it would have been reasonable to suppose that they both might be under Gestapo surveillance. One may very well conclude that by the time the bomb was planted in the conference room at Hitler's East Prussian H.Q. the conspiracy had used up all its due allotment of luck; and the error of leaving so much to be handled individually by Stauffenberg was underlined by the fact that, having lost one hand and two fingers of the other in North Africa – hence his relegation to H.Q. duties – the would-be assassin had difficulty manipulating the pliers required to prime the bombs, and though supplied with two bombs, had time only to prime one before going into the conference room.[11]

II. Social Cohesion in the Third Reich: Seduction

Though the executions and imprisonments must have touched almost every family in Hitler's Germany, there was no breakdown such as occurred in many countries in the First World War, and in Italy in the Second World War. While it is true that the Gestapo, much better staffed even if not better organized than comparable organs in the earlier war, held down the level of dissent, the level of dissent achieved, judging by the numbers of prosecutions and detention orders, was far higher than any other regime could have sustained, yet seems rather to have strengthened the commitment of those not implicated, in a reflex of obstinacy and intolerance that suggests psychic reserves of bitterness directed as much against self as against outsiders.

An important difference between 1918 and 1945 was that the German administration was able to maintain food supplies almost till the last. A British Foreign Office official visiting Germany shortly after the capitulation reported:

> The population more healthy looking, better dressed, and showing less sign of strain than one would have expected, even in the most heavily damaged areas.

He evidently discussed this with members of the occupation forces:

> there is general agreement that the Germans are by no means exhausted by their struggles and their defeat. The general impression is that they are less defeatist and more self-reliant than the French, less war-weary than the British.

The fact was that, with adequate food supplies, and despite over two million war-dead and hundreds of thousands of permanently mutilated, the vast majority of the German population had been less physically touched by the horrors they had unleashed than any other European population save that of Sweden. One may observe today that the town cemeteries filled with tragic memorials to Germany's war dead coexist with suburbs encrusted with ornate

---

[11] Rudolf Semmler *Goebbels The Man Next to Hitler* (1947) p. 40, diary 19 Dec. 1942; Gille Perrault *The Red Orchestra* (1968) p. 106, 199, 215; Tatiana Metternich *Tatiana: Five Passports in a Shifting Europe* (1976) p. 202: for her sister cf *The Berlin Diaries of Marie 'Missie' Vassiltchikov* (1985) p. 83, 1 Aug. 1943; this book, originally written in English, might have been subtitled 'Sloane Ranger in the Third Reich'. For the final conference cf Zeller *Flame of Freedom* p. 272, and for the details for the priming and planting of the bomb cf Hoffmann *History of the German Resistance* p. 398–9, 405–6, 666 n. 15: it seems however that the principal reason why the second bomb was not primed was that Stauffenberg was interrupted by Feldwebel Werner Vogel, who had been sent to hurry him up. Peter Hoffmann 'Colonel Claus von Stauffenberg in the German Resistance to Hitler: Between East and West' *Historical Journal* vol. 31 (1988) p. 629–650 at p. 650 comments on the impracticality of the arrangements made for the Putsch: this article generally argues that in any case the plotters had no rational expectation of obtaining new foreign policy options for Germany by removing Hitler.

Jugendstil ironwork; the one paid for the survival of the other. In Britain there are fewer war graves, but the cropped metalwork stumps on front garden walls throughout the vast acreage of nineteenth-century suburbia, representing thousands of tons of wrought iron railings requisitioned to make armaments, provide an enduring reminder of wartime sacrifices and privations.[12]

The German people's will to resist had undoubtedly been strengthened by the dread of Russian Bolshevism and by the Anglo-American insistence on an unconditional surrender which would deliver the eastern half of the Reich to the Communists. The Bolshevik bogey, though much emphasized by the Nazis, was not a Nazi creation. Essentially it even predated Bolshevism. The October 1917 revolution had revived two phobias which are already identifiable in the eighteenth century: the chilling vision of a society which combined unlimited imperialist ambition with unlimited supplies of inhumanly regimented manpower; and the spectre of a total abolition of private property, the sequestration of all that one had worked for, saved up or inherited. In 1919 even Britain had borne witness to how close these nightmares came to the most cherished fear and preoccupations of middle-class society; and the Germans, long before Hitler, had always been geographically much closer to the threat. The Nazis needed only to build on this.

Except in the heady days following the fall of France the war had never been very popular in Germany, and the Nazi party as an institution, or group of public figures, quickly lost such credibility as it had gained in the 1930s – and even as early as 1934 and 1935 it had been noted that the initial magic of the Nazi regime seemed to have worn off and that resentment of the party dictatorship was more open. Many prominent Nazis disgraced themselves during the war, particularly Hess by his flight to Scotland in May 1941 and Göring by the successive failures of the Luftwaffe. Less widely known, though not without influence, were the suspension of Julius Streicher from his duties as Gauleiter of Franconia in 1940, the expulsion from the party of Joseph Wagner, Gauleiter of Silesia in 1942 – he had wanted a church

[12] Public Record Office FO 371/46933/C 3858 printed report Sir William Strang to Foreign Secretary 13 July 1945.

The German government had become seriously concerned regarding the break-down of food supplies by March 1945 (cf Marlis G. Steinert *Capitulation 1945: The Story of the Dönitz Regime* (1969) p. 4, 124–5 and cf p. 218–221). Nevertheless one assumes that by the early spring most of the food for the coming months had already been imported and distributed to the regions, though the breakdown of the transportation network obviously caused local difficulties. At this stage government activity in this sphere was largely a matter of paper exercises, with the actual situation varying enormously from district to district. Newsreel footage of looting by starving German mobs in the British-occupied zone appears to have been staged (cf Nicholas Pronay 'Defeated Germany in British Newsreels, 1944–45' in K.R.M. Short and Stephen Dolezel ed. *Hitler's Fall: The Newsreel Witness* (1988) p. 28–49 at p. 31–2). After the German surrender however the food situation even in the more fortunate areas deteriorated considerably.

wedding for his daughter and her SS fiancé, an ideological lapse which led eventually to his disappearance into a concentration camp – and the dismissal for incompetence of Karl Heinrich, Gauleiter of Kurhessen, in September 1944. Generally speaking Hitler's loyalty to his Gauleiters was not justified by their actual contribution to the solidity of the regime and some of them were not even politically reliable: Fritz Wächtler, Gauleiter of Bayreuth, was summarily executed by the SS as a defeatist in the last weeks of the war and Joseph Bürckel, Gauleiter of Westmark – earlier called Saarpfalz – having objected to his *Gau* become a battle zone, either shot himself at the SS's insistence (or with their assistance) in September 1944, or else died after a well-timed illness. Non-party members were often more loyal than party veterans; though in the late spring of 1943 Mussolini set up the 'M' division, on the model of the Waffen-SS as an instrument to defend the Fascist Revolution, the Waffen-SS gained less distinction in this particular role than its Italian counterpart; it was a regular army unit under a career officer, Otto-Ernst Remer, which played the decisive part in putting down the 20 July *Putsch*, and after the war Remer, though he had never been a party member, became briefly the most prominent neo-Nazi leader in West Germany before fleeing to Egypt in 1952 to escape a jail sentence and to pursue the struggle against World Jewry in the Middle East.[13]

As the war moved towards its catastrophic end, the German leadership seems to have lost interest in their former rhetoric of innovation and renewal and concentrated their energies on a struggle which, like a modern Sword and Sorcery novel, seemed to be set in some kind of historical Never-Never Land. Goebbels noted:

> I am reading memoranda by Gneisenau and Scharnhorst about preparations for expansion of the people's war in 1808. At that time things were precisely as they are to today and we must defend ourselves against the enemy using the same methods as were in vogue before the wars of liberation.

Frederick the Great, Barbarossa and the Nibelungs also took on a new topicality. Like Britain in 1940, fired by journalistic memories of the Spanish Armada and the resistance to Napoleon, Germany in 1944–1945 felt that it had been there before.[14]

It is instructive to compare Hitler, the leader who maintained his leadership, with Mussolini, the leader who was ousted, and to see how differently they comported themselves during the final months of their two superficially similar

---

[13] Arthur Geoffrey Dickens *Lübeck Diary* (1947) p. 14, 16 May 1945 (recollecting pre-war visits to Germany) and Public Record Office FO 371/18858/C 6332 D. St. Clair Gainer, consul-general at Munich to Foreign Office 28 August 1935; Peter Hüttenberger *Die Gauleiter: Studie zum Wandel des Machtgefüges in der NSDAP* (Stuttgart 1969) p. 208–9, 220; ibid. p. 210–211. For Remer see Robert Wistrich *Who's Who in Nazi Germany* (1982) p. 244–5.

[14] Hugh Trevor-Roper ed. *The Goebbels Diaries: The Last Days* (1978) p. 26, 2 March 1945.

regimes. While Mussolini tried to rally support to his government by a round of speech-making, culminating in an address from the balcony of the Palazzo Venezia on 5 May 1943, Hitler withdrew increasingly into the claustrophobic privacy of his various military headquarters. His last visit to an Army Group H.Q. was on 8 September 1943; his last big broadcast speech was at the Munich *Löwenbräukeller* two months later; his last public speech was at a gathering of industrial leaders at Obersalzberg, on 4 July 1944 ('uneasy and disordered speech,' Speer wrote later, '. . . hardly any applause'); his last broadcast, a cursory and uninspiring effort, was on 30 January 1945, the twelfth anniversary of his accession to power. Basically, after Stalingrad, he withdrew himself from the limelight. Goebbels thought this was a major error:

> The situation is such that only a word from the Führer can relieve the crisis of morale in which the people is plunged at the moment. I regard it as a great mistake that the Führer does not speak. Even if at the moment we have no victory to which we can point, the Führer could still say something; it not only in victory that one should speak but in misfortune as well.

But perhaps Hitler knew what he was doing: certainly he knew his people would not forget he was there.[15]

In reality it is difficult to see what more Hitler could have done to rally support, though in any case he did not much care: 'If the war is lost, the people will be lost also', he said. 'The nature of this struggle permits no consideration for the population to be taken.' But perhaps he also perceived that it was not really necessary to whip up support; he had so established himself as the symbol of Germany's regeneration in the years 1933–1940, had become so pervasive a presence in the imagination of his people, that it would have been self-indulgently theatrical to parade himself as Mussolini did. After Stalingrad there was no time for doubts or distractions or looking over one's shoulder; Hitler set himself to be an example of myopic devotion to duty and millions of his adopted countrymen eagerly followed his example as an alternative to reflecting on the implications of what they were doing. When he had toured the country in the 1930s he had seen in the adoring eyes of the people a pledge to follow him to the ends of the universe, and the promise of those earlier years was duly fulfilled in the scorched and shattered boulevards of Hamburg, Berlin and Dresden and in those other communities which will always seem synonyms of evil rather than actual places, Auschwitz, Sobibor and Treblinka.[16]

---

[15] F.W. Deakin *The Brutal Friendship: Mussolini, Hitler and the Fall of Italian Fascism* (1962) p. 316–323; Max Domarus ed. *Hitler Reden und Proklamationen, 1932–1945* (Munich 1963) p. 2050, 2113, 2195; Joachim Fest *Hitler* (Harmondsworth 1982 edit.) p. 673, 676; Albert Speer *Inside the Third Reich* (1970) p. 360, Trevor-Roper ed. *Goebbels Diaries* p. 309, 3 April 1945.

[16] Speer *Inside the Third Reich* p. 440, 456–7.

III. Wartime Leadership

Hitler and his personal ascendancy, in fact, represented the solution of the problem of command and control which had plagued the belligerent governments during the First World War.

Despite its scale the Second World War was dominated by personalities as no previous conflict had been. It was a war, not of Empires, but of Dictatorships. It might be argued that this was, if not simply the workings of coincidence, no more than the correlation of the disparate results of the 1914–1918 war:– international instability resulting from the First World War leading to renewed conflict, internal instability resulting form the First World War leading to dictatorship. It is indeed true that the Stalin regime in Russia and (with a four-year time lag) the Mussolini regime in Italy grew directly out of the social crisis of the 1914–1918 war. And it was part of the Nazi repudiation of Weimar that the Hitler regime should present itself as a rebuilding and regeneration consequent on the disaster of 1918: note for example the emphasis of the opening titles of Leni Riefenstahl's propaganda film *The Triumph of the Will*:

> Sept. 4 1934
> 20 years after the outbreak of the World War
> 16 years after the beginning of German suffering and sorrow
> 19 months after the beginning of German's rebirth.

Many of the young men who responded most constructively to the new conditions of the First World War turned to ultra-right politics: Fuller, the pioneer theorist of Blitzkrieg, Graham Seton Hutchison the machine-gunner, airmen like Hermann Göring and Rudolf Berthold, who, after becoming Germany's sixth ranking ace with 44 aerial victories led a Freikorps group, *Eiserne Schar Berthold* till caught by Leftists and strangled with the ribbon of his *Pour le mérite* order. Major Mannock's violently anti-establishment view had a definitely proto-fascist tinge and it is difficult to believe that if he had survived the war he would have remained in Ramsay Macdonald's Labour Party; Sir Oswald Mosley too was a pilot in the Royal Flying Corps, while the flight training of Mussolini's coadjutor Italo Balbo was interrupted by the Caporetto disaster; the French air ace René Fonck, a Republican Democrat Left deputy in the *Chambre* after the First World War, was arrested as a pro-German collaborator at the end of the Second World War, and so on. But a number of innovatory and historically anomalous regimes – of which Hitler's was merely the most extreme – owed their establishment not to the catastrophe of 1918 but to the traumatic aftermath of the 1929–1931 world economic crisis, a crisis which though shaped was by no means provoked by the First World War. Hitler in Germany and Dollfuss in Austria erected nationalist dictatorships on the ruins of their national economies; in Hungary the government of Gyula Gömbös began to push the ultra-conservative Horthy regency in the direction of right-radicalism. But the failure of the traditional party system was evident in countries which did not slide into overt dictatorship. In Britain a minority Labour administration dissolved and part of the remnants, placing 'country before party', formed a coalition with the Conservatives and a Liberal splinter group. In Belgium a government of 'technicians' was formed. In the United States Franklin D. Roosevelt attempted to transform the system of federal government, fighting a running battle with the conservatives of his own party; the war had already broken out in Europe when he was elected to an unprecedented third term. The regimes in Austria and Belgium were of course swept away by the advance of the Nazis but Britain and the United States, in combating this advance, relied on what was essentially a continuation of the governments that had evolved in the 1930s. In the U.S. there was no change at all; in Britain the coalition was enlarged but remained dominated by the elements that had come to the fore in the final months of the National Government regime established in 1931.[17]

Even before the war, and increasingly during it, much was made of the difference between the democratic system championed by Churchill and Roosevelt and the tyranny of Hitler and Mussolini; yet to a large extent this was a question merely of forms, at a time when forms had lost their real significance.

The tyrant with the most absolute power was not Hitler the Führer or Mussolini the Duce, but Joseph Stalin, who, up till May 1941, was merely General Secretary of the Communist Party of the Soviet Union, without office in the government: it was only according to people like Beatrice Webb that he had less power than Roosevelt. Stalin was alone amongst the dictators in having achieved his dominant position as a result of a murderous civil war and a completed social revolution. As far as dates were concerned he had ruled about the same length of time as Mussolini, but he had inherited from Lenin an already established revolutionary regime whereas Mussolini had had to build his from scratch so that it had not been till 1924, perhaps not till 1929, that the Italian dictator had achieved his unchallengeable position in Italian politics; and even then it was not absolute. Stalin's rule, like that of Hitler and Mussolini, depended heavily on propaganda and indoctrination, but in view of the way Fascism melted away in Italy in 1943 it may be questioned whether indoctrination can be the monocausal explanation for a system's survival or strength. Stalin had also had time to do two things which Mussolini did not even attempt and for which Hitler had had time, by 1939, only to make a tentative, conservative beginning. First Stalin killed a lot of people. He destroyed an entire class – the peasant proprietors – and the upper reaches of several professions, most notably the military; his victims in the great purge of the late 1930s included 13 out of 15 army commanders,

[17] For Berthold see Bruce Robertson ed. *Air Aces of the 1914–1918 War* (Letchworth 1959) p. 179–180; for Mannock's political views see Frederick Oughton ed. *The Personal Diary of Major Edward 'Mick' Mannock* (1966) p. 15–16, 19, 153–4 n. 32, 161–2 n. 88.

50 out of 57 corps commanders, 154 out of 186 divisional commanders and over 36,000 other officers. The scale of his mass-murders is exceeded only by Hitler's massacre of the Jews, but while part of the loathsomeness of Hitler's Final Solution is that so many Germans took care not to know what was going on, Stalin's murdering, especially the later stages aimed at the military, was accompanied by a stage-managed blaze of publicity. Quite apart from the psychological impact, the terror, relief, bewilderment, disorientation and depression of the survivors, no-one could have been left in any doubt as to the Communist government's absolute 100 per cent commitment to change and Stalin's absolute 100 per cent control of the process; Hitler, incidentally, was a great admirer of Stalin's purges. But, secondly, the urban and industrial sector of the economy developed apace. Russia was materially transformed between 1922 and 1941, whereas in Italy, though the rhetoric changed and became more strident, little was achieved beyond the destruction of a few picturesque slums in Rome and some drainage and irrigation schemes in the more retarded areas; the vast majority of the Italian population experienced neither purges nor industrialization, but merely a few new uniforms to add piquancy to old shortages and frustrations, and a more punctual train service.[18]

Hitler, in the six and a half years of his peacetime government, went further than Mussolini but nothing like as far as Stalin. Up till the outbreak of war the rigging of trials was not immeasurably worse than what might happen in a parliamentary regime – the trial of Sacco and Vanzetti in the U.S. might be compared to that of Marinus van der Lubbe, the alleged Reichstag arsonist – and the concentration camps were relatively small (21,000 detainees in mid-1939 compared to 108,685 prisoners in 226 regular jails). Hitler's economic policies had a shorter term, a more limited objective, than Stalin's; Germany was already an advanced industrial society and the objective was, first to put it back to work, and secondly, to rearm. With private consumption held down, Hitler's reflation of the German economy largely limited the possibility of social mobility to within the framework of the party; Nazism had a psychological impact that was backed up by a material transformation that was probably less than in Britain in the same period, and certainly much less than in the Soviet Union. Hence the emphasis on the *Volksgemeinschaft* (racial community) which according to Hitler, 'means the community of effective labour . . . the unity of all interests . . . the elimination of private citizenship'. Many Germans would have appreciated a little more attention to the elimination of inequalities of wealth and privilege but Hitler's priorities precluded any overhaul of economic and professional elites such as

[18] Figures for the decimation of the Soviet officer corps are taken from Robert Conquest *The Great Terror: a Reassessment* (1990) p. 450, cf Louis P. Lochner ed. *The Goebbels Diaries* (1948) p. 278, 8 May 1943.

had been achieved so homicidally by Stalin; Hitler *needed* his generals, and even the civilian administration was infiltrated rather than jacobinized.[19]

Both Mussolini and Hitler (unlike Stalin) came to power by manipulating a parliamentary system, which they did not control, though their regimes mytholigized the *Marcia su Roma* (March on Rome) and the *Machtergreifung* (Seizure of Power) as much as the Soviet Union mythologized the October Revolution. Mussolini indeed took two years to consolidate his grip on the Italian parliament and never achieved absolute control of the state. Vittorio Emanuele remained nominally *capostato*; though invincibly reticent just as he had been with regard to the First World War ministries, when he chose to intervene it was with decisive effect, just as in pre-Mussolini times. Mussolini complained of 'dragging empty freight cars' and in March 1939 was brought to exclaim: 'If Hitler had had a dickhead of a King between his feet he would never have been able to take Austria and Czechoslovakia'. In June 1939, smarting with resentment at Vittorio Emanuele's graceless behaviour at the ceremonial handing over of the constitution of Albania (newly acquired by Italy), Mussolini announced, 'I am now considering whether we ought to finish the House of Savoy'. But more than three years later he had to confess to Himmler, 'There are three of us in Rome: myself, the King, and the Pope'.[20]

Partly because of the monarchy, Mussolini did not even have absolute sway over his own party and his own appointed colleagues; though he weakened the Fascist party locally and nationally by dismissing nearly all the leaders who showed most energy and initiative, and appointed himself to all the most important ministerial portfolios so as not to set up rival foci of influence in Rome, he was ultimately voted out of office by the Grand Council of the party he had created, and dismissed by the King whose older prestige he had chafed against in vain. That was not Hitler's style: even Stauffenberg's bomb did not shift him. There was always something of the burlesque actor about Mussolini; he never convinced, never managed to fascinate – 'win the love of' is perhaps the required expression – collaborators of the order of Göring, Goebbels, Bormann, Speer. Behind the overlarge personality there was an uncertainty of purpose, and an astonishingly poor grasp of

[19] Ruge and Schumann *Dokumente* p. 142–3; David Schoenbaum *Hitler's Social Revolution: Class and Status in Nazi Germany, 1933–1939* (1967) p. 61. For frequency of criticism of continuing social inequalities in Nazi Germany see Steinert *Hitler's War and the Germans* p. 122, 125–6, 155: Otto Ohlendorf, who was responsible for the surveys on which Steinert's book is based, was particularly interested in this issue.

[20] Malcolm Muggeridge ed. *Ciano's Diary 1939–1943* (1947) p. 93, 25 May 1939, and p. 98, 3 June 1939: this translation has 'empty baggage cars' but the version 'empty freight cars' seems to have established itself (Galeazzo Ciano *Diario* (2 vols Milan 1948 edit.) vol. 1 p. 106, 111 has 'vagoni vuoti'): Muggeridge ed. *Ciano's Diary* p. 56, 27 March 1939 gives 'a nincompoop of a King': Ciano *Diario* vol. 1 p. 67 gives 'testa di c . . . di Re', 'c . . .' obviously having been *cazzo* in the original; Muggeridge ed. *Ciano's Diary* p. 99, 3 June 1939: Deakin *Brutal Friendship* p. 55, record of meeting between Himmmler and Mussolini 11 Oct. 1942.

practical realities. Hitler's judgement was often exceptionally penetrating and backed by a remarkable grasp of technical detail, only failing (though then disastrously) when dealing with other countries; Mussolini fluffed two of the most important arrangements relating to the domestic security of his regime, keeping the police and OVRA (political police) independent of party control, and dismissing the very local officials who, when they reappeared as delegates at the Verona Congress in November 1943, turned out to be the most besottedly loyal; in both cases the intention was to avoid the danger of party rivals and the result was the failure to develop a party organization that could defend his revolution in emergency.

Yet perhaps the difference between Hitler and Mussolini was also a difference of cultures and opportunities. The larger-than-life-size but not quite serious Mussolini suited the Italians' love of theatre; they enjoyed the rhetoric and the flourishes and the spectacle and the trains one could set one's watch by, for no previous Italian government had offered them even so much, and they accepted the bluster and the bullying by the police and the unrelieved poverty because no other government had offered anything else. As the more idealistic participants of the March on Rome were squeezed out, and memories of the communal sacrifices of the First World War faded, the commitment to fundamental changes became progressively weaker, and though Mussolini continued to talk of such changes until his overthrow and subsequent resurrection as head of the Repubblica Sociale Italiana under German protection, he seemed more or less satisfied to accept the limitations on his position, for want of the compulsion and the vision to change it. Hitler in Germany was in some ways much less symbolically appropriate – one still wonders what can have been the psychological appeal for the Germans of someone so drearily lower-middle-class and, what was worse, *Austrian* – but his awful psychotic purposefulness fitted in with a culture that seems, even today, to emphasize commitment and purpose and to nurse grievances, more than any other in Europe. The two dictators thus had little in common other than their two dictatorships – only the name in fact.

Roosevelt's pre-war regime resembles that of Hitler and Mussolini in that it emphasized change, though reform and reconstruction rather than revolution. Even his rhetoric had similar militaristic overtones. Referring in his inaugural address to the need to reduce unemployment, Roosevelt spoke of 'treating the task as we would treat the emergency of war' and announced, 'I assume unhesitatingly the leadership of this great army of our people dedicated to a disciplined attack on our common problems'. Seven years later he felt able to tell the American people: 'We have carried on an offensive on a broad front against social and economic inequalities and abuses which had made our society weak.' There is in fact a detectable similarity between Roosevelt's governmental style and that of Hitler: the same dislike of career officials, especially diplomats, the same organizing of decision-making structures so as to keep the final say in policy in his own hands, the same proliferation of overlapping jurisdictions necessitating constant appeal to his arbitration. On the other hand, though it is probable that Hitler and Mussolini, if they had sought free democratic reelection in 1936–1938, would have been successful – the most that could be claimed against the officially registered 95 per cent Yes vote in Germany's March 1936 plebiscite was that in reality 25 per cent had voted No 'in the old Communist areas of Berlin' – only Roosevelt bothered to renew his popular mandate: and his government, controversial, divisive, and in the absence of peacetime censorship criticized more bitterly than any previous American government, was successful in being reelected. Again, like Hitler, there was something almost sinisterly inappropriate about Roosevelt as a national leader:

> the great torso, the huge and splendid head, the magnificent frame, immobile, anchored to a sofa or a chair, carried from room to room, just able to seem to stand when held firmly up, while the poor withered legs and feet, like those of a cloth doll, are nothing but a mockery.

Roosevelt took on a role that seemed to require the personality of an Abraham Lincoln; but perhaps the amazing sincerity he was able to switch on made up for the leg irons, the cigarette holder, the Harvard drawl he affected to conceal his deviousness. Or perhaps in the desperate days of 1932 the American people looked only for a symbol of tradition and of a courage which could transcend crippling disability.[21]

IV. Winston Churchill: His Finest Hour

All these men were symbols, of differing kinds and with differing success; but the most strikingly symbolic figure of all was Winston Churchill, the pedigree British bulldog come to life.

A paper written in September 1939 by government Chief Whip David Margesson or one of his associates claimed of Neville Chamberlain and his standing in the eyes of the British public:

> They see in him a reflection of themselves and . . . therefore feel that he is one they can understand and can trust.
>
> The ordinary Englishman sees in him an ordinary Englishman like himself; one who has been in business in a small way and has made a little – but not much – money; one who has been happily married and brought up a family of which the world knows little; one who wears the same business-suit everyday, the black coat and vest, the striped trousers, the laced boots, and carries the

---

[21] *The Public Papers and Addresses of Franklin D. Roosevelt* (13 vols New York 1938–50) vol. 2 p. 13, 14, Inaugural Address 4 March 1933; ibid. vol. 9 p. 237 'Fireside chat' 26 May 1940; William Carr *Poland to Pearl Harbour: The Making of the Second World War* (1985) p. 15–16 for comparison of Roosevelt's and Hitler's governing style; William E. Dodd and Martha Dodd *Ambassador Dodd's Diary, 1933–1938* (1941) p. 333, 30 March 1936; Harold Macmillan *War Diaries: Politics and War in the Mediterranean, January 1943–March 1945* (1984) p. 318, 5 Dec. 1943. Roosevelt had been struck down by polio in 1921 and never recovered the use of his legs.

same umbrella whether he is walking on a cloudless morning in the Park with Mrs Chamberlain (which he does everyday at the same hour) or whether he is flying across Europe to meet a dictator and settle the affairs of nations.

It quickly transpired of course that the mood which had made Chamberlain seem so right as natural leader in 1937–1938 had changed, and amidst the escapist distractions of world war the average Englishman no longer wished to be reminded of business gents descending from commuter trains at Waterloo Station. Churchill's superior symbolic quality had been widely appreciated even while he was serving under Chamberlain as First Lord of the Admiralty during the first months of the war, and Chamberlain, with his lugubrious, llama-like features and his umbrella was increasingly seen as the living representation of what had gone wrong at Munich, eventually becoming a kind of counter-symbol of bureaucratic timidity, visionless conservatism and moral platitude, attacked even – or especially – by pre-war admirers who could never forgive him for once having given official authority to their own short-sightedness.[22]

Only twenty-one years separated the two world wars but apart from the ultra-reticent Vittorio Emanuele and Philippe Pétain, the aged hero of Verdun who was recalled to lead the French in their hour of tragedy in 1940, Churchill was the only leader in any country during the Second World War to have held a position of first-rate importance in the previous conflict (Roosevelt had been assistant Secretary of the Navy in the Woodrow Wilson administration, the Hungarian regent Horthy had commanded the Habsburg fleet within the fastnesses of Pola harbour, and Ion Antonescu, the Rumanian *Conducator*, had been chief of operations – *Şeful Biuroului Operaţiilor* – in the Rumanian general staff, with the rank of major, in 1917: but none of these positions can be described as possessing really decisive importance). Churchill had also become the most widely-read authority on the First World War, his best-selling study *The World Crisis* serving moreover as a convincing vindication of his Gallipoli policy; the strategy of Robertson and Haig had few defenders and the lengthy volumes of Lloyd George's *War Memoirs*, though effective as a demolition job on the British military leadership, served more to cut into Lloyd George's own reputation than into the sales of Churchill's book. By 1940 therefore Churchill had more credibility as a war leader in the public mind than could have seemed possible in 1916. In long retrospect a professional iconoclast like Malcolm Muggeridge could refer sneeringly to 'the old sets, the old lines, the old cast, most of whom were decidedly shaky and creaky by this time, but could still manage to get through their lines – just. So tatty a show, to be kept going, required a truly seasoned and outstanding impresario'. Indeed, as befitted the circumstances there was a *déjà vu*, hackneyed element in all the most cherished rhetoric

---

[22] Arthur Marwick *The Home Front: The British and the Second World War* (1976) p. 13 quoting Margesson Papers, Churchill College Cambridge.

of 1940, but to emphasize the spurious, stagey element of Churchill's war leadership would be to deny the apparent seriousness of the situation he confronted, especially during the summer and autumn after the fall of France. The important point about symbols, in the end, is their timeliness and the topicality of their appeal.[23]

Within a couple of weeks of replacing Chamberlain as Prime Minister, Churchill found himself with the task of leading his nation in the greatest crisis of its history. Initially due allowance had to be made for the fact that France was still an ally of seemingly formidable potential; on 27 May 1940 Churchill told the War Cabinet, 'he would not join France in asking for terms; but if he were told what the terms offered were, he would be prepared to consider them'. But even by that stage the orders were going out to take down all sign-posts, to dig up all milestones, to obliterate all places names, so as to deny information to the German parachutists who were daily expected. On the B.B.C. newsreaders began identifying themselves at the beginning of their reading of the news, in case Fifth Columnists or even invading forces gained control of broadcasting studios. Internment of aliens had begun on 12 May; by the end of May Mosley and the leadership of the British Union of Fascists had been rounded up; a government circular of 29 July 1940 advised local authorities to suspend and investigate officials who were 'out of sympathy with the national cause' and who had 'exercised a disturbing and upsetting influence calculated to impede the national war effort'. At the same time some of the most outspoken pre-war defenders of fascist dictatorship such as G. Ward Price of *The Daily Mail* and Beverley Nichols of *The Sunday Chronicle* began taking the lead in publishing hysterical accusations against refugees from Germany and Austria. The crisis brought to Britain the politicization of the private and personal, more precisely the annihilation of the barrier between private and public, which was characteristic of the totalitarian, especially the Nazi spirit. Persons like John Strachey who had made themselves conspicuous by their campaigning for a juster society, or like Duff Cooper who had spoken out before the war against the dictatorships, hastily evacuated their children to Canada to prevent their falling into the hands of the Gestapo. The country prepared itself for the last and decisive stages of a titanic struggle: Churchill told the Commons:

> We shall fight on the beaches, we shall fight on the landing grounds, we shall fight in the fields and in the streets, we shall fight in the hills, we shall hit them over the head with bottles – for we have nothing else – we shall never surrender.

Chains of pillboxes began to be constructed on the outskirts of towns in the southern and eastern counties. A *levée en masse*, subsequently famous as the Home Guard, was mobilized; the availability of large numbers of First World War veterans facilitated this but was not always an advantage: 'in one company

---

[23] Malcolm Muggeridge *Chronicles of Wasted Time* (2 vols 1972–3) vol. 2 p. 76.

in East Sussex there are six different generals all dressed up as generals', the Commons were informed on 2 July. The preparation of equipment to spray mustard gas on the beachheads from light bombers was speeded up. (Stocks of such equipment had been available previously but had been abandoned in France.) On 5 July Lord Beaverbrook, Minister for Aircraft Production, appealed to the 'Women of Britain', for their aluminium cooking utensils, promising, 'We will turn your pots and pans into Spitfires and Hurricanes'. In a broadcast on 10 July the Marchioness of Reading, head of the Women's Voluntary Service said:

> we can all have the tiny thrill of thinking as we hear the news of an epic battle in the air 'Perhaps it was my saucepan that made a part of that Hurricane'.

Vast quantities of saucepans were quickly accumulated: 'The fact that the shops were filled with aluminium pots and pans was churlishly pointed out by some sour-pusses, but it made no difference'. The saucepans (often much missed subsequently in working-class kitchens) were token of an almost hysterical unanimity. There was hardly any thought of capitulation. Hitler's peace offer of 19 July was spontaneously and contemptuously rejected by a B.B.C. announcer within the hour, without reference to the Foreign Office, though Hitler's previous offer, in October 1939, had been considered by the government with the greatest care. The whole nation was ready for Hitler's worst.[24]

[24] Public Record Office CAB 65/13 p. 180, 27 May 1940; Peter Fleming *Invasion 1940* (1957) p. 60, 108; London Borough of Hackney, Archives Department SN/EMER/2 between pp. 106 and 107 copy of Ministry of Health Circular 29 July 1940 (as there has never been a Ministry of the Interior in Britain it was the Ministry of Health which at this time handled most aspects of the relations between central and local government). The Ministry of Health copy of this circular is in Public Record Office HLG 51/568, a file dealing specifically with the question of Conscientious Objectors in local government employment. Reading this circular in the Hackney Archives, it gives the impression of being a mandate for a witch-hunt in the nation's town halls, but in the context of the other papers in HLG 51/568 it seems extremely moderate; Wells City Council had decided to suspend Conscientious Objectors without pay as early as 17 June 1940 and by 15 August 1940 29 councils including Middlesbrough, Ebbw Vale, Bermondsey, Paignton, Richmond and Leamington, had decided to *dismiss* the Conscientious Objectors in their employ (cf various items in HLG 51/568). These blanket dismissals were absolutely contrary to the spirit of the government circular which laid down that, 'The first principle to be observed is that in this country no person should be penalized for the mere holding of an opinion', and that dismissal should only be resorted to in the case of someone who 'has been guilty of more than mere foolishness or indiscretion'. See also Rachel Barker *Conscience, Government and War: Conscientious Objection in Great Britain, 1939–45* (1982) p. 59–77; *Hansard: House of Commons* vol. 361 col. 796, speech by Churchill 4 June 1940: the muttered interjection about hitting the Germans with bottles – not in *Hansard* – is reported in James Lansdale Hodson *Home Front* (1944) p. 296, 14 Feb. 1943; Henry Wills *Pillboxes: A Study of U.K. Defences 1940* (1985) p. vii, p. 46–7; *Hansard House of Commons* vol. 362, col. 645, remark by Vernon Bartlett on generals in the Home Guard, 2 July 1940; Public Record Office AIR 14/609 passim; Norman Longmate *How We Lived Then: A History of Everyday Life during the Second World War* (1971) p. 280; Arthur Christiansen *Headlines All My Life* (1961) p. 189. For the careful consideration given Hitler's October 1939 peace offer cf David Dilks ed. *Diaries of Sir Alexander Cadogan, 1938–1945* London 1971 p. 221–4.

Britain had faced invasion before, in 1588 and 1804–1805, but the previous occasions had not come so soon after having been ignominiously ejected from the continent. The brief campaign in France had used up most of the Army's modern equipment – much of it abandoned in the suburbs of Dunkirk:

	Shipped to France, 1939–1940	Brought home
Field guns and other artillery	2,794	322
Tanks	c.720	22
Other vehicles	68,618	4,739
Ammunition	109,000 tons	32,303 tons
Petrol	166,000 tons	1,071 tons
Other supplies	449,000 tons	33,060 tons

But of course plenty more was rolling out of the factories and the Americans sent quantities of material, including 22,000 machine guns and 55,000 Thompson sub-machine guns to replace the 11,000 machine guns lost in France. It is even possible that the chief weakness of Britain's defences was their lack of coordination; there was no overall inter-service commander-in-chief and within the Royal Air Force and the Royal Navy there was no clear chain of authority integrating the different commands (e.g. Bomber Command, Coastal Command, Fighter Command; Home Fleet, Dover, Portsmouth, Plymouth etc.) This lack of integration may have been part of the reason why Churchill and his colleagues failed to appreciate the fact that the Wehrmacht, precisely because it was so much vaster and more formidably armed than the forces available to Philip II or Napoleon Bonaparte, would have faced insuperable difficulties simply in crossing the channel in sufficient strength. Churchill, with his indifference to logistics and his instinct for overdramatization, allowed himself to be persuaded as much as anybody else, that the situation was worse than it truly was. Indeed, 'his appeal to his countrymen to fight it out was made more passionate by his sense of the drama of this hour in history'.[25]

Of course Churchill was not alone in his sense of drama. 'We were in the final, people were saying, and playing at home', it was recalled; but more often the parallels that occurred (at least to the better educated) were literary or historical. 'There was more than a touch of the address before Agincourt in the air, a secret satisfaction that if it was coming we were to be the chosen, we few, we happy few', wrote Margery Allingham. The critic James Agate noted on 17 June, 'France has surrendered, and this country is back in 1805, 1667, 1588, 1066, or 55 B.C.'. Henry Channon, M.P., later very critical of Churchill's rhetoric, wrote in his diary, 'we are living as people did during the

[25] L.F. Ellis *The War in France and Flanders, 1939–1940* (1953) p. 327; M.M. Postan *British War Production* (1952) p. 117; Lord Moran [C.M. Wilson] *Winston Churchill: The Struggle for Survival, 1940–1965* (1966) p. 782 for quotation concluding this paragraph.

French Revolution – every day is a document, every hour history'. They found themselves, the Lord Mayor of London informed the people of the United States, 'the very bulwark of civilisation and freedom as we know it. It is the greatest responsibility that the world has ever known', and J.B. Priestley, in his much listened-to Sunday night broadcasts, announced:

> Just now we're not really obscure persons tucked away in our offices and factories, villas and back streets; we're the British people being attacked and fighting back; we're in the great battle for the future of our civilization; and so instead of being obscure and tucked away, we're bang in the middle of the world's stage with all the spotlights focused on us; we're historical personages, and it's possible that distant generations will find inspiration, when their time of trouble comes, in the report in their history books of our conduct at this hour.

The Times Literary Supplement joined in with a poem by Dorothy L. Sayers:

> This is the war that England knows,
>   When all the world holds but one man –
> King Philip of the galleons,
> Louis, whose light outshone the sun's,
>   The conquering Corsican;
>
> When Europe, like a prison door,
>   Clangs; and the swift, enfranchised sea
> Runs narrower than a village brook;
> And men who love us not, yet look
>   To us for liberty;
>
> When no allies are left, no help
>   to count upon from alien hands,
> No waverers remain to woo,
> No more advice to listen to,
>   And only England stands.

This became something of a pop-classic; Noël Coward, who had somehow missed it in *The Times Literary Supplement*, picked up a copy in General Wavell's quarters during a tour of the Middle East and read it to the troops in his concert the same evening. (It may have been a little inconsistent of Coward to remonstrate with Wavell afterwards concerning his taste for Macaulay.) The isolationist, anti-foreigner note of Sayers's poem, while not entirely in keeping with Churchill's opinions, was fairly typical of the then current mood: it had been reported at the time of the French surrender, 'Many people express relief (of a quite unrealistic kind) that at last, "There are no more Allies"', and even the King wrote, 'Personally I feel happier now that we have no allies to be polite to & to pamper'. Though this was not Churchill's view, he must have shared Dorothy Sayers's perception of the historical parallels, for he gave them classic statement in a broadcast some nights later:

> We must regard the next week or so as a very important period in our history. It ranks with the days when the Spanish Armada was approaching the Channel

and Drake was finishing his game of bowls; or when Nelson stood between us and Napoleon's Grand Army at Boulogne. We have read all about this in the history books; but what is happening now is on a far greater scale and of far more consequence to the life and future of the world and its civilization than these brave old days of the past.[26]

As Churchill's doctor noted, 'He still says a piece, but for perhaps the first time in his life he seems to see things through the eyes of the average man'. Of course there was something a little incongruous in Churchill, the grandson of an English duke and of a noted American patron of the turf, posing as the embodiment of the common man. Even his loyal wife pointed out, 'He knows nothing of the life of ordinary people. He's never been in a bus, and only once on the Underground'. When he told his entourage:

The way to lose the war is to try to force the British public into a diet of milk, oatmeal, potatoes, etc., washed down on gala occasions with a little lime juice,

his views derived less from personal experience of the privations of rationing than from Nat Gubbins's column in *The Sunday Express*; later his efforts to restore the manufacture of ice-cream were less successful than his urging that the ban on sending flowers by rail should be lifted, the sending of flowers in England being a distinctly middle-class custom. His Vee for Victory finger sign excited first the resentment of his uncomprehending and insulted lower-class audiences, then their ridicule: they rarely imitated it. 'They heard in his Edwardian twang (as Orwell called it) not the voice of equality but that of a ruling class more deeply entrenched than that represented by their haw-haw officers', recalled Anthony Burgess. The famous cigars merely provoked the envy of soldiers starved of decent tobacco; they were not allowed in close enough to see that his underwear was of pink silk.[27]

It was perhaps not inappropriate that at the Finest Hour of the nation which had produced Chaucer, Shakespeare, Milton, Defoe, Gibbon, Wordsworth,

[26] Henry Longhurst *My Life and Soft Times* (1971) p. 136; Margery Allingham *The Oaken Heart* (1941) p. 198–9; James Agate *Ego 4: Yet More of the Autobiography of James Agate* (1940) p. 262; Robert Rhodes James ed. *Chips: The Diaries of Sir Henry Channon* (1967) p. 259, 20 June 1940; *Times* 23 Sept. 1940 p. 2b, text of broadcast to New York by Sir William Coxen, Lord Mayor of London, 21 Sept. 1940; J.B. Priestley *Postscripts* (1940) p. 69 (broadcast 8 Sept. 1940); *Times Literary Supplement* 7 Sept. 1940 p. 445; James Brabazon, *Dorothy L. Sayers: The Life of a Courageous Woman* (1981) p. 187, and cf Noël Coward *Autobiography* London 1987 p. 489–490; Ian McLaine *Ministry of Morale: Home Front Morale and the Ministry of Information in World War II* (1979) p. 74; John W. Wheeler-Bennett *King George VI: His Life and Reign* (1965) p. 460; Robert Rhodes James ed. *Winston S. Churchill: His Complete Speeches, 1897–1963* (8 vols New York 1974) vol. 6 p. 6276 broadcast 11 Sept. 1940.

[27] Moran *Churchill: The Struggle for Survival* p. 13, 24 Dec. 1941; ibid. p. 247, April 1945; John Colville *The Fringes of Power: Downing Street Diaries, 1939–1955* (1985) p. 196, 14 July 1940; Winston S. Churchill *The Second World War* (6 vols 1948–54) vol. 4 p. 796, minute of 22 Sept. 1942, and p. 832, minute of 3 March 1943, cf Longmate *How We Lived Then* p. 299; Anthony Burgess *Little Wilson and Big God* (1987) p. 305.

Dickens and Tennyson the leader should be no mean writer, a wordsmith like Hitler but at a higher professional level, who had often lived only by his pen and had worked in every genre, even novel and film. In the First World War even non-combatant writers had been unable to ignore the fact of the war, though in retrospect there can be little doubt that much the most important writing of the 1914–1918 period was produced by frontline soldiers; but though the Second World War produced no Owen, no Rosenberg, no Sassoon (and perhaps rather too many Edmund Blundens), it does seem that the influence of the war on writers was far more pervasive. Even Virginia Woolf wrote an article, in a suitably ironic and belittling tone, entitled 'Thoughts on Peace in an Air Raid':

> The drone of the planes is now like the sawing of a branch overhead. Round and round it goes, sawing at a branch directly above the house ... A bomb drops. All the windows rattle ... The searchlights, wavering across the flat, have picked up the plane now. From this window one can see a little silver insect turning and twisting in the light. The guns go pop, pop, pop.

One recalls that Jane Austen had, to a large extent, edited the world war of her day out of her writing, except that the militia is embodied to provide undesirable husbands and naval prize money is forthcoming to endow suitable ones. But it was perhaps because the writers of the 1940s nearly all took a positive, constructive, supportive, socially acceptable attitude to the war (unlike the best of their First World War predecessors) that the literature of the period bores later generations with the earnestness of its submission (perhaps prostitution) to the public objectives of the regime. Some of the best-known books of the period, still in print more than a generation later, were popular histories; *The Times Literary Supplement*'s review of Arthur Bryant's *The Years of Endurance* (describing the first part of the struggle against Napoleon) began, 'By something more than coincidence, the pattern of English warfare against the conquerors of Europe repeats itself on the loom of the centuries', and ends, '"Drum-and-trumpet history" is after all the history of the people'. There were also a number of striking historical films with a more-than-nationalistic slant; *The Prime Minister*, completed in December 1940, released in March 1941, had Disraeli in the Winston Churchill role of patriotic leader and Gladstone as Chamberlain, preaching peace and retrenchment while clearly in the pocket of the party establishment and the industrialists. *The Young Mr. Pitt*, completed in December 1941 and released in June 1942, had a different slant at this later stage of the war: 'Pitt is Churchill, but a Churchill recast on MoI [Ministry of Information] lines', writes one post-war critic: another refers to it as a 'topical allegory in which the arch-demon is transferred from Nürnberg to Corsica', and certainly Herbert Lom, who played Napoleon, seemed much more central European than Mediterranean. *Forever and a Day*, a tribute by British expatriates resident in Hollywood, directed by René Clair and Cedric Hardwicke and others, even uses the Blitz to frame a family saga touching on Napoleon's

threatened invasion in 1804 and 1805. As already indicated Churchill favoured
the use of history as current propaganda; when appointing R.A. Butler to the
Board of Education in 1941 he instructed him, 'Tell the children that Wolfe
won Quebec', and though still reduced to tears by his fifth viewing of the film
Lady Hamilton he was nevertheless able to inform his entourage, 'Gentlemen,
I thought this film would interest you, showing great events similar to those
in which you have been taking part'.[28]

One might wonder if there was not, in this pop-historical nostalgia, in the
déjà vu quality of Britain's wartime propaganda generally, and in the figure
of Churchill himself, a kind of elegiac celebration, perhaps the hegemonic
system's first acknowledgement of intimations of coming change. The fact is
however that a historical perspective was not the monopoly of the embattled
British. If anything the use of history was even more blatant in the Soviet
Union, for example in the Kukryniksy group's poster, 'Napoleon suffered
defeat and so will the conceited Hitler', and Viktor Ivanov and Olga Byrova's
poster showing what appear to be girls in winter combat gear attacking with
automatic weapons past two monuments, one bearing an eagle symbol, and
the other the words, '1812: Glory, Honour, Remembrance', with the spectral
figure of Kutuzov looming in the background and the caption, '"May the
example of our great predecessors inspire you in this war" – Stalin'. When in
1942 the Soviet government established a new decoration for military valour it
was named the Order of Suvorov after the great eighteenth-century general. In
the same vein, during the final days of the Third Reich Hitler told Goebbels:

> It must be our ambition to set an example today on which later generations can
> model themselves in similar crises and times of stress, just as today we must
> take our cue from the heroes of past history.

A few weeks later Goebbels directed the press:

> The cultural section of our newspapers is not to become a little bourgeois refuge
> for war-weary brothers. These columns too must use every method to assist in
> reinforcing our national resistance and our war morale. The particular job of the
> cultural editor is to express in lofty, varied language what has been said in the
> political section on the military and political struggle of the day ... Discussion
> of Clausewitz's writings, descriptions of the Second Punic War, comments on

---

[28] Virginia Woolf *Collected Essays* (4 vols 1966–7) vol. 4 p. 173–177, quotations from
p. 174, 176; *Times Literary Supplement* 14 Nov. 1942 p. 558; Anthony Aldgate and Jeffrey
Richards *Britain Can Take It: The British Cinema in the Second World War* (Oxford 1986)
p. 147 and Robert F. Moss *The Films of Carol Reed* (1987) p. 133 quoting Andrew Sarris
'Carol Reed in the Context of His Times' *Film Culture* vol. 2 no. 4 (1956) p. 16; R.A. Butler
The Art of the Possible (1971) p. 90; Dilks ed. *Diaries of Sir Alexander Cadogan* p. 396–7,
8 August 1941: cf also William Armstrong ed. *With Malice Toward None: A War Diary by
Cecil H. King* (1970) p. 222, 3 June 1943. Churchill also found time to write the introduction
to an edition of *The War Speeches of William Pitt the Younger*, published by Oxford University
Press in 1940.

Mommsen's *Roman History*, dissertations on Frederick the Great's letters and writings, the careers of great warlike geniuses all through history.[29]

Now obviously, in a species endowed with the power of recollection, historical events are part of the equipment with which current developments are perceived and manipulated. In the normal course of events it would probably be the historical occurrences which people have themselves witnessed which would seem most relevant ('Memories of August 1914 Cast their Shadow Across the Fateful Session of Today' ran the headline of a parliamentary report in *The Daily Telegraph* at the time of Munich). As events became more extreme and exceptional one would need to go further afield – even perhaps as far back as the time of Hannibal and Scipio Africanus, as Goebbels suggested. Yet these historical analogies have, historically speaking, a somewhat minimal informational value and cannot be seen as tapping pre-existing reservoirs of historical sentiment and knowledge, bearing in mind that the majority of people in western society normally show only the most cursory interest in events prior to their birth. It is possible therefore that the function of the historical analogies was not to create a healthy awareness of continuities and parallels, but to help conceal the essential differences between the past and the present and to divert attention from the essential novelty of new developments. The myth-making basic to Nazism and Fascism has already been adverted to: perhaps it was no less important in the notionally more open system over which Churchill presided.[30]

As has already been indicated, one of the fundamental paradoxes of Nazism was its combination of unashamed elitism and emphasis on the essential equality of everyone within the racial community. It can be argued that the pressure of war mobilization threw Britain into an almost identical situation. In the First World War, despite the key role of Lloyd George in British public life, social justice had not generally been seen as relevant to winning the war; if anything the war fostered a Social Darwinistic atmosphere reminiscent of the earlier nineteenth century, with various lady busy-bodies and manor-house do-gooders snatching at new opportunities to assert social power. The way in which regulation of distribution and consumption came last in 1918, after the regulation of practically everything else, suggests that the reason for the delay in establishing regulation of consumption was political rather than administrative. Partly because of the lessons learnt in 1918, partly because of the greater power of the Labour Party in 1940, partly because of the emphasis on the ideological nature of the war necessitated by the ideological stance of the enemy dictatorships, matters were organized on a much more

---

[29] Trevor-Roper ed. *Goebbels Diaries* p. 102, 11 March 1945; ibid. p. 307, 3 April 1945; cf also the American poster 'AMERICANS will *always* fight for liberty' showing modern troops labelled '1943' on the right, and, more faintly on the left, ragged soldiers of the George Washington's era labelled '1778'.

[30] *Daily Telegraph* 28 Sept. 1938 p. 12d-f;

egalitarian basis in the Second World War. Despite the extension of controls in so many areas, there was even a new freedom of expression with regard to criticism of the existing social order; political and social themes which had been banned before 1939 by the semi-official censorship of the British film industry became familiar topics in wartime films. But inevitably old class antagonisms and prejudices did not disappear over night. When the Labour Home Secretary, Herbert Morrison, dismissed two classic establishment types, Sir Warren Fisher, former Permanent Secretary of the Treasury, since 1940 a Special Commissioner in the London Civil Defence Region, and Colonel Thomas Blatherwick, C.B., D.S.O., M.C., T.D., D.L., J.P., since 1939 a Deputy Commissioner in the North Western Region, there was a chorus of approval, and Evelyn Walkden told the House of Commons of the 'enormous postbag' of complaints he had received about 'half the people in charge at the different war stations in the country' and how, unlike Tory M.P.s, 'we know more about our people because we have had to live among them ever since we were born'. (Walkden, though MP. for a Yorkshire constituency, had been born in Lancashire and lived in the stockbroker belt of Surrey.) Expressions of opinion from the opposite point of view were not encouraged: Lieutenant Colonel R.C. Bingham D.S.O., an old-Etonian, was sacked from his command of No. 168 Officer Cadets Training Unit for writing to *The Times* that officers from the 'middle, lower middle, and working classes' having no experience of management 'have very largely fallen down in their capacity as Army officers'. Yet while denting old snobberies, if only slightly, the war created new snobberies of its own. In the sexual rat-race, for example, even nubile members of the Women's Royal Naval Service considered that 'R.A.F. officers rated tops, being classified in turn by rank and number of decorations: naval officers came second and Brown Jobs a long way behind'. The mere fact of the vast expansion of the armed forces extended the influence of hierarchy and inequality of status; the nature of the new warfare of the technological era, with its special elite arms such as commandos, submariners, airmen, involved the privileging of certain groups: Bomber Command pilots for example were given fried eggs (at that time a rare delicacy) for breakfast when they went on a mission, and, less officially, had access to unlimited supplies of 100-octane aviation spirit and the services of their aircraft ground crew for the sports cars they used when off duty, at a time when most private citizens had been obliged to lay up their cars for the duration. Clearly the egalitarianism of the war was largely a matter of outward forms. Churchill was perhaps the perfect symbol of the paradoxical inner reality. We may read of him in his private secretary's diary, gloating over the paintings by Old Masters adorning the prime ministerial country residence, Chequers, including 'a little Rubens in the dining room about which Winston went into ecstasies ... At about 4.00 we left Chequers and went to look at the R.A.F. establishment at Halton, by which the P.M. was obviously bored'. This was not quite how the leader of an embattled democracy was supposed to behave; but then the appropriate leader for an embattled democracy would have been a lower-middle-class version of

Neville Chamberlain. Churchill obviously represented something much more complex, multi-faceted and profound.[31]

One thing which made Churchill rather an unexpected leader for a democracy at war was that, beyond a passion for parliamentary tradition, he had very little feeling for democracy, but a colossal interest in war. 'There is always the quite inescapable suspicion that he loves war, which broke Neville Chamberlain's better heart', Channon noted in his diary. The Canadian premier, Mackenzie King, on meeting Churchill, 'rather put off by a strain of violence in the Prime Minister'. Kennedy, the Director of Military Operations at the War Office, applied to Churchill the passage in the Book of Job:

> He saith among the trumpets, Ha, Ha!; and he smelleth the battle afar off, the thunder of the captains, and the shouting.

Indeed Churchill was fascinated by war, and always had been. He had first come to the public eye as a war correspondent, then as a war hero after his escape from the Boers, and had retained something of the *Boy's Own* adventure hero while at the Admiralty. On manoeuvres with the German army in 1909 he had written to his wife:

> Much as the war attracts me & fascinates my mind with its tremendous situations – I feel more deeply every year – & can measure the feeling here in the midst of arms – what vile and wicked folly and barbarism it all is.

But on the eve of the First World War he confessed the real truth:

> I am interested, geared up & happy. Is it not horrible to be built like that? The preparations have a hideous fascination for me.

After little more than a year of this earlier conflict he was forced out of the Admiralty on a wave of public revulsion and it was perhaps the one real tragedy of his life that he had not had a greater share in the direction of the war after 1915. The Second World War was not merely Germany's second chance: it was Churchill's. 'It took Armageddon to make me Prime Minister', he boasted; and yet behind him there stood a people who shared his eagerness to confront the last judgement.[32]

[31] Nicholas Pronay and Jeremy Crofts 'British Film Censorship and Propaganda Policy during the Second World War' in James Curran and Vincent Porter ed. *British Cinema History* (1983) p. 144–163 at p. 150–1; *Hansard: House of Commons* vol. 379 col. 578–9, speech by Evelyn Walkden 21 April 1942; *Times* 15 Jan. 1941 p. 5f; J. Maclaren-Ross *Memoirs of the Forties* London 1965 p. 104; Eric Williams *The Tunnel* (1951) p. 54 and cf Anthony Bartley *Smoke Trails in the Sky: From the Journals of a Fighter Pilot* (1984) p. 42, 62; Colville *Fringes of Power* p. 195, 14 July 1940.

[32] Rhodes James ed, *Chips* p. 259, 20 June 1940; Moran *Churchill: The Struggle for Survival* p. 19 31 Dec. 1941; John Kennedy *The Business of War: The War Narrative of Major-General Sir John Kennedy* ed. Bernard Fergusson (1957) p. 62, cf *Job* c.39 v.25 Randolph S. Churchill and Martin Gilbert *Winston S. Churchill* (8 vols 1966–88) vol. 2 companion volume **p. 912, Churchill to Clementine Churchill 15 Sept. 1909; ibid. vol. 3 p. 31 same to same 28 July 1914; Lord Boothby *Recollections of a Rebel* (1978) p. 145.

V. Churchill as War Leader

As war leader, Churchill upstaged even the traditional state figurehead, the King, as the focus of national esteem. Despite the efforts of enthusiasts like G. Wilson Knight, the famous Shakespearian critic (then a master at Stowe), to launch an integrated royalist-christian-democratic revival, despite the well-publicized visits of King George VI and Queen Elizabeth to working-class areas immediately after (and sometimes, disconcertingly, immediately before) extra-heavy German air raids, public attention to the sovereign declined steadily: 22.7 per cent of Mass Observation's diarists listened to the King's Christmas broadcast in 1939, only 9.3 per cent in 1941; even during the Blitz, when he was perhaps at his most popular, the King's appearance in cinema newsreels provoked applause only one time out of three, whereas Hitler was almost invariably hissed and booed. Despite Churchill's sentimental reverence for the institution of monarchy, George VI also had less influence behind the scenes than former monarchs. Beaverbrook was appointed Minister of Aircraft Production despite the King's warning of 'the effect likely to be produced in Canada', and his objections to making Brendan Bracken a privy councillor were also brushed aside. This was not because George VI was a less able person than his father: it was simply that the conditions of power had changed.[33]

The implications of Churchill's national figurehead role were not lost on critical observers. Sir Alexander Cadogan, permanent head of the Foreign Office, was not above referring to Churchill as 'our Dictator', or 'that baby Dictator'. Tom Jones, formerly deputy secretary to the Cabinet, is reported to have said:

> if Winston Churchill had been born ten years later he would, in the 1930s, have made England a fascist state, ranged with the other fascist powers; but ... he was too old a man with roots too firmly rooted in the Victorian aristocratic traditions to adopt so alien a philosophy.

But some officials were prepared to admit that, 'in order to wage war Democracies had to convert themselves into Dictatorships', and beyond the purlieus of Whitehall it was not unknown for punch-ups to start in public bars because someone said, 'Churchill and Hitler are all the same'.[34]

[33] The British Library has a typescript of Wilson Knight's 'A Royal Propaganda' (1956) which is an important source for Wilson Knight's wartime ideals; Philip Ziegler *Crown and People* (1978) p. 70; Jeffrey Richards and Dorothy Sheridan ed. *Mass-Observation at the Movies* (1987) p. 162, 213; Colville *Fringes of Power* p. 131, 14 May 1940; ibid. p. 145, 1 June 1940.

George VI was able in 1945 to deflect the appointment of Hugh Dalton as Foreign Secretary in the new Labour government; but this was possible less perhaps because of the Labour leadership's traditional sycophancy towards the sovereign than because the war was practically over and peacetime conditions and conventions were coming back into force.

[34] Dilks ed. *Diaries of Sir Alexander Cadogan* p. 339, 12 Dec. 1940, p. 347, 3 Jan. 1941 and cf A.J.P. Taylor ed. *My Darling Pussy: The Letters of Lloyd George and Frances Stevenson, 1913–41* (1975) p. 233, 235 Frances Stevenson to Lloyd George 26 and 29 Sept. 1940; James

continued

Even Churchill's wife enjoyed reminding her husband that 'except for the King, the Archbishop of Canterbury & the Speaker, you can sack anyone & everyone', and some of Churchill's less firmly anchored associates were thought to have come even closer to adopting the views increasingly prevalent on the continent:

> I suspect that the real attitude towards Hitler of our Lords Beaverbrook and Rothermere is a mixture of envy and admiration, mingled with wonder how a hysterical house painter had got so much further towards his aim, in spite of lack of capital, than they have achieved.

And it was not only right-wing press barons who were seduced by the mirage of total power; it was Ernie Bevin who was responsible for the prosecution of hundreds of miners for absenteeism and disobedience at work – and it was Herbert Morrison who summarily dismissed Sir Warren Fisher for publicly denouncing one of Morrison's petty tyrannies: though Morrison was only accused of 'Prussianism' by the Civil Service Clerical Association, the word 'dictator' was at least mentioned when the matter was discussed in the House of Commons.[35]

One of the features of Churchill's government which most resembled the Hitler and Mussolini systems was his monopolizing of the civilian direction of the war. Though he seems initially to have thought in terms of a small War Cabinet and a Defence Committee in regular touch with the service chiefs of staff, by 1942 the practice was that he alone dealt with the military leaders on operational questions; the heads of the service ministries were excluded

continued

Lees-Milne *Ancestral Voices* (1975) p. 271, diary 22 Nov. 1943 – this is a second-hand report of Jones's views, but perfectly credible; Colville *Fringes of Power* p. 150, 6 June 1940 quoting Sir George Clerk, formerly ambassador in Paris. Mr R.M. Greenwold informs me that he remembers his father coming home from the pub one lunch-time in 1940 or 1941, very depressed and anxious after witnessing a fight provoked by someone remarking, 'Churchill and Hitler are all the same': he was afraid that if called to give evidence in court it would come out that this was exactly his own opinion. In July 1941 a woman was sentenced to five years penal servitude for telling two soldiers; 'Hitler was a good ruler, a better man than Churchill': Churchill himself thought five years excessive: Gilbert *Winston S. Churchill* vol. 6 p. 895 fn. 3.

[35] Gilbert *Winston S. Churchill* vol. 6 p. 588, Clementine Churchill to Winston Churchill 27 June 1940; Imperial War Museum: Letters of General Sir Campbell Clarke to Brigadier G. Macleod Ross p. 54, 11 Jan. 1940; *Hansard: House of Commons* vol. 383 col. 1736–7 statement by Bevin 15 Oct. 1942; *Hansard: House of Commons* vol. 379 col. 571 letter from Civil Service Clerical Association quoted by Sir Waldron Smithers 21 April 1942; ibid. col. 575 speech by George Griffiths in same debate. The term 'Prussianism' had been introduced into the question by Fisher himself in a letter to *The Manchester Guardian* 23 March 1942. See Bernard Donoghue and G.W. Jones *Herbert Morrison: Portrait of a Politican* (1973) p. 300–301 for a fuller account, but one written entirely from Morrison's point of view. One wonders how far Churchill's impression of his Labour colleagues during the wartime coalition helped to inspire his much-criticized party political broadcast on 4 June 1945 in which he claimed that Labour Government would necessarily involve 'some form of Gestapo, no doubt very humanely directed in the first instance'.

from the War Cabinet, which became essentially a forum on the overall shape of the war at the more-than-military level, and the Defence Committee effectively ceased to have any directing influence. While Churchill's intimates were putting it about that he 'has the theory that the Prime Minister is nothing more than Chairman of the Cabinet', the ageing Lloyd George was complaining:

> My War Cabinet was a real Council of State. I had in it men of the calibre of Balfour, Bonar Law, Milner, Curzon and Smuts, to whom I could and did turn for advice. Hankey, Amery, Grigg and Kerr were members of my secretariat. I listened to them all. No one in this War Cabinet or secretariat knows anything about war except Churchill, He will listen to no-one but himself.

In the late spring of 1941, after the fall of Greece, Hankey, although a minister (Chancellor of the Duchy) found himself agreeing with complaints that Churchill 'is running the war as a Dictator'. Haining, the Vice-Chief of the Imperial General Staff, was 'very anxious about the complete subservience of the C.O.S.s [Chiefs of Staff] to Churchill'; Kennedy, the Director of Military Operations, was 'very anxious' about 'Supreme Control'. Early in May 1941 Hankey told the Marquess of Salisbury that the war was being run 'by a Dictator', and at the end of the month Hankey lunched with his old boss, Lloyd George: 'We both agreed that Churchill's War Cabinet of "Yes-men" was hopeless'. In March 1942, having been sacked from the Cabinet, Hankey lectured the House of Lords on Lloyd George's War Cabinet, announcing 'There were no "Yes men" or "No men" – horrid terms!' Needless to say these grumbles had as much effect as the sneers of the German generals about Corporal Hitler.[36]

'No one in this War Cabinet or secretariat knows anything about war except Churchill', Lloyd George had complained; and indeed Churchill did know a lot about war, in much the same way as he knew a lot about English Literature. Whether this knowledge was organized on any solid foundations was another matter. Sir Alan Brooke, the Chief of the Imperial General Staff from 1942, wrote after the war:

---

[36] Nigel Nicolson ed. *Harold Nicolson: Diaries and Letters* (3 vols.1966–8) vol. 2 p. 103, 18 July 1940 cf Boothby *Recollections of a Rebel* p. 150; Stephen Roskill *Hankey: Man of Secrets* (3 vols 1970–4) vol. 3 p. 497, diary 22 April 1941; ibid. vol. 3 p. 499, 28 April 1941; ibid. vol. 3 p. 501, 1 May 1941; ibid. vols. 3 p. 503, 5 May 1941; *Hansard: House of Lords* vol. 122 col. 444, speech by Hankey 25 March 1942.

There is a considerable body of testimony as to how much better Lloyd George was than Churchill as chairman of the Cabinet and government leader; see for example John Barnes and David Nicholson ed. *The Leo Amery Diaries* (2 vols.1980–8) vol. 2 p. 1021, 23 Nov. 1944 and p. 1034, 26 March 1945. I think there can be little doubt that Lloyd George was far more accomplished at chairing meetings, picking the minds of better-informed persons on subjects in which he had no interest, and generally demonstrating the talents desirable for success in the committee room; Churchill's problem had always been that he had too many ideas of his own: not a characteristic likely to commend him to colleagues like Hankey and Amery whose advice he avoided listening to.

The President [Roosevelt] had no great military knowledge and was aware of this fact and consequently relied on Marshall and listened to Marshall's advice ... My position was very different. Winston never had the slightest doubt that he had inherited all the military genius of his great ancestor, Marlborough ... To wean him away from [his] wilder plans required superhuman efforts.

This was not simply the Army view. 'How he works in such complete ignorance & disregard for facts beats me', Sir Andrew Cunningham, the First Sea Lord, confided to his diary. But Kennedy, Brooke's assistant on the Imperial General Staff on the military operations side, read Arthur Bryant's *The Years of Endurance* (about Britain and the war against the French Revolution) and concluded:

Pitt and his Ministers were immensely more ignorant of strategy than Churchill and his War Cabinet ... Churchill appeared a paragon in strategic matters as compared with Pitt.

Edmonds, the official historian of Haig's campaigns on the Western Front and no great admirer of Lloyd George's leadership of the War Cabinet in 1916–1918, considered that the Second World War showed 'the inestimable advantage of sympathetic political leadership of a soldier of war experience, Mr Churchill instead of the amateur misdirection of a windy party politician'. And perhaps it was not simply gush or egregious ignorance which led Mountbatten, on his appointment to command in South East Asia, to write to Churchill:

I would not have felt competent to take this on if I had not had the rare privilege of being allowed to sit for 18 months at the feet of the greatest master of strategy this century has produced.[37]

Objectively there is much to be said for the view that, despite having been shot at in four continents, Churchill was a strategic maverick, and that whenever he managed to rush through one of his own pet schemes it almost invariably resulted in a cock-up. The expedition to seize the French base at Dakar, for example, was apparently dreamed up by Edward Spears, the head of the British mission to General de Gaulle, by de Gaulle himself and by Churchill's personal assistant Desmond Morton, but received Churchill's enthusiastic sponsorship – and failed ignobly. The occupation of the Dodecanese Islands in the autumn of 1943, despite the unfavourable position with regard to air support, was Churchill's personal inspiration, presented with the usual flourish of rhetoric: 'This is a time to think of

---

[37] Arthur Bryant *The Turn of the Tide, 1939–1943* (1957) p. 415, Brooke's post-war notes; British Library Add. 52578 f. 1 Andrew Cunningham diary 6 Jan, 1945; Kennedy *Business of War* p. 353, October 1944; King's College London, Edmonds Papers III 13/4 verso; Philip Ziegler *Mountbatten* (1985) p. 223–4, Mountbatten to Churchill 28 Aug. 1943: though note Mountbatten's use of a similar line of flattery with Chiang Kai-shek: Barbara Tuchman *Sand against the Wind: Stillwell and the American American Experience in China, 1911–45* (1970) p. 395.

Clive and Peterborough and Rooke's men taking Gibraltar'. Once occupied, the islands were attacked and reoccupied by the Germans with humiliating ease, enabling Kennedy to remark sourly, 'This is a good example of the price we have to pay occasionally for Winston's confidence in his own military judgement'.[38]

In fact the professionals never quite forgot Churchill's most celebrated blunder which had ruined him in 1915. It was remarked of the plan to send troops to northern Norway in February 1940, 'its inception smacks all to alarmingly of Gallipoli', and Admiral Keyes's verdict afterwards was, 'The Gallipoli tragedy has been followed step by step'. At the time of the Dakar expedition, as one naval officer recalled, 'The word "Dardanelles" was in the minds if not on the lips of the planning Staff'. Even the Americans picked up the idea: Major-General John P. Lucas, commanding the American landing at Anzio, which had been intending to outflank the German positions south of Rome, noted in his diary:

> I feel like a lamb being led to the slaughter . . . the whole affair has a strong odor of Gallipoli and apparently the same amateur was still on the coach's bench.

But Churchill saw the parallel of Anzio and Gallipoli too, and with perhaps a juster perception of the resemblance of the two failures:

> They did at Anzio what Stopford did at Suvla Bay: clung to the beaches and failed to establish positions inland as they could well have done.

It was, arguably, the inadequacies of the professionals on the spot which made it desirable to blame everything on an amateur in Whitehall.[39]

'He is still thinking of his books', sneered one official, and Channon complained, 'We might as well have Macaulay or even Caruso as Prime Minister'. But the idea that Churchill as war leader was simply led astray by his imagination and 'blasted rhetoric' simply tends to smoke-screen the failings of those whose job it was to assist him. It was Churchill, not the Chiefs of Staff, who was blamed for the string of defeats beginning in North Africa and Greece and culminating with the surrender of Singapore and the evacuation of Burma. 'I do not think you can divorce the almost unending and unbroken sequence of strategic disasters from this mixture of the political and military elements in your war machine', Leslie Hore-Belisha told the Commons in May 1942 in an attack on Churchill's role in strategic planning. In reality all these

---

[38] Arthur Marder *Operation 'Menace': The Dakar Expedition and the Dudley North Affair* (1976) p. 14–17; Gilbert *Winston S. Churchill* vol. 7 p. 503 Churchill to Sir H. Maitland Wilson 13 Sept. 1943; Kennedy *Business of War* p. 313, diary 17 Nov. 1943.

[39] Brian Bond ed. *Chief of Staff: The Diaries of Lieutenant-General Sir Henry Pownall* (2 vols 1972–4) p. 282, 9 Feb. 1940; *Hansard: House of Commons* vol. 360 col. 1127, speech by Keyes 7 May 1940; Marder *Operation 'Menace'* p. 27 quoting a letter by T.C. Crease (formerly of Naval Intelligence) to Marder 22 Nov. 1973; Martin Blumenson 'General Lucas at Anzio (1944)', in Kent Roberts Greenfield ed. *Command Decisions* (New York 1959) p. 224–272, at p. 225 quoting Lucas's diary 9 Jan 1944; Colville *Fringes of Power* p. 674, 8 Aug. 1953.

disasters could be attributed to Churchill's mistake in accepting professional advice, and much of the friction, especially with the irascible Brooke, was the result of his constant efforts to push against the conservative margins, dogmatic abstractions and short-sighted cautiousness of his service leaders. Churchill was by no means completely insensitive to the organizational problems of modern warfare; when the American commander in the Far East, Douglas MacArthur, communicated his views on the desirability of sending all available Anglo-American forces to the Russian Front, he commented, 'The General's ideas about the European theatre are singularly untroubled by considerations of transport and distance', but he was baffled by his professional advisers' unrelenting barrage of counter-arguments against his own suggestions, which were usually much more moderate than MacArthur's. On one occasion he remarked:

you may take the most gallant sailor, the most intrepid airman, or the most audacious soldier, put them at a table together – what do you get? *The sum total of their fears!*

Later, infuriated by the cumbersomeness of military planning procedures, he minuted:

The best thing would be to form a Sacred Legion of about 1,000 Staff Officers and let them set an example to the troops in leading some particularly desperate attack.

The British High Command was indeed extra-ordinarily desk bound. The Chiefs of Staff – i.e. first Sea Lord, C.I.G.S. and Chief of Air Staff – met most days, usually in the morning, at the War Cabinet offices; each one-and-a-half or two-hour session required, according to Portal, three or four hours of preparatory reading. Portal, while Chief of Air Staff, attended (and checked the minutes of) approximately 2,000 Chiefs of Staff meetings, read 5,830 Chiefs of Staff memos, dictated at least 765 memos for Churchill, and generally worked a fourteen-hour day. At the suggestion of Sir Archibald Sinclair, the Secretary of State for Air, he instituted monthly meetings with the A.O.C.-in-C.s of the home commands (i.e. Bomber Command, Fighter Command, Coastal Command etc.) in 1942 but dropped them by the end of the year as taking up too much time. He never visited an air base. It can hardly be said that the results were not commensurate with this stupendous intellectual effort, but one does sometimes suspect that if Portal and Brooke had not been working their way so dedicatedly through that mass of paper they might have had the time to collaborate more whole-heartedly with Churchill in seeking ways of winning the war with less delay and cost.[40]

---

[40] Colville *Fringes of Power* p. 132, 16 May 1940 quoting Arthur Rucker, Chamberlain's private secretary; Rhodes James ed. *Chips* p. 334, 2 July 1942; Colville *Fringes of Power* p. 132, 16 May 1940, quoting Churchill's private secretary E.A. Seal for the phrase 'blasted rhetoric', *Hansard: House of Commons* vol. 380 col. 257–8, speech by Leslie Hore-Belisha 20 May 1942;
continued

VI. Civil and Military in Britain

In many instances Churchill was unable to impose his vision and imaginative fire on the vast military bureaucracy which Portal and Brooke represented. In 1941 James Burnham claimed, 'The war of 1914 was the last great war of capitalist society; the war of 1939 is the first great of managerial society': this is perhaps too glib but one does nevertheless see in Churchill something of the Victorian eccentric engaged in a struggle with Organization Man. The fact that this struggle never took on the bitterness of Lloyd George's contest with Haig and Robertson can perhaps be attributed to his commanding personality and upper-class background: the armed forces' capacity to fall out with and sabotage civilian direction had if anything increased since 1918, as is shown by the strange case of Leslie Hore-Belisha.[41]

Hore-Belisha, having given his name to the Belisha Beacons at zebra crossings while Minister of Transport, was appointed Secretary of State for War in 1937. To begin with he relied very heavily on the advice of Captain Liddell Hart, which undoubtedly disturbed some of the old fogies at the War Office, though since Liddell Hart had his admirers within the upper ranks of the Army the increasing antipathy of the generals to Hore-Belisha cannot be blamed simply on his association with the ex-Army Education Corps captain. More important was that Hore-Belisha talked about reform and changes, and even pushed a few reforms through, but in doing so convinced the soldiers that his object was less the improvement of the army than self-advertisement and the promotion of his political career. The soldiers were undoubtedly assisted in their recognition of Hore-Belisha's self-seeking showmanship and not-quite gentlemanly ambition by the fact that he was a Jew. He had been brought up by a stepfather whose own parents had been an Indian army colonel and a vicar's daughter, he had played rugby at Clifton and had been a major on the G.H.Q. staff in Salonica by the time he was twenty-five: but he was a Jew and looked it.

One of Hore-Belisha's most important though least fortunate acts as War Secretary was to appoint John Standish Surtees Prendergast Vereker, sixth Viscount Gort V.C. as Chief of the Imperial General Staff. Subsequently – especially after the debacle in Belgium in May 1940 in which Gort had figured (or failed to figure) as G.O.C.-in-C. – other senior generals took care to point out that Gort was a complete dud. 'I had little confidence in Gort's leadership

continued
Public Record Office PREM 3/158/5/100 Churchill to Ismay for Chiefs of Staff 5 July 1943; Harold Macmillan *War Diaries: Politics and War in the Mediterranean, January 1943–May 1945* (1984) p. 25, 16 Nov. 1943; James Leasor and Sir Leslie Hollis *War at the Top* (1959) p. 245, Churchill to Hillis May 1944; Denis Richards *Portal of Hungerford* (1977) p. 173–5, 181, cf J.R.M. Butler, M. Howard, J. Ehrman, J.M.A. Gwyer, N.A. Gibbs *Grand Strategy* (6 vols 1956–76) vol 6 p. 330–331.
    [41] James Burnham *The Managerial Revolution: What Is Happening in the World* (New York 1941) p. 176.

in the event of attack,' wrote Brooke: 'his brain was geared to details the whole time'. Ironside noted, 'Gort doesn't even begin to know how to run the bigger things'. Sir Philip Neame, who was the only man ever to win both the V.C. and an Olympic gold medal and who was deputy Chief of General Staff at Gort's G.H.Q. in France in 1939 and 1940, recorded, 'I gave Gort no marks at all as a C.-in-C. He had the mentality of a Guards platoon commander'. The fact that Churchill seriously considered reappointing Gort as Chief of the Imperial General Staff in October 1941 by no means serves to counter these views, since Churchill's judgement of soldiers was usualy as erratic as his assessment of politicians was sound.[42]

Hore-Belisha, when looking around for a new C.I.G.S. in the autumn of 1937, had asked Liddell Hart, 'Is there anyone who isn't tame? I want a real gangster'. In proposing Gort's appointment to Chamberlain, Hore-Belisha claimed that Gort 'is the most dynamic personality I have met in the Army, and . . . is bred in an independent school'. Later Hore-Belisha was stimulated, positively thrilled by Gort's management style: 'When he went through the list of generals and colonels with Gort, the latter marked nearly 99 per cent as unfit for their jobs'. Yet within a few weeks he was alluding to Gort as 'the most reactionary' of the new Army Council, and referring to Gort as 'a Lord' and 'a V.C.' as justification for having appointed him. At lunch with Liddell Hart in March 1939 Hore-Belisha said, 'more than once that "Gort had no brain at all". He was only a façade. He could not grasp any problem. H-B could not understand how Gort had gained his reputation'. Later he claimed that he had wanted Gort to confine himself to outdoors activities with the troops, while entrusting the C.I.G.S's administrative duties to a suitable deputy: 'I knew he wouldn't make a good C.I.G.S. and he didn't. But I wanted to get him known'. That, at least, was the Hore-Belisha story when Gort looked like being a successful G.O.C.-in-C. in France: but of course Gort turned out to be a failure there as well.[43]

The reason why Hore-Belisha appointed Gort was that Liddell Hart was convinced that Gort was brilliant, and persuaded Hore-Belisha that this was the case:

His military reading was much wider than most soldiers – he was one of the few I knew who studied the French Army's manuals – and he was very sensitive to any tendency to regard him as a gallant V.C., rather than an intellectual soldier.

[42] Bryant *Turn of the Tide* p. 80–81; R. Macleod and D. Kelly ed. *The Ironside Diaries* (1962) p. 83, 24 July 1939; John Smyth *Leadership in War, 1939–1945: The Generals in Victory and Defeat* (Newton Abbot 1974) p. 32 Neame to Smyth; 2 Feb. 1972, Gilbert *Winston S. Churchill* vol. 6 p. 1234. G.O.C.-in-C. stands for General Officer Commanding-in-Chief.

[43] [B.H. Liddell Hart] *The Memoirs of Captain Liddell Hart* (2 vols 1965) vol. 2 p. 37 Hore-Belisha to Liddell Hart 15 Oct. 1937; R.J. Minney ed. *The Private Papers of Hore-Belisha* (1960) p. 69 Hore-Belisha to Chamberlain 23 Nov. 1937; *Liddell Hart Memoirs* vol. 2 p. 78, diary 11 Dec. 1937; ibid. vol. 2 p. 89, 29 Jan. 1938 and p. 109, 5 April 1938; ibid. vol. 227, 27 March 1939; Kennedy *Business of War* p. 4–5, 37.

Liddell Hart had known Gort for nearly twenty years, and regarded him as 'an intensely serious student' whose letters 'amply refute' any estimate of Gort as someone promoted above his intellectual level. And indeed Gort's intelligent, balanced, painstaking letters to Liddell Hart, now preserved at the Liddell Hart Centre, King's College London, do support Liddell Hart's claim. He was so impressed, indeed, that he had sections of Gort's letters typed out, including a thirteen-page, 'Discussion by Letter with Gort on the questions raised in the articles "DEFENCE OR ATTACK?" by BHLH which were published in *The Times*, October 25, 26 & 27, 1937' – it may be noted that this discussion occurred at precisely the time Liddell Hart was engaged in selling Gort to Hore-Belisha.[44]

Liddell Hart's (and Hore-Belisha's) misunderstanding of Gort is a good example of the mistakes intellectual theorists make when confronted by the anomalies of real life. Because, when he so wished, Gort could write intelligent and thoughtful letters, Liddell Hart thought he was an intellectual. He wasn't. He seems rather to have been a schizoid personality – an impression confirmed by a curious feral expression round his eyes, visible especially in photographs where he appears together with Hore-Belisha. What he really wanted to be, as his military colleagues were better able to appreciate than Liddell Hart, was Peter Pan commanding an infantry platoon. When appointed to lead the British Expeditionary Force at the outbreak of war he was thrilled to be escaping from Whitehall and 'kept saying "Isn't it *grand* to be going to the War!" ... like a schoolboy going off for the holidays'. He was not intellectually out of his depth as C.I.G.S or G.O.C.-in-C. – merely psychologically.[45]

It is not remarkable that such a man acquiesced in, possibly connived at, possibly even inspired, a campaign against Hore-Belisha which eventually led to Hore-Belisha's dismissal and, as subsequently transpired, the ruin of his political career; but it seems that the moving force in this was not Gort himself but his Chief of General Staff in France, Henry Pownall. Pownall was the conventional-minded military bureaucrat personified and a doughty battler for the preservation of his caste. As early as June 1939 he was confiding to his diary, 'If ... the Army Council will only stand together they'll be able to keep H-B in order if not to break him'. In January 1940, according to Pownall:

> He was already an enemy at our back, that was clearly proved when he started Lloyd George tactics (for he was clearly modelling himself on Ll.G.) within three months of the outbreak of war.

The pretext for the High Command's discontent was Hore-Belisha's complaints of the slow progress made in building defences on the Western Front,

---

[44] *Liddell Hart Memoirs* vol. 2 p. 35; ibid. vol. 1 p. 40–41 cf King's College London, Liddell Hart Papers 1/322/62 and 63.

[45] Kennedy *Business of War* p. 20.

but this was only a pretext. The Secretary of State for War was, in Pownall's view, 'a menace to the proper conduct of the war on land and a thoroughly evil man'. Although Montgomery's considered assessment of Pownall was that he was 'completely useless', he and his cronies were deft enough to mobilize such a spate of not-quite-behind-the-scenes complaints against Hore-Belisha and hints of loss of confidence within the Army that Chamberlain was forced to tell him 'there existed a strong prejudice against him for which I could not hold him altogether blameless', and offered him the Board of Trade – which Hore-Belisha refused. The validity of the generals' claim that getting rid of Hore-Belisha was necessary to enable them to get on with the war may be judged by their failure to do so once he was sacked. The whole story, obscure as the details remain, indicates the kind of thing that might have happened to Churchill if he had had a less firm grip.[46]

Churchill remembered Lloyd George even better than Pownall; he remembered that Lloyd George had won his feud with Robertson. And it was not his style to shy away from trouble. Consequently he had no hesitation in denouncing the 'jealousy and cliquism' of senior officers, and their parallel pursuit of vendetta and cover-up. His unsuccessful efforts to save Dowding in the R.A.F have already been described. Not all of his interventions were entirely justified. The failure of Britain's campaign in Norway in 1940 inspired him to write:

> I hope before any fresh appointment is given to General Auchinleck, the whole story of the slack and feeble manner in which the operations at Narvik were conducted, and the failure to make an earlier assault on Narvik Town will be considered ... I regard the operations at Narvik as a shocking example of costly over-caution and feebleness ... the question of disciplinary action against General Mackesy must also be considered. Rewards to brave and skilful

[46] Bond ed. *Chief of Staff: Pownall Diaries* vol. 1 p. 208, 12 June 1939; ibid. vol. 1 p. 274, 11 Jan. 1940; ibid. vol. 1 p. 277, 17 Jan. 1940; Nigel Hamilton *Monty: The Making of a General, 1887–1942* (1981) p. 395; see generally A.J. Trythall 'The Downfall of Leslie Hore-Belisha' in *The Second World War: Essays in Military and Political History* (1982) p. 121–141. For Lloyd George's comments and recognition of the partial analogy with his own experience see A.J. Sylvester *Life with Lloyd George: The Diary of A.J. Sylvester, 1931–45* ed. Colin Cross, (1975) p. 256, 6 Jan. 1940.
Although material printed in *The Private Papers of Hore-Belisha* suggests that Chamberlain was personally rather fond of Hore-Belisha, I am told by Dr Richard Cockett that Chamberlain's intimate correspondence with his sisters indicates exactly the contrary. Two articles by Henry Newnham in *Truth*, an organ of the Conservative Research Department and of Sir Joseph Ball, one of Chamberlain's most trusted supporters, denounced Hore-Belisha with particular savagery on 12 January 1940 (p. 29–30) and 19 January 1940 (p. 53). The second article was followed by a reprint of the first, in response to 'requests literally by the thousand'. These articles dealt sharply with Hore-Belisha's career as a promoter of companies which quickly went bust: Dr Cockett's surmise is that Chamberlain offered Hore-Belisha the Board of Trade to shut him up, and to avoid the press comment which would arise if Hore-Belisha was ignominiously relegated to the back benches, and that when Hore-Belisha refused demotion within the Cabinet, *Truth* was commissioned to print a hatchet job aimed at totally discrediting him.

officers have no meaning unless severe and public punishment is also inflicted on those who fall below the standard of determination without which we cannot win this war.

Auchinleck, a sound, sensible general though possibly already promoted out of his class, survived: as G.O.C. Southern Command later in the year he would have had tactical control of the land forces confronting a German invasion, and he was still around to provoke Churchill's further dissatisfaction as G.O.C.-in-C. Middle East in 1942. Mackesy was bowler-hatted. He was soon appointed to Liddell Hart's old job of military correspondent of *The Daily Telegraph*, which suggests he was regarded with some sympathy in London; cautious he certainly had been, but he had also been hampered in northern Norway by climatic conditions of which Churchill had no conception. The idea that Mackesy should be court-martialled *pour encourager les autres* was in any case not one that was politically viable in the twentieth century; though in the following year Edward Hulton of *Picture Post* called for 'a remorseless dismissal of failures, accompanied where necessary by prosecutions', such demands were inevitably brushed aside as gutter journalism.[47]

Churchill was almost equally unsuccessful in the case of Major-General Percy Hobart, though in this instance he was seeking to reinstate a victim of military prejudice rather than to sack one of the profession's stalwarts. At the beginning of the war Hobart had been in Egypt commanding Britain's only armoured division, and having previously been Director of Military Training at the War Office seemed in line for honourable promotion. Like Dowding in the R.A.F. his crime had essentially been one of doctrine: he had broken ranks in his profession. He was in fact much more of a fanatic about tanks than Dowding was about Home Defence. After a confused signal exercise and loss of temper Henry Maitland Wilson, G.O.C.-in-C. Egypt reported officially:

> I have no confidence in the ability of Major-General P.C.S. Hobart, C.B., D.S.O., O.B.E., M.C. to Command the Armoured Division to my satisfaction . . .
>
> His tactical ideas are based on the invincibility and invulnerability of the tank to the exclusion of the employment of other arms in correct proportion.
>
> Being self-opinionated and lacking in stability . . . [his] personality does not make for harmonious working.

Hobart was placed on half-pay, but the German victory in France made it appear that his ideas might be worth consideration and Sir Frederick Pile, another tank expert though now side-tracked to command Britain's A.A. defences, drew him to Churchill's attention. The Army establishment rallied

---

[47] Gilbert *Winston S. Churchill* vol. 6 p. 435 n. 1 Churchill to Eden 30 May 1940; *Picture Post* 21 June 1941 p. 13. There seems to have been no counterpart in Britain to the public outcry (and campaign of hate mail) directed against Admiral Kimmel and General Short in the U.S. after Pearl Harbor: John Toland *Infamy: Pearl Harbor and its Aftermath* London 1982 p. 46–7.

against Hobart as one man. Brooke, then G.O.C.-in-C. Home Forces, insisted Hobart was 'too wild'. Dill, the C.I.G.S., described Hobart to Churchill as 'impatient, quick-tempered, hot-headed, intolerant and inclined to see things as he wished them to be instead of as they are'. After meeting Hobart, Churchill informed Dill:

> I am not at all impressed by the prejudices against him in certain quarters. Such prejudices attach frequently to persons of strong personality and original view. In this case General Hobart's original views have been only too tragically borne out . . . I have carefully read your note to me and the summary of the case for and against General Hobart. We are now at war, fighting for our lives, and we cannot afford to confine Army appointments to persons who have excited no hostile comment in their career.

A few days later he told Dill in conversation, 'Remember it isn't only the good boys who help to win wars, it is the sneaks and the stinkers as well'. Hobart himself made difficulties, wanting his former seniority in the Army List so as 'to restore my honour', but he was eventually re-employed to train a division of tanks specially equipped to carry out anomalous tasks – crossing canals and clearing minefields and so on. Since the division was not intended to be employed as a tactical unit this was an important but far from glamorous task, and at the end of the war, when many generals once junior to him received promotions and decorations, Hobart was left with the rank of major-general, which he had had for nine years.[48]

After the war an American general commented:

> the bitterness, personal and professional jealousy, the complete lack of under-standing, and even hatred, which existed among some of the American commanders and staffs, I could never condone. If similar feelings existed among the British, their natural reserve prevented it from ever coming to my attention.

Evidently Britain's public-school-educated officers were more inhibited than, for example, George Patton, who after his appointment to command in Sicily noted with regard to his professional rival Mark Clark:

> Saw Clark – he was as sour as a pickle. I think I have passed him, and am amused at all the envy and hatred I wasted on him and many others. Looking back, men seem less vile.

Nevertheless such bitternesses did exist in the British forces and seem to have had a much greater influence on careers than was the case, for example, in

[48] K.J. Macksey *Armoured Crusader: A Biography of Major-General Sir Percy Hobart* (1967) p. 170–171; ibid. p. 185; Colville *Fringes of Power* p. 262, 11 Oct. 1940; Gilbert *Winston S. Churchill* vol. 6 p. 862 Dill to Churchill 15 Oct. 1940; ibid. vol. 6 p. 862 Churchill to Dill 19 Oct. 1940; Colville *Fringes of Power* p. 275, 23 Oct. 1940; Macksey *Armoured Crusader* p. 186 fn, 188–190. See also Capt. Alec Cunningham-Reid's denunciation of 'old school tie' predominance, 22 July 1941, *Hansard: House of Commons* vol. 373 col.853–8.

the German Army. German institutional groups tend to be intensely and nakedly competitive, and German people, with the possible exception of the Prussian military aristocracy, a good deal less bottled up and buttoned down than the British stereotype of them would suggest: consequently the running of the armed forces involved a great deal of screaming and shouting, desk banging, door slamming and paranoid sulking. Apart from Hitler's personal contribution this was not particularly the result of the vulgar influence of the Nazis – Waffen-SS officers more than once acted as mediators between feuding generals of the regular Army – nor was it a by-product of defeat: in May 1940 a row between Heinz Guderian and Ewald von Kleist, his immediate superior, led to Guderian resigning, and the Army Group commander had to send another senior general to sort things out; in North Africa Rommel seems to have been convinced throughout that the High Command was working to effect his failure, and so on. But somehow the bad tempers and the paranoia in the German Army seemed to go together with higher professional standards.[49]

Churchill was no more able to combat the institutional prejudices of the armed forces with regard to individuals like Dowding and Hobart than he was to ginger up the cautious planning of the professional staffs. The fact was that even a man of Churchill's phenomenal energy and force could not prevail against the dead weight of the rigidifying military bureaucracies. If the professionals at least responded politely to his interventions it was because they continued to respect him as 'a magnificent leader', 'the ideal leader of the Nation in these times', not because he restrained himself from overstepping the mark in the way Lloyd George was thought to have done in 1917 and 1918. Churchill was perhaps even less of a restrained person than Lloyd George – 'At times you could kiss his feet – at others you feel you could kill him', Admiral Sir Dudley Pound once remarked – but he had a much clearer sense than Lloyd George of constitutional proprieties, and even if his critics sometimes saw him as a dictator, this was a role he consistently

---

[49] J.K. Truscott Jr. *Command Missions: A Personal Story* (New York 1954) p. 539; Martin Blumenson ed. *The Patton Papers* (2 vols Boston 1972–4) vol. 2 p. 220, diary 14 April 1943; Kenneth Macksey *Guderian: Panzer General* (1975) p. 112–3; B.H. Liddell Hart *The Rommel Papers* (1953) p. 139–140, 512–3. But see the study 'The Psychological Foundations of the Wehrmacht' by Lt.-Col. H.V. Dicks R.A.M.C. Public Record Office WO 241/1 p. 14–16 for a rather different picture.

The insidious nature of old boy networks and professional vendettas within elite institutional groups means that there is comparatively little reliable documentation of this phenomenon, but see *Liddell Hart Memoirs* vol. 2 p. 64–5fn. for the tarnished career of Major-General Edward Tollemache: urging his officers not to open fire during the General Strike, he was shouted down by a popular senior officer who exclaimed, 'Bloody balls – take it from me and shoot the bastards down', and had the dashed bad taste to report the incident to H.Q. For the apparent vendetta of General Sir Thomas Blamey and the Australian Staff Corps against Major-General Gordon Bennett see Frank Legg *The Gordon Bennett Story* (Sydney 1965) p. 296–7. Unpleasants goings on in the Canadian army in the First World War are documented in H.A. Bruce *Politics and the Army Medical Corps* (Toronto 1919).

and contemptuously rejected. Ultimately, he wanted his colleagues to stand up for themselves and disagree with him, not because he enjoyed arguments – though he obviously did – but because he thought that was the British and constitutional way. Brooke, Portal and the others understood this, and admired Churchill for it. But perhaps this mutual respect and admiration (so conspicuously lacking in the First World War) was part of the problem.[50]

VII. Civil and Military in Germany and Japan

Personalities aside, the general structure of war leadership was essentially the same in America, in Russia, in Germany and in Italy as in Britain. As Alfred Jodl was afterwards to point out:

> Ever since war began to assume an ever more total character, that is, ever since it relentlessly drew the entire state, with all its functions, together with every citizen, regardless of occupation, sex, or age, into its orbit, the strategic leadership of war has developed into so universal a function that it has come to include every aspect of state leadership, thereby exceeding the limits of purely military responsibilities.

This was implicitly recognized everywhere but in Japan. Everywhere except in Japan therefore the civilian leadership both participated in detailed strategic policy-making and had the final say in the decisions. Perhaps the individual style most resembling Churchill's was that of Stalin. Though his senior officers had reason to fear for their lives in his presence as even Hitler's did not, he was receptive to other people's ideas and, having become the most powerful man in the world, disinclined to act the *prima donna*. Mussolini, too, though suspicious of professional military men, was occasionally prepared to take advice, though some of his key strategic decisions were made without consultation and in the face of subsequent professional objections. Roosevelt, the most distant from the combat zone in terms of miles and communications (and the only one of the war leaders never to have fought in a war), exercised the lightest control, with the least concern for details and the least personal conflict with his chiefs of staff, though his impact on the overall strategic shape of the war was, from 1942 onward, greater than any other leader's. Curiously he saw much less of his service chiefs than other war leaders: Brooke noted that Marshall, the U.S. Army Chief of Staff, told him, 'he frequently did not see him [Roosevelt] for a month or six weeks. I was fortunate if I did not see Winston for six hours'. Marshall indeed avoided intimate contact with the Preident, later recalling, 'I was at Hyde Park for the first time at his funeral'

---

50 British Library Add. 52561 f. 18 Pound to Sir Andrew Cunningham 20 Sept. 1940; ibid. cf 33 same to same, 1 Dec. 1940; Stephen Roskill *Churchill and the Admirals* (1977) p. 215 quoting the diary of A.V. Alexander, First Lord of the Admiralty, 10 June 1942.

– Hyde Park being Roosevelt's private residence. Nevertheless Roosevelt kept his hand on the tiller throughout.[51]

At the other extreme was Hitler. The strained relations of the military and civilian leadership in Germany in the Second World War were not at all after the model of the embittered military-civilian partnership of the First World War. In the earlier conflict the problem arose from the inadequacy of the existing command structure at the top, and the *OHL* (Army High Command), in grasping at ultimate authority, was embarked on a new and revolutionary course, as is evident from the nature of Ludendorff's quasi-dictatorship. Under the Nazis the generals were not competing as rivals, merely attempting to resist the encroachments of Hitler. Hitler indeed can be said to have fused, or even *confused*, the roles of military and civilian leadership; from 1942 he devoted almost all his time and energy to the tactical management of the war, in a way the other leaders and even their chiefs of general staff never dreamt of, while at the same time neglecting almost totally the need to coordinate the Home Front. Nevertheless his conduct differed from the other national leaders essentially only in degree. The other leaders reserved to themselves the crucial decisions, while Hitler assumed that even the disposition of a battalion was crucial. They argued with their service chiefs but attended to their advice; Hitler shouted and sulked but even at the very end he occasionally listened. They coordinated the military and civilian sector of the war economy; Hitler dealt with the problem by pretending it did not exist, while making sure nobody else could tackle it.

Hitler had never expected complete cooperation from the German Army even before the war, as is evident from his removal of the Army commander-in-chief Werner Fritsch and the chief of staff Ludwig Beck. Once the war broke out he was consistently bored and irritated by the cautious conservative strategic thinking of their successors Brauchitsch and Halder. He began to seek alternative advice. He talked of the *OKW*, the Armed Forces High Command, as if it was a coordinating body superior to the three branches of the armed forces: 'We have got a Defence Staff. We have got an organization the envy of every other country in the world, the OKW. No one else has such a thing'. In reality the *OKW* became, after September 1942, merely a kind of alternative *OKH* (Army High Command) under General Alfred Jodl, the head of the Operations Staff; while the Army High Command handled the war with Russia, Jodl's *OKW* Operations Staff assumed responsibility for Western Europe, though it remained dependent on the Army High Command

[51] Percy Ernst Schramm *Hitler: The Man and the Military Leader* ed. Donald S. Detwiler (London 1972) p. 195–204 Appendix II 'Memorandum Dictated in 1946 by General Jodl on Hitler's Military Leadership', at p. 196; Seweryn Bialer ed. *Stalin and his Generals: Soviet Military Memoirs of World War II* (Boulder 1984) p. 34–42; Bryant *Turn of the Tide* p. 302 fn. 1; Forrest C. Pogue 'The Wartime Chiefs of Staff and the President' in Monte D. Wright and Laurence J. Paszek ed. *Soldiers and Statesmen* (Washington 1973; U.S.A.F. Symposium 1970) p. 69–85 at p. 72–3.

for military intelligence evaluations and other services. Yet Jodl was on such bad terms with Zeitzler, Halder's successor as chief of staff in the Army High Command, that they did not attend each other's conferences, so that only Hitler was fully informed of the overall picture of the various fronts. The tendency for administrative functions to be exercised by competing and uncoordinated bodies was a characteristic of Nazi government and is usually explained in terms of the Nazi's doctrinaire approval of Social Darwinistic competition; but this explanation misses the point that the newer bodies always developed because of Hitler's dissatisfaction with the performance of the older bodies, and the peculiarity of the Nazis is that they never, till the very end, abolished any government departments, the corollary of their disdain for conventional organization being a lack of interest in or appetite for reorganization.[52]

From late 1942 Hitler's working relationship with the generals deteriorated rapidly; the discovery of the extent of military involvement in the attempted 20 July 1944 *Putsch* merely completed a process already very far advanced. On the other hand the appointment of SS-supremo Heinrich Himmler to command the home armies after the *Putsch* was prescribed probably less by the disloyalty of possibly alternative appointees from within the regular army than by the consideration that only a party heavy-weight, in fact only the Reichsführer-SS, could handle in appropriate style the final stages of the *Götterdämmerung* which now seemed inevitable. Even at the very end Hitler did not repudiate the professionals completely: his appointed successor as head of state, Grand Admiral Dönitz, was a professional to his finger tips.

To some extent the essential fact of a split between Nazi party and military was a post-war fabrication, cooked up by the army staff's apologists at Mondorf, under the guidance of Franz Halder. There had been a split of course, as the 20 July *Putsch* showed, but it was not between the Nazis and the Army as such, and many of the conspirators were not even soldiers. At the same time it was not only the Nazi Party that was objected to by the soldiers. Even before the war ended, when it was still unsafe to make direct accusations against party functionaries, some of the

---

[52] [Walter] Warlimont 'Commentary on a Study of OKW', in Donald S. Detwiler ed. *World War II German Military Studies* (24 vols New York 1979) vol 6 p. 1–142 at p. 56, cf Matthew Cooper *The German Army, 1933–1945* (1978) p. 192; Walter Warlimont *Inside Hitler's Headquarters, 1939–1945* (1964) p. 466, diary 1 Sept. 1944; Warlimont 'Commentary' in Detwiler ed. *German Military Studies* vol 6 p. 83, 88, 94.

In reality the Chiefs of Staff organizations in Britain and the U.S. fulfilled a coordinating function far more successfully than the *OKW* (*Oberkommando der Wehrmacht*): as the German Navy was comparatively very small and the Luftwaffe staff had failed to establish itself as an independent entity it is difficult to see what the *OKW* was supposed to coordinate in any case, and being composed chiefly of Army officers mainly supplemented the *OKH* (*Oberkommando des Heeres*) staff. In Italy there was a *Capo di Stato Maggiore Generale* superior to the general staffs of each of the three armed services but planning and consultation was not organized on the elaborate scale adopted in Britain and the U.S.

generals were preparing documentation to prove that their failures were the result of incorrect institutional arrangements vis-à-vis civilian officials; Georg Thomas, the former *OKW* war economy head, blamed the breakdown of his working relationship with Speer's armaments ministry not on Speer himself – that would have we been too risky an allegation, even though it would probably have been the truth – but on the state secretary and other officials in Speer's ministry. He wrote of the witch-hunt (*Kesseltrieben*) against him by Speer's underlings and seemed to regard his position in the *OKW* as incompatible with responsibility to a civilian ministry, though of course comparable arrangements were quite common in, for example, the Britain armed services and procurement departments. Though Thomas was in fact in sympathy with the military resistance to Hitler, it seems that his objection was to civilian, rather than Nazi, interference with his department.[53]

Jodl, whose functions related increasingly to tactical rather than strategic planning, had been scathing before the war on the subject of military leaders who could not accept the role allotted to them by their civilian superiors:

> The General Staff is obsessed with memories of the past and instead of doing what it is told and getting on with its military job, thinks it is responsible for political decisions.

Later, during the war, he seems to have given up the implied distinction and began to make explicitly political speeches, even, for example, at a meeting of Reichsleiters and Gauleiters in Munich in November 1943 when he lectured the assembled party hierarchs on, 'The strength of the revolutionary idea', on how Hitler had been 'predetermined by fate to lead our people to a brighter future' and how 'we will be victorious, because we must be victorious, otherwise, the history of the world would have lost its meaning' ('wir siegen werden, weil wir siegen müssen, denn sonst hätte die Weltgeschichte ihren Sinn verloren') a piece of Nazi logic if ever there was one. The circumstance that many generals, including Jodl, had serious doubts about the war situation from 1943 onwards does not remove the fact that very many of them collaborated with the Nazis, to the utmost of their ability and energy, till the very end: it was in more senses than one that these men were the heirs of the Ludendorff tradition.[54]

The one belligerent government where there was a fundamental lack of central coordination was that of Japan. Japan's government in the late 1930s and early 1940s has been compared to that of Wilhelmine Germany. Jodl, though confused as to details, understood the essential point when he wrote in 1946:

53 Georg Thomas *Geschichte der deutschen Wehr-und-Rüstungs Wirtschaft, 1918–1943/5* ed. Wolfgang Birkenfeld, (Boppard-am-Rhein 1966) p. 308, 310–311, 314. *Kesseltreiben* is, literally, a *battue*, a driving of game animals into a confined area so they can be killed more easily.

54 Warlimont *Inside Hitler's H.Q.* p. 14, quoting Jodl's diary for 10 Aug. 1938; *Trial of the Major War Criminals before the International Military Tribunal* (42 vols Nuremberg 1947–9) vol 37 p. 632–668: the longer quotation is from p. 668.

Only in Japan, which in this respect simply had not kept pace with the times, did the military machinery fight its way to political power and lead the country – though divided and without a strong political hand – in a war that was waged not as a a means of politics, but rather with politics being made to serve as handmaiden of war.[55]

Up till 1940 the Japanese armed forces had had a veto on any government because of the constitutional arrangement that the ministers of war and of marine had to be serving officers and therefore subject to the orders of their respective High Commands; but governments headed by generals had collapsed in 1937 and in 1940 because of their inability to handle the Lower House of the Diet. Hideki Tojo, the former minister of war, became premier in October 1941. He denied that his was a 'dictatorial government' like those of Hitler, Mussolini, Roosevelt and Churchill – the list is Tojo's – 'my position in the Japanese state is essentially different from theirs'. This was in fact true. He could resign with his whole government, but he was unable to dismiss any of his colleagues individually. He was unable to subordinate the armed forces to his control – he was not even told of the disastrous defeat at Midway for a month. He was unable to silence criticism of his government in the Army, in the press, or even at public meetings. When Nakano Seigo, a leading critic of Tojo's government in the Diet, killed himself under mysterious circumstances in October 1943, the government requested that the funeral should be in private: instead 20,000 people attended. Though political parties had been suppressed in 1940, Tojo, having no mass movement behind him, lacked the means even to rig an election; in the 1942 General Election – Japan and the U.S.A. were the only major belligerents to poll during the war – over a third of the votes went to candidates opposing the government-sponsored list, though admittedly some of these were independent ultra-rightists who functioned as a pro-government ginger group. Despite the government's energetic propaganda against the contamination of western influences, the study of European literature thrived at the universities: in 1943 there were at least fourteen graduation theses on Thomas Hardy and Professor M. Ohsawa published the first of a series of papers 'The War Literature of T. Hardy' in *Studies in English Literature*. Wartime Japan may have been authoritarian, but it lacked the institutional machinery to be totalitarian.[56]

[55] For the comparison of Tojo's Japan and Wilhelmine Germany see e.g. Masao Maruyama *Thought and Behaviour in Modern Japanese Politics* (Oxford 1969) p. 115 and Stanley G. Payne *Fascism: Comparison and Definition* (Madison 1980) p. 164; Schramm *Hitler: The Man and the Military Leader* p. 196–7, Jodl's memo of 1946.

[56] Ben-Ami Shillony *Politics and Culture in Wartime Japan* (Oxford 1981) p. 11; ibid. p. 29–31; Saburo Ienaga *Japan's Last Wars: World War II and the Japanese, 1931–1945* (Oxford 1979) p. 39; Shillony *Politics and Culture* p. 47–9 and cf p. 50 for Nakano's funeral; ibid. p. 26 for the 1942 election.

There was a general election in Canada in the spring of 1940, held to strengthen the Mackenzie King government, and in Australia there were general elections in September 1940 and October 1941, the first weakening and the second defeating the government. All three of these elections

continued

When Japan's war effort began to fail it was from within the Army that criticism was most vocal, and finally leading to the fall of Tojo's government. The fact that Tojo was a general, and Army chief of staff, as well as prime minister, does not alter the essential resemblance to the civilian-military feuds of the First World War; Tojo fell precisely because he failed to represent the military point of view to the army's satisfaction. The Japanese phenomenon of *gekokujo*, the 'rule of the higher by the lower' prevents one from identifying any really important individual ring-leaders in the army opposition to Tojo; the Japanese believed that, 'The great propelling force of a strong army emanates from the middle stratum' and senior generals – even Tojo himself – were in part only figureheads for pressure groups of middle-grade officers. But then of course part of the significance of Ludendorff and Hindenburg, Cadorna, Joffre, Robertson and Haig in the First World War was that they were seen as representing much more than their own individual wills; is only superficially a paradox that Tojo, as a general, should play the Bethmann-Hollweg rather than the Ludendorff role in Japan's re-run of the German Second Reich.[57]

At first glance of course Tojo's claim that Churchill's and Roosevelt's were as much 'dictatorial governments' as Hitler's or Mussolini's seems monstrous; compared to the situation in Japan, or in any of the First World War governments, the claim seems more valid. The seed of totalitarianism which had germinated in the matrix of the First World War burst into flower in the Second World War; indeed a striking proof of the theory that the 1939–1945 war was no more than a continuation of 1914–1918 is the way the leadership crisis of the 1914–1918 period was decisively resolved in 1939–1945. In a longer perspective this development may simply be a stage in the evolution from national wars fought without effective national leadership, as in 1793–1815, to wars fought by national leaders determined to survive in their bunkers while the nation as such perishes in the nuclear holocaust outside. The cycle is not yet completed however; we will know better where we are going when we have got there, and a book like this one cannot be more than an attempt at an interim report.

continued
were fought with the assumption of the essential remoteness of the world war. John Curtin's Labour government came to power after the October 1941 election in time to meet the Japanese bringing the war to Australia's doorstep. Another election in June 1943 was a landslide for Curtin's war government. Similarly the July 1943 general election in South Africa was a major victory for the ruling party led by Jan Christian Smuts, though in the September 1943 general election in New Zealand the Government was only returned with a reduced majority.

There was also a general election in German-occupied Denmark.

I am grateful to Professor Harunori of the Aichi University of Education and to Professor James Goldstein who provided me with a bibliography of Hardy studies in wartime Japan. There seems something sublime in Professor S. Morioka lecturing on 'The Tragedy of Thomas Hardy' to the Tenth General Conference of the Japan Society of English Literature in the year of Singapore and Midway.

[57] For *gekokujo* see Eric Larrabee *Commander-in-Chief: Frankin Delano Roosevelt, his Lieutenants and their War* (1987) p. 68, quoting the semi-official newspaper *Nichi-Nichi*.

Envoi

Let there be no specious rant about this in the future, as there has been all too much in the past. What we have fought for all these four years, watching our generation wither month after month, is not Belgium, nor Serbia, nor France; no abstract principle of justice, no political theory, no imperial scheme; but England, her life and existence. Could we have done it else? If in saving England we succeeded in freeing Belgium, so much to the good; yet all the time, as we rode through these poor people commending us to God, I caught myself wishing that the language they spoke, and the flags they waved, had been my own.

Duff Hart Davis ed. *End of an Era: Letters and Journals of Sir Alan Lascelles, 1887–1920* (1986), p. 256: 9 November 1918; Lascelles, a staff officer with Britain's 1st Cavalry Brigade, describing the welcome he and his companions received from the liberated Belgians.

Index

This is primarily an index of personal names but also includes, on a selective basis, battles, cities and countries, film titles, newspapers and periodicals, official organizations, the names of certain types of aeroplane and other weapons, and topics such as 'medals' and 'riots'.